PRINCIPLES OF
INTERNATIONAL MARKETING

MICHAEL R. CZINKOTA

Georgetown University

University of Birmingham, UK

ILKKA A. RONKAINEN

Georgetown University

SOUTH-WESTERN
CENGAGE Learning™

Australia • Brazil • Japan • Korea • Mexico • Singapore • Spain • United Kingdom • United States

SOUTH-WESTERN
CENGAGE Learning

Principles of International Marketing, 9th Edition
Michael R. Czinkota and Ilkka A. Ronkainen

Vice President of Editorial, Business:
Jack W. Calhoun

Vice President/Editor-in-Chief: Melissa Acuña

Executive Editor: Michael Roche

Developmental Editor: Erin Guendelsberger

Editorial Assistant: Shanna Shelton

Executive Marketing Manager:
Kimberly Kanakes

Senior Marketing Coordinator: Sarah Rose

Senior Marketing Communications Manager:
Sarah Greber

Production Manager: Jennifer Ziegler

Content Project Management: Pre-Press PMG

Managing Media Editor: Pamela Wallace

Media Editor: John Rich

Frontlist Buyer, Manufacturing:
Miranda Klapper

Production Service: Pre-Press PMG

Copyeditor: Pre-Press PMG

Compositor: Pre-Press PMG

Senior Art Director: Stacy Shirley

Internal Designer: Pre-Press PMG

Cover Image: © Shutterstock

Photo Permissions Editor: Deanna Ettinger

Permissions Editor: Timothy Sisler

Library of Congress Control Number: 2009929199

International Student Edition ISBN-13: 978-1-4390-4137-6
International Student Edition ISBN-10: 1-4390-4137-7

Cengage Learning International Offices

Asia
cengageasia.com
tel: (65) 6410 1200

Australia/New Zealand
cengage.com.au
tel: (61) 3 9685 4111

Brazil
cengage.com.br
tel: (011) 3665 9900

India
cengage.co.in
tel: (91) 11 30484837/38

Latin America
cengage.com.mx
tel: +52 (55) 1500 6000

UK/Europe/Middle East/Africa
cengage.co.uk
tel: (44) 207 067 2500

Represented in Canada by Nelson Education, Ltd.
nelson.com
tel: (416) 752 9100 / (800) 668 0671

For product information: **www.cengage.com/international**
Visit your local office: **www.cengage.com/global**
Visit our corporate website: **www.cengage.com**

Printed in the Canada
1 2 3 4 5 6 7 13 12 11 10 09

To Ilona and Margaret Victoria—MRC
To Susan, Sanna, and Alex—IAR

Thank you for reading our book! Practicing international marketing and writing a text on the subject have much in common. The focus is on delighting the customer; it is a lot of work; the competition is tough; and it's fun to succeed. It is therefore with great pleasure that we present the ninth edition of *Principles of International Marketing* to you.

Over the years, we have always made key improvements in our new editions, but never before has it been so important to bring out a revised text. There has been unprecedented change. When domestic economic activities are down, international marketing is down as well, only much more so. Austerity brings changes in production and consumption patterns and introduces new dimensions into the decision-making process. The role of governments is growing by leaps and bounds, making them key entities to dictate the direction and strength of international marketing activities. There is a rising tendency to restrict imports, and encourage exports, in order to keep home industries safe and gradually reduce global imbalances.

In dire economic times, international marketers are a key agent of social change, providing insight and knowledge that helps society understand the trade-offs and consequences of actions and thus make good decisions.

The challenge is great. Nations around the world attempt to stabilize and revitalize their economies. Typically, each nation's emphasis rests with domestic issues. But, any international intervention of one nation is likely to rapidly affect other countries and may trigger economic and policy responses. Once introduced, protectionism can quickly become contagious and be emulated around the world. The prevalence of a market economy is not automatically understood any more. Key tenets of the marketing discipline, such as risk, profit, competition, and ownership, are being redefined and reassessed.

International marketers develop the knowledge and talents that serve to disentangle the competing priorities confronting individuals, companies, and governments. They explain the principle that nations must be able and willing to buy each other's goods if world economies are to blossom. They can show how competition and consumer choice are crucial to the achievement of a higher level of well being.

By having field-specific knowledge, by understanding the effect of culture and emotions, and by sitting at the table and making their contribution, international marketers help to ensure a better world. When there is some disagreement and some sparring, we ask you to apply to international marketers the great scholar Ludwig von Wittgenstein's statement: "A philosopher who is not taking part in discussions is like a boxer who never goes into the ring."

It is essential to focus on international marketing now. In academia we see great increases in student enrollment—they want to stock up on knowledge and capabilities during bad times in order to be ready for the good ones. Companies and governments need to do the same. In times of slack resources one can explore new market opportunities and new customs and customers. When economic conditions get better, one can convert that capability into market results and receive a payoff for all the prior research and preparation. International marketing is a vital economic stimulus. Our recognition and presentation of all these issues makes this ninth edition of *Principles of International Marketing* the best one yet!

We reflect many new dimensions, emotions and boundaries, which affect the discipline. Here are the key features that make this book stand out:

- We paint a broader picture of the implications of adapting or rejecting a market orientation. In doing so, we highlight ethical issues and discuss the shortcomings encountered in corporate transparency and executive veracity.

- We provide deep data analysis and support. For example, we discuss all economic regions, offering comparative benchmarks not only from the economically advanced world but also from China, Australia, Kenya, and Brazil.

- We cover the full spectrum of international marketing, from start-up operations to the formation of virtual alliances. We offer a thorough discussion of the operations of multinational corporations, but also present a specific focus on the activities of small and medium-sized firms, which are increasingly major players in the international market and will be the employers of many students.

- We provide a hands-on analysis of the growing interaction between government and business. We have served in government positions and advised international marketer. This policy orientation greatly enhances the managerial relevance of this book.

- We cover both the theory and the application of international marketing. Based on our personal research record and business experience, we can offer research insights from around the globe and show how corporations are adjusting to the marketplace realities of today.

- We acknowledge and give clear examples of how the world has changed in an era of terrorism, hostility, and distrust. We look at the marketing repercussions of these changes on people management, sourcing policies, cargo security, inventory management, and port utilization. However, we also draw on our work with corporations to find new forms of collaboration and network building without compromising safety or security.

- We address the concerns of emerging and developing markets throughout the text. We present the issue of underserved markets, with a population of four billion, and also suggest how these people and countries can become greater participants in marketing efforts.

- We examine international marketing from a truly global perspective. By addressing, confronting, and analyzing the existence of different environments, expectations, and market conditions, we highlight the need for awareness, sensitivity, and adaptation.

- We integrate the e-commerce and Web impact on the international marketer. We discuss the revolutionary changes in communication between firms and their customers and suppliers, and present the latest consequences for international market research and market entry.

Personal Support

Most important, we personally stand behind our product and we will work hard to delight you. Should you have any questions or comments on this book, you can contact us, talk to us, and receive feedback from us.

Michael R. Czinkota
(202) 687-4204
czinkotm@georgetown.edu

Ilkka A. Ronkainen
(202) 687-3788
ronkaii@georgetown.edu

Organization

The text is designed primarily of the advanced undergraduate student with prior exposure to the marketing field. Because of its in-depth coverage, it also presents an excellent challenge for graduate instruction and executive education.

The text is divided into four parts. First, the core concepts of international marketing are outlined, and the environmental forces that the international marketer has to consider are discussed. The second part focuses on international market entry and development. We cover strategic planning for internationalization, organizing for implementation, preparing through research, and executing the entry. Part Three addresses the elements of the marketing mix that are most important for firms at an initial level of international experience. Part Four discusses the marketing management issues most relevant to the expanded global operations of multinational corporations. We conclude with a new chapter on the future of International Marketing, based on our own Delphi study of policy makers, business executives, and researchers in the European Union, Asia, Africa and the Americas. We also offer an appendix on international employment opportunities.

Both the instructor and the student can work with this text in two ways. One alternative is to cover the material sequentially, progressing from the initial international effort to multinational activities. In this way, marketing dimensions such as distribution, promotion, and pricing are covered in the order in which they are most relevant for the particular level of expertise within the firm. Another approach is to use the text in a parallel manner, by pairing comparable chapters from Parts two, Three, and Four. In this way, the primary emphasis can be placed on the functional approach to international marketing.

Key Features

The ninth edition reflects the highly dynamic nature of international marketing. We offer a perspective on the shift in the role of market forces and the impact of this revolution on international marketers in terms of outreach, research, and competition. Our *Principles of International Marketing* vignettes reflect state-of-the-art corporate practices with a substantial emphasis on the environment and sustainability. We have included links to the Web sites of companies, data sources, governments, international organizations, and monitors of international marketing issues.

Our focus on the physical environment and geography is strong. Updated maps provide context in terms of social and economic data. An appendix directly addresses the relationship between geography and international marketing. New text components, marketplaces, and several cases specifically focus on the environment and the opportunities, challenges, and ambiguities that it poses to international marketers.

This edition gives increased attention to developing economies and economies in transition. In Part One, international organizations such as the World Bank, the World Trade Organization, the International Monetary Fund, and the United Nations are covered, along with the public debate surrounding these institutions. We have increased the focus on ethics and corporate citizenship in this section and strengthened our discussion of intellectual property rights.

We broaden our highlights of emerging markets by systematically addressing the bottom of the income pyramid. Our revised strategy section is now linked directly with organization, implementation, and research concerns. We have recast the chapter on market entry and expansion to include a wider variety of ways in which firms go global. All of these strategies are now integrated into one chapter, organized around our model of the internationalization process.

The marketing mix discussions now include new technologies and their impact. For example, we present the effect of consumer generated media, such as blogs, on-line communities and opportunities presented by international marketing through mobile devices. We offer specific sections on outsourcing by involving partners in research and design, on the effect of terrorism on international transportation, and the reconfiguration of web-based services. New also is the focus on how local companies can defend against global players and win, and our emphasis on sponsorship and ambush marketing. The final chapter and appendix on international employment opportunities helps students prepare for the implementation steps yet to come.

Innovative Learning Tools

Contemporary Realism
Each chapter offers three current International Marketplace boxes. They focus on real marketing situations, including the environment and sustainability, and help students understand and absorb the presented materials. The instructor can highlight the boxes to exemplify theory or use them as mini-cases for class discussion.

Research Emphasis

A special effort has been made to provide current research information and data from around the world. Chapter notes are augmented by lists of relevant recommended readings incorporating the latest research findings. In addition, a wide variety of sources and organizations that provide international information are offered in the text. These materials enable the instructor and the student to go beyond the text when desired.

Internet Focus

The Internet, electronic commerce, and the World Wide Web affect all of international marketing. We highlight how the way of reaching customers and suppliers has changed given the new technology. We explain the enhanced ability of firms to position themselves internationally in competition with other larger players. We offer insights into the electronic marketing research process and present details of how companies cope with new market realities. Whenever appropriate, we direct readers to Internet resources that can be useful in obtaining up-to-date information. Each chapter also provides several Internet questions in order to offer training opportunities that make use of the Internet.

Geography

This edition contains several maps, covering the social, economic, and political features of the world. In addition, several chapters have maps particularly designed for this book, which integrate the materials discussed in the text and reflect a truly "global" perspective. These maps enable the instructor to visually demonstrate concepts such as socioeconomic variables or exposure to terrorism. An appendix, dealing specifically with the impact of geography on international marketing, is part of Chapter 1.

Cases

Following each part of the text are a variety of cases. Fourteen of the twenty-nine cases are either new or updated especially for this edition. These cases present students with real business situations and cover international marketing conditions from around the world. All cases address the activities of actual or former companies and cover a broad geographic spectrum. In addition, nine video cases further help to enliven classroom activity. Challenging questions accompany each case, permitting in-depth discussion of the materials covered in the chapters.

Ancillary Package

Instructor's Manual

Available on the password-protected instructor's resource Web site, the text is accompanied by an in-depth *Instructor's Manual,* devised to provide major assistance to the professor. The material in the manual includes the following:

- **Discussion Guidelines** For each chapter, specific teaching objectives and guidelines are developed to help stimulate classroom discussion.
- **End-of-Chapter Questions** Each question is fully developed in the manual to accommodate different scenarios and experience horizons. In addition, each chapter has Internet-based exercises in order to offer students the opportunity to explore the application of new technology to international marketing on their own.
- **Cases** A detailed case-chapter matrix is supplied that delineates which cases are most appropriate for each area of the international marketing field. In addition, case and video case discussion questions are answered in detail.

Test Bank

Available on the password-protected instructor's resource Web site, the revised and updated Test Bank includes a variety of multiple choice, true/false, and short answer questions, which emphasize the important concepts presented in each chapter. The Test Bank questions vary in levels of difficulty so that instructors can tailor their testing to meet their specific needs.

Exam View (Computerized) Test Bank

Available on the web site www.cengage.com/international, ExamView contains all of the questions in the printed Test Bank. This program consists of easy-to-use test creation software. Instructors can add or edit questions, instructions, and answers, and select questions (randomly or numerically) by previewing them on the screen. Instructors can also create and administer quizzes online, whether over the Internet, a local area network (LAN), or a wide area network (WAN).

PowerPoint Presentation Slides

Available on the Web site, the PowerPoint Lecture Presentation enables instructors to customize their own multimedia classroom presentations. The package includes select figures and tables from the text, as well as outside materials to supplement chapter concepts. Material is organized by chapter, and can be modified or expanded for individual classroom use. PowerPoint presentations are also easily printed to create customized Transparency Masters.

Web Site www.cengage.com/international

Visit the test Web site to find instructor's support materials, as well as study resources that will help students practice and apply the concepts they have learned in class.

Student Resources

- Crossword puzzles that use glossary terms and definitions arranged by chapter, for extra review of key terms found in the text.
- Interactive Quizzes
- Internet Exercises

Instructor Resources

- Downloadable Instructor's Manual files
- Downloadable PowerPoint presentation files
- Downloadable Test Bank files

DVD Videos

A video package has been prepared to correspond with the key concepts taught in the text. These Videos, featuring companies such as BP and Doc Martens, coincide with the video cases found at the end of each part in the text. Professors can assign the cases after presenting videos in class or use these cases to simply illustrate a key point.

We are deeply grateful to Professor Victoria Crittenden of Boston College, who has joined us with a major effort in this new edition. Her work was instrumental in introducing new research and societal dimensions and in ensuring timely completion of the project. Prof. Crittenden was always very helpful and a great pleasure to work with. Of equal importance, her input truly made a difference. Thank you!

We are also grateful to all the professors, students, and professionals using this book. Your interest demonstrates the need fore more knowledge about international marketing. As our market, you are telling us that our product adds value to your lives. As a result, you add value to ours. Thank you! We also thank the many reviewers for their constructive and imaginative comments and criticisms, which were instrumental in making this edition even better.

Jo Ann L. Asquith
St. Cloud State University

Thomas Belich
University of Minnesota

John Besaw, Ph.D.
University of Washington-Tacoma

Andrew J. Czaplewski
University of Colorado at Colorado Springs

Yara DeAndrade
Webster University

Matt Elbeck
Troy University

Ken Fairweather
LeTourneau University

Thomas F. List
Saginaw Valley State University

Drew Martin
University of Hawaii at Hilo

Paul Myer
University of Maine

Frank Novakowski
Davenport University

Tagi Sagafi-nejad
Texas A&M International University

Milena Simic
Missouri Valley College

Kevin E. Voss
Oklahoma State University

A. N. M. Waheeduzzaman
Texas A&M University-Corpus Christi

Theodore O. Wallin
Whitman School of Management

Wendel Weaver
Oklahoma Wesleyan University

Mark D. Woodhull, Ph.D.
Schreiner University

We remain indebted to the reviewers and survey respondents of this and earlier editions of this text:

Sanjeev Agarwal
Iowa State University

Zafar Ahmed
Texas A&M—Commerce

Lyn S. Amine
St. Louis University

Jessica M. Bailey
The American University

Subir Bandyopadhyay
Indiana University Northwest

Warren Bilkey
University of Wisconsin

Katharine A. Bohley Hubbard
University of Indianapolis

S. Tamer Cavusgil
Michigan State University

Samit Chakravorti
Florida International University

Shih-Fen Chen
Kansas State University

Alex Christofides
Ohio State University

Farok J. Contractor
Rutgers University

Robert Dahlstrom
University of Kentucky

Paul Dowling
University of Utah

Carl E. Dresden
Coastal Carolina University

John Dyer
University of Miami

Luiz Felipe
IBMEC Business School (Rio de Janeiro, Brazil)

Dr. John P. Fraderich
Southern Illinois University—Carbondale

Roberto Friedmann
University of Georgia

Shenzhao Fu
University of San Francisco

Jim Gentry
University of Nebraska

Donna Goehle
Michigan State University

Needlima Gogumala
Kansas State University

Peter J. Gordon
Southeast Missouri State University

Paul Groke
Northern Illinois University

Andrew Gross
Cleveland State University

John Hadjimarcou
University of Texas at El Paso

Hari Hariharan
DePaul University

Braxton Hinchey
University of Lowell

Carol Howard
Oklahoma City University

Basil Janavaras
Mankato State University

Denise Johnson
University of Louisville

Sudhir Kale
Arizona State University

Ceyhan Kilic
DePaul University

Hertha Krotkoff
Towson State University

Kathleen La Francis
Central Michigan University

Ann L. Langlois
Palm Beach Atlantic University

Trina Larsen
Drexel University

Edmond Lausier
University of Southern California

Bertil Liander
University of Massachusetts

Mushtaq Luqmani
Western Michigan University

Isabel Maignan
Florida State University

James Maskulka
Lehigh University

James McCullouch
Washington State University

Fred Miller
Murray State University

Joseph Miller
Indiana University

Mark Mitchell
University of South Carolina—Spartanburg

Tomasz Mroczkowski
American University

Amit Mukherjee
Auburn University

Henry Munn
California State University, Northridge

Cheryl Nakata
University of Illinois—Chicago

Jacob Naor
University of Maine, Orono

Urban Ozanne
Florida State University

Tony Peloso
Queensland University of Technology (Australia)

Ilsa Penaloza
University of Connecticut

Zahir A. Quraeshi
Western Michigan University

John Ryans
Kent State University

F. J. Sarknas
Duquesne University

Regina P. Schlee
Seattle Pacific University

Matthew Sim
Temesek Business School (Singapore)

James Spiers
Arizona State University

Odile J. Streed
Concordia College

Janda Swinder
Kansas State University

Ray Taylor
Villanova University

Tyzoon T. Tyebjee
Santa Clara University

Robert Underwood
Virginia Polytechnic Institute and State University

Robert Weigand
University of Illinois at Chicago

John Wilkinson
University of South Australia

Sumas Wongsunopparat
University of Wisconsin—Milwaukee

Nittaya Wongtada
Thunderbird

Van R. Wood
Texas Tech University

Many thanks to all the colleagues and students who have helped us sharpen our thinking by cheerfully providing challenging comments and questions. In particular, we thank Bernard LaLonde, The Ohio State University; Tamer Cavusgil, Georgia State University; James Wills, University of Hawaii; Svetla Marinova, University of Birmingham; Urs Baldegger and Stefan Güldenberg; Hochschule Liechtenstein.

Many colleagues, friends, and business associates graciously gave their time and knowledge to clarify concepts; provide us with ideas, comments, and suggestions; and deepen our understanding of issues. Without the direct links to business and policy that you have provided, this book could not offer its refreshing realism. In particular, we are grateful to Secretaries Malcolm Baldridge, C. William Verity, Clayton Yeutter, and William Brock for the opportunity to gain international business policy experience and to William Morris, Paul Freedenberg, and J. Michael Farrell for enabling its implementation. We also thank William Casselman of Stairs Dillenbeck Kelly Merle and Finley, Robert Conkling, Lew Cramer of the Utah World Trade Center, Mark Dowd of IBM, David Danjczek, Veikko Jaaskelainen, and Reijo Luostarinen of HSE. A special tip of the hat goes to Eugene Markowski and son for all their insights into international financial changes.

We also thank the colleagues who have generously written new cases to contribute to this new edition of our book. They are Professor Svetla Marinova of the University of Birmingham, Professor Lluis Renart of IESE, Hannu Serisito of HSE, and Professor Thomas Cooke of Georgetown University.

Valuable research assistance was provided by our student research elite team. They made important and substantive contributions to this book. They pursued research information with tenacity and relentlessness; they organized and analyzed research materials, prepared drafts of vignettes and cases, and reinforced everyone on the third floor of Old North with their can-do spirit. They are Sugy Choi, Kenny Krupa, Dafina Nikolova, and Christel Tham, all of Georgetown University.

A very special word of thanks to the people at Cengage. Mike Roche has the vision but hasn't lost his hands-on approach. Erin Guendelsberger supported the lengthy process of writing a text with her input and feedback. Stacy Shirley created the outstanding design and Deanna Ettinger and Timothy Sisler provided art research and permission coordination.

Foremost, we are grateful to our families, who have truly participated in our labors. Only the patience, understanding, and love of Ilona and Margaret Victoria Czinkota and Susan, Sanna, and Alex Ronkainen enabled us to have the energy, stamina, and inspiration to write this book.

Michael R. Czinkota
Ilkka A. Ronkainen
Washington, DC
August 2009

Michael R. Czinkota presents international marketing and business issues at the Graduate School and the Robert Emmett McDonough School of Business at Georgetown University and the Birmingham Business School in the United Kingdom. He has held professional appointments at universities in Asia, Australia, Europe, and the Americas.

Dr. Czinkota served in the U.S. government as Deputy Assistant Secretary of Commerce. He also served as head of the U.S. Delegation to the OECD Industry Committee in Paris and as senior advisor for Export Controls.

His background includes ten years of private-sector business experience as a partner in a fur trading firm and in an advertising agency. His research has been supported by the U.S. government, the National Science Foundation, the Organization of American States, and the the American Management Association. He was listed as one of the three most published contributors to international business research in the world by the *Journal of International Business Studies,* and has written several books, including Key Shifts in *International Business: Adjusting to a new world*, (with I. Ronkainen and M. Kotabe, Businessexpertspress.com) and *Mastering Global Markets* (Cengage).

Dr. Czinkota served on the Global Advisory Board of the American Marketing Association, the Global Council of the American Management Association, and the Board of Governors of the Academy of Marketing Science. He is on the editorials boards of *Journal of Academy of Marketing Science, Journal of International Marketing, and Asian Journal of Marketing.* He is a contributor to the *Washington Times*, the *Korea Times* and the *Handelsblatt* in Germany.

For his work in international business and trade policy, he was named a Distinguished Fellow of the Academy of Marketing Science, a Fellow of the Chartered Institute of Marketing, and a Fellow of the Royal Society of Arts in the United Kingdom. He has been awarded honorary degrees from the Universidad Pontificia Madre y Maestra in the Dominican Republic and the Universidad del Pacifico in Lima, Peru.

He serves on several corporate boards and has worked with corporations such as AT&T, IBM, GE, Nestlé, and US WEST. He advises the Executive Office of the President of the United States, the United Nations, and the World Trade Organization. Dr. Czinkota is often asked to testify before the United States Congress.

Dr. Czinkota was born and raised in Germany and educated in Austria, Scotland, Spain, and the United States. He studied law and business administration at the University of Erlangen-Nürnberg and was awarded a two-year Fulbright Scholarship. He holds an MBA in international business and a Ph.D. in logistics from The Ohio State University.

Ilkka A. Ronkainen is a member of the faculty of marketing and international business at the School of Business at Georgetown University. From 1981 to 1986 he served as Associate Director and from 1986 to 1987 as Chairman of the National Center for Export-Import Studies. Currently, he directs Georgetown University's Hong Kong Program.

Dr. Ronkainen serves as docent of international marketing at the Helsinki School of Economics. He was visiting professor at HSE during the 1997–88 and 1991–92 academic years and continues to teach in its Executive MBA, International MBA, and International BBA programs. He is currently the chair holder at the Saastamoinen Foundation Professorship in International Marketing.

Dr. Ronkainen holds a Ph.D. and a master's degree from the University of South Carolina as well as an M.S. (Economics) degree from the Helsinki School of Economics.

Dr. Ronkainen has published extensively in academic journals and the trade press. He is a coauthor of a number of international business and marketing texts, including *Best Practices in International Marketing and Mastering Global Markets* (Thomson). He serves on the review boards of the *Journal of Business Research, International Marketing Review, and Journal of Travel Research, and has reviewed for the Journal of International Marketing* and *the Journal of International Business Studies*. He served as the North American coordinator for the European Marketing Academy, 1984–90. He was a member of the board of the Washington International Trade Association from 1981 to 1986 and started the association's newsletter, *Trade Trends*.

Dr. Ronkainen has served as a consultant to a wide range of U.S. and international institutions. He has worked with entities such as IBM, the Rand Organization, and the Organization of American States. He maintains close relations with a number of Finnish companies and their internationalization and educational efforts.

PART 4

THE GLOBAL MARKETING MIX

VIDEO CASES

CONTENTS

PART 2

INTERNATIONAL MARKET ENTRY AND DEVELOPMENT

PART 3

EXPORT MARKETING MIX

PART 4

THE GLOBAL MARKETING MIX

VIDEO CASES

THE INTERNATIONAL MARKETING ENVIRONMENT

PART ONE INTRODUCES THE INTERNATIONAL TRADE FRAMEWORK AND ENVIRONMENT. IT HIGHLIGHTS THE NEED FOR INTERNATIONAL MARKETING ACTIVITIES AND EXPLORES RECENT DEVELOPMENTS IN WORLD TRADE AND GLOBAL MARKETS, INCLUDING AN OVERVIEW OF REGIONAL AND INTERNATIONAL TRADE AGREEMENTS. THESE CHAPTERS ARE LARGELY DEVOTED TO MACRO-ENVIRONMENTAL FORCES THAT FIRMS AND MANAGERS MUST BE AWARE OF WHEN CONDUCTING BUSINESS INTERNATIONALLY. IN ORDER TO BE SUCCESSFUL, THE MARKETER MUST ADAPT TO FOREIGN ENVIRONMENTS AND MUST BE ABLE TO RESOLVE CONFLICTS STEMMING FROM DIFFERENCES IN CULTURAL, ECONOMIC, POLITICAL, AND LEGAL FACTORS.

CHAPTER ONE

THE GLOBAL MARKETING IMPERATIVE

The International MARKETPLACE

1.1

A New Outlook for Markets, Marketers, and Marketing

Financial turmoil and market uncertainty set new directions for businesses and people around the world. There maybe many new goals and expectations, but there also will be competing values when it comes to their implementation.

It is crucial to reconcile the apparent conflict between responsible economic behavior of citizens and the responsible government leadership of an economy. For example, in many countries the message of "save more," has been a shining beacon for economic stability. Yet it is much more difficult to emphasize the necessarily complementary message of "spend less." Active consumer expenditures are important to keep the economy going. Rapid and sudden declines in an industry—say, in automotive sales—due to too much consumer caution, carries major displacement disadvantages. One also needs to prevent individuals and society from becoming cheap. Greater selectivity based on quality should be a key focus of enlightened self interest.

More government emphasis also means less reliance on market forces. But if one does not use market signals, there needs to be the development of leading indicators to help guide decision-making. New and different non-market criteria encourage the productivity of think tanks, government offices and universities, and provide for greater flexibility. At the same time, there will be an increase in policy errors, performance uncertainty, and outcome disputes.

Less faith in free markets affects currency values and exchange rates. Government intervention instead of market adjustment is often quick and severe. Such extraterritorial application of policy goals can be a new obstacle for foreign trade and investment relations and perhaps even provide for less market access.

There are new thoughts going beyond the traditional concepts of risk, competition, profit, and private property, issues which form the core dimensions of capitalism. For example, the risk/reward relationship may become less central to decision-making. A reduction in incentives for competition may lead to more harmony but perhaps also reduce the speed of innovation. More creative thinking about property rights will provide for more flexibility in the development of medications but may precipitate the migration of pharmaceutical firms. Less private ownership of the means of production may promote social goals but reduce their flexibility and institute the primacy of government objectives over voluntary resource allocation.

Revising the mechanics of a traditional pinball machine may be a useful analogy: Currently, when a player achieves a high score in competition, the machine issues that player an extra ball—allowing the winner to further extend his lead. Now consider what would happen if, instead, the player who has fallen behind receives the extra ball in order to catch up with leader. Such a shift is not necessarily uninteresting, but it produces very different rules and outcomes of the game.

There are also changed expectations for higher standards of virtue, vision, and veracity by individuals, corporations, and government in order to maintain faith and confidence. Such values cannot be created overnight but rather require gradual shifts in perspectives and cultures. Perhaps here is a substantial and new opportunity for business education to blaze new trails.

Policy priorities may be new, and economic emphasis may shift, but market forces will remain important. They need to be guided by global leadership and not sidetracked by narrow concerns and self interest which often work like barnacles and algae on the hull of a ship.

They slow down movement, reduce flexibility, and make action more difficult. Market forces need the support of marketers with personal inner strength, skills, and morality. These qualities are essential for long-term leadership for the common good. They offer the freedom of almost unlimited growth potential.

SOURCES: M. R. Czinkota, "Competing Economic Aspiration," *The Korea Times,* Nov. 9, 2008; M. R. Czinkota and I. A. Ronkainen, "Trends and Indications in International Business: A Delhi approach," *Management International Review,* Spring 2009.

You are about to begin an exciting, important, and necessary task: the exploration of international marketing. International marketing is exciting because it combines the science and the art of business with many other disciplines. Economics, anthropology, cultural studies, geography, history, languages, jurisprudence, statistics, demographics, and many other fields combine to help you explore the global market. Different business environments will stimulate your intellectual curiosity, which will enable you to absorb and understand new phenomena. International marketing has been compared by many who have been active in the field to the task of mountain climbing: challenging, arduous, and exhilarating.

International marketing is important because the world has become globalized. Increasingly, we all are living up to the claim of the Greek philosopher Socrates, who stated, "I am a citizen, not of Athens or Greece, but of the world." International marketing takes place all around us every day, has a major effect on our lives, and offers new opportunities and challenges. After reading through this book and observing international marketing phenomena, you will see what happens, understand what happens, and, at some time in the future, perhaps even make it happen. All of this is much better than to stand by and wonder what happened.

International marketing is necessary because, from a national standpoint, economic isolationism has become impossible. Failure to participate in the global marketplace assures a nation of declining economic capability and its citizens of a decrease in their standard of living. Successful international marketing, however, holds the promise of an improved quality of life, a better society, and more efficient business transactions, *The International Marketplace 1.1* highlights how global market forces and marketers need to adjust to a changing environment, but also clarifies how market forces and marketers are the critical catalysts between individuals, businesses, and society.

This chapter is designed to increase your awareness of what international marketing is about. It describes current levels of world trade activities, projects future developments, and discusses the repercussions on countries, institutions, and individuals worldwide. Both the opportunities and the threats that spring from the global marketplace are highlighted, and the need for an international "marketing" approach on the part of individuals and institutions is emphasized.

This chapter ends with an explanation of the major organizational thrust of this book, which is a differentiation between the beginning internationalist and the multinational corporation. This theme ties the book together by taking into account the concerns, capabilities, and goals of firms that will differ widely based on their level of international expertise, resources, and involvement. The approach to international marketing taken here will therefore permit you to understand the entire range of international activities and allow you easily to transfer your acquired knowledge into practice.

What International Marketing Is

In brief, **international marketing** consists of the activity, institutions, and processes across national borders that create, communicate, deliver, and exchange offerings that have value for stakeholders and society. International marketing has forms ranging from export–import trade to licensing, joint ventures, wholly owned subsidiaries, turnkey operations, and management contracts.

As this definition indicates, international marketing very much retains the basic marketing tenets of "value" and "exchange." There is also the focus on stakeholders and society whose present positions are to be improved. The fact that a transaction takes place across national borders highlights the difference between domestic and international marketing. The international marketer is subject to a new set of macroenvironmental factors, to different constraints, and to quite frequent conflicts resulting from different laws, cultures, and societies. The basic principles of marketing still apply, but their applications, complexity, and intensity may vary substantially. It is in the international marketing field where one can observe most closely the role of marketing as a key agent of societal change and as a key instrument for the development of societally responsive business strategy. When we look, for example, at the emerging market economies of China and Russia, we can see the many new challenges confronting international marketing. How does the marketing concept fit into these societies? How can marketing contribute to economic development and the improvement of society? How should distribution systems be organized? How should the price mechanism work? Similarly, in the areas of social responsibility and ethics, the international marketer is faced with a multicultural environment of differing expectations and often inconsistent legal systems when it comes to monitoring environmental pollution, maintaining safe working conditions, copying technology or trademarks, or paying bribes.[1] In addition, the long-term repercussions of marketing actions need to be understood and evaluated in terms of their societal impact, using not just today's criteria, but considering also the long term retrospective of future affected parties. These are just a few of the issues that the international marketer needs to address. The capability to master these challenges successfully affords a company the potential for new opportunities and high rewards. *The International Marketplace 1.2* shows how Sony Ericsson uses its leadership in the green marketing field to achieve business success.

The emphasis on stakeholders and society at large indicates the need for the marketer to look beyond narrow self-interest and to understand that there are many parties touched by

The International MARKETPLACE

ENVIRONMENT & SUSTAINABILITY

1.2

Environment and Sustainability: An Environmental Warranty

Environmental concerns have become a global phenomenon. Air pollution, deforestation, and many other environmental problems are now of concern to many. Consumers are buying more biodegradable products even if they are more expensive. Going green is vogue.

Many corporations have chosen to support environmentally-minded projects. They also attempt to do business with minimal detrimental impact on the natural environment. Going green is a fashionable tool. With green marketing, companies can become more socially responsible, follow government regulations, and respond to changing consumer preferences.

Sony Ericsson has launched the idea of an environmental warranty which basically says " . . . when any Sony Ericsson product is taken to a designated collection point, Sony Ericsson will recycle this product in an environmentally friendly way."

What is unique about this particular program is that the initiative is an international attempt. Phones can be purchased in any part of the world and dropped off at any collection point. Participating countries range from India, Taiwan, Singapore, Mexico, USA, China, and Thailand. Sony Ericsson has already established collection points in 500 different areas. Convenience is a key selling point.

Sony Ericsson was recognized by Greenpeace in 2008 for its ban of hazardous chemicals in its products. In 2007, the company sold 100 million phones. Many of its sales can be attributed to the innovative and diverse marketing strategy it uses. The director of corporate responsibility, Elaine Weidman says: "Around the globe, top managers and CEOs are talking about climate issues. Five years ago, this wasn't the case. There is increased awareness of social and environmental issues, and they are closely connected to financial performance."

SONY ERICSSON EMPHASIZES "GREEN" PRACTICES IN ITS ADVERTISING.

SOURCES: **http://www.ericsson.com/solutions/news/2007/q4/20071016_carbon.shtml**
Ericsson ranks high in the Carbon Disclosure Project's latest index (press release)
http://biz.thestar.com.my/news/story.asp?file=/2008/10/3/business/2176458&sec=business

marketing. Willing or unwilling, they all participate in the outcome of the marketing effort and their interests must be considered.

International marketing also focuses on the need to create, communicate, and deliver value internationally. These dimensions indicate that marketing internationally is an activity that needs to be pursued, often aggressively. Those who do not participate in the transactions are still exposed to international marketing and subject to its changing influences. The international marketer is part of the exchange and recognizes the constantly changing nature of transactions. This need for adjustment, for comprehending change, and, in spite of it all, for successfully delivering value highlights the fact that international marketing is as much art as science.

To achieve success in the art of international marketing, it is necessary to be firmly grounded in its scientific aspects. Only then will individual consumers, policymakers, and business executives be able to incorporate international marketing considerations into their thinking and planning. Only then will they be able to consider international issues and repercussions and make decisions based on answers to questions such as:

- Does my market have borders?
- Should I obtain my supplies domestically or from abroad?
- What marketing adjustments are or will be necessary?
- What threats from global competition should I expect?
- How can I work with these threats to turn them into opportunities?
- What are my strategic global alternatives?

If all these issues are integrated into each decision made by individuals and by firms, international markets can become a source of growth, profit, needs satisfaction, and quality of life that would not have existed for them had they limited themselves to domestic activities. The purpose of this book is to aid in this decision process.

The Importance of World Trade

World trade has assumed an importance heretofore unknown to the global community. In past centuries, trade was conducted internationally but never before did it have the broad and simultaneous impact on nations, firms, and individuals that it has today. Within five years alone, world trade in merchandise has expanded from $6.2 trillion in 2000 to over $15.1 trillion in 2008. World trade in services has expanded from $1.5 trillion to $3.3 trillion in the same period of time. That represents a growth of more than 100 percent for trade in both merchandise and services![2] Such economic growth is exceptional, particularly since, as Exhibit 1.1 shows, global growth of trade has typically outperformed the growth of domestic economies in the past few decades. Many countries and firms have found it highly desirable to become major participants in international marketing.

The Iron Curtain has disintegrated, offering a vast array of new marketing opportunities—albeit amid uncertainty. Firms invest on a global scale, with the result that entire industries shift their locations. International specialization and cross-sourcing have made production much more efficient. New technologies have changed the way we do business, allowing

Exhibit 1.1

Growth of World Output in Trade (1997–2008)

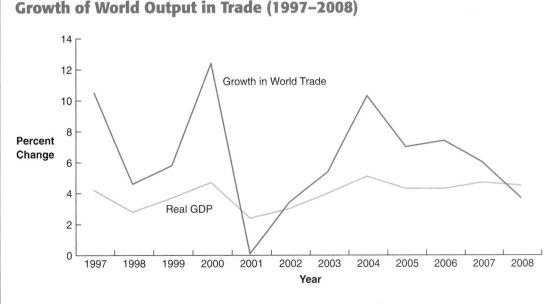

SOURCE: *International Monetary Fund, World Economic Outlook 2008, Statistical Appendix.*

us to both supply and receive products from across the world by using the Internet. As a result, consumers, union leaders, policymakers, and sometimes even the firms themselves are finding it increasingly difficult to define where a particular product has been made. There are trading blocs such as the European Union in Europe, NAFTA in North America, Mercosur in Latin America, and ASEAN in Asia. These blocs encourage trade relations between their members, but, through their rules and standards, they also affect the trade and investment flows of nonmember countries.

Individuals and firms have come to recognize that they are competing not only domestically but also globally. World trade has given rise to global linkages of markets, technology, and living standards that were previously unknown and unanticipated. At the same time, it has deeply affected domestic policy-making and has often resulted in the emergence of totally new opportunities as well as threats to firms and individuals. *The International Marketplace 1.3* provides an example.

Global Linkages

World trade has forged a network of global linkages that bind us all—countries, institutions, and individuals—much more closely than ever before. These linkages were first widely recognized during the worldwide oil crisis of 1970, but they continue to increase. A drought in Brazil and its effect on coffee production and prices is felt around the world. The 2004 tsunami in the Indian Ocean resulted in massive casualties in South Asia, caused worldwide disruptions in manufacturing and trade, and devastated the tourism industry of many countries. For example, in the Maldives, which are located more than 2,500 kilometers

---

The International
MARKETPLACE
1.3

Outsourcing: The End or the Beginning?

The global financial crisis of 2008 brought down corporations in developing and developed countries. In Gurgaon, India, the entrepreneur Manoj Malhotra worries a lot about whether his once thriving outsourcing company will be able to handle the financial crisis. Will American and Western European companies still want to do business with him? The financial crisis that started in America could cause him a crisis at his home thousands of mile away.

Since the 1980s, corporations in developed nations have been sending entire business functions and management roles to developing countries. Companies have been outsourcing by using efficient call centers for technical support, information technology, and software support. Multinational companies cut costs while developing countries benefit from an upsurge in jobs and income. In light of the financial crisis the question is whether or not outsourcing will be affected. Most call centers depended on a significant amount of business from former financial giants that have had to significantly scale back. Other companies, like Lehman Brothers, are no longer in existence. Without their biggest clients, how

can outsourcing firms continue to thrive? Indians like Malhotra may have a bitter laugh at their common joke: "when America sneezes, [our] industry will catch a cold here in India."

However, other perspectives suggest different conclusions. Wall Street now has a serious need to cut costs. Financial services have to resort to more offshore outsourcing in order to do their budgeting efficiently. In 2008, faith in the US dollar strengthened due to the world-wide credit crunch. A strong US dollar makes it difficult to hire US labor and encourages the usage of international labor.

While most outsourcing originally took place in India and China, wages in these two countries are beginning to rise. There is now a rapid increase in the usage of Eastern European and Southeast Asian labor. Many of the new players have very educated populations. Ironically, Malhotra's biggest concern then may be losing business to the East rather than losing business from the West.

SOURCES: **http://www.pcworld.com/businesscenter/ article/151517/india_outsource_will_be_hit_by_us_ financial_crisis.html; http://www.forbes.com/fdc/welcome_ mjx.shtml; http://www.washingtonpost.com/wp-dyn/ content/article/2008/10/AR25/2008102501861.html**

(1.6 kilometers = 1 mile) from the quake's epicenter, tourism is the largest industry, contributing 28 percent of its GDP of $1.59 billion.[3] The distant quake caused a tsunami (large ocean wave) which caused $300 million in property damage. The damage also resulted in a 3.6% contraction of GDP.[4] The combined effects of hurricanes Katrina and Rita on the Gulf Coast of the United States in the fall of 2005 caused the production loss of nearly 75 million barrels of oil, or 13.6 percent of the annual oil production in the Gulf of Mexico. The result was a spike in the price of gasoline worldwide, which raised the transportation costs for countless industries and businesses.[5] The financial crisis of 2008 has demonstrated how these linkages have caused shortcoming in funds, credits, and loans that affect the entire global economy. Even countries

DISASTER CAN HAVE DRAMATIC EFFECTS ON SUPPLY AND DEMAND. THE COMBINED EFFECTS OF HURRICANES KATRINA AND RITA ON THE GULF COAST LED TO OIL PRODUCTION LOSSES AND A SPIKE IN GASOLINE PRICES. THE PICTURED OIL TANKS WERE DAMAGED BY KATRINA.

that considered themselves as distanced and independent from any particular economic event in far away countries found, to their unexpected chagrin, that their firms, budgets, and plans were deeply affected.

These linkages have also become more intense on an individual level. Communication has built new international bridges, be it through music or international programs transmitted by CNN, BBC, Al Arabiya, and other networks. New products have attained international appeal and encouraged similar activities around the world—where many of us wear jeans, dance to the same music on our iPods, and eat kebobs, curry, and sushi. Transportation linkages let individuals from different countries see and meet each other with unprecedented ease. Common cultural pressures result in similar social phenomena and behavior—for example, more dual-income families are emerging around the world, which leads to more frequent, but also more stressful, shopping.[6]

World trade is also bringing about a global reorientation of corporate processes, which opens up entirely new horizons. Never before has it been so easy to gather, manipulate, analyze, and disseminate information—but never before has the pressure been so great to do so. Ongoing global technological innovation in marketing has direct effects on the efficiency and effectiveness of all business activities. Products can be produced more quickly, obtained less expensively from sources around the world, distributed at lower cost, and customized to meet diverse clients' needs. As an example, only a decade ago, it would have been thought impossible for a firm to produce parts for a car in more than one country, assemble the car in yet another country, and sell it in still other nations. Today, such global investment strategies coupled with production and distribution sharing are becoming a matter of routine. Of course, as *The International Marketplace 1.3* explains, these changes increase the level of global competition, which in turn increases the challenge of staying in a leadership position.

Advances in technology also allow firms to separate their activities by content and context. Firms can operate in a "market space" rather than a marketplace[7] by keeping the content while changing the context of a transaction. For example, a newspaper can be distributed online globally rather than house-to-house on paper, thereby allowing outreach to entirely new customer groups.

The level of global investment is at an unprecedented high. The shifts in financial flows have had major effects. They have resulted in the buildup of international debt by governments, affected the international value of currencies, provided foreign capital for firms, and triggered major foreign direct-investment activities. Societies can grow concerned about these shifts. For example, in the United States, the Patriot Act defines critical infrastructure as systems and assets so vital that any breakdown in them "would have a debilitating impact on security, national economic security, national public health, or safety." A resulting national strategy developed for the protection of such critical infrastructure eleven sectors: agriculture and food, water, public health, emergency services, defense industrial bases, telecommunications, energy, transportation, banking and finance, chemical industry and hazardous material, and postal services and shipping. The "key assets" identified in the report are: national monuments and icons, nuclear power plants, dams, government facilities, and commercial key assets.[8] The fact that there is increasing foreign investment in such key assets indicates that nations, firms, and people grow more and more dependent on one another.

This interdependence, however, is not stable. On almost a daily basis, realignments taking place on both micro and macro levels make past trade orientations at least partially obsolete. For example, for the first 200 years of its history, the United States looked to Europe for markets and sources of supply. Today, U.S. two-way trade with Asia far outpaces U.S. trade with Europe. The participants in international marketing also are changing their roles. For example, the International Monetary Fund (IMF) was founded in 1944 to help restructure impoverished economies. More recently, however, the fund has been assisting nations that used to be categorized as "wealthy," such as Iceland. It appears to become increasingly difficult to differentiate between "rich" and "poor": For example, based on its foreign currency reserves of $2 trillion, China easily qualifies for the upper echelons of the wealthy countries. However, the nation's GDP per capita would still let it be classified as a developing nation.

Not only is the environment changing, but the pace of change is accelerating as well. Atari's Pong was first introduced in the early 1980s; today, action games and movies are made with computerized humans. The first office computers emerged in the mid-1980s; today, home computers have become commonplace. E-mail was introduced to a mass market only in the 1990s; today, many college students hardly ever send personal notes using a stamp and envelope.[9]

These changes and the speed with which they come about significantly affect countries, corporations, and individuals. One change is the role participants play. For example, the United States accounted for nearly 25 percent of world merchandise exports in the 1950s, but by 2005 this share had declined to less than half of that. Also, the way countries participate in world trade is shifting. In the past two decades the role of primary commodities in international trade has dropped precipitously, while the importance of manufactured goods has increased. Exhibit 1.2 shows how substantial the growth rates for export trade have been. Of course, one needs to consider the base from which this growth has taken place. Here the European Union, China, and the United States are the consistent leaders. Most important, the growth in the overall volume and value of both merchandise and services trade has had a major impact on firms, countries, and individuals.

Domestic Policy Repercussions

The effects of closer global linkages on the economics of countries have been dramatic. Policymakers have increasingly come to recognize that it is very difficult to isolate domestic economic activity from international market events. Decisions that once were clearly in the domestic purview have now become subject to revision by influences from abroad, and domestic policy measures are often canceled out or counteracted by the activities of global market forces.

A lowering of interest rates domestically may make consumers happy or may be politically wise, but it quickly becomes unsustainable if it results in a major outflow of funds to countries that offer higher interest rates. Agricultural and farm policies, which historically have been strictly domestic issues, are suddenly thrust into the international realm. Any policy consideration must now be seen in light of international repercussions due to influences from global trade and investment.

To some extent, the economic world as we knew it has been turned upside down. For example, trade flows traditionally have been used to determine currency flows and therefore the level of the exchange rate. In the more recent past, **currency flows** took on a life of their own. Independent of trade, they set exchange rates, which are the values of currencies relative to each other. These **exchange rates** in turn have now begun to determine the level of trade. Governments that wish to counteract these developments with monetary policies

Exhibit **1.2**

Growth in Exports 2000–2008

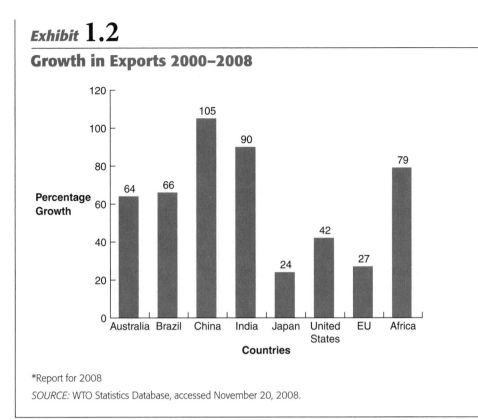

*Report for 2008

SOURCE: WTO Statistics Database, accessed November 20, 2008.

find that currency flows outnumber trade flows by 100 to 1. Also, private-sector financial flows vastly exceed the financial flows that can be marshaled by governments, even when acting in concert. Major economic change can be swift and harsh, and its cause may be difficult to identify. An analogy might consist of persons traveling in a giant plastic bubble filled with vital air. Suddenly the bubble begins to shrink, the air escapes, but the passengers don't find the rupture, nor are they able to replenish the air sufficiently. Rash reaction may lead to mistakes and unintended consequences, but no reaction will lead to a hard landing.

Constant rapid technological change and vast advances in communication permit firms and countries to quickly emulate innovation and counteract carefully designed plans. As a result, governments are often powerless to implement effective policy measures, even when they know what to do.

Policymakers therefore find themselves with increasing responsibilities yet with fewer and less effective tools to carry out these responsibilities. At the same time that more parts of a domestic economy are vulnerable to international shifts and changes, these parts are becoming less controllable. The global market imposes increasingly tight limits on national economic regulation and sovereignty.

To regain some of their power to influence events, policymakers have sought to restrict the impact of global trade and financial flows by erecting barriers, charging tariffs, designing quotas, and implementing other import regulations. How ever, these measures too have been restrained by international agreements that regulate trade restrictions, particularly through the World Trade Organization (WTO) (**http://www.wto.org**). Global trade has therefore changed many previously held notions about nation-state sovereignty and extraterritoriality. The same interdependence that has made us more affluent has also left us more vulnerable. Be cause this vulnerability is spread out over all major trading nations, however, some have credited international marketing with being a pillar of international peace. Clearly, closer economic relations can result in many positive effects. At the same time, however, interdependence brings with it risks, such as dislocations of people and economic resources and a decrease in a nation's capability to do things its own way. Given the ease—and sometimes the desirability—of blaming a foreign rather than a domestic culprit for economic failure, it may well also be a key task for the international marketer to stimulate societal acceptance of the long-term benefits of interdependence.

Opportunities and Challenges in International Marketing

To prosper in a world of abrupt changes and discontinuities, of newly emerging forces and dangers, of unforeseen influences from abroad, firms need to prepare themselves and develop active responses. New strategies need to be envisioned, new plans need to be made, and the way of doing business needs to be changed. The way to obtain and retain leadership, economically, politically, or morally, is—as the examples of Rome, Constantinople, and London have amply demonstrated—not through passivity but rather through a continuous, alert adaptation to the changing world environment. To help a country remain a player in the world economy, governments, firms, and individuals need to respond aggressively with innovation, process improvements, and creativity.[10]

The growth of global business activities offers increased opportunities. International activities can be crucial to a firm's survival and growth. By transferring knowledge around the globe, an international firm can build and strengthen its competitive position. Firms that heavily depend on long production runs can expand their activities far beyond their domestic markets and benefit from reaching many more customers. Market saturation can be avoided by lengthening or rejuvenating product life cycles in other countries. Production sites once were inflexible, but now plants can be shifted from one country to another and suppliers can be found on every continent. Cooperative agreements can be formed that enable all parties to bring their major strengths to the table and emerge with better products, services, and ideas than they could produce on their own. In addition, research has found that multinational corporations face a lower risk of insolvency and pay higher wages than do domestic companies.[11] For example, in the United States, jobs supported by goods exports pay 13–16 percent above the average wage.[12] At the same time, international marketing enables consumers all over the world to find greater varieties of products at lower prices and to improve their lifestyles and comfort.[13]

International opportunities require careful exploration. What is needed is an awareness of global developments, an understanding of their meaning, and a development of capabilities to adjust to change. Firms must adapt to the international market if they are to be successful.

One key facet of the marketing concept is adaptation to the environment, particularly the market. Even though many executives understand the need for such an adaptation in their domestic market, they often believe that international customers are just like the ones the firm deals with at home. It is here that many firms commit grave mistakes that lead to inefficiency, lack of consumer acceptance, and sometimes even corporate failure. As *The International Marketplace 1.4* explains, there are quite substantial differences in this world between consumer groups.

Firms increasingly understand that many of the key difficulties encountered in doing business internationally are marketing problems. Judging by corporate needs, a background in international marketing is highly desirable for business students seeking employment, not only for today but also for long-term career plans.

Many firms do not participate in the global market. Often, managers believe that international marketing should only be carried out by large multinational corporations. It is true that there are some very large players from many countries active in the world market. But smaller firms are major players, too. For example, 50 percent of German exports are created by firms with 19 or fewer employees.[14] Just over 97.3 percent of U.S. exporters are small and medium-sized enterprises, with two-thirds of U.S. exporters having less than 20 employees.[15] Increasingly we find smaller firms, particularly in the computer and telecommunications industries, that are born global, since they achieve a worldwide presence within a very short time.[16]

Those firms and industries that are not participating in the world market have to recognize that in today's trade environment, isolation has become impossible. Willing or unwilling, firms are becoming participants in global business affairs. Even if not by choice, most firms and individuals are affected directly or indirectly by economic and political developments that occur in the international marketplace. Those firms that refuse to participate are relegated to react to the global marketplace and therefore are unprepared for harsh competition from abroad.

The International
MARKETPLACE

1.4

Global Consumers in the New Millennium

One of the drives behind the move toward global marketing strategies has been the notion that consumer needs are becoming more alike around the world. Yet drastic differences in the development of various regions of the world remain, and they are bound to continue into the new century.

Such differences warrant substantial differentiation in marketing tactics and strategies. Here are just a few examples of what a baby in the Western world and a baby in the less-developed world may face upon birth.

The Western Baby:

- In Switzerland she will live to the age of 84, while he will live to the age of 79.
- In the Netherlands there is a 100 percent chance that she will use adequate sanitation.
- In the United States her family's annual income will likely be around $36,110.

- In Canada, he will share one square mile with eight other people.
- In Italy she will be living in a city, as 68 percent of the population does.

The Baby in the Lesser-Developed World:

- In Sierra Leone she will live to the age of 49, while he will live to the age of 48.
- In Niger there is a 20 percent chance that she will use adequate sanitation.
- In Uganda her family's annual income is likely to be about $1.360.
- In China he will share one square km with 352 other people.
- In India she will be living in a rural area, as 72 percent of the population does.

SOURCE: **www.prb.org** Publication Reference Bureau. September 29, 2008.

Some industries have recognized the need for international adjustments. Farmers understand the need for high productivity in light of stiff international competition. Computer makers, and firms in other technologically advanced industries, have learned to forge global relationships to stay in the race. Firms in the steel, textile, and leather sectors have shifted production, and perhaps even adjusted their core business, in response to overwhelming onslaughts from abroad. Other industries in some countries have been caught unaware and have been unable to adjust. The result is the extinction of firms or entire industries, such as VCRs in the United States and coal mining and steel smelting in other countries.

The Goals of This Book

This book aims to make you a better, more successful participant in the international marketplace by providing information about what is going on in international markets and by helping you to translate knowledge into successful business transactions. By learning about both theory and practice, you can obtain a good conceptual understanding of the field of international marketing as well as become firmly grounded in the realities of the global marketplace. Therefore, this book approaches international marketing in the way the manager of a firm does, reflecting different levels of international involvement and the importance of business–government relations.

Firms differ widely in their international activities and needs, depending on their level of experience, resources, and capabilities. For the firm that is just beginning to enter the global market, the level of knowledge about international complexities is low, the demand on time is high, expectations about success are uncertain, and the international environment is often inflexible. Conversely, for a multinational firm that is globally oriented and employs thousands of people on each continent, much more leeway exists in terms of resource availability, experience, and information. In addition, the multinational firm has the option of responding

International Trade as a Percentage of Gross Domestic Product

SOURCE: Based on **http://www.worldbank.org/** accessed April 16, 2009.

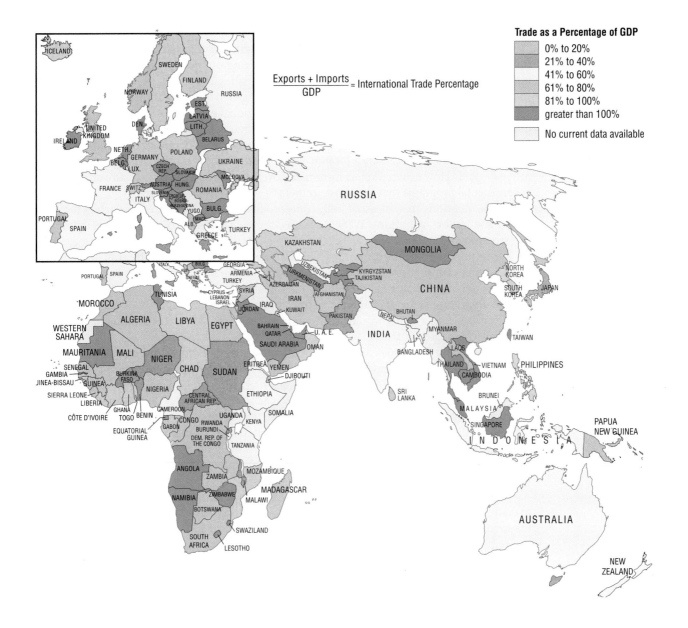

Trade as a Percentage of GDP

0% to 20%
21% to 40%
41% to 60%
61% to 80%
81% to 100%
greater than 100%

No current data available

$$\frac{\text{Exports} + \text{Imports}}{\text{GDP}} = \text{International Trade Percentage}$$

creatively to the environment by shifting resources or even shaping the environment itself. For example, the heads of large corporations have access to government ministers to plead their case for a change in policy, an alternative that is rarely afforded to smaller firms.

To become a large international corporation, however, a firm usually has to start out small. Similarly, to direct far-flung global operations, managers first have to learn the basics. The structure of this text reflects this reality by presenting initially a perspective of the business environment, which covers national marketing and policy issues and their cultural, economic, financial, political, and legal dimensions.

Subsequently, the book discusses in detail the beginning internationalization of the firm. The emphasis is on the needs of those who are starting out and the operational questions that are crucial to success. Some basic yet essential issues addressed are: What is the difference between domestic and international marketing? Does the applicability of marketing principles change when they are transferred to the global environment? How do marketers find out whether there is a market for a product abroad without spending a fortune in time and money on research? How can the firm promote its products in foreign markets? How do marketers find and evaluate a foreign distributor, and how do they make sure that their firm gets paid? How can marketers minimize government red tape yet take advantage of any governmental programs that are of use to them?

These questions are addressed both conceptually and empirically, with a strong focus on export and import operations. We will see how the international com mitment is developed and strengthened within the firm.

Once these important dimensions have been covered, we make the transition to the multinational corporation. The focus is now on the transnational allocation of resources, the coordination of multinational marketing activities, and the attainment of global synergism. Finally, emerging issues of challenge to both policy makers and multinational firms, such as countertrade, marketing to economies in transition, and the future outlook of the global market, are discussed.

All the marketing issues are considered in relation to national policies so as to familiarize you with the divergent forces at play in the global market. Governments' increased awareness of and involvement with international marketing require managers to be aware of the role of governments and also to be able to work with them in order to attain marketing goals. Therefore, the continued references in the text to business–government interaction demonstrate a vital link in the development of international marketing strategy. In addition, we give full play to the increased ability of firms to communicate with a global market. Therefore, we develop and offer, for firms both small and large, our ideas and strategies for viable participation in electronic commerce.

We expect that this gradual approach to international marketing will permit you not only to master another academic subject, but also to become well versed in both the operational and the strategic aspects of the field. The result should be a better understanding of how the global market works and the capability to participate in the international marketing imperative.

Summary

Over the last few decades, international trade in merchandise has expanded at astounding rates to reach over $15.1 trillion in 2008. In addition, trade in services has grown at particularly high rates within the last decade to reach almost $3.3 trillion in 2008. As a result, nations are much more affected by international business than in the past. Global linkages have made possible investment strategies and marketing alternatives that offer tremendous opportunities. Yet these changes and the speed of change also can represent threats to nations and firms.

On the policy front, decision makers have come to realize that it is very difficult to isolate domestic economic activity from international market events. Factors such as currency exchange rates, financial flows, and foreign economic actions increasingly render the policymaker powerless to implement a domestic agenda. International interdependence, which has contributed to greater affluence, has also increased our vulnerability.

Both firms and individuals are greatly affected by international trade. Whether willing or not, they are participating in global business affairs. Entire industries have been threatened in their survival as a result of international trade flows and have either adjusted to new market realities or left the market. Some individuals have lost their workplace and experienced reduced salaries. At the same time, global business changes have increased the opportunities available. Firms can now reach many more customers, product life cycles have been lengthened, sourcing policies have become variable, new jobs have been created, and consumers all over the world can find greater varieties of products at lower prices.

To benefit from the opportunities and deal with the adversities of international trade, business needs to adopt the international marketing concept. The new set of macroenvironmental factors has to be under stood and responded to in order to let international markets become a source of growth, profit, and needs satisfaction.

Key Terms

international marketing
global linkages

currency flows
exchange rates

Questions for Discussion

1. What are the recent trends in world trade? Will expansion of world trade in the future follow these trends?

2. Does increased world trade mean increased risk?

3. What impact do global linkages have on firms and consumers?

4. Can you think of examples of international marketing contributing to world peace?

5. Describe some opportunities and challenges in international marketing created by new advances in information technology.

Internet Exercises

1. Using World Trade Organization data (http://www.wto.org), identify the following: (a) the top ten exporting and importing countries in world merchandise trade and (b) the top ten exporting and importing countries of commercial services.

2. Please compare the top ten exporting countries to each other. Highlight similarities and differences, considering factors such as geographic location, population, Gross Domestic Product, and inflation. Financial indicators are available online from the World Bank, World Trade Organization, and International Monetary Fund.

Recommended Readings

Bhagwati, Jagdish. *In Defense of Globalization.* Oxford: Oxford University Press, 2008.

Friedman, Thomas. *Hot, Flat, and Crowded.* New York: Farrar, Strauss, Giroux, 2008.

Morris, Charles. *The Trillion Dollar Meltdown.* New York: Public Affairs, 2008.

Soros, George. *The New Paradigm for Financial Markets: the Credit Crisis of 2008 and what it means.* New York, Public Affairs, 2008.

Stiglitz, Joseph E. *Making Globalization Work.* New York: W.W. Norton, 2008.

BASICS OF MARKETING

This appendix provides a summary of the basic concepts in marketing for the reader who wishes to review them before applying them to international marketing. The American Marketing Association defines **marketing** as "the activity, set of institutions, and processes for creating, communicating, delivering, and exchanging offerings that have value for customers, clients, partners, and society at large."[1]

It is useful to focus on the definition's components to fully understand its meaning. Marketing as an *activity* indicates the proactive nature of the discipline, with a specific thrust that gives direction to its user. *Sets of institutions and processes* highlights that there are inside and outside participants in the marketing effort and that the activity goes beyond a single transaction. *Creating, communicating, and delivering* emphasizes that the marketing discipline takes leadership in its activities from beginning to end and that the art and the practical implementation dimensions of the discipline are crucial in their simultaneity. The fact that there are an "exchange" and "offerings" involved is a crucial dimension setting marketing apart from other disciplines and other forms of resource acquisition. Each party gives up something of value and receives something of equal (or even perceived higher) value. It is important to recognize the powerful effect of the "offering," which highlights the voluntary nature of the exchange and signifies the existence of freedom of choice. Carrying out the exchange is then designed to achieve satisfaction with the transaction.

Value for customers, clients, partners, and society at large presents the core focus of marketing. Physicians have as their overriding principle the Hippocratic oath "do no harm." Marketers should consider any action under the prism of "are my stakeholders better off"? There is both a dyadic and plurilateral (many sided) aspect to marketing. Is an individual interaction between, say, the firm and its customers? Of course, but there are also the relationships among the customers themselves, and the consequences of the marketing effort for other parties, such as suppliers, distributors, investors, or family members, who can play the role of both clients and partners. All of these form part of a network that is defined by the interactions and relationships between its members and creates the society in which we live.

Since marketers will be major influencers on this relationship they need to take into account the repercussions that their actions are likely to have on these linkages.

Relationships are key, since they are indicative of the fact that actions build upon each other and are instrumental in forging bonds and inflaming disagreements. The marketer therefore cannot see any product or effort as an isolated event. Rather it has to be understood as a component of an entire series of steps that define the bridge between entities. Using this perspective, marketing has a very broad mission. The discipline is not narrowly confined to relationships that emerge when money is exchanged for goods. Rather, marketing has its application just as well when there is performance of a service (say, coaching Little League or fundraising for a charity) in exchange for obtaining a good feeling and a sense of fulfillment.

The fact that marketing develops and adds value is critical. Marketing needs to be seen, after all, in the context of a planned and purposeful activity. It seeks a definite, favorable outcome for the participants of the marketing pursuit. Again, it is important to recognize that this benefit need not be seen strictly in terms of mammon. Rather, the organization itself is the one that defines what it determines to be beneficial. Therefore, there is ample room for both macro benefits, such as "more positive images of our country," as well as micro benefits, such as "increase desire to participate in project," in addition to the business benefits customarily seen to be in the purview of organizations. As a result, marketing finds a full range of applicability in not-for-profit areas, such as medicine, the arts, or government areas typically wrongfully excluded from the need for marketing. The various stakeholders are also indicative of this breadth of marketing in that it gives recognition to others who have an interest in either the process or the outcome of marketing activities.

As you can see, this definition packs a lot of punch, and lets marketing make a major contribution to the welfare of individuals and organizations. Nevertheless, based on our view of marketing, we will expand this definition on several dimensions. First, we believe that the terms *create*, *deliver*, and *value* overemphasize transactions as one-time events. Therefore, we add the terms *maintain* and *value stream* to highlight the long-term nature of marketing that encourages customers to continue to come back. We also believe that, as the scope of marketing is broadened, societal goals need to be added to individuals and organizations, properly reflecting the overarching reach and responsibility of marketing as a social change agent that responds to and develops social concerns about the environment, technology, and ethics. Equally important is the need to specifically broaden our marketing understanding beyond national borders. Today, sourcing and supply linkages exist around the globe, competition emerges from all corners of the earth, and marketing opportunities evolve worldwide. As a result, many crucial dimensions of marketing need to be reevaluated and adapted in a global context.

Based on these considerations, our expanded definition of marketing is "an organizational function and a set of processes for creating, communicating, delivering, and maintaining value streams to consumers and for managing customer relationships in ways that benefit the organization, its stakeholder, and society in the context of a global environment."[2]

The concepts of satisfaction and exchange are at the core of marketing. For an exchange to take place, two or more parties must come together in person, through the mail, or through technology, and they must communicate and deliver things of perceived value. Potential customers should be perceived as information seekers who evaluate marketers' efforts in terms of their own drives and needs. When the offering is consistent with their needs, they tend to choose the product; if it is not, they choose other alternatives. A key task of the marketer is to recognize the ever-changing nature of needs and wants. Increasingly, the goal of marketing has been expanded from sensing, serving, and satisfying individual customers to taking into consideration the long-term interests of society.

Marketing is not limited to business entities but involves governmental and nonbusiness units as well. Marketing techniques are applied not only to goods but also to ideas (for example, a "Made in Japan" campaign) and to services (for example, international advertising agencies). The term *business marketing* is used for activities directed at other businesses, governmental entities, and various types of institutions. Business marketing accounts for well over 50 percent of all marketing activities.

Strategic Marketing

The marketing manager's task is to plan and execute programs that will ensure a long-term competitive advantage for the company. This task has two integral parts: (1) the determining of specific target markets and (2) marketing management, which consists of developing and operationalizing marketing mix elements to best satisfy the needs of individual target markets.

Target Market Selection

Characteristics of intended target markets are of critical importance to the marketer. These characteristics can be summarized by eight Os: occupants, objects, occasions, objectives, outlets, organization, operations, and opposition.[3]

Occupants are targets of the marketing effort. The marketer must determine which customers to approach and also define them along numerous dimensions, such as demographics (age, sex, and nationality, for example), geography (country or region), psychographics (attitudes, interests, and opinions), or product-related variables (usage rate and brand loyalty, for example). Included in this analysis must be the major influences on the occupants during their buying processes.

Objects are what is being bought at present to satisfy a particular need. Included in this concept are physical objects, services, ideas, organizations, places, and persons.

Occasions are moments when members of the target market buy the product or service. This characteristic is important to the marketer because a product's consumption may be tied to a particular time period—for example, imported beer and a festival.

Objectives are the motivations behind the purchase or adoption of the marketed concept. A computer manufacturer markets not hardware but solutions to problems. Additionally, many customers look for hidden value in the product they purchase, which may be expressed, for example, through national origin of the product or through brand name.

Outlets are places where customers expect to be able to procure a product or to be exposed to messages about it. Outlets include not only the entities themselves but also spots within a particular place. Although aseptic packaging made it possible to shelve milk outside the refrigerated area in supermarkets, customers' acceptance of the arrangement was not automatic: the product was not where it was supposed to be. In the area of services, outlet involves (1) making a particular service available and communicating its availability, and (2) selecting the particular types of facilitators (such as brokers) who bring the parties together.

Organization describes how the buying or acceptance of a (new) idea takes place. Organization expands the analysis beyond the individual consumer to the decision-making unit (DMU). The DMU varies in terms of its size and its nature from relatively small and informal groups like a family to large groups (more than ten people) to formal buying committees. Compare, for example, the differences between a family buying a new home-entertainment center and the governing board at a university deciding which architectural firm to use. In either case, to develop proper products and services, the marketer should know as much as possible about the decision-making processes and the roles of various individuals.

Operations represent the behavior of the organization buying products and services. Increasingly, industrial organizations are concentrating their purchases with fewer suppliers and making longer-term commitments. Supermarkets may make available only the leading brands in a product category, thereby complicating the marketer's attempts to place new products in these outlets.

Opposition refers to the competition to be faced in the marketplace. The nature of competition will vary from direct product-type competition to competition from other products that satisfy the same need. For example, Prince tennis rackets face a threat not only from other racket manufacturers but also from any company that provides a product or service for leisure-time use. Competitive situations will vary from one market and from one segment to the next. Gillette is number one in the U.S. market for disposable razors, with Bic a distant runner-up; however, elsewhere, particularly in Europe, the roles are reversed. In the long term, threats may come from outside the industry in which the marketer operates. As an example, digital watches originated in the electronics industry rather than the watch industry.

Analyzing Kotler's eight Os, and keeping in mind other uncontrollable factors in the environment (cultural, political, legal, technological, societal, and economic), the marketer must select the markets to which efforts will be targeted. In the short term, the marketer has to adjust to these environmental forces; in the long term, they can be manipulated to some extent by judicious marketing activity. Consumerism, one of the major forces shaping marketing activities, is concerned with protecting the consumer whenever an exchange relationship exists with any type of organization. Manifestations of the impact of consumerism on marketing exist in labeling, product specifications, promotional campaigns, recycling expectations, and demands for environmentally friendly products.

Because every marketer operates in a corporate environment of scarcity and comparative strengths, the target market decision is a crucial one. In some cases, the marketer may select only one segment of the market (for example, motorcycles of 1,000+ cc) or multiple segments (for example, all types of motorcycles), or the firm may opt for a very broad approach to the market (for example, any two-wheeled conveyance, with or without an engine, with or without a cover, usable for one or more passengers).

Marketing Management

The marketing manager, having analyzed the characteristics of the target market(s), is in a position to specify the mix of marketing variables that will best serve each target market. The variables the marketing manager controls are known as the elements of the marketing mix, or the four Ps: product, price, place, and promotion.[4] Each consists of a submix of variables, and policy decisions must be made on each.

Product policy is concerned with all the elements that make up the good, service, or idea that is offered by the marketer. Included are all possible tangible characteristics (such as the core product and packaging) and intangible character istics (such as branding and warranties). Many products are a combination of a concrete product and the accompanying service; for example, in buying an Otis elevator, the purchaser buys not only the product but an extensive service contract as well.

Pricing policy determines the cost of the product to the customer—a point some where between the floor created by the costs to the firm and the ceiling created by the strength of demand. An important consideration of pricing policy is pricing within the channel of distribution; margins to be made by the middlemen who assist in the marketing effort must be taken into account. Discounts to middlemen include functional, quantity, seasonal, and cash discounts, as well as promotional allowances. An important point to remember is that **price** is the only revenue-generating element of the marketing mix.

Distribution policy covers the **place** variable of the marketing mix and has two components: channel management and logistics management. Channel management is concerned with the entire process of setting up and operating the contractual organization, consisting of various types of middlemen (such as wholesalers, agents, retailers, and facilitators). Logistics management is focused on providing product availability at appropriate times and places in the marketing channel.[5] Place is the most long term of all the marketing mix elements; it is the most difficult to change in the short term.

Communications policy uses **promotion tools** to interact with customers, middle men, and the public at large. The communications element consists of these tools: advertising, sales promotion, personal selling, and publicity. Because the purpose of all communications is to persuade, this is the most visible and sensitive of the marketing mix elements.

Blending the various elements into a coherent program requires trade-offs based on the type of product or service being offered (for example, detergents versus fighter aircraft), the stage of the product's life cycle (a new product versus one that is being revived), and resources available for the marketing effort (money and personnel), as well as the type of customer at whom the marketing efforts are directed.

The Marketing Process

The actual process of marketing consists of four stages: analysis, planning, implementation, and control.

Analysis begins with collecting data on the eight Os and using various quantitative and qualitative techniques of marketing research. Data sources will vary from secondary to primary, internal to external (to the company), and informal to formal. The data are used to determine company opportunities by screening a plethora of environmental opportunities. The company opportunities must then be checked against the company's resources to judge their viability. The key criterion is competitive advantage.

Planning refers to the blueprint generated to react to and exploit the opportunities in the marketplace. The planning stage involves both long-term strategies and short-term tactics. A marketing plan developed for a particular market includes a situation analysis, objectives and goals to be met, strategies and tactics, and cost and profit estimates. Included in the activity is the formation of a new organizational structure or adjustments in the existing one to prepare for the execution of the plan.

Implementation is the actual carrying out of the planned activity. If the plans drawn reflect market conditions, and if they are based on realistic assessments of the company's fit into the market, the implementation process will be a success. Plans must take into account unforeseeable changes within the company and environmental forces, and allow for corresponding changes to occur in implementing the plans.

For this reason, concurrently with implementation, **control mechanisms** must be put into effect. The marketplace is ever dynamic and requires the monitoring of environmental forces, competitors, channel participants, and customer receptiveness. Short-term control tools include annual plan control (such as comparing actual sales to quota), profitability control, and efficiency control. Long-term control is achieved through comprehensive or functional audits to make sure that marketing not only is doing things right but is doing the right things. The results of the control effort provide valuable input for subsequent planning efforts.

These marketing basics do not vary, regardless of the type of market one is planning to enter or to continue operating within. They have been called the "technical universals" of marketing.[6] The different environments in which the marketing manager must operate will give varying emphases to the variables and will cause the values of the variables to change.

Key Terms

marketing	place	planning
product policy	promotion tools	implementation
price	analysis	control mechanisms

GEOGRAPHICAL PERSPECTIVES ON INTERNATIONAL MARKETING

The globalization of business has made geography indispensable for the study of international marketing. Without significant attention to the study of geography, critical ideas and information about the world in which business occurs will be missing.

Just as the study of business has changed significantly in recent decades, so has the study of geography. Once considered by many to be simply a descriptive inventory that filled in blank spots on maps, geography has emerged as an ana lytical approach that uses scientific methods to answer important questions.

Geography focuses on answering "Where?" questions. Where are things located? What is their distribution across the surface of the earth? An old aphorism holds, "If you can map it, it's geography." That statement is true, because we use maps to gather, store, analyze, and present information that answers "Where?" questions. Identifying where things are located is only the first phase of geographic inquiry. Once locations have been determined, "Why?" and "How?" questions can be asked. Why are things located where they are? How do different things relate to one another at a specific place? How do different places relate to each other? How have geographic patterns and relationships changed over time? These are the questions that take geography beyond mere description and make it a powerful approach for analyzing and explaining geographical aspects of a wide range of different kinds of problems faced by those engaged in international marketing.

Geography answers questions related to the location of different kinds of economic activity and the transactions that flow across national boundaries. It provides insights into the natural and human factors that influence patterns of production and consumption in different parts of the world. It explains why patterns of trade and exchange evolve over time. And because a geographic per spective emphasizes the analysis of processes that result in different geographic patterns, it provides a means for assessing how patterns might change in the future.

NOTE: This appendix was contributed by Thomas J. Baerwald. Dr. Baerwald is a senior science advisor and geography program director at the National Science Foundation in Arlington, Virginia. He is coauthor of *Prentice-Hall World Geography* (2006)—a best-selling geography textbook.

SOURCE: Darrell Delamaide, The New Superregions of Europe (New York: Dutton, 1995); Joel Garreau, The Nine Nations of North America (New York: Houghton Mifflin Co., 1989).

Geography has a rich tradition. Classical Greeks, medieval Arabs, enlightened European explorers, and contemporary scholars in the United States and elsewhere have organized geographic knowledge in many different ways. In recent decades, however, geography has become more familiar and more relevant to many people because emphasis has been placed on five fundamental themes as ways to structure geographic questions and to provide answers for those questions. Those themes are (1) location, (2) place, (3) interaction, (4) movement, and (5) region. The five themes are neither exclusive nor exhaustive. They complement other disciplinary approaches for organizing information, some of which are better suited to addressing specific kinds of questions. Other questions require insights related to two or more of the themes. Experience has shown, however, that the five themes provide a powerful means for introducing students to the geographic perspective. As a result, they provide the structure for this discussion.

Location

For decades, people engaged in real estate development have said that the value of a place is a product of three factors: location, location, and location. This statement also reflects the importance of location for international marketing. Learning the location and characteristics of other places has always been important to those interested in conducting business outside their local areas. The drive to learn about different areas, especially their resources and potential as markets, has stimulated geographic exploration throughout history. Explorations of the Mediterranean by the Phoenicians, Marco Polo's journey to China, and voyages undertaken by Christopher Columbus, Vasco da Gama, Henry Hudson, and James Cook not only improved general knowledge of the world but also expanded business opportunities.

Assessing the role of location requires more than simply determining specific locations where certain activities take place. Latitude and longitude often are used to fix the exact location of features on the earth's surface, but to simply describe a place's coordinates provides relatively little information about that place. Of much greater significance is its location relative to other features. The city of Singapore, for example, is between 1 and 2 degrees North latitude and is just west of 104 degrees East longitude. Other locational characteristics are far more important if you want to understand why Singapore has emerged as such an important locale for international business. Singapore is at the southern tip of the Malay Peninsula near the eastern end of the Strait of Malacca, a critical shipping route connecting the Indian Ocean with the South China Sea. For almost 150 years, this location made Singapore an important center for trade in the British Empire. After it attained independence in 1965, Singapore's leaders diversified its economy and complemented trade in its bustling port with numerous manufacturing plants that export products to nations around the world. Singapore quickly became one of the world's leading manufacturers of disk drives and other electronic components, using its pivotal location on global air routes to quickly ship these light-weight, high-value goods around the world. The same locational advantages have spurred its rise in recent decades as a business and financial services center for eastern Asia.

An understanding of the way location influences business therefore is critical for the international marketing executive. Without clear knowledge of an enterprise's location relative to its suppliers, to its market, and to its competitors, an executive operates like the captain of a fogbound vessel that has lost all navigational instruments and is heading for dangerous shoals.

Place

In addition to its location, each place has a diverse set of characteristics. Although many of those characteristics are present in other places, the ensemble makes each place unique. The characteristics of places—both natural and human—profoundly influence the ways that business executives in different places participate in international economic transactions.

Natural Features

Many of the characteristics of a place relate to its natural attributes. Geologic characteristics can be especially important, as the presence of critical minerals or energy resources may make a place a world-renowned supplier of valuable products. Gold and diamonds help make South Africa's economy the most prosperous on that continent. Rich deposits of iron ore in southern parts of the Amazon Basin have made Brazil the world's leading exporter of that commodity, while Chile remains a preeminent exporter of copper. Coal deposits provided the foundation for massive industrial development in the eastern United States, in the Rhine River Basin of Europe, in western Russia, and in northeastern China. Because of abundant pools of petroleum beneath desert sands, standards of living in Saudi

Arabia and nearby nations have risen rapidly to be among the highest in the world.

The geology of a place also shapes its terrain. People traditionally have clustered in lower, flatter areas, because valleys and plains have permitted the agri cultural development necessary to feed the local population and to generate surpluses that can be traded. Hilly and mountainous areas may support some people, but their population densities are invariably lower. Terrain also plays a critical role in focusing and inhibiting the movement of people and goods. Business leaders throughout the centuries have capitalized on this fact. Just as feudal masters sought control of mountain passes in order to collect tolls and other duties from traders who traversed an area, modern executives maintain stores and offer services near bridges and at other points where terrain slows down travel.

The terrain of a place is related to its hydrology. Rivers, lakes, and other bodies of water influence the kinds of economic activities that occur in a place. In general, abundant supplies of water boost economic development, because water is necessary for the sustenance of people and for both agricultural and industrial production. Locations like Los Angeles and Saudi Arabia have prospered despite having little local water, because other features offer advantages that more than exceed the additional costs incurred in delivering water supplies from elsewhere. While sufficient water must be available to meet local needs, overabundance of water may pose serious problems, such as in Bangladesh, where development has been inhibited by frequent flooding.

The character of a place's water bodies also is important. Smooth-flowing streams and placid lakes can stimulate transportation within a place and connect it more easily with other places, while waterfalls and rapids can prevent navigation on streams. The rapid drop in elevation of such streams may boost their potential for hydroelectric power generation, however, thereby stimulating development of industries requiring considerable amounts of electricity. Large plants producing aluminum, for example, are found in the Tennessee and Columbia river valleys of the United States and in Quebec and British Columbia in Canada. These plants refine materials that originally were extracted elsewhere, especially bauxite and alumina from Caribbean nations like Jamaica and the Dominican Republic. Although the transport costs incurred in delivery of these materials to the plants is high, those costs are more than offset by the presence of abundant and inexpensive electricity.

Climate is another natural feature that has profound impact on economic activity within a place. Many activities are directly affected by climate. Locales blessed with pleasant climates have become popular recreational havens, attracting tourists whose spending fuels the local economy. Florida, the Côote d'Azur of France, the Crimean Peninsula of Ukraine, and the "Gold Coast" of northeastern Australia are just a few examples of popular tourist destinations whose primary attribute is a salubrious climate.

Agricultural production is also influenced by climate. The average daily and evening temperatures, the amount and timing of precipitation, the timing of frosts and freezing weather, and the variability of weather from one year to the next all influence the kinds of crops grown in an area. Plants producing bananas and sugar cane flourish in moist tropical areas, while cooler climates are more conducive for crops such as wheat and potatoes. Climate influences other industries as well. The aircraft manufacturing industry in the United States developed largely in warmer, drier areas, where conditions for test flights were more beneficial throughout the year. In a similar way, major rocket-launching facilities have been placed in locations where climatic conditions are most favorable. As a result, the primary launch site of the European Space Agency is not in Europe at all, but rather in the South American territory of French Guiana. Climate also affects the length of the work day and the length of economic seasons. For example, in some regions of the world, the construction industry can build only during a few months of the year because permafrost makes construction prohibitively expensive the rest of the year. Construction demand can be spurred by climate-related disasters, however, as occurred following massive devastation along the central Gulf Coast in the southern U.S.

Variations in **soils** have a profound impact on agricultural production. The world's great grain-exporting regions, including the central United States, the Prairie Provinces of Canada, the "Fertile Triangle" stretching from central Ukraine through southern Russia into northern Kazakhstan, and the Pampas of northern Argentina, all have been blessed with mineral-rich soils made even more fertile by humus from natural grasslands that once dominated the landscape. Soils are less fertile in much of the Amazon Basin of Brazil and in central Africa, where heavy rains leave few nutrients in upper layers of the soil. As a result, few commercial crops are grown.

The interplay between climate and soils is especially evident in the production of wines. Hundreds of varieties of grapes have been bred in order to take advantage of the different physical characteristics of various places. The wines fermented from these grapes are shipped around the world to consumers, who differentiate among various wines based not only on the grapes but also on the places where they were grown and the conditions during which they matured.

Human Features

The physical features of a place provide natural resources and influence the types of economic activities in which people engage, but its human characteristics also are critical. The **population** of a place is important because farm production may require intensive labor to be successful, as is true in rice-growing areas of eastern Asia. The skills and qualifications of the population also play a role in determining how a place fits into global economic affairs.

Although blessed with few mineral resources and a terrain and climate that limit agricultural production, the Swiss have emphasized high levels of education and training in order to maintain a labor force that manufactures sophisticated products for export around the world. In recent decades, Japan and smaller nations such as South Korea and Taiwan have increased the productivity of their workers to become major industrial exporters.

As people live in a place, they modify it, creating a **built environment** that can be as important as or more important than the natural environment in economic terms. The most pronounced areas of human activity and their associated structures are in cities. In nations around the world, cities grew dramatically during the twentieth century. Much of the growth of cities has resulted from the migration of people from rural areas. This influx of new residents broadens the labor pool and creates vast new demand for goods and services. As urban populations have grown, residences and other facilities have replaced rural land uses. Executives seeking to conduct business in foreign cities need to be aware that the geographic patterns found in their home cities are not evident in many other nations. For example, in the United States, wealthier residents generally have moved out of cities, and as they established their residences, stores and services followed. Residential patterns in the major cities of Latin America and other developing nations tend to be reversed, with the wealthy remaining close to the city center while poorer residents are consigned to the outskirts of town. A store-location strategy that is successful in the United States therefore may fail miserably if transferred directly to another nation without knowledge of the different geographic patterns of that nation's cities.

Interaction

The international marketing professional seeking to take advantage of opportunities present in different places learns not to view each place separately. The way a place functions depends on the presence and form of certain charac teristics as well as the interactions among them. Fortuitous combinations of features can spur a region's economic development. The presence of high-grade supplies of iron ore, coal, and limestone powered the growth of Germany's Ruhr Valley as one of Europe's foremost steel-producing regions, just as the proximity of the fertile Pampas and the deep channel of the Rio de la Plata combined to make Buenos Aires the leading economic center in southern South America.

Interactions among different features change over time within a place, and as they do, so does that place's character and economic activities. Human activities can have profound impacts on natural features. The courses of rivers and streams are altered as dams are erected and meanders are straightened. Soil fertility can be improved through fertilization. Vegetation is transformed, with naturally growing plants replaced by crops and other varieties that require careful management.

Many human modifications have been successful. For centuries, the Dutch have constructed dikes and drainage systems, slowly creating polders—land that once was covered by the North Sea but that now is used for agricultural production. But other human activities have had disastrous impacts on natural features. A large area in Ukraine and Belarus was rendered uninhabitable by radioactive materials leaked from the Chernobyl reactor in 1986. In countless other places around the globe, improper disposal of wastes has seriously harmed land and water resources. In some places, damage can be repaired, as has happened in rivers and lakes of the United States following the passage of measures to curb water pollution in the latter third of the 20th century, but in other locales, restoration may be impossible. At times, human activity can have counterproductive results for unforeseen reasons. In large parts of Bangladesh and the West Bengal state of India, arsenic concentrations in drinking water drawn from wells is far above acceptable levels, and increasing numbers of residents are exhibiting signs of arsenic poisoning. Ironically, the wells were drilled to provide a supposedly safer alternative to the highly polluted surface water on which residents previously relied.

Growing concerns about environmental quality have led many people in more economically advanced nations to call for changes in economic systems that harm the natural environment. Concerted efforts are under way, for example, to halt the destruction of forests in the Amazon Basin, thereby preserving the vast array of different plant and animal species in the region and saving vegetation that can help moderate the world's climate. Cooperative ventures have been established to promote selective harvesting of nuts, hardwoods, and other products taken from natural forests. Furthermore, an increasing number of restaurants and grocers are refusing to purchase beef raised on pastures that are established by clearing forests.

Market mechanisms have also been developed to try to facilitate environmentally friendly practices. Emissions trading has emerged as an administrative approach that can be instituted by a central unit to limit the overall level of pollution that is released in the area under that administrative unit's authority. The administrative unit can be a local government, state, nation, or even a set of nations. Based on historical patterns and other factors, maximum emission levels are established for subunits in the area. If some subunits expect to exceed the upper limits established for them, they can purchase credits from other subunits whose emissions are below their limits. This system provides incentives for subunits that have higher emissions levels to reduce their pollution in order to reduce costs, while other subunits may seek to reduce their emissions even more in order to reap income from the sale of additional credits. The system has been implemented across a range of geographic scales. The state of Illinois established an emissions reduction market system in the Chicago area in 2000 through which more than 100 major polluters trade credits in order to reduce the emission of volatile organic compounds. Starting in 2003, nine northeastern states in the United States sought to collectively limit carbon dioxide emissions. The European Union's 27 member nations instituted a greenhouse gas emission trading scheme in 2005 to limit overall emissions across Europe. Emissions trading is envisioned as a way to help the world's nations stabilize atmosheric greenhouse gas concentrations in accordance with the terms of the **Kyoto Protocol**, which was signed in 1997. This protocol called for reductions in the emission of carbon dioxide and five other greenhouse gases. The U.S. Senate in 1997 and the Bush administration since 2001 objected to the Kyoto Protocol because it did not seek to limit emissions from all industrializing nations. Opponents of the Kyoto Protocol argue that this places an unfairly heavy economic burden on the U.S., which emits about one quarter of the world's greenhouse gases.

As with so many other geographical relationships, the nature of human–environmental interaction changes over time. With technological advances, people have been able to modify and adapt to natural features in increasingly sophisticated ways. The development of air conditioning has permitted people to function more effectively in torrid tropical environments, thereby enabling the populations of cities such as Houston, Rio de Janeiro, and Jakarta to multiply many times over in recent decades. Owners of winter resorts now can generate snow artificially to ensure favorable conditions for skiers. Advanced irrigation systems now permit crops to be grown in places such as the southwestern United States, northern Africa, and Israel. The use of new technologies may cause serious problems over the long run, however. Extensive irrigation in large parts of the U.S. Great Plains has seriously depleted groundwater supplies. In central Asia, the diversion of river water to irrigate cotton fields in Kazakhstan and Uzbekistan has reduced the size of the Aral Sea by more than one-half since 1960. In future years, business leaders may need to factor into their decisions the additional costs asso ciated with the restoration of environmental quality after they have finished using a place's resources.

Other business leaders may have to deal with issues associated with the social, ecological, and ethical dimensions the associated with genetically modified foods and organisms. These products are created by combining genes from different organisms in order to achieve certain desirable qualities. In 2003, researchers estimated that 7 million farmers in 18 countries grew genetically altered crops, especially herbicide- and insecticide-resistant soybeans, corn, cotton, and canola. Other crops have been engineered to have greater nutritional value. The rapid growth in genetic modification of crops has led to concerns regarding potential introduction of new allergens, the unintended transfer of genes through cross-pollination, and potentially adverse impacts on other organisms. As a result, some nations have prohibited their own farmers from producing genetically modified crops as well as the importation of such products grown elsewhere. The need for accurate labeling of products so that consumers know what kinds of products they are buying will be an issue that international marketers will need to address in the future.

Movement

Whereas the theme of interaction encourages consideration of different characteristics within a place, movement provides a structure for considering how different places relate to each other. International marketing exists because movement permits the transportation of people and goods and communication of information and ideas among different places. No matter how much people in one place want something found elsewhere, they cannot have it unless transportation systems permit the good to be brought to them or allow them to move to the location of the good.

The location and character of transportation and communication systems long have had powerful influences on the economic standing of places. Especially significant have been places on which transportation routes have focused. Many ports evolved to be prosperous cities because they channeled the movement of goods and people between ocean and inland waterways. New York became the largest city in North America because its harbor provided sheltered anchorage for ships crossing the Atlantic and the Hudson River provided access leading into the interior of the continent. In eastern Asia, Hong Kong grew under similar circumstances, as British traders used its splendid harbor as an exchange point for goods moving in and out of southern China.

Businesses also have succeeded at well-situated places along overland routes. The fabled oasis of Timbuktu has been an important trading center for centuries because it had one of the few dependable sources of water in the Sahara. Chicago's ascendancy as the premier city of the U.S. heartland came when its early leaders engineered its selection as the termination point for a dozen railroad lines converging from all directions. Not only did much of the rail traffic moving through the region have to pass through Chicago, but passengers and freight passing through the city had to be transferred from one line to another. This process generated numerous jobs and added considerably to the wealth of many businesses in the city.

In addition to the business associated directly with the movement of people and goods, other forms of economic activity have become concentrated at critical points in the transportation network. Places where transfers from one mode of transportation to another were required often were chosen as sites for manufacturing activities. Buffalo was the most active flour-milling center in the United States for much of the twentieth century because it was the point where Great Lakes freighters carrying wheat from the northern Great Plains and Canadian prairies were unloaded. Rather than simply transfer the wheat into rail cars for shipment to the large urban markets of the northeastern United States, millers transformed the wheat into flour in Buffalo, thereby reducing the additional handling of the commodity.

Global patterns of resource refining also demonstrate the wisdom of careful selection of sites with respect to transportation systems. Some of the world's largest oil refineries are located at places like Bahrain and Houston, where pipe lines bring oil to points where it is processed and loaded onto ships in the form of gasoline or other distillates for transport to other locales. Massive refinery complexes also have been built in the Tokyo and Nagoya areas of Japan and near Rotterdam in the Netherlands to process crude oil brought by giant tankers from the Middle East and other oil-exporting regions. For similar reasons, the largest new steel mills in the United States are near Baltimore and Philadelphia, where iron ore shipped from Canada and Brazil is processed. Some of the most active aluminum works in Europe are beside Norwegian fjords, where abundant local hydroelectric power is used to process imported alumina.

Favorable location along transportation lines is beneficial for a place. Conversely, an absence of good transportation severely limits the potential for firms to succeed in a specific place. Transportation patterns change over time, however, and so does their impact on places. Some places maintain themselves because their business leaders use their size and economic power to become critical nodes in newly evolving transportation networks. New York's experience provides a good example of this process. New York became the United States' foremost business center in the early nineteenth century because it was ideally situated for water transportation. As railroad networks evolved later in that century, they sought New York connections in order to serve its massive market. During the twentieth century, a complex web of roadways and major airports reinforced New York's supremacy in the eastern United States. In similar ways, London, Moscow, and Tokyo reasserted themselves as transportation hubs for their nations through successive advances in transport technology.

Failure to adapt to changing transportation patterns can have harmful impacts on a place. During the middle of the nineteenth century, business leaders in St. Louis discouraged railroad construction, seeking instead to maintain the supremacy of river transportation. Only after it became clear that railroads were the mode of preference did St. Louis officials seek to develop rail connections for the city, but by then it was too late; Chicago had ascended to a dominant position in the region. For about 30 years during the middle part of the twentieth century, airports at Gander (Newfoundland, Canada) and Shannon (Ireland) became important refueling points for transatlantic flights. The development of planes that could travel nonstop for much longer distances returned those places to sleepy oblivion.

Continuing advances in transportation technology have effectively "shrunk" the world. Just a few centuries ago, travel across an ocean took harrowing months. As late as 1873, readers marveled when Jules Verne wrote of a hectic journey around the world in 80 days. Today's travelers can fly around the globe in less than 80 hours, and the speed and dependability of modern modes of transport have transformed the ways in which business is conducted. Modern manufacturers have transformed the notion of relationships among suppliers, manufacturers, and markets. Automobile manufacturers, for example, once maintained large stockpiles of parts in assembly plants that were located near the parts plants or close to the places where the cars would be sold. Contemporary auto assembly plants now are built in places where labor costs and worker productivity are favorable and where governments have offered attractive inducements. They keep relatively few parts on hand, calling on suppliers for rapid delivery of parts as they are needed when orders for new cars are received. This "just-in-time" system of production leaves manufacturers subject to disruptions caused by work stoppages at supply plants and to weather-related delays in the transportation system, but losses associated with these infrequent events are more than offset by reduced opera ting costs under normal conditions.

The role of advanced technology and its effect on international marketing are even more apparent with respect to advances in communications systems. Sophisticated forms of telecommunication that began more than 170 years ago with the telegraph have advanced through the telephone to facsimile transmissions and electronic mail networks. As a result, distance has practically ceased to be a consideration with respect to the transmission of information. Whereas information once moved only as rapidly as the person carrying the paper on which the information was written, data and ideas now can be sent instantaneously almost anywhere in the world.

These communication advances have had a staggering impact on the way that international marketing is conducted. They have fostered the growth of multi national corporations, which operate in diverse sites around the globe while maintaining effective links with headquarters and regional control centers. International financial operations also have been transformed because of communication advances. Money and stock markets in New York, London, Tokyo, and Frankfurt now are connected by computer systems that process transactions around the clock. As much as any other factor, the increasing mobility of money has enabled modern business executives to engage in activities around the world.

Region

In addition to considering places by themselves or how they relate to other places, regions provide alternative ways to organize groups of places in more meaningful ways.

A region is a set of places that share certain characteristics. Many regions are defined by characteristics that all of the places in the group have in common. When economic characteristics are used, the delimited regions include places with similar kinds of economic activity. Agricultural regions include areas where certain farm products dominate. Corn is grown throughout the "Corn Belt" of the central United States, for example, although many farmers in the region also plant soybeans and many raise hogs. Regions where intensive industrial production is a prominent part of local economic activity include the manufacturing belts of the northeastern United States, southern Canada, northwestern Europe, and southern Japan.

Regions can also be defined by patterns of movement. Transportation or communication linkages among places may draw them together into configurations that differentiate them from other locales. Studies by economic geographers of the locational tendencies of modern high-technology industries have identified complex networks of firms that provide products and services to each other. Because of their linkages, these firms cluster together into well-defined regions. The "Silicon Valley" of northern California, the "Western Crescent" on the outskirts of London, and the "Technopolis" of the Tokyo region all are distinguished as much by connections among firms as by the economic landscapes they have established.

Economic aspects of movement may help define functional regions by establishing areas where certain types of economic activity are more profitable than others. In the early nineteenth century, German landowner Johann Heinrich von Thünen demonstrated how different costs for transporting various agricultural goods to market helped to define regions where certain forms of farming would occur. Although theoretically simple, patterns predicted by von Thünen can still be found in the world today. Goods such as vegetables and dairy products that require more intensive production and are more expensive to ship are produced closer to markets, while less demanding goods and commodities that can be transported at lower costs come from more remote production areas. Advances in transportation have dramatically altered such regional patterns. Once, a New York City native enjoyed fresh vegetables and fruits only in the summer and early autumn when New Jersey, upstate New York, and New England producers brought their goods to market. Today, New Yorkers buy fresh produce year-round, with new shipments flown in daily from Florida, California, Chile, Columbia, and even more remote locations during the colder months.

Governments have a strong impact on the conduct of business, and the formal borders of government jurisdictions often coincide with the functional boundaries of economic regions. The divisive character of these lines on the map has been altered in many parts of the world in recent decades. The formation of common markets and free trade areas in Western Europe, North America, and other parts of the world has dramatically changed the patterns and flows of economic activity, and similar kinds of formal restructuring of relationships among nations likely will continue into the next century. As a result, business analysts increasingly need to consider regions that cross international boundaries.

Some analysts have identified regional structures that transcend national boundaries. In a book titled *The Nine Nations of North America*, Joel Garreau identified a set of regions based on economic activities and cultural outlooks. Seven of Garreau's nine regions include territory in at least two nations. In the Southwest, "Mexamerica" recognized the bicultural heritage of Anglo and Hispanic groups and the increasingly close economic ties across the U.S.–Mexican border that were spurred by the maquiladora and other export-oriented programs. The evolution of this region as a distinctive collection of places has been accelerated by the decade-long operation of the North American Free Trade Agreement (NAFTA). Another cross-national region identified by Garreau was "The Islands," a collection of nations in the Caribbean for which Miami has become the functional "capital." Many business leaders seeking to tap into this rapidly growing area have become knowledgeable of the laws and customs of those nations. They often have done so by employing emigres from those nations who may now be U.S. citizens but whose primary language is not English and whose outlook on the region is multinational. The establishment of the Central American Free Trade Agreement (CAFTA) linking the United States, Guatemala, El Salvador, Honduras, Costa Rica, Nicaragua, and the Dominican Republic likely will further strengthen links across many of the nations in this region.

In a similar vein, Darrell Delamaide divided Europe into ten regions based on economic, cultural, and social affinities that have evolved over centuries. His vision of Europe challenges regional structures that persist from earlier times. Seen by many as a single region known as Eastern Europe, the formerly communist nations west of what once was the Soviet Union are seen by Delamaide as being part of five different "super regions": "The Baltic League," a group of nations clustered around the Baltic Sea;—"Mitteleuropa," the economic heartland of northern Europe; "The Slavic Federation," a region dominated by Russia with a common Slavic heritage; "The Danube Basin," a melange of places along and near Europe's longest river; and "The Balkan Peninsula," a region characterized by political turmoil and less-advanced economies.

The ideas posed by Garreau and Delamaide have been controversial, but the value of their ideas is measured not in terms of the "accuracy" of the regional structures they presented, but rather by their ability to lead more people to take a geographic perspective of the modern world and the way it functions. The regions defined by Garreau and Delamaide are not those described by traditional geographers, but they reflect the views of many business leaders who have learned to look across national boundaries in their search for opportunities. As marketing increasingly becomes international, the most successful entrepreneurs will be the ones who complement their business acumen with effective application of geographic information and principles.

For online activities, visit the following Web sites:

http://state.gov
http://www.state.gov/www/s/int/rls/4250.htm

Key Terms

geologic characteristics	climate	built environment
terrain	soils	Kyoto Protocol
hydrology	population	

THE ECONOMIC ENVIRONMENT

And Now for the Next One Billion Consumers

During the first fifty years of the info-tech era, more than one billion people have come to use computers, the vast majority in the developed markets of Europe, North America, and Australasia. Those markets have become increasingly saturated and do not provide the needed growth. Computer sales increased a mere 6 percent per year between 2005 and 2008. The next billion consumers have to be found in the emerging markets of the 21st century: China, India, Russia, South Africa, and Brazil. Sales in info-tech are expected to increase by 11 percent per year over the next five years, fueled mostly by the burgeoning ranks of millions of middle-class consumers. These newly wealthy consumers are showing preferences for fashionable brands as well as for features every bit as sophisticated as their developed-country counterparts.

The challenges of succeeding in the emerging markets are forcing the established global players to come up with innovative new approaches. Areas in which fundamental rethinking is required include the following:

- *Design.* Solutions have to be simpler and more durable. TVS Electronics, an Indian printer manufacturer, is producing devices for India's 1.2 million small shops. They are an all-in-one computer, cash register, and inventory-management system. They can be operated with icons, because many of the clerks are illiterate. They have to be robust to withstand the elements, such as heat and dust.

- *Innovation.* Marketers have to innovate for the peculiarities of emerging markets. Electricity may often be unavailable and unreliable. Hewlett-Packard adjusted to this by designing a small solar panel to charge digital printers for itinerant photographers in India. In South Africa, HP is working with a solar fabric that is cheaper and less fragile.

- *Business Development.* Old strategies may have to be adjusted. IBM figures that it can do well in China only by supplying technology to local companies. It developed a low-cost, $12 microprocessor and a simple network computer for China's Culturecom, which is selling computers and Internet access services in the country's rural areas.

- *Competition.* Companies such as Cisco, Dell, and Microsoft dominate global markets. However, many new challengers are using their low costs and intimate knowledge of local, or similar emerging markets, to expand their businesses. Chinese network systems company Huawei can charge 50 percent less than Cisco and has made sales in markets in Africa and Europe.

- *Pricing.* Pressure on prices can lead to innovative solutions in financing. Poland needed to modernize its motor vehicle driver's licensing system but could not afford it. Hewlett-Packard

© UDO WEITZ/BLOOMBERG NEWS/LANDOV

THAI BUDDHIST MONKS EXAMINE LAPTOP COMPUTERS. THE NEXT BILLION COMPUTER CONSUMERS HAVE TO BE FOUND IN THE EMERGING MARKETS OF THE 21ST CENTURY.

agreed to install Poland's new computer system in exchange for a cut of the fees drivers pay each time they get a new license or renew an old one.

While the first billion customers may have created a sector with annual revenues of more than $1 trillion, sales for the second billion will not reach the same level. Lower prices in these markets may put pressure on prices everywhere. However, staying out of these markets is not an option.

Unconventional thinking will have to be the norm rather than an exception. Philippino mobile-telephony providers

Globe Telecom and Smart Communications use initiatives, ranging from educational programs to food and medical assistance, that benefit the whole community to encourage local leaders to safeguard cell towers and protect company employees.

SOURCES: Christopher Beshouri, "A Grassroots Approach to Emerging-Market Consumers," *McKinsey Quarterly* (no. 4, 2006): 28–36; Tarun Khanna, Krishna Palepu, and Jayant Sinha, "Strategies that Fit Emerging Markets," *Harvard Business Review* 83 (June 2005): 63–76; and "Tech's Future," *Business Week,* September 27, 2004, 82–89.

The assessment of a foreign market environment should start with the evaluation of economic variables relating to the size and nature of the markets. Because of the large number of worthwhile alternatives, initial screening of markets should be done efficiently yet effectively enough, with a wide array of economic criteria, to establish a preliminary estimate of market potential. One of the most basic characterizations of the world economy is provided in Exhibit 2.1, which incorporates many of the economic variables pertinent to marketers.

The **Group of Five**—listed in Exhibit 2.1 as the United States, Britain, France, Germany, and Japan—consists of the major industrialized countries of the world. This group is sometimes expanded to the **Group of Seven** (by adding Italy and Canada) and to the **Group of Ten** (by adding Sweden, the Netherlands, and Belgium). It may also be expanded to encompass the members of the Organization for Economic Cooperation and Development, OECD (which consists of 30 countries: Western Europe, the United States, Australia, Canada, Czech Republic, Hungary, Japan, Mexico, New Zealand, Poland, Slovakia, South Korea, and Turkey).

Important among the middle-income developing countries are the newly industrialized countries (NICs), which include Singapore, Taiwan, Korea, Hong Kong, Brazil, and Mexico (some propose adding Malaysia and the Philippines to the list as well). Some of these NICs will earn a new acronym, RIC (rapidly industrializing country). Over the past 20 years, Singapore has served as a hub, providing critical financial and managerial services to the Southeast Asian

Exhibit **2.1**

The Global Economy

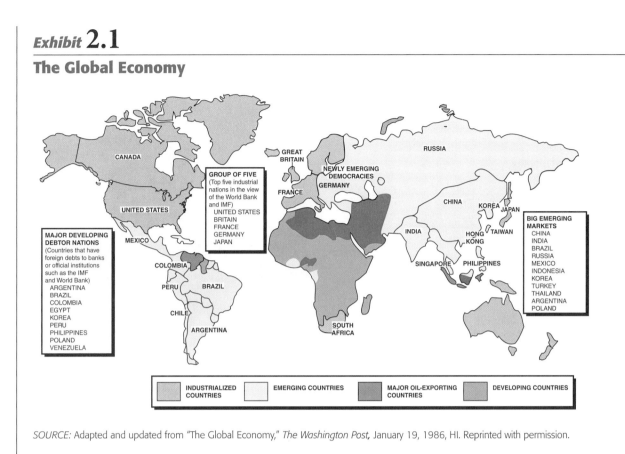

SOURCE: Adapted and updated from "The Global Economy," *The Washington Post*, January 19, 1986, HI. Reprinted with permission.

markets. Singapore has successfully attracted foreign investment, mostly regional corporate headquarters and knowledge-intensive industries, and has served as one of the main gateways for Asian trade. Its exports have reached well over 300 percent of GDP.[1]

The major oil-exporting countries, in particular the eleven members of the Organization of Petroleum Exporting Countries (OPEC) and countries such as Russia, are dependent on the price of oil for their world market participation. A relatively high dollar price per barrel (as high as $140 in 2008) works very much in these countries' favor, while lower prices (as low as $40 in 2009) cause significant economic hardship.

Many of the emerging economies will depend on the success of their industrialization efforts in the years to come, even in the case of resource-rich countries that may find commodity prices being driven down by humanmade substitutes. This applies especially to the BRIC (Brazil, Russia, India, China) group. China has become the world's largest exporter of textiles since beginning to increase production in the 1980s. Despite an image of hopeless poverty, India has nearly 300 million middle-class consumers, more than Germany. However, as shown in *The International Marketplace 2.1,* these countries, which constitute the majority of the world's population, may also provide the biggest potential market opportunity for marketers in the twenty-first century.[2] Even if they lack the scale of the BRICs, eleven (also known as the "Next 11") countries can rival the G7 in time.[3] These include Bangladesh, Egypt, Indonesia, Iran, Korea, Mexico, Nigeria, Pakistan, Philippines, Turkey, and Vietnam.

In less-developed countries, debt problems and falling commodity prices make market development difficult. Africa, the poorest continent, owes the rest of the world $200 billion, an amount equal to three-quarters of its GNP and nearly four times its annual exports. Another factor contributing to the challenging situation is that only 1 percent of the world's private investment goes to sub-Saharan Africa.[4]

In the former centrally planned economies, dramatic changes have been under way for the last fifteen years. A hefty capital inflow has been key to modernizing the newly emerging democracies of both Central and Eastern Europe. Desperately needed will be Western technology, management, and marketing know-how to provide better jobs and

Top World Economies (GDP in milliondollars US)*

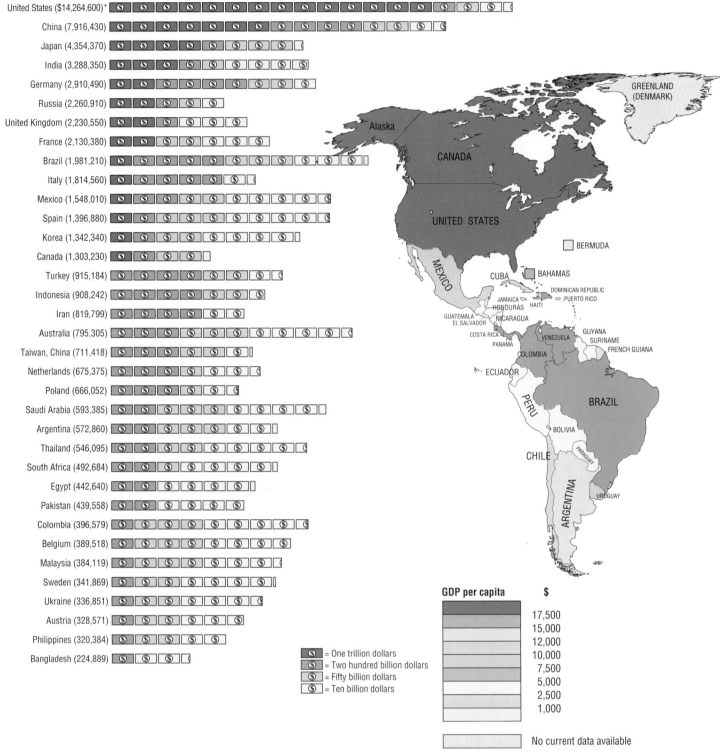

*GDP calculated by Purchasing Power Parity (PPP).

SOURCE: Based on World Economic Outlook Database, April 2007. (Washington: International Monetary Fund).

put more locally made and imported consumer goods in the shops. Within the groups, prospects vary: The future for countries such as Hungary, the Baltics, the Czech Republic, and Poland looks far better than it does for Russia, as they reap the benefits of membership in the European Union.[5]

Classifications of markets will vary by originator and intended use. Marketers will combine economic variables to fit their planning purposes by using those that relate directly to the product and/or service the company markets, such as the market's ability to buy. For example, a company marketing electrical products (from power generators to appliances) may take into account both general country considerations—such as population, GNP, geography, manufacturing as a percentage of national product, infrastructure, and per capita income—and narrower industry-specific considerations of interest to the company and its marketing efforts, such as extent of use of the product, total imports, and U.S. or EU share of these imports.

The discussion that follows is designed to summarize a set of criteria that helps identify foreign markets and screen the most opportune ones for future entry or change of entry mode. Discussed are variables on which information is readily available from secondary sources such as international organizations, individual governments, and private organizations or associations.

World Bank and United Nations publications and individual countries' *Statistical Abstracts* provide the starting point for market investigations. The more developed the market, the more data available. Data are available on past developments as well as on projections of broader categories such as population and income. Euromonitor, for example, publishes *World Consumer Income & Expenditure Patterns,* which covers 49 countries around the world.

Market Characteristics

The main dimensions of a market can be captured by considering variables such as those relating to the population and its various characteristics, infrastructure, geographical features of the environment, and foreign involvement in the economy.

Population

The total world population exceeded six billion people in 1999 and is expected to close in on eight billion by 2025. The number of people in a particular market provides one of the most basic indicators of market size and is, in itself, indicative of the potential demand for certain staple items that have universal appeal and are generally affordable. As indicated by the data in Exhibit 2.2, population is not evenly divided among the major regions of the world; Asia holds over half the world's population.

These population figures can be analyzed in terms of marketing implications by noting that countries belonging to the European Union (EU) constitute 85 percent of the Western European population, and with the expansion of the EU in 2007, the percentage rose to 95. The two largest entities in Asia, China and India, constitute nearly 70 percent of Asia's population. The greatest population densities are also to be found in Europe, providing the international marketer with a strategically located center of operation and ready access to the major markets of the world.

Population figures themselves must be broken down into meaningful categories in order for the marketer to take better advantage of them. Because market entry decisions may lie in the future, it is worthwhile to analyze population projections in the areas of interest and focus on their possible implications. Exhibit 2.2 includes United Nations projections that point to a population explosion, but mainly in the developing countries. Northern Europe will show nearly zero population growth for the next 30 years, whereas the population of Africa will triple. Even in the low- or zero-growth markets, the news is not necessarily bad for the international marketer. Those in the 25 to 45 age group, whose numbers are increasing, are among the most affluent consumers of all, having formed family units and started to consume household goods in large quantities as they reach the peak of their personal

Exhibit **2.2**

World Population: Present and the Shape of Things to Come

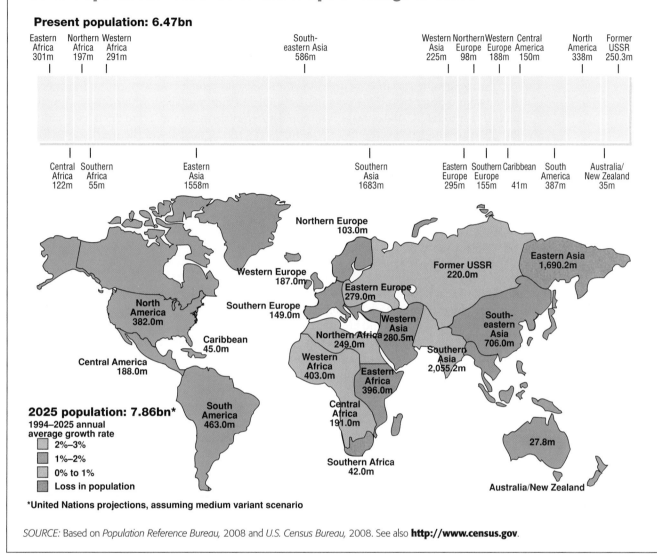

Present population: 6.47bn

| Eastern Africa 301m | Northern Africa 197m | Western Africa 291m | South-eastern Asia 586m | Western Asia 225m | Northern Europe 98m | Western Europe 188m | Central America 150m | North America 338m | Former USSR 250.3m |

| Central Africa 122m | Southern Africa 55m | Eastern Asia 1558m | Southern Asia 1683m | Eastern Europe 295m | Southern Europe 155m | Caribbean 41m | South America 387m | Australia/ New Zealand 35m |

Northern Europe 103.0m

Western Europe 187.0m

Southern Europe 149.0m

Eastern Europe 279.0m

Former USSR 220.0m

Eastern Asia 1,690.2m

North America 382.0m

Caribbean 45.0m

Central America 188.0m

Northern Africa 249.0m

Western Asia 280.5m

Southern Asia 2,055.2m

South-eastern Asia 706.0m

Western Africa 403.0m

Eastern Africa 396.0m

Central Africa 191.0m

South America 463.0m

2025 population: 7.86bn*
1994–2025 annual average growth rate
■ 2%–3%
■ 1%–2%
■ 0% to 1%
■ Loss in population

27.8m

Southern Africa 42.0m

Australia/New Zealand

*United Nations projections, assuming medium variant scenario

SOURCE: Based on *Population Reference Bureau,* 2008 and *U.S. Census Bureau,* 2008. See also **http://www.census.gov**.

earnings potential. Early in this century, they are expected to start spending more on leisure goods and health care and related services.[6]

To influence population growth patterns, governments will have to undertake, with the help of private enterprise, quite different social marketing tasks. These will range from promoting and providing incentives for larger families (in Scandinavia, for example) to increased family planning efforts (in Thailand, for example). Regardless of the outcome of such government programs, current trends will further accelerate the division of world markets into the "haves" and the "have-nots." More adjustment capability will be required on the part of companies that want to market in the developing countries because of lower purchasing power of individuals and increasing government participation in the marketing of basic products. However, as the life expectancy in a market extends and new target markets become available, international marketers may be able to extend their products' life cycles by marketing them abroad.

Depending on the marketer's interest, population figures can be classified to show specific characteristics of their respective markets. Age distribution and life expectancy correlate heavily with the level of development of the market. Industrialized countries, with their increasing median age and a larger share of the population above 65, will open unique opportunities for international marketers with new products and services. For example, Kimberly-Clark markets its Depend line for those with incontinence problems both in Europe and North America.

Interpretation of demographics will require some degree of experiential knowledge. As an example, which age categories of females should be included in an estimate of market potential for a new contraceptive? This would vary from the very early teens in the developing countries to higher age categories in developed countries, where the maturing process is later.

An important variable for the international marketer is the size of the household. A **household** describes all the persons, both related and unrelated, who occupy a housing unit.[7] Within the EU, the average household size has shrunk from 2.9 to 2.5 persons in the last 25 years and is expected to decline further.[8] One factor behind the overall growth in households, and the subsequent decline in the average size, has been the increase in the numbers of divorced and sole survivor households. One-person households are most common in Norway and Germany. This compares strikingly with countries such as Colombia, where the average household size is six. With economic development usually bringing about more, but smaller-sized, households, international marketers of food products, appliances, and household goods have to adjust to patterns of demand; for example, they may offer single-serving portions of frozen foods and smaller appliances.

The increased urbanization of many markets has distinctly changed consumption patterns. Urban populations as a percentage of the total will vary from a low of 10 percent in Burundi to a high of 97 percent in Belgium. The degree of urbanization often dictates the nature of the marketing task the company faces, not only in terms of distribution but also in terms of market potential and buying habits. Urban areas provide larger groups of consumers who may be more receptive to marketing efforts because of their exposure to other consumers (the demonstration effect) and to communication media. In markets where urbanization is recent and taking place rapidly, the marketer faces additional responsibility as a change agent, especially when incomes may be low and the conditions for the proper use of the products may not be adequate. This is especially true in countries where rapid industrialization is taking place, such as Greece, Spain, and Portugal.

When using international data sources, the international marketer must recognize that definitions of a construct may vary among the many secondary sources. The concept of **urbanization**, for example, has different meanings depending on where one operates. In the United States, an urban area is defined as a place of 2,500 or more inhabitants; in Sweden, it is a built-up area with at least 200 inhabitants with no more than 200 meters between houses; in Mauritius, it is a town with proclaimed legal limits. Comparability, therefore, is concerned with the ends and not the means (or the definition).

Income

Markets require not only people but also purchasing power, which is a function of income, prices, savings, and credit availability. World markets can be divided into four tiers of consumers based on broad measures of income, as shown in Exhibit 2.3. Tier 1 consists of 100 million consumers from around the world. Typically, this means consumers in developed markets, such as the OECD, but also includes the rich elites in developing markets. Tier 2 consists of the lower-income segments in developed markets, while Tier 3 includes the rising middle-class consumers in emerging markets. Tier 4 is home to the average consumer in developing markets.

Apart from basic staple items, for which population figures provide an estimate, income is most indicative of the market potential for most consumer and industrial products and services. For the marketer to make use of information on gross domestic products of various nations, further knowledge is needed on distribution of income. Per capita GDP is often used as a primary indicator for evaluating purchasing power. This figure shows great variation between countries, as indicated by Luxembourg's $79,400 and Ethiopia's $700. The wide use of GDP figures can be explained by their easy availability, but they should nevertheless be used with caution. In industrialized countries, the richest 10 percent of the population consume 20 percent of all goods and services, whereas the respective figure for the developing countries

Exhibit 2.3

World Economic Pyramid

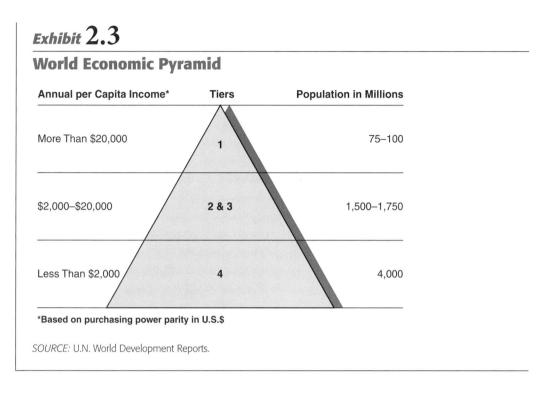

Annual per Capita Income*	Tiers	Population in Millions
More Than $20,000	1	75–100
$2,000–$20,000	2 & 3	1,500–1,750
Less Than $2,000	4	4,000

*Based on purchasing power parity in U.S.$

SOURCE: U.N. World Development Reports.

may be as high as 50 percent.[9] In some markets, income distribution produces wide gaps between population groups. The more developed the economy, the more income distribution tends to converge toward the middle class.

The international marketer can use the following classification as a planning guide:

1. Very low family incomes. Subsistence economies tend to be characterized by rural populations in which consumption relies on personal output or barter. Some urban centers may provide markets. Example: Cameroon.

2. Very low, very high family incomes. Some countries exhibit strongly bimodal income distributions. The majority of the population may live barely above the subsistence level, but there is a strong market in urban centers and a growing middle class. The affluent are truly affluent and will consume accordingly. Examples: India, Mexico.

3. Low, medium, high family incomes. Industrialization produces an emerging middle class with increasing disposable income. The very low and very high income classes tend to remain for traditional reasons of social class barriers. Example: Portugal.

4. Mostly medium family incomes. The advanced industrial nations tend to develop institutions and policies that reduce extremes in income distribution, resulting in a large and comfortable middle class able to purchase a wide array of both domestic and imported products and services. Example: Denmark.

Although the national income figures provide a general indication of a market's potential, they suffer from various distortions. Figures available from secondary sources are often in U.S. dollars. The per capita income figures may not be a true reflection of purchasing power if the currencies involved are distorted in some way. For example, fluctuations in the value of the U.S. dollar may distort real-income and standard-of-living figures. The goods and services in different countries have to be valued consistently if the differences are to reflect real differences in the volumes of goods produced. The use of **purchasing power parities (PPP)** instead of exchange rates is intended to achieve this objective. PPPs show how many units of currency are needed in one country to buy the amount of goods and services that one unit of currency will buy in another country. Exhibit 2.4 provides GDP data based on PPPs for selected countries.

In addition, using a monetary measure may not be a proper and all-inclusive measure of income. For example, in developing economies where most of the consumption is either self-produced or bartered, reliance on financial data alone would seriously understate the

Exhibit 2.4

Gross Domestic Product per Capita Adjusted to Purchasing Power Parities for Selected Countries, 2007, in Dollars

Highest			Lowest		
1.	Qatar	87,600	229.	Zimbabwe	200
2.	Luxembourg	79,400	210.	Afghanistan	1,000
6.	Norway	53,300	196.	Bangladesh	1,400
9.	Ireland	46,600	190.	Kenya	1,700
10.	United States	45,800	173.	Uzbekistan	2,400
13.	Hong Kong	42,000	168.	Vietnam	2,600
15.	Switzerland	40,100	167.	India	2,600
19.	Canada	38,600	163.	Philippines	3,200
23.	Australia	37,300	158.	Indonesia	3,600
27.	Finland	36,000	146.	Bolivia	4,400
29.	United Kingdom	35,000	139.	Egypt	5,000
30.	Germany	34,100	135.	Bhutan	5,200
34.	Japan	33,500	132.	China	5,400
35.	European Union	32,700	106.	Brazil	9,500
40.	Taiwan	30,100	103.	World	10,000

SOURCE: CIA Factbook, available at **http://www.cia.gov/cia/publications/factbook**

standard of living. Further, several of the service-related items (for example, protective services and travel), characteristic of the industrialized countries' national income figures, do not exist for markets at lower levels of development.

Moreover, the marketer will have to take into consideration variations in market potential in individual markets. Major urban centers in developing countries may have income levels comparable to those in more developed markets, while rural areas may not have incomes needed to buy imported goods.

In general, income figures are useful in the initial screening of markets. However, in product-specific cases, income may not play a major role, and startling scenarios may emerge. Some products, such as motorcycles and television sets in China, are in demand regardless of their high price in relation to wages because of their high prestige value.

Some products are in demand because of their foreign origin. As an example, European luxury cars have lucrative markets in countries where per capita income figures may be low but there are wealthy consumers who are able and willing to buy them. For example, Mercedes-Benz's target audience in India is families earning 1 million rupees (approximately $20,000). Earnings at that level, due to a much higher level of disposable income, are enough for a lifestyle to rival that of a U.S. or European family with an income three times higher.[10] Further, the lack of income in a market may preclude the marketing of a standardized product but, at the same time, provide an opportunity for an adjusted product. A packaged goods company, confronted with considerable disparity in income levels within the same country, can adapt product size or product features. By substituting cheaper parts and materials, successful international marketers can make both consumer and industrial products more affordable in less affluent markets and therefore reach a wider target audience.

© ARNO BURGI/DPA/LANDOV

MERCEDES-BENZ TARGET AUDIENCE IN INDIA IS FAMILIES EARNING 1 MILLION RUPEES (APPROXIMATELY $20,000).

Consumption Patterns

Depending on the sophistication of a country's data collection systems, economic data on consumption patterns can be obtained and analyzed. The share of income spent on necessities will provide an indication of the market's development level as well as an approximation of how much money the consumer has left for other purchases. Engel's laws provide some generalizations about consumers' spending patterns and are useful generalizations when precise data are not available. They state that as a family's income increases, the percentage spent on food will decrease, the percentage spent on housing and household operations will be roughly constant, and the amount saved or spent on other purchases will increase. Private expenditure comparisons reveal that the percentage spent on food in 2007 varied from 6.8 percent in the United States to 46 percent in Indonesia (see Exhibit 2.5).

In Western Europe, expenditures on clothing typically account for 5 to 9 percent of all spending, but in poorer countries the proportion may be lower. In some low-wage areas, a significant proportion of clothing is homemade or locally made at low cost, making comparisons not entirely accurate. Eastern European households spend an inordinate proportion of their incomes on foodstuffs but quite a low proportion on housing. The remaining, less absolutely central areas of consumption (household goods, leisure, and transportation) are most vulnerable to short-term cancellation or postponement and thus serve as indicators for the strength of confidence in the market in general.

Exhibit 2.5

Consumer Spending by Category as Percent of Total, 2007

Countries	Food and Non-alcoholic Beverages	Clothing and Footwear	Household Goods and Services	Housing	Leisure and Education	Transport and Communications	Hotels/ Catering
Argentina	20.0	7.1	6.7	15.6	8.6	16.1	7.3
Australia	10.5	3.6	5.5	17.0	11.5	14.7	7.9
Brazil	24.5	3.3	5.1	15.1	3.3	18.1	2.6
Canada	9.1	4.1	8.5	22.2	9.5	16.4	6.7
China	34.8	8.6	4.9	12.2	2.9	12.6	3.8
Colombia	27.8	4.3	5.0	14.5	5.0	16.3	6.5
Eastern Europe*	26.3	7.3	6.2	17.2	6.9	14.7	4.0
Western Europe*	11.9	6.3	6.8	22.3	10.7	17.1	9.1
India	36.5	4.3	4.0	12.0	1.9	17.8	2.6
Indonesia	45.6	4.1	6.0	16.2	1.9	4.7	5.0
Japan	15.9	3.0	3.6	25.1	11.3	14.2	7.6
Mexico	24.1	3.0	7.6	13.7	2.6	19.0	7.2
Nigeria	40.3	7.3	4.1	18.6	2.2	9.5	1.2
Singapore	8.3	3.2	6.5	15.2	11.0	20.1	7.6
South Korea	15.4	4.0	3.8	17.3	7.0	16.5	7.2
Thailand	24.9	7.4	5.5	7.5	6.5	19.7	7.2
United States	6.8	4.4	4.7	17.3	9.0	13.0	6.1
Russia	28.6	9.5	8.1	12.8	7.2	16.1	4.1
Finland	12.2	4.8	5.8	25.2	11.5	15.4	5.8
Germany	11.3	5.1	6.7	24.5	9.5	16.2	5.1
Spain	13.6	5.0	5.0	16.5	9.4	14.7	19.2
UK	9.0	5.5	5.4	20.0	11.6	16.6	10.6

*Eastern Europe includes Belarus, Bulgaria, Croatia, Czech Republic, Estonia, Hungary, Latvia, Lithuania, Poland, Romania, Russia, Slovakia, Slovenia, Ukraine. Western Europe includes Austria, Belgium, Denmark, Finland, France, Germany, Greece, Ireland, Italy, Netherlands, Norway, Portugal, Spain, Sweden, Switzerland, Turkey, United Kingdom.

SOURCE: Compiled from Global Market Information Database.

In large markets, such as China, India, and the United States, marketers need to exercise care in not assuming uniformity across regions. In China, for example, marked differences exist between geographic markets and consumers in urban and rural markets. Nearly 60 percent of PCs sold find customers in the economically developed east, north, and south, especially in the big coastal cities. In the submarket of servers, the share is even higher at 65 percent. Urban consumers spend 2.5 times more on food and 10 times more on entertainment than their rural counterparts. This does not mean that inland urban markets and rural areas are without opportunity. Massive investments by the central and provincial governments have linked these areas to the coastal ports and export/import markets by multilane highways, in their attempt to close some of the income gaps between regions in China.[11]

Data on product saturation or diffusion—information on the percentage of households in a market that own a particular product—allow a further evaluation of market potential. Exhibit 2.6 presents the percentage of households that own certain appliances and indicates that saturation levels in the markets for which the data exist are quite high. This does not necessarily indicate lack of market potential; replacement markets or the demand for auxiliary products may offer attractive opportunities to the international marketer. Low rates of diffusion should be approached cautiously, because they can signal a market opportunity or lack thereof resulting from low income levels, use of a substitute product, or lack of acceptance. As an example of lack of acceptance, the time-saving feature of microwave ovens may not be as attractive in more tradition-bound societies as it is in the United States or the EU. Similarly, consumers in some markets replace their appliances with the same brand more than 80 percent of the time.

General consumption figures are valuable, but they must be viewed with caution because they may conceal critical product-form differences; for example, appliances in European households tend to be smaller than their U.S. counterparts. Information about existing product usage can nevertheless provide indirect help to international marketers. As an example, a large number of telephones, and their even distribution among the population or a target group, may allow market research via telephone interviewing.

A problem for marketers in general is **inflation**; varying inflation rates complicate this problem in international markets. Many of the industrialized countries, such as the United States, Germany, and Japan, have recently been able to keep inflation rates at single-digit levels, while some have suffered from chronic inflation (Exhibit 2.7). Inflation affects the ability of both industrial customers and consumers to buy and also introduces uncertainty into both the marketer's planning process and consumers' buying habits. In high-inflation markets, the marketer may have to make changes in the product (more economical without compromising quality), promotion (more rational), and distribution (more customer involvement) to meet customer needs and maintain demand. In response to rapidly escalating prices, a government will often invoke price controls. The setting of maximum prices for products may cause the international marketer to face unacceptable profit situations, future investments may not be made, and production may even have to be stopped.

Infrastructure

The availability and quality of an infrastructure is critically important in evaluating marketing operations abroad. Each international marketer will rely heavily on services provided by the local market for transportation, communication, and energy as well as on organizations participating in the facilitating functions of marketing: marketing communications, distributing, information, and financing. Indicators such as steel consumption, cement production, and electricity production relate to the overall industrialization of the market and can be used effectively by suppliers of industrial products and services. As an example, energy consumption per capita may serve as an indicator of market potential for electrical markets, provided evenness of distribution exists over the market. Yet the marketer must make sure that the energy is affordable and compatible (in terms of current and voltage) with the products to be marketed.

The existence and expansion of basic infrastructure has contributed significantly to increased agricultural output in Asia and Latin America. The Philippines has allocated 5 percent of agricultural development funds to rural electrification programs. On a similar level, basic

Exhibit 2.6

Percentage of Households Owning Selected Appliances

	USA	Belgium	Denmark	France	Germany	Italy	Netherlands	Spain	Sweden	Switzerland	United Kingdom	China	Japan
Car	93.15	78.47	73.28	78.98	91.73	75.59	72.03	76.29	92.09	49.1	75.15	2.98	81.78
CD Player	59.6	68.01	90.05	24.45	87.08	13.21	87.76	41.68	84.27	59.84	86.77	2.26	68.51
Dishwasher	58.93	53.09	51.45	37.11	58.74	39.33	44.28	26.68	61.82	80.79	31.98	1.43	57.41
Freezer	37.11	70.78	92.42	51.62	76.17	47.16	75.16	50.53	98.72	67.3	59.77	0.55	34.95
Microwave Oven	85.64	87.04	59.97	52.82	39.02	36.22	77.33	42.29	74.89	59.11	89.01	0.47	90.64
Personal Computer	72.75	53.08	76.27	40.32	55.9	28.88	71.79	26.12	57.91	63.5	48.33	15.69	49.14
Refrigerator	99.47	99.8	98.85	86.57	90.41	87.2	98.95	88.49	99.26	99.05	98.59	6.7	97.75
Telephone	85.86	96.47	96.46	89.22	99.38	97.29	92.18	82.31	99.08	98.65	94.23	27.13	87.41
Television	99.61	99.57	92.53	95.94	97.31	95.97	98.65	98.55	97.09	96.94	98.25	46.37	99
Tumble Dryer	69.42	30.32	50.09	27.58	43.99	18.07	68.05	16.63	38.51	39.02	56.13	1.74	36.94
Vacuum Cleaner	99.28	99.04	95.14	96.6	99.59	84.96	94.53	70.57	96.42	99.68	91.41	1.92	99.75
Washing Machine	82.32	88.34	80.04	98.59	98.17	97.99	97.17	83.61	79.23	78.73	96.02	2.59	99.34

SOURCE: Compiled from *International Marketing Data and Statistics 2004* (London: Euromonitor, 2004), table 15.7.

Exhibit **2.7**

Consumer Price Index for Selected Countries

Country	1998	2001	2004	2007
Argentina	0.92	−1.07	4.42	8.8
Australia	0.85	4.38	2.34	2.5
Bangladesh	6.97	1.39	3.16	9.1
Brazil	3.20	6.86	6.60	3.6
Canada	0.99	2.53	1.83	2.1
China (PRC, excl. Hong Kong)	−0.84	0.34	3.99	4.8
Ecuador	36.10	37.68	2.74	2.3
Egypt	4.18	2.27	11.27	9.3
France	0.67	1.63	2.13	1.5
Ghana	14.62	32.91	12.63	15.5
India	13.23	3.68	3.77	6.4
Japan	0.66	−0.73	−0.01	0.1
Mexico	15.93	6.36	4.69	4.8
Romania	59.10	34.47	11.88	7.1
South Africa	6.88	5.70	1.39	2.3
South Korea	7.54	4.03	3.61	6.1
Turkey	84.64	54.40	8.60	8.8
United States	1.55	2.83	2.68	2.9
United Kingdom	3.42	1.82	2.96	4.3
Venezuela	35.78	12.53	12.75	18.7

SOURCE: Compiled data from *International Financial Statistics* (Washington, DC: International Monetary Fund, various editions). © International Monetary Fund; **http://www.imf.org**.

roads are essential to moving agricultural products. In many parts of Africa, farmers are more than a day's walk from the nearest road. As a result, measures to improve production without commensurate improvements in transportation and communications are of little use because the crops cannot reach the market. In addition, the lack of infrastructure cuts the farmers off from new technology, inputs, and ideas.

Transportation networks by land, rail, waterway, or air are essential for physical distribution. An analysis of rail traffic by freight tons per kilometer offers a possible way to begin an investigation of transportation capabilities; however, these figures may not always indicate the true state of the system. China's railway system carries five times as much freight as India's does, which is an amazing feat considering that only 20 percent of the network is doubletracked and that it is shared by an ever-growing amount of passenger traffic. In spite of the railway's greater use, the international marketer has to rely on other methods of distribution. The tremendous logistics challenge has made national distribution in China slow and constrained expansion from the major urban population centers of Guangzhou, Shanghai, and Beijing.[12] With the same type of caution, the number of passenger cars as well as buses and trucks can be used to analyze the state of road transportation and transportation networks.

Communication is as important as transportation. The ability of a firm to communicate with entities both outside and within the market can be estimated by using indicators of the communications infrastructure: telephones, computers, broadcast media, and print media in use. Wireless technology is changing the world landscape in communications in many ways. The number of mobile phone connections passed the 2 billion mark in 2005 and the 4 billion subscribers level was passed by the end of 2008.[13] Developed, emerging, and developing markets will require different adjustments by marketers. As several markets have achieved greater than 100 percent penetration, handset vendors and network operators have to provide new features such as cameras, MP3 music, and mobile TV. New growth will come from markets such as China, India, Eastern Europe, Latin America, and Africa. By the end of 2008, China had 600 million subscribers and India's growth reached 334 million. The introduction of prepaid service in Latin America led mobile subscriptions to rise from 2 million in 1998 to 400 million in 2008, turning two in three Latin Americans into users.[14]

The diffusion of Internet technology into core business processes and into the lifestyles of consumers has been rapid, especially in industrialized countries. The number of Internet hosts (computers through which users connect to the network) has increased to 541.7 million by 2008, up from 56.2 million in 1999.[15] The total number of people using the Internet is difficult to estimate. Estimates in early 2009 put the number at 1.46 billion (see Exhibit 2.8). There are naturally significant differences within regions as well; for example, within the European Union, the Nordic countries have penetration rates of 70 percent, while new members, such as Poland, are at less than 30 percent.[16] Given the changes expected in the first years of the twenty-first century, all the estimates indicating explosive growth may be low. The number of users will start evening out around the globe, with new technologies assisting. Computers priced at less than $500 or even $200 will boost global computer ownership and subsequent online activity. Developments in television, cable, phone, and wireless technologies not only will make the market broader but will also allow for more services to be delivered more efficiently. For example, with the advent of third-generation mobile communications technology, systems will have 100-fold increase in data transfer, allowing the viewing of videos on mobile phones.[17] Television will also become a mainstream Internet access method of the future. While the interactive TV market served only 3 million viewers in Europe and North America in 1999, the estimates are for 270 million subscribers by 2009.[18] The growth in international opportunities is leading to a rapid internationalization of search engines, as shown in *The International Marketplace 2.2*.

The careful assessment of infrastructure spells out important marketing opportunities. While 2 billion people in Asia are without electricity and only 16 in 1,000 have access to a telephone, the Asian market is the most keenly watched by marketers. According to one estimate, between 1994 and 2000, Asian countries (excluding Japan) spent $1.5 trillion on power, transportation, telecommunications, water supplies, and sanitation.[19] The booming middle class in cities such as Bangkok will ensure that cellular phone sales continue at a record pace. With increasing affluence comes an increasing need for energy. General Electric estimates that China will place orders for 168,000 megawatts in additional power-generating capacity and India more than 70,000 megawatts; the corresponding figure in the United States is 154,000.

Data on the availability of commercial (marketing-related) infrastructure are often not readily available. Data on which to base an assessment may be provided by government sources, such as Overseas Business Reports; by trade associations, such as the Business Equipment Manufacturers' Association or the American Chambers of Commerce; and by trade publications, such as *Advertising Age*. The more extensive the firm's international involvement, the more it can rely on its already existing support network of banks, advertising agencies, and distributors to assess new markets.

Exhibit 2.8

World Internet Usage, 2008

World Regions	Population (2008 Est.)	Population % of the World	Internet Usage, Latest Data	% Population (Penetration)	Usage % of World	Usage Growth 2000–2008
Africa	955,206,348	14.3%	51,065,630	5.3%	3.5%	1,031.2%
Asia	3,776,181,949	56.6%	578,538,257	15.3%	39.5%	406.1%
Europe	800,401,065	11.9%	384,633,765	48.1%	26.3%	266.0%
Middle East	197,090,443	2.9%	41,939,200	21.3%	2.9%	1,176.8%
North America	337,167,248	5.0%	248,241,969	73.6%	17.0%	129.6%
Latin America/Caribbean	576,091,673	8.6%	139,009,209	24.1%	9.5%	669.3%
Oceania/Australia	33,981,562	0.4%	20,204,331	59.5%	1.4%	165.1%
World Total	6,676,120,288	100%	1,463,632,361	21.9%	100.0%	305.5%

SOURCE: Internet World Stats, **http://internetworldstats.com/stats.htm**, accessed January 2, 2009.

The International MARKETPLACE

The International Pay-Per-Click Market

Pay per click (PPC) is an Internet advertising model used on search engines, advertising networks, and content website—such as blogs—where advertisers only pay when a user actually clicks on an advertisement to visit the advertisers' website. It has become a battlefield between global players and their local challengers.

China

In China, e-commerce and online payment platforms are well developed and have a large number of users. The numbers will soon surpass U.S. figures and, in 2008 alone, Chinese marketers continued to grow spending at approximately 8 percent. The Chinese search engine market is expected to see a compound annual growth of 30 percent from 2006 to 2010. Within 10 years, China is expected to be the most important online ad and commerce market in the world. In China, Baidu is considered the leading search engine. Market shares for 2008 are: Baidu 60.9 percent, Google 27 percent, and Sogou 3.1 percent.

Baidu's early success is attributed to its MP3 search engine. With Baidu, there are various well known controversies regarding corruption. One of the big ones is strong players must have strong governmental relations that may translate to foreign companies (like Google) never having equal footing in the Chinese market. With Baidu, issues related to poor search quality have also been documented.

Japan

Japan has one of the highest Internet penetrations. Approximately 67.7 percent of Japan's population has access to the Internet. Japan has approximately $5.7 billion in the online advertising market out of a global market estimated at $45 billion. By 2011, Internet advertising is projected to grow to $7.5 billion, including $1.28 billion for mobile ads and $2.26 billion for PPC ads. In Japan, Yahoo! is predominant. The Japanese market share breakdown shows Yahoo! at 76 percent and Google at 54 percent.

In July 2008, Yahoo! Japan had ten times as many monthly page views (21.9 billion) as Google (2.2 billion) and almost twice as many monthly unique Japanese visitors (46 million for Yahoo! versus 26 million for Google). In terms of search volume, one can only speculate because Japanese search engines don't disclose search volume figures. In Japan, more than half of the Internet users access the web via mobile devices, and the country is ranked number 3 in terms of total web population at 94 million. This equals the web populations of Germany and the UK combined.

Russia

Internet penetration in Russia is about 25 percent. The Russian Internet market has been experiencing rapid development, with its audience growing 25 percent during the past year. Search related ads revenue is expected to rise from $200 million in 2007 to approximately $1 billion by 2010. The largest search engine in the Russian market is called the Yandex (contained within a web portal). The two predominant players in the Russian market are Yandex (at 47.4 percent) and Google (at 34 percent). In 2006, Google had a 5 percent market share but has since managed to capture one-third of the Russian paid search market.

Marketing Considerations for International PPC

In targeting international markets, it is prudent to use a company located in the specific geographic area one is interested in. A company with "boots on the ground" will have knowledge in language, culture, and marketing jargon and will be able to localize content, as opposed to merely translating it from one language to another.

Currently, there are good deals to be had in other countries. For example, clicks costs are cheaper on the Yandex and Baidu than on Google in the U.S. and UK. In markets like China and Russia, the influence of government is an important consideration. The ruling bodies of both countries have been known to interfere in business. Having said this, China's government seems to be encouraging and supporting Internet and technology-related industries.

SOURCES: Mona Eleissely, "Getting to Know International PPC Markets," *Search Engine Land*, November 3, 2008, available at **http://searchengineland.com/getting-to-know-international-ppc-markets-14955.php**; and Nick Wilsdon, ed., *Global Search Report 2007*, available at **http://www.e3internet.com/downloads/global-search-report-2007.pdf**; **http://www.comscore.com/press/release.asp?press=2176**.

Impact of the Economic Environment on Social Development

Many of the characteristics discussed are important beyond numbers. Economic success comes with a price tag. All the social traumas that were once believed endemic only to the West are now hitting other parts of the world as well. Many countries, including the nations of Southeast Asia, were able to achieve double-digit growth for decades while paying scant attention to problems that are now demanding treatment: infrastructure limits, labor shortages, demands for greater political freedom, environmental destruction, urban congestion, and even the spread of drug addiction.[20]

Because of the close relationship between economic and social development, many of the figures can be used as social indicators as well. Consider the following factors and their significance: share of urban population, life expectancy, number of physicians per capita, literacy rate, percentage of income received by the richest 5 percent of the population, and percentage of the population with access to electricity. In addition to these factors, several other variables can be used as cultural indicators: number of public libraries, registered borrowings, book titles published, and number of daily newspapers. The **Physical Quality of Life Index (PQLI)** is a composite measure of the level of welfare in a country. It has three components: life expectancy, infant mortality, and adult literacy rates.[21] The three components of the PQLI are among the few social indicators available to provide a comparison of progress through time in all of the countries of the world.

Differences in the degree of urbanization of target markets in lesser-developed countries influence international marketers' product strategies. If products are targeted only to urban areas, products need minimal adjustments, mainly to qualify them for market entry. However, when targeting national markets, firms may need to make extensive adaptations to match more closely the expectations and the more narrow consumption experiences of the rural population.

In terms of infrastructure, improved access in rural areas brings with it an expansion of nonfarm enterprises such as shops, repair services, and grain mills. It also changes customs, attitudes, and values. As an example, a World Bank study on the impact of rural roads of Yucatán in Mexico found that roads offered an opportunity for enlarging women's roles by introducing new ideas, education, medical care, and economic alternatives to maize cultivation.[22] In particular, women married later, had fewer children, and pursued more nondomestic activities. The same impact has been observed with increased access to radio and television. These changes can, if properly understood and utilized, offer major new opportunities to the international marketer.

As societies attain a certain level of wealth, income becomes less of a factor in people's level of contentment. Emotional well-being may be determined by the quality of social relationships, enjoyment at work, job stability, and overall conditions in the country (such as democratic institutions). Countries like Mexico and Denmark score high on a national well-being index, while Zimbabwe and Russia are among the lowest.[23]

The presence of multinational corporations, which by their very nature are change agents, will accelerate social change. If government control is weak, the multinational corporation bears the social responsibility for its actions. In some cases, governments restrict the freedom of multinational corporations if their actions may affect the environment. As an example, the Indonesian government places construction restrictions (such as building height) on hotels in Bali to avoid the overcrowding and ecological problems incurred in Hawaii when that state vigorously developed its tourism sector.

Regional Economic Integration

Economic integration has been one of the main economic developments affecting world markets since World War II. Countries have wanted to engage in economic cooperation to use their respective resources more effectively and to provide larger markets for member-country producers. Some integration efforts have had quite ambitious goals, such as political integration;

some have failed as the result of perceptions of unequal benefits from the arrangement or parting of ways politically. Exhibit 2.9, a summary of the major forms of economic cooperation in regional markets, shows the varying degrees of formality with which integration can take place. These economic integration efforts are dividing the world into trading blocs. Of the 32 groupings in existence, some have superstructures of nation-states (such as the European Union), some (such as ASEAN Free Trade Area) are multinational agreements that are currently more political than economic. Some are not trading blocs per se, but work to further them. The Free Trade Area of the Americas (FTAA) is a foreign-policy initiative to further democracy in the hemisphere through incentives to capitalistic development and trade liberalization. Blocs are joining bigger blocs as in the case of the Asia Pacific Economic Cooperation, which brings partners together from multiple continents (including NAFTA, AFTA, and individual countries such as Australia, China, Japan, and Russia).[24] With an impasse in the Doha Round of WTO negotiations, more countries are turning to bilateral agreements with 205 of them in effect.

Success of these blocs, from their establishment to future expansion institutionally and geographically, will depend (1) on leadership of selected countries (i.e., every bloc needs an "engine"); (2) their proximity in terms of geography, culture, administrative dimensions, and basis economic factors; and (3) their commitment to regional cooperation. For example, the biggest trading partners for any of the European Union member nations are other EU countries. Countries that have traditionally not traded with each other or have relations driven by animosities (e.g., in South Asia) have a more challenging time in implementing economic integration.

Levels of Economic Integration

Free Trade Area

The **free trade area** is the least restrictive and loosest form of economic integration among nations. In a free trade area, all barriers to trade among member countries are removed. Goods and services are freely traded among member countries. No discriminatory taxes,

Exhibit **2.9**

Forms of Economic Integration in Regional Markets

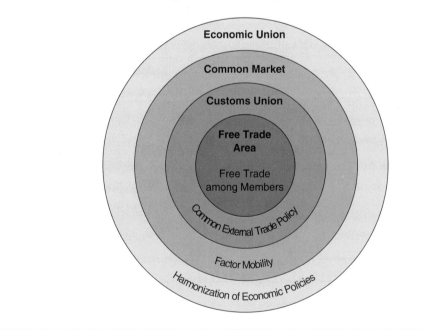

quotas, tariffs, or other barriers are allowed. Sometimes a free trade area is formed only for certain classes of goods and services. For example, before NAFTA, the United States and Canada already had sectoral free trade agreements such as that for automobiles. A notable feature of free trade areas is that each member country continues to set its own policies in relation to nonmembers. This means that each member is free to set any tariffs or other restrictions that it chooses on trade with countries outside of the free trade area. Among such arrangements are the European Free Trade Area (EFTA) and the North American Free Trade Agreement (NAFTA). As an example of the freedom members have in terms of their policies toward nonmembers, Mexico has signed a number of bilateral free trade agreements with other blocs (the European Union) and nations (Chile) to both improve trade and to attract investment.

Customs Union

The **customs union** is one step further along the spectrum of economic integration. As in the free trade area, members of the customs union dismantle barriers to trade in goods and services among members. In addition, however, the customs union establishes a common trade policy with respect to nonmembers. Typically, this takes the form of a common external tariff, whereby imports from nonmembers are subject to the same tariff when sold to any member country. The Southern African Customs Union is the oldest and most successful example of economic integration in Africa.

Common Market

The **common market** amounts to a customs union covering the exchange of goods and services, the prohibition of duties in exports and imports between members, and the adoption of a common external tariff with respect to nonmembers. In addition, factors of production (labor, capital, and technology) are mobile among members. Restrictions on immigration and cross-border investment are abolished. The importance of **factor mobility** for economic growth cannot be overstated. When factors of production are mobile, then capital, labor, and technology may be employed in their most productive uses.

Despite the obvious benefits, members of a common market must be prepared to cooperate closely in monetary, fiscal, and employment policies. Furthermore, although a common market will enhance the productivity of members in the aggregate, it is by no means clear that individual member countries will always benefit. Because of these difficulties, the goals of common markets have proved to be elusive in many areas of the world, notably Central and South America and Asia. In the mid-1980s, the European Community (EC) embarked on an ambitious effort to remove the barriers between the then twelve member countries to free the movement of goods, services, capital, and people. The process was ratified by the passing of the **Single European Act** in 1987 with the target date of December 31, 1992, to complete the internal market. In December 1991, the EC agreed in Maastricht that the so-called 1992 process would be a step toward cooperation beyond the economic dimension. While many of the directives aimed at opening borders and markets were completed on schedule, some sectors, such as automobiles, took longer to open up.

Economic Union

The creation of a true **economic union** requires integration of economic policies in addition to the free movement of goods, services, and factors of production across borders. Under an economic union, members will harmonize monetary policies, taxation, and government spending. In addition, a common currency is to be used by members. This could be accomplished, de facto, by a system of fixed exchange rates. Clearly, the formation of an economic union requires members to surrender a large measure of their national sovereignty to supranational authorities in communitywide institutions such as the European Parliament. The final step would be a **political union** calling for political unification. The ratification of the Maastricht Treaty in late 1993 by all of the twelve member countries of the EC created the **European Union**, effective January 1, 1994. The treaty (jointly with the Treaty of Amsterdam in 1997) set the foundation for economic and monetary union (EMU) with the establishment of the euro (€) as a common currency by January 1, 1999.

International Groupings

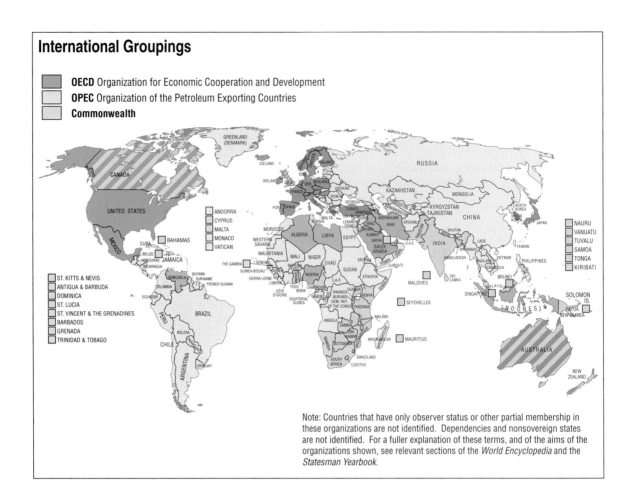

- **OECD** Organization for Economic Cooperation and Development
- **OPEC** Organization of the Petroleum Exporting Countries
- **Commonwealth**

Note: Countries that have only observer status or other partial membership in these organizations are not identified. Dependencies and nonsovereign states are not identified. For a fuller explanation of these terms, and of the aims of the organizations shown, see relevant sections of the *World Encyclopedia* and the *Statesman Yearbook*.

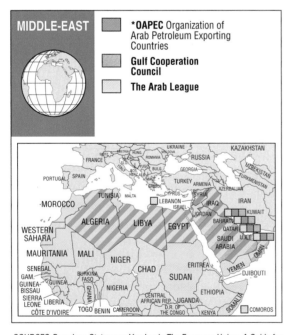

MIDDLE-EAST

- ***OAPEC** Organization of Arab Petroleum Exporting Countries
- **Gulf Cooperation Council**
- **The Arab League**

EUROPE

- **EU** European Union
- Countries interested in **EU** membership

SOURCES: Based on *Statesman Yearbook; The European Union: A Guide for Americans*, 2006, **http://www.eurounion.org/infores/euguide/euguide.htm**; "Afrabet Soup," *The Economist*, February 10, 2001, p. 77, **http://www.economist.com**.

*Eritrea, Venezuela, and India were recently added as "observers."

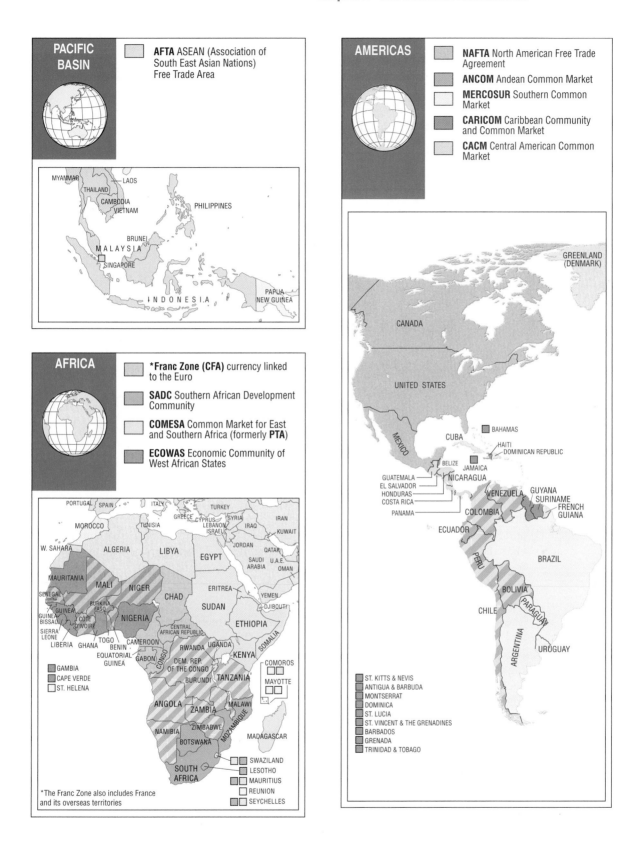

© ISTOCKPHOTO.COM/MARIA TOUTOUDAKI

IN 1999, THE EURO BECAME THE COMMON CURRENCY FOR A NUMBER OF EU COUNTRIES.

Fifteen EU countries are currently part of "Euroland" (Austria, Belgium, Cyprus, Finland, France, Germany, Greece, Holland, Ireland, Italy, Luxembourg, Malta, Portugal, Slovenia, and Spain). In addition, moves would be made toward a political union with common foreign and security policy as well as judicial cooperation.[25] Efforts to tie the members closer together through a Constitution for Europe have, however, failed.

European Integration

The most important implication of the freedom of movement for products, services, people, and capital within the EU is the economic growth that is expected to result. Several specific sources of increased growth have been identified. First, there will be gains from eliminating the transaction costs associated with border patrols, customs procedures, and so forth. Second, economic growth will be spurred by the economies of scale that will be achieved when production facilities become more concentrated. Third, there will be gains from more intense competition among European companies. Firms that were monopolists in one country will now be subject to competition from firms in other member countries. The introduction of the euro is expected to add to the efficiencies, especially in terms of consolidation of firms across industries and across countries. Furthermore, countries in Euroland will enjoy cheaper transaction costs and reduced currency risks, and consumers and businesses will enjoy price transparency and increased price-based competition. Marketer reactions to the euro will be discussed further in Chapter 17.

The enlargement of the EU has become one of the most debated issues. In 2004, the EU expanded to 25 members, accepting eight Central European and two Mediterranean countries to the Union. Despite some of the uncertainties about the future cohesiveness of the EU, new nations want to join. Bulgaria and Romania joined in 2007, and Croatia's, Macedonia's, and Turkey's memberships are pending. The agreement on the European Economic Area (EEA) extends the Single Market of the EU to three of the four EFTA countries (Iceland, Liechtenstein, and Norway, with Switzerland opting to develop its relationship with the EU through bilateral agreements).[26]

The integration has important implications for firms within and outside Europe because it poses both threats and opportunities, benefits and costs. There will be substantial benefits for those firms already operating in Europe. These firms will gain because their operations in one country can now be freely expanded into others and their products may be freely sold across borders. In a borderless Europe, firms will have access to approximately 493 million consumers. Substantial economies of scale in production and marketing will also result. The extent of these economies of scale will depend on the ability of the marketers to find pan-regional segments or to homogenize tastes across borders through promotional activity. There are challenges as well. Nokia's decision to close down a major production facility for mobile devices in Bochum, Germany, and to move its manufacturing to more cost-competitive regions in Europe (such as Cluj in Romania) met with a hailstorm of protests from the German government and individual citizens.[27]

For firms from nonmember countries, there are various possibilities depending on the firm's position within the market. Exhibit 2.10 provides four different scenarios with proposed courses of action. Well-established U.S.-based multinational marketers such as H.J. Heinz and Colgate-Palmolive will be able to take advantage of the new economies of scale. For example, 3M plants earlier turned out different versions of the company's products for various markets. Now, the 3M plant in Wales, for example, makes videotapes and videocassettes for all of Europe. Colgate-Palmolive has to watch out for competitors, like Germany's Henkel, in the brutally competitive detergent market. At the same time, large-scale retailers, such as France's Carrefour and Germany's Aldi group, are undertaking their own efforts to exploit the situation with hypermarkets supplied by central warehouses with computerized inventories. Their procurement policies have to be met by companies like Heinz. Many multinationals are developing pan-European strategies to exploit the emerging situation; that is, they are standardizing their products and processes to the greatest extent possible without compromising local input and implementation.

A company with a foothold in only one European market is faced with the danger of competitors who can use the strength of multiple markets. Furthermore, the elimination of barriers may do away with the company's competitive advantage. For example, more than half of the 45 major European food companies have traditionally been in just one or two of the individual European markets and seriously lag behind broader-based U.S. and Swiss firms. Similarly, automakers PSA and Fiat are nowhere close to the cross-manufacturing presence of Ford and GM. The courses of action include expansion through acquisitions or

Exhibit 2.10

Proposed Company Responses to European Integration

Company Status	Challenges	Response
Established multinational market/multiple markets	Exploit opportunities from improved productivity Meet challenge of competitors Cater to customers/intermediaries doing same	Pan-European strategy
Firm with one European subsidiary	Competition Loss of niche	Expansion Strategic alliances Rationalization Divestment
Exporter to Europe	Competition Access	European branch Selective acquisition Strategic alliance
No interest	Competition at home Lost opportunity	Entry

SOURCE: Developed from John F. Magee, "1992: Moves Americans Must Make," *Harvard Business Review* 67 (May–June 1989): 78–84.

mergers, formation of strategic alliances, rationalization by concentrating only on business segments in which the company can be a pan-European leader, and finally, divestment.

Exporters will need to worry about maintaining their competitive position and continued access to the market. Small and mid-sized U.S. companies account for more than 60 percent of U.S. exports to the EU. Their success, despite the high value of the dollar making exports more expensive, is based on the relationships they have developed with their customers, especially in high-tech.[28] Companies with a physical presence may be in a better position to assess and take advantage of the developments. Internet systems provider WatchGuard Technologies has almost doubled its staff in Europe, from 12 to 20, in the wake of September 11 and increasing concern about viruses. In some industries, marketers do not see a reason either to be in Europe at all or to change from exporting to more involved modes of entry. Machinery and machine tools, for example, are in great demand in Europe, and marketers in these companies say they have little reason to manufacture there.

The term **Fortress Europe** has been used to describe the fears of many, especially U.S. firms, about a unified Europe. The concern is that while Europe dismantles internal barriers, it will raise external ones, making access to the European market difficult for U.S. and other non-EU firms. In a move designed to protect European farmers, for example, the EU has occasionally banned the import of certain agricultural goods from the United States. The EU has also called on members to limit the number of American television programs broadcast in Europe. Finally, many U.S. firms are concerned about the relatively strict domestic content rules passed by the EU. These rules require certain products sold in Europe to be manufactured with European inputs. One effect of the perceived threat of Fortress Europe has been increased direct investment in Europe by U.S. firms. Fears that the EU will erect barriers to U.S. exports and fears of the domestic content rules governing many goods have led many U.S. firms to initiate or expand European direct investment.

North American Integration

Although the EU is undoubtedly the most successful and best-known integrative effort, North American integration efforts, although only a few years old, have gained momentum and attention. What started as a trading pact between two close and economically well-developed allies has already been expanded conceptually to include Mexico, and long-term plans call for further additions. However, North American integration is for purely economic reasons; there are no constituencies for political integration.

The ratification of NAFTA created the world's largest free market with 450 million consumers and a total output of $15.7 trillion, slightly smaller than the EEA.[29] The pact marked a bold departure: Never before had industrialized countries created such a massive free trade area with a developing-country neighbor.

Since Canada stood to gain very little from NAFTA (its trade with Mexico is 1 percent of its trade with the United States), much of the controversy centered on the gains and losses for the United States and Mexico. Proponents argued that the agreement gives U.S. firms access to a huge pool of relatively low-cost Mexican labor at a time when demographic trends are resulting in labor shortages in many parts of the United States. At the same time, many new jobs are created in Mexico. The agreement gives firms in both countries access to millions of additional consumers, and the liberalized trade flows resulted in higher economic growth in both countries. The top 20 exports and imports between Mexico and the United States are in virtually the same industries, indicating intra-industry specialization and building of economies of scale for global competitiveness.[30] Overall, the corporate view toward NAFTA was overwhelmingly positive.

Opposition to NAFTA centered on issues relating to labor and the environment. Unions in particular worried about job losses to Mexico, given its lower wages and work standards; some estimated that 6 million U.S. workers were vulnerable to migration of jobs. Similarly, any expansion of NAFTA was perceived as a threat. Distinctive features of NAFTA are the two-side agreements that were worked out to correct perceived abuses in labor and the environment in Mexico. The North American Agreement on Labor Cooperation (NAALC) was set up to hear complaints about worker abuse, and the Commission on Environmental Compliance was established to act as a public advocate on the environment. These side agreements have had little impact, however, and have almost no enforcement power.[31]

After a remarkable start in increased trade and investment, NAFTA suffered a serious setback due to a significant devaluation of the Mexican peso in 1995 and its negative impact on trade. Critics argue that too much was expected too fast of a country whose political system and economy were not ready for open markets. In response, advocates argue that there was nothing wrong with the Mexican real economy and that the peso crisis was a political one that would be overcome with time.

Trade among Canada, Mexico, and the United States has increased by 50 percent since NAFTA took effect, exceeding $930 billion in 2007.[32] Reforms have turned Mexico into an attractive market in its own right. Mexico's gross domestic product has been expanding by more than 3 percent every year since 1989, and exports to the United States have doubled since 1986 to $166.5 billion in 2008. By institutionalizing the nation's turn to open its markets, the free trade agreement has attracted considerable new foreign investment (well over $100 billion since NAFTA began). The United States has benefited from Mexico's success. U.S. exports to Mexico ($114.8 billion) are double those to Japan. While the surplus of $1.3 billion in 1994 had turned to a deficit of $111.5 billion in 2004, these imports have helped Mexico's recovery and will, therefore, strengthen NAFTA in the long term. Furthermore, U.S. imports from Mexico have been shown to have much higher U.S. content than imports from other countries.[33] Cooperation between Mexico and the United States is expanding beyond trade and investment. For example, binational bodies have been established to tackle issues such as migration, border control, and drug trafficking.[34]

Among the U.S. industries to benefit are computers, autos and auto parts, petro-chemicals, financial services, and aerospace. Aerospace companies such as Boeing, Honeywell, Airbus Industrie, and GE Aircraft Engines have recently made Mexico a center for both parts manufacture and assembly. Aerospace is now one of Mexico's largest industries, second only to electronics, with 10,000 workers employed.[35] In Mexico's growth toward a more advanced society, manufacturers of consumer goods will also stand to benefit. NAFTA has already had a major impact on the emergence of new retail chains, many of which were developed to handle new products from abroad.[36] Not only have U.S. retailers, such as Wal-Mart, expanded to and in Mexico, but Mexican retailers, such as Grupo Gigante, have entered the U.S. market.[37] Wal-Mart's use of lower tariffs, physical proximity, and buying power are changing the Mexican retail landscape, as shown in *The International Marketplace 2.3*.

Free trade produces both winners and losers. Although opponents concede that the agreement spurred economic growth, they point out that segments of the U.S. economy have been harmed by the agreement. Wages and employment for unskilled workers in the United States decreased because of Mexico's low-cost labor pool. U.S. companies have been moving operations to Mexico since the 1960s. The door was opened when Mexico liberalized export restrictions to allow for more so-called **maquiladoras**, plants that make goods and parts or process food for export to the United States. The supply of labor in the maquiladoras was plentiful, the pay and benefits low, and the work regulations lax by U.S. standards. In the last two decades, maquiladoras evolved from low-end garment or small-appliance assembly outfits to higher-end manufacturing of big-screen TVs, computers, and auto parts. The factories shipped $80 billion worth of goods (half of Mexican exports), almost all of it to the United States. But the arrangement is in trouble. The NAFTA treaty required Mexico to strip maquiladoras of their duty-free status by 2001. Tariff breaks formerly given to all imported parts, supplies, equipment, and machinery used by foreign factories in Mexico now apply only to inputs from Canada and Mexico. This effect is felt most by Asian factories because Mexico still imports a large amount of components from across the Pacific (for example, 97 percent of components for TVs assembled in Tijuana are imported, most from Asia). European companies felt less of an effect because of Mexico's free trade agreement with the EU, which eliminated tariffs gradually by the end of 2007.[38] Wages have also been rising with the result of some low-end manufacturers of apparel and toys moving production to Asia. While the Mexican government is eager to attract maquiladora investment, it is also keen to move away from using cheap labor as a central element of competitiveness. Furthermore, many of the companies employing maquiladoras have also come under criticism for their wage practices.[39]

Despite U.S. fears of rapid job loss due to companies sending business south of the border, recent studies declare job gains and losses a near washout. The good news is that

The International MARKETPLACE

NAFTA Reshaping Retail Markets

Wal-Mart saw the promise of the Mexican market in 1991 when it stepped outside of the United States for the first time by launching Sam's Clubs in 50–50 partnership with Cifra, Mexico's largest retailer at that time. The local partner was needed to provide operational expertise in a market significantly different in culture and income from Wal-Mart's domestic one. Within months, the first outlet—a bare-bones unit that sold bulk items at just above wholesale prices—was breaking all Wal-Mart records in sales. While tariffs still made imported goods pricey, "Made in the USA" merchandise also started appearing on the shelves.

After NAFTA took effect in 1994, tariffs tumbled, unleashing pent-up demand in Mexico for U.S.-made goods. The trade treaty also helped eliminate some of the transportation headaches and government red tape that had kept Wal-Mart from fully realizing its competitive advantage. NAFTA resulted in many European and Asian manufacturers setting up plants in Mexico, giving the retailer cheaper access to more foreign brands.

Wal-Mart's enormous buying power has kept it ahead of its Mexican competitors who are making similar moves. Because Wal-Mart consolidates its orders for all goods it sells outside of the United States, it can wring deeper discounts from suppliers than its local competitors. Wal-Mart Mexico has repeatedly exploited NAFTA and other economic forces to trigger price wars. For example, rather than pocket the windfall that resulted when tariffs on Lasko brand floor fans fell from 20 percent to 2 percent, price cuts took place equal to the tariff reductions.

Behind Wal-Mart's success are increasingly price-conscious consumers. The greater economic security of NAFTA has helped tame Mexico's once fierce inflation. The resulting price stability has made it easier for Mexican consumers to spot bargains. In addition, Wal-Mart's clean, brightly lit interiors, orderly and well-stocked aisles, and consistent pricing policies are a relief from the chaotic atmosphere that still prevails in many local stores.

Wal-Mart's aggressive tactics have resulted in complaints as well. In 2002, Mexico's Competition Commission was asked to probe into reports that Wal-Mart exerts undue pressure on suppliers to lower their prices. Local retailers, such as Comerci, Gigante, and Soriana, have seen their profits plummet but are forced to provide prices competitive to Wal-Mart's. In addition, they have engaged in aggressive rehauls of their operations. Soriana, for example, took out ads in local newspapers warning about

WAL-MART'S ENORMOUS BUYING POWER HAS KEPT IT AHEAD OF ITS MEXICAN COMPETITORS.

"foreign supermarkets" when regulators fined a Wal-Mart in Monterrey because a shelf price did not match the price on the checkout receipt.

Mexican retailers are not just playing a defensive game. Gigante has opened nine stores in the Los Angeles area and aims to become the most popular supermarket among California's 11 million Latinos, most of whom are from Mexico and connect with the stores. Latinos boast a collective disposable income of $450 billion a year, with much of it going toward food. "The big chains gave Gigante the opportunity to come in here," said Steven Soto, head of the Mexican-American Grocers Association, a trade group that represents some 18,000 Latino store managers and owners. "The chains did not understand how to market to our community." Given that food tastes are the last things to change with immigrants, Gigante's product choices (e.g., chorizo and carnitas), placements (e.g., produce close by the entrance), and decor have made it a success. Some local players are focusing on relatively uncontested rural markets in a similar fashion to the way Wal-Mart was able to grow in the United States against Kmart and Sears in its time. Soriana and Chedraui have avoided Mexico City until recently, opting instead to build a presence and refine their approaches in rural areas, where their customer knowledge is greatest.

SOURCES: Dante Di Gregorio, Douglas Thomas, and Fernan Gonzalez de Castilla, "Competition Between Emerging Markets and Multinational Firms: Wal-Mart and Mexican Retailers," *International Journal of Management* 25 (September 2008): 532–545; "Grocer Grande," *Time Inside Business,* April 2003, A3–A10; "War of the Superstores," *Business Week,* September 23, 2002, 60; "How Well Does Wal-Mart Travel?" *Business Week,* September 3, 2001, 82–84; "How NAFTA Helped Wal-Mart Reshape the Mexican Market," *The Wall Street Journal,* August 31, 2001, A1–A2; and Vijay Govindarajan and Anil K. Gupta, "Taking Wal-Mart Global: Lessons from Retailing's Giant," *Strategy and Business,* fourth quarter, 1999, 45–56.

free trade will create higher-skilled and better-paying jobs in the United States as a result of growth in exports. As a matter of fact, jobs in U.S. exporting firms tend to pay 10 to 15 percent more than the jobs they have replaced. Losers have been U.S. manufacturers of auto parts, furniture, and household glass; sugar, peanut, and citrus growers; and seafood and vegetable producers. The U.S. Labor Department has certified 316,000 jobs as threatened or lost due to trade with Mexico and Canada. At the same time, the U.S. economy has added some 20 million jobs in the years since NAFTA. The fact that job losses have been in more heavily unionized sectors has made these losses politically charged. In most cases, high Mexican shipping and inventory costs will continue to make it more efficient for many U.S. industries to serve their home market from U.S. plants. Outsourcing of lower-skilled jobs is an unstoppable trend for developed economies such as the United States. However, NAFTA has given U.S. firms a way of taking advantage of cheaper labor while still keeping close links to U.S. suppliers. Mexican assembly plants get 82 percent of their parts from U.S. suppliers, while factories in Asia are using only a fraction of that.[40] Without NAFTA, entire industries might be lost to Asia rather than just the labor-intensive portions.

Integration pains extend to other areas as well. Approximately 85 percent of U.S.–Mexican trade moves on trucks. Under NAFTA, cross-border controls on trucking were to be eliminated by the end of 1995, allowing commercial vehicles to move freely in four U.S. and six Mexican border states. But the U.S. truckers, backed by the Teamsters Union, would have nothing of this, arguing that Mexican trucks were dangerous and exceeded weight limits. The union also worried that opening of the border would depress wages, because it would allow U.S. trucking companies to team up with lower-cost counterparts in Mexico. In 2001, however, the NAFTA Arbitration Panel ruled that Mexican trucks must be allowed to cross U.S. borders and the U.S. Senate approved a measure that allows Mexican truckers to haul cargo provided they meet strict inspection and safety rules.[41] Yet, even 8 years later the trading issue continues to be controversial and a source of trade conflict. On the Mexican side, truckers are worried that if the border opens, U.S. firms will simply take over the trucking industry in Mexico. First trials of cross-border trucking were still waiting to start in 2008.

Countries dependent on trade with NAFTA countries are concerned that the agreement would divert trade and impose significant losses on their economies. Asia's continuing economic success depends largely on easy access to the North American markets, which account for more than 25 percent of annual export revenue for many Asian countries. Lower-cost producers in Asia are likely to lose some exports to the United States if they are subject to tariffs but Mexican firms are not and may, therefore, have to invest in NAFTA.[42] Similarly, many in the Caribbean and Central America have always feared that the apparel industries of these regions will be threatened as would much-needed investments.

NAFTA may be the first step toward a hemispheric bloc, although nobody expects it to happen anytime soon. It took more than three years of tough bargaining to reach an agreement between the United States and Canada—two countries with parallel economic, industrial, and social systems. The challenges of expanding free trade throughout Latin America will be significant. As a first step, Chile was scheduled to join as a fourth member in 1997. However, the membership has not materialized due to U.S. political maneuvering, and Chile has since entered into bilateral trade agreements with both Canada and Mexico and joined

Mercosur as an associate member. This has meant that U.S. marketers are reporting trade deals lost to Canadian competitors, who are free of Chile's 11 percent tariffs.[43] Overall, many U.S. marketers fear that Latin Americans will start moving closer to Europeans if free trade discussions throughout the hemisphere are not seen to progress. For example, both Mercosur and Mexico have signed free-trade agreements with the EU.[44] Since of hemispheric free-trade negotiations to achieve the Free Trade Area of the Americas (FTAA) stalled, the United States only has free trade arrangements with Chile, Colombia, and Panama. The Central America–Dominican Republic–United States Free Trade Agreement (CAFTA–DR) of 2005 includes seven signatories: the United States, Costa Rica, Dominican Republic, El Salvador, Guatemala, Honduras, and Nicaragua.

Other Economic Alliances

Perhaps the world's developing countries have the most to gain from successful integrative efforts. Because many of these countries are also quite small, economic growth is difficult to generate internally. Quite a few have adopted policies of **import substitution** to foster economic growth. An import substitution policy involves developing industries to produce goods that were formerly imported. Many of these industries, however, can be efficient producers only with a higher level of production than can be consumed by the domestic economy. Their success, therefore, depends on accessible export markets made possible by integrative efforts.

Integration in Latin America

Before the signing of the U.S.–Canada Free Trade Agreement, all the major trading bloc activity had taken place elsewhere in the Americas. However, none of the activity in Latin America has been hemispheric; that is, Central America had its structures, the Caribbean nations had theirs, and South America had its own different forms. However, for political and economic reasons, these attempts have never reached set objectives. In a dramatic transformation, these nations sought free trade as a salvation from stagnation, inflation, and debt. In response to these developments, Brazil, Argentina, Uruguay, and Paraguay set up a common market called MERCOSUR (Mercado Común del Sur).[45] Despite their own economic challenges and disagreements over trade policy, the MERCOSUR members and the two associate members, Bolivia and Chile, have agreed to economic-convergence targets similar to those the EU made as a precursor to the euro. These are in areas of inflation, public debt, and fiscal deficits. Bolivia, Colombia, Ecuador, and Peru have formed the Andean Common Market (ANCOM) and are also associate members of MERCOSUR (as is Chile). Many Latin nations are realizing that if they do not unite, they will become increasingly marginal in the global market. In approaching the EU with a free trade agreement, MERCOSUR members want to diversify their trade relationships and reduce their dependence on U.S. trade. Venezuela's recent addition to the group has experts wondering if MERCOSUR will reorient itself as a political force.

It has been likened to the European Union, but with an area of 12 million square kilometers (4.6 million square miles), it is four times as big. The bloc's combined market encompasses more than 250 million people and accounts for more than three-quarters of the economic activity on the continent. MERCOSUR is the world's fourth largest trading bloc.

When Venezuela joined MERCOSUR, it was required to resign from ANCOM, as Bolivia will have to do if it is admitted. This is because MERCOSUR'S charter does not allow its member nations to have FTAs with non-member nations. Bolivia, however, has said that it will not leave ANCOM. ANCOM and MERCOSUR leaders have discussed the possibility of allying to form a South American Community of Nations, modeled on the European Union, but those talks have not progressed quickly.

The Free Trade Area of the Americas (FTAA) is a policy initiative to bring together five major blocs in the Western hemisphere to compete more effectively against Europe and Asia. It was supposed to be in effect in 2005, but due to political changes in South America and disputes over agriculture and intellectual property rights, there is little chance for a comprehensive trade agreement in the foreseeable future.[46] As a matter of fact, an alternative has arisen in opposition to the U.S.-led FTAA. ALBA, the Bolivarian Alternative for the People of Our America (led by Venezuela) focuses more on social welfare and economic aid than trade liberalization. Ideally, the larger countries would have agreed to consider giving smaller and lesser-developed countries more time to reduce tariffs, to open their economies to foreign investment, and to adopt effective laws in areas such as antitrust, intellectual property rights, bank regulation, and prohibitions on corrupt business practices. At the same time, the less-developed countries would agree to include labor and environmental standards in the negotiations.[47]

Free market reforms and economic revival up to now have had marketers ready to export and to invest in Latin America. For example, Brazil's opening of its computer market has resulted in Hewlett-Packard establishing a joint venture to produce PCs. In the past, Kodak dealt with Latin America through eleven separate country organizations, but has since streamlined its operations to five "boundaryless" companies organized along product lines and taking advantage of trading openings, and has created centralized distribution, thereby making deliveries more efficient and decreasing inventory carrying costs.[48]

Integration in Asia

Development in Asia has been quite different from that in Europe and in the Americas. While European and North American arrangements have been driven by political will, market forces may force more formal integration on Asian politicians. The fact that regional integration is increasing around the world may drive Asian interest to it for pragmatic reasons. First, European and American markets are significant for the Asian producers, and some type of organization or bloc may be needed to maintain leverage and balance against the two other blocs. Second, given that much of the Asian trade growth is from intraregional trade, having common understandings and policies will become necessary. Future integration will most likely use the frame of the most established arrangement in the region, the Association of Southeast Asian Nations (ASEAN). Before late 1991, ASEAN had no real structures, and consensus was reached through informal consultations. In October 1991, ASEAN members announced the formation of a customs union called ASEAN Free Trade Area (AFTA). The ten member countries agreed to reduce tariffs to a maximum level of 5 percent by 2003 and to create a customs union by 2010. Even a common currency has been proposed. Skepticism about the lofty targets has been raised about the group's ability to follow the example of the EuropeanUnion given the widely divergent levels of economic development (e.g., Singapore versus Laos) and the lack of democratic institutions (especially in Myanmar). ASEAN has also agreed to economic cooperation with China, Japan, and South Korea (the so-called ASEAN + 1 and ASEAN + 3 arrangements), as well as with India.

The Malaysians have pushed for the formation of the East Asia Economic Group (EAEG), which would add Hong Kong, Japan, South Korea, and Taiwan to the membership list. This proposal makes sense, because without Japan and the rapidly industrializing countries of the region such as South Korea and Taiwan, the effect of the arrangement would be nominal. Japan's reaction has been generally negative toward all types of regionalization efforts, mainly because it has the most to gain from free trade. However, part of what has been driving regionalization has been Japan's reluctance to foster some of the elements that promote free trade, for example, reciprocity. Should the other trading blocs turn against Japan, its only resort may be to work toward a more formal trade arrangement in the Asia-Pacific area.

Another formal proposal for cooperation would start building bridges between two emerging trade blocs. Some individuals have publicly called for a U.S.-Japan common market. Given the differences on all fronts between the two countries, the proposal may be quite unrealistic at this time. Negotiated trade liberalization will not open Japanese markets because of major institutional differences, as seen in many rounds of successful negotiations but totally unsatisfactory results. The only solution, especially for the U.S. government, is to forge better cooperation between the government and the private sector to improve competitiveness.[49]

In 1988, Australia proposed the Asia Pacific Economic Cooperation (APEC) as an annual forum to maintain a balance in negotiations. The proposal calls for ASEAN members to be joined by Australia, New Zealand, Japan, South Korea, Canada, Chile, Mexico, and the United States. Originally, the model for APEC was not the EU, with its Brussels bureaucracy, but the Organization for Economic Cooperation and Development (OECD), which is a center for research and high-level discussion. However, APEC has now established an ultimate goal of achieving free trade in the area among its developed members by 2010 and among its developing members by 2020.[50]

Economic integration has also taken place on the Indian subcontinent. In 1985, seven nations of the region (India, Pakistan, Bangladesh, Sri Lanka, Nepal, Bhutan, and the Maldives) launched the South Asian Association for Regional Cooperation (SAARC). Cooperation has been limited to relatively noncontroversial areas, such as agriculture and regional development, and is hampered by political disagreements.

Integration in Africa and the Middle East

Africa's economic groupings range from currency unions among European nations and their former colonies to customs unions between neighboring states. In addition to wanting to liberalize trade among members, African countries want to gain better access to European and North American markets for farm and textile products. Given that most of the countries are too small to negotiate with the other blocs, alliances have been the solution. In 1975, sixteen West African nations attempted to create a megamarket large enough to interest investors from the industrialized world and reduce hardship through economic integration. The objective of the Economic Community of West African States (ECOWAS) was to form a customs union and eventually a common market. Although many of its objectives have not been reached, its combined population of 160 million represents the largest economic entity in sub-Saharan Africa. Other entities in Africa include the Common Market for Eastern and Southern Africa (COMESA), the Economic Community of Central African States (CEEAC), the Southern African Customs Union, the Southern African Development Community (SADC), and some smaller, less globally oriented blocs such as the Economic Community of the Great Lakes Countries, the Mano River Union, and the East African Community (EAC). Most member countries are part of more than one block (for example, Tanzania is a member in both the EAC and SADC). The blocs, for the most part, have not been successful due to small memberships and lack of economic infrastructure to produce goods to be traded within the blocs. Moreover, some of the blocs have been relatively inactive for substantial periods of time while their members endure internal political turmoil or even warfare amongst each other.[51] In 2002, African nations established the African Union (AU) for regional cooperation. Eventually, plans call for a pan-African parliament, a court of justice, a central bank, and a shared currency.[52]

Countries in the Arab world have made some progress in economic integration. The Arab Maghreb Union ties together Algeria, Libya, Mauritania, Morocco, and Tunisia in northern Africa. The Gulf Cooperation Council (GCC) is one of the most powerful of any trade groups. The per capita income of its six member states (Bahrain, Kuwait, Oman, Qatar, Saudi Arabia, and the United Arab Emirates) is in the ninetieth percentile in the world. The GCC was formed in 1980 mainly as a defensive measure due to the perceived threat from the Iran-Iraq war. Its aim is to achieve free trade arrangements with the EU and EFTA. A proposal among GCC members calls for the creation of a common currency by 2010. A strong regional currency would help the GCC become a viable trading bloc, able to compete in the new global environment. Two key elements required to create a common currency are underway: the dismantling of trade barriers among members and the creation of a GCC member bank.[53]

A listing of the major regional trade agreements is provided in Exhibit 2.11.

Economic Integration and the International Marketer

Regional economic integration creates opportunities and potential problems for the international marketer. It may have an impact on a company's entry mode by favoring direct investment, because one of the basic rationales of integration is to generate favorable conditions for local production and intraregional trade. By design, larger markets are created, with

Exhibit **2.11**

Major Regional Trade Agreements

AFTA	**ASEAN Free Trade Area**
	Brunei, Cambodia, Indonesia, Laos, Malaysia, Myanmar, Philippines, Singapore, Thailand, Vietnam
ANCOM	**Andean Common Market**
	Bolivia, Colombia, Ecuador, Peru
APEC	**Asia Pacific Economic Cooperation**
	Australia, Brunei, Canada, Chile, China, Hong Kong, Indonesia, Japan, Malaysia, Mexico, New Zealand, Papua New Guinea, Peru, Philippines, Russia, Singapore, South Korea, Taiwan, Thailand, Vietnam, United States
CACM	**Central American Common Market**
	Costa Rica, El Salvador, Guatemala, Honduras, Nicaragua
CARICOM	**Caribbean Community**
	Antigua and Barbuda, Bahamas, Barbados, Belize, Dominica, Grenada, Guyana, Jamaica, Montserrat, St. Kitts–Nevis, St. Lucia, St. Vincent and the Grenadines, Suriname, Trinidad-Tobago
ECOWAS	**Economic Community of West African States**
	Benin, Burkina Faso, Cape Verde, Gambia, Ghana, Guinea, Guinea- Bissau, Ivory Coast, Liberia, Mali, Mauritania, Niger, Nigeria, Senegal, Sierra Leone, Togo
EFTA	**European Free Trade Association**
	Iceland, Liechtenstein, Norway, Switzerland
EU	**European Union**
	Austria, Belgium, Bulgaria, Cyprus, Czech Republic, Denmark, Estonia, Finland, France, Germany, Greece, Hungary, Ireland, Italy, Latvia, Lithuania, Luxembourg, Malta, Netherlands, Poland, Portugal, Romania, Slovakia, Slovenia, Spain, Sweden, United Kingdom
GCC	**Gulf Cooperation Council**
	Bahrain, Kuwait, Oman, Qatar, Saudi Arabia, United Arab Emirates
LAIA	**Latin American Integration Association**
	Argentina, Bolivia, Brazil, Chile, Colombia, Cuba, Ecuador, Mexico, Paraguay, Peru, Uruguay, Venezuela
MERCOSUR	**Southern Common Market**
	Argentina, Brazil, Paraguay, Uruguay, Venezuela
NAFTA	**North American Free Trade Agreement**
	Canada, Mexico, United States
SAARC	**South Asian Association for Regional Cooperation**
	Bangladesh, Bhutan, India, Maldives, Nepal, Pakistan, Sri Lanka
SACU	**Southern African Customs Union**
	Botswana, Lesotho, Namibia, South Africa, Swaziland

For information, *see* **http://www.aseansec.org**; **http://www.apec.org**; **http://www.caricom.org**; **http://www .eurunion.org**; **http://www.mercosur.org.uy**; and **http://www.nafta.org**.

potentially more opportunity. Harmonization efforts may result in standardized regulations, which, in turn, affect production and marketing efforts in a positive manner.

Decisions regarding integrating markets must be assessed from four different perspectives: the range and impact of changes resulting from integration, development of strategies to relate to these changes, organizational changes needed to exploit these changes, and strategies to influence change in a more favorable direction.[54]

Effects of Change

The first task is to envision the outcome of the change. Change in the competitive landscape can be dramatic if scale opportunities can be exploited in relatively homogeneous demand conditions. This could be the case, for example, for industrial goods, consumer durables such as cameras and watches, and professional services. The international marketer will have to take into consideration varying degrees of change readiness within the markets themselves; that is, governments and other stakeholders, such as labor unions, may oppose the liberalization of competition, especially when national champions such as airlines, automobiles, energy, and telecommunications are concerned. However, with deregulation, monopolies have had to transform into competitive industries. In Germany, for example, the price of long-distance calls has fallen 40 percent, forcing the former monopolist, Deutsche Telekom, to streamline its operations and seek new business abroad. By fostering a single market for capital, the euro is pushing Europe closer to a homogeneous market in goods and services, thereby exerting additional pressure on prices.[55]

Strategic Planning

The international marketer will then have to develop a strategic response to the new environment to maintain a sustainable long-term competitive advantage. Those companies already present in an integrated market should fill in gaps in European product/market portfolios through acquisitions or alliances to create a regional or global company. It is increasingly evident that even regional presence is not sufficient and companies need to set their sights on presence beyond that. In industries such as automobiles, mobile communications, and retailing, blocs in the twenty-first century may be dominated by two or three giants, leaving room only for niche players. Those with currently weak positions, or no presence at all, will have to create alliances for market entry and development with established firms. General Mills created Cereal Partners Worldwide with Nestlé to establish itself in Europe and to jointly develop new-market opportunities in Asia. An additional option for the international marketer is to leave the market altogether if it cannot remain competitive because of new competitive conditions or the level of investment needed. For example, Bank of America sold its operations in Italy to Deutsche Bank after it discovered the high cost of becoming a pan-European player.

Reorganization

Whatever changes are made, they will require company reorganization.[56] Structurally, authority will have to become more centralized to execute regional programs. In staffing, focus will have to be on individuals who understand the subtleties of consumer behavior across markets and are therefore able to evaluate the similarities and differences between cultures and markets. In developing systems for the planning and implementation of regional programs, adjustments have to be made to incorporate views throughout the organization. If, for example, decisions on regional advertising campaigns are made at headquarters without consultation with country operations, resentment from the local marketing staff could lead to less-than-optimal execution. The introduction of the euro will mean increased coordination in pricing as compared to the relative autonomy in price setting enjoyed by country organizations in the past. Companies may even move corporate or divisional headquarters from the domestic market to be closer to the customer or centers of innovation. For example, after Procter & Gamble's reorganization, its household care business unit is headquartered in Brussels, Belgium.

Lobbying

International managers, as change agents, must constantly seek ways to influence the regulatory environment in which they have to operate. Economic integration will create its own powers and procedures similar to those of the EU commission and its directives. The international marketer is not powerless to influence both of them; as a matter of fact, a passive approach may result in competitors gaining an advantage or it may put the company at a disadvantage. For example, it was very important for the U.S. pharmaceutical industry to obtain tight patent protection as part of the NAFTA agreement; therefore, substantial time and money were spent on lobbying both the executive and legislative branches of the U.S. government. Often, policymakers rely heavily on the knowledge and experience of the private sector to carry out their own work. Influencing change will therefore mean providing industry information, such as test results, to the policymakers. Many marketers consider lobbying a public relations activity and therefore go beyond the traditional approaches. Lobbying will usually have to take place at multiple levels simultaneously; within the EU, this means the European Commission in Brussels, the European Parliament in Strasbourg, or the national governments within the EU. Marketers with substantial resources have established their own lobbying offices in Brussels, while smaller companies get their voices heard through joint offices or their industry associations. In terms of lobbying, U.S. firms have an advantage because of their experience in their home market; however, for many European firms, lobbying is a new, yet necessary, skill to be acquired. Culture does play a role in lobbying in Brussels versus lobbying in Washington, D.C. One does not have to grapple with 20 different languages in Washington as you do in Brussels. Although English is increasingly imposing itself as the *lingua franca* in Brussels, significantly, many MEPs Members of European Parliament still value being approached in their native language. Internal political cultures are starkly different too. While U.S.-style politics tend to be polarized around bi-partisanship and highly adversarial, Brussels politics draw on a wider array of parties and specific national issues that are often deeply rooted in a country's governance culture (e.g., British laissez-faire versus French command and control).[57] At the same time, marketers operating in two or more major markets (such as the EU and North America) can work to produce more efficient trade through, for example, mutual recognition agreements (MRAs) on standards.

Emerging Markets

Broadly defined, an emerging market is a country making an effort to change and improve its economy with the goal of raising its performance to that of the world's more advanced nations.[58] Improved economies can benefit emerging-market countries through higher personal income levels and better standards of living, more exports, increased foreign-direct investment, and more stable political structures. Developed countries benefit from the development of human and natural resources in emerging markets through increased international trading.

Although opinions on which countries are emerging markets differ, the Big Emerging Markets are China, India, Brazil, Argentina, and Indonesia. The data provided in Exhibit 2.12 compares selected emerging markets with each other on dimensions indicating market potential. The biggest emerging markets display the factors that make them strategically important: favorable consumer demographics, rising household incomes and increasing availability of credit, as well as increasing productivity resulting in more attractive prices.[59] As computer-factory workers in China and software programmers in India increase their incomes, they become consumers. The number of people with the equivalent of $10,000 in annual income will double, to 2 billion, by 2015—and 900 million of those newcomers to the consumer class will be in emerging markets. GE, for example, expects to get as much as 60 percent of its revenue growth from emerging markets over the next decade.[60]

Mere size and growth do not guarantee an emerging market's overall appeal and potential. The growth rates may be consistently higher than in developed markets but they may be subject to greater volatility. For example, Russia, Brazil, and Argentina all faced severe financial crises between the years of 1999–2001. Evident in the data is the role of political risk; that is, government interference in entry and market development situations. The Russian government blocked a landmark investment of German engineering company Siemens in OAO Power Machines on antitrust grounds, as the government tightened its control on industries it deems vital to the country's interests. The Russian government has also barred foreign-owned companies from bidding for its oil and metal deposits.[61] In other instances, emerging-market governments have leveraged their position as hosts to foreign investors. The Chinese government has tried to impose their own standards on new technologies, such as EVD for video-disk players and Red Flag Linux for operating systems. The rationale behind this "techno-nationalism" is that China is tired of foreign patent fees for products made and sold domestically (in this case, $4.50 per unit to six Japanese companies that developed the underlying DVD technology).[62] In Brazil, it took a Dutch telecommunications company six months and eight government agency approvals before obtaining a temporary business license.[63]

Exhibit 2.12

Market Potential of 27 Emerging Markets, 2008*

Countries	Market Size		Market Growth Rate		Market Intensity		Market Consumption Capacity		Commercial Infrastructure		Economic Freedom		Market Receptivity		Country Risk		Overall Index
	Rank	Index	Rank	Index	Rank	Index	Rank	Index	Rank	Index	Rank	Index	Rank	Index	Rank	Index	Rank
Hong Kong	25	1	9	35	1	100	1	100	4	96	2	95	1	100	2	88	1
China	1	100	1	100	25	9	20	44	18	41	27	1	17	6	13	47	2
Singapore	27	1	2	49	10	53	14	53	5	89	5	80	2	84	1	100	3
Taiwan	11	5	20	16	7	58	5	81	1	100	4	80	6	30	3	83	4
Korea, South	6	11	24	10	6	61	2	92	2	97	7	75	10	19	6	64	5
Czech Rep.	23	1	22	15	15	48	4	82	3	96	3	81	9	20	5	65	6
Hungary	26	1	25	4	3	68	3	89	7	83	6	75	8	21	9	60	7
Mexico	7	11	16	21	9	54	22	29	15	52	9	64	3	83	12	51	8
Israel	24	1	27	1	2	72	9	68	8	78	8	70	4	39	7	63	9
Poland	15	4	21	16	12	52	7	72	6	85	11	63	16	8	8	60	10
India	2	39	3	46	23	22	13	56	24	26	18	43	25	2	16	40	11
Russia	3	27	19	19	22	26	12	59	10	63	26	11	19	6	15	41	12
Turkey	9	7	8	37	14	48	15	49	14	53	17	45	20	6	19	28	13
Malaysia	20	3	14	23	24	19	18	44	9	67	16	46	5	32	11	52	14
Chile	21	2	23	14	18	39	24	9	13	55	1	100	12	13	10	60	15
Thailand	17	4	10	34	19	39	16	47	17	48	21	32	11	19	17	39	16
Argentina	13	5	6	37	5	61	21	33	11	59	14	49	23	3	26	2	17
Philippines	12	5	13	23	4	67	19	44	22	33	19	43	13	13	23	18	18
Indonesia	5	12	12	25	20	37	10	63	23	30	20	43	21	4	24	15	19
Saudi Arabia	14	4	17	21	27	1	8	69	12	56	24	17	14	9	4	65	20
Egypt	16	4	7	37	16	45	11	61	21	35	25	16	18	6	20	28	21
South Africa	8	7	11	27	13	49	27	1	25	19	10	64	7	22	14	46	22
Brazil	4	22	26	4	21	37	25	8	16	49	13	51	27	1	18	32	23
Pakistan	10	6	18	20	8	56	6	73	26	18	22	22	26	1	25	9	24
Peru	22	2	4	46	17	39	23	24	27	1	12	57	24	2	22	22	25
Colombia	19	3	15	22	11	53	26	3	20	40	15	48	22	4	21	23	26
Venezuela	18	3	5	41	26	4	17	47	19	41	23	18	15	8	27	1	27

*rank order among 27
All numbers represent
Market Intensity = private consumption as a percent of GDP
Market Consumption Capacity = share of middle-class income
Commercial Infrastructure = composite of factors such as mobile subscribers and Internet hosts
Market Receptivity = trade as a percent of GDP
SOURCE: Global Edge, available at **http://globaledge.msu.edu/resourceDesk/mpi/**.

Another concern is the current and future competition from emerging-market companies. Chinese companies have been able to develop powerful global brands in a very short period of time. Some have been developed from the domestic base in a step-by-step manner (e.g., Haier in appliances and Geely in cars) or through acquisitions of existing global brands (such as TCL in TVs and Lenovo in computers).[64] Another concern is based on economic and national security. Companies such as GE, Microsoft, Cisco, and Intel all have established R&D operations in China, thereby training foreign scientists and possibly giving the omnipresent Chinese government access to proprietary technologies.[65]

Given that emerging markets differ from each other in substantial ways, appropriate strategies have to be developed for each. As shown in Exhibit 2.13, Brazil, China, India, and Russia are quite different when measured on marketing-related dimensions. Surveys show that Chinese consumers value convenience, followed by spaciousness and comfort of stores and selection they offer. Carrefour, Wal-Mart, and Metro have all done very well in China's new retail environment.[66] In Latin America, however, companies that have tried to

Exhibit **2.13**

Marketing Contexts for Key Emerging Markets

Brazil	China	India	Russia
Modes of entry			
Both greenfield investments and acquisitions are possible. Companies team up with local partners to gain local expertise.	Government permits both greenfield and acquisitions. Acquired companies may have been state-owned and have hidden liabilities. Alliances allow for aligning interests with all levels of government.	Restrictions in some sectors make joint ventures necessary. Red tape hinders companies in sectors where the government does not allow foreign investment.	Both greenfield and acquisitions are possible but difficult. Companies form alliances to gain access to government and local inputs.
Product development/intellectual property rights			
Local design capability exists. IPR disputes with the United States exist in some sectors.	Imitation and piracy abound. Penalties for violation vary by province and level of corruption.	Some local design capability is available. IPR problems with the United States exist in some industries. Regulatory bodies monitor product quality and fraud.	Strong local design capability but an ambivalent attitude toward IPR. Sufficient regulatory authority exists, but enforcement is patchy.
Supplier base and logistics			
Suppliers are available with-MERCOSUR. A good network of highways, airports, and ports exists.	Several suppliers have strong manufacturing capabilities, but few vendors have advanced technical capabilities. Road network is well developed and port facilities are excellent.	Suppliers are available, but their quality and depend-ability vary greatly. Roads are in poor condition. Ports and airports are under-developed.	Companies can rely on local companies for basic supplies. The European region has decent logistics networks, trans-Ural does not.
Brand perceptions and management			
Consumers accept both local and global brands. Global as well as local agencies are present.	Consumers prefer to buy products from American, European, and Japanese companies. Multinational ad agencies dominate.	Consumers buy both local and global brands. Global ad agencies are present, but they have been less successful than locals.	Consumers prefer global brands in automobiles and high tech. Local brands thrive in food and beverages. Some local and global ad agencies are present.

SOURCE: Adapted from Tarun Khanna, Krishna Palepu, and Jayant Sinha, "Strategies that Fit Emerging Markets," *Harvard Business Review* 83 (June 2005), pp. 68, 69.

export supermarket and hypermarket models from developed markets have faced strong competition from small-scale retailers—the shops, street markets, and small independent supermarkets that are an integral part of Latin culture.[67]

A number of strategic choices are available but most of them require recognizing the idiosyncracies of the market. Whatever the strategy, the marketer has to make sure to secure the company's core competencies while being innovative.[68] An example of such an approach is provided in *The International Marketplace 2.4*.

Adjust Entry Strategy

GM entered the Russian market to produce SUVs in a joint venture with AvtoVAZ, Russia's largest car maker. Russia is one of the eight large markets that will grow substantially in the future. GM chose to use a joint venture to secure a local engineering source to eliminate many of the risks that lead to failure in emerging markets. Since the car, the Niva, is 100 percent designed in Russia, the cost of engineering is substantially lower than what GM would have had to pay in Europe. Relying completely on local content protects GM from any protective scheme that the government may impose. Controlling the costs allows GM to, in

The International MARKETPLACE

2.4

The Cisco Playbook for Emerging Markets

Early in the 21st century, Cisco (which sells everything from million-dollar routers to $300,000 videoconferencing systems to set-top boxes for cable TV) approached emerging markets in the same simplistic way as most developed-market companies did: it had a few sales offices and distributors but no specialized effort. Today, over $4.5 billion of its total $39 billion in sales come from emerging markets, such as Saudi Arabia, Turkey, and Poland.

Win the Government, Business Will Follow

Cisco CEO John Chambers and emerging-markets chief Paul Mountford focus on selling "country transformation" plans to heads of state and top ministers. Since governments often drive these massive investment initiatives, success there converts into equipment sales at companies building the nation's infrastructure.

Sell More than Technology

Rather than just peddle its wide array of products, Cisco focuses on working with governments on broad issues. In Saudi Arabia, for example, the government had trouble managing the many pilgrims who visit Mecca. Cisco brought in consultants and partners to build an online system that allows travelers to secure a visa and hotel room in hours rather than weeks.

Charity Pays

Chambers and Cisco have won big points in the Middle East and elsewhere by getting involved in philanthropic efforts. In Jordan, the company helped launch training programs to boost the skills of the poverty-stricken. It is also giving away its high-end videoconferencing systems, which can cost up to $300,000 per location, to all Middle Eastern heads of state, including Israel's Prime Minister.

Hire Well-Connected Locals

Cisco doesn't just hire locals: It recruits top power brokers. In Turkey, it recently brought in the former chairman of Türk Telekom, the dominant phone carrier in the country. In Saudi Arabia, Mountford hired as the country's chief Badr Al Badr, a well-known entrepreneur and son of a leading adviser to the king.

Create Jobs

With half of its population under 21, Saudi Arabia needs to create millions of jobs to absorb those entering the labor force and build a modern economy. Cisco has agreed to invest $265 million in the country over five years. Most of that is going to establish Networking Academy training centers where locals learn everything from repairing routers to network design. The Saudi centers have had 13,700 students so far.

Create and Adapt Products for Local Needs

Cisco has a campus in Bangalore, India, from which teams of engineers can be dispatched to cater to different market needs. For example, a Web site in Turkey allows small textile companies to bid on a variety of contracts. The customized products are then marketed to potential buyers in other, similar countries.

SOURCE: "Cisco's Brave New World," *Businessweek,* November 24, 2008, 56–68.

---

turn, provide a car at the pricing point (approximately $12,000) that consumers are willing to pay for a GM-branded vehicle. Another benefit of GM's strategy is securing an existing dealer network. An added benefit for GM is its ability to export the NIVA to other emerging markets using the Daewoo network (acquired by GM earlier).[69] Chinese consumers typically want to lay their hands on computers before they buy them. That means the best way to reach them is via vast retailing operations, the strength of local players Lenovo and Founder Electronics, which both rank ahead of Dell. Dell's computers are sold in nearly 3,000 outlets of the Gome and Suning electronics store chains. To maintain its core approach, Dell set up kiosks to demonstrate its SmartPC and other products and allow for orders from these kiosks.[70]

Manage Affordability

Volkswagen, which arrived in 1984, and General Motors, which established its operations in 1997, have dominated the Chinese auto markets. However, they are now facing competition offering more economically priced cars. The reason for the shift in purchasing preferences is that the typical buyer has changed. Only a few years ago, the majority of purchases were made by state-owned companies, for whom price was not the critical criterion. Currently, most buyers are individuals who want the best deal for their money. To respond, GM has introduced the $8,000 Chevy Spark but will focus on the higher-end market with its Cadillac line.[71] A critical battleground is emerging for companies in the "good-enough" market segment, home of reliable-enough products at low-enough prices to attract the fastest-growing segment of mid-level Chinese customers. This may mean that rather than paying a 70 to 100 percent premium for a global brand, the customer is only willing to pay 20 to 30 percent.[72]

Invest in Distribution

Kodak has nearly 8,000 photo stores across China, one of the country's largest retail operations. The company taps the desire of many Chinese to run their own businesses while helping them negotiate setting up their operations. One Kodak campaign offered all of the necessary photo-development equipment, training, and a store license for 99,000 yuan ($12,000). Kodak negotiated a deal with the Bank of China and other big banks to arrange financing for individuals lacking capital. These programs are part of Kodak's big bet when it bought three debt-laden state enterprises and many of their workers for $1 billion. In return, no other companies in the industry were allowed into China for four years.[73]

Build Strong Brands

A common characteristic across all emerging markets is the appeal of recognizable brands. While it is easiest for international marketers to extend their global brands to emerging markets, some companies such as Danone acquire companies but continue selling the products under original names. Adding a new quality dimension to well-established brands, consumer loyalty is ensured. Furthermore, this strategy can generate favor among Chinese officials who may not want to see local brands go under. In 2005, Wahaha was honored one of "Most Favorite Chinese Brands" by CCTV. Danone has started making a local water brand, Wahaha, into a global brand.[74]

Developing Markets

The time may have come to look at the four billion people in the world who live in poverty, subsisting on less than $2,000 a year.[75] Not only is this segment a full two-thirds of the current market place, but it is expected to grow to six billion by 2040. Despite initial skepticism about access and purchasing power, marketers are finding that they can make profits while having a positive effect on the sustainable livelihoods of people not normally considered potential customers.[76] However, it will require radical departures from the traditional business models; for example, new partnerships (ranging from local governments to non-profits) and new pricing structures (allowing customers to rent or lease rather than buy and providing new financing choices for purchases). Hewlett-Packard has an initiative called World e-Inclusion that, working with a range of global and local partners, aims to sell, lease, or donate a billion dollars worth of satellite-powered computer products and services to markets in Africa, Asia, Eastern Europe, Latin America, and the Middle East.[77] To engage with beta communities in Senegal, Hewlett-Packard partnered with Joko, Inc., a company founded by revered Senegalese pop star Youssou n'Dour.

Five elements of success are required for an international marketer to take advantage of and thrive in developing markets.[78]

Research

The first order of business is to learn about the needs, aspirations, and habits of targeted populations for whom traditional intelligence gathering may not be the most effective. For example, just because the demand for land lines in developing countries was low, it would have been wrong to assume that little demand for phones existed. The real reasons were that land lines were expensive, subscribers had to wait for months to get hooked up, and lines often went down due to bad maintenance, flood, and theft of copper cables. Mobile phones have been a solution to that problem. Subscriptions increased 67 percent in sub-Saharan Africa in 2004, as compared with 10 percent in Western Europe.[79]

Creating Buying Power

Without credit, it is impossible for many of the developing-country consumers to make major purchases. Programs in **microfinance** have allowed consumers, with no property as collateral, to borrow sums averaging $100 to make purchases and have retail banking services available to them. Lenders such as GrameenBank in Bangladesh and Compartamos in Mexico have helped millions of families to escape poverty. Excellent payment records (e.g., only 0.56 percent of the loans are even days late at Compartamos), have started attracting companies such as Citicorp to microfinancing, through underwriting microfinance bonds in markets such as Peru.[80]

Tailoring Local Solutions

In the product area, companies must combine advanced technology with local insights. Hindustan Lever (part of Unilever) learned that low-income Indians, usually forced to settle for low-quality products, wanted to buy high-end detergents and personal care products, but could not afford them in the quantities available. In response, the company developed extremely low-cost packaging material and other innovations that allowed for a product priced in pennies instead of the $4 to $15 price of the regular containers. The same brand is on all of the product forms, regardless of packaging. Given that these consumers do not shop at supermarkets, Lever employs local residents with pushcarts who take small quantities of the sachets to kiosks.[81]

Improving Access

Due to economic and physical isolation of poor communities, providing access can lead to a thriving business. In Bangladesh (with income levels of $200), GrameenPhone Ltd. leases access to wireless phones to villagers. Every phone is used by an average of 100 people and generates $90 in revenue a month—two or three times the revenues generated by wealthier users who own their phones in urban areas.[82] Similarly, the Jhai Foundation, an American-Lao foundation, is helping villagers in Laos with Internet access. The first step, however, was to develop an inexpensive and robust computer. The computer has no moving, and very few delicate, parts. Instead of a hard disk, it relies on flash-memory chips, and instead of an energy-guzzling glass cathode ray tube, its screen is a liquid-crystal display.[83] The XO-1, previously known as the $100 Laptop, is an inexpensive laptop computer intended to be distributed to 150 million children in developing countries around the world. The laptop was developed by One Laptop Per Child, a non-profit organization, and manufactured by Quanta Computer. Originally intended to run on open-source software, OLPC has reached an agreement for the use of Microsoft's Windows XP operating system. The agreement with OLPC underscores Microsoft's eagerness to market its software in emerging markets, where it has tried to seed Windows in schools—the target of OLPC's machines. The $3 price represents a big discount to what the company charges in the U.S. Recently, Microsoft has also done $3 software deals in Russia, Libya, and Egypt.[84]

Shaping Aspirations

The biggest challenges in developing markets are in providing essential services. In this sense, developing markets can be ideal settings for commercial and technological innovation. With significant demand for mobile handsets in developing countries, both Nokia and Motorola have developed models that sell for as little as $25. They are ideally suited to match consumer demand for inexpensive phones with the features, quality, and brand names consumers want. Emerging low-cost producers from China cannot match the volume or the brand franchises of the global players. While gross margins on these phones may be as little as 15 percent (as compared with 33 percent at the high end), the big volumes can establish scale economies that reduce costs even for high-end models.[85] Global marketers are very often the only ones that can realistically make a difference in solving some of the problems in developing markets. Developing new technologies or products is a resource-intensive task and requires knowledge transfer from one market to another. Without multinationals as catalysts, nongovernmental organizations, local governments, and communities will continue to flounder in their attempts to bring development to the poorest nations in the world.[86]

The emergence of these markets presents a great growth opportunity for companies. It also creates a chance for business, government, and civil society to join together in a common cause to help the aspiring poor to join the world market economy. Lifting billions of people from poverty may help avert social decay, political chaos, terrorism, and environmental deterioration that is certain to continue if the gap between the rich and poor countries continues to widen. For example, Coca-Cola has introduced "Project Mission" in Botswana to launch a drink to combat anemia, blindness, and other afflictions common in poorer parts of the world. The drink, called Vitango, is like the company's Hi-C orange-flavored drink, but it contains 12 vitamins and minerals chronically lacking in the diets of people in developing countries. The project satisfies multiple objectives for the Coca-Cola Company. First, it could help boost sales at a time when global sales of carbonated drinks are slowing, and, second, it will help in establishing relationships with governments and other local constituents that will serve as a positive platform for brand Coca-Cola. The market for such nutritional drinks may be limited, but they are meant to offer Coca-Cola a role of good corporate citizen at a time when being perceived as such is increasingly important for multinational corporations.[87]

Summary

Economic variables relating to the various markets' characteristics—population, income, consumption patterns, infrastructure, geography, and attitudes toward foreign involvement in the economy—form a starting point for assessment of market potential for the international marketer. These data are readily available but should be used in conjunction with other, more interpretive data, because the marketer's plans often require a long-term approach. Data on the economic environment produce a snapshot of the past; in some cases, old data are used to make decisions affecting operations two years in the future. Even if the data are recent, they cannot themselves indicate the growth and the intensity of development. Some economies remain stagnant, plagued by natural calamities, internal problems, and lack of export markets, whereas some witness booming economic development.

Economic data provide a baseline from which other more market/product–specific and even experiential data can be collected. Understanding the composition and interrelationships between economic indicators is essential for the assessment of the other environments and their joint impact on market potential. The international marketer needs to understand the impact of the economic environment on social development.

The emergence of economic integration in the world economy poses unique opportunities for and challenges to the international marketer. Eliminating barriers between member markets and erecting new ones vis-à-vis nonmembers will call for adjustments in past strategies to fully exploit the new situations. In the late 1980s and early 1990s, economic integration increased substantially. The signing of the North American Free Trade Agreement produced the largest trading bloc in the world, whereas the Europeans are moving in their cooperation beyond the pure trade dimension. New trading blocs and the expansion of the existing ones will largely depend on future trade liberalization and political will within and among countries.

As developed markets have matured, marketers are looking at both emerging and developing markets for their future growth. To succeed, marketers will have to be innovative, pioneer new ways of doing business, and outmaneuver local competitors, many of them intent on becoming global players themselves.

Key Terms

Group of Five	Physical Quality of Life Index (PQLI)	political union
Group of Seven	free trade area	European Union
Group of Ten	customs union	Fortress Europe
household	common market	maquiladoras
urbanization	factor mobility	import substitution
purchasing power parities (PPP)	Single European Act	microfinance
inflation	economic union	

Questions for Discussion

1. Place these markets in the framework that follows.

a. Indonesia	g. Turkey	m. Peru
b. Mozambique	h. Spain	n. Jamaica
c. India	i. Singapore	o. Poland
d. Bangladesh	j. Nigeria	p. United Kingdom
e. Niger	k. Algeria	q. Iraq
f. Brazil	l. Zambia	r. Saudi Arabia

	Income Level		
	Low	**Middle**	**High**
TRADE STRUCTURE			
Industrial			
Developing			
· Semi-Industrial			
· Oil-Exporting			
· Primary Producing			
· Populous South Asia			
· Least Developed			

2. Using available data, assess the market potential for (a) power generators and (b) consumer appliances in (1) the Philippines, (2) Jordan, and (3) Portugal.

3. From the international marketer's point of view, what are the opportunities and problems caused by increased urbanization in developing countries?

4. Comment on this statement: "A low per capita income will render the market useless."

5. What can a marketer do to advance regional economic integration?

6. Explain the difference between a free trade area and a common market. Speculate why negotiations were held for a North American Free Trade Agreement rather than for a North American Common Market.

Internet Exercises

1. Compare and contrast two different points of view on expanding trade by accessing the Web site of The Business Roundtable—an industry coalition promoting increased interaction to and from world markets (http://www.brtable.org)—and the AFL-CIO, American Federation of Labor–Congress of Industrial Organizations (http://www.aflcio.org).

2. Why do marketers engage in major projects in developing countries, such as Hewlett-Packard's e-inclusion project (http://www.hp.com/e-inclusion/en/index.html). Outline both the short-term and long-term benefits.

Recommended Readings

Business Guide to Mercosur. London: Economist Intelligence Unit.

Current issues of *Country Monitor, Business Europe, Business East Europe, Business Asia, Business Latin America, Business China*.

The European Union: A Guide for Americans, 2008 edition. Available at http://www.eurunion.org/infores/euguide/euguide.htm.

Folsom, Ralph H. *NAFTA and Free Trade in the Americas in a Nutshell*. St. Paul, MN: Thomson/West, 2008.

International Marketing Data and Statistics 2008. London: Euromonitor, 2008.

Ohmae, Kenichi. *Next Global Stage: Challenges and Opportunities in Our Borderless World*. Philadelphia: Wharton School Publishing, 2005.

The World in Figures. London: Economist Publications, 2008.

World Development Report 2008. New York: Oxford University Press, 2008.

Yearbook of International Trade Statistics. New York: United Nations, 2008.

TRADE POLICY AND INSTITUTIONS

The International
MARKETPLACE

3.1

A Trade Negotiator's Glossary: What They Said and What They Really Meant

"An ambitious proposal"
(It is unlikely to get any support.)

"An innovative proposal"
(This one really is out of the trees.)

"This paper is unbalanced."
(It does not contain any of our views.)

"This proposal strikes a good balance."
(Our interests are completely safeguarded.)

"I should like to make some brief comments."
(You have time for a cup of coffee.)

"We will be making detailed comments at a later stage."
(Expect that your posting will be over before you hear from us.)

"This paper contains some interesting features."
(I am going to give you some face-saving reasons why it should be withdrawn.)

"The paper will provide useful background to our discussions."
(I haven't read it.)

"We need transparency in the process."
(I am worried that I won't be included in the back-room negotiations.)

"English is not my mother tongue."
(I am about to give you a lecture on a fine point of syntax.)

"The delegate of…spoke eloquently on this subject."
(I haven't the faintest idea what he or she means.)

"A comprehensive paper"
(It's over two pages in length and seems to have an awful lot of headings.)

SOURCE: Anonymous

The international environment is changing rapidly. Firms, individuals, and policy-makers are affected by these changes. These changes offer new opportunities but also represent new challenges. Although major economic and security shifts will have a profound impact on the world, coping with them successfully through imagination, investment, and perseverance can produce a new, better world order and an improved quality of life.

This chapter begins by highlighting the importance of trade to humankind. Selected historical developments that were triggered or influenced by international trade are delineated. Subsequently, more recent trade developments are presented, together with the international institutions that have emerged to regulate and facilitate trade. As *The International Marketplace 3.1* shows, the attempts by nations to negotiate trade terms and regulate international trade can be tedious and bureaucracy-ridden.

The chapter will analyze and discuss the country position in the world trade environment and explain the impact of trade. Various efforts undertaken by governments to manage trade by restricting or promoting exports, imports, technology transfer, and investments will be described. Finally, the chapter will present a strategic outlook for future developments in trade relations.

The Historical Dimension

Many peoples throughout history have gained preeminence in the world through their trade activities. Among them were the Etruscans, Phoenicians, Egyptians, Chinese, Spaniards, and Portuguese. To underscore the role of trade, we will take a closer look at some selected examples.

One of the major world powers in ancient history was the Roman Empire. Its impact on thought, knowledge, and development can still be felt today. Even while expanding their territories through armed conflicts, the Romans placed primary emphasis on encouraging international business activities. The principal approaches used to implement this emphasis were the **Pax Romana**, or the Roman Peace, and the common coinage. The Pax Romana ensured that merchants were able to travel safely on roads that were built, maintained, and protected by the Roman legions and their affiliated troops. The common coinage, in turn, ensured that business transactions could be carried out easily throughout the empire. In addition, Rome developed a systematic law, central market locations through the founding of cities, and an excellent communication system that resembled an early version of the Pony Express; all of these measures contributed to the functioning of the international marketplace and to the reduction of business uncertainty. As a result, economic well-being within the empire rose sharply compared to the outside.

Soon, city-nations and tribes that were not part of the empire wanted to share in the benefits of belonging. They joined the empire as allies and agreed to pay tribute and taxes. Thus, the immense growth of the Roman Empire occurred through the linkages of business rather than through the marching of its legions and warfare. Of course, the Romans had to engage in substantial efforts to facilitate business

THE ROMAN EMPIRE DEVELOPED A SYSTEMATIC LAW, CENTRAL MARKET LOCATIONS THROUGH THE FOUNDING OF CITIES, AND AN EXCELLENT COMMUNICATION SYSTEM. THESE MEASURES CONTRIBUTED TO THE FUNCTIONING OF THE INTERNATIONAL MARKETPLACE.

in order to make it worthwhile for others to belong. For example, when pirates threatened the seaways, Rome, under Pompeius, sent out a large fleet to subdue them. The cost of international distribution, and therefore the cost of international marketing, was substantially reduced because fewer goods were lost to pirates. As a result, goods could be made available at lower prices, which, in turn, translated into larger demand. Of course, only few things are new under the sun. As you can see in the *International Marketplace 3.2*, even today, pirates still threaten the sea ways.

The fact that international business was one of the primary factors holding the empire together can also be seen in its decay. When "barbaric" tribes overran the empire, it was not mainly through war and prolonged battles that Rome lost ground. The outside tribes were actually attacking an empire that was already substantially weakened, because it could no longer offer the benefits of affiliation. Former allies no longer saw any advantage in being associated with the Romans and willingly cooperated with the invaders, rather than face prolonged battles.

In a similar fashion, one could interpret the evolution of European feudalism to be a function of trade and marketing. Because farmers were frequently deprived of their harvests as a result of incursions by other (foreign) tribes, or even individuals, they decided to band together and provide for their own protection. By delivering a certain portion of their "earnings" to a protector, they could be assured of retaining most of their gains. Although this system initially worked quite well in reducing the cost of production and the cost of marketing, it did ultimately result in the emergence of the feudal system, which, perhaps, was not what the initiators had intended it to be.

Interestingly, the feudal system encouraged the development of a closed-state economy that was inwardly focused and ultimately conceived for self-sufficiency and security. However, medieval commerce still thrived and developed through export trade. In Italy, the Low

---

The International MARKETPLACE   3.2

The Modern Day Pirate

There are circumstances in which legal rules fail to keep situations under control and cause major setbacks to international trade. If an area represents basically ungoverned space due to continuous illegal activity, corporations must bear the cost if they have to do business there. More than two millennia ago Pompeius, the Roman General and Consul, needed to equip a fleet to subdue pirates that disrupted the shipping of goods. In 2008, large scale piracy has returned to Somali waters with a major effect on shipping costs.

In one year alone, seventy-three attacks on ships occurred in the Gulf of Aden, making it the most dangerous water to cross. The Gulf of Aden connects the Indian Ocean to the Red Sea, making it a vital pathway for 20,000 ships per year. Over four percent of the world's oil supply is transported across the gulf. Somali pirates have changed how business is conducted there.

These pirates are equipped with some of the best weaponry and transportation, using speedboats with grenades. Despite the fact the countries like Yemen, India, and members of the European Union have sent warships

to assist the U.S. Navy to protect ships, the pirates are very active. Somali pirates received ransom money in October 2008 from South Korea and Thailand in order to release cargo ships. In 2008, ransom payments will surpass $50 million.

These Somali pirates are able to escape to most powerful navies in the world due to their weapons and their knowledge of the environment. Companies simply pay the ransom money in order to avoid harm to their cargo and crew members. The shipping alternative would be extremely expensive. It would require that ships go around the Cape of Good Hope of South Africa, a route which is thousands of miles longer. Running a ship costs $20,000 to $30,000 a day, according to Noel Choong, head of the International Maritime Bureau's piracy reporting center. So until countries can secure the waters of the Gulf of Aden, and ransom costs remain below the cost of re-routing ships, Somali pirates will continue to reap their profits.

SOURCES: **http://news.yahoo.com/s/ap/20081019/ ap_on_re_af/af_somalia_piracy_1**; September 11th, 2008, *The Washington Post*, "World's Navies Scramble to Curb Upturn in Piracy."; September 27th, 2008, *The Washington Post*, "100 Hostages Held by Somali Pirates."

Countries, and the German Hanse towns, the impetus for commerce was provided by East–West trade. Profits from the spice trade through the Middle East created the wealth of Venice and other Mediterranean ports. Europe also imported rice, oranges, dyes, cotton, and silk. Western European merchants in turn exported timber, arms, and woolen clothing in exchange for these luxury goods. A remaining legacy of this trade is found in the many English and French words of Arabic origin, such as divan, bazaar, artichoke, orange, jar, and tariff.[1]

The importance of trade has not always persisted, however. For example, in 1896, the Empress Dowager Tz'u-hsi, in order to finance the renovation of the summer palace, impounded government funds that had been designated for Chinese shipping and its navy. As a result, China's participation in world trade almost came to a halt. In the subsequent decades, China operated in almost total isolation, without any transfer of knowledge from the outside, without major inflow of goods, and without the innovation and productivity increases that result from exposure to international trade.

The effect of turning away from international trade was highlighted during the 1930s. The Smoot-Hawley Act raised duties to reduce the volume of imports into the United States, in the hopes that this would restore domestic employment. The result, however, was a raising of duties and other barriers to imports by most other trading nations as well. These measures were contributing factors in the subsequent worldwide depression and the collapse of the world financial system, which in turn set the scene for World War II.

International marketing and international trade have also long been seen as valuable tools for foreign policy purposes. The use of economic coercion—for example, by nations or groups of nations—can be traced back as far as the time of the Greek city-states and the Peloponnesian War or, in more recent times, to the Napoleonic wars. Combatants used blockades to achieve their goal of "bringing about commercial ruin and shortage of food by dislocating trade."[2] Similarly, during the Civil War in the United States, the North consistently pursued a strategy of denying international trade opportunities to the South and thus deprived it of export revenue needed to import necessary products. In the 1990s, the Iraqi invasion of Kuwait resulted in a trade embargo of Iraq by the United Nations, with the goal of reversing the aggression. Following government suppression of civil protests in Uzbekistan, the European Union imposed a series of sanctions against the country. These included travel bans for top Uzbeki officials, and include a ban on the sale or transfer to Uzbekistan of arms, military equipment, or any other equipment that might be used for internal repression.[3] Although such deprivations of trade do not often bring about policy change, they can have a profound impact on the standard of living of a nation's citizens.

Global Division

After 1945, the world was sharply split ideologically into West and East, a division that had major implications for trade relations. The Soviet Union, as the leader of the Eastern bloc, developed the Council for Mutual Economic Assistance (CMEA or COMECON), which focused on developing strong linkages among the members of the Soviet bloc and discouraged relations with the West. The United States, in turn, was the leading proponent of creating a "Pax Americana," or American peace, for the Western world, driven by the belief that international trade was a key to worldwide prosperity. Many months of international negotiations in London, Geneva, and Lake Success (New York) culminated on March 24, 1948, in Havana, Cuba, with the signing of the charter for an International Trade Organization (ITO).

This charter, a series of agreements among 53 countries, was designed to cover international commercial policies, domestic business practices, commodity agreements, employment and reconstruction, economic development and international investment, and a constitution for a new United Nations agency to administer the whole. In addition, a General Agreement on Tariffs and Trade was initiated, with the purpose of reducing tariffs among countries, and international institutions such as the World Bank and the International Monetary Fund were created.

Even though the International Trade Organization incorporated many farsighted notions, most nations refused to ratify it, fearing its power, its bureaucratic size, and its threat to national sovereignty. As a result, the most forward-looking approach to international trade never came about. However, other organizations conceived at the time are still in existence and have made major contributions toward improving international trade.

Transnational Institutions Affecting World Trade

World Trade Organization (WTO) (http://www.wto.org)

The World Trade Organization has its origins in the General Agreement on Tariffs and Trade (GATT), to which it became the successor organization in January of 1995. In order to better understand the emergence of the WTO, a brief review of the GATT is appropriate. The GATT has been called "a remarkable success story of a postwar international organization that was never intended to become one."[4] It began in 1947 as a set of rules for nondiscrimination, transparent procedures, and settlement of disputes in international trade. One of the most important tools is the Most-Favored Nation (MFN) clause, which calls for each member country of the GATT to grant every other member country the most favorable treatment it accords to any other country with respect to imports and exports. In effect, MFN is the equal opportunity clause of international trade. Over time, the GATT evolved into an institution that sponsored successive rounds of international trade negotiations with a key focus on a reduction of prevailing high tariffs.

Early in its existence, the GATT achieved the liberalization of trade in 50,000 products, amounting to two-thirds of the value of the trade among its participants. In subsequent years, special GATT negotiations such as the Kennedy Round and the Tokyo Round further reduced trade barriers and developed improved dispute-settlement mechanisms, better provisions dealing with subsidies, and a more explicit definition of rules for import controls.

In spite of, or perhaps because of, these impressive gains, GATT became less effective over time. Duties had already been drastically reduced—for example, the average U.S. tariff rate fell from 26 percent in 1946 to an average of 3.6 percent by 2008.[5] Further reductions are therefore unlikely to have a major impact on world trade. Most imports either enter the United States duty free or are subject to low tariffs. The highest tariffs apply mainly to imports of agri-food and tobacco products, as well as clothing, textiles, and footwear. In these industries, tariffs tend to increase with the degree of processing.[6]

Many nations developed new tools for managing and distorting trade flows, nontariff tools that were not covered under GATT rules. Examples are "voluntary agreements" to restrain trade, bilateral or multilateral special trade agreements such as the multifiber accord that restricts trade in textiles and apparel, and other nontariff barriers. Also, GATT, which was founded by 24 like-minded governments, was designed to operate by consensus. As membership grew, this consensus rule often led to a stalemate of many GATT activities.

After many years of often contentious negotiations, the Uruguay Round accord was finally ratified in January of 1995. As part of this ratification, a new institution, the World Trade Organization, was created, which now is the umbrella organization responsible for overseeing the implementation of all the multilateral agreements negotiated in the Uruguay Round and those that will be negotiated in the future.[7] The GATT has ceased to exist as a separate institution and has become part of the WTO, which also is responsible for the General Agreement on Trade in Services (GATS), agreements on trade-related aspects of intellectual property rights (TRIPS), and trade-related investment measures (TRIMS), and administers a broad variety of international trade and investment accords. As of December 2008, the WTO had 153 members, with Cape Verde being the newest, as can be seen in *The International Marketplace 3.3.*

The creation of the WTO has greatly broadened the scope of international trade agreements. Many of the areas left uncovered by

THE CREATION OF THE WORLD TRADE ORGANIZATION HAS BROADENED THE SCOPE OF INTERNATIONAL TRADE AGREEMENTS AND MADE TRADE AND INVESTMENT FLOWS AROUND THE WORLD MORE EFFICIENT.

© FABRICE COFFRINI/AFP/GETTY IMAGES

The International
MARKETPLACE

3.3

Accessing the Hallowed Halls of the WTO

On July 23, 2008, after 8 years of negotiation, the General Council of the World Trade Organization (WTO) welcomed Cape Verde, making it the 153rd member of the WTO. Cape Verde is an archipelago located in the Atlantic Ocean, off the west coast of Africa. The road to accession is by no means an easy one.

Becoming a member of the WTO requires compliance with WTO policies that span a broad spectrum of government and private sector alike. Among many other considerations, in order to join, the Cape Verde committed to a tariff ceiling of between zero and 55%. There was also the promise of an average maximum tariff of 15% for industrial goods. The country also made specific commitments so that persons from abroad could offer their services in Cape Verde.

While compliance with WTO standards may be initially costly, it can have great payoffs in the long run. First, states that become members of the WTO are granted Most-Favored Nation (MFN) status, which gives them equal treatment with all other members of the Organization. Second, companies looking to locate part of their operations abroad can expect certain legal guarantees from WTO members. For example, members of the

WTO are required to adopt the Agreement on Trade-Related Aspects of Intellectual Property Rights (TRIPS). TRIPS covers topics such as how intellectual property rights should be applied, how countries should enforce intellectual property laws, and how members of the WTO should settle disputes regarding intellectual property. In an age of rampant privacy and copyright infringements, corporations are increasingly wary of countries with poor intellectual property protection. In addition, both consumers and corporations are guaranteed certain health guidelines, because member nations must adopt agreements on sanitary and phytosanitary measures (sanitary measures relate to human and animal health, while phytosanitary measures apply to plants). These regulate things such as the maximum allowable pesticide residues in crops and salmonella levels in chicken. Outbreaks of mad cow disease and avian flu have highlighted the need for countries to have a uniform procedure for dealing with food and livestock emergencies.

SOURCES: WTO Press Releases, Accession of Cape Verde, Accessed on November 23, 2008; Global Trade Negotiations Home Page, **http://www.cid.harvard.edu/cidtrade/gov/russiagov.html**, accessed December 3, 2005; "WTO General Council Successfully Adopts Saudi Arabia's Terms of Accession," **http://www.wto.org/english/news_e/pres05_e/ pr420_e.htm** accessed December 3, 2005.

the GATT, such as services and agriculture, are now addressed at least to some degree by international rules, speedier dispute settlement procedures have been developed, and the decision-making process has been streamlined. Even though the WTO will attempt to continue to make decisions based on consensus, provisions are now made for decisions to be made by majority vote if such consensus cannot be achieved.

The WTO makes major contributions to improved trade and investment flows around the world. However, a successful WTO may well infringe on the sovereignty of nations. For example, more streamlined dispute settlements mean that decisions are made more quickly and that nations in violation of international trade rules are confronted more often. Negative WTO decisions affecting large trading nations are likely to be received with resentment. Some governments intend to broaden the mandate of the WTO to also deal with social causes and issues such as labor laws, competition, and emigration freedoms. Since many nations fear that social causes can be used to devise new rules of protectionism against their exports, the addition of such issues may become a key reason for divisiveness and dissent within the WTO.[8] Outside groups such as nongovernmental organizations and special interest alliances believe that international trade and the WTO represent a threat to their causes.

In 2001, a new round of international trade negotiations was initiated. Because the agreement to do so was reached in the city of Doha (Qatar), the negotiations are now called the "Doha Round." The aim was to further hasten implementation of liberalization, particularly to help impoverished and developing nations. In addition, the goal was to expand the role of the WTO to encompass more of the trade activities in which there were insufficient rules for their definition and structure. This was due to either purposeful exclusion of governments in earlier negotiations or new technology changing the global marketplace. Examples include trade in agricultural goods, antidumping regulations, and electronic commerce.

The negotiations were largely marked by disagreement between developed and developing economies. The most divisive issue continued to be agricultural tariffs and subsidies. While there were many attempts at compromise, the parties never came close enough for an agreement. After 8 years of ongoing meetings, concessions and dissent, the negotiations continue.[9]

Unless trade advocates and the WTO are supported by their member governments and other outside stakeholders in trade issues, there is unlikely to be major progress on further liberalization of trade and investment. It will therefore be important to have the WTO focus on its core mission, which is the facilitation of international trade and investment, while ensuring that an effective forum exists to afford a hearing and subsequent achievements for concerns surrounding the core.

International Monetary Fund (IMF) (http://www.imf.org)

The International Monetary Fund (IMF), conceived in 1944 at Bretton Woods in New Hampshire, was designed to provide stability for the international monetary framework. It obtained funding from its members, who subscribed to a quota based on expected trade patterns and paid 25 percent of the quota in gold or dollars and the rest in their local currencies. These funds were to be used to provide countries with protection against temporary fluctuations in the value of their currency. Therefore, it was the original goal of the IMF to provide for fixed exchange rates between countries.

The perhaps not so unintended result of using the U.S. dollar as the main world currency was a glut of dollar supplies in the 1960s. This forced the United States to abandon the gold standard and devalue the dollar and resulted in flexible or floating exchange rates in 1971. However, even though this major change occurred, the IMF as an institution has clearly contributed toward providing international liquidity and to facilitating international trade.

Over time, the IMF system has experienced substantial pressures. In the 1980s, some of this pressure was triggered by the substantial debts incurred by less-developed countries as a result of overextended development credits and changes in the cost of energy. In the 1990s, major additional pressure resulted from the financial requirements of the former socialist countries searching for funds to improve their economies. Twelve former Soviet republics joined the IMF. Major currency fluctuations among old customers have also stretched the resources of the IMF.

In 2005, the IMF agreed to write off $3.3 billion of debt owed to it by virtually all of the world's 20 poorest nations.[10] In 2008, the Fund needed to take on entirely new activities designed to stabilize the global financial system and to develop a global economic stimulus. In light of the worldwide slowdown of economies, the IMF needed to go beyond its traditional customers of emerging markets and developing economies. Even already accomplished market economies, such as Iceland, required financial help. In order to ensure that a local stimulus would not be suffocated by global restrictions, the Fund worked to ensure simultaneous expansions in economies. The overall goal of new short-term lending facilities became to rapid establishment of liquidity and the development of new trust, in order to extinguish the crisis of confidence.[11]

As a result of all these global financial needs, the future role of the IMF may be very different. If the institution can mobilize its members to provide the financial means for an active role, its past accomplishments may pale in view of the new opportunities. At the same time, however, the new orientation will also require a rethinking of the rules under which the IMF operates. For example, it is quite unclear whether stringent economic rules and performance measures are equally applicable to all countries seeking IMF assistance. New economic conditions that have not been experienced to date may require different types of approaches. Also, perhaps the link between economic and political stability will magnify but also change the mission of the IMF.

ONE KEY TASK OF THE WORLD BANK IS TO REDUCE WORLD POVERTY.

World Bank (http://www.worldbank.org)

The World Bank's official name is the International Bank for Reconstruction and Development. It was formed in 1944 to aid countries suffering from the destruction of war. After completing this process most successfully, it has since taken on the task of aiding world development. With new nations emerging from the colonial fold of the world powers of the early twentieth century, the bank has made major efforts to assist fledgling economies to participate in a modern economic trade framework. More recently, the bank has begun to participate actively with the IMF to resolve the debt problems of the developing world and to bring a market economy to the former members of the Eastern bloc.

Major debates surround the effectiveness of the bank's expenditures. In the 1970s and 1980s, funds were invested into infrastructure projects in developing countries, based on the expectation that such investment would rapidly propel the economies of these nations forward. However, in retrospect, it appears that many of these funds were squandered by corrupt regimes, and that many large projects have turned into white elephants—producing little in terms of economic progress. In addition, some projects have had major negative side effects for the recipient nations. For example, the highway through the rain forest in Brazil has mainly resulted in the migration of people to the area and is upsetting a very fragile ecological balance.

The World Bank tries now to reorient its outlook, focusing more on institution building and the development of human capital through investments into education and health. Key performance criteria are now: The sustainability of growth and development; the addressing of higher commodity prices; agricultural assistance in times of higher food prices; opening world trade to all countries and greater participation of rising economic powers and developing nations in the bank's governance.[12]

Regional Institutions

The WTO, IMF, and World Bank operate on a global level. Regional changes have also taken place, based on the notion that trade between countries needs to be encouraged. Of particular importance was the formation of **economic blocs** that integrated the economic and political activities of nations.

The concept of regional integration was used more than 170 years ago when Germany developed the Zollverein to remove internal customs barriers. Its modern-day development began in 1952 with the establishment of the European Coal and Steel Community, which was designed to create a common market among six countries in coal, steel, and iron. Gradually, these nations developed a Customs Union and created common external tariffs. The ultimate goal envisioned was the completely free movement of capital, services, and people across national borders and the joint development of common international policies. Over time, the goals have been largely attained. The European Union (EU) now represents a formidable market size internally and market power externally, and the well-being of all EU members has increased substantially since the bloc's formation.

Similar market agreements have been formed by other groups of nations. Examples are the North American Free Trade Agreement (NAFTA), the Mercosur in Latin America, and the Gulf Cooperation Council (GCC). These unions were formed for different reasons and operate with different degrees of cohesiveness as appropriate for the specific environment. They focus on issues such as forming a customs union, a common market, an economic union, or a political union.

Simultaneous with these economic bloc formations, the private sector has begun to develop international trade institutions of its own. Particularly when governments are not quick enough to address major issues of concern to global marketers, business has taken the lead by providing a forum for the discussion of such issues. One example is the Transatlantic Business Dialogue (TBD), which is a non-governmental organization composed of business leaders from Europe and the United States. Recognizing the inefficiency of competing and often contradictory standards and lengthy testing procedures, this group is working to achieve mutual recognition agreements on an industry basis. The executives of leading international firms that participate in this organization attempt to simplify global marketing by searching for ways to align international standards and regulations.

The activities of all these institutions demonstrate that the joining of forces internationally permits better, more successful international marketing activities, results in an improved standard of living, and provides an effective counterbalance to large economic blocs. Just as in politics, trade has refuted the old postulate of "the strong is most powerful alone." Nations have come to recognize that trade activities are of substantial importance to their economic well-being. Over the long term, the export activities of a nation are the key to the inflow of imports and therefore to the provision of choice, competition, and new insights. In the medium and long run, the balance of payments has to be maintained. In the short run, "an external deficit can be financed by drawing down previously accumulated assets or by accumulating debts to other countries. In time, however, an adjustment process must set in to eliminate the deficit."[13]

The urgency of the adjustment will vary according to the country in question. Some countries find it very hard to obtain acceptance for an increasing number of IOUs. Others, like the United States, can run deficits of trillions of dollars and are still a preferred borrower because of political stability, perceived economic security, and the worldwide use of the U.S. dollar as a reserve and business reference currency. Such temporary advantages can change, of course. Before the rise of the dollar, the British pound was the reserve currency of choice for many years.

Trade Positions Compared

Over the years, international trade positions have changed substantially when measured in terms of world market share. For example, in the 1950s, U.S. exports composed 25 percent of total world exports. Since then, this share has declined precipitously. It is not that U.S. exports have actually dropped during that time. The history of the U.S. success in world market share began with the fact that the U.S. economy was not destroyed by the war. Because other countries had little to export and a great need for imports, the U.S. export position was powerful. Over time, however, as other trade partners entered the picture and aggressively obtained a larger world market share for themselves, U.S. export growth was not able to keep pace with total world export growth. Exhibit 3.1 shows the world share of exports and imports of various trading countries and regions. Notable is the degree to which U.S. imports exceed exports.

Another important development is the rise of China's trade position. In just one decade, China increased its trade in merchandise more than four times. China now runs a trade surplus with the world's three major economic centers: The United States, the European Union and Japan. China also replaced Mexico as the United States' second most important trading partner and is now the fourth largest market for U.S. exports.[14]

The impact of international trade and marketing on individuals is highlighted when trade is scrutinized from a per-capita perspective. Exhibit 3.2 presents this information on a comparative basis. From this table, the extent to which imports exceed exports in the United States is quite evident. Per capita, the value of exports is only 64 percent that of imports. On the other hand, for Brazil the exports exceed the imports per capita by 28 percent. It is important to note that statistics for the European Union (EU) have been

Exhibit 3.1

Merchandise Exports and Imports as a Percentage of World Total, 2008

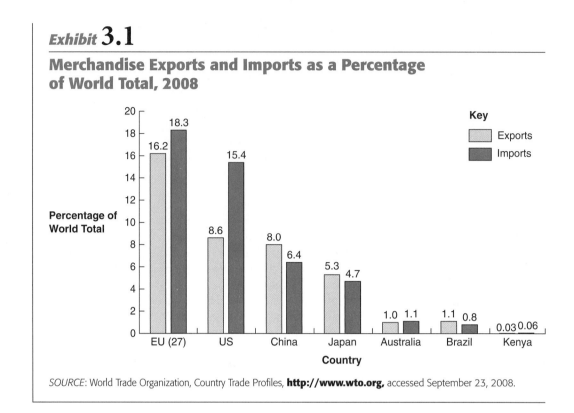

SOURCE: World Trade Organization, Country Trade Profiles, **http://www.wto.org,** accessed September 23, 2008.

Exhibit 3.2

Exports and Imports of Goods and Services per Capita for Selected Countries, 2008 (in U.S. $)

Country	Exports per Capita	Imports per Capita
EU*	4,068	4,390
Australia	7,600	8,330
Brazil	830	650
China	810	680
Japan	6,030	5,670
Kenya	160	240
United States	4,800	7,450

*Excludes intra-EU trade

SOURCE: Based on World Trade Organization, Statistics Database, Country Profiles, **http://www.wto.org,** accessed September 23, 2008.

changing drastically in recent years, mainly due to the addition of new countries with economies of varying strengths.

A Diagnosis of the U.S. Trade Position

The developments just enumerated foster the question: Why did these shifts occur? We should not attribute changes in U.S. trade performance merely to temporary factors such as the value of the dollar, the subsidization of exports from abroad, or the price of oil.

We need to search further to determine the root causes for the decline in U.S. international competitiveness.

Since World War II, it has been ingrained in the minds of American policymakers that the United States is the leading country in world power and world trade. Together with this opinion came the feeling that the United States should assist other countries with their trade performance because without American help, they would never be able to play a meaningful role in the world economy. At the same time, there was admiration for "Yankee ingenuity"—the idea that U.S. firms were the most aggressive in the world. Therefore, the U.S. private sector appeared not to need any help in its international trade efforts.

The result of this overall philosophy was a continuing effort to aid countries abroad in their economic development. At the same time, no particular attention was paid to U.S. domestic firms. This policy was well conceived and well intentioned and resulted in spectacular successes. Books written in the late 1940s describe the overwhelming economic power of the United States and the apparently impossible task of resurrecting foreign economies. Comparing those texts with the economic performance of countries such as Japan and Germany today demonstrates that the policies of helping to stimulate foreign economies were indeed crowned by success.

These policies were so successful that no one wished to tamper with them. The United States continued to encourage trade abroad and not to aid domestic firms throughout the 1990s. Although the policies were well conceived, the environment to which they were applied was changing. In the 1950s and early 1960s, the United States successfully encouraged other nations again to become full partners in world trade. However, U.S. firms were placed at a distinct disadvantage when these policies continued for too long.

U.S. firms were assured that "because of its size and the diversity of its resources, the American economy can satisfy consumer wants and national needs with a minimum of reliance on foreign trade."[15] The availability of a large U.S. domestic market and the relative distance to foreign markets resulted in U.S. manufacturers simply not feeling a compelling need to seek business beyond national borders. Subsequently, the perception emerged within the private sector that exporting and international marketing were too risky, complicated, and not worth it.

This perception also resulted in increasing gaps in international marketing knowledge between managers in the United States and those abroad. Whereas business executives in most countries were forced, by the small size of their markets, to look very quickly to markets abroad and to learn about cultural sensitivity and market differences, most U.S. managers remained blissfully ignorant of the global economy. Similarly, U.S. education did not make knowledge about the global business environment, foreign languages, and cultures an area of major priority.

Given such lack of global interest, inadequacy of information, ignorance of where and how to market internationally, unfamiliarity with foreign market conditions, and complicated trade regulations, the private sector became fearful of conducting international business activities.

However, conditions have changed. Most institutions of higher learning have recognized the responsibilities and obligations that world leadership brings with it. Universities and particularly business programs are emphasizing the international dimension, not only in theory but also in practice. Many schools are offering opportunities for study abroad, designing summer programs with global components, and expecting a global orientation from their students.

Managers have also grown more intense in their international commitment. Many newly founded firms are global from very early on, giving rise to the term **born global**.[16] Electronic commerce has made it more feasible to reach out to the global business community, whether the firm be large or small. The U.S. Department of State offers training in business–government relations to new ambassadors and instructs them to pay close attention to the needs of the U.S. business community.

In effect, the interest given to international markets as both an opportunity for finding customers and sources of supply is growing. As a result, the need for international marketing expertise can be expected to rise substantially as well.

The Impact of Trade and Investment

The Effect of Trade

Exports are important in a macroeconomic sense, in terms of balancing the trade account. Exports are special because they can affect currency values and the fiscal and monetary policies of governments, shape public perception of competitiveness, and determine the level of imports a country can afford. The steady erosion of the U.S. share of total world exports has had more than purely optical repercussions. It has also resulted in a merchandise **trade deficit**, which has been continuous since 1975. In 1987, the United States posted a then-record trade deficit with imports of products exceeding exports by more than $171 billion. Due to increases in exports, the merchandise trade deficit declined in the following years, only to climb again to record heights in 2008 by reaching $856 billion.[17] Such large trade deficits are unsustainable in the longer run.[18]

These trade deficits have a major impact on the United States and its citizens. They indicate that a country, in its international activities, is consuming more than it is producing. One key way to reduce trade deficits is to increase exports. Such an approach is highly beneficial for various reasons.

Exports can be instrumental in creating jobs. For example, in the United States, export-related employment is 39.5 percent in the domestic computer and electronics industry and 34 percent in the leather industry.[19] One billion dollars worth of exports supports the creation, on average, of 11,500 jobs.[20] Increases in exports can therefore become a major contributor to economic growth.

Equally important, through exporting, firms can achieve **economies of scale**. By broadening its market reach and serving customers abroad, a firm can produce more and do so more efficiently. As a result, the firm may achieve lower costs and higher profits both at home and abroad. Through exporting, the firm also benefits from market diversification. It can take advantage of different growth rates in different markets and gain stability by not being overly dependent on any particular market. Exporting also lets the firm learn from the competition, makes it sensitive to different demand structures and cultural dimensions, and proves its ability to survive in a less-familiar environment in spite of higher transaction costs. All these lessons can make the firm a stronger competitor at home.[21]

On the import side, firms become exposed to new competition, which may offer new approaches, better processes, or better products and services. In order to maintain their market share, firms are forced to compete more effectively by improving their own products and activities. Consumers in turn receive more choices when it comes to their selection. The competitive pressures exerted by imports also work to keep quality high and prices low.

The Effect of International Investment

International marketing activities consist not only of trade but of a spectrum of involvement, much of which results in international direct investment activities. Such investment activities can be crucial to a firm's success in new and growing markets.

For decades, the United States was the leading foreign direct investor in the world. U.S. multinationals and subsidiaries sprouted everywhere. Today, however, international firms from many countries increasingly invest around the world.

Foreign direct investment is extensive in many U.S. industries. Almost one in seven U.S. manufacturing employees works for a **foreign affiliate**, which is a U.S. firm of which foreign entities own at least 10 percent. However, the foreign ownership is not equally distributed across all industries. Foreign direct investment tends to be concentrated in specific sectors, where the foreign investors believe they are able to contribute the best and benefit the most from their investment.

Overall, foreign affiliates account for more than 5.8 million jobs in the U.S.,[22] with employees in the U.S. chemical industry leading with more than 288,000 employees and a share of 32.2 percent of total employment.[23] As a result of foreign investment, some individuals and policymakers may grow concerned about dependency on foreign owners, even though firm proof for the validity of such concern has been difficult to establish.

To some extent, these foreign direct investments substitute for trade activities. As a result, firms operating only in the domestic market may be surprised by the onslaught of foreign competition and, unprepared to respond quickly, may lose their domestic market share. However, the substitution for trade is far from complete. In many instances, foreign affiliates themselves are major participants in trade. They may import raw materials or components and export some of their output.

Even though theory suggests an open investment policy that welcomes foreign corporations, some degree of uneasiness exists about the rapid growth of such investment. Therefore, many countries review major incoming investment projects as to their effect and desirability. For example, in the United States, the government review is done by an interagency committee called the Committee for Foreign Investments in the United States (CFIUS). This committee primarily scrutinizes foreign investment activities from the standpoint of their impact on U.S. national security, and occasionally denies them. For example, the United States moved to block the acquisition of American oil company UNOCAL by the China National Offshore Oil Corporation. In the EU, France has come under criticism for its protectionist stance against foreign investors when the French government acted to prevent Aventis, a pharmaceutical company, from being acquired by Swiss-owned Novartis.[24]

A general restriction of foreign investments might well be contrary to the general good of a country's citizens. Domestic industries may be preserved, but only at great peril to the free flow of capital and at substantial cost to consumers. A restriction of investments may permit more domestic control over industries, yet it also denies access to foreign capital and often innovation. This in turn can result in a tightening up of credit markets, higher interest rates, and a decrease in willingness to adapt to changing world market conditions.

Policy Responses to Trade Problems

The word *policy* implies that there is a coordinated set of continuous activities in the legislative and executive branches of government to attempt to deal with U.S. international trade. Unfortunately, such concerted efforts only rarely come about. Policy responses have consisted mainly of political ad hoc reactions, which over the years have changed from deep regret to protectionism. Whereas in the last century most lawmakers and administration officials simply regretted the lack of U.S. performance in international markets, more recently, industry pressures have forced increased action.

Restrictions of Imports

In light of persistent trade deficits, growing foreign direct investment, and the tendency by some firms and industries to seek legislative redress for failures in the marketplace, the U.S. Congress has increasingly been willing to provide the president with more powers to restrict trade. Many resolutions have also been passed and legislation enacted admonishing the president to pay closer attention to trade. However, most of these admonitions provided only for an increasing threat against foreign importers, not for better conditions for U.S. exporters. The power of the executive to improve international trade opportunities for U.S. firms through international negotiations and a relaxation of rules, regulations, and laws has become increasingly restricted over time.

A tendency has also existed to disregard the achievements of past international negotiations. For example, in Congress an amendment was attached to protectionistic legislation, stipulating that U.S. international trade legislation should not take effect if it is not in conformity with internationally negotiated rules. The amendment was voted down by an overwhelming majority, demonstrating a legislative lack of concern for such international trade agreements. There has also been a tendency to seek short-term political favors domestically in lieu of long-term international solutions. Trade legislation has become increasingly oriented to specific trading partners and specific industries. The United States often attempts to transfer its own trade laws abroad, in areas such as antitrust or export controls, resulting

The Global Environment: A Source of Conflict between Developed and Less-Developed Nations

DESERTIFICATION
High degree of desertification hazard
Moderate degree of desertification hazard

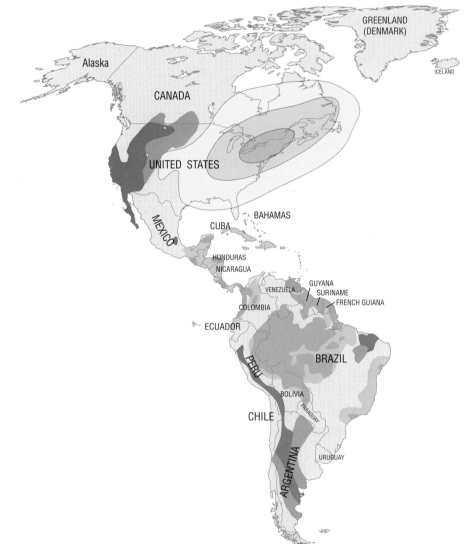

SOURCE: Based on *Environment Atlas.*

RAINFOREST DESTRUCTION
Present distribution of forest area
Former extent of rainforest

ACID DEPOSITION
Estimated acidity of precipitation in the Northern Hemisphere
Slightly acid rain
Acid rain
Very acid rain

in bilateral conflicts. During international trade negotiations, U.S. expectations regarding production costs, social structure, and cultural patterns are often expected to be adopted in full abroad.

Yet, in spite of all these developments, the United States is still one of the strongest advocates of free trade, to which its large volume of imports and ongoing trade deficit attest. Although this advocacy is shared, at least officially, by nations around the world, governments have become very creative in designing and implementing trade barriers, examples of which are listed in Exhibit 3.3.

One typical method consists of "voluntary" import restraints that are applied selectively against trading partners. Such measures have been used mainly in areas such as textiles, automobiles, and steel. Voluntary restrictions, which are, of course, implemented with the assistance of severe threats against trading partners, are intended to aid domestic industries to reorganize, restructure, and recapture their trade prominence of years past. They fail to take into account that importers may not have caused the economic decline of the domestic industry.

The steel industry provides a good example. World steel production capacity and supply clearly exceed world demand. This is the result both of overly ambitious industrial development projects motivated by nationalistic aspirations and of technological innovation. However, a closer look at the steel industries of developed nations shows that demand for steel has also been reduced. In the automobile industry, for example, fewer automobiles are being produced, and they are being produced differently than ten years ago. Automobiles are more compact, lighter, and much more fuel efficient as a result of changing consumer preferences, government regulation, and higher oil prices. The weight of automobiles has been reduced by up to 40 percent from the 1970's.[25] Accordingly, less steel is needed for its production. In addition, many components formerly made of steel are now being replaced by components made from other materials such as plastic. If imports of steel were to be totally eliminated, the steel industries would still not regain the sales lost from a substantial change in the automotive industry.

Exhibit **3.3**

Trade Barriers

There are literally hundreds of ways to build a barrier.
The following list provides just a few of the trade barriers that exporters face.

- Special Import authorization
- Restrictions on data processing
- Voluntary export restraints
- Advance import deposits
- Taxes on foreign exchange deals
- Preferential licensing applications
- Excise duties
- Licensing fees
- Discretionary licensing
- Trade restriction on e-commerce
- Anti-competitive practices
- Burdensome marketing rules
- Green barriers
- Discriminatory tax measures
- Failure to protect copyrights and patents

- Country quotas
- Testing, labeling
- Seasonal prohibitions
- Health and sanitary prohibitions
- Certification
- Foreign exchange licensing
- Barter and countertrade requirements
- Customs surcharges
- Stamp taxes
- Consular invoice fees
- Taxes on transport
- Export subsidies

SOURCE: Adapted from Crowell and Mooring, Report to the Directorate General Trade of the European Commission, Interim Evaluation of the European Union's Trade Barrier Regulation, 2005 and Office of the United States Trade Representative, 2008 National Trade Estimate Report on Foreign Trade Barriers, Washington. DC, March 28, 2008. For more information, refer to **http://www.ustr.gov/**

THE DEMAND FOR STEEL HAS BEEN REDUCED. IN THE AUTOMOBILE INDUSTRY, FOR EXAMPLE, FEWER AUTOMOBILES ARE BEING PRODUCED AND THEY CONTAIN LESS STEEL.

If countries do not use the subtle mechanism of voluntary agreements, they often resort to old-fashioned tariffs. For example, Japanese heavy motorcycles imported into the United States were assessed a duty of 49.4 percent. This regulation kept the last U.S. producer of motorcycles, the Harley-Davidson Company, in business. Even though these tariffs have since been removed—and one year early at that—one can rightfully question whether the cost imposed on U.S. consumers who preferred foreign products during the four years of tariff imposition was justified. Even though average tariffs have been substantially reduced, their specific application can still have a major effect on trade flows.

A third major method by which trade has been restricted is through **nontariff barriers**. Compared with tariffs or even subsidies, which are visible and at least force products to compete for market acceptance on dimensions other than price, some nontariff barriers are much more difficult to detect, prove, and quantify. For example, these barriers may be government or private-sector "buy domestic" campaigns, which affect importers and foreign direct investors. Other nontariff barriers consist of providing preferential treatment to domestic bidders over foreign bidders, using national standards that are not comparable to international standards, placing emphasis on design rather than performance, and providing for general difficulties in the market entry of foreign products. Most famous in this regard are probably the measures implemented by France. To stop or at least reduce the importation of foreign video recorders, France ruled that all of them had to be sent through the customs station at Poitiers. This customshouse was located in the middle of the country, was woefully understaffed, and was open only a few days each week. In addition, the few customs agents at Poitiers insisted on opening each package separately in order to inspect the merchandise. Within a few weeks, imports of video recorders in France came to a halt. The French government, however, was able to point to international agreements and to the fact that officially all measures were in full compliance with the law.

The primary result of all of these trade restrictions is that many actions are taken that are contrary to what we know is good for the world and its citizens. Industries are preserved, but only at great peril to the world trade framework and at substantial cost to consumers. The direct costs of these actions are hidden and do not evoke much public complaint because they are spread out over a multitude of individuals. Yet, these costs are real and burdensome and directly affect the standard of living of individuals and the competitiveness of firms.

For example, if agricultural subsidies and tariffs were eliminated in the Doha Round of trade negotiations, the gains to the world economy by 2015 have been estimated to be $287 billion annually! These gains do not necessarily mean that prices would decrease. The elimination of artificial distortions would increase the prices for some agricultural goods. For example, projections show that cotton prices would increase by 21 percent, but the increase would primarily benefit the countries of Sub-Saharan Africa, currently one of the poorest regions in the world.[26]

Export Promotion Efforts

Many countries provide export promotion assistance to their firms. Key reasons for such assistance are the national need to earn foreign currency, the encouragement of domestic employment, and the increase in domestic economic activity. Many forms of export promotion can be seen as government distortion of trade since government support simply results in a subsidization of profitability or reduction of risk. Yet, there are instances where such intervention may be justified. Government support can be appropriate if it annuls unfair foreign practices, increases market transparency and therefore contributes to the better functioning of markets,[27] or helps overcome, in the interest of long-term national competitiveness, the short-term orientation of firms.[28]

The U.S. Department of Commerce provides companies with an impressive array of data on foreign trade and marketing developments. Its Commercial Service provides a link with U.S. businesses in terms of information flow and market assistance. Efforts are made to coordinate the activities of diverse federal agencies. As a result of these efforts, a national network of export assistance centers has been created, capable of providing one-stop shops for exporters in search of export counseling and financial assistance. In addition, an official interagency advocacy network was created that helps U.S. companies win overseas contracts for large government purchases abroad. A variety of agencies now collaborate in order to continue to improve services to U.S. exporters.

In terms of comparative efforts, however, U.S. export promotion activities still lag far behind the support provided by other major industrial nations. Many countries also provide substantial levels of private-sector support, which exists to a much lesser degree in the United States. Even more importantly, of the total U.S. export promotion expenditures, the largest portion (almost 50 percent) continues to go to the agricultural sector, and relatively few funds are devoted to export counseling and market research for manufacturing and service firms. However, it also needs to be considered that WTO regulations sharply restrict the ability of governments to promote their manufacturing export—though the opportunity for the promotion of service exports is substantially less regulated.

A new focus has come about in the area of export financing. Policymakers have increasingly recognized that U.S. business may be placed at a disadvantage if it cannot meet the subsidized financing rates of foreign suppliers. The Export-Import Bank of the United States, charged with the mission of aggressively meeting foreign export-financing conditions, has in recent years even resorted to offering **mixed aid credits**. These take the form of loans composed partially of commercial interest rates and partially of highly subsidized developmental aid interest rates. The bank has also launched a major effort to reach out to smaller-sized businesses and assist in their export success.

Tax legislation that inhibited the employment of Americans by U.S. firms abroad has also been altered to be more favorable to U.S. firms. In the past, U.S. nationals living abroad were, with some minor exclusion, fully subject to U.S. federal taxation. Because the cost of living abroad can often be quite high—rent for a small apartment can approach the range of $4,000-plus per month—this tax structure often imposed a significant burden on U.S. firms and citizens, and companies frequently were not able to send U.S. employees abroad. However, as the result of a tax code revision that allows a substantial amount of income (up to $85,700 in 2007) to remain tax-free,[29] more Americans can now be posted abroad. In their work they may specify the use of U.S. products and thus enhance the competitive opportunities of U.S. firms.

One other export promotion development was the passage of the Export Trading Company Act of 1982. Intended to be the U.S. response to Japanese *sogoshoshas,* or international trading firms, this legislation permits firms to work together to form **export consortia**.

The basic idea was to provide the foreign buyer with a one-stop shopping center in which a group of U.S. firms could offer a variety of complementary and competitive products. By exempting U.S. firms from current antitrust statutes, and by permitting banks to cooperate in the formation of these ventures through direct capital participation and the financing of trading activities, the government hoped that more firms could participate in the international marketplace. Although this legislation was originally hailed as a masterstroke and a key measure in turning around the decline in U.S. competitiveness abroad, it has not attracted a large number of successful firms. It appears that the legislation may not have provided sufficient incentive for banks, export service firms, or exporters to participate. Banks simply may find domestic profit margins to be more attractive and safe; export service firms may be too small; and exporters themselves may be too independent to participate in such consortia.

A Strategic Outlook for Trade and Investment Policies

All countries have international trade and investment policies. The importance and visibility of these policies have grown dramatically as international trade and investment flows have become more relevant to the well-being of most countries. Given the growing links among countries, it will be increasingly difficult to consider domestic policy without looking at international repercussions.

A U.S. Perspective

The U.S. need is for a positive trade policy rather than reactive, ad hoc responses to specific situations. **Protectionistic legislation** can be helpful, provided it is not enacted. Proposals in Congress, for example, can be quite useful as bargaining chips in international negotiations. If passed and signed into law, however, protectionistic legislation can result in the destruction of the international trade and investment framework.

It has been suggested that a variety of regulatory agencies could become involved in administering U.S. trade policy. Although such agencies could be useful from the standpoint of addressing narrowly defined grievances, they carry the danger that commercial policy will be determined by a new chorus of discordant voices. Shifting the power of setting trade and investment policy from the executive branch to agencies or even states could give the term *New Federalism* a quite unexpected meaning and might cause progress at the international negotiation level to grind to a halt. No U.S. negotiator can expect to retain the goodwill of foreign counterparts if he or she cannot place issues on the table that can benegotiated without constantly having to check back with various authorities.

In light of continuing large U.S. trade deficits, there is much disenchantment with past trade policies. Disappointment with past trade negotiations is mainly the result of overblown expectations. Too often, the public has mistakenly expected successful trade negotiations to affect the domestic economy in a major way, even though the issue addressed or resolved was only of minor economic importance. Yet, cumulatively and over time, the decrease in international tariffs and non-tariff barriers has dramatically affected the economic well being of consumers.

In light of global changes, U.S. trade policy does need to change. Rather than treating trade policy as a strictly "foreign" phenomenon, it must be recognized that it is mainly domestic economic performance that determines global competitiveness. Therefore, trade policy must become more domestically oriented at the same time that domestic policy must become more international in vision. Such a new approach should pursue at least five key goals. First, the nation must improve the quality and amount of information government and business share to facilitate competitiveness. Second, policy must encourage collaboration among companies in such areas as goods and process technologies. Third, U.S. industry collectively must overcome its export reluctance and its short-term financial orientation. Fourth, the United States must invest in its people, providing education and training suited to the competitive challenges of the twenty-first century. Finally, the executive branch must be given authority by Congress to negotiate international agreements with a reasonable certainty that the negotiation outcome will not be subject to minute amendments. Therefore, renewal of **trade promotion authority**, which gives Congress the right to accept or reject trade treaties and agreements, but reduces the amendment procedures, is very important. Such authority is instrumental for new, large-scale trade accords such as the Doha Round to succeed.

It will also be necessary to achieve a new perspective on government–business relations. In previous decades, government and business stayed at arm's length, and it was seen as inappropriate to involve the government in private-sector activities. Now, however, closer government–business collaboration is seen as one key to enhanced competitiveness. More mutual listening to each other and joint consideration of the long-term domestic and international repercussions of policy actions and business strategy can indeed pay off. Perhaps it will make both business and government more responsive to each other's needs. At least it will reduce the failures that can result from a lack of collaboration and insufficient understanding of linkages.

An International Perspective

From an international perspective, trade and investment negotiations must continue. In doing so, trade and investment policy can take either a multilateral or bilateral approach. **Bilateral negotiations** are carried out mainly between two nations, while **multilateral negotiations** are carried out among a number of nations. The approach can also be broad, covering a wide variety of goods, services, or investments, or it can be narrow in that it focuses on specific problems.

In order to address narrowly defined trade issues, bilateral negotiations and a specific approach seem quite appealing. Very specific problems can be discussed and resolved expediently. However, to be successful on a global scale, negotiations need to produce winners. Narrow-based bilateral negotiations require that there be, for each issue, a clearly identified winner and loser. Therefore, such negotiations have less chance for long-term success, because no one wants to be the loser. This points toward multilateral negotiations on a broad scale, where concessions can be traded off among countries, making it possible for all participants to emerge and declare themselves as winners. The difficulty lies in devising enough incentives to bring the appropriate and desirable partners to the bargaining table. One area that would benefit greatly from multilateral negotiations is the regulation of e-commerce and the Internet as described in *The International Marketplace 3.4* (for more on e-commerce, see Chapter 9).

Policymakers must be willing to trade off short-term achievements for long-term goals. All too often, measures that would be beneficial in the long term are sacrificed to short-term expediency to avoid temporary pain and the resulting political cost. Given the increasing links among nations and their economies, however, such adjustments are inevitable. In the recent past, trade and investment volume continued to grow for everyone. Conflicts were minimized and adjustment possibilities were increased manyfold. In times of increasing competition and resource scarcity, however, conflicts are likely to increase significantly. Thoughtful economic coordination will therefore be required among the leading trading nations. Such coordination will result to some degree in the loss of national sovereignty.

New mechanisms to evaluate restraint measures will also need to be designed. The beneficiaries of trade and investment interference are usually clearly defined and have much to gain, whereas the losers are much less visible, which will make coalition building a key issue. The total cost of policy measures affecting trade and investment flows must be assessed, must be communicated, and must be taken into consideration before such measures are implemented.

The affected parties need to be concerned and join forces. The voices of retailers, consumers, wholesalers, and manufacturers all need to be heard. However, the different groups promoting government intervention or subsidies also will need to clearly demonstrate what they will deliver in exchange for government action. A specific performance plan will then need to be developed in order to assure the continued wise use of resources. Such steps will place government action and corporate expectations in a context that is transparent and acceptable to consumers.

The International MARKETPLACE

3.4

The Trade Reality of E-commerce

The Internet presents an opportunity for businesses and individuals to collaborate and communicate faster and cheaper than ever before. However, the new technology also poses challenges to modern policymakers, businesses, and consumers. As more information is stored online and more people purchase with their computers, security is becoming a major problem. Hackers have been able to use security holes in Web sites and databases to steal information, including credit card and social security numbers. They have also attacked personal, corporate, and government computers connected to the Internet by exploiting weaknesses in operating systems and browser security. With the globalization of technology, hacking becomes much more than a simple break-in and entry. Who has the legal jurisdiction in these cases? Is it the country in which the computer that was hacked into is located? The country from which the hacker is attacking? Or the country in which the company is based? Many nations have yet to develop laws regarding internet crimes and the existing laws vary greatly between nations.

In the past, consumers were able to buy foreign products through distributors and retailers in their home country. Today, they can skip intermediaries entirely and buy the product directly from the manufacturer over the Internet. But what happens if a consumer buys a product from a relatively little known company and the product is defective, or the consumer is hurt by the product? Many countries have fairly extensive consumer protection laws, but many do not. Can the consumer sue based on the laws of his or her country, or on the laws of the country where the company is headquartered? Given the differences in legal theories and damage awards, should corporations be concerned about lawsuits from every country in the world?

One landmark for e-commerce was the internet portal Yahoo! Case. Some French web surfers chose to sell Nazi artifacts. The Ligue International Contre le Racism et 1-Antisemitisme (LICRA) and the Union of French Jewish Students (UEJF) took legal action in order to stop Yahoo! From selling these artifacts. They were able to sue under the French laws that prohibited any type of incitation or promotion of Nazi memorabilia.

Some critics of e-commerce have suggested that it be regulated by the World Trade Organization. In 2005, the WTO actually did take action in regard to the international online gambling industry. Nonetheless, as of 2008, WTO has not made much progress in e-commerce regulation. Dispute settlements are left up to national courts. The technology is difficult to keep up with and there is a lack of government constituents. As e-commerce becomes more popular, however, some steps to protect people's security and privacy will be needed.

SOURCES: Global Reach, **http://glreach.com/eng/ed/art/2004.-ecommerce.php3**, accessed December 16, 2005; **http://www.iacis.org/iis/2007_iis/PDFs/Ivy.pdf**, accessed Novermber 23, 2008; **http://www.onestopclick.com/news/E-commerce-is-'business-channel-of-the-future'_18796870.html**, accessed November 23, 2008.

Summary

International trade has often played a major role in world history. The rise and fall of the Roman Empire and the emergence of feudalism can be attributed to trade. Since 1945, the Western nations have made concerted efforts to improve the trade environment and expand trade activities. In order for them to do so, various multinational organizations, such as the WTO, the IMF, and the World Bank, were founded. In addition, several economic blocs such as the EU, NAFTA, and Mercosur were formed. Many of these organizations have been very successful in their mission, yet new realities of the trade environment demand new types of action.

Recall from Chapter 1 that the last few decades have been marked by tremendous growth in world trade. In addition, there have been significant changes in the trade positions of many countries. For example, the United States' share of world exports has declined precipitously from 25 percent in the 1950s, while China's share in world trade has risen substantially in the last few years alone. Furthermore, foreign direct investment has come to play an important role in the world economy.

The WTO is the key forum for trade disputes and negotiations. However, there are growing tensions between developed and developing countries, particularly in the sphere of agriculture.

Despite calls for trade liberalization, some policymakers intend to enhance trade performance by threatening the world with increasing protectionism. The danger of such a policy lies in the fact that world trade would

shrink and standards of living would decline. Protectionism cannot, in the long run, prevent adjustment or increase productivity and competitiveness. It is therefore
important to improve the capability of firms to compete

internationally, to provide an international trade framework that facilitates international marketing activities,
but also to keep in mind the displacement consequences
of trade, which may require adjustment preparations.

Key Terms

Pax Romana	foreign direct investment	protectionistic legislation
economic blocs	foreign affiliate	trade promotion authority
born global	nontariff barriers	bilateral negotiations
trade deficit	mixed aid credits	multilateral negotiations
economies of scale	export consortia	

Questions for Discussion

1. Why is international trade important to a nation?
2. Give examples of the effects of the "Pax Americana."
3. Discuss the role of "voluntary" import restraints in international marketing.
4. Provide examples of multilateral versus bilateral trade agreements.
5. How have consumer demands changed international trade?
6. Discuss the impact of import restrictions on consumers.
7. Does foreign direct investment have an effect on trade?

Internet Exercises

1. What is the major role played by the World Bank today? Check http://www.worldbank.org to report on key projects.
2. Determine the latest exports per capita for a country of your choice not listed in Exhibit 3.3 (use data from http://www.imf.org and http://www.un.org).
3. Compare the discussion of industry/country trade barriers from the perspective of the European Union and the United States (http://ec.europa.eu/trade and www.ustr.gov).

Recommended Readings

Aaronson, S. and Zimmerman, J., *Trade Imbalance: The Struggle to Reconcile Human Rights Concerns in Trade Policy Making.* Cambridge University Press, 2008.

Finger, Michael J. *Institutions and Trade Policy.* Northampton MA: Edward Elgar, 2002.

Mann, Catherine, *Accelerating the Globalization of America: The Next Wave of Information Technology.* Peterson Institute for International Economics, Washington D.C., 2007.

McCue, Sarah. *Farce to Force: Building Profitable E-Commerce Strategies.* Mason, OH: Thomson Higher Education, 2006.

Odell, John, ed. *Negotiating Trade: Developing Countries in the WTO and NAFTA.* Cambridge; England: Cambridge University Press, 2006.

Razeen, Sally, *New Frontiers in Free Trade: Globalization's future and Asia's Rising Role.* The Cato Institute, Washington D.C., 2008.

THE CULTURAL ENVIRONMENT

The International
MARKETPLACE

Cultural Imperialism Does Not Sell in International Markets

The dominance of U.S. cultural exports is felt everywhere. Of the 50 worldwide highest-grossing films by 2008, all were U.S. productions. *Kung Fu Panda* (which came in at thirty-sixth) had grossed $631.5 million in its first year and had been the top earner of the year in diverse markets such as Singapore ($4.3 million), Lithuania ($493,000), and Argentina ($5.8 million). Given the marketing power of Hollywood, many are worried that diversity will not survive and that the end result of globalization will be "Americanization." Quite the opposite is actually taking place in the entertainment world and international market for popular culture.

In television, during the initial stage of the life cycle, the domestic industry has only fledgling production and cheap imports—primarily from the United States—to fill the time slots. With time, however, homegrown production develops and its market share increases. The top TV show in South Africa is *Generations* (a soap opera); in France, it is *Julie Lescaut* (a police series); and in Brazil, it is *O Clone* (a soap opera). The more the world globalizes, the more people want entertainment that reflects their own culture. U.S. shows do have their niche, as well. Blockbuster Hollywood action movies, cartoons (easy to dub), and certain hit series travel well across cultural barriers. The number one hit among German teenagers is *Buffy im Bann der Dämonen,* while Chinese children enjoy newly introduced Mickey Mouse cartoons. However, on a broader scale, U.S. content providers are having to think about how to refashion their exports.

Art Attack, an art show for Disney Channel (which is seen around the world), included 216 episodes shot in 26 different languages. A single format (a set that features oversized paint pots and paint brushes, in fuchsia pink and lime green) is reshaped for each country to give it a local feel. About three-fifths of each show is made up of shared footage: close-ups of the hands of one artist (British). The rest of the show is filmed separately for each country, with the heads and shoulders of local presenters seamlessly edited in. Even though the local presenters are all flown into one central studio in the United Kingdom, the show costs only one-third of what it would take to produce separately for each country. Local viewers in each place consider the show to be theirs.

In Europe, a number of developments seem to conspire to favor U.S. films. The spread of multiplex cinemas has increased attendance, but the multiplexes tend to show more U.S. movies. Hollywood blockbusters, such as *King Kong* or *Star Wars: Episode III—Revenge of the Sith,* are made with budgets beyond the Europeans' wildest dreams. Marketing spending, too, has soared, doubling since the mid-1990s to an average of $34 million per movie. Finally, U.S. studios have become increasingly dependent on overseas revenues and are investing more to push their movies in foreign markets. Lately, French moviemakers, who have long resented the overwhelming popularity of Hollywood movies on their home turf, have begun to fight back. *Le Fabuleux Destin d'Amélie Poulain,* a French-made romantic comedy, recaptured the French box office to the tune of $37.7 million in receipts. It was one of four French films released in 2001 that sold more than five million tickets, beating a

KUNG FU PANDA WAS THE TOP EARNER OF THE YEAR IN DIVERSE MARKETS SUCH AS SINGAPORE, LITHUANIA, AND ARGENTINA.

In 2001, French-language films enjoyed their best year in the United States, grossing $28 million—small by overall standards but a huge improvement over $6.8 million in 2000. In 2005, however, the results were more modest. *Après Vous* grossed $81 million and *High Tension* $6 million worldwide. The U.S. audience for foreign films in general comes squarely from the youth market, a dramatic change from the art-house crowd of the past. To reach this audience, studios use the Internet as a marketing tool, offering prizes as well as trailers and synopses.

Top local programming created around the world is making its way into the United States, too. Most shows on Univision, America's Spanish-language TV network, including the hugely popular telenovelas, are made by Mexico's Televisa. As a matter of fact, the success of telenovelas is often celebrated as an example of reverse cultural imperialism. The BBC, while expanding its own programming in the United States, coproduces much of the natural-history content on Discovery. Even Arte, a Franco-German culture channel, is no stranger to American airwaves.

The trade in entertainment is no longer a one-way street making all who watch and listen clones of one another. Much of the U.S. content going abroad is adjusted to its markets, as is the material coming into the United States. Britain's *Bob the Builder* has hammered his way into U.S. homes and the homes of 29 other countries but with the loss of his Staffordshire accent; since its introduction in May 2001, 2.9 million videos of this animated series have been sold.

record set in 1947. For the first time in decades, French films stood their ground against American imports. With higher budgets and better production values, the new films were created by a wave of young directors with Hollywood experience. What is even more interesting is that films that have success in their home markets are also more acceptable to the big-money U.S. market.

SOURCES: Ibsen Martinez, "Romancing the Globe," *Foreign Policy,* November/December 2005, 48–56; "Score One for the PG Crowd," *The San Diego Union-Tribune,* April 10, 2005, B7; "Think Local: A Survey of Television," *The Economist,* April 13, 2002, 12–14; "Culture in Peril? Mais Oui," *Fortune,* May 13, 2002, 51; "The American Connection," *The Washington Post,* May 25, 2002, E1–E2; "Rebels Without a Cause," *The Economist,* April 27, 2002, 65; "At Vivendi Universal, A French Evolution," *The Washington Post,* April 24, 2002, E1, E3.

The ever-increasing level of world trade, opening of markets, enhanced purchasing power of customers, and intensifying competition all have allowed and even forced marketers to expand their operations. The challenge for the marketing manager is to handle the differences in values and attitudes, and subsequent behavioral patterns that govern human interaction, on two levels: first, as they relate to customer behavior and, second, as they affect the implementation of marketing programs within individual markets and across markets.

For years, marketers have been heralding the arrival of the global customer, an individual or entity that would both think and purchase alike the world or region over.[1] These universal needs could then be translated into marketing programs that would exploit these similarities. However, if this approach were based on the premise of standardization, a critical and fatal mistake would be made. Overseas success is very much a function of cultural adaptability: patience, flexibility, and tolerance for others' beliefs.[2]

To take advantage of global markets or global segments, marketers are required to have or attain a thorough understanding of what drives customer behavior in different markets and to detect the extent to which similarities exist or can be achieved through marketing efforts.

For example, no other group of emerging markets in the world have as much in common as those in Latin America. They largely share a Spanish language and heritage; the Portuguese language and heritage are close enough to allow Brazilians and their neighbors to communicate easily. The Southern Florida melting pot, where Latin Americans of all backgrounds mix in a blend of Hispanic cultures, is in itself a picture of what Latin America can be. Tapping into the region's cultural affinities through a network scale approach (e.g., regional hubs for production and preproduction, and pan-Latin brands) is not only possible but advisable.[3] As appliance makers such as Whirlpool study the habits and preferences of consumers in different countries, they develop specialized appliances (e.g., grinders for coffee and spices) and features (e.g., a fifth burner for ranges). Interestingly, as cooking habits have extended to include food from other cultures—from pizza to pot roast to tortillas—the new features have found new adopters. For example, non-Latinos want griddle cook tops for pancakes as well as fajitas.[4]

In expanding their presence, marketers will acquire not only new customers but new partners as well. These essential partners, whose efforts are necessary for market development and penetration, include agents, distributors, other facilitating agents (such as advertising agencies and law firms), and, in many cases, the government. Expansion will also mean new employees or strategic alliance partners whose motivations will either make or break marketing programs. Thus understanding the hot buttons and turnoffs of these groups becomes critical.

In the past, marketing managers who did not want to worry about the cultural challenge could simply decide not to do so and concentrate on domestic markets. In today's business environment, a company has no choice but to face international competition. In this new environment, believing that concern about culture and its elements is a waste of time often proves to be disastrous. An understanding allows marketers to determine when adaptation may be necessary and when commonalities allow for regional or global approaches, as seen in *The International Marketplace 4.1.* Understanding culture is critical not only in terms of getting strategies right but also for ensuring that implementation by local operations is effective.

Cultural differences often are the subject of anecdotes, and business blunders may provide a good laugh. Cultural diversity must be recognized not simply as a fact of life but as a positive benefit; that is, differences may actually suggest better solutions to challenges shared across borders. Cultural competence must be recognized as a key marketing skill.[5] Adjustments will have to be made to accommodate the extraordinary variety in customer preferences and work practices, by cultivating the ability to detect similarities and to allow for differences. Ideally, this means that successful ideas can be transferred across borders for efficiency and adapted to local conditions for effectiveness. For example, in one of his regular trips to company headquarters in Switzerland, the general manager of Nestlé Thailand was briefed on a promotion for a cold coffee concoction called Nescafé Shake. The Thai group swiftly adopted and adapted the idea to their regional operations. It designed plastic containers to mix the drink and invented a dance, the Shake, to popularize the product.[6] Cultural incompetence, however, can easily jeopardize millions of dollars in wasted negotiations, potential purchases, sales and contracts, and customer relations. Furthermore, the internal efficiency of a firm may be weakened if managers, employees, and intermediaries are not "on the same wavelength."

The intent of this chapter is first to analyze the concept of culture and its various elements and then to provide suggestions for meeting the cultural challenge.

Culture Defined

Culture gives an individual an anchoring point—an identity—as well as codes of conduct. Of the more than 160 definitions of culture analyzed by Alfred Kroeber and Clyde Kluckhohn, some conceive of culture as separating humans from nonhumans, some define it as communicable knowledge, and some see it as the sum of historical achievements produced by humanity's social life.[7] All the definitions have common elements: Culture is learned, shared, and transmitted from one generation to the next. Culture is primarily passed on by parents to their children but also by social organizations, special-interest groups, the government, the schools, and religious institutions. Common ways of thinking and behaving that are developed are then reinforced through social pressure. Geert Hofstede calls this the "collective programming of the mind."[8] Culture is also multidimensional, consisting of a number of common elements that are interdependent. Changes occurring in one of the dimensions will affect the others as well.

For the purposes of this text, **culture** is defined as an integrated system of learned behavior patterns that are distinguishing characteristics of the members of any given society. It includes everything that a group thinks, says, does, and makes—its customs, language, material artifacts, and shared systems of attitudes and feelings. The definition therefore encompasses a wide variety of elements, from the materialistic to the spiritual. Culture is inherently conservative, resisting change and fostering continuity. Every person is encultured into a particular culture, learning the "right way" of doing things. Problems may arise when a person encultured in one culture has to adjust to another one. The process of **acculturation**— adjusting and adapting to a specific culture other than one's own—is one of the keys to success in international operations.

Edward T. Hall, who has made some of the most valuable studies on the effects of culture on business, makes a distinction between high and low context cultures.[9] In **high context cultures**, such as Japan and Saudi Arabia, context is at least as important as what is actually said. The speaker and the listener rely on a common understanding of the context. In **low context cultures**, however, most of the information is contained explicitly in the words. North American cultures engage in low context communications. Unless we are aware of this basic difference, messages and intentions can easily be misunderstood. If performance appraisals of marketing personnel are to be centrally guided or conducted in a multinational corporation, those involved must be acutely aware of cultural nuances. One of the interesting differences is that the U.S. system emphasizes the individual's development, whereas the Japanese system focuses on the group within which the individual works. In the United States, criticism is more direct and recorded formally, whereas in Japan it is more subtle and verbal. What is not being said can carry more meaning than what is said.

Few cultures today are as homogeneous as those of Japan and Saudi Arabia. Elsewhere, intracultural differences based on nationality, religion, race, or geographic areas have resulted in the emergence of distinct subcultures. The international manager's task is to distinguish relevant cross-cultural and intracultural differences and then to isolate potential opportunities and problems. Good examples are the Hispanic subculture in the United States and the Flemish and the Walloons in Belgium. For example, IKEA's research in the United States found that Latin families wanted bigger dining room tables to accommodate bigger families.[10] On the other hand, borrowing and interaction between national cultures may lead to narrowing gaps between cultures. Here the international business entity will act as a **change agent** by introducing new products or ideas and practices. Although this may consist of no more than shifting consumption from one product brand to another, it may lead to massive social change in the manner of consumption, the type of products consumed, and social organization.

The example of Kentucky Fried Chicken in India illustrates the difficulties marketers may have in entering culturally complex markets. Even though the company opened its outlets in two of India's most cosmopolitan cities (Bangalore and New Delhi), it found itself the target of protests by a wide range of opponents. KFC could have alleviated or eliminated some of the anti-Western passions by taking a series of preparatory steps. First, rather than opting for more direct control, KFC should have allied with local partners for advice and support. Second, KFC should have tried to appear more Indian rather than using high-profile advertising with Western ideas. Indians are quite ambivalent toward foreign culture, and ideas usable elsewhere do not work well in India. Finally, KFC should have planned for reaction by competition that came from small restaurants with political clout at the local level.[11]

In some cases, the international marketer may be accused of **cultural imperialism**, especially if the changes brought about are dramatic or if culture-specific adaptations are not made in the marketing approach. There is a growing fear among many countries that globalization is bringing a surge of foreign products across their borders that will threaten their cultural heritage. In 2005, the United Nations Educational, Scientific, and Cultural Organization passed the Convention on the Protection and Promotion of Diversity of Cultural

Expressions, which declares the right of countries to "maintain, adopt, and implement policies and measures that they deem appropriate for the protection and promotion of music, art, language, and ideas as well as cultural activities, goods and services."[12] Some countries, such as Brazil, Canada, France, and Indonesia, protect their cultural industries through restrictive rules and subsidies. France's measures include, for example, "prix unique du livre," a limitation on the percent of discount on books (to support small publishing houses and help maintain small bookstores); quotas on non-French movies on French national TV channels and mandatory financing of films by TV channels (as a provision in their license) as well as for French music on radio channels; and "avance sur recettes" or "fonds de soutien," a state financial advance on all French films.[13] Such subsidies have allowed the French to make 200 films a year, twice as many as the United Kingdom. Similar measures have been taken to protect geographic indications; for example, signs on goods that have a specific geographic origin and possess qualities or a reputation due to that place of origin (as seen in *The International Marketplace 4.2*). Some countries have started taking measures to protect their traditions in areas such as medicine, in which the concern is biopiracy of natural remedies.[14]

The International MARKETPLACE

ENVIRONMENT & SUSTAINABILITY   4.2

Cultural Sustainability: Protecting Feta and Mozzarella

In October 2005, the European Court of Justice brought to a close one of the most controversial disputes over geographic indications, removing the right of any non-Greek EU producers to use the name Feta for cheese. The Court decided that Feta fulfilled the requirements of a destination of origin because the name referred to an agricultural product from a defined geographical area and reflected characteristics specific to that area and its processing and preparation. All other non-Greek Feta producers had to change the name of their cheese by 2007.

If European negotiators in the World Trade Organization get their way, food names associated with specific regions—Parma ham from Italy, Stilton cheese from the United Kingdom, and Marsala wine from Italy—would be reserved solely for companies located in the respective regions. EU officials argue that mozzarella, for example, is made according to exacting standards only in that particular part of Italy.

The EU Commission summarized the European point of view in this way: "Geographical indications offer the best protection to quality products which are sold by relying on their origin and reputation and other special characteristics linked to such an origin. They reward investment in quality by our producers. Abuses in other countries undermine the heritage of EU products and create confusion among consumers." Furthermore, Europeans fear that they may not be able to use their own names selling abroad in the future. A company in Canada, for example, could trademark a product named for a European place, preventing the rightful European

originator from selling his goods in that market. The European Union has adopted geographic-indication laws governing over 600 products sold inside the EU. Now the EU wants to expand such a list worldwide and establish a multilateral register to police it.

For many, the European idea is bald-faced protectionism and has no merit on protecting cultural values. "This does not speak of free trade; it is about making a monopoly of trade," said Sergio Marchi, Canada's ambassador to the WTO. "It is even hard to calculate the cost and confusion of administering such a thing." Others argue that the Europeans are merely trying to cover up for inefficient production practices. Some even make the argument that multinational companies are the ones who have built up the value of many of the product names on the list—not the small producers in the regions in question.

The debate is still in its early stages. The definition of geographic indications is not altogether clear in that some countries want to protect the adjectives found on product labels (such as "tawny" or "ruby" to describe Portuguese port wine). Other countries have their own lists as well; for example, India wants basmati rice to be protected even though "basmati" is not a place name. Examples of geographical indications from the United States include: *FLORIDA* for oranges; *IDAHO* for potatoes; *VIDALIA* for onions; and *WASHINGTON STATE* for apples.

SOURCES: "Greek Cheese Gets EU Protection," Marketing News, November 15, 2005, 15; "Food Fight!" Time Europe, September 8, 2003, 32–33; "WTO Talks: EU Steps Up Bid for Better Protection of Regional Quality Products," EU Institutions Press Releases, August 28, 2003, DN:IP/03/1178; "Ham and Cheese: Italy Wins EU Case," CNN.com, May 20, 2003; "Europe Says, 'That Cheese is No Cheddar!'" The Wall Street Journal, February 13, 2003, B1; "USTR Supports Geographic Indications for Drinks," Gourmet News, January, 2003, 3. See also **http://www.geographicindications.com**.

Even if a particular country is dominant in a cultural sector, such as the United States in movies and television programming, the commonly suggested solution of protectionism may not work. Although the European Union has a rule that 40 percent of the programming has to be domestic, anyone wanting a U.S. program can choose an appropriate channel or rent a video. Quotas will also result in behavior not intended by regulators. U.S. programming tends to be scheduled during prime time, while the 60 percent of domestic programming may wind up being shown during less attractive times. Furthermore, quotas may also lead to local productions designed to satisfy official mandates and capture subsidies that accompany them. Recently, a question has been raised of whether movies produced by foreign-owned companies would be eligible for government subsidies.

Popular culture is not only a U.S. bastion. In many areas, such as pop music and musicals, Europeans have had an equally dominant position worldwide. For example, the United Kingdom exported 3,795 hours of television programming in 2004 as compared to Netherlands' 2,569 and the United States' 2,236.[15] Furthermore, no market is only an exporter of culture. Given the ethnic diversity in the United States (as in many other country markets), programming from around the world is made readily available. Many of the greatest successes among cultural products in the last five years in the United States have been imports; e.g., in television programming, *Pop Idol* is a British concept, as is the best-seller in children's literature, the Harry Potter series. In cartoons, Pokémon hails from Japan. Global marketers and media have made it possible for national and regional artists to break into worldwide markets, especially the U.S. and European markets. Thailand's Tata Young has been signed by SONY BMG to be groomed for global stardom.[16]

The worst scenario for marketers is when they are accused of pushing alien behaviors and values—along with products and promotions—into other cultures, which can result in consumer boycotts and even destruction of property. McDonald's, KFC, Coca-Cola, Disney, and Pepsi, for example, have all drawn the ire of anti-American demonstrators for being icons of globalization. Similarly, noisy boycotts and protests targeted many multinational companies in the wake of the situation in Iraq. In the United States, those protests were aimed at French and Germans, while opponents of the war focused on U.S. companies.[17]

The Elements of Culture

The study of culture has led to generalizations that may apply to all cultures. Such characteristics are called cultural universals, which are manifestations of the total way of life of any group of people. These include such elements as bodily adornments, courtship, etiquette, family gestures, joking, mealtimes, music, personal names, status differentiation, and trade.[18] These activities occur across cultures, but their manifestation may be unique in a particular society, bringing about cultural diversity. Common denominators can indeed be found, but the ways in which they are actually accomplished may vary dramatically. Even when a segment may be perceived to be similar across borders, such as in the case of teenagers and the affluent, cultural differences make marketers' jobs challenging. For example, European teens resent being treated as Americans with an accent by U.S. companies.[19]

Observation of the major denominators summarized in Exhibit 4.1 suggests that the elements are both material (such as tools) and abstract (such as attitudes). The sensitivity

Exhibit **4.1**

Elements of Culture

Language	Manners and customs
· Verbal	Material elements
· Nonverbal	Aesthetics
Religion	Education
Values and attitudes	Social institutions

and adaptation to these elements by an international firm depends on the firm's level of involvement in the market—for example, licensing versus direct investment—and the product or service marketed. Naturally, some products and services or management practices require very little adjustment, whereas others have to be adapted dramatically.

Language

A total of 6,912 known living languages exist in the world, with 311 being spoken in the United States, 297 in Mexico, 13 in Finland, and 241 in China.[20] The European Union has 23 official languages for its bureaucracy. Interestingly, a total of 96 percent of the world's languages are spoken by just 4 percent of the world's population. Language has been described as the mirror of culture. Language itself is multidimensional by nature. This is true not only of the spoken word but also of what can be called the nonverbal language of international business. Messages are conveyed by the words used, by the way the words are spoken (for example, tone of voice), and by nonverbal means such as gestures, body position, and eye contact.

Very often, mastery of the language is required before a person is acculturated to a culture other than his or her own. Language mastery must go beyond technical competency, because every language has words and phrases that can be readily understood only in context. Such phrases are carriers of culture; they represent special ways a culture has developed to view some aspect of human existence.

Language capability serves four distinct roles in international marketing.[21]

1. Language aids in information gathering and evaluation efforts. Rather than rely completely on the opinions of others, the manager is able to see and hear personally what is going on. People are far more comfortable speaking their own language, and this should be treated as an advantage. The best intelligence on a market is gathered by becoming part of the market rather than observing it from the outside. For example, local managers of a multinational corporation should be the firm's primary source of political information to assess potential risk.

2. Language provides access to local society. Although English may be widely spoken, and may even be the official company language, speaking the local language may make a dramatic difference. For example, firms that translate promotional materials and information are seen as being serious about doing business in the country.

3. Language capability is increasingly important in company communications, whether within the corporate family or with channel members. Imagine the difficulties encountered by a country manager who must communicate with employees through an interpreter.

4. Language provides more than the ability to communicate. It extends beyond mechanics to the interpretation of contexts.

The manager's command of the national language(s) in a market must be greater than simple word recognition. Consider, for example, how dramatically different English terms can be when used in Australia, the United Kingdom, or the United States. In negotiations, for U.S. delegates "tabling a proposal" means that they want to delay a decision, whereas their British counterparts understand the expression to mean that immediate action is to be taken. If the British promise something "by the end of the day," this does not mean within 24 hours, but rather when they have completed the job. Additionally, they may say that negotiations "bombed," meaning that they were a success; to a U.S. manager, this could convey exactly the opposite message. Similar challenges occur with other languages and markets. Swedish is spoken as a mother tongue by 8 percent of the population in Finland, where it has idioms that are not well understood by Swedes. Goodyear has identified five different terms for the word *tires* in the Spanish-speaking Americas: *cauchos* in Venezuela, *cubiertas* in Argentina, *gomas* in Puerto Rico, *neumaticos* in Chile, and *llantas* in most of the other countries in the region.[22]

An advertising campaign presented by Electrolux highlights the difficulties in transferring advertising campaigns between markets. Electrolux's theme in marketing its vacuum cleaners, "Nothing Sucks Like an Electrolux," is interpreted literally in the United Kingdom, but in the United States, the slang implications would interfere with the intended message. The danger exists of translingual homonyms; an innocent word may have a strong resemblance to another word not used in polite company in another country. For example, global elevator maker Kone wanted to ensure correct pronunciation of its name and added an accent (Koné) to its name in French-speaking countries to avoid controversy. Toyota Motor behaved similarly in changing its MR2 model to Spider. Other features of language have to be considered as well. In a Lucky Goldstar ad, adaptation into Arabic was carried out without considering that Arabic reads from right to left. As a result, the creative concept in this execution was destroyed.

The role of language extends beyond that of a communications medium. Linguistic diversity often is an indicator of other types of diversity. In Quebec, the French language has always been a major consideration of most francophone governments because it is one of the clear manifestations of the identity of the province that separates it from the English-speaking provinces. The Charter of the French Language states that the rights of the francophone collectivity are, among others, the right of consumers to be informed and served in French. The Bay, a major Quebec retailer, spends $8 million annually on its translation operations. It even changed its name to La Baie in appropriate areas. Similarly, in trying to battle English as the *lingua franca,* the French government has tried to ban the use of any foreign term or expression wherever an officially approved French equivalent exists (e.g., *mercatique,* not *un brainstorming*).[23] This applies also to Web sites that bear the ".fr" designation; they have to be in the French language. Similarly, the Hong Kong government is promoting the use of Cantonese rather than English as the language of commerce.

Other countries have taken similar measures. Germans have founded a society for the protection of the German language from the spread of "Denglish." Poland has directed that all companies selling or advertising foreign products use Polish in their advertisements, while some people in India—with its 800 dialects—scorn the use of English as a lingua franca since it is a reminder of British colonialism.[24]

Despite the fact that English is encountered daily by those on the Internet, the "e" in e-business does not translate into "English." In a survey, European users highlighted the need to bridge the culture gap. One third of the senior managers said they will not tolerate English online, while less than 20 percent of the German middle managers and less than 50 percent of the French ones believe they can use English well. Fully three-quarters of those surveyed considered that being forced to use nonlocalized content on the Internet had a negative impact on productivity.[25] A truly global portal works only if online functions are provided in a multilingual and multicultural format. Starting in late 2007, Internet users have been able to use addresses in 11 languages that do not use the Roman alphabet. Russians, for example, are able to type in Web addresses entirely in Cyrillic characters instead of having to revert to English. The change has also involved languages such as Chinese, Arabic, and Korean. These are a billion people on the Internet; this move will accelerate the incorporation of the next billion.

Dealing with the language problem invariably requires the use of local assistance. A good local advertising agency and a good local market research firm can prevent many problems. When translation is required, as when communicating with suppliers or customers, care should be taken in selecting the translator or translation software. One of the simplest methods of control is **back-translation**—the translating of a foreign language version back to the original language by a different person from the one who made the first translation. This approach may help to detect only omissions and blunders, however. To assess the quality of the translation, a complete evaluation with testing of the message's impact is necessary.[26] In essence this means that international marketers should never translate words but emotion, which then, in turn, may well lead to the use of completely different words.

Language also has to be understood in its historic context. In Germany, Nokia launched an advertising campaign for the interchangable covers for its portable phones using the theme "*Jedem das Seine*" ("to each his own"). The campaign was withdrawn after the American Jewish Congress pointed out that the same slogan was found on the entry portal to Buchenwald, a Nazi-era concentration camp.[27] The Indian division of Cadbury-Schweppes incensed Hindu society by running an advertisement comparing its Temptations chocolate to war-torn Kashmir. The ad carried a tag line: "I'm good. I'm tempting. I'm too good to share. What am I?

Religions of the World: A Part of Culture

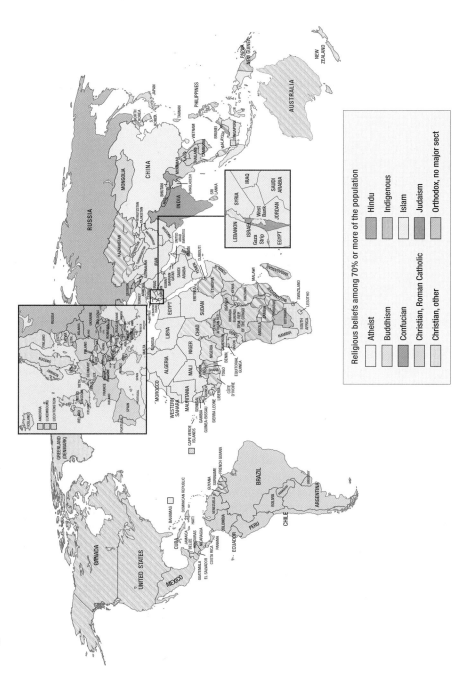

Religious beliefs among 70% or more of the population

- Atheist
- Buddhism
- Confucian
- Christian, Roman Catholic
- Christian, other
- Hindu
- Indigenous
- Islam
- Judaism
- Orthodox, no major sect

SOURCE: Based on *The World Factbook*, 2008.

Cadbury's Temptations or Kashmir?" The ad featured a map of Kashmir to highlight the point, and it also first appeared on August 15th, Indian Independence Day.[28]

Nonverbal Language

Managers must analyze and become familiar with the hidden language of foreign cultures.[29] Five key topics—time, space, material possessions, friendship patterns, and business agreements—offer a starting point from which managers can begin to acquire the understanding necessary to do business in foreign countries. In many parts of the world, time is flexible and not seen as a limited commodity; people come late to appointments or may not come at all. In Hong Kong, for example, it is futile to set exact meeting times, because getting from one place to another may take minutes or hours depending on the traffic. Showing indignation or impatience at such behavior would astonish an Arab, Latin American, or Asian.

In some countries, extended social acquaintance and the establishment of appropriate personal rapport are essential to conducting business. The feeling is that one should know one's business partner on a personal level before transactions can occur. Therefore, rushing straight to business will not be rewarded, because deals are made not only on the basis of the best product or price, but also on the entity or person deemed most trustworthy. Contracts may be bound on handshakes, not lengthy and complex agreements—a fact that makes some, especially Western, businesspeople uneasy.

Individuals vary in the amount of space they want separating them from others. Arabs and Latin Americans like to stand close to people they are talking with. If a U.S. executive, who may not be comfortable at such close range, backs away from an Arab, this might incorrectly be taken as a negative reaction. Also, Westerners are often taken aback by the more physical nature of affection between Slavs—for example, being kissed by a business partner, regardless of sex.

International body language must be included in the nonverbal language of international business. For example, a U.S. manager may, after successful completion of negotiations, impulsively give a finger-and-thumb OK sign. In southern France, the manager will have indicated that the sale is worthless, and in Japan that a little bribe has been asked for; the gesture is grossly insulting to Brazilians. An interesting exercise is to compare and contrast the conversation styles of different nationalities. Northern Europeans are quite reserved in using their hands and maintain a good amount of personal space, whereas Southern Europeans involve their bodies to a far greater degree in making a point.

Religion

In most cultures, people find in religion a reason for being and legitimacy in the belief that they are part of a larger context. To define religion requires the inclusion of the supernatural and the existence of a higher power. Religion defines the ideals for life, which in turn are reflected in the values and attitudes of societies and individuals. Such values and attitudes shape the behavior and practices of institutions and members of cultures, and are the most challenging for the marketer to adjust to. When Procter & Gamble launched its Biomat laundry detergent in Israel, it found Orthodox Jews (15 percent of the population) a challenge since they do not own traditional media such as television sets. The solution was to focus on the segment's core belief that they should aid those less fortunate. A Biomat truck equipped with washing machines traveled around key towns. People would donate their clothing, and Biomat would wash and distribute them to the needy. As a result, the brand's share has grown 50 percent among the segment.[30]

Religion provides the basis for transcultural similarities under shared beliefs and behavior. The impact will vary depending on the strength of the dominant religious tenets. While religion's impact may be quite indirect in Protestant Northern Europe, its impact in countries where Islamic fundamentalism is on the rise (such as Algeria) may be profound. The impact of these similarities will be assessed in terms of the dominant religions of the world: Christianity, Islam, Hinduism, Buddhism, and Confucianism. Other religions may have smaller numbers of followers, such as Judaism with 14 million followers around the world, but their impact is still significant due to the many centuries during which they have influenced world history. While some countries may officially have secularism, such as Marxism-Leninism, as a state belief (for example, China, Vietnam, and Cuba), traditional religious beliefs still remain a powerful force in shaping behavior. International marketing managers must be aware of the differences not only among the major religions but also within them. The impact of these divisions may range from hostility, as in Sri Lanka, to barely perceptible but long-standing suspicion, as in many European countries where Protestant and Catholic are the main divisions. With some religions, such as Hinduism, people may be divided into groups, which determines their status and to a large extent their ability to consume.

Christianity has the largest following among world religions, with more than 2 billion people. While there are many significant groups within Christianity, the major ones are Catholicism and Protestantism. A prominent difference between the two of them is their attitude toward making money. While Catholicism has questioned it, the Protestant ethic has emphasized the importance of work and the accumulation of wealth for the glory of God. At the same time, frugality is stressed and the residual accumulation of wealth from hard work has formed the basis for investment. It has been proposed that this is the basis for the development of capitalism in the Western world, and for the rise of predominantly Protestant countries to world economic leadership in the twentieth century.

Major holidays are often tied to religion. Holidays will be observed differently from one culture to another, and the same holiday may have different connotations. Christian cultures observe Christmas and exchange gifts on either December 24 or 25, with the exception of the Dutch, who exchange gifts on St. Nicholas Day, December 6. Tandy Corporation, in its first year in the Netherlands, targeted its major Christmas promotion for the third week of December with less than satisfactory results. The international marketing manager must see to it that local holidays, such as Mexico's Dìa De Los Muertos (October 31 to November 2), are taken into account in the scheduling of events ranging from fact-finding missions to marketing programs.

Islam, which reaches from the west coast of Africa to the Philippines and across a wide band that includes Tanzania, central Asia, western China, India, and Malaysia, has more than 1.2 billion followers.[31] Islam is also a significant minority religion in many parts of the world, including Europe. It plays a pervasive role in the life of its followers, referred to as Muslims, through the *shari'ah* (law of Islam). This is most obvious in the five stated daily periods of prayer, fasting during the holy month of Ramadan, and the pilgrimage to Mecca, Islam's holy city. While Islam is supportive of entrepreneurship, it nevertheless strongly discourages acts that may be interpreted as exploitation. Islam also lacks discrimination, except for those outside the religion. Some have argued that Islam's basic fatalism (that is, nothing happens without the will of Allah) and traditionalism have deterred economic development in countries observing the religion.

One of the fastest growing segments in the financial sector is Islamic banking. In Shariah-compliant banking, lenders may not charge interest and investors cannot make money from industries such as gambling, alcohol, pork, and pornography. Currently there are over 250 Islamic financial institutions managing funds of over $200 billion.[32]

The role of women in business is tied to religion, especially in the Middle East, where women are not able to function as they would in the West. The effects of this are numerous; for example, a firm may be limited in its use of female managers or personnel in these areas, and women's role as consumers and influencers in the consumption process may be different. Except for food purchases, men make the final purchase decisions. Access to women in Islamic countries may only be possible through the use of female sales personnel, direct marketing, and women's specialty shops.[33]

Religion affects the marketing of products and service delivery. When beef or poultry is exported to an Islamic country, the animal must be killed in the *halal* method and certified appropriately. Recognition of religious restrictions on products (for example, alcoholic beverages) can reveal opportunities, as evidenced by successful launches of several nonalcoholic beverages in the Middle East. Other restrictions may call for innovative solutions. A challenge for the Swedish firm that had the primary responsibility for building a traffic system to Mecca was that non-Muslims are not allowed access to the city. The solution was to use closed-circuit television to supervise the work. Given that Islam considers interest payments usury, bankers and Muslim scholars have worked to create interest-free banking products that rely on lease agreements, mutual funds, and other methods to avoid paying interest.[34]

Hinduism has 860 million followers, mainly in India, Nepal, Malaysia, Guyana, Suriname, and Sri Lanka. In addition to being a religion, it is also a way of life predicated on the caste, or class, to which one is born. While the caste system has produced social stability, its impact on business can be quite negative. For example, if one cannot rise above one's caste, individual effort is hampered. Problems in workforce integration and coordination may become quite severe. Furthermore, the drive for business success may not be forthcoming because of the fact that followers place value mostly on spiritual rather than materialistic achievement.

The family is an important element in Hindu society, with extended families being the norm. The extended family structure will have an impact on the purchasing power and consumption of Hindu families. Market researchers, in particular, must take this into account in assessing market potential and consumption patterns.

Buddhism, which extends its influence throughout Asia from Sri Lanka to Japan, has 360 million followers. Although it is an offspring of Hinduism, it has no caste system. Life is seen as an existence of suffering, with achieving nirvana, a state marked by an absence of desire, as the solution to suffering. The emphasis in Buddhism is on spiritual achievement rather than worldly goods.

Confucianism has over 150 million followers throughout Asia, especially among the Chinese, and has been characterized as a code of conduct rather than a religion. However, its teachings that stress loyalty and relationships have been broadly adopted. Loyalty to central authority and placing the good of a group before that of the individual may explain the economic success of Japan, South Korea, Singapore, and the Republic of China. It also has led to cultural misunderstandings: In Western societies there has been a perception that the subordination of the individual to the common good has resulted in the sacrifice of human rights. The emphasis on relationships is very evident when developing business ties in Asia. The preparatory stage may take years before the needed level of understanding is reached and actual business transactions can take place.

Values and Attitudes

Values are shared beliefs or group norms that have been internalized by individuals.[35] Attitudes are evaluations of alternatives based on these values. The Japanese culture raises an almost invisible—yet often unscalable—wall against all *gaijin,* foreigners. Many middle-aged bureaucrats and company officials, for example, feel that buying foreign products is unpatriotic. The resistance therefore is not so much against foreign products as it is against those who produce and market them. As a result, foreign-based corporations have had difficulty in hiring university graduates or midcareer personnel because of bias against foreign employers. Dealing in China and with the Chinese, the international marketing manager will have to realize that marketing has more to do with cooperation than competition. The Chinese believe that one should build the relationship first and, if that is successful, transactions will follow. The relationship, or *guanxi,* is a set of exchanges of favors to establish trust.[36]

The more rooted values and attitudes are in central beliefs (such as religion), the more cautiously the international marketing manager has to move. Attitude toward change is basically positive in industrialized countries, whereas in more tradition-bound societies, change is viewed with great suspicion, especially when it comes from a foreign entity.

To counter the perceived influence of Mattel's Barbie and Ken dolls on Iranian values, a government agency affiliated with Iran's Ministry of Education is marketing its own Dara and Sara dolls. The new products, a brother and sister, are modeled on Iranian school-book characters. Sara is dressed in a white headscarf covering black or brown curls. A popular outfit is a full-length, flower-dotted chador, which covers the doll from head to toe. One toy seller explained that playing with Mattel's golden-haired, skimpily dressed Barbie may lead girls to grow up into women who reject Iranian values.[37]

Cultural attitudes are not always a deterrent to foreign business practices or foreign goods. Japanese youth, for instance, display extremely positive attitudes toward Western goods, from popular music to Nike sneakers to Louis Vuitton haute couture to Starbuck's lattes. Even in Japan's faltering economy, global brands are able to charge premium prices if they are able to tap into cultural attitudes that revere imported goods. Similarly, attitudes of U.S. youth toward Japanese "cool" have increased the popularity of authentic Japanese "manga" comics and animated cartoons. Pokémon cards and Hello Kitty are examples of Japanese products that caught on in the United States almost as quickly as in Japan.[38]

While products that hit the right cultural buttons can be huge successes in foreign markets, not all top brands will translate easily from one culture to another. For example, while the Disneyland concept worked well in Tokyo, it had a tougher time in Paris. One of the main reasons was that while the Japanese have positive attitudes toward American pop culture, the Europeans are quite content with their own cultural values and traditions.[39] In Hong Kong, Disney's success is expected to be based on it being American with foreignness being part of the appeal.[40]

Manners and Customs

Changes occurring in manners and customs must be carefully monitored, especially in cases that seem to indicate narrowing of cultural differences between peoples. Phenomena such as McDonald's and Coke have met with success around the world, but this does not mean that the world is becoming Westernized. Modernization and Westernization are not at all the same, as can be seen in Saudi Arabia, for example.

Understanding manners and customs is especially important in negotiations, because interpretations based on one's own frame of reference may lead to a totally incorrect conclusion. To negotiate effectively abroad, one needs to read correctly all types of communication. U.S. executives often interpret inaction and silence as a negative sign, so Japanese executives tend to expect their U.S. counterparts to lower prices or sweeten the deal if they just say as little as possible. Even a simple agreement may take days to negotiate in the Middle East, because the Arab party may want to talk about unrelated issues or do something else for a while. The abrasive style of Russian negotiators, and their usual last-minute change requests, may cause astonishment and concern on the part of ill-prepared negotiators. And consider the reaction of a U.S. businessperson if a Finnish counterpart were to propose the continuing of negotiations in the sauna. Preparation is needed not only in the business sense but in a cultural sense as well. Some of the potential areas in which marketers may not be prepared include: (1) insufficient understanding of different ways of thinking; (2) insufficient attention to the necessity of saving face; (3) insufficient knowledge and appreciation of the host country—history, culture, government, and image of foreigners; (4) insufficient recognition of the decision-making process and the role of personal relations and personalities; and (5) insufficient allocation of time for negotiations.[41]

One instance when preparation and sensitivity are called for is in the area of gift giving. Exhibit 4.2 provides examples of what to give and when. An ideal gift is one that represents

Exhibit 4.2

When and What to Give as Gifts

China	India	Japan	Mexico	Saudi Arabia
Chinese New Year (January or February)	*Hindu Diwali festival (October or November)*	*Oseibo (Jan. 1)*	*Christmas/New Year*	*Id al-Fitr (December or January)*
✓ Modest gifts such as coffee table books, ties, pens	✓ Sweets, nuts, and fruit; elephant carvings; candleholders	✓ Scotch, brandy, Americana, round fruit such as melons	✓ Desk clocks, fine pens, gold lighters	✓ Fine compasses to determine direction for prayer, cashmere
✗ Clocks, anything from Taiwan	✗ Leather objects, snake images	✗ Gifts that come in sets of four or nine	✗ Sterling silver items, logo gifts, food baskets	✗ Pork and pigskin, liquor

✓ recommended
✗ to be avoided

SOURCE: Kate Murphy, "Gifts without Gaffes for Global Clients," *Business Week* (December 6, 1999): 153.

the giver's own culture while being sensitive to the recipient's. For example, a Finn may give a Suunto compass to a Saudi business partner (to help him determine the direction for daily prayers). Giving gifts that are easily available in that country (e.g., chocolates to a Swiss) is not advisable. Some gifts are not suitable: clocks or other time pieces are symbols of death in China, while handkerchiefs symbolize tears in Latin America and Korea. Gifts are an important part of relationship management during visits and a way of recognizing partners during holidays. Care should be taken with the way the gift is wrapped; for example, it should be in appropriately colored paper. If delivered in person, the actual giving has to be executed correctly; in China, this is done by extending the gift to the recipient using both hands.[42] It should be noted, however, that many companies in the United States have policies that do not allow the giving and receiving of gifts.

Managers must be concerned with differences in the ways products are used. The international manager must ask, "What are we selling?" "What are the use benefits we should be providing?" and "Who or what are we competing against?" Campbell Soup has targeted China as one of the markets with the strongest growth potentials for soup. However, homemade soups account for 99 percent of the consumption. With this in mind, Campbell's prices have been kept at an attractive level and the product is promoted on convenience. Care should be taken not to assume cross-border similarities even if many of the indicators converge. For example, a jam producer noted that the Brazilian market seemed to hold significant potential because per capita jelly and jam consumption was one-tenth that of Argentina, clearly a difference not justified by obvious factors. However, Argentines consume jam at tea time, a custom that does not exist in Brazil. Furthermore, Argentina's climate and soil favor growing wheat, leading it to consume three times the amount of bread Brazil does.[43]

Package sizes and labels must be adapted in many countries to suit the needs of the particular culture. In Mexico, for example, Campbell's sells soup in cans large enough to serve four or five because families are generally large. In Britain, where consumers are more accustomed to ready-to-serve soups, Campbell's prints "one can makes two" on its condensed soup labels to ensure that shoppers understand how to use it.

Approaches that might be rarely taken in the United States or Europe could be recommended in other regions; for example, Conrad Hotels (the international arm of Hilton) experienced low initial occupancy rates at its Hong Kong facility until the firm brought in a feng shui man. These traditional "consultants" are foretellers of future events and the unknown through occult means and are used extensively by Hong Kong businesses, especially for advising about where to locate offices and how to position office equipment.[44] In Conrad's case, the suggestion was to move a piece of sculpture outside of the hotel's lobby because one of the characters in the statue looked like it was trying to run out of the hotel.[45] At Disneyland Hong Kong, the feng shui master rotated the front gate, repositioned cash registers, and ordered boulders set in key locations to ensure the park's prosperity.[46]

Meticulous research plays a major role in avoiding these types of problems. Concept tests determine the potential acceptance and proper understanding of a proposed new product. **Focus groups**, each consisting of eight to twelve consumers representative of the proposed target audience, can be interviewed and their responses used to check for disasters and to fine-tune research findings. The most sensitive types of products, such as consumer packaged goods, require consumer usage and attitude studies as well as retail distribution studies and audits to analyze the movement of the product to retailers and eventually to households. H.J. Heinz Co. uses focus groups to determine what consumers want in ketchup in the way of taste and image. U.S. consumers prefer a relatively sweet ketchup while Europeans go for a spicier variety. In Central Europe and Sweden, Heinz sells a hot ketchup in addition to the classic variety. In addition to changes in the product, the company may need to promote new usage situations. For example, in Greece this may mean running advertisements showing how ketchup can be poured on pasta, eggs, and cuts of meat. While some markets consider Heinz's U.S. origin a plus, there are others where it has to be played down. In Northern Europe, where ketchup is served as an accompaniment to traditional meatballs and fishballs, Heinz deliberately avoids reminding consumers of its heritage. The messages tend to be health related.[47]

In-depth studies are also used to study consumer needs across markets. Intel, for example, has a team of 10 ethnographers traveling the world to find out how to redesign existing products or to come up with new ones to fit different cultures and demographic groups.

The adjustment to cultural variables in the marketplace may have to be long term and accomplished through trial and error. For example, U.S. retailers have found that Japanese consumers are baffled by the warehouse-like atmosphere of the U.S-style retail outlets. When Office Depot reduced the size of its Tokyo store by a third and crammed the merchandise closer together, sales remained at the same level as before.[48]

Material Elements

Material culture results from technology and is directly related to the way a society organizes its economic activity. It is manifested in the availability and adequacy of the basic economic, social, financial, and marketing **infrastructures**. The basic economic infrastructure consists of transportation, energy, and communications systems. Social infrastructure refers to housing, health, and educational systems. Financial and marketing infrastructures provide the facilitating agencies for the international firm's operation in a given market in terms of, for example, banks and research firms. In some parts of the world, the international firm may have to be an integral partner in developing the various infrastructures before it can operate, whereas in others, it may greatly benefit from their high level of sophistication.

The level of material culture can be a segmentation variable if the degree of industrialization of the market is used as a basis. For companies selling industrial goods, such as General Electric, this can provide a convenient starting point. In developing countries, demand may be highest for basic energy-generating products. In fully developed markets, time-saving home appliances may be more in demand.

While infrastructure is often a good indicator of potential demand, goods sometimes discover unexpectedly rich markets due to the informal economy at work in developing nations. In Kenya, for example, where most of the country's 30 million population live on less than a dollar a day, more than 770,000 people have signed up for mobile phone service during the last two years; wireless providers are scrambling to keep up with demand. Leap-frogging older technologies, mobile phones are especially attractive to Kenya's thousands of small-business entrepreneurs—market stall owners, taxi drivers, and even hustlers who sell on the sidewalks. For most, income goes unreported, creating an invisible wealth on the streets. Mobile phones outnumber fixed lines in Kenya, as well as in Uganda, Venezuela, Cambodia, South Korea, and Chile. This development is attractive for marketers as well, given the expense of laying land lines.

Again, however, the advent of new technologies must be culturally calibrated, as seen in *The International Marketplace 4.3*. Voice mail, while available, is not used to any significant degree in China. On the one hand, many Chinese do not comprehend the need to return phone calls or to respond to customers (having worked for state-owned companies before). Chinese workers tend to be away from their desks most of the day, conducting business in the traditional, face-to-face Asian style. On the other hand, Chinese do not leave messages either, expecting to talk to a live person.[49]

Technological advances have probably been the major cause of cultural change in many countries. For example, the increase in leisure time so characteristic in Western cultures has been a direct result of technological development. Workers in Germany have pushed for a 35-hour work week. Increasingly, consumers are seeking more diverse products—including convenience items—as a way of satisfying their demand for a higher quality of life and more leisure time. For example, a Gallup survey in China found that 44 percent of the respondents were saving to buy electronic items and appliances, second only to saving for a rainy day.[50] Marketers able to tailor and market their products to fit the new lifestyle, especially in emerging markets, stand to reap the benefits. Consumers around the world are showing greater acceptance of equipment for personal use, reflected in increased sales of mobile phones and small computers as well as increased Internet use. With technological advancement also comes **cultural convergence**. Black-and-white television sets extensively penetrated the U.S. market more than a decade before they reached similar levels in Europe and Japan. With color television, the lag was reduced to five years. With videocassette recorders, the difference was only three years, but this time the Europeans and the Japanese led the way while U.S. consumers concentrated on cable systems. With the compact disc, penetration rates were even after only one year. Today, with MTV available by satellite around the world, no lag exists at all.[51]

The International
MARKETPLACE

4.3

Mobile Payments Across the Globe?

Mobile payment services (m-payments) enable consumers to pay for goods and services from their bank account using their mobile phone. These services have evolved over time from using voice or short message services (SMS) to initiate and settle a transaction to the present-day use of a phone for one-step instant purchases. The convenience for consumers is significant in that they avoid using cash or credit cards, and, with prepaid services, avoid monthly bills. Services are secure in that an alphanumeric password is required for authentication. In addition, direct payments from the customer's account means that spending power is not limited to the amount of credit available on the phone account.

However, while analysts predicted that m-payments would account for as much as $15 billion by 2010, m-payments have taken off in Japan and Korea but failed to reach estimated potential within the European Union and the United States. Reasons for this can be found in the lack of readiness in existing technology, unwillingness of the various stakeholders (banks, credit card issuers, handset makers, and telecommunication companies) to collaborate, as well as cultural variables in terms of existing usage patterns and perceptions of risk and relative advantage of a new technology.

The chief driver of mobile innovation in Japan is NTT DoCoMo. Its market power is so significant that it can impose new systems from the top down, as it did with the introduction of the i-mode (which allowed consumers to use their phones for everything from trading stocks and checking movie times to playing games, instant messaging, and downloading Hello Kitty characters). While the i-mode did not include m-payments, it laid the groundwork for that continuous innovation. M-payment capability was added by using SONY's contactless chips, which allow payment by passing the phones over a sensor. The key to success is NTT DoCoMo's dominance in the market. Customers have transitioned easily to adding making payments with their phones. Merchants wanted to tap into the large and growing market, especially when they were subsidized by NTT DoCoMo in buying the needed new technology. In Korea, the three

big operators (SK Telecom, KTF, and LG Telecom) have collaborated with credit card companies, which are taking care of the financing and operations.

In the European Union and the United States, payment cards are already deeply embedded in consumer behavior; consumers may not be eager to move away from a familiar system, and they may not have thought of using phones as payment devices. In markets where mobile diffusion is high (such as the Nordic countries) or in countries where cash still accounts for a majority of retail transactions (e.g., Germany and Central Europe), chances may be better. In Central Europe, for example, merchants may be eager to switch to cashless systems at the expense of handling currency. At the same time, all of the stakeholders need to demonstrate to mobile phone users that m-payments are much more attractive than other familiar payment schemes. The bundle of convenience items (safe, secure, available, fast, transparent) needs to be packaged and sold to target groups.

None of the North American nor European players have the market power of their Asian counterparts. Cooperation among banks, credit card issuers, handset makers, and retailers will be essential. One such attempt, SIMPAY, an alliance set up by Orange, Vodafone, T-Mobile, and Telefónica Móviles, to allow consumers to charge small purchases to their mobile phone bills, closed in 2005 after 18 months of operation. One of the main reasons was the lack of sufficient volume to cover collection costs.

Despite uneven global acceptance, Arthur D. Little predicts a tenfold increase in mobile payment transactions, to reach $37 billion by 2008.

SOURCES: Roman Friedrich, Johannes Bussman, Olaf Acker, and Niklas Dietrich, "Making Mobile Payment Work for Everyone," *Strategy and Business Resilience Report*, September 22, 2005, available at **http://www.strategy-business.com**; Lucy Sherriff, "Simpay Halts Mobile Commerce Project," *The Register*, June 27, 2005, available at **http://www.theregister.co.uk/2005/06/27/simpay_halts_project/**; "M-payments Making Inroads," *Arthur D. Little's Global M-payment Update 2005*, Boston, MA: Arthur D. Little, 2005; "M-payments Predicted to Be Worth £20 billion in 2008," *New Media Age*, August 5, 2004, 11; Malte Krueger and Gérard Carat, "M-payments and the Role of Telcos," *Electronic Payment Systems Observatory Newsletter*, number 2, 2000, 4–7. See also **http://www.nttdocomo.com/corebiz/interconnected/felicaContent.html**.

Material culture—mainly the degree to which it exists and how much it is esteemed—will have an impact on marketing decisions. Many exporters do not understand the degree to which U.S. consumers are package-conscious; for example, cans must be shiny and beautiful. On the other hand, packaging problems may arise in other countries due to lack of certain materials, different specifications when the material is available, different line-fill machinery, and immense differences in quality and consistency of printing ink, especially in developing markets. Even the ability of media to reach target audiences will be affected by ownership of radios, television sets, and personal computers.

Aesthetics

Each culture makes a clear statement concerning good taste, as expressed in the arts and in the particular symbolism of colors, form, and music. What is and what is not acceptable may vary dramatically even in otherwise highly similar markets. Sex in advertising is an example. In an apparent attempt to preserve the purity of Japanese womanhood, Japanese advertisers frequently turn to blonde, blue-eyed foreign models to make the point. In introducing the shower soap Fa from the European market to the North American market, Henkel also extended its European advertising campaign to the new market. The main difference was to have the young woman in the waves don a bathing suit rather than be naked, as in the German original.

Color is often used as a mechanism for brand identification, feature reinforcement, and differentiation. In international markets, colors have more symbolic value than in domestic markets. Black, for instance, is considered the color of mourning in the United States and Europe, whereas white has the same symbolic value in Japan and most of the Far East. A British bank interested in expanding its operations to Singapore wanted to use blue and green as its identification colors. A consulting firm was quick to tell the client that green is associated with death there. Although the bank insisted on its original choice of colors, the green was changed to an acceptable shade.[52] Similarly, music used in broadcast advertisements is often adjusted to reflect regional differences.

International firms have to take into consideration local tastes and concerns in designing their facilities. They may have a general policy of uniformity in building or office space design, but local tastes may often warrant modifications. Respecting local cultural traditions may also generate goodwill toward the international marketer. For example, McDonald's painstakingly renovated a seventeenth-century building for its third outlet in Moscow. History may also play a role. The Shanghai World Financial Center (developed largely by the Japanese Mori Building Corporation) became the tallest structure in China in 2008 at 492 meters / 1,641 feet. The most distinctive feature in the design of the building is an opening at the peak (the functional reason of which is to allow airflow). The opening originally was meant to be a circular moon gate, but the intended design met with opposition from the Chinese who saw it resembling the rising sun design of the Japanese flag. It was replaced by a trapezoidal hole featuring an observation deck on the hundredth floor.

Education

Education, either formal or informal, plays a major role in the passing on and sharing of culture. Educational levels of a culture can be assessed using literacy rates and enrollment in secondary or higher education, information available from secondary data sources. International firms also need to know about the qualitative aspects of education, namely, varying emphases on particular skills, and the overall level of the education provided. Japan and the Republic of Korea, for example, emphasize the sciences, especially engineering, to a greater degree than do Western countries.

© AP PHOTO/GREG BAKER

THE SHANGHAI WORLD FINANCIAL CENTER BECAME THE TALLEST STRUCTURE IN CHINA IN 2008; THE MOST DISTINCTIVE FEATURE IN THE DESIGN OF THE BUILDING IS AN OPENING AT ITS PEAK.

Educational levels will have an impact on various business functions. Training programs for a production facility will have to take the educational backgrounds of trainees into account. For example, a high level of illiteracy will suggest the use of visual aids rather than printed manuals. Local recruiting for sales jobs will be affected by the availability of suitably trained personnel. In some cases, international firms routinely send locally recruited personnel to headquarters for training.

The international marketing manager may also have to be prepared to fight obstacles in recruiting a suitable sales force or support personnel. For example, the Japanese culture places a premium on loyalty, and employees consider themselves to be members of the corporate family. If a foreign firm decides to leave Japan, employees may find themselves stranded midcareer, unable to find a place in the Japanese business system. University graduates are therefore reluctant to join all but the largest and best known of foreign firms.[53]

If technology is marketed, the level of sophistication of the product will depend on the educational level of future users. Product adaptation decisions are often influenced by the extent to which targeted customers are able to use the product or service properly.

Social Institutions

Social institutions affect the ways in which people relate to each other. The family unit, which in Western industrialized countries consists of parents and children, in a number of cultures is extended to include grandparents and other relatives. This will have an impact on consumption patterns and must be taken into account, for example, when conducting market research.

The concept of kinship, or blood relations between individuals, is defined in a very broad way in societies such as those in sub-Saharan Africa. Family relations and a strong obligation to family are important factors to be considered in human resource management in those regions. Understanding tribal politics in countries such as Nigeria may help the manager avoid unnecessary complications in executing business transactions.

The division of a particular population into classes is termed social stratification. Stratification ranges from the situation in Northern Europe, where most people are members of the middle class, to highly stratified societies such as India, in which the higher strata control most of the buying power and decision-making positions.

An important part of the socialization process of consumers worldwide is reference groups. These groups provide the values and attitudes that become influential in shaping behavior. Primary reference groups include the family, coworkers, and other intimate groupings, whereas secondary groups are social organizations in which less-continuous interaction takes place, such as professional associations and trade organizations. Besides socialization, reference groups develop an individual's concept of self, which manifests itself, for example, through the use of products. Reference groups also provide a baseline for compliance with group norms through either conforming to or avoiding certain behaviors.

Social organization also determines the roles of managers and subordinates and the way they relate to one another. In some cultures, managers and subordinates are separated explicitly and implicitly by various boundaries ranging from social class differences to separate office facilities. In others, cooperation is elicited through equality. For example, Nissan USA has no reserved parking spaces and no private dining rooms, everyone wears the same type of white coveralls, and the president sits in the same room with a hundred other white-collar workers. The fitting of an organizational culture for internal marketing purposes to the larger context of a national culture has to be executed with care. Changes that are too dramatic may cause disruption of productivity or, at the minimum, suspicion.

While Western business practice has developed impersonal structures for channeling power and influence through reliance on laws and contracts, the Chinese emphasize getting on the good side of someone and storing up political capital with him or her. Things can get done without this capital, or *guanxi,* only if one invests enormous personal energy, is willing to offend even trusted associates, and is prepared to see it all melt away at a moment's notice.[54] For the Chinese, contracts form a useful agenda and a symbol of progress, but obligations come from relationships. McDonald's found this out in Beijing, where it was evicted from a central building after only two years despite having a twenty-year contract. The incomer had strong *guanxi,* whereas McDonald's had not kept its relationships in good repair.[55]

Sources of Cultural Knowledge

The concept of cultural knowledge is broad and multifaceted. **Cultural knowledge** can be defined by the way it is acquired. Objective or **factual information** is obtained from others through communication, research, and education. **Experiential knowledge**, on the other hand, can be acquired only by being involved in a culture other than one's own. A summary of the types of knowledge needed by the international manager is provided in Exhibit 4.3. Both factual and experiential information can be general or country-specific. In fact, the more a manager becomes involved in the international arena, the more he or she is able to develop a meta-knowledge, that is, ground rules that apply to a great extent whether in Kuala Lumpur, Malaysia, or Asunción, Paraguay. Market-specific knowledge does not necessarily travel well; the general variables on which the information is based do.

In a survey on how to acquire international expertise, managers ranked eight factors in terms of their importance, as shown in Exhibit 4.4. These managers emphasized the experiential acquisition of knowledge. Written materials were indicated to play an important but supplementary role, very often providing general or country-specific information before operational decisions must be made. Interestingly, many of today's international managers have precareer experience in government, the Peace Corps, the armed forces, or missionary service. Although the survey emphasized travel, a one-time trip to London with a stay at a large hotel and scheduled sight-seeing tours does not contribute to cultural knowledge in a significant way. Travel that involves meetings with company personnel, intermediaries, facilitating agents, customers, and government officials, on the other hand, does contribute.

Exhibit 4.3

Types of International Information

Source of Information	Type of Information	
	General	Country-Specific
Objective	Examples: • Impact of GDP • Regional integration	Examples: • Tariff barriers • Government regulations
Experiential	Example: • Corporate adjustment to internationalization	Examples: • Product acceptance • Program appropriateness

Exhibit 4.4

Managers' Rankings of Factors Involved in Acquiring International Expertise

Factor	Considered Critical	Considered Important
1. Assignments overseas	85%	9%
2. Business travel	83	17
3. Training programs	28	57
4. Non-business travel	28	54
5. Reading/Web	22	72
6. Graduate courses	13	52
7. Pre-career activities	9	50
8. Undergraduate courses	0.5	48

SOURCE: Data collected by authors from 110 executives by questionnaire, February, 2003. Original study by Stephen J. Kobrin, *International Expertise in American Business* (New York: Institute of International Education, 1984), 38.

However, from the corporate point of view, the development of a global capability requires experience acquisition in more involved ways. This translates into foreign assignments and networking across borders, for example through the use of multicountry, multicultural teams to develop strategies and programs. At Nestlé, for example, managers shuffle around a region (such as Asia or Latin America) at four- to five-year intervals and may have tours at headquarters for two to three years between such assignments. This allows these managers to pick up ideas and tools to be used in markets where they have not been used or where they have not been necessary up to now. In Thailand, where supermarkets are revolutionizing consumer-goods marketing, techniques perfected elsewhere in the Nestlé system are being put to effective use. These experiences will then, in turn, be used to develop newly emerging markets in the same region, such as Vietnam.

Various sources and methods are available to the manager for extending his or her knowledge of specific cultures. Most of these sources deal with factual information that provides a necessary basis for market studies. Beyond the normal business literature and its anecdotal information, specific country studies are published by governments, private companies, and universities. The U.S. Department of Commerce's (**http://www.ita.doc.gov**) *Country Commercial Guides* cover 133 countries, while the Economist Intelligence Unit's (**http://www.eiu.com**) *Country Reports* cover 180 countries. *Culturegrams* (**http://www.culturegrams.com**), which detail the customs of peoples of 187 countries, are published by the Center for International and Area Studies at Brigham Young University. Many facilitating agencies—such as advertising agencies, banks, consulting firms, and transportation companies—provide background information on the markets they serve for their clients: for example, Runzheimer International's (**http://www.runzheimer.com**) international reports on employee relocation and site selection for 44 countries, the Hong Kong and Shanghai Banking Corporation's (**http://www.hsbc.com**) *Business Profile Series* for 22 countries in the Asia-Pacific, and *World Trade* magazine's (**http://www.worldtrademag.com**) "Put Your Best Foot Forward" series, which covers Europe, Asia, Mexico/Canada, and Russia.

Many of the marketer's facilitators are equipped for advising the marketer on the cultural dimensions of their efforts. Their task is not only to avoid cultural mistakes but also to add culture as an ingredient of success in the program. See Exhibit 4.5 for an example of such a service provider.

Blunders that could have been avoided with factual information about a foreign market are generally inexcusable. A manager who travels to Taipei without first obtaining a visa and is therefore turned back has no one else to blame. Other oversights may lead to more costly mistakes. For example, Brazilians are several inches shorter than the average U.S. consumer, but this was not taken into account when Sears erected American-height shelves that block Brazilian shoppers' view of the rest of the store.

International business success requires not only comprehensive fact finding and preparation, but also an ability to understand and fully appreciate the nuances of different cultural traits and patterns. Gaining this **interpretive knowledge** requires "getting one's feet wet" over a sufficient length of time.

Cultural Analysis

To try to understand and explain differences among cultures and subsequently in cross-cultural behavior, the marketer can develop checklists and models showing pertinent variables and their interaction. An example of such a model is provided in Exhibit 4.6. This model is based on the premise that all international business activity should be viewed as innovation and as producing change processes.[56] After all, exporters and global marketers introduce, from one country to other cultures, marketing practices as well as products and services, which are then perceived to be new and different. Although many question the usefulness of such models, they do bring together, into one presentation, all or most of the relevant variables that have an impact on how consumers in different cultures may perceive, evaluate, and adopt new behaviors. However, any manager using such a tool should periodically cross-check its results with reality and experience.

Exhibit 4.5

An Example of Culture Consulting

If this picture offends you, we apologize. If it doesn't, perhaps we should explain. Because, although this picture looks innocent enough, to the Asian market, it symbolizes death. But then, not every one should be expected to know that.

That's where we come in. Over the last 17 years interTrend has been guiding clients to the Asian market with some very impressive results. Clients like State Farm, Toyota, AT&T, JCPenney, Remy Martin, Northwest Airlines, The Gas Company, Gilead, and Western Union have all profited from our knowledge of this country's fastest growing and most affluent cultural market. And their success has made us one of the largest Asian advertising agencies in the country.

We can help you as well. Give us a call or E-mail us at jon@intertrend.com. We can share some more of our trade secrets. We can also show you how we've helped our clients succeed in the Asian market. And that's something that needs no apology.

interTrend Communications
555 E. Ocean Blvd. 9th Floor
Long Beach, CA 90802
562.733.1888   fax 562.733.1889

OOOOPS.

building relationships, building brands

COURTESY: INTERTREND COMMUNICATIONS

The key variable of the model is propensity to change, which is a function of three constructs: (1) cultural lifestyle of individuals in terms of how deeply held their traditional beliefs and attitudes are, and also which elements of culture are dominant; (2) change agents (such as international marketers and their practices) and strategic opinion leaders (for example, social elites); and (3) communication about the innovation from commercial sources, neutral sources (such as government), and social sources, such as friends and relatives.

Exhibit 4.6

A Model of Cross-Cultural Behavior

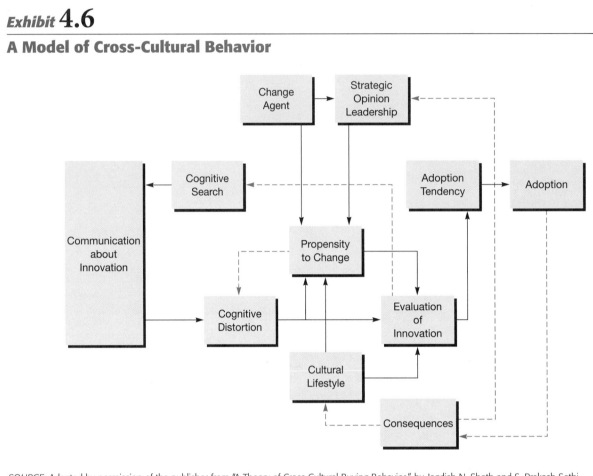

SOURCE: Adapted by permission of the publisher from "A Theory of Cross-Cultural Buying Behavior," by Jagdish N. Sheth and S. Prakash Sethi, in *Consumer and Industrial Buying Behavior,* eds. Arch G. Woodside, Jagdish N. Sheth, and Peter D. Bennett, 1977, 373. Copyright 1977 by Elsevier Science Publishing Co., Inc.

It has been argued that differences in cultural lifestyle can be accounted for by four major dimensions of culture.[57] These dimensions consist of (1) individualism (e.g., "I" consciousness versus "we" consciousness), (2) power distance (e.g., level of equality in a society), (3) uncertainty avoidance (e.g., need for formal rules and regulations), and (4) masculinity (e.g., attitudes toward achievement, roles of men and women). Exhibit 4.7 presents a summary of twelve countries' positions along these dimensions. A fifth dimension has also been added to the list to distinguish cultural differences: long-term versus short-term orientation.[58] All the high-scoring countries on this fifth dimension (not shown in the Exhibit) are Asian (e.g., China, Hong Kong, Taiwan, Japan, and South Korea), while most Western countries (such as the United States and Britain) have low scores. Some have argued that this cultural dimension may explain the Japanese marketing success based on market-share (rather than short-term profit) motivation in market development.

Knowledge of similarities along these four dimensions allows us to cluster countries and regions and establish regional and national marketing programs.[59] An example is provided in Exhibit 4.8, in which the European market is segmented along cultural lines for the development of programs. Research has shown that the takeoff point for new products (i.e., when initial sales turn into mass market sales) is six years on the average in Europe. However, in Northern Europe new products take off almost twice as fast as they do in southern Europe. Culturally, consumers in Cluster 1 are far more open to new ideas. Cluster 2, consisting of southern Europe, displays the highest uncertainty avoidance and should therefore be targeted with risk-reducing marketing programs such as extended warranties and return privileges.[60] It is important to position the product as a continuous innovation that does not require radical changes in consumption patterns.[61] Since the United States highly regards

Exhibit **4.7**

Culture Dimension Scores for Twelve Countries
(0 = Low; 100 = High)

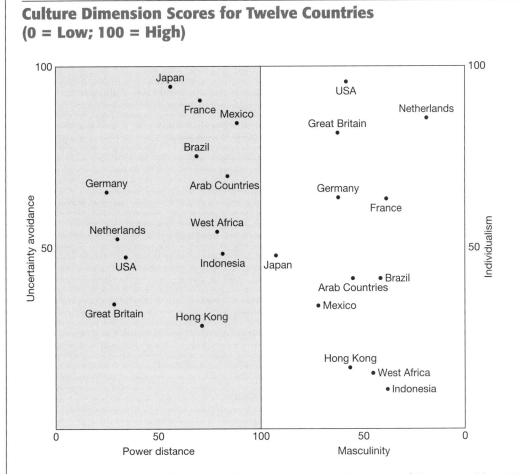

SOURCE: Data for the figure derived from Geert Hofstede, "Management Scientists Are Human," *Management Science* 40 (no. 1, 1994): 4–13.

Exhibit **4.8**

Culture-Based Segmentation

	Cultural Characteristics					
	Size (Million)	Power Distance	Uncertainty Avoidance	Individualism	Masculinity	Illustrative Marketing Implications
Cluster 1 Austria, Germany, Switzerland, Italy, Great Britain, Ireland	203	Small	Medium	Medium-High	High	Preference for "high-performance" products, use "successful-achiever" theme in advertising, desire for novelty, variety and pleasure, fairly risk-averse market.
Cluster 2 Belgium, France, Greece, Portugal, Spain, Turkey	182	Medium	Strong	Varied	Low-Medium	Appeal to consumer's status and power position, reduce perceived risk in product purchase and use, emphasize product functionality.
Cluster 3 Denmark, Sweden, Finland, Netherlands, Norway	37	Small	Low	High	Low	Relatively weak resistance to new products, strong consumer desire for novelty and variety, high consumer regard for "environmentally friendly" marketers and socially conscious firms.

SOURCE: Sudhir H. Kale, "Grouping Euroconsumers: A Culture-Based Clustering Approach," *Journal of International Marketing* 3 (no. 3, 1995): 42. Reprinted by permission.

individualism, promotional appeals should be relevant to individual empowerment. Also, in order to incorporate the lower power distance, messages should be informal and friendly. In opposite situations, marketing communications must emphasize that the new product is socially accepted. However, if the product is imported, it can sometimes utilize global or foreign cultural positioning. For example, in china, individualism is often used for imported products but almost never for domestic ones.[62] Similarly, channel choice is affected by cultural factors. Firms in societies emphasizing individualism are more likely to choose channel partners based on objective criteria, whereas firms at the opposite end would prefer to deal with other firms whose representatives they consider to be friends.[63] When negotiating in Germany, one can expect a counterpart who is thorough, systematic, very well prepared, but also rather dogmatic and therefore lacking in flexibility and compromise. Great emphasis is placed on efficiency. In Mexico, however, the counterpart may prefer to address problems on a personal and private basis rather than on a business level. This means more emphasis on socializing and conveying one's humanity, sincerity, loyalty, and friendship. Also, the differences in pace and business practices of the region have to be accepted. Boeing found in its annual study on world aviation safety that countries with both low individualism and substantial power distances had accident rates 2.6 times greater than at the other end of the scale. These findings will naturally have an impact on training and service operations of airlines.

Communication about the innovation takes place through the physical product itself (samples) or through a new policy in the company. If a new practice, such as quality circles or pan-regional planning, is in question, results may be communicated in reports or through word-of-mouth by the participating employees. Communication content depends on the following factors: the product's or policy's relative advantage over existing alternatives; compatibility with established behavioral patterns; complexity, or the degree to which the product or process is perceived as difficult to understand and use; trialability, or the degree to which it may be experimented with and not incur major risk; and observability, which is the extent to which the consequences of the innovation are visible.

Before the product or policy is evaluated, information about it will be compared with existing beliefs about the circumstances surrounding the situation. Distortion will occur as a result of selective attention, exposure, and retention. As examples, anything foreign may be seen in a negative light, another multinational company's efforts may have failed, or the government may implicitly discourage the proposed activity. Additional information may then be sought from any of the input sources or from opinion leaders in the market.

Adoption tendency refers to the likelihood that the product or process will be accepted. Individualism has a significant positive relationship and uncertainty avoidance a negative relationship with acceptance and diffusion rates of new products.[64] Similar findings have been reached on the penetration of e-commerce in different markets.[65] If an innovation clears the hurdles, it may be adopted and slowly diffused into the entire market. An international manager has two basic choices: adapt company offerings and methods to those in the market or try to change market conditions to fit company programs. In Japan, a number of Western companies have run into obstructions in the Japanese distribution system, where great value is placed on established relationships; everything is done on the basis of favoring the familiar and fearing the unfamiliar. In most cases, this problem is solved by joint venturing with a major Japanese entity that has established contacts. On occasion, when the company's approach is compatible with the central beliefs of a culture, the company may be able to change existing customs rather than adjust to them. Initially, Procter & Gamble's traditional hard-selling style in television commercials jolted most Japanese viewers accustomed to more subtle approaches. Now the ads are being imitated by Japanese competitors. However, this should not be interpreted to mean that Japanese advertising will adapt necessarily to the influence of Western approaches. The emphasis in Japan is still on who speaks rather than on what is spoken. That is why, for example, Japan is a market where Procter & Gamble's company name is presented, as well as the brand name of the product, in the marketing communication for a brand rather than using only the product's brand name, which is customary in the U.S. and European markets.[66]

Although models like the one in Exhibit 4.7 may aid in strategy planning by making sure that all variables and their linkages are considered, any analysis is incomplete without the basic recognition of cultural differences. Adjusting to differences requires putting one's own cultural values aside. James E. Lee proposes that the natural **self-reference criterion**—the unconscious reference to one's own cultural values—is the root of most international business problems.[67] However, recognizing and admitting this are often quite difficult. The following analytical approach is recommended to reduce the influence of one's own cultural values:

1. Define the problem or goal in terms of domestic cultural traits, habits, or norms.
2. Define the problem or goal in terms of foreign cultural traits, habits, or norms. Make no value judgments.
3. Isolate the self-reference criterion influence in the problem and examine it carefully to see how it complicates the problem.
4. Redefine the problem without the self-reference criterion influence and solve for the optimal goal situation.

This approach can be applied to product introduction. If Kellogg Co. wants to introduce breakfast cereals into markets where breakfast is traditionally not eaten or where consumers drink very little milk, managers must consider very carefully how to instill this new habit. The traits, habits, and norms of breakfast are quite different in the United States, France, and Brazil, and they have to be outlined before the product can be introduced. In France, Kellogg's commercials are aimed as much at providing nutrition lessons as they are at promoting the product. In Brazil, the company advertised on a soap opera to gain entry into the market, because Brazilians often emulate the characters of these television shows. A further example is provided in *The International Marketplace 4.4*.

The International MARKETPLACE

4.4

Anyone For Flatbread?

Food is arguably one of the most culture-sensitive categories. How is it possible for a company whose main line of business is in the production of corn-flour and related products to be a player in markets beyond Mexico, where corn is plentiful and tortillas are a staple? Gruma, a company headquartered in Monterrey, Mexico, is a $2.5 billion international powerhouse transcending to markets as diverse as the United States, Mexico, Central America, Venezuela, and more recently, Europe. The Company began operations in Mexico in 1949. Its objective was to modernize the traditional Mexican masa and tortilla industry—which is an activity of huge economic and social significance—through an industrial, ecological, and more efficient process. Because of its constant research and development efforts, Gruma developed proprietary technology that has allowed the company to position itself as the worldwide leader in corn flour and tortilla production, in production cost, and product quality.

Gruma's success has come in part from the realization that its product is a *carrier* of local tastes and it is the company's job to adapt that carrier to local tastes. Ultimately, Gruma's most versatile and marketable product has proven to be not a food, but a process—more specifically, the ability to roll any kind of flour, from corn

to wheat to rice, into salable flatbread. Most people from India do not eat corn tortillas, but they do eat a flatbread called naan, made from wheat, which Gruma sells in the United Kingdom and plans to sell in India. The Chinese don't have much taste for corn tortillas either, but they buy wraps made by Gruma for Peking duck and plum sauce.

At the same time, Gruma is using a combination of psychographics and "chefmanship" to establish market potential, in particular to determine if consumers are willing to try something new, and specifically, are they willing to try a new product. People in certain markets are looking for healthier, less fattening food and are thus open to products like Gruma's wheat flour sandwich wraps. Other markets are becoming faster-paced, and so flatbread, which can be eaten on the run without utensils, is a good fit. In still other areas, such as China, people seem predisposed to experimentation. They want to try new things. Tortillas are more expensive in China than traditional sandwich bread, but they are growing in popularity nonetheless.

In many European countries, however, such as Portugal, Spain, Italy, Greece, and France, where the food is healthy and the eating habits are good, it's harder to make inroads. Because Italians have very traditional eating habits, quick-serve restaurants that offer flatbread were not successful for many years. But when these quick-serve restaurants

GRUMA'S MOST MARKETABLE PRODUCT HAS PROVEN TO BE NOT A FOOD, BUT A PROCESS—THE ABILITY TO ROLL ANY KIND OF FLOUR, FROM CORN TO WHEAT TO RICE, INTO SALABLE FLATBREAD. GRUMA CREATES SPECIALIZED FLATBREAD TO ACCOMMODATE LOCAL TASTES.

appeared in tourist destinations such as Rome, Venice, and Florence, local resistance ebbed. Tourists frequented the restaurants and ate flatbread, and the local Italians became curious and wanted to try it themselves, particularly the younger Italians.

Similar sensitivities have to be applied in single-market efforts as well. In Texas, for example, people generally like fluffier tortillas than those sold in the rest of the U.S. In California they like elastic tortillas, and in Arizona

they like chewy tortillas. Through research, Gruma marketers learned that each of those areas had been settled predominantly by Mexicans from a particular region, where variations in the local quality of tortilla manufacturing ingrained certain preferences.

SOURCES: Jairo Senise, "Who is Your Next Customer?" *eNews of Strategy and Business,* September 28, 2007, 1–4; and Alonzo Martinez and Ronald Haddock, "The Flatbread Factor," *Strategy and Business,* Spring 2007, 1–14. See also **www.gruma.com**.

Analytical procedures require constant monitoring of changes caused by outside events as well as the changes caused by the business entity itself. Controlling **ethnocentrism**—the belief that one's own culture is superior to others—can be achieved only by acknowledging it and properly adjusting to its possible effects in managerial decision making. The international manager needs to be prepared and able to put that preparedness to effective use.[68]

The Training Challenge

International managers face a dilemma in terms of international and intercultural competence. U.S. firms' lack of adequate foreign language and international business skills has resulted in lost contracts, weak negotiations, and ineffectual management. A UNESCO study of ten- and fourteen-year-old students in nine countries placed U.S. teens next to last in their comprehension of foreign cultures. The terrorist attacks of September 11, 2001, for instance, alerted the U.S. government not only to the national lack of competence in foreign language skills, but to the nation's failure to educate its population to cultural sensibilities at home and around the world.[69]

The increase in overall international activity of firms has increased the need for cultural sensitivity training at all levels of the organization. Today's training must take into consideration not only outsiders to the firm but interaction within the corporate family as well. However inconsequential the degree of interaction may seem, it can still cause problems if proper understanding is lacking. Consider, for example, the date 11/12/06 on a message; a European will interpret this as the eleventh of December, but in the United States it is the twelfth of November.

Some companies try to avoid the training problem by hiring only nationals or well-traveled executives for their international operations. This makes sense for the management of overseas operations but will not solve the training need, especially if transfers to a culture unfamiliar to the manager are likely. International experience may not necessarily transfer from one market to another.

To foster cultural sensitivity and acceptance of new ways of doing things within the organization, management must institute internal education programs. These programs may include (1) culture-specific information (e.g., data covering other countries, such as videopacks and culturegrams), (2) cultural general information (e.g., values, practices, and assumptions of countries other than one's own), and (3) self-specific information (e.g., identifying one's own cultural paradigm, including values, assumptions, and perceptions about others).[70] One study found that Japanese assigned to the United States receive mainly language training as preparation for the task. In addition, many companies use mentoring whereby an individual is assigned to someone who is experienced and who will spend the required time squiring and explaining. Talks given by returnees and by visiting lecturers hired specifically for the task round out the formal part of training.[71] At Samsung, several special interest groups were formed to focus on issues such as Japanese society and business practices, the Chinese economy, changes in Europe, and the U.S. economy. In addition, groups also explored cutting-edge business issues, such as new technology and marketing strategies. And for the last few years, Samsung has been sending the brightest junior employees abroad for a year.[72]

The objective of formal training programs is to foster the four critical characteristics of preparedness, sensitivity, patience, and flexibility in managers and other personnel. These programs vary dramatically in terms of their rigor, involvement, and, of course, cost.[73] A summary of these programs is provided in Exhibit 4.9.

Environmental briefings and cultural orientation programs are types of **area studies** programs. These programs provide factual preparation for a manager to operate in, or work with people from, a particular country. Area studies should be a basic prerequisite for other types of training programs. Alone, they serve little practical purpose because they do not really get the manager's feet wet; in other words, action learning is the key.[74] Other, more involved programs contribute the context in which to put facts so that they can be properly understood.

The **cultural assimilator** is a program in which trainees must respond to scenarios of specific situations in a particular country. These programs have been developed for the Arab countries, Iran, Thailand, Central America, and Greece. The results of the trainees' assimilator experience are evaluated by a panel of judges. This type of program has been used in particular in cases of transfers abroad on short notice.

When more time is available, managers can be trained extensively in language. This may be required if an exotic language is involved. **Sensitivity training** focuses on enhancing a manager's flexibility in situations that are quite different from those at home. The approach is based on the assumption that understanding and accepting oneself is critical to understanding a person from another culture. While most of the methods discussed are best delivered in face-to-face settings, Web-based training is becoming more popular, as seen in *The International Marketplace 4.5.*

Finally, training may involve **field experience**, which exposes a manager to a different cultural environment for a limited amount of time. Although the expense of placing and maintaining an expatriate is high (and, therefore, the cost of failure is high), field experience

Exhibit 4.9

Cross-Cultural Training Methods

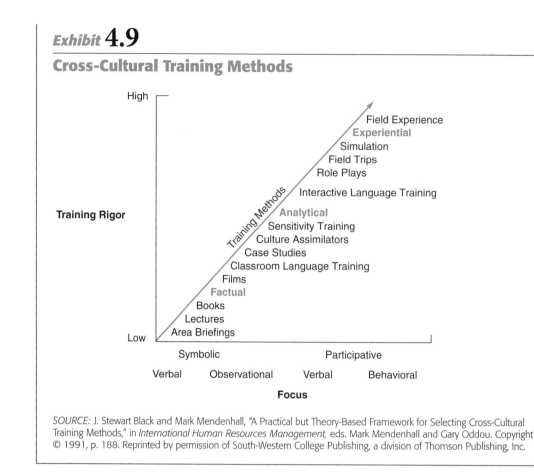

SOURCE: J. Stewart Black and Mark Mendenhall, "A Practical but Theory-Based Framework for Selecting Cross-Cultural Training Methods," in *International Human Resources Management*, eds. Mark Mendenhall and Gary Oddou. Copyright © 1991, p. 188. Reprinted by permission of South-Western College Publishing, a division of Thomson Publishing, Inc.

The International
MARKETPLACE   4.5

Online Cultural Training

Managers heading abroad to negotiate a deal, relocating to a foreign environment, or multicultural teams working within large organizations are just some of the scenarios that benefit from cross-cultural training. Skimping on training in this area can be potentially hazardous. For example, those going to Japan unprepared for high levels of etiquette and ceremony risk offending valuable clients. Employees who move to Hong Kong are often responsible for working with multiple countries and therefore require the know-how to work in a variety of cultural settings.

However, it is nearly impossible to cover such complex cross-cultural training in one- or two-day training periods. Furthermore, such training costs in excess of $1,000 per head per day. Therefore, many organizations are adding online training following the face-to-face classroom training in order to gain continuous and

additional training. Many of the programs use the following elements:

1. **Detailed Scenarios.** Much of the training material consists of a detailed, realistic story that is tied into elements of the learner's background; i.e., the session becomes more than a briefing. It becomes a narrated experience full of learning moments for participants. This is made possible by the ability of the Web to store and circulate a lot of information instantaneously around the world.

2. **Gradual Delivery.** The ability to control the flow of information to the participant supports the learning process in a number of ways. First, the participant is allowed to fit the training into his or her schedule. Second, the real-life flow of information is mimicked and a higher degree of realism is achieved.

3. **Support.** A set of detailed materials is provided to the participants 24 hours a day. At any hour and at any location, participants can check their perceptions

against the materials, reinforce learning from a dimly recalled lesson, or seek feedback on an important point or issue.

4. **Relevant Exercises.** Participants can be provided topical exercises and activities, the level of which can be adjusted depending on how the participant has invested in the training.

5. **Online Discussions.** Sessions can be simulcast to hundreds of participants around the world. The lack of face-to-face interaction can be remedied by having discussion groups where participants can share their experiences with one another. The pooled learning experience is stronger than the experience with one solitary participant.

The following case highlights some of the points made:

Joe Schmed is a marketing representative for a pharmaceutical company. His company has just undertaken a joint venture with a pan-Asian pharmaceutical company based in Kuala Lumpur. In order to develop a successful sales plan, over the next six months Joe will travel to Southeast Asia at least eight times. The first trip will be in two weeks. However, Joe lacks the time to take two full days out of his schedule for a traditional training program. Since his undergraduate major was in Asian studies, Joe feels that his cultural understanding is quite adequate. Nevertheless, he would like to brush up on some of his knowledge and gain a better understanding of Asian business. Logging on, he enters a training course, completing parts of it as he finds time—on airplanes and after work, for example.

Online cross-cultural programs focus on preparing international managers for the host of business scenarios encountered overseas. Training is often specific to a location, priming managers for posts in the Asia Pacific, Latin America, Europe, or the Middle East. Using a range of training tools, from case studies to web-based activities and exercises, programs cover such topics as intercultural adaptation, recognizing differences in communication styles, negotiation strategies, and practical information aspects of business and daily life.

SOURCES: Ross Bentley, "It Pays to Be a Cross-Culture Vulture," *Personnel Today*, January 23, 2007, 8; Jessica Caplan, "Innovations in intercultural tyraining," *China Staff*, November 2004, 14; Mike Bowler, "Online Learning is Fastest Growing Segment of Higher Education," *Knight Ridder Tribune Business News,* August 17, 2003, 1; "On-Line Learning," Special Advertising Section, Fortune, July 1, 2002, S1–S19; Peter T. Burgi and Brant R. Dykehouse, "On-Line Cultural Training: The Next Phase," *International Insight,* Winter 2000, 7–10. See also **http://www.runzheimer.com** and **http://www.iorworld.com**.

is rarely used in training. One field experience technique that has been suggested when the training process needs to be rigorous is the host-family surrogate. This technique places a trainee (and possibly his or her family) in a domestically located family of the nationality to which they are assigned.[75]

Regardless of the degree of training, preparation, and positive personal characteristics, a manager will always remain foreign. A manager should never rely on his or her own judgment when local managers can be consulted. In many instances, a manager should have an interpreter present at negotiations, especially if the manager is not completely bilingual. Overconfidence in one's language capabilities can create problems.

Making Culture Work for Marketing Success

Culture should not be viewed as a challenge but as an opportunity that can be exploited.[76] This requires, as has been shown in this chapter, an understanding of the differences and their fundamental determinants. Differences can quite easily be dismissed as indicators of inferiority or approaches to be changed; however, the opposite may actually be the case. Best practice knows no one particular origin, nor should it acknowledge boundaries. *The International Marketplace 4.6* demonstrates how the Walt Disney Company has responded to global cultural issues. The following rules serve as a summary of how culture and its appreciation may serve as a tool to ensure marketing success.

- **Embrace local culture.** Many corporate credos include a promise to be the best possible corporate citizens in every community operated in.[77] For example, in 3M's plant near Bangkok, Thailand, a Buddhist shrine, wreathed in flowers, pays homage

The International
MARKETPLACE

Romancing the Globe

Of all the brands in the world, there is none more consistent than Disney, which stands for "family magic," whether in Penang, Pisa, or Peoria. This does not mean, however, that a cookie-cutter approach of transplanted products from the United States work in key markets such as China, India, Latin America, Russia, and South Korea. Global markets want more than homogeneous, plain-vanilla products and services—they want them are in tune with local and regional preferences.

For the last ten years, the Walt Disney Company has made it a priority to build its international business in television, movies, retail, and theme parks with the goal of half of profits to come from overseas by 2010 (in 2006, the percentage was 25). The main approach of getting to the goal is by **embracing local culture**.

Disney's theme park in Hong Kong, which opened in 2005, suffered a 30 percent drop in attendance in its second year, largely due to not appealing to mainland Chinese audiences. The first big opportunity to reverse the trend is a stroke of astrological fortune: the year 2008 is the year of the rat, allowing Disney to proclaim it the Year of the Mouse. The Disneyland Chinese New Year campaign featured a logo with the Chinese character for luck flipped upside down (a New Year tradition), with mouse ears added on top. Inside the park, dumplings

and turnip cakes are featured on the menus. The parade down Main Street, USA, is being joined by the "Rhythm of Life Procession," featuring a dragon dance and puppets of birds, flowers, and fish, set to traditional Chinese music.

Disney's efforts to give its Hong Kong park a more Chinese character reflect a broader effort by the company to **understand local culture**. Research is conducted in the homes of Chinese consumers, who are asked about their knowledge of the Disney brand and their lifestyles as busy families. As a result, for example, Disneyland ads feature one child (Chinese government limits most couples to just one child), two parents, and two grandparents (many households are extended ones) sharing branded Disney activities, such as watching a movie or giving a plush version of the mouse as a gift.

Adapting products and processes to local markets is a key ingredient of successful global strategy. The gods of wealth, longevity, and happiness have been added to the Hong Kong Disneyland gang. To support the marketing efforts of the theme park, Disney has expanded its TV, online, and film businesses in China. "The Secret of the Magic Gourd" was the first-ever movie made just for Chinese audiences. The movie also meant a departure from Disney's obsession with going it alone in that they worked with local experts (including the state-run China

© TED ALJIBE/AFP/GETTY IMAGES

DISNEY'S THEME PARK IN HONG KONG SUFFERED A 30 PERCENT DROP IN ATTENDANCE IN ITS SECOND YEAR, LARGELY DUE TO INSUFFICIENT APPEAL TO MAINLAND CHINESE CUSTOMERS.

Film Group) to produce the culturally customized product.

The role of **local employees** is critical in gaining cultural knowledge. Disney has given more power to local managers to develop completely local approaches, to adapt U.S. franchises and make local versions of them, or build interest in U.S. shows such as "Hannah Montana" and "Kim Possible." It is also important to help local employees understand their foreign employers. Chinese executives and staff benefit from visits to Burbank, California, and interaction with Disney executives from around the world to combine Disney and Chinese values.

The same processes are being replicated in the other emerging markets targeted by Disney. Local versions of "High School Musical" for India, Latin America, and Russia are part of Disney's $100 million investment in movies outside of the United States designed to generate larger profits from markets with further growth potential. The cast for the Indian version of "High School Musical" was chosen in an "American Idol"-style competition. To create interest, Disney aired a dubbed version of the American movie and launched "My School Rocks," a dance competition featuring "High School Musical" songs. A CD of the movie soundtrack with Hindi lyrics and Indian instruments has been successful due to a low retail cost.

SOURCES: "Main Street, H. K.," *The Wall Street Journal*, January 23, 2008, B1–B2; "Disney Rewrites Script to Win Fans in India," *The Wall Street Journal*, June 11, 2007, A1, A10; Ibsen Martinez, "Romancing the Globe," *Foreign Policy*, November/December 2005, 48–56.

to the spirits that Thais believe took care of the land prior to the plant's arrival. Showing sensitivity to local custom helps local acceptance and builds employee morale. More importantly, it contributes to a deeper understanding of the market and keeps the marketer from inadvertently doing something to alienate constituents.

- **Build relationships.** Each market has its own unique set of constituents who need to be identified and nurtured. Establishing and nurturing local ties at the various stages of the market-development cycle develops relationships that can be invaluable in expansion and countering political risk. 3M started its preparations for entering the China market soon after President Nixon's historic visit in 1972. For ten years, company officials visited Beijing and entertained visits of Chinese officials to company headquarters in Minneapolis–St. Paul. Such efforts paid off in 1984, when the Chinese government made 3M the first wholly owned venture in the market. Many such emerging markets require long-term commitment on the part of the marketer.

- **Employ locals to gain cultural knowledge.** The single best way to understand a market is to grow with it by developing human resources and business partnerships along the way. Of the 7,500 3M employees in Asia, fewer than ten are from the United States. As a matter of fact, of the 34,000 3M employees outside of the United States, fewer than 1 percent are expatriates. The rest are locals who know local customs and the purchasing habits of their compatriots. In every way possible, locals are made equals with their U.S. counterparts. For example, grants are made available for 3M employees to engage in the product-development process with concept and idea development.

- **Help employees understand you.** Employing locals will give a marketer a valuable asset in market development; that is, in acculturation. However, these employees also need their own process of adjustment (i.e., "corporatization") to be effective. At any given time, more than 30 of 3MAsian technicians are in the United States, where they learn the latest product and process advances while gaining insight into how the company works. Also, they are able to develop personal ties with people they may work with. Furthermore, they often contribute by infusing their insights into company plans. Similar schemes are in place for distributors. Distributor advisory councils allow intermediaries to share their views with the company.

- **Adapt products and processes to local markets.** Nowhere is a company's commitment to local markets as evident as in its product offering. Global, regional, and purely local products are called for, and constant and consistent product-development efforts on a market-by-market basis are warranted to find the next global success. When the sales of 3M's famous Scotchbrite cleaning pads were languishing in

Southeast Asia, company researchers interviewed housewives and domestic help to determine why. They found that traditionally floors are scrubbed with the help of the rough shells of coconuts. 3M responded by making its cleaning pads brown and shaping them like a foot. In China, a big seller for 3M is a composite to fill tooth cavities. In the United States, dentists pack a soft material into the cavity and blast it with a special beam of light, making it as hard as enamel in a matter of seconds. In China, dentists cannot afford this technology. The solution was an air-drying composite that hardens in a matter of minutes, but at a reasonable expense to the dental customer.

- **Coordinate by region.** The transfer of best practice is critical, especially in areas that have cultural similarities. When 3M designers in Singapore discovered that customers used its Nomad household mats in their cars, they spread the word to their counterparts throughout Asia. The company encourages its product managers from different parts of Asia to hold regular periodic meetings and share insights and strategies. The goal of this cross-pollination is to come up with regional programs and "Asianize," or even globalize, a product more quickly. Joint endeavors build cross-border esprit de corps, especially when managers may have their own markets' interests primarily at heart.[78]

Summary

Culture is one of the most challenging elements of the international marketplace. This system of learned behavior patterns characteristic of the members of a given society is constantly shaped by a set of dynamic variables: language, religion, values and attitudes, manners and customs, aesthetics, technology, education, and social institutions. An international manager, to cope with this system, needs both factual and interpretive knowledge of culture. To some extent, the factual can be learned; the interpretation comes only through experience.

The most complicated problems in dealing with the cultural environment stem from the fact that we cannot learn culture—we have to live it. Two schools of thought exist in the business world on how to deal with cultural diversity. One is that business is business the world around, following the model of Pepsi and McDonald's. In some cases, globalization is a fact of life; however, cultural differences are still far from converging.

The other school proposes that companies must tailor business approaches to individual cultures. Setting up policies and procedures in each country has been compared to an organ transplant; the critical question centers on acceptance or rejection. The major challenge to the international manager is to make sure that rejection is not a result of cultural myopia or even blindness.

The internationally successful companies all share an important quality: patience. They have not rushed into situations but rather built their operations carefully by following the most basic business principles. These principles are to know your challenger, know your audience, and know your customer.

Key Terms

culture	focus groups	experiential knowledge
acculturation	in-depth studies	interpretive knowledge
high context cultures	infrastructures	self-reference criterion
low context cultures	cultural convergence	ethnocentrism
change agent	social stratification	area studies
cultural imperialism	reference groups	cultural assimilator
cultural universals	cultural knowledge	sensitivity training
back-translation	factual information	field experience

Questions for Discussion

1. Comment on the assumption, "If people are serious about doing business with you, they will speak English."

2. You are on your first business visit to Germany. You feel confident about your ability to speak the language (you studied German in school and have taken a refresher course), and you decide to use it. During introductions, you want to break the ice by asking *"Wie geht's?"* and insisting that everyone call you by your first name. Speculate as to the reaction.

3. What can a company do to culture-sensitize its staff?

4. What can be learned about a culture from reading and attending to factual materials? Given the tremendous increase in international marketing activities, where will companies in a relatively early stage of the internationalization process find the personnel to handle the new challenges?

5. Management at a U.S. company trying to market tomato paste in the Middle East did not know that, translated into Arabic, tomato paste is "tomato glue." How could they have known in time to avoid problems?

6. Give examples of how the self-reference criterion might be manifested.

Internet Exercises

1. Various companies, such as GMAC Global Relocation Services, are available to prepare and train interna tional marketers for the cultural challenge. Using their Web site (http://www. gmacglobalrelocation.com), assess its role in helping the international marketer.

2. Compare and contrast an international marketer's home pages for presentation and content; for example, Coca-Cola (http://www.coca-cola.com) and its Japanese version (http://www.cocacola. co.jp). Are the differences cultural?

Recommended Readings

Axtell, Roger E. *Do's and Taboos around the World.* New York: John Wiley & Sons, 1993.

Brett, Jeanne. *Negotiating Globally: How to Negotiate Deals, Resolve Disputes, and Make Decisions across Cultures.* New York: Jossey-Bass, 2001.

Brislin, R. W., W. J. Lonner, and R. M. Thorndike, *Cross-Cultural Research Methods.* New York: John Wiley & Sons, 1973.

Carte, Penny and Chris Fox. *Bridging the Culture Gap: A Practical Guide to International Business Communication.* New York: Kogan, 2004.

Cellich, Claude and Subhash Jain. *Global Business Negotiations.* Mason, OH: Thomson South-Western, 2003.

Hofstede, Geert. *Culture's Consequences: Comparing Values, Behaviors, Institutions and Organizations across Nations.* London: Sage Publications, 2003.

Lewis, Richard D. *When Cultures Collide.* London: Nicholas Brealey Publishing, 2000.

Trompenaars, Fons, and Charles Hampden-Turner. *Riding the Waves of Culture.* New York: Irwin, 1998.

THE LEGAL AND POLITICAL ENVIRONMENT

The Dawning of the Age of the Bicycle

In 1932, at the onset of the global automotive age, George Lansbury—the Leader of the British Labor Party, opened the Royal Lightweight Cycling, Hiking, and Camping Exhibition with an ode to the bicycle. He stated that it would be a bad day for humanity, when we ceased to use our limbs for transport. "It was a good thing that some machinery should be so adapted that men and women could use their own limbs, and he was glad to see this rebirth of interest in cycling."

Lansbury's words have proven eerily prophetic, as the contemporary world grapples with mounting oil costs, concerns about the environment, the availability of renewable resources, urban congestion, and the health effects of sedentary societies with rising obesity rates. In light of these trends, it would appear that the humble bicycle is set for a comeback. The past decade has indeed witnessed a doubling of cyclists in urban centers from Berlin to Portland, and global bicycle production has increased steadily. Antony Lo—President of the world's largest bike manufacturer—Taiwan's Giant, said in an interview, *"High-priced gasoline is here to stay. I tell my people we are just at the beginning of a very big cycling boom."* This optimism is especially justified with consumers around the world eager to cut back on their transportation costs.

Business leaders are taking heed. For example, Schwinn Bicycles and Toshiba announced a strategic collaborative agreement in 2008, aimed at increasing their combined market share of the electric bike (or eBike) market. eBikes are bicycles driven by battery-powered electric motors. Their sales have jumped about 20 percent since 2005 and their popularity is projected to continue to increase, especially in developing countries with a burgeoning middle class. Under the Toshiba-Schwinn agreement, riders would be able to recharge their Schwinn eBikes in 30 minutes through a standard electric outlet, or in one-eighth of the time of competing electric bikes.

Despite the solid economic and ecological rationale supporting a resurgence of bicycling, it would appear that some countries are paying closer attention than others. Northern Europe and Japan have undertaken large-scale policy measures to promote bicycle commuting, while North America, Australia, and Britain have lagged behind. In the developing world, most notably its two most populous nations, China and India, consumers are discarding bikes in favor of cars.

The policy measures that entice commuters to give the bicycle a try are simple and straightforward: bike-for-hire stations, bike-friendly infrastructure, secure bike parking and convenient access to public transportation, combined with high automobile taxes, congestion-zone fees, and assorted monetary incentives/disincentives. The Netherlands spearheaded such policies decades ago, and as a result, 27 percent of all trips there are by bike. In the United States, efforts to encourage bicycle use are gaining momentum. At the local government level, Pasadena offers a cash rewards program for frequent bikers and a $500 subsidy to eBike purchasers. On the federal

© ISTOCKPHOTO.COM/CAN BALCIOGLU

THE PAST DECADE HAS WITNESSED A DOUBLING OF CYCLISTS IN URBAN CENTERS FROM BERLIN TO PORTLAND, AND GLOBAL BICYCLE PRODUCTION HAS INCREASED STEADILY.

level, Representative Blumenauer (D-OR) heads the Congressional Bike caucus and attempts to promote pro-bike legislation through the Federal Transportation Bill.

However, the global future of the bicycle is not without its challenges. In the developing world, economic growth often means a populist reaction against cycling. Nalin Sinha, New Delhi program director for a nonprofit transportation group, summed up the anti-bike trend in India, by saying; "People want cars, as it indicates development, progress, and that you are more influential…" The traffic composition of his home city has changed drastically over the past two decades, with bicycles accounting for about 4 percent of all transportation, down from 60 percent. A similar trend is

evident in China, where the bike fleet has been steadily declining, while private car ownership has more than double over the past ten years. The future challenge for both marketers and policy makers would be how to overcome the populist anti-bike sentiments in the world's developing economies and persuade their rapidly growing consumer base to again give bikes a chance.

SOURCES: "Bicycle Boom," *The Guardian*, Nov. 14, 1932; Harden, Blaine, "For Bicyclists, a Widening Patchwork World," *The Washington Post*, August 31, 2008; Whelan, Carolyn, "Electric Bikes are Taking Off," *International Herald Tribune*, March 14, 2007; "Schwinn and Toshiba Collaborate to Dramatically Alter the Electric Bike Market," Interbike 2008, Sept. 24th, 2008, **http://reviews .roadbikereview.com/intebike/**, Retrieved Nov. 10, 2008; Peirce, Neal, "Year of the Bicycle," *National Academy of Public Administration*, March 2, 2008.

Much as most managers would like to ignore them, political and legal factors often play a critical role in international marketing activities. The interpretation and application of regulations can sometimes lead to conflicting and even misleading results. Even the best business plans can go awry as a result of unexpected political or legal influences, and the failure to anticipate these factors can be the undoing of an otherwise successful business venture. Exhibit 5.1 ranks the factors that affect a country's investment climate; note that inefficient government bureaucracy dominates the concerns of firms. However, variations in political and legal environments can also offer new opportunities to international marketers, as *The International Marketplace 5.1* shows.

Of course, a single international political and legal environment does not exist. The business executive must be aware of political and legal factors on a variety of levels. For example, although it is useful to understand the complexities of a host country's legal system, such knowledge does not protect against a home-country-imposed export embargo.

The study of the international political and legal environment must therefore be broken down into several subsegments. Many researchers do this by separating the legal from the political. This separation—although perhaps analytically useful—is somewhat artificial because laws are generally the result of political decisions. Here no attempt will be made to separate legal and political factors, except when such a separation is essential.

Exhibit 5.1

Environmental Shortcomings of the Investment Climate

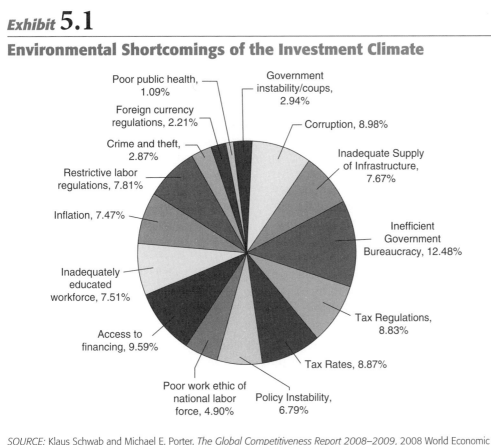

Poor public health, 1.09%

Government instability/coups, 2.94%

Foreign currency regulations, 2.21%

Corruption, 8.98%

Crime and theft, 2.87%

Restrictive labor regulations, 7.81%

Inadequate Supply of Infrastructure, 7.67%

Inflation, 7.47%

Inefficient Government Bureaucracy, 12.48%

Inadequately educated workforce, 7.51%

Access to financing, 9.59%

Tax Regulations, 8.83%

Tax Rates, 8.87%

Poor work ethic of national labor force, 4.90%

Policy Instability, 6.79%

SOURCE: Klaus Schwab and Michael E. Porter, *The Global Competitiveness Report 2008–2009*, 2008 World Economic Forum, Geneva, **www.weforum.org/pdf/GCR08/GCR08.pdf**, accessed November 3, 2008.

Instead, this chapter will examine the political-legal environment from the manager's point of view. In making decisions about his or her firm's international marketing activities, the manager will need to concentrate on three areas: the political and legal circumstances of the home country; those of the host country; and the bilateral and multilateral agreements, treaties, and laws governing the relations between host and home countries.

Home Country Legal and Political Environment

No manager can afford to ignore the policies and regulations of the country from which he or she conducts international marketing transactions. Wherever a firm is located, it will be affected by government policies and the legal system.

Many of these laws and regulations may not be designed specifically to address international marketing transactions, yet they can have a major impact on a firm's opportunities abroad. Minimum wage legislation, for example, affects the international competitiveness of a firm using production processes that are highly labor intensive. The cost of domestic safety regulations may significantly affect the pricing policies of firms in their international marketing efforts. For example, U.S. legislation that created the **Environmental Superfund** requires payment by chemical firms based on their production volume, regardless of whether the production is sold domestically or exported. As a result, these firms are at a disadvantage internationally when exporting their commodity-type products because they must compete against foreign firms that are not required to make such a payment in their home countries and therefore have a cost advantage.

Other legal and regulatory measures, however, are clearly aimed at international marketing activities. Some may be designed to help firms in their international efforts. The lack of enforcement of others may hurt the international marketer. For instance, many firms are concerned about the lack of safeguards for intellectual property rights in developing countries, an issue discussed later in this chapter.

Another area in which governments may attempt to aid and protect the international marketing efforts of companies is gray market activities. Gray market goods are products that enter markets in ways not desired by their manufacturers. Companies may be hurt by their own products if they reach the consumer via uncontrolled distribution channels.

Apart from specific areas that result in government involvement, the political environment in most countries tends to provide general support for the international marketing efforts of the country's firms. For example, a government may work to reduce trade barriers or to increase trade opportunities through bilateral and multilateral negotiations. Such actions will affect individual firms to the extent that they affect the international climate for free trade.

Often, however, governments also have specific rules and regulations restricting international marketing. Such regulations are frequently political in nature and are based on the fact that governments believe commerce to be only one objective among others, such as foreign policy and national security. Four main areas of governmental activities are of major concern to the international marketer here: embargoes or trade sanctions, export controls, import controls, and the regulation of international business behavior.

Embargoes and Sanctions

The terms trade sanctions and embargoes as used here refer to governmental actions that distort the free flow of trade in goods, services, or ideas for decidedly adversarial and political, rather than strictly economic, purposes. Exhibit 5.2 illustrates the sanctions currently maintained by the U.S. against China. Human rights conditions in the country, as well as the threat of weapons proliferation, are the concerns of the U.S. administration that help maintain these sanctions in place. Advocates of sanctions regard them as an important weapon of foreign policy. Skeptics question whether sanctions are effective, and whether the costs they impose are worth the benefits.[1]

Exhibit 5.2

U.S. Sanctions Against China

The U.S. goods trade deficit with China was $256.3 billion in 2007. U.S. goods exports in 2007 were $65.2 billion. Corresponding U.S. imports from China were $321.5 billion.

- Limits on U.S. foreign assistance
- U.S. "No" votes or abstention in the international banks
- Ban on Overseas Private Investment Corporation programs
- Ban on export of defense articles or defense services
- Ban on import of munitions or ammunition
- Ban on procurement of goods and services listed on the munitions list in the International Trafficking in Arms Regulations
- Denial of Generalized System of Preferences status
- Substantial export controls on dual-use items, particularly satellites, nuclear technology, and computers
- Suspension of export licenses for crime control and detection instruments and equipment
- Export and licensing restrictions on targeted entities found to have engaged in proliferation of missiles and weapons of mass destruction (or related technology)
- Presidential authority to restrict Chinese military companies and Chinese government-affiliated businesses from developing commercial activities inside the United States

SOURCES: Rennack, Dianne E. *"China: Economic Sanctions,"* Congressional Research Service Report, p. 2, updated February 1, 2006; **http://fas.org/sgp/crs/row/RL31910.pdf**, accessed Nov. 3, 2008. "2008 National Trade Estimate Report on Foreign Trade Barriers," Office of the United States Trade Representative, March 28th, 2008, **http://www.ustr.gov/ assets/Document_Library/Reports_Publications/2008/2008_NTE_Report/asset_uplod_file930_14640.pdf**, accessed Nov. 17, 2008.

Trade sanctions were already used in the thirteenth century by the Hansa league, an association of north German merchants with grievances against Norway. Over the years, economic sanctions and embargoes have become an often-used foreign policy tool for many countries. Reasons for the impositions are varied, ranging from human rights to nuclear nonproliferation to terrorism (see the section on terrorism later in this chapter). The range of sanctions imposed can be quite broad. Examples are elimination of credits and prohibition of financial transactions. Typically, the intent is to bring commercial interchange to a complete halt.

The League of Nations set a precedent for the international legal justification of economic sanctions by subscribing to a covenant that provided for penalties or sanctions for breaching its provisions. The members of the League of Nations did not intend to use military or economic measures separately, but the success of the blockades of World War I fostered the opinion that "the economic weapon, conceived not as an instrument of war but as a means of peaceful pressure, is the greatest discovery and most precious possession of the League."[2] The basic idea was that economic sanctions could force countries to behave peacefully in the international community.

The idea of the multilateral use of economic sanctions was again incorporated into international law under the charter of the United Nations, but greater emphasis was placed on the enforcement process. Once decided upon, sanctions are mandatory, even though each permanent member of the Security Council can veto efforts to impose sanctions. The charter also allows for sanctions as enforcement action by regional agencies such as the Organization of American States, the Arab League, and the Organization of African Unity, but only with the Security Council's authorization.

The apparent strength of the United Nations enforcement system soon turned out to be flawed. Stalemates in the Security Council and vetoes by permanent members often led to a shift of emphasis to the General Assembly, which does not have the power to enforce. Further, concepts such as "peace" and "breach of peace" are seldom perceived in the same way by all members, and thus no systematic sanctioning policy developed in the United Nations. As a result, sanctions have frequently been imposed unilaterally in the hope of changing a particular country's government, or at least its policies. Unilateral imposition, however, tends to have major negative effects on the firms in the country that is exercising sanctions, since the only result is often a simple shift in trade.

Another key problem with unilateral imposition of sanctions is that they typically do not produce the desired result. Sanctions may make the obtaining of goods more difficult or expensive for the sanctioned country, yet achievement of the purported objective almost never occurs. In order to work, sanctions need to be imposed multilaterally. Only when virtually all nations in which a product is produced agree to deny it to a target can there be a true deprivation effect. Without such denial, sanctions do not have much bite. Yet to get all producing nations to agree can be quite difficult. Typically, individual countries have different relationships with the country subject to the sanctions due to geographic or historic reasons, and therefore cannot or do not want to terminate trade relations.

Sudan is a poignant example of the importance of a unified sanctions regime. For years, news of atrocities in Sudan's Darfur region have been splashed across TV screens all over the world. The United States spearheaded sanctions in 1997 with a trade embargo and an asset freeze against the Sudanese government. The goal was to force Sudan's leadership to improve its human rights record and to put an end to genocide in the country.

Over the following decade, the global public became increasingly aware of the widespread human rights abuses in the region. Grassroots organizations around the world placed increased pressure on their governments to join the sanctions endeavor. The United Nations Security Council passed two resolutions, including an assets freeze and arms embargo, and has since dispatched a peace-keeping force to the region. However, initiatives to expand the scope of the sanctions regime against Sudan have met staunch opposition from Russia and China, who have economic interests in the oil-rich country.[3] Many human rights organizations and independent analysts believe that unless the global community presents a unified front to the Sudanese government and imposes real economic punishment for continued repression, the situation in Darfur will continue to deteriorate.[4] Sanctions can represent a powerful international policy measure, but their effectiveness is a function of the global political will and unity that underpins them.

One key concern with sanctions is the fact that governments often consider them as being free of cost. However, even though they may not affect the budget of governments, sanctions imposed by governments can mean significant loss of business to firms. One estimate claims that the economic sanctions held in place by the United States annually costs the country some $20 billion in lost exports and that the success rate of all U.S. sanctions where the United States was part of a sanction coalition approached 30 percent.[5]

Due to these costs, the issue of compensating the domestic firms and industries affected by these sanctions needs to be raised. Yet, trying to impose sanctions slowly or making them less expensive to ease the burden on these firms undercuts their ultimate chance for success. The international marketing manager is often caught in this political web and loses business as a result. Frequently, firms try to anticipate sanctions based on their evaluations of the international political climate. Even when substantial precautions are taken, firms may still suffer substantial losses due to contract cancellations. However, this can be seen as the cost of one's government's support for an open global trading and investing environment.

Export Controls

Many nations have **export control systems**, which are designed to deny or at least delay the acquisition of strategically important goods by adversaries. Most of these systems make controls the exception rather than the rule, with exports taking place independently from politics. The United States, however, differs substantially from this perspective in that exports are considered to be a privilege rather than a right, and exporting is seen as an extension of foreign policy.

The legal basis for export controls varies across nations. For example, in Germany, armament exports are covered in the so-called War Weapons List, which is a part of the War Weapons Control Law. The exports of other goods are covered by the German Export List. **Dual-use items**, which are goods useful for both military and civilian purposes, are then controlled by the Joint List of the European Union.[6]

U.S. laws control all exports of goods, services, and ideas. It is important to note here that an export of goods occurs whenever goods are physically transferred from the United States. Services and ideas, however, are deemed exported whenever transferred to a foreign national, regardless of location. Permitting a foreign national from a controlled country to have access to a highly sensitive computer program in the United States is therefore deemed to be an export. The effect of such a perspective can be major, particularly on universities and for international students.

The U.S. export control system is based on the Export Administration Act, administered by the Department of Commerce, and the Arms Expert Control Act, administered by the Department of State. The Commerce Department focuses on exports in general, while the State Department covers products designed or modified for military use, even if such products have commercial applicability. The determinants for controls are national security, foreign policy, short supply, and nuclear nonproliferation.

In order for any export from the United States to take place, the exporter needs to obtain an export license. The administering government agencies have, in consultation with other government departments, drawn up a list of commodities whose export is considered particularly sensitive. In addition, a list of countries differentiates nations according to their political relationship with the United States. Finally, a list of individual firms that are considered to be unreliable trading partners because of past trade-diversion activities exists for each country.

After an export license application has been filed, government specialists match the commodity to be exported with the commerce control list, a file containing information about products that are either particularly sensitive to national security or controlled for other purposes. The product is then matched with the country of destination and the recipient company. If no concerns regarding any of the three exist, an export license is issued. Control determinants and the steps in the decision process are summarized in Exhibit 5.3.

This process may sound overly cumbersome, but it does not apply in equal measure to all exports. Most international business activities can be carried out under NLR conditions, which stands for "no license required." NLR provides blanket permission to export.

Exhibit **5.3**

The U.S. Export Control System

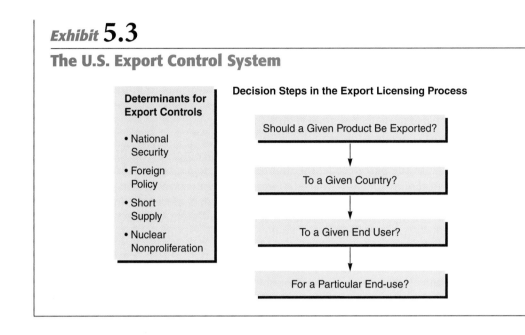

Determinants for Export Controls

- National Security
- Foreign Policy
- Short Supply
- Nuclear Nonproliferation

Decision Steps in the Export Licensing Process

- Should a Given Product Be Exported?
- To a Given Country?
- To a Given End User?
- For a Particular End-use?

Products can be freely shipped to most trading partners provided that neither the end user nor the end use involved are considered sensitive. However, the process becomes more complicated when products incorporating high-level technologies and countries not friendly to the United States are involved. The exporter must then obtain an export license, which consists of written authorization to send a product abroad.

The international marketing repercussions of export controls are important. It is one thing to design an export control system that is effective and that restricts those international business activities subject to important national concerns. It is, however, quite another when controls lose their effectiveness and when one country's firms are placed at a competitive disadvantage with firms in other countries whose control systems are less extensive or even nonexistent.

In some instances, the heavy-handed implementation of export regulations can have dramatic and far-reaching effects. The government of Argentina has learned this lesson the hard way. Following a controversial tax increase on grain exports, in addition to previous price controls and heavy state intervention, farmers and anti-government protesters took to the streets. This, in turn, caused fuel and food shortages in parts of the country. Considering that soy accounts for a quarter of Argentina's total exports and has largely been the backbone of its economic growth over the last five years, the new tax was controversial at best. In addition to eroding the government's popularity, it led to a crash in the Argentinean stock and bond markets and drove up the global price of soybeans.[7] When a government sets out to impose export restrictions in an attempt to "redistribute the wealth," as was the case with Argentina, it needs to pay careful attention to the Pandora's box of economic inefficiencies and social unrest that it could unleash.

A New Environment for Export Controls

Today's international environment continues to highlight the importance of export controls. Restricting the flow of materials can be crucial in avoiding the proliferation of weapons of mass destruction; reducing flows of technological knowledge can reduce the sophistication of armaments used by insurgent groups; financial controls can inhibit funding for terrorist training.

Nowadays, the principal focus of export controls rests on the Third World. A number of countries from this region want chemical and nuclear weapons, as well as the technology to make use of them. Even if a country already has dangerous weaponry, export controls can reduce the opportunity for its deployment. Today's export controls use a "tactical balance" approach affecting specific hotspots, rather than the "strategic balance" approach exercised during the era of U.S.–Soviet global deterrence. Iran is a prominent example of export control issues. Its efforts to implement a nuclear program have caused much consternation in the global community. Intense negotiations included threats of additional controls and sanctions. The UN Security Council's five permanent members and Germany pledged to establish full relations and economic cooperation with Iran in exchange for suspension of enrichment-related and reprocessing activities. While this commitment diffused the crisis, most analysts believe that this is not the last the world has seen of Iran's nuclear ambitions.[8] Export controls are likely to remain an important tool in the arsenal of international policy makers, as they strive to contain dangers in the world at large.

Major change has also resulted from the increased **foreign availability** of high-technology products. In the past decade, the number of participants in the international trade field has grown rapidly. In earlier decades, industrializing countries mainly participated in world trade due to wage-based competition. Today, they are increasingly focused on technology-based competition. As a result, high-technology products are available worldwide from many sources. The broad availability makes any product denial more difficult to enforce. If a nation does control the exports of widely available products, it imposes a major competitive burden on its firms.

Enormous technical progress has also brought about a radical change in computer architecture. Instead of having to replace a personal computer or a workstation with a new computer, one can simply exchange microprocessors or motherboards with new, more efficient ones. Furthermore, today's machines can be connected to more than one microprocessor and users can customize and update configurations almost at will. A user simply acquires additional chips from whomever and uses expansion slots to enhance the capacity of his or her computer.

The question arises as to how much of the latest technology is required for a country to engage in "dangerous" activity. For example, nuclear weapons and sophisticated delivery systems were developed by the United States and the Soviet Union long before supercomputers became available. Therefore, it is reasonable to assert that researchers in countries working with equipment that is less than state-of-the-art, or even obsolete, may well be able to achieve a threat capability that can result in major destruction and affect world safety.

From a control perspective, there is also the issue of equipment size. Supercomputers and high-technology items used to be fairly difficult to hide and any movement of such products was easily detectable. Nowadays, state-of-the-art technology has been miniaturized. Much leading-edge technological equipment is so small that it can fit into a briefcase, and most equipment is no larger than the luggage compartment of a car. Given these circumstances, it has become difficult to closely supervise the transfer of such equipment.

There is a continuing debate about what constitutes military-use products, civilian-use products, and dual-use products, and the achievement of multilateral agreement on such classifications. Increasingly, goods are of a dual-use nature, meaning that they are commercial products that have potential military applications.[9] Examples are exported trucks that can be used to transport troops, or the exports of supplies to a pesticide factory that, some years later, is revealed to be a poison gas factory.[10] It is difficult enough to define weapons clearly. It is even more problematic to achieve consensus among nations regarding dual-use goods.

Conflicts can result from the desire of nations to safeguard their own economic interests. Due to different industrial structures, these interests vary across nations. For example, Germany, with a strong world market position in machine tools, motors, and chemical raw materials, will think differently about controls than a country such as the United States, which sees computers as an area of its competitive advantage.

The rise in international awareness of the threat of terrorism has led to a renewed importance of global export controls. In recent years, many policies have been targeted to better focus on the dangers of proliferation and terrorist attack. This has helped to differentiate more sharply between those high-tech products that need to be controlled, and those that don't; an overall easing of export control policies in the technology field has resulted. U.S. administration export control policy is increasingly based on a "stick and carrot" approach, showing preferential treatment to countries better aligned with U.S. policy goals. It can therefore be said that the role of export controls, as well as their sophistication, has intensified.

Import Controls

In these countries, either all imports or the imports of particular products are controlled through tariff and nontariff mechanisms. **Tariffs** place a tax on imports and raise prices. Nontariff barriers like **voluntary restraint agreements** are self-imposed restrictions and cutbacks aimed at avoiding punitive trade actions from the host. **Quota systems** reduce the volume of imports accepted by a country. The final effect of all these actions is a quantitative reduction of imports.

For the international marketer, such restrictions may mean that the most efficient sources of supply are not available because government regulations restrict importation from those sources. The result is either second-best products or higher costs for restricted supplies. This in turn means that the customer receives inferior service and often has to pay significantly higher prices, and that the firm is less competitive when trying to market its products internationally.

Policymakers are faced with several problems when trying to administer import controls. First, most of the time such controls exact a huge price from domestic consumers. Even though the wide distribution of the burden among many consumers may result in a less obvious burden, the social cost of these controls may be damaging to the economy and subject to severe attack by individuals. However, these attacks are counteracted by pressures from protected groups that benefit from import restrictions. For example, although citizens of the European Union may be forced—because of import controls—to pay an elevated price for all agricultural products they consume, agricultural producers in the region benefit from higher levels of income. Achieving a proper trade-off is often difficult, if not impossible, for the policymaker.

A second major problem resulting from import controls is the **downstream change** in import composition that results from these controls. For example, if the import of copper ore is restricted, either through voluntary restraints or through quotas, firms in copper-producing countries may opt to shift their production systems and produce copper wire instead, which they then export. As a result, initially narrowly defined protectionist measures may have to snowball in order to protect one downstream industry after another.

A final major problem that confronts the policymaker is that of efficiency. Import controls that are frequently designed to provide breathing room to a domestic industry either to grow or to recapture its competitive position often turn out not to work. Rather than improve the productivity of an industry, such controls provide it with a level of safety and a cushion of increased income yet let the drive for technological advancement fall behind. Alternatively, supply may respond to artificial stimulation and grow far beyond demand.

Regulation of International Business Behavior

Home countries may implement special laws and regulations to ensure that the international business behavior of their firms is conducted within the legal, moral, and ethical boundaries considered appropriate. The definition of appropriateness may vary from country to country and from government to government. Therefore, such regulations, their enforcement, and their impact on firms can differ substantially among nations.

Several major areas in which nations attempt to govern the international marketing activities of its firms are **boycotts**, whereby firms refuse to do business with someone, often for political reasons; antitrust measures, wherein firms are seen as restricting competition; and corruption, which occurs when firms obtain contracts with bribes rather than through performance. Arab nations, for example, have developed a blacklist of companies that deal with Israel. Even though enforcement of the blacklisting has decreased, some Arab customers still demand from their suppliers assurances that the source of the products purchased is not Israel and that the company does not do any business with Israel. The goal of these actions clearly is to impose a boycott on business with Israel. The U.S. government in turn, because of U.S. political ties to Israel, has adopted a variety of laws to prevent U.S. firms from complying with the Arab boycott. These laws include a provision to deny foreign income tax benefits to companies that comply with the boycott and also require notification of the U.S. government in case any boycott requests are received. U.S. firms that comply with the boycott are subject to heavy fines and denial of export privileges.

Boycott measures put firms in a difficult position. Caught in a web of governmental activity, they may be forced to either lose business or pay fines. This is particularly the case if a firm's products are competitive yet not unique, so that the supplier can opt to purchase them elsewhere. Heightening of such conflict can sometimes force companies to withdraw operations entirely from a country.

The second area of regulatory activity affecting international marketing efforts of firms is antitrust laws. These can apply to the international operations of firms as well as to domestic business. In the European Union, for example, the Commission watches closely when any firm buys an overseas company, engages in a joint venture with a foreign firm, or makes an agreement with a competing firm. The Commission evaluates the effect these activities will have on competition and has the right to disapprove such transactions. However, given the increased globalization of national economies, some substantial rethinking is going on regarding the current approach to antitrust enforcement. One could question whether any country can still afford to define the competition only in a domestic sense or whether competition has to be seen on a worldwide scale. Similarly, one can wonder whether countries will accept the infringement on their sovereignty that results from the extraterritorial application of any nation's law abroad.

There are precedents for making special allowances for international marketers with regard to antitrust laws. In the United States, for example, the Webb-Pomerene Act of 1918 excludes from antitrust prosecution those firms that are cooperating to develop foreign markets. This act was passed as part of an effort to aid U.S. export efforts in the face of strong foreign competition by oligopolies and monopolies. The exclusion of international marketing activity from antitrust regulation was further enhanced by the Export Trading Company Act of 1982, which does not expose cooperating firms to the threat of treble damages. It was specifically designed to assist small- and medium-sized firms in their export efforts by permitting them to join forces in their international market development activities. Due to ongoing globalization of production, competition, and supply and demand, it would appear that over time the application of antitrust laws to international marketing activities must be revised to reflect global rather than national dimensions.

Another area in which some governments regulate international marketing actions concerns bribery and corruption. The United States has taken a lead on this issue by passing laws in the sphere of ethics that affect U.S. firms operating overseas. The effects of corrupt practices and governmental intervention on international marketing are explored later in this chapter.

Host Country Legal and Political Environment

The host country environment, both political and legal, affects the international marketing operations of firms in a variety of ways. A good manager will understand the country in which the firm operates so that he or she is able to work within the existing parameters and can anticipate and plan for changes that may occur.

Political Action and Risk

Firms usually prefer to conduct business in a country with a stable and friendly government, but such governments are not always easy to find. Managers must therefore continually monitor the government, its policies, and its stability to determine the potential for political change that could adversely affect corporate operations.

There is political risk in every nation, but the range of risks varies widely from country to country. **Political risk** is defined as the risk of loss when investing in a given country caused by changes in a country's political structure or policies, such as tax laws, tariffs, expropriation of assets, or restriction in repatriation of profits. For example, a company may suffer from such loss in the case of expropriation or tightened foreign exchange repatriation rules, or from increased credit risk if the government changes policies to make it difficult for the company to pay creditors.[11] In general, political risk is lowest in countries that have a history of stability and consistency. Political risk tends to be highest in nations that do not have this sort of history. In a number of countries, however, consistency and stability that were apparent on the surface have been quickly swept away by major popular movements that drew on the bottled-up frustrations of the population. Three major types of political risk can be encountered: **ownership risk**, which exposes property and life; **operating risk**, which refers to interference with the ongoing operations of a firm; and **transfer risk**, which is mainly encountered when attempts are made to shift funds between countries. Political risk can be the result of government action, but it can also be outside the control of government. The types of actions and their effects are classified in Exhibit 5.4.

A major political risk in many countries involves conflict and violent change. A manager will want to think twice before conducting business in a country in which the likelihood of such change is high. To begin with, if conflict breaks out, violence directed toward the firm's property and employees is a strong possibility. Guerrilla warfare, civil disturbances, and terrorism often take an anti-industry bent, making companies and their employees potential targets. Oil workers appear to be especially vulnerable and have frequently been the victims of murder and kidnapping, since some of their operations are located in politically volatile parts of the globe, such as Nigeria, Sudan, and Colombia. For example, in May, 2008, guerrillas in Nigeria's oil-rich Niger delta kidnapped a Chevron transport tanker and its eleven-member crew. Nigeria is Africa's biggest oil-producing nation, but pipeline bombings and attacks against oil workers by militants demanding a bigger share of the profits have reduced output by a quarter over the past ten years.[12]

In many countries, particularly in the developing world, coups d'état can result in drastic changes in government. The new government may attack foreign multinational corporations

Exhibit 5.4

Exposure to Political Risk

Contingencies May Include:	Loss May Be the Result of:	
	The actions of legitimate government authorities	Events caused by factors outside the control of government
The involuntary loss of control over specific assets without adequate compensation	• Total or partial expropriation • Forced divestiture • Confiscation • Cancellation or unfair calling of performance bonds	• War • Revolution • Terrorism • Strikes • Extortion
A reduction in the value of a stream of benefits expected from the foreign-controlled affiliate	• Nonapplicability of "national treatment" • Restriction in access to financial, labor, or material markets • Controls on prices, outputs, or activities • Currency and remittance restrictions • Value-added and export performance requirements	• Nationalistic buyers or suppliers • Threats and disruption to operations by hostile groups • Externally induced financial constraints • Externally imposed limits on imports or exports

SOURCES: José de la Torre and David H. Neckar, "Forecasting Political Risks for International Operations," in H. Vernon-Wortzel and L. Wortzel, *Global Strategic Management: The Essentials,* 2nd ed. (New York: John Wiley and Sons, 1990), 195. Copyright © 1990 John Wiley and Sons. Reprinted by permission of John Wiley and Sons, Inc.

as remnants of the Western-dominated colonial past, as has happened in Cuba, Nicaragua, and Iran. Even if such changes do not represent an immediate physical threat to firms and their employees, they can have drastic effects. The past few decades have seen such coups in the countries of Ghana, Ethiopia, and Venezuela, to name a few. These coups have seriously impeded the conduct of international marketing.

Less dramatic but still worrisome are changes in government policies that are caused not by changes in the government itself but by pressure from nationalist or religious factions or widespread anti-Western feeling. As local businesses become more developed, patriotic feelings can breed new enterprises to compete with global corporations, as *The International Marketplace 5.2* shows. The aware manager will work to anticipate these changes and plan for ways to cope with them.

The International MARKETPLACE

5.2

From Mecca-Cola to Afri-Cola

Coca-Cola Co. and PepsiCo Inc. have long basked in the unbeatable advantage of representing not a drink, but a lifestyle. They connote the American experience not necessarily reflective of everyday U.S. realities, but imagined nonetheless by millions across the globe: one's own house, with a white fence; a car; a swimming pool; a benevolent golden retriever and 1.7 healthy, happy children. An inherent marketing tool these corporations have at their disposal, therefore, is the reputation of the United States as a land of success and as a standard to be imitated.

Lately, however, this reputation has begun to change. Some people connect "Americanism" to exploitation, military aggression, and scandalous MTV programs. One economic response to this reputation shift has occurred in the cola market. Alternative cola companies have sprung up outside the USA, gaining global market share and popularity as they ride the wave of anti-Americanism.

Alternatives to Coke and Pepsi in the Middle East and Central America are not an entirely new phenomenon. Iran's Zamzam Cola, for example, had been Pepsi's partner company until 1979. After the Islamic revolution, Zamzam's contract with Pepsi was terminated, and its operation taken over by a state charity called the Foundation of the Dispossessed, which proceeded to make Zamzam carbonated beverages a staple across the Middle East. However, until recently, such upstarts were not known outside their regions of origin, leaving the firstborn Coca-Cola's global prevalence intact. Now, Zamzam is being sold in nearly every country with a substantial Muslim population, including France, the UK, and Canada.

Although imitator corporations use the idealism of the public in their marketing techniques—making beverages appealing through brand names like Mecca-Cola—they are grounded solidly in reality. Tunisian-born Tawfiq Mathlouthi is a lawyer by profession; outraged by U.S. actions in Iraq, he decided that economic competition was the only

TO FOUNDER MATHLOUTHI, THE ACT OF DRINKING MECCA-COLA IS A PEACEFUL PROTEST.

© CONTENT MINE INTERNATIONAL/ALAMY

meaningful way to protest U.S. policy. Launching Mecca-Cola in Paris in 2002, he found himself expanding the brand to fifty-four countries by 2003. To Mathlouthi, the act of drinking Mecca-Cola in itself is a peaceful protest. His Web site tagline reads: "No drinking stupid. Drink with commitment!"

Inca Kola is another example of the same trend, symbolizing South American resentment of local culture's subversion to "westernization" and "Americanization." Named after an ancient civilization of the region, this drink offers a poignant combination of historic reverence and modern flavor. It is the child of the Corporación Jose R. Lindley S.A. (JR Lindley), a bottler and marketer of soft drinks that launched this creation in Peru in 1935. Inca Kola's introduction resulted in rapid growth. In 2000, a strategic alliance was even formed with the Coca-Cola Group, indicating that the American corporation did not feel able to enter a market already captured by a local provider. Inca Kola continues to hold a lion's market share (26%) in its home country, while retaining an identity and taste distinct from those of its American business partner.

Of course, one must differentiate between a soft-drink alternative, potentially motivated by anti-American sentiments, and one inspired by good old-fashioned profit-seeking and the desire to promote local industry, occasionally with somewhat humorous results. For example, the organizers of the 2007 G8 international summit in Germany banned Pepsi and Coco-Cola from the event. Bewildered journalists and participants were offered Afri-Cola instead. For those unfamiliar with this giant of the global soft drink industry, Afri-Cola is a local soda, bottled in a village near Heiligendamm—the town hosting the summit. It has been around since 1931 and sells approximately 12 million drinks a year. By contrast, Coca-Cola sells about 3.4 billion units annually in Germany alone. When asked about the selection, catering manager Jarste Weuffen said: "It's a regional product and we wanted to plug a local beverage."

SOURCES: "Coca-Cola is canned," *The Sun*, June 9, 2007; Arundhati Parmar, "Drink Politics," *Marketing News,* February 15, 2004; "Inca Kola," *Wikipedia: The Free Encyclopedia,* **http://en.wikipedia .org/wiki/Inca_Kola**, accessed August 27, 2005.

What sort of changes in policy result from the various events described? The range of possible actions is broad. All of them can affect international marketing operations, but not all are equal in weight. We have learned that companies have to fear violence against employees, and that violence against company property is quite common. Also common are changes in policy that take a strong nationalist and antiforeign investment stance. The most drastic steps resulting from such policy changes are usually confiscation and expropriation.

An important governmental action is **expropriation**, which is the seizure of foreign assets by a government with payment of compensation to the owners. Expropriation has appealed to some countries because it demonstrated nationalism and immediately transferred a certain amount of wealth and resources from foreign companies to the host country. It did have costs to the host country, however, to the extent that it made other firms more hesitant to invest in the country. Expropriation does provide compensation to the former owners. However, compensation negotiations are often protracted and result in settlements that are frequently unsatisfactory to the owners. For example, governments may offer compensation in the form of local, nontransferable currency or may base the compensation on the book value of the firm. Even though firms that are expropriated may deplore the low levels of payment obtained, they frequently accept them in the absence of better alternatives.

The use of expropriation as a policy tool has sharply decreased over time. Apparently, governments have come to recognize that the damage inflicted on themselves through expropriation exceeds the benefits.[13]

Confiscation is similar to expropriation in that it results in a transfer of ownership from the foreign firm to the host country. However, its effects are even harsher in that it does not involve compensation for the firm. Some industries are more vulnerable than others to confiscation and expropriation because of their importance to the host country's economy and their lack of ability to shift operations. For this reason, sectors such as mining, energy, public utilities, and banking have been targets of such government actions.

Confiscation and expropriation constitute major political risks for foreign investors. Other government actions, however, are nearly as damaging. Many countries are turning from confiscation and expropriation to more subtle forms of control such as **domestication**. The goal of domestication is the same, to gain control over foreign investment, but the method is different. Through domestication, the government demands partial transfer of ownership and management responsibility and imposes regulations to ensure that a large share of the product is locally produced and a larger share of the profit is retained in the country.

Domestication can have profound effects on the international marketer for a number of reasons. First, if a firm is forced to hire nationals as managers, poor cooperation and communication can result. If the domestication is imposed within a very short time span, corporate operations overseas may have to be headed by poorly trained and inexperienced local managers. Further, domestic content requirements may force a firm to purchase supplies and parts locally, which can result in increased costs, inefficiency, and lower-quality products, thus further damaging a firm's competitiveness. Export requirements imposed on companies may also create havoc for the international distribution plan of a corporation and force it to change or even shut down operations in other countries. Finally, domestication will usually shield the industry within one country from foreign competition. As a result, inefficiencies will be allowed to grow due to a lack of market discipline. In the long run, this will affect the international competitiveness of an operation abroad and may become a major problem when, years later, the removal of domestication is considered by the government.

Most businesses operating abroad face a number of other risks that are less dangerous, but probably more common, than the drastic ones already described. Host governments that face a shortage of foreign currency sometimes will impose controls on the movement of capital in and out of the country. Such controls may make it difficult for a firm to remove its profits or investments from the host country. Sometimes, exchange controls are also levied selectively against certain products or companies in an effort to reduce the importation of goods that are considered to be a luxury or unnecessary. Such regulations are often difficult to deal with because they may affect the importation of parts, components, or supplies that are vital for production operations. Restrictions on such imports may force a firm either to alter its production program or, worse yet, to shut down its entire plant. Prolonged negotiations with government officials may be necessary in order to reach a compromise agreement on what constitutes a "valid" expenditure of foreign currency resources. Because the goals of government officials and corporate managers may often be quite different, such compromises, even when they can be reached, may result in substantial damage to the international marketing operations of a firm.

Countries may also raise the tax rates applied to foreign investors in an effort to control the firms and their capital. On occasion, different or stricter applications of the host country's tax codes are implemented for foreign investors. The rationale for such measures is often an apparent underpayment of taxes by such investors, when comparing their payments to those of long-established domestic competitors. Overlooked is the fact that new investors in foreign lands tend to "**overinvest**" by initially buying more land, space, and equipment than is needed and by spending heavily so that facilities are state-of-the-art. This desire to accommodate future growth and to be highly competitive in the early investment stages will, in turn, produce lower profits and lower tax payments. Yet over time, these investment activities should be very successful, competitive, and job-creating. Selective tax increases for foreign investors may result in much-needed revenue for the coffers of the host country, but they can severely damage the operations of the foreign investors. This damage, in turn, may result in decreased income for the host country in the long run.

The international marketing manager must also worry about **price controls**. In many countries, domestic political pressures can force governments to control the prices of imported products or services, particularly in sectors that are considered to be highly sensitive from a political perspective, such as food or health care. If a foreign firm is involved in these areas, it is a vulnerable target of price controls because the government can play on its people's nationalistic tendencies to enforce the controls. Particularly in countries that suffer from high inflation and frequent devaluations, the international marketer may be forced to choose between shutting down the operation or continuing production at a loss in the hope of recouping that loss once the government chooses to loosen or remove its price restrictions. How a firm can adjust to price controls is discussed in greater detail later in the book.

Managers face political and economic risk whenever they conduct business overseas, but there may be ways to lessen the risk. Obviously, if a new government that is dedicated to the removal of all foreign influences comes into power, a firm can do little. In less extreme cases, however, managers can take actions to reduce the risk if they understand the root causes of the host country policies. Most important is the accumulation and appreciation of factual information about a country's history, political background, and culture before making a long-term investment decision. Also, a high degree of sensitivity by a firm and its employees to country-specific approaches and concerns are important dimensions that help a firm to blend into the local landscape rather than stand out as a foreign object.

Adverse governmental actions are usually the result of a host country's nationalism, desire for independence, and opposition to colonial remnants. If a country's citizens feel exploited by foreign firms, government officials are more likely to take antiforeign action. To reduce the risk of government intervention, a firm needs to demonstrate that it is concerned with the host country's society and that it considers itself an integral part of the host country rather than simply an exploitative foreign corporation. Ways to do this include intensive local hiring and training practices, good pay, philanthropy, and more societally useful investment. In addition, a company can form joint ventures with local partners to demonstrate a willingness to share its benefits with nationals. Although such actions will not guarantee freedom from risk, they will certainly lessen the exposure to it.

Corporations can also protect against political risk by closely monitoring political developments. Increasingly, private-sector firms offer assistance in such monitoring activities, permitting the overseas corporation to discover potential trouble spots as early as possible and react quickly to prevent major losses. Firms can also take out insurance to cover losses due to political risk. Most industrialized countries offer insurance programs for their firms doing business abroad. In Germany, for example, Hermes Kreditanstalt provides exporters with insurance. In the United States, the Overseas Private Investment Corporation (OPIC) can cover three types of risk: currency inconvertibility insurance, which covers the inability to convert profits, debt service, and other remittances from local currency into U.S. dollars; expropriation insurance, which covers the loss of an investment due to expropriation, nationalization, or confiscation by a foreign government; and political violence insurance, which covers the loss of assets or income due to war, revolution, insurrection, or politically motivated civil strife, terrorism, and sabotage. Rates vary by country and industry, but for $100 of coverage per year for a manufacturing project, the base rate is $0.25–0.45 for protection against inconvertibility, $0.50–$0.70 to protect against expropriation, and $0.70–1.10 to protect against political violence.[14] Usually, insurance policies do not cover commercial risks and, in the event of a claim, cover only the actual loss—not lost profits. In the event of a major political upheaval, however, risk insurance can be critical to a firm's survival.

Clearly, the international marketer must consider the likelihood of negative political factors in making decisions on conducting business overseas. On the other hand, host country political and legal systems can have a positive impact on the conduct of international business. Many governments, for example, encourage foreign investments, especially if they believe that the investment will produce economic and political benefits domestically. Some governments have opened up their economy to foreign investors, placing only minimal constraints on them, in the hope that such policies will lead to rapid economic development. Others have provided for substantial subsidization of new investment activities in the hope that investments will generate additional employment. The international marketer, in his or her investment decision, can and should therefore also pay close attention to the extent and forms of incentives available from foreign governments. Although international marketing decisions should be driven by free market forces, these decisions may change if incentives are offered.

In this discussion of the political environment, laws have been mentioned only to the extent that they appear to be the direct result of political changes. However, each nation has laws regarding marketing, and the international manager must understand their effects on the firm's efforts.

Legal Differences and Restraints

Countries differ in their laws as well as in their implementation of these laws. For example, the United States has developed into an increasingly litigious society, in which institutions and individuals are quick to take a case to court. As a result, court battles are often protracted and costly, and simply the threat of a court case can reduce marketing opportunities. In contrast, Japan's legal tradition tends to minimize the role of the law and of lawyers. Some possible reasons include the relatively small number of courts and attorneys; the delays, the costs, and the uncertainties associated with litigation; the limited doctrines of plaintiffs' standing and rights to bring class action suits; the tendency of judges to encourage out-of-court settlements; and the easy availability of arbitration and mediation for dispute resolution.

Some estimates suggest that the number of lawyers in the United States is as much as 48 times higher than in Japan, based on the fact that Japan has only about 23,000 fully licensed lawyers.[15] However, comparisons can be misleading because officially registered lawyers in Japan perform a small fraction of the duties performed by American lawyers. After accounting for the additional roles of American lawyers, the number of "lawyers" in Japan appears to be approximately one-tenth of that in the United States. Different perceptions and legal practices can lead to substantially different approaches to communication and conflict resolution.

Over the millennia of civilization, many different laws and legal systems have emerged. King Hammurabi of Babylon codified a series of judges' decisions into a body of law. Hebrew law was the result of the dictates of God. Legal issues in many African tribes were settled through the verdicts of clansmen. A key legal perspective that survives today is that of **theocracy**, which has faith and belief as its key focus and is a mix of societal, legal, and spiritual guidelines. Examples are Hebrew law and Islamic law (*Shariáh*), which are the result of scripture, prophetic utterances and practices, and scholarly interpretations.[16]

While these legal systems are important to society locally, from an international business perspective the two major legal systems worldwide can be categorized into common law and code law. **Common law** is based on tradition and depends less on written statutes and codes than on precedent and custom. Common law originated in England and is the system of law found today in the United States.

On the other hand, **code law** is based on a comprehensive set of written statutes. Countries with code law try to spell out all possible legal rules explicitly. Code law is based on Roman law and is found in the majority of the nations of the world. In general, countries with the code law system have much more rigid laws than those with the common law system. In the latter, courts adopt precedents and customs to fit the cases, allowing the marketer a better idea of the basic judgment likely to be rendered in new situations.

The International MARKETPLACE
5.3

The Archbishop and the Law

Rowan Williams is the archbishop of Canterbury and the spiritual leader of the approximately 80 million member global Anglican Church. He stirred up some controversy when he examined the role of *Shariáh* in British life. *Shariáh* is the body of Islamic religious law that is based on the Koran, the words and actions of the Prophet Mohammad, and the rulings of Islamic scholars. It typically finds is application mainly in Muslim countries.

The archbishop suggested that, with a population of more than 2 million Muslims in Great Britain, *Shariáh* already figures prominently in the lives of many. For example, informal neighborhood councils provide rulings on family issues such as divorce; banks, such as HSBC, already market mortgages that comply with *Shariáh* rules

of lending. Perhaps Muslims in Britain would be more comfortable and willing to build a more constructive relationship with their fellow citizens if they could choose *Shariáh* law for the settling of civil disputes.

Many commentators, including the British Prime Minister Gordon Brown, strongly opposed such thinking. There was the feeling that such a move would undermine British values and laws and substantially weaken the position of women. Perhaps not since Thomas Becket ran afoul of King Henry II in 1170 was there such controversy surrounding the archbishop and the law.

SOURCES: Karla Adam, "Archbishop Defends Remarks on Islamic Law in Britain," *The Washington Post,* February 12, 2008, A11; "Archbishop of Canterbury: Sharia law unavoidable in Britain," *Christian Today,* February 7, 2008; Matthew Lynn, "Archbishop Williams is Wrong Back Sharia Law," *Bloomberg.Com,* February 28, 2008.

Although wide in theory, the differences between code law and common law and their impact on the international marketer are not always as broad in practice. For example, many common law countries, including the United States, have adopted commercial codes to govern the conduct of business.

Host countries may adopt a number of laws that affect a company's ability to market. To begin with, there can be laws affecting the entry of goods, such as tariffs and quotas. Also in this category are **antidumping laws**, which prohibit below-cost sales of products, and laws that require export and import licensing. In addition, many countries have health and safety standards that may, by design or by accident, restrict the entry of foreign goods. Japan, for example, has particularly strict health standards that affect the import of pharmaceuticals. Rather than accepting test results from other nations, the Japanese government insists on conducting its own tests, which are time consuming and costly. It claims that these tests are necessary to reflect Japanese peculiarities. Yet some importers and their governments see these practices as thinly veiled protectionist barriers.

A growing global controversy surrounds the use of genetic technology. Governments are increasingly devising new rules that affect trade in genetically modified products. For example, Australia introduced a mandatory standard for foods produced using biotechnology, which prohibits the sale of such products unless the food has been assessed by the Australia New Zealand Food Authority.

Other laws may be designed to protect domestic industries and reduce imports. For example, Russia assesses high excise taxes on goods such as cigarettes, automobiles, and alcoholic beverages—and provides a burdensome import licensing and quotas regime for alcohol and products containing alcohol to depress Russian demand for imports. In the case of automobiles, combined tariffs, VAT, and excise duties can increase import prices by 70 percent.[17]

Very specific legislation may also exist to regulate where a firm can advertise or what constitutes deceptive advertising. Many countries prohibit specific claims by marketers comparing their product to that of the competition and restrict the use of promotional devices. Some countries regulate the names of companies or the foreign language content of a product's label. Even when no laws exist, the marketer may be hampered by regulations. For example, in many countries, governments require a firm to join the local chamber of commerce or become a member of the national trade association. These institutions in turn may have internal regulations that set standards for the conduct of business and may be seen as quite confining to the international marketer.

Finally, the enforcement of laws may have a different effect on national and on foreign marketers. For example, the simple requirement that an executive has to stay in a country until a business conflict is resolved may be a major burden for the international marketer.

Influencing Politics and Laws

To succeed in a market, the international marketer needs much more than business know-how. He or she must also deal with the intricacies of national politics and laws. Although a full understanding of another country's legal and political system will rarely be possible, the good manager will be aware of the importance of this system and will work with people who do understand how to operate within the system.

Many areas of politics and law are not immutable. Viewpoints can be modified or even reversed, and new laws can supersede old ones. Therefore, existing political and legal restraints do not always need to be accepted. To achieve change, however, there must be some impetus for it, such as the clamors of a constituency. Otherwise, systemic inertia is likely to allow the status quo to prevail.

The international marketer has various options. One approach may be to simply ignore prevailing rules and expect to get away with it. Pursuing this option is a high-risk strategy because of the possibility of objection and even prosecution. A second, traditional option is to provide input to trade negotiators and expect any problem areas to be resolved in multilateral negotiations. The drawback to this option is, of course, the quite time-consuming process involved.

A third option involves the development of coalitions or constituencies that can motivate legislators and politicians to consider and ultimately implement change. This option can be pursued in various ways. One direction can be the recasting or redefinition of issues. Often, specific **terminology** leads to conditioned but inappropriate responses. For example, before China's accession to the World Trade Organization, the country's trade status with the United States had been highly controversial for many years. The U.S. Congress had to decide annually whether to grant "Most-Favored Nation" (MFN) status to China. The debate on this decision was always very contentious and acerbic and was often framed around the question of why China deserved to be treated the "most favored way." Lost in the debate was the fact that the term "most favored" was simply taken from WTO terminology and indicated only that trade with China would be treated no worse than with any other country. Only when the terminology was changed from MFN to NTR, or "normal trade relations," was the controversy about special treatment eliminated.[18]

Beyond terminology, marketers can also highlight the direct linkages and their cost and benefit to legislators and politicians. For example, the manager can explain the employment and economic effects of certain laws and regulations and demonstrate the benefits of change. The picture can be enlarged by including indirect linkages. For example, suppliers, customers, and distributors can be asked to participate in delineating to decision makers the benefit of change. Such groups can be quite influential. For example, it has been suggested that it was the community of Indian businesses working as information technology suppliers to U.S. firms that exerted substantial pressure on their government to work toward finding a resolution to the Kashmiri conflict. If so, this is an encouraging example of the benefits of globalization.[19]

Developing such coalitions is not an easy task. Companies often seek assistance in effectively influencing the government decision-making process. Such assistance usually is particularly beneficial when narrow economic objectives or single-issue campaigns are needed. Typical providers of this assistance are **lobbyists**. Usually, these are well-connected individuals and firms that can provide access to policymakers and legislators.

Lobbying firms tend to be located in state, national, or regional capitals. Their experience and networks can help in presenting corporate concerns to decision makers. In doing so, new information and insights can be provided to policy makers and decisions can be precipitated more rapidly.

Lobbying is very valuable to the international marketer, as is evidenced by the large number of lobbyists and their high compensation. For example, the number of U.S. lobbyists working on behalf of foreign entities is estimated to be in the thousands. Brazil has held on average nearly a dozen contracts per year with U.S. firms covering trade issues. Brazilian citrus exporters and computer manufacturers have hired legal and public relations firms to provide them with information on relevant legislative activity. The Banco do Brasil lobbied for the restructuring of Brazilian debt and favorable banking regulations.

A key factor in successful lobbying is the involvement of local citizens and companies. Typically, legislators are only willing to take positions on important issues if they are supported by or at least not opposed by their constituents. Therefore, it is important to demonstrate how a particular issue affects a decision maker's domestic constituents. For example, to ward off negative legislation it may be helpful to point out how many jobs are created by a firm's foreign investment, or how export-intensive such an investment can be.

Although representation of the firm's interests to government decision makers and legislators is entirely appropriate, the international marketer must also consider any potential side effects. Major questions can be raised if such representation becomes very strong or is seen as reflecting a conflict of interest. For example, former chancellor Schröder of Germany took on the representation of a Russian pipeline corporation. There was substantial concern about his representing a cause that he had championed and approved as chancellor only months before. There is an unease with revolving door issues involving former policy makers working on behalf of clients who were subject to their previous official decisions, or of lobbyists spending large amounts of money to further their cause. Due to the reality or perception of inappropriateness, some countries have passed legislation that restricts lobbying activities. In the United States, for example, policy makers are limited in the extent of hospitality they can accept, ex-policy makers are barred from approaching their former colleagues for at least one year, and involvement in former decision areas is restricted even longer. It is important to abide by these rules, and to ensure that public perception sees the process as reasonable and fair. Otherwise, short-term gains may be far outweighed by long-term negative repercussions if the international marketer is perceived as exerting too much political influence.

The International Environment

In addition to the politics and laws of both the home and the host countries, the international marketer must consider the overall international political and legal environment. Relations between countries can have a profound impact on firms trying to do business internationally.

International Politics

The effect of politics on international marketing is determined by both the bilateral political relations between home and host countries and the multilateral agreements governing the relations among groups of countries.

The government-to-government relationship can have a profound effect, particularly if it becomes hostile. Numerous examples exist of the linkage between international politics and international marketing. One such example involves British-Icelandic relations, following the Icelandic government's 2008 decision to assume control of three of the country's largest banks hit hard by the global credit crunch. Iceland initiated a deposit freeze that affected deposits of approximately £4.5 billion from British citizens. The British government promptly used its anti-terror law to seize an estimated £4 billion of Icelandic resources, which, in turn, forced Iceland to cover the losses of British depositors at a cost to Icelandic taxpayers of more than £2.2 billion. With a population base of only 300,000 people, such new debt was huge. While the U.K. chose to adopt this "stick" approach, the Dutch government secured a commitment from Iceland to pay back its savers using a different tactic, perhaps more conducive to long-term good neighborly relations. It offered to loan Iceland the money.[20]

A more recent example of government-to-government conflict was presented by the Helms-Burton Act. Passed in response to the shooting down of two unarmed small planes by the Cuban Air Force, this U.S. legislation granted individuals the right to sue, in U.S. courts, subsidiaries of those foreign firms that had invested in properties confiscated by the Cuban government in the 1960s. In addition, managers of these firms were denied entry into the United States. Many U.S. trading partners strongly disagreed with this legislation. In response, Canada proposed suing U.S. firms that had invested in properties taken from royalists in 1776, and the European Union threatened to permit European firms to counter-sue subsidiaries of U.S. firms in Europe and to deny entry permits to U.S. executives. To date, U.S. presidents have signed a waiver that bars enforcement of the Act.

International political relations do not always have harmful effects on international marketers. If bilateral political relations between countries improve, business can benefit. A good example is the thawing of relations between the West and the countries of the former Soviet bloc. Political warming has opened up completely new frontiers for U.S. international marketers in Hungary, Poland, and Russia. Activities such as selling computers, which would have been considered treasonous only a few years ago, are now routine.

The international marketer needs to be aware of political currents worldwide and attempt to anticipate changes in the international political environment, good or bad, so that his or her firm can plan for them. Sometimes, however, management can only wait until the emotional fervor of conflict has subsided and hope that rational governmental negotiations will let cooler heads prevail.

International Law

International law plays an important role in the conduct of international business. Although no enforceable body of international law exists, certain treaties and agreements respected by a number of countries profoundly influence international business operations. As an example, the World Trade Organization (WTO) defines internationally acceptable economic practices for its member nations. Although it does not deal directly with individual firms, it does influence them indirectly by providing a more stable and predictable international market environment.

In addition to multilateral agreements, firms are affected by bilateral treaties and conventions. The United States, for example, has signed bilateral treaties of friendship, commerce, and navigation (FCN) with a wide variety of countries. These agreements generally define the rights of U.S. firms doing business in the host country. They normally guarantee that the U.S. firms will be treated by the host country in the same manner in which domestic firms are treated. Although these treaties provide for some stability, they can be canceled when relationships worsen.

The international legal environment also affects the marketer to the extent that firms must concern themselves with jurisdictional disputes. Because no single body of international law exists, firms usually are restricted by both home and host country laws. If a conflict occurs between contracting parties in two different countries, a question arises concerning which country's laws will be followed. Sometimes the contract will contain a jurisdictional clause, which settles the matter. If not, the parties to the dispute can follow either the laws of the country in which the agreement was made or those of the country in which the contract will have to be fulfilled. Deciding on the laws to be followed and the location to settle the dispute are two different decisions. As a result, a dispute between a U.S. exporter and a French importer could be resolved in Paris with the resolution based on New York State law.

The parties to a business transaction can also choose either arbitration or litigation. Litigation is usually avoided for several reasons. It often involves extensive delays and is very costly. In addition, firms may fear discrimination in foreign countries. Companies therefore tend to prefer conciliation and arbitration because these processes result in much quicker decisions. Arbitration procedures are often spelled out in the original contract and usually provide for an intermediary who is judged to be impartial by both parties. Frequently, intermediaries will be representatives of chambers of commerce, trade associations, or third-country institutions. For example, the rules of the international chamber of commerce in Paris are frequently used for arbitration purposes.

International Terrorism and Marketing

Terrorism is the systematic use (or threat) of violence aimed at attaining a political goal and conveying a political message. International terrorism seeks to do this across national borders.[21] While it has existed for centuries, terrorism's global impact has changed significantly in recent years: improved means of transportation lead to an omnipresence never previously experienced. The rise of terrorist incidents in Western nations, often carried out by foreign nationals, brings terrorism to countries once considered immune. Global mass media, meanwhile, have ensured the visibility of terrorist events, spreading fear and creating irrational expectations of localized attacks.

Terrorists direct their strikes at business far more than any other target.[22] Businesses need to be easily accessible and able to conduct transactions with many new persons every day; this introduces a level of vulnerability that is not typically encountered by government offices. Exhibit 5.5 shows the frequency of terrorist attacks in different geographic regions. Bombings are most common, followed by armed assaults, kidnapping, vandalism, and hijacking.

While always regrettable, terrorism nevertheless creates new opportunities for firms in a few industries like construction, security, and information technology. For most companies, however, terrorism results in reduced revenues or increased costs, and managers must prepare for this. Terrorists intend to affect supply and demand in order to shatter existing economic systems; this brings about both direct and indirect effects. The direct consequences to business are the immediate costs levied on individual firms. While harm is clear to individual firms, from a societal perspective, the direct effects tend to be less consequential than the indirect ones. The latter accumulate over time, and are often not apparent immediately.

Exhibit **5.5**

Patterns of Global Terrorism

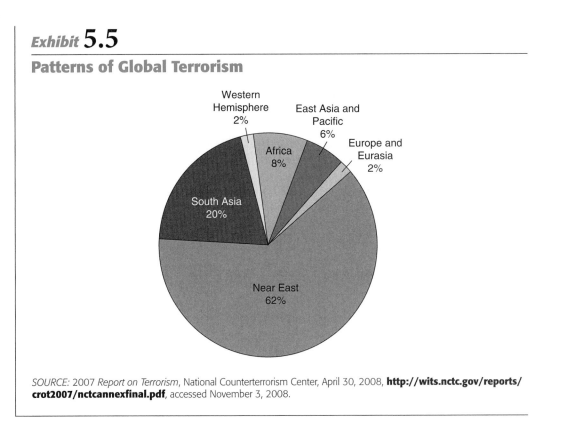

SOURCE: 2007 *Report on Terrorism*, National Counterterrorism Center, April 30, 2008, **http://wits.nctc.gov/reports/crot2007/nctcannexfinal.pdf**, accessed November 3, 2008.

The indirect negative consequences of terrorism begin with macroeconomic phenomena, such as the real or perceived decline in per-capita income, purchasing power, and stock market values. In the wake of a terror event, these trends cause a fall in the subjective (perceived) security of the nation. Buyers become uncertain about the state of their nation's economy, and a sharp reduction in demand for both consumer and industrial goods follows—a phenomenon which we call the **chill effect**.

A further effect on enterprises may be the failures in power, communication, transport, and other infrastructure due to actual physical damage incurred at the terrorists' hands. Indirectly, this leads to unpredictable shifts and interruption in the supply of inputs, resources, and services. Finally, international terrorism often causes tension between the countries whose citizens or property is involved; the deterioration of transnational relationships can affect foreign buyer and seller attitudes, and thus the marketing activities of firms doing business abroad.

One key side-effect of terrorism can be the government policies and laws it brings about. In order to make a country less vulnerable, politicians often enact restrictions on the business environment. New regulations in customs clearance may delay the supply of inputs, increase the administrative burden, and require firms to invest in new procedures. Transaction costs generally increase, and the commercial environment may be altered in ways that are more harmful to business than the terrorist attack itself might have been. For example, stricter regulations and increased security measures in the United States, following 9/11, have generated large losses in cross-border trade and tourism.

From a global perspective, these effects are present for many firms, even those that are geographically remote from any location directly affected by terrorism. Today's climate of global commerce involves countless interactions with customers and distributors; producers and marketers often rely on entire networks of diverse suppliers. Such exposure to a variety of actors leaves firms vulnerable to events that take place nearby as well as at a distance. Even firms perceived as having little international involvement may depend on the receipt of imported goods, and therefore risk experiencing shortages or delays of input if economies abroad are disrupted.

In the wake of a terrorist event, physical damage must be undone, security arrangements enhanced, and risk premiums reassessed. In order to do this effectively, an enterprise must establish its priorities, quantify risk, and outline response scenarios ahead of an actual attack. It is important to note that in today's global climate, firms must aim for more than mere survival. Instead, businesses must offer assured continuity to stakeholders. Flexibility to withstand shock, as well as the continuity of existing business relationships, must be the principal goal of any global firm. In addition to being economically necessary, persistent business activity is a major step in denying terrorists their goals.[23] Exhibit 5.6 shows a model of corporate preparedness for terrorist attack.

There are several obstacles to successful corporate strategy in mitigating terrorism. The first lies in frequent mistakes of global management: Managers of foreign subsidiaries may shunt any terrorism concerns to headquarters. At the same time, executives at headquarters often frame terrorism only in local terms and look to local managers for tackling possible repercussions. As a result, costs incurred from growing precautionary measures cannot be defrayed efficiently throughout the enterprise, and wholesale closure of international operations may follow.

In addition, terrorist risk is difficult to assess in an integrated global economy. If supply chains are complex and multinational, the effects of terrorism can potentially spread across the globe from an initially local focus. For most firms, the costs of averting terrorism are hard to quantify and even harder to justify to key stakeholders. In an era when the mandates of the Sarbanes-Oxley Act (see upcoming section on Corporate Governance) are straining corporate budgets, top executives put a greater premium on meeting financial performance benchmarks than on addressing vague political risks.

Exhibit 5.6

A Model of Corporate Preparedness for Terrorism

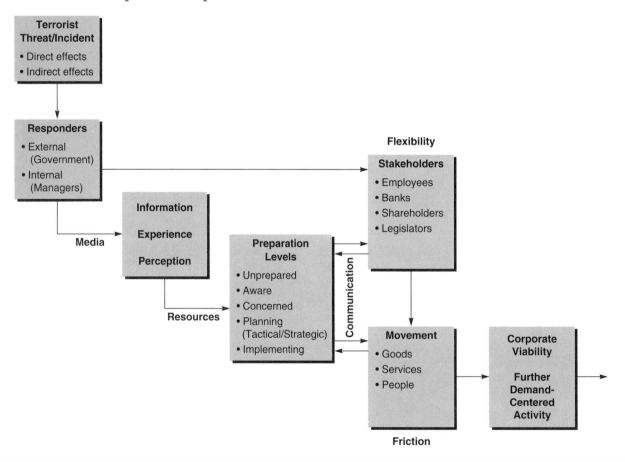

An important consideration is that individual assessment of vulnerability changes based on individual information, experience, and perception of an event. Over time, these impressions shift, resulting in potentially faulty managerial decisions. Ironically, the greater the tragedy, the more likely people are to discount it as an aberration, once confidence is restored and normal activities are resumed. Widespread underestimation of the likelihood of future recurrences results. Managers are therefore tempted to rest comfortably in the belief that any future attack will not affect their company and not lead to widespread personal repercussions.

Over time, terrorism will increasingly influence the evaluation and selection of markets, particularly those located abroad. Thus far, for instance, developing nations have proven to be most vulnerable to economic and consumption downturns following terror events.

In a volatile world, marketing managers are the frontline response to business disruption. Although all corporate areas are likely to be affected by terrorist activity, the marketing field, which constitutes a key liaison with the world outside the firm, is likely to be under the most pressure. Marketers deal specifically with the activities of supply and demand that terrorists aim to destroy, and are thus confronted with terrorism on a daily basis. Devising new distribution and logistics avenues in the case of attack, responding with pricing strategies to market dislocations, and communicating the firm's position to buyers and suppliers are all marketing activities.[24]

In some cases, marketers may choose to pursue a strategy of working with customer segments less sensitive to terrorism. For instance, in the months following September 11th, marketers in the hotel industry focused their selling efforts on regional rather than national or international business. Oftentimes, sales are perceived to be safer in domestic and thus familiar markets. However, staying domestic is becoming difficult as a long-term strategy in our increasingly globalized world.

Marketers tend to have the clearest understanding of the mutual corporate dependence so critical for effective planning. For example, when determining the need for specific emergency inputs, marketers will not only look for the source of such inputs. They will also be able to analyze the existing relationships and networks, and devise incentives to ensure that the supplier will actually provide goods and services to the firm. Dry runs and simulations can then be used by marketers to develop expectations about long-term effects and to see whether the system works as planned. Without such considerations, a plan for input contingency is akin to identifying the location of gas stations as the principal remedy for a fuel shortage, without keeping in mind that the stations need to be resupplied to stay open, and need to be willing to provide the gasoline for a client pulling in.

On the supply side, marketers deal with communication with customers and suppliers, devise campaigns to present information, provide direction, and alter any misperceptions. Marketers are the experts who implement steps to address imbalances and create new incentives by changing corporate pricing, packaging, or sizing. Goods or services whose price is strongly affected by changing information flows and perceptions of risk are highly susceptible to the indirect consequences of terrorism. Insurance coverage is an example. Actual or perceived terrorist threats tend to create upward pressure on the pricing of particularly vulnerable offerings. Prices may also experience a certain "stickiness," that is, under conditions of inability to predict the occurrence of terrorism or its indirect effects, once raised, prices may not be decreased. Conversely, firms in certain industries may feel pressure to lower prices in order to induce reluctant buyers to maintain or increase their buying activities. Through their actions, marketers can reverse an emerging softness in demand, rally joint responses, and avoid the occurrence of unintended consequences. With their understanding of the long-term repercussions of terrorism, marketers can also be instrumental in formulating alternative corporate strategies, for example, the shift from an investment-based foreign market expansion to an export-based one.

The continuing efforts of marketers to understand cultural issues are also highly useful for devising terminology and persuasive encouragement. Studies tell us that there are major cultural differences between and even within nations. International marketing, through its linkages via goods, services, ideas, and communications, can achieve important assimilations of value systems. Marketers know that culture and values are learned, not genetically implanted. As life's experiences grow more international and more similar, so do values. Therefore, every time international marketing forges a new linkage in thinking and provides for new exchanges of goods or services, new progress is made in shaping a greater global commonality in values. It may well be that international marketing's ability to align global values, and the subsequent greater ease of countries, companies, and individuals to build bridges among themselves, may eventually become the field's greatest gift to the world.[25]

Ethical Issues

Corporate governance, responsibility, intellectual property rights, and corruption all fall under the ethical obligations experienced by multinational enterprises today. Whether following the most ethical route in business dealings matters in the long run is, in many ways, a difficult question. Historically, the answer has depended on the environment and outcomes. Nineteenth century textile mills in the United States, for instance, flagrantly violated today's standards for workers' rights (including living wages, maximum weekly working hours, and safe working conditions). However, they did much to move U.S. industrialization forward. It was a fire in one such mill in New York—in which 146 workers died because employers had locked all the exits from the factory—that spurred safety drives by U.S. labor unions. Similarly, the credit conflagration that started in the United States in 2007 provoked considerable global public debate and legislation concerning responsible and ethical lending practices and banking oversight.

Today, one issue concerning corporate ethics is the divide between the "first world" and less-developed countries. Should emerging economies follow the same course experienced by the United States and Europe in their industrial history? Or should they be aided and, on occasion, forced by developed nations to skip the mishaps of the Western experience, and industrialize under more stringent modern-day standards?

Restrictions may hinder progress by excessively curbing business practices with ethical requirements. In addition, corporate practices are far from perfect in the world's most advanced countries themselves. Some even claim that a focus on ethics is a thin disguise for protectionism. Finally, globalization raises an interesting concern: When investing abroad, should firms from a developed country with stringent ethical laws be allowed to use looser local principles to their advantage?

The following sections may shed some light on the nature, focus, and concerns of the ethical dimension in modern-day businesses abroad.

Corporate Governance and Responsibility

The relationships among stakeholders that determine and control the strategic direction and performance of an organization are called **corporate governance**.[26] A system of corporate governance must be established to ensure that decisions are made and interests are represented properly for all stakeholders. The structure, conduct, and methods used in the assessment of company behavior vary dramatically across countries. Key elements of corporate governance, however, remain the transparency of a firm's operations, its financial results, and the principles by which it measures sales, expenses, assets, and liabilities.

For some, the overriding objective of corporate governance is to optimize returns to shareholders over time. In order to achieve this, good governance practices focus the attention of the company's board of directors on strategies that ensure corporate growth and increase equity value. In addition, corporate governance frameworks typically protect shareholder rights and ensure their equitable treatment, provide for timely and accurate disclosure of all the company's material matters, and ensure the board of directors' accountability to the company and its shareholders.

Others interpret corporate governance as dealing with stakeholders (such as employees, customers, banks, etc.) who are affected by corporate decisions. For them, the providers of capital are only one of various constituencies to satisfy.

Exhibit **5.7**

Comparative Corporate Governance Regimes

Regime Basis	Characteristics	Examples
Market-based	Efficient equity markets; Dispersed ownership	United States, United Kingdom, Canada, Australia
Family-based	Management & ownership is combined; Family/majority and minority shareholders	Hong Kong, Indonesia, Malaysia, Singapore, Taiwan, France
Bank-based	Government influence in bank lending; Lack of transparency; Family control	Korea, Germany
Government affiliated	State ownership of enterprise; Lack of transparency; No minority influence	China, Russia

SOURCE: Based on J. Tsui and T. Shieh, "Corporate Governance in Emerging Markets: An Asian Perspective," in *International Finance and Accounting Handbook,* 3rd ed., Frederick D. S. Choi, ed. (Hoboken, NJ: Wiley, 2004), 24.4–24.6.

The separation of ownership from management, and the various cultural views on stakeholders' identity and significance, all affect corporate governance and lead to different practices across countries, economies, and cultures. Exhibit 5.7 illustrates variants of corporate governance structures classified by regime and ownership. The major factors driving global corporate governance principles and practices are financial market development, the degree of separation between management and ownership, and transparency.

Proponents of a market-based regime emphasize the benefit of forces that result from interplaying supply and demand. Price signals adjust activities instead of government intervention, and create an environment of respect for profitability and private property. In exchange for the chance to derive proceeds, investors allocate resources to the most productive and efficient uses. In order for such allocations to take place, however, trust must exist between managers and investors. In return for their financial inputs, managers must provide stakeholders with their best efforts to secure gains on the supplied capital.

In this sense, managers can be seen as marketing their corporate virtue, vision, and potential for economic gain to potential investors. It is therefore of vital interest to them that bribery, corruption, and obscurity be eliminated, allowing relationships of trust and commitment to be forged between firms and individual sources of money.[27] This takes on additional importance as investment experiences globalization. Transparency must reign not only within a country, but also across borders to foreign business partners.

As firms become increasingly multinational, governments respond by increasing global cooperation to achieve the same principles of taxation and corporate ethics laws across nations. This serves to slowly eliminate tax issues like the shifting of income from high-into low-tax countries, or the shielding of income from taxation by holding profits in tax havens.

Aside from responsibility to stakeholders, corporations are often expected to fulfill certain obligations and exhibit conscientious behavior toward the societies in which they operate. Such obligations often include environmental safety and efficiency, reasonable working conditions and wages, and concerns about layoffs, healthcare, and family care. The European Union has surpassed most of the world in both cultural friendliness to and actual implementation of such programs. In 1995, the president of the European Commission joined with leading European companies to found CSR Europe, a business network aimed at helping companies integrate corporate social responsibility (CSR) with daily business practices. Meanwhile, *The International Marketplace 5.4* shows that environmental concerns are often important not only for ethical, but also for practical, reasons.

The International MARKETPLACE

ENVIRONMENT & SUSTAINABILITY

5.4

Does Pollution Matter?

Economic development in China leads to numerous benefits, like a rise in GDP and popular welfare levels. However, it has also caused significant environmental challenges. To fuel its rapid industrialization, China consumes record amounts of coal as it builds new factories and energy plants. It has become the world's second largest emitter of greenhouse gases; in the next ten years, it is even expected to surpass the United States, which holds first place.

This may seem like a concern mainly for the Chinese government and for international environmental protection agencies. However, lately the destruction of China's ecosystem has become a threat for multinational corporations as well. A lack of transparent laws concerning the environment has caused instability in the local workforce. The latter, in turn, creates uncertainty about the future and increases the risk faced by any multinational enterprise wishing to enter a developing market. Recent events in rural Huaxi, China, have presented an example.

Factories in Huaxi not only emit dangerous substances into the air, but also discharge harmful chemicals into local water systems. The pollution of waterways, in turn, threatens both the health and lifestyle of local farmers: crops grown with contaminated irrigation become substandard in quality and low in quantity. Local officials, meanwhile, can be bribed into turning a blind eye to polluters to spur economic growth. Such laxity on their part could be viewed as an opportunity for foreign companies: they could now utilize China's resources

and cheap labor force without the limits and costs of environmental protection. However, the local populace is increasingly unwilling to live with the environmental decision. A staged sit-in by farmers from Huaxi villages in front of a new factory led to clashes with the police. Yet the persistence of the farmers helped them win, and persuaded the local government to close the factory.

Although the factory in Huaxi belonged to the Chinese government, a multinational firm's manufacturing facility could potentially meet with the same fate. If local interests are capable of manipulating regulations, a multinational's production facility could easily be closed. A sudden change in laws (or their implementation) could threaten the entire input supply structure of an international company, particularly if its international subsidiaries depend on each other for resources and inputs.

Is it therefore better that an international corporation come into China with stricter environmental laws than those existent in China itself? Should a firm adopt the local culture (including bribing) to be more in tune with local customs? Huaxi proves that even with government support corporations are vulnerable to the concerns of other stakeholders.

SOURCES: Emily Rauhala, "The Richest Reds in China," *Time*, April 4, 2008, **http://www.time.com/time/world/article/0.8599,1728126,00.html**, accessed November 17, 2008; Edward Cody, "For Chinese, Peasant Revolt Is Rare Victory," *Washington Post*, June 13, 2005, **www.washingtonpost.com/wp-dyn/content/article/2005/06/12/AR2005061201531.html**, accessed January 15, 2006; Cindy Sui, "China's Economic Development Creating Dire Consequences on Environment," **http://www.petroleumworld.com/story05060305.htm**, accessed January 15, 2006.

Intellectual Property

The development of a new product or technique by a corporation can be a lucrative endeavor, opening the door to a variety of benefits, such as a larger customer base, increased market share, or a reduction in production costs. However, innovation is also a vulnerable process. Statistics regarding the survival rates of new businesses vary from source to source; however, the probability for a new enterprise to fail in the first three years of existence can be as high as 85%.[28] This makes it important that an enterprise be able to recoup its investments into new products, including its research and development costs. However, competitors can make this more difficult if they are able to copy the innovation, thereby reducing the originator's market share and ability to profit. Finally, as "copycat" enterprises often try to beat the originator through lower prices, they wind up producing inferior products.

The term **intellectual property (IP)** refers to a legal entitlement of exclusive rights to use an idea, piece of knowledge, or invention. The subject of such legal claims must be a product of the mind—an intangible, but potentially profitable form of property. In the past, intellectual property laws were usually territorial, meaning that the registration and enforcement of rights to certain knowledge had to be pursued separately in each country. Recently, however, IP laws have become increasingly harmonized across nations. TRIPs, or the WTO *Agreement on Trade-Related Aspects of Intellectual Property Rights,* was a significant step in this direction. Adopted in 1994, it introduced intellectual property law into the international trade system for the first time; included were minimum standards for copyrights, appellations of geographic origin, industrial designs, trademarks, and even trade secrets. Unlike other international agreements on the subject, TRIPS has powerful enforcement mechanisms (like trade sanctions) at its disposal. Its requirements apply equally to all WTO member states; developing countries are given more time to implement necessary changes. However, the act's fairness with regards to developing nations and their ability to patent is frequently contested.

Intellectual property is of key concern to various industries. For several years, the European Union had struggled to reach a consensus regarding online music copyright laws—something it was finally able to achieve in July of 2008. Up to that point, music rights were sold separately in each European country, effectively preventing online music retailers, such as iTunes, from setting up a single service store for all of Europe. Instead, separate licenses had to be obtained from each member state, forcing iTunes to make considerable adjustments for each market in Europe. The change in regulations removes a major obstacle to iTunes' expansion. Not everybody is excited about the possibility of a pan-European music market. Some artists have protested that selling music rights across the EU might reduce their royalties. They have threatened to boycott the reform by refusing to allow their work to be played. More than 220 singers, musicians, and composers, including the Bee Gees' Robin Gibb, Sade, Julio Iglesias, and Mark Knopfler, have signed a petition stating that pan-European music licensing will stifle creativity.[29]

Another, more ethically charged issue with intellectual property rights is the availability of medicine. Many life-saving vaccines and remedies were initially developed by private enterprises; examples include the AIDS cocktail and Tamiflu (today's only birdflu-fighting drug). The issue, then, is whether a corporation ought to retain all rights to manufacture the drug, even in times when its supply cannot satisfy world demand, or when its prices are too high for those who need its product. Most patent laws permit, for a limited period of time, a corporation to refuse the manufacture of generic versions for its product. This provides it with the benefit of monopolizing an indispensable commodity.

Multinational corporations have been criticized for exercising this right particularly in the case of the AIDS cocktail, given the numbers and the typical poverty of those infected with the disease. Cipla, India's third largest drug company, is one of many third-world producers who has offered to make the cocktail at a "humanitarian price"—one significantly lower than that negotiated by the UN for impoverished African countries. However, three large multinationals (one British, one German, and one American) hold the patents for the drugs involved. In South Africa, the country with the largest number of HIV infections, the firms have filed lawsuits against local generic producers of the cocktail. However, in light of mounting public outrage, they were forced to drop the lawsuits in order to extricate themselves from what had become a large-scale PR morass. An unidentified drug company representative reportedly said: "People ask me, how we could have been so stupid as to sue Nelson Mandela?"[30]

Bribery and Corruption

In many countries, payments or favors are a way of life, and a "greasing of the wheels" is expected in return for government services. In the past, many U.S. companies doing business internationally routinely paid bribes or did favors for foreign officials in order to gain contracts. In the 1970s, major national debates erupted over these business practices, led by arguments that U.S. firms should provide ethical and moral leadership, and that contracts won through bribes do not reflect competitive market activity. As a result, the Foreign Corrupt Practices Act (FCPA) was passed in 1977, making it a crime for U.S. firms to bribe foreign officials for business purposes.

A number of U.S. firms have complained about the act, arguing that it hinders their efforts to compete internationally against companies from countries that have no such antibribery laws. In-depth research supports this claim by indicating that in the years after the antibribery legislation was enacted, U.S. business activity in those countries in which government officials routinely received bribes declined significantly.[31] The problem is one of ethics versus practical needs and, to some extent, of the amounts involved. For example, it may be difficult to draw the line between providing a generous tip and paying a bribe in order to speed up a business transaction. Many business managers argue that one country should not apply its moral principles to other societies and cultures in which bribery and corruption are endemic. If they are to compete internationally, these managers argue, they must be free to use the most common methods of competition in the host country. Particularly in industries that face limited or even shrinking markets, such stiff competition forces firms to find any edge possible to obtain a contract.

On the other hand, applying different standards to management and firms, depending on whether they do business abroad or domestically, is difficult to envision. Also, bribes may open the way for shoddy performance and loose moral standards among managers and employees and may result in a spreading of generally unethical business practices. Unrestricted bribery could result in a concentration on how best to bribe rather than on how best to produce and market products.

The international manager must carefully distinguish between reasonable ways of doing business internationally—including compliance with foreign expectations—and outright bribery and corruption. To assist the manager in this task, revisions were made in the 1988 Trade Act to clarify the applicability of the Foreign Corrupt Practices legislation. These revisions clarify when a manager is expected to know about violation of the act, and a distinction is drawn between the facilitation of routine governmental actions and governmental policy decisions. Routine actions concern issues such as obtaining permits and licenses, processing governmental papers such as visas and work orders, providing mail and phone service, and loading and unloading cargo. Policy decisions refer mainly to situations in which obtaining or retaining contracts is at stake. One researcher differentiates between **functional lubrication** and individual greed. With regard to functional lubrication, he reports the "express fee" charged in many countries, which has several characteristics: the amount is small, it is standardized, and it does not stay in the hands of the official who receives it but is passed on to others involved in the processing of the documents. The express service is available to anyone, with few exceptions. By contrast, in the process driven by "individual greed," the amount depends on the individual official and is for the official's own personal use.[32] Although the facilitation of routine actions is not prohibited, the illegal influencing of policy decisions can result in the imposition of severe fines and penalties.

The issue of global bribery has taken on new momentum. In 1995, the Organization of American States (OAS) (**http://www.oas.org**) officially condemned bribery. The Organization for Economic Cooperation and Development (OECD) (**http://www.oecd.org**) in 1999 agreed to change the bribery regulations among its member countries not only to prohibit the tax deductibility of improper payments, but to prohibit such payments altogether. Similarly, the World Trade Organization has, for the first time, decided to consider placing bribery rules on its agenda. A good portion of this progress can be attributed to the public work done by Transparency International (TI). This nonprofit organization regularly publishes information about the perception of corruption in countries around the globe. In addition, TI also reports on countries whose firms are most and least likely to offer bribes—as shown in Exhibit 5.8.

In 2002, U.S. President George W. Bush signed into law the **Sarbanes-Oxley Act**, intended to protect investors by improving the accuracy and reliability of corporate disclosures. The act covers issues like corporate responsibility, financial transparency, and accounting oversight. Major provisions include the certification of financial reports by CEOs and CFOs, and a requirement for publicly traded companies to furnish annual reports on the reliability of their internal financial reporting structures. This was considered a highly significant change to U.S. security laws.

However, there are questions regarding the law's effectiveness and the cost-benefit rationale for compliance. Some estimate that the cost of being a publicly-traded company

Exhibit 5.8

Corruption Perception Index*

Least Corrupt			Most Corrupt		
Rank	**Country**	**CPI Score**	**Rank**	**Country**	**CPI Score**
1	Denmark	9.3	180	Somalia	1.0
1	New Zealand	9.3	178	Myanmar	1.3
1	Sweden	9.3	178	Iraq	1.3
4	Singapore	9.2	177	Haiti	1.4
5	Finland	9.0	176	Afghanistan	1.5
5	Switzerland	9.0	173	Sudan	1.6
7	Iceland	8.9	173	Guinea	1.6
7	Netherlands	8.9	173	Chad	1.6
9	Australia	8.7	171	Equatorial Guinea	1.7
9	Canada	8.7	171	Congo, (DRC)	1.7

*A country's Corruption Perception Index shows the degree of corruption perceived by business people and country analysts. Possible scores range from 10 (very clean) to 0 (highly corrupt). The top ten least corrupt and most corrupt countries are shown above, along with their world ranks and CPI scores.

SOURCE: *Corruption Perception Index 2008,* Dr. J. Graf for Transparency International, University of Passau, Germany, **http://www.transparency.org**, accessed November 2, 2008.

doubled within a few months of the law's enactment, from $1.3 million to $2.5 million. Business leaders have also expressed concerns about disclosing too much information to the competition.[33]

However, the act seems to be effective in changing the way companies operate in the developing world—a fortunate and unexpected side-effect of a law targeting domestic business relations. By requiring corporate directors and CEOs to personally certify their companies' internal controls, and by making executives who provide false certifications criminally liable, the law inadvertently led to the emergence of an entire industry of global compliance auditors. These auditors are effective in finding the "offshore intermediaries" that help companies to sidestep the 1977 Foreign Corrupt Practices Act (which prohibited payoffs to foreign officials). The result has been a sharp increase in the number of companies cleaning up their overseas procedures and self-reporting illegal payments overseas.

A major issue that is critical for international marketers is that of general standards of behavior and ethics. Increasingly, public concerns are raised about such issues as global warming, pollution, and moral behavior. However, these issues are not of the same importance in every country. What may be frowned on or even illegal in one nation may be customary or at least acceptable in others. For example, cutting down the Brazilian rain forest may be acceptable to the government of Brazil, but scientists, concerned consumers, and environmentalists may object vehemently because of the effect of global warming and other climatic changes. The export of U.S. tobacco products may be legal but results in accusations of exporting death to developing nations. China may use prison labor in producing products for export, but U.S. law prohibits the importation of such products. Mexico may permit the use of low safety standards for workers, but the buyers of Mexican products may object to the resulting dangers. In the area of moral behavior, firms are increasingly not just subject to government rules, but are also held accountable by the public at large. For example, issues such as child labor, inappropriately low wages, or the running of sweat shops are raised by concerned individuals and communicated to customers. Firms can then be subject to public scorn, consumer boycotts, and investor scrutiny if their actions are seen as reprehensible, and run the danger of losing much more money than they gained by engaging in such practices.

Summary

The political and legal environment in the home country, the environment in the host country, and the laws and agreements governing relationships among nations are all important to the international marketer. Compliance with them is mandatory in order to do business abroad successfully. Such laws can control exports and imports both directly and indirectly and can also regulate the international business behavior of firms, particularly in the areas of boycotts, antitrust, corruption, and ethics.

To avoid the problems that can result from changes in the political and legal environment, the international marketer must anticipate changes and develop strategies for coping with them. Whenever possible, the manager must avoid being taken by surprise and thus not let events control business decisions.

On occasion, the international marketer may be caught between clashing home and host country laws. In such instances, the firm needs to conduct a dialogue with the governments in order to seek a compromise solution. Alternatively, managers can encourage their government to engage in government-to-government negotiations to settle the dispute. By demonstrating the business volume at stake and the employment that may be lost through such governmental disputes, government negotiators can often be motivated to press hard for a settlement of such intergovernmental difficulties. Finally, the firm can seek redress in court. Such international legal action, however, may be quite slow and, even if resulting in a favorable judgment for the firm, may not be adhered to by the government against which the judgment is rendered.

In the final analysis, a firm conducting business internationally is subject to the vagaries of political and legal changes and may lose business as a result. The best the manager can do is to be aware of political influences and laws and strive to adopt them as far as possible.

Key Terms

Environmental Superfund	downstream change	common law
intellectual property rights	boycotts	code law
gray market	political risk	antidumping laws
trade sanctions	ownership risk	terminology
embargoes	operating risk	lobbyists
export control systems	transfer risk	chill effect
dual-use items	expropriation	corporate governance
export license	confiscation	intellectual property
foreign availability	domestication	functional lubrication
tariffs	overinvest	Sarbanes-Oxley Act
voluntary restraint agreements	price controls	
quota systems	theocracy	

Questions for Discussion

1. Discuss this statement: "High political risk requires companies to seek a quick payback on their investments. Striving for such a quick payback, however, exposes firms to charges of exploitation and results in increased political risk."

2. How appropriate is it for governments to help drum up business for their companies abroad? Should commerce be completely separate from politics?

3. Discuss this statement: "The national security that export control laws seek to protect may be threatened by the resulting lack of international competitiveness of firms."

4. After you hand your passport to the immigration officer in country X, he misplaces it. A small "donation" would certainly help him find it again. Should you give him money? Is this a business expense to be charged to your company? Should it be tax deductible?

5. Discuss the advantages and disadvantages of common versus code law for the international marketer.

6. The United States has been described as a "litigious" society. How does frequent litigation affect the international marketer, particularly in comparison with the situation in other countries?

7. What are your views on lobbying efforts by foreign firms?

8. Discuss how changes in technology have affected the effectiveness of U.S. export control policy.

Internet Exercises

1. Summarize the U.S. export licensing policy toward Cuba. (Go to http://www.bis.doc.gov.)

2. What are the key components of the anticorruption agreements passed by the European Union, the Organization of American States, and the United Nations? (Go to http://www.oecd.org/ or http://www.transparency.org.)

Recomended Readings

Annual Report on the OECD Guidelines for Multinational Enterprises 2007: Corporate Responsibility in the Financial Sector, Paris: Organization for Economic Cooperation and Development, 2008.

Askari, Hossein, John Forrer, Hildy Teegan, and Jiawen Yang. *Economic Sanctions: Examining Their Philosophy and Efficacy.* Westport, CT: Praeger Publishers, 2004.

Brigadier General USA (Ret) Russell Howard, Reid Sawyer, Natasha Bajema, *Terrorism and Counterterrorism: Understanding the New Security Environment, Readings and Interpretations,* McGraw-Hill/Dushkin; 3rd edition, 2008.

Hirschhorn, Eric. The Export Control Embargo Handbook, 2nd ed. New York: Oceana, 2005.

Hufbauer, Gary C., Jeffrey J. Schott, Kimberly Ann Elliott and Barbara Oegg, *Economic Sanctions Reconsidered,* 3rd ed. (Washington, DC: Peterson Institute, May 30, 2008).

Lambsdorff, Johann Graf, *The Institutional Economics of Corruption and Reform: Theory, Evidence and Policy,* Cambridge University Press, 2008.

U.S. Department of Commerce, Bureau of Industry Security, *Annual Report 2007,* available online at: http://www.bis.doc.gov/news/2008/annreport07/bis_annual_report07.pdf.

CHINA: FORGING A GLOBAL REPUTATION

The 2008 Summer Olympics Games, with the motto "One World, One Dream," was a testament by China that it was capable of hosting the world's grandest athletic event despite western criticism of its one-party communist government. The world watched in excitement as athletes set new world records and accomplished amazing physical feats. China had developed a new identity as a more hospitable and accommodating country. However, positive views of the Olympics found counterbalance in two major scandals. The first occurred in 2007 when Chinese manufacturers were found to have used lead paint in the production of many children's toys. The 2008 Beijing Games helped ease the tension created by this issue. However, the second major scandal, dubbed the 2008 Chinese milk scandal, nearly eclipsed the gains China had made earlier that summer.

Lead Paint in Chinese Manufactured Toys

In early August of 2007, Fisher-Price issued a recall of approximately 967,000 toys in the U.S.[1] The recall came after the Mattel subsidiary learned that the paint used in some toys manufactured between April and July of 2007 was contaminated by lead. Mattel later would recall an additional 9.5 million toys in the U.S. and 11 million in other countries throughout the world. This larger recall was issued after it was found that lead paint was used in toys manufactured from May of 2003 to November of 2007.[2] Among the recalled items were the classic Sesame Street toys and Barbie dolls.

Companies such as RC2 Corp (famous for its Thomas & Friends toy line), Hasbro (known for its Easy-Bake Ovens), and Marvel all required recalls due to the use of lead in paint. The underlying issue for all four companies was a lack of quality-control testing. In Mattel's case, its primary manufacturer, Lee Der Industrial, had contracted out toy painting to another company. Although not the company that used lead paint, Lee Der neglected to conduct quality-control testing even though it was capable of doing so.

Lead paint is commonly used in China because it lowers costs. Chinese factories claim that rising demands to cut costs by American companies such as Mattel have forced manufactures to turn to cheaper substitutes such as leaded paint. Lead paint cuts costs to nearly a third of what costs would be if unleaded paint was used.[3] Moreover, China has copious amounts of industrial paint that contain high levels of lead. Because it is easy to obtain excess industrial paint, toy factories often use it.[4] The drive to reduce costs has resulted in insufficient funding for testing and other measures to ensure quality control.[5]

The Chinese government responded with relatively severe punishments by banning some toy manufacturers from exporting their products. Lee Der and RC2 Corp's manufacturer Hansheng Wood Products were among those no longer permitted to export their manufactured toys.[6] Several other toy factories also were shut down for knowingly using lead paint.[7] And the Chinese government arrested and imposed harsh prison sentences on factory managers and business executives. This was done in order to reassure consumers that quality control in China is a primary concern. The increasing pressure by the government to admit responsibility for these problems and fix them have had drastic impacts; for example, the owner of Lee Der Industrial committed suicide in August 2007 shortly after the major recalls were announced.[8]

Chinese law is tougher than U.S. law in its regulations for paint. While the U.S. allows for 600 ppm of lead in paint, Chinese law allows for only 90 ppm.[9] Recall testing showed some manufactured toys were in clear violation of both regulations. These recalls and quality control violations led the U.S. to change its toy import policies. The U.S. Congress has established new testing standards to ensure quality.[10] Many toy stores in the U.S. and around the world pulled toys made in China off their shelves in order to ensure consumer safety.

These toy recalls also set off a shockwave through the worldwide toy industry. Toy manufacturers all over the world, particularly in Southeast Asia, were subjected to quality control testing. Further testing discovered that many other countries, not just China, were in violation of quality regulations.[11]

Many experts predict, however, that these recalls will not have any long term effect on Chinese toy exports. U.S. Toy Industry Association President Carter Keithley

SOURCE: This case study was written by Professor Michael Czinkota and Kenneth Adam Krupa, student of the Edmund A. Walsh School of Foreign Service at Georgetown University.

Exhibit **1**

NEWS from CPSC

U.S. Consumer Product Safety Commission

Office of Information and Public Affairs   **Washington, DC 20207**

FOR IMMEDIATE RELEASE	**Firms Recall Hotline: (800) 916-4498**
August 2, 2007	CPSC Recall Hotline: (800) 638-2772
Release #07-257	CPSC Media Contact: (301) 504-7908

Fisher-Price Recalls Licensed Character Toys Due To Lead Poisoning Hazard

WASHINGTON, D.C.—The U.S. Consumer Product Safety Commission, in cooperation with the firms named below, today announced a voluntary recall of the following consumer product. Consumers should stop using recalled products immediately unless otherwise instructed.

Name of Product: Sesame Street, Dora the Explorer, and other children's toys

Units: About 967,000

Importer: Fisher-Price Inc., of East Aurora, N.Y.

Hazard: Surface paints on the toys could contain excessive levels of lead. Lead is toxic if ingested by young children and can cause adverse health effects.

Incidents/Injuries: None reported.

Description: The recalled involves various figures and toys that were manufactured between April 19, 2007 and July 6, 2007 and were sold alone or as part of sets. The model names and product numbers for the recalled toys, which are all marked with "Fisher-Price," are listed below. The toys may have a date code between 109-7LF and 187-7LF marked on the product or packaging.

Sold at: Retail stores nationwide from May 2007 through August 2007 for between $5 and $40.

Manufactured in: China

Remedy: Consumers should immediately take the recalled toys away from children and contact Fisher-Price. Consumers will need to return the product and will receive a voucher for a replacement toy of the consumer's choice (up to the value of the returned product).

Consumer Contact: For additional information contact Fisher-Price at (800) 916-4498 anytime or visit the firm's Web site at *www.service.mattel.com*

Product List:

---

said that only 0.3 percent of toys imported to the U.S. from China were contaminated.[12] Given that 80 percent of American toys are imported from China,[13] U.S. toy importers are not likely to shift from Chinese export suppliers. Chinese toy exports are unlikely to falter for the same reason that led to lead paint being used: costs. From that perspective, China remains one of the few countries in the world where the costs for mass producing toys remains reasonable.[14]

Tainted Milk

One year after the toy recalls, the Beijing Olympics came and went. Chinese export quality control violations, however, persist. Allegations of poor standards arose in the dairy industry. Chinese baby formula producers had used an additive known as melamine in their products. Melamine was added in order to increase the protein count in watered-down milk. Like the use of lead paint, milk was watered down in China because of costs. Small-scale consumption of melamine is not usually harmful, but prolonged exposure may cause kidney stones and possibly even kidney failure, ultimately resulting in death.

Although the issue gained international notoriety only after the Olympics, the first sick infants were taken to Chinese hospitals in the beginning of the summer of 2008. Parents were quick to discover that the problem was with the baby formula. A few parents even lobbied their local governments to help pressure the dairy companies to take action to help sick infants and prevent further illness. Parents received little help and babies continued to consume contaminated milk. Most of the tainted baby formula emanated from the diary producer Sanlu.

By December of 2008, six deaths and nearly 300,000 ill infants were attributed to the contaminated milk powder found in baby formulas. The government again responded with relatively severe punishments. Many factories and stores were closed after it was discovered that they were responsible for manufacturing and distributing the contaminated milk products. In addition, many food regulatory officials were dismissed.[15]

China's food quality control received stark criticism because the baby formula debacle was not the first melamine scandal in Chinese consumables. A similar problem occurred in 2007 when pet food was also found to contain melamine. Pet food was recalled in the U.S. after many household animals became sick. Although the vast majority of infant deaths and illnesses were in China and not spread worldwide as in the pet food incident, the world still responded with its own measures to insure quality control and consumer safety. The U.S. Food and Drug Administration started its own quality control initiatives in China for the first time.[16] Moreover, the European Union prohibited Chinese dairy imports altogether and increased quality control testing of other imports.[17] International corporations also installed measures to protect consumers. In September 2008, Starbucks China cut ties with its dairy supplier Mengniu and shifted to using soy as a short-term solution.[18] In October 2008, Wal-Mart started enforcing new regulatory standards to insure the quality of its products.[19]

The Chinese government was also blasted for reports that it had always known about this problem and did not act. Many dairy farmers in China claim that it was well known their products were often watered down and needed additives to pass nutrition testing. However, bribery kept farmers from calling attention to this practice.[20]

The Chinese Government has come under further scrutiny after reports that it forbade media reporting on the incident. It stressed the importance of masking national problems in order to promote the Olympics and improve its international image. Analysts speculate that this incident and the cover-up spearheaded by the Chinese government are examples of the China Communist Party's corruption and inability to maintain quality control over its export industry.[21]

What to Do Next?

China's quality-control testing remains an issue, despite these two export scandals.[22] However, America has continued to rely on China for production of low-cost goods. Even after the lead paint incident, Chinese exports to the United States grew by double digits in 2007. Imports to the EU from China increased by nearly 30 percent in 2007.[23]

The demand for low cost, high-quality products has left many corporations with few production locations to choose from. While some companies, specifically in Europe, continue production at home, few in other countries are capable of doing so. The lower production costs in China have made it an attractive country to produce in. Some analysts argue that the world will continue to rely on China as the major supplier of manufactured goods since recalls will not drive away investors or companies. China will only be watched until it has established an internationally suitable quality control standard.[24]

Questions for Discussion

1.   Can consumer goods from China be trusted?

2.   How can retailers ensure that their products are safe?

3.   Has increased globalization increased product risk?

THE CATFISH DISPUTE

The U.S. Catfish Industry

The cultivation of water plants and animals for human use started thousands of years ago. Globally, aquaculture's growth more than doubled in the 1990s (to more than 35 million tons a year). To meet the demand for improved quality protein sources, scallops, oysters, salmon, and catfish are being raised in controlled environments. Farm-raised fish is of high quality and, unlike ocean-caught fish, is available all year long.

U.S. aquaculture production has grown more than 49 percent since 1991.[1] Aquaculture is the fastest growing segment of agriculture in the United States. Farmed seafood makes up about a third of the seafood consumed in the United States. About two thirds of the shrimp and salmon and almost all of the catfish and trout consumed by Americans is raised in ponds.[2]

Thick-skinned, whiskered, wide-mouthed wild catfish can be found in the wild in channels and rivers of the southern United States Wild catfish is typically described as pungent, bony, and muddy. However, as a result of aquaculture technology, catfish is now an economical farm-raised species that tastes mild. Catfish are raised in clay-based ponds filled with fresh water pumped from underground wells. They are fed an enriched, high-protein grain-based food. Their firm, white flesh can convey strong flavors and stands up to a variety of cooking techniques, which makes it suit virtually any ethnic cuisine.[3]

Americans consumed about 275 million kilograms (more than 600 million pounds) of catfish in 2000,[4] most of which came from 150,000 acres of catfish ponds in the United States, mainly located in Mississippi, Arkansas, and Louisiana. The U.S. catfish industry is estimated to turn over $4 billion worth of fish product a year. Catfish is especially popular in Southern dishes, but its use has been growing also in the Midwest. Filets are now available in New York supermarkets and fish stores. One recent poll placed catfish as the country's third favorite seafood, beaten only by shrimp and lobster.[5]

The Issue

The United States is a leading market for Vietnamese catfish (followed by Hong Kong, the EU, and Australia). In 2001 the United States produced 270.5 million kilograms (597 million pounds) and imported about 3.7 million kilograms (8.2 million pounds) of catfish out of which ninety percent, about 3.2 million kilograms (7 million pounds), came from Vietnam. By the end of 2001 prices for U.S. catfish had dropped to 50 cents a pound, about 15 cents below the cost of production and about 30 cents below the price of 2000. U.S. producers blamed the Vietnamese for the falling prices.[6]

Vietnamese catfish exporters and importers in turn blame U.S. producers for dragging down prices. They say that the Americans are mainly at fault for expanding inventories up to 30 percent, a figure obtained from the National Agricultural Statistics Service (**http://www. usda.gov/nass**). Vietnamese fish importers also claim that American catfish growers are to blame for their own difficulties because they sell the domestic fish in only a few states. "It is the failure to adequately market the product effectively throughout the United States," says Andrew Forman, president of Boston-based Infinity Seafood, LLC. According to a report by Consulting Trends International, a California-based consulting firm, the price drop is "primarily the result of higher domestic catfish inventories in the United States, which will depress prices through the end of 2001 and 2002."

The American catfish industry tripled in size from 1985 to 2001. Hugh Warren, vice president of the Catfish Institute of America, says that this growth was strictly due to the industry's marketing effort of $50 million. He feels that importers get a free ride.[7] The U.S. industry offers 15,000 jobs that earn $8 an hour in the poorest parts of America. These jobs are being "stolen" by cheap Vietnamese imports.[8]

The U.S.-Vietnam Bilateral Trade Agreement (BTA), approved by Congress, was signed by the two countries on July 13, 2000. The BTA, signed by President George W. Bush in 2001, opened the door for increased bilateral trade. In the very first year, trade between the two countries doubled. The BTA reduction in tariffs resulted in an increase from 5 million pounds of frozen fillets in 1999 to 34 million pounds in 2002—capturing 20 percent of the U.S. market.

One major exception to the framework of the BTA is the lack of a formal and neutral dispute settlement mechanism. The BTA provides for a "Joint Committee on Development of Economic and Trade Relations." The Committee is given the power to serve as a forum for consultation over problems regarding the agreement.

In an attempt to change this situation, American catfish farmers, industry associations, and supporting organizations came to Washington to call on officials at the State Department, the Commerce Department, the Food and Drug Administration, and Congress for help. They waged an advertising campaign against their Vietnamese competitors in order to convince the public that Vietnamese catfish is low quality and raised in dirty waters.[9]

SOURCE: This case was written by Professors Michael R. Czinkota and Thomas B. Cooke, Georgetown University McDonough School of Business, assisted by graduate student Armen S. Hovhannisyan, Georgetown University School of Foreign Service.

Congressional Reaction: The Labeling Dispute

The support from Congress was swift. In December 2001 an amendment was added to an appropriations bill that barred the Food and Drug Administration (FDA) from spending money "to allow admission of fish or fish products labeled in whole or in part with the term 'catfish' unless the fish is from the *Ictaluridae* family." The senators from the South, who introduced a labeling bill, claimed Vietnamese fish to be as different scientifically from catfish "as cow from a yak."[10] Supporting a different view, Senator Phil Gramm (R-TX) characterized the Vietnamese catfish as follows: "Not only does it look like a catfish, but it acts like a catfish. And the people who make a living in fish science call it a catfish. Why do we want to call it anything other than a catfish?"[11] This meant that the FDA needed to identify different kinds of catfish.

In January 2002, under Congress' direction, the Food and Drug Administration (FDA) published "Guidance for Industry" regulations on how the imported fish should be labeled. Under the regulation, Flat Whiskered Fish is an acceptable substitute for Flat Whiskered Catfish; but Katfish or Cat Fish are not. Instead, importers, restaurants, and grocery stores will have to use a name such as "basa," which is another name to call catfish from the *Pangasius* (*Pangasiidae*) family. The 2002 U.S. Farm Act prohibited non-*ictaluridae* fish from being marketed and sold as "catfish" in the U.S.

While U.S. catfish producers were counting on the labeling decision to decrease sales of Vietnamese catfish, the result was just the opposite, as sales of Vietnamese "basa" or "tra" actually increased. It seemed that the term "basa" had a special marketplace intrigue to it.

The amendment and the regulation were not good news for a number of concerned players (restaurants, consumers, and people in the catfish industry). An article appearing in *The Far Eastern Economic Review* (December 6, 2001) noted that declining prices in the U.S. caused U.S. catfish producers to report a 30 percent (2001–02) decline in the average earnings from a kilogram of catfish. As the owner of Piazza's Seafood World, a New Orleans based importer, put it: "Nobody in the U.S. owns the word 'catfish.'"[12] However, Vietnam was still free to export catfish to the U.S., as long as it was called something other than catfish—that is, until the special tariffs arrived.

When Is a Catfish a Catfish?

In order to identify different kinds of catfish, the FDA sought expert help on the question. Before promulgating its regulation, it consulted Dr. Carl J. Ferraris of the ichthyology department at the California Academy of Sciences. Dr. Ferraris's response was that there was no scientific justification to treat or rename catfish from Vietnam differently than that of the United States.[13]

According to U.S. catfish farmers, the only true catfish belongs to the family with the Latin name *Ictaluridae*. The Vietnamese variety is in the family *Pangasiidae,* which are "freshwater catfishes of Africa and southern Asia." Vietnamese catfish farmers claim that they have created a new agricultural industry, turning their rice and soybean fields into profitable fish farms in the poor regions of the country. By giving up crops, they gave up heavy use of chemical fertilizers and pesticides, which is good for the environment. They also gave up agriculture subsidies at a time when lawmakers wanted to get the government out of farming.[14]

U.S. catfish farmers say their catfish is raised in purified water ponds, which have to be tested by federal agencies and meet the standards of the Catfish Institute. The U.S. catfish industry must go through inspections from 17 federal agencies (including the Department of Commerce, the Food and Drug Administration, and the Environmental Protection Agency). By contrast, the Vietnamese imports have only to meet FDA approval.[15] The Vietnamese catfish are raised in cages that float in marshes in the Mekong River; some of the senators from the South talk about the possibility of toxins from Vietnam in that "dirty" river.[16]

Department of Commerce and International Trade Commission

Less than a year after winning the Congressional labeling regulation, the Catfish Farmers of America (CFA) applied to the U.S. government for additional protection. It seems that the labeling decision was not having the desired result. By this time the Vietnamese share of the U.S. market had actually dropped to 12 percent. But that 12 percent was seen as continuing to drive down the cost (and profits) of catfish in the United States. The request to the International Trade Commission (ITC) was for import tariffs as high as 191 percent.

In addressing the anti-dumping complaint from the CFA, the Department of Commerce (DOC) relied on certain necessary assumptions. In assuming that Vietnam was a non-market economy (and not looking at the Vietnamese seafood industry separately), the DOC used data from India and Bangladesh to establish what would be a "fair price" for Vietnam's exports of catfish to the United States. The initial decision of the DOC was to impose tariffs ranging from 38 percent to 64 percent on four Vietnamese exporters. The subsequent step was for the ITC to confirm the DOC's actions.

In February 2003, Vietnam halted exports of catfish to the U.S. At the time of the announcement, prices of Vietnamese catfish had increased by more than 20 percent in the U.S. market. Nguyen Huu Dung, General Secretary of the Vietnamese Association of Seafood Exporters and Producers (VASEP) noted that "we are forced to stop exporting frozen catfish fillets because our U.S. importers cannot afford to pay the high tariffs."

Vietnamese seafood businesses and producers were quick to denounce the actions of the DOC. The Vietnam Ministry of Trade, Ministry of Fisheries, and VASEP called the actions an "act of protectionism." Rather than wait for the ITC to confirm the decision of the DOC, VASEP offered to resolve the dispute by voluntarily offering an export quota in lieu of tariffs. The offer to settle fell on deaf ears in the United States and the ITC imposed tariffs of up to 64 percent on "basa" or "tra." The ITC's final vote on July 23, 2003 was 4-0.

An editorial appearing in *The New York Times* (July 26, 2003) condemned the action of the ITC by referring to the decision as "a final flourish of hypocrisy to its efforts to crush the Vietnamese catfish industry under a mountain of protectionism." In an earlier editorial (July 22) the publication noted that any decision upholding tariffs would make Vietnam become "yet another case study in the way the United States, Europe, and Japan are rigging global trade rules so they remain the only winners."

The Issue and Free Trade

Vietnam's catfish industry provides a useful example of how global cooperation can enhance participation in global business. An Australian importer, for example, taught the Vietnamese how to fillet catfish, French researchers worked with a local university on low-cost breeding techniques, and Vietnam's leading catfish exporters depended on industrial equipment from the United States.[17] However, a stumbling U.S. economy has made American farmers, along with many others in a number of industries, very sensitive to surging imports,

and the catfish dispute represents a case of domestic politics' alignment against free market forces.[18] Critics in both Vietnam and the United States say that the catfish issue is an example of protectionism and hypocrisy, undermining the free-trade policies most recently espoused by the United States at the World Trade Organization talks in Doha.

"After spending years encouraging the Vietnamese that open trade is a win-win situation, it would be a shame if immediately after the trade agreement is signed the U.S. shifts to a protectionist 'we win, you lose' approach on catfish," says Virginia Foote, president of the US–Vietnam Trade Council in Washington.[19]

In the ongoing dispute over how to manage global trade, agriculture and its cousin aquaculture are very sensitive issues. Industrial nations use farm policy not only to promote their agribusinesses overseas but also to protect their markets and farmers at home. European countries have used their agricultural subsidies to defend their countryside from urban invasion, whereas developing countries try to raise their standard of living by breaking into those markets with less expensive products.

Questions for Discussion

1. Was it fair for the Vietnamese catfish importers to step in and capture market share while the market has been expanded due to the significant efforts and investments of the domestic industry? How should quality considerations (if quality differences exist) be reconciled?

2. The label regulation would probably make consumers pay a higher price than they would have paid otherwise. Is this right?

3. Can any industry in the United States influence lawmakers to take decisions in their favor?

IKEA

IKEA, the world's largest home furnishings retail chain, was founded in Sweden in 1943 as a mail-order company and opened its first showroom ten years later. From its headquarters in Almhult, IKEA has since expanded to worldwide sales of $27 billion from 253 outlets in 37 countries (see Exhibit 1). In fact, the second store that IKEA built was in Oslo, Norway. Today, IKEA operates large warehouse showrooms in Sweden, Norway, Denmark, Holland, France, Belgium, Germany, Switzerland, Austria, Canada, the United States, Saudi Arabia, and the United Kingdom. It has smaller stores in Kuwait, Australia, Hong Kong, Singapore, the Canary Islands, and Iceland. A store near Budapest, Hungary, opened in 1990, followed by outlets in Poland, the Czech Republic, and the United Arab Emirates in 1991 and Slovakia in 1992, followed by Taiwan in 1994, Finland and Malaysia in 1996, and mainland China in 1998. IKEA first appeared on the Internet in 1997 with the World Wide Living Room Web site. The first store in Russia opened in March of 2000 and in Greece and Israel in 2001. Turkey was added in 2005. Five stores have been opened in Japan after 2006. The IKEA Group's new organization has three regions: Europe, North America, and Asia and Australia.

The international expansion of IKEA has progressed in three phases, all of them continuing at the present time: Scandinavian expansion, begun in 1963; West European expansion, begun in 1973; and North American expansion, begun in 1976. Of the individual markets, Germany is the largest, accounting for 15 percent, followed by the U.S. at 10 percent of company sales. The phases of expansion are detectable in the worldwide sales shares depicted in Exhibit 2. "We want to bring the IKEA concept to as many people as possible," IKEA officials have said. The company estimates that over 1.25 million people visit its showrooms daily. Similarly, IKEA websites attract 450 million visitors per year.

The IKEA Concept

Ingvar Kamprad, the founder, formulated as IKEA's mission to "offer a wide variety of home furnishings of good design and function at prices so low that the majority of people can afford to buy them." The principal target market of IKEA, which is similar across countries and regions in which IKEA has a presence, is composed of people who are young, highly educated, liberal in their cultural values, white-collar workers, and not especially concerned with status symbols.

IKEA follows a standardized product strategy with a universally accepted assortment around the world. Today, IKEA carries an assortment of thousands of different home furnishings that range from plants to pots, sofas to soup spoons, and wine glasses to wallpaper. The smaller items are carried to complement the bigger ones. IKEA has limited manufacturing of its own but designs all of its furniture. The network of subcontracted manufacturers numbers nearly 1,300 in over 53 countries. The top five purchasing countries are China (21 percent), Poland (17 percent), Italy (8 percent), Sweden (6 percent), and Germany (6 percent).

IKEA's strategy is based on cost leadership secured by contract manufacturers, many of whom are in low-labor-cost countries and close to raw materials, yet accessible to logistics links. Extreme care is taken to match manufacturers with products. Ski makers—experts in bent wood—have been contracted to make armchairs, and producers of supermarket carts have been contracted for durable sofas. High-volume production of standardized items allows for significant economies of scale. In exchange for long-term contracts, leased equipment, and technical support from IKEA, the suppliers manufacture exclusively at low prices for IKEA. IKEA's designers work with the suppliers to build savings-generating features into the production and products from the outset. If sales continue at the forecasted rate, by 2010 IKEA will need to source twice as much material as today. Since Russia is a major source of lumber, IKEA aims to turn it into a major supplier of finished products in the future.

IKEA has acquired some of its own production capacity in the last few years, constituting 10 percent of its total sales. While new facilities were opened in 2000 in Latvia, Poland, and Romania to bring the total number to 30, IKEA plans to have its own production not exceed 10 percent, mainly to secure flexibility.

SOURCES: This case, prepared by Ilkka A. Ronkainen, is based on "First IKEA Furniture Manufacturing Facility to open in Danville," *Reuters* April 30, 2008; Kerry Capell, "How a Swedish Retailer Became a Global Cult Brand," *Business Week*, November 14, 2005, 96–106; "Create IKEA. Make Billions, Take Bus," *Fortune*, May 3, 2004, 44; Lisa Margonelli, "How IKEA Designs Its Sexy Price Tags," *Business 2.0*, October 2002, 108; "Furnishing the World," *Economist*, November 19, 1994, 79; Richard Norman and Rafael Ramirez, "From Value Chain to Value Constellation: Designing Interactive Strategy," *Harvard Business Review* 71 (July/August 1993): 65–77; "IKEA's No-Frills Strategy Extends to Management Style," *Business International*, May 18, 1992, 149–150;

Bill Saporito, "IKEA's Got 'Em Lining Up," *Fortune*, March 11, 1991, 72; Rita Martenson, "Is Standardization of Marketing Feasible in Culture-Bound Industries? A European Case Study," *International Marketing Review* 4 (Autumn 1987): 7–17; Eleanor Johnson Tracy, "Shopping Swedish Style Comes to the U.S.," *Fortune*, January 27, 1986, 63–67; Mary Krienke, "IKEA—Simple Good Taste," *Stores*, April 1986, 58; Jennifer Lin, "IKEA's U.S. Translation," *Stores*, April 1986, 63; "Furniture Chain Has a Global View," *Advertising Age*, October 26, 1987, 58; Bill Kelley, "The New Wave from Europe," *Sales & Marketing Management*, November 1987, 46–48. Updated information available from **http://www.ikea.com**.

Exhibit 1

IKEA's International Expansion

Catalog Year	Outlets[a]	Countries[a]	Coworkers[a]	Circulation	Turnover
1954	1	1	15	285,000	3,000,000[c]
1964	2	2	250	1,200,000	79,000,000[c]
1974	10	5	1,500	13,000,000	616,000,000[c]
1984	66	17	8,300	45,000,000	6,770,000,000[c]
1990	95	23	16,850	n.a.	19,400,000,000[c]
1995	131	27	30,500	n.a.	4,000,000,000[d]
2002	175	32	65,000	110,000,000[b]	11,000,000,000[d]
2005	226	33	90,000	160,000,000[b]	15,212,000,000[d]
2008	253	37	127,800	200,000,000[b]	21,200,000,000[d]

[a]Stores/countries being opened by 2008.
[b]Estimate.
[c]In Swedish crowns.
[d]In Euro.

SOURCE: IKEA U.S., Inc.

Exhibit 2

IKEA's Worldwide Sales Expressed as Percentages of Turnover by Market Unit

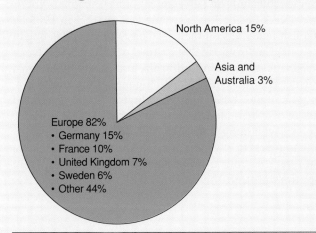

North America 15%

Asia and Australia 3%

Europe 82%
• Germany 15%
• France 10%
• United Kingdom 7%
• Sweden 6%
• Other 44%

Manufacturers are responsible for shipping the components to large distribution centers, for example, to the central one in Almhult. These twelve distribution centers then supply the various stores, which are in effect miniwarehouses.

IKEA consumers have to become "prosumers"—half producers, half consumers—because most products have to be assembled. The final distribution is the customer's responsibility as well. Although IKEA expects its customers to be active participants in the buy-sell process, it is not rigid about it. There is a "moving boundary" between what consumers do for themselves and what IKEA employees will do for them. Consumers save the most by driving to the warehouses themselves, putting the boxes on the trolley, loading them into their cars, driving home, and assembling the furniture. Yet IKEA can arrange to provide these services at an extra charge. For example, IKEA cooperates with car rental companies to offer vans and small trucks at reasonable rates for customers needing delivery service. Additional economies are reaped from the size of the IKEA outlets; the blue-and-yellow buildings average 300,000 square feet (28,000 square meters) in size. IKEA stores include baby-sitting areas and cafeterias and are therefore intended to provide the value-seeking, car-borne consumer with a complete shopping destination. IKEA managers state that their competitors are not other furniture outlets but all attractions vying for the consumers' free time. By not selling through dealers, the company hears directly from its customers.

Management believes that its designer-to-user relationship affords an unusual degree of adaptive fit. IKEA has "forced both customers and suppliers to think about value in a new way in which customers are also suppliers (of time, labor information, and transportation), suppliers are also customers (of IKEA's business and technical services), and IKEA itself is not so much a retailer as the central star in a constellation of services." Exhibit 3 provides a presentation of IKEA's value chain.

Although IKEA has concentrated on company-owned, larger-scale outlets, franchising has been used in areas in which the market is relatively small or where uncertainty may exist as to the response to the IKEA concept. These markets include Hong Kong and the United Arab Emirates. IKEA uses mail order in Europe and Canada but has resisted expansion into the United States, mainly because of capacity constraints.

Exhibit 3

IKEA's Value Chain

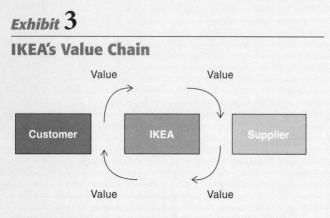

SOURCE: Richard Norman and Rafael Ramirez, "From Value Chain to Value Constellation: Designing Interactive Strategy," *Harvard Business Review* 71 (July/August 1993): 72.

IKEA offers prices that are 30 to 50 percent lower than fully assembled competing products. This is a result of large-quantity purchasing, low-cost logistics, store location in suburban areas, and the do-it-yourself approach to marketing. IKEA's prices do vary from market to market, largely because of fluctuations in exchange rates and differences in taxation regimes, but price positioning is kept as standardized as possible. IKEA's operating margins of approximately 10 percent are among the best in home furnishings (as compared to 5 percent at U.S. competitor Pier l Imports and 7.7 percent at Target). This profit level has been maintained while the company has cut prices steadily. For example, the Klippan sofa's price has decreased by 40 percent since 1999.

IKEA's promotion is centered on the catalog. The IKEA catalog is printed in 52 editions in 27 languages and has a worldwide circulation of 200 million copies. The catalogs are uniform in layout except for minor regional differences. The company's advertising goal is to generate word-of-mouth publicity through innovative approaches. The IKEA concept is summarized in Exhibit 4.

IKEA in the Competitive Environment

IKEA's strategic positioning is unique. As Exhibit 5 illustrates, few furniture retailers anywhere have engaged in long-term planning or achieved scale economies in production. European furniture retailers, especially those in Sweden, Switzerland, Germany, and Austria, are much smaller than IKEA. Even when companies have joined forces as buying groups, their heterogeneous operations have made it difficult for them to achieve the same degree of coordination and concentration as IKEA. Because customers are usually content to wait for the delivery of furniture, retailers have not been forced to take purchasing risks.

The value-added dimension differentiates IKEA from its competition. IKEA offers limited customer assistance but creates opportunities for consumers to choose (for example, through informational signage), transport, and assemble units of furniture. The best summary of the competitive situation was provided by a manager at another firm: "We can't do what IKEA does, and IKEA doesn't want to do what we do."

IKEA in the United States

After careful study and assessment of its Canadian experience, IKEA decided to enter the U.S. market in 1985 by establishing outlets on the East Coast and, in 1990, one in Burbank, California. In 2008, a total of 37 stores (twelve in the Northeast, eight in California, and others in Arizona, Florida, Georgia, Illinois, Michigan, Minnesota, Ohio, Oregon, Texas, Utah, and Washington State) generated sales of over $4 billion. The stores employ 13,000 workers. The overwhelming level of success in 1987 led the company to invest in a warehousing facility near Philadelphia that receives goods from Sweden as well as directly from suppliers around the world. Plans call for five to six

Exhibit 4

The IKEA Concept

Target Market:	"Young people of all ages"
Product:	IKEA offers the same products, which are distinctively Swedish/Scandinavian in design, worldwide. The number of active articles is 9,500. Each store carries a selection of these 9,500, depending on outlet size. The core range is the same worldwide. Most items have to be assembled by the customer. The furniture design is modern and light.
Distribution:	IKEA has built its own distribution network. Outlets are outside the city limits of major metropolitan areas. Products are not delivered, but IKEA cooperates with car rental companies that offer small trucks. IKEA offers mail order in Europe and Canada.
Pricing:	The IKEA concept is based on low price. The firm tries to keep its price-image constant.
Promotion:	IKEA's promotional efforts are mainly through its catalogs. IKEA has developed a prototype communications model that must be followed by all stores. Its advertising is attention-getting and provocative. Media choices vary by market.

Exhibit 5

Competition in Furniture Retailing

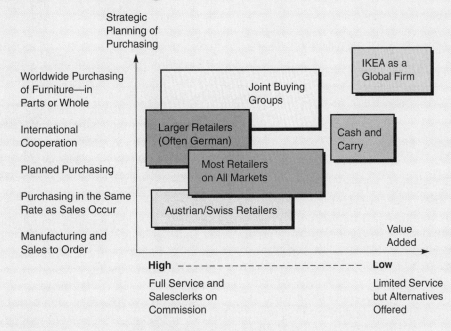

SOURCE: Rita Martenson, "Is Standardization of Marketing Feasible in Culture-Bound Industries? A European Case Study," *International Marketing Review* 4 (Autumn 1987): 14.

additional stores annually over the next 25 years, concentrating on the northeastern United States and California. The goal is 50 U.S. outlets by 2010. IKEA's first U.S. manufacturing operation opened in 2008 in Virginia.

Success today has not come without compromises. "If you are going to be the world's best furnishing company, you have to show you can succeed in America, because there is so much to learn here," said Goran Carstedt, head of North American operations. Whereas IKEA's universal approach had worked well in Europe, the U.S. market proved to be different. In some cases, European products conflicted with American tastes and preferences. For example, IKEA did not sell matching bedroom suites that consumers wanted. Kitchen cupboards were too narrow for the large dinner plates needed for pizza. Some Americans were buying IKEA's flower vases for glasses.

Adaptations were made. IKEA managers adjusted chest drawers to be an inch or two deeper because consumers wanted to store sweaters in them. Sales of chests increased immediately by 40 percent. In all, IKEA has redesigned approximately a fifth of its product range in North America. Today, 45 percent of the furniture in the stores in North America is produced locally, up from 15 percent in the early 1990s. In addition to not having to pay expensive freight costs from Europe, this has also helped to cut stock-outs. And because Americans hate standing in lines, store layouts have been changed to accommodate new cash registers. IKEA offers a more generous return policy in North America than in Europe, as well as next-day delivery service.

In hindsight, IKEA executives are saying they "behaved like exporters, which meant not really being in the country.... It took us time to learn this." IKEA's adaptation has not meant destroying its original formula. Their approach is still to market the streamlined and contemporary Scandinavian style to North America by carrying a universally accepted product range but with a mind on product lines and features that appeal to local preferences. The North American experience has caused the company to start remixing its formula elsewhere as well. Indeed, now that Europeans are adopting some American furnishing concepts (such as sleeper sofas), IKEA is transferring some American concepts to other markets such as Europe.

Questions for Discussion

1. What has allowed IKEA to be successful with a relatively standardized product and product line in a business with strong cultural influence? Did adaptations to this strategy in the North American market constitute a defeat to its approach?

2. Which features of the "young people of all ages" are universal and can be exploited by a global/regional strategy?

3. Is IKEA destined to succeed everywhere it cares to establish itself?

CAR FINANCING IN CHINA

In China, car financing is a lot like the unification of North and South Korea. Just about everyone wants it to happen. But before that can happen, first you need to sweep away the landmines.

—Mike Dunne, *Automotive News*

China and the WTO

After 15 years of negotiations, China formally became a member of the World Trade Organization (WTO) on December 11, 2001. During this time China had been gradually liberalizing most of its trade and investment policies, making the official admission largely symbolic. More than anything, WTO membership signals China's commitment to establish clear and enforceable nondiscriminatory rules to conduct business in and with the country. For example, China's trademark and copyright laws were brought in line with international standards in October 2001. In a similar fashion, many companies established their strategies in the 1990s based on the assumption that China would gain entry into the WTO and are now ready to execute those plans.

Given China's unwillingness to show progress on political reform, the commitment to structural economic reforms has been particularly noteworthy. A constitutional amendment in 1999 legitimized private capital and granted private firms the same legal rights as state-owned enterprises, which laid a foundation for sustained, market-based growth. The private sector has grown to 40 percent of GDP with over 30 percent of the workforce. New jobs created in the private sector account for 38 percent of all new formal employment, rising to 56 percent in urban areas. The significance of this is more pronounced given layoffs in the state-owned enterprise sector.

China has been the fastest growing economy in the last ten years, with annual real GDP growth averaging 10.8 percent. While average national GDP per capita is $2,500, urban populations (such as those in Shanghai and Guangzhou) enjoy incomes of over $9,000 (a point at which consumption increases dramatically). This has meant that urban households can afford color TVs (96 percent have

them), phones (76 percent), and mobile phones (28 percent). Similar wealth is gradually (albeit slowly) spreading to rural areas as well. Furthermore, purchasing on credit is gaining acceptance among young urban consumers.

China's integration into the world economy has resulted in spectacular numbers both in trade and in investment. China's foreign trade volume is expected to reach $2.5 trillion in 2010, making it the second largest trade country in the world. In 2008, Sino–U.S. trade volume reached $302 billion. While the lowering of trade barriers may permit more sales of foreign goods in China in the future, the rush by many companies from the Americas and Europe to manufacture in China for export may maintain China's trade imbalance with these trading partners. With Asian countries, however, China has been running a trade deficit since 2000 and will continue to be a source of demand as markets liberalize.

China received more foreign direct investment (FDI) in the 1990s than any country in the world except for the United States. The inflows have amounted to over $60 billion per year in the last five years, as shown in Exhibit 1. In 2007, inflows totalled $74.8 billion. One of the most popular sectors of this investment has been automobile production (Exhibit 2). Planned capacity had already exceeded 2.75 million units in 1999, when actual auto sales reached 565,000 units.

China's FDI has not only come at the expense of the rest of Asia, however. FDI inflows go to areas (within a region and a country) with comparative advantages—some to areas with abundant labor, some to areas with technological skills. With China leading in terms of inward investment flows, it may emerge as a hub for interregional demand for goods and services. Countries such as Japan will have to reorient themselves to focus on research and development, design, software, and high-precision manufactured goods.

Of economic significance is China's effort to stabilize its currency in the last five years. While officially described as a managed float, the currency (*yuan renminbi*) is effectively pegged to a basket of currencies. This has resulted in China being immune to currency fluctuations that have wreaked havoc among emerging markets such as Mexico, Indonesia, Russia, Brazil, and Argentina. However, due to China's increasing foreign exchange reserves, strong

SOURCES: This case was compiled by Ilkka A. Ronkainen using publicly available materials. These include: "China Now 2nd Largest Auto Market in World After US," Reuters, January 13, 2006, accessed at **http://www.reuters. com/news/**; "DaimlerChrysler Plans to Tap into China's Car-Loan Market," *The Wall Street Journal*, November 2, 2005, A8; "New Cultural Revolution in China: Cars on Credit," *The Wall Street Journal*, August 19, 2004, A11; "Businness Digest," *Far Eastern Economic Review*, February 5, 2004, 23; "China Clears Car-Financing Ventures," *The Wall Street Journal*, December 30, 2003, A8; "Motor Nation," *Business Week*, June 17, 2002, 44–45; Gong Zhenzheng, "Auto Price Wars Start to Rev Up," *China Daily*, January 22, 2002, 5; Joe Studwell,

The China Dream (New York: Atlantic Monthly Press, 2002), chapter 7, note 29; "China's Carmakers Flattened by Falling Tariffs," *Business Week*, December 3, 2001; Mike Dunne, "Car Loans: Ready, Set, Go?" *Automotive News International*, September 1, 2000, 33; "Why Auto Financing Is Difficult in China," *Access Asia*, November 24, 2001; "Shanghai Leads in Efforts to Build Personal Credit for Chinese," Xinhua News Agency, July 20, 2000; "First Auto-Finance Firms to Be Launched in Early 2002," *Access Asia*, December 6, 2001; and Danny Hakim, "All That Easy Credit Haunts Detroit Now," *The New York Times*, January 6, 2002, section 3, page 1. For further information, see **http://www.gmacfs.com** and **http://www.fordcredit.com**.

Exhibit 1

Foreign Direct Investment in China 1983–2007

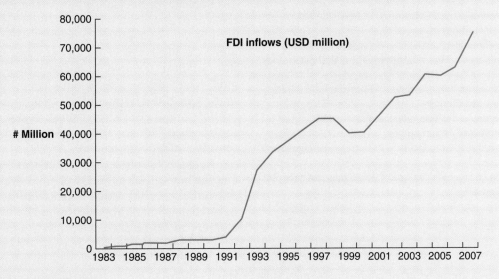

SOURCE: http://www.chinability.com.

Exhibit 2

Top 20 Foreign-Invested Enterprises in China by Sales

Rank	Foreign-Invested Enterprise	Sales Value (RMB billion)
1	Shanghai Volkswagen Co. Ltd.	56.7
2	Hongfujin Precision Industries (Shenzhen) Co. Ltd.	54.8
3	FAW-Volkswagen Automotive Co., Ltd.	49.0
4	Dafeng Computer (Shanghai) Co. Ltd.	47.8
5	Motorola (China) Electronics Co. Ltd.	38.6
6	Shanghai General Motors Co. Ltd.	34.7
7	Great Wall International Information Products (Shenzhen) Co., Ltd.	29.1
8	Shanghai Hewlett-Packard Co. Ltd.	28.7
9	CNOOC China Co. Ltd.	27.0
10	Dell (China) Co. Ltd.	25.2
11	EMB International Trading (Shanghai) Co., Ltd.	24.3
12	Huaneng Power International, Inc.	23.5
13	Guangzhou Honda Automobile Co., Ltd.	22.3
14	Lenovo (Beijing) Co., Ltd.	17.4
15	West Pacific Petrochemical Co., Ltd., Dalian	15.8
16	Maanshan Iron & Steel Co., Ltd.	15.7
17	Ocean Crown Logistics (Shanghai) Co. Ltd.	15.1
18	Dong Feng Motor Co., Ltd.	13.3
19	Nokia (China) Investment Co. Ltd.	12.8
20	Seagate Technology	

SOURCE: "China Data: A Macro Snapshot of China," *The China Business Review*, May–June 2005, 21.

capital inflows, and current account surplus, as well as pressure from Asian countries (especially Japan), the currency has come under appreciation pressure. However, with trade liberalization due to WTO membership, the higher value of the *renminbi* would aggravate the shock on domestic companies that compete with imports as well as on exporters who must compete in the global market (often on the basis of price). Chinese authorities have acknowledged the need for financial and currency liberalization, but the damaging impact of rising currency in the short term will most likely keep the currency regime of pegging unchanged. This will naturally result in low currency risk for investors.

It has been widely assumed that large corporations in particular from around the world would benefit from the liberalization measures undertaken and committed to by China (Exhibit 3). For example, the Motion Picture Association estimated that lifting the barriers to film distribution would result in $80 million in revenues, in addition to another $120 million from sales and rentals of videos (which would no longer be plagued by rampant piracy). Some sectors, such as banking and insurance, are expected to make especially strong moves as markets open up. Foreign insurers can now operate beyond the two cities they were originally limited to and were allowed nationwide access in 2005. Similar liberalization occurred in the retail sector, allowing companies such as Wal-Mart and Carrefour to develop their chains throughout the country. Majority ownership in Chinese companies is now possible, as is the choice of joint venture partners.

Because many imports now face no tariff barriers (and the remaining ones are to be eliminated by 2010) or nontariff barriers (many quotas were eliminated on accession and the rest by 2005), and because trading and

Exhibit 3

China's WTO Obligations

- **2001:** After membership, China opened new cities to foreign banks for local currency business.
- **2002:** China eliminated restrictions on where foreign law firms may operate and the number of offices that can be opened.
- **2004:** Foreign companies permitted to provide health and group insurance to Chinese.
- **2005:** U.S. eliminated Chinese textile quotas but adopted measures to prevent import surges.
- **2006:** China reduced auto tariffs to 25% from current 80% to 100%.
- **2007:** Foreign companies can hold 49% in telecom services (voice) joint ventures.

SOURCE: "China Begins Career as a WTO Member," *The Washington Post*, December 11, 2001, A14.

distribution rights are now provided, business questions focus on the timetable for change. Most business leaders have been quite realistic in not expecting substantive changes immediately but have committed to long-term planning. In some sectors, competition has already heated up given consumer expectations of more and less expensive choices.

China's transformation must be seen in the context of political change, that is slow in countries such as China. Adverse effects of WTO membership are expected in terms of output and employment in sectors such as agriculture, financial services, and in general "less-competitive industries" which are typically dominated by state-owned enterprises. For example, agricultural employment is forecast to fall by 11 million, while a substantial share of the 1.7 million workers in the four largest state-owned banks are in jeopardy. These factors have contributed to the government wanting to move with caution in allowing for change in the post-WTO environment. Furthermore, any dramatic change will probably face opposition from regional or local government officials who may see themselves as protectors of local interests.

There are already examples of the challenges to be faced as the WTO agreement is implemented at industrial and regional levels. Companies wanting to exploit the world's largest mobile telecommunications market were promised a 49 percent stake in domestic operators. But to obtain this, companies have found that waiting periods for official approval are between 270 to 310 days and that any local partner must put up 75 percent of 1 billion *renminbi* before permission is granted. This will mean that the number of joint-venture partners is considerably smaller than expected, and is possibly limited to state-owned entities. In a similar fashion, banks have found their aspirations dampened. Under the WTO agreement, foreign banks were able to offer *renminbi* banking services to Chinese corporate clients in 2004 and Chinese

consumers starting in 2007. New regulations stipulate that foreign banks can only open one branch per year which, given that many are starting from scratch (only 158 branches of foreign banks existed in 2001) and given the tens of thousands of branches currently held by local entities (for example, the Bank of China has 15,200), creates a daunting task. Foreign branches are required to have 1 billion *renminbi* in operating capital to conduct a full range of services, an amount considered discriminatory by those hoping to develop the sector. Exporters have found delays in certifications for their products to enter the China market, especially in areas that are sensitive, such as agriculture.

The expectation is that disputes and problems will emerge but will be solved over time. A parallel can be drawn between the United States and its trading partners (such as the European Union and Canada), which continue to have disagreements within the WTO framework. The extent of the challenges will depend on China's economic health and its ability to absorb the competitive shocks of WTO membership. Of concern for politicians will be the growing gap between the haves and the have-nots (especially the urban and the rural), and the costs of reforming the state sector causing social unrest and challenging the legitimacy of the political structures.

The western world has had a commercial fascination with China for the last 2,000 years. The latest wave of interest started in 1979 with the official opening of China, culminating in the official acceptance of China as the 143rd member of the WTO. Companies will continue to speculate on what sales might be achieved if only a fraction of the Chinese population would buy their products or services.

China's economic stature will undoubtedly continue to grow. Increased investment will make China a production base for the world as global companies put their best practices to work in the largest emerging market in the world. For the United States, this may mean losses of more than 600,000 jobs and a widening trade deficit with China which, in turn, may result in growing tensions between two world superpowers. At the corporate level, the huge investments have meant that while efforts in China may be profitable, they are not earning their cost of capital (which many multinationals calculate at 15 percent).

Those companies interested in entering China primarily to exploit its domestic market may have more freedom to do so (such as having control of their own distribution or the ability to provide financing) but will continue to face the same challenges as before the WTO agreement. It is no longer enough to extend products and services (however famous their brand names may be) without adjusting to local market conditions. While foreign players are dominant in sectors such as beverages, film, and personal care, local companies still dominate in televisions, refrigerators, and washing machines despite the presence of multinational companies. Multinationals may bring their best practices to China, but local firms are quick to copy those practices and with their inherent advantages are able to compete effectively. While some doubt these Chinese companies will be competitive in global markets due to the lack of success factors such as global brands, some companies are already dominant in commodity-based sectors. Qingdao-based appliance maker Haier already has a 40 percent market share in small refrigerators and is planning to expand its base in the United States to, among other things, learn to be more effective at home. Car imports from China totalled $8.5 billion in 2007.

Changes in the Chinese Car Market

A full-scale price war between car makers in China broke out in the first months of 2002. The phenomenon was a result of Chinese consumers' delays in buying cars throughout 2001 as well as increased imports following China's tariff cuts as part of the WTO agreement. The slashing of tariffs in the car sector was the biggest in any sector (from 80 percent to 50 percent now and down to 25 percent by 2006).

Consumers had been waiting for cheaper cars for years, and this dream became a reality through the effects of the WTO agreement. For example, the Buick Sail's pre-WTO price was $13,855 but dropped to $12,040, with further decreases possible as domestic makers lower their prices to maintain competitive advantage. The price war was ignited when Tianjin Automotive Industry Group slashed prices of all of its Xiali compact cars by 9,000 to 23,000 *yuan* ($1,084–$2,771). More than 3,600 are reported to have been sold during the first four days after the price cut. Chang'an Suzuki, a joint venture between Chongqing-based Chang'an Motor and Japan's Suzuki Motors, cut its prices by 20 percent. Analysts estimated that domestic car makers of vehicles priced at less than 150,000 *yuan* ($18,070) would have to reduce prices, although car makers such as Shanghai General Motors and Shanghai Volkswagen would try to hold on and let dealers engage in price promotions. Even with the price decreases, comparable cars cost far less in Europe, a fact not lost on the Chinese consumer.

Car makers already producing in China are bracing for intense competition. As the Chinese government phases out regulations as to what models to produce, General Motors (GM), Volkswagen (VW), Ford, Honda, and Toyota all plan to launch models aimed at quality- and cost-conscious consumers. With the new market freedoms, car makers will have to focus on customer desires more than ever before.

Eventually, lower prices and wider choice should create a thriving auto industry. Car sales increased from 900,000 units in 2002 and hit the 6-million unit mark by 2006 making China the second largest auto market after the United States. Car sales have been slowing, however, due in part to the central government's crackdown on easy auto credit to help cool an overheating Chinese economy.

Current Market Structure for Car Financing in China

In 2005, most Chinese consumers paid cash for cars, with only 20 percent financing their purchases. More than 20 percent were financing their purchases before new government restrictions. In contrast, U.S. auto purchasers finance between 65 to 93 percent of all units purchased, depending on the make.

China is still a very small market for auto financing and for consumer credit in general. There are a number of reasons behind the small market size. Auto financing was not permitted by the government before 1998. From 1998 to 2004, only four state-owned and two private banks were authorized by the Chinese government to provide loans, with interest rates regulated by the government. These include Bank of China, China's oldest bank, as well as China Construction Bank. These institutions had onerous requirements to gain approval for a loan, including: (1) collateral other than the car (home, deposits at the bank) valued at 100 to 120 percent of the amount of the loan, (2) a guarantor, (3) proof of income and tax payments (not onerous in and of itself, but many Chinese underreport income and taxes to an extent that verifiable income is insufficient for loan repayment), (4) a marriage certificate, (5) an official estimate of the value of the vehicle, and (6) mandated vehicle purchase through an "approved" retailer. This meant that nearly one-third of car buyers opted to quit the process rather than complete it. Even with the onerous requirements, results have not been promising: since 1998, default rates have ranged from 10 to 30 percent. Reasons include bad credit checks and disgruntled buyers who refuse to pay off loans after declines in prices for models they had purchased.

In late 2003, the Chinese government granted permission to non-financial and foreign firms to start providing auto-financing operations. The central government saw personal credit as a way to stimulate consumer spending and take some of the burden off the government's traditional means of stimulating the economy, expensive infrastructure projects. By the end of 2005, China had six auto financing firms, some of which are wholly-owned (e.g., Ford, Toyota, and Volkswagen), some joint ventures (e.g., GM with Shanghai Automotive Industry Group, and PSA with the Bank of China). DaimlerChrysler announced its financing operations in late 2005 to boost sales of its Mercedes E-class and Chrysler 300C produced in China.

The infrastructure is not yet fully developed for car financing. Most vehicle regulatory agencies do not allow liens or security interests in autos that are registered for personal use. Laws and regulations are not consistently in place to protect insurance companies when investing in loans or underwriting loan risks. Repossession procedures are not generally codified. Where rules exist, the Public Security Bureau must effect repossession and will decide resale value on repossessed vehicles.

Regional differences are significant. While the industry is still in its infancy, Shanghai is the most advanced both in terms of amounts of consumer credit and the systems in place. For example, GM's venture limited its operations initially to Shanghai, where a credit bureau keeps computer records that shortened credit checks to a few hours. The urban populations of the east will play a major role in the change process because of their increasing wealth and nontraditional attitudes toward buying on credit. Foreign interest in the market for car financing is predicated on the long-term potential of the market, influenced by China's membership in the WTO. While government rules made market entry possible in theory already prior to January 2002, setting up operations is still challenging. Auto financing companies are only allowed to have one office, which may present logistics challenges. Government rules mandate loans denominated in *renminbi* (the local currency, "people's money"). Furthermore, foreign entities can count on local competition from existing and new government-owned institutions as well as private entities. China's banks have more than 10 trillion yuan ($1.2 trillion) in deposits and are eager to put it into use. Yafei Auto Chain General Store—with default rates at less than 2 percent and 90 percent regional market share—is a chain of auto dealerships that gets preferential treatment from the Beijing government and enjoys exclusive underwriting support from the China People's Life Insurance Company.

The WTO agreement caused a drop in the tariffs of imported cars from a range of 70 to 80 percent of the list price to 50 to 60 percent. By 2006, duties sank another 25 percent—enough to put cars within the reach of China's upper middle class.

Expected Market Changes in Car Financing in China

All indications are that auto financing in China in the 21st century will be a lucrative business both at the macro level and the micro level. Only a very small share of China's total consumption is made through consumer credit. In an effort to fuel economic growth, Chinese officials have stated that they are working toward percentages of consumption from credit more in line with the western world. Most of the western economies average between 20 and 25 percent of consumption through consumer credit.

Urban incomes increased 75 percent between 1997 and 2008, to an annual level of $5,000. GDP per capita in Beijing, Guangzhou, and Shanghai exceeds $9,000. Rural incomes, which are a third of the urban incomes, in comparison, increased only modestly in the same time frame. Most experts agree that automotive purchases generally and automotive finance specifically expand rapidly after crossing the $3,000 per capita GDP threshold.

Consensus estimates for the car financing market—both for personal and business use—are 20 percent of the expected unit sales. This number is expected to increase by 40 to 60 percent over a five-year period, resulting in a $3.25 billion market.

All indications are that Chinese consumers' aversion to debt is waning—at least in the cities of the south and east. Estimates for consumer lending in general can be extrapolated from analogous evidence. In 1995, 15,000 individuals in Shanghai borrowed 570 million *yuan* worth of mortgages. By 2004, 76 percent of new bank loans went to property, of which 72.8 billion *yuan* was for personal housing mortgages.

The industry is dependent on accurate and timely information as well as a transparent system of operation. Shanghai Credit Information Services has emerged as a reliable source of credit information for more than 5 million Chinese. Rules for recording liens and repossession and remarketing of vehicles are now in place in Shanghai and Beijing (albeit in their infancy and open to local interpretation).

Options for Market Entry and Development

There are four ways that auto finance companies can set up in China:

- Automakers can launch an auto-financing services subsidiary;
- Banks (Chinese) can set up special auto financing institutions;
- Nonbanking financial institutions owned by enterprise groups can form an auto financing company; or
- Existing lending consortia can provide financing services for auto companies' sales divisions.

GMAC's Competitive Position

GMAC and the other financing arms of carmakers were at an obvious disadvantage in relation to home-country institutions because the market was reserved for Chinese institutions until January 2002. GMAC previously acted in an advisory capacity to GM's Shanghai JV manufacturing facility, which, in turn, has set up relationships with official government lending institutions (such as China Construction Bank and the Bank of Shanghai).

GMAC's competitive position vis-à-vis the other foreign companies appears to be solid for a number of reasons:

- GM is one of the largest corporate FDI contributors to China in the world and has a substantial partnership with the government;
- GMAC has numerous manufacturing partners to leverage—SGM, Jinbei GM (which produces the Chevrolet S-10 pickup and Blazer SUV), and Wuling (GM has an equity stake in the largest producer of mini-cars for the Chinese market). These partners deliver the second highest number of FDI autos in the market—just behind VW and far ahead of Ford Motor Credit and Peugeot; and
- GMAC has numerous GM-network partners to leverage (Isuzu, Suzuki, Fiat, Fuji Heavy Industries).

GMAC's expertise in auto lending generally and in the following ancillary areas critical to doing business in China should allow for the business to get up and running. It has extensive experience in auto lending in developing markets without efficient infrastructure; for example, it has experience in India, which has no credit bureaus and state involvement in repossession and remarketing. Partnering with other private and quasi-state-run institutions such as Fannie Mae, GMAC subsidiaries (GMAC Mortgage, GMAC Commercial Mortgage and Residential Funding Corporation) have developed expertise in profitable loan securitization, profitable (mortgage) loan servicing, and profitable receivables (purchase and sale), giving them the necessary skills to work together with third parties and governmental units. Finally, market presence in many other countries in the Asia-Pacific region gives GMAC the human resources necessary for China expansion. These offices are staffed with a broad array of third-country expatriates from China and other cultures who have better insight into the Chinese market than do GMAC's U.S.-based staff.

Despite the overwhelming external and internal opportunities, challenges exist as well. Ford's and GM's credit ratings were downgraded by Moody's and Standard & Poor's in 2001, forcing the automakers out of commercial paper and into other, more expensive forms of funding. Their no- or low-interest loans and cheap leases intended to pump up sales since then have threatened the financial health of the carmakers' credit arms. For example, GMAC North America's huge success with 0 percent financing during 2001 Q4's "Keep America Rolling" and the 2005 "Employee Discount for Everyone," campaigns ate up significant resources. Effectively, GMAC may be out of cash for big market-entry investments and equity investment from the parent company, when GM as a whole faces an unfunded pension liability and reduced cash flow that is critical for reinvestment into future product programs. Ford Motor Credit is facing even bigger problems given its more aggressive lending practices in the recent past.

Implications for Global Operations

A carmaker's captive financing arm exists for two reasons: to assist in delivering additional cars and trucks to consumers, and to provide a superior return on investment and cash flow to its sole stockholder. While still extremely risky and lacking in short-term profit, the China market is still valued by carmakers because of its market potential for sales and because of the potential it displays for their financing arms in terms of auto finance and mortgages. The question is how to deliver on the promise and the mandate. No company can adopt a wait-and-see attitude any longer.

Questions for Discussion

1. Suggest reasons for a company to enter the Chinese market for auto financing.

2. What is the most prudent mode of entry and market development for a car-financing arm of an auto maker?

3. Where should a company make its moves and with what type of products?

4. What should a company do to influence the positive change in China in its favor?

SHOULD DUBAI TAKE OVER U.S. PORTS?

On February 13, 2006, the shareholders of Peninsular & Oriental Steam Navigation Co., of London (P&O), confirmed sale of their company to DP World (Dubai Ports World). Through this act, the management of port operations in five U.S. ports also came under DP World's purview. On March 9, DP World announced that it would divest the US port operations.

The intervening 25 days saw a flurry of activity in the United States, with politicians of all shades of opinion, news programs, administration officials, and assorted experts debating the pros and cons of the deal. The outcome of the deal was seen to have much larger implications than mere port management. It raised issues of national security, the investments of petrodollars around the world, U.S. policy towards foreign investment, political risk, and the attitudes of Americans towards Arabs.

DP World, a Dubai Company

Since 1999, DP World, a Dubai government owned company, had begun a strategy of aggressive growth. With the acquisition of P&O, it became the world's second largest port operator, with operations in 13 countries, including China, India, Germany, Australia, UK, and the Dominican Republic. The acquisition of P&O was the successful outcome of a bidding war against Singapore's PSA International (a unit of Temasek Holdings) for $6.8 billion. (DP World's revenues and profit figures are not publicly accessible.)

Dubai was the second largest of a federation of seven semi-autonomous city states, which became the United Arab Emirates in 1971. It has a population of about 4 million, of whom only about 20% are citizens. Like most of the other countries in the region, Dubai depends on a large number of expatriate workers from South Asia (India, Pakistan and Bangladesh) to run the country. It has also attracted a number of Britons, Australians, and Americans who have come to work or retire.

Dubai attempts to balance the demands of being a small Middle Eastern state with its desire to play a larger role in the world. The UAE is a part of the Arab League's boycott of Israel in place since the early 1990s, although it ignores it in practice. It also does not recognize U.S. sanctions against Iran. As the UAE does not have any direct links with Israel, products are not shipped directly from Israel, but are allowed to enter from third countries.

Unlike some of its neighboring states, Dubai gets only a small share of its income from oil and has worked hard over the years to build the country as a business hub and tourism destination. It does not have income taxes. Dubai is a popular shopping center in the region with glitzy malls, extravagant hotels, and amusement parks. All major luxury brands of the world have outlets there. Apart from tourism, it is also the regional headquarters of many of the world's large financial institutions. Dubai built its port to world-class levels, and it also operates the biggest airline of the area, Emirates Air. More than 500 US companies operate in the UAE.

The Dubai government has been using its oil revenues to make major investments around the world. It has purchased hotels and property in the United States and the UK. They recently purchased a $1 billion stake in Daimler-Chrysler AG, and became the third largest shareholder.[1]

Given its strategic geographic location and small size, the country has tried to maintain good relations with countries, both the region and outside. It stayed neutral during the Iran–Iraq war in the 1980s. The UAE is considered a key ally by the U.S. administration. It cooperates militarily, hosting U.S. naval vessels (since its ports are capable of receiving large aircraft carriers and nuclear submarines), and it also has an airbase for refueling U.S. military planes. Out of about $126 million received as international donations towards the Hurricane Katrina reconstruction effort in the south, the UAE is said to have contributed $100 million.[2]

On the other hand, two of the hijackers who participated in the September 11, 2001, terrorist attack in the U.S. were from the UAE. Even earlier, UAE was one of three countries (apart from Pakistan and Saudi Arabia) who officially recognized the Taliban regime in Afghanistan. The UAE was also seen as a transit point for Iran and Pakistan to move contraband nuclear materials, and its banking facilities are believed to be used by terrorist groups. After the terrorist attack in the United States, the country had worked hard to strengthen controls on its financial system.

Investment in U.S. Ports

Through this purchase, the operations by P&O in five ports in the United States passed on to DP World's hands. These included: New York/New Jersey, Philadelphia, Baltimore, Miami, and New Orleans. Of these, the New York/New Jersey and Miami terminals are considered the more attractive ones, and in these two, P&O shared ownership with other operators. Apart from the five marine terminal operations, P&O's operations in the US include cargo handling and cruise ship services in 22 ports.[3]

The management of the five ports was not the first venture of DP World in the United States. In a previous deal, DP World had purchased the international terminal business of CSX Corp. of Jacksonville, Florida, for $1.15 billion, in December 2004.

All foreign investment in the United States needs to be approved by the Committee on Foreign Investment in the United States. This body, referred to as the CFIUS, was set up in 1975 in response to a surge in foreign investments. The initial focus was on investments in defense-related industries. The late 1980s saw a lot of debate about increasing Japanese investments, and inresponse, the U.S. Congress passed the Exon-Florio Amendment to the Defense Production Act of 1950, which empowered the president to block foreign acquisition proposals on grounds of national security. This role was assigned to the CFIUS. The CFIUS comes under the Department of the Treasury, and is an interagency committee chaired by the Department's Secretary. There are 12 members, including the Secretaries of State, Defense, Commerce, and Homeland Security; the Attorney General; the Director of the Office of Management and Budget; the U.S. Trade Representative; the Chairman of the Council of Economic Advisers; the Assistant to the President for Economic Policy; the Assistant to the President for National Security; and the Director of the Office of Science and Technology. On receipt of application, a 30-day review is initiated (each agency undertakes its independent investigation), and in some cases, an additional 45-day period for investigation is allowed, after which the CFIUS makes a recommendation to the President. The Committee since 1988 has reviewed about 1600 transactions. Of these, only about 25 were investigated further.

P&O and DP World retained the services of lawyers in Washington, DC, and approached CFIUS on October 17 for informal consultations and to seek their support. This is normal practice, and often a lot of the work involved in such reviews is undertaken before a formal application. The company had two briefings with the committee. After the deal with P&O was formalized, DP World on December 16, 2005, made its application to CFIUS and the acquisition was approved on January 16, 2006.[4] The company, at that time, also put forward a package of commitments on security, such as allowing U.S. officials to examine company records and check the background of its employees, and to separate the port terminal operations from the rest of the country.

When DP World's deal was announced on November 29, 2005, Eller & Co., which managed the Miami port in partnership with P&O and provided stevedoring services, filed cases in Miami and London to stop the deal. It argued that its business would be affected because it felt some companies would withdraw business from the port if DP World managed it. It said the deal threatened the national security of the United States, and argued that the deal was a breach of the joint venture it had with P&O. Eller, from before, had a dispute with P&O, which it felt was seeking to increase control of Continental Stevedoring and Terminals, Inc., a subsidiary of Eller and the firm with whom P&O had the venture.[5]

Apart from the lawsuits, Eller retained the services of a lobbyist in Washington, Joe Muldoon, who began researching the issues involved in the P&O acquisition and contacted several legislators in February, when they returned from their January recess. One of those senators was Charles Schumer, Democrat from New York (where one of the ports is situated), who was on the Banking Senate Committee. Meanwhile, the Associated Press also contacted Schumer and issued a report making a connection between the acquisition, the country of Dubai, terrorists, and the vulnerability of the ports to terrorism, much as the lawsuits of Eller had done.[6]

Politicians of different hues were quick to react to the deal. Schumer addressed a press conference along with the families of those who suffered from the terrorist attack of September 11, 2001, calling on the president to step in and prevent the deal. On February 17, 2006, Senator Hillary Clinton, the other senator from New York and a Democrat said, "Our port security is too important to place in the hands of foreign governments." Even Republicans were opposed to the deal, saying "Dubai can't be trusted with our critical infrastructure" and "it is my intention to lay the foundation to block the deal."[7] Senator Lindsey Graham (Republican) said, "It's unbelievably tone-deaf politically . . . four years after 9/11, to entertain the idea of turning port security over to a company based in the UAE, [a country that] vows to destroy Israel."[8]

Some political observers felt that the President's low standing in public opinion polls due to dissatisfaction with the progress in the war in Iraq was making some Republican lawmakers challenge and distance themselves from him in preparation for their own re-election battles in November 2006.

News commentators began to raise alarms about the deal. On the same day that P&O announced its purchase, Lou Dobbs, a business anchor on CNN News Channel, said, "A country with ties to the September 11 terrorists could soon be running significant operations at some of our most important and largest seaports with full blessing of the Bush White House."[9] Mr. Dobbs was known for taking a nationalist position on issues like immigration and outsourcing, and their effects on jobs in the United States. Several radio talk shows picked up the story, filling the airwaves with different interpretations. Moreover, many among the public and security professionals who had been concerned that the government had not been doing enough for port safety and scanning of containers found the DP World situation another example of a government that was slackening on security. Reports suggested that legislators were being flooded on their Blackberries (portable email devices) by comments from their staffers, constituents, and others.

In an effort to manage the debate around the deal, the federal administration clarified that it had asked for and received additional security commitments from DP World before giving its clearance. An Israeli shipping company, ZIM Integrated Shipping Services Ltd., even sent a letter to U.S. senators stating that they have used the services of DP World at Dubai and have had no concern about their level of security.[10]

Officials also clarified that security screening was not the responsibility of the commercial port operators but that of U.S. law enforcement agents. However, the misperception that the Middle East company would be responsible for port security persisted in the public impression and was repeated in talk shows. There was even confusion in the airwaves with some commenting that the Middle East was taking over the ports (rather than port operations).

Ports and Container Operations

Container shipping was pioneered by a U.S. company, Sea Land, in the 1950s. However, during the 1980s, U.S. companies found it difficult to face the competition from companies that were operating under flags of convenience and were thus subject to less stringent tax and regulatory policies, and used cheaper labor. The shipping industry had been global for some time. None of the major global container shipping companies is U.S. owned; these businesses generate returns over the long term that U.S. companies, under pressure for quarterly performance targets, are unable to meet. Shipping companies often have subsidiaries to manage terminals, in order to facilitate the cargo they carry. About 80 percent of global cargo was handled by five companies around the world, headquartered in Hong Kong (Hutchi Whampoa), Singapore (PSA International), Dubai (DP World), Denmark (A.P. Moler-Maersk AS), and Germany (Eurogate).

Port authorities that are set up by local governments own most ports. The authorities lease a terminal to an individual company, which is responsible for port management and operations such as moving the containers from the ships to the warehouses.

Large ports have multiple terminals, and different companies operate these. At the Los Angeles port, companies from China, Denmark, Japan, Singapore, and Taiwan manage the terminals. The big ports of the United States, namely, Los Angeles, Long Beach, and Oakland in California and New York/New Jersey, handle about half of all containers that pass through the US. At these ports, foreign companies (some of whom are owned by foreign governments) handle about 80 percent of the container terminals.

The purchase of P&O by DP World gave it control over terminal operations at New York/New Jersey, Philadelphia, Baltimore, Miami, and New Orleans. Other companies, some of whom are foreign, run other terminals in these ports.

Security[11]

The global nature of the shipping industry means that any security effort requires the cooperation of various governments, ship owners, and all participants along the commercial supply chain.

Within the United States, irrespective of who operates the terminal, whether a U.S. or a foreign company, security at the ports (including inspection of containers) is the responsibility of federal agencies such as the U.S. Coast Guard and U.S. Customs and Border Protection. The Coast Guard is also authorized to inspect a vessel at sea or at the harbor entrance. About 26,000 containers arrive at U.S. ports every day, and customs agents inspect about 5 percent of them. About 37 percent of containers that leave the ports for the highways are screened. Security in the area surrounding the ports is part of the responsibility of the local police.

There are several areas that can do with strengthening to improve security, and they have very little to do with who manages port operations. There is a voluntary program operated by the U.S. government to protect incoming shipments. Many companies have signed up for this, under which the companies develop voluntary security procedures to protect the shipment from the factory to the port. In return, their cargo is processed at a faster pace at the port. Shipments from companies that don't take part in the program may not always be inspected. Even for those who do participate, security is not perfect as the cargo may be open to tampering in transit.

About 40 ports around the world ship about 80 percent of the cargo entering the United States. At the port of shipment, the carrier is required to electronically provide the manifest (list of items, name of the shipper and importer) at least 24 hours before loading. This list is analyzed in a screening center in the United States, and Customs Agents who identify any suspicious items can ask their counterparts at the port of dispatch to screen the containers. However, the U.S. Government Accountability Office reports that as of 2005 about one-third of the containers were not being analyzed, and about 25 percent of those identified as high-risk were not being inspected. Scanners and radiation detectors to screen every single container are available and their use was estimated to add about $20 to the container.

Opposition Gathers Momentum

Faced with rising criticism, DP World also had a crew of lobbyists and attorneys working on its behalf in Washington, DC. Officials of its embassy were working closely with people like Senator John Warner (Republican), who was in favor of the deal. Legislation was also being planned to allow the deal subject to conditions such as the terminals being operated by U.S. citizens.

When some members of Congress threatened to pass legislation blocking the sale, President Bush responded on February 21 by saying that he would veto it. He also said that he learned about the deal only after it was approved by his administration. Expressing concern about the debates around the deal, he was quoted as saying, "I want those who are questioning to step up and explain why all of a sudden a Middle Eastern company is held to a different standard than a [British] company. I am trying to [say] to the people of the world, 'We'll treat you fairly.'"[12]

With political objections mounting, DP World on February 26 requested a fresh 45-day review of the deal and offered to hold the American operations separate until the review was completed. The administration agreed to undertake the review. By end of February, a CBS News Poll revealed that 70 percent of participants said that a UAE company should not be permitted to operate U.S. shipping ports.[13]

Although the federal administration had taken a hard stand initially in supporting the deal, the opposition from within the President's party was strong. Both the leader of the party in the Senate and the Speaker in the House were opposed to the President on the issue. The Governor of New Jersey, Jon Corzine, planned a federal lawsuit blocking the handover of the Port of Newark to DP World.

Although the U.S. operations accounted for only about 10 percent of P&O's profits, DP World was keen on the making the deal work. The U.S. operations of the company were the destinations of cargo from its more significant holdings in Asia, and the company wanted this as a foothold to expand its U.S. operations in the future. Its COO, Mr. Ted Bilkey, told a U.S. news channel, "We'll do anything possible to make sure this deal goes through."[14]

In keeping with this, the company, on March 7, offered three Republican senators a package of security measures titled "Proposed solution to the DP World Issue."[15] These proposals, which were in addition to the commitments the company made earlier in January, included the following:

- Paying for screening devices at all current and future ports the company operates around the world.

- Giving the Department of Homeland Security the right to disapprove the choice of Chief Executive, board members, security officials, and all senior officers.

- A "supermajority" of the board would be U.S. citizens.

- All records pertaining to its security operations would be maintained on U.S. soil and these records would be turned over at the request of the U.S. government.

- Its U.S. subsidiary, now managed by a British citizen, would in the future also only be headed by a U.S. or British citizen.

- A Security and Financial Oversight Board would be established, headed by a prominent U.S. citizen, which would report annually to the Department of Homeland Security.

Some observers felt that this was truly extraordinary for a foreign company to offer. Although such an offer, if made earlier, may have swayed the debate, by the time it came, positions had already hardened. On March 8, the House Appropriations Committee voted 62 to 2 to block the DP World deal. To make the president's threat of a veto more difficult, the Committee attached this as an amendment to a spending bill for the wars in Iraq and Afghanistan. The next day, the Republican congressional leaders conveyed to the president that Congress would kill the deal.

The Bush administration then conveyed a request to Dubai's ruler to sever the U.S. operations in order to allay fears in the United States about security. Officials in the UAE saw this as a situation where President Bush was incurring a loss of face in his dealings with the Congress. Consequently, DP World on March 9, 2006, offered to divest the U.S. port operations.

Protectionism

As the public debates wore on, many started wondering if a bout of protectionism was beginning to sweep the developed world. Economic theory provides for a justification for protection to select industries under the "infant industry" argument. When countries engage in international trade, they face competition from well-established players in different parts of the world. If a country has a "weak" industry, it may collapse in the face of such competition through imports. In such a situation, the domestic industry may be protected through tariffs or quotas until such time when the firms in that industry are able to stand on their own feet. In recognition of this argument, the WTO rules often allow developing countries more time to implement international agreements so that their domestic firms have the time to make the adjustments.

The "infant industry" argument was stretched in March 2002 when the United States, in support of its domestic steel industry, instituted tariffs on imports to enable the steel firms to adjust to lower-cost competition from overseas. Although the United States steel industry was not an "infant," the tariffs were a means of protection to enable an industry in transition.

Recent incidents have raised concerns as to whether national security is now being used as an excuse to bring in protectionism. In July 2005, China National Offshore Oil Corp. (CNOOC), a Chinese government-owned company, was involved in bidding against Chevron Corp. to acquire Unocal Corp., an oil and natural gas company. Many U.S. lawmakers began tying the deal to China's approach to free trade, its military expansion, and energy policy. CNOOC subsequently dropped out of the race, and many believed that the political risk of its proposed acquisition was part of the reason. In March 2005, IBM's sale of its personal computer business to Lenovo Group, Inc., of China was cleared by CFIUS, after a full investigation and several concessions on the structuring of the deal were made by IBM—such as separation of Chinese and U.S. employees in the research facility.

Europe has been seeing its own version of protectionism within the EU, negating the fundamental principles of the formation of the EU. France, in December 2004, identified 11 industries that it considered "strategic" and announced that foreign (outside France, even if within EU) takeovers of companies in these sectors would be subject to heightened scrutiny. The EU Commission was concerned about this development.

Foreign investment is an integral part of the U.S. economy. Foreign investment in the United States has been about $530 billion in the last three years, and U.S. companies invested about $252 billion overseas. Continued foreign investment funded the current account deficit, compensated for the low savings rate in the country, and kept long-term interest rates low.[16] Clyde Prestowitz, President of the Economic Strategy Institute, commented that the United States needs a "net inflow of capital of $3 billion a day to keep the economy afloat."[17]

Impact on Pending Issues

The DP World incident put a crimp on other pending issues. The United States had been engaged in free trade talks with the UAE since March 2005. The fifth round, which was to begin on March 10, was postponed on grounds that both sides needed more time to prepare; both sides denied that the ports issue had anything to do with the postponement. Bilateral trade between the two countries amounted to about $10 billion in 2005, of which about 80 percent was U.S. exports. The U.S. side would like the UAE to revise its investment laws, which presently require foreign companies that want access to the local market to enter into joint ventures in which the Emirates partner will have 51 percent ownership, or alternatively to have local agents.

Bill Reinsch, the President of the National Foreign Trade Council in the United States, representing more than 300 companies engaged in international trade, felt that the ports issue would make it harder for the U.S. Administration to accomplish its goals in the Middle East: "The message [from the United States] is that we're not distinguishing between countries that help us in the war on terrorism and countries that don't. So the obvious question is why cooperate with the United States, if [they are] going to treat you as a terrorist anyway?"[18]

In January 2006, independent of the ports deal, President Bush nominated David Sanborn, DPWorld's Director of Operations for Europe and Latin America, to head the U.S. Maritime Administration. The Maritime Administration maintains data on port traffic and runs the Merchant Marine Academy. Subsequently, his nomination was put on hold due to the controversy; finally Sanborn, a retired naval officer, withdrew his nomination in March.[19]

Although the decision by DP World to offer the U.S. operations for sale defused the crisis, the momentum about the need for policy changes continued among the lawmakers who continued holding hearings and proposing bills. There was a call for more transparency and accountability by CFIUS. One set of bills wanted to give more oversight to Congress through more reports being given to it by CFIUS, and transferring jurisdiction over CFIUS from the Treasury to Homeland Security. This would shift the balance of the intent of scrutiny. Another proposal would make the 45-day investigation required for all proposals in "critical" sectors including agriculture, telecommunication, and banking, and accounting for about 25 percent of all investment in the country.

Some Congressmen had even begun wondering if there was a need for broader legislation which would ban foreign companies from owning or managing critical infrastructure, which would include ports, roads, telecommunications, airlines, broadcasting, shipping, technology firms, water facilities, and even U.S. Treasury securities. Even under current law, in the case of U.S. airlines, foreign ownership is restricted to 25 percent of voting stock and 45 percent of total stock. Moreover, only U.S. citizens can exercise actual control over airline operations.

Future Repercussions

DP World said it would conduct the sale of its U.S. operations in an orderly manner and not incur any economic loss. There were only a few companies with experience in marine terminal operations in the United States. Eller & Co. expressed an interest in making an offer.

Mr. Mohammed Sharaf, DP World's Chief Executive, said that the reaction in the United States to their purchase of P&O came as a shock to him: "Since Dubai has been a close friend of the United States for three decades, and a staunch ally in the fight against terrorism, and since we at DP World have been serving the U.S. Navy directly since 1990, the misunderstanding came as a real shock. Even with 20:20 hindsight, it's hard to think what we could have done differently."[20]

President Bush, talking to newspaper editors, said he was "concerned about a broader message this issue could send to our friends and allies around the world, particularly in the Middle East."[21] His fears seem to have been realized. Many in the Middle East were upset andbelieved that DP World was being singled out because it was an Arab company. "They preach about a capitalisteconomy where everyone's free to do as they wish, but now they're just trying to come up with any excuse topaint the country with terrorism," said Ahmed el-Leithy, a construction engineer in Dubai.[22]

Mr. Maurice Flanagan, President of the Emirates Group, which runs the fast-growing Emirates Air airline, commented "[The ports issue] is rather a slap in the face." The company has extensive dealings with U.S. companies, buying Boeing planes and GE jet engines, but was not expected to retaliate by taking its business elsewhere.[23]

A post-mortem of the DP World debacle caused some to wonder if a reason for the fiasco was the inept handling of the issues by the administration. It was being handled at very low levels, and should have been quickly escalated in the early stages to higher levels given the sensitivity of the issues. For the long term, clarity in the area of national security and its implications for foreign investment in the United States would be welcomed by investors.

There were certainly mixed signals emanating from the administration. In late March of 2006, the U.S. government appointed Hutchison Whampoa, Ltd., to use its radiation screening equipment to screen containers in order to detect nuclear material at the port in Bahamas. The company manages terminals at the port. Yet, about three years ago, a subsidiary of Hutchison was prevented from buying a part of the bankrupt U.S. telecom company Global Crossing on grounds of national security. Li Ka Shing, owner of Hutchison, is a well-known businessmen and is also considered close to the Chinese government.

In April 2005, an Indian telecom company, VSNL, was permitted to acquire the undersea cable assets of Tyco Global Network. It was subjected to stringent scrutiny by CFIUS and signed agreements, among others, allowing for court-authorized wiretaps and scrutiny of all its employees. The company is said to have recommended to the Government of India to have similar scrutiny of foreign investments into India, and this proposal is under active consideration.[24]

The more immediate impact of the DP World fiasco was apparent. On the anvil was Dubai International Capital's scheduled purchase of Doncasters, a privately held British aerospace manufacturer that works on U.S. weapons programs. This deal had been put on an extensive 45-day investigation as of mid-March 2006. When France's Alcatel announced its merger agreement with Lucent of the United States on April 2, 2006, it said it plans to form an independent U.S. subsidiary to handle some American government contracts. This subsidiary would be separately managed by a board comprising three U.S. citizens acceptable to the U.S. government.

Several broader issues arise out of DP World's experience in the United States. While political risk is frequently attributed to locations with unstable political environments, it is relevant even in a mature stable environment and should be a concern in all foreign investment decisions. The question is: How can it be managed? The attributions about the region that a Dubaibased company could not shake may have a lesson for governments in how they project their image overseas. Finally, even as industries become more global, they would have to deal with national concerns and arguments that suggest divergence rather than convergence.

CLOSING THE MG ROVER PLANTS: THE AFTEREFFECTS

Background

The closure of the MG Rover plant at Longbridge, Birmingham, England in April 2005 was one of the largest industrial failures seen in the UK for some 20 years, with around 6,300 workers losing their jobs when MG Rover went into administration, and several thousand more affected in the supply chain. The scale of the job losses in an already economically disadvantaged region and the loss of the last remaining British-owned car manufacturer combined to highlight the consequences of the ongoing decline of manufacturing and the associated human costs of structural change.

By February 2006, of the 6,300 unemployed resulting directly from the collapse, around 4,000 were back in work (90% of whom were working full-time). A further 667 were in training or awaiting training, 398 had received training but were still not working, 530 were not working and had not received any training, 443 had unknown destinations, and 257 had claimed alternative benefits after claiming Job Seekers' Allowance (RTF, 2006).

This Report

This report presents findings on where people now live and work relative to before the closure. It also provides a survey that investigates their lives.

Key Findings

Key points from the report's findings are:

- Most workers are now in full time employment on permanent contracts;
- Most employees have witnessed a significant drop in salary relative to their MG Rover wage, on average a fall of £5,640 (adjusted for inflation), but post MG Rover salaries are highly differentiated;
- Managers are earning about the same as they were at MG Rover, just £1,280 more (adjusted for inflation). Those now working in some service sectors took average cuts of more than £6,000 per annum compared to their final salaries at MG Rover;
- 25% reported being in debt or needing to draw on savings and 36% were just about managing;
- 66% of all ex-MG Rover workers reported being financially worse off now;
- Those who found re-employment sooner use similar skills to those they used at MG Rover and earn more than other ex-MG Rover workers;
- Of those who were still unemployed eight months post closure, 80% underwent some forms of training;
- Overall, 60% of all workers received some form of training or educational support, with 40% taking up the offer of free training;
- Workers who took up training reported higher satisfaction and less of a decline in health than those who did not receive any form of training;
- Workers re-employed sooner reported higher levels of overall job quality with higher life satisfaction and lower anxiety levels.

Overall, the vast majority of ex-workers surveyed (90%) are back at work, with most in full-time work on permanent contracts. Behind this "success story," workers nevertheless reported difficulties in finding a job, with the main perceived barriers being age, skills and experience, and the simple fact that there were too many people applying for the same jobs (not a surprise given the scale of job losses at MG Rover and the level of unemployment in parts of Birmingham when the plant closed). In overcoming such barriers to find work, personal initiative and networks have been the key to ex-workers finding jobs.

The jobs that ex-MG Rover workers have found are highly diversified, with only 30% working in manufacturing and a mix of both lower and higher occupational status. The gross average salary of workers has decreased (on average by £5,640, adjusted for inflation, for workers in full-time employment) even three years after closure. A third of respondents have actually reported an increase in salary. People who found work in four sectors—wholesale and retail, real estate and business services, education, and health and social work—took average cuts of more than £6,000 in annual income (adjusted for inflation).

This case was derived from: Bailey, David, Caroline Chapain, Michelle Mahdon, and Rebecca Fauth. "Life after Longbridge: Three Years on. Pathways to re-employment in a restructuring economy." *University of Birmingham Economic & Social Research Council* (November 2008): 1-66. **http://www.theworkfoundation.com/assets/does/MG_Rover_2008.pdf,** accessed November 9, 2008.

Job satisfaction was higher for those who had received some form of training relative to those in our sample who had not. Only a third of ex-workers surveyed felt that their current job was better than the one they had at MG Rover. Nearly half felt that their job was worse than the one they had at MG Rover. Nevertheless, a majority of workers still liked the work that they do and expected to be doing it for the foreseeable future.

Some Policy Implications

Much work was done by the RDA Advantage West Midlands and other agencies before the MG Rover closure in diversifying the supply chain and economy. This work may have "saved" many as 10,000–12,000 jobs in the supply chain (Bailey and MacNeill, 2008).

When MG Rover finally closed in 2005, the MG Rover Task Force Mark II was able to hit the ground running on the day of the announcement of the closure. Such advance preparation could work well in future closure situations, since it is unlikely that a future closure would happen without at least some prior warning. This lesson points toward the need for good "institutional memory" of how to work in such a situation and having a permanent capacity to deal with such situations. Keeping knowledge available would help with advanced planning and avoid "fire fighting" in the future.

Our research has identified three "pathways" back into re-employment, looking at different groups of workers (those employed by three months after the closure, those employed eight months on, and those still unemployed at eight months but in employment by three years after the closure). The impact of the closure across these groups has varied, suggesting a greater degree of differentiation in support may be appropriate in similar situations in the future. Such tailored support would combine help psychologically, in making training and education available and accessible, enabling mobility (both in occupational and physical terms), counseling and support regarding finance and debt, and help for partners to retrain and/or enter work.

Questions for Discussion

1. How do you evaluate the outcomes described in the case?
2. Should workers be forced to change industries?
3. What key dimensions would you evaluate to determine success?

INTERNATIONAL MARKET ENTRY AND DEVELOPMENT

PART TWO FOCUSES ON THE FRAMEWORK OF GOING GLOBAL. IT BEGINS BY PRESENTING THE OVERALL STRATEGIC OPTIONS AND THEIR IMPLEMENTATION BY THE FIRM, WHICH PROVIDES THE FRAMEWORK FOR THE SUBSEQUENT DEVELOPMENT OF THE TEXT. THIS SETTING OF THE STAGE IS FOLLOWED BY THE DEVELOPMENT OF THE KNOWLEDGE BASE THROUGH MARKETING RESEARCH, WHICH ENSURES THAT THE COMPANY NOT ONLY DOES THINGS RIGHT BUT ALSO DOES THE RIGHT THINGS. THEN WE CONCENTRATE ON MARKET ENTRY, PRIMARILY THROUGH EXPORTING AND OTHER LOW-COST, LOW-RISK INTERNATIONAL EXPANSION ALTERNATIVES, FOLLOWED BY THE SYSTEMATIC MULTINATIONAL EXPANSION OF INTERNATIONALLY MORE EXPERIENCED FIRMS.

STRATEGIC PLANNING

Appliance Makers on a Global Quest

The $70 billion home appliance market (expected to grow to $120 billion by 2010) is undergoing major consolidation and globalization. Many U.S.-based manufacturers are faced in their home markets with increased competition from foreign companies, such as the world's largest appliance maker, Electrolux, and newcomers such as China's Haier and Kelon. In addition, industry fundamentals in the United States are rather gloomy: stagnating sales, rising raw material prices, and price wars. On the other hand, markets abroad are full of opportunities. The European market, for example, is growing quite fast, and the expansion of the European Union has made establishing business there even more attractive. Market potential is significant as well: While 65 percent of U.S. homes have dryers, only 18 percent of Europeans have them. Markets in Latin America and Asia are showing similar trends as well; for example, only 15 percent of Brazil's households own microwave ovens compared with 91 percent in the United States. However, expansion was slowed down considerably by the financial crises of 1997–2002 and 2008–2009.

To take advantage of this growth, appliance makers have formed strategic alliances and made acquisitions. General Electric entered into a joint venture with Britain's General Electric PLC, and in its strategic shift to move the company's "center of gravity" from the industrialized world to Asia and Latin America, joint ventures were established in India with Godrej and in Mexico with Mabe. A strictly North American manufacturer before 1989,

Whirlpool purchased the appliance business of Dutch giant N. V. Phillips. Whirlpool's move gave it ten plants on the European continent and some popular appliance lines, which is a major asset in a region characterized by loyalty to domestic brands. Today, Whirlpool is third in European market share after Electrolux and Bosch-Siemens. The company ranks first in the Americas, and while it only has a one percent market share in Asia, it is the region's largest Western appliance maker. Whirlpool's advantage in Brazil, for example, is the strong loyalty it has earned in 40 years of operations (which it lacks in some Asian markets). In the last five years, Whirlpool has expanded its operations in Eastern and Central Europe as well as South Africa, thus extending its total reach to 170 countries worldwide.

Product differences present global marketers with a considerable challenge. The British favor front-loading washing machines, while the French swear by top-loaders. The French prefer to cook their food at high temperatures, causing grease to splatter onto oven walls, which calls for self-cleaning ovens. This feature is in less demand in Germany, where lower temperatures are traditionally used. Manufacturers are hoping that European integration will bring about cost savings and product standardization. The danger to be avoided is the development of compromise products that in the end appeal to no one. Joint ventures present their share of challenges to the global marketers. For example, in Whirlpool's Shanghai facility, teams of American, Italian, and Chinese technicians must work through three interpreters to set up production.

Although opportunities do exist, competition is keen. Margins have suffered as manufacturers (more than 300 in

Europe alone) scrape for business. The major players have decided to compete in all the major markets of the world. "Becoming a global appliance player is clearly the best use of our management expertise and well-established brand line-up," Whirlpool executives have said. Whirlpool's long-term goal is to leverage its global manufacturing and brand assets strategically across the world.

The most recent entrants into the global home appliance markets are China's Haier and Kelon, both mainly in refrigerators and air conditioners, industries in which China's technology is up to world standards. Haier's market share globally is still small (2.8 percent) compared to Whirlpool's (11.3 percent) and Electrolux's (8.2 percent), but the company is on an ambitious growth trajectory. While no foreign brand has made it big in the U.S. major-appliance market (mainly due to lack of brand recognition and distribution presence), Haier is currently selling 250 models of appliances through big retailers such as Wal-Mart and Costco and over 1,000 independent dealers. The company claims to have 50 percent of the

HAIER IS THE SECOND LARGEST MAKER OF REFRIGERATORS IN THE WORLD AND RANKS SIXTH IN OVERALL APPLIANCE SALES.

U.S. market for small refrigerators (for offices and dorm rooms). The approach is to build brands with lower prices and dependable quality and move upscale with time. Haier is already the second largest maker of refrigerators in the world and ranks sixth in overall appliance sales.

Further consolidation in the industry occurred in late 2005, when Maytag was acquired by Whirlpool after a bidding war that included Haier. Apart from blocking a major global competitor, Whirlpool's $13 billion in annual sales expanded by Maytag's $4.7 billion. In 2008, when GE announced it would spin off its appliance unit for up to $8 billion, five possible buyers emerged, each wanting to boost its global position: LG, a South Korean electronics and telecommunications giant; Haier; Contoladora Mabe., a successful Mexico-based appliance firm that is partly owned by GE (and already makes appliances for other brand-name firms—including GE); Electrolux AB, a Stockholm-based company that parlayed its success in high-end vacuum cleaners into a broader success in home appliances; and Arcelik Anonim Sirketi, an appliance maker based in Istanbul, Turkey, that does business throughout the world—including in the United States.

SOURCES: "Will GE's Appliances Suffer Under a New Owner?" *The Wall Street Journal,* June 16, 2008, A11; William Patalon III, "GE Home Appliance Unit Sale Underscores Again that Corporations and Investors Alike Must Go Global to Succeed," *Money Morning,* May 29, 2008, available at **www.moneymorning.com**; "Maytag Corp.; Shareholders Approve the Sale of Company to Whirlpool," *The Wall Street Journal,* December 25, 2005, A1; "China's Power Brands," *Business Week,* November 8, 2004, 77–84; "Haier's Purpose," The *Economist,* March 20, 2004, 72; Joshua Kurlantzick, "Making It in China," U.S. *News & World Report,* October 7, 2002, 44–49; Jonathan Sprague, "Haier Reaches Higher," *Fortune,* September 16, 2002, 43–46; "Chinese Multinationals Aim to Be Just That," *The Wall Street Journal,* January 28, 2002, A1; Russell Flannery, "China Goes Global," *Forbes,* August 6, 2001, 35–38; **http://www.whirlpool.com**; **http://www.ge.com**; and **http://www.haieramerica.com**.

Global Marketing

Many marketing managers have to face the increasing globalization of markets and competition described in *The International Marketplace 6.1.* The rules of survival have changed since the beginning of the 1980s when Theodore Levitt first coined the phrase *global marketing.*[1] Even the biggest companies in the biggest home markets cannot survive on domestic sales alone if they are in global industries such as cars, banking, consumer electronics, entertainment, pharmaceuticals, publishing, travel services, or home appliances. They have to be in all major markets to survive the shakeouts expected to leave three to five players per industry at the beginning of the twenty-first century.[2]

Globalization reflects a business orientation based on the belief that the world is becoming more homogeneous and that distinctions between national markets are not only fading but, for some products, will eventually disappear. As a result, companies need to globalize their international strategy by formulating it across markets to take advantage of underlying market, cost, environmental, and competitive factors. This has meant, for example, that Chinese companies (in categories ranging from auto parts and appliances to telecommunications) have entered the main markets of the world, such as Europe and North America, to become global powerhouses.[3] Having a global presence ensures viability against other players, both local and global, in the home market as well.

As shown in Exhibit 6.1, global marketing can be seen as the culmination of a process of international market entry and expansion. Before globalization, marketers utilized a country-by-country multidomestic strategy to a great extent, with each country organization operated as a profit center. Each national entity markets a range of different products and services targeted to different customer segments, utilizing different marketing strategies with little or no coordination of operations between countries.

However, as national markets become increasingly similar and scale economies become increasingly important, the inefficiencies of duplicating product development and manufacture in each country become more apparent and the pressure to leverage resources and coordinate activities across borders gains urgency. Similarly, the increasing number of customers operating globally, as well as the same or similar competitors faced throughout the major markets, adds to the need for strategy integration.

It should be noted that global leverage means balancing three interests: global, regional, and local. In many cases, the exploitation of commonalities is best executed on a regional basis, given that some differences remain between groups of markets.[4] The same strategic principles apply to developing and implementing global and regional strategy. Naturally, the more a marketer can include the local dimension to efforts in each individual market, the more effective the strategy tends to be.[5] For example, consumers may prefer a global brand that has been adapted to the needs of local usage conditions. While the approach is localized, the global resources of a marketer provide the brand with a winning edge (e.g., in terms of quality or quality perceptions).

Exhibit 6.1

Global Marketing Evolution

Phase 1	Phase 2	Phase 3
Leverage of domestic capabilities: foreign market entry Objective: economies of scale	Expansion of foreign market presence Objective: economies of scope	Coordination of global operations Objective: exploit synergies throughout network
Corporate Actions		
Driven opportunistically, often by approach of distributor or customer	Slower domestic growth creates greater pressure for foreign sales growth	Product the broadened, new emphasis on full-line service rather than proprietary technology
Constrained by lack of funding (domestic growth still priority investment), so low cost entry	New lines carried, sales mix broadens and reflects national market	Global account management
Risk minimized by entering close markets (geographically, culturally, economically)	Search for new customer segments, requiring new management skills	Coordination mechanisms (Global Task Forces) Learning transferred between countries
Entry based on core products with technical superiority	Countries develop own marketing programs	Headquarters introduces global branding, packaging
	New applications sought	Requires common culture
	Decentralization of R & D, production	
	Regional management reflects foreign experience	

SOURCE: Adapted from Susan P. Douglas and C. Samuel Craig, "Evolution of Global Marketing Strategy: Scale, Scope, and Synergy," *Columbia Journal of World Business* 24 (Fall 1989): 47–58, and George S. Yip, *Total Global Strategy II*, Upper Saddle River, NJ: Pearson, 2002, chapter 1.

Globalization Drivers

Both external and internal factors will create the favorable conditions for development of strategy and resource allocation on a global basis. These factors can be divided into market, cost, environmental, and competitive factors.[6]

Market Factors

The world customer identified by Ernst Dichter more than 40 years ago has gained new meaning today.[7] For example, Kenichi Ohmae has identified consumers in the **triad** of North America, Europe, and the Asia-Pacific region, whom marketers can treat as a single market with similar consumption habits.[8] Over a billion in number, these consumers have similar educational backgrounds, income levels, lifestyles, use of leisure time, and aspirations. One reason given for the similarities in their demand is a level of purchasing power (ten times greater than that of the developing markets or even emerging economies) that translates into higher diffusion rates for certain products. Another reason is that developed infrastructures—diffusion of telecommunication and common platforms such as Microsoft Windows and the Internet—lead to attractive markets for other goods and services. Emerging and developing markets have been able to leapfrog into the newest technologies, closing significant gaps of the past. Products can therefore, be designed to meet similar demand conditions throughout the triad and beyond. These similarities also enhance the transferability of other marketing elements. For example, mobile subscribers in BRIC countries rank entertainment, gaming, and music sites among their top categories while European and U.S. users rank e-mail, weather and news, and sports highest. The reason for the difference is that BRIC residents often do not have the home PCs, cable TV, and iPods that Westerners do, and thus use phones for entertainment purposes.[9]

At the same time, channels of distribution are becoming more global; that is, a growing number of retailers are now showing great flexibility in their strategies for entering new geographic markets.[10] Some are already world powers (e.g., Benetton and McDonald's), whereas others are pursuing aggressive growth (e.g., ALDI, Toys, 'Я' Us, and IKEA). Also noteworthy are cross-border retail alliances, which expand the presence of retailers to new markets quite rapidly. The presence of global and regional channels makes it more necessary for the marketer to rationalize marketing efforts.

Cost Factors

Avoiding cost inefficiencies and duplication of effort are two of the most powerful globalization drivers. A single-country approach may not be large enough for the local business to achieve all possible economies of scale and scope as well as synergies, especially given the dramatic changes in the marketplace. Take, for example, pharmaceuticals. In the 1970s, developing a new drug cost about $16 million and took four years. The drug could be produced in Britain or the United States and eventually exported. Now, developing a drug costs as much as $1 billion and takes as long as 12 years, with competitive efforts close behind. For the leading companies, annual R&D budgets can run to $5 billion. Only global products for global markets can support that much risk.[11] Size has become a major asset, which partly explains the many mergers and acquisitions in industries such as aerospace, pharmaceuticals, and telecommunications. The paper industry has undergone major regional consolidation between 1998 and 2008, as shown in Exhibit 6.2, as companies from North America and Europe in particular consolidated their positions in a scale-driven sector.[12] In the heavily contested consumer goods sectors, launching a new brand may cost as much as $100 million, meaning that companies such as Unilever and Procter & Gamble are not going to necessarily spend precious resources on one-country projects.

In many cases, expanded market participation and activity concentration can accelerate the accumulation of learning and experience. General Electric's philosophy is to be first or second in the world in a business or to get out. This can be seen, for example, in its global effort to develop premium computed tomography (CT), a diagnostic scanning system. GE swapped its consumer electronics business with the French Thomson

Exhibit 6.2

Consolidation in the Paper Industry, 1998–2008

Acquirer	Target	Value	Date Announced
Sappi (South Africa)	M-Real (Finland)	$1.1 billion	9/29/08
Abitibi-Consol. (Canada)*	Bowater (U.S.)*	$8 billion	10/29/07
Koch Industries (U.S.)	Georgia-Pacific (U.S.)	$13.2 billion	11/13/05
Chuetsu Pulp & Paper (Japan)	Mitsubishi Paper (Japan)	$2.4 billion	1/31/05
Semapa (Portugal)	Portucel (Portugal)	$1.9 billion	7/6/04
Weyerhaeuser (U.S.)	Willamette Industries (U.S.)	$6.2 billion	1/28/02
MeadWestvaco (U.S.)*	Mead (U.S.)*	$3.2 billion	8/29/01
Norske Skogindustrier (Norway)	Fletcher Challenge Paper (New Zealand)	$2.5 billion	4/03/00
Smurfit-Stone (U.S.)	St. Laurent Paperboard (Canada)	$1.0 billion	2/23/00
Stora Enso (Finland)	Consolidated Papers (U.S.)	$3.9 billion	2/22/00
International Paper (U.S.)	Champion Int'l (U.S.)	$5.7 billion	2/17/00
Abitibi-Consol. (Canada)	Donohue (Canada)	$4.0 billion	2/11/00
Weyerhaeuser (U.S.)	MacMillan Bloedel (Canada)	$2.3 billion	6/21/99
Int'l Paper (U.S.)	Union Camp (U.S.)	$5.9 billion	11/24/98
Stora (Sweden)*	Enso Oyj (Finland)*	Undisclosed	6/02/98

* Merger of equals

SOURCES: "Sappi Acquires Coated Graphic Paper Business from M-Real," *PR Newswire*, September 29, 2008; Donald Granholm, "Industry Consolidation, Escalating Cost of Materials Push Paper Prices Higher," *Nashua Corporation*, available at **www.nashua.com**; "Koch Industries Agrees to Buy Georgia-Pacific," *The Wall Street Journal*, November 14, 2005, A3; "Paper Merger Attains Size without Adding Huge Debt," *The Wall Street Journal*, August 30, 2001, B4; and "Stora Enso to Buy Consolidated Papers," *The Wall Street Journal*, February 23, 2000, A3, A8. See also **http://www.storaenso.com**; and Robert Frank, "The Emerging Global Paper Industry," **http://www.worldleadersinprint.com**.

for Thomson's diagnostic imaging business. At the same time, GE established GE Medical Systems Asia in Tokyo, anchored on Yokogawa Medical Systems, 75 percent of which is owned by GE.

Environmental Factors

As shown earlier in this text, government barriers have fallen dramatically in the last years to further facilitate the globalization of markets and the activities of marketers within them. For example, the forces pushing toward a pan-European market are very powerful: The increasing wealth and mobility of European consumers (favored by the relaxed immigration controls), the accelerating flow of information across borders, the introduction of new products where local preferences are not well established, and the common currency.[13] Also, the resulting removal of physical, fiscal, and technical barriers is indicative of the changes that are taking place around the world on a greater scale.

At the same time, rapid technological evolution is contributing to the process. For example, Ford Motor Company is able to accomplish its globalization efforts by using new communications methods, such as teleconferencing, intranet, and CAD/CAM links, as well as travel, to manage the complex task of meshing car companies on different continents.[14] Newly emerging markets will benefit from advanced communications by being able to leapfrog stages of economic development. Places that until recently were incommunicado in China, Vietnam, Hungary, or Brazil are rapidly acquiring state-of-the-art telecommunications, especially in mobile telephony, that will let them foster both internal and external development.[15]

A new group of global players is taking advantage of today's more open trading regions and newer technologies. "Mininationals" or "Born Globals" (newer companies with sales between $200 million and $1 billion) are able to serve the world from a handful of bases, compared with having to build a presence in every country as the established multinational corporations once had to do. Their smaller bureaucracies have also allowed these mininationals to move swiftly to seize new markets and develop new products—a key to global success.[16]

The lessons from these new-generation global players are to (1) keep focused and concentrate on being number one or two in a niche; (2) stay lean by having small headquarters to save on costs and to accelerate decision-making; (3) take ideas from wherever they can be found and solutions to wherever they are needed; (4) take advantage, regardless of nationality, of employees' ideas and experience to globalize thinking; and (5) solve customers' problems by involving them rather than pushing standardized solutions on them.[17] For example, Cochlear, an Australian firm specializing in implants for the profoundly deaf, exports 95 percent of its output and maintains its technological lead through strong links with hospitals and research units around the world.[18]

An example of this phenomenon in the area of social marketing is provided in *The International Marketplace 6.2.*

Competitive Factors

Many industries are already dominated by global competitors that are trying to take advantage of the three sets of factors mentioned earlier. To remain competitive, the marketer may have to be the first to do something or to be able to match or preempt competitors' moves. Products are now introduced, upgraded, and distributed at rates unimaginable a decade ago. Without a global network, a marketer may run the risk of seeing carefully researched ideas picked off by other global players. This is what Procter & Gamble and Unilever did to Kao's Attack concentrated detergent, which they mimicked and introduced into the United States and Europe before Kao could react.

With the triad markets often both flat in terms of growth and fiercely competitive, many global marketers are looking for new markets and for new product categories for growth. Nestlé, for example, is setting its sights on consumer markets in fast-growing Asia, especially China, and has diversified into pharmaceuticals by acquiring Alcon and by becoming a major shareholder in the world's number-one cosmetics company, the French L'Oreal.

The International MARKETPLACE

6.2

Born Globals and Social Sustainability

Atsumasa Tochisako founded Microfinance International in June 2003, following a 27-year career at the Bank of Tokyo-Mitsubishi that included assignments in four Latin American countries. Mr. Tochisako realized that microlending has the potential to be both a commercially attractive business and to serve as a form of high impact developmental assistance.

He also knew that remittances from immigrants in industrialized countries provide the largest source of capital to many developing countries, often exceeding any other source of capital inflow and representing up to 20 percent of GDP in some countries. Applying his banking experience and the world-renowned financial expertise of the team he assembled, he designed a business model that links remittances with microfinance for the benefit of immigrants in the United States and their families in developing countries.

MFI was global from its birth with operations in the United States and El Salvador. Since then, it has expanded to more than ten Latin American countries and further extended its

reach by allowing multinational financial institutions to use its proprietary Internet-based settlement platform.

Social enterprises are born global for three reasons. First, social problems, such as disease, malnutrition, poverty, and illiteracy, exist on a large scale in many developing countries. Second, the resources (funds, institutions, and governance systems) are mainly in the developed world. Third, global for-profit social enterprises that tackle specific conditions can often be adapted to other similar countries and situations. For example, The Lapdesk Company with the support of corporations, international agencies, and NGOs is tackling classroom desk shortages. In contrast to the conventional school desk, which is expensive and unsuited to outside schooling and overcrowded classrooms, the portable Lapdesk offers a cost-effective, creative, and proven solution suitable to any type of environment where schooling is conducted. The program has been extended from its African origins to India and Latin America.

SOURCES: Daniel J. Isenberg, "How Social Entrepreneurs Think Global," *Harvard Business Review* 86 (December 2008): 110; **www.mfi-corp.com**; and **www.lapdesk.co.za**.

Between 1985 and 2000, Nestlé spent $26 billion on acquisitions, and another $18 billion from 2001 to 2002.[19] Since then, the company has focused its acquisitions on the ice-cream and drinks sectors by buying Mövenpick, Powwow, Dreyers, and Valio. Future acquisitions may include Hershey of the United States or the British Cadbury.[20]

Market presence may be necessary to execute global strategies and to prevent others from having undue advantage in unchallenged markets. Caterpillar faced mounting global competition from Komatsu but found out that strengthening its products and operations was not enough to meet the challenge. Although Japan was a small part of the world market, as a secure home base (no serious competitors), it generated 80 percent of Komatsu's cash flow. To put a check on its major global competitor's market share and cash flow, Caterpillar formed a heavy-equipment joint venture with Mitsubishi to serve the Japanese market.[21] Similarly, when Unilever tried to acquire Richardson-Vicks in the United States, Procter & Gamble saw this as a threat to its home market position and outbid its archrival for the company. International Paper prevented Finland's United Paper Mills from acquiring Champion International to protect its market position as the leading paper maker in North America and the world.

The Outcome

The four globalization drivers have affected countries and industrial sectors differently. While some industries are truly globally contested, such as paper and soft drinks, some others, such as government procurement, are still quite closed and will open up as a decades-long evolution. Commodities and manufactured goods are already in a globalized state, while many consumer goods are accelerating toward more globalization. Similarly, the leading trading nations of the world display far more openness than low-income countries, thus advancing the state of globalization in general. The expansion of the global trade arena is summarized in Exhibit 6.3. The size of the market estimated to be global in the early twenty-first century is well over $21 billion, boosted by new sectors and markets that will become available. For example, while financially unattractive in the short to medium term, low-income markets may be beneficial in learning the business climate, developing relationships, and building brands for the future. Hewlett-Packard, through its e-Inclusion initiative, is looking at speech interfaces for the Internet, solar applications, and cheap devices that connect with the Web.[22]

Exhibit 6.3

The Global Landscape by Industry and Market

Industry

		Commodities and scale-driven goods	Consumer goods and locally delivered goods and services	Government services
Country	**Triad***	Established arena Globalized in 1980s		
	Emerging countries†	Growing arena Globally contestable today		
	Low-income countries‡	Closed arena Still blocked or lacking significant opportunity		

Global ← → Local

More globalized ↑ / ↓ Less globalized

*30 OECD countries from North America, Western Europe, and Asia; Japan and Australia included
†70 countries with middle income per capita, plus China and India ($2,000–$20,000)
‡100 countries of small absolute size and low income per capita (< $2,000)

SOURCES: Adapted and updated from Jane Fraser and Jeremy Oppenheim, "What's New about Globalization," *The McKinsey Quarterly* 33 (no. 2, 1997): 173; and Jagdish N. Sheth and Atul Parkatiyar, "The Antecedents and Consequences of Integrated Global Marketing," *International Marketing Review* 18 (no. 1, 2001): 16–29.

Leading companies by their very actions drive the globalization process. There is no structural reason why soft drinks should be at a more advanced stage of globalization than beer and spirits, which remain more local, except for the opportunistic behavior of Coca-Cola. Similarly, Nike and Adidas have driven their businesses in a global direction by creating global brands, a global customer segment, and a global supply chain. By creating a single online trading exchange for all their parts and suppliers, General Motors, Ford, and Chrysler created a worldwide market of $240 billion in automotive components.[23]

The Strategic Planning Process

Given the opportunities and challenges provided by the new realities of the marketplace, decision makers have to engage in strategic planning to match markets with products and other corporate resources more effectively and efficiently, to strengthen the company's long-term competitive advantage. While the process has been summarized as a sequence of steps in Exhibit 6.4, many of the stages can occur simultaneously. Furthermore, feedback as a result of evaluation and control may restart the process at any stage.

It has been shown that for globally committed marketers, formal strategic planning contributes to both financial performance and nonfinancial objectives.[24] These benefits include raising the efficacy of new-product launches, cost reduction efforts, and improving product quality and market share performance. Internally, these efforts increase cohesion and improve on understanding different units' points of view. The process will have to keep three broad dimensions in mind: (1) the potential benefits for the company in the short versus the long-term; (2) the costs in terms of management time and process realignment; as well as (3) the presence of the necessary management resources to undertake the endeavor.[25]

Exhibit 6.4

Global Strategy Formulation

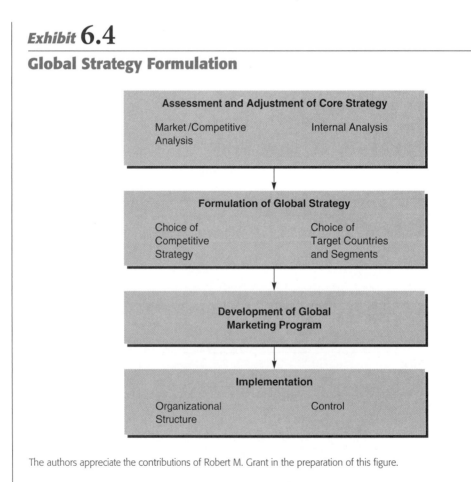

The authors appreciate the contributions of Robert M. Grant in the preparation of this figure.

Imbedded in this planning has to be the selection of the types of power the company wants to exercise in the global marketplace. In business, hard power refers to the use of scale, financial might, or the use of low-cost position to win market access and share. Increasingly, marketers will also have to incorporate **soft power** into their tool kits. Soft power refers to the capability of attracting and influencing all stakeholders whether through energetic brands, heroic missions, distinctive talent development, or an inspirational corporate culture.[26]

Understanding and Adjusting the Core Strategy

The planning process has to start with a clear definition of the business for which strategy is to be developed. Generally, the strategic business unit (SBU) is the unit around which decisions are based. In practice, SBUs represent groupings organized around product-market similarities based on (1) needs or wants to be met, (2) end user customers to be targeted, or (3) the product or service used to meet the needs of specific customers. For a global marketer such as Black & Decker, the options may be to define the business to be analyzed as the home improvement business, the do-it-yourself business, or the power tool business. Ideally, these SBUs should have primary responsibility and authority in managing their basic business functions.

This phase of the planning process requires the participation of executives from different functions, especially marketing, production, finance, distribution, and procurement. Geographic representation should be from the major markets or regions as well as from the smaller, yet emerging, markets. With appropriate members, the committee can focus on product and markets as well as competitors whom they face in different markets, whether they are global, regional, or purely local. Heading this effort should be an executive with highest-level experience in regional or global markets; for example, one global firm called on the president of its European operations to come back to headquarters to head the global planning effort. This effort calls for commitment by the company itself, both in calling on the best talent to participate in the planning effort and later in implementing their proposals.

It should be noted that this assessment against environmental realities may mean a dramatic change in direction and approach. For example, the once-separate sectors of computing and mobile telephony will be colliding and the direction of future products is still uncertain. The computer industry believes in miniaturizing the general-purpose computer, while the mobile-phone industry believes in adding new features (such as photo-messaging, gaming, and location-based information) to its existing products.[27] The joint venture between Ericsson and Sony aims at taking advantage of this trend, something that neither party could have done on its own.

Market and Competitive Analysis

For global marketers, planning on a country-by-country basis can result in spotty worldwide market performance. The starting point for global strategic planning is to understand that the underlying forces that determine business success are common to the different countries that the firm competes in. Planning processes that focus simultaneously across a broad range of markets provide global marketers with tools to help balance risks, resource requirements, competitive economies of scale, and profitability to gain stronger long-term positions.[28] On the demand side this requires an understanding of the common features of customer requirements and choice factors. In terms of competition, the key is to understand the structure of the global industry in order to identify the forces that will drive competition and determine profitability.[29]

For any automobile company, for example, strategy begins not with individual national markets, but with understanding trends and sources of profit in the global automobile market. What are the trends in world demand? What are the underlying trends in lifestyles and transportation patterns that will shape customer expectations and preferences with respect to safety, economy, design, and performance? What is the emerging structure of the industry, especially with regard to consolidation among both automakers and their suppliers? What will determine the intensity of competition between the different automakers?

The level of excess capacity (currently about 40 percent in the worldwide auto industry) is likely to be a key influence.[30] If competition is likely to intensify, which companies will emerge as winners? An understanding of scale economies, the state of technology, and the other factors that determine cost efficiency is likely to be critically important.

Internal Analysis

Organizational resources have to be used as a reality check for any strategic choice, in that they determine a company's capacity for establishing and sustaining competitive advantage within global markets. Industrial giants with deep pockets may be able to establish a presence in any market they wish, while more thinly capitalized companies may have to move cautiously. Human resources may also present a challenge for market expansion. A survey of multinational corporations revealed that good marketing managers, skilled technicians, and production managers were especially difficult to find. This difficulty is further compounded when the search is for people with cross-cultural experience to run future regional operations.[31]

At this stage it is imperative that the company assess its own readiness for the necessary moves. This means a rigorous assessment of organizational commitment to global or regional expansion, as well as an assessment of the product's readiness to face the competitive environment. In many cases this has meant painful decisions of focusing on certain industries and leaving others. For example, Nokia, the world's largest manufacturer of mobile phones, started its rise in the industry when a decision was made at the company in 1992 to focus on digital cellular phones and to sell off dozens of other product lines (such as personal computers, automotive tires, and toilet tissue). By focusing its efforts on this line, the company was able to bring to market new products quickly, build scale economies into its manufacturing, and concentrate on its customers, thereby communicating a commitment to their needs. Nokia's current 40 percent market share allows it the best global visibility of and by the market.[32] Its size also allows it to deal with low-cost challengers in an aggressive manner. In China, which is the company's single largest market, it faced a challenge from Ningbo Bird: appealing new designs for the country's young target

IN CHINA, NOKIA FACED A CHALLENGE FROM NINGBO BIRD, WHO WAS ABLE TO PROVIDE APPEALING NEW DESIGNS FOR THE COUNTRY'S YOUNG TARGET AUDIENCE. IN RESPONSE, NOKIA DEVELOPED NEW TRENDY PHONES.

audience. In response, Nokia developed trendier phones and, in order to sell them, radically expanded its sales and distribution network.[33]

Formulating Global Marketing Strategy

The first step in the formulation of global strategy is the choice of competitive strategy to be employed, followed by the choice of country markets to be entered or penetrated further.

Choice of Competitive Strategy

In dealing with the global markets, the marketing manager has three general choices of strategies, as shown in Exhibit 6.5: (1) cost leadership, (2) differentiation, or (3) focus.[34] A focus strategy is defined by its emphasis on a single industry segment within which the orientation may be toward either low cost or differentiation. Any one of these strategies can be pursued on a global or regional basis, or the marketer may decide to mix and match strategies as a function of market or product dimensions.

In pursuing cost leadership, the global marketer offers an identical product or service at a lower cost than the competition. This often means investment in scale economies and strict control of costs, such as overhead, research and development, and logistics. Differentiation, whether it is industry-wide or focused on a single segment, takes advantage of the marketer's real or perceived uniqueness in elements such as design or after-sales service. It should be noted, however, that a low-price, low-cost strategy does not imply a commodity situation.[35] Although Japanese, U.S., and European technical standards differ, mobile phone manufacturers like Motorola and Nokia design their phones to be as similar as possible to hold down manufacturing costs. As a result, they can all be made on the same production line, allowing the manufacturers to shift rapidly from one model to another to meet changes in demand and customer requirements. In the case of IKEA, the low-price approach is associated with clear positioning and a unique brand image focused on a clearly defined target audience of "young people of all ages." Similarly, marketers who opt for high differentiation cannot forget the monitoring of costs. One common denominator of consumers around the world is their quest for value for their money. With the availability of information increasing and levels of education improving, customers are poised to demand even more of their suppliers.

Most global marketers combine high differentiation with cost containment to enter markets and to expand their market shares. Flexible manufacturing systems using mostly standard components and total quality management measures that reduce the occurrence of defects are allowing marketers to customize an increasing amount of their production while at the same time saving on costs. Global activities will in themselves permit the exploitation of scale economies not only in production but also in marketing activities, such as advertising.

Exhibit 6.5

Competitive Strategies

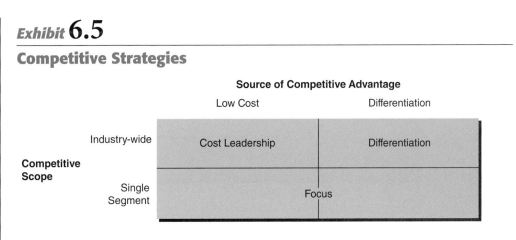

SOURCE: Michael Porter, *Competitive Advantage: Creating and Sustaining Superior Performance* (New York: Free Press, 1998), chapter 1.

Country-Market Choice

A global strategy does not imply that a company should serve the entire globe. Critical choices relate to the allocation of a company's resources between different countries and segments.

The usual approach is first to start with regions and further split the analysis by country. Many marketers use multiple levels of regional groupings to follow the organizational structure of the company, e.g., splitting Europe into northern, central, and southern regions that display similarities in demographic and behavioral traits. An important consideration is that data may be more readily available if existing structures and frameworks are used.[36]

Various portfolio models have been proposed as tools for this analysis. They typically involve two measures—internal strength and external attractiveness.[37] As indicators of internal strength, the following variables have been used: relative market share, product fit, contribution margin, and market presence, which would incorporate the level of support by constituents as well as resources allocated by the company itself. Country attractiveness has been measured using market size, market growth rate, number and type of competitors, and governmental regulation, as well as economic and political stability.

An example of such a matrix is provided in Exhibit 6.6. The 3 × 3 matrix on country attractiveness and company strength is applied to the European markets. Markets in the invest/grow position will require continued commitment by management in research and development, investment in facilities, and the training of personnel at the country level. In cases of relative weakness in growing markets, the company's position may have to be strengthened (through acquisitions or strategic alliances) or a decision to divest may be necessary. For example, General Mills signed a complementary marketing arrangement with Nestlé to enter the European market dominated by its main global rival, Kellogg's. This arrangement allowed General Mills effective market entry and Nestlé more efficient utilization of its distribution channels in Europe, as well as entry to a new product market. The alliance has since resulted in the formation of Cereal Partners Worldwide, which has a combined worldwide market share of 21 percent and sells its products in more than 130 countries.[38]

Exhibit **6.6**

Example of a Market-Portfolio Matrix

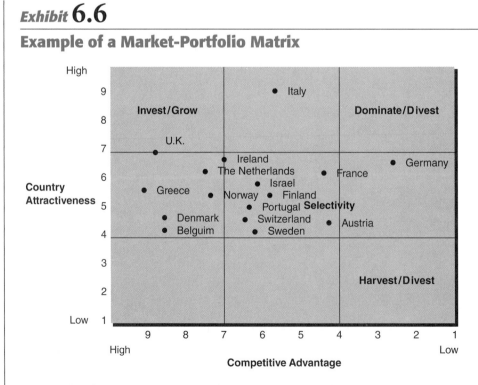

SOURCE: Adapted from Gilbert D. Harrell and Richard O. Kiefer, "Multinational Market Portfolios in Global Strategy Development," *International Marketing Review* 10 (no. 1, 1993): 60–72.

In choosing country markets, a company must make decisions beyond those relating to market attractiveness and company position. A market expansion policy will determine the allocation of resources among various markets. The basic alternatives are concentration on a small number of markets and diversification, which is characterized by growth in a relatively large number of markets. Expansion strategy is determined by market-, mix-, and company-related factors, listed in Exhibit 6.7. Market-related factors determine the attractiveness of the market in the first place. With high and stable growth rates only in certain markets, the firm will likely opt for a concentration strategy, which is often the case for innovative products early in their life cycle. If demand is strong worldwide, as the case may be for consumer goods, diversification may be attractive. If markets respond to marketing efforts at increasing rates, concentration will occur; however, when the cost of market share points in any one market becomes too high, marketers tend to begin looking for diversification opportunities.

The uniqueness of the product offering with respect to competition is also a factor in expansion strategy. If lead time over competition is considerable, the decision to diversify may not seem urgent. Very few products, however, afford such a luxury. In many product categories, marketers will be affected by spillover effects. Consider, for example, the impact of satellite channels on advertising in Europe or in Asia, where ads for a product now reach most of the market. The greater the degree to which marketing mix elements can be standardized, the more diversification is probable. Overall savings through economies of scale can then be utilized in marketing efforts. Finally, the objectives and policies of the company itself will guide the decision-making on expansion. If extensive interaction is called for with intermediaries and clients, efforts are most likely to be concentrated because of resource constraints.

The conventional wisdom of globalization requires a presence in all of the major markets of the world. In some cases, markets may not be attractive in their own right but may have some other significance, such as being the home market of the most demanding customers, thereby aiding in product development, or being the home market of a significant competitor (a preemptive rationale). For example, Procter & Gamble rolled its Charmin bath tissue into European markets in 2000 to counter an upsurge in European paper products sales by its global rival Kimberly-Clark.[39] European PC makers, such as Germany's Maxdata, are taking aim at the U.S. market based on the premise that if they can compete with the big multinationals (Dell, Hewlett-Packard, and Gateway) at home, there is no reason why they cannot be competitive in North America as well.[40]

Exhibit 6.7

Factors Affecting the Choice between Concentration and Diversification Strategies

Factor	Diversification	Concentration
MARKET		
Market growth rate	Low	High
Sales stability	Low	High
Sales response function	Decreasing	Increasing
Extent of constraints	Low	High
MARKETING		
Competitive lead time	Short	Long
Spillover effects	High	Low
Need for product adaptation	Low	High
Need for communication adaptation	Low	High
Economies of scale in distribution	Low	High
Program control requirements	Low	High

SOURCE: Adapted from Igal Ayal and Jehiel Zif, "Marketing Expansion Strategies in Multinational Marketing," *Journal of Marketing* 43 (Spring 1979): 89.

Therefore, for global marketers three factors should determine country selection: (1) the stand-alone attractiveness of a market (e.g., China in consumer products due to its size), (2) global strategic importance (e.g., Finland in shipbuilding due to its lead in technological development in vessel design), and (3) possible synergies (e.g., entry into Latvia and Lithuania after success in the Estonian market, given the market similarities).

Segmentation

Effective use of segmentation, that is, the recognition that groups within markets differ sufficiently enough to warrant individual marketing mixes, allows global marketers to take advantage of the benefits of standardization (such as economies of scale and consistency in positioning) while addressing the unique needs and expectations of a specific target group. This approach means looking at markets on a global or regional basis, thereby ignoring the political boundaries that otherwise define markets in many cases. The identification and cultivation of such intermarket segments is necessary for any standardization of marketing programs to work.[41]

The emergence of segments that span markets is already evident in the world marketplace. Global marketers have successfully targeted the teenage segment, which is converging as a result of common tastes in sports and music fueled by their computer literacy, travels abroad, and, in many countries, financial independence.[42] Furthermore, a media revolution is creating a common fabric of attitudes and tastes among teenagers. Today, satellite TV and global network concepts such as MTV are both helping create this segment and providing global marketers access to the teen audience around the world. For example, Reebok used a global ad campaign to launch its Instapump line of sneakers in the United States, Germany, Japan, and 137 other countries. Given that teenagers around the world are concerned with social issues, particularly environmentalism, Reebok has introduced a new ecological climbing shoe made from recycled and environmentally sensitive materials. Similarly, two other distinct segments have been detected to be ready for a pan-regional approach. One includes trendsetters who are wealthier and better educated and tend to value independence, refuse consumer stereotypes, and appreciate exclusive products. The second one includes Europe's businesspeople who are well-to-do, regularly travel abroad, and have a taste for luxury goods.

Despite convergence, global marketers still have to make adjustments in some of the marketing mix elements for maximum impact. For example, while Levi's jeans are globally accepted by the teenage segment, European teens reacted negatively to the urban realism of Levi's U.S. ads. Levi's converted its ads in Europe, drawing on images of a mythical America.[43] Similarly, segment sizes vary from one market to another even in cohesive regions such as Europe. The value-oriented segment in Germany accounts for 32 percent of the grocery sales but only 9 percent in the United Kingdom and 8 percent in France.[44]

The greatest challenge for the global marketer is the choice of an appropriate base for the segmentation effort. The objective is to arrive at a grouping or groupings that are substantial enough to merit the segmentation effort (for example, there are nearly 230 million teenagers in the Americas, Europe, and the Asia-Pacific, with the teenagers of the Americas spending nearly $60 billion of their own money yearly) and are reachable as well by the marketing effort (for example, the majority of MTV's audience consists of teenagers).

The possible bases for segmentation are summarized in Exhibit 6.8. Marketers have traditionally used environmental bases for segmentation. However, using geographic proximity, political system characteristics, economic standing, or cultural traits as a stand-alone basis may not provide relevant data for decision making. Using a combination of them, however, may produce more meaningful results. One of the segments pursued by global marketers around the world is the middle-class family. Defining the composition of this global middle class is tricky, given the varying levels of development among nations in Latin America and Asia. However, some experts estimate that 25 percent of the world population enjoy middle-class lives, some 300 million in India alone.[45] Using household income alone may be quite a poor gauge of class. Income figures ignore vast differences in international purchasing power. Chinese consumers, for example, spend less than 5 percent of their total outlays on rent, transportation, and health, while a typical U.S. household spends 45 to 50 percent. Additionally, income distinctions do not reflect education or values—two increasingly

Exhibit 6.8

Bases for Global Market Segmentation

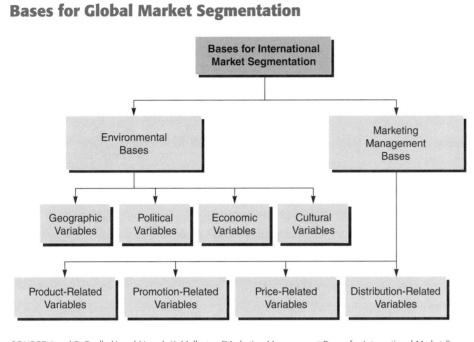

SOURCE: Imad B. Baalbaki and Naresh K. Malhotra, "Marketing Management Bases for International Market Segmentation: An Alternate Look at the Standardization/Customization Debate," *International Marketing Review* 10 (no. 1, 1993): 19–44. Reprinted with permission.

important barometers of middle-class status. A global segmentation effort using cultural values is provided in *The International Marketplace 6.3*.

It has also been proposed that markets that reflect a high degree of homogeneity with respect to marketing mix variables could be grouped into segments and thereby targeted with a largely standardized marketing strategy. Whether bases related to product, promotion, pricing, or distribution are used, their influence should be related to environmentally based variables. Product-related bases include the degree to which products are culture-based, which stage of the life cycle they occupy, consumption patterns, and attitudes toward product attributes (such as country of origin), as well as consumption infrastructure (for example, telephone lines for modems). The growth of microwave sales, for example, has been surprising in low-income countries; however, microwaves have become status symbols and buying them more of an emotional issue. Many consumers in these markets also want to make sure they get the same product as available in developed markets, thereby eliminating the need in many cases to develop market-specific products. Adjustments will have to made, however. Noticing that, for reasons of status and space, many Asian consumers put their refrigerators in their living rooms, Whirlpool makes refrigerators available in striking colors such as red and blue.

With promotion, customers' values and norms set the baseline for global versus regional versus local solutions. The significant emphasis on family relationships among many Europeans and North Americans creates a multiregional segment that can be exploited by consumer-goods and consumer-services marketers (such as car marketers or telecommunications service providers). On the pricing side, dimensions such as customers' price sensitivity may lead the marketer to go after segments that insist on high quality despite high price in markets where overall purchasing power may be low, to ensure global or regional uniformity in the marketing approach. Affordability is a major issue for customers whose buying power may fall short for at least the time being. Offering only one option may exclude potential customers of the future who are not yet part of a targeted segment; companies like Procter & Gamble and Unilever offer an array of products at different price

The International MARKETPLACE

6.3

Segmenting Global Markets by Cultural Values

Three critical factors—nationality, demographics, and values—play major roles in determining the nature and evolution of global consumer markets. But their importance relative to one another depends on the product or service category with which marketers are dealing. Core values go much deeper than behavior or attitude, and they determine, at a basic level, people's choices and desires over the long term. Behavior changes quickly in response to outside forces of all kinds, including whether a person got a good night's sleep or how long the line is at the grocery store. Although slower to change, attitudes also are prone to external influences. Core values, on the other hand, are intrinsic to a person's identity and inherent beliefs. By appealing to people's inner selves, it's possible to influence their outer selves—their purchase behavior.

As part of a Roper Reports Worldwide Global Consumer Survey, 1,000 people were interviewed in their homes in each of 35 countries. As part of their responses, they ranked 56 values by the importance they hold as guiding principles in their lives. Among adults, six global values segments emerged, residing in all 35 countries, but to varying degrees in each. Interestingly, the largest values

segment across the globe focuses on the material world, while the second largest centers on the soul.

Although most people fall into a particular category, some values cut across many categories and countries. For example, "protecting the family" ranks in the top 10 for all six groups. All 35 countries rank family in their top five guiding principles, except for Indonesia, which ranks respecting ancestors as number one. All the Asian countries surveyed place family in their top two. Protecting the family was given top value in 22 countries, including the United States. A country-by-country analysis reveals that Great Britain leads the world in wanting to protect the family, Brazil has the most fun seekers, Saudi Arabia ranks first in faith, the Netherlands has the highest percentage worldwide in esteeming honesty, and Korea is the global front-runner in valuing health and fitness.

The research shows that people in different segments generally pursue different activities, buy different products, and use different media. Knowing which segments dominate in a country helps with marketing efforts and enables advertisers to tailor their message to those parts of the population most likely to buy. Profiles of the values segments around the world give marketers the tools to refine their strategies, identify potential consumers, reinforce loyal customer bases, and buffer them against competitive moves.

Segment	Characteristics	Geographics
Strivers	More likely to be men; place more emphasis on material and professional goals	One-third of people in developing Asia; one-quarter in Russia and developed Asia
Devouts	22 percent of adults; women more than men; tradition and duty are paramount	Africa, Asia, Middle East; least common in Europe
Altruists	18 percent of adults; larger portion of females; interested in social issues and welfare of society; older	Latin America and Russia
Intimates	15 percent of population; personal relationships and family take precedence	Europeans and North Americans
Fun Seekers	12 percent of population; youngest group	Disproportionately more in developed Asia
Creatives	10 percent worldwide; strong interest in education, knowledge, and technology	Europe and Latin America

SOURCE: Tom Miller, "Global Segments from 'Strivers' to 'Creatives,'" *Marketing News*, July 20, 1998, 11. Reprinted with permission. See also **http://www.gfkamerica.com/products/roper_reports_worldwide.htm**.

points to attract them and to keep them as they move up the income scale.[46] As distribution systems converge, for example, with the increase of global chains, markets can also be segmented by outlet types that reach environmentally defined groups. For example, toy manufacturers may look at markets not only in terms of numbers of children but by how effectively and efficiently they can be reached by global chains such as Toys 'Я' Us, as opposed to purely local outlets.

Global Marketing Program Development

Decisions need to be made regarding how best to utilize the conditions set by globalization drivers within the framework of competitive challenges and the resources of the firm. Marketing-related decisions will have to be made in four areas: (1) the degree of standardization in the product offering, (2) the marketing program beyond the product variable, (3) location and extent of value-adding activities, and (4) competitive moves to be made.

This development effort has to combine three elements: (1) adaptation by maximizing the marketer's local relevance; (2) aggregation by leveraging cross-border resources; and (3) arbitrage by exploiting differences between local and regional markets by placing marketing activities where they are most efficiently executed and by making competitive moves where they deliver the maximum impact.[47]

Product Offering

Globalization is not equal to standardization except in the case of the core product or the technology used to produce the product. The need to localize varies by product. Fashion or fashion products depend for their appeal on sameness. Information technology products are susceptible to power requirements, keyboard configurations (e.g., Europe alone may require 20 different keyboards), instruction-manual language, and warning labels compliant with local regulations.[48] Product standardization may result in significant cost savings upstream. For example, Stanley Works' compromise between French preferences for handsaws with plastic handles and "soft teeth" and British preferences for wooden handles and "hard teeth"—to produce a plastic-handled saw with "hard teeth"—allowed consolidation for production and resulted in substantial economies of scale. Most automakers have reduced the number of platforms they offer worldwide to achieve greater economies of scale. For example, Toyota has reduced the number of its platforms from 11 to 6. This is not to reduce variety but to deliver it more cost effectively.[49] Shania Twain's double CD *Up!* is an example of catering to multiple segments at the same time: both disks contained the same 19 tracks, but one with the effects pop fans appreciate, and the other with country dimensions. A third disk with "an Asian, Indian vibe" replaced the country disk in Europe.[50]

Marketing Approach

Nowhere is the need for the local touch as critical as in the execution of the marketing program. Uniformity is sought especially in elements that are strategic in nature (e.g., positioning), whereas care is taken to localize necessary tactical elements (e.g., distribution). This approach has been called **glocalization**. For example, Unilever achieved great success with a fabric softener that used a common positioning, advertising theme, and symbol (a teddy bear) but differing brand names (e.g., Snuggle, Cajoline, Kuschelweich, Mimosin, and Yumos) and bottle sizes. Gillette Co. scored a huge success with its Sensor shaver when it was rolled out in the United States, Europe, and Japan with a common approach based on the premise that men everywhere want the same thing in a shave. Although the language of its TV commercials varied, the theme ("the best a man can get") and most of the footage were the same. A comparison of the marketing mix elements of two global marketers is given in Exhibit 6.9. Notice that adaptation is present even at Coca-Cola, which is acknowledged to be one of the world's most global marketers.

Location of Value-Added Activities

Globalization strives to reduce costs by pooling production or other activities or exploiting factor costs or capabilities within a system. Rather than duplicating activities in multiple, or even all, country organizations, a firm concentrates its activities. Nokia's over 20,000 research & development people work in centers in 12 different countries, including Finland, Germany, Hungary, and China. The company has also entered into development agreements with operators (such as France Telecom and Vodafone) to bring innovations to market more efficiently.[51] Many global marketers have established R&D centers next to key production facilities so that concurrent engineering can take place every day on the factory floor. To enhance the global exchange of ideas, the centers have joint projects and are in real-time contact with each other.

Exhibit 6.9

Globalization of the Marketing Mix

Marketing Mix Elements	Adaptation		Standardization	
	Full	Partial	Full	Partial
Product design			C	N
Brand name			C	N
Product positioning		N	C	
Packaging				C/N
Advertising theme		N	C	
Pricing		N		C
Advertising copy	N		C	C
Distribution	N	C		
Sales promotion	N	C		
Customer service	N	C		

Key: C = Coca-Cola; N = Nestlé.

SOURCE: Adapted from John A. Quelch and Edward J. Hoff, "Customizing Global Marketing," *Harvard Business Review*, May–June 1986 (Boston: Harvard Business School Publishing Division), 61.

The quest for cost savings and improved transportation and transfer methods has allowed some marketers to concentrate customer service activities rather than having them present in all country markets. For example, Sony used to have repair centers in all the Scandinavian countries and Finland; today, all service and maintenance activities are actually performed in a regional center in Stockholm, Sweden. Similarly, MasterCard has teamed up with Mascon Global in Chennai, India, where MasterCard's core processing functions—authorization, clearing, and settlement—for worldwide operations are handled.[52]

To show commitment to a given market, both economically and politically, centers may be established in these markets. Philips Electronics has chosen China as their Asian center for global product research and development.[53]

Competitive Moves

A company with regional or global presence will not have to respond to competitive moves only in the market where it is being attacked. A competitor may be attacked in its profit sanctuary to drain its resources, or its position in its home market may be challenged.[54] When Fuji began cutting into Kodak's market share in the United States, Kodak responded by drastically increasing its advertising in Japan and created a new subsidiary to deal strictly with that market.

Cross-subsidization, or the use of resources accumulated in one part of the world to fight a competitive battle in another, may be the competitive advantage needed for the long term.[55] One major market lost may mean losses in others, resulting in a domino effect. Jockeying for overall global leadership may result in competitive action in any part of the world. This has manifested itself in the form of "wars" between major global players in industries such as soft drinks, automotive tires, computers, and cellular phones. The opening of new markets often signals a new battle, as happened in the 1990s in Russia, in Mexico after the signing of the North American Free Trade Agreement, and in Vietnam after the normalization of relations with the United States. Given their multiple bases of operation, global marketers may defend against a competitive attack in one country by countering in another country or, if the competitors operate in multiple businesses, countering in a different product category altogether. In the mobile phone category, the winners in the future will be those who can better attack developing and emerging markets with cheaper phones, while providing Internet-based devices elsewhere.[56]

In a study of how automakers develop strategies that balance the conflicting pressures of local responsiveness and regional integration in Europe, Japanese marketers were found to practice standardization in model offerings but selectively respond to differences in market conditions by manipulating prices and advertising levels.[57]

Implementing Global Marketing

The successful global marketers of the future will be those who can achieve a balance between local and regional/global concerns. Marketers who have tried the global concept have often run into problems with local differences. Especially early on, global marketing was seen as a standardized marketing effort dictated to the country organizations by headquarters. For example, when Coca-Cola re-entered the Indian market in 1993, it invested most heavily in its Coke brand, using its typical global positioning, and saw its market leadership slip to Pepsi. Recognizing the mistake, Coke re-emphasized a popular local cola brand (Thums Up) and refocused the Coke brand advertising to be more relevant to the local Indian consumer.[58] In the past ten years, Coca-Cola has been acquiring local soft-drink brands (such as Inca Cola in Peru), which now account for 10 percent of company sales.[59]

Challenges of Global Marketing

Pitfalls that handicap global marketing programs and contribute to their suboptimal performance include market-related reasons, such as insufficient research and a tendency to overstandardize, as well as internal reasons, such as inflexibility in planning and implementation.

If a product is to be launched on a broader scale without formal research as to regional or local differences, the result may be failure. An example of this is Lego A/S, the Danish toy manufacturer, which decided to transfer sales promotional tactics successful in the U.S. market unaltered to other markets, such as Japan. This promotion included approaches such as "bonus packs" and gift promotions. However, Japanese consumers considered these promotions wasteful, expensive, and not very appealing.[60] Going too local has its drawbacks as well. With too much customization or with local production, the marketer may lose its import positioning. For example, when Miller Brewing Company started brewing Löwenbräu under license in the United States, the brand lost its prestigious import image. Often, the necessary research is conducted only after a product or a program has failed.

Globalization by design requires a balance between sensitivity to local needs and deployment of technologies and concepts globally. This means that neither headquarters nor independent country managers can alone call the shots. If country organizations are not part of the planning process, or if adoption is forced on them by headquarters, local resistance in the form of the not-invented-here syndrome (NIH) may lead to the demise of the global program or, worse still, to an overall decline in morale. Subsidiary resistance may stem from resistance to any idea originating from the outside or from valid concerns about the applicability of a concept to that particular market. Without local commitment, no global program will survive.

Localizing Global Marketing

The successful global marketers of the new century will be those who can achieve a balance between country managers and global product managers at headquarters. This balance may be achieved by a series of actions to improve a company's ability to develop and implement global strategy. These actions relate to management processes, organization structures, and overall corporate culture, all of which should ensure cross-fertilization within the firm.[61]

Management Processes In the multidomestic approach, country organizations had very little need to exchange ideas. Globalization, however, requires transfer of information between not only headquarters and country organizations but also between the country organizations themselves. By facilitating the flow of information, ideas are exchanged and organizational values strengthened. Information exchange can be achieved through periodic meetings of marketing managers or through worldwide conferences to allow employees to discuss their issues and local approaches to solving them. IBM, for example, has a Worldwide Opportunity Council, which sponsors fellowships for employees to listen to business cases from around the world and develop global platforms or solutions. IBM has found that some country organizations find it easier to accept input from other country organizations than that coming directly from headquarters. The approach used at Levi Strauss & Co. is described in *The International Marketplace 6.4.*

The International
MARKETPLACE

Finding the Fit Overseas

Twice a year, Levi Strauss & Co. calls together managers from its worldwide operations for a meeting of the minds. In sessions that could be described as a cross between the United Nations general assembly and MTV, the participants brainstorm and exchange ideas on what seems to work in their respective markets, regionally or globally. If a marketing manager finds an advertising campaign appealing, he or she is encouraged to take it back home to sell more Levi's blue jeans.

All told, Levi's marketing approach epitomizes a slogan that is becoming popular among companies around the world: Think globally, act locally. Levi's has deftly capitalized on the Levi's name abroad by marketing it as an enshrined piece of Americana, and foreign consumers have responded by paying top dollar for the product. An Indonesian commercial shows Levi's-clad teenagers cruising around Dubuque, Iowa, in 1960s convertibles. In Japan, James Dean serves as a centerpiece in virtually all Levi's advertising. Overseas, Levi's products have been positioned as an upscale product, which has meant highly satisfactory profit margins. To protect the image, Levi's has avoided the use of mass merchants and discounters in its distribution efforts.

Levi's success turns on its ability to fashion a global strategy that does not stifle local initiative. It is a delicate balancing act, one that often means giving foreign managers the freedom needed to adjust their tactics to meet the changing tastes of their home markets. In Brazil, Levi's prospers by letting local managers call the

LEVI'S SUCCESS TURNS ON ITS ABILITY TO FASHION A GLOBAL STRATEGY THAT DOES NOT INHIBIT LOCAL INITIATIVE. PICTURED IS A LEVI'S STORE IN BANGALORE, INDIA.

shots on distribution. For instance, Levi's penetrated the huge, fragmented Brazilian market by launching a chain of 400 Levi's Only stores, some of them in tiny rural towns. Levi's is also sensitive to local tastes in Brazil, where it developed the Feminina line of jeans exclusively for women, who prefer ultratight jeans. What Levi's learns in one market can often be adopted in another. The Dockers line of chino pants and casual wear originated in the company's Argentine unit and was applied to loosely cut pants by Levi's Japanese subsidiary. The company's U.S. operation adopted both in 1986, and the line now generates significant North American as well as European revenues. In 2002, Dockers unveiled its Go Khaki with Stain Defender line in the United States followed by a quick roll-out in other major markets. In 2003, the company launched the Levi Strauss Signature brand, aimed at giving value-conscious consumers high-quality and fashionable clothing from a company they trust.

Headquarters managers exercise control where necessary. To protect Levi's cherished brand identity and image of quality, the company has organized its foreign operations as subsidiaries rather than relying on a patchwork of licensees. It is important for a brand to have a single face; it cannot be controlled if there are 20 to 25 licensees around the world interpreting it in different ways. The company also keeps ahead of its competition by exporting its pioneering use of computers to track sales and manufacturing.

The company has also launched a reorganization to focus more on consumer needs. Levi's Web site has been redesigned to feature a virtual dressing room, custom-tailored jeans ordering, and virtual salespeople who offer tips on matching outfits.

Levi's continues to focus on global sales with its three divisions—the Americas (NAFTA plus Latin America); Europe, Middle East, and Africa; and Asia-Pacific—employing 10,500 people worldwide. The Americas contributed 59 percent of its sales; Europe, the Middle East, and Africa 24 percent; and Asia-Pacific 17 percent of $4.2 billion in total sales in 2006.

SOURCES: "How Levi Strauss Rekindled the Allure of Brand America," *World Trade*, March 2005, 28; Michele Orecklin, "Look, Ma, No Stains," *Time*, December 9, 2002, 64–65; "Levi Strauss & Co. Fiscal 2006 Financial Results," at **http://www.levistrauss.com**; Alice Z. Cuneo, "Levi Strauss Begins 1st Online Sales Effort," *Advertising Age*, November 23, 1998, 18; "For Levi's, a Flattering Fit Overseas," *Business Week*, November 5, 1990, 76–77.

Part of the preparation for becoming global has to be personnel interchange. Many companies encourage (or even require) midlevel managers to gain experience abroad during the early or middle stages of their careers. The more experience people have in working with others from different nationalities—getting to know other markets and surroundings—the better a company's global philosophy, strategy, and actions will be integrated locally.

The role of headquarters staff should be that of coordination and leveraging the resources of the corporation. For example, this may mean activities focused on combining good ideas that come from different parts of the company to be fed into global planning. Many global companies also employ world-class advertising and market research staffs whose role should be to consult subsidiaries by upgrading their technical skills, and to focus their attention not only on local issues but also on those with global impact.

Globalization calls for the centralization of decision-making authority far beyond that of the multidomestic approach. Once a strategy has been jointly developed, headquarters may want to permit local managers to develop their own programs within specified parameters and subject to approval, rather than forcing them to adhere strictly to the formulated strategy. For example, Colgate Palmolive allows local units to use their own ads, but only if they can prove they beat the global "benchmark" version. With a properly managed approval process, effective control can be exerted without unduly dampening a country manager's creativity.

Overall, the best approach against the emergence of the NIH syndrome is utilizing various motivational policies, such as (1) ensuring that local managers participate in the development of marketing strategies and programs for global brands, (2) encouraging local managers to generate ideas for possible regional or global use, (3) maintaining a product portfolio that includes local as well as regional and global brands, and (4) allowing local managers control over their marketing budgets so that they can respond to local customer needs and counter global competition (rather than depleting budgets by forcing them to participate only in uniform campaigns). Acknowledging this local potential, global marketers can pick up successful brands in one country and make them cross- border stars. Since Nestlé acquired British candy maker Rowntree Mackintosh, it has increased its exports by 60 percent and made formerly local brands, such as After Eight dinner mints, into pan-European hits. When global marketers get their hands on an innovation or a product with global potential, rolling it out in other regions or worldwide is important.

Organization Structures Various organization structures have emerged to support the globalization effort. Some companies have established global or regional product managers and their support groups at headquarters. Their tasks are to develop long-term strategies for product categories on a worldwide basis and to act as the support system for the country organizations. This matrix structure focused on customers, which has replaced the traditional country-by-country approach, is considered more effective in today's global marketplace according to companies that have adopted it.

Whenever a product group has global potential, firms such as Procter & Gamble, 3M, and Henkel create strategic-planning units to work on the programs. These units, such as 3M's EMATs (European Marketing Action Teams), consist of members from the country organizations that market the products, managers from both global and regional headquarters, and technical specialists.

To deal with the globalization of customers, marketers are extending national account management programs across countries, typically for the most important customers.[62] In a study of 165 multinational companies, 13 percent of their revenues came from global customers (revenues from all international customers were 46 percent). While relatively small, these 13 percent come from the most important customers who cannot be ignored.[63] AT&T, for example, distinguishes between international and global customers and provides the global customers with special services, including a single point of contact for domestic and international operations and consistent worldwide service. Honeywell provides global account services for multinational customers who want to specify the types of process-control equipment that can be installed in their facilities worldwide in order to ensure common quality standards and minimize variations in operating and training procedures.[64] Executing **global account management** programs builds relationships not only with important customers but also allows for the development of internal systems and interaction. It will require, however, a new organizational overlay and demands new ways of working for anyone involved in marketing to global customers. One of the main challenges is in evaluating and rewarding sales efforts. If Nokia sells equipment to Telefonica in Brazil, should the sale be credited to the sales manager in Brazil or to the global account manager for Telefonica? The answer in most cases is to double count the credit.[65]

Corporate Culture Corporate culture affects and is affected by two dimensions: the overall way in which the company holds its operations together and makes them a single entity, and the commitment to the global marketplace. For example, Panasonic (Formerly Matshushita) has a corporate vision of being a "possibility-searching company" with four specific objectives: (1) business that creates new lifestyles based on creativity and convenience; (2) technology based on artificial intelligence, fuzzy logic, and networking technology; (3) a culture based on heterogeneity; and (4) a structure to enable both localization and global synergy. Overall, this would mean a company in which individuals with rich and diversified knowledge share similar ideals and values.[66]

An example of a manifestation of the global commitment is a global identity that favors no specific country (especially the "home country" of the company). The management features several nationalities, and whenever terms are assembled, people from various country organizations get represented. The management development system has to be transparent, allowing non-national executives an equal chance for the fast track to top management.[67] Whirlpool's corporate profile states the following: "Beyond selling products around the world, being a global home-appliance company means identifying and respecting genuine national and regional differences in customer expectations, but also recognizing and responding to similarities in product development, engineering, purchasing, manufacturing, marketing and sales, distribution, and other areas." Companies that exploit the efficiencies from these similarities will outperform others in terms of market share, cost, quality, productivity, innovation, and return to shareholders. In truly global companies, very little decision-making occurs that does not support the goal of treating the world as a single market. Planning for and execution of programs take place on a worldwide basis.

The pressure to be global and local at the same time has to be addressed through developing talent. Leading companies systematically identify global talent sources while building name recognition in the labor market to assist in wooing potential recruits. They also develop global training programs and manage careers carefully over many years (including expatriate assignments). Finally, the companies have to implement appropriate compensation and mobility policies to ensure that the best talent is always available regardless of a job's location.[68]

For marketers from emerging markets, achieving cultural integration to facilitate market penetration on a global scale can be daunting task. Many Chinese managers have limited fluency in English, which is increasingly the language of global business. Secondly, Chinese cultural traits—such as avoiding direct confrontation, having few boundaries between work and personal life, and maintaining an emphasis on seniority and relationships—have to be addressed through approaches such as regular meetings and training programs.[69]

The Local Company in the Global Environment

The global marketplace presents significant challenges but also opportunities for local firms.[70] As global marketers such as Boeing, Honda, McDonald's, and Volkswagen expand their presence, there are local companies that must defend their positions or lose out. They can no longer rely on the government to protect or support them. If selling out or becoming a part of a bigger global entity is not an acceptable option, the local marketer will have to build on an existing competitive advantage or adopt a creative growth strategy globally. To counter the significant resources of global marketers (such as powerful brands and sizable promotional budgets), the local company can compete successfully in the local market by emphasizing the perceived advantages of its product and marketing.[71] More proactively, the local company can pursue its own globalization strategy through segments that have similar features to the local marketer's home market or segments that global marketers have not catered to.

Strategies available to the local company depend on both external and internal realities. The degree and strength of globalization in an industry will determine the pressure that the local marketer will be under. Internally, the extent to which the company's assets are transferable (as opposed to having only local relevance) will determine the opportunity dimension. Exhibit 6.10 provides a summary of the options to be considered.

In markets where a local company has enjoyed government protection, the liberalization of markets as a result of economic integration or WTO membership may mean hardship for the local company. A dodger may have to rethink its entire strategy. With the collapse of Communism and introduction of free-market reforms, the Czech carmaker Škoda found its models to be outdated and with little appeal in comparison to Western makes that became available for consumers. The company became part of the largest privatization deals in Eastern Europe in its sale to Volkswagen in 1991. Rather than being merged with VW's operations, Škoda has followed VW's formula for success: performance-oriented management, cooperative labor relations, utilitarian marketing, and an emphasis on design. It has benefited from wholesale implementation of the latest technologies and working practices and has been able to leapfrog into leaner and more intelligent supply and distribution networks. With sales in 85 countries, Škoda is a leading emerging global brand in one of the most competitive industries.[72]

A defender is a local company that has assets that give it a competitive advantage only in its home market. Ideally, this asset is something that an entering global marketer cannot easily replicate; for example, channel penetration, or a product line that has a strong local-customer franchise. Many believed that small local retailers in Latin America would be swept away with the sector's consolidation and the entry of global players such as Carrefour. This has been the case in developed markets, where small retailers have retained only 10–20 percent of the consumer packaged-goods market as large retailers have expanded. In Latin America, however, their share has remained at 45–61 percent, because they are not only meeting the needs of emerging consumers, but in many ways are serving them better. For emerging-market consumers, price is not the determining factor of retailer choice; it is the total cost of purchases (including cost of transportation, time, the burden of carrying purchases, and ability to store purchased items).[73] Similarly, while U.S. chocolate companies Mars and Hershey's have established only a marginal presence in Latin America with their larger chocolate bars, Arcor and Nacional de Chocolates have maintained their businesses selling bite-sized chocolates that are affordable to low-income consumers, cater to their tastes, and can be bought in remote rural stores.[74]

If a local company's assets are transferable, the company may be able to compete head-on with the established global players worldwide. While Airbus and Boeing have been

Exhibit 6.10

Competitive Strategies for Local Companies

		Competitive assets	
		Customized to home market	Transferable abroad
Pressures to globalize in the industry	High	**Dodger** Sells out to a global player or becomes part of an alliance	**Contender** Upgrades capabilities to match globals in niches
	Low	**Defender** Leverages local assets in segments where globals are weak	**Extender** Expands into markets similar to home base

SOURCE: Adapted from Niraj Dawar and Tony Frost, "Competing with the Giants: Survival Strategies for Local Companies in Emerging Markets," *Harvard Business Review* 77 (March–April 1999): 119–129.

competing by developing and launching ever-bigger aircraft, the niche for jets that carry 70 to 110 passengers has been left open for others. In the last ten years, the number of regional jet routes has grown 1,000 percent in Europe and 1,400 percent in North America. Much of that increase has come from commuter airlines that the majors own or contract with to connect smaller markets with their hubs. The **contender** that has taken advantage of the increased demand is Brazil's Embraer, which has challenged the market leader, Canada's Bombardier. When demand took off faster than expected, Bombardier could not meet demand, thus opening the door for Embraer. Currently, Brazil's lower labor costs allow Embraer to undercut its competitor on prices.[75]

Extenders are able to exploit their success at home as a platform for expansion elsewhere. This calls for markets or segments that are similar in terms of customer preferences; for example, sizable expatriate communities. The number of Indians in the United States has doubled in the last ten years to 2.5 million, making them the largest and fastest-growing Asian minority.[76] This will provide an opportunity for Bollywood to extend its marketing beyond India. Televisa from Mexico, Venevisíon from Venezuela, and Globo TV in Brazil have emerged as leading producers and marketers of telenovelas, especially to culturally close markets in Europe.[77] Some local marketers have been seasoned in competing against global players and subsequently extended their market presence to new markets abroad. Jollibee Foods Corporation challenged McDonald's in its home market of the Philippines with products and services customized to local tastes and has subsequently expanded its presence to other markets with sizable Filipino communities, such as Hong Kong and California. Jollibee now has 24 restaurants operating in 7 countries and continues to grow.[78]

Multiple strategies are available to local marketers when global markets and marketers challenge them. The key is to innovate, rather than imitate, and exploit the inherent competitive advantages over global players. A six-part strategy for success has been proposed.[79] First, given that local companies have an inherent familiarity with their own marketplace, they should create customized products and services. E-commerce site Dangdang edged out Amazon in China by recognizing the country's poor credit-card payment infrastructure and developing the best cash-settlement system. Second, the local marketer can develop approaches that overcome key obstacles. Grupo Elektra, a leading Mexican retailer, provides financing to cater to low-income Mexican consumers. The retailer has 4,000 loan officers to visit prospective borrowers' homes and establish credit worthiness. Third, local companies can utilize the latest technologies for advantage. Brazil Gol airline issues e-tickets and promotes online sales for cost efficiency. Customers without internet access can use kiosks or approach attendants with wireless-enabled pocket PCs to process check-ins. Fourth, local companies can scale up their operations swiftly not just locally but also regionally, even globally. Chinese auto parts company Wanxiang has used its production know-how gained in China to revive a number of U.S. producers. Fifth, local companies can often exploit low-cost labor. Chinese dairy companies such as Mengniu and Yili are successful examples in categories where a relatively high proportion of the cost structure and capital goes to production and logistics, and where customer needs change less frequently. Finally, local companies need to invest in talent to sustain their growth and expansion. The successful players promise and deliver accelerated careers, a chance to contribute meaningfully, and a meritocratic corporate culture.[80]

Summary

Globalization has become one of the most important strategy issues for marketing managers in the last ten years. Many forces, both external and internal, are driving companies to globalize by expanding and coordinating their participation in foreign markets. The approach is not standardization, however. Marketers may indeed occasionally be able to take identical technical and marketing concepts around the world, but most often, concepts must be customized to local tastes. Internally, companies must make sure that country organizations around the world are ready to launch global products and programs as if they had been developed only for their markets. Firms that are able to exploit commonalities across borders and do so with competent marketing managers in country organizations are able to see the benefits in their overall performance.[81]

Marketing managers need to engage in strategic planning to better adjust to the realities of the new marketplace. Understanding the firm's core strategy (i.e., what business they are really in) starts the process, and this assessment may lead to adjustments in what business the company may want to be in. In formulating global strategy for the chosen business, the decision makers have to assess and make choices about markets and competitive strategy to be used in penetrating them. This may result in the choice of one particular segment across markets or the exploitation of multiple segments in which the company has a competitive advantage. In manipulating and implementing the marketing mix for maximum effect in the chosen markets, the old adage, "think globally, act locally," becomes a critical guiding principle both as far as customers are concerned and in terms of country organization motivation. While local marketers may have an advantage based on their better understanding of the market, for long-term competitiveness they may also become involved in the global marketplace. This is typically most feasible by exploiting a particular niche in which they have a cost advantage or cultural edge.

Key Terms

triad	cross-subsidization	defender
concentration	not-invented-here syndrome (NIH)	contender
diversification	global account management	extender
glocalization	dodger	

Questions for Discussion

1. What is the danger in oversimplifying the globalization approach? Would you agree with the statement that "if something is working in a big way in one market, you better assume it will work in all markets"?

2. In addition to teenagers as a global segment, are there possibly other such groups with similar traits and behaviors that have emerged worldwide?

3. Suggest ways in which a global marketer is better equipped to initiate and respond to competitive moves.

4. Why is the assessment of internal resources critical as early as possible in developing a global strategic plan?

5. What are the critical ways in which the multidomestic and global approaches differ in country-market selection?

6. Outline the basic reasons why a company does not necessarily have to be large and have years of experience to succeed in the global marketplace.

Internet Exercises

1. Using the material available at Unilever's Web site (http://www.unilever.com), suggest ways in which Unilever's business groups can take advantage of global and regional strategies due to interconnections in production and marketing.

2. Whirlpool's goal is "a Whirlpool product in every home, everywhere." Using its Web site, http://www.whirlpoolcorp.com/about/vision_and_strategy/default.asp, describe what needs to take place for this vision to become a reality.

Recommended Readings

Arnold, David. *Mirage of Global Markets: How Globalizing Companies Can Succeed as Markets Localize.* Englewood Cliffs, NJ: Prentice-Hall, 2003.

Birkinshaw, Julian, and Michael Mol. *Giant Steps in Management: Innovations that Change the Way You Work.* Englewood Cliffs, NJ: Prentice Hall, 2009.

The Economist Intelligence Unit. *151 Checklists for Global Management.* New York: The Economist Intelligence Unit, 1993.

Feist, William R., James A. Heely, Min H. Lau, and Roy L. Nersesian. *Managing a Global Enterprise.* Westport, CT: Quorum, 1999.

Grant, Robert M. *Cases in Contemporary Strategy Analysis.* Oxford, England: Blackwell, 2005.

Grosse, Robert E., ed. *Thunderbird on Global Business Strategy.* New York: Wiley Investment, 2000.

Inkpen, Andrew, and Kannan Ramaswamy. *Global Strategy: Creating and Sustaining Advantage Across Borders.* Oxford: Oxford University Press, 2005.

Irwin, Douglas A. *Free Trade under Fire.* Princeton, NJ: Princeton University Press, 2005.

Kanter, Rosabeth Moss. *World Class.* New York: Simon & Schuster, 1997.

Lindsey, Brink. *Against the Dead Hand: The Uncertain Struggle for Global Capitalism.* New York: John Wiley & Sons, 2001.

Prahalad, C. K., and M. S. Krishnan. *The New Age of Innovation: Driving Co-Created Value*

Through Global Networks. New York: McGraw-Hill, 2008.

Rosensweig, Jeffrey. *Winning the Global Game: A Strategy for Linking People and Profits.* New York: Free Press, 2007.

Schwab, Klaus, Michael Porter, and Xavier Sala-Martin. *The Global Competitiveness Report 2003–2004.* Oxford, England: Oxford University Press, 2004.

Scott, Allen J. *Regions and the World Economy: The Coming Shape of Global Production, Competition, and Political Order.* Oxford, England: Oxford University Press, 2000.

Soros, George. *George Soros on Globalization.* New York: Public Affairs, 2005.

Stiglitz, Joseph E. *Making Globalization Work.* New York: W.W. Norton & Co., 2006.

MARKETING ORGANIZATION, IMPLEMENTATION, AND CONTROL

The International
MARKETPLACE

7.1

Procter & Gamble: Organized to Innovate

Globalization is at the heart of Procter & Gamble's structuring of its organization. This global structure replaced a region-driven apparatus with the goal of making employees stretch themselves and speed up innovation as well as moving products and processes across borders.

There are five key elements to the organizational structure:

- Global Business Units (GBUs). P&G moved from business units based on geographic regions to three GBUs based on product lines. This will drive greater innovation and speed by centering global strategy and profit responsibility on brands, rather than on geographics.

- Market Development Organizations (MDOs). The company established seven MDO regions that will tailor global programs to local markets and develop marketing strategies to build P&G's entire business based on superior local consumer and customer knowledge.

- Global Business Services (GBS). GBS brings business activities such as accounting, human resource systems, order management, and information technology into a single global organization to provide these services to all P&G business units at best-in-class quality, cost, and speed. They will be in the following locations: Americas (San Jose, Costa Rica); Europe, Middle East, Africa (Newcastle, United Kingdom); and Asia (Manila, Philippines).

- Corporate Functions. P&G has redefined the role of corporate staff. Most have moved into new business units, with the remaining staff refocused on developing cutting-edge new knowledge and serving corporate needs. For example, the company decentralized its 3,600-person information technology department so that 97 percent of its members now work in P&G's individual product, market, and business teams or are part of GBS, which provides shared services such as infrastructure to P&G units. The remaining 3 percent are still in corporate IT. In addition, 54 "change agents" have been assigned to work across the four GBUs to lead cultural and business change by helping teams work together more effectively through greater use of IT—in particular, real-time collaboration tools. Future plans have called for some of these functions to be outsourced.

- Culture. Changes to P&G's culture should create an environment that produces bolder, mind-stretching goals and plans; bigger innovations; and greater speed. For example, the reward system has been redesigned to better link executive compensation with new business goals and results.

P&G has balanced and focused its GBUs to create units of about the same size. Health and Well-being; Household Care; and Beauty each command $17 billion in worldwide sales. MDOs, GBS, and Corporate Functions were combined into Global Operations.

How the organization works can be highlighted with an example. The GBUs define the equity, or what a brand

Procter & Gamble's Organizational Structure

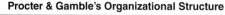

Global Business Units	Market Development Organizations	Global Business Services	Corporate Functions
• Health and Well-being • Household Care • Beauty	• North America • Latin America • Western Europe • Central Eastern Europe/ Middle East/Africa • ASEAN/India/Australia • Northeast Asia • Greater China	• Global Enabling Team • Regional Leadership Team • Global Process Owners	• Customer Business Development • Finance & Accounting • IT • Legal • Product Supply • R&D • Human Resources • Marketing • Consumer & Market Knowledge

stands for. The Pantene brand, for example, gives a customer healthy, shiny hair, and a Pantene Team within the Health, Baby, and Family Care GBU is charged with building on this. It starts with product initiatives or upgrades, which ideally would be launched simultaneously around the world. It includes a marketing campaign that communicates the same fundamental benefit around the world, and it includes manufacturing the product against global formula and package specifications. The MDOs then ensure Pantene excels in their region. In the United States, this could mean focusing on Club Stores, which might entail partnering with the GBU to develop large packaging that the outlet demands to maximize value for their shoppers. Conversely, the focus in Latin America might be to develop the smallest possible package (like a sachet), as consumers in that region want to minimize their out-of-pocket costs. The outcome should be the same overall brand equity, but very different executions by region. The GBS Center in Costa Rica would be providing support for both the U.S. and Latin America MDOs in this example (and for any other brand business team from these regions). Some of the services would include accounting, employee benefits and payroll, order management and product logistics, and systems operations. Those working directly on the business teams would likely determine the amount of Corporate Function (CF) support. Each function would want to ensure that they are capitalizing on the latest thinking or methodologies for each discipline. In this capacity, think of CF as a consulting group ready to provide service if called upon.

In the past, when a product was introduced, it might have taken years for it to be available worldwide, since management in each region was responsible for the product's launch there, including everything from test marketing to getting products onto retailers' shelves. Collaborative technologies, including chat rooms on the company's intranet, are transforming the company's conservative culture to one that encourages employees to be candid, test boundaries, and take chances.

As with any change of consequence, challenges have arisen in the implementation of the structure as well. The

THE GLOBAL BUSINESS UNITS (GBUS) DEFINE WHAT A BRAND STANDS FOR. THE PANTENE BRAND, FOR EXAMPLE, CONNOTES HEALTHY, SHINY HAIR.

projected $2 billion in savings also resulted in 9,600 layoffs. Furthermore, many positions have new reporting structures and even new locations. More than half of the executives at the various levels are in new jobs. Physical transfers have been significant as well; for example, 1,000 people were moved to Geneva from around Europe and another 200 to Singapore from various Asian locations. Furthermore, the changed reporting structures have raised concerns as well; for example, Household Care reports to Brussels. Personnel transferred to MDOs suddenly had no brands to manage and had to think across borders. The change from a U.S.-centric company to a global one was a substantial demand in a short period of time and has required adjustments by those affected and in the timetables set.

SOURCES: Procter & Gamble Annual Report, 2008; "It Was a No-Brainer," Fortune, February 21, 2005, 96–102; *Procter & Gamble 2004 Annual Report,* 11; "P&G Profits by Paradox," *Advertising Age,* February 24, 2004, 18–19, 31; Sonoo Singh, "P&G Opens Up Its Doors and Its Ears," *Marketing Week,* February 13, 2003, 21; Jack Neff, "Does P&G Still Matter?" *Advertising Age,* September 25, 2000, 48–56; "Rallying the Troops at P&G," *The Wall Street Journal,* August 31, 2000, B1, B4; "P&G Jump-Starts Corporate Change," *Internetweek,* November 1, 1999, 30; "All around the World," *Traffic World,* October 11, 1999, 22–24; "Organization 2005 Drive for Accelerated Growth Enters Next Phase," P&G News Releases, June 9, 1999, 1–5; and "Procter & Gamble Moves Forward with Reorganization," *Chemical Market Reporter,* February 1, 1999, 12. See also **http://www.pg.com**.

© DIBYANGSHU SARKAR/AFP/GETTY IMAGES

As companies evolve from purely domestic entities to multinationals, their organizational structure and control systems must change to reflect new strategies. With growth comes diversity in terms of products and services, geographic markets, and personnel, leading to a set of challenges for the company. Two critical issues are basic to addressing these challenges: (1) the type of organization that provides the best framework for developing worldwide strategies, while at the same time maintaining flexibility with respect to individual markets and operations, and (2) the type and degree of control to be exercised from headquarters to maximize total effort. Organizational structures and control systems have to be adjusted as market conditions change, as seen in *The International Marketplace 7.1*. While some units are charged with the development of strong global brands, others are charged with local adaptation and creating synergies across programs.

This chapter will focus on the advantages and disadvantages of the organizational structures available, as well as their appropriateness at various stages of internationalization. A determining factor is where decision-making authority within the organizational structures will be placed. The roles of different entities of the organization need to be defined, including how to achieve collaboration among these units for the benefit of the entire global organization. The chapter will also outline the need for devising a control system to oversee the international operations of the company, emphasizing the control instruments needed in addition to those used in domestic business, as well as the control strategies of multinational corporations. The appropriateness and eventual cost of the various control approaches will vary as the firm expands its international operations. Overall, the objective of the chapter is to study intraorganizational relationships in the firm's attempt to optimize competitive response in areas most critical to its business.

Organizational Structure

The basic functions of an organization are to provide (1) a route and locus of decision-making and coordination, and (2) a system for reporting and communications. Increasingly, the coordination and communication dimensions have to include learning from the global marketplace through the company's different units.[1] These networks are typically depicted in the organizational chart.

Organizational Designs

The basic configurations of international organizations correspond to those of purely domestic ones; the greater the degree of internationalization, the more complex the structures can become. The core building block is the individual company operating in its particular market. However, these individual companies need to work together for maximum effectiveness—thus, the need for organizational design. The types of structures that companies use to manage foreign activities can be divided into three categories based on the degree of internationalization:

1. Little or no formal organizational recognition of international activities of the firm. This category ranges from domestic operations handling an occasional international transaction on an ad hoc basis to separate export departments.

2. International division. Firms in this category recognize the ever-growing importance of international involvement.

3. Global organizations. These can be structured by product, area, function, process, or customer.

Hybrid structures may exist as well, in which one market may be structured by product, another by area. Matrix organizations have emerged in large multinational corporations to combine product, regional, and functional expertise. As worldwide competition has increased dramatically in many industries, the latest organizational response is networked global organizations in which heavy flows of technology, personnel, and communication take place between strategically interdependent units, to establish greater global integration.

The ability to identify and disseminate best practices throughout the organization is an important competitive advantage for global companies. For example, a U.S. automaker found that in the face of distinctive challenges presented by the local environment, Brazilian engineers developed superior seals, which the company then incorporated in all its models worldwide.[2] The increasing enthusiasm for outsourcing has put new demands on managing relationships with independent partners. Boeing, for example, holds a partners' council meeting every six weeks, and has set up a network that makes it possible for designers (both at Boeing and suppliers) to work on the same up-to-the-minute database. Virtual meetings with colleagues in different time zones take place throughout the day.[3]

Little or No Formal Organization

In the very early stages of international involvement, domestic operations assume responsibility for international marketing activities. The share of international operations in the sales and profits of the corporation is initially so minor that no organizational adjustment takes place. No consolidation of information or authority over international sales is undertaken or is necessary. Transactions are conducted on a case-by-case basis either by the resident expert or quite often with the help of facilitating agents, such as freight forwarders.

As demand from the international marketplace grows and interest within the firm expands, the organizational structure will reflect it. An export department appears as a separate entity. This may be an outside export management company—that is, an independent company that becomes the de facto export department of the firm. This is an indirect approach to international involvement, in that very little experience is accumulated within the firm itself. Alternatively, a firm may establish its own export department, hiring a few seasoned individuals to take full responsibility for international activities. Organizationally, the department may be a subdepartment of marketing (as shown in Exhibit 7.1) or may have equal ranking with the various functional departments. This choice will depend on the importance assigned to overseas activities by the firm. Because the export department is the first real step for internationalizing the organizational structure, it should be a full-fledged marketing organization and not merely a sales organization; that is, it should have the resources for market research and market-development activities (such as trade show participation).

Exhibit 7.1

The Export Department Structure (TAL Apparel)

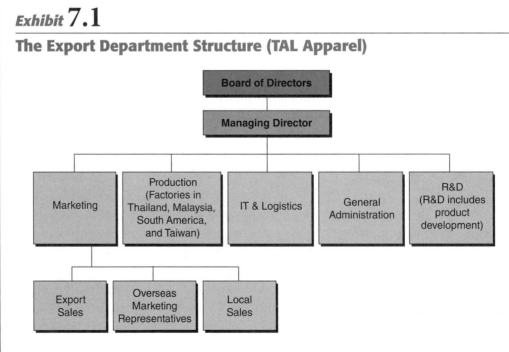

NOTE: TAL Apparel is based in Hong Kong, with over 100 employees. Its major customers include Marks & Spencer, Goldlion, and Giordano.

SOURCE: Hong Kong Chamber of Commerce.

Licensing is the international entry mode for some firms. Responsibility for licensing may be assigned to the R&D function despite its importance to the overall international strategy of the firm. A formal liaison among the export, marketing, production, and R&D functions should be formed for the maximum utilization of licensing.[4] A separate manager should be appointed if licensing becomes a major activity for the firm.

As the firm becomes more involved in foreign markets, the export department structure will become obsolete. The firm may then undertake joint ventures or direct foreign investment, which require those involved to have functional experience. The firm therefore typically establishes an international division.

Some firms that acquire foreign production facilities pass through an additional stage in which foreign subsidiaries report directly to the president or to a manager specifically assigned this duty. However, the amount of coordination and control that is required quickly establishes the need for a more formal international organization in the firm.

The International Division

The international division centralizes in one entity, with or without separate incorporation, all of the responsibility for international activities, as illustrated in Exhibit 7.2. The approach aims to eliminate a possible bias against international operations that may exist if domestic divisions are allowed to independently serve international customers. In some cases, international markets have been found to be treated as secondary to domestic markets. The international division concentrates international expertise, information flows concerning foreign market opportunities, and authority over international activities. However, manufacturing and other related functions remain with the domestic divisions in order to take advantage of economies of scale.

Exhibit **7.2**

The International Division Structure (Timberland)

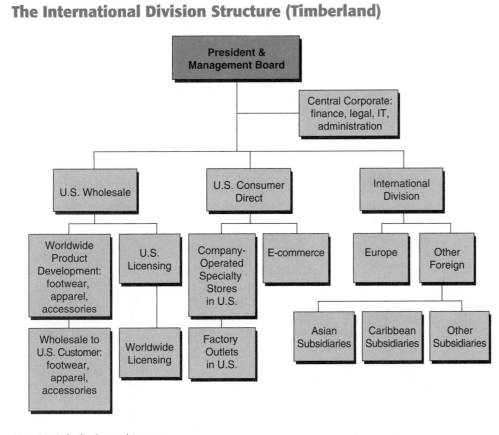

SOURCE: Timberland Annual Reports.

To avoid situations in which the international division is at a disadvantage in competing for production, personnel, and corporate services, corporations need to coordinate between domestic and international operations. Coordination can be achieved through a joint staff or by requiring domestic and international divisions to interact in strategic planning and to submit the plans to headquarters. Further, many corporations require and encourage frequent interaction between domestic and international personnel to discuss common challenges in areas such as product planning. Coordination is also important because domestic operations may be organized along product or functional lines, whereas international divisions are geographically oriented.

International divisions best serve firms with few products that do not vary significantly in terms of their environmental sensitivity, and when international sales and profits are still quite insignificant compared with those of the domestic divisions.[5] Companies may outgrow their international divisions as their international sales grow in significance, diversity, and complexity. European companies used international divisions far less than their U.S. counterparts due to the relatively small size of their domestic markets. Royal Dutch Shell or Philips, for example, would have never grown to their current prominence by relying on the Dutch market alone. While international divisions were still popular among U.S. companies in the 1980s and 1990s, globalization of markets and the increased share of overseas sales have made international divisions less suitable than global structures.[6] For example, Loctite, a leading marketer of sealants, adhesives, and coatings, moved from having an international division to being a global structure in which the company is managed by market channel (e.g., industrial automotive and electronics industry), to enable Loctite employees to synergize efforts and expertise worldwide.[7]

Global Organizational Structures

Global structures have grown out of competitive necessity. In many industries, competition is on a global basis, with the result that companies must have a high degree of reactive capability.

Five basic types of global structures are available:

1. Global product structure, in which product divisions are responsible for all manufacture and marketing worldwide
2. Global area structure, in which geographic divisions are responsible for all manufacture and marketing in their respective areas
3. Global functional structure, in which the functional areas (such as production, marketing, finance, and personnel) are responsible for the worldwide operations of their own functional areas
4. Global customer structure, in which operations are structured based on distinct worldwide customer groups
5. Mixed—or hybrid—structure, which may combine the other alternatives

Product Structure   The product structure is the one that is most used by multinational corporations.[8] This approach gives worldwide responsibility to strategic business units for the marketing of their product lines, as shown in Exhibit 7.3. Most consumer product firms utilize some form of this approach, mainly because of the diversity of their products. One of the major benefits of the approach is improved cost efficiency through centralization of manufacturing facilities. This is crucial in industries in which competitive position is determined by world market share, which in turn is often determined by the degree to which manufacturing is rationalized.[9] Adaptation to this approach may cause problems because it is usually accompanied by consolidation of operations and plant closings. A good example is Black & Decker, which rationalized many of its operations in its worldwide competitive effort against Makita, the Japanese power tool manufacturer. Similarly, Goodyear reorganized itself into a single global organization with a complete business team approach for tires and general products. The move was largely prompted by tightening worldwide competition.[10] In a similar move, Ford merged its large and culturally distinct European and North American auto operations by vehicle platform type to make more efficient use of its engineering and product development resources against rapidly globalizing rivals.[11] The Ford Fusion was designed by one team of engineers for worldwide markets.

Exhibit 7.3

The Global Product Structure (Kodak)

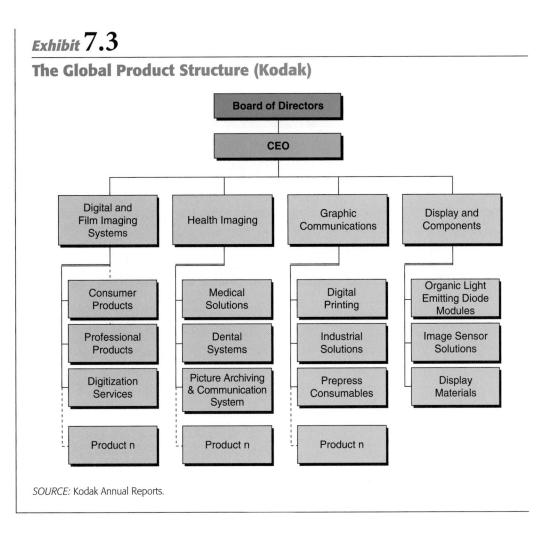

SOURCE: Kodak Annual Reports.

Another benefit is the ability to balance the functional inputs needed by a product and to react quickly to product-specific problems in the marketplace. Even smaller brands receive individual attention. Product-specific attention is important because products vary in terms of the adaptation they need for different foreign markets. All in all, the product approach ideally brings about the development of a global strategic focus in response to global competition.

At the same time, this structure fragments international expertise within the firm because a central pool of international experience no longer exists. The structure assumes that managers will have adequate regional experience or advice to allow them to make balanced decisions. Coordination of activities among the various product groups operating in the same markets is crucial to avoid unnecessary duplication of basic tasks. For some of these tasks, such as market research, special staff functions may be created and then hired by the product divisions when needed. If product managers lack an appreciation for the international dimension, they may focus their attention on only the larger markets, often with emphasis on the domestic markets, and fail to take the long-term view.

Area Structure   The second most frequently adopted approach is the area structure, illustrated in Exhibit 7.4. The firm is organized on the basis of geographical areas; for example, operations may be divided into those dealing with North America, the Far East, Latin America, and Europe. Regional aggregation may play a major role in this structuring; for example, many multinational corporations have located their European headquarters in Brussels, where the EU has its headquarters. The inevitability of a North American trading bloc led to the creation of Campbell Soup Co.'s North American division, which replaced the U.S. operation as the power center of the company. Organizational changes were also made at 3M Company as a result of NAFTA, with the focus on three concepts: simplification,

Exhibit 7.4

The Global Area Structure (Honda)

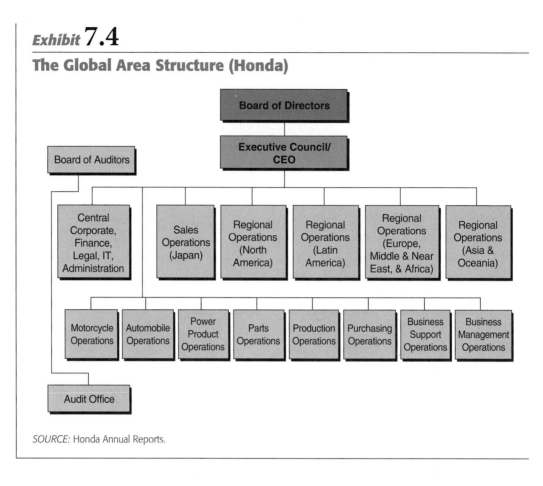

SOURCE: Honda Annual Reports.

linkage, and empowerment. As an example, this means that new-product launches are coordinated throughout North America, with standardization of as many elements as is feasible and prudent. The driver of the choice can also be cultural similarity, such as in the case of Asia, or historic connections between countries, such as in the case of combining Europe with the Middle East and Africa. As new markets emerge, they may first be delegated to an established country organization for guidance with the ultimate objective of having them be equal partners with others in the organization. When Estonia regained its independence and started its transformation to a market economy, many companies assigned their country organization in Finland the responsibility of the Estonian unit's development. In Latvia's case, the Swedish country organization got the job. Since then, the development of new markets such as the "Stans" (e.g., Kazakhstan and Turkmenistan) has been delegated to country organizations in Russia, Turkey, or Dubai.

The area approach follows the marketing concept most closely because individual areas and markets are given concentrated attention. If market conditions with respect to product acceptance and operating conditions vary dramatically, the area approach is the one to choose. Companies opting for this alternative typically have relatively narrow product lines with similar end uses and end users. However, expertise is most needed in adapting the product and its marketing to local market conditions. Once again, to avoid duplication of effort in product management and in functional areas, staff specialists—for product categories, for example—may be used.

Without appropriate coordination from the staff, essential information and experience may not be transferred from one regional entity to another. Also, if the company expands in terms of product lines, and if end markets begin to diversify, the area structure may become inappropriate.

Some marketers may feel that going into a global product structure may be too much too quickly and opt, therefore, to have a regional organization for planning and reporting purposes. The objective may also be to keep profit or sales centers of similar size at similar levels in the corporate hierarchy. If a group of countries has small sales compared with other country operations, they can be consolidated into a region. The benefits of a regional operation and regional headquarters are more efficient coordination of programs across the region (as opposed to globally), a management more sensitized to country-market operations in the region, and the ability for the region's voice to be heard more clearly at global headquarters (as compared to what an individual, especially smaller, country operation could achieve).[12]

Functional Structure

Of all the approaches, the **functional structure** is the most simple from the administrative viewpoint because it emphasizes the basic tasks of the firm—for example, manufacturing, sales, and research and development. This approach, illustrated in Exhibit 7.5, works best when both products and customers are relatively few and similar in nature. Because coordination is typically the key problem, staff functions have been created to interact between the functional areas. Otherwise, the company's marketing and regional expertise may not be exploited to the fullest extent.

A variation of this approach is one that uses processes as a basis for structure. The **process structure** is common in the energy and mining industries, where one corporate entity may be in charge of exploration worldwide and another may be responsible for the actual mining operation.

Customer Structure

Firms may also organize their operations using the **customer structure**, especially if the customer groups they serve are dramatically different—for example, consumers versus businesses versus governments. Catering to these diverse groups may require the concentration of specialists in particular divisions. The product may be the same, but the buying processes of the various customer groups may differ. Governmental buying is characterized by bidding, in which price plays a larger role than when businesses are the buyers. However, products and solutions are increasingly developed around capabilities, such as networked communications, that can be used by more than one service or agency.[13] Similarly, in financial institutions, it is important to know whether customers who signed up for one service are already customers for other services being provided by the institution.[14]

Exhibit *7.5*

The Global Functional Structure (NetLogic Microsystems)

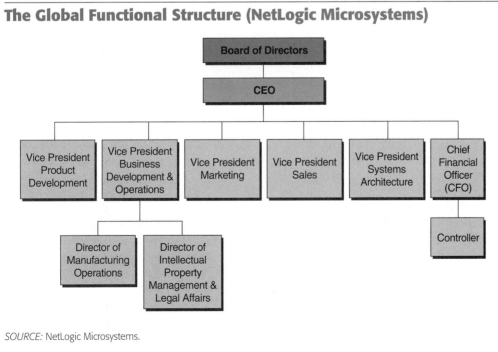

SOURCE: NetLogic Microsystems.

Mixed Structure

Mixed, or hybrid, organizations also exist. A mixed structure combines two or more organizational dimensions simultaneously. It permits attention to be focused on products, areas, or functions, as needed. This approach may occur in a transitionary period after a merger or an acquisition, or it may come about because of a unique customer group or product line (such as military hardware). It may also provide a useful structure before the implementation of the matrix structure.[15]

Organization structures are, of course, never as clear-cut and simple as they have been presented here. Whatever the basic format, inputs are needed for product, area, and function. One alternative, for example, might be an initial product structure that would eventually have regional groupings. Another alternative might be an initial area structure with eventual product groupings. However, in the long term, coordination and control across such structures become tedious.

Matrix Structure

Many multinational corporations—in an attempt to facilitate planning, organizing, and controlling interdependent businesses, critical resources, strategies, and geographic regions—have adopted the matrix structure.[16] Business is driven by a worldwide business unit (for example, photographic products or commercial and information systems) and implemented by a geographic unit (for example, Europe or Latin America). The geographical units, as well as their country subsidiaries, serve as the "glue" between autonomous product operations.

Organizational matrices integrate the various approaches already discussed, as the Philips example in Exhibit 7.6 illustrates. The product divisions (which are then divided into 60 product groups) have rationalized manufacturing to provide products for continent-wide markets rather than lines of products for individual markets. These product groups adjust to changing market conditions; for example, the components division has been slated to be merged into the other divisions due to lack of stand-alone profitability.[17] Philips has three general types of country organizations: In "key" markets, such as the United States, France, and Japan, product divisions manage their own marketing as well as manufacturing. In "local business" countries, such as Nigeria and Peru, the organizations function as importers from product divisions, and if manufacturing occurs, it is purely for the local market. In "large" markets, such as Brazil, Spain, and Taiwan, a hybrid arrangement is used depending on the size and situation. The product divisions and the national subsidiaries interact together in a matrix-like configuration, with the product divisions responsible for the globalization dimension and the national subsidiaries responsible for local representation and coordination of common areas of interest, such as recruiting. The matrix structure manager has functional, product, and resource managers reporting to him or her. The approach is based on team building and multiple command, each team specializing in its own area of expertise. It provides a mechanism for cooperation among country managers, business managers, and functional managers on a worldwide basis through increased communication, control, and attention to balance in the organization.

The matrices used vary according to the number of dimensions needed. Dow Chemical's matrix is three-dimensional, consisting of six geographic areas, three major functions (marketing, manufacturing, and research), and more than 70 products. The matrix approach helps cut through enormous organizational complexities by building in a provision for cooperation among business managers, functional managers, and strategy managers. However, the matrix requires sensitive, well-trained middle managers who can cope with problems that arise from reporting to two bosses—a product line manager and an area manager. Every management unit may have some sort of multidimensional reporting relationship, which may cross functional, regional, or operational lines. On a regional basis, group managers in Europe report administratively to a vice president of operations for Europe. But functionally, they report to group vice presidents at global headquarters.

Many companies have found the matrix structure problematic. The dual reporting channel easily causes conflict; complex issues are forced into a two-dimensional decision framework; and even minor issues may have to be resolved through committee discussion.[18] Ideally, managers should solve problems themselves through formal and informal

Exhibit 7.6

The Global Matrix Structure (Philips)

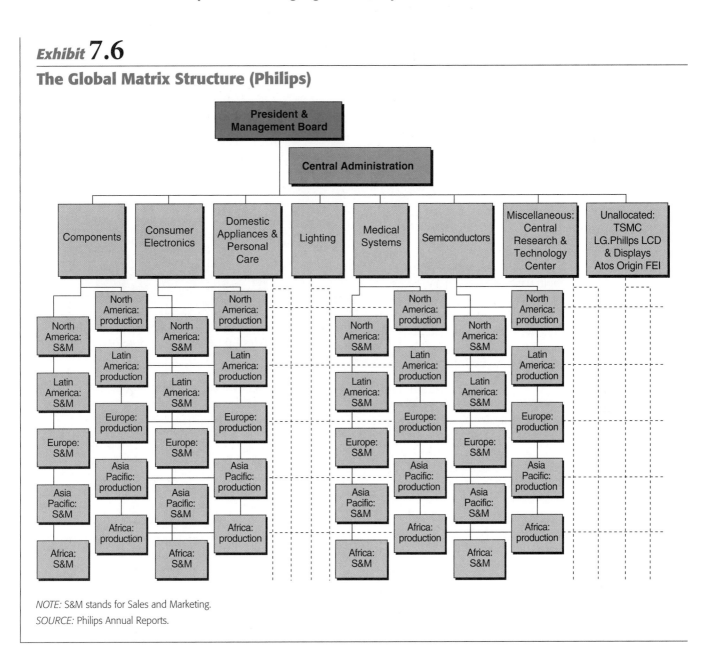

NOTE: S&M stands for Sales and Marketing.

SOURCE: Philips Annual Reports.

communication; however, physical and psychic distance often make that impossible. Especially when competitive conditions require quick reaction, the matrix, with its inherent complexity, may actually lower the reaction speed of the company. As a result, authority has started to shift in many organizations from area to product, although the matrix may still officially be used. At the same time, approaches to increase collaboration have been focused on, as seen in *The International Marketplace 7.2.*

Evolution of Organizational Structures

Companies develop new structures in stages as their product diversity develops and the share of foreign sales increases.[19] At the first stage are autonomous subsidiaries reporting directly to top management, followed by the establishment of an international division. With increases in product diversity and in the importance of the foreign marketplace, companies develop global structures to coordinate subsidiary operations and rationalize worldwide production. As global corporations have faced pressures to adapt to local market conditions while trying to rationalize production and globalize competitive reaction, many have opted for the matrix structure. Ideally, the matrix structure probably allows a corporation to best meet the challenges of global markets: to be global and local, big and small, decentralized

The International MARKETPLACE

Beyond the Matrix

Royal Philips Electronics of the Netherlands is one of the world's biggest electronics companies, as well as the largest in Europe, with 128,000 employees in over 60 countries and sales in 2007 of $36 billion. In the past 60 years, it has had three major phases of change in its organizational structure.

The company was one of the earliest champions of the matrix structure. After World War II, the organizational structure consisted of both national organizations and product divisions. Every division in a given country would report to the head of Philips in that country but also to the division's head at headquarters. This network was loosely held together by coordinating committees designed to resolve any conflicts between the basic reporting structures.

By the 1990s, environmental complexities had rendered the structure inefficient. Accountability and credit were difficult to assign and require. For example, who was to be held responsible for the profit-and-loss account—the country manager or the product head? The subsequent reorganization created a number of units with worldwide responsibility for groups of the company's businesses (e.g., consumer electronics and lighting products). The national offices became subservient to these units, built around products and based at headquarters.

In the 21st century, changes have been made that are not necessarily evident in organizational charts. For example, a chief marketing officer has been appointed to help counter criticism of technology and new-product bias at the expense of customer orientation. Under an initiative

PHILIPS WAS ONE OF THE EARLIEST CHAMPIONS OF THE MATRIX STRUCTURE.

called "One Philips," the company has introduced a number of low-key changes. Employees are encouraged to work on cross-cultural and cross-functional teams. New awards have been instituted for employees who have created value for the company by collaborating with others outside of their immediate units. Transfers across geographic entities as well as product units are expected as an explicit requirement for advancement. Top executives at Philips have argued that up to 80 percent of the desired changes will come about through readjustment of attitudes, the rest from using appropriate incentives, most of them not directly monetary. To accelerate these changes, Philips brought together its top 1,000 managers for a series of workshops designed to find ways to cut through organizational barriers.

SOURCE: "The Matrix Master," *The Economist*, January 21, 2006, 4. See also **http://www.philips.com**.

with centralized reporting, by allowing the optimizing of businesses globally and maximizing performance in every country of operation.[20] The evolutionary process is summarized in Exhibit 7.7.

A gateway model to reduce the tension between global integration and local responsiveness has been proposed.[21] As new markets emerge, the need to manage increased complexity is necessary. For example, 10 gateway countries could serve as hubs for the developed markets and another 10 countries might perform the same role for emerging markets. Each hub would serve the gateway market as well as other similar markets. For example, the German hub might manage Austria, Hungary, and Switzerland; Brazil would support Argentina, Bolivia, Chile, Paraguay, and Uruguay. The non-hub countries would usually feature only customer contact and service. Some countries would cover all aspects of corporate activity, while others might gradually build capabilities beyond sales. The executive committee of the company would consist of leaders with diverse experience from all of the hubs across the key countries of the developed and developing world.

Whatever the choice of organizational arrangement may be, the challenge of people having to work in silos remains. Employee knowledge tends to be fragmented with one unit's

Exhibit 7.7

Evolution of International Structures

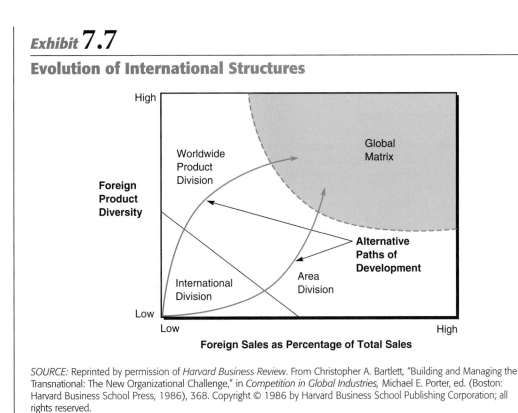

experience and know-how inaccessible to other units. Therefore, the wheel gets reinvented at considerable cost to the company and frustration to those charged with tasks. Information technology can be used to synchronize knowledge across even the most complicated and diverse organizations.[22] At Procter & Gamble, for example, brand managers have use of a standardized, worldwide ad-testing system which allows them access to every ad the company has ever run, providing examples for the needs that may have to be met at a particular time. Once knowledge transfer is established, what may be needed is a form of organization in which individuals and teams decide for themselves what to do, but are accountable for the results.[23]

Implementation

Organizational structures provide the frameworks for carrying out marketing decision-making. However, for marketing to be effective, a series of organizational initiatives are needed to develop marketing strategy to its full potential; that is, secure implementation of such strategies at the national level and across markets.[24]

Locus of Decision Making

Organizational structures themselves do not indicate where the authority for decision making and control rests within the organization, nor will they reveal the level of coordination between units. The different levels of coordination between country units are summarized in Exhibit 7.8. Once a suitable form of structure has been found, it has to be made to work by finding a balance between the center and the country organizations.

If subsidiaries are granted a high degree of autonomy, the result is termed decentralization. In decentralized systems, controls are relatively loose and simple, and the flows between headquarters and subsidiaries are mainly financial; that is, each subsidiary operates as a profit center. On the other hand, if controls are tight and if strategic decision making is concentrated at headquarters, the result is termed centralization. Firms are typically neither totally centralized nor totally decentralized. Increasingly, companies do not want

Exhibit 7.8

Levels of Coordination

Level	Description
5. Central control	No national structures
4. Central direction	Central functional heads have line authority over national functions
3. Central coordination	Central staff functions in coordinating role
2. Coordinating mechanisms	Formal committees and systems
1. Informal cooperation	Functional meetings: exchange of information
0. National autonomy	No coordination between decentralized units, which may even compete in export markets

Level 5 = highest; Level 0 = lowest. Most commonly found levels are 1–4.

SOURCE: Norman Blackwell, Jean-Pierre Bizet, Peter Child, and David Hensley, "Creating European Organizations That Work," in *Readings in Global Marketing*, Michael R. Czinkota and Ilkka A. Ronkainen, eds. (London: The Dryden Press, 1995), 376–385.

constituents to think they are from anywhere in particular nor do they want to be perceived as having a home base in each of the markets where they operate. For example, Lenovo's main corporate functions are divided between Beijing, Singapore, and Raleigh, N.C.[25] Some functions, such as finance, lend themselves to more centralized decision making, whereas other functions, such as promotional decisions, lend themselves to far less. Research and development is typically centralized in terms of both decision making and location, especially when basic research work is involved. In many cases, however, variations in decision making are product- and market-based; for example in Unilever's new organization launched in 2005, managers of global business units are responsible for brand management and product development, and managers of regional market development organizations are responsible for sales, trade marketing, and media choices.[26]

Allowing maximum flexibility at the country-market level takes advantage of the fact that subsidiary management knows its market and can react to changes quickly. Problems of motivation and acceptance are avoided when decision makers are also the implementors of the strategy. On the other hand, many marketers faced with global competitive threats and opportunities have adopted global strategy formulation, which by definition requires some degree of centralization. What has emerged as a result can be called **coordinated decentralization**. This means that overall corporate strategy is provided from global or regional headquarters, but subsidiaries are free to implement it within the range established in consultation between headquarters and the subsidiaries.

However, moving into this new mode may raise significant challenges. Among these systemic difficulties are a lack of widespread commitment to dismantling traditional national structures, driven by an inadequate understanding of the larger, global forces at work. Power barriers—especially if the personal roles of national managers are under threat of being consolidated into regional organizations—can lead to proposals being challenged without valid reason. Finally, some organizational initiatives (such as multicultural teams or corporate chat rooms) may be jeopardized by the fact that people do not have the necessary skills (e.g., language ability) or that an infrastructure (e.g., intranet) may not exist in an appropriate format.[27]

One particular case is of special interest. Organizationally, the forces of globalization are changing the country manager's role significantly. With profit-and-loss responsibility, oversight of multiple functions, and the benefit of distance from headquarters, country managers enjoyed considerable decision-making autonomy as well as entrepreneurial initiative. Today, however, many companies have to emphasize the product dimension of the product-geography matrix, which means that the power has to shift at least to some extent from country managers to worldwide strategic business unit and product line managers. Many of the previously local decisions are now subordinated to global strategic moves. However, regional and local brands still require an effective local management component. Therefore, the future country manager will have to have diverse skills (such as government relations and managing entrepreneurial teamwork) and wear many hats in balancing the needs of the operation for which the manager is directly responsible with those of the entire region or strategic business unit.[28] To emphasize the importance of the global/regional dimension in the country manager's portfolio, many companies have tied the country manager's compensation to the way the company performs globally or regionally, not just in the market for which the manager is responsible.

Factors Affecting Structure and Decision Making

The organizational structure and locus of decision making in multinational corporations are determined by a number of factors. They include (1) the degree of involvement in international operations, (2) the business(es) in which the firm is engaged (in terms, for example, of products marketed), (3) the size and importance of the markets, and (4) the human resource capability of the firm.[29]

The effect of the degree of involvement on structure and decision making was discussed earlier in the chapter. With low degrees of involvement by the parent company, subsidiaries can enjoy high degrees of autonomy as long as they meet their profit targets. The same situation can occur in even the most globally involved companies, but within a different framework. As an example, consider Philips USA, which generates one-third of the company's worldwide sales. Even more important, it serves a market that is on the leading edge of digital media development. Therefore, it enjoys an independent status in terms of local policy setting and managerial practices but is nevertheless within the parent company's planning and control system.

The firm's country of origin and the political history of the area can also affect organizational structure and decision making. For example, Swiss-based Nestlé, with only 1 to 2 percent of its sales in the small domestic market, has traditionally had a highly decentralized organization. Moreover, events of the past 90 years, particularly during the two world wars, have often forced subsidiaries of European-based companies to act independently in order to survive.

The type and variety of products marketed will have an effect on organizational decisions. Companies that market consumer products typically have product organizations with high degrees of decentralization, allowing for maximum local flexibility. On the other hand, companies that market technologically sophisticated products, such as General Electric's turbines, display centralized organizations with worldwide product responsibilities.

Going global has recently meant transferring world headquarters of important business units abroad. For example, Philips has moved headquarters of several of its global business units to the United States, including taking its Digital Video Group, Optimal Storage, and Flat Panel Display activities to Silicon Valley.

Apart from situations that require the development of an area structure, the characteristics of certain markets or regions may require separate arrangements for the firm. Upon entry, AT&T China was made the only one of 20 divisions in the world to be based on geography rather than on product or service line. Furthermore, it was the only one to report directly to the CEO.[30]

The human factor in any organization is critical. Managers both at headquarters and in the subsidiaries must bridge the physical and psychic distances separating them. If subsidiaries have competent managers who rarely need to consult headquarters about their problems, they may be granted high degrees of autonomy. In the case of global organizations, subsidiary management must understand the corporate culture because subsidiaries must sometimes make decisions that meet the long-term objectives of the firm as a whole but that are not optimal for the local market.

The Networked Global Organization

No international structure is ideal, and some have challenged the wisdom of even looking for an ideal one. They have called attention to new processes that would, in a given structure, develop new perspectives and attitudes to reflect and respond to complex demands of the opposite forces of global integration and local responsiveness. Rather than a question of which

Exhibit **7.9**

The Networked Global Organization

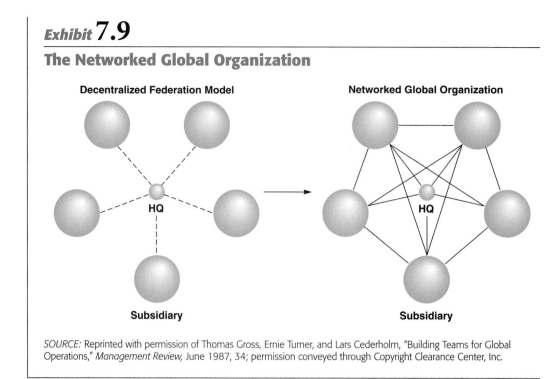

SOURCE: Reprinted with permission of Thomas Gross, Ernie Turner, and Lars Cederholm, "Building Teams for Global Operations," *Management Review,* June 1987, 34; permission conveyed through Copyright Clearance Center, Inc.

structural alternative is best, the question is thus one of how best to take into account the different perspectives of various corporate entities when making decisions. In structural terms, nothing may change. As a matter of fact, Philips still has its basic matrix structure, yet major changes have occurred in internal relations. The basic change was from a decentralized federation model to a networked global organization; the effects are depicted in Exhibit 7.9. This approach allows for the internal glocalization of strategic planning and implementation.[31]

Companies that have adopted the approach have incorporated the following three dimensions into their organizations: (1) the development and communication of a clear corporate vision, (2) the effective management of human resource tools to broaden individual perspectives and develop identification with corporate goals, and (3) the integration of individual thinking and activities into the broad corporate agenda.[32] The first dimension relates to a clear and consistent long-term corporate mission that guides individuals wherever they may work in the organization. IBM has established three values for the 21st century: dedication to every client's success, innovation that matters (for the company and the world), and trust and personal responsibility in all relationships.[33] The second dimension relates both to developing global managers who can find opportunities in spite of environmental challenges and to creating a global perspective among country managers. The last dimension refers to tackling the "not-invented-here" syndrome to co-opt possibly isolated, even adversarial managers into the corporate agenda.

For example, in an area structure, units (such as Europe and North America) may operate quite independently, sharing little expertise and information with the others. While they are supposed to build links to headquarters and other units, they may actually be building walls. To tackle this problem, Nissan established four management committees, meeting once a month, to supervise regional operations. Each committee includes representatives of the major functions (e.g., manufacturing, marketing, and finance), and the committees (for Japan, Europe, the United States, and general overseas markets) are chaired by Nissan executive vice presidents based in Japan. The CEO attends the committee meetings periodically but regularly.[34]

The network avoids the problems of duplication of effort, inefficiency, and resistance to ideas developed elsewhere by giving subsidiaries the latitude, encouragement, and tools to pursue local business development within the framework of the global strategy. Headquarters considers each unit as a source of ideas, skills, capabilities, and knowledge that can be utilized for the benefit of the entire organization. This means that the subsidiaries must be upgraded from the role of implementation and adaptation to that of contribution and partnership in the development and execution of worldwide strategies. Efficient plants may be converted into international production centers, innovative R&D units may become centers of excellence (and thus role models), and leading subsidiary groups may be given a leadership role in developing new strategy for the entire corporation.

Centers of excellence can emerge in three formats: charismatic, focused, or virtual. Charismatic centers of excellence are individuals who are internationally recognized for their expertise in a function or an area. The objective is primarily to build through an expert, via a mentoring relationship, a capability in the firm that has been lacking. The most common types are focused centers of excellence that are based on a single area of expertise, be it technological or product-based. The center has an identifiable location from which members provide advice and training. In virtual centers of excellence, the core individuals live and work around the world and keep in touch through electronic means and meetings. The knowledge of dispersed individuals is brought together, integrated into a coherent whole, and disseminated throughout the firm.[35]

Promoting Internal Cooperation

The global marketing entity in today's environment can be successful only if it is able to move intellectual capital within the organization; that is, take ideas and move them around faster and faster.[36]

One of the tools for moving ideas is teaching. The focus is on teachable points of view; that is, an explanation of what a person knows and believes about what it takes to succeed in his or her business.[37] For example, GE's Jack Welch coined the term "boundarylessness" to describe the way people can act without regard to status or functional loyalty and look for better ideas from anywhere. Top leadership of GE spends considerable time at training centers interacting with up-and-comers from all over the company. Each training class is given a real, current company problem to solve, and the reports can be career makers (or breakers).[38]

A number of benefits arise from this approach. A powerful teachable point of view can reach the entire company within a reasonable period by having students become teachers themselves. At PepsiCo, the CEO passed his teachable point on to 110 executives, who then passed it on to 20,000 people within 18 months. Second, participants in teaching situations are encouraged to maintain the international networks they develop during the sessions.

Teachers do not necessarily need to be top managers. When General Electric launched a massive effort to embrace e-commerce, many managers found that they knew little about the Internet. Following a London-based manager's idea to have an Internet mentor, GE encourages all managers to have one for a period of training each week.[39]

Another method to promote internal cooperation for global marketing implementation is the use of international teams or councils. In the case of a new product or program, an international team of managers may be assembled to develop strategy. Although final direction may come from headquarters, the input has included information on local conditions, and implementation of the strategy is enhanced because local managers were involved from the beginning. This approach has worked even in cases that, offhand, would seem impossible because of market differences. Both Procter & Gamble and Henkel have successfully introduced pan-European brands for which strategy was developed by European strategy teams. These teams consisted of local managers and staff personnel to smooth eventual implementation and to avoid unnecessarily long and disruptive discussion about the fit of a new product to individual markets.

On a broader and longer-term basis, companies use councils to share **best practice**, an idea that may have saved money or time, or a process that is more efficient than existing ones. Most professionals at the leading global marketing companies are members of multiple councils.

While technology has made teamwork of this kind possible wherever the individual participants may be, technology alone may not bring about the desired results; "high-tech" approaches inherently mean "low touch," sometimes at the expense of results. Human relationships are still paramount.[40] A common purpose is what binds team members to a particular task, and can only be achieved through trust, achievable through face-to-face meetings. At the start of its 777 project, Boeing brought members of the design team from a dozen different countries to Everett, Washington, giving them the opportunity to work together for up to 18 months. Beyond learning to function effectively within the company's project management system, they also shared experiences that, in turn, engendered a level of trust between individuals that later enabled them to overcome obstacles raised by physical separation. The result was a design and launch in 40 percent less time than for comparable projects.

The term *network* also implies two-way communications between headquarters and subsidiaries and between subsidiaries themselves. This translates into intercultural communication efforts focused on developing relationships.[41] While this communication can take the form of newsletters or regular and periodic meetings of appropriate personnel, new technologies are allowing marketers to link far-flung entities and eliminate traditional barriers of time and distance. Intranets integrate a company's information assets into a single and accessible system using Internet-based technologies such as E-mail, newsgroups, and the World Wide Web. For example, employees at Levi Strauss & Co. can join an electronic discussion group with colleagues around the world, watch the latest Levi's commercials, or comment on the latest marketing program or plan.[42] IBM has opened an online suggestion box called "Think Place" where ideas are logged for all to see and improve upon. Of the first 4,500 to appear in 2005, 300 were implemented. In many companies, the annual videotaped greeting from management has been replaced by regular and frequent E-mails (called e-briefs at GE). The benefits of intranets are (1) increased productivity, in that there is no longer lag time between an idea and the information needed to implement it; (2) enhanced knowledge capital that is constantly updated and upgraded; (3) facilitated teamwork, enabling online communication at insignificant expense; and (4) incorporation of best practice at a moment's notice by allowing marketing managers and sales personnel to make to-the-minute decisions anywhere in the world. The technology is increasingly available to create a culture of collaboration both within companies and with pertinent outside constituents.[43]

The networked approach is not a structural adaptation but a procedural one that requires a change in management mentality. Adjustment is primarily in the coordination and control functions of the firm. While there is still considerable disagreement as to which of the approaches works, some measures have been shown to correlate with success, as seen in *The International Marketplace 7.3*.

The Role of Country Organizations

Country organizations should be treated as a source of supply as much as they are considered a source of demand. Quite often, however, headquarters managers see their role as the coordinators of key decisions and controllers of resources and perceive subsidiaries as implementors and adapters of global strategy in their respective local markets. Furthermore, all country organizations may be seen as the same. This view severely limits the utilization of the firm's resources, by not using country organizations as resources and by depriving country managers of possibilities of exercising their creativity.[44]

The role that a particular country organization can play depends naturally on that market's overall strategic importance as well as the competencies of its organization. From these criteria, four different roles emerge (see Exhibit 7.10).

The role of strategic leader can be played by a highly competent national subsidiary located in a strategically critical market. The country organization serves as a partner of headquarters in developing and implementing strategy. For example, a strategic leader market may have products designed specifically with it in mind. Nissan's Z-cars have always been designated primarily for the U.S. market, starting with the 240Z in the 1970s to the 350Z introduced in 2002.[45]

A contributor is a country organization with a distinctive competence, such as product development or regional expertise. Increasingly, country organizations are the source of new products. These range from IBM's breakthroughs in superconductivity research, generated

The International
MARKETPLACE

7.3

Characteristics of Success

A survey of chief executive officers of 43 leading U.S. consumer companies, made by McKinsey & Co., sheds light on organizational features that distinguish internationally successful companies. Companies were classified as more or less successful compared to their specific industry average, using international sales and profit growth over a five-year period as the most important indicators of success.

The survey results indicate certain distinctive traits that are correlated with high performance in international markets. The following are moves that companies can make to enhance prospects for international success:

- Differentiate treatment of international subsidiaries
- Let product managers in subsidiaries report to the country general manager
- Have a worldwide management development program

- Make international experience a condition for promotion to top management
- Have a more multinational management group
- Support international managers with global electronic networking capabilities
- Manage cross-border acquisitions particularly well
- Have overseas R&D centers
- Remain open to organizational change and continuous self-renewal

In general, successful companies coordinate their international decision making globally, with more central direction than less successful competitors, as seen in the following exhibit. This difference is most marked in brand positioning, package design, and price setting. The one notable exception is an increasing tendency to decentralize product development.

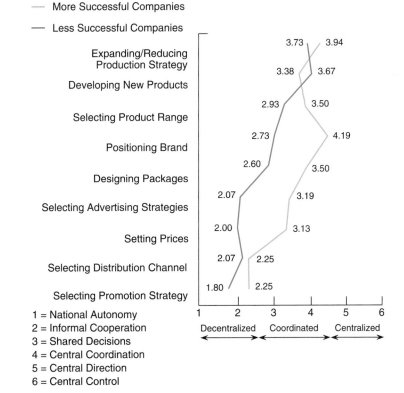

Key
— More Successful Companies
— Less Successful Companies

Expanding/Reducing Production Strategy — 3.73 / 3.94
Developing New Products — 3.38 / 3.67
Selecting Product Range — 2.93 / 3.50
Positioning Brand — 2.73 / 4.19
Designing Packages — 2.60 / 3.50
Selecting Advertising Strategies — 2.07 / 3.19
Setting Prices — 2.00 / 3.13
Selecting Distribution Channel — 2.07 / 2.25
Selecting Promotion Strategy — 1.80 / 2.25

1 = National Autonomy
2 = Informal Cooperation
3 = Shared Decisions
4 = Central Coordination
5 = Central Direction
6 = Central Control

1 2 3 4 5 6
Decentralized Coordinated Centralized

SOURCE: Adapted from Ingo Theuerkauf, David Ernst, and Amir Mahini, "Think Local, Organize...?" in *Best Practices in International Business,* Michael R. Czinkota and Ilkka A. Ronkainen, eds. (Mason, OH: South-Western, 2001), 249–255.

Exhibit 7.10

Roles for Country Organizations

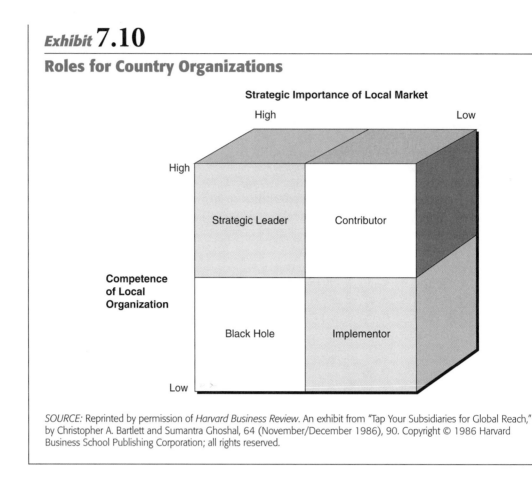

in its Zurich lab, to low-end innovations like Procter & Gamble's liquid Tide, made with a fabric-softening compound developed in Europe. Similarly, country organizations may be assigned as worldwide centers of excellence for a particular product category, for example, ABB Strömberg in Finland for electric drives, a category for which it is a recognized world leader.[46] Similarly, companies such as Carrier, IBM, and Hewlett-Packard use their units in Finland to penetrate the Russian market.[47]

The critical mass for the international marketing effort is provided by **implementors**. These country organizations may exist in smaller, less-established markets in which corporate commitment to market development is less. The presence in these markets is typically through a sales organization. Although most entities fill this role, it should not be slighted: Implementors provide the opportunity to capture economies of scale and scope that are the basis of a global strategy.

The **black hole** is a situation that the international marketer has to work out of. A company may be in a "black hole" situation because it has read the market incorrectly (for example, Philips focused its marketing efforts in the North American market on less-expensive items instead of the up-market products that have made the company's reputation worldwide)[48] or because government may restrict its activities (for example, Citibank being restricted in terms of activities and geography in China). If possible, the marketer can use strategic alliances or acquisitions to change its competitive position. Whirlpool established itself in the European Union by acquiring Philips' white goods' operation, and has used joint ventures to penetrate the Chinese market. If governmental regulations hinder the scale of operations, the firm may use its presence in a major market as an observation post to keep up with developments before a major thrust for entry is executed (for example, with China's WTO membership, the financial services sector opened up in 2008).

Depending on the role, the relationship between headquarters and the country organization will vary from loose control based mostly on support to tighter control in making sure strategies are implemented appropriately. Yet in each of these cases, it is imperative that country organizations have enough operating independence to cater to local needs and to provide motivation to the country managers. For example, an implementor should provide input in the development of a regional or a global strategy or program. Strategy formulation should ensure that appropriate implementation can be achieved at the country level.

Good ideas can, and should, come from any country organization. To take full advantage of this, individuals at the country level have to feel that they have the authority to pursue ideas in the first place and that they can see their concepts through to commercialization.[49] In some cases, this may mean that subsidiaries are allowed to experiment with projects that would not be seen as feasible by headquarters. For example, developing products for small-scale power generation using renewable resources may not generate interest in Honeywell's major markets and subsidiaries but may well be something that one of its developing-country subsidiaries should investigate.

Control

The function of the organizational structure is to provide a framework in which objectives can be met. A set of instruments and processes is needed, however, to influence the behavior and performance of organization members to meet the goals. Controls focus on actions to verify and correct actions that differ from established plans. Compliance needs to be secured from subordinates through various means of coordinating specialized and interdependent parts of the organization.[50] Within an organization, control serves as an integrating mechanism. Controls are designed to reduce uncertainty, increase predictability, and ensure that behaviors originating in separate parts of the organization are compatible and in support of common organizational goals despite physical, psychic, and temporal distances.

The critical issue is the same as with organizational structure: What is the ideal amount of control? On the one hand, headquarters needs information to ensure that international activities contribute maximum benefit to the overall organization. On the other hand, controls should not be construed as a code of law and allowed to stifle local initiative.

This section will focus on the design and functions of control instruments available for the international marketer, along with an assessment of their appropriateness. Emphasis will be placed on the degree of formality of controls used.

Types of Controls

Most organizations display some administrative flexibility, as demonstrated by variations in the application of management directives, corporate objectives, or measurement systems. A distinction should be made, however, between variations that have emerged by design and those that are the result of autonomy. The one is the result of management decision, whereas the other has typically grown without central direction and is based on emerging practices. In both instances, some type of control will be exercised. Here, we are concerned only with controls that are the result of headquarters initiative rather than consequences of tolerated practices. Firms that wait for self-emerging controls often find that such an orientation may lead to rapid international growth but may eventually result in problems in areas of product-line performance, program coordination, and strategic planning.[51]

Whatever the system, it is important in today's competitive environment to have internal benchmarking. Benchmarking relays organizational learning and sharing of best practices throughout the corporate system to avoid the costs of reinventing solutions that have already been discovered. A description of the knowledge transfer process by which this occurs is provided in *The International Marketplace 7.4.*

Three critical features are necessary in sharing best practice. First, there needs to be a device for organizational memory. For example, at Xerox, contributors to solutions can send their ideas to an electronic library where they are indexed and provided to potential adopters in the corporate family. Second, best practice must be updated and adjusted to new situations. For example, best practice adopted by the company's Chinese office will be modified and customized, and this learning should then become part of the database. Finally, best practice must be legitimized. This calls for a shared understanding that exchanging knowledge across units is valued in the organization and that these systems are important

The International
MARKETPLACE

International Best Practice Exchange

As growing competitive pressures challenge many global firms, strategies to improve the transfer of best practice across geographically dispersed units and time zones becomes critical. The premise is that a company with the same product range targeting the same markets pan-regionally should be able to use knowledge gained in one market throughout the organization. The fact is, however, that companies use only 20 percent of their most precious resources—knowledge, in the form of technical information, market data, internal know-how, and processes and procedures. Trying to transfer best practices internationally amplifies the problem even more. However, a corporate environment that creates informal cooperation in addition to the more formal, builds the necessary trust—and subsequently the critical mass—to share knowledge.

Copier maker Xerox (formerly Rank Xerox), with over 60 subsidiaries, is working hard to make better use of the knowledge, corporatewide. A 35-person group identified nine practices that could be applicable throughout the group. These ranged from the way the Australian subsidiary retains customers to Italy's method of gathering competitive intelligence to a procedure for handling new major accounts in Spain. These practices were thought to be easier to "sell" to other operating companies, were considered easy to implement, and would provide a good return on investment.

Three countries were much quicker in introducing new products successfully than others. In the case of France, this was related to the training given to employees. The subsidiary gave its sales staff three days of hands-on

practice, including competitive benchmarking. Before they attended the course, salespeople were given reading materials and were tested when they arrived. Those remaining were evaluated again at the end of the course, and performance reports were sent to their managers.

The difficult task is to achieve buy-in from the other country organizations. Six months might be spent in making detailed presentations of the best practices to all the companies and an additional three years helping them implement the needed changes. It is imperative that the country manager is behind the proposal in each subsidiary's case. However, implementation cannot be left to the country organizations after the concept has been presented. This may result in the dilution of both time and urgency and with possible country-specific customization that negates comparisons and jeopardizes the success of the change.

With time, these projects become codified into programs. Focus 500 allows the company's top 500 executives to share information on their interactions with customers and industry partners. Project Library details costs, resources, and cycle times of more than 2,000 projects, making it a vital resource in assuring Six Sigma in project management. PROFIT allows salespeople to submit hot selling tips—with cash incentives for doing so.

SOURCES: Philip Evans and Bob Wolf, "Collaboration Rules," *Harvard Business Review* 83 (July–August 2005): 96–104; Kristine Ellis, "Sharing Best Practices Globally," *Training,* July 2001, 34–38; Michael McGann, "Chase Harnesses Data with Lotus Notes," *Bank Systems and Technology* 34 (May 1997): 38; "Rank Xerox Aims at Sharing Knowledge," *Crossborder Monitor* (September 18, 1996): 8; "World-Wise: Effective Networking Distinguishes These 25 Global Companies," *Computerworld,* August 26, 1996, 7; See also Xerox Online Fact Book, available at **http://www.xerox.com**.

mechanisms for knowledge exchange. An assessment of how effectively employees share information with colleagues and utilize the databases can also be included in employee performance evaluations.

In the design of the control system, a major decision concerns the object of control. Two major objects are typically identified: output and behavior.[52] Output controls consist of balance sheets, sales data, production data, product line growth, or a performance review of personnel. Measures of output are accumulated at regular intervals and forwarded from the foreign operation to headquarters, where they are evaluated and critiqued based on comparisons to the plan or budget. Behavioral controls require the exertion of influence over behavior after, or ideally before, it leads to action. This influence can be achieved, for example, by providing sales manuals to subsidiary personnel or by fitting new employees into the corporate culture.

To institute either of these measures, corporate officials must decide on instruments of control. The general alternatives are bureaucratic/formalized control or cultural control. **Bureaucratic controls** consist of a limited and explicit set of regulations and rules that outline

Exhibit 7.11

Comparison of Bureaucratic and Cultural Control Mechanisms

Object of Control	Type of Control		Characteristics of Control
	Pure Bureaucratic/ Formalized Control	Pure Cultural Control	
Output	Formal performance reports	Shared norms of performance	HQ sets short-term performance target and requires frequent reports from subsidiaries
Behavior	Company policies, manuals	Shared philosophy of management	Active participation of HQ in strategy formulation of subsidiaries

SOURCES: Peter J. Kidger, "Management Structure in Multinational Enterprises: Responding to Globalization," *Employee Relations,* August 2001, 69–85; and B. R. Baliga and Alfred M. Jaeger, "Multinational Corporations: Control Systems and Delegation Issues," *Journal of International Business Studies* 15 (Fall 1984): 28.

desired levels of performance. **Cultural controls**, on the other hand, are much less formal and are the result of shared beliefs and expectations among the members of an organization. A comparison of the two types of controls and their objectives is provided in Exhibit 7.11. It can be argued that instilling the marketing approach (i.e., customer orientation) will have to rely more on behavioral dimensions since an approach focused on outputs may put undue pressure on short-term profits.[53]

Bureaucratic/Formalized Control

The elements of bureaucratic/formalized controls are (1) an international budget and planning system, (2) the functional reporting system, and (3) policy manuals used to direct functional performance. **Budgets** are short-term guidelines in such areas as investment, cash, and personnel, whereas **plans** refer to formalized long-range programs with more than a one-year horizon. The budget and planning process is the major control instrument in headquarters-subsidiary relationships. Although systems and their execution vary, the objective is to achieve the best fit possible with the objectives and characteristics of the firm and its environment.

The budgetary period is typically one year because budgets are tied to the accounting systems of the company. The budget system is used for four main purposes: (1) allocation of funds among subsidiaries; (2) planning and coordination of global production capacity and supplies; (3) evaluation of subsidiary performance; and (4) communication and information exchange among subsidiaries, product organizations, and corporate headquarters.[54] Long-range plans, on the other hand, extend over periods of two to ten years, and their content is more qualitative and judgmental in nature than that of budgets. Shorter periods, such as two years, are the norm because of the uncertainty of diverse foreign environments.

Although firms strive for uniformity, this may be comparable to trying to design a suit to fit the average person. The budget and planning processes themselves are formalized in terms of the schedules to be followed.

Control can also be seen as a mechanism to secure cooperation of local units. For example, while a company may grant substantial autonomy to a country organization in terms of strategies, headquarters may use allocation of production volume as a powerful tool to ensure compliance. Some of the ways for headquarters to gain cooperation of country organizations are summarized in Exhibit 7.12. Some of the methods used are formal, such as approval of strategic plans and personnel selection, while some are more informal, including personal contact and relationships as well as international networking.[55]

Since the frequency and types of reports to be furnished by subsidiaries are likely to increase due to globalization, it is essential that subsidiaries see the rationale for the often time-consuming task. Two approaches, used in tandem, can facilitate the process: participation and feedback. Involving the preparers of reports in their ultimate use serves to avoid the

Exhibit 7.12

Securing Country-Organization Cooperation

Extent of use of . . .

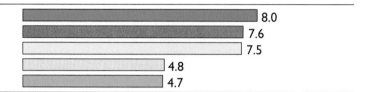

Approval of local budgets	8.0
Compensation for job performance	7.6
Evaluation of job performance	7.5
Allocation of production capacity/volume	4.8
Financial contribution from HQ	4.7

Among 35 MNCs.
0 to 10 scale (0 = "Never used" and 10 = "Always used")

SOURCE: Henry P. Conn and George S. Yip, "Global Transfer of Critical Capabilities," in *Best Practices in International Business,* Michael R. Czinkota and Ilkka A. Ronkainen, eds. (Mason, OH: South-Western, 2001): 256–274.

perception at subsidiary levels that reports are "art for art's sake." When this is not possible, feedback about results and consequences is an alternative. Through this process, communication is also enhanced.

On the behavioral front, headquarters may want to guide the way in which subsidiaries make decisions and implement agreed-upon strategies. U.S.-based multinational companies, relying heavily on manuals for all major functions, tend to be far more formalized than their Japanese and European counterparts.[56] The manuals are for functions such as personnel policies for recruitment, training, motivation, and dismissal. The use of policy manuals as a control instrument correlates with the level of reports required from subsidiaries.

Cultural Control

In countries other than the United States, less emphasis is placed on formal controls, which are viewed as rigid and too quantitatively oriented. Rather, the emphasis is on corporate values and culture, and evaluations are based on the extent to which an individual or entity fits in. Cultural controls require an extensive socialization process, and informal, personal interaction is central to the process. Substantial resources must be spent to train the individual to share the corporate culture, that is, "the way things are done at the company."[57] Adding to this need is the increasing cultural diversity at companies. For example, people of 120 different nationalities work at Nokia, and 45 percent of senior management are not Finnish.[58] To build common vision and values, managers spend a substantial amount of their first months at Matsushita in what the company calls "cultural and spiritual training." They study the company credo, the "Seven Spirits of Matsushita," and the philosophy of the founder, Konosuke Matsushita. Then they learn how to translate these internalized lessons into daily behavior and operational decisions. Although more prevalent in Japanese organizations, many Western entities have similar programs, for example, Philip's "organization cohesion training" and Unilever's "indoctrination." This corporate acculturation will be critical to achieve the acceptance of possible transfers of best practice within the organization, as seen in *The International Marketplace 7.5*.[59]

The primary instruments of cultural control are the careful selection and training of corporate personnel and the institution of self-control. The choice of cultural controls rather than bureaucratic controls can be justified if the company enjoys a low turnover rate. Cultural controls are thus applied, for example, when companies offer lifetime or long-term employment, as many Japanese firms do.

In selecting home country nationals and, to some extent, third-country nationals, global companies are exercising cultural control. They assume that these managers have already internalized the norms and values of the company and that they tend to run a country operation with a more global view. In some cases, the use of headquarters personnel to ensure

The International
MARKETPLACE

7.5

Corporate Acculturation

Toyota has 580 different companies with 299,300 employees around the world, 51 factories outside of Japan, and sells nearly 9 million cars in more than 170 countries. What holds these operations together and makes them part of a cohesive entity is a strong corporate culture.

The "Toyota Way" has seven distinct elements: (1) *Kaizen,* the process of continuous improvement that has Toyota employees coming back to work each day determined

Fresher Air

Fuel Efficiency

Smooth Ride

Quietness

What will your reason be?

Hybrid Synergy Drive, delivers in more ways than one. Fresher air is the result of the lowest CO_2 emissions in its class*. Its fuel efficiency is demonstrated by its ability to travel 650 miles on a single tank of petrol, and its electric motor can take you from 0 to 62 mph in just 10.9 seconds. And just when you thought it could not get any better, the Torque on Demand Control uses the high-output electric motors to deliver a responsive, smooth and quiet acceleration. Will you choose it for yourself, for the earth, or both? Hybrid Synergy Drive. What will your reason be?

HYBRID SYNERGY DRIVE

www.HybridSynergyDrive.com

TODAY **TOMORROW TOYOTA**

All figures quoted refer to Toyota Prius with Hybrid Synergy Drive. Official Fuel Consumption Figures for the Prius 1.5 Hybrid in mpg (l/100 km): Urban – 56.5 (5.0), Extra-Urban – 67.3 (4.2), Combined – 65.7 (4.3), CO_2 – 104 g/km. * Lowest CO_2 emissions than all other vehicles in the upper medium segment, according to SMMT annual CO_2 report 2006 market overview.

© IMAGE COURTESY OF ADVERTISING ARCHIVES

TOYOTA'S VAST OPERATIONS ARE HELD TOGETHER BY A STRONG CORPORATE CULTURE.

to perform better than the day before; (2) *Genchi genbustu,* which expects fact-based consensus building on defining challenges; (3) *Kakushin,* which focuses on radical innovation in terms of technologies and models; (4) *Challenge,* which spurs employees to see obstacles not as something undesirable but as ways to reach improvements; (5) *Teamwork,* to facilitate sharing knowledge with others and putting the company's interests before those of the individual; (6) *Respect,* for other people, not just as people but for their skills and special knowledge; and (7) *Customers first, dealers second—and manufacturer last,* with the realization that customers pay salaries, not the company.

Ultimately, employees reach a point of "emotional fortitude," where their behavior is consistent with the organization's objectives. In the West, where individualism is at a higher level, it is more difficult for employees to absorb this. Emulating Toyota is not about copying any one practice, it is about creating a culture.

SOURCES: Hirotaka Takeuchi, Emi Osono, and Norihiko Shimizu, "The Contradictions that Drive Toyota's Success," *Harvard Business Review* 86 (June 2008): 96–105; Thomas A. Stewart and Anand P. Raman, "Lessons from Toyota's Long Drive," *Harvard Business Review* 85 (July/August 2007): 74–82; "Inculcating Culture," *The Economist,* January 21, 2006, 11; see also **http://www.toyota.co.jp/en/index_company.html**.

uniformity in decision making may be advisable. Expatriates are used in subsidiaries not only for control purposes but also for initiating change and to develop local talent. Companies control the efforts of management specifically through compensation, promotion, and replacement policies.

When the expatriate corps is small, headquarters can exercise control through other means. Management training programs for overseas managers as well as visits to headquarters will indoctrinate individuals to the company's way of doing things. Similarly, visits to subsidiaries by headquarters teams will promote a sense of belonging. These may be on a formal basis, as for a strategy audit, or less formal—for example, to launch a new product. Some innovative global marketers assemble temporary teams of their best talent to build local skills. IBM, for example, drafted 50 engineers from its facilities in Italy, Japan, New York, and North Carolina to run three-week to six-month training courses on all operations carried on at its Shenzhen facility in China. After the trainers left the country, they stayed in touch by E-mail, so whenever the Chinese managers have a problem, they know they can reach someone for help. The continuation of support has been as important as the training itself.[60]

Corporations rarely use one pure control mechanism. Rather, emphasis is placed on both quantitative and qualitative measures. Corporations are likely, however, to place different levels of emphasis on the types of performance measures and on the way the measures are taken. To generate global buy-in, annual bonuses have shifted away from the employee's individual unit and toward the company as a whole. This sends a strong signal in favor of collaboration across all boundaries. Other similar approaches to motivate and generate changes in thinking exist. At BP, for example, individual performance assessments exclude the effects of price of oil and foreign exchange because they are outside of the employee's control.[61]

Exercising Control

Within most corporations, different functional areas are subject to different guidelines. The reason is that each function is subject to different constraints and varying degrees of those constraints. For example, marketing as a function has traditionally been seen as incorporating many more behavioral dimensions than does manufacturing or finance. As a result, many multinational corporations employ control systems that are responsive to the needs of the function. Yet such differentiation is sometimes based less on appropriateness than on personality. One researcher hypothesized that manufacturing subsidiaries are controlled more intensively than sales subsidiaries because production more readily lends itself to centralized direction, and technicians and engineers adhere more firmly to standards and regulations than do salespeople.[62]

Similarly, the degree of control imposed will vary by subsidiary characteristics, including its location. For example, since Malaysia is an emerging economy in which managerial talent is in short supply, headquarters may want to participate more in all facets of decision making. If a country-market witnesses economic or political turmoil, controls may also be tightened to ensure the management of risk.[63]

In their international operations, U.S.-based multinational corporations place major emphasis on obtaining quantitative data. Although this allows for good centralized comparisons against standards and benchmarks, or cross-comparisons between different corporate units, several drawbacks are associated with the undertaking. In the international environment, new dimensions—such as inflation, differing rates of taxation, and exchange rate fluctuations—may distort the performance evaluation of any given individual or organizational unit.

For the global corporation, measuring whether a business unit in a particular country is earning a superior return on investment relative to risk may be irrelevant to the contribution an investment may make worldwide or to the long-term results of the firm. In the short term, the return may even be negative.[64] Therefore, the control mechanism may quite inappropriately indicate reward or punishment. Standardizing the information received may be difficult if the environment fluctuates and requires frequent and major adaptations. Further complicating the issue is the fact that, although quantitative information may be collected monthly, or at least quarterly, environmental data may be acquired annually or "now and then," especially when crisis seems to loom on the horizon.

To design a control system that is acceptable not only to headquarters but also to the organization and individuals abroad, a firm must take great care to use only relevant data. Major concerns, therefore, are the data collection process and the analysis and utilization of data. Evaluators need management information systems that provide for maximum comparability and equity in administering controls. The more behaviorally based and culture-oriented controls are, the more care that needs to be taken.

In designing a control system, management must consider the costs of establishing and maintaining it and weigh the costs against the benefits to be gained. Any control system will require investment in a management structure and in systems design. As an example, consider the costs associated with cultural controls: Personal interaction, use of expatriates, and training programs are all quite expensive. Yet these expenses may be justified in savings through lower employee turnover, an extensive worldwide information system, and a potentially improved control system.[65] Moreover, the impact goes beyond the administrative component. If controls are erroneous or too time-consuming, they can slow or misguide the strategy implementation process and thus the overall capability of the firm. The result will be lost opportunity or, worse, increased threats. In addition, time spent on reporting takes time away from other tasks. If reports are seen as marginally useful, the motivation to prepare them will be low. A parsimonious design is therefore imperative. The control system should collect all the information required and trigger all the intervention necessary but should not create a situation that resembles the pulling of strings by a puppeteer.

The impact of the environment must also be taken into account when designing controls. First, the control system should measure only dimensions over which the organization has control. Rewards or sanctions make little sense if they are based on dimensions that may be relevant for overall corporate performance but over which no influence can be exerted, for example, price controls. Neglecting the factor of individual performance capability would send wrong signals and severely impede the motivation of personnel. Second, control systems should harmonize with local regulations and customs. In some cases, however, corporate behavioral controls have to be exercised against local customs even though overall operations may be affected negatively. This type of situation occurs, for example, when a subsidiary operates in markets where unauthorized facilitating payments are a common business practice.

Corporations are faced with major challenges to adequately control systems in today's business environment. With an increase in local (government) demands for a share in the control of companies established, controls can become tedious, especially if the multinational company is a minority partner. Even in a merger, such as the one between Air France and KLM—or in a new entity formed by two companies, as when Toyota and GM formed NUMMI—the backgrounds of the partners may be sufficiently different to cause problems in terms of the controls.

Summary

The structures and control mechanisms needed to operate internationally define relationships between the firm's headquarters and subsidiaries and provide the channels through which these relationships develop. The most fundamental test of organizational design is whether there is a fit with the company's overall marketing strategy and whether it reflects the strengths of the entities within the organization.[66]

International firms can choose from a variety of organizational structures, ranging from a domestic operation that handles ad hoc export orders to a full-fledged global organization. The choice will depend primarily on the degree of internationalization of the firm, the diversity of international activities, and the relative importance of product, area, function, and customer variables in the process. Whatever the choice of structure may be, implementation of the planned strategies is a critical factor determining success. Companies typically realize only 60 percent of their strategies' potential value due to factors such as organizational silos and culture blocking execution.[67] To close the strategy-to-performance gap, the buy-in of all units is necessary. Of these, the primary one is the use of subsidiaries as resources, not merely as implementors of headquarters strategy.

The control function is of increasing importance because of the high variability in performance that results from divergent local environments, and the need to reconcile local objectives with the corporate goal of synergism. It is important to grant autonomy to country organizations so that they can be responsive to local market needs, but it is equally important to ensure close cooperation between units.

Control can be exercised through bureaucratic means, emphasizing formal reporting and evaluation of benchmark data. It can also be exercised through a cultural control process in which norms and values are understood by individuals and entities that compose the corporation. U.S. firms typically rely more on bureaucratic controls, whereas multinational corporations headquartered in other countries frequently control operations abroad through informal means and rely less on stringent measures.

The execution of controls requires great sensitivity to behavioral dimensions and to the environment. The measurements used must be appropriate and must reflect actual performance rather than marketplace vagaries. Entities should be measured only on factors over which they have some degree of control.

Key Terms

product structure	decentralization	contributor
area structure	centralization	implementors
functional structure	coordinated decentralization	black hole
process structure	glocalization	bureaucratic controls
customer structure	best practice	cultural controls
mixed structure	intranets	budgets
matrix structure	strategic leader	plans

Questions for Discussion

1. Firms differ, often substantially, in their organizational structures even within the same industry. What accounts for these differences in their approaches?

2. Discuss the benefits gained in adopting a matrix approach in terms of organizational structure.

3. What changes in the firm and/or in the environment might cause a firm to abandon the functional approach?

4. Is there more to the "not-invented-here" syndrome than simply hurt feelings on the part of those who believe they are being dictated to by headquarters?

5. How can systems that are built for global knowledge transfer be used as control tools?

6. "Implementors are the most important country organizations in terms of buy-in for effective global marketing strategy implementation." Comment.

Internet Exercises

1. Improving internal communications is an objective for networked global organizations. Using the Web site of the Lotus Development Corporation (http://www.ibm.com/itsolutions/collaboration) and its section on case studies, outline how marketers have used the Lotus Notes and Domino to interactively share information.

2. Using company and product information available on its Web site, determine why Siemens (http://w1.siemens.com/about/en/management-structure.htm) has opted for global product/business structures for its organization.

Recommended Readings

Bartlett, Christopher, and Sumantra Ghoshal. *Managing across Borders*. Cambridge, MA: Harvard Business School Press, 2002.

Bartlett, Christopher, Sumantra Ghoshal, and Paul Beamish. *Transnational Management: Text, Cases, and Readings in Cross-Border Management*. New York: McGraw-Hill, 2007.

Cairncross, Frances. *The Company of the Future*. Cambridge, MA: Harvard Business School Press, 2003.

Chisholm, Rupert F. Developing Network Organizations: Learning from Practice and Theory. Boston: Addison-Wesley, 1997.

Doz, Yves, Jose Santos, and Peter Williamson. *From Global to Metanational: How Companies Win in the Knowledge Economy*. Cambridge, MA: Harvard Business School Press, 2001.

Galbraith, Jay R. *Designing Matrix Organizations That Actually Work: How IBM, Procter & Gamble, and Other Design for Success*. New York: Jossey-Bass, 2008.

Ghoshal, Sumantra, and Christopher Bartlett. *The Individualized Corporation: A Fundamentally New Approach to Management*. New York: Harper Business, 1999.

Govindarajan, Vijay, Anil K. Gupta, and C. K. Prahalad. *The Quest for Global Dominance: Transforming Global Presence into Global Competitive Advantage*. New York: Jossey-Bass, 2008.

Govindarajan, Vijay, and Robert Anthony. *Management Control Systems*. New York: McGraw-Hill/Irwin, 2006.

Kluge, Jurgen, Wolfram Stein, and Thomas Licht. *Knowledge Unplugged: The McKinsey & Company Global Survey on Knowledge Management*, London: Palgrave Macmillan, 2002.

McCall, Morgan W., and George P. Hollenbeck. *Developing Global Executives*. Cambridge, MA: Harvard Business School Press, 2002.

Pasternak, Bruce A., and Albert J. Viscio. The Centerless Corporation: A New Model for Transforming our Organization for Growth and Prosperity. New York: Simon and Schuster, 1999.

Pfeffer, Jeffrey, and Robert I. Sutton. *The Knowing-Doing Gap: How Smart Companies Turn Knowledge into Action*. Cambridge, MA: Harvard Business School Press, 2000.

Stewart, Thomas A. *The Wealth of Knowledge: Intellectual Capital and the Twenty-first Century Organization*. New York: Doubleday, 2003.

RESEARCH

The International
MARKETPLACE

8.1

The Internet: A Virtual Word of Mouth

The Internet has many implications for modern-day consumer behavior, since it has enabled one of the most powerful marketing methods of all time—word of mouth in virtual form. As more people around the world are turning to a computer screen for news, entertainment, and shopping, the marketing community is searching for new ways to target them. One of the fastest-growing forms of online media are the so-called social media, which encompass social networking sites, such as MySpace, Facebook, and Twitter, blogs, and virtual interest-based communities. According to a Morgan Stanley report, 16 percent of time spent online by all Internet users is devoted to "social connections." Approximately half of all social networkers use sites to learn more about brands or products that they like or have had an online friend recommend a brand or product to them.

The reach of social media has been extending internationally at a rapid pace. For example, Facebook, which has emerged as the most-trafficked social media site in the world, has been translated into over 35 languages, with 65 more in development as of 2008. MySpace has over 110 million monthly active users around the globe and has been localized in more than 20 international territories. In addition to the global social networking sites, local sites are springing up around the world and growing in popularity, such as Japan's Mixi.JP and India's Orkut.

Marketing researchers acknowledge the importance of using "social media," as an integral tool for research and marketing activities, such as successful brand-building. However, there is a notable lack of consensus on how to harness the marketing power of online consumer communities. Because social networking sites are relatively new and flexible, marketers are unsure of how to approach the online consumer. A study by Coremetrics determined that 78 percent of marketers believe that social media can be used to gain a competitive edge, yet fewer than 8 percent have budgets devoted to them.

A product search on MySpace or Facebook yields a list of recommendations and comments directly from consumers, complete with reviews and personal experiences. A new term, the "Momentum Effect," has been coined to quantify the impact that a brand has within a social network, reflecting the "word-of-mouth" power of online consumer communication. For certain brands, such as adidas and Electronic Arts, more than 70 percent of their marketing return on investment can be attributed to the "Momentum Effect." Social networking sites are an emerging force to be reckoned with in the marketing community, both in terms of accumulating data on consumer preference and effectively targeting them. The companies that find a way to successfully harness the marketing power of Facebook and MySpace will be in the best position to cater to the consumer of the future.

SOURCES: Beth Snyder Bulik, "Is Your Consumer Using Social Media?" *Advertising Age*, May 5, 2008, Volume 79, Issue 18; Ian Schafer, "We Better Start Monetizing Social Media Before It's Too Late," *Advertising Age*, May 5, 2008, Volume 79, Issue 18; Beth Snyder Bulik, "Know Your Visual DNA? Research Gets Social-Net Bug," *Advertising Age*, May 21, 2007, Volume 78, Issue 21; Facebook Statistics, **http://facebook.com/press/info.php?statistics**, retrieved December 2, 2008; MySpace Statistics on Techradar, **http://techradar1.wordpress.com/2008/01/11/facebookmyspace-statistics/**, retrieved December 2, 2008.

Even though most managers recognize the need for domestic marketing research, the single most important cause for failure in the international marketplace is insufficient preparation and information. Major mistakes often occur because the firm and its managers do not have an adequate understanding of the business environment. Hindsight, however, does not lead to an automatic increase in international marketing research. Many firms either do not believe that international market research is worthwhile or face manpower and resource bottlenecks that impede such research. The increase in international marketing practice is also not reflected in the orientation of the articles published in key research journals.[1] Yet building a good knowledge base is a key condition for subsequent marketing success. To do so, one needs to accumulate data and information through research. Two basic forms of research are available to the firm: primary research, where data are collected for specific research purposes, and secondary research, where data that have already been collected are used. This chapter will first outline secondary research issues, focusing primarily on ways to obtain basic information quickly, ensuring that the information is reasonably accurate, and doing so with limited corporate resources. Later, primary research and its ways of answering more in-depth questions for the firm are covered together with the development of a decision-support system.

Defining the Issue

The American Marketing Association (AMA) defines marketing research as "the function that links the consumer, customer, and public to the marketer through information— information used to identify and define marketing opportunities and problems; generate, refine, and evaluate marketing actions; monitor marketing performance; and improve understanding of marketing as a process. Marketing research specifies the information required to address these issues, designs the method for collecting information, manages and implements the data collection process, analyzes the results, and communicates the findings and their implications."[2]

This very broad statement highlights the fact that research is the link between marketer and market, without which marketing cannot function. It also emphasizes the fact that marketing actions need to be monitored and outlines the key steps of the research process.

Another definition states that marketing research is the "systematic and objective identification, collection, analysis and dissemination for the purpose of improving decision making related to the identification and solution of problems and opportunities in marketing."[3] This statement is more specific to research activities for several reasons: It highlights the need for systematic work, indicating that research should be the result of planned and organized activity rather than coincidence. It stresses the need for objectivity and information, reducing the roles of bias, emotions, and subjective judgment. Finally, it addresses the need for the information to relate to specific problems. Marketing research cannot take place in a void; rather, it must have a business purpose.

International marketing research must also be linked to the decision-making process within the firm. The recognition that a situation requires action is the factor that initiates the decision-making process. The problem must then be defined. Often, symptoms are mistaken for causes; as a result, action determined by symptoms may be oriented in the wrong direction.

International and Domestic Research

The tools and techniques of international marketing research are said by some to be exactly the same as those of domestic marketing research, and only the environment differs. However, the environment is precisely what determines how well the tools, techniques, and concepts apply to the international market. Although the objectives of marketing research may be the same, the execution of international research may differ substantially from the process of domestic research. As a result, entirely new tools and techniques may need to be developed. The four primary differences are new parameters, new environments, an increase in the number of factors involved, and a broader definition of competition.

New Parameters

In crossing national borders, a firm encounters parameters not found in domestic marketing. Examples include duties, foreign currencies and changes in their value, different modes of transportation, international documentation, and port facilities. A firm that has done business only domestically will have had little or no prior experience with these requirements and conditions. Information about each of them must be obtained in order for management to make appropriate business decisions. New parameters also emerge because of differing forms of international operations. For example, a firm can export, it can license its products, it can engage in a joint venture, or it can carry out foreign direct investment.

New Environments

When deciding to go international in its marketing activities, a firm exposes itself to an unfamiliar environment. Many of the assumptions on which the firm was founded and on which its domestic activities were based may not hold true internationally. Firms need to learn about the culture of the host country and its demographics, understand its political system, determine its stability, and appreciate differences in societal structures and language. In addition, they must fully comprehend pertinent legal issues in the host country to avoid operating contrary to local legislation. They should also incorporate the technological level of the society in the marketing plan and understand the economic environment. In short, all the assumptions formulated over the years in the domestic market must be reevaluated. This crucial point has often been neglected, because most managers were born into the environment of their domestic operations and have subconsciously learned to understand the constraints and opportunities of their business activities. The process is analogous to learning one's native language. Growing up with a language makes speaking it seem easy. Only in attempting to learn a foreign language do we begin to appreciate the complex structure of languages, the need for rules, and the existence of different patterns.

Number of Factors Involved

Going international often means entering into more than one market. As a result, the number of changing dimensions increases geometrically. Even if every dimension is understood, management must also appreciate the interaction between them. Because of the sheer number of factors, coordination of the interaction becomes increasingly difficult. The international marketing research process can help management with this undertaking.

Broader Definition of Competition

By entering the international market, the firm exposes itself to a much greater variety of competition than existed in the domestic market. For example, when expanding the analysis of an island's food production from a local to an international level, fishery products compete not only with other fishery products but also with meat or even vegetarian substitutes. Similarly, firms that offer labor-saving devices in the domestic marketplace may suddenly face competition from cheap manual labor abroad. Therefore, the firm must, on an ongoing basis, determine the breadth of the competition, track the competitive activities, and, finally, evaluate the actual and potential impact on its own operations.

Recognizing the Need for Research

To serve a market efficiently, firms must learn what customers want, why they want it, and how they go about filling their needs. To enter a market without conducting marketing research places firms, their assets, and their entire operation at risk. Even though most firms recognize the need for domestic marketing research, this need is not fully understood for international marketing activities. Often, decisions concerning entry and expansion into overseas markets and the selection and appointment of distributors are made after a cursory subjective assessment of the situation. The research done is less rigorous, less formal, and less quantitative than for domestic marketing activities. Many business executives appear to view foreign market research as relatively unimportant.

A major reason that firms are reluctant to engage in international marketing activities is the lack of sensitivity to differences in consumer tastes and preferences. Managers tend to assume that their methods are both best and acceptable to all others. This is fortunately not true. What a boring place the world would be if it were!

A second reason is a limited appreciation for the different marketing environments abroad. As *The International Marketplace 8.1* shows, understanding and communicating with consumers is essential to company success and growth. Often, managers incorrectly believe that national or geographic boundaries indicate cultural homogeneity. In addition, firms are not prepared to accept that distribution systems, industrial applications and uses, the availability of media, or advertising regulations may be entirely different from those in the home market. Barely aware of the differences, many firms are unwilling to spend money to find out about them.

A third reason is the lack of familiarity with national and international data sources and the inability to use them if obtained. As a result, the cost of conducting international marketing research is seen as prohibitively high and therefore not a worthwhile investment relative to the benefits to be gained.[4] There is wider information collection and more data availability, and the expanding research base also includes more countries than those traditionally researched in marketing, namely the United States and Europe. In addition, the Internet makes international marketing research much easier and much less expensive. Therefore, growing access to the Internet around the world will make research more accessible as well.

Finally, firms often build up their international marketing activities gradually, frequently on the basis of unsolicited orders. Over time, actual business experience in a country or with specific firms may be used as a substitute for organized research.

Yet, international marketing research is important. It permits management to identify and develop strategies for internationalization. This task includes the identification, evaluation, and comparison of potential foreign market opportunities and subsequent market selection. Second, research is necessary for the development of a marketing plan. The requirements for successful market entry and market penetration need to be determined. Subsequently, the research should define the appropriate marketing mix for each international market and should maintain continuous feedback in order to fine-tune the various marketing elements. Finally, research can provide management with foreign market intelligence to help it anticipate events, take appropriate action, and prepare for global changes.

The Benefits of Research

To carry out international research, firms require resources in terms of both time and money. For the typical smaller firm, those two types of resources are its most precious and scarce commodities. To make a justifiable case for allocating resources to international marketing research, management must understand what that value of research will be. This is even more important for international market research than for domestic market research because the cost tends to be higher. The value of research in making a particular decision may be determined by applying the following equation:

$$V(dr) - V(d) > C(r)$$

where

　$V(dr)$ is the value of the decision with the benefit of research;
　$V(d)$ is the value of the decision without the benefit of research;

and

　$C(r)$ is the cost of research.

Obviously, the value of the decision with the benefit of research should be greater than the value of the decision without research, and the value increase should exceed the cost of the research. Otherwise, international marketing research would be a waste of resources. It may be difficult to quantify the individual values because often the risks and benefits are not easy to ascertain. Realistically, companies and their marketing researchers are often quite pragmatic: their research decisions are guided by research objectives, but constrained by resources.[5] The use of decision theory permits a comparison of alternative research strategies.[6]

Determining Research Objectives

Research objectives will vary from firm to firm because of the views of management, the corporate mission, and the marketing situation. In addition, the information needs of firms are closely linked with the level of existing international expertise. The firm may therefore wish to start out by determining its internal level of readiness to participate in the global market. This includes a general review of corporate capabilities such as personnel resources and the degree of financial exposure and risk that the firm is willing and able to tolerate. Existing diagnostic tools can be used to compare a firm's current preparedness on a broad-based level.[7] Knowing its internal readiness, the firm can then pursue its objectives with more confidence.

Going International: Exporting

The most frequent objective of international market research is that of foreign-market opportunity analysis. When a firm launches its international activities, basic information is needed to identify and compare key alternatives. The aim is not to conduct a painstaking and detailed analysis of the world on a market-by-market basis but instead to utilize a broad-brush approach. Accomplished quickly at low cost, this can narrow down the possibilities for international marketing activities. There are 193 countries in the world, and an evaluation of each one is difficult and time-consuming. There are two ways to evaluate foreign markets, country ranking and clustering, and both should be used. Indexing and ranking countries by their market appeal to a specific business or project is the first step. Clustering countries into similar groups for screening and evaluation is essential for further development and planning of strategies once a specific country is chosen.[8]

Such an approach should begin with a cursory analysis of general market variables such as total and per capita GDP, GDP growth, mortality rates, and population figures. Although these factors in themselves will not provide detailed market information, they will enable the researcher to determine whether the corporation's objectives might be met in those markets. For example, expensive labor-saving consumer products may not be successful in the People's Republic of China because their price may be a significant proportion of the annual salary of the customer, and the perceived benefit to the customer may be only minimal. Such cursory evaluation will help reduce the number of markets to be considered to a more manageable number—for example, from 193 to 25.

Next, the researcher will require information about each individual market for a preliminary evaluation. This information typically identifies the fastest-growing markets, the largest markets for a particular product, market trends, and market restrictions. Although precise and detailed information for each product probably cannot be obtained, it is available for general product categories.

Government restrictions on markets must also be considered. For example, the large population of China would have presented a great market for citrus imports from its relatively close neighbor, Australia. However, due to a citrus canker outbreak in Australia, the importation of its citrus fruit has been prohibited by the Chinese government.[9] A cursory overview will screen markets quickly and reduce the number of markets subject to closer investigation.

At this stage, the researcher must select appropriate markets. The emphasis will shift to focus on market opportunities for a specific product or brand, including existing, latent, and

Exhibit **8.1**

A Sequential Process of Researching Foreign Market Potentials

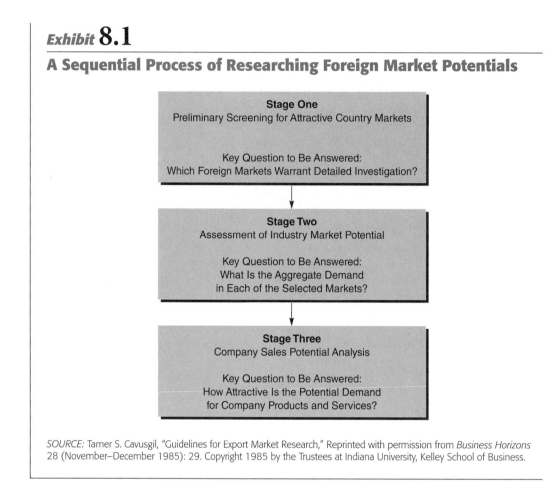

Stage One
Preliminary Screening for Attractive Country Markets

Key Question to Be Answered:
Which Foreign Markets Warrant Detailed Investigation?

Stage Two
Assessment of Industry Market Potential

Key Question to Be Answered:
What Is the Aggregate Demand
in Each of the Selected Markets?

Stage Three
Company Sales Potential Analysis

Key Question to Be Answered:
How Attractive Is the Potential Demand
for Company Products and Services?

SOURCE: Tamer S. Cavusgil, "Guidelines for Export Market Research," Reprinted with permission from *Business Horizons* 28 (November–December 1985): 29. Copyright 1985 by the Trustees at Indiana University, Kelley School of Business.

incipient markets. Even though the aggregate industry data have already been obtained, general information is insufficient to make company-specific decisions. For example, the market demand for medical equipment should not be confused with the potential demand for a specific brand. In addition, the research should identify demand-and-supply patterns and evaluate any regulations and standards. Finally, a competitive assessment needs to be made that matches markets with corporate strengths and provides an analysis of the best market potential for specific products. Exhibit 8.1 offers a summary of the various stages in the determination of market potential.

Going International: Importing

When importing, firms shift their major focus from supplying to sourcing. Management must identify markets that produce desired supplies or materials or that have the potential to do so. Foreign firms must be evaluated in terms of their capabilities and competitive standing.

The importer needs to know, for example, about the reliability of a foreign supplier, the consistency of its product or service quality, and the length of delivery time. Information obtained through the subsidiary office of a bank or through one's embassy can be very helpful. Information from business rating services and recommendations from current customers are also very useful in evaluating the potential business partner.

In addition, government rules must be scrutinized as to whether exportation from the source country is possible. For example, India may set limits on the cobra handbags it allows to be exported, and laws protecting cultural heritage may prevent the exportation of pre-Columbian artifacts from Latin American countries. The international manager must also analyze domestic restrictions and legislation that may prohibit the importation of certain goods into the home country. Even though a market may exist in the United States for foreign umbrella handles, for example, quotas may restrict their importation in order to protect domestic industries. Similarly, even though domestic demand may exist for ivory, its importation may be illegal because of worldwide legislation enacted to protect wildlife. Firms must also consider the risks of imports, such as disruption or terrorism. Such occurrences can cause major dislocations in corporate planning and order fulfillment.

Market Expansion

Research objectives may include obtaining detailed information for penetrating a market, for designing and fine-tuning the marketing mix, or for monitoring the political climate of a country so that the firm can expand its operation successfully. The better defined the research objective is, the better the researcher will be able to determine the information requirements and thus conserve time and financial resources of the firm.

Determining Secondary Information Requirements

Using the research objective as a guide, the researcher will be able to pinpoint the type of information needed. For example, if only general initial market information is required, macro data such as world population statistics will be sufficient. If research is to identify market restraints, then information is required about international accords and negotiations in the WTO. Alternatively, broad product category, production, and trade figures may be desired in order to pinpoint general market activities. For the fine-tuning of a marketing mix, very specific detailed product data may be necessary. This often entails gathering data on both a macro and micro level. On the macro level, these are typically tariff and nontariff information, and data on government trade policy. On the micro level, these tend to be data on local laws and regulations, local standards and specifications, distribution systems, and competitive activities.

Sources of Data

Secondary data for international marketing research purposes are available from a wide variety of sources. The major ones are briefly reviewed here. In addition, Appendix A to this chapter lists a wide variety of publications and organizations that monitor international issues.

Governments

Of all data sources, governments typically have the greatest variety of data available. This information provided by governments addresses either macro or micro issues or offers specific data services. Macro information includes population trends, general trade flows between countries, and world agricultural production. Micro information includes materials on specific industries in a country, their growth prospects, and their foreign trade activities. Specific data services might provide custom-tailored information responding to the detailed needs of a firm. Alternatively, some data services may concentrate on a specific geographic region. More information about selected government publications and research services is presented in Appendix A to this chapter. *The International Marketplace 8.2* explains some of the information services offered by the European Union.

Most countries have a wide array of national and international trade data available. Increasingly these data are available on the Internet, which makes them much more current than ever before. Closer collaboration between governmental statistical agencies also makes the data more accurate and reliable, since it is now much easier to compare data such as bilateral exports and imports to each other. These information sources are often available at embassies and consulates, whose mission includes the enhancement of trade activities. A country's commercial counselor or commercial attaché can provide the information available from these sources.

International Organizations

International organizations often provide useful data for the researcher. The *Statistical Yearbook* produced by the United Nations (UN) contains international trade data on

The International
MARKETPLACE

8.2

What If You Need Information on Europe?

With the expanding economic and political union within Europe, official information resources are becoming more centralized. A short sampling of government sources of information helpful to international managers targeting the EU are reviewed below. All of them are accessible through EUROPA (**http://europa.eu.it**), which is the portal site of the European Union.

The EU Day by Day

"The EU Day by Day" is aimed principally at journalists and other people professionally involved in the information industry. It contains links to the virtual press rooms of the various EU institutions and information on major upcoming events.

Activities

"Activities" sets out the Union's activities by subject, giving an overview of the policies as well as more detailed information for students and professionals.

Institutions

"Institutions" provides a general introduction to each of the institutions and to European decision-making procedures. It also contains links to the institutions' homepages.

The EU at a Glance

"The EU at a Glance" is aimed at the general public and sets out to provide clear answers to key questions concerning such things as the objectives of the European Union, European citizens' rights, and the history of the EU.

Documents

"Documents" provides access to the conclusions of European Councils, the General Report on the activities of the European Union, and the Bulletin of the European Union. Other documents, such as the Official Journal, the Treaties, and documents on current legislation and legislation under preparation may be obtained via EUR-Lex.

Services

"Services" is a gateway to various databases, information services, and official publications about the European Union. It also provides access to the latest statistics and the list of information relays in the European Union.

SOURCE: EUROPA—Gateway to the European Union, **http://europa.eu/index_en.htm**, accessed November 29, 2008.

products and provides information on exports and imports by country. Because of the time needed for worldwide data collection, the information is often dated. Additional information is compiled and made available by specialized substructures of the UN. Some of these are the UN Conference on Trade and Development (**http://www.unctad.org**), which concentrates primarily on international issues surrounding developing nations, such as debt and market access; the UN Center on Transnational Corporations; and the International Trade Centre (**http://www.intracen.org**). The *World Atlas,* published by the World Bank (**http://www.worldbank.org**), provides useful general data on population, growth trends, and GDP figures. The World Trade Organization (**http://www.wto.org**) and the Organization for Economic Cooperation and Development (OECD) (**http://www.oecd.org**) also publish quarterly and annual trade data on their member countries. Organizations such as the International Monetary Fund (**http://www.imf.org**) and the World Bank publish summary economic data and occasional staff papers that evaluate region- or country-specific issues in depth.

Service Organizations

A wide variety of service organizations that may provide information include banks, accounting firms, freight forwarders, airlines, and international trade consultants. Frequently, they are able to provide data on business practices, legislative or regulatory requirements, and political stability as well as basic trade data. Although some of this information is available without charge, its basic intent is to serve as an "appetizer." Much of the initial information is quite general in nature; more detailed answers often require an appropriate fee.

Trade Associations

Associations such as world trade clubs and domestic and international chambers of commerce (for example, the American Chamber of Commerce abroad) can provide valuable information about local markets. Often, files are maintained on international trade issues and trends affecting international marketers. Useful information can also be obtained from industry associations. These groups, formed to represent entire industry segments, often collect from their members a wide variety of data that are then published in an aggregate form. The information provided is often quite general in nature because of the wide variety of clientele served. It can provide valuable initial insights into international markets, since it permits a benchmarking effort through which the international marketer can establish how it is faring when compared to its competition. For example, an industry summary that indicates firm average exports to be 10 percent of sales, and export sales growth to take place mainly in Asia, allows a better evaluation of a specific firm's performance by the international marketer.

Directories and Newsletters

Many industry directories are available on local, national, and international levels. These directories primarily serve to identify firms and to provide very general background information such as the name of the chief executive officer, the address and telephone number, and some information about a firm's products. The quality of a directory depends, of course, on the quality of input and the frequency of updates. Some of the directories are becoming increasingly sophisticated and can provide quite detailed information to the researcher.

Many newsletters are devoted to specific international issues such as international trade finance, international contracting, bartering, countertrade, international payment flows, and customs news. Published by banks or accounting firms in order to keep their clientele current on international developments, newsletters usually cater to narrow audiences but can provide important information to the firm interested in a specific area.

Electronic Information Services

When information is needed, managers often cannot spend a lot of time, energy, or money finding, sifting through, and categorizing existing materials. Consider laboring through every copy of a trade publication to find out the latest news on how environmental concerns are affecting marketing decisions in Mexico. With electronic information services, search results can be obtained almost immediately. International online computer database services, numbering in the thousands, can be purchased to supply information external to the firm, such as exchange rates, international news, and import restrictions. Most database hosts do not charge any sign-up fee and request payment only for actual use. The selection of initial database hosts depends on the choice of relevant databases, taking into account their product and market limitations, language used, and geographical location.

A large number of databases and search engines provide information about products and markets. Many of the main news agencies through online databases provide information about events that affect certain markets. Some databases cover extensive lists of companies in given countries and the products they buy and sell. A large number of databases exist that cover various categories of trade statistics. The main economic indicators of the UN, IMF, OECD, and EU are available online. Standards institutes in most of the G8 nations (Canada, France, Germany, Italy, Japan, Russia, U.K., and the United States) provide online access to their databases of technical standards and trade regulations on specific products.

In the United States, "Global Business Opportunities" and "National Trade Data Bank" (NTDB) are published by the U.S. Department of Commerce. They contain information on international commerce from federal agencies, including trade leads, exchange rates, market and country research, and contact databases. For example, Country Commercial Guides report the political, economic, and commercial environment of foreign countries. The Global Trade Directory gives detailed information on products, services, and industries offered by local, regional, national, and global companies. Foreign Reports on Economic Policy and Trade Practices provide comparative analyses of the economic policies and trade practices of countries with whom the United States has significant economic and trade relationships.[10]

Using data services for research means that researchers do not have to leave their offices, going from library to library to locate the facts they need. Many online services have late-breaking information available within 24 hours. These research techniques are cost-effective as well. Stocking a company's library with all the books needed to have the same amount of data that is available online or with CD-ROM would be too expensive and space-consuming. However, there are also drawbacks. In spite of the ease of access to data on the Internet, search engines cover only a portion of international publications. Also, they are heavily biased toward the English language. As a result, sole reliance on electronic information may cause the researcher to lose out on valuable input.[11] Electronic databases should therefore be seen as only one important dimension of research scrutiny.

Other Firms

Often, other firms can provide useful information for international marketing purposes. Firms appear to be more open about their international than about their domestic marketing activities. On some occasions, valuable information can also be obtained from foreign firms and distributors.

Evaluating Data

Before obtaining secondary data, the researcher needs to evaluate their appropriateness for the task at hand. As the first step of such an evaluation, the quality of the data source needs to be considered with a primary focus on the purpose and method of the original data collection. Next, the quality of the actual data needs to be assessed, which should include a determination of data accuracy, reliability, and recency. Obviously, outdated data may mislead rather than improve the decision-making process. In addition, the compatibility and comparability of the data need to be considered. Since they were collected with another purpose in mind, we need to determine whether the data can help with the issue of concern to the firm. In international research it is also important to ensure that data categories are comparable to each other in order to avoid misleading conclusions. For example, the term *middle class* is likely to have very different implications for income and consumption patterns in different parts of the world.

Analyzing and Interpreting Secondary Data

After the data have been obtained, the researcher must use his or her research creativity to make good use of them. This often requires the combination and cross tabulation of various sets of data or the use of proxy information in order to arrive at conclusions that address the research objectives. A **proxy variable** is a substitute for a variable that one cannot directly measure. For example, the market penetration of personal music devices, such as the iPod, can be used as an indicator of the number of tracks that can be sold online. Similarly, in an industrial setting, information about plans for new port facilities may be useful in determining future containerization requirements. Also, the level of computerization of a society may indicate the future need for software.

The researcher must go beyond the scope of the data and use creative inferences to arrive at knowledge useful to the firm. However, such creativity brings risks. Once the interpretation and analysis have taken place, a consistency check must be conducted. The researcher should always cross-check the results with other possible sources of information or with experts.

In addition, the researcher should take another look at the research methods employed and, based on their usefulness, determine any necessary modifications for future projects. This will make possible the continuous improvement of international market research activities and enables the corporation to learn from experience.

Data Privacy

The attitude of society toward obtaining and using both secondary and primary data must be taken into account. Many societies are increasingly sensitive to the issue of data privacy, and the concern has grown exponentially as a result of e-business. Readily accessible databases may contain information valuable to marketers, but they may also be considered privileged by individuals who have provided the data. The European Union has passed a number of regulations on privacy and electronic communications. These maintain high standards of data privacy to ensure the free flow of data throughout its member states.

For example, the European Union requires member states to block transmission of data to non-EU countries if these countries do not have domestic legislation that provides for a level of protection judged adequate by the European Union. These laws restrict access to lifestyle information and its use for segmentation purposes. It is particularly difficult for direct marketers to obtain international access to voter rolls, birth records, or mortgage information. There are key differences between the European and the U.S. perspective on data privacy. The EU law permits companies to collect personal data only if the individuals consent to the collection, know how the data will be used, and have access to databases to correct or erase their information. The U.S. approach strictly safeguards data collected by banks and government agencies. However, it also recognizes that most personal data such as age or zip code are collected because someone is trying to sell something. Consumers who are annoyed by such data requests or sales pitches can only refuse to provide the information, throw out the junk mail, or request to be taken off telemarketers' call list.

Increasingly, however, the desire for personal privacy, particularly in the context of business contacts, is growing in value in the United States. Firms must inform their customers of privacy policies and inform them of the right to deny the use of their personal information. Therefore, the gap in policies is likely to shrink.

In order to settle conflicts between divergent government policies, companies are increasingly likely to encourage global privacy rules for managing information online and to seek international certification to assure users. Overall, the international marketer must pay careful attention to the privacy laws and expectations in different nations and to possible consumer reactions to the use of data in the marketing effort.

The Primary Research Process

Primary research is conducted to fill specific information needs. The research may not actually be conducted by the firm with the need, but the work must be carried out for a specific research purpose. Primary research therefore goes beyond the activities of secondary data collection, which often cannot supply answers to the specific questions posed. Conducting primary research internationally can be complex due to different environments, attitudes, and market conditions. Yet, it is precisely because of these differences that such research is necessary. Nonetheless, at this time, marketing research is still mainly concentrated in the industrialized nations of the world. Global marketing research expenditures were estimated to be $18.9 billion in 2004. Of that amount, more than 80 percent was spent in the United States and in the European Union.[12]

Primary research is essential for the formulation of strategic marketing plans. One particular area of research interest is international market segmentation. Historically, firms segmented international markets based on macro variables such as income per capita or consumer spending on certain product categories. Increasingly, however, firms recognize that segmentation variables, such as lifestyles, attitudes, or personality, can play a major role in identifying similar consumer groups in different countries, which can then be targeted across borders. One such group could consist, for example, of educationally elite readers who read *Scientific American, Time, Newsweek, The Financial Times,* and *The Economist.* Members in this group are likely to have more in common with one another than with their fellow citizens.[13] Alternatively, in marketing to women, it is important to understand the degree to which they have entered the workforce in a country and how women in different economic segments make or influence purchase decisions. In order to identify these groups and to devise ways of meeting their needs, primary international market research is indispensable.

Determining Information Requirements

Specific research questions must be formulated to determine precisely the information that is sought. The following are examples of such marketing questions:

- What is the market potential for our furniture in Indonesia?
- How much does the typical Nigerian consumer spend on soft drinks?
- What will happen to demand in Brazil if we raise our product price along monthly inflation levels?
- What effect will a new type of packaging have on our "green" consumers in Germany, France, and England?

Only when information requirements are determined as precisely as possible will the researcher be able to develop a research program that will deliver a useful product.

Industrial versus Consumer Research

The researcher must decide whether to conduct research with consumers or with industrial users. This decision will in part determine the size of the universe and respondent accessibility. For example, consumers are usually a very large group and can be reached through interviews at home or through intercept techniques. On the other hand, the total population of industrial users may be smaller and more difficult to reach. Further, cooperation by respondents may be quite different, ranging from very helpful to very limited. In the industrial setting, differentiating between users and decision makers may be much more important because their personality, their outlook, and their evaluative criteria may differ widely.

Determining Research Administration

The major issues in determining who will do the research are whether to use a centralized, coordinated, or decentralized approach and whether to engage an outside research service.

Degree of Research Centralization

The level of control that corporation headquarters exercises over international marketing research activities is a function of the overall organizational structure of the firm and the nature and importance of the decision to be made. The three major approaches to international research organization are the centralized, coordinated, and decentralized approaches.

The centralized approach clearly affords the most control to headquarters. All **research specifications** such as focus, thrust, and design are directed by the home office and are forwarded to the local country operations for implementation. The subsequent analysis of gathered information again takes place at headquarters. Such an approach can be quite valuable when international marketing research is intended to influence corporate policies and strategy. It also ensures that all international market studies remain comparable to one another. On the other hand, some risks exist. For example, headquarters management may not be sufficiently familiar with the local market situation to be able to adapt the research appropriately. Also, headquarters cultural bias may influence the research activities. Finally, headquarters staff may be too small or insufficiently skilled to provide proper guidance for multiple international marketing research studies.

A coordinated research approach uses an intermediary such as an outside research agency to bring headquarters and country operations together. This approach provides for more interaction and review of the international marketing research plan by both headquarters and the local operations and ensures more responsiveness to both strategic and local concerns. If the intermediary used is of high quality, the research capabilities of a corporation can be greatly enhanced through a coordinated approach.

The decentralized approach requires corporate headquarters to establish the broad thrust of research activities and to then delegate the further design and implementation to the specific countries. The entire research is then carried out locally under the supervision of the specific country operation, and only a final report is provided to headquarters. This approach has particular value when international markets differ significantly, because it permits detailed adaptation to local circumstances. However, implementing research activities on a country-by-country basis may cause unnecessary duplication, lack of knowledge transference, and lack of comparable results.

A country's operations may not be aware of research carried out by corporate units in other countries and may reinvent the wheel. This problem can be avoided if a proper intracorporate flow of information exists so that local units can check whether similar information has already been collected elsewhere within the firm. Corporate units that operate in markets similar to one another can then benefit from the exchange of research findings.

Local units may also develop their own research thrusts, tools, and analyses. A researcher in one country may, for example, develop a creative way of dealing with a nonresponse problem. This new technique could be valuable to company researchers who face similar difficulties in other countries. However, for the technique to become widely known, systems must be in place to circulate information to the firm as a whole.

Finally, if left to their own devices, researchers will develop different ways of collecting and tabulating data. As a result, findings in different markets may not be comparable, and potentially valuable information about major changes and trends may be lost to the corporation.

International marketing research activities will always be carried out subject to the organizational structure of a firm. Ideally, a middle ground between centralization and decentralization will be found, one that permits local flexibility together with an ongoing exchange of information within the corporation. As the extent of a firm's international activities grows, the exchange of information becomes particularly important, because global rather than local optimization is the major goal of the multinational corporation.

Outside Research Services

One major factor in deciding whether or not to use outside research services is, of course, the size of the international operations of a firm. No matter how large a firm is, however, it is unlikely to possess specialized expertise in international marketing research for every single market it currently serves or is planning to serve. Rather than overstretch the capabilities of its staff or assert a degree of expertise that does not exist, a corporation may wish to delegate the research task to outside groups. This is particularly the case when corporate headquarters have little or no familiarity with the local research environment. Exhibit 8.2 provides an example of such a situation. The use of outside research agencies may be especially appropriate for large-scale international marketing research or when highly specialized research skills are required. Increasingly, marketing research agencies operate worldwide, in order to accommodate the research needs of their clients. Exhibit 8.3 provides information about the top 25 global research organizations and their international activities. More than half of these are non–U.S. firms, demonstrating the growing global importance of marketing research.

The selection process for outside research providers should emphasize the quality of information rather than the cost. Low price is no substitute for data pertinence or accuracy.

Before a decision is made, the capabilities of an outside organization should be carefully evaluated and compared with the capabilities available in-house and from competing firms. Although general technical capabilities are important, the prime selection criterion should be previous research experience in a particular country and a particular industry. Some experience is transferable from one industry or country to another; however, the more the corporation's research needs overlap with an agency's past research accomplishment, the more likely it is that the research task will be carried out satisfactorily. Although the research may be more difficult to administer, multinational corporations should consider subcontracting each major international marketing research task to specialists, even if research within one country is carried out by various international marketing research agencies as a result. To have experts working on a problem is usually more efficient than to conserve corporate resources by centralizing all research activities with one service provider, who is only marginally familiar with key aspects of the research. However, if different firms carry out the research, it becomes very important to ensure that data are comparable. Otherwise, the international firm will not be able to transfer lessons learned from one market to another.

Exhibit **8.2**

Research Agencies Understand the Importance of Cultural Adaptation

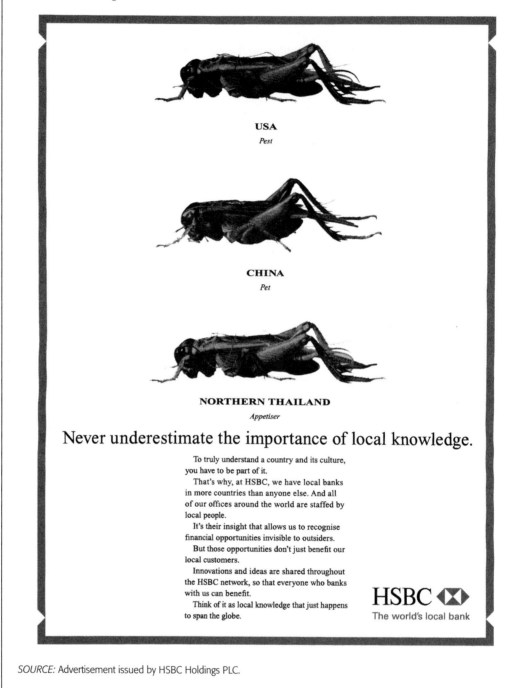

SOURCE: Advertisement issued by HSBC Holdings PLC.

Determining the Research Technique

Selection of the research technique depends on a variety of factors. First, the objectivity of the data sought must be determined. Standardized techniques are more useful in the collection of objective data than of subjective data. *Unstructured data* will require more open-ended questions and more time than structured data. Since the willingness and ability of respondents to spend the time and provide a free-form response are heavily influenced by factors such as culture and education, the prevailing conditions in the country and segments to be studied need to be understood in making these decisions. Whether the data are to be collected in the

Exhibit 8.3

Top 25 Global Market Research Firms

RANK 2007	2006	Organization	Headquarters	Parent Country	Web Site	Number of Countries with Subsidiaries/Branch Offices[1]	Research Only Fulltime Employees[2]	Global Research Revenue[3] (US $ in million)	Percent Change from 2006[4]	Revenue from Outside Parent Country (US $ in million)	Percent Revenue from Outside Home Country
1	1	The Nielsen Co.	New York	USA	nielsen.com	108	33,171	$4,220.0	12.7%	$2,047.0	48.5%
2	2	IMS Health Inc.	Norwalk, Conn.	USA	imshealth.com	76	7,950	2,192.6	6.0	1,391.6	63.5
3	3	Taylor Nelson Sofres plc	London	UK	tnsglobal.com	80	15,267	2,137.2	5.4	1,754.6	82.1
4	5	GfK AG	Nuremberg, Germany	Germany	gfk.com	63	9,070	1,593.2	5.8	1,195.3	75.0
5	4	The Kantar Group*	London & Fairfield, Conn.	UK	kantargroup.com	61	7,100	1,551.4	2.7	1,024.6	66.0
6	6	Ipsos Group SA	Paris	France	ipsos.com	56	8,088	1,270.3	9.1	1,125.5	88.6
7	7	Synovate	London	UK	synovate.com	57	5,801	867.0	7.8	813.3	93.8
8	8	IRI	Chicago	USA	infores.com	8	3,655	702.0	5.6	261.0	37.2
9	9	Westat Inc.	Rockville, Md.	USA	westat.com	1	1,906	467.8	10.4	–	–
10	10	Arbitron Inc.	New York	USA	arbitron.com	2	1,130	352.1	6.9	13.6	3.9
11	11	INTAGE Inc.**	Tokyo	Japan	intage.co.jp	2	1,666	281.1	7.5	2.5	0.9
12	12	J.D. Power and Associates*	Westlake Village, Calif.	USA	jdpa.com	8	875	260.5	12.0	76.0	29.2
13	13	Harris Interactive Inc.	Rochester, N.Y.	USA	harrisinteractive.com	7	1,336	226.8	-1.7	66.0	29.1
14	14	Maritz Research	Fenton, Mo.	USA	maritzresearch.com	4	806	223.3	3.0	35.9	16.1
15	15	The NPD Group Inc.	Port Washington, N.Y.	USA	npd.com	13	1,120	211.1	11.7	50.7	24.0
16	17	Opinion Research/Guideline Group	Omaha, Neb.	USA	infousa.com	7	1,235	202.2	7.5	87.1	43.1
17	16	Video Research Ltd.**	Tokyo	Japan	videor.co.jp	3	386	169.6	-1.1	0.2	0.1
18	18	IBOPE Group	São Paulo	Brazil	ibope.com.br	16	1,743	116.5	0.4	25.0	21.5
19	19	Lieberman Research Worldwide	Los Angeles	USA	lrwonline.com	4	324	87.5	11.7	16.4	18.7
20	21	comScore Inc.	Reston, Va.	USA	comscore.com	5	452	87.2	31.5	10.1	11.6
21	*	Cello Research & Consulting	London	UK	cellogroup.co.uk	2	400	79.9	11.0	38.8	48.6
22	*	Market Strategies Intl.	Livonia, Mich.	USA	marketstrategies.com	2	311	61.8	10.8	6.0	9.7
23	*	BVA Group	Paris	France	bva.fr	4	620	55.6	-0.3	2.7	4.9
24	*	OTX	Los Angeles	USA	otxresearch.com	2	191	54.5	35.6	3.7	6.8
25	22	Dentsu Research Inc.	Tokyo	Japan	dentsuresearch.co.jp	1	116	54.2	-10.4	–	–
		Total					104,719	$17,525.4	7.7%	$10,047.6	57.3%

*Estimated by Top 25

**For fiscal year ending March 2008

[1] Includes countries that have subsidiaries with an equity interest or branch offices, or both.

[2] Includes some nonresearch employees.

[3] Total revenue that includes nonresearch activities for some companies are significantly higher. This information is given in the individual company profiles.

[4] Rate of growth from year to year has been adjusted so as not to include revenue gains or losses from acquisitions or divestitures. See company profiles for explanation. Rate of growth is based on home country currency and includes currency exchange effects.

SOURCE: Marketing News, 08/15/08, **http://www.marketingpower.com/ResourceLibrary/Publications/MarketingNews/2008/42/13/2008%20Hono25.pdf**, accessed Dec. 3, 2008.

real world or in a controlled environment also must be decided. Finally, a decision needs to be made as to whether the research is to collect historical facts or gather information about future developments. This is particularly important for consumer research because firms frequently desire to determine consumers' future intentions to purchase a certain product.

Cultural and individual preferences, which vary significantly among nations, play a major role in determining research techniques. U.S. managers frequently prefer to gather large quantities of hard data through surveys, which provide numbers that can be manipulated statistically and directly compared to other sets of data. In some other countries managers appear to prefer the "soft" approach. For example, much of Japanese-style market research relies heavily on two kinds of information: soft data obtained from visits to dealers and other channel members and hard data about shipments, inventory levels, and retail sales.

Once the structure of the type of data sought has been determined, a choice must be made among the types of research instruments available. Each provides a different depth of information and has its unique strengths and weaknesses.

Interviews

Interviews with knowledgeable persons can be of great value to a corporation desiring international marketing information. Because bias from the individual may be part of the findings, the intent should be to obtain in-depth information rather than a wide variety of data. Particularly when specific answers are sought to very narrow questions, interviews can be most useful.

Focus Groups

Focus groups are a useful research tool resulting in interactive interviews. A group of informed persons is gathered for a limited period of time (two to four hours). Usually, the ideal size for a focus group is seven to ten participants. A specific topic is introduced and thoroughly discussed by all group members. Because of the interaction, hidden issues are sometimes raised that would not have been addressed in an individual interview. The skill of the group leader in stimulating discussion is crucial to the success of a focus group. Discussions are often recorded on tape and subsequently analyzed in detail. Focus groups, like in-depth interviews, do not provide statistically significant information; however, they can be helpful in providing information about perceptions, emotions, and other nonovert factors. In addition, once individuals are gathered, focus groups are highly efficient in terms of rapidly accumulating a substantial amount of information. With the advances occurring in the communications field, focus groups can also be carried out internationally, with interaction between groups.

When conducting international research via focus groups, the researcher must be aware of the importance of culture in the discussion process. Not all societies encourage frank and open exchange and disagreement among individuals. Status consciousness may result in situations in which the opinion of one is reflected by all other participants. Disagreement may be seen as impolite, or certain topics may be taboo.

Observation

Observation techniques require the researcher to play the role of a nonparticipating observer of activity and behavior. Observation can be personal or impersonal—for example, mechanical. Observation can be obtrusive or inobtrusive, depending on whether the subject is aware or unaware of being observed. In international marketing research, observation can be extremely useful in shedding light on practices not previously encountered or

FOCUS GROUPS ARE A USEFUL RESEARCH TOOL RESULTING IN INTERACTIVE INTERVIEWS.

understood. This aspect is particularly valuable for the researcher who is totally unfamiliar with a market or market situation, and can be quickly achieved through, for example, participation in a trade mission. Finding employees with personal experience and observations about international markets can be very beneficial for employers. *The International Marketplace 8.3* shows how the state of Utah is benefiting from the international exposure of its citizens.

Observation can also help in understanding phenomena that would have been difficult to assess with other techniques. For example, Toyota sent a group of its engineers and designers to southern California to unobtrusively observe how women get into and operate their cars. They found that women with long fingernails have trouble opening the door and operating various knobs on the dashboard. Based on their observations, Toyota engineers and designers were able to observe the women's plight and redraw some of the automobile exterior and interior designs.[14]

Conducting observations can also have its pitfalls. For example, people may react differently to the discovery that their behavior has been observed. The degree to which the observer has to be familiarized or introduced to other participants may vary. The complexity of the task may differ due to the use of multiple languages. To conduct in-store research in Europe, for example, store checks, photo audits of shelves, and store interviews must be scheduled well in advance and need to be preceded by a full round of introductions of the researchers to store management and personnel. In some countries, such as Belgium, a researcher must remember that four different languages are spoken and their use may change from store to store.

The International
MARKETPLACE   8.3

Excellence in International Research

The Church of Jesus Christ of Latter-day Saints, commonly known as the Mormon Church, was organized by Joseph Smith in 1830 in New York. It has grown into an organization with 12 million members and congregations throughout the world and is currently increasing at an average rate of about 1 million new members every three years. It generates close to $6 billion in annual income from its non-church-related businesses and enterprises and has $30 billion in assets. One of its key growth strategies is to send many of its members abroad as missionaries. Therefore, the church has thousands of young and experienced travelers, returning with foreign language skills and intercultural understanding. Indeed Utah, where the Mormon population is highly concentrated, has speakers fluent in 90 percent of the world's written languages, and 30 percent of its U.S.-born adult males speak a second language. Due to its large and globally educated workforce, Utah is successfully attracting businesses such as Intel, eBay, American Express, and Goldman Sachs.

Young Mormon followers, 19 to 22 years of age, are expected to go on a mission abroad for 18 to 24 months. There are currently approximately 60,000 full-time missionaries serving in more than 330 mission districts around the world. Most missionaries learn new languages during their brief stay at the missionary training centers, where about 50 different languages are taught, and become fully proficient during their stay abroad. In any country in which they are located, missionaries go door to door, promoting their religion and indirectly developing their sales skills. Young individuals are completely immersed in the host culture, live among local families, and therefore have a personal understanding of the people of the country. Individuals with such extensive experience abroad can be great resources to their companies as sources of global knowledge. Their personal insight into local cultures can help enlighten employers about marketing abroad.

CEOs in Utah note the diverse foreign language experience, high ethics, and family-oriented attitudes of the Mormon workforce as significant factors in the success of their businesses. Employers look for individuals who are not only well rounded but have a specific area of expertise. Having a workforce that knows foreign languages and has the experience of living abroad adds to a company's ability to research international markets.

SOURCES: "Utah CEOs Cite Cost Advantages, Ethics and Local Workforce as Top Reasons to Locate Companies Here," *PR Newswire US*, November 3, 2005; Earl Fry, Wallace McCarlie, Derek Wride, and Stacey Sears, "Mapping Globalization along the Wasatch Front," Pacific Council on International Policy, **http://www.pacificcouncil.org**, accessed February 19, 2008; Eric Johnson, "Get The Fire: Young Mormon Missionaries Abroad," Mormonism Research Ministry, **www.mrm.org**, accessed February 22, 2008.

The research instruments discussed so far—interviews, focus groups, and observation—are useful primarily for gathering **qualitative data**. The intent is not to amass data or to search for statistical significance, but rather to obtain a better understanding of given situations, behavioral patterns, or underlying dimensions. The researcher using these instruments must be cautioned that even frequent repetition of the measurements will not lead to a statistically valid result. Yet, statistical validity often is not the major focus of corporate international marketing research. Rather, it is the better understanding, description, and prediction of events that have an impact on marketing decision making. When **quantitative data** are desired, surveys are appropriate research instruments.

Surveys

Survey research is useful in providing the opportunity to quantify concepts. In the social sciences, the cross-cultural survey is generally accepted as a powerful method of hypothesis testing. Surveys are usually conducted via questionnaires that are administered personally, by mail, or by telephone. Use of the survey technique presupposes that the population under study is able to comprehend and respond to the questions posed. Also, particularly in the case of mail and telephone surveys, a major precondition is the feasibility of using the postal system or the widespread availability of telephones. In many countries, only limited records are available about dwellings, their location, and their occupants. In Venezuela, for example, most houses are not numbered but rather are given individual names like "Casa Rosa" or "El Retiro." In some countries, street maps are not even available. As a result, it becomes virtually impossible to reach respondents by mail.

In other countries, obtaining a correct address may be easy, but the postal system may not function well. The Italian postal service, for example, has suffered from scandals that exposed such practices as selling undelivered mail to paper mills for recycling.

Telephone surveys may also be inappropriate if telephone ownership is rare. In such instances, any information obtained would be highly biased even if the researcher randomizes the calls. In some instances, telephone networks and systems may also prevent the researcher from conducting surveys. Frequent line congestion and a lack of telephone directories are examples. There are also great variations between countries or regions of countries in terms of unlisted telephone numbers or for cellular phones. For example, the percentage of households with unlisted telephone numbers varies widely by country and even city.

Surveys can be hampered by social and cultural constraints. Recipients of letters may be illiterate or may be reluctant to respond in writing. In some nations, entire population segments—for example, women—may be totally inaccessible to interviewers. One must also assess the purpose of the survey in the context of the population surveyed. It has been argued, for example, that one should not rely on consumer surveys for new product development information. Key reasons are the absence of responsibility—the consumer is sincere when spending but not when talking; conservative attitudes—ordinary consumers are conservative and tend to react negatively to a new product; vanity—it is human nature to exaggerate and put on a good appearance; and insufficient information—the research results depend on the product characteristics information that is given to survey participants and that may be incomplete or unabsorbed.[15]

In spite of all these difficulties, however, the survey technique remains a useful one because it allows the researcher to rapidly accumulate a large quantity of data amenable to statistical analysis. Even though quite difficult, **international comparative research** has been carried out very successfully between nations, particularly if the environments studied are sufficiently similar so that the impact of uncontrollable macrovariables is limited. However, even in environments that are quite dissimilar, in-depth comparative research can be carried out.[16] Doing so may require a country-by-country adjustment of details while preserving the similarity of research thrust. For example, researchers have reported good results in mail surveys conducted simultaneously in Japan and the United States after adjusting the size of the return envelope, outgoing envelope, address style, signature, and cover letter to meet specific societal expectations.[17] With constantly expanding technological capabilities, international marketers will be able to use the survey technique more frequently in the future. Exhibit 8.4 provides an overview of the extent of the Internet technology available to help the international research process.

Exhibit 8.4

Internet Penetration around the Globe

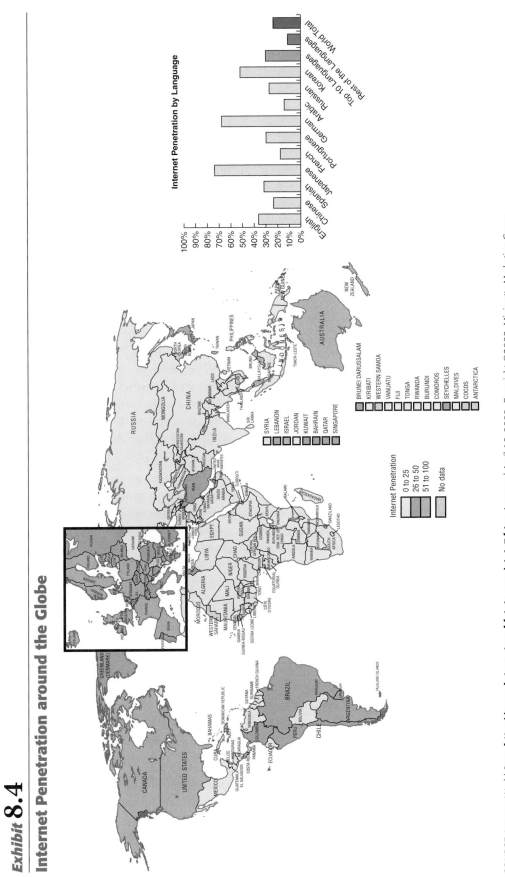

SOURCE: Internet World Stats, **http://www.internetworldstats.com/stats7.htm**. Accessed April 16, 2009. Copyright ©2009, Miniwatts Marketing Group.

Designing the Survey Questionnaire

International marketing surveys are usually conducted with questionnaires. These questionnaires should contain questions that are clear and easy to comprehend by the respondents, as well as easy for the data collector to administer. Much attention must therefore be paid to question format, content, and wording.

Question Format

Questions can be structured or unstructured. Structured questions typically allow the respondents only limited choice options. Unstructured (or open-ended) questions permit the capture of more in-depth information, but they also increase the potential for interviewer bias. Even at the cost of potential bias, however, open-ended questions are quite useful in cross-cultural surveys, because they make allowance for the frame of reference of the respondents and can even permit the respondents to set their own frame of reference.

Another question format decision is the choice between direct and indirect questions. Societies have different degrees of sensitivity to certain questions. Questions related to the income or age of a respondent may be accepted differently in different countries. Also, the social desirability of answers may vary. In some cultures, questions about employees, performance, standards, and financing are asked directly of a respondent, while in others, particularly in Asia or the Middle East, these questions are thought to be rude and insulting.[18] As a result, the researcher must be sure that the questions are culturally acceptable. This may mean that questions that can be asked directly in some cultures will have to be asked indirectly in others. For example, rather than ask "How old are you?" one could ask "In what year were you born?"

The researcher must also be sure to adapt the complexity of the question to the level of understanding of the respondent. For example, a multipoint scaling method, which may be effectively used in a developed country to discover the attitudes and attributes of company executives, may be a very poor instrument if used among rural entrepreneurs. It has been found that demonstration aids are useful in surveys among poorly educated respondents.[19]

The question format should also ensure data equivalence in international marketing research. This requires categories used in questionnaires to be comparatively structured. In a developed country, for example, a white-collar worker may be part of the middle class, whereas in a less-developed country, the same person would be part of the upper class. Before using categories in a questionnaire, the researcher must therefore determine their appropriateness in different environments. This is particularly important for questions that attempt to collect attitudinal, psychographic, or lifestyle data, since cultural variations are most pronounced in these areas. For example, pizza may be chic in Asia but a convenience food in the United States, or a bicycle may be recreational in some regions while being a basic mode of transportation in others.[20]

Question Content

Major consideration must be given to the ability and willingness of respondents to supply the answers. The knowledge and information available to respondents may vary substantially because of different educational levels and may affect their ability to answer questions. Further, societal demands and restrictions may influence the willingness of respondents to answer certain questions. For various reasons, respondents may also be motivated to supply incorrect answers. For example, in countries where the tax collection system is consistently eluded by taxpayers, questions regarding level of income may deliberately be answered inaccurately. Distrust in the researcher, and the fear that research results may be passed on to the government, may also lead individuals to consistently understate their assets. Because of government restrictions in Brazil, for example, individuals will rarely admit to owning an imported car. Nevertheless, when one observes the streets of Rio de Janeiro, a substantial number of foreign cars are seen. The international market researcher is unlikely to change the societal context of a country. The objective of the content planning process should therefore be to adapt the questions to societal constraints.

Question Wording

The impact of language and culture is of particular importance when wording questions. The goal for the international marketing researcher should be to ensure that the potential for misunderstandings and misinterpretations of spoken or written words is minimized. Both language and cultural differences make this issue an extremely sensitive one in the international marketing research process. As a result, attention must be paid to the translation equivalence of verbal and nonverbal questions that can change in the course of translation. One of this book's authors, for example, used the term *group discussion* in a questionnaire for Russian executives, only to learn that the translated meaning of the term was "political indoctrination session."

The key is to keep questions clear by using simple rather than complex words, by avoiding ambiguous words and questions, by omitting leading questions, and by asking questions in specific terms, thus avoiding generalizations and estimates.[21] To reduce problems of question wording, it is helpful to use a **translation-retranslation approach**. The researcher formulates the questions, has them translated into the language of the country under investigation, and subsequently has a second translator return the foreign text to the researcher's native language. Through the use of this method, the researcher can hope to detect possible blunders. As demonstrated in *The International Marketplace 8.4* translation mistakes are easy

---

The International
MARKETPLACE   8.4

Check Your Translations!

All sorts of things can go wrong when a company translates its advertising into foreign languages. Kentucky Fried Chicken's slogan "Finger-lickin' good" was translated into the less appetizing "Eat your fingers off" in Chinese. Ford launched the Ford Fiera in Spanish-speaking Latin-American countries not knowing that "fiera" means "ugly old woman." The Italian brand of mineral water Traficante didn't sell so well either, being translated into "drug dealer" in Spanish. Advertising mistakes receive a fair amount of attention in the media and the international business world when they occur, but many people never stop to think about what would happen if a company unknowingly committed translation errors much earlier—in the research phase.

The possibility of disaster due to such errors is in many ways even greater than in the advertising stage, because research findings are often used to determine a firm's strategy or for new product development. A translation blunder that goes undiscovered at this stage could set a company on the wrong track entirely. Imagine spending millions of dollars to develop a new product or to enter a new market only to find that your company's surveys had asked the wrong questions!

Researchers at the Pew Research Center for the People and the Press in Washington, DC, are not new to international research. They have been conducting public opinion research around the globe for more than a decade. Their findings related to attitudes toward the press, politics, and public policy issues are regularly cited in the media. However, the company received an unwelcome

surprise when it translated one of its worldwide polls into 63 languages and then back into English. As it turns out, the ride to the foreign languages and back again was a bit bumpier than they had imagined.

For example, in Ghana, the original phrase "married or living with a partner" was first translated into one of the country's tribal languages as "married but have a girlfriend," and the category "separated" became "There's a misunderstanding between me and my spouse." The original version of a questionnaire to be used in Nigeria had similar problems: "American ideas and customs" came out "the ideology of America and border guards" (get it, customs? border guards?) and the phrase "success in life is pretty much determined by forces outside our control" initially read "Goodness in life starts with blessings from one's personal god." In the original Nigerian Yoruba version, "fast food" had been translated to "microwave food" and "the military" became "herbalist/medicine man." Not quite the same thing, is it?

Fortunately, the meanings were corrected in the final translation of the questionnaire, said the Center's director Andrew Kohut. The lesson? Multinational researchers, check your translations!

SOURCES: "Translation Mistakes," *Marketing Solutions Inc.,* Terri Morrison and Wayne Conaway, "Bite the Wax Tadpole," *Getting through Customs,* **www.industryweek.com/articles/bite_the_wax_tadpole_1744.aspx/**, accessed April 13, 2009; Richard Morin, "Words Matter," *The Washington Post,* January 19, 2003, B5; Ian Dow, "Your ad is a tad mad," *The Scottish Daily Record,* October 5, 2002, 8; Global Attitude Report, "What the World Thinks in 2002," December 4, 2002 (from the Pew Research Center for the People and the Press).

to make. An additional safeguard is the use of alternative wording. Here the researcher uses questions that address the same issue but are worded differently and that resurface at various points in the questionnaire in order to check for consistency in question interpretation by the respondents.

In spite of superb research planning, a poorly designed instrument will yield poor results. No matter how comfortable and experienced the researcher is in international research activities, an instrument should always be pretested. Ideally, such a pretest is carried out with a subset of the population under study. At least a pretest with knowledgeable experts and individuals should be conducted. Even though a pretest may mean delays and additional cost, the risks of poor research are simply too great for this process to be omitted.

Developing the Sampling Plan

To obtain representative results, the researcher must reach representative members of the population under study. Many methods that have been developed in industrialized countries for this purpose are useless abroad. For example, address directories may simply not be available. Multiple families may live in one dwelling. Differences between population groups living, for example, in highlands and lowlands may make it imperative to differentiate these segments. Lack of basic demographic information may prevent the design of a sampling frame. In instances in which comparative research addresses very different areas, for example China and North America, it may be virtually impossible to match samples.[22]

The international marketing researcher must keep in mind the complexities of the market under study and prepare his or her sampling plan accordingly. Often, samples need to be stratified to reflect different population groups, and innovative sampling methods need to be devised in order to assure representative and relevant responses. For example, a survey concerning grocery shopping habits might require data from housewives in one country, but from domestic help in another.[23]

Data Collection

The international marketing researcher must check the quality of the data collection process. In some cultures, questionnaire administration is seen as useless by the local population. Instruments are administered primarily to humor the researcher. In such cases, interviewers may cheat quite frequently. Spot checks on the administration procedures are vital to ensure reasonable data quality. A **realism check** of data should also be used. For example, if marketing research in Italy reports that very little spaghetti is consumed, the researcher should perhaps consider whether individuals responded to their use of purchased spaghetti rather than homemade spaghetti. The collected data should therefore be compared with secondary information and with analogous information from a similar market in order to obtain a preliminary understanding of data quality.

Analyzing and Interpreting Primary Data

Interpretation and analysis of accumulated information are required to answer the research questions that were posed initially. The researcher should, of course, use the best tools available and appropriate for analysis. The fact that a market may be in a less-developed country does not preclude the collection of good data and the use of good analytical methods. On the other hand, international researchers should be cautioned against using overly sophisticated tools for unsophisticated data. Even the best of tools will not improve data quality. The quality of data must be matched with the quality of the research tools to achieve appropriately sophisticated analysis and yet not overstate the value of the data.

Presenting Research Results

The primary focus in the presentation of research results must be communication. In multinational marketing research, communication must take place not only with management at headquarters but also with managers in the local operations. Otherwise, little or no transference of research results will occur, and the synergistic benefits of a multinational operation are lost. To minimize time devoted to reading reports, the researcher must present results clearly and concisely. In the worldwide operations of a firm, particularly in the communication efforts, lengthy data and analytical demonstrations should be avoided. The availability of data and the techniques used should be mentioned, however, so that subsidiary operations can receive the information on request.

The researcher should also demonstrate in the presentation how research results relate to the original research objective and fit with overall corporate strategy. At least schematically, possibilities for analogous application should be highlighted. These possibilities should then also be communicated to local subsidiaries, perhaps through a short monthly newsletter. A newsletter format, ideally distributed through an intranet, can be used regardless of whether the research process is centralized, coordinated, or decentralized. The only difference will be the person or group providing the input for the newsletter. It is important to maintain such communication in order for the entire organization to learn and to improve its international marketing research capabilities.

Follow-Up and Review

Now that the research has been carried out, appropriate managerial decisions must be made based on the research, and the organization must absorb the research. For example, if it has been found that a product needs to have certain attributes to sell well in Latin America, the manager must determine whether the product development area is aware of this finding and the degree to which the knowledge is now incorporated into new product projects. Without such follow-up, the role of research tends to become a mere "staff" function, increasingly isolated from corporate "line" activity and lacking major impact on corporate activity. If that is the case, research will diminish and even be disregarded—resulting in an organization at risk.

Research on the Web

The growing use of technology has given rise to new marketing research approaches that allow consumers to be heard more often and permit firms to work much more effectively at their customer-listening skills. The evolution of marketing research on the web has been both dramatic and rapid! The rise in Internet usage and capabilities has catapulted marketing research from a Web 1.0 model in which researchers have taken traditional primary data collection methods online (for example, surveys/questionnaires in which specific questions are asked) to a Web 2.0 model in which users generate the content of the data collected.[24]

The increasing degree to which the World Wide Web truly lives up to its name is making it possible for international marketers to use this medium in their research efforts. With low barriers to entry, understanding consumers worldwide is now an option for almost any company. As a market researcher, the internet serves as a portal to reach out to consumers in a low-cost fashion. For example, product details, pictures of products, brand logos, and shopping environments can be portrayed with graphics and sounds—thus bringing the issues to be researched much closer to the respondent.

In the Web 1.0 online research model, surveys can be administered either through E-mail or via a website. An E-mail survey format eliminates the need for printing and postage. This is especially critical due to the fact that mailing surveys internationally can be very costly. As a result, larger and geographically diverse audiences can be the focus of inquiry. If surveys are posted on a site, they can be of the pop-up nature, where visitors can be targeted specifically. Companies that utilize the web for administering traditional surveys internationally are Qualtrics (**www.qualtrics.com**), Zoomerang (**www.zoomerang.com**), Zogby International (**www.zogby.com**), and Harris (**www.harrisinteractive.com**). Research indicates that there is a higher and faster response rate to electronic inquiries. In addition, the process of data entry can be structured so that responses are automatically fed into data analysis software.[25]

However, it would be too simplistic to assume that the digitalization of survey content is all that it takes to go global on the Web. There are cultural differences that must be taken into account by the researcher. Global visitors to a site should encounter research that is embedded in their own cultural values, rituals, and symbols. Testimonials or encouragement should be delivered by culture-specific heroes. For example, a website might first offer a visitor from Korea the opportunity to become part of a product user community. A low-context visitor from the United States may in turn be exposed immediately to product features.[26] Other suggestions for constructing successful Web surveys are to include only the most important questions, keep the total number of questions to 30 or fewer, limit the number of screens respondents have to navigate through, keep response time to less than 10 to 15 minutes, inform each respondent of the time needed to complete the survey, and give an incentive to take the survey that relates directly to the company's product that respondents are being asked to evaluate.[27]

Another trend in the Web 1.0 world has been the use of social networks to access particular consumer groups. With the popularity and growth in the number of social networking sites, market researchers can post pop-up and banner ads on these sites directing particular target audiences to online surveys. There are a number of worldwide social networking sites, such as Facebook, MySpace, Twitter, Bebo, LinkedIn, Ning, Classmates, and Flickr. The benefits for market research on these social networking sites are numerous: highly targeted markets (can specify demographics of respondent), real-time results (results within an hour), simple interface and ease-of-use, over millions of potential users for less than $50 U.S., opensource software to allow researchers to customize surveys, and respondents can be actively or passively recruited. The major benefit to the networking site is a fee for each completed survey.[28]

The recent company acquisitions and geographical expansion within the social networking marketplace signal the importance that businesses are placing on the wealth of interactions within these sites. For example, New Corp. has bought MySpace, Microsoft purchased a stake in Facebook, and AOL purchased Bebo. Facebook is opening an international headquarters in Ireland and Bebo, headquartered in California (USA), has millions of users in Britain, Italy, France, Germany, Spain, and the Netherlands.[29] This industry activity is a signal of the move from Web 1.0 to Web 2.0 market research.

In one of the first Web 2.0 moves, Facebook and Vizu[30] challenged traditional research methods by offering polling, which is a new way to find quick answers to simple questions. With Facebook Polling or Vizu's Power Polls, all a user has to do is create a question and specify a sample size. For as little as $50 U.S. per 100 interviews, users can have results in their account in just a few hours. In this paradigm, the research is not designed before it begins, but occurs over a series of polls.[31] Unlike the use of social networks to *access* respondents, the online survey is moved *into the existing* social network. Users can actually view real-time results, which increase their perception of value with respect to the interaction.[32] Herein, however, lies some of the limitations of Web 2.0 market research efforts: reliability (lack of respondent screening), sampling (are the right people answering?), and methodology (single-response poll format, does not currently offer statistically significant results).[33]

Communispace was one of the first online market researchers to fully engage in the Web 2.0 research space. This company established a new online community dedicated solely to market research. These online communities mimic traditional focus groups in the amount of qualitative information made available to the market researcher.[34] The company touts some of its biggest success stories as those related to Hallmark's Shoebox cards, Unilever's AXE products, GlaxoSmithKline's launch of alli, and Kraft's South Beach Diet products.[35]

The future of online marketing research is evolving as the capabilities on the internet evolve. While traditional marketing research tools will not be replaced in the near term by online research methods, the world is the marketplace in the 21st century and access to consumer opinions worldwide is critical for business success. Web-based research is a natural for gathering consumer information quickly and cost-effectively.

The International Information System

Many organizations have data needs going beyond specific international marketing research projects. Most of the time, daily decisions must be made, and there is neither time nor money for special research. An information system already in place is needed to provide the decision maker with basic data for most ongoing decisions. Corporations have responded by developing marketing decision support systems. Defined as "an integrated system of data, statistical analysis, modeling, and display formats using computer hardware and software technology," such a system serves as a mechanism to coordinate the flow of information to corporate managers for decision-making purposes.[36]

To be useful to the decision maker, the system needs various attributes. First, the information must be *relevant*. The data gathered must have meaning for the manager's decision-making process. Second, the information must be *timely*. It is of little benefit to the manager if decision information help that is needed today does not become available until a month from now. To be of use to the international decision maker, the system must therefore feed from a variety of international sources and be updated frequently. For multinational corporations, this means a real-time linkage between international subsidiaries and a broad-based ongoing data input operation.

Third, information must be *flexible*—that is, it must be available in the forms needed by management. A marketing decision support system must therefore permit manipulation of the format and combining of the data. Therefore, great effort must be expended to make diverse international data compatible with and comparable to each other. Fourth, information contained in the system must be *accurate*. This attribute is particularly relevant in the international field because information quickly becomes outdated as a result of major changes. Obviously, a system is of no value if it provides incorrect information that leads to poor decisions. Fifth, the system's information bank must be reasonably *exhaustive*. Because of the interrelationship between variables, factors that may influence a particular decision must be appropriately represented in the information system. This means that the marketing decision support system must be based on a broad variety of factors. Finally, to be useful to managers, the system must be *convenient,* both to use and to access. Systems that are cumbersome and time-consuming to reach and to use will not be used enough to justify corporate expenditures to build and maintain them.

More international information systems are being developed successfully due to progress in computer technology in both hardware and software. To build an information system, corporations use the internal data that are available from divisions such as accounting and finance and also from their subsidiaries. In addition, many organizations put mechanisms in place to enrich the basic data flow. Three such tools are environmental scanning, Delphi studies, and scenario building.

Environmental Scanning

Any changes in the business environment, whether domestic or foreign, may have serious repercussions on the marketing activities of the firm. Corporations therefore should understand the necessity for tracking new developments and obtaining continuous updates. To carry out this task, some large multinational organizations have formed environmental scanning groups.

Environmental scanning activities are useful to continuously receive information on political, social, and economic affairs internationally; on changes of attitudes held by public institutions and private citizens; and on possible upcoming alterations in international markets.

The precision required for environmental scanning varies with its purpose. Whether the information is to be used for mind stretching or for budgeting, for example, must be taken into account when constructing the framework and variables that will enter the scanning process. The more immediate and precise the exercise is to be in its application within the corporation, the greater the need for detailed information. At the same time, such heightened precision may lessen the utility of environmental scanning for the strategic corporate purpose, which is more long-term in its orientation.

Environmental scanning can be performed in various ways. One method consists of obtaining factual input regarding many variables. For example, the U.S. Census Bureau collects, evaluates, and adjusts a wide variety of demographic, social, and economic characteristics of foreign countries. Estimates for all countries of the world are developed, particularly on economic variables, such as labor force statistics, GDP, and income statistics, but also on health and nutrition variables. Similar factual information can be obtained from international organizations such as the World Bank or the United Nations.

Frequently, corporations believe that such factual data alone are insufficient for their information needs. Particularly for forecasting future developments, other methods are used to capture underlying dimensions of social change. One significant method is **content analysis**. This technique investigates the content of communication in a society and entails literally counting the number of times preselected words, themes, symbols, or pictures appear in a given medium. It can be used productively in international marketing to monitor the social, economic, cultural, and technological environment in which the marketing organization is operating.

Corporations can use content analysis to pinpoint upcoming changes in their line of business, and new opportunities, by attempting to identify trendsetting events. For example, the Alaska oil spill by the tanker *Exxon Valdez* resulted in entirely new international concern about environmental protection and safety, reaching far beyond the incident itself.

Environmental scanning is conducted by a variety of groups within and outside the corporation. Frequently, small corporate staffs are created at headquarters to coordinate the information flow. In addition, subsidiary staff can be used to provide occasional intelligence reports. Groups of volunteers are also formed to gather and analyze information worldwide and feed individual analyses back to corporate headquarters, where they can be used to form the "big picture."

Finally, it should be kept in mind that internationally there may be a fine line between tracking and obtaining information and misappropriating corporate secrets. With growing frequency, governments and firms claim that their trade secrets are being obtained and abused by foreign competitors. The perceived threat from economic espionage has led to accusations of government spying networks trying to undermine the commercial interests of companies.[37] Information gatherers must be sensitive to these issues in order to avoid conflict or controversy.

Delphi Studies

To enrich the information obtained from factual data, corporations resort to the use of creative and highly qualitative data-gathering methods. Delphi studies are one such method. These studies are particularly useful in the international marketing environment because they are "a means for aggregating the judgments of a number of . . . experts . . . who cannot come together physically."[38] This type of research approach clearly aims at qualitative rather than quantitative measures by aggregating the information of a group of experts. It seeks to obtain answers from those who know instead of seeking the average responses of many with only limited knowledge.

Typically, Delphi studies are carried out with groups of about 30 well-chosen participants who possess particular in-depth expertise in an area of concern, such as future developments in the international trade environment. These participants are asked via mail to identify the major issues in the area of concern. They are also requested to rank their statements according to importance and explain the rationale behind the order. Next, the aggregated information is returned to all participants, who are encouraged to state clearly their agreements or disagreements with the various rank orders and comments. Statements can be challenged, and in another round, participants can respond to the challenges. After several rounds of challenge and response, a reasonably coherent consensus is developed.

The Delphi technique is particularly valuable because it uses the mail or facsimile method of communication to bridge large distances and therefore makes individuals quite accessible at a reasonable cost. It does not suffer from the drawback of ordinary mail investigations: lack of interaction among the participants. One drawback of the technique is that it requires several steps, and therefore months may elapse before the information is obtained. Even though the increasing availability of electronic mail may hasten the process, the researcher must be cautious to factor in the different penetration and acceptance levels of such technology. One should not let the research process be driven by technology to the exclusion of valuable key informants who utilize less sophisticated methods of communication.

Also, substantial effort must be expended in selecting the appropriate participants and in motivating them to participate in this exercise with enthusiasm and continuity. When obtained on a regular basis, Delphi information can provide crucial additions to the factual data available for the marketing information system. In this book, the final chapter has largely been designed based on a Delphi study carried out by the authors.

Scenario Building

Some companies use **scenario analysis** to look at different configurations of key variables in the international market. For example, economic growth rates, import penetration, population growth, and political stability can be varied. By projecting such variations for medium- to long-term periods, companies can envision completely new environmental conditions. These conditions are then analyzed for their potential domestic and international impact on corporate strategy.

Of major importance in scenario building is the identification of crucial trend variables and the degree of their variation. Frequently, key experts are used to gain information about potential variations and the viability of certain scenarios.

A wide variety of scenarios must be built to expose corporate executives to multiple potential occurrences. Ideally, even far-fetched variables deserve some consideration, if only to build worst-case scenarios.

Scenario builders also need to recognize the nonlinearity of factors. To simply extrapolate from currently existing situations is insufficient. Frequently, extraneous factors may enter the picture with a significant impact. Finally, in scenario building, the possibility of joint occurrences must be recognized because changes may not come about in an isolated fashion but may be spread over wide regions. An example of a joint occurrence is the indebtedness of developing nations. Although the inability of any one country to pay its debts would not present a major problem for the international banking community, large and simultaneous indebtedness may well pose a problem of major severity. Similarly, given large technological advances, the possibility of" obsolescence of current technology must also be considered. For example, quantum leaps in computer development and new generations of computers may render obsolete the technological investment of a corporation or even a country.

For scenarios to be useful, management must analyze and respond to them by formulating contingency plans. Such planning will broaden horizons and may prepare management for unexpected situations. Familiarization in turn can result in shorter response times to actual occurrences by honing response capability. The difficulty, of course, is to devise scenarios that are unusual enough to trigger new thinking yet sufficiently realistic to be taken seriously by management.[39]

The development of an international information system is of major importance to the multinational corporation. It aids the ongoing decision process and becomes a vital corporate tool in carrying out the strategic planning task. Only by observing global trends and changes will the firm be able to maintain and increase its international competitive position. Many of the data available are quantitative in nature, but attention must also be paid to qualitative dimensions. Quantitative analysis will continue to improve as the ability to collect, store, analyze, and retrieve data increases through the use of high-speed computers. Nevertheless, qualitative analysis should remain a major component of corporate research and strategic planning.

Summary

Constraints of time, resources, and expertise are the major inhibitors of international marketing research. Nevertheless, firms need to carry out planned and organized research in order to explore global market alternatives successfully. Such research needs to be closely linked to the decision-making process.

International market research differs from domestic research in that the environment, which determines how well tools, techniques, and concepts apply, is different abroad. In addition, the manager needs to deal with new parameters, such as duties, exchange rates, and international documentation, a greater number of interacting factors, and a much broader definition of the concept of competition.

Given the scarcity of resources, companies beginning their international effort often need to use data that have already been collected—that is, secondary data. Such data are available from governments, international organizations, directories, trade associations, or online databases.

To respond to specific information requirements, firms frequently need primary research. The researcher needs to select an appropriate research technique to collect the information needed. Sensitivity to different international environments and cultures will guide the researcher in deciding whether to use interviews, focus groups, observation, surveys, · or experimentation as data collection techniques. In addition to traditional data gathering tools, Web-based surveys can be faster at bringing better quality results. The same sensitivity applies to the design of the research instrument, where issues such as question format, content, and wording are decided. Also, the sampling plan needs to be appropriate for the local environment in order to ensure representative and useful responses.

Once the data have been collected, care must be taken to use analytical tools appropriate for the quality of data collected, so that management is not misled about the sophistication of the research. Finally, the research results must be presented in a concise and useful form so that

management can benefit in its decision making, and implementation of the research needs to be tracked.

To provide ongoing information to management, an international information support system is useful. Such a system will provide for the systematic and continuous gathering, analysis, and reporting of data for decision-making purposes. It uses a firm's internal information and gathers data via environmental scanning, Delphi studies, or scenario building, thus enabling management to prepare for the future and hone its decision-making skills.

Key Terms

foreign-market opportunity analysis	international comparative research	translation-retranslation approach
proxy variable	structured/unstructured questions	realism check
research specifications	direct/indirect questions	Web-based research
qualitative data	social desirability	content analysis
quantitative data	data equivalence	scenario analysis

Questions for Discussion

1. Discuss the possible shortcomings of secondary data.

2. Why would a firm collect primary data in its international marketing research?

3. Discuss the trade-offs between centralized and decentralized international marketing research.

4. How is international market research affected by differences in language?

5. Compare the use of telephone surveys in the United States and in Egypt.

6. What are some of the crucial variables you would track in an international information system?

7. How has information technology affected international marketing research?

Internet Exercises

1. What were the industries and countries against which the United States filed antidumping actions last year? (Check http://www.usitc.gov.)

2. Where would it be most difficult to conduct business due to a high degree of corruption? (Check http://www.transparency.org.)

Recommended Readings

Baker, Donald, and Carol Terry, *Internet Research—Illustrated Fourth Edition*, Course Technology; Fourth edition, 2008.

Bush , Robert P., David Ortinau, and Joseph Hair Jr., *Marketing Research,* McGraw Hill Higher Education; Fourth edition, 2008.

Bradley, Nigel, *Marketing Research: Tools and Techniques,* Oxford University Press, 2007.

Scott, David Meerman, *The New Rules of Marketing and PR: How to Use News Releases, Blogs, Podcasting, Viral Marketing, and Online Media to Reach Buyers Directly*, Wiley, 2007.

Zikmund, William, *Essentials of Marketing Research,* South-Western College Pub; Third edition, 2007.

Roberts, Mary Lou, *Internet Marketing: Integrating Online and Offline Strategies*, Atomic Dog; Second edition 2007.

INFORMATION SOURCES FOR MARKETING ISSUES

European Union

EUROPA
The umbrella server for all institutions
http://www.europa.eu.int

CORDIS
Information on EU research programs
http://www.cordis.lu

Council of the European Union
Information and news from the Council, with sections covering Common Foreign and Security Policy (CFSP) and Justice and Home Affairs
http://ue.eu.int

Court of Auditors
Information notes, annual reports, and other publications
http://eca.europa.eu/portal/page/portal/eac_main_pages/splash_page

Court of Justice
Overview, press releases, publications, and full-text proceedings of the court
http://europa.eu.int/cj/en/index.htm

Citizens Europe
Covers rights of citizens of EU member states
http://www.c-o-e.net

Delegation of the European Commission to the United States
Press releases, EURECOM: Economic and Financial News, EU-U.S. relations, information on EU policies and Delegation programs
http://www.eurunion.org/eu/

Euro
The Single Currency
http://ec.europa.eu/economy_finance/the_euro/index_en.htm?cs_mid=2946

EUDOR (European Union Document Repository)
Bibliographic database
http://ec.europa.eu/eclasF

European Bank for Reconstruction and Development
One Exchange Square
London EC2A 2JN
United Kingdom
http://www.ebrd.com

European Centre for the Development of Vocational Training
Information on the Centre and contact information
http://www.cedefop.europa.eu/

European Environment Agency
Information on the mission, products and services, and organizations and staff of the EEA
http://www.eea.europa.eu

European Investment Bank
Press releases and information on borrowing and loan operations, staff, and publications
http://www.eib.org

European Medicines Agency
Information on drug approval procedures and documents of the Committee for Proprietary Medicinal Products and the Committee for Veterinary Medicinal Products
http://www.emea. europa.eu/

European Monetary Institute
Name: European Central Bank
http://www.ecb.int/home/html/index.en.html

EuroStat
Statistical Information on Europe
http://epp.eurostat.ec.europa.eu

European Training Foundation
Information on vocational education and training programs in Central and Eastern Europe and Central Asia
http://www.etf.europa.enlweb.nsf?Open

European Union
200 Rue de la Loi
1049 Brussels, Belgium
and
2300 M Street NW
Washington, DC 20037
http://www.eurunion.org/eu/

Office of Harmonization for the Internal Market
Guidelines, application forms, and other information for registering an EU trademark
http://www.oami.europa.eu

United Nations

Conference of Trade and Development
Palais des Nations
8-14, Av. de la Paix
1211 Geneva 10
Switzerland
http://www.un.org

Department of Economic and Social Development
1 United Nations Plaza
New York, NY 10017
http://www.un.org/esa/

UNCTAD—United Nations Conference on Trade and Development
http://ww.unctad.org/

Industrial Development Organization
Room DC1–1118
1 United Nations Plaza
New York, NY 10017
and

Post Office Box 300
Vienna International Center
A-1400 Vienna, Austria
http://www.unido.org

International Trade Centre
UNCTAD/WTO
54–56 Rue de Mountbrillant
CH-1202 Geneva
Switzerland
http://www.intracen.org

United Nations Educational, Scientific
and Cultural Organization
2 United Nations Plaza, Suite 900
New York, NY 10017
http://www.unesco.org

UN Publications
Room DC2-853
2 United Nations Plaza
New York, NY 10017
http://unp.un.org

U.S. Government

Agency for International Development
Office of Business Relations
Washington, DC 20523
http://www.usaid.gov

Department of Agriculture
1400 Independence Ave., S.W.
Washington, DC 20250
http://www.usda.gov

Department of Commerce
Herbert C. Hoover Building
14th Street and Constitution Avenue
NW
Washington, DC 20230
http://www.commerce.gov

Department of State
2201 C Street NW
Washington, DC 20520
http://www.state.gov

Department of the Treasury
15th Street and Pennsylvania
Avenue NW
Washington, DC 20220
http://www.ustreas.gov

Federal Trade Commission
6th Street and Pennsylvania
Avenue NW
Washington, DC 20580
http://www.ftc.gov

FedStats
http://www.fedstats.gov

International Trade Commission
500 E Street SW
Washington, DC 20436
http://www.usitc.gov

Small Business Administration
409 Third Street SW
Washington, DC 20416
http://www.sbaonline.sba.gov

U.S. Census Bureau
http://www.census.gov

U.S. Customs and Border Protection
1300 Pennsylvania Ave. NW
Washington, DC 20229
http://www.cbp.gov

U.S. Trade and Development Agency
1000 Wilson Blvd., Suite 1600
Arlington, VA 22209
http://www.ustda.gov

World Fact Book
**http://www.cia.gov/library/
publications/the-world-
factbook/**

World Trade Centers Association
420 Lexington Ave.
Suite 518
New York, NY 10170
**http://world.wtca.org/portal/site/
wtcaonline**

Council of Economic Advisers
http://www.whitehouse.gov/cea

Department of Defense
http://www.defenselink.mil/

Department of Energy
http://www.energy.gov

Department of Interior
http://www.doi.gov

Department of Labor
http://www.dol.gov

Department of Transportation
http://www.dot.gov

Environmental Protection Agency
http://www.epa.gov

National Trade Data Bank
http://www.stat-usa.gov

National Economic Council
http://www.whitehouse.gov/nec

Office of Management and Budget
http://www.whitehouse.gov/omb/

Office of the U.S. Trade Representative
http://www.ustr.gov/

Overseas Private Investment
Corporation
http://www.opic.gov/

Selected Organizations

Academy for Educational Development
1825 Connecticut Ave. NW
Washington, DC 20009-5721
http://www.aed.org

American Bankers Association
1120 Connecticut Avenue NW
Washington, DC 20036
http://www.aba.com

American Bar Association
Section of International Law and
Practice
321 N. Clark St.
Chicago, IL 60654-7598
and
740 15th St. NW
Washington, DC 20005-1019
http://www.abanet.org/intlaw/

American Management Association
http://www.amanet.org

American Marketing Association
311 S. Wacker Drive, Suite 5800
Chicago, IL 60606
http://www.marketingpower.com

American Petroleum Institute
1220 L Street NW
Washington, DC 20005-4070
http://www.api.org

Asia-Pacific Economic Cooperation
Secretariat
35 Heng Mui Keng Terrace
Singapore 1196169
**http://www.apec.org/apec/about_
apec/apec_secretariat.html**

Asian Development Bank
6 ADB Ave.
Mandaluyong City 1550
Philippines
http://www.adb.org

Association of South East Asian
   Nations (ASEAN)
Publication Office
c/o The ASEAN Secretariat
70A, Jalan Sisingamangaraja
Jakarta 12110
Indonesia
http://www.aseansec.org

Better Business Bureau
http://www.bbb.org

Canadian Market Data
**http://www.strategis.ic.gc.ca/
   ic_wp-pa.htm**

Chamber of Commerce of the
   United States
1615 H Street NW
Washington, DC 20062
http://www.uschamber.org

Commission of the European
   Communities to the
   United States
2300 M Street NW
Washington, DC 20037
http://www.eurunion.org/eu/

Conference Board
845 Third Avenue
New York, NY 10022
http://www.conference-board.org

Deutsche Bundesbank
Hauptverwaltung Frankfurt am Main
Postfach 11 12 32
60047 Frankfurt/Main
http://www.bundesbank.de

Electronic Industries Alliance
2001 Pennsylvania Avenue NW
Washington, DC 20004
http://www.eia.org

Export-Import Bank of the United
   States
811 Vermont Avenue NW
Washington, DC 20571
http://www.exim.gov

Federal Reserve Bank of New York
33 Liberty Street
New York, NY 10045
http://www.ny.frb.org

Gallup Organization
http://www.gallup.com/Home.aspx

Greenpeace
http://www.greenpeace.org

Iconoculture
http://iconoculture.com

Inter-American Development Bank
1300 New York Avenue NW
Washington, DC 20577
http://www.iadb.org

International Bank for Reconstruction
   and Development (World Bank)
1818 H Street NW
Washington, DC 20433
http://www.worldbank.org

International Monetary Fund
700 19th Street NW
Washington, DC 20431
http://www.imf.org

International Telecommunication Union
Place des Nations
Ch-1211 Geneva 20
Switzerland
http://www.itu.int

IRSS (Institute for Research in Social
   Science)
**http://www.irss.unc.edu/odum/jsp/
   content_node.jsp?nodeid=7**

LANIC (Latin American Network
   Information Center)
http://www1.lanic.utexas.edu

Marketing Research Society
111 E. Wacker Drive, Suite 600
Chicago, IL 60601
Michigan State University
   globalEDGE
**http://globaledge.msu.edu/
   resourceDesk/**

National Association of Manufacturers
1331 Pennsylvania Avenue NW
Suite 1500
Washington, DC 20004
http://www.nam.org

National Federation of Independent
   Business
1201 F St. NW
Suite 200
Washington, DC 20004
http://www.nfib.com

Organization for Economic
   Cooperation and Development
2, rue Andre Pascal
F-75775 Paris Cedex 16
France
   and

2001 L Street NW, Suite 700
Washington, DC 20036
http://www.oecd.org

Organization of American States
17th and Constitution Avenue NW
Washington, DC 20006
http://www.oas.org

The Roper Center for Public Opinion
   Research
http://www.ropercenter.uconn.edu

Transparency International
Alt-Moabit 96
10559 Berlin
Germany
http://www.transparency.org

Indexes to Literature

Business Periodicals Index
H.W. Wilson Co.
950 University Avenue
Bronx, NY 10452

New York Times Index
http://www.nytimes.com

Public Affairs Information Service
   Bulletin
11 W. 40th Street
New York, NY 10018
http://www.virtualref.com

Wall Street Journal Index
http://online.wsj.com/public/us

Directories

American Register of Exporters and
   Importers
38 Park Row
New York, NY 10038

Arabian Year Book
Dar Al-Seuassam Est. Box 42480
Shuwahk, Kuwait

Directories of American Firms
   Operating in Foreign Countries
World Trade Academy Press
Uniworld Business Publications Inc.
50 E. 42nd Street
New York, NY 10017

The Directory of International Sources
   of Business Information
Pitman
128 Long Acre
London WC2E 9AN, England

Encyclopedia of Associations
Gale Research Co.
Book Tower
Detroit, MI 48226

Polk's World Bank Directory
R.C. Polk & Co.
2001 Elm Hill Pike
P.O. Box 1340
Nashville, TN 37202

Verified Directory of Manufacturer's
    Representatives
MacRae's Blue Book Inc.
817 Broadway
New York, NY 10003

World Guide to Trade Associations
K.G. Saur & Co.
175 Fifth Avenue
New York, NY 10010

Periodic Reports, Newspapers, Magazines

Advertising Age
711 Third Ave.
New York, NY 10017-4036
http://www.adage.com

Advertising World
University of Texas at Austin
Department of Advertising
CMA 7142
Austin, TX 78712
**http://www.advertising.utexas.edu/
    world/**

Barron's
University Microfilms International
300 N. Zeeb Road
Ann Arbor, MI 48106
http://online.barrons.com

Business Week
McGraw-Hill Publications Co.
1221 Avenue of the Americas
New York, NY 10020
http://www.businessweek.com

Commodity Trade Statistics
United Nations Publications
1 United Nations Plaza
Room DC2–0853
New York, NY 10017
http://comtrade.un.org/

Conference Board Record
Conference Board Inc.
845 Third Avenue
New York, NY 10022

Customs and Border Protection Bulletin
U.S. Customs Service
1301 Constitution Avenue NW
Washington, DC 20229
**http://cbp.gov/xp/cgov/trade/legal/
    bulletins_decisions/**

The Dismal Scientist
http://www.economy.com/dismal

The Economist
Economist Newspaper Ltd.
25 St. James Street
London SWIA 1HG, England
http://www.economist.com

Export America
U.S. Department of Commerce
14th Street and Constitution
    Avenue NW
Washington, DC 20230
**http://www.export.gov/
    exportamerica/**

The Financial Times
Bracken House
10 Cannon Street
London EC4P 4BY, England
http://www.ft.com

Forbes
Forbes, Inc.
60 Fifth Avenue
New York, NY 10011
http://www.forbes.com

Fortune
Time, Inc.
Time & Life Building
1271 Avenue of the Americas
New York, NY 10020
http://www.fortune.com

Global Trade and Transportation
North American Publishing Co.
401 N. Broad Street
Philadelphia, PA 19108

Industrial Marketing Management
Elsevier
Reed Elsevier Group
1-3 Strand
London
WC2N 5JR
UK

*International Encyclopedia of the Social
    Sciences*
Cengage Learning
27500 Drake Rd.
Farmington Hills, MI 48331

International Financial Statistics
International Monetary Fund
Publications Unit
700 19th Street NW
Washington, DC 20431
http://www.imf.org

Investor's Daily
http://www.investors.com

Journal of Commerce
33 Washington Street
Newark, NJ 07102
http://www.joc.com

Lexis-Nexis Legal Express Info
    Service
http://www.michie.com

Sales and Marketing Management
Bill Communications Inc.
633 Third Avenue
New York, NY 10017
http://salesandmarketing.com

Trade Finance
1401 Constitution Ave. NW
Washington, DC 20230

Wall Street Journal
200 Liberty Street
New York, NY 10281
http://online.wsj.com

World Wide Web Virtual Law
    Library
http://www.vlib.org/Law

*World Trade Center Association
    (WTCA) Directory*
60 East 42nd Street
Suite 1901
New York, NY 10048
http://www.wtca.com

*Media Guide International:
    Business/Professional
    Publications*
Directories International Inc.
150 Fifth Avenue, Suite 610
New York, NY 10011

World Wide Web Virtual Law
    Library
www.vlib.org/Law

Selected Trade Databases

Trade Publication References with Bibliographic Keywords

Agris
Biocommerce Abstracts & Directory
Findex
Frost (short) Sullivan Market
Research Reports
Marketing Surveys Index
McCarthy Press Cuttings Service
Paperchem
PTS F & S Indexes
Trade and Industry Index

Trade Publication References with Summaries

ABI/Inform
Arab Information Bank
Asia-Pacific
BFAI
Biobusiness
CAB Abstracts
Chemical Business Newbase
Chemical Industry Notes
Caffeeline
Delphes
InfoSouth Latin American
    Information System
Management Contents
NTIS Bibliographic Data Base
Paperchem
PIRA Abstract
PSTA
PTS Marketing & Advertising
Reference Service
PTS PromtRapra Abstracts
Textline
Trade & Industry ASAP
World Textiles

Full Text of Trade Publications

Datamonitor Market Reports
Dow Jones News
Euromonitor Market Direction
Federal News Service
Financial Times Business Report
File
Financial Times Fulltext
Globefish
ICC Key Notes Market Research
Investext

McCarthy Press Cuttings Service
PTS Promt
Textline
Trade & Industry ASAP

Statistics

Agrostat (diskette only)
Arab Information Bank
ARI Network/CNS
Comext/Eurostat
Comtrade
FAKT-German Statistics
Globefish
IMF Data
OECD Data
Piers Imports
PTS Forecasts
PTS Time Series
Reuters Monitor
Trade Statistics
Tradstat World Trade Statistics
TRAINS (CD-ROM being developed)
U.S. I/E Maritime Bills of Lading
U.S. Imports for Consumption
World Bank Statistics

Price Information

ARI Network/CNS
Chemical Business Newsbase
COLEACP
Commodity Options
Commodities 2000
Market News Service of ITC
Nikkei Shimbun News Database
Reuters Monitor
UPI
U.S. Wholesale Prices

Company Registers

ABC Europe Production Europe
Biocommerce Abstracts & Directory
CD-Export (CD-ROM only)
Company Intelligence
D&B Dun's Market Identifiers (U.S.A.)
D&B European Marketing File
D&B Eastern Europe
Dun's Electronic Business Directory
Firmexport/Firmimport
Hoppenstedt Austria
Hoppenstedt Benelux
Hoppenstedt Germany
Huco-Hungarian Companies

ICC Directory of Companies
Kompass Asia/Pacific
Kompass Europe (EKOD)
Mexican Exporters/Importers
Piers Imports
Polu-Polish Companies
SDOE
Thomas Register
TRAINS (CD-ROM being developed)
UK Importers
UK Importers (DECTA)
U.S. Directory of Importers
U.S. I/E Maritime Bills of Lading
World Trade Center Network

Trade Opportunities, Tenders

Business
Federal News Service
Huntech-Hungarian Technique
Scan-a-Bid
Tenders Electronic Daily
World Trade Center Network

Tariffs and Trade Regulations

Celex
ECLAS
Justis Eastern Europe (CD-ROM only)
Scad
Spearhead
Spicer's Centre for Europe
TRAINS (CD-ROM being developed)
U.S. Code of Federal Regulations
U.S. Federal Register
U.S. Harmonized Tariff Schedule

Standards

BSI Standardline
Noriane/Perinorm
NTIS Bibliographic Data Base
Standards Infodisk ILI (CD-ROM only)

Shipping Information

Piers Imports
Tradstat World Trade Statistics
U.S. I/E Maritime Bills of Lading

Others

Fairbase
Ibiscus

THE STRUCTURE OF A COUNTRY COMMERCIAL GUIDE

The U.S. Commercial Service

The following is an example of governmental research made available to firms. Country commercial guides provide a condensed and business-focused overview of business customs, conditions, contacts, and opportunities. Using such guides can be of major help in getting started in unfamiliar territory.

Guide for Doing Business in Austria

Table of Contents

- Cellular phones
- Internet

   I.   Transportation

   J.   Language

   K.   Health
- Water
- Emergencies
- Pharmacies

   L.   Local Time, Business Hours, and Holidays

   M.   Temporary Entry of Materials and Personal Belongings

   N.   Web Resources

Chapter 9   **Contacts, Market Research, and Trade Events**

   A.   Contacts
- Austrian Government Agencies
- Austrian Trade Associations/Chambers of Commerce
- Austrian Commercial Banks/Branch Offices of Austrian Banks in the U.S.
- Washington-Based U.S. Government Contacts

   B.   Market Research

   C.   Trade Events

SOURCE: Doing Business in Austria, U.S. Department of Commerce and U.S. Department of State, Washington, D.C. 2008, **http://www.buyusa.gov/austria/doing_business_in_austria.html**.

MARKET ENTRY AND EXPANSION

Market Entry Mired in Conflict

Hangzhou Wahaha Group, with 70 subsidiaries and 40 manufacturing sites, owns one of the best known brands of bottled water, fruit juices, and children's drinks, under the Wahaha trademark, in China. Groupe Danone is a French multinational company that owns major brands in dairy products and water such as Donnon, Activia, Stonyfield Farm, and Evian. In 1996, Danone and Wahaha signed a cooperative agreement to establish five joint venture companies. For Danone, it was an opportunity to enter into the highly regulated Chinese marketplace. For Wahaha, Danone's financial investment enabled it to double its production output by upgrading its production facilities. *Forbes* magazine went so far as to describe the partnership as a showcase example of a joint venture between two international companies. During the financial crises in Asia, Danone went on to purchase additional shares of the Wahaha holdings and ultimately ended up with a 51 percent stake in, by then, 39 Danone-Wahaha joint ventures.

Unfortunately, the relationship between Wahaha and Danone did not go smoothly. Critical to the 1996 joint venture agreement was that the Wahaha brand be transferred to the joint ventures between Danone and Wahaha. However, by 2007, Danone had accused Wahaha of operating independent companies and selling products identical to those sold by the joint venture companies. Thus, Danone accused its partner of defrauding it and filed over 30 lawsuits, claiming that Wahaha had violated the

A JOINT VENTURE BETWEEN WAHAHA AND DANONE BEGAN WELL BUT ENDED BADLY.

terms of the joint venture contract and illegally used the Wahaha trademark in countries such as China, France, Italy, and the United States.

At the heart of the legal issue was the ownership of the Wahaha brand. The Hangzhou Wahaha Group claimed that the trademark transfer to the joint venture had never gotten approval from China's state trademark office.

Thus, according to the Wahaha Group, the brand transfer had failed and the brand transfer agreement had expired by the time Danone was charging the company with irregularities. In August of 2008, the Hangzhou Intermediate People's Court denied Danone's appeal against a December 2007 arbitration ruling that found that the Wahaha trademark belonged to the Hangzhou Wahaha Group.

Within ten years this joint venture went from being espoused as one of the most successful Sino-French enterprises to a prolonged battle between the two partners. The battle has left dark clouds over both companies. The founder of Wahaha eventually resigned, saying that Danone had launched a smear campaign against him and his family. Danone was taking its public blows for not placing any of its executives at Wahaha's headquarters in Hangzhou and for not taking an active role in the day-to-day operations of the joint venture. If nothing else, both companies have hopefully learned the roles of trust and engagement in international joint ventures.

SOURCES: Thomson Reuters, "Wahaha Believes Arbitration in Stockholm Critical in Disputes with Danone," *Reuters*, September 23, 2008, **http://www.reuters.com/article/pressRelease/ idUS119232+23-Sep-2008+PRN2080923**, retrieved December 16, 2008; David Barboza and James Kanter, *The New York Times*, June 13, 2007, **http://www.nytimes .com/2007/06/13/business/worldbusiness/13danone .html**, retrieved December 15, 2008; "Wahaha in Danone Arbitration Move," *BBC News*, June 18, 2007, **http://www.bbc.co.uk/go/ pr/fr/-/2/hi/business/6763215.stm**, retrieved December 16, 2008; "Danone to Appeal Wahaha Trade Mark Decision," *Asia Law*, September 2008, **http://www.asialaw.com/Article/ 2004999/Danone-to-appeal-Wahaha-trade-mark-decision .html**, retrieved December 15, 2008.

A s *The International Marketplace 9.1* shows, doing business internationally provides opportunities for companies to unite their strengths to create a stronger, more market-ready company. Groupe Danone provided financial capital to a strong local brand in China, enabling Wahaha to increase the offering of its strong brand. Thus, Danone gained easy entry into the Chinese market, and Wahaha received the cash it needed to grow and improve its operations. Unfortunately, the saga of the two companies shows how an international alliance can go astray. However, international expansion can be very rewarding and may turn out to be the key to prosperity for corporations and employees. Firms that export grow faster, are more productive, and have employees who tend to earn more.[1] Even though some firms go international from the start, most of them do so gradually. New activities in an unfamiliar environment increase a firm's risk. Therefore, companies must prepare their activities and adjust to the needs and opportunities of international markets in order to become long-term participants.

This chapter discusses the activities that take place within the firm preparing to enter the international market. It focuses on the basic stimuli for internationalization and on the internal and external change agents that activate these stimuli. The concerns and preoccupations of firms as they begin their international marketing operations are discussed. Finally expansion strategies, such as franchising, licensing, and foreign direct investment, are presented. Exhibit 9.1 provides a model of the international entry and expansion process. It shows what triggers and inhibits international expansion and outlines the subsequent discussion of this chapter.

Stimuli to Internationalize

In most business activities, one factor alone rarely accounts for any given action. Usually a mixture of factors results in firms taking steps in a given direction. This is true of internationalization; there are a variety of stimuli both pushing and pulling firms along the international path. Exhibit 9.2 lists the major motivations to go international, differentiated into proactive and reactive motivations. Proactive motivations represent stimuli to attempt strategic change. Reactive motivations influence firms that respond to environmental shifts by changing their activities over time. In other words, proactive firms go international because they want to, while reactive ones go international because they have to.

Exhibit **9.1**

A Model of International Entry and Expansion

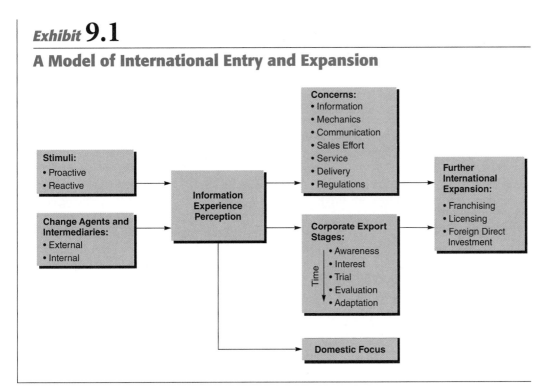

Exhibit **9.2**

Why Firms Go International

Proactive Stimuli	Reactive Stimuli
· Profit advantage Profit advantage	· Competitive pressures
· Unique products	· Overproduction
· Technological advantage	· Declining domestic sales
· Exclusive information	· Excess capacity
· Economies of scale	· Saturated domestic markets
· Market size	· Proximity to customers and ports

Proactive Stimuli

Profits provide the strongest incentive to become involved in international marketing. Management may perceive international sales as a potential source of higher profit margins or of added-on profits. Of course, the perceived profitability from going international may not match actual profitability because of such factors as high start-up costs, sudden shifts in exchange rates, or insufficient market research.

A second major stimulus results either from *unique products* or a *technological advantage.* A firm's goods or services may not be widely available from international competitors or may offer technological advances in a specialized field. Uniqueness can provide a competitive edge and result in major business success abroad. Again, real and perceived advantages should be differentiated. Many firms believe that theirs are unique products or services, even though, on a global level, this may not be the case. The intensity of marketing's interaction with the research and development function, as well as the level of investment into R&D, has been shown to have a major effect on the success of exported products.[2] One issue to consider is how long such a technological or product advantage will continue. Historically, a firm with a competitive edge could count on being the sole supplier to international markets for years to come. This type of advantage, however, has shrunk dramatically because of competing technologies and imitation due to insufficient protection of intellectual property rights.

Exclusive market information is another proactive stimulus. This includes knowledge about foreign customers, marketplaces, or market situations that is not widely shared by other firms. Such knowledge may result from a firm's international research, special contacts, or by being in the right place at the right time (for example, recognizing a good business situation during a vacation trip). Although exclusivity can serve well as an initial stimulus to go international, it rarely provides for sustained motivation. Over time competitors will catch up with the information advantage of the firm, particularly in light of the growing ease of global information access.

A major proactive motivation are *economies of scale*. The *size* of the international market may enable the firm to increase its output and slide down more rapidly on the learning curve. Increased production for the international market can also help reduce the cost of production for domestic sales.[3] Research by the Boston Consulting Group showed that a doubling of output can reduce production costs up to 30 percent!

Reactive Stimuli

Here firms respond to changes and pressures in the business environment rather than blaze new trails. In reaction to *competitive pressures,* a firm may fear losing domestic market share to competing firms or losing foreign markets permanently to new competitors. However, insufficient preparation may result in a hasty market entry and a quick withdrawal.

Overproduction is a major reactive motivation. Historically, during downturns in the domestic business cycle, markets abroad provided an ideal outlet for high inventories. Such market expansion often does not represent commitment by management, but rather a temporary safety-valve activity. Instead of developing an international marketing perspective by adjusting the marketing mix to needs abroad, firms stimulate export sales with short-term price cuts.[4] As soon as the domestic market demand returns to previous levels, international marketing activities are curtailed or even terminated. Firms that have used such a strategy once may encounter difficulties when trying it again, because many foreign customers are not interested in temporary or sporadic business relationships. The lessons learned, and the increased synchronization of the major industrial economies, may well decrease the importance of this motivation over time.

Stable or declining domestic sales, whether measured in sales volume or market share, also stimulate firms. Products marketed by the firm domestically may be in the declining stage of the product life cycle; thus, the firm may opt to prolong the life of the product by expanding the market. In the past, such efforts often met with success in developing nations because their customers only gradually reached a level of need already attained by customers in industrialized nations. Increasingly, however, global lag times are quite short. Nevertheless, developing nations often still have very good use for products for which the demand in the industrialized world is already on the decline. This holds particularly true for high-technology items that are outdated by the latest innovations. Such "just-dated" technology—for example, slightly obsolete medical equipment—can be highly useful to economic development and offer vast progress.

Excess capacity can be a powerful motivation. If equipment is not fully utilized, international expansion can help achieve broader distribution of fixed costs. Alternatively, if all fixed costs are assigned to domestic production, the firm can penetrate international markets with a pricing scheme that focuses mainly on variable costs. Such a strategy may result in the offering of products abroad at a cost lower than at home, which may trigger dumping charges. In the long run, fixed costs recovery needs to ensure the replacement of production equipment used for international marketing activities.

The stimulus of a *saturated domestic market* is similar to that of declining domestic sales. Again, firms can use the international market to prolong the life cycle of their product and of their organization.

A final major reactive motivation is *proximity to customers and ports*. Physical closeness to foreign markets can encourage the international activities of a firm. This factor is much less prevalent in North America than in many other countries, since most American firms are situated far away from the border. Consider a typical 200-mile activity radius of U.S. firms, which would likely mean doing business in another state. In Europe, however, such a radius makes most firms international, simply because their neighbors are so close. As an example, a European company operating in the heart of Belgium needs to go only 50 miles to be in multiple foreign markets.

In this context, the concept of **psychological distance** needs to be understood. Psychological distance refers to the lack of symmetry between growing international markets with respect to cultural variables, legal factors, and other societal norms. Geographic closeness to foreign markets may not translate into real or perceived closeness to the foreign customers since a foreign market that is geographically close may be psychologically distant. For example, research has shown that U.S. firms perceive Canada to be much closer psychologically than Mexico. Two major issues frame the context of psychological distance. First, some of the distance seen by firms is based on perception rather than reality. For example, German firms may view the Austrian market simply as an extension of their home market due to so many superficial similarities, just as many U.S. firms may see the United Kingdom as psychologically very close due to the similarity in language. However, the attitudes and values of managers and customers may vary substantially between markets. Too much of a focus on the similarities may let the firm lose sight of the differences. Many Canadian firms have incurred high costs in learning this lesson when entering the United States.[5] At the same time, closer psychological proximity does make it easier for firms to enter markets. Therefore, for firms new to international marketing, it may be advantageous to begin this new activity by entering the psychologically closer markets first in order to gather experience before venturing into markets that are farther away.[6]

Overall, the more successful international firms are motivated by proactive—that is, firm-internal—factors. The motivations of firms do not seem to shift dramatically over the short term but are rather stable. For the reader who seeks involvement in international markets and searches for good corporate opportunities, an important consideration should be whether a firm is proactive or reactive.

Change Agents

Someone or something within the firm must initiate change and shepherd it through to implementation. This intervening individual or variable is here called a **change agent**. Change agents in the internationalization process are shown in Exhibit 9.3.

Exhibit 9.3

Change Agents in the Internationalization Process

Internal	External
• Enlightened management	• Demand
• New management	• Competition
• Significant internal event	• Domestic distributors
	• Service firms
	• Business associations
	• Governmental activities
	• Export intermediaries
	- Export management companies
	- Trading companies

Internal Change Agents

The type and quality of *management* is key to a firm's international activities. Dynamic management is important when firms take their first international steps. Over the long term, management commitment and management's perceptions and attitudes are also good predictors of export success.[7] Key also are the international experience and exposure of management.[8] Managers who have lived abroad, know foreign languages, or are particularly interested in foreign cultures are likely, sooner rather than later, to investigate whether international marketing opportunities would be appropriate for their firm. Managerial urge reflects the desire, drive, and enthusiasm toward international marketing activities. This enthusiasm can exist simply because managers like to be part of a firm that operates internationally. They may like international travel—for example, to call on a major customer in the Bahamas during a cold winter month. Or the urge to internationalize may simply reflect entrepreneurial zeal—a desire for continuous market growth and expansion.[9]

This conclusion has largely been formulated by reverse deduction: The managers of firms that are unsuccessful or inactive in the international marketplace usually exhibit a lack of commitment to international marketing. International markets cannot be penetrated overnight—to succeed in them requires substantial market development activity, market research, and the identification of and response to new market factors. Therefore, a high level of commitment is crucial to endure setbacks and failure. It is important to involve all levels of management early on in the international planning process. Any international venture must be incorporated into the firm's strategic management process. A firm that sets no strategic goals is less likely to achieve long-term success.[10] It is also important to establish a specific structure in which someone has the responsibility for international activities. Without such responsibility, the focus necessary for success is lost. Just one person assigned part-time can explore international opportunities successfully.

Another major change agent is a *significant internal event*. The development of a new product that can be useful abroad can serve as such an event, as can the receipt of new information about current product uses. As an example, a manufacturer of hospital beds learned that beds it was selling domestically were being resold in a foreign country. Further, the beds sold abroad for more than twice the price that they were fetching at home. This new information triggered a strong interest by the company's management to enter international markets.

In small and medium-sized firms (firms with fewer than 250 employees), the initial decision to go international is usually made by the president, with substantial input from the marketing department. The implementation of this decision usually becomes primarily the responsibility of marketing personnel. The strategic evaluation of international marketing activities is typically carried out again by the president of the firm. This makes the president and the marketing department the leading internal change agents.

External Change Agents

The primary outside influence on a firm's decision to go international is foreign *demand*. Inquiries from abroad and other expressions of demand have a powerful effect on initial interest in entering the international marketplace. Unsolicited international orders are one major factor that encourage firms to begin exporting. In the United States, such orders have been found to account for more than half of all cases of export initiation by small and medium-sized firms. Through their Web sites, firms can easily become unplanned participants in the international market. Customers from abroad can visit the site and place an international order, even though a firm's plans may have been strictly domestic. Thus, a company can unexpectedly find itself an exporter.[11] We call such firms **accidental exporters**. While good fortune may have initiated the export activity, over the longer term the firm must start planning how to systematically increase its international expansion or, at least, how to make more of these accidents happen.

Another major change agent may actually be the *competition*. Just as firms respond to competitive pressures from other companies, statements by executives from competing firms may serve as change agents. Therefore, formal and informal meetings among managers from different firms at trade association meetings, conventions, or business roundtables often trigger major change.

Domestic distributors also initiate change. To increase their international distribution volume, they encourage purely domestic clients to participate in the international market. This is true not only for exports but also for imports.

Banks and other *service firms,* such as accounting offices, can alert domestic clients to international opportunities. Although these service providers have historically followed their major multinational clients abroad, increasingly they are establishing a foreign presence and then urging domestic clients to expand their market reach.

Chambers of commerce and other *business associations* that interact with firms locally can frequently heighten international marketing interests. These organizations function as secondary intermediaries, by sponsoring the presence and encouragement of other managers.

Government efforts on the national or local level can also serve as a major change agent. In light of the contributions exports make to growth, employment, and tax revenue, governments are active in encouraging and supporting exports. In the United States, the Department of Commerce is particularly involved in export promotion. Frequently, district officers, with the help of voluntary groups such as District Export Councils, visit firms and analyze their international marketing opportunities. In addition, many states have formed economic development agencies that assist companies by providing information, displaying products abroad, and sometimes even helping with financing.

Going International

For many firms, internationalization is a gradual process. Particularly in small markets, however, firms may very well be **born global**, founded for the explicit purpose of marketing abroad because the domestic economy is too small to support their activities. There are three major methods to enter new markets. These are export, licensing and franchising, and foreign direct investment.

Export

In some countries, more than a third of exporting firms commenced their export activities within two years of establishment.[12] Such start-up, or **innate exporters**, play a growing role in an economy's international trade involvement. In addition, firms with a strong e-commerce focus may also be gaining rapid global exposure due to the ease of outreach and access. Such rapid exposure, however, should not be confused with actual internationalization, since it may often take a substantial amount of time to translate exposure into international business activities and strategic corporate acceptance.

In most instances today, firms begin their operations in the domestic market. From their home location, they gradually expand, and, over time, some of them become interested in the international market. The development of this interest typically appears to proceed in several stages, as shown in Exhibit 9.4.

Exhibit **9.4**

Key Corporate Export Stages

- Awareness
- Interest
- Trial
- Evaluation
- Demand
- Adaptation

In each one of these stages, firms are measurably different in their capabilities, problems, and needs.[13] Initially, the vast majority of firms are not even aware of the international marketplace. Frequently, management will not even fill an unsolicited export order. Should unsolicited orders or other international market stimuli continue over time, however, a firm may gradually become aware of international market opportunities. While such awareness is unlikely to trigger much business activity, it can lead management to gradually become interested in international activities. Eventually, firms will answer inquiries, participate in export counseling sessions, attend international trade fairs and seminars, and even begin to fill unsolicited export orders.

Prime candidates among firms to make this transition from aware to interested are those companies that have a track record of domestic market expansion. In the next stage, the firm gradually begins to explore international markets. Management is willing to consider the feasibility of exporting. In this trial, or exploratory stage, the firm begins to export systematically, usually to psychologically close countries. However, management is still far from being committed to international marketing activities.

After some export activity, typically within two years of the initial export, management is likely to conduct an evaluation of its export efforts. Key questions concern the fulfillment of expectations. Are our products as unique as we thought they were, and are we making enough money on our exports? If a firm is disappointed with its international performance it may withdraw from these activities. Alternatively, it can continue as an experienced small exporter. Success can also lead to the process of export adaptation. Here a firm is an experienced exporter to a particular country and adjusts its activities to changing exchange rates, tariffs, and other variables. Management is ready to explore the feasibility of exporting to additional countries that are psychologically farther away. Frequently, this level of adaptation is reached once export transactions comprise 15 percent of overall sales volume. Planning for export marketing becomes incorporated into the strategy of the firm.

The population of exporting firms within these stages does not remain stable. Researchers of U.S. firms have found that in any given year, 15 percent of exporters will stop exporting by the next year, while 10 percent of nonexporters will enter the foreign market. The most critical junctures for the firm are the points at which it begins or ceases exporting.[14]

As can be expected, firms in different stages are faced with different problems. Firms at the export awareness and interest stages are primarily concerned with operational matters such as information flow and the mechanics of carrying out international business transactions. They understand that a totally new body of knowledge and expertise is needed and try to acquire it. Companies that have already had some exposure to international markets via trial or evaluation begin to think about tactical marketing issues such as communication and sales effort. Finally, firms that have reached the export adaptation phase are mainly strategy- and service-oriented. They worry about longer-range issues such as service delivery and regulatory changes. One can recognize that increased sophistication in international markets translates into increased application of marketing knowledge on the part of firms. The more they become active in international markets, the more firms recognize that a marketing orientation is internationally just as essential as it is in the domestic market.

Firms who choose to export their products may do so in a number of different ways. They may export directly or use export intermediaries such as export management companies or trading companies. They can also sell to a domestic firm that in turn sells abroad. For example, many products sold to multinational corporations are used as input for their global sales.

Market intermediaries specialize in bringing firms or their goods and services to the global market. Often, they have detailed information about the competitive conditions in certain markets or they have personal contacts with potential buyers abroad. They can also evaluate credit risk, call on customers abroad, and manage the physical delivery of the product. Two key intermediaries are export management companies and trading companies.

Export Management Companies

Export management companies (EMCs) are domestic firms that perform international marketing services as commission representatives or as distributors for several other firms. Most EMCs are quite small. They are frequently formed by one or two principals with experience in international marketing or in a particular geographic area.

EMCs have two primary forms of operation. They either take title to goods and operate internationally on their own account, or they perform services as agents. As an agent, an EMC is likely to have a contractual relationship, which specifies exclusivity agreements and sales quotas. In addition, price arrangements and promotional support payments are agreed on.[15] Because EMCs often serve a variety of clients, their mode of operation may vary from client to client and from transaction to transaction. An EMC may act as an agent for one client, whereas for another client, or even for the same one on a different occasion, it may operate as a distributor.

For the export management company concept to work, both parties must recognize the delegation of responsibilities, the costs associated with these activities, and the need for information sharing and cooperation. On the manufacturer's side, use of an EMC is a major channel commitment. This requires a thorough investigation of the intermediary, a willingness to cooperate on a prolonged basis, and proper rewards. The EMC in turn must adopt a flexible approach to the export relationship. As access to the Internet is making customers increasingly sophisticated, export management companies must ensure that they continue to deliver true value added. They must acquire, develop, and deploy resources, such as new knowledge about foreign markets or about export processes, in order to lower their client firm's export-related transaction costs.[16] The EMC must show that the service is worth the cost.

Trading Companies

Another major exporting intermediary is the trading company. The concept was originated by European trading houses, such as the Fuggers, and was soon formalized by the monarchs. Hoping to expand their power and wealth, kings chartered traders with exclusive trading rights and protection by the naval forces in exchange for tax payments. Today, the most famous trading companies are the *sogoshosha* of Japan. Names like Sumitomo, Mitsubishi, Mitsui, and C. Itoh have become household words around the world. These general trading companies play a unique role in world commerce by importing, exporting, countertrading, investing, and manufacturing. Because of their vast size, they can benefit from economies of scale and survive on very low profit margins.

Four major reasons have been given for the success of the Japanese *sogoshosha*. First, these firms are organized to gather, evaluate, and translate market information into business opportunities. By making large investments in their information systems, these firms have developed a strategic information advantage. Second, their vast transaction volume provides them with cost advantages. For example, they can negotiate preferential transportation rates. Third, these firms serve large markets around the world and have transaction advantages. They can benefit from unique opportunities, such as barter trade in which they exchange goods for goods. Finally, *sogoshosha* have access to vast quantities of capital, both within Japan and in the international capital markets. With their financial advantage they can carry out transactions that are larger and riskier than is feasible for other firms.

For many decades, the emergence of trading companies was commonly believed to be a Japan-specific phenomenon. Over time, however, prodded by government legislation, successful trading companies have also emerged in countries as diverse as Brazil, South Korea, and Turkey.

Export trading company (ETC) legislation designed to improve the export performance of small and medium-sized firms in the United States permits bank participation in trading companies and reduces the antitrust threat to joint export efforts. An ETC can apply for a Certificate of Review from the U.S. Department of Commerce that provides antitrust pre-clearance for specific export activities. Businesses are encouraged to join together for a certificate to export or offer export services.

Bank participation in ETCs was intended to allow better access to capital. The relaxation of antitrust provisions in turn was to enable firms to share the cost of international market entry. As an example, in case a warehouse is needed to support foreign-market penetration, one firm alone does not have to bear all the costs.

Although ETCs seem to offer major benefits to U.S. firms wishing to penetrate international markets, they have not been used very extensively. As of 2009, certificates were held by 75 individuals, companies, and associations. Yet these certificates cover more than

3,000 firms, mainly because the various trade associations have applied for certification for all of their members.[17]

Firms participating in trading companies by joining or forming them need to consider the difference between product- and market-driven activities. Firms have a tendency to use a trading company to dispose of their existing merchandise. International success, however, depends primarily on market demand. Trading companies must therefore accomplish a balance between the demands of the market and the supply of the members in order to be successful. Information must be collected on the needs and wants of foreign customers. It must then be disseminated to participating firms and help must be provided in implementing change. Otherwise, lack of responsiveness to market demand will limit international success.

E-Commerce

Many companies increasingly choose to market their products internationally through e-commerce, the ability to offer goods and services over the Web. The growth of e-commerce has led to increased revenue for many companies. There are a variety of ways in which companies can market their products over the internet. One key option is the development of corporate websites. Many companies initially become exporters because of unsolicited international orders. In order to encourage more orders from foreign consumers, companies should accept international means of payment and have the ability to ship their product internationally. In addition, companies need to consider the ever-growing population of non–English speakers on the Web. Websites should be offered in several different languages. However, having a website translated and kept up to date may be costly and time-consuming. If the site is well developed, it will naturally lead to the expectations that order fulfillment will be of equal caliber. Therefore, any World Wide Web strategy has to be tied closely to the company's overall growth strategy in world markets.

Companies can also enter e-commerce by exporting through a variety of business-to-consumer and business-to-business forums. For example, consumers and businesses alike can sell their products on the online auction site eBay (**http://www.ebay.com**). Businesses who would like to target the Chinese market can use China's Alibaba (**http://www.alibaba.com**), whose slogan is "Global trade starts here." Alibaba, in particular, targets small and medium-sized businesses who would like to export to China, and Chinese businesses looking to expand domestically. In 2008, Alibaba.com Limited was the world's leading business-to-business e-commerce company with 36 million registered users from over 240 countries and regions.[18]

There are a variety of new concerns if a firm uses e-commerce to enter the international marketplace. Due to international time differences, firms must be ready to provide 24-hour order taking and customer support service, have the regulatory and customs-handling expertise to deliver internationally, and have an understanding of global marketing environments for the further development of business relationships. Many companies choose to use the capabilities of air carriers such as UPS, DHL, and FedEx, who offer a range of support services such as order fulfillment, delivery, customs clearance, and supply chain management. There are some legal concerns for e-businesses, such as export controls laws, especially if they market strategically important products or software. Firms must also consider privacy, security, and intellectual property regulations. The EU's privacy measures are much more stringent than those of the United States and thus may impact U.S. companies looking to do business in Europe. Furthermore, companies need to be able to protect their customers from identity theft and other online scams.

As seen in Exhibit 9.5, internet usage worldwide is growing rapidly. Africa and the Middle East have experienced substantial increase in usage since the beginning of the 21st century. But each of those regions still has significant room for growth, as do other regions around the world. As use of the internet grows, e-commerce will become an even more important venue for commercial activity. It can be expected that countries will implement more laws concerning business transactions over the internet, and that the international community as a whole will develop standards, either outside or inside the World Trade Organization, for conducting e-commerce.

Exhibit **9.5**

Internet Usage Statistics

World Internet Usage and Population Statistics

World Regions	Population (2008 Est.)	Internet Users Dec. 1, 2000	Internet Usage (2008 EST.)	% Population (Penetration)	Usage % of World	Usage Growth 2000–2008
Africa	955,206,348	4,514,400	51,065,630	5.3%	3.5%	1,031.2%
Asia	3,776,181,949	114,304,000	578,538,257	15.3%	39.5%	406.1%
Europe	800,401,065	105,096,093	384,633,765	48.1%	26.3%	266.0%
Middle East	197,090,443	3,284,800	41,939,200	21.3%	2.9%	1,176.8%
North America	337,167,248	108,096,800	248,241,969	73.6%	17.0%	129.6%
Latin America/Caribbean	576,091,673	18,068,919	139,009,209	24.1%	9.5%	669.3%
Oceania/Australia	33,981,562	7,620,480	20,204,331	59.5%	1.4%	165.1%
WORLD TOTAL	6,676,120,288	360,985,492	1,463,632,361	21.9%	100.0%	305.5%

SOURCE: **http://www.internetworldstats.com**. Copyright © 2001–2008, Miniwatts Marketing Group.

Licensing and Franchising

Licensing and franchising are market expansion alternatives used by all types of firms, large and small. They offer flexibility and reflect the needs of the firm and the market. A small firm, for example, uses licensing to access intellectual property owned by a foreign business or to expand without much capital investment. A multinational corporation may use the same strategy to rapidly enter foreign markets in order to take advantage of new conditions and foreclose opportunities for its competition.

Licensing

Under a **licensing** agreement, one firm, the licensor, permits another to use its intellectual property in exchange for compensation designated as a royalty. The recipient firm is the licensee. The property might include patents, trademarks, copyrights, technology, technical know-how, or specific marketing skills. *The International Marketplace 9.2* describes how three companies have entered into a licensing agreement that brings together one company's established customer base, another company's distribution expertise, and yet another's product knowledge.

Assessment of Licensing

As an international entry strategy, licensing requires neither capital investment nor knowledge or marketing strength in foreign markets. Royalty income provides an opportunity to obtain an additional return on research and development investments already incurred. Licensing offers a proven concept that reduces the risk of R&D failures, the cost of designing around the licensor's patents, or the fear of patent infringement litigation. Furthermore, ongoing licensing cooperation and support enables the licensee to benefit from new developments.

Licensing reduces the exposure to both government intervention and terrorism, since the licensee is typically a local company. It allows a firm to test a foreign market without major investment of capital or management time. It can also preempt a market for the competition, especially if the licensor's resources permit full-scale involvement only in selected markets. A final reason for growing licensing activities is the increase in global protection of intellectual property rights, which makes companies more willing to transfer proprietary knowledge internationally.[19] A strong foreign partner then becomes a local force with a distinct interest in rooting out unlicensed activities.

The International
MARKETPLACE

9.2

Will a Manufacturing, Marketing, and Distribution Licensing Agreement Grow the International Market for Tazo Tea?

Tea is one of the oldest beverages in the world and the second most consumed beverage worldwide (water being the first). Approaches to drinking tea have evolved from as far back as 2372 B.C. In 1904 teabags largely replaced loose tea leaves, in the 1940s instant tea and mixes appeared, and the 1980s saw the advent of ready-to-drink tea (RTD). For aesthetic reasons, RTD teas have been sold in glass bottles. However, the future appears to lie with plastic and aluminum packaging, and packaging attributes are critical to the growth of the RTD tea market since convenience and availability will be the critical demand drivers of this market. Along with these packaging attributes, however, is the fact that tea is perceived to be healthful and the consumption of healthy products is a trend that has worldwide appeal.

Tapping into this underdeveloped and potential growth market are major international players Unilever, PepsiCo, and Starbucks. In 1991, Unilever and PepsiCo entered into a joint venture, the Pepsi/Lipton Tea Partnership (PLP), with each company having 50 percent ownership. The PLP quickly became the leading distributor of RTD tea in the United States. In 2003, the Pepsi Lipton International (PLI) joint venture took the RTD tea product into over 40 countries and experienced double-digit volume growth. Building on these two joint ventures, the two companies expanded on their international partnership in 2007. The intent with the 2007 expansion of the international joint venture was to further leverage complementary strengths of Unilever's Lipton brand and tea product knowledge with PepsiCo's bottling and distribution network. The expansion added 11 new countries to Unilever and Lipton's RTD tea business, essentially more than doubling the RTD tea volume and propelling the partnership into the leadership spot in the global RTD tea business.

With strong growth expected in the RTD tea marketplace, neither company was, however, taking any time to bask in the leadership spot. In 2008, PepsiCo and Unilever entered into a licensing agreement for the manufacturing, marketing, and distribution of Starbucks Tazo Tea ready-to-drink-beverages. In 1994, Starbucks and PepsiCo formed the North American Coffee Partnership (NAC).

STARBUCKS HAS BEEN SUCCESSFUL WITH CREATING AN ESTABLISHED BASE OF TAZO CONSUMERS.

This joint venture focused on the RTD coffee business in the United States via the development and distribution of Starbucks bottled products such as Frappuccino, Doubleshot espresso, and Doubleshot Energy + Coffee. With over 100 unique tea, fruit, and herbal beverages, Tazo was acquired by Starbucks in 1999, and Tazo is the exclusive tea offered in Starbucks coffeehouses.

Starbucks has been successful with building an established base of Tazo consumers. A licensing agreement with the Pespi/Lipton Tea Partnership (PLP) for the manufacturing, marketing, and distribution of the Tazo brand of tea in ready-to-drink packaging sets the stage for all three companies to take advantage of a worldwide growing tea marketplace.

SOURCES: Aninditta Savitry, "The US Ready-to-Drink Team Market: Trends and Compe-tea-tion," *Beverage Aisle*, April 1, 2001, **http://www.allbusiness.com/retail-trade/eating-drinking-places-eating/4126352-1.html**, retrieved January 7, 2009; "Tea and the Ready-to-Drink Tea in the U.S.," *Packaged Facts*, November 1, 2007, **http://www.packagedfacts.com/Tea-RTD-1282368/**, retrieved January 7, 2009; "Starbucks, Pepsi, and Unilever Partner to Grow the Tazo Tea Ready-to-Drink Business," *istockAnalyst,* August 19, 2008, **http://www.istockanalyst.com/article/viewiStockNews/articleid/2527986**, retrieved December 17, 2008; "Unilever and PepsiCo to Expand Ready-to-Drink Tea Joint Venture," September 14, 2007, **http://www.unileverusa.com/ourcompany/newsandmedia/pressreleases/2007/Unilever_and_Pepsico_to_expand_ready-to-drink_tea_joint_venture.asp**, retrieved January 7, 2009; "Starbucks, Pepsi and Unilever Partner to Grow the Tazo Tea Ready-to-Drink Business," August 19, 2008, **http://www.starbucks.com/aboutus/pressdecs.asp?id=891**, retrieved December 17, 2008.

Licensing is not without disadvantages. It leaves most international marketing functions to the licensee. As a result, the licensor gains only limited expertise and may not even gain any advantages when it comes to market entry itself. In exchange for the royalty, the licensor may actually create its own competitor not only in the markets for which the agreement was made but also in third markets.

Licensing has come under criticism from supranational organizations, such as the United Nations Conference on Trade and Development (UNCTAD). It has been alleged that licensing lets multinational corporations (MNCs) capitalize on older technology. Such technology, however, may be in the best interest of the recipient. Guinness Brewery, for example, in order to produce Guinness Stout in Nigeria, licensed equipment that had been used in Ireland at the turn of the twentieth century. This equipment had additional economic life in Nigeria because it presented a good fit with local needs.

Principal Issues in Negotiating Licensing Agreements

The key issues in negotiating licensing agreements include the scope of the rights conveyed, compensation, licensee compliance, dispute resolution, and the term and termination of the agreement.[20] Clear agreements reduce trouble down the road.

The rights conveyed are product and/or patent rights. Defining their scope involves specifying the technology, know-how, or show-how to be included, the format, and guarantees. An example of format specification is an agreement on whether manuals will be translated into the licensee's language.

Compensation issues may be heavily argued. The licensor wants to cover (1) **transfer costs**, which are all variable costs incurred in transferring technology to a licensee and all ongoing costs of maintaining the agreement, (2) **R&D costs** incurred in researching and developing the licensed technology, and (3) **opportunity costs** incurred in the foreclosure of other sources of profit, such as exports or direct investment. To cover these costs, the licensor wants a share of the profits generated from the use of the license.

Compensation can take the form of running royalties, such as 5 percent of the licensee sales, and/or up-front payments, service fees, and disclosure fees (for proprietary data). Sometimes, government regulations restrict royalty payments. In such instances, the know-how transferred can be capitalized and payments can be profits or dividends.

Licensee compliance in the agreement should address: (1) export control regulations, (2) confidentiality of the intellectual property and technology provided, and (3) record keeping and provisions for licensor audits. Finally, the term, termination, and survival of rights must be specified.

Trademark Licensing

Trademark licensing permits use of the names or logos of designers, literary characters, sports teams, and movie stars on merchandise such as clothing. British designer Laura Ashley started the first major furniture licensing program. Coca-Cola licensed its name to Murjani to be used on blue jeans, sweatshirts, and windbreakers. The licensors can obtain large revenues with little effort, whereas the licensees can produce a branded product that consumers will recognize immediately. Fees can range between 7 and 12 percent of net sales for merchandising license agreements.[21]

Both licensor and licensee may run into difficulty if the trademark is used for a product too far removed from the original success or if the licensed product casts a shadow on the reputation of the licensor. In licensing a trademark, consumer perceptions have to be researched to understand the effect on the brand's position.

Franchising

In **franchising**, a parent company (the franchiser) grants another, independent entity (the franchisee) the right to do business in a specified manner. This right can take the form of selling the franchiser's products or using its name, production, preparation, and marketing techniques, or its business approach. The major forms of franchising are manufacturer-retailer systems (such as car dealerships), manufacturer-wholesaler systems (such as soft drink companies), and service firm–retailer systems (such as lodging services and fast food outlets). Product/trade franchising emphasizes the product or commodity to be sold, while business format franchising focuses on ways of doing business.

Franchising's origins are in Bavaria, but it has been adopted by various types of businesses in many countries. Franchises exist across many different industries, but the

Exhibit 9.6

Fast Food in Jakarta, Indonesia

© AP PHOTO/FIRDIA LISNAWATI

ones perhaps most visible to consumers are in the restaurant and food service industry. Exhibit 9.6 shows an example of a U.S. fast food franchise that has successfully entered the Hong Kong market. Franchisers from around the world are penetrating international markets. For example, 24 percent of British and 30 percent of French franchisers are active outside their home countries.[22] In Vietnam one can encounter several Asian-owned franchises such as the South Korea–based Burger Khan, Thailand's Five Star Chicken, and Japan's Lotto Burger.[23]

The typical reasons for the international expansion of franchise systems are market potential, financial gain, and saturated domestic markets. From a franchisee's perspective, the franchise is beneficial because it reduces risk by implementing a proven concept. In Malaysia, for example, the success rate in the franchise business is 90 percent, compared to a 20 percent success rate of all new businesses.[24]

From a government perspective, franchising does not replace exports or export jobs. From a recipient-country view, franchising requires little outflow of foreign exchange, and the bulk of the profit generated remains within the country.[25]

One key franchising concern is the need for standardization, without which many of the benefits of the transferred know-how are lost. Typically, such standardization will include the use of a common business name, similar layout, and similar production or service processes. Apart from leading to efficient operations, all of these factors will also contribute to a high degree of international recognizability. Standardization, however, does not mean 100 percent uniformity. Adjustments in the final product need to take local market conditions into account. For example, fast-food outlets in Europe often need to serve beer and wine to be attractive to the local clientele. In order to enter the Indian market, where cows are considered sacred, McDonald's has developed nonbeef burgers.

Another issue is the protection of the total business system that a franchise offers. Once a business concept catches on, local competition may emerge quite quickly with an imitation of the product, the general style of operation, and even with a similar name.

Selection and training of franchisees present another concern. Although the local franchisee knows the market best, the franchiser still needs to understand the market for

Exhibit **9.7**

Key Impediments to International Franchising

- Meeting and training qualified and reliable franchisees overseas
- Security and protection of industrial property and trademarks in foreign countries
- Keeping current with market prospects overseas
- Familiarity with business practices overseas
- Foreign government regulations on business operations
- Foreign regulations or limitations on royalty fees
- Negotiation with foreign franchisees
- Foreign regulations or limitations on entry of franchise business
- Collection and transfer of franchise fee
- Control of quality or quantity of product or service
- Providing technical support overseas
- Pricing franchise for a foreign market
- Promotion and advertising opportunities for franchise overseas
- Sourcing and availability of raw materials, equipment, and other products
- Shipping and distribution of raw materials required to operate a foreign franchise
- Financing franchise operations overseas
- Shipping and handling of equipment needed to operate a foreign franchise

SOURCE: Adapted from Ben L. Kedia, David J. Ackerman, and Robert T. Justis, "Changing Barriers to the Internationalization of Franchising Operations: Perceptions of Domestic and International Franchisors," *The International Executive* 37 (July/August 1995): 329–348.

product adaptation purposes and operational details. There may be complications in selecting appropriate advertising media, effective copy testing, effective translation of the franchiser's message, and the use of appropriate sales promotion tools. Exhibit 9.7 summarizes research findings regarding the challenges faced in international franchising.

To encourage better-organized and more successful growth, many companies turn to the master franchising system, wherein foreign partners are selected and awarded the rights to a large territory in which they in turn can subfranchise. As a result, the franchiser gains market expertise and an effective screening mechanism for new franchises, while reducing costly mistakes.[26]

Foreign Direct Investment

Foreign direct investment (FDI) represents international investment flows that acquire properties and plants. The international marketer makes such investments to create or expand a long-term interest in an enterprise with some degree of control. Portfolio investment in turn focuses on the purchase of stocks and bonds internationally. Portfolio investment is of primary concern to the international financial community.

Foreign direct investments have grown rapidly. With financial investments alone burgeoning from billions in the late 1960s to trillions by the mid-2000s, it is not surprising that FDI is the largest source of external finance for developing countries. This amounts to around 33 percent of GDP, compared to approximately 10 percent in 1980. Additionally, the impact on overall productivity is phenomenal. For example, the foreign affiliates of close to 64,000 transnational corporations (TNCs) generate 53 million jobs.[27] The United States plays a major role in global investments. At the end of 2007, U.S.-owned assets abroad were $17.6 billion, compared to $14.4 billion at the end of 2006. Foreign-owned assets in the United States were $20.1 billion at the end of 2007, compared to $16.6 billion in 2006.[28] Exhibit 9.8 shows how the U.S. net international investment position has changed over time. Foreign direct investment has clearly become a major avenue for international market entry and expansion.

U.S. Net International Investment Position at Year-end

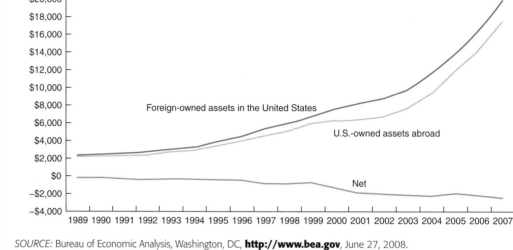

SOURCE: Bureau of Economic Analysis, Washington, DC, **http://www.bea.gov**, June 27, 2008.

Major Foreign Investors

The United Nations defines multinational corporations as "enterprises which own or control production or service facilities outside the country in which they are based."[29] This definition makes all foreign direct investors multinational corporations. Yet large corporations are the key players. Exhibit 9.9 lists 50 of the world's biggest and most important companies according to Forbes "Global 2000" list of companies. These 50 companies have the best composite ranking based on sales, profits, assets, and market value. Overall, however, there are 60 countries and 72 million people represented in Forbes' global 2000 list. The global 2000 companies account for $30 trillion in revenues, $2.4 trillion in profits, and $119 trillion in assets.[30] Their market value exceeds the equivalent of more than half of global GDP. These firms appear to benefit from a greater ability to cope with new, unfamiliar situations.[31]

Many of the large multinationals operate in well over 100 countries. For some, their original home market accounts for only a fraction of their sales. For example, the Dutch company Philips, the Swedish SKF, and the Swiss Nestlé sell less than 5 percent of their total sales in their home country. In some firms, even the terms *domestic* and *foreign* have fallen into disuse. Others are working to consider issues only from a global perspective. For example, in management meetings of ABB (Asea Brown Boveri), individuals get fined $100 every time the words *foreign* and *domestic* are used.

Through their investment, multinational corporations bring economic vitality and jobs to their host countries and often pay higher wages than the average domestically oriented firms.[32]

At the same time, however, trade follows investment. This means that foreign direct investors often bring with them imports on an ongoing basis. The flow of imports in turn may contribute to the weakening of a nation's international trade position.

Reasons for Foreign Direct Investment

Marketing Factors

Marketing considerations and the corporate desire for growth are major causes for the increase in foreign direct investment. Even large domestic markets limit growth, which typically means greater responsibilities and more pay for those who contribute to it.

Exhibit **9.9**

Top Global Performers

Rank	Company	Country	Industry	Sales ($Bil)	Profits ($Bil)	Assets ($Bil)	Value ($Bil)
1	HSBC Holdings	United Kingdom	Banking	146.50	19.13	2,348.98	180.81
2	General Electric	United States	Conglomerates	172.74	22.21	795.34	330.93
3	Bank of America	United States	Banking	119.19	14.98	1,715.75	176.53
4	JPMorgan Chase	United States	Banking	116.35	15.37	1,562.15	136.88
5	ExxonMobil	United States	Oil & Gas Operations	358.60	40.61	242.08	465.51
6	Royal Dutch Shell	Netherlands	Oil & Gas Operations	355.78	31.33	266.22	221.09
7	BP	United Kingdom	Oil & Gas Operations	281.03	20.60	236.08	204.94
8	Toyota Motor	Japan	Consumer Durables	203.80	13.99	276.38	175.08
9	ING Group	Netherlands	Insurance	197.93	12.65	1,932.15	75.78
10	Berkshire Hathaway	United States	Diversified Financials	118.25	13.21	273.16	216.65
10	Royal Bank of Scotland	United Kingdom	Banking	108.45	14.62	3,807.51	76.64
12	AT&T	United States	Telecommunications Services	118.93	11.95	275.64	210.22
13	BNP Paribas	France	Banking	116.16	10.71	2,494.41	81.90
14	Allianz	Germany	Insurance	139.12	10.90	1,547.48	80.30
15	Total	France	Oil & Gas Operations	199.74	19.24	165.75	181.80
16	Wal-Mart Stores	United States	Retailing	378.80	12.73	163.38	198.60
17	Chevron	United States	Oil & Gas Operations	203.97	18.69	148.79	179.97
18	American Intl Group	United States	Insurance	110.06	6.20	1,060.51	118.20
19	Gazprom	Russia	Oil & Gas Operations	81.76	23.30	201.72	306.79
20	AXA Group	France	Insurance	151.70	7.75	1,064.67	70.33
21	Banco Santander	Spain	Banking	72.26	10.02	1,332.72	113.27
22	ConocoPhillips	United States	Oil & Gas Operations	171.50	11.89	177.76	129.15
23	Goldman Sachs Group	United States	Diversified Financials	87.97	11.60	1,119.80	67.16
24	Citigroup	United States	Banking	159.23	3.62	2,187.63	123.44
25	Barclays	United Kingdom	Banking	79.70	8.76	2,432.34	62.43
26	EDF Group	France	Utilities	81.60	7.69	271.66	170.81
27	E.ON	Germany	Utilities	94.04	9.86	200.84	126.22
28	ENI	Italy	Oil & Gas Operations	119.27	13.70	128.15	127.38
29	Petrobras-Petróleo Brasil	Brazil	Oil & Gas Operations	87.52	11.04	129.98	236.67
30	PetroChina	China	Oil & Gas Operations	88.24	18.21	111.70	546.14
31	Procter & Gamble	United States	Household & Personal Products	79.74	11.13	144.40	203.67
32	Deutsche Bank	Germany	Diversified Financials	95.50	7.45	1,485.58	56.27
33	UniCredit Group	Italy	Banking	63.67	7.19	1,077.21	77.46
34	Telefónica	Spain	Telecommunications Services	82.40	13.00	143.13	138.42
35	Mitsubishi UFJ Financial	Japan	Banking	49.49	7.50	1,591.56	98.14
36	Volkswagen Group	Germany	Consumer Durables	149.00	5.64	210.88	90.23
37	IBM	United States	Software & Services	98.79	10.42	120.43	157.62
38	ArcelorMittal	Luxembourg	Materials	105.22	10.37	133.65	108.82
38	Daimler	Germany	Consumer Durables	145.11	5.82	199.77	85.16
40	BBVA-Banco Bilbao Vizcaya	Spain	Banking	54.34	8.94	733.14	78.29
41	Wells Fargo	United States	Banking	53.59	8.06	575.44	96.37
42	ICBC	China	Banking	37.48	6.31	961.65	289.57
43	Credit Suisse Group	Switzerland	Diversified Financials	83.72	7.53	1,194.75	50.85
44	HBOS	United Kingdom	Banking	100.32	8.10	1,336.17	44.84
45	Crédit Agricole	France	Banking	101.59	6.49	1,662.60	45.73
45	Nestlé	Switzerland	Food Drink & Tobacco	94.76	9.38	99.06	188.11
47	Fortis	Netherlands	Diversified Financials	121.19	5.46	1,020.98	49.04
48	Verizon Communications	United States	Telecommunications Services	93.47	5.65	186.96	104.27
49	France Telecom	France	Telecommunications Services	77.31	9.20	137.09	87.89
50	Siemens	Germany	Conglomerates	103.20	5.42	126.72	118.47

SOURCE: **http://www.forbes.com/lists/2008/18/biz_2000global08_The-Global-2000_Rank.html**.

Corporations therefore seek wider market access in order to maintain and increase their sales. This objective can be achieved most quickly through acquisitions abroad.

Corporations also attempt to obtain low-cost resources and ensure their sources of supply. Finally, once the decision is made to invest internationally, the investment climate plays a major role. Firms will seek to invest where their investment is most protected and has the best chance to flourish.

Foreign direct investment permits corporations to circumvent current barriers to trade and operate abroad as a domestic firm, unaffected by duties, tariffs, or other import restrictions. For example, research on Japanese foreign direct investment in Europe found that a substantial number of firms have invested there in order to counteract future trade friction.[33]

Customers may insist on domestic goods and services, as a result of nationalistic tendencies, as a function of cultural differences, or for strategic planning and security purposes.[34] Having the origin of a product associated with a specific country may also bring positive effects with it, particularly if the country is known for the particular product category. An investment in a Swiss dairy firm by a cheese producer is an example.

Firms have been categorized as resource seekers, market seekers, and efficiency seekers.[35] Resource seekers search for either natural resources or human resources. Natural resources typically are based on mineral, agricultural, or oceanographic advantages. Companies seeking human resources typically search for either low-cost labor or highly skilled labor. The value of labor resources may change over time and lead to corporate relocations. For example, in the 1980s, many non-European firms invested in the low-wage countries of Portugal, Spain, and Greece. The major political changes of the 1990s, however, shifted the investment interest to Hungary, the former East Germany, and the Czech Republic, where wages were even lower.

Corporations primarily in search of better opportunities to enter and expand within markets are market seekers. Particularly when markets are closed or access is restricted, corporations have a major incentive to invest rather than export. Efficiency seekers attempt to obtain the most economic sources of production. They frequently have affiliates in multiple markets with highly specialized product lines or components, and exchange their production in order to maximize the benefits to the corporation. The reasons why firms engage in foreign investment can change over time.

A second major cause for the increase in foreign direct investment is the result of derived demand, which is the result of the move abroad by established customers. Large multinational firms like to maintain their established business relationships and, therefore, frequently encourage their suppliers to follow them abroad. As a result, a few initial investments can lead to a series of additional investments. For example, advertising agencies may move to service foreign affiliates of their domestic clients. Similarly, engineering firms, insurance companies, and law firms may provide their services abroad. Some suppliers invest abroad out of fear that their clients might find better sources abroad and therefore begin to import the products or services they currently supply.

Government Incentives

Governments are under pressure to provide jobs for their citizens. Foreign direct investment can increase employment and income. Countries such as Ireland have been promoting government incentive schemes for foreign direct investment for decades. Increasingly, state and local governments promote investment by sending out investment missions or opening offices abroad in order to inform local businesses about the beneficial investment climate at home.

Government incentives are mainly of three types: fiscal, financial, and nonfinancial. Fiscal incentives are specific tax measures designed to attract the foreign investor. They typically consist of special depreciation allowances, tax credits or rebates, special deductions for capital expenditures, tax holidays, and other reductions of the tax burden on the investor. Financial incentives offer special funding for the investor by providing land or buildings, loans, loan guarantees, or wage subsidies. Nonfinancial incentives consist of guaranteed government purchases; special protection from competition through tariffs, import quotas, and local content requirements; and investments in infrastructure facilities.

Incentives may slightly alter the advantage of a region. By themselves, they are unlikely to spur an investment decision if proper market conditions do not exist. Consequently, when individual states or regions within a country offer special incentives to foreign direct investors, they may be competing against each other for a limited pie rather than increasing the size of the pie. Furthermore, a question exists about the extent to which new jobs are actually created by foreign direct investment. Because many foreign investors import equipment, parts, and even personnel, the expected benefits in terms of job creation may often be either less than initially envisioned or only temporary. One additional concern arises from domestic firms already in existence. Since their "old" investment typically does not benefit from incentives designed to attract new investment, established firms may feel disadvantaged when competing against the newcomer.

A Perspective on Foreign Direct Investors

Foreign direct investors, and particularly multinational corporations, are viewed with a mixture of awe and dismay. Governments and individuals praise them for bringing capital, economic activity, employment, and for transferring technology and managerial skills. These actions encourage competition, market choice, and competitiveness.

At the same time, investment may lead to dependence. Just as the establishment of a corporation can create all sorts of benefits, its disappearance can also take them away again. Very often, international direct investors are accused of draining resources from their host countries. By employing the best and the brightest, they are said to deprive domestic firms of talent, thus causing a **brain drain**. Once they have hired locals, multinational firms are often accused of not promoting them high enough.

By raising money locally, multinationals can starve smaller capital markets. By bringing in foreign technology, they are viewed either as discouraging local technology development or as perhaps transferring only outmoded knowledge. By increasing competition, they are declared the enemy of domestic firms. There are concerns about foreign investors' economic and political loyalty toward their host government, and a fear that such investors will always protect only their own interests and those of their home governments. And, of course, their sheer size, which sometimes exceeds the financial assets of the government, makes foreign investors suspect.

Clearly, a love–hate relationship can exist between governments and the foreign investor. Corporate experts may be more knowledgeable than government employees. Particularly in developing countries, this knowledge advantage may offer opportunities for exploitation. There seems to be a distinct "liability of foreignness" affecting both firms and governments. As Exhibit 9.10 shows, there are firms that try to inform markets and governments about foreign companies' contributions to the local economy.

Exhibit **9.10**

The American International Automobile Dealers Association

© PRNEWSFOTO/AMERICAN INTERNATIONAL AUTOMOBILE DEALERS ASSOCIATION

An array of guidelines for international corporate behavior have been published by organizations such as the United Nations, the Organization for Economic Cooperation and Development, and the International Labor Organization. They address the behavior of foreign investors in such areas as employment practices, consumer and environmental protection, political activity, and human rights. While the social acceptability of certain practices may vary among nations, the foreign investor should transfer the best business practices across nations. The multinational firm should be a leader in improving standards of living around the world. It will be managerial virtue, vision, and veracity combined with corporate openness, responsiveness, long-term thinking, and truthfulness that will determine the degrees of freedom and success of global business in the future.[36] *The International Marketplace 9.3* describes how Vietnam is mandating that all foreign direct investors now adhere to strict laws regarding sustainable projects.

Types of Ownership

A corporation's ownership choices can range from 100 percent ownership to a minority interest. The different levels of ownership will affect corporate flexibility, ability to control business plans and strategy, and exposure to risk. Some firms appear to select specific foreign ownership structures based on their experience with similar structures in the past.[37] In other words, they tend to keep using the same ownership model. However, the ownership decision should be a strategic response to corporate needs or a consequence of government regulation.

The International
MARKETPLACE

 **ENVIRONMENT & SUSTAINABILITY**   **9.3**

Foreign Direct Investments in Vietnam: The Good and the Bad

Often referred to as the "next Asian Tiger," Vietnam had 1,171 new foreign direct investment (FDI) projects in 2008. These investments were valued at over $64 billion, almost double the value of FDI in 2007. Including the large gains in 2008, Vietnam has a total of around 9,700 licensed foreign direct investment projects, with total registered capital of around $150 billion. The move to a market economy is positioning Vietnam as a dynamic and influential player in Southeast Asia.

The biggest FDI projects in 2008 were: (1) the *Son Duong Port and Steel Complex* begun in July of 2008 by Formosa, a Taiwanese group; (2) a project by a Brunei company called the *New City Vietnam Tourism Project,* which is a complex of hotels, office buildings, restaurants, healthcare centers, and sports clubs; (3) the *Ho Tram Tourism and Resort Complex* under development by Asian Coast Development Ltd. based in Canada; (4) the *Vietnam International University Township Project* started in July 2008 by Malaysian-based Berjaya Land Berhad; (5) a resort by an affiliate of USA-based Starbay Holding Group, called *Cua Dai Beach Resort*; (6) a tourism complex, the *5-Star Complex,* by the American group Good Choice; (7) *TA Associates International Project,* office buildings and living facilities by a group out of

Singapore; and (8) the *Urban, Hotel, Trade and Service Complex* by Water Front Ltd. based in Singapore.

Such rapid FDI activity, however, has not been without oversight. The Ministry of Planning and Investment's Foreign Investment Agency has stated clearly that it appreciates foreign companies that contribute to Vietnam's social activities and adhere to environmental protection regulations. As such, 40 foreign investment companies are selected annually as recipients of the Sai Gon Times Top 40 Awards, where the selection criteria includes a contribution to community development through social, charitable, and environmental preservation programs. The companies come from a variety of industries, with four actually receiving the award in consecutive years. My Duc Ceramics is a leading tile manufacturer and was the first company in Vietnam to be certified with ISO 9001:2000 and ISO 14001:2004 quality assurance. The My Duc Ceramics' staff members are trained in Europe, with Italian technicians present in the Vietnamese factory developing breakthrough products. Nam Con Son Pipeline is a partnership among three companies, ONGC-Videsh, BP, and Statoil. This FDI has formulated a plan for successful development of gas reserves. Hikosen Cara produces clothing, home accessories, and other textile-related products. The company's head office is in Japan. Phu My 3 BOT Power, Vietnam's first build-operate-transfer power plant, is one of Vietnam's most important power projects and plays a critical role in the government's plan to develop a clean and dependable power generation sector. The Phu My 3 BOT Power Company is a consortium of BP, Sojitz Corp., SembCorp Utilities of Singapore, and Kyushu Electric Power of Japan.

Unfortunately, not all of Vietnam's FDI projects operate in a sustainable manner. In October 2008, a large Taiwanese-owned factory, Vedan Vietnam, was closed after it was found to be dumping over 80,000 cubic feet of untreated wastewater daily into the Thi Vai River. This 14-year producer of monosodium glutamate (MSG) was discovered to have an underground pipeline network that pumped the untreated water into the river. This waste water contained high contents of molasses and chemicals, which is in violation of the country's Environmental Protection Law. The damage to the river's ecosystem was deemed almost irreversible.

In any developing country, there are risks associated with rapid industrialization. Yet it appears that the Vietnamese government recognizes the need for sustainable economic growth and is preparing itself to welcome only environmentally-friendly investors by imposing strong sanctions against violators.

SOURCES: "Top Eight FDI Projects 2008," *Vietnam Business Finance*, January 8, 2009, **http://www.vnbusinessnews.com/2009/01/top-eight-fdi-projects-2008.html**, retrieved January 8, 2009; "Vietnam—Programming Framework 2004–2009," *Canadian International Development Agency*, **http://www.acdi-cida.gc.ca/CIDAWEB/acdicida.nsf/En/JUD-3210321-L8L**, retrieved January 8, 2009; "Top 40 Companies Received Awards for Sustainability," *Vietnam Business Finance*, December 14, 2008, **http://www.vnbusinessnews.com/2008/12/top-40-companies-receive-awards-for.html**, retrieved January 8, 2009; *My Duc Ceramics*, **http://myduc.com**, retrieved January 8, 2009; John Mueller, "Nam Con Son Players Step on the Gas," *Asian Oil and Gas*, January 1, 2002, **http://www.oilonline.com/news/features/aog/20020101.Nam_Con_.8083.asp**, retrieved January 8, 2009; *Hikosen Cara*, **http://hikosen-cara.com**, retrieved January 8, 2009; Sian Green, "Phu My 3: A Model BOT," *Power Engineering International*, September 2004, **http://pe.articles.printthis.clickability.com/pt/cpt?action=cpt&title=Power+Engineering+International+Phu+My+3%3A+a+model+BOT&expire=&urlID=25182391&fb=Y&url=thhp%3A%2F%2Fpepei.pennnet.com%2Fdisplay_article%2F212244%2F17%2F ARTCL%Fnone%Fnone%2F1%FPhu-My-3%3A-a-model-BOT%2F&partnerID=1405**, retrieved January 8, 2009; Chua Siew Joo, "Vietnam Implements Regulations for Environmental Sustainability," *Vietnam Briefing*, October 8, 2008, **http://www.vietnam-briefing.com/news/vietnam-implements-regulations-sustainability.html**, retrieved January 8, 2009; Tran Van Minh, "Vietnam Shuts Taiwanese Plant for Dumping Wastewater," *The China Post*, October 8, 2008, **http://www.chinapost.com.tw/asia/vietnam/2008/10/08/177829/Vietnam-shuts.htm**, retrieved January 8, 2009.

Full Ownership

Many firms prefer to have 100 percent ownership. Sometimes, this is the result of ethnocentric considerations, based on the belief that no outside entity should have an impact on management. At other times, the issue is one of principle.

To make a rational decision about the extent of ownership, management must evaluate how important total control is for the success of its international marketing activities. Often, full ownership may be a desirable, but not a necessary, prerequisite for international success. At other times, interdependencies between local operations and headquarters may require total control. Since the international environment is quite hostile to full ownership by multinational firms it is important to determine whether these reasons are important enough to warrant a sole ownership policy or whether the needs of the firm can be accommodated with other arrangements.

Commercial activities under the control of foreigners are frequently believed to reflect the wishes, desires, and needs of headquarters abroad much more than those of the domestic economy. Governments fear that domestic economic policies may be counteracted by such firms, and employees are afraid that little local responsibility and empathy exist at headquarters. A major concern is the "fairness" of profit repatriation, or transfer of profits, and the extent to which firms reinvest into their foreign operations. Governments often believe that transfer pricing mechanisms are used to amass profits in a place most advantageous for the firm and that, as a consequence, local operations often show very low levels of performance. By reducing the foreign control of firms, they hope to put an end to such practices.

Ownership can be limited either through outright legal restrictions or through measures designed to make foreign ownership less attractive—such as limitations on profit repatriation. The international marketer is therefore frequently faced with the choice of either accepting a reduction in control or of losing the opportunity to operate in the country.

General market instability can also serve as a major deterrent to full ownership of foreign direct investment. Instability may result from political upheavals or changes in regimes. More often, it results from threats of political action, complex and drawn-out bureaucratic procedures, and the prospect of arbitrary and unpredictable alterations in regulations after the investment decision has been made.[38]

Joint Ventures

Joint ventures are collaborations of two or more organizations for more than a transitory period.[39] As equity stake participants, the partners share assets, risks, and profits, though equality of partners is not necessary. The partners' contributions to the joint venture can vary widely and can consist of funds, technology, know-how, sales organizations, or plants and equipment.

Advantages of Joint Ventures

The two major reasons for joint ventures are governmental and commercial. Government restrictions are designed to reduce the extent of control that foreign firms can exercise over local operations. As a basis for defining control, most countries have employed percentage levels of ownership. Over time, the thresholds of ownership that define control have decreased as it became apparent that even small, organized groups of stockholders may influence control of an enterprise. At the same time, many countries also recognize the competitive benefits of foreign direct investment and permit more control of local firms by foreign entities.

Equally important to the formation of joint ventures are commercial considerations. Joint ventures can pool resources and lead to a better outcome for each partner than if they worked individually. This is particularly the case when each partner has a specialized advantage in areas that benefit the joint venture. For example, a firm may have new technology available, yet lack sufficient capital to carry out foreign direct investment on its own. By linking efforts with a partner, the technology can be used more quickly and market penetration is easier. Similarly, if one of the partners has an already established distribution system, a greater volume of sales can be achieved more rapidly.

Joint ventures also permit better relationships with local organizations—government, local authorities, or labor unions. If the local partner can bring political influence to the undertaking, the new venture may be eligible for tax incentives, grants, and government support and may be less vulnerable to political risk. Negotiations for certifications or licenses may be easier with authorities. Relationships with the local financial establishment may enable the joint venture to tap local capital markets. The greater experience—and therefore greater familiarity—with the culture and environment of the local partner may enable the joint venture to be more aware of cultural sensitivities and to benefit from greater insights into changing market conditions and needs.

Disadvantages of Joint Ventures

Problem areas in joint ventures, as in all partnerships, involve implementing the concept and maintaining the relationship. This was evident in the Danone-Wahaha joint venture described earlier. Joint venture regulations are often subject to substantial interpretation and arbitrariness. Major problems can arise due to conflicts of interest, problems with disclosure of sensitive information, and disagreement over how profits are to be shared; these are typically the result of a lack of communication and planning before, during, and after the formation of the venture. In some cases, managers are interested in launching the venture but are too little concerned with actually running the enterprise. In other instances, managers dispatched to the joint venture by the partners may feel differing degrees of loyalty to the venture and its partners.[40] The joint venture may, for example, identify a particular market as a profitable target, yet the headquarters of one of the partners may already have plans for serving this market, plans that would require competing against its own joint venture. Reconciling such conflicts of loyalty is one of the greatest human resource challenges for joint ventures.[41]

Strategic Alliances

One special form of joint ventures consists of strategic alliances, or partnerships, which are arrangements between two or more companies with a common business objective. Unlike the more rigid joint venture, the great advantage of strategic alliances is their ongoing flexibility, since they can be formed, adjusted, and dissolved rapidly in response to changing conditions. In essence, strategic alliances are networks of companies, which collaborate in the achievement of a given project or objective. Partners for one project may well be fierce competitors for another.

Alliances can range from information cooperation in the market development area to joint ownership of worldwide operations. For example, Texas Instruments has reported agreements with companies such as IBM, Hyundai, Fujitsu, Alcatel, and L. M. Ericsson, using such terms as "joint development agreement," "cooperative technical effort," "joint program for development," "alternative sourcing agreement," and "design/exchange agreement for cooperative product development and exchange of technical data."

Market development is one reason for the growth in such alliances. In Japan, Motorola is sharing chip designs and manufacturing facilities with Toshiba to gain greater access to the Japanese market. Another focus is spreading the cost and risk inherent in production and development efforts. Texas Instruments and Hitachi have teamed up to develop the next generation of memory chips. The costs of developing new jet engines are so vast that they force aerospace companies into collaboration; one such consortium was formed by United Technologies' Pratt & Whitney division, Britain's Rolls Royce, Motoren-und-Turbinen Union from Germany, Fiat of Italy, and Japanese Aero Engines. Some alliances are also formed to block or co-opt competitors.[42] For example, Caterpillar formed a heavy equipment joint venture with Mitsubishi in Japan to strike back at its main global rival, Komatsu, in its home market.

Companies must carefully evaluate the effects of entering such a coalition, particularly with regards to strategy and competitiveness. The most successful alliances are those that match the **complementary strengths** of partners to satisfy a joint objective. Often the partners have different product, geographic, or functional strengths, which the alliance can build on in order to achieve success with a new strategy or in a new market. They can then either operate jointly as equals or have one partner **piggyback** by making use of the other's strengths. For example, Pepsi has combined its marketing prowess for canned beverages with Lipton's strong brand position for tea in order to jointly sell canned iced tea beverages.[43] Firms also can have a reciprocal arrangement whereby each partner provides the other access to its market. The New York Yankees and Manchester United sell each others' licensed products and develop joint sponsorship programs. International airlines have started to share hubs, coordinate schedules, and simplify ticketing. Star Alliance (joining airlines such as United and Lufthansa) and Oneworld (British Airways and American Airlines) provide worldwide coverage for their customers both in the travel and shipping communities.

In a **management contract**, the supplier brings together a package of skills that will provide an integrated service to the client without incurring the risk and benefit of ownership. The activity is quite different from other contractual arrangements because people actually move and directly implement the relevant skills and knowledge in the client organization.[44]

Management contracts have clear benefits for the client. They can provide organizational skills that are not available locally, expertise that is immediately available rather than built up, and management assistance in the form of support services that would be difficult and costly to replicate locally. In addition, the outside involvement is clearly limited. When a turnkey project is online, the system will be totally owned, controlled, and operated by the customer. As a result, management contracts are seen by many governments as a useful alternative to foreign direct investment and the resulting control by nondomestic entities.

Similar advantages exist for the supplier. The risk of participating in an international venture is substantially lowered because no equity capital is at stake. At the same time, a significant amount of operational control can be exercised. Being on the inside represents a strategic advantage in influencing decisions. In addition, existing know-how that has been built up with significant investment can be commercialized. Frequently, the impact of fluctuations in business volume can be reduced by making use of experienced personnel who otherwise would have to be laid off. Accumulated service knowledge and comparative advantage should be used internationally. Management contracts permit a firm to do so.

In a dynamic business environment, alliances must be able to adjust to market conditions. Any agreement should therefore provide for changes in the original concept so that the venture can grow and flourish. In light of growing international competition and the rising cost of innovation in technology, strategic alliances are likely to continue their growth in the future.

Government Consortia

One form of cooperation takes place at the industry level and is typically characterized by government support or even subsidization. Usually, it is the reflection of escalating cost and a governmental goal of developing or maintaining global leadership in a particular sector. A new drug, computer, or telecommunication switch can cost more than $1 billion to develop and bring to market. To combat the high costs and risks of research and development, research consortia have emerged in the United States, Japan, and Europe. Since the passage of the Joint Research and Development Act of 1984 (which allows both domestic and foreign firms to participate in joint basic research efforts without the fear of antitrust action), well over 100 consortia have been registered in the United States. These consortia pool their resources for research into technologies ranging from artificial intelligence and electric car batteries to semiconductor manufacturing.

The European Union has several megaprojects to develop new technologies, under the names BRITE, COMET, ESPRIT, EUREKA, RACE, and SOKRATES. Japanese consortia have worked on producing the world's highest-capacity memory chip, and other advanced computer technologies. On the manufacturing side, the formation of Airbus Industries secured European production of commercial jets. The consortium of the European Aeronautic Defence and Space Company (EADS), which emerged from the link-up of the German DaimlerChrysler Aerospace AG, the French Aerospatiale Matra, and CASA of Spain has become a prime global competitor.[45]

Summary

Most companies become gradually involved in international markets, though some are born global. A variety of internal and external factors expose them to the international market. Employees and management serve as particularly important change agents. After becoming aware of international marketing opportunities, companies progress through the corporate export stages, and may choose to retreat to a purely domestic focus or to increase the scope of their international activities through a variety of different means.

Firms may employ third parties, such as export management companies or trading companies, or they may break into the global marketplace using the technology of the Internet. If a firm wants to establish an international presence it can also license its products, open global franchises, or directly invest into a region of the world. These expansion alternatives involve varying degrees of risk, and varying degrees of control that a company may exercise over its international ventures. Firms' involvement in international markets may also be legally limited by the extent to which a country allows foreign ownership of assets. Companies looking to go abroad need to consider a variety of factors—such as mechanics, corporate structure, strategic goals, logistics, cost, and regulations—before they expand.

Key Terms

safety-valve activity	e-commerce	derived demand
psychological distance	licensing	fiscal incentives
change agent	transfer costs	financial incentives
accidental exporters	R&D costs	nonfinancial incentives
born global	opportunity costs	brain drain
innate exporters	trademark licensing	profit repatriation
awareness	franchising	joint ventures
interest	master franchising system	strategic alliances
trial	foreign direct investment (FDI)	complementary strengths
evaluation	portfolio investment	piggyback
adaptation	resources seekers	management contract
sogoshosha	market seekers	research consortia
export trading company (ETC)	efficiency seekers	

Questions for Discussion

1. Discuss the difference between a proactive and a reactive firm.

2. Discuss the impact of the Internet and e-commerce in making a firm global.

3. What is meant by the term "born global"?

4. Why might a firm choose to retreat to a domestic focus?

5. Explain the difference between franchising, licensing, and foreign direct investment, in terms of ownership, control, and risk.

6. From a government standpoint, what kind of investment is most beneficial to a country?

7. Discuss the benefits and drawbacks of strategic partnerings at the corporate level.

Internet Exercises

1. What programs does the Export-Import Bank (http://www.exim.gov) offer that specifically benefit small businesses trying to export? What benefits can be derived from each?

2. Use the United Nations Conference on Trade and Development FDI Database (available under the Statistics option at http://www.unctad.org) to research the foreign direct investment profile of a country or region of your choice.

Recommended Readings

Braken, Steven and Harry Garretson (Editors). *Foreign Direct Investment and the Multinational Enterprise.* Cambridge, MA: MIT Press, 2008.

Comm, Joel. *Click Here to Order: Stories of the World's Most Successful Internet Marketing Entrepreneurs.* Garden City, NY: Morgan James Publishing, 2008.

Kaynak, Erdener and Jorma Larimo. *Contemporary Euromarketing: Entry and Operational Decision Making.* New York, NY: Routledge, 2007.

Klossek, Andreas. *Market Entry and Expansion through International Joint Ventures.* Germany: VDM Verlag, 2008.

Konigsberg, Alexander S. *International Franchising,* 3rd edition. Huntington, NY: Juris Publishing, Inc., 2008.

Meiners, Roger E., Al H. Ringleb, Frances L. Edwards, and Charles Lako. *The Legal & Ethical Environment of Business and E-commerce at the International, National, And State Level.* Washington, D.C.: Thompson Publishing Group, Inc., 2006.

Robertson, Christopher J. and Andrew Watson. "Corruption and Change: The Impact of Foreign Direct Investment," *Strategic Management Journal,* 25: 385–396, 2004.

Weiss, Kenneth D. *Building an Import/Export Business.* Hoboken, NJ: Wiley, 2007.

STARTING AN IMPORT/EXPORT BUSINESS

So you're interested in an import/export business. Perhaps you're in the same position I was five months ago and have no previous experience in the field. Where do you begin? In August, I began an independent study on U.S. whiskey exports to Vietnam with Georgetown Professor Michael Czinkota, one of the authors of this book. We decided to keep notes on the process and share some suggestions here so that future generations of students could benefit from our work. I'll take you through the process of how in five months I went from knowing absolutely nothing about import/export to obtaining exclusive rights to export Wasmund's, a brand of single malt whiskey, to Vietnam.

Preliminary Research: See Where Google Takes You

The first step is to begin preliminary research on the topic and bridge the information gap. Utilize all of the resources at your disposal, such as websites, books, and personal contacts, to glean introductory information on the subject. Get on Google, type in "import export business" and see where the URL links lead you. I clicked my way to an article by Entrepreneur.com titled, "How to Start an Import/Export Business."[1] The article gave first-timers like me a picture of what life was like in the business, covering topics such as expenses, potential income, and what a typical day might look like. Next, surf Amazon and see if you can find a book that interests you. I found *Building an Import/Export Business* by Kenneth Weiss to be a helpful overview of what I was getting myself into. Finally, set up informational interviews with family, friends, and any other contacts familiar with the business. Valuable contacts are oftentimes just an introduction away. I learned that a couple of classmates had family import/export businesses in Columbia and Kenya. I set up meetings with them to ask them questions about their family businesses. After three to four weeks of preliminary research, I had a basic understanding of the key components of an import/export business.

Leverage Your School

Students should make sure to take advantage of the resources available to them through their schools. There is a wealth of information, resources, and contacts to tap into during this short window of academic life. You will find that courses, students, and professors have much to offer. If your university doesn't specifically have a class on import/export, then find professors that have experience in the field and see if they are interested in doing an independent study with you. It's likely that there are professors at your school who have import/export experience. Do some research and find the professor that best matches your particular area of interest.

I sent Georgetown Professor Michael Czinkota an email saying that I was interested in an independent study on import/export. He replied asking for my resume and for my thoughts on what it was that I wanted to accomplish with such a study. Through my preliminary research I had a few products in mind and knew that I specifically wanted to work in Asia. After some discussion, we agreed that I would have a two part project. The first part would be research-based and would study consumer perception and acceptance of import—specifically in Asia. The second part would involve the study of (and the practical application of) exporting Wasmund's single malt whiskey to Vietnam. Wasmund's is based in northern Virginia and had distribution in the U.S. and Europe but was not available in Asia.

Fellow students are also a great resource and should not be overlooked. Campuses and business schools are becoming increasingly international. Take advantage of the fact that there are people from all over the world studying at your university. Reach out to some of them and build friendships. If you are genuinely interested in them, their country, their culture, and their food, it's a good opportunity to build a mutually beneficial relationship where you can both learn from and help each other.

SOURCES: This case study was contributed by Mike Kim, graduate student of the McDonough School of Business at Georgetown University (2009).

Explore Your Contacts

It's important to take some time and give careful thought to your contacts. Spend a few minutes putting together a list of all the relevant contacts you can think of. Doing so may help identify opportunities that you never knew existed. Earlier I stated: "Valuable contacts are oftentimes just an introduction away." For example, through Ambassador Mark Palmer, one of my mentors, I was able to get an introduction to an executive at the Distilled Spirits Council of the United States (DISCUS), the national trade association. Additionally, as I explored my contacts, I found that through one of my classmates in the Georgetown MBA program, I was one introduction away from the Vietnamese Trade Counselor to Germany.[2] He was formerly the Trade Counselor to Italy and had experience with importing alcohol to Vietnam. Your contacts may not be as strong as mine or they may be better, but the point is to explore them to see where they might lead.

Identify Potential Products and Countries

Now it's time to move beyond the preliminary search and narrow the research. I wanted to start focusing on specific products and countries. Some of my questions were: What products stand out as interesting? Were there any countries that piqued interest? What opportunities seemed to be the most viable? There were a number of products that I was considering, such as seafood, clothing, and sand (used for construction). However, the lowest hanging fruit seemed to be exporting American whiskey to Asia. Wasmund's was interested in exporting to Asia—now I just had to do the market research to see if American whiskey was a good product for Vietnam.

Market Research

Market research is a critical component of import/export. A person cannot succeed until they first understand the consumer and the market.

Market research can be done in various ways. It can be done informally, by setting up a format where you can test your product. For example, I did whiskey "tastings" with Vietnamese people in the U.S. and asked for their thoughts on Wasmund's. I gave samples to Vietnamese classmates, professionals, and even people at the trade office. An even more effective method would be to travel to the country and set up tasting events there to see how consumers respond to the product.

Additionally, market research can be gathered through public data available online. An internet search on "distilled spirits Vietnam" brings up relevant reports. I went to the DISCUS website[3] and entered "Vietnam" in the search box and found a number of reports and press releases. A press release titled "Vietnam's WTO Membership Will Significantly Reduce Spirits Tariffs" announced that Vietnam would be reducing tariffs on imported spirits from 65 percent to 45 percent. As a result, it was anticipated that distilled spirits imports would be on the rise.

Government resources can also be very helpful when it comes to market research. There are online resources such as email updates on the **http://www.export.gov** website. The Department of Commerce (DOC)[4] has Country Commercial Guides[5] available that provide detailed information about doing business in a certain country. The 2008 Vietnam Country Commercial Guide is over a hundred pages long and has a wealth of country-specific information.

The U.S. International Trade Commission[6] also provides valuable data. I was able to obtain data through a report on U.S. distilled spirits exports to Vietnam. I learned that there were $0 U.S. whiskey exports in 2006 and 2007.[7] In 2008, there were $300,000 dollars of whiskey exports in the first quarter alone. This increase is due both to Vietnam joining the WTO in 2007 and more favorable consumer perception of American whiskey.

Information can also be gathered by meeting with people at the DOC or your government's trade ministry. If you are in the Washington, D.C., area, it will be easier to take advantage of government resources. If you are not, this is still possible through the internet, email, and phone. Try to schedule a meeting (in person or over the phone) with the industry specialist for the area you are considering and the desk officer for the country you want to export to. For those that hit a roadblock here, my advice is be persistent and leverage any contacts that might effect an introduction. I sent an email to a Georgetown alumnus that I once met in passing. He was a Deputy Assistant Secretary at the DOC and agreed to arrange a meeting between me and the industry specialist for distilled spirits. (It's important to note here that these are very busy people who are overloaded with requests for meetings. Naturally, they want to devote their time to prospects with the most potential. It is important to sell yourself and your business throughout the process.)

I put on a suit and tie and went over to the DOC for a meeting with the industry specialist. Three important things happened during that meeting: 1) I gained some industry-specific knowledge about distilled spirits; 2) the specialist gave me reports, such as the 2007 Vietnam Retail Food Sector Report,[8] as well as historical data on the amount of U.S. alcohol exports to Vietnam, 3) I received an introduction to the Vietnam desk officer at the DOC.

While the specialist gave me great information about the distilled spirits industry, the Vietnam desk officer gave me helpful information about the industry in Vietnam. In our meeting, we discussed specifics such as tariffs and consumption tax related to my product. We also talked about the overall potential for whiskey in Vietnam and the marketing that would be required to launch a new product.

Define Your Business and Connect the Dots

The end goal of doing the above-mentioned research is to arrive at a point where you can define your potential business. In order to do so, you need a product, a seller in one country, and a buyer in another country. It is said that the hardest part of import/export is finding a buyer. At this point, I had identified a product and a seller in the States. Now I had to find a buyer and distributor in Vietnam. There are three ways to find a buyer and distributor: l) through your government's export assistance activities (e.g., in the U.S., the DOC's Export Assistance Center); 2) through the foreign trade office of the country you are trying to export to; 3) through other organizations and individual contacts.

In the following section, I'll walk you through how each of these groups can help you identify a distributor.

U.S. Export Assistance Center

The Export Assistance Center (EAC) is the commercial service arm of the DOC designed to help U.S. citizens with their import/export business. There are local EAC offices throughout the country and the nearest office can easily be located through the website.[9] An EAC can help in a variety of ways, but its bread and butter is to help find distributors in the target country. Note that there are fees associated with using EAC's services. To give you an idea, there is a charge of $700 to set up one day of meetings with four to six potential distributors in the target country.

While the DOC may be the most helpful government agency, don't forget to connect with other groups. The Department of the Treasury has an International Trade Division that can provide information as well. I emailed the program manager at the Alcohol and Tobacco Tax and Trade Bureau and received a response with some information on the industry in Vietnam. In addition, there may be industry-specific organizations. Since I was dealing with distilled spirits, the USDA Foreign Agricultural Service became a valuable contact. If your product is in the food and beverage industry, this will be a helpful group as well.

Foreign Trade Offices

Next, I called the Vietnamese trade counselor in Washington, D.C. I had a personal introduction and was able to set up a meeting fairly easily. If you are not able to see the trade counselor, it should be feasible to meet with one of the commercial attaches at the office.[10] Vietnam also has an import/export counseling center in New York. These foreign government resources can provide country-specific information and can also suggest distributors. Depending on your product and circumstances, they can most likely recommend several possibilities. For some industries, they will already have a prepared list of distributors.

It is probably a good strategy to try and find a distributor through a dual strategy, utilizing both the EAC and the foreign trade office. In a country like Vietnam, the foreign trade office might be biased towards State Owned Enterprise distributors, while the EAC may have stronger relationships with private distributors.

Trade Associations and Individual Contacts

Alternative ways to find distributors are through individual contacts or other organizations. For example, as mentioned earlier, DISCUS is the national trade association for distilled spirits. It has an international program for promotional events in places such as China, Vietnam, and South Korea. That is one way to introduce your product to a market and possibly link up with a distributor. Other potentially helpful groups are the American Chamber of Commerce and the Association of Southeast Asian Nations.

Negotiations and Legal Agreement

At this point, I wanted to make sure I was in agreement with my business partners regarding pay and any other legal issues, such as exclusivity. The first thing to discuss was how I would be paid. Working as an agent or middle-person, 15–25 percent commission is typical. Another option involves the company selling the product to you at a certain price and letting you decide the retail price in the foreign market. We agreed that I would buy the products at a certain price and whatever margin I sold the products at would constitute my commission. I was shooting for 15 percent.

Exclusivity was the next item on the agenda. It was important for me to have exclusive rights for Vietnam. If I was going to put in much of the work up front to create a business there, I wanted to insure an opportunity to be rewarded for my work. Exclusivity for the local distributor is another issue. Some distributors may ask for exclusive rights to distribute the product in a country. Some minimum level of sales typically needs to be reached in order to receive exclusivity.

Marketing is the final major piece to discuss. If the distributor has a retail presence it may not require any marketing support. Alternatively, they may say, "We'll take this product but only if you provide us with marketing support." The question is: Who will pay this fee? I am currently suggesting that Wasmund's provide minimal marketing support at first, with the distributor marketing the product in its retail locations.

International Travel: Meeting Potential Distributors

Finally, it's time to travel to the country and meet with the potential distributors. I'll be traveling to Vietnam as soon as I graduate in May. While in the country, I'll be meeting with both the EAC-suggested distributors[11] and those proposed by the Vietnam trade office.

When meeting with the distributors, it's important to have an in-depth understanding of pricing. They will want to know the CIF price, which is the price of the products when they arrive at the port in Vietnam (this includes costs such as shipping and insurance). I'll need to have enough of an understanding to know how low I am willing to go during negotiations. In addition, I will need to be prepared to discuss how various shipment sizes will determine the cost per case.

I'll also have to decide how to get samples of the product there for the initial trip. This entails researching customs issues so as to make sure samples of the product aren't stuck at entry points. Some of the potential distributors may be able to help with this process and ensure that the samples get there without any problems.

Try a Shipment

During your visit, if you are fortunate enough to find a good distributor, the next step is to try a shipment. If my meetings in Vietnam go well, we'll try shipping some cases of Wasmund's single malt whiskey to Asia for the first time. International trade is a fun business. If you have a curiosity about international markets, like to travel internationally, and don't mind risk, this could be the business for you. As with most things, the best way to learn is to get your hands dirty and give it a try. The points outlined above should give you some clarity on how to get started. Good luck!

Questions/Action Points

1. Complete preliminary research on possible import/export activities. What countries and industries caught your interest?

2. Put together a contact list and set up some informational interviews.

3. Define a potential business. Name a potential product, seller, and buyer.

4. Leverage government resources such as the Department of Commerce and the nearest Export Assistance Center for information on the industry and country.

5. Identify some potential distributors through the three methods mentioned in this case study (DOC, EAC, and other organizations).

WATER FROM ICELAND

Stan Otis was in a contemplative mood. He had just hung up the phone after talking with Roger Morey, vice president of Citicorp. Morey had made him an offer in the investment banking sector of the firm. The interview had gone well, and Citicorp management was impressed with Stan's credentials from a major northeastern private university. "I think you can do well here, Stan. Let us know within a week whether you accept the job," Morey had said.

The three-month search had paid off well, Stan thought. Yet an alternative plan complicated the decision to accept the position.

Stan had returned several months before from an extended trip throughout Europe, a delayed graduation present from his parents. Among other places, he had visited Reykjavik, Iceland. Even though he could not communicate well, he found the island enchanting. What particularly fascinated him was the lack of industry and the purity of the natural landscape. In particular, he felt the water tasted extremely good. Returning home, he began to consider making this water available in the United States.

The Water Market in the United States

In order to consider the possibilities of importing Icelandic water, Stan knew that he first had to learn more about the general water market in the United States. Fortunately, some former college friends were working in a market research firm. Owing Stan some favors, these friends furnished him with a consulting report on the water market.

The Consulting Report

Bottled water has a 19 percent share of total non-alcoholic beverage consumption, excluding milk, in the United States in 2007. Bottled water has more than a 16 percent share of total beverage consumption in the United States. The overall distribution of market share is shown in Exhibit 1 and Exhibit 2. Primary types of water available for human consumption in the United States are treated or processed water, mineral water, sparkling or ettervescent water, and spring well water.

Treated or processed water comes from a well stream or central reservoir supply. This water usually flows as tap water and has been purified and fluoridated.

Mineral water is spring water that contains a substantial amount of minerals, which may be injected or occur naturally. Natural mineral water is obtained from underground water strata or a natural spring. The composition of the water at its source is constant, and the source discharge and temperature remain stable. The natural content of the water at the source is not modified by an artificial process.

Sparkling or effervescent water is water with natural or artificial carbonation. Some mineral waters come to the surface naturally carbonated through underground gases but lose their fizz on the surface with normal pressure. Many of these waters are injected with carbon dioxide later on.

Enhanced waters are bottled waters that contain components that are acclaimed to enhance a particular physical aspect. For example, Propel Fitness Water, made by PepsiCo, is a popular brand of enhanced water that boasts its ability to increase hydration.

Minerals are important to the taste and quality of water. The type and variety of minerals present in the water can make it a very healthy and enjoyable drink. The combination of minerals present in the water determines its relative degree of acidity. The level of acidity is measured by the pH factor. A pH 7 rating indicates a neutral water. A higher rating indicates that the water contains more solids, such as manganese calcium, and is said to be "hard." Conversely, water with a lower rating is classified as "soft." Most tap water is soft, whereas the majority of commercially sold waters tend to be hard.

Water Consumption in the United States

Tap water has generally been inexpensive, relatively pure, and plentiful in the United States. Traditionally, bottled water has been consumed in the United States by the very wealthy. In the past several years, however, bottled water has begun to appeal to a wider market.

SOURCES: This study was prepared by Professor Michael R. Czinkota. The author is grateful for the input from Professor Ingjaldur Hannibalsson and the students at the University of Iceland. Assistance form Kenneth Adam Krupa, undergraduate student of the Edmund A. Walsh School of Foreign Service at Georgetown University, is acknowledged. This study was prepared using the following background material: International Bottled Water Association, Beverage Marketing Corporation, Beverage Aisle, 2002. We also gathered statistics from "Non-alcoholic Beverages: The Market-US-April 2008," Mintel Oxygen (London: Mintel International Group Ltd.), http://academic.mintel.com/, accessed March 2, 2009, "Bottled Water-US-December 2008," Mintel Oxygen (London: Mintel International Group Ltd.), http://academic.mintel.com/, accessed March 2, 2009 and the World Fact Book.

Exhibit **1**

Sales in U.S. $ Million and Market Share of U.S. Non-alcoholic Beverage Sales, 2007*

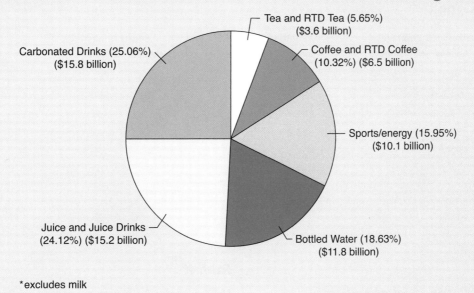

Tea and RTD Tea (5.65%)
($3.6 billion)

Coffee and RTD Coffee
(10.32%) ($6.5 billion)

Carbonated Drinks (25.06%)
($15.8 billion)

Sports/energy (15.95%)
($10.1 billion)

Juice and Juice Drinks
(24.12%) ($15.2 billion)

Bottled Water (18.63%)
($11.8 billion)

*excludes milk

SOURCE: Mintel's estimates based on: Bureau of Labor Statistics, Consumer Expenditure Surveys, Information Resource, Inc. InfoScan® Reviews™
Date Accessed: March 2, 2009

Exhibit **2**

U.S. Bottled Water Market Per Capita Consumption Per Year 1997–2007

Year	Gallons Per Capita Per Year	Annual Percentage Change
1997	13.5	–
1998	14.7	8.3%
1999	16.2	10.2%
2000	16.7	3.5%
2001	18.2	8.6%
2002	20.1	10.6%
2003	21.6	7.2%
2004	23.2	7.5%
2005	25.4	9.7%
2006	27.6	8.4%
2007	29.3	6.4%

SOURCE: Beverage Marketing Corporation
Data Accessed: March 2, 2009

The two main reasons for this change are:

1. An increasing desire to avoid excess consumption of caffeine, sugar, and other substances in coffee and soft drinks
2. Affluence in society

Bottled water consumers are found chiefly in the states of California, Texas, Florida, New York and Arizona. Consumers in California, Texas, Florida, New York, and Arizona account for 70 percent of the bottled water consumption in the United States, with California consuming the most.

Nationwide, consumption is estimated to be nearly 30 gallons per capita per year. Sales from bottled water increased by nearly $1.7 billion from 2005 to 2007. Bottled water sales grew more than any other beverage, except for sports/energy beverages. As Exhibit 3 shows, per capita consumption of bottled water steadily increased from 2001 to 2006.

Exhibit 4 shows the volume of bottled water sold. It rose from only 354.3 million gallons in 1976 to nearly 8.8 billion gallons in 2007, an almost twenty-five fold increase. From 2002 to 2007, bottled water volume increased almost 4 billion gallons, a 75 percent increase.

The volume of bottled water sold in the U.S. (nonsparkling, sparkling, and imported) rose from 4.7 billion gallons in 2000 to 8.8 billion gallons in 2007, roughly an 86.7 percent increase in just seven years. Consumption of nonsparkling water increased 6.8 percent from 2006 to 2007, while consumption of domestic sparkling increased 6.3 percent. Overall, as demonstrated by Exhibit 5, nonsparkling water holds the lion's share of the market.

Exhibit 3

U.S. Per Capita Consumption of Carbonated Soft Drinks, Bottled Water, and Sports Drinks, 2001–2006

Years	Carbonated Beverages		Bottled Water		Sports Drinks	
	Gallons	% Change	Gallons	% Change	Gallons	% Change
2001	54.3	−0.4	19.3	8.4	2.8	12
2002	54.2	−0.2	21.2	9.8	3.1	10.7
2003	53.8	−0.7	22.1	4.2	3.2	3.2
2004	53.7	−0.2	23.8	7.7	3.4	6.2
2005	52.7	−1.9	26.1	9.7	4.1	20.6
2006	50.4	−4.4	27.6	5.7	4.5	9.8

SOURCE: Mintel/Beverage Marketing Corp./*Beverage World*
Date Accessed: March 2, 2009

Exhibit 4

U.S. Bottled Water Market Volume, 1976–2007

Year	Millions of Gallons	Year	Millions of Gallons
1976	354	1995	3,167
1980	605	2002	5,033
1985	1,214	2005	7,507
1990	2,237	2007	8,828

SOURCE: Beverage Aisle, Table and graph data taken from *Beverage Aisle,* 11 (no 8): 38. August 15, 2002. Figures are determined based upon industry contracts with the help of Adams Business Media. Figures from 2005 and 2007 are determined from data from the *Beverage Marketing Corporation* and the *U.S. Census Bureau.*
Date Accessed: March 2, 2009

The most popular type of bottled water is convenience/PET still water with sales growing almost 11 percent from 2006 to 2008. PET stands for polyethylene terephthalate and is a common component in synthetic materials. Examples of convenience/PET water include 20 ounce water bottles. This increase can be attributed to the popularity of a portable healthy drink. Both Jug/bulk still water (not easily transportable and typically left in the left in the home for multiple uses) and sparkling/mineral water sales fell 6 and 2 percent, respectively, between 2006 and 2008. Sparkling/mineral water sales fell nearly 3 percent due to rising prices. On the other hand, Jug/bulk still water was most likely substituted by tap water as households shifted to using tap water because of its very low cost and improving purity. Some reports claim that substituting tap water will cost only $0.50 per year.[1] FDA law also subjects city tap water to thorough filtration and high chemical standards, whereas bottled water is not required to undergo the same treatment. Moreover, given that bottled water

Exhibit 5

U.S. Market Share of Bottled Water by Segment in 2007 (Based on Volume)

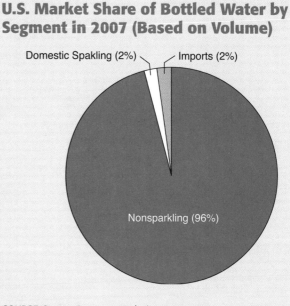

Domestic Spakling (2%) · Imports (2%) · Nonsparkling (96%)

SOURCE: Source: *Beverage Marketing Corporation*
Date Accessed: March 2, 2009

is an industry, companies often lobby for legislation to reduce standards.[2] Lowering standards would ultimately lower costs.

It should be noted, however, that there is a growing demand for enhanced waters. Enhanced waters appeal to consumers for their high-vitamin and low-calorie content. Consumers are often unaware that enhanced waters contain lots of sugar, thus defeating their desire to consume a healthy drink.

According to Exhibit 6, the forecasted sales of bottled water for 2011 are approximately $15.3 billion, an estimated 21 percent increase in sales from 2008.

Exhibit 6

Forecast of U.S. Non-Alcoholic Beverage Sales, 2008–2011

Beverage Type	Sales at current prices, 2008 $million	Sales at current prices, 2009 $million	Sales at current prices, 2010 $million	Sales at current prices, 2011 $million
Carbonated drinks	16,006	16,178	16,354	16,536
Juice and juice drinks	15,123	15,056	14,989	14,918
Bottled water	12,641	13,520	14,411	15,341
Sports/Energy	11,186	12,323	13,477	14,681
Coffee and RTD Coffee	6,931	7,391	7,857	8,343
Tea and RTD tea	3,991	4,412	4,839	5,284

SOURCE: Mintel estimates
Date Accessed: March 2, 2009

Imports of bottled water to the U.S. rose 34.9 percent from 2000 to 2007 from 137.9 to 186.0 million gallons (Exhibit 7). The leading country importing water to the United States is France, with 24.5 percent share of total bottled water imports in 2005, which fell from 53.12 percent in 2001. In 2005 Canada was second with 22.7 percent market share, which is about a 4 percent increase since 2001. Ranked eighth, bottled water from Iceland holds roughly 0.6 percent market share.

Among producers, Nestlé Waters North America is the strong leader with a 27 percent market share in 2008, a 1 percent from 2007. Most of its market share comes from its still water distribution. Its sales are driven primarily by Poland Spring, Nestlé Pure Life, Arrowhead, and Deer Park. The Coca-Cola Company holds 24.5 percent of the market, a 0.3 percent increase from 2007. The Coca-Cola Company's market share is mainly comprised of Dasani and Evian. The market share of PepsiCo is 15 percent, a 1.5 decrease from 2007. Its sales are mainly comprised of Aquafina. Refer to Exhibit 8 for details.

Overall, U.S. bottled water consumption has risen and is projected to continue to grow 12 percent in the next five years after adjusting for inflation. However, the 2008 financial crisis has many producers anticipating actual decreased consumption in the following years as bottled water sales only grew by 0.6 percent in 2008. To try to entice consumers, the industry has worked to appear more environmentally friendly. Many consumer groups have attacked bottled water manufacturers for being wasteful and detrimental to the environment for not using decomposable bottles. To curb such criticism, companies such as Nestlé and PepsiCo have introduced new "eco-shape" bottles that have reduced plastic content by 30 percent.[3] However, the growth of the market for bottled water could continue to shrink in following years.

Exhibit 7

U.S. Bottled Water Market by Segments

	Nonsparkling		Sparkling		Imports		Total	
Year	Volume	Change	Volume	Change	Voume	Change	Volume	Change
1990	1,988	–	176	–	74	–	2,237	–
1995	2,906	46.2%	164	–6.8%	97	31.1%	3,168	41.6%
2000	4,443	52.9%	144	–12.2%	138	42.3%	4,725	49.1%
2005	7,171	61.4%	185	28.5%	183	32.6%	7,523	59.2%
2007	8,435	17.6%	201	8.6%	186	1.6%	8,823	17.3%

*All volume figures reported in millions of gallons
SOURCE: Beverage Marketing Corporation
Date Accessed: March 2, 2009

Exhibit 8

Sales of Bottled Water Companies, from 2007 to 2008*

	52 weeks ending on November 4, 2007		52 weeks ending on November 2, 2008		% change in market share from 2007 to 2008
	$million	% market share	$million	% market share	
Nestlé S.A.	1,478	28.5	1,392	27.2	−1.3
Coca-Cola Co.	1,254	24.2	1,252	24.5	0.3
PepsiCo Inc.	857	16.5	770	15.1	−1.5
Crystal Geyser Water Co.	153	3	153	3	0
Private label	1,076	20.8	1,112	21.8	1
Other	367	7.1	430	8.4	1.3
Total	5,185	100	5,109	100	0

*Excluding sales from Wal-Mart

SOURCE: Mintel based on Information Resources, Inc. InfoScan® Reviews™

Date Accessed: March 2, 2009

Additional Research

Further exploring his import idea, Stan Otis gathered information on various other marketing facets. One of his main concerns was government regulations.

Bottled Water Regulations in the United States

The bottled water industry in the United States is regulated and controlled at two levels—by the federal government and by various state governments. Some states, such as California and Florida, impose even stricter regulations on bottled water than they are required to follow under the federal regulations. Others, such as Arizona, do not regulate the bottled water industry beyond the federal requirements. About 75 percent of bottled water is obtained from springs, artesian wells, and drilled wells. The other 25 percent comes from municipal water systems, which are regulated by the Environmental Protection Agency (EPA). All bottled water is considered food and is thus regulated by the Food and Drug Administration (FDA). Under the 1974 Safe Drinking Water Act, the FDA adopted bottled water standards compatible with EPA'S standards for water from public water systems. As the EPA revises its drinking water regulations, the FDA revises its drinking water regulations, the FDA is required to revise its standards for bottled water or to explain in the Federal Register why it decided not to do so. The FDA requires bottled water products to be clean and safe for human consumption, processed and distributed under sanitary conditions, and produced in compliance with FDA good manufacturing practices. In addition, domestic bottled water producers engaged in interstate commerce are subject to periodic, unannounced FDA inspections.

These standards are regularly maintained with so-called sanitary surveys. Moreover, private testing performed by bottled water manufacturers must be kept on company record for a period of no less than 2 years.

In 2006, the EPA enacted the Ground Water Rule that calls for better testing and measures against fecal contaminates. Recently, the FDA has proposed to test source water with the similar standards as bottled water. Most notably, the FDA wants to test source water from coliform, and, should coliform be detected, the source water would be further tested for E. coli.

In 1991, an investigation by the U.S. House Energy and Commerce Committee found that 25 percent of the higher-priced bottled water comes from the same sources as ordinary tap water, another 25 percent of producers were unable to document their sources of water, and 31 percent exceeded limits of microbiological contamination. The Committee faulted the FDA with negligent oversight. In response, the FDA established, in November 1995, definitions for artesian water, groundwater, mineral water, purified water, sparkling bottled water, sterile water, and well water in order to ensure fair advertising by the industry. These results went into effect in May 1996. They include specification of the mineral content of water that can be sold as mineral water. Previously, mineral water was not regulated by the FDA, which resulted in varying standards for mineral water across states. In addition, under these rules, if bottled water comes from a municipal source, it must be labeled to indicate its origin.

The Icelandic Scenario

Iceland is highly import-dependent with an estimated $6.181 billion in imports compared to an estimated $4.793 billion in exports in 2007, according to the World Fact Book. In terms of products exported, it has little diversity and is dangerously dependent on its fish crop and world fish prices. Until 2008, the country utilized a policy that had, for the past four years, helped economic growth. An Icelandic Export Board had been created and charged with developing new products for exports and aggressively promoting them abroad.

The Ministry of Commerce, after consulting the Central Bank, has the ultimate responsibility in matters concerning import and export licensing. The Central Bank is responsible for the regulation of foreign exchange transactions and exchange controls, including capital controls. It is also responsible for ensuring that all foreign exchange due to residents is surrendered to authorized banks. All commercial exports require licenses. The shipping documents must be lodged with an authorized bank. Receipts exchanged for exports must be surrendered.

All investments by nonresidents in Iceland are subject to individual approval. The participation of nonresidents in Icelandic joint venture companies may not exceed 49 percent. Nonresident-owned foreign capital entering in the form of foreign exchange must be surrendered.

Iceland is a member of the United Nations, the European Free Trade Association, and the World Trade Organization. Iceland enjoys "most favored nation" status with the United States. Under this designation, mineral and carbonated water from Iceland is subject to a tariff of 0.33 cents per liter, and natural (still) water is tariff-free.

As a result of the 2008 financial crisis, great strain has been placed on Icelandic trade—particularly imports. Although the Central Bank of Iceland has worked to boost international trade in the past, imports have been restricted. Imports are limited to necessities—such as food—as the government tries to curb the entrance of foreign currency into its economy.

The Icelandic banking system was crippled as the country's three largest banks collapsed. Meanwhile, the value of its currency fell sharply because of high inflation rates and low financial reserves. Iceland's stock exchange (OMX Nordic Iceland Exchange) plummeted amidst the crisis. The government was further troubled by civil unrest, as Icelanders protested for the government to claim responsibility and to restore the economy.

Despite the international trade strain placed on Iceland as a result of the crisis and stagnation of American demand for bottled water, Icelandic Glacial bottled water from Reykjavik, Iceland, might still see substantial penetration of the U.S. market. In 2007, beverage giant Anheuser-Busch (before being acquired by InBev) developed a plan to distribute Icelandic Glacial bottled water to the widespread U.S. market by 2008. However, in early 2009, the now Anheuser-Busch InBev sold InBev USA, which could potentially hinder the distribution plan of Icelandic Glacial bottled water.

Questions for Discussion

1. Is there sufficient information to determine whether importing water from Iceland would be a profitable business? If not, what additional information is needed to make a determination?

2. Is the market climate in the United States conducive to water imports from Iceland?

3. What are some possible reasons for the fluctuation in the market share held by imports over the past ten years?

4. Should the U.S. government be involved in regulating bottled water products?

DAMAR INTERNATIONAL

Damar International, a fledgling firm importing handicrafts of chiefly Indonesian origin, was established in Burke, Virginia, a suburb of Washington, DC. Organized as a general partnership, the firm is owned entirely by Dewi Soemantoro, its president, and Ronald I. Asche, its vice president. Their part-time, unsalaried efforts and those of Soemantoro's relatives in Indonesia constitute the entire labor base of the firm. Outside financing has been limited to borrowing from friends and relatives of the partners in Indonesia and the United States.

Damar International estimates that its current annual sales revenues are between $20,000 and $30,000. Although the firm has yet to reach the break-even point, its sales revenues and customer base have expanded more rapidly than anticipated in Damar's original business plan. The partners are generally satisfied with results to date and plan to continue to broaden their operations.

Damar International was established to capitalize on Soemantoro's international experience and contacts. As the daughter of an Indonesian Foreign Service officer, Soemantoro spent most of her youth and early adulthood in western Europe and has for the past 18 years resided in the United States. Her immediate family, including her mother, now resides in Indonesia. In addition to English and Malay, Soemantoro speaks French, German, and Italian. Although she has spent the past four years working in information management in the Washington area, first for MCI and currently for Records Management Inc., her interest in importing derives from the six years she spent as a management consultant. In this capacity, she was frequently called on to advise clients about importing clothing, furniture, and decorative items from Indonesia. At the urging of family and friends, she decided to start her own business. While Soemantoro handles the purchasing and administrative aspects of the business, Asche is responsible for marketing and sales.

Damar International currently imports clothing, high-quality brassware, batik accessories, wood carvings, and furnishings from Indonesia. All of these items are handcrafted by village artisans working in a cottage industry. Damar International estimates that 30 percent of its revenues from the sale of Indonesian imports are derived from clothing, 30 percent from batik accessories, and 30 percent from wood carvings, with the remainder divided equally between brassware and furnishings. In addition, Damar markets in the eastern United States sell comparable Thai and Philippine handcrafted items imported by a small

California firm. This firm in turn markets some of Damar's Indonesian imports on the West Coast.

Most of Damar's buyers are small shops and boutiques. Damar does not supply large department stores or retail chain outlets. By participating in gift shows, trade fairs, and handicraft exhibitions, the firm has expanded its customer base from the Washington area to many locations in the eastern United States.

In supplying small retail outlets with handcrafted Indonesian artifacts, Damar is pursuing a niche strategy. Although numerous importers market similar mass-produced, manufactured Indonesian items chiefly to department stores and chain retailers, Damar knows of no competitors that supply handcrafted artifacts to boutiques. Small retailers find it difficult to purchase in sufficient volume to order directly from large-scale importers of mass-produced items. More importantly, it is difficult to organize Indonesian artisans to produce handcrafted goods in sufficient quantity to supply the needs of large retailers.

Damar's policy is to carry little if any inventory. Orders from buyers are transmitted by Soemantoro to her family in Indonesia, who contract production to artisans in the rural villages of Java and Bali. Within broad parameters, buyers can specify modifications of traditional Indonesian wares. Frequently, Soemantoro cooperates with her mother in creating designs that adapt traditional products to American tastes and to the specifications of U.S. buyers. Soemantoro is in contact with her family in Indonesia at least once a week by telex or phone to report new orders and check on the progress of previous orders. In addition, Soemantoro makes an annual visit to Indonesia to coordinate policy with her family and maintain contacts with artisans.

Damar also fills orders placed by Soemantoro's family in Indonesia. The firm, in essence, acts as both an importer and an exporter despite its extremely limited personnel base. In this, as well as with its source of financing, Damar is highly atypical. The firm's great strength, which allows it to fill a virtually vacant market niche with extremely limited capital and labor resources, is clearly the Soemantoro family's nexus of personal connections. Without the use of middlemen, this single bicultural family is capable of linking U.S. retailers and Indonesian village artisans and supplying products that, while unique, are specifically oriented to the U.S. market.

Damar's principal weakness is its financing structure. There are limits to the amount of money that can be borrowed from family and friends for such an enterprise. Working capital is necessary because the Indonesian artisans must be paid before full payment is received from

SOURCE: This case was prepared by Michael R. Czinkota and Laura M. Gould.

U.S. buyers. Although a 10 percent deposit is required from buyers when an order is placed, the remaining 90 percent is not due until 30 days from the date of shipment F.O.B. Washington, DC. Yet, the simplicity of Damar's financing structure has advantages: To date, it has been able to operate without letters of credit and their concomitant cost and paperwork burdens.

One major importing problem has been the paperwork and red tape involved in U.S. customs and quota regulations. Satisfying these regulations has occasionally delayed fulfillment of orders. Furthermore, because the Indonesian trade office in the United States is located in New York rather than Washington, assistance from the Indonesian government in expediting such problems has at times been difficult to obtain with Damar's limited personnel. For example, an order was once delayed in U.S. customs because of confusion between the U.S. Department of Commerce and Indonesian export authorities concerning import stamping and labeling. Several weeks were required to resolve the problem.

Although Damar received regulatory information directly from the U.S. Department of Commerce when it began importing, its routine contact with the government is minimal because regulatory paperwork is contracted to customs brokers.

One of the most important lessons that the firm has learned is the critical role of participating in gift shows, trade fairs, and craft exhibitions. Soemantoro believes that the firm's greatest mistake was not attending a trade show in New York. By connecting with potential buyers, both through trade shows and "walk-in scouting" of boutiques,

Damar has benefited greatly from helpful references from existing customers. Buyers have been particularly helpful in identifying trade fairs that would be useful for Damar to attend. Here too, the importance of Damar's cultivation of personal contacts is apparent.

Similarly, personal contacts offer Damar the possibility of diversifying into new import lines. Through a contact established by a friend in France, Soemantoro is currently planning to import handmade French porcelain and silk blouses.

Damar is worried about sustained expansion of its Indonesian handicraft import business because the firm does not currently have the resources to organize large-scale cottage-industry production in Indonesia. Other major concerns are potential shipping delays and exchange rate fluctuations.

Questions for Discussion

1. Evaluate alternative expansion strategies for Damar International in the United States.

2. Discuss Damar's expansion alternatives in Indonesia and France and their implications for the U.S. market.

3. How can Damar protect itself against exchange rate fluctuations?

4. What are the likely effects of shipment delays on Damar? How can these effects be overcome?

EXPORT MARKETING MIX

PART THREE FOCUSES ON THE COMPANY THAT IS CONSIDERING WHETHER TO FILL AN UNSOLICITED EXPORT ORDER, ON THE MANAGER WHO WANTS TO FIND OUT HOW THE CURRENT PRODUCT LINE CAN BE MARKETED ABROAD, AND ON THE FIRM SEARCHING FOR WAYS TO EXPAND ITS CURRENTLY LIMITED INTERNATIONAL ACTIVITIES. IT CONCENTRATES ON LOW-COST, LOW-RISK INTERNATIONAL EXPANSION, WHICH PERMITS A FIRM TO ENTER THE GLOBAL MARKET WITHOUT AN EXTRAORDINARY COMMITMENT OF HUMAN AND FINANCIAL RESOURCES. THE READER WILL SHARE THE CONCERNS OF SMALL AND MEDIUM-SIZED FIRMS THAT NEED INTERNATIONAL MARKETING ASSISTANCE MOST AND THAT SUPPLY THE LARGEST EMPLOYMENT OPPORTUNITY, BEFORE PROGRESSING TO THE ADVANCED INTERNATIONAL MARKETING ACTIVITIES DESCRIBED IN PART FOUR.

PRODUCT ADAPTATION

The International
MARKETPLACE

10.1

Build-A-Bear: Customized Standardization to Meet Worldwide Customer Desires

Build-A-Bear Workshop was founded in St. Louis, Missouri (USA) in 1997. By 2009, the company operated more than 400 company-owned and franchise stores worldwide. The stores were located in:

North America:	Canada and North America
Europe:	Belgium, Denmark, France, Germany, Ireland, Norway, Russian Federation, Sweden, Netherlands, and United Kingdom
Asia-Pacific:	Australia, Japan, Singapore, South Korea, Taiwan, Thailand, and United Arab Emirates
Africa:	South Africa

Build-A-Bear Workshop was founded on the concept that teddy bears are a tangible symbol of love, security, and friendship—worldwide! The origin of the teddy bear supposedly began in 1903 when President Teddy Roosevelt would not shoot a bear cub while hunting. The spared animal was thereafter referred to as the Teddy Bear.

As an interactive retail workshop, Build-A-Bear Workshop customers experience each phase of the bear-making process. Upon entering the retail store, customers progress through eight stages (stations at the store): Choose Me, Hear Me, Stuff Me and Heart Stuff, Stitch Me, Fluff Me, Dress Me, Name Me, and Take Me Home. Each of these stations engages the customer in the construction of a personalized bear.

© UK ALAN KING/ALAMY

BUILD-A-BEAR WORKSHOP STORES PERMIT DETAILED CUSTOMIZATION AND ARE LOCATED IN NORTH AMERICA, EUROPE, ASIA-PACIFIC, AND AFRICA.

The company's global strategy was released in 2002, when it announced plans to open international stores in Japan, Australia, and Canada. In a short five to six years, the company has more than 400 stores in 20 countries. Stores located in the United States, Puerto Rico, Canada, France, and the United Kingdom are company-owned and operated. In other countries, the global strategy is to grant an exclusive franchise per country. The franchisor is responsible for opening and operating all franchise locations within the country.

The product strategy behind the teddy bears at Build-A-Bear Workshop is consistent worldwide—with customers always following the bear-making process via the stations in the store. Thus, the process, worldwide, is standardized. Then, customers worldwide customize their bears to suit their own interests—whether it is making a sports fanatic bear or one for a special occasion, such as a Valentine's Day. Internationally, the company has adapted bears/furry friends and outfits/accessories to match the desires of local customers.

One need only visit the company's website to see the degree of adaptation that the company has engaged in. Customers first select the country and sometimes the language. For example, a visitor to the United States site can select between English and Español; a visitor to the Canadian site can select either English or Français. Sites in other countries are posted in the country's native language.

Thus, the company has taken a product concept that apparently originated in the United States, standardized the production process worldwide, and customized the product to meet the desires of consumers worldwide. Ultimately, Build-A-Bear Workshop mass produces customized products.

SOURCES: **http://www.buildabear.com**; Matt Slovick, "Want a Teddy Bear? Built It, Too," *Washingtonpost.com*, September 1, 1999, **http://www.washingtonpost.com/wp-srv/style/shopping/features/buildabear.htm**, retrieved February 13, 2009.

Because meeting and satisfying customer needs and expectations is the key to successful marketing, research findings on market traits and potential should be used to determine the optimal degree of customization needed in products and product lines relative to incremental cost of the effort. As seen in *The International Marketplace 10.1,* mass customization is a growing option. Adapting to new markets should be seen not only in the context of one market but also as to how these changes can contribute to operations elsewhere. A new feature for a product or a new line item may have applicability on a broader scale, including the market that originated the product.[1]

Take the Boeing 737, for example. Due to saturated markets and competitive pressures, Boeing started to look for new markets in the Middle East, Africa, and Latin America for the 737 rather than kill the program altogether. To adjust to the idiosyncrasies of these markets, such as softer and shorter runways, the company redesigned the wings to allow for shorter landings and added thrust to the engines for quicker takeoffs. To make sure that the planes would not bounce even if piloted by less experienced captains, Boeing redesigned the landing gear and installed low-pressure tires to ensure that the plane would stick to the ground after initial touchdown. In addition to becoming a success in the intended markets, the new product features met with approval around the world and made the Boeing 737 the best-selling commercial jet in history.

This chapter is concerned with how the international marketer should adjust the firm's product offering to the marketplace, and it discusses the influence of an array of both external and internal variables. A delicate balance has to be achieved between the advantages of standardization and those of localization to maximize export performance. The challenge of intellectual property violation will be focused on as a specialty topic. International marketers must be ready to defend themselves against theft of their ideas and innovations.

Product Variables

The core of a firm's international operations is a product or service. This product or service can be defined as the complex combination of tangible and intangible elements that distinguishes it from the other entities in the marketplace, as shown in Exhibit 10.1. The firm's success depends on how good its product or service is and on how well the firm is able to differentiate the product from the offerings of competitors. Products can be differentiated by their composition, by their country of origin, by their tangible features such as packaging or quality, or by their augmented features such as warranty. Further, the positioning of the product in consumers' minds (for example, Volvo's reputation for safety) will add to its perceived value. The **core product**—for example, the ROM BIOS component of a personal computer or the recipe for a soup—may indeed be the same as or highly similar to those of competitors, leaving the marketer with the other tangible and **augmented features** of the product with which to achieve differentiation. Winnebago Industries, a leading exporter of

Exhibit **10.1**

Elements of a Product

SOURCE: Adapted from Philip Kotler, *Marketing Management,* 11th ed., 408. © 2003. Reprinted by permission of Pearson Education, Inc., Upper Saddle River, New Jersey.

motor homes, is finding increased interest in Europe for its "American-styled" recreation vehicles, or RVs, that offer more features and options, such as automatic transmission and air conditioning, than those made available by local competitors. The only significant modifications made today are the conversion of the electrical system and installation of European-made kitchen appliances familiar to the customer. Furthermore, European buyers are assured that they will receive the same quality of product and service as customers in the United States.[2]

To the potential buyer, a product is a complete cluster of value satisfactions. A customer attaches value to a product in proportion to its perceived ability to help solve problems or meet needs. This will go beyond the technical capabilities of the product to include intangible benefits sought. In Latin America, for example, great value is placed on products made in the United States. If packaging is localized, then the product may no longer have the "*EEUU*" appeal that motivates customers to choose the product over others, especially over local competitors. In some cases, customer behavior has to be understood from a broader perspective. For example, while Chinese customers may view Japanese products quite positively regarding their quality, historic animosity toward Japan may prevent them from buying Japanese goods or cause them to prefer goods from other sources.[3] Given such dramatic variation from market to market, careful assessment of product dimensions is called for.

Standardization versus Adaptation

The first question, after the internationalization decision has been made, concerns the product modifications that are needed or warranted. A firm has four basic alternatives in approaching international markets: (1) selling the product as is in the international marketplace, (2) modifying products for different countries and/or regions, (3) designing new products for foreign markets, and (4) incorporating all the differences into one flexible

Exhibit **10.2**

Standardization versus Adaptation

Factors Encouraging Standardization	Factors Encouraging Adaptation
• Economies of scale in production	• Differing use conditions
• Economies in product R&D	• Government and regulatory influences
• Economies in marketing	• Differing consumer behavior patterns
• "Shrinking" of the world marketplace/economic integration	• Local competition
• Global competition	• True to the marketing concept

product design and introducing a global product. Different approaches for implementing these alternatives exist. For example, a firm may identify only target markets where products can be marketed with little or no modification. A large consumer products marketer may have in its product line for any given markets global products, regional products, and purely local products. Some of these products developed for one market may later be introduced elsewhere, including the global marketer's "home" market. The Dockers line of casual wear originated at Levi Strauss's Argentine unit and was applied to loosely cut pants by Levi's Japanese subsidiary. The company's U.S. operation later adopted both, making Dockers the number-one brand in the category in the United States. Similar success has followed in over 50 country markets entered since.[4] Occasionally, the international marketplace may want something that the domestic market discards. By exporting chicken cuts that are unpopular (e.g., dark meat) or would be hauled off to landfills (such as chicken feet), U.S. poultry producers earn well over $1 billion annually from Russian and Chinese markets.[5]

The overall advantages and drawbacks of standardization versus adaptation are summarized in Exhibit 10.2. The benefits of standardization—that is, selling the same product worldwide—are cost savings in production and marketing. In addition to these economies of scale, many point to economic integration as a driving force in making markets more unified. As a response to integration efforts around the world, especially in Europe, many international marketers are indeed standardizing many of their marketing approaches, such as branding and packaging, across markets. Similarly, having to face the same competitors in the major markets of the world will add to the pressure of having a worldwide approach to international marketing. However, in most cases, demand and usage conditions vary sufficiently to require some changes in the product or service itself.

Coca-Cola, Levi's jeans, and Colgate toothpaste have been cited as evidence that universal product and marketing strategy can work. Yet the argument that the world is becoming more homogenized may actually be true for only a limited number of products that have universal brand recognition and minimal product knowledge requirements for use.[6] Although product standardization is generally increasing, there are still substantial differences in company practices, depending on the products marketed and where they are marketed. As shown in Exhibit 10.3, industrial products such as steel, chemicals, and agricultural equipment tend to be less culturally grounded and warrant less adjustment than consumer goods. Similarly, marketers in technology-intensive industries such as scientific instruments or medical equipment find universal acceptability for their products.[7] Within consumer products, luxury goods and personal care products tend to have high levels of standardization while food products do not.

Adaptation needs in the industrial sector may exist even though they may not be overt. As an example, capacity performance is seen from different perspectives in different countries. Typically, the performance specifications of a German product are quite precise; for example, if a German product is said to have a lifting capacity of 1,000 kilograms, it will perform precisely up to that level. The U.S. counterpart, however, is likely to maintain a safety factor of 1.5 or even 2.0, resulting in a substantially higher payload capacity. Buyers of

Exhibit 10.3

Strategic Adaptation to Foreign Markets

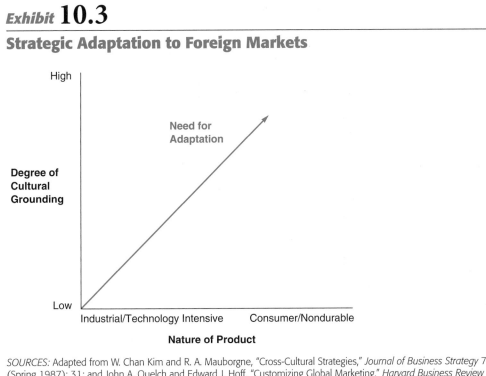

SOURCES: Adapted from W. Chan Kim and R. A. Mauborgne, "Cross-Cultural Strategies," *Journal of Business Strategy* 7 (Spring 1987): 31; and John A. Quelch and Edward J. Hoff, "Customizing Global Marketing," *Harvard Business Review* 64 (May–June 1986): 92–101.

Japanese machine tools have also found that these tools will perform at the specified levels, not beyond them, as would their U.S.-made counterparts. Technology gaps in industrial markets may require adaptation to bridge them, at least for the short term.[8]

Consumer goods generally require product adaptation because of their higher degree of cultural grounding. The amount of change introduced in consumer goods depends not only on cultural differences but also on economic conditions in the target market. Low incomes may cause pressure to simplify the product to make it affordable in the market. For example, Unilever learned that low-income Indians, usually forced to settle for low-quality products, wanted to buy high-end detergents and personal care products but could not afford them in available formats. In response, the company developed extremely low-cost packaging material and other innovations that allowed the distribution of single-use sachets costing the equivalent of pennies rather than the $5 regular-sized containers. Having the same brand on both product formats builds long-term loyalty for the company.[9]

Beyond the dichotomy of standardization and adaptation exist other approaches. The international marketer may design and introduce new products for foreign markets in addition to the firm's relatively standardized "flagship" products and brands. Some of these products developed specifically for foreign clients may later be introduced elsewhere, including in the domestic market. For example, IKEA introduced sleeper sofas in the United States to cater to local tastes but has since found demand for the concept in Europe as well.

Even companies that are noted for following the same methods worldwide have made numerous changes in their product offerings. Coca-Cola introduces 30 to 40 new products per year, the majority of which are never marketed outside of the country of introduction.[10] Although Colgate toothpaste is available worldwide, the company also markets some products locally, such as a spicy toothpaste formulated especially for the Middle East. McDonald's serves abroad the same menu of hamburgers, soft drinks, and other foods that it does in the United States, and the restaurants look the same. But McDonald's has also tried to tailor its product to local styles; for example, in Japan, the chain's trademark character, known as Ronald McDonald in the United States, is called Donald McDonald because it is easier to pronounce that way. Menu adjustments include beer in Germany and wine in France, mutton burgers in India, and rye-bread burgers in Finland.

Increasingly, companies are attempting to develop global products by incorporating differences regionally or worldwide into one basic design. This is not pure standardization, however. To develop a standard in the United States, for example, and use it as a model for other markets is dramatically different from obtaining inputs from the intended markets and using the data to create a standard. What is important is that adaptability is built into the product around a standardized core. The international marketer attempts to exploit the common denominators, but local needs are considered from product development to the eventual marketing of the product. Car manufacturers like Ford and Nissan may develop basic models for regional, or even global, use, but they allow for substantial discretion in adjusting the models to local preferences.

Factors Affecting Adaptation

In deciding the form in which the product is to be marketed abroad, the firm should consider three sets of factors: (1) the market(s) that have been targeted, (2) the product and its characteristics, and (3) company characteristics, such as resources and policy. For most firms, the key question linked to adaptation is whether the effort is worth the cost involved—in adjusting production runs, stock control, or servicing, for example—and the investigative research involved in determining, for example, features that would be most appealing. For most firms, the expense of modifying products should be moderate. In practice, this may mean, however, that the expense is moderate when modifications are considered and acted on, whereas modifications are considered but rejected when the projected cost is substantial.

Studies on product adaptation show that the majority of products have to be modified for the international marketplace one way or another. Changes typically affect packaging, measurement units, labeling, product constituents and features, usage instructions, and, to a lesser extent, logos and brand names.[11]

There is no panacea for resolving questions of adaptation. Many firms are formulating decision-support systems to aid in product adaptation, and some consider every situation independently. Exhibit 10.4 provides a summary of the factors that determine the need

Exhibit 10.4

Factors Affecting Product-Adaptation Decisions

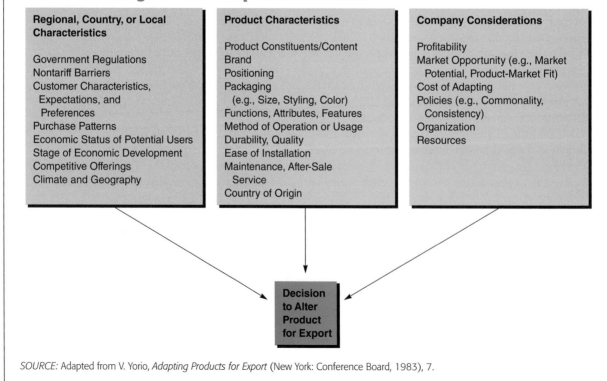

Regional, Country, or Local Characteristics	Product Characteristics	Company Considerations
Government Regulations Nontariff Barriers Customer Characteristics, Expectations, and Preferences Purchase Patterns Economic Status of Potential Users Stage of Economic Development Competitive Offerings Climate and Geography	Product Constituents/Content Brand Positioning Packaging (e.g., Size, Styling, Color) Functions, Attributes, Features Method of Operation or Usage Durability, Quality Ease of Installation Maintenance, After-Sale Service Country of Origin	Profitability Market Opportunity (e.g., Market Potential, Product-Market Fit) Cost of Adapting Policies (e.g., Commonality, Consistency) Organization Resources

Decision to Alter Product for Export

SOURCE: Adapted from V. Yorio, *Adapting Products for Export* (New York: Conference Board, 1983), 7.

for either **mandatory** or **discretionary product adaptation**. All products have to conform to the prevailing environmental conditions, over which the marketer has no control. These relate to legal, economic, and climatic conditions in the market. Further adaptation decisions are made to enhance the exporter's competitiveness in the marketplace. This is achieved by matching competitive offers, catering to customer preferences, and meeting demands of local distribution systems.

The adaptation decision will also have to be assessed as a function of time and market involvement. The more exporters learn about local market characteristics in individual markets, the more they are able to establish similarities and, as a result, standardize their marketing approach, especially across similar markets. This market insight will give the exporters legitimacy with the local representatives in developing a common understanding of the extent of standardization versus adaptation.[12]

The Market Environment

Government Regulations

Government regulations often present the most stringent requirements. Some of the requirements may serve no purpose other than political (such as protection of domestic industry or response to political pressures). Because of the sovereignty of nations, individual firms need to comply but can influence the situation by lobbying, directly or through their industry associations, for the issue to be raised during trade negotiations. Government regulations may be spelled out, but firms need to be ever vigilant in terms of changes and exceptions.

Sweden was the first country in the world to enact legislation against most aerosol sprays on the grounds that they may harm the atmosphere. The ban, which went into effect January 1, 1979, covers thousands of hair sprays, deodorants, air fresheners, insecticides, paints, waxes, and assorted sprays that use Freon gases as propellants. It does not apply to certain medical sprays, especially those used by people who suffer from asthma. The Swedish government, which has one of the world's most active environmental protection departments, was the first to take seriously warnings by scientists that continued release of these chemicals could eventually degrade the earth's ozone layer. As a matter of fact, certain markets, such as Sweden and California, often serve as precursors of changes to come in broader markets and should, therefore, be monitored by marketers.

Although economic integration usually reduces discriminatory governmental regulation, some national environmental restrictions may stay in place. For example, a ruling by the European Court of Justice let stand Danish laws that require returnable containers for all beer and soft drinks. These laws seriously restrict foreign brewers, whose businesses are not on a scale large enough to justify the logistics system necessary to handle returnables.[13] A poll of 4,000 European companies found that burdensome regulatory requirements (e.g., need to ensure that products confirm to national requirements) affecting exports made the United Kingdom the most difficult market to trade with in the EU.[14]

Government regulations are probably the single most important factor contributing to product adaptation and, because of bureaucratic red tape, often the most cumbersome and frustrating factor to deal with. In some cases, government regulations have been passed and are enforced to protect local industry from competition from abroad. In early 2000, the EU decided to limit the use of older commercial aircraft that have "hush kit" mufflers on their engines to cut down airplane noise. U.S. marketers saw a two-dimensional threat in this new regulation: what the EU was really trying to do was keep out U.S. goods (hush kits are typically U.S. made) and, in forcing airlines to buy new aircraft, to direct them to buy European Airbus rather than U.S. Boeing planes.[15]

Some government regulations for adaptation may be controversial both within the company and with some of its constituents, including home governments. Google was forced by the Chinese government to establish a new site, Google.cn, the contents of which are censored by Google in accordance with government preferences. Although a warning label informs the user of the arrangement, the company was criticized for its collaboration to curtail the free flow of information.[16]

Nontariff Barriers

Nontariff barriers include product standards, testing or approval procedures, subsidies for local products, and bureaucratic red tape. The nontariff barriers affecting product adjustments usually concern elements outside the core product. For example, France requires the use of the French language in any offer, presentation, or advertisement, whether written or spoken, in instructions for use and in specification or guarantee terms for goods or services, as well as for invoices and receipts.

Because nontariff barriers are usually in place to keep foreign products out and/or to protect domestic producers, getting around them may be the toughest single problem for the international marketer. The cost of compliance with government regulations is high. The U.S. Department of Commerce estimates that a typical machine manufacturer can expect to spend between $50,000 and $100,000 a year on complying with foreign standards. For certain exports to the European Union, that figure can reach as high as $200,000.[17] As an example, Mack International has to pay $10,000 to $25,000 for a typical European engine certification. Brake system changes to conform with other countries' regulations run from $1,500 to $2,500 per vehicle. Wheel equipment changes will cost up to $1,000 per vehicle. Even with these outlays and the subsequent higher price, the company is still able to compete successfully in the international marketplace.

Small companies with limited resources may simply give up in the face of seemingly arbitrary harassment. For example, product testing and certification requirements have made the entry of many foreign companives into Japanese markets quite difficult, if not impossible.[18] Japan requires testing of all pharmaceutical products in Japanese laboratories, maintaining that these tests are needed because the Japanese may be physiologically different from Americans or Swiss. Similarly, foreign ski products were kept out because Japanese snow was somehow unique. Many exporters, rather than try to move mountains of red tape, have found ways to accommodate Japanese regulations. U.S. cookie marketers, for example, create separate product batches to meet Japanese requirements and avoid problems with the Japanese Health and Welfare Agency.

With a substantial decrease in tariff barriers, nontariff forms of protectionism have increased. On volume alone, agriculture dominates the list. The United States and the EU have fought over beef produced with the aid of hormones. Although it was declared safe for consumption by UN health authorities, the Europeans have banned the importation of such beef and demand appropriate labeling as a precondition for market entry. In a similar debate, an international trade agreement was reached in 2000 that requires the labeling of genetically modified food in the world market. This will mean that U.S. farmers have to separate the increasingly controversial foods from the overall supply.[19]

One way to keep a particular product or producer out of a market is to insist on particular standards. Since the EU chose ISO 9000 as a basis to harmonize varying technical norms of its member states, some of its trading partners have accused it of erecting a new trade barrier against outsiders.[20] ISO 9000, created by the International Organization for Standardization (ISO), is a set of technical standards designed to offer a uniform way of determining whether manufacturing plants and service organizations implement and document sound quality procedures. The ISO itself does not administer or regulate these standards; that job is left to the 160 countries that have voluntarily adopted them. The feeling that ISO registration is a trade barrier comes from the Europeans' earlier start and subsequent control of the program. There were 951,486 ISO registrations by 2008[21] and the five-year period between 2003 and 2008 experienced an almost doubling of certificates worldwide. There is no legal requirement to adopt the standards; however, many agree that these guidelines are already determining what may be sold to and within the EU and increasingly around the world. This is especially true for products for which there are safety or liability issues, or that require exact measurements or calibration, such as medical or exercise equipment.

The International Organization for Standardization also issued the first standards on environmental management, the ISO 14000 series in 1996. The standards, which basically

Exhibit **10.5**

Top 10 Countries for ISO 9000 and ISO 14000 Certificates

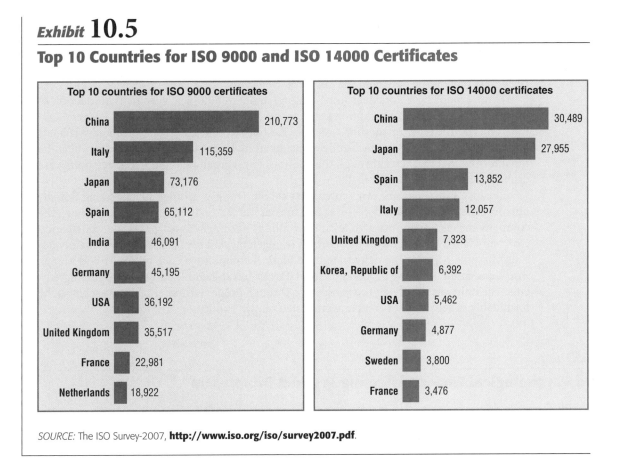

SOURCE: The ISO Survey-2007, **http://www.iso.org/iso/survey2007.pdf**.

require that a firm design an environmental management system, do provide benefits for the adopters such as substantial efficiencies in pollution control (e.g., packaging) and a better public image.[22] However, these standards can also serve as a nontariff barrier if advanced nations impose their own requirements and systems on developing countries that often lack the knowledge and resources to meet such conditions. The adoption rate has increased more rapidly in the last few years to 154,572 by 2008. Exhibit 10.5 provides an overview of the top 10 countries worldwide in terms of ISO 9000 and ISO 14000 certificates at the end of 2007.

Customer Characteristics, Expectations, and Preferences

The characteristics and behavior of intended customer groups are as important as governmental influences on the product adaptation decision. Even when the benefits sought are quite similar, the physical characteristics of customers may dictate product adaptation. Quaker Oats' extension of the Snapple soft drink product to Japan suffered from lack of fit on three dimensions: the glass bottles the drink comes in are almost twice the size that Japanese customers are used to; the product itself was too sweet for the palate; and the Japanese did not feel comfortable with the sediment that characteristically collects at the bottom of the bottle.[23] GE Medical Systems has designed a product specifically for Japan in addition to computerized tomography scanners produced for the U.S. market. The unit is smaller because Japanese hospitals are smaller than most U.S. facilities but also because of the smaller size of Japanese patients. Similarly, Tefal, the world leader in cookware, makes available pans with detachable handles in Japan enabling storage in the traditionally tighter spaces of Japanese kitchens. The general expectation is that products are economical in purchase, use, and maintenance.[24]

Product decisions of consumer-product marketers are especially affected by local behavior, tastes, attitudes, and traditions—all reflecting the marketer's need to gain customers' approval. This group of variables is critical in that it is the most difficult to quantify but is nevertheless essential in making a go/no-go decision. The reason most Europeans who wear western boots buy those made in Spain may be that U.S. footwear manufacturers are unaware of style-conscious Europeans' preference for pointed toes and narrow heels. They view U.S.-made boots as "practical, but not interesting." Similarly, the U.S. Mint has been unable to penetrate the Asian market with its gold coins, which are 22 carat (.916 pure), because customers there value pure gold (i.e., 24 carat, .999 pure).

Three groups of factors determine cultural and psychological specificity in relation to products and services: consumption patterns, psychosocial characteristics, and general cultural criteria. The types of questions asked in Exhibit 10.6 should be answered and systematically recorded for every product under consideration. Use of the list of questions will guide the international marketer through the analysis, ensuring that all the necessary points are dealt with before a decision is made.

Because Brazilians are rarely breakfast eaters, Dunkin' Donuts is marketing doughnuts in Brazil as snacks and desserts and for parties. To further appeal to Brazilians, the company makes doughnuts with local fruit fillings like papaya and guava. Campbell Soup Company failed in Brazil with its offerings of vegetable and beef combinations, mainly because Brazilians prefer the dehydrated products of competitors such as Knorr and Maggi; Brazilians could use these products as soup starters but still add their own flair and ingredients. The only way of solving this problem is through proper customer testing, which can be formidably expensive for a company interested only in exports.

Exhibit 10.6

Cultural and Psychological Factors Affecting Product Adaptation

I. Consumption Patterns
  A. Pattern of Purchase
   1. Is the product or service purchased by relatively the same consumer income group from one country to another?
   2. Do the same family members motivate the purchase in all target countries?
   3. Do the same family members dictate brand choice in all target countries?
   4. Do most consumers expect a product to have the same appearance?
   5. Is the purchase rate the same regardless of the country?
   6. Are most of the purchases made at the same kind of retail outlet?
   7. Do most consumers spend the same amount of time making the purchase?
  B. Pattern of Usage
   1. Do most consumers use the product or service for the same purpose or purposes?
   2. Is the product or service used in different amounts from one target area or country to another?
   3. Is the method of preparation the same in all target countries?
   4. Is the product or service used along with other products or services?

II. Psychosocial Characteristics
  A. Attitudes toward the Product or Service
   1. Are the basic psychological, social, and economic factors motivating the purchase and use of the product the same for all target countries?
   2. Are the advantages and disadvantages of the product or service in the minds of consumers basically the same from one country to another?
   3. Does the symbolic content of the product or service differ from one country to another?
   4. Is the psychic cost of purchasing or using the product or service the same, whatever the country?
   5. Does the appeal of the product or service for a cosmopolitan market differ from one market to another?
  B. Attitudes toward the Brand
   1. Is the brand name equally known and accepted in all target countries?
   2. Are customer attitudes toward the package basically the same?
   3. Are customer attitudes toward pricing basically the same?
   4. Is brand loyalty the same throughout target countries for the product or service under consideration?

III. Cultural Criteria
   1. Does society restrict the purchase and/or use of the product or service to a particular group?
   2. Is there a stigma attached to the product or service?
   3. Does the usage of the product or service interfere with tradition in one or more of the targeted markets?

SOURCE: Adapted from Steuart Henderson Britt, "Standardizing Marketing for the International Market," *Columbia Journal of World Business* 9 (Winter 1974): 32–40. Copyright © 1974 Columbia Journal of World Business. Reprinted with permission.

Often, no concrete product changes are needed, only a change in the product's positioning. Positioning refers to consumers' perception of a brand as compared with that of competitors' brands, that is, the mental image that a brand, or the company as a whole, evokes. A brand's positioning, however, may have to change to reflect the differing lifestyles of the targeted market. Coca-Cola has renamed Diet Coke in many countries Coke Light, and subtly shifted the promotional approach from "weight loss" to "figure maintenance." Coca-Cola positioned its product as a soft drink that would help people feel and look their best rather than one solely centered around weight loss. The company hoped that consumers would perceive these characteristics just by looking at the product's graphics regardless of the name it bore.

On occasion, market realities may cause a shift in the product's positioning. Panda, a northern European chocolate and candy maker, had to place its licorice products in the United Kingdom in healthcare stores after finding traditional channels at British daily-goods retailers blocked by competition.

Health- and beauty-care products often rely on careful positioning to attain a competitive advantage. Timotei shampoo, which is Unilever's brand leader in that category, has a natural-looking image with a focus on mildness and purity. Because people around the world have different hair, Timotei's formula varies, but it always has the same image. The selling of "lifestyle" brands is common for consumer goods for which differentiation may be more difficult. Lifestyles may be more difficult for competitors to copy, but they fare also more susceptible to changes in fashion.[25]

Even the export of TV culture, which is considered by many as a local product, can succeed abroad if concepts are adjusted to reflect local values. By 2006, Muppets were being seen in over 140 countries, including 20 coproductions reflecting local languages, customs, and educational needs. The Russian version of *Sesame Street* is 70 percent locally produced and features Aunt Dasha, a quintessential Russian character who lives in a traditional cottage and spouts folklore and homespun wisdom. In China, new characters were added for local color (such as Little Berry, "Xiao Mei"). The creators of the joint Israeli–Palestinian production, called *Sesame Stories,* hope that the exploits of Dafi, a purple Israeli Muppet, and Haneen, an orange Palestinian one, will help teach mutual respect and understanding by exposing children to each other's culture and breaking down stereotypes.[26] When the Arab satellite network MBC started broadcasting the Simpsons, "Al Shamsoon" had replaced Homer's Duff beer with soda, hot dogs with Egyptian beef sausages, donuts with cookies called kahk, and Moe's Bar had been written out completely.[27]

Exhibit 10.7

Boeing Looked for New Markets for the 737

© IMAGINECHINA VIA AP IMAGES

Economic Development

Management must take into account the present stage of economic development of the overseas market. As seen in *The International Marketplace 10.2*, as a country's economy advances, buyers are in a better position to buy and to demand more sophisticated products

---

The International MARKETPLACE

10.2

Economic Development Critical in Growth Strategies of Luxury Goods Companies

Economic development is changing the way luxury goods marketers are thinking about growth opportunities. While emerging markets currently account for only around 20 percent of luxury goods sales, companies such as Louis Vuitton, Gucci, and Hermes are counting on developing markets to provide a strong source of revenue for the future, particularly as markets in the United States and Europe face an economic downturn.

In 2008, sales of luxury goods in the emerging markets of Russia, China, and India were expected to provide healthy profits—with projections of up to one-third of luxury goods going into these three markets by 2018. For example, Moet & Chandon champagne by Louis Vuitton had exceptional growth in Russia, China, and India in 2007, and the company was setting the stage for Tag Heuer to overtake Omega and Rado for the number one spot in the Indian premium watch market. This stage-setting involved the opening of 30 Tag Heuer boutiques by 2009.

Unlike the Western attitude of "don't flaunt your money," the up and coming middle and upper class in these emerging markets see luxury brands as the easiest way to announce to the world that "they've made it and want everyone to know." In India alone there are millions of these rising "flaunters" who have come from little or no income but are now rising fast in the income category. The Chinese aspiration embodied in the phrase "you are what you buy" currently extends to only about the top two percent of the Chinese population. However, this number is supposed to grow to around 150 million urban middle class by 2025. These consumers are on the verge of being ready and willing to spend—and spend big.

Luxury manufacturers and retailers have already begun paving the way for this growth in spending. The August 2008 issue of *Vogue India* had 16 pages of luxury products on display. Interestingly, the products were not exhibited by popular models or members of the upper echelon of India. Instead, the products were modeled by "regular" Indians—that group of rising flaunters that luxury goods companies are targeting for future growth.

The $100 Fendi baby bib was worn by a toddler in rumpled clothes being held by a toothless woman, the

LUXURY GOODS MARKETERS, LIKE ROLEX, ARE SEARCHING FOR GROWTH OPPORTUNITIES IN EMERGING MARKETS.

$10,000 Hermès Birkin handbag was worn by a mother riding sidesaddle on a motorbike along with her husband and child, and the $200 Burberry umbrella was carried by a barefoot, toothless man. While it may be difficult to imagine how a country with 455 million people who live on less than $1.25 a day will ever be the hot spot for luxury goods, efforts such as those by *Vogue* are examples of the early stages of building brand awareness in areas with a growing middle class.

Actions such as these in emerging markets depict the level of market understanding that businesses must have with regard to economic development. Luxury goods marketers have found a strong potential for their products and want to be well-established in the aspirational set when the time is right!

SOURCES: Jennifer Fishbein, "The People Want Champagne and Watches," *Business Week*, February 6, 2008, **http://www .businessweek.com/globalbiz/content-feb2008026_690656 .htm**, retrieved December 11, 2008; Alison Smale, "For Sales of Luxury Goods, Emerging Markets may not Offset any U.S. Downturn, Analysts Say," *International Herald Tribune*, November 28, 2007, **http://www.iht.com/articles/2007/11/28/business/emerge. php**, retrieved February 13, 2009; "Worldwide Luxury Goods Market Growth Projected to Slow Substantially by End of Year and Head into Recession in 2009," *Bain & Company press release*, October 29, 2008, **http://www.bain.com/bainweb?About/press_release_ detail.asp?id=26657&menu_url=for_the_media.asp**, retrieved February 13, 2009; Heather Timmons, "Trying to Sell Luxury Goods Amid Stark Poverty," *International Herald Tribune*, September 1, 2008, **http://www.iht.com/articles/2008/09/01/business/vogue .php**, retrieved February 13, 2009; **http://www.fibre2fashion .com**, retrieved December 11, 2008.

and product versions. With broad country considerations in mind, the firm can determine potentials for selling certain kinds of products and services. This means managing affordability in a way that makes the marketer's products accessible. For example, C&A, an apparel retailer from Holland, has been able to build a successful business in Latin American countries because it offers reasonable-quality goods at various price points—the best $10, $20, $30 dresses on the market. In Brazil, two-thirds of its sales are to families with incomes below $8,000 per year.[28]

In some cases, the situation in a developing market may require backward innovation; that is, the market may require a drastically simplified version of the firm's product due to lack of purchasing power or usage conditions. It may have to be simple and capable of operating in harsh environments. India's TVS Electronics, for example, has developed a new all-in-one business machine designed especially for small shopkeepers in developing markets. It is part cash register, part computer, and able to tolerate heat, dust, and power outages.[29]

Buying power will affect packaging in terms of size and units sold in a package. In developing markets, products such as cigarettes and razor blades are often sold by the piece so that consumers with limited incomes can afford them. Soft drink companies have introduced four-can packs in Europe, where cans are sold singly even in large stores. On the other hand, products oriented to families, such as food products, appear in larger sizes in developing markets. Pillsbury packages its products in six- and eight-serving sizes for developing countries, whereas the most popular size in the North American market is for two.

Economic conditions may change rapidly, thus warranting change in the product or the product line. During the Asian currency crisis, McDonald's replaced french fries with rice in its Indonesian restaurants due to cost considerations. With the collapse of the local rupiah, potatoes, the only ingredient McDonald's imports to Indonesia, quintupled in price. In addition, a new rice and egg dish was introduced to maintain as many customers as possible despite the economic hardship.[30]

Competitive Offerings

Monitoring competitors' product features, as well as determining what has to be done to meet and beat them, is critical. Competitive offerings may provide a baseline against which the firm's resources can be measured—for example, what it takes to reach a critical market share in a given competitive situation. An analysis of competitors' offerings may reveal holes in the market or suggest avoiding certain market segments. American Hospital Supply, a Chicago-based producer of medical equipment, adjusts its product in a preemptive way by making products that are hard to duplicate. As a result, the firm achieved increases of about 40 percent per year in sales and earnings in Japan over a ten-year period. The products are so specialized that it would be hard for Japanese firms to duplicate them on a mass production basis.

In many markets, the international marketer is competing with global players and local manufacturers and must overcome traditional purchasing relationships and the certainty they provide. What is needed is a niche-breaking product that is adjusted to local needs. TeleGea has had success in Japan because its technology (which has been adjusted to support Asian languages) automates the service-fulfillment process for telecom companies, cutting their delivery costs more than 30 percent.[31]

Climate and Geography

Climate and geography will usually have an effect on the total product offering: the core product; tangible elements, mainly packaging; and the augmented features. Some products, by design, are vulnerable to the elements. Marketing of chocolate products is challenging in hot climates, which may restrict companies' options. Cadbury Schweppes has its own display cases in shops, while Toblerone has confined its distribution to air-conditioned outlets. Nestlé's solution was to produce a slightly different Kit Kat chocolate wafer for Asia with reduced fat content to raise the candy's melting point. The international marketer must consider two sometimes contradictory aspects of packaging for the international market. On the one hand, the product itself has to be protected against longer transit times and possibly for longer shelf life; on the other hand, care has to be taken that no nonallowed preservatives are used. One firm experienced this problem when it tried to sell Colombian guava paste in the United States. Because the packaging could not withstand the longer distribution channels and the longer time required for distribution, the product arrived in stores in poor condition and was promptly taken off the shelves. If a product is exposed to a lot of sunshine and heat as a result of being sold on street corners, as may be the case in developing countries, marketers are advised to use special varnishing or to gloss the product wrappers. Without this, the coloring may fade and make the product unattractive to the customer.

Product Characteristics

Product characteristics are the inherent features of the product offering, whether actual or perceived. The inherent characteristics of products and the benefits they provide to consumers in the various markets make certain products good candidates for standardization, others not. Consumer nondurables, such as food products, generally show the highest amount of sensitivity toward differences in national tastes and habits. Consumer durables, such as cameras and home electronics, are subject to far more homogeneous demand and more predictable adjustment (for example, adjustment to a different technical system in television sets and videotape recorders). Industrial products tend to be more shielded from cultural influences. However, substantial modifications may sometimes be required—in the telecommunications industry, for example—as a result of government regulations and restraints.

Product Constituents and Content

The international marketer must make sure products do not contain ingredients that might be in violation of legal requirements or religious or social customs. As an example, DEP Corporation, a Los Angeles manufacturer with $19 million annual sales of hair and skin products, takes particular pains to make sure that no Japan-bound products contain formaldehyde—an ingredient commonly used in the United States but illegal in Japan. To ensure the purity of the Japanese batches, the company repeatedly cleans and sterilizes the chemical vats, checks all ingredients for traces of formaldehyde, and checks the finished product before shipment. When religion or custom determines consumption, ingredients may have to be replaced in order for the product to be acceptable. In Islamic countries, for example, animal fats have to be replaced by ingredients such as vegetable shortening. In deference to Hindu and Muslim beliefs, McDonald's "Maharaja Mac" is made with mutton in India.

Digital technology is making it easy and inexpensive to substitute product placements in country or region-specific versions of the same movie. Dr. Pepper's logo appeared on a refrigerator in the U.S. version of *Spiderman 2,* whereas overseas the logo belonged to Mirinda, a fruit-flavored soft drink brand that Pepsico markets outside the United States.[32]

Branding

Brand names convey the image of the product or service. The term **brand** refers to a name, term, symbol, sign, or design used by a firm to differentiate its offerings from those of its competitors. Brands are one of the most easily standardized items in the product offering; they may allow further standardization of other marketing elements such as promotional items. The brand name is the vocalizable part of the brand, the brand mark the nonvocalizable part (for example, Camel's "camel"). The brand mark may become invaluable when the product itself cannot be promoted but the symbol can be used. As an example, Marlboro cannot be advertised in most European countries because of legal restrictions on cigarette advertising; however, Philip Morris features advertisements showing only the Marlboro cowboy, who is known throughout the world. Unfortunately, most brands do not have such recognition. The term *trademark* refers to the legally protected part of the brand, indicated by the symbol ®. Increasingly, international markets have found their trademarks violated by counterfeiters who are illegally using or abusing the brand name of the marketer.

The international marketer has a number of options in choosing a branding strategy. The marketer may choose to be a contract manufacturer to a distributor (the generics approach) or to establish national, regional, or worldwide brands. The use of standardization in branding is strongest in culturally similar markets; for example, for U.S. marketers this means Canada and the United Kingdom. Standardization of product and brand do not necessarily move hand in hand; a regional brand may well have local features, or a highly standardized product may have local brand names.[33]

The establishment of worldwide brands is difficult; how can a consumer marketer establish world brands when it sells 800 products in more than 200 countries, most of them under different names? This is Gillette's situation. A typical example is Silkience hair conditioner, which is sold as Soyance in France, Sientel in Italy, and Silkience in Germany. Many companies have, however, massive standardization programs of brand names, packaging, and advertising.[34] Standardizing names to reap promotional benefits can be difficult, because a particular name may already be established in each market and the action may raise objections from local constituents. Despite the opposition, globalizing brands presents huge opportunities to cut costs and achieve new economies of scale.[35]

The psychological power of brands is enormous. Brands are not usually listed on balance sheets, but they can go further in determining success than technological breakthroughs by allowing the marketer to demand premium prices.[36] Brand loyalty translates into profits despite the fact that favored brands may not be superior by any tangible measure. New brands may be very difficult and expensive to build, and as a result, the company may seek a tie-in with something that the customer feels positively toward. For instance, a small Hong Kong–based company markets a hair care product line called American No. 1 because the market prefers U.S. products.

Brand names often do not travel well. Semantic variations can hinder a firm's product overseas. Even the company name or the trade name should be checked out. For instance, Mirabell, the manufacturer of the genuine Mozart Kugel (a chocolate ball of marzipan and nougat), initially translated the name of its products as "Mozart balls" but has since changed the name to the "Mozart round."[37] Most problems associated with brands are not as severe but require attention nevertheless. To avoid problems with brand names in foreign markets, NameLab, a California-based laboratory for name development and testing, suggests these approaches:[38]

1. Translation. Little Pen Inc. would become La Petite Plume, S.A., for example.

2. Transliteration. This requires the testing of an existing brand name for connotative meaning in the language of the intended market. Toyota's MR2 brand faced a challenge in French-speaking countries due to the pronunciation of "MR2" and emphasized the Spyder designation to defuse the connotation. In other instances, positive connotations are sought, as shown in *The International Marketplace 10.3*.

3. Transparency. This can be used to develop a new, essentially meaningless brand name to minimize trademark complexities, transliteration problems, and translation complexities. (Sony is an example.)

4. Transculture. This means using a foreign-language name for a brand. Vodkas, regardless of where they originate, should have Russian-sounding names or at least Russian lettering, whereas perfumes should sound French.

Brands are powerful marketing tools; for example, the chemicals and natural ingredients in any popular perfume retailing for $140 an ounce may cost less than $3.

Packaging

Packaging serves three major functions: protection, promotion, and user convenience. The major consideration for the international marketer is making sure the product reaches the ultimate user in the form intended. Packaging will vary as a function of transportation mode, transit conditions, and length of time in transit. Because of the longer time that products spend in channels of distribution, firms in the international marketplace, especially those exporting food products, have had to use more expensive packaging materials and/or more expensive transportation modes. The solution of food processors has been to utilize airtight, reclosable containers that reject moisture and other contaminants.

Pilferage is a problem in a number of markets and has forced companies to use only shipping codes on outside packaging.[39] With larger shipments, containerization has helped alleviate the theft problem. An exporter should anticipate inadequate, careless, or primitive loading methods. The labels and loading instructions should be not only in English but also in the market's language as well as in symbols.

The International MARKETPLACE

10.3

When There Is More to a Name

Products in Asia often carry brand names that are translated from their original names. They are either direct translations (which result in a different-sounding but same-meaning name in the local language) or phonetic (which result in the same sound but likely different meaning). Given the globalization of markets, marketers not only need to decide whether to translate their brand names but also must consider the form, content, style, and image of such translations.

In Europe and the Americas, brand names such as Coca-Cola and Sharp have no meaning in themselves, and few are even aware of the origins of the name. But to Chinese-speaking consumers, brand names include an additional dimension: meaning. Coca-Cola means "tasty and happy" and Sharp stands for "treasure of sound."

Chinese and Western consumers share similar standards when it comes to evaluating brand names. Both appreciate a brand name that is catchy, memorable, and distinct, and says something indicative of the product. But, because of cultural and linguistic factors, Chinese consumers expect more in terms of how the names are spelled, written, and styled and whether they are considered lucky. When Frito-Lay introduced Cheetos in the Chinese market, it did so under a Chinese name that translates as "Many Surprises"; in Chinese *qi duo*—roughly pronounced "chee-do."

Other similar examples include:

BMW "宝马·"—precious horse

Benz "奔驰·"—speedy: fast speed

Budweiser "百威"—hundreds of power and influence

Heineken "喜力"—happy and powerful

Rejoice "·飘柔"—waving and softening

Windows "·视窗"—a window of vision

J&J "·强生"—strong life

Gucci "古姿"—classic pose

Ikea "宜家"—pleasant home

Canon "佳能"—perfect capability

Ricoh "理光"—neatening light

百事可乐
(A hundred happy things)

© USED WITH PERMISSION OF PEPSICO

声宝
(Treasure of sound)

© USED WITH PERMISSION OF SHARP

A name is like a work of art, and the art of writing (*shu fa*—calligraphy) has had a long tradition all over Asia. Reading Chinese relies more on the visual processes, whereas reading English is dominated by phonological processes (affecting, for example, the processing of features such as font style and color). A name has to look good and be rendered in appealing writing, thereby functioning like a logo or trademark. Companies will consequently have to take into account this dimension of Chinese and Chinese-based languages such as Korean, Japanese, and Vietnamese when they create corporate and brand names and related communications strategies.

In a study of Fortune 500 companies in China and Hong Kong, the vast majority of marketers were found to localize their brand names using, for the most part, transliteration (such as that used by Cheetos).

SOURCES: Nader Tavassoli and Jin K. Han, "Auditory and Visual Brand Identifiers in Chinese and English," *Journal of International Marketing* 10 (no. 2, 2002): 13–28; F. C. Hong, Anthony Pecotich, and Clifford J. Schultz, "Brand Name Translation: Language Constraints, Product Attributes, and Consumer Perceptions in East and Southeast Asia," *Journal of International Marketing* 10 (no. 2, 2002): 29–45; June N. P. Francis, Janet P. Y. Lam, and Jan Walls, "The Impact of Linguistic Differences on International Brand Name Standardization," *Journal of International Marketing* 10 (no. 1, 2002): 98–116; Eugene Sivadas, "Watching Chinese Marketing, Consumer Behavior," *Marketing News*, July 20, 1998, 10; "The Puff, the Magic, the Dragon," *The Washington Post*, September 2, 1994, B1, B3; and "Big Names Draw Fine Line on Logo Imagery," *South China Morning Post*, July 7, 1994, 3.

The promotional aspect of packaging relates mostly to labeling. The major adjustments concern bilingual legal requirements, as in the case of Canada (French and English), Belgium (French and Flemish), and Finland (Finnish and Swedish). Even when the same language is spoken across markets, nuances will exist requiring labeling adaptation. Ace Hardware's Paint Division had to be careful in translating the world "plaster" into Spanish. In Venezuela, *friso* is used, while Mexicans use *yeso*. In the end, *yeso* was used for the paint labels, because the word was understood in all of Latin America.[40] Governmental requirements include more informative labeling on products. Inadequate identification, failure to use the needed languages, or inadequate or incorrect descriptions printed on the labels may cause problems. If in doubt, a company should study competitors' labels.

User convenience is a priority in packaging decisions. Containers need to be strong enough to withstand the logistics challenge, yet must open easily for the consumer. Nestlé, for example, has packaging teams around the world working on improvements and market-specific adjustments. Some are as simple as deeper indentations in the flat end of candy wrappers in Brazil making opening them easier, or deeper notches on single-serve packages of Nescafé in China. A new glue was introduced for Smarties tubes in the United Kingdom to ensure a louder clicking sound when opened.[41]

Package aesthetics must be a consideration in terms of the promotional role of packaging. This mainly involves the prudent choice of colors and package shapes. African nations, for example, often prefer bold colors, but flag colors may be alternately preferred or disallowed. Red is associated with death or witchcraft in some countries. Color in packaging may be faddish. White is losing popularity in industrialized countries because name brands do not want to be confused with generic products, usually packaged in white. Black, on the other hand, is increasingly popular and is now used to suggest quality, excellence, and "class." Package shapes may serve an important promotional role as well. When Grey Goose, a French brand of vodka, researched its international market entry, the development of the bottle took center stage. The company finally settled on a tall (taller than competition) bottle that was a mélange of clear glass, frosted glass, a cutaway of geese in flight, and the French flag.[42] *The International Marketplace 10.4* provides an example of how such packaging issues were addressed by Lipton Ice Tea.

Package size varies according to purchasing patterns and market conditions. For instance, a six-pack format for soft drinks may not be feasible in certain markets because of the lack of refrigeration capacity in households. Quite often, overseas consumers with modest or low discretionary purchasing power buy smaller sizes or even single units in order to stretch a limited budget. For example, the smallest size of laundry detergent available in Latin American supermarkets is 500 grams, while sizes as small as 150 grams may be in demand (and carried by small retailers).[43] The marketer also has to take into consideration perceptions concerning product multiples. In the West, the number 7 is considered lucky, whereas 13 is its opposite. In Japan, the ideogram for the number 4 can also be read as "death." Therefore, consumer products in multiples of four have experienced limited sales. On the other hand, 3 and 5 are considered lucky numbers.

Marketers are wise to monitor packaging technology developments in the world marketplace. A major innovation was in aseptic containers for fruit drinks and milk. Tetra Pak International, the $6.5-billion Swedish company, converted 40 percent of milk sales in Western Europe to its aseptic packaging system, which keeps perishables fresh for five months without refrigeration. The company claimed 5 percent of the fruit juice packaging market and 20 percent of the fruit drink market in the United States. Today, it markets its technologies in over 150 countries.[44]

Finally, the consumer mandate for marketers to make products more environmentally friendly also affects the packaging dimension, especially in terms of the 4 Rs: redesign, reduce, recycle, and reuse. The EU has strict policies on the amounts of packaging waste that are generated and the levels of recycling of such materials.[45] Depending on the packaging materials (20 percent for plastics and 60 percent for glass), producers, importers, distributors, wholesalers, and retailers are held responsible for generating the waste. In Germany, which has the toughest requirements, all packaging must be reusable or recyclable, and packaging must be kept to a minimum needed for proper protection and marketing of the product. Exporters to the EU must find distributors who can fulfill such requirements and agree how to split the costs of such compliance.

The International
MARKETPLACE

10.4

The Re-Packaging of Lipton Ice Tea

Ready-to-drink beverages are popular around the world. To compete in this crowded world of drinks and brands, companies will attempt to use a product's package design as a way to connect with consumers. Essentially, the packaging helps the brand become the benchmark by which the consumer judges all other brands.

Recognizing the importance of packaging in establishing its Lipton tea product in the global marketplace, Pepsi Lipton International (PLI) began to focus on the bottle that the consumer holds in his or her hand. The marketing team at PLI wanted to differentiate its tea product from carbonated beverages and use the bottle to establish tea as a product with a "natural vitality" appeal. The challenge, however, was that each country has its own packaging requirements. Thus, country specific packaging requirements could vary by available technology, physical bottle size, material configuration, filling type, and suppliers. But the marketing team was determined to use a three-dimensional form (the bottle) as a way to communicate Lipton Tea's vitality—an "unwinding energy" for the 18- to 29-year-old target market.

The packaging design challenge was to remain consistent throughout the world and with various types of fill processes (hot fit, aseptic, or glass). Thus, consistency could not mean that each and every country had the exact same packaging. The marketing team needed a design that would convey the iconic nature of the branding process, while adapting to meet the needs of the local market. To achieve this, the design group utilized "implied ergonomics" instead of "actual ergonomics." That is, the package needed to project a good feeling when it was in the hands of the consumer—a feeling that sent the signal that the product could go anywhere with the consumer.

To accomplish its packaging objectives, PLI turned to 4sight Inc, which is a team of experienced product development and structural packaging specialists. Working together, PLI and 4sight created a sustainable and lightweight package that had a first-of-its-kind flex-grip handle. This contemporary bottle could be manufactured in different countries, using the latest technology and production processes, while eliminating 20 millions pounds of waste.

© AP IMAGES/PRNEWSFOTO/PEPSI-COLA COMPANY

The bottle was test-marketed in China, since the Chinese market held similar beliefs about packaging and because the bottling unit in China did not require a change in technology. Following the successful test-market launch in China, the new bottle was distributed into Eastern Europe. The bottle's acceptance in these markets was encouraging, enabling worldwide bottle launches. From Eastern Europe, the bottle design was introduced into Southeast Asia, Latin America, and Australia.

The ability to communicate the message, worldwide, that Lipton Tea was a premium product that was better than the average carbonated soft drink was critical to long-term, global success of the product. The package had to convey that the product was worth a price premium. To accomplish this, companies like PLI spend a lot of time, energy, and dollars on utilizing the package as the brand icon known worldwide.

SOURCES: Jonathan Ford, "Design Trend or Design Icon?" *Beverage World*, June 2007, 103; Erika Flynn, "Lipton's Global Repackaging," *Brand Packaging*, August 2008, 26–30; "Lipton Russia's Refreshing Change," *Beverage World*, June 2007, 103; **http://www.4sightinc.com**.

Throughout all of this, however, the company has to ensure that the product packaging conveys the brand message. *The International Marketplace 10.4* describes how Pepsi Lipton International accomplished this.

Appearance

Adaptations in product styling, color, size, and other appearance features are more common in consumer marketing than in industrial marketing. Color plays an important role in the way consumers perceive a product, and marketers must be aware of the signal being sent by the product's color.[46] Color can be used for brand identification—for example, the yellow of Hertz, red of Avis, and green of National. It can be used for feature reinforcement; for example, Honda adopted the color black to give its motorcycles a Darth Vader look, whereas Rolls

Royce uses a dazzling silver paint that denotes luxury. Colors communicate in a subtle way in developed societies; they have direct meaning in more traditional societies. For instance, in the late 1950s, when Pepsi Cola changed the color of its coolers and vending machines from deep regal blue to light ice blue, the result was catastrophic in Southeast Asia. Pepsi had a dominant market share, which it lost to Coca-Cola because light blue is associated with death and mourning in that part of the world. IKEA has found that Latin families prefer bold colors to the more subdued Scandinavian preferences, and want to display numerous pictures in elaborate frames.[47] AVG Inc., a California-based provider of technology for theme-park rides, had to change the proposed colors of a ride it designed for a park outside Beijing because the client felt they conveyed the wrong attitude for the ride. Instead the client wanted the colors to be "happy" ones.[48] The only way companies can protect themselves against incidents of this kind is through thorough on-site testing, or, as in AVG's case, on-site production.

Method of Operation or Usage

The product as it is offered in the domestic market may not be operable in the foreign market. One of the major differences faced by appliance manufacturers is electrical power systems. In some cases, variations may exist even within a country, such as Brazil. An exporter can learn about these differences through local government representatives or various trade publications such as the U.S. Department of Commerce publication *Electric Current Abroad*.[49] However, exporters should determine for themselves the adjustments that are required by observing competitive products or having their product tested by a local entity.

Many complicating factors may be eliminated in the future through standardization efforts by international organizations and by the conversion of most countries to the metric system. When Canada adopted the metric system in 1977–1978, many U.S. companies were affected. Perfect Measuring Tape Company in Toledo, for example, had to convert to metric if it wanted to continue selling disposable paper measuring tape to textile firms in Canada. Once the conversion was made, the company found an entire world of untapped markets. It was soon shipping nearly 30 percent of its tape to overseas markets as disparate as Australia and Zimbabwe. More than 2,000 U.S. businesses use the metric system in research and development (e.g., Eastman Kodak) and marketing (e.g., Procter & Gamble's Scope mouthwash is sold in incremental liter bottles) to take advantage of global economies of scale.[50]

Products that rely heavily on the written or spoken language have to be adapted for better penetration of the market. For example, SPSS, Inc., the marketer of statistical software, localizes both DOS and Windows for German, English, Kanji, and Spanish. Producing software in the local language has also proven to be a weapon in the fight against software piracy.

An exporter may also have to adapt the product to different uses. MicroTouch Systems, which produces touch-activated computer screens for video poker machines and ATMs, makes a series of adjustments in this regard. Ticket vending machines for the French subway need to be waterproof, since they are hosed down. Similarly, for the Australian market, video poker screens are built to take a beating because gamblers there take losing more personally than anywhere else.[51]

The international marketer should be open to ideas for new uses for the product being offered. New uses may substantially expand the market potential of the product. For example, Turbo Tek, Inc., which produces a hose attachment for washing cars, has found that foreign customers have expanded the product's functions. In Japan, Turbo-Wash is used for cleaning bamboo, and the Dutch use it to wash windows, plants, and the sidings of their houses.[52] To capture these phenomena, observational research, rather than asking direct questions, may be the most appropriate approach. This is especially true in emerging and developing markets, in order to understand how consumers relate to products in general and to the marketer's offer in particular.

Quality

Many Western exporters must emphasize quality in their strategies because they cannot compete on price alone. Many new exporters compete on value in the particular segments they have chosen. In some cases, producers of cheaper Asian products have forced international marketers to reexamine their strategies, allowing them to win contracts on the basis of technical advantage. To maintain a position of product superiority, exporting firms must invest in research and development for new products as well as manufacturing methods. For example, Sargent and Burton, a small Australian producer of high-technology racing boats, invested in CAD/CAM technology to develop state-of-the-art racing boats that have proven successful in international competition against sophisticated overseas entries.[53]

Marketers themselves may seek endorsement of their efforts from governmental or consumer organizations. Many car exporters to the United States (e.g., the Koreans) have become more popular in the market by doing well in J.D. Power and other car rankings, a fact that may then be used in promotional efforts. However, China's initial efforts to sell cars to the European Union and the United States is drawing scrutiny regarding the quality, especially safety, of their exports.[54]

Increasingly, many exporters realize that they have to meet international quality standards to compete for business abroad and to win contracts from multinational corporations. Foreign buyers, especially in Europe, are requiring compliance with international ISO 9000 quality standards. For example, German electronics giant Siemens requires ISO compliance in 50 percent of its supply contracts and is encouraging other suppliers to conform. This has helped eliminate the need to test parts, which saves time and money. DuPont began its ISO drive after losing a big European order for polyester films to an ISO-certified British firm. However, many exporters still have grave misunderstandings about the certification process and its benefits.[55]

Many exporters may overlook the importance of product quality, especially when entering a developing market. While Fedder, the largest U.S. manufacturer of room air conditioners, had planned to market its most up-to-date air conditioners in China, it quickly discovered that even that was not going to be enough. The reason was that many Chinese buyers want a more sophisticated product than the standard unit sold in the United States. In China, it is a major purchase, and therefore often a status symbol. The Chinese also want special features such as remote control and an automatic air-sweeping mechanism.[56]

Service

When a product sold overseas requires repairs, parts, or service, the problem of obtaining, training, and holding a sophisticated engineering or repair staff is not easy. If the product breaks down, and the repair arrangements are not up to standard, the image of the product will suffer. In some cases, products abroad may not even be used for their intended purpose and may thus require modifications not only in product configuration but also in service frequency. For instance, snow plows exported from the United States are used to remove sand from driveways in Saudi Arabia. Closely related to servicing is the issue of product warranties. Warranties not only are instructions to customers about what to do if the product fails within a specified period of time, but also are effective promotional tools.

Country-of-Origin Effects

The country of origin of a product, typically communicated by the phrase "Made in (country)," has a considerable influence on the quality perceptions of a product. The manufacture of products in certain countries is affected by a built-in positive or negative stereotype of product quality. These stereotypes become important when important dimensions of a product category are also associated with a country's image.[57] For example, if an exporter has a positive match of quality and performance for its exports, the country of origin should be a prominent feature in promotional campaigns. If there is a mismatch, the country of origin may have to be hidden through the adoption of a carefully crafted brand name (e.g., a Hong Kong–based apparel company chose the name Giordano), or the product sold with the help of prestigious partners whose image overshadows concerns about negative country-of-origin perceptions. This issue may be especially important to emerging countries, which need to increase exports, and for importers, who source products from countries different from those where they are sold.[58] In some markets, however, there may be a tendency to reject domestic goods and embrace imports of all kinds.

When the country of origin does matter to consumers, it is in the exporter's best interest to monitor consumers' perceptions. For example, many consumers around the world perceive Nokia as a Japanese brand, which does not have a negative impact on the company despite the incorrect appropriation, and has led to no action by Nokia. However, a Japanese car maker Daihatsu suffered in the U.S. market at the time of its launch because it was perceived as a Korean brand. For this and other reasons, Daihatsu is no longer in the U.S. but concentrates its efforts on Latin America.

Some products have fared well in the international marketplace despite negative country-of-origin perceptions. For example, Belarus tractors (manufactured both in Belarus and Russia) have fared well in Europe and the United States not only because of their reasonable price tag but also because of their ruggedness. Only the lack of an effective network has hindered the company's ability to penetrate Western markets to a greater degree.[59]

Country-of-origin effects lessen as customers become more informed. Also, as more countries develop the necessary bases to manufacture products, the origin of the products becomes less important. This can already be seen with so-called hybrid products (for example, a U.S. multinational company manufacturing the product in Malaysia). The argument has been made that with the advent of more economic integration, national borders become less important.[60] However, many countries have started strategic campaigns to improve their images to promote exports and in some cases to even participate in joint promotional efforts. In some cases, this means the development of new positive associations rather than trying to refute past negative ones.[61]

French and Italian trade and consumer groups are lobbying the European Union to require mandatory place-of-origin labels. The issue has become a sensitive one for high-end European fashion houses that are starting to make products oveaseas in low-cost countries.[62]

Company Considerations

Product adaptation is an international marketing tool that serves a variety of strategic needs. In addition to the need to cater to market differences and to compete effectively with others in these markets, the role of product adaptation is also to reach internal goals more effectively.[63]

The issue of product adaptation most often climaxes in the question "Is it worth it?" The answer depends on the firm's ability to control costs, correctly estimate market potential, and finally, secure profitability, especially in the long term. The costs of product adaptation may be recouped through higher export performance. Arguments to the contrary exist as well. While new markets, such as those in central Europe, may at present require product adaptation, some marketers may feel that the markets are too small to warrant such adjustments and may quite soon converge with western European ones, especially in light of their EU membership. Sales of a standard product may be smaller in the short term, but long-term benefits will justify the adoption of this approach.[64] However, the question that used to be posed as "Can we afford to do it?" should now be "Can we afford not to do it?"

The decision to adapt should be preceded by a thorough analysis of the market. Formal market research with primary data collection and/or testing is warranted. From the financial standpoint, some firms have specific return-on-investment levels to be satisfied before adaptation (for instance, 25 percent), whereas some let the requirement vary as a function of the market considered and also the time in the market—that is, profitability may be initially compromised for proper market entry.

Most companies aim for consistency in their marketing efforts. This translates into the requirement that all products fit in terms of quality, price, and user perceptions. An example of where consistency may be difficult to control is in the area of warranties. Warranties can be uniform only if the use conditions do not vary drastically and if the company is able to deliver equally on its promise anywhere it has a presence.

A critical element of the adaptation decision has to be human resources; that is, individuals to make the appropriate decisions. Individuals are needed who are willing to make risky decisions and who know about existing market conditions. Many companies benefit from having managers from different (types of) countries, giving them the experience and the expertise to make decisions between standardization and adaptation.

Product Counterfeiting

Counterfeit goods are any goods bearing an unauthorized representation of a trademark, patented invention, or copyrighted work that is legally protected in the country where it is marketed. The International Trade Commission estimated that U.S. companies lose a total of $200–250 billion every year because of product counterfeiting and other infringement of intellectual property.[65] Hardest hit are the most innovative, fastest-growing industries, such as computer software, pharmaceuticals, and entertainment. In 2007, the software, publishing, and distribution industries lost more than $47 billion due to software theft.[66] Worldwide, more than 35 percent of all software is illegally copied, with the percentage rising to over 90 percent in countries such as Bangladesh, Sri Lanka, Zimbabwe, and Moldova.

The practice of product counterfeiting has spread to high-technology products and services from the traditionally counterfeited products: high-visibility, strong brand name consumer goods. In addition, previously the only concern was whether a company's product was being counterfeited; now, companies have to worry about whether the raw materials and components purchased for production are themselves real.[67] The European Union estimates that trade in counterfeit goods now accounts for 2 percent of total world trade. The International Chamber of Commerce estimates the figure at 5–7 percent. In general, countries with lower per capita incomes, higher levels of corruption in government, and lower levels of involvement in the international trade community tend to have higher levels of intellectual property violation.[68]

Counterfeiting problems occur in three ways and, depending on the origin of the products and where they are marketed, require different courses of action. Approximately 75 percent of counterfeit goods are estimated to be manufactured outside the United States, and 25 percent are either made in this country or imported and then labeled here. Problems originating in the United States can be resolved through infringement actions brought up in federal courts. Counterfeit products that originate overseas and that are marketed in the United States should be stopped by the customs barrier. Enforcement has been problematic because of the lack of adequate personnel and the increasingly high-tech character of the products. When an infringement occurs overseas, action can be brought under the laws of the country in which it occurs. The sources of the largest number of counterfeit goods are China, Brazil, Taiwan, Korea, and India, which are a problem to the legitimate owners of intellectual property on two accounts: the size of these countries' own markets and their capability to export. For example, Nintendo estimates its annual losses to video-game piracy at $700 million, with the origin of the counterfeits mainly in China. In one series of raids in China, 3 million illegal copies of game software for Game Boys were seized.[69] Countries in Central America and the Middle East are typically not sources but rather markets for counterfeit goods. Counterfeiting is a pervasive problem in terms not only of geographic reach but of the ability of the counterfeiters to deliver products, and the market's willingness to buy them.

The first task in fighting intellectual property violation is to use patent application or registration of trademarks or mask works (for semiconductors). The rights granted by a patent, trademark, copyright, or mask work registration in the United States confer no protection in a foreign country. There is no such thing as an international patent, trademark, or copyright. Although there is no shortcut to worldwide protection, some advantages exist under treaties or other international agreements. These treaties, under the World Intellectual Property Organization (WIPO), include the Paris Convention for the Protection of Industrial Property, the Patent Cooperation Treaty, the Berne Convention for the Protection of Literary and Artistic Works, and the Universal Copyright Convention, as well as regional patent and trademark offices such as the European Patent Office. Applicants are typically granted international protection throughout the member countries of these organizations.[70]

After securing valuable intellectual property rights, the international marketer must act to enforce, and have enforced, these rights. Four types of action against counterfeiting are legislative action, bilateral and multilateral negotiations, joint private sector action, and measures taken by individual companies, as shown in Exhibit 10.8. It is essential that all the parties interact to gain the most effect. For example, the pharmaceutical industry lobbied to make sure that provisions for patent protection in the NAFTA agreement were meticulously spelled out.

Exhibit 10.8

Measures to Combat Counterfeiting

	Public Sector	Private Sector
Legislative	TRIPS Section 301 Action	Input to Trade Negotiation Lobbying
Cooperation and Liaison	Conventions	Industry Organizations
Enforcement	Customs Services Task Forces	Task Forces Private Investigation
Prevention	Education	Education/Publicity Strategic Alliances Marketing Strategy Assessment and Application

SOURCE: Ilkka A. Ronkainen, "Protecting Intellectual Property Rights: Public and Private Sector Interaction," working paper, Georgetown University, February 2006.

In the legislative arena, the Omnibus Tariff and Trade Act of 1984 amended Section 301 of the Trade Act of 1974 to clarify that the violation of intellectual property rights is an unreasonable practice within the statute. The act also introduced a major carrot-and-stick policy: The adequacy of protection of intellectual property rights of U.S. manufacturers is a factor that will be considered in the designation of Generalized System of Preferences (GSP) benefits to countries. The United States has denied selected countries duty-free treatment on goods because of lax enforcement of intellectual property laws.

The Trademark Counterfeiting Act of 1984 made trading in goods and services using a counterfeit trademark a criminal rather than a civil offense, establishing stiff penalties for the practice. The Semiconductor Chip Protection Act of 1984 clarified the status and protection afforded to semiconductor masks, which determine the capabilities of the chip. Protection will be available to foreign-designed masks in the United States only if the home country of the manufacturer also maintains a viable system of mask protection. The Intellectual Property Rights Improvement Act requires the U.S. Trade Representative to set country-specific negotiating objectives for reciprocity and consideration of retaliatory options to assure intellectual property protection. The United States imposed punitive tariffs on $39 million of Brazilian imports to retaliate against Brazil's refusal to protect U.S. pharmaceutical patents. The United States has threatened to take China's lack of progress against piracy to the World Trade Organization.[71]

The U.S. government is seeking to limit counterfeiting practices through bilateral and multilateral negotiations as well as education. A joint International Trade Administration and Patent and Trademark Office action seeks to assess the adequacy of foreign countries' intellectual property laws and practices, to offer educational programs and technical assistance to countries wishing to establish adequate systems of intellectual property protection, to offer educational services to the industry, and to review the adequacy of U.S. legislation in the area. Major legislative changes have occurred in the past few years in, for example, Taiwan and Singapore, where penalties for violations have been toughened. The WTO agreement includes new rules on intellectual property protection, under the Trade-Related

Aspects of Intellectual Property Rights (TRIPS) agreement. Under them, trade-related intellectual property will enjoy 20 years of protection. More than 100 countries have indicated they will amend their laws and improve enforcement. Violators of intellectual property will face retaliation not only in this sector, but in others as well.[72] Similarly, the NAFTA agreement provides extensive patent and copyright protection.

A number of private-sector joint efforts have emerged in the battle against counterfeit goods. In 1978, the International Anti-Counterfeiting Coalition was founded to lobby for stronger legal sanctions worldwide. The coalition consists of 375 members. The International Chamber of Commerce established the Counterfeit Intelligence and Investigating Bureau in London, which acts as a clearinghouse capable of synthesizing global data on counterfeiting.

In today's environment, companies are taking more aggressive steps to protect themselves. The victimized companies are losing not only sales but also goodwill in the longer term if customers believe they have the real product rather than a copy of inferior quality. In addition to the normal measures of registering trademarks and copyrights, companies are taking steps in product development to prevent knockoffs of trademarked goods. For example, new authentication materials in labeling are extremely difficult to duplicate. Some companies, such as Disney, have tried to legitimize offenders by converting them into authorized licenses. These local companies would then be a part of the fight against counterfeiters, because their profits would be the most affected by fakes.

Many companies maintain close contact with the government and the various agencies charged with helping them. Computer makers, for example, loan testing equipment to customs officers at all major U.S. ports, and company attorneys regularly conduct seminars on how to detect pirated software and hardware. Other companies retain outside investigators to monitor the market and stage raids with the help of law enforcement officers. For example, when executives at WD-40 Co., the maker of an all-purpose lubricant, realized a counterfeit version of their product was being sold in China, they launched an investigation and then approached local authorities about the problem. Offending retailers were promptly raided and, in turn, led police to the counterfeiter.[73]

The issue of intellectual property protection will become more important for the United States and the EU in future years. It is a different problem from what it was a decade ago, when the principal victims were manufacturers of designer items. Today, the protection of intellectual property is crucial in high technology, one of the strongest areas of U.S. competitiveness in the world marketplace. The ease with which technology can be transferred and the lack of adequate protection of the developers' rights in certain markets make this a serious problem.[74]

Summary

Marketers may routinely exaggerate the attractiveness of international markets, especially in terms of their similarity. Despite the dramatic impact of globalization as far as market convergence is concerned, distances, especially cultural and economic, challenge the marketer to be vigilant.[75] The international marketer must pay careful attention to variables that may call for an adaptation in the product offering. The target market will influence the adaptation decision through factors such as government regulation and customer preferences and expectations. The product itself may not be in a form ready for international market entry in terms of its brand name, its packaging, or its appearance. Some marketers make a conscious decision to offer only standardized products; some adjust their offerings by market.

Like the soft drink and packaged-goods marketers that have led the way, the newest marketers of world brands are producing not necessarily identical products, but recognizable products. As an example, the success of McDonald's in the world marketplace has been based on variation, not on offering the same product worldwide. Had it not been for the variations, McDonald's would have limited its appeal unnecessarily and would have been far more subject to local competitors' challenges.

Firms entering or participating in the international marketplace will certainly find it difficult to cope with the conflicting needs of the domestic and international markets. They will be certain to ask whether adjustments in their product offerings, if the marketplace requires them, are worthwhile. There are, unfortunately, no magic formulas for addressing the problem of product adaptation. The answer seems to lie in adopting formal procedures to assess products in terms of the markets' and the company's own needs.

The theft of intellectual property—ideas and innovations protected by copyrights, patents, and trademarks—is a critical problem for many industries and countries, accelerating with the pace of market globalization.[76] Governments have long argued about intellectual property protection, but the lack of results in some parts of the world has forced companies themselves to take action on this front.

Key Terms

core product
augmented features
mandatory/discretionary product
    adaptation

positioning
backward innovation
brand

Generalized System of Preferences
    (GSP)

Questions for Discussions

1. Comment on the statement "It is our policy not to adapt products for export."

2. What are the major problems facing companies, especially smaller ones, in resolving product adaptation issues?

3. How do governments affect product adaptation decisions of firms?

4. Are standards like those promoted by the International Organization for Standardization (see http://www.iso.ch) a hindrance or an opportunity for exporters?

5. Is any product ever the same everywhere it is sold?

6. Propose ways in which intellectual property piracy could be stopped permanently.

Internet Exercises

1. How can marketers satisfy the 4 Rs of environmentally correct practice? See, for example, the approaches proposed by the Duales System Deuschland (www.gruener-punkt.de).

2. The software industry is the hardest hit by piracy. Using the Web site of the Business Software Alliance (http://www.bsa.org), assess how this problem is being tackled.

Recommended Readings

Chadha, Radha and Paul Husband. *The Cult of Luxury Brand: Inside Asia's Love Affair with Luxury.* London: Nicholas Brealey Publishing, 2007.

Czinkota, Michael R., Ilkka A. Ronkainen, and Bob Donath. *Mastering Global Markets: Strategies for Today's Trade Globalist.* Mason, OH: Thomson South-Western, 2004.

Levitt, Theodore. *The Marketing Imagination.* New York: Free Press, 1986.

Phillips, Tim. *Knockoff: The Deadly Trade in Counterfeit Goods: The True Story of the World's Fastest Growing Crime Wave.* London: Kogan Page, 2007.

Smith, Preston G. *Flexible Product Development: Building Agility for Changing Markets.* Hoboken, NJ: Jossey-Bass, 2007.

Tisch, Jonathan M. *Chocolates on the Pillow aren't Enough: Reinventing the Customer Experience.* Hoboken, NY: Wiley, 2007.

EXPORT PRICING

The International
MARKETPLACE

Now for the Hard Part: Getting Paid for Exports

Smaller exporters often do not have the luxury that big corporations have to weigh risks of doing business abroad and to investigate the creditworthiness of foreign customers. The result may be a hard lesson about the global economy: Foreign sales do not help much when you cannot collect the bill.

More often than not, exporters will do less checking on an international account than they will on a domestic customer. For example, a U.S. fan blade manufacturer with less than $10 million in revenue was left with an overdue payment of $127,000 owed by an African customer. Before shipping the goods, the company had failed to call any of the customer's credit references. These turned out to be nonexistent—just like the company itself.

The simple guideline of selling only in countries where you are most likely to get paid may not be enough, given that collection periods for some of the more attractive markets may be long (see table). However, in many cases, basic information about the economic and political conditions in markets may be enough to warrant caution. Old World Industries Inc., a midsized maker of antifreeze fluid and other automotive products, found that out after selling 500,000 gallons of antifreeze to a customer in a newly emerging market. After two years, Old World was still waiting to be paid in full, because the foreign bank it dealt with had trouble obtaining U.S. dollars despite the country's strengthening foreign reserve position.

The length of time required for U.S. companies in different industries to collect on the average bill varies dramatically. The data in the table are for the second half of 2005 as reported by members of the Foreign Credit Interchange Bureau. The number of days for Argentina has increased dramatically in recent years due to currency restrictions placed on importers. For some countries, such as Pakistan, no number is available because all transactions are on a cash-in-advance or letter-of-credit basis.

Country	Number of Days
Kenya	210
Italy	136
Argentina	119
Canada	100
Switzerland	85
Brazil	83
United Kingdom	75
Germany	72
Mexico	69
Japan	59
Taiwan	59
Finland	54

SOURCES: Data updated by interview with FCIB, February 8, 2006; "Congratulations, Exporter! Now about Getting Paid . . ." *Business Week,* January 17, 1994, 98; and "Small Firms Hit Foreign Obstacles in Billing Overseas," *The Wall Street Journal,* December 8, 1992, B2.

This chapter will focus on the pricing decision from the exporter's point of view: the setting of export price, terms of sale, and terms of payment. The setting of export prices is complicated by factors such as increased distance from the markets, currency fluctuations, governmental policies such as duties, and typically longer and different types of channels of distribution. In spite of new factors influencing the pricing decision, the objective remains the same: to create demand for the marketer's offerings and to do so profitably in the long term. In achieving this, financing arrangements for export transactions are critical for two reasons: to secure sales and to combat various types of risk. As *The International Marketplace 11.1* shows, the most crucial assurance a firm will want in its export process is getting paid.

Two special considerations in export pricing—leasing and dumping—are discussed at the end of this chapter. Foreign market pricing (by subsidiaries) and intracompany transfer pricing, that is, pricing for transactions between corporate entities, will be discussed in Chapter 17.

Price Dynamics

Price is the only element of the marketing mix that is revenue generating; all the others are costs. It should therefore be used as an active instrument of strategy in the major areas of marketing decision making. Price serves as a means of communication with the buyer by providing a basis for judging the attractiveness of the offer. It is a major competitive tool in meeting and beating close rivals and substitutes. Competition will often force prices down, whereas intracompany financial considerations have an opposite effect. Prices, along with costs, will determine the long-term viability of the enterprise.[1]

Price should not be determined in isolation from the other marketing mix elements. It may be used effectively in positioning the product in the marketplace—for example, JLG, the world leader in self-propelled aerial work platforms used at construction sites, is able to charge premium prices because its products are powered by nonpolluting hydrogen fuel cells.[2] The feasibility range for price setting established by demand, competition, costs, and legal considerations may be narrow or wide in a given situation (for example, the pricing of a commodity versus an innovation). Regardless of how narrow the gap allowed by these factors, however, pricing should never be considered a static element. The marketer's ultimate goal is to make the customer as inelastic as possible; that is, the customer should prefer the marketer's offer even at a price premium.

Similarly, pricing decisions cannot be made in isolation from the other functions of the firm. Effective financial arrangements can significantly support the marketing program if they are carefully formulated between the finance and marketing areas. Sales are often won or lost on the basis of favorable credit terms to the buyer. With large numbers of competent firms active in international markets, financing packages—often put together with the help of governmental support—have become more important. Customers abroad may be prepared to accept higher prices if they can obtain attractive credit terms.

A summary of international pricing situations is provided as a matrix in Exhibit 11.1. Pricing challenges—such as pricing for a new market entry, changing price either as an attack strategy or in response to competitive changes, and multiple-product coordination in cases of related demand—are technically the same as problems encountered in domestic markets. The scope of these pricing situations will vary according to the degree of foreign involvement and the type of market encountered.

In first-time pricing, the general alternatives are (1) skimming, (2) following the market price, and (3) penetration pricing. The objective of **skimming** is to achieve the highest possible contribution in a short time period. For an exporter to use this approach, the product has to be unique, and some segments of the market must be willing to pay the high price. As more segments are targeted and more of the product is made available, the price is gradually lowered. The success of skimming depends on the ability and speed of competitive reaction.

If similar products already exist in the target market, **market pricing** can be used. The final customer price is determined based on competitive prices, and then both production

Exhibit **11.1**

International Pricing Situations

Pricing Situation	International Involvement		
	Exporting	Foreign-Market Pricing	Intracompany Pricing
First-Time Pricing			
Changing Pricing			
Multiple-Product Pricing			

SOURCES: Elements of the model adopted from Howard Forman and Richard A. Lancioni, "International Industrial Pricing Strategic Decisions and the Pricing Manager: Some Key Issues," *Professional Pricing Society,* October 9, 1999, at **http://www.pricingsociety.com/pdf-4-index/international-industrial-pricing.pdf**; and Helmut Becker, "Pricing: An International Marketing Challenge," in *International Marketing Strategy,* eds. Hans Thorelli and Helmut Becker (New York: Pergamon Press, 1980): 203–215.

and marketing must be adjusted to the price. This approach requires the exporter to have a thorough knowledge of product costs, as well as confidence that the product life cycle is long enough to warrant entry into the market. It is a reactive approach and may lead to problems if sales volumes never rise to sufficient levels to produce a satisfactory return. Although firms typically use pricing as a differentiation tool, the international marketing manager may have no choice but to accept the prevailing world market price.

When **penetration pricing** is used, the product is offered at a low price intended to generate volume sales and achieve high market share, which would compensate for a lower per-unit return. One company found, for example, that a 20 percent reduction in average pricing roughly doubled the demand for its product.[3] This approach typically requires mass markets, price-sensitive customers, and decreasing production and marketing costs as sales volumes increase. The basic assumption of penetration pricing is that the lower price will increase sales, which may not always be the case. This approach can also be used to discourage other marketers from entering the market.

Price changes are called for when a new product is launched, when a change occurs in overall market conditions (such as a change in the value of the billing currency), or when there is a change in the exporter's internal situation, such as costs of production. An exporter may elect not to change price even though the result may be lower profitability. However, if a decision is made to change prices, related changes must also be considered. For example, if an increase in price is required, it may at least initially be accompanied by increased promotional efforts. Price changes usually follow changes in the product's stage in the life cycle. As the product matures, more pressure will be put on the price to keep the product competitive despite increased competition and less possibility of differentiation.

With multiple-product pricing, the various items in the line may be differentiated by pricing them appropriately to indicate, for example, an economy version, a standard version, and the top-of-the-line version. One of the products in the line may be priced to protect against competitors or to gain market share from existing competitors. The other items in the line are then expected to make up for the lost contribution of such a "fighting brand."

Although foreign market pricing and intracompany pricing are discussed later in conjunction with global pricing challenges, they do have an impact on the exporter as well. For example, distributors in certain markets may forgo certain profit margins in exchange for exclusivity. This may mean that the exporter will have to lower prices to the distributor and take less profit to ensure sales and to remain competitive, or, if the market conditions warrant it, to move into more direct distribution.[4] Similarly, the exporter, in providing products to its own sales offices abroad, may have to adjust its transfer prices according to foreign exchange fluctuations. Exporters with operations across multiple diverse markets will have to align and coordinate prices to minimize problems such as gray-market imports.[5]

The Setting of Export Prices

In setting the export price, a company can use a process such as the one summarized in Exhibit 11.2. The setting of export price is influenced by both internal and external factors, as well as their interaction.[6] Internal factors include the company's philosophy, goals,

Exhibit 11.2

Stages in Setting of Export Prices

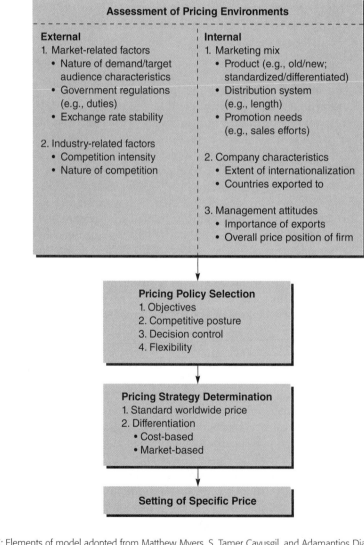

SOURCES: Elements of model adopted from Matthew Myers, S. Tamer Cavusgil, and Adamantios Diamantopoulos, "Antecedents and Actions of Export Pricing Strategy: A Conceptual Framework and Research Propositions," *European Journal of Marketing* 36 (numbers 1/2, 2002): 159–189; Barbara Stöttinger, "Strategic Export Pricing: A Long and Winding Road," *Journal of International Marketing* 9 (no. 1, 2001): 40–63; S. Tamer Cavusgil, "Pricing for Global Markets," *Columbia Journal of World Business* 31(Winter 1996): 66–78; and Alfred R. Oxenfeld, "Multistage Approach to Pricing," *Harvard Business Review* 38 (July/August 1960): 120–132.

and objectives; the costs of developing, producing, and marketing the export product; and the nature of the exporter's product and industry. External factors relate to international markets in general or to a specific target market in particular and include such factors as customer, regulatory, competitive, and financial (mainly foreign exchange) characteristics. The interaction of these elements causes pricing opportunities and constraints in different markets. For example, company management may have decided to challenge its main foreign competitor in the competitor's home market. Regulation in that market requires expensive product adaptation, the cost of which has to be absorbed now for the product to remain competitive.

As in all marketing decisions, the intended target market will establish the basic premise for pricing. Factors to be considered include the importance of price in customer decision making (in particular, the ability to pay), the strength of perceived price-quality relationships, and potential reactions to marketing-mix manipulation by marketers. For example, an exporter extending a first-world product to an emerging market may find its potential unnecessarily limited and thus opt for a new version of a product that costs a fraction of the original version. Customers' demands will also have to be considered in terms of support required by the intermediary. The marketing mix must be planned to match the characteristics of the target market. Pricing will be a major factor in determining the desired brand image as well as the distribution channels to be used and the level of promotional support required. Conversely, mix elements affect pricing's degrees of freedom. If the use of specialty channels is needed to maintain product positioning, price will be affected.

Pricing policies follow from the overall objectives of the firm for a particular target market and involve general principles or rules that a firm follows in making pricing decisions.[7] Objectives include profit maximization, market share, survival, percentage return on investment, and various competitive policies such as copying competitors' prices, following a particular competitor's prices, or pricing so as to discourage competitors from entering the market. For example, an exporter entering a new market may allow wholesalers and retailers above-normal profit margins to encourage maximum sales volume, geographic distribution, and loyalty. Loctite Corporation, in marketing adhesives for industrial uses, requires a highly technical selling effort from distributors and uses higher-than-average compensation packages to secure their services. These types of demands are common especially in the early stages of the export effort and may have to be satisfied to gain market penetration. They should be phased out later on, however, with sales volume increases making up for the difference.[8]

Where and how decisions are made is also an important part of an exporter's pricing policy. The degree to which the pricing decision should be localized is a function of competitive conditions and economic conditions, such as inflation. The more dissimilarity and uncertainty a market displays, the more local pricing decision has to be pushed. The inherent conflicts between local sales (focused on volume generation) and upper management (focused on profitability) have to be settled as well.[9] This is especially true in terms of pricing flexibility; in other words, the willingness to adjust prices under certain circumstances, such as competitive changes or currency fluctuations.

Export Pricing Strategy

The general price-setting strategies in international marketing are a standard worldwide price and dual pricing, which differentiates between domestic and export prices. Two approaches exist within each of these general strategies: cost-based, which is relatively simple to establish and implement, and market-based, in which the focus is on customer demand and competition. In general, the more involved the company is in exports, the more likely they are to use market-driven methods, whereas those new to exports prefer the cost-driven methods.

The **standard worldwide price** may be the same price regardless of the buyer (if foreign product or foreign marketing costs are negligible) or may be based on average unit costs of fixed, variable, and export-related costs. Uniform pricing is advisable when customers worldwide are aware of the prices charged, and when there is little chance of differentiating the product or the service to warrant price differences.

Exhibit 11.3

Export Pricing Alternatives

Production Costs	Standard	Cost Plus	Marginal Cost
Materials	2.00	2.00	2.00
Fixed costs	1.00	1.00	0.00
Additional foreign product costs	0.00	0.10	0.10
Production overhead	0.50	0.50	0.00
Total production costs	3.50	3.60	2.10
U.S. marketing costs	1.50	0.00	0.00
General and administrative	0.75	0.75	0.00
Foreign marketing	0.00	1.00	1.00
Other foreign costs	0.00	1.25	1.25
Subtotal	5.75	6.60	4.35
Profit margin (25%)	1.44	1.65	1.09
Selling price	7.19	8.25	5.44

SOURCE: Adapted from Lee Oster, "Accounting for Exporters," *Export Today* 7 (January 1991): 28–33.

In **dual pricing**, domestic and export prices are differentiated, and two approaches to pricing products for export are available: cost-driven and market-driven methods. If a cost-based approach is decided upon, the marketer can choose between the **cost-plus method** and the **marginal cost method**. The cost-plus strategy is the true cost, fully allocating domestic and foreign costs to the product. Although this type of pricing ensures margins, the final price may be so high that the firm's competitiveness is compromised. This may cause some exporters to consider a flexible cost-plus strategy, which allows for variations in special circumstances.[10] Discounts may be granted, depending on the customer, the size of the order, or the intensity of competition. Changes in prices may also be put into effect to counter exchange rate fluctuations. Despite these allowances, profit is still a driving motive, and pricing is more static as an element of the marketing mix.

The marginal cost method considers the direct costs of producing and selling products for export as the floor beneath which prices cannot be set. Fixed costs for plants, R&D, and domestic overhead as well as domestic marketing costs are disregarded. An exporter can thus lower export prices to be competitive in markets that otherwise might have been beyond access. On certain occasions, especially if the exporter is large, this may open a company to dumping charges, because determination of dumping may be based on average total costs, which are typically considerably higher. A comparison of the cost-oriented methods is provided in Exhibit 11.3. Notice how the rigid cost-plus strategy produces the highest selling price by full-cost allocation.

Market-differentiated pricing calls for export pricing according to the dynamic conditions of the marketplace. For these firms, the marginal cost strategy provides a basis, and prices may change frequently due to changes in competition, exchange rate changes, or other environmental changes. The need for information and controls becomes crucial if this pricing alternative is to be attempted. Exporters are likely to use market-based pricing to gain entry or better penetration in a new market, ignoring many of the cost elements, at least in the short term.

While most exporters, especially in the early stages of their internationalization, use cost-plus pricing, it usually does not lead to desired performance.[11] It typically leads to pricing too high in weak markets and too low in strong markets by not reflecting prevailing market conditions. But as experience is accumulated, the process allows for more flexibility and is more market-driven. Care has to be taken, however, that the cost of implementing a pricing-adaptation strategy does not outweigh the advantages of having a more adapted price.[12]

Interestingly, exporters have been found to differ in their pricing approaches by their country of origin. For example, Korean firms price more competitively in international markets than domestically, while U.S. firms seem to consider costs and profits more in setting their export prices.[13]

Overall, exporters see the pricing decision as a critical one, which means that it is typically taken centrally under the supervision of top-level management. In addition to product quality, correct pricing is seen as the major determinant of international marketing success.[14]

Export-Related Costs

In preparing a quotation, the exporter must be careful to take into account and, if possible, include unique export-related costs. These are in addition to the normal costs shared with the domestic side. They include the following:

1. The cost of modifying the product for foreign markets

2. Operational costs of the export operation: personnel, market research, additional shipping and insurance costs, communications costs with foreign customers, and overseas promotional costs

3. Costs incurred in entering the foreign markets: tariffs and taxes; risks associated with a buyer in a different market (mainly commercial credit risks and political risks); and risks from dealing in other than the exporter's domestic currency—that is, foreign exchange risk

The combined effect of both clear-cut and hidden costs results in export prices that far exceed domestic prices. The cause is termed **price escalation**. In the case of Geochron, the marketer of world time indicators, the multilayered distribution system with its excessive markups makes the price of a $1,300 clock exceed $3,800 in Japan.[15]

Four different export scenarios are compared with a typical domestic situation in Exhibit 11.4. The first case is relatively simple, adding only the CIF (cost, insurance, freight) and tariff charges. The second adds a foreign importer and thus lengthens the foreign part of the distribution channel. In the third case, a **value-added tax (VAT)**, such as those used within the European Union, is included in the calculations. This is imposed on the full export selling price, which represents the "value added" to or introduced into the country from abroad. In Italy, for example, where most food items are taxed at 2 percent, processed meat is taxed at 18 percent because the government wants to use the VAT to help reduce its trade deficit. The fourth case simulates a situation typically found in less-developed countries where distribution channels are longer. Lengthy channels can easily double the landed (CIF) price.

Complicating price escalation in today's environment may be the fact that price increases are of different sizes across markets. If customers are willing to shop around before purchasing, the problem of price differentials will make distributors unhappy and could result in a particular market's being abandoned altogether.

Price escalation can be overcome through creative strategies, depending on what the demand elasticities in the market are. Typical methods, such as the following, focus on cost cutting:

1. Reorganize the channel of distribution. The example in Exhibit 11.5, based on import channels for spaghetti and macaroni in Japan, shows how the flow of merchandise through the various wholesaling levels has been reduced to only an internal wholesale distribution center, resulting in savings of 25 percent and increasing the overall potential for imports. Shortening of channels may, however, bring about other costs such as demands for better discounts if a new intermediary takes the role of multiple previous ones.

2. Adapt the product. The product itself can be reformulated by including less expensive ingredients or unbundling costly features, which can be made optional. Remaining features, such as packaging, can also be made less expensive. If price escalation causes price differentials between markets, the product can be altered to avoid cross-border price shopping by customers. For example, Geochron alters its clocks' appearance from one region to another.

Exhibit 11.4

Export Price Escalation

International Marketing Channel Elements and Cost Factors	Domestic Wholesale-Retail Channel	Export Market Cases			
		CASE 1 Same as Domestic with Direct Wholesale Import CIF/Tariff	**CASE 2** Same as 1 with Foreign Importer Added to Channel	**CASE 3** Same as 2 with VAT Added	**CASE 4** Same as 3 with Local Foreign Jobber Added to Channel
Manufacturer's net price	6.00	6.00	6.00	6.00	6.00
+ Insurance and shipping cost (CIF)	—	2.50	2.50	2.50	2.50
= Landed cost (CIF value)	—	8.50	8.50	8.50	8.50
+ Tariff (20% on CIF value)	—	1.70	1.70	1.70	1.70
= Importer's cost (CIF value + tariff)	—	10.20	10.20	10.20	10.20
+ Importer's margin (25% on cost)	2.55	2.55	2.55	2.55	2.55
+ VAT (16% on full cost plus margin)	—	—	—	2.04	2.04
= Wholesaler's cost (= importer's price)	6.00	10.20	12.75	14.79	14.79
+ Wholesaler's margin (331/3% on cost)	2.00	3.40	4.25	4.93	4.93
+ VAT (16% on margin)	—	—	—	.79	.79
= Local foreign jobber's cost (= wholesale price)	—	—	—	—	20.51
+ Jobber's margin (331/3% on cost)	—	—	—	—	6.84
+ VAT (16% on margin)	—	—	—	—	1.09
= Retailer's cost (= wholesale or jobber price)	8.00	13.60	17.00	20.51	28.44
+ Retailer's margin (50% on cost)	4.00	6.80	8.50	10.26	14.22
+ VAT (16% on margin)	—	—	—	1.64	2.28
= Retail price (what consumer pays)	12.00	20.40	25.50	32.41	44.94
Percentage price escalation over domestic		70%	113%	170%	275%
Percentage price escalation over Case 1			25%	59%	120%
Percentage price escalation over Case 2				27%	76%
Percentage price escalation over Case 3					39%

SOURCE: Helmut Becker, "Pricing: An International Marketing Challenge," in *International Marketing Strategy,* eds. Hans Thorelli and Helmut Becker (New York: Pergamon Press, 1980), 215.

3. Use new or more economical tariff or tax classifications. In many cases, products may qualify for entry under different categories that have different charges levied against them. The marketer may have to engage in a lobbying effort to get changes made in existing systems, but the result may be considerable savings. For example, when the U.S. Customs Service ruled that multipurpose vehicles were light trucks and, therefore, subject to 25 percent tariffs (and not the 2.5 percent levied on passenger cars), Britain's Land Rover had to argue that its $75,000+ luxury vehicle, the Range Rover, was not a truck. When the United States introduced a luxury tax (10 percent of the part of a car's price that exceeded $33,000), Land Rover worked closely with the U.S. Internal Revenue Service to establish that its vehicles were trucks (since trucks were free of such tax). Before it got its way, however, it had to make slight adjustments in the vehicle, since the IRS defines a minimum weight for trucks at 6,000 lbs. Land Rover's following-year model weighed in at 6,019 lbs.[16]

4. Assemble or produce overseas. In the longer term, the exporter may resort to overseas sourcing or eventually production. Through foreign sourcing, the exporter may accrue an additional benefit to lower cost: **duty drawbacks**. An exporter may be refunded up to 99 percent of duties paid on imported goods when they are exported or incorporated in articles that are subsequently exported within five years of the importation.[17] Levi Strauss, for example, imports zippers from China that are sewn into the company's

Exhibit 11.5

Distribution Adjustment to Decrease Price Escalation

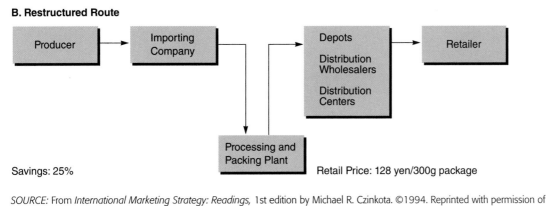

A. Conventional Route

Producer → Import Agent → Processing and Packing Plant → Primary Wholesaler → Intermediary Wholesaler → Small Wholesaler → Retailer

Retail Price: 170 yen/300g package

B. Restructured Route

Producer → Importing Company → Processing and Packing Plant → Depots (Distribution Wholesalers, Distribution Centers) → Retailer

Savings: 25%

Retail Price: 128 yen/300g package

SOURCE: From *International Marketing Strategy: Readings,* 1st edition by Michael R. Czinkota. ©1994. Reprinted with permission of South-Western, a division of Thomson Higher Education: **http://www.thomsonrights.com**.

jackets and jeans in the United States. The amount that Levi's reclaims can be significant, because the duty on zippers can climb to 30 percent of the product's value.[18]

If the marketer is able to convey a premium image, it may then be able to pass the increased amounts to the final price.

Appropriate export pricing requires the establishment of accounting procedures to assess export performance. Without such a process, hidden costs may bring surprises. For example, negotiations in the Middle Eastern countries or Russia may last three times longer than the average domestic negotiations, dramatically increasing the costs of doing business abroad. Furthermore, without accurate information, a company cannot combat phenomena such as price escalation.

Terms of Sale

The responsibilities of the buyer and the seller should be spelled out as they relate to what is and what is not included in the price quotation and when ownership of goods passes from seller to buyer. **Incoterms** are the internationally accepted standard definitions for terms of sale set by the International Chamber of Commerce (ICC) since 1936. The Incoterms 2000 (for the next ten years) went into effect on January 1, 2000, with significant revisions to better reflect changing transportation technologies and the increased use of electronic communications.[19] Although the same terms may be used in domestic transactions, they gain new meaning in the international arena. The terms are grouped into four categories, starting with the terms whereby the seller makes the goods available to the buyer only at the seller's own premises (the "E"-terms), followed by the group whereby the seller is called upon to deliver the goods to a carrier appointed by the buyer (the "F"-terms). Next are the "C"-terms, whereby the seller has to contract for carriage but without assuming the risk of

Exhibit 11.6

Selected Trade Terms (Incoterms)

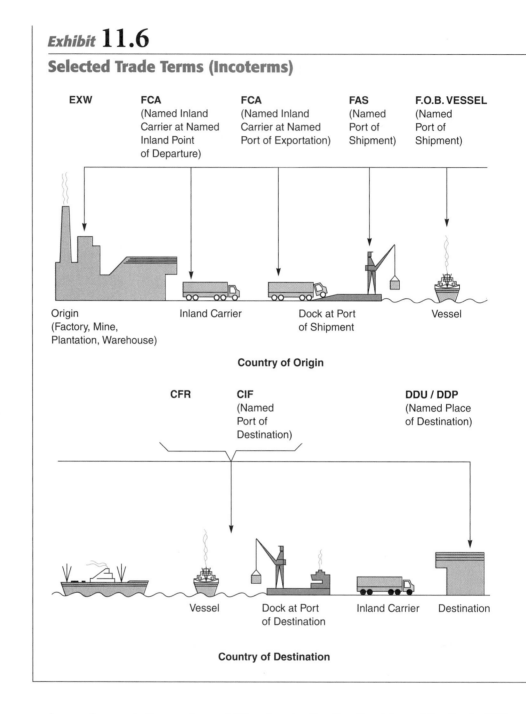

Country of Origin

Country of Destination

loss or damage to the goods or additional costs after the dispatch, and finally the "D"-terms, whereby the seller has to bear all costs and risks to bring the goods to the destination determined by the buyer. The most common of the Incoterms used in international marketing are summarized in Exhibit 11.6. Incoterms are available in 31 languages.

Prices quoted *ex-works (EXW)* apply only at the point of origin, and the seller agrees to place the goods at the disposal of the buyer at the specified place on the date or within the fixed period. All other charges are for the account of the buyer.

One of the new Incoterms is *free carrier (FCA)*, which replaced a variety of FOB terms for all modes of transportation except vessel. FCA (named inland point) applies only at a designated inland shipping point. The seller is responsible for loading goods into the means of transportation; the buyer is responsible for all subsequent expenses. If a port of exportation is named, the costs of transporting the goods to the named port are included in the price.

Free alongside ship (FAS) at a named port of export means that the exporter quotes a price for the goods, including charges for delivery of the goods alongside a vessel at the port.

The seller handles the cost of unloading and wharfage; loading, ocean transportation, and insurance are left to the buyer.

Free on board (FOB) applies only to vessel shipments. The seller quotes a price covering all expenses up to, and including, delivery of goods on an overseas vessel provided by or for the buyer.

Under *cost and freight (CFR)* to a named overseas port of import, the seller quotes a price for the goods, including the cost of transportation to the named port of debarkation. The cost of insurance and the choice of insurer are left to the buyer.

With cost, insurance, and freight *(CIF)* to a named overseas port of import, the seller quotes a price including insurance, all transportation, and miscellaneous charges to the point of debarkation from the vessel. If other than waterway transport is used, the terms are *CPT* (carriage paid to) or *CIP* (carriage and insurance paid to).

With *delivered duty paid (DDP)*, the seller delivers the goods, with import duties paid, including inland transportation from import point to the buyer's premises. With *delivered duty unpaid (DDU)*, only the destination customs duty and taxes are paid by the consignee. Ex-works signifies the maximum obligation for the buyer; delivered duty paid puts the maximum burden on the seller.

Careful determination and clear understanding of terms used, and their acceptance by the parties involved, are vital if subsequent misunderstandings and disputes are to be avoided not only between the parties but also within the marketer's own organization.[20]

These terms are also powerful competitive tools. The exporter should therefore learn what importers usually prefer in the particular market and what the specific transaction may require. An inexperienced importer may be discouraged from further action when receiving a price quote of "ex-plant Jessup," Maryland, whereas "CIF Helsinki" covers all expenses up to the part in Helsinki, which will enable the Finnish importer to easily handle the remaining costs because they are incurred in a familiar environment.

Increasingly, exporters are quoting more inclusive terms. The benefits of taking charge of the transportation on either a CIF or DDP basis include the following: (1) exporters can offer foreign buyers an easy-to-understand "delivered cost" for the deal; (2) by getting discounts on volume purchases for transportation services, exporters cut shipping costs and can offer lower overall prices to prospective buyers; (3) control of product quality and service is extended to transport, enabling the exporter to ensure that goods arrive to the buyer in good condition; and (4) administrative procedures are cut for both the exporter and the buyer.[21] These benefits are highlighted in *The International Marketplace 11.2.*

When taking control of transportation costs, however, the exporter must know well in advance what impact the additional costs will have on the bottom line. If the approach is implemented incorrectly, exporters can be faced with volatile shipping rates, unexpected import duties, and restive customers. Most exporters do not want to go beyond the CIF quotation because of uncontrollables and unknowns in the destination country. Whatever terms are chosen, the program should be agreed to by the exporter and the buyer(s) rather than imposed solely by the exporter.

Freight forwarders are useful in determining costs, preparing quotations, and making sure that unexpected changes do not cause the exporter to lose money. Freight forwarders are useful to the exporter not only as facilitators and advisors but also in keeping down some of the export-related costs. Rates for freight and insurance provided to freight forwarders may be far more economical than to an individual exporter because of large-volume purchases, especially if export sales are infrequent. Some freight forwarders can also provide additional value-added services, such as taking care of the marketer's duty-drawback receivables.

Terms of Payment

Export credit and terms add another dimension to the profitability of an export transaction. The exporter has in all likelihood already formulated a credit policy that determines the degree of risk the firm is willing to assume and the preferred selling terms. The main objective is to meet the importer's requirements without jeopardizing the firm's financial goals.

The International
MARKETPLACE

Penetrating Foreign Markets by Controlling Export Transport

Companies that once sought short-term customers to smooth out recessions are searching for every means to get an edge over rivals in foreign markets. To achieve that, they are increasingly concerned about controlling quality and costs at every step, including the transportation process.

International transport costs are far higher than domestic shipping expenses. International ocean transport typically accounts for 4 to 20 percent of the product's delivered cost but can reach as high as 50 percent for commodity items. That makes transport a factor in situations in which a single price disadvantage can cause a sale to be lost to a competitor.

Still, most U.S. companies continue to abdicate responsibility for export shipping—either because they lack sophistication or simply because they do not want to be bothered. Increasingly, however, companies like Deere & Co. are paying for, controlling, and often insuring transport from their factories either to foreign ports or to the purchasing companies' doorsteps. This means that they are shipping on a DDP basis.

Deere exports premium-quality farm and lawn equipment worldwide. For years, it has insisted on overseeing transportation because it boosts sales, cuts costs, and ensures quality. "We have a long-term relationship with our dealers. It is in our best interest to do the transport job," says Ann Salaber, an order control manager in the export order department.

One goal of Deere's approach to transportation is to ensure that equipment is delivered to customers in good condition—a factor that Deere considers central to its image as a quality producer. The goal is to avoid cases like the one in which an inexperienced customer insisted on shipping a tractor himself. The tractor was unwittingly put on a ship's deck during a long, stormy sea voyage and arrived in terrible shape.

The process also helps when Deere tractor windows are inadvertently broken during transport. Because Deere closely monitors the tractors, it can quickly install new windows at the port and avoid the huge cost of flying replacements to a customer as far away as Argentina.

INCREASINGLY, COMPANIES LIKE DEERE & CO. ARE PAYING FOR, CONTROLLING, AND INSURING TRANSPORT FROM THEIR FACTORIES TO FOREIGN PORTS OR THEIR CUSTOMER'S DOORSTEPS.

Cost is an important consideration as well. Depending on where a $150,000 combine is shipped, transport costs can range between $7,500 and $30,000, or between 5 and 20 percent of delivered cost. Deere's ability to buy steamship space in volume enables it to reduce transport costs by 10 percent. That in turn enables it to cut the combine's delivered cost by between $750 and $3,000. "That adds up," says Salaber. Because of those savings, "you do not have to discount so much, and Deere gets more profit."

SOURCES: Toby B. Gooley, "Incoterms 2000: What the Changes Mean to You," *Logistics Management and Distribution Report* 39 (January 2000): 49–51; "How Badly Will the Dollar Whack the U.S.?" *Business Week*, May 5, 1997; Gregory L. Miles, "Exporter's New Bully Stick," *International Business*, December 1993, 46–49; **http://www.iccwbo.org; and http://www.deere.com**.

The exporter will be concerned over being paid for the goods shipped and will therefore consider the following factors in negotiating terms of payment: (1) the amount of payment and the need for protection, (2) terms offered by competitors, (3) practices in the industry, (4) capacity for financing international transactions, and (5) relative strength of the parties involved.[22] If the exporter is well established in the market with a unique product and accompanying service, price and terms of trade can be set to fit the exporter's desires. If, on the other hand, the exporter is breaking into a new market or if competitive pressures call for action, pricing and selling terms should be used as major competitive tools. Both parties have their own concerns and sensitivities; therefore, this very basic issue should be put on the negotiating table at the very beginning of the relationship.

The basic methods of payment for exports vary in terms of their attractiveness to the buyer and the seller, from cash in advance to open account or consignment selling. Neither of the extremes will be feasible for longer-term relationships, but they do have their use in certain situations. For example, in the 1999–2000 period very few companies were exporting into Russia except on a cash-in-advance basis, due to the country's financial turmoil. A marketer may use multiple methods of payment with the same buyer. For example, in a distributor relationship, the distributor may purchase samples on open account, but orders have to be paid for with a letter of credit. These methods are depicted in the risk triangle presented in Exhibit 11.7.

The most favorable term to the exporter is **cash in advance** because it relieves the exporter of all risk and allows for immediate use of the money. It is not widely used, however, except for smaller, first-time transactions or situations in which the exporter has reason to doubt the importer's ability to pay. Cash-in-advance terms are also found when orders are for custom-made products, because the risk to the exporter is beyond that of a normal transaction. In some instances, the importer may not be able to buy on a cash-in-advance basis because of insufficient funds or government restrictions.

A **letter of credit** is an instrument issued by a bank at the request of a buyer. The bank promises to pay a specified amount of money on presentation of documents stipulated in the letter of credit, usually the bill of lading, consular invoice, and a description of the goods.[23] Letters of credit are one of the most frequently used methods of payment in international transactions. Exhibit 11.8 summarizes the process of obtaining a letter of credit and the relationship between the parties involved.

Letters of credit can be classified among three dimensions:

1. Irrevocable versus revocable. An irrevocable letter of credit can neither be canceled nor modified without the consent of the beneficiary (exporter), thus guaranteeing payment. According to the new rules drawn by the International Chamber of Commerce, all letters of credit are considered irrevocable unless otherwise stated.[24]

Exhibit 11.7

Methods of Payment for Exports

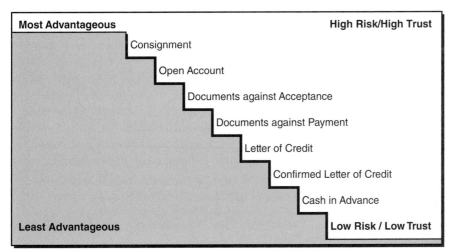

SOURCE: Adapted from Chase Manhattan Bank, *Dynamics of Trade Finance* (New York: Chase Manhattan Bank, 1984), 5.

Exhibit 11.8

Letter of Credit: Process and Parties

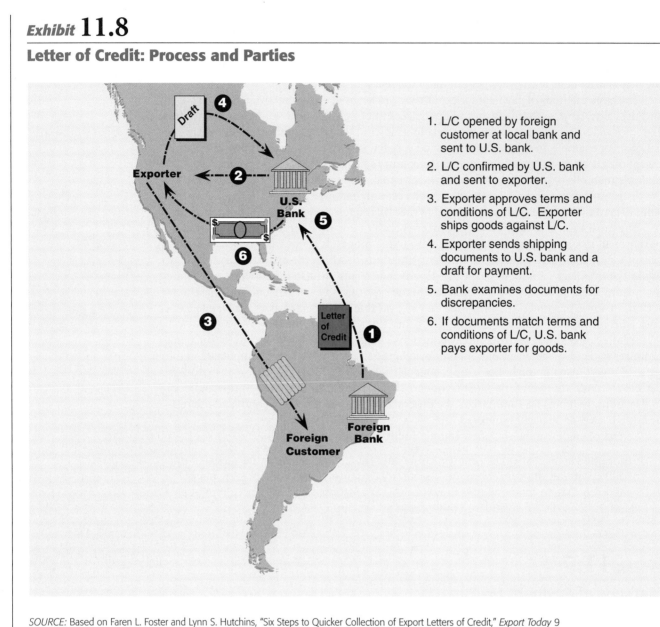

1. L/C opened by foreign customer at local bank and sent to U.S. bank.
2. L/C confirmed by U.S. bank and sent to exporter.
3. Exporter approves terms and conditions of L/C. Exporter ships goods against L/C.
4. Exporter sends shipping documents to U.S. bank and a draft for payment.
5. Bank examines documents for discrepancies.
6. If documents match terms and conditions of L/C, U.S. bank pays exporter for goods.

SOURCE: Based on Faren L. Foster and Lynn S. Hutchins, "Six Steps to Quicker Collection of Export Letters of Credit," *Export Today* 9 (November–December 1993): 26–30.

2. Confirmed versus unconfirmed. In the case of a U.S. exporter, a U.S. bank might confirm the letter of credit and thus assume the risk, including the transaction (exchange) risk. The single best method of payment for the exporter in most cases is a confirmed, irrevocable letter of credit. Banks may also assume an advisory role but not assume the risk; the underlying assumption is that the bank and its correspondent(s) are better able to judge the credibility of the bank issuing the letter of credit than is the exporter.

3. Revolving versus nonrevolving. Most letters of credit are nonrevolving, that is, they are valid for the one transaction only. In case of established relationships, a revolving letter of credit may be issued.

Exhibit 11.9 provides an example of a letter of credit.

The letter of credit provides advantages to both the exporter and the importer, which explains its wide use. The approach substitutes the credit of the bank for the credit of the buyer and is as good as the issuing bank's access to dollars. In custom-made orders, an

Exhibit 11.9

Letter of Credit

	:47A/ADDITIONAL C	1) INSURANCE IS COVERED BY BUYER. 2) PLUS ORMINUS 10 PCT ON CREDIT AMOUNT AND QUANTITY IS ACCEPTABLE

NPS WORLD TRADE BANCORP

NINA PINTA SANTA MARIA

0556   29PNBPUS33APIIL6264190547
1756   20BOTKSGXAXX0607854525

      * THE BANK OF ERATOSTHENES
      * LISBON, PORTUGAL

      700 02

:27	/SEQUENCE OF A/1
:40A	/FORM OF DOCU: IRREVOCABLE
:20	/DOCUMENTARY: 655-210-482267
:31C	DATE OF ISSUE: APR 29 2006
:31D	/DATE AND PLA: OCT 21 2006

USA

:50	/APPLICANT:	:JPP ALTO DURO PTE LTD RUA CASTILHO, 70 LISBON, PORTUGAL 2-DTR 1350-058
:59	/BENEFICIARY::	WORKS PLASTIQUE INTERNATIONAL 2345 MILLWOOD CIRCLE CHARLOTTE, NORTH CAROLINA 21261 U.S.A
:32B/VAL/AMOUNT		: USD ****************39,100.00
:41D/AVAILABLE WD		: ANY BANK BY NEGOTIATION
:42C DRAFTS AT...		:SIGHT FOR FULL INVOICE COST AND MARKED AS BEING DRAWN UNDER THIS CREDIT.
:42D/DRAWEE:		:ISSUING BANK
:43P/PARTIAL SHIP		:ALLOWED
:44TTRANSSSHIPMENT		:ALLOWED
44A:		LOADING ON BOARD/DISPATCH/TAKING IN CHARGE AT/FROM.... ANY EUROPEAN PORT
:48B/FOR TRANSPORT		:LISBON
:44C/LATEST DATE		:SEP 30 2006
:45A/DESCRIPTION		:43 M/TONS "NAVIGATOR" 4 HOLES PREE-PUNCHED
		CNF
:46A/DOCUMENTS RE		:1) SIGNED COMMERCIAL INVOICES IN QUADRUPLICATE. 2) FULL SET (3/3) CLEAN ON BOARD OCEAN BILLS OF LADING MADE OUT TO ORDER OF SHIPPER AND BLANK ENDORSED MARKED "FREIGHT PREPAID" AND NOTIFY APPLICANT.
		3) PACKING LIST IN QUADRUPLICATE

	3) SHIPMENT MUST BE EFFECTED AS FOLLOWS:
	A) 21.5M/TONS OF MERCHANDISE MUST BE EFFECTED NOT LATER THAN END OF JUNE 2006.
	B) 21.5M/TONS OF MERCHANDISE MUST BE EFFECTED NOT LATER THAN END OF SEPTEMBER 2006.
:71B/CHARGES	: ALL BANK CHARGES OUTSIDE LISBON ARE FOR BENEFICIARY'S ACCOUNT.
:49/CONFIRMATION	:WITHOUT
78/INSTRUCTIONS	1) UPON RECEIPT OF DOCUMENTS IN ORDER, WE SHALL REMIT DRAFT AMOUNT AS INSTRUCTED BY THE NEGOTIATING BANK.
	2) COURIER ALL DOCUMENTS TO U.S. IN TWO CONSECUTIVE LOTS.
	3) EACH NEGOTIATION MUST BE ENDORSED ON THESE REVERSE OF THIS CREDIT
	4) NEGOTIATING BANK MUST CERTIFY COMPLIANCE WITH ALL TERMS OF CONDITIONS OF THIS CREDIT.
27/BANK INFO	(THIS CREDIT IS SUBJECT TO UCP 1993 REVISION PUBLICATION NO.500).
MAC : FA11B280 CHK	:66A-358B077C2
SW990910557094-2000	

Note: The parties and transactions depicted are fictious examples and are not intended to represent any known institution or activity.

irrevocable letter of credit may help the exporter secure pre-export financing. The importer will not need to pay until the documents have arrived and been accepted by the bank, thus giving an additional float. The major caveat is that the exporter has to comply with all the terms of the letter of credit.[25] For example, if the documents state that shipment is made in crates measuring $4 \times 4 \times 4$ and the goods are shipped in crates measuring $4 \times 3 \times 4$, the bank will not honor the letter of credit. If there are changes, the letter of credit can be amended to ensure payment. Importers have occasionally been accused of creating discrepancies to slow down the payment process or to drive down the agreed-upon price.[26] In some cases, the exporter must watch out for fraudulent letters of credit, especially in the case of less-developed countries. In these cases, exporters are advised to ship only on the basis of an irrevocable letter of credit, confirmed by their bank, even after the credentials of the foreign contact have been established.

With the increasing amount of e-commerce, things will have to change. Solutions include online issuance and status reporting on letters of credit, creating a worldwide network of electronic trade hubs, and offering a smart card that will allow participating companies to transact financial business online.[27] For example, TradeCard is an online service for B2B (business-to-business) exchanges. Once an exporter and importer have agreed on the terms, the buyer creates an electronic purchase order, which specifies the terms and conditions. Once it is in electronic format, the seller formally agrees to the contract. The purchase order is stored in TradeCard's database. The system then creates both a commercial invoice and a packing list, and a promise of payment is included with the invoice for the seller. A third-party logistics provider sends proof of delivery electronically to TradeCard, which then debits the buyer's account and credits the seller's account.[28] Trade portals now support document creation and transmission, and make it possible for all parties to the transaction to exchange information on the same secure site. For example, Wachovia Bank's CyberXport Service lets exporters receive and review advised letters of credit as soon as Wachovia receives them. The enhanced information flow makes it possible to minimize and eliminate discrepancies.[29]

The letter of credit is a promise to pay but not a means of payment. Actual payment is accomplished by means of a **draft**, which is similar to a personal check. Like a check, it is an order by one party to pay another. Most drafts are documentary, which means that the buyer must obtain possession of various shipping documents before obtaining possession of the goods involved in the transaction. Clean drafts—orders to pay without any other documents—are mainly used by multinational corporations in their dealings with their own subsidiaries and in well-established business relationships.

In **documentary collection** situations, the seller ships the goods, and the shipping documents and the draft demanding payment are presented to the importer through banks acting as the seller's agent. The draft, also known as the bill of exchange, may be either a sight draft or a time draft (Exhibit 11.10). A sight draft documents against payment and is payable on presentation to the drawee, that is, the party to whom the draft is addressed. A time draft

Exhibit 11.10

Draft

| NPS WORLD TRADE BANCORP | | customer draft |
| NINA PINTA SANTA MARIA | | |

| Tenor | Date |
| 90 Days Date | April 29, 2006 |

| Pay to the order of | Amount |
| NPS World Trade Bancorp | $100,000 |

| Amount in words | |
| One Hundred Thousand and no/100 dollars | |

| To | Firm Name |
| NPS World Trade Bancorp | |

Drawn Under _____   Authorized Signature _____

Note: The parties and transactions depicted are fictious examples and are not intended to represent any known institution or activity.

SOURCE: © R. Alcorn/Thomson

documents against acceptance and allows for a delay of 30, 60, 90, 120, or 180 days. When a time draft is drawn on and accepted by a bank, it becomes a **banker's acceptance**, which is sold in the short-term money market. Time drafts drawn on and accepted by a business firm become trader's acceptances, which are normally not marketable. A draft is presented to the drawee, who accepts it by writing or stamping a notice of acceptance on it. With both sight and time drafts, the buyer can effectively extend the period of credit by avoiding receipt of the goods. A date draft requires payment on a specified date, regardless of the date on which the goods and the draft are accepted by the buyer.

To illustrate, an exporter may have a time draft accepted by Citibank for $1 million to be paid in 90 days. Like many exporters who extend credit for competitive reasons, the firm may have immediate need for the funds. It could contact an acceptance dealer and sell the acceptance at a discount, with the rate depending on the market rate of interest. If the annual interest rate was 6 percent, for example, the acceptance could be sold for $985,222 ($1 million divided by 1.015).

Even if the draft is not sold in the secondary market, the exporter may convert it into cash by **discounting**. To discount the draft simply means that the draft is sold to a bank at a discount from face value. If the discounting is with recourse, the exporter is liable for the payment to the bank if the importer defaults. If the discounting is without recourse, the exporter will not be liable even if the importer does not pay the bank. Discounting without recourse is known as factoring or, in the case of higher credit risk and longer-term receivables, forfaiting.

The normal manner of doing business in the domestic market is **open account** (open terms). The exporter selling on open account removes both real and psychological barriers to importing. However, no written evidence of the debt exists, and the exporter has to put full faith in the references contacted. Worst of all, there is no guarantee of payment. If the debt turns bad, the problems of overseas litigation are considerable. Bad debts are normally easier to avoid than to rectify. In emerging countries, importers will usually need proof of debt in the application to the central bank for hard currency, which will not allow them to deal on an open-account basis. It may be more expedient to send the documents through a bank via direct collections, which can reduce the process by several days or even weeks.[30] For more involved marketers with units abroad, internal transactions are normally handled on an open-account basis.

The most favorable term to the importer is **consignment selling**, which allows the importer to defer payment until the goods are actually sold. This approach places all the burden on the exporter, and its use should be carefully weighed against the objectives of the transaction. If the exporter wants entry into a specific market through specific intermediaries, consignment selling may be the only method of gaining acceptance by intermediaries. The arrangement will require clear understanding as to the parties' responsibilities—for example, which party is responsible for insurance until the goods have actually been sold. If the goods are not sold, returning them will be costly and time-consuming; for example, there is getting through customs or paying, avoiding paying, or trying to get refunds on duties. Due to its burdensome characteristics, consignment is not widely used.

Getting Paid for Exports

The exporter needs to minimize the risk of not being paid if a transaction occurs. The term **commercial risk** refers primarily to the insolvency of, or protracted payment default by, an overseas buyer. Commercial defaults, in turn, usually result from deterioration of conditions in the buyer's market, fluctuations in demand, unanticipated competition, or technological changes. These naturally emerge domestically as well, but the geographic and cultural distances in international markets make them more severe and more difficult to anticipate. In addition, noncommercial or **political risk** is completely beyond the control of either the buyer or the seller. For example, the foreign buyer may be willing to pay but the local government may use every trick in the book to delay payment as far into the future as possible.

These challenges must be addressed through actions by either the company itself or support systems. The decision must be an informed one, based on detailed and up-to-date information in international credit and country conditions. In many respects, the assessment of a buyer's creditworthiness requires the same attention to credit checking and financial analysis as for domestic buyers; however, the assessment of a foreign private buyer is complicated by some of the following factors:

1. Credit reports may not be reliable.

2. Audited reports may not be available.

3. Financial reports may have been prepared according to a different format.

4. Many governments require that assets be annually reevaluated upward, which can distort results.

5. Statements are in local currency.

6. The buyer may have the financial resources in local currency but may be precluded from converting to dollars because of exchange controls and other government actions.

More than one credit report should be obtained (from sources such as the one in Exhibit 11.11), and it should be determined how each credit agency obtains its reports. They may use the same correspondent agency, in which case it does the exporter no good to obtain the same information from two sources and to pay for it twice. Exhibit 11.12 provides a summary of the major sources of credit information. Where private-sector companies (such as Dun & Bradstreet or Veritas) are able to provide the needed credit information, the services of the U.S. Department of Commerce's International Company Profiles (ICP) are not available. Local credit reporting agencies, such as Profancresa in Mexico, may also provide regional services (in this case, throughout Latin America). With the growth of e-commerce, a company may want to demonstrate its creditworthiness to customers and suppliers in a rapid and secure fashion. The Coface Group (of which Veritas is the information arm in

Exhibit **11.11**

Providers of International Credit Information

SOURCE: Courtesy of the U.S. Commercial Service (**http://www.export.gov**); copyright © Dun & Bradstreet and The Guild Group.

Exhibit 11.12

Sources of International Credit Information

	Response Time	Service Offerings	Presence	Remarks
Dun & Bradstreet http://www.dnb.com	Many nonsubscription-based reports, in electronic copies, readily available for U.S. customers by online purchase; shipment delays on printed reports depending on location; non-U.S. customers can access online database by subscription; certain delays on customized information	• Credit information, both standardized and customized • Country risk reports for 132 countries available online, costing $350 on the average	8,000 employees worldwide (including all other D&B business), covering 130 million companies in 214 countries	Core strength in small and medium-size enterprises, with 87% of active files in its U.S. database being small companies with less than 10 staff; industry standard, with the largest worldwide company coverage
FCIB-NACM http://www.fcibglobal.com	Same day for already-available reports (excluding shipment); customized credit reports can take from a few days to three weeks; no online database	• Country risk reports cost $100 each for members and $125 for nonmembers • Credit reports • Business credit magazines • Seminars and conferences for export groups	More than 1000 members in 55 countries. Two main offices in the United States and UK, with country representatives in Europe, Canada, Mexico, and China	Services focus on exports business; membership costs $840, fees for industry-focus export groups range from $125 to $515
@rating http://www.cofacerating.com	Online focus, instantaneous access of information	• Free online check of company's reliability and financial soundness • Free country risk assessment and rating • Fee-based information reports • Fee-based @rating quality labeling service	78,000 clients worldwide. Presence in 99 countries, 5 continents, covering 41 million companies	Most efficient and least costly resource, but analysis may lack depth; aim to become standard Web-based rating system, supported by the EU
International Company Profiles http://www.ita.doc.gov	About 10 days of processing time, depending on complexity of information and availability from existing database; no online service, thus adding delays from shipment, depending on location	• Company background check, including financial status, management profile, and company potential • $500–700 for each company report	151 international offices in 85 countries, with 1,800 employees	Focus on serving small and mid-sized companies in the United States; analysis is U.S.-centric because service provider is part of U.S. Department of Commerce
Local Credit Agencies or Trade Councils	Varies	• Focus on information of local companies	Locally	Quality varies, with limited scope in international marketing
Bank Reports	Slower	• Company background	None (client)	Limited in scope

SOURCE: Interviews with company and organization personnel and corporate data, February 2006 and February 2009.

the Americas) introduced the "@rating" system, available on the World Wide Web and designed to assess a company's performance in paying its commercial obligations.[31]

Beyond protecting oneself by establishing creditworthiness, an exporter can match payment terms to the customer. In the short term, an exporter may require payment terms that guarantee payment. In the long term, the best approach is to establish a relationship of mutual trust, which will ensure payment even if complications arise during a transaction.[32] Payment terms need to be stated clearly and followed up effectively. If prompt payment is not stressed and enforced, some customers will assume they can procrastinate, as we saw in *The International Marketplace 11.1*.

Should a default situation occur in spite of the preparatory measures discussed above, the exporter's first recourse is the customer. Communication with the customer may reveal a misunderstanding or error regarding the shipment. If the customer has financial or other concerns or objections, rescheduling the payment terms may be considered. Third-party intervention through a collection agency may be needed if the customer disputes the charges. For example, the Total Credit Management Group, a cooperative of leading credit and collection companies in 46 countries, can be employed. Only when further amicable demands are unwarranted should an attorney be used.[33]

Managing Foreign Exchange Risk

Unless the exporter and the importer share the same currency (as is the case in the 17 countries of Euroland), exchange rate movements may harm or benefit one or the other of the parties. *The International Marketplace 11.3* shows some of the currency effects. If the price is quoted in the exporter's currency, the exporter will get exactly the price it wants but may lose some sales due to lack of customer orientation. If the exporter needs the sale, the invoice may be in the importer's currency, and the exchange risk will be the burden of the exporter. Some exporters, if they are unable to secure payment in their own currency, try to minimize the risk by negotiating shorter terms of payment, such as 10 or 15 days. Exchange risks may be a result of an appreciating or depreciating currency or result from a revaluation or devaluation of a currency by a central bank. Assume that a U.S. importer bought $250,000 or €208,750 worth of goods from a German company, which agreed to accept U.S. dollars for payment in 90 days. At the time of the quotation, the exchange rate for $1 was €0.835, whereas at the time of payment, it had changed to €0.820. This means that the German exporter, instead of receiving €208,750, winds up with €206,250.

Two types of approaches to protect against currency-related risk are proposed: (1) risk shifting, such as foreign currency contractual hedging, and/or (2) risk modifying, such as manipulating prices and other elements of a marketing strategy.

When invoicing in foreign currencies, an exporter cannot insulate itself from the problems of currency movements, but it can at least know how much it will eventually receive by using the mechanism of the **forward exchange market**. In essence, the exporter gets a bank to agree to a rate at which it will buy the foreign currency the exporter will receive when the importer makes payment. The rate is expressed as either a premium or a discount on the current spot rate. A fixed rate allows the exporter to budget effectively without currency fluctuations eroding profit margins.[34] The risk still remains if the exchange rate does not move as anticipated, and the exporter may be worse off than if it had not bought forward. Although forward contracts are the most common foreign currency contractual hedge, other financial instruments and derivatives, such as currency options and futures, are available. An **option** gives the holder the right to buy or sell foreign currency at a prespecified price on or up to a prespecified date. The difference between the currency options market and the forward market is that the transaction in the former gives the participant the right to buy or sell, whereas a transaction in the forward market entails a contractual obligation to buy or sell. This means that if an exporter does not have any or the appropriate amount of currency when the contract comes due, it would have to go into the foreign exchange markets to buy the currency, potentially exposing itself to major losses if the currency has appreciated in the meanwhile. The greater flexibility in the options contract makes it more expensive, however. The currency **futures** market is conceptually similar to the forward market; that is, to buy

The International
MARKETPLACE

11.3

One's Opportunity, Another's Squeeze

Since early 2002, the weaker U.S. dollar has given U.S. exporters an edge both abroad and at home, by making dollar-valued goods cheaper than those produced in the stronger-currency markets such as Europe and Japan. The 30 percent decline versus the euro, for example, has provided many exporters with new opportunities, from higher profits to expanding product lines and market entries.

Purafil, an Atlanta-based maker of air-purification systems, has won a number of major contracts abroad, including $500,000 deals in Canada and Spain, attributing the success to the dollar's value. The weaker dollar has not only resulted in more sales but has allowed the company to raise its prices as much as 15 percent in dollar terms without losing its ability to compete against rivals in euro markets. Superior Products of Cleveland, which sells 2,500 different types of gas fittings and assemblies, has seen its exports grow 65 percent in the last few years with new markets in Europe, such as Italy. During the strong-dollar period, Superior bought some of its valves from Germany and then sold them in the United States under its own brand name. However, with the euro's appreciation, Superior has found that making these products in-house is more economical. The German supplier has responded by reducing prices, recognizing that its former customer may be emerging as a major competitor in the crucial U.S. equipment market.

Bison Gear & Engineering, a small manufacturer of power-transmission equipment in St. Charles, Illinois, shut down an assembly and warehouse operation in the Netherlands as a result of the strong dollar. The machinery from Europe was packed in shipping containers and sent to back to Illinois. The equipment is now being used in Bison's U.S. plant to supply growing demand, including a revival in Europe. The company is reconsidering reopening a European operation. Applied Robotics of Glenville, NY, has increased its euro-based exports to 40 percent of its sales. It has opened a subsidiary in Belgium that handles sales and technical support for the products sold in Europe.

Currency markets have not helped all U.S. exporters. A full 60 percent of the U.S. trade deficit is with Asian countries, a region where the currencies have not moved favorably against the dollar. China's currency policy keeps the yuan renminbi artificially low and gives the Chinese an additional edge in the global marketplace. In some cases, the declining dollar has a downside. Certain types of specialized machinery are only available from producers in Europe or Japan, which means that U.S. buyers pay more for those items.

While many exporters have seen the lower dollar open doors to new markets, they cannot count on currency changes to carry their businesses into the future. "It's dangerous to bet on the dollar," says one export manager. "You need to be low-cost and very efficient, no matter where the dollar is."

SOURCES: "U.S. Exporters Face Harsh Climate," *The Wall Street Journal,* May 2, 2005, A2; "In Canada, Efficiency is Survival," *The Wall Street Journal,* March 28, 2005, A14; "Weaker Dollar May be Starting to Lift U.S. Exports," *The Wall Street Journal,* February 11, 2005, A1, A5; "Weak Dollar, Strong Sales," The Wall Street Journal, January 20, 2005, B1, B2; Nelson D. Schwartz, "The Dollar in the Dumps," *Fortune,* December 13, 2004, 113–116; "Region's Exporters Love Strong Euro," *Business Review,* July 16, 2004, 15–16; and "Beware of the Super Euro," *Business Week,* May 19, 2003, 52–53. See also **http://www.purafil.com**; **http://www.superiorprod.com**; **http://www.bisongear.com**; and **http://www.arobotics.com**.

futures on the British pound sterling implies an obligation to buy in the future at a prespecified price. However, the minimum transaction sizes are considerably smaller on the futures market. Forward quotes apply to transactions of $1 million or more, whereas on the futures market transactions will typically be well below $100,000. The market, therefore, allows relatively small firms engaged in international trade to lock in exchange rates and lower their risk. Forward contracts, options, and futures are available from banks (such as UBS and JPMorgan Chase), the Chicago Mercantile Exchange, and the Philadelphia Stock Exchange.

U.S. exporters have faced both high and low values of the dollar with respect to other currencies in the past ten years: low values in the early to mid-1990s, high values since then until early 2002, and lower values of as much as 30 percent from then on. When the exporter's domestic currency is weak, strategies should include stressing the price advantage to customers and expanding the scale and scope of the export operation. Sourcing can be shifted to domestic markets and the export price can be subjected to full-costing. However, under the opposite scenario, the exporter needs to engage in nonprice competition, minimizing the price dimension as much as possible. Costs should be reduced by every means, including enhancing productivity. At this time, the exporter should prioritize efforts to markets that show the greatest returns. Marketers may also attempt to protect themselves by manipulating leads and lags in export and import payments or receivables in anticipation

Exhibit 11.13

Exporter Strategies under Varying Currency Conditions

Weak	Strong
1. Stress price benefits	1. Nonprice competition
2. Expand product line	2. Improve productivity/cost reduction
3. Shift sourcing to domestic market	3. Sourcing overseas
4. Exploit all possible export opportunities	4. Prioritize exports
5. Cash-for-goods trade	5. Countertrade with weak currency countries
6. Full-costing	6. Marginal-cost pricing
7. Speed repatriation	7. Slow collections
8. Minimize expenditure in local currency	8. Buy needed services abroad
	9. Maximize expenditures in home currency

SOURCE: Adapted from S. Tamer Cavusgil, "Unraveling the Mystique of Export Pricing," *Business Horizons* 31 (May–June 1988): 54–63.

of either currency revaluations or devaluations. This, however, will require thorough market knowledge and leverage over overseas partners. Alternatives available to marketers under differing currency conditions are summarized in Exhibit 11.13.

Whatever the currency movements are, the marketer needs to decide how to adjust pricing to international customers in view of either a more favorable or an unfavorable domestic currency rate. A European exporter, during a strong euro, has three alternatives. First, making no change in the euro price would result in a less favorable price in foreign currencies and, most likely, lower sales, especially if no corrective marketing steps are taken. Second, the export price could be decreased in conjunction with increases in the value of the euro to maintain stable export prices in foreign currencies. This first alternative is an example of **pass-through**, while the second alternative features the **absorption** approach; that is, the increase in the price is absorbed into the margin of the product, possibly even resulting in a loss. For pass-through to work, customers have to have a high level of preference for the exporter's product. In some cases, exporters may have no choice but to pass most of the increase to the customer due to the cost structure of the firm. Exporters using the absorption approach have as their goal long-term market-share maintenance, especially in a highly competitive environment.

The third alternative is to pass through only a share of the increase, maintaining sales if possible while at the same time preserving profitability. According to a study on exporter responses to foreign-exchange rate changes over the period of 1973 to 1997, Japanese exporters have the highest tendency to dampen the effects of exchange-rate fluctuations in foreign-currency export prices in both directions by adjusting their home-currency prices.[35] Furthermore, Japanese exporters put a larger emphasis on stabilizing the foreign currency prices of their exports during a weak yen than when the yen is strong. German exporters display completely the opposite behavior. The data in Exhibit 11.14 for German and Japanese auto exports support these findings for the period, when the dollar appreciated against the German mark and the Japanese yen.

The strategic response depends on market conditions and may result in different strategies for each market or product. Destination-specific adjustment of mark-ups in response to exchange-rate changes have been referred to as **pricing-to-market**.[36] For example, a mark-up change will be more substantial in a price-sensitive market and/or product category. In addition, the exporter needs to consider the reactions of local competitors, who may either keep their prices stable (hoping that price increases in imports will improve their position) or increase their prices along with those of imports in search of more profits. U.S. automakers were criticized for raising their domestic prices at a time when Japanese imports were forced up by the higher value of the yen. Instead of trying to capture more market share, the automakers went for more profits.[37] If the exporter faces a favorable domestic currency rate, pass-through means providing international customers with a more favorable price, while

Exhibit **11.14**

Absorption versus Pass-Through: Japanese and German Automarketer Behavior

Model	Real Dollar Appreciation	Real Retail Price Change in U.S. Market
Honda Civic 2-Dr. Sedan	39%	−7%
Nissan 200 SX 2-Dr.	39	−10
Toyota Cressida 4-Dr.	39	6
BMW 320i 2-Dr. Sedan	42	−8
BMW 733i 4-Dr. Sedan	42	−17
Mercedes 300 TD Sta. Wgn.	42	−39

SOURCE: Joseph A. Gagnon and Michael M. Knetter, "Markup Adjustment and Exchange Rate Fluctuations: Evidence from Panel Data on Automobile Exports," *Journal of International Money and Finance* 14 (no. 2, 1995): 289–310. Copyright © 1995, with permission from Elsevier.

absorption means that the exporter keeps the export price stable and pockets a higher level of profits.

Some exporters prefer price stability to the greatest possible degree and allow mark-ups to vary in maintaining stable local currency prices. Harley-Davidson, for example, maintains its price to distributors as long as the spot exchange rate does not move more than plus or minus 5 percent from the rate in effect when the quote was made. If the movement is an additional 5 percentage points in either direction, Harley and its distributors will share the costs or benefits. Beyond that the price will have to be renegotiated to bring it more in line with current exchange rates and the economic and competitive realities of the market.[38] During times of exchange-rate gains, rather than lower the price, some exporters use other support tools (such as training and trade deals) with their distributors or customers, on the premise that increasing prices after a future currency swing in the opposite direction may be difficult.

Beyond **price manipulation**, other adjustment strategies exist. They include the following:

1. Market refocus. If lower values of the target market currencies make exporting more difficult by, for example, making collection times longer, marketers may start looking at other markets for growth. For example, U.S. construction industry sales to Mexico grew by nearly 150 percent after markets in Thailand and Indonesia dried up due to the Asian financial crisis.[39] In some cases, the emphasis may switch to the domestic market, where market share gain at the expense of imports may be the most efficient way to grow. Currency appreciation does not always lead to a dire situation for the exporter. Domestic competitors may depend very heavily on imported components and may not able to take advantage of the currency-related price pressure on the exporter. The manufacturing sectors of Indonesia, Malaysia, Philippines, and Thailand use over 30 percent imported parts and raw materials in the production process.[40]

2. Streamlined operations. The marketer may start using more aggressive methods of collection, insisting on letters of credit and insurance to guarantee payments. Some have tightened control of their distribution networks by cutting layers or taking over the responsibility from independent intermediaries. On the product side, marketers may focus on offerings that are less sensitive to exchange-rate changes.

3. Shift in production. Especially when currency shifts are seen as long-term, marketers will increase direct investment. With the high value of the yen, Japanese companies shifted production bases to lower-cost locations or closer to final customers. Matsushita Electric, for example, moved a substantial share of its production to Southeast Asian countries, while earthmoving-equipment maker Komatsu launched a $1 billion joint venture with Texas-based Dresser Industries to build equipment in the United States. Remaining units in Japan will focus on research and development, design, software, and high-precision manufactured goods.[41]

In some cases, even adverse developments in the currency market have not had an effect on international markets or marketers. During the currency crisis in Asia, U.S. oil toolmakers and oil-field service companies were never hurt by the high value of the dollar because their expertise was in demand. Similarly, many U.S. firms such as IBM did not suffer because their exported products are both built and sold in other countries. In some cases, imported goods may be in demand because no domestic production exists, which is the case in the United States with consumer goods such as electronics and cameras.

Sources of Export Financing

Except in the case of larger companies that may have their own financing entities, most international marketers assist their customers abroad in securing appropriate financing. Export financing terms can significantly affect the final price paid by buyers. Consider, for example, two competitors for a $1 million sale. Exporter A offers an 8 percent interest rate over a ten-year payment period, while B offers 9 percent for the same term. Over the ten years, the difference in interest is $55,000. In some cases, buyers will award a contract to the provider of cheaper credit and overlook differences in quality and price.

Financing assistance is available from both the private and the public sectors. The international marketer should assess not only domestic programs but also those in other countries. For example, Japan and Taiwan have import financing programs that provide exporters added potential in penetrating these significant markets.[42]

Commercial Banks

Commercial banks the world over provide trade financing depending on their relationship with the exporter, the nature of the transaction, the country of the borrower, and the availability of export insurance. This usually means that financing assistance is provided only to first-rate credit risks, leaving many U.S. exporters to report major problems in enlisting assistance from U.S. commercial banks. Furthermore, some U.S. banks do not see international trade finance as part of their core competence. Although the situation has improved, exporters still continue to complain about lack of export financing as it pertains to developing countries, financing high technology, or lending against foreign receivables. Many exporters complain that banks will not deal with them without a guarantee from the Ex-Im Bank of rock-solid collateral, such as property and/or equipment.

However, as the share of international sales and reach of companies increases, banking relationships become all the more important, a fact that is also noted by banks themselves. Many banks offer enhanced services, such as electronic services, which help exporters monitor and expedite their international transactions to customers who do a certain amount of business with them. As with all suppliers, the more business done with a bank, the higher the level of service, usually at a better price. As the relationship builds, the more comfortable bankers feel about the exporter's business and the more likely they will go out of their way to help, particularly with difficult transactions. For example, before the credit crunch, Silicon Valley Bank in San Jose, California, financed fledgling technology exporters, while Capitol Bank in Los Angeles provided export and import financing to companies doing business in Taiwan and South Korea. It is clear that the development of an effective credit policy requires teamwork between the company's marketing and finance staffs and its bankers.

In addition to using the types of services a bank can provide as a criterion of choice, an exporter should assess the bank's overseas reach.[43] This is a combination of the bank's own network of facilities and correspondent relationships. While money-center banks can provide the greatest amount of coverage through their own offices and staff, they still use correspondents in regions outside the main banking or political centers of foreign markets. For example, Citibank has a worldwide correspondent network of 5,000 institutions in addition to its facilities in more than 100 countries.

Some banks have formed alliances to extend their reach to markets that their customers are entering. Some regional banks develop relationships with global banks that have strong correspondent networks in place in emerging markets. Other banks have no intention of establishing branches abroad, and rely only on strong alliances with, or ownership by, foreign banks. Foreign banks can provide a competitive advantage to exporters because of their home-country connections and their strong global networks. For example, Commerzbank, Germany's second-largest private-sector bank, has 5,000 banks in 50 countries in North America, the Far East, Latin America, South America, Africa, and Eastern Europe to support its international trade financing activities.[44] Regardless of the arrangement, the bank's own branches or correspondents play an important role at all stages of the international transaction, from gathering market intelligence about potential new customers to actually processing payments. Additional services include reference checks on customers in their home markets and suggestions for possible candidates to serve as intermediaries.

Forfaiting and Factoring

Forfaiting provides the exporter with cash at the time of the shipment. In a typical forfait deal, the importer pays the exporter with bills of exchange or promissory notes guaranteed by a leading bank in the importer's country. The exporter can sell them to a third party (for example, Citicorp) at a discount from their face value for immediate cash. The sale is without recourse to the exporter, and the buyer of the notes assumes all the risks. The discount rate takes into account the buyer's creditworthiness and country, the quality of the guaranteeing bank, and the interest cost over the term of the credit.

The benefits to the exporter are the reduction of risk, simplicity of documentation (because the documents used are well known in the market), and 100 percent coverage, which official sources such as export-import banks do not provide. In addition, forfaiting does not involve either content or country restrictions, which many of the official trade financing sources may have.[45] The major complaints about forfaiting center on availability and cost. Forfaiting is not available where exporters need it most, that is, the high-risk countries. Furthermore, it is usually a little more expensive than public sources of trade insurance.

Certain companies, known as **factoring** houses, may purchase an exporter's receivables for a discounted price (2 to 4 percent less than face value). Factors not only buy receivables but also provide the exporter with a complete financial package that combines credit protection, accounts-receivable bookkeeping, and collection services to take away many of the challenges that come with doing business overseas.[46] Arrangements are typically with recourse, leaving the exporter ultimately liable for repaying the factor in case of a default. Some factors accept export receivables without recourse but require a large discount.

The industry is dominated by a dozen major players, most of which are subsidiaries of major banks. One leader is the CIT Group, 44 percent owned by Dai-Ichi Kangyo Bank of Japan, which has won the President's "E" Award for its excellence in export service.[47] However, with the increase in companies looking for factoring services, independent factors are also emerging. Factors can be found through the Commercial Finance Association or through marketing facilitators whose clients use factors.

Although the forfaiting and factoring methods appear similar, they differ in three significant ways: (1) factors usually want a large percentage of the exporter's business, while most forfaiters work on a one-shot basis; (2) forfaiters work with medium-term receivables (over 180 days to 5 years), while factors work with short-term receivables; and (3) factors usually do not have strong capabilities in the developing countries, but since forfaiters usually require a bank guarantee, most are willing to deal with receivables from these countries. Furthermore, forfaiters work with capital goods, factors typically with consumer goods.[48]

Official Trade Finance[49]

Official financing can take the form of either a loan or a guarantee, including credit insurance. In a loan, the government provides funds to finance the sale and charges interest on those funds at a stated fixed rate. The government lender accepts the risk of a possible default. In a guarantee, a private-sector lender provides the funds and sets the interest rate, with the government assuring that it will reimburse the lender if the loan is unpaid. The government is providing not funds but rather risk protection. The programs provide assurance that the governmental agency will pay for a major portion of the loss should the foreign buyer default on payment. The advantages are significant: (1) protection in the riskiest part of an exporter's business (foreign sales receivables), (2) protection against political and commercial risks over which the exporter does not have control, (3) encouragement to exporters to make competitive offers by extending terms of payment, (4) broadening of potential markets by minimizing exporter risks, (5) the possibility of leveraging exporter accounts receivable, and (6) through the government guarantee, the opportunity for commercial banks to remain active in the international finance arena.[50]

Because credit has emerged as an increasingly important component in export selling, governments of most industrialized countries have established entities that insure credit risks for exports. Officially supported export credit agencies (ECAs), such as the French Coface or German Hermes, are organizations whose central purpose is to promote national trade objectives by providing financial support for national exports. ECAs benefit from varying degrees of explicit or implicit support from national governments. Some ECAs are divisions of government trade missions. Other ECAs operate as autonomous or even private institutions, but most require a degree of recourse to national government support.

The Export-Import Bank of the United States (Ex-Im Bank) was created in 1934 and established as an independent U.S. government agency in 1945. The purpose of the bank is "to aid in financing and facilitating exports." Since its inception, Ex-Im Bank has supported more than $400 billion in U.S. export sales. The Ex-Im Bank supports short-, medium-, and long-term financing to creditworthy international customers (both in the private and public sectors), as well as working capital guarantees to U.S. exporters. Special initiatives exist for environmental exports, small business, and lending directly to municipalities in certain countries.

The data and examples in *The International Marketplace 11.4* highlight the programs available for exporters—pre-export, short term, medium term, and long term. One of the greatest impediments small businesses experience in attempting to fulfill export orders is a lack of working capital to build necessary inventory for the export order. If the local bank is reluctant to make such financing available (because the exporter might have reached its borrowing limit, for example), the Working Capital Guarantee Program is available.

The ability to offer financing or credit terms is often critical in competing for, and winning, export contracts. Increasingly, foreign buyers expect suppliers to offer open account or unsecured credit terms rather than requiring letters of credit, which may be expensive. Yet for small exporters, extending credit terms to foreign customers may represent an unacceptable risk, especially when the exporter's bank is unwilling to accept foreign receivables as collateral for working lines of credit. The solution is export credit insurance, wherein, for a reasonable premium, an institution (e.g., an insurance company or an ECA) guarantees payment to the seller if the buyer defaults. The short-term credit-insurance business is dominated by five major players, which account for more than 75 percent of the world market: Coface, Euler, Gerling, Hermes, and NCM.[51]

Ex-Im Bank also guarantees to provide repayment protection for private-sector loans to creditworthy buyers of U.S. goods and services. Guarantees, both for the medium and long term, are backed in full by the U.S. government. The fee schedule is determined by country risk and repayment terms of the transaction. Medium-term guarantees (not to exceed seven years) are typically used by commercial banks that do not want exposure in a certain country or that have reached their internal exposure limit in a given country. For long-term guarantees, projects are usually large (in excess of $100 million), and commercial banks may not want such exposure for long periods of time in one country or in a particular industry sector. Ex-Im may act as a lender directly to the foreign buyer. The majority (typically 85 percent or more) of the project must be U.S.-produced goods and services.

In addition to the ECAs, other public-sector supporters exist as well. In the United States, the Overseas Private Investment Corporation (OPIC) offers investment guarantees comparable to those offered by the Ex-Im Bank to manufacturers who wish to establish facilities in less-developed countries, either by themselves or as a joint venture

The International
MARKETPLACE

Inside the EX-IM Bank

Pre-export   Penn Anderson Equipment Co. of Oakmont, Penn., a small business manufacturer of equipment that tests the efficiency of fuel, air, and lube filters on gasoline automobile engines, had been experiencing a very slow business period until it received a $417,000 order from a buyer in China. But although Penn Anderson had a letter of credit from the Bank of China and had a proven capability to perform under foreign contracts, the three-employee company did not have the working capital needed to build the machinery for Pingyuan Machine Factory in China. Penn Anderson owner Carl Michael had worked with Ex-Im Bank successfully in the past on exports to Saudi Arabia, Egypt, and China. So he approached PNC Bank to apply for an Ex-Im Bank–guaranteed working capital loan that would enable him to build the test equipment. Given the contract in place, Michael's successful history as an exporter, and the support Ex-Im Bank would provide under its Working Capital Guarantee Program, PNC agreed to a $315,000 short-term working capital line of credit.

Short term   Southwest Windpower Inc., a small business manufacturer of battery-charging wind-powered generators with factories in Flagstaff, Ariz., and Duluth, Minn., has used Ex-Im Bank's environmental export credit insurance since 1996 to sell its products to small foreign distributors in developing markets, including Brazil, Hungary, Turkey, India, and South Africa, among others. Ex-Im Bank's insurance enables the company to offer its foreign buyers open account terms, which enables buyers to place larger orders. More than 50 percent of the company's revenues come from export sales and its products are sold in more than 50 countries. In the past 16 years, the company has produced more than 60,000 wind generators to produce electricity for telecom munications towers, remote homes and schools, off-shore platforms, and a variety of other applications.

Medium term   A $13.7 million Ex-Im Bank Loan Guarantee enabled exporter Marubeni America Corp., San Francisco, to sell oncology medical equipment supplied by GE Healthcare, Waukesha, Wisc., and other U.S. suppliers to a leading Turkish hospital. Hacettepe Universitesi, located in Ankara, used the linear accelerator, comput erized tomography scanners, magnetic resonance

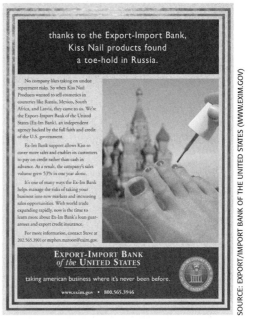

thanks to the Export-Import Bank, Kiss Nail products found a toe-hold in Russia.

No company likes taking on undue repayment risks. So when Kiss Nail Products wanted to sell cosmetics in countries like Russia, Mexico, South Africa, and Latvia, they came to us. We're the Export-Import Bank of the United States (Ex-Im Bank), an independent agency backed by the full faith and credit of the U.S. government.

Ex-Im Bank support allows Kiss to cover more sales and enables its customers to pay on credit rather than cash in advance. As a result, the company's sales volume grew 53% in one year alone.

It's one of many ways the Ex-Im Bank helps manage the risks of taking your business into new markets and increasing sales opportunities. With world trade expanding rapidly, now is the time to learn more about Ex-Im Bank's loan guarantees and export credit insurance.

For more information, contact Steve at 202.565.3901 or stephen.marron@exim.gov.

EXPORT-IMPORT BANK
of the **UNITED STATES**

taking american business where it's never been before.

www.exim.gov • 800.565.3946

imaging, and other equipment to upgrade and expand its oncology facilities. The guaranteed lender on the export sale was Citigroup.

Long term   Ex-Im Bank approved a direct loan of up to $70.2 million to support the export by Caterpillar Inc., Peoria, Ill., and other U.S. suppliers of equipment and services to build a new international airport near Quito, Ecuador. The airport will be located 24 kilometers outside of Quito at a lower elevation than the existing airport, with a longer runway to accommodate larger aircraft. Project company Quiport, will design, build, operate, and maintain the airport. Quiport is owned by sponsors Aecon Construction Group, Inc., of Canada; Andrade Guiterrez Concessoes S.A. of Brazil; ADC Management, Ltd., of the British Virgin Islands; and HAS Development Corp. of Texas. The transaction is structured as a limited recourse project financing, a type of private financing in which repayment comes from project revenues. Participating with Ex-Im Bank as senior lenders are Export Development Canada (EDC), the Inter-American Development Bank (IDB), and the U.S. Overseas Private Investment Corp. (OPIC).

SOURCE: Export-Import Bank of the United States, **http://www.exim.gov**.

with local capital. The programs involve either (1) direct loans, (2) loan guarantees to U.S. institutional lenders, or (3) political risk insurance against currency inconvertibility, expropriation or takeover, and physical damage resulting from political strife. The Agency for International Development (AID) administers most of the foreign economic assistance programs of the United States, and since many of them require that purchases be made from the United States, exporters can use this support mechanism. The U.S. Department of Agriculture's Commodity Credit Corporation (CCC) operates export credit guarantee programs to provide agricultural exporters or financial institutions a guarantee that they will be repaid for export financing to foreign buyers. The Small Business Administration (SBA) has two programs to assist small businesses in starting export operations: the working capital program and the international trade loan program.[52]

In addition to country-specific entities, the exporter will find it worthwhile to monitor the activities of multilateral institutions such as the United Nations and the World Bank Group as well as regional development banks (such as the Inter-American Development Bank and the Asian Development Bank). They specialize in financing investment activities and can provide valuable leads for future business activity. In a typical year, the United Nations purchases $3 billion of goods and services with 12 percent coming from U.S. companies. For example, Igloo Corp. sells annually $200,000 worth of picnic coolers to the United Nation's Children's Fund for the transportation of temperature sensitive vaccines in tropical climates.

Price Negotiations

The final export price is negotiated in person or electronically. Since pricing is the most sensitive issue in business negotiations, the exporter should be ready to discuss price as part of a comprehensive package and should avoid price concessions early on in the negotiations.[53]

An importer may reject an exporter's price at the outset in the hopes of gaining an upper hand or obtaining concessions later on. These concessions include discounts, an improved product, better terms of sales/payment, and other possibly costly demands. The exporter should prepare for this by obtaining relevant information on the target market and the customer, as well as by developing counterproposals for possible objections. For example, if the importer states that better offers are available, the exporter should ask for more details on such offers and try to convince the buyer that the exporter's total package is indeed superior. In the rare case that the importer accepts the initial bid without comment, the exporter should make sure the extended bid was correct by checking the price calculations and the Incoterm used. Furthermore, competitive prices should be revisited to ascertain that the price reflects market conditions accurately.

During the actual negotiations, pricing decisions should be postponed until all of the major substantive issues have been agreed upon. Since quality and reliability of delivery are the critical dimensions of supplier choice (in addition to price), especially when long-term export contracts are in question, the exporter may want to reduce pressure on price by emphasizing these two areas and how they fit with the buyer's needs.

Leasing

Organizational customers frequently prefer to lease major equipment, making it a $220 billion industry. About 30 percent of all capital goods (50 percent of commercial aircraft) are leased in the United States, with eight out of ten companies involved in leasing.[54] Although a major force in the United States, Japan, and Germany, leasing has grown significantly elsewhere as well; for example, one of the major international trade activities of Russia, in addition to shipping and oil, is equipment leasing. The Russians view leasing not only as a potential source of hard currency but also as a way of attracting customers who would be reluctant to buy an unfamiliar product.

Trade liberalization around the world is expected to benefit lessors both through expected growth in target economies and through the eradication of country laws and regulations hampering outside lessors. For example, the NAFTA agreement and the pent-up demand for machinery, aircraft, and heavy equipment for road building has provided a promising opportunity for U.S. leasing companies in Mexico.[55]

For the marketing manager who sells products such as printing presses, computers, forklift trucks, and machine tools, leasing may allow penetration of markets that otherwise might not exist for the firm's products if the firm had to sell them outright. Balance-of-payment problems have forced some countries to prohibit or hinder the purchase and importation of equipment into their markets; an exception has been made if the import is to be leased. In developing countries, the fact that leased products are serviced by the lessor may be a major benefit because of the shortage of trained personnel and scarcity of spare parts. At present, leasing finances over $40 billion in new vehicles and equipment each year in developing countries. The main benefit for the lessor is that total net income, after charging off pertinent repair and maintenance expenses, is often higher than it would be if the unit was sold.

In today's competitive business climate, traditional financial considerations are often only part of the asset-financing formula. Many leasing companies have become more than a source of capital, developing new value-added services that have taken them from asset financiers to asset managers or forming relationships with others who can provide these services. In some cases, lessors have even evolved into partners in business activities. El Camino Resources, Ltd., targets high-growth, technology-dependent companies such as Internet providers and software developers for their hardware, software, and technical services needs, including e-commerce as well as Internet and intranet development.[56]

Dumping

Inexpensive imports often trigger accusations of dumping—that is, selling goods overseas for less than in the exporter's home market or at a price below the cost of production, or both. Charges of dumping range from those of Florida tomato growers, who said that Mexican vegetables were being dumped across the border, to those of the Canadian Anti-Dumping Tribunal, which ruled that U.S. firms were dumping radioactive diagnostic reagents in Canada. Such disputes have become quite common, especially in highly competitive industries such as computer chips, ball bearings, and steel. From 1999 to 2004, U.S. steelmakers faced increasing competition from abroad, especially from Asia, with many foreign competitors selling at subsidized low prices. As a result the U.S. government imposed tariffs of 30 percent on imports.[57] A group of U.S. manufacturers called the American Furniture Manufacturers for Legal Trade accused Chinese wood bedroom furniture manufacturers of selling their products in the United States market below cost. They and other industry watchers have blamed cheaper imports for job losses in U.S. furniture manufacturing. As a result, the U.S. Department of Commerce determined that dumping had occurred and duties averaging 6.65 percent were imposed on Chinese imports.[58] In the United States, foreign companies found guilty of dumping not only have to pay higher tariffs, but the government has also distributed the proceeds to affected U.S. competitors.[59] The World Trade Organization has ruled that this practice violates international trade rules because it allows U.S. companies to benefit twice from anti-dumping rules.

Dumping ranges from predatory dumping to unintentional dumping. **Predatory dumping** refers to a tactic whereby a foreign firm intentionally sells at a loss in another country in order to increase its market share at the expense of domestic producers, which amounts to an international price war. **Unintentional dumping** is the result of time lags between the dates of sales transaction, shipment, and arrival. Prices, including exchange rates, can change in such a way that the final sales price turns out to be below the cost of production or below the price prevailing in the exporter's home market. It has been argued that current dumping laws, especially in the United States, do not take into adequate account such developments as floating exchange rates, which make dumping appear to be more widespread.

In the United States, domestic producers may petition the government to impose antidumping duties on imports alleged to be dumped. The duty is imposed if the International Trade Administration within the Department of Commerce determines that sales have occurred at less than fair market value and if the U.S. International Trade Commission finds that domestic industry is being, or is threatened with being, materially injured by the imports. The remedy is an **antidumping duty** equal to the dumping margin. International agreements and U.S. law provide for **countervailing duties**, which may be imposed on imports that are found to be subsidized by foreign governments and which are designed to offset the advantages imports would otherwise receive from the subsidy. The WTO reports that a total of 162 antidumping measures were taken in 2007 by India, 149 by the European Union, and 229 by the United States. The worldwide total of such administrative shelter actions was 1,274 during that year.[60] As more developing and emerging markets are reducing tariffs to comply with WTO agreements, they are switching to antidumping penalties to protect domestic players. For example, U.S. exporters faced 53 active investigations in China in 2007.[61]

Governmental action against dumping and subsidized exports violating WTO rules may result in hurting the very industries seeking relief. Action against Russian or Brazilian steel, for example, resulted in retaliatory measures against U.S. steelmakers, who themselves export billions of dollars' worth of steel products. European governments also threatened to retaliate against U.S. exports of other products. Furthermore, imposing tariffs on imports such as steel causes hardship to other industries. For example, steel tariffs will cause the costs of producing automobiles in the United States to rise.

In some cases, dumping suits have strong competitive motivations; for example, to discourage an aggressive competitor by accusing it of selling at unfair prices. Antidumping and unfair subsidy suits have led in some cases to formal agreements on voluntary restraints, whereby foreign producers agree that they will supply only a certain percentage of the U.S. market. One such arrangement is the semiconductor trade agreements signed by the United States and Japan, which required the Japanese to stop selling computer chips below cost and to try to increase sales of foreign-made computer chips in Japan.

To minimize the risk of being accused of dumping (as well to be protected from dumping), the marketer can focus on value-added products and increase differentiation by including services in the product offering. If the company operates in areas made sensitive by virtue of the industry (such as electronics) or by the fact that local competition is economically vulnerable yet powerful with respect to the government, it may seek to collaborate with local companies in gaining market access, for example.[62]

Summary

The status of price has changed to that of a dynamic element of the marketing mix. This has resulted from both internal and external pressures on business firms. Management must analyze the interactive effect that pricing has on the other elements of the mix, and how pricing can assist in meeting the overall goals of the marketing strategy.

The process of setting an export price must start with the determination of an appropriate cost baseline, and should include variables such as export-related costs to avoid compromising the desired profit margin. The quotation needs to spell out the respective responsibilities of the buyer and the seller in getting the goods to the intended destination. The terms of sale indicate these responsibilities but may also be used as a competitive tool. The terms of payment have to be clarified to ensure that the exporter will indeed get paid for the products and services rendered. Facilitating agents such as freight forwarders and banks are often used to absorb some of the risk and uncertainty in preparing price quotations and establishing terms of payment.

Exporters also need to be ready to defend their pricing practices. Competitors may petition their own government to investigate the exporter's pricing to determine the degree to which it reflects costs and prices prevailing in the exporter's domestic market.

Key Terms

skimming	cash in advance	futures
market pricing	letter of credit	pass-through
penetration pricing	draft	absorption
standard worldwide price	documentary collection	pricing-to-market
dual pricing	banker's acceptance	price manipulation
cost-plus method	discounting	forfaiting
marginal cost method	open account	factoring
market-differentiated pricing	consignment selling	predatory dumping
price escalation	commercial risk	unintentional dumping
value-added tax (VAT)	political risk	antidumping duty
duty drawbacks	forward exchange market	countervailing duties
Incoterms	option	

Questions for Discussion

1. Propose scenarios in which export prices are higher/lower than domestic prices.

2. What are the implications of price escalation?

3. Discuss the use of the currency of quotation as a competitive tool.

4. Argue for the use of more inclusive shipping terms from the marketing point of view.

5. Suggest different importer reactions to a price offer and how you, as an exporter, could respond to them.

6. Who is harmed and who is helped by dumping?

Internet Exercises

1. Assess the international trade financing commitment of different commercial banks, such as Citibank (http://www.citibank.com), Chase (http://www.chase.com), and Silicon Valley Bank (http://www.svb.com).

2. The International Trade Administration monitors cases filed against U.S. exporters on charges of dumping, to assist them in the investigations and their subsequent defense. Using their data on such cases (http://trade.gov/fairtrade/index.asp), focus on a few countries (e.g., EU, Canada, South Africa, Japan) and assess what industries seem to come under the most scrutiny.

Recommended Readings

Connor, John M. *Global Price Fixing*. Springer, Berlin: 2009.

Contino, Richard M., and Tony Valmis, eds. *Handbook of Equipment Leasing: A Deal Maker's Guide*. New York: AMACOM, 2006.

Czinkota, Michael R., Ilkka A. Ronkainen, and Marta Ortiz-Buonafina. *The Export Marketing Imperative*. Mason, OH: Thomson/South-Western, 2004.

Hart, Rupert M. *Recession Storming: Thriving in Downturns through Superior Marketing, Pricing, and Product Strategies*. Scotts Valley: CreateSpace, 2008.

Monroe, Kent B. *Pricing: Making Profitable Decisions*. New York: McGraw-Hill, 2003.

Nagle, Thomas T., and Reed K. Holden. *The Strategy and Tactics of Pricing: A Guide to Profitable Decision Making*. Englewood Cliffs, NJ: Prentice-Hall, 2005.

U.S. Department of Commerce. *A Basic Guide to Exporting 10th edition*. Washington D.C.: International Trade Administration, 2009.

Vermulst, Edwin. *The WTO Anti-Dumping Agreement*. Oxford University Press, USA, 2006.

MARKETING COMMUNICATION

Audi Promotes Vehicles, Despite Tough Economic Times

Facing a difficult economic environment, but assuming that the competition would cut back on marketing expenditures, Audi announced plans to increase its U.S. marketing budget by around 15 percent for 2009. While the company does not disclose its actual budgeted dollars for marketing communications, the company planned to spend more in the United States than ever before.

The U.S. marketing budget decisions came on the heels of a couple of outstanding years for this German auto-maker. The company's goal is to become the most successful premium car manufacturer in the world by 2015. It plans to do this by producing high quality automobiles, with a sustainable economic approach in mind. The company is driven by the principle of "Progressive Performance." This principle is based on the company's efforts in meeting the environmental demands of today's marketplace. The goal, according to Audi, is to "strike a perfect balance between performance, safety, low pollution of the environment, and recyclability."

This balance relies on three major components of the Audi car. One, aluminum is one of the preferred materials for making an Audi lighter and more agile. From a recycling viewpoint, aluminum can be fed back into the materials cycle with virtually zero loss of quality at the end of the car's life. Two, the drive train in an Audi, powered by petrol and diesel engines, offers the potential for savings by ensuring that the car's power is delivered at the optimum engine operating point. Three, the design

AUDI'S GOAL IS TO BECOME THE MOST SUCCESSFUL PREMIUM CAR MANUFACTURER IN THE WORLD BY 2015. PICTURED IS THE NEW AUDI TT RS.

of an Audi allows for the fuel efficiency of each car to be maximized. Included in the design is a concern about recyclability. But the question then becomes whether Audi's emphasis on sustainability will capture the hearts and souls of the "green" thinkers. Added to that is the question of whether or not these green thinkers reside in the high-end car marketplace.

Audi's largest export market is the United States, followed by the United Kingdom and China (excluding Hong Kong). Audi management planned to invest heavily in the brand in the United States marketplace and to dedicate money to three major areas: television commercials, online, and with dealer advertising groups. None of Audi's money in America will go toward incentives, since the company believes that they destroy the value of the brand.

In its advertising, Audi plans to target mega-events. The company spent almost $3 million for a commercial during the Super Bowl. Additionally, the company wants to become the hot car for Hollywood—and not just for Hollywood drivers. The company plans to have a fleet of Audis to lend to stars and directors. In *Iron Man,* Audi had three vehicles in starring roles, and *Transporter 3* was described as a two-hour commercial for the Audi luxury sedan A8.

But will getting America talking about Audi via movie placement and cool commercials pay off in terms of sales in a recessionary economy? Will consumers relate the pricey car and pricey promotions to sustainability?

SOURCES: Kate Linebaugh, "Audi Plans to Boost Marketing Budget in U.S. by 15 Percent," *The Wall Street Journal,* November 19, 2008, **http://online.wsj.com/article/ SB122714587029643285.html**, retrieved December 11, 2008; April Wortham, "Audi to Boost U.S. Marketing Budget," *Automotive News Europe,* January 9, 2009, **http://www.autonews.com/ article/20090109/COPY/301099731**, retrieved February 8, 2009; **http://www.audi.co.uk/etc/medialib/cms4imp/ audi2/uk/Products/about_audi/Environment.Par.0002 .File.pdf**, retrieved February 9, 2009; "Annual Press Conference: Audi Remains on Course for Success," *Audi AG,* February 28, 2007, **http://www.audiworld.com/news/07/audi-on-course- for-success/content.shtml**, retrieved February 8, 2009; Ron Grover, "Audi: Putting its Models in Movie Roles," *Business Week,* November 27, 2008, **http://www.businessweek.com/ technology/content/nov2008/tc20081126_092112.htm**, retrieved December 11, 2008.

As seen in *The International Marketplace 12.1,* effective communication is particularly important in international marketing because of the geographic and psychological distances that separate a firm from its intermediaries and customers. By definition, communication is a process of establishing a "commonness" of thought between a sender and a receiver.[1] This process extends beyond the conveying of ideas to include persuasion and thus enables the marketing process to function more effectively and efficiently. Ideally, marketing communication is a dialogue that allows organizations and consumers to achieve mutually satisfying exchange agreements. This definition emphasizes the two-way nature of the process, with listening and responsiveness as integral parts. A relationship has to be established from the beginning and deepened over time. The majority of communication is verbal, but nonverbal communication and the concept of silent languages must also be considered because they often create challenges for international marketers.

This chapter will include an overview of the principles of marketing communications in international markets. Because face-to-face, buyer–seller negotiations are possibly the most fundamental marketing process,[2] guidelines for international business negotiations are discussed first. Second, the chapter will focus on the management of the international communications mix from the exporter's point of view. Because the exporter's alternatives may be limited by the entry mode and by resources available, the tools and the challenges are quite different from those of the multinational entity. We discuss the promotional approaches used by global marketers in Chapter 18.

The Marketing Communications Process

As shown in the communications model presented in Exhibit 12.1, effective communications requires three elements—the sender, the message, and the receiver—connected by a message channel. The process may begin with an unsolicited inquiry from a potential customer or as a planned effort by the marketer. Whatever the goal of the communications process, the sender needs to study receiver characteristics before encoding the message in order to achieve maximum impact. **Encoding** the message simply means converting it into symbolic form that is properly understood by the receiver. This is not a simple task, however. For example, if an e-commerce site's order form asks only for typical U.S.-type address information, such as a zip code, and does not include anything for other countries, the would-be buyer abroad will interpret this as unwillingness to do business outside the United States. Similarly, if an export price is quoted on an ex-works basis (that includes only the cost of goods sold in the price), the buyer may not be interested in or be able to take responsibility for the logistics process and will go elsewhere.

The message channel is the path through which the message moves from sender (source) to receiver. This link that ties the receiver to the sender ranges from sound waves conveying

Exhibit **12.1**

The Marketing Communications Process

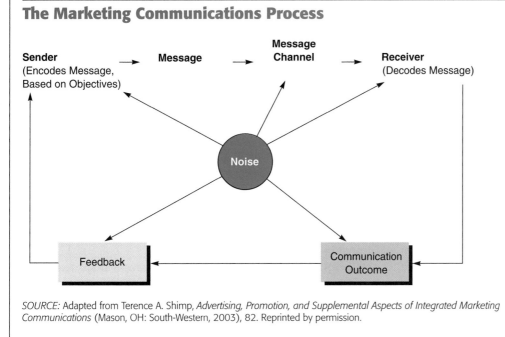

SOURCE: Adapted from Terence A. Shimp, *Advertising, Promotion, and Supplemental Aspects of Integrated Marketing Communications* (Mason, OH: South-Western, 2003), 82. Reprinted by permission.

the human voice in personal selling to transceivers or intermediaries such as print and broadcast media. Although technological advances (for example, video conferencing and the Internet) may have made buyer–seller negotiations more efficient, the fundamental process and its purpose have remained unchanged. Face-to-face contact is still necessary for two basic reasons. The first is the need for detailed discussion and explanation, and the second is the need to establish the rapport that forms the basis of lasting business relationships. Technology will then support in the maintenance of the relationship.

The message channel also exists in mass communications. Complications in international marketing may arise if a particular medium does not reach the targeted audience, which is currently the case for Internet communications, for example, due to varying online penetration rates around the world.[3] Other examples of complications are the banning of advertising for certain product categories, such as for cigarettes in most of Europe, and the fact that some marketing practices may not be allowed, such as direct selling in China.

Once a sender has placed a message into a channel or a set of channels and directed it to the intended destination, the completion of the process is dependent on the receiver's **decoding**—that is, transforming the message symbols back into thought. If there is an adequate amount of overlap between sender characteristics and needs reflected in the encoded message and receiver characteristics and needs reflected in the decoded message, the communications process has worked.

A message moving through a channel is subject to the influence of extraneous and distracting stimuli, which interfere with the intended accurate reception of the message. This interference is referred to as **noise**. In the international marketing context, noise might be a bad telephone connection, failure to express a quotation in the inquirer's system of currency and measurement, or lack of understanding of the recipient's environment—for example, having only an English-language Web site. A U.S. company got a message from its Thai client complaining of an incomplete delivery: an order of 85,000 units was four short! When the U.S. company shipped in bulk, the number of units was estimated by weight. In Thailand, however, labor is cheap and materials expensive, allowing the client to hand count shipments. The solution was to provide a slight overage in each shipment without incurring a major expense but achieving customer satisfaction.[4] Similarly, a valid inquiry from overseas may not be considered seriously by an international marketer because of noise consisting of low-quality paper, grammatical errors, or a general appearance unlike domestic correspondence.

The international marketer should be most alert to cultural noise. The lack of language skills may hinder successful negotiations, whereas translation errors may render a promotional campaign or brochure useless. Similarly, nonverbal language and its improper interpretation may cause problems. While eye contact in North America and Europe may be direct, the cultural style of the Japanese may involve markedly less eye contact.[5]

The success of the **outcome** is determined by how well objectives have been met in generating more awareness, a more positive attitude, or increased purchases. For example, the development of sales literature in the local language and reflective of the product line offered may result in increased inquiries or even more sales. While call centers abroad may provide significant cost savings, their use has to be benchmarked against customer-service standards, expectations, and overall goodwill towards the company.[6]

Regardless of whether the situation calls for interpersonal or mass communications, the collection and observation of **feedback** is necessary to analyze the success of the communications effort. The initial sender–receiver relationship is transposed, and interpretative skills similar to those needed in developing messages are needed. To make effective and efficient use of communications requires considerable strategic planning. Examples of concrete ways in which feedback can be collected are inquiry cards and toll-free numbers distributed at trade shows to gather additional information. Similarly, the Internet allows marketers to track traffic flows and to install registration procedures that identify individuals and track their purchases over time.[7]

International Negotiations

When international marketers travel abroad to do business, they are frequently shocked to discover the extent to which the many variables of foreign behavior and custom complicate their efforts.[8] Given that most negotiations are face to face, they present one of the most obvious and immediate challenges to be overcome. This means that international marketers have to adjust their approaches to establishing rapport, information exchange, persuasion, and concession making if they are to be successful in dealing with their clients and partners, such as intermediaries.[9] The consequences of failure are quickly seen in profits not realized and increases in nonrecoverable expenses, as well as decreased motivation of the international negotiators.[10]

The two biggest dangers faced in international negotiations are parochialism and stereotyping. Parochialism refers to the misleading perception that the world of business is becoming ever more American and that everyone will behave accordingly. This approach leads to stereotyping in explaining remaining differences. Stereotypes are generalizations about any given group, both positive and negative. For example, a positive stereotype has a clear influence on decisions to explore business options, whereas a negative stereotype may lead to a request to use a low-risk payment system, such as a letter of credit.[11] In a similar fashion, seemingly familiar surroundings and situations may lull negotiators into a false sense of security. This may be true for a U.S. negotiator in the United Kingdom or Australia thinking that the same language leads to the same behavioral patterns, or even in a far-off market if the meeting takes place in a hotel belonging to a large multinational chain.

The level of adjustment depends on the degree of cultural familiarity the parties have and their ability to use that familiarity effectively. For example, in China, the ideal negotiator is someone who has an established relationship with the Chinese and is trusted by them.[12] This is especially true in making the initial contact or stepping in if problems emerge. However, Chinese-Americans or overseas Chinese may be less effective in leading a negotiation. Where the Chinese are often willing to make an exception for visitors, they will expect ethnic Chinese to accept the Chinese way of doing things. The ideal team would, therefore, include a non-Chinese who understands the culture and an ethnic-Chinese individual. Together, the two can play "good guy–bad guy" roles and resist unreasonable demands.[13] If neither party is familiar with the counterpart's culture, outside facilitators should be employed.

With the increased use of the Internet, the question arises as to its use in international negotiations. Using the e-dimension does allow the exporter to overcome distances, minimize social barriers (e.g., age, gender, status), obtain instant feedback, negotiate from a home base, and do so with a number of parties simultaneously. However, it cannot be used in isolation, given the critical role of building trust in negotiations. Additionally, its extensive use may restrict much of the interaction to focusing mostly on price. The Internet is effective in the exchange of information and for possible clarification during the course of the process.[14] It should be noted that technology is only gradually making its way to such use; lack of the necessary tools and mind-set may challenge the Internet's use for this purpose.

Stages of the Negotiation Process

The process of international business negotiations can be divided into five stages: the offer, informal meetings, strategy formulation, negotiations, and implementation.[15] Which stage is emphasized and the length of the overall process will vary dramatically by culture. The negotiation process can be a short one, with the stages collapsing into one session, or a prolonged endeavor taking weeks. The differences between northern and southern Europe highlight this. Northern Europe, with its Protestant tradition and indoor culture, tends to emphasize the technical, the numerical, and the tested. Careful prenegotiations preparations are made. Southern Europe, with its Catholic background and open-air lifestyle, tends to favor personal networks, social contexts, and flair. Meetings in the South are often longer, but the total decision process may be faster.[16]

The offer stage allows the two parties to assess each other's needs and degree of commitment. The initiation of the process and its progress are determined to a great extent by background factors of the parties (such as objectives) and the overall atmosphere (for example, a spirit of cooperativeness). As an example, many European buyers may be skittish about dealing with a U.S. exporter, given the number of U.S. companies that are perceived to be focused on short-term gains or that leave immediately when the business environment turns sour.

After the buyer has received the offer, the parties meet to discuss the terms and get acquainted. In many parts of the world (Asia, the Middle East, southern Europe, and Latin America), informal meetings may often make or break the deal. Foreign buyers may want to ascertain that they are doing business with someone who is sympathetic and whom they can trust. For example, U.S. exporters to Kuwait rank the strength of the business relationship ahead of price as the critical variable driving buying decisions.[17] In some cases, it may be necessary to utilize facilitators (such as consultants or agents) to establish the contact.

Both parties have to formulate strategies for formal negotiations. This means not only careful review and assessment of all the factors affecting the deal to be negotiated but also preparation for the actual give-and-take of the negotiations. For example, U.S. negotiators were found to express more satisfaction with the outcome if it maximized joint gain, while Hong Kong Chinese negotiators are happier when they achieve outcome parity. This is evidence that cultural values (e.g., harmonious relationships for the Chinese) create the environment in which negotiation tactics are selected.[18] Thus, managers should consciously and carefully consider competitive behaviors of clients and partners. Especially in the case of governmental buyers, it is imperative to realize that public-sector needs may not necessarily fit into a mold that the marketer would consider rational. Negotiators may not necessarily behave as expected; for example, the negotiating partner may adjust behavior to the visitor's culture.

The actual face-to-face negotiations and the approach used in them will depend on the cultural background and business traditions prevailing in different countries. The most commonly used are the competitive and collaborative approaches.[19] In a competitive strategy, the negotiator is concerned mainly about a favorable outcome at the expense of the other party, while in the collaborative approach focus is on mutual needs, especially in the long term. For example, an exporter accepting a proposal that goes beyond what can be realistically delivered (in the hopes of market entry or renegotiation later) will lose in the long term. To deliver on the contract, the exporter may be tempted to cut corners in product quality or delivery, eventually leading to conflict with the buyer.

The choice of location for the negotiations plays a role in the outcome as well. Many negotiators prefer a neutral site. This may not always work, for reasons of resources or parties' perceptions of the importance of the deal. The host does enjoy many advantages, such as lower psychological risk due to familiar surroundings. Guests may run the risk of cultural shock and being away from professional and personal support systems. These pressures are multiplied if the host chooses to manipulate the situation with delays or additional demands. Visiting teams are less likely to walk out; as a matter of fact, the pressure is on them to make concessions. However, despite the challenges of being a guest, the visitor has a chance to see firsthand the counterpart's facilities and resources, and to experience culture in that market. In addition, visiting a partner, present or potential, shows commitment to the effort.[20]

Negotiator characteristics (e.g., gender, race, or age) may work for or against the exporter in certain cultures. It is challenging to overcome stereotypes, but well-prepared negotiators can overcome these obstacles or even make them work to their advantage. For example, a female negotiator may use her uniqueness in male-dominated societies to gain better access to decision makers.[21] It may be easier for a Westerner to interact with younger Chinese for the simple reason that their educational backgrounds, behavioral styles, and objectives are more similar than those of the old cadres.[22]

How to Negotiate in Other Countries[23]

A combination of attitudes, expectations, and habitual behavior influences negotiation style. Although some of the following recommendations may go against the approach used at home, they may allow the negotiator to adjust to the style of the host-country negotiators.

1. *Team assistance.* Using specialists will strengthen the team substantially and allow for all points of view to be given proper attention. Further, observation of negotiations can be valuable training experience for less-experienced participants. Whereas Western teams may average two to four people, a Chinese negotiating team may consist of up to ten people.[24] A study on how U.S. purchasing professionals conduct negotiations abroad revealed that while the vast majority believed a small team (two to five individuals) was ideal, they also said their teams were often outnumbered by their international counterparts.[25] Even if there are intragroup disagreements during the negotiations, it is critical to show one face to the counterparts and handle issues within the team privately, outside the formal negotiations.

2. *Traditions and customs.* For newcomers, status relations and business procedures must be carefully considered with the help of consultants or local representatives. For example, in highly structured societies, such as Korea, great respect is paid to age and position.[26] It is prudent to use informal communication to let counterparts know, or ask them about, any prestigious degrees, honors, or accomplishments by those who will be facing one another in negotiations. What seem like simple rituals can cause problems. No first encounter in Asia is complete without an exchange of business cards. Both hands should be used to present and receive cards, and respect should be shown by reading them carefully.[27] One side should be translated into the language of the host country.

3. *Language capability.* Ideally, the international marketing manager should be able to speak the customer's language, but that is not always possible. A qualified individual is needed as part of a marketing team to ensure that nothing gets lost in the translation, literally or figuratively. Whether the negotiator is bilingual or an interpreter is used, it might be a good gesture to deliver the first comments in the local language to break the ice. The use of interpreters allows the negotiator longer response time and a more careful articulation of arguments. If English is being used, a native speaker should avoid both jargon and idiomatic expressions, avoid complex sentences, and speak slowly and enunciate clearly.[28] An ideal interpreter is one who briefs the negotiator on cultural dimensions, such as body language, before any meetings. For example, sitting in what may be perceived as a comfortable position in North America or Europe may be seen by the Chinese as showing a lack of control of one's body and, therefore, of one's mind.

4. *Determination of authority limits.* Negotiators from North America and Europe are often expected to have full authority when they negotiate in the Far East, although their local counterparts seldom if ever do. Announcing that the negotiators do not have the final authority to conclude the contract may be perceived negatively; however, if it is used as a tactic to probe the motives of the buyer, it can be quite effective. It is important to verify who does have that authority and what challenges may be faced in getting that decision. In negotiating in Russia, for example, the international marketer will have to ascertain who actually has final decision-making authority—the central, provincial, or local government—especially if permits are needed.

5. *Patience.* In many countries, such as China, business negotiations may take three times the amount of time that they do in the United States and Europe. Showing impatience in countries such as Brazil or Thailand may prolong negotiations rather than speed them up. Also, U.S. executives tend to start relatively close to what they consider a fair price in their negotiations, whereas Chinese negotiators may start with "unreasonable" demands and a rigid posture.[29]

6. *Negotiation ethics.* Attitudes and values of foreign negotiators may be quite different from those that a U.S. marketing executive is accustomed to. Being tricky can be valued in some parts of the world, whereas it is frowned on elsewhere. For example, Western negotiators may be taken aback by last-minute changes or concession requests by Russian negotiators.[30]

7. *Silence.* To negotiate effectively abroad, a marketer needs to read correctly all types of communication. U.S. businesspeople often interpret inaction and silence as a negative sign. As a result, Japanese executives tend to expect that they can use silence to get them to lower prices or sweeten the deal. Finns may sit through a meeting expressionless, hands folded and not moving much. There is nothing necessarily negative about this; they show respect to the speaker with their focused, dedicated listening.[31]

8. *Persistence.* Insisting on answers and an outcome may be seen as a threat by negotiating partners abroad. In some markets, negotiations are seen as a means of establishing long-term commercial relations, not as an event with winners and losers. U.S. negotiators are likely to refer to written agreements and expertise during the negotiations as a function of their national culture, whereas Asians may focus more on relationship commitment. Confrontations are to be avoided because minds cannot be changed at the negotiation table; this has to be done informally. Face is an important concept throughout the Far East.

9. *Holistic view.* Concessions should be avoided until all issues have been discussed, so as to preclude the possibility of granting unnecessary benefits to the negotiation partners. Concessions traditionally come at the end of bargaining. This is especially true in terms of price negotiations. If price is agreed on too quickly, the counterpart may want to insist on too many inclusions for that price.

10. *The meaning of agreements.* What constitutes an agreement will vary from one market to another. In many parts of the world, legal contracts are still not needed; as a matter of fact, reference to legal counsel may indicate that the relationship is in trouble. For the Chinese, the written agreement exists mostly for the convenience of their Western partners and represents an agenda on which to base the development of the relationship.[32]

When a verbal agreement is reached, it is critical that both parties leave with a clear understanding of what they have agreed to. This may entail only the relatively straightforward act of signing a distributor agreement, but in the case of large-scale projects, details must be explored and spelled out. In contracts that call for cooperative efforts, the responsibilities of each partner must be clearly specified. Otherwise, obligations that were anticipated to be the duty of one contracting party may result in costs to another. For example, foreign principal contractors may be held responsible for delays that have been caused by the inability of local subcontractors (whose use might be a requisite of the client) to deliver on schedule.

Marketing Communications Strategy

The international marketing manager has the responsibility of formulating a communications strategy for the promotion of the company and its products and services. The basic steps of such a strategy are outlined in Exhibit 12.2.

Few, if any, firms can afford expenditures for promotion that is done as "art for art's sake" or only because major competitors do it. The first step in developing communications strategy is therefore assessing what company or product characteristics and benefits should be communicated to the export market. This requires constant monitoring of the various environments and target audience characteristics. For example, Volvo has used safety and quality as its primary themes in its worldwide promotional campaigns since the 1950s. This approach has provided continuity, repetition, and uniformity in positioning Volvo in relation to its primary competitors: Mercedes-Benz (prestige) and BMW (sportiness).

Absolut started exporting its vodka to the United States in 1979 with 45,000 cases and an introductory promotion effort by its distributors, Carillon Importers, Ltd. At the time, import vodka sales were almost nonexistent and Absolut's brand name was unknown. With a very small budget ($750,000) and the capability to do only print advertising, Carillon's agency, TBWA, set about to establish brand awareness. Since then, the ads have featured a full-page shot of the bottle and a two-word headline.[33] In 2008, vodka was a hot category for the alcohol marketplace. Second only to Smirnoff in the United States, Absolut sales grew by seven percent in 2006 (equal to an almost 700,000 case increase) and the vodka had 98 percent brand awareness in the United States consumer market. In the United States, Absolut owns about 11 percent of the total vodka market.[34] Certain rules of thumb can be followed in evaluating resources to be allocated for export communications efforts. The exporter has to operate in foreign markets according to the rules of the marketplace, which in the United States, for example, means high promotion costs—perhaps 30 percent of exports or even more during the early stage of entry. With heavily contested markets, the level of spending may even have to increase over time. For example, Absolut's media expenditures in 2008 were almost $23 million.[35]

Because of monetary constraints that most exporters face, promotional efforts should be concentrated on key markets. For example, European liquor marketers traditionally concentrate their promotional efforts on the United States, where volume consumption is greatest, and Great Britain, which is considered the world capital of the liquor trade. A specific objective might be to spend more than the closest competitors do in the

Exhibit 12.2

Steps in Formulating Marketing Communications Strategy

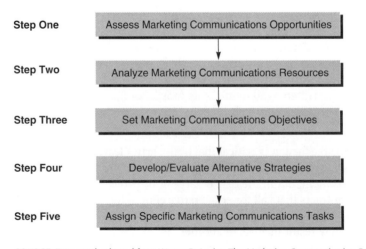

SOURCE: Framework adapted from Wayne DeLozier, *The Marketing Communication Process* (New York: McGraw-Hill, 1976), 272.

U.S. market. In the United States, for example, this would require a new import brand, aimed at the lower-price segment, to spend at the minimum $10 million during the rollout year.[36] In some cases, an exporter will have to limit this to one country, even one area, at a time to achieve set goals with the available budget. International campaigns require patient investment; the market has to progress through awareness, knowledge, liking, preference, and favorable purchase intentions before payback begins. Payback periods of one or two years cannot be realistically expected. For many exporters, a critical factor is the support of the intermediary. Whether a distributor is willing to contribute a $3 million media budget or a few thousand dollars makes a big difference. In some cases, intermediaries take a leading role in the promotion of the product in a market. In the case of Absolut, for example, Carillon Importers has been credited with the creative advertising widely acknowledged as a primary reason for the brand's success. However, as described in *The International Marketplace 12.2*, even these ads can run amok.

The International MARKETPLACE 12.2

When Absolut Did Not Depict the Absolute Truth

Absolut Vodka experienced the power of the Internet first hand in 2008 with an ad targeted solely to consumers in Mexico. Tapping into the national pride of Mexicans, the company's Mexico City–based advertising agency, Teran/TBWA, created a billboard and press campaign that featured a colorful map in which much of the southwestern United States was located in Mexico. In the advertisement, the southern border of the USA was redrawn to resemble historical times in which states such as California and Texas were part of Mexico. While Mexicans might have gotten a good chuckle out of the ad, residents of the United States were not pleased.

Initially, commentator Michelle Malkin posted the Mexican ad on her blog site, michellemalkin.com. Soon after, the ad news was picked up by drudgereport.com, the site that broke the Monica Lewinsky story years ago. Both of these sites are thought to have tremendous viral abilities. This was proven true when the ad story posted on the sites began inciting outrage among citizens of the United States—many of whom were Absolut consumers.

Bloggers in the United States were angered over the ad's depiction, with many demanding a boycott of Absolut, some even threatening to pour their remaining Absolut down the drain! Organizations fighting illegal immigration also launched boycotts of Absolut vodka. The National Illegal Immigration Boycott Coalition (NIIBC) and the Americans for Legal Immigration (ALIPAC) claimed that global companies like Absolut were trying to cash in on the threat of a separatist movement in the United States. The ad appeared at a time when the United States was building up its border security and on the heels of the collapse of a comprehensive immigration reform that had evoked considerable emotional debate. American-made SKYY vodka saw the opportunity to send out a press release that took a shot at Absolut. According to SKYY vodka spokesperson Dave Karraker, "Like SKYY vodka, the residents of states like California, Texas, and Arizona are exceptionally proud of the fact that they are from the United States of America. To imply that they might be interested in changing their mailing address, as our competitor seems to be suggesting in their advertising, is a bit presumptuous."

The backlash from the ad's debut in Mexico and ultimate infiltration into the hands of consumers in the United States appeared to come as a surprise to the Swedish company. According to a statement left on the company's consumer inquiry line, "In no way was it meant to offend or disparage, nor does it advocate an altering of borders, nor does it lend support to any anti-American sentiment, nor does it reflect immigration issues." As a global company, Absolut saw first-hand that ads have no borders—anything designed for residents of one country will, in today's technological age, end up in the hands of consumers worldwide—from Mexico to the United States to Australia—all in one day!

SOURCES: David Usborne, "Storm in a Shot Glass as Advert Redraws Map of Americas," *The Independent*, April 8, 2008, **http://www.independent.co.uk/news/world/americas/storm-in-a-shot-glass-as-advert-redraws-map-of-americas-805764**, retrieved February 10, 2009; "Mexico Reconquers California? Absolut Drinks to That!" *LA Plaza blogs, Los Angeles Times*, April 2008, **http://latimesblogs.latimes.com/laplaza/2008/04/mexico-reconque.html**, retrieved February 10, 2009; "Absolut's 'Mexico U.S.' Map Angers Many," *Newsmax*, April 14, 2008, **http://www.newsmax.com/insidecover/Absolut_mexico_Map/2008/04/14/87761.html**, retrieved February 10, 2009; Ioan Grillo, "A Vodka Tonic for Mexico's Loss?" *Time*, April 8, 2008, **http://www.time.com/time/world/article/0,8599,1728801,00.html**, retrieved February 10, 2009; "California in Mexico? Absolut-ly," *Reuters, Brisbane Times*, April 8, 2008, **http://www.brisbanetimes.com.au/articles/2008/04/08/1207420359230.html**, retrieved February 10, 2009; "Vodka Maker Apologizes for Ad Depicting Southwest as Part of Mexico," *Associated Press, Fox News*, April 7, 2008, **http://www.foxnews.com/story/0,2933,346964,00.html**, retrieved February 10, 2009.

In most cases, however, the exporter should retain some control of the campaign rather than allow intermediaries or sales offices a free hand in the various markets operated. Although markets may be dissimilar, common themes and common objectives need to be incorporated into the individual campaigns. For example, Duracell, the world leader in alkaline batteries, provides graphics—such as logos and photos—to country operations. Although many exporters do not exert pressure to conform, overseas distributors take advantage of annual meetings to discuss promotional practices with their head office counterparts.

Alternative strategies are needed to spell out how the firm's resources can be combined and adapted to market opportunities. The tools the international marketer has available to form a total communications program for use in the targeted markets are referred to as the **promotional mix**. They consist of the following:

1. *Advertising:* Any form of nonpersonal presentation of ideas, goods, or services by an identified sponsor, with predominant use made of *mass* communication, such as print, broadcast, or electronic media, or *direct* communication that is pinpointed at each business-to-business customer or ultimate consumer using computer technology and databases.

2. *Personal selling:* The process of assisting and persuading a prospect to buy a good or service or to act on an idea through use of person-to-person communication with intermediaries and/or final customers.

3. *Publicity:* Any form of nonpaid, commercially significant news or editorial comment about ideas, products, or institutions.

4. *Sales promotion:* Direct inducements that provide extra product value or incentive to the sales force, intermediaries, or ultimate consumers.

5. *Sponsorship:* The practice of promoting the interests of the company by associating it with a specific event (typically sports or culture) or a cause (typically a charity or a social interest).

The use of these tools will vary by company and by situation. Although all Harley-Davidson motorcycles are on allocation in overseas markets, their promotion focuses on postpurchase reinforcement. Owners, in turn, become a powerful promotional tool for Harley-Davidson through word-of-mouth communication. The company also sells "motor clothes," illustrated in catalogs. Copies are made for overseas dealers, who cannot afford to translate and reprint them, and they pass them on to their customers with notes that not all items are available or permissible in their markets.[37]

The choice of tools leads to either a push or a pull emphasis in marketing communications. **Push strategies** focus on the use of personal selling. Despite its higher cost per contact, personal selling is appropriate for the international marketing of industrial goods, which have shorter channels of distribution and smaller target populations than do consumer goods. Governmental clients are typically serviced through personal selling efforts. Some industries, such as pharmaceuticals, traditionally rely on personal selling to service the clientele.

On the other hand, **pull strategies** depend on mass communications tools, mainly advertising. Advertising is appropriate for consumer-oriented products with large target audiences and long channels of distribution. Of its promotional budget, Absolut has traditionally spent up to 85 percent in print media in the United States, with the balance picked up by outdoor advertising, mainly billboards. The base of the advertising effort has been formed by magazines such as *Sports Illustrated, Vanity Fair, Business Week, Rolling Stone, Esquire, Time,* and *Newsweek.* However, starting in 2006, the company's online spending has increased to 20 percent of the annual media budget, with the new domain building on an online community and more interactive content.

No promotional tool should be used in isolation or without regard to the others; hence, we see a trend toward **integrated marketing communications**. Promotional tools should be coordinated according to target market and product characteristics, the size of the promotional budget, the type and length of international involvement, and control considerations. As an example, industrial purchasing decisions typically involve eight to eleven people. Because a salesperson may not reach all of them, the use of advertising may be necessary to influence the participants in the decision-making process. In addition, steps must be taken to have information readily available to prospects who are interested in the exporter's products. This can be achieved with the development of a Web site and participating in trade shows.

Exhibit 12.3 provides an example of an advertising campaign for a disk-drive exporter. While the company's ads in its home market focus on product benefits and technical excellence, the approach taken in Asia was much softer. Under the theme "Unique ideas are often the most enduring," the objective was to increase original equipment makers'

Exhibit **12.3**

Advertising Campaign for a Disk-Drive Exporter

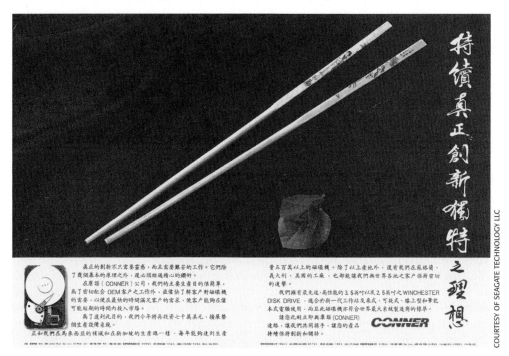

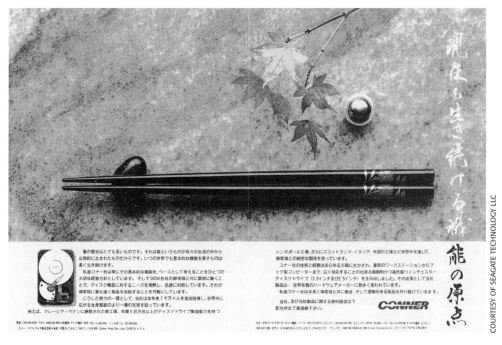

awareness of the company's products and the fact that it designed them in close cooperation with its customers. The Chinese ad pictured bone Chinese chopsticks on black cloth, while the Japanese version showed enameled Japanese (pointed) chopsticks on a marble slab to appeal to different aesthetics.

Finally, specific marketing communications tasks must be assigned, which may require deciding on a division of labor with foreign intermediaries or with other exporters for co-operative communications efforts. For example, Ernie Ball, the maker of Gauge, Slinky, and Earthwood guitar strings, cooperates closely with its distributors in the marketing of its products. Local distributors have adapted U.S. programs to their markets, such as Battle of Bands for Europe, which is the largest live music promotion in the industry. The company also uses the Internet for contest promotions such as the best guitarist and the best bassist.[38] Cooperative programs allow the exporter control of the promotional effort while getting distribution partners to contribute to the effort financially.

In cases in which the locally based intermediaries are small and may not have the resources to engage in promotional efforts, the exporter may suggest dealer-participatory programs. In exchange for including the intermediaries' names in promotional material without any expense to them—for example, in announcing a sweepstakes—the exporter may request increased volume purchases from the intermediaries.

Communications Tools

The main communications tools used by exporters to communicate with the foreign market-place from their domestic base are business and trade journals, directories, direct advertising, the Internet, trade fairs and missions, and personal selling. If the exporter's strategy calls for a major promotional effort in a market, it is advisable either to use a domestic agency with extensive operations in the intended market or to use a local agency and work closely with the company's local representatives in media and message choices.

Because the promoter–agency relationship is a close one, it may be helpful if the exporter's domestic agency has an affiliate in the target foreign market. The management function and coordination can be performed by the agency at home, while the affiliate can execute the program as it seems appropriate in that market. An exporter, if it has a sufficient budget, may ask its domestic agency to set up a branch overseas. Some exporters, especially those that have a more significant presence overseas, leave the choice of the agency to local managers. If a local agency is to be chosen, the exporter must make sure that coordination and coop-eration between the agency and the exporter's domestic agency can be achieved. Whatever the approach used, the key criterion must be the competence of the people who will be in charge of the creation and implementation of the promotional programs.

Business/Trade Journals and Directories

Many varied business and trade publications, as well as directories, are available to the exporter. Some, such as *Business Week, Fortune, The Economist, The Wall Street Journal,* and *Financial Times,* are standard information sources worldwide. Extensions of these are their regional editions; for example, *The Asian Wall Street Journal* or *Business Week— Europe.* Trade publications can be classified as (1) horizontal, which cater to a particular job function cutting across industry lines, such as *Purchasing World* or *Industrial Distribution,* and (2) vertical, which deal with a specific industry, such as *Chemical Engineering* or *International Hospital Supplies.* These journals are global, regional, or country-specific in their approaches. Many U.S.-based publications are available in national language editions, with some offering regional buys for specific export markets—for example, the Spanish edition of *Feed Management,* titled *Alimentos Balanceados Para Animales.*

The exporter should also be aware of the potential of government-sponsored publica-tions. For example, *Commercial News USA,* published by the U.S. Department of Commerce, is an effective medium for the marketer interested in making itself and its products known worldwide for a modest sum. For as little as $895, an exporter can reach 400,000 potential buyers in 145 countries through the publication, distributed to recipients free of charge 6 times a year.[39]

Directories provide a similar tool for advertising efforts. Many markets feature exporter yellow pages, some of which offer online versions in addition to the traditional print ones. For example, *The Export Yellow Pages* offers U.S. firms a means to promote their businesses worldwide at no cost (if they just want to be listed), and at low cost for an advertisement or link to their e-mail or homepage. Some of the directories are country-specific. For example, BellSouth*Guia Internacional* allows exporters to showcase their products to 425,000 Latin American and Caribbean importers.[40] A number of online directories, such as *Internet International Business Exchange* (**http://www.imex.com**), provide the exporter the opportunity to have banner ads (i.e., ads placed on frequently visited Web sites) for $100 to $390 a month. Examples of international trade publications and directories are provided in Exhibit 12.4.

The two main concerns when selecting media are effectiveness in reaching the appropriate target audience(s) and efficiency in minimizing the cost of doing so, measured in terms of cost per thousand. If the exporter is in a position to define the target audience clearly (for example, in terms of demographics or product-related variables), the choice of media will be easier. In addition, consideration should be given to how well a given medium will work with the other tools the exporter wishes to employ. For example, advertisements in publications and directories may have the function of driving customers and prospects to the exporter's Web site.[41]

In deciding which publications to use, the exporter must apply the general principles of marketing communications strategy. Coverage and circulation information is available from Standard Rate & Data Service (**http://www.srds.com**). SRDS provides a complete list of

Exhibit 12.4

Example of International Trade Publications and Directories

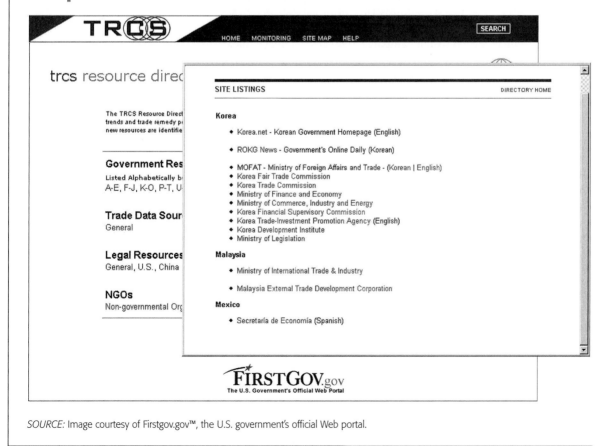

SOURCE: Image courtesy of Firstgov.gov™, the U.S. government's official Web portal.

international publications (more than 100,000 media properties in all) in the International Section of the *Business Publication,* and audit information similar to that on the U.S. market is provided for countries such as the United Kingdom, Italy, France, Austria, Switzerland, Germany, Mexico, and Canada. Outside these areas, the exporter has to rely on the assistance of publishers or local representatives. Actual choices are usually complicated by lack of sufficient funds and concern over the information gap. The simplest approach may be to use U.S. publishers, in which the exporter may have more confidence in terms of rates and circulation data. If a more localized approach is needed, a regional edition or national publication can be considered. Before advertising is placed in an unfamiliar journal, the marketer should analyze its content and overall quality of presentation.

Direct Marketing

The purpose of direct marketing is to establish a relationship with a customer in order to initiate immediate and measurable responses.[42] This is accomplished through direct-response advertising, telemarketing, and direct selling.

Direct mail is by far the dominant direct-response medium, but some advertising is also placed in mass media, such as television, magazines, and newspapers. Direct mail can be a highly personalized tool of communication if the target audience can be identified and defined narrowly. Ranging from notices to actual samples, it allows for flexibility in the amount of information conveyed and in its format. Direct mail is directly related in its effectiveness to the availability and quality of the mailing lists. Mailing lists may not be available around the world in the same degree that they are in, say, the United States. However, more and better lists are surfacing in Asia, Latin America, and the Middle East. In addition, reliable, economical, global postal service has become available.[43] Philips Broadband, which markets cable television equipment, has used its international mailings to support its broad schedule of trade shows, many of which are in developing regions.

Even when mailing lists are available, they may not be as up-to-date or as precise as the international marketer would desire. In China, for example, lists are available to send literature directly to factories, ministries, professional societies, research institutes, and universities. However, such mailings can be extremely costly and produce few results. An effective and efficient direct-mail campaign requires extensive market-by-market planning of materials, format, and mode of mailing.

Catalogs are typically distributed to overseas customers through direct mail, although many catalogs have online versions as well. Their function is to make the exporter's name known, generate requests for further information, stimulate orders, and serve as a reminder between transactions. Catalogs are particularly useful if a firm's products are in a highly specialized field of technology and if only the most highly qualified specialists are to be contacted. In many markets, especially the developing ones, people may be starving for technology information and will share any mailings they receive. Due to this unsatisfied demand, a very small investment can reach many potential end users.

The growing mail-order segment is attracting an increasing number of foreign entrants to markets previously dominated by local firms. However, because consumers are wary of sending orders and money to an unknown company overseas, the key to market penetration is a local address. In Japan, L. L. Bean, the U.S. outdoor clothing merchandiser, works through McCann Direct, the specialized direct-marketing division of McCann-Erickson Hakuhodo Inc., Japan's largest foreign advertising agency. Bean places ads for its catalogs in Japanese media, orders for catalogs are sent to McCann Direct, and McCann Direct then forwards the addresses to Bean's headquarters in Maine, where all the orders for catalogs or goods are filled.[44] Despite the economic promise of emerging markets such as China, India, and Russia, the development of direct marketing is constrained by negative attitudes toward Western business practices and problems with distribution networks and marketing support systems, as well as bureaucratic obstacles.[45]

Traditional direct mail is undergoing major change. New types of mail services (e.g., Global Express Mail) enable companies to deal with their customers more efficiently when customers buy through catalogs or electronic means. New electronic media will assume an increasing share in the direct-response area. However, direct marketing will continue to grow as a function of its targetability, its measurability, and the responsiveness of consumers to direct marketing efforts.

In the past, U.S. marketers thought that country-specific offices were almost essential to bringing their companies closer to overseas customers. Now with functioning telecommunication systems and deregulation in the industry, **telemarketing** (including sales, customer service, and help-desk-related support) is flourishing throughout the world. A growing number of countries in Latin America, Asia, and Europe are experiencing growth in this area as consumers are becoming more accustomed to calling toll-free numbers and more willing to receive calls from marketers.

In Europe, companies using this service publicize their assigned local phone numbers on television or print ads, direct mailings, catalogs, or Web sites, and then the calls are routed to a call center. The number and location of such call centers will depend on a variety of issues, such as what the distribution area of the product is, what the costs of operation are, how important local presence is, and how important certain capabilities are, such as language and the ability to handle calls from various time zones.[46] Argentine, Brazil, and Costa Rica are choices for Central and Latin American call center operations, India and the Philippines for Asia, while Belgium, Holland, Ireland, Portugal, and some of the new EU countries are leading locations in Europe (Exhibit 12.5).[47] If only one center is used in Europe, for example, access to a multilingual workforce is a major factor in selecting the location. When a call comes in, the name of the country in which the call originates is displayed above the switchboard so that it can be taken by an operator who speaks the language(s) native to that country.

Call center activity has developed more slowly in emerging markets than it has in North America and Europe, mostly because of infrastructural reasons and cultural resistance to the new form of communicating with business.[48] However, new technologies are helping to overcome such resistance. **Database marketing** allows the creation of an individual relationship with each customer or prospect. For example, a call center operator will know a customer's background with the company or overall purchasing habits. Care has to be taken not to violate privacy regulations or sensitivities. The development of the needed databases through direct mail or the Internet will advance the use of telemarketing.

Exhibit 12.5

An Example of an International Call Center

FOR PAN-EUROPEAN CALL CENTERS, **PTT TELECOM HAS THE ANSWER.**

Whether you're looking to establish, expand, or enhance your European presence, look to PTT Telecom Netherlands to provide the seamless telecommunications services your company can depend on. ■ Only PTT Telecom Netherlands provides a 99.9% call completion rate, fastest call set-up times, and the lowest call failure rate in all of Europe. ■ We also offer distinct advantages unique to the Netherlands: a highly trained workforce (over 75% of our Call Center agents speak 3 or more languages), and a sophisticated distribution infrastructure (49% of the Fortune 500 companies have European distribution centers located here). ■ In fact, working with our sister KPN companies, we can provide you with cost-effective, seamless solutions for your entire European enterprise. ■ From turnkey call center solutions to invoice and collection services, warehousing, distribution and fulfillment, call 800.777.6842. ■ Find out how PTT Telecom Netherlands can bring Europe together for you.

kpn telecom
A KPN COMPANY
Visit us on the internet. http://www.dutch-tele.com/us/

Some exporters see the use of call centers as a preliminary step to entering an international market with a deeper presence such as a sales office.

Internet[49]

Having a Web site is seen as necessary if for no other reason than image; lack of a Web presence may convey a negative image to the various constituents of the marketer. The Web site should be linked to the overall marketing strategy and not just be there for appearance's sake. This means having a well-designed and well-marketed site.[50] Quality is especially critical if customers use the Web site to find more information or clarification, as triggered by the exporter's other communications efforts such as advertisements or telemarketing efforts.

Having a Web presence will support the exporter's marketing communications effort in a number of ways. First, it allows the company to increase its presence in the marketplace and to communicate its overall mission and information about its marketing mix. Second, the Internet will allow 24-hour access to customers and prospects. Providing important information during decision making can help the customer clarify the search. The potential interactivity of the Web site (e.g., in providing tailor-made solutions to the customer's concerns) may provide a competitive advantage as the customer compares alternative sites. For example, the Web site for apparel marketer Lands' End allows consumers to identify their body type and then mix and match clothing items that suit them.[51] Interactivity is also critical when the site is designed, in determining what features to include (e.g., should sites adjust to different dialects of a language in a region?).

Third, the Internet can improve customer service by allowing customers to serve themselves when and where they choose. This is an area where an exporter's Web presence can reduce overall communications costs in the most significant way. Naturally, the exporter must have the necessary capacity to serve all interested customers through the Web site, especially if there is an increase in interest and demand. An important dimension of customer service is after-sales service to solve consumer problems and to facilitate the formation of consumer groups. A Web forum where customers can exchange news and views on product use will not only facilitate product research, but it also will build loyalty among consumers.

The fourth advantage is the ability of the exporter to gather information, which has its uses not only in research but also in database development for subsequent marketing efforts. While the data collected may be biased, they are also very inexpensive to collect. If the data are used to better cater to existing customers, then data collected through Internet interaction are the best possible.

The fifth advantage of the Internet is the opportunity to actually close sales. This function is within the realm of e-commerce. It will require a significant commitment on the part of the exporter in terms of investment in infrastructure to deliver not only information but also the product to the customer. E-commerce is discussed in more detail in Chapter 13.

In addition to communications with customers, the Internet provides the possibility to communicate with internal constituents. Exporters may have part of their Web sites set up with detailed product and price information that only their agents, representatives, or distributors have access to. Especially when changes are called for, this is an efficient way of communicating about them without having to mail or fax each and every overseas party. Web sites can also be used in the recruitment of intermediaries and partners. P&D Creative, a manufacturer of environmentally safe cleaning products, uses its site (**http://pdcreativeinc.com**) to attract intermediaries. The company promotes its site in search engines and internationally oriented newsgroups and provides information of special interest to intermediaries.

Internet strategy is not restricted to the exporter's own Web site. The exporter needs to determine with which portals, such as AOL (**http://www.aol.com**) or Yahoo! (**http://www.yahoo.com**), or with what type of hyperlinks with related products or services, such as Internet International Business Exchange (**http://www.imex.com**), to negotiate for banner advertising on those sites.

The challenges faced by exporters in Internet-based communications are related to the newness of the medium and the degree to which adjustments need to be made for each market served. A very large portion of the world population has yet to adopt the Internet, and its users have a distinct profile. In some cases this might match the exporter's intended target market (such as for online music); however, in many cases Internet diffusion has yet to reach the targeted customer.

While English-only Web sites can deliver information and support to some international customers, having local-language sites and registering with local search engines demonstrate appropriate market and cultural sensitivity. It takes 20 languages to reach 90 percent of the web's worldwide users.[52] The choice of languages will depend on the target audience. The most popular languages are English, French, Spanish, German, Japanese, and Chinese. For some, a dialect must be specified; for example, Spanish has three main variants: European, Mexican, and South American. The exporter needs also to determine which pages have to be modified. Pages that emphasize marketing, sales, and corporate identity are normally the ones chosen.[53]

While the exporter's local Web sites may (and for global product or service offerings, should) be quite similar in terms of aesthetics, adjustments should also be made for such dimensions as depth of product line and level of market presence. Customers who are familiar with the Internet may access information about products and services before purchasing them and may visit sites in several countries. Second-generation technology is increasing the interactivity of advertising on the Web. Given that individuals around the world have different information needs, varying levels of company and product familiarity, and different user capabilities, exporters can adjust their Web sites' content and develop paths tailored to each group of customers or even to an individual customer. Overall, the incorporation of the Internet into the exporter's marketing strategy will enhance market orientation, marketing competence, and eventually marketing performance.[54]

Marketers using the Web as an advertising medium will have to be concerned about market-by-market differences in regulations. For example, Germany sued Benetton (**http://www.benetton.com**) for "exploiting feelings of pity" with one of its "United Colors of Benetton" campaigns.[55] Finally, online communications strategy should also include provisions for technological development. Hand-held devices such as mobile phones and video iPods may present a new media opportunity provided that consumers are willing to watch entertainment, and the advertising that supports it, on a small screen.[56]

Trade Shows and Missions

Marketing goods and services through trade shows is a European tradition that dates back at least as far as A.D. 1240. After sales force costs, trade shows are one of the most significant cost items in marketing budgets. Although they are usually associated with industrial firms, some consumer-products firms are represented as well. Typically, a trade show is an event at which manufacturers, distributors, and other vendors display their products or describe their services to current and prospective customers, suppliers, other business associates, and the press.[57] The International Automotive Services Industries Show and the International Coal Show, for example, run eight hours a day for three days, plus one or two preview days, and register 25,000 attendees. In the consumer goods area, expositions are the most common type of show. Tickets are usually sold; typical expositions include home/garden, boat, auto, stereo, and antiques. Although a typical trade show or typical participant does not exist, an estimated $75,000 is allocated for each show, and the median manufacturer or distributor attends nine or ten shows annually. The number of days spent at trade shows averages 2.4, and the hours per day are 8.6.[58]

Whether an exporter should participate in a trade show depends largely on the type of business relationship it wants to develop with a particular country. More than 16,000 trade shows create an annual $50 billion in business worldwide.[59] A company looking only for one-time or short-term sales might find the expense prohibitive, but a firm looking for long-term involvement may find the investment worthwhile. Arguments in favor of participation include the following:

1. Some products, by their very nature, are difficult to market without providing the potential customer a chance to examine them or see them in action. Trade fairs provide an excellent opportunity to introduce, promote, and demonstrate new products. Auto shows, such as the ones in Detroit, Geneva, and Tokyo, feature "concept" cars to gauge industry and public opinion. Recently, many of these new models have been

environmentally friendly, such as being 90 percent recyclable. The world's premier mobile telephony event, 3GSM World Congress, has nearly 1,000 marketers showcasing their latest mobile products, services, and solutions.[60]

2. An appearance at a show produces goodwill and allows for periodic cultivation of contacts. Beyond the impact of displaying specific products, many firms place strong emphasis on "waving the company flag" against competition. This facet also includes morale boosting of the firm's sales personnel and distributors.

3. The opportunity to find an intermediary may be one of the best reasons to attend a trade show. A show is a cost-effective way to solicit and screen candidates to represent the firm, especially in a new market. Copylite Products of Ft. Lauderdale used the CeBIT computer-and-automation show in Hannover, Germany, to establish itself in Europe. The result was a distribution center in Rotterdam and six distributors covering eight countries. Its $40,000 investment in the trade show has reaped millions in new business.[61]

4. Attendance is one of the best ways to contact government officials and decision makers, especially in China. For example, participation in the Chinese Export Commodities Fair, which is held twice a year in Guangzhou, China, is "expected" by the host government.

5. Trade fairs provide an excellent chance for market research and collecting competitive intelligence. The exporter is able to view most rivals at the same time and to test comparative buyer reactions. Trade fairs provide one of the most inexpensive ways of obtaining evaluative data on the effectiveness of a promotional campaign.

6. Exporters are able to reach a sizable number of sales prospects in a brief time period at a reasonable cost per contact. According to research by Hannover Messe, more than 86 percent of all attendees represent buying influences (managers with direct responsibility for purchasing products and services). Of equal significance is the fact that trade show visitors are there because they have a specific interest in the exhibits.[62] Similarly, suppliers can be identified. One U.S. apparel manufacturer at the International Trade Fair for Clothing Machinery in Cologne paid for its participation by finding a less expensive thread supplier.[63]

On the other hand, the following are among the reasons cited for nonparticipation in trade fairs:

1. High costs. These can be avoided by participating in events sponsored by the U.S. Department of Commerce or exhibiting at U.S. trade centers or export development offices. An exporter can also lower costs by sharing expenses with distributors or representatives. Further, the costs of closing a sale through trade shows are estimated to be much lower than for a sale closed through personal representation.

2. Difficulty in choosing the appropriate trade fairs for participation. This is a critical decision. Because of scarce resources, many firms rely on suggestions from their foreign distributors on which fairs to attend and what specifically to exhibit. Caterpillar, for example, usually allows its foreign dealers to make the selections for themselves. In markets where conditions are more restricted for exporters, such as China, Caterpillar in effect serves as the dealer and thus participates itself.

3. For larger exporters with multiple divisions, the problem of coordination. Several divisions may be required to participate in the same fair under the company banner. Similarly, coordination is required with distributors and agents if joint participation is desired, which requires joint planning.

Trade show participation is too expensive to be limited to the exhibit alone. A clear set of promotional objectives would include targeting accounts and attracting them to the show with preshow promotion using mailings, advertisements in the trade journals, or Web site information. Contests and giveaways are effective in attracting participants to the company's exhibition area. Major customers and attractive prospects often attend, and they should be acknowledged, for example, by arranging for a hospitality suite.[64] Finally, a system is needed to evaluate post-show performance and to track qualified leads.

Exporters may participate in general or specialized trade shows. General trade fairs are held in Hannover, Germany and Milan, Italy. (See *The International Marketplace 12.3* for an overview of a relative newcomer to the trade show industry.) An example of a specialized one is Retail Solutions, a four-day trade show on store automation held in London. Participants planning to exhibit at large trade shows may elect to do so independently or as part of a national pavilion. For small and medium-sized companies the benefit of a group pavilion

---

The International
MARKETPLACE
12.3

Dubai's International Direct Selling Festival

Dubai, a 37-year old city, is one of the seven emirates located in the United Arab Emirates (UAE). According to promotional material about Dubai, the city is home to many of the world's largest and best attractions. For example, the city boasts of the world's tallest tower (Burj Dubai), the world's largest shopping mall (Dubai Mall), the world's only 7-star hotel (Burj Al Arab), and the world's first manmade marina (Dubai Marina). A fast-growing destination for tourists and expatriates, the city is supported by a large service and hospitality infrastructure. Dubai is truly an emerging market.

Approximately 85 percent of the UAE population—Dubai in particular—consists of expatriates. A high percentage of these expats are classified as middle-class, Rapid expansion in the UAE has served to drive up the inflation rate, and it is believed that these middle-class residents will want to increase their incomes. Given its growth opportunities, the UAE has become a breeding ground for direct selling companies. With a 2008 worldwide sales figure of around $110 billion the industry employs approximately 60 million salespeople.

In May of 2008, Dubai held its first International Direct Selling Festival. The festival had 45 exhibitors, over 350 conference participants, and approximately 3000 visitors from 35 countries. It was estimated that 60 percent of the attendees were from outside the UAE. According to reports, 95 percent of the companies participating in the 2008 festival ultimately launched offices in the UAE.

The success of the 2008 expo and conference led to immediate planning for the next festival. The 2009 festival was organized jointly by the Direct Selling Educational Institute (DSEI) in Dubai and Links Group, an events-based management company in Dubai. Exhibitors for the festival were international direct selling companies, multi-level marketing and network marketing companies, teleshopping TV companies, and service providers (such as financial/legal/IT advisors, advertising and PR companies, and office supply companies). Visitors to the

DUBAI'S FIRST INTERNATIONAL DIRECT SELLING FESTIVAL HAD 45 EXHIBITORS, OVER 350 CONFERENCE PARTICIPANTS, AND APPROXIMATELY 3000 VISITORS FROM 35 COUNTRIES.

trade show included direct sellers, network marketers, distributors, students, and anyone looking to make additional income. The international draw for the trade show, however, truly came from its visitor base, with visitors from countries such as Saudi Arabia, Oman, Qatar, Bahrain, Iran, Kuwait, India, Jordan, Lebanon, Malaysia, Singapore, Turkey, and Egypt.

Putting together a trade show such as Dubai's International Direct Selling Festival requires effort on the part of many trade show partners. As noted, DSEI and Linkviva Events were two major players. Another major event partner was The Box, which specializes in storage and logistics. Naturally, a marketing communications event such as this would not be complete without media. Tambi Studios was the media production firm that focused on telling the success stories about the festival. Ultimately, the goal of all of these event partners was to legitimize the direct selling industry in the UAE and garner a piece of the revenue available from direct selling.

SOURCES: World Federation of Direct Selling Association, **http://www.wfdsa.org/**, retrieved February 5, 2009; Dubai Second International Direct Selling Festival Expo and Conference, **http://www.directsellingfestival.com/**, retrieved February 5, 2009; "Direct Selling News Europe Update," *Direct Selling News*, January 2009, 50.

is in both cost and ease of the arrangements. These pavilions are often part of governmental export-promotion programs. Even foreign government assistance may be available; for example, the Japanese External Trade Organization (JETRO) helps non-Japanese companies participate in the country's two largest trade shows.

Other promotional events that the exporter can use are trade missions, seminar missions, solo exhibitions, video/catalog exhibitions, and virtual trade shows. **Trade missions** can be U.S. specialized trade missions or industry-organized, government-approved (IOGA) trade missions, both of which aim at expanding the sales of U.S. goods and services and the establishment of agencies and representation abroad. The U.S. Department of Commerce is actively involved in assistance of both types. **Seminar missions** are events in which eight to ten firms are invited to participate in a one- to four-day forum, during which the team members conduct generic discussions on technological issues—that is, follow a soft-sell approach. This is followed up by individual meetings with end users, government agencies, research institutions, and other potentially useful contacts. Individual firms may introduce themselves to certain markets by proposing a technical seminar there. Synopses of several alternative proposed lectures, together with company details and the qualifications of the speakers, must be forwarded to the proper body, which will circulate the proposals to interested bodies and coordinate all the arrangements. The major drawback is the time required to arrange for such a seminar, which may be as much as a year. **Solo exhibitions** are generally limited to one, or at the most, a few product themes and are held only when market conditions warrant them. Philips's approach is the Philips Electronics Circus, which features three interconnected tents equipped with the company's latest technology. The idea is to let consumers experience the latest technology, thus helping to boost brand recognition and sales.[65] **Video/catalog exhibitions** allow exporters to publicize their products at low cost. They consist of 20 to 35 product presentations on videotapes, each lasting five to ten minutes. They provide the advantage of actually showing the product in use to potential customers. **Virtual trade shows** enable exporters to promote their products and services over the Internet and to have electronic presence without actually attending a trade show.[66] Trade leads and international sales interests are collected and forwarded by the sponsor to the companies for follow-up. The information stays online for 365 days for one flat fee. For example, BuyUSA (an online environment sponsored by the U.S. Department of Commerce) offers exporters the opportunity to show their company profile, logo, product listings, Web site link, and catalog in a virtual trade zone. The virtual trade zone is promoted heavily at the trade shows actually attended by the department, giving buyers at the show a chance to review company information for possible contact.[67]

Personal Selling

Personal selling is the most effective of the promotional tools available to the marketer; however, its costs per contact are high. The average cost of sales calls may vary from $200 to $1,100, depending on the industry and the product or service. Personal selling allows for immediate feedback on customer reaction as well as information on markets.

The exporter's sales effort is determined by the degree of internationalization in its efforts, as shown in Exhibit 12.6. As the degree of internationalization advances, so will the exporter's own role in carrying out or controlling the sales function.

Indirect Exports

When the exporter uses indirect exports to reach international markets, the export process is externalized; in other words, the intermediary, such as an EMC, will take care of the international sales effort. While there is no investment in international sales by the marketer, there is also no, or very little, learning about sales in the markets that buy the product. The sales effort is basically a domestic one directed at the local intermediary. This may change somewhat if the marketer becomes party to an ETC with other similar producers. Even in that case, the ETC will have its own sales force and exposure to the effort may be limited. Any learning that takes place is indirect; for example, the intermediary may advise the marketer of product adaptation requirements to enhance sales.

Exhibit **12.6**

Levels of Exporter Involvement in International Sales

Type of Involvement	Target of Sales Effort	Level of Exporter Involvement	Advantage/ Disadvantage
Indirect exports	Home-country–based intermediary	Low	+ No major investment in international sales – Minor learning from/control of effort
Direct exports	Locally based intermediary	Medium	+ Direct contact with local market – Possible gatekeeping by intermediary
Integrated exports	Customer	High	+ Generation of market-specific assets – Cost/risk

SOURCE: Framework adapted from Reijo Luostarinen and Lawrence Welch, *International Operations of the Firm* (Helsinki, Finland: Helsinki School of Economics, 1990), chapter 1.

Direct Exports

At some stage, the exporter may find it necessary to establish direct contact with the target market(s), although the ultimate customer contact is still handled by locally based intermediaries, such as agents or distributors. Communication with intermediaries must ensure both that they are satisfied with the arrangement and that they are equipped to market and promote the exporter's product appropriately. Whatever the distribution arrangement, the exporter must provide basic selling aid communications, such as product specification and data literature, catalogs, the results of product testing, and demonstrated performance information—everything needed to present products to potential customers. In some cases, the exporter has to provide the intermediaries with incentives to engage in local advertising efforts. These may include special discounts, push money, or cooperative advertising. Cooperative advertising will give the exporter's product local flavor and increase the overall promotional budget for the product. However, the exporter needs to be concerned that the advertising is of sufficient quality and that the funds are spent as agreed.

For the marketer–intermediary interaction to work, four general guidelines have to be satisfied.[68]

1. Know the sales scene. Often what works in the exporter's home market will not work somewhere else. This is true especially in terms of compensation schemes. In U.S. firms, incentives and commission play a significant role, while in most other markets salaries are the major share of compensation. The best way to approach this is to study the salary structures and incentive plans in other competitive organizations in the market in question.

2. Research the customer. Customer behavior will vary across markets, meaning the sales effort must adjust as well. ECA International, which sells marketing information worldwide based on a membership concept (companies purchase memberships to both participate in information gathering and receive appropriate data), found that its partners' sales forces could not sell the concept in Asia. Customers wanted instead to purchase information piece by piece. Only after research and modification of the sales effort was ECA able to sell the membership idea to customers.

3. Work with the culture. Realistic objectives have to be set for the salespeople based on their cultural expectations. This is especially true in setting goals and establishing measures such as quotas. If either of these is set unrealistically, the result will be frustration for both parties. Cultural sensitivity also is required in situations where the exporter has to interact with the intermediary's sales force—in training situations, for example.[69] In some cultures, such as those in Asia, the exporter is expected to act as a teacher and more or less dictate how things are done, while in some others, such as

in Northern Europe, training sessions may be conducted in a seminar-like atmosphere of give and take.

4. Learn from your local representatives. If the sales force perceives a lack of fit between the marketer's product and the market, as well as inability to do anything about it, the result will be suboptimal. A local sales force is an asset to the exporter, given its close contact with customers. Beyond daily feedback, the exporter is wise to undertake two additional approaches to exploit the experience of local salespeople. First, the exporter should have a program by which local salespeople can visit the exporter's operations and interact with the staff. If the exporter is active in multiple markets of the same region, it is advisable to develop ways to put salespeople in charge of the exporter's products in different markets to exchange ideas and best practice. Naturally, it is in the best interest of the exporter also to make regular periodic visits to markets entered.

An approach that requires more commitment from the exporter is to employ its own sales representatives, whose main function is to represent the firm abroad to existing and potential customers and to seek new leads. It is also important to sell with intermediaries, by supporting and augmenting their efforts. This type of presence is essential at some stage of the firm's international involvement. Other promotional tools can facilitate foreign market entry, but eventually some personal selling must take place. A cooperative effort with the intermediaries is important at this stage, in that some of them may be concerned about the motives of the exporter in the long term. For example, an intermediary may worry that once the exporter has learned enough about the market, it will no longer need the services of the intermediary. If these suspicions become prevalent, sales information may no longer flow to the exporter in the quantity and quality needed.

Integrated Exports

In the final stage of export-based internationalization, the exporter internalizes the effort through either a sales office in the target market or a direct contact with the buyer from home base. This is part of the exporter's perceived need for increased **customer relationship management**, where the sales effort is linked to call-center technologies, customer-service departments, and the company's Web site. Advancements in 3G networks, VoIP (voice-over-Internet protocol), and dual-mode handsets will bring new opportunities to account management, and real-time reporting tools will enable managers to gain insight into the sales process like nothing previously seen.

The establishment of a sales office does not have to mean an end to the use of intermediaries; the exporter's salespeople may be dedicated to supporting intermediaries' sales efforts. At this stage, expatriate sales personnel, especially those needed to manage the effort locally or regionally, may be used. The benefits of expatriates are their better understanding of the company and its products, and their ability to transfer best practice to the local operation. With expatriate management, the exporter can exercise a high amount of control over the sales function. Customers may also see the sales office and its expatriate staff as a long-term commitment to the market. The challenges lie mostly in the fit of the chosen individual to the new situation. The cost of having expatriate staff is considerable, approximately 2.5 times the cost at home, and the availability of suitable talent may be a problem, especially if the exporting organization is relatively small.[70]

The role of personal selling is greatest when the exporter sells directly to the end user or to governmental agencies, such as foreign trade organizations. Firms selling products with high price tags (such as Boeing commercial aircraft) or companies selling to monopsonies (such as Seagrams liquor to certain Northern European countries, where all liquor sales are through state-controlled outlets) must rely heavily on person-to-person communication, oral presentations, and direct-marketing efforts. Many of these firms can expand their business only if their markets are knowledgeable about what they do. This may require corporate advertising and publicity generation through extensive public relations efforts.

Whatever the sales task, effectiveness is determined by a number of interrelated factors. One of the keys to personal selling is the salesperson's ability to adapt to the customer and the selling situation.[71] This aspect of selling requires cultural knowledge and empathy; for example, in the Middle East, sales presentations may be broken up by long discussions of topics that have little or nothing to do with the transaction at hand. The characteristics of the buying task, whether routine or unique, have a bearing on the sales presentation. The exporter may be faced by a situation in which the idea of buying from a foreign entity is the biggest obstacle in terms of the risks perceived. If the exporter's product does not provide a clear-cut relative advantage over that of competitors, the analytical, interpersonal skills of the salesperson are needed to assist in the differentiation. A salesperson, regardless of the market, must have a thorough knowledge of the product or service. The more the salesperson is able to apply that knowledge to the particular situation, the more likely it is that he or she will obtain a positive result. The salesperson usually has front-line responsibility for the firm's customer relations, having to handle conflict situations such as the parent firm's bias for domestic markets and thus the possibility that shipments of goods to foreign clients receive low priority.

Summary

Effective communication is essential in negotiating agreements. To maximize the outcome of negotiations with clients and partners from other cultural backgrounds, international marketers must show adjustment capability to different standards and behaviors. Success depends on being prepared and remaining flexible, whatever the negotiation style in the host country.

Effective and efficient communication is needed for the dual purpose of (1) informing prospective customers about the availability of products or services and (2) persuading customers to opt for the marketer's offering over those of competitors. Within the framework of the company's opportunities, resources, and objectives, decisions must be made about whether to direct communications to present customers, potential customers, the general public, or intermediaries. Decisions must be made on how to reach each of the intended target audiences without wasting valuable resources. A decision also has to be made about who will control the communications effort: the exporter, an agency, or local representatives. Governmental agencies are the best sources of export promotion support, which is essential in alleviating the environmental threats perceived by many exporters.

The exporting international marketer must also choose tools to use in the communications effort. Usually, two basic tools are used: (1) mass selling through business and trade journals, direct mail, the Internet, trade shows and missions, and (2) personal selling, which brings the international marketer face-to-face with the targeted customer.

Key Terms

encoding	push strategies	trade missions
decoding	pull strategies	seminar missions
noise	integrated marketing	solo exhibitions
outcome	communications	video/catalog exhibitions
feedback	telemarketing	virtual trade shows
promotional mix	database marketing	customer relationship management

Questions for Discussion

1. What is potentially harmful in going out of one's way to make clients feel comfortable by playing down status distinctions such as titles?

2. Discuss this statement: "Lack of foreign-language skills puts U.S. negotiators at a disadvantage."

3. Compare and contrast the usefulness to a novice exporter of elements of the promotional mix.

4. Why do exporters usually choose U.S.-based services when placing advertisements to boost export sales specifically?

5. Some exporters report that they value above all the broad exposure afforded through exhibiting at a trade show, regardless of whether they are able to sell directly at the event. Comment on this philosophy.

6. What specific advice would you give to an exporter who has used domestic direct marketing extensively and wishes to continue the practice abroad?

Internet Exercises

1. The success of CeBIT in Hannover has prompted Deutsche Messe AG to market the CeBIT concept outside Germany using the slogan "CeBIT Worldwide Events." Using http://www.cebit.de, suggest a rationale for this.

2. Will the availability of *The Export Yellow Pages* on the Internet add to its ability to "offer U.S. firms a means to promote their businesses worldwide" and "attract appropriate foreign customers"? The service is available at http://www.exportyellowpages.com/.

Recommended Readings

Granered, Erik. *Global Call Centers: Achieving Outstanding Customer Service Across Cultures and Time Zones.* London: Nicholas Brealey Publishing, 2004.

Kirchgeorg, Manfred, Wernger M. Dornscheidt, Wilhelm Giese, and Nobert Stoeck. *Trade Show Management.* Germany: Gabler, 2006.

Lee, Catherine. *The New Rules of International Negotiation: Building Relationships, Earning Trust, and Creating Influence Around the World.* Franklin Lakes, New Jersey: Career Press, 2007.

Nelson, Carl. *Import/Export: How to Take Your Business Across Borders.* Columbus, Ohio: McGraw-Hill, 2008.

Parker, Philip M. *The 2007–2012 Outlook for Direct Selling Establishments in India.* San Diego, California: ICON Group International, Inc., 2006.

Schmidt, Wallace V., Roger Conaway, Susan S. Easton, and William J. Wardrope. *Communicating Globally: Intercultural Communication and International Business.* Thousand Oaks, California: Sage Publications, Inc., 2007.

CHAPTER THIRTEEN

DISTRIBUTION MANAGEMENT

The International MARKETPLACE

13.1

The Distribution and Export of Made-in-Italy Food Products

Italy is the sixth largest economy in the world, with a gross domestic product of $1.8 trillion and per capita annual income of $31,000. The country has the fifth highest population density in Europe but has few natural resources, since much of the land is unsuited for farming. The farming that is done in Italy is indigenous to the northern and southern parts of the country. Grains, sugar beets, and soybeans are produced primarily in the northern part of Italy. The southern part of the country tends to produce fruits, vegetables, and durum wheat. Even with much of the hilly, mountainous terrain unsuitable for farming, there are almost one and a half million Italians engaged in farming. The vast majority of these workers are on small farms that average only seven hectares.

Eating is a part of the Italian culture, and Italians truly enjoy their food. This is evidenced by the fact that food purchases comprise around 20 percent of disposable income. Healthy food products account for much of this spending. Imported healthy food products are consumed mainly in northern Italy. Many of these healthy food products are produced in southern and central Italy by around 500 small- to medium-sized Italian food producers. These are non-corporate, cooperative, small-scale organic farmers, and they face constant pressure from large corporations with their "super crop" harvesting abilities. Large corporations such as Monsanto, DuPont, Sandoz,

Ciba-Geigy, and Northrup King spend billions of dollars in the development of genetically-modified crops.

Slow Food International is an activist group founded in Italy in 1986. The group focuses upon preserving traditional agro-processing methods and indigenous foods that are in danger of dying out in favor of modern, mass-produced food and encourages consumers to buy from local organic food producers. Slow Food is against the commercial planting of genetically engineered crops, and this position has been supported by officials of the Italian government.

The European Union has stringent requirements guaranteeing the standards of all food products. Quality designators include the Protected Designation of Origin (PDO), Protected Geographical Indication (PGI), and Traditional Specialty Guaranteed (TSG). These designations are intended to promote and protect names of quality agricultural products. L' Arcadia Srl capitalizes on this lack of support for genetically-modified foods and distributes Made-in-Italy food products throughout Italy and exports to countries in Europe and Asia. L' Arcadia boasts both PDO and PGI products, as well as niche products linked closely to Slow Food's designation for high-quality foods.

L' Arcadia distributes and exports food categories such as fresh vegetables, truffles and mushrooms, seafood, meats and salami, and cheese and creams. Use of agencies such as TradeReady makes exporting these Made-in-Italy products easier. TradeReady is a European business-to-business marketplace that provides a listing and searching service for company and trade offers. This listing/searching service is free of charge, supporting over 100,000 importers and exporters in almost 200 countries. The goal is to help buyers and suppliers find each other easily, connect cost effectively, and trade efficiently.

Facilitating agencies enable small companies such as L' Arcadia to engage in international distribution that otherwise might not be possible with limited company resources. With the European Union's stringent requirements around genetically-modified foods, small- and medium-sized

farmers can export healthy food products to other countries in which consumers hold similar food consumption beliefs.

SOURCES: "Background Note: Italy," U.S. Department of State, Bureau of European and Eurasian Affairs, June 2008, **http://www .state.gov/r/pa/ei/bgn/4033.htm**, retrieved February 20, 2009; Carl Crittenden, "The Battle over Genetically Modified Crops in Italy," unpublished document, March 2006; Dana Biasetti, "Italy Exporter Guide Annual 2005," USDA Foreign Agricultural Services, September 30, 2005, **http://rome.usembassy.gov/agtrade.files/ Export2005.pdf**, retrieved February 20, 2009; Slow Food, **http:// www.slowfood.com**, retrieved February 20, 2009; L'Arcadia Srl, **http://www.larcadia.com**, retrieved February 9, 2009; **http:// www.tradeready.net**.

Channels of distribution provide the essential linkages that connect producers and customers. The links are intracompany and extracompany entities that perform a number of functions. Optimal distribution systems are flexible and are able to adjust to market conditions over both the short and long terms. In general, companies use one or more of the following distribution systems: (1) the firm sells directly to customers through its own field sales force or through electronic commerce; (2) the company operates through independent **intermediaries**, usually at the local level; or (3) the business depends on an outside distribution system that may have regional or global coverage. Producers often rely on intermediaries, as seen in *The International Marketplace 13.1*, to facilitate the location of companies interested in distributing products.

A channel of distribution should be seen as more than a sequence of marketing institutions connecting producers and consumers; it should be a team working toward a common goal.[1] Too often intermediaries are mistakenly perceived as temporary market-entry vehicles and not the partners with whom marketing efforts are planned and implemented. The intermediary is often the de facto marketing arm of the producer/originator. In today marketing environment, being close to customers, be they the final consumer or intermediary, and solving their problems is vital to bringing about success. When its office supplies superstore customer kicked off a joint venture in Australia, 3M dispatched two employees to its Australian subsidiary to educate that division on the special needs of a superstore.

Since most marketers cannot or do not want to control the distribution function completely, structuring channel relationships becomes a crucial task. The importance of this task is further compounded by the fact that the channel decision is the most long-term of the marketing mix decisions in that, once established, it cannot easily be changed. In export marketing, a new dimension is added to the task: the export channel decision, in addition to making market-specific decisions. An experienced exporter may decide that control is of utmost importance and choose to perform tasks itself and incur the information collection and adaptation costs. An infrequent exporter, on the other hand, may be quite dependent on experienced intermediaries to get its product to markets. Whether export tasks are self-performed or assigned to export intermediaries, the distribution function should be planned so that the channel will function as one rather than as a collection of different or independent units.

The decisions involved in the structuring and management of the export channel of distribution are discussed first, including an evaluation of a distribution challenge presented by parallel imports. The chapter will end with a discussion of the steps needed in preparation for e-commerce. Logistics issues will be discussed in detail in Chapter 16.

Channel Structure

A generalization of channel configurations for consumer and industrial products as well as services is provided in Exhibit 13.1. Channels can vary from direct, producer-to-consumer types to elaborate, multilevel channels employing many types of intermediaries, each serving

Exhibit 13.1

Channel Configuration

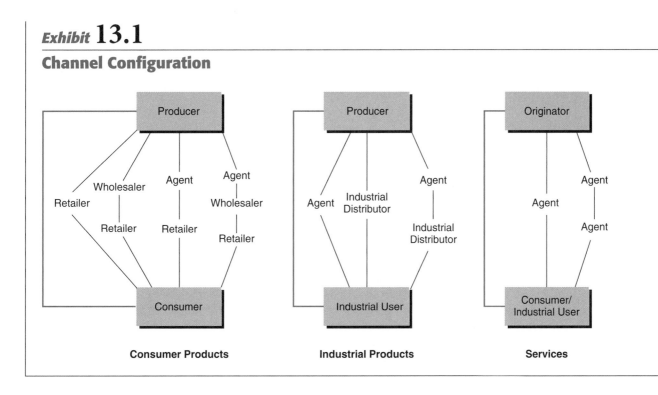

a particular purpose. For example, Canadian software firms enter international markets by exporting directly from Canada (40 percent), by opening their own sales offices (14 percent), by entering into cooperative arrangements with other exporters (15 percent), by using a local distributor or a value-adding reseller (13 percent), or by a mixture of modes (17 percent).[2] British firms, on the other hand, exported directly in 60 percent of the cases, 8 percent opened a foreign sales office, 5 percent used an agent, and the remainder entered a cooperative export effort such as piggybacking, in which the exporter uses another company's channel to enter a foreign market.[3] Software makers use the Internet to communicate with foreign counterparts and to find new partners. Firms also derive substantial benefits from delivering value-added services to users over the Internet.[4] However, the Internet has limited capability to substitute for personal sales.

Channel configurations for the same product will vary within industries, even within the same firm, because national markets quite often have unique features. This may mean dramatic departures from accepted policy for a company. For example, to reach the British market, which is dominated by a few retailers such as J. Sainsbury, Tesco, and ASDA, marketers such as Heinz may have to become suppliers to these retailers' private-label programs in addition to making their own efforts.[5] A firm's international market experience will also cause variation in distribution patterns. AMPAK, a manufacturer of packaging machinery, uses locally based distributors in markets where it is well established. Others are entered indirectly by using domestically based intermediaries: either by using the services of trading companies or through selling to larger companies, which then market the products alongside their own.

The connections made by marketing institutions are not solely for the physical movement of goods. They also serve as transactional title flows and informational communications flows. Rather than unidirectional, downward from the producer, the flows are usually multidirectional, both vertical and horizontal. As an example, the manufacturer relies heavily on the retailer population for data on possible changes in demand. Communications from retailers may be needed to coordinate a cooperative advertising campaign instituted by a manufacturer. The three flows—physical, transactional, and informational—do not necessarily take place simultaneously or occur at every level of the channel. Agent intermediaries, for example, act only to facilitate the information flow; they do not take title and often do not physically handle the goods. Similarly, electronic intermediaries, such as amazon.com, have to rely on facilitating agents to perform the logistics function of their operation.

Because only a few products are sold directly to ultimate users, an international marketer has to decide on alternative ways to move products to chosen markets. The basic marketing functions of exchange, physical movement, and various facilitating activities must be performed, but the marketer may not be equipped to handle them. Intermediaries can therefore be used to gain quick, easy, and relatively low-cost entry to a targeted market.

Channel Design

The term *channel design* refers to the length and the width of the channel employed.[6] Length is determined by the number of levels, or different types, of intermediaries. In the case of consumer products, the most traditional is the producer–wholesaler–retailer–customer configuration. Channel width is determined by the number of institutions of each type in the channel. An industrial goods marketer may grant exclusive distribution rights to a foreign entity, whereas a consumer goods marketer may want to use as many intermediaries as possible to ensure intensive distribution.

Channel design is determined by factors that can be summarized as the 11 Cs, listed in Exhibit 13.2. These factors are integral to both the development of new marketing channels and the modification and management of existing ones. Their individual influences will vary from one market to another, and seldom, if ever, can one factor be considered without the interactive effects of the others. The marketer should use the 11 Cs checklist to determine the proper approach to reach intended target audiences before selecting channel members to fill the roles. The first three factors are givens, since the firm must adjust to the existing structures. The other eight are controllable to a certain extent by the international marketer.

Customer Characteristics

The demographic and psychographic characteristics of targeted customers will form the basis for channel design decisions. Answers to questions such as what customers need—as well as why, when, and how they buy—are used to determine ways in which the products should be made available to generate a competitive advantage. As an example, Anheuser-Busch entered Japan when Suntory, one of the country's largest liquor distillers, acquired the importing rights. Suntory's marketing plan stressed distribution of Budweiser in discos, pubs, and other night spots where Japan's affluent, well-traveled youth gather. Young people in Japan are influenced by U.S. culture and adapt themselves more readily to new products than do older Japanese. Taking advantage of this fact, Suntory concentrated its efforts on one generation, and on-premise sales led to major off-premise (retail outlet) sales as well.

In the early stages of product introduction, the international marketer may concentrate efforts on only the most attractive markets and later, having attained a foothold, expand distribution. When Kronenbourg, one of the best-selling beers in Europe, entered the U.S. market, distribution was initiated in New York City and then extended to the metropolitan area.

Exhibit **13.2**

Determinants of Channel Structure and Relationships

External	Internal
Customer characteristics	Company objectives
Culture	Character
Competition	Capital
	Cost
	Coverage
	Control
	Continuity
	Communication

The reason was the area's prominence in both domestic and imported beer consumption. The national rollout took place five years later. In the industrial sector, certain industries cluster geographically, allowing the international marketer to take a more direct approach.

Customer characteristics may cause the same product to be distributed through two different types of channels. Many industrial goods marketers' sales, such as those of Caterpillar, are handled by individual dealers, except when the customer might be the central government or one of its entities, in which case sales are direct from the company itself. Furthermore, primary target audiences may change from one market to another. For example, in Japan, McDonald's did not follow the U.S. pattern of locating restaurants in the suburbs. The masses of young pedestrians that flood Japanese cities were more promising than affluent but tradition-minded car owners in the suburbs.

In business-to-business marketing, the adoption of e-commerce provides new opportunities for international marketers. New export markets can be accessed by expanding network and customer bases. At the same time, the explosive growth of the Internet poses a direct threat and challenge to traditional intermediaries, leading possibly to elimination, or disintermediation.[7]

Culture

In planning a distribution system, the marketer must analyze existing channel structures, or what might be called **distribution culture**. As an example, the manner in which Japanese channels of distribution are structured and managed presents one of the major reasons for the apparent failure of foreign firms to establish major market penetration in Japan.[8] In any case, and in every country, international marketers must study distribution systems in general and the types of linkages between channel members for their specific type of product. Usually, the international marketer has to adjust to existing structures to gain distribution. However, as seen in *The International Marketplace 13.2*, companies will take a risk and utilize their own channel strategies in foreign markets.

The International
MARKETPLACE

13.2

Hennes & Mauritz Retails in Japan

In September of 2008, Hennes & Mauritz (H&M) opened its first retail store in Japan. Unlike other international fashion brands, H&M followed a green field strategy, choosing to open a 100 percent wholly-owned subsidiary in the Japanese marketplace. The first H&M store opened in the Ginza district, with other stores opening in Tokyo's fashion district of Harajuku and Shibuya.

H&M was founded in 1947 by Erling Persson, a salesperson from a small town in Sweden. With an average annual growth rate of 20 percent, the company's core business concept is to offer fashion and quality at a good price. With this core business concept, H&M is often referred to as the "king of fast fashion" and is know as the provider of quick-to-market trendy clothes. H&M has around 800 suppliers, mass produces its products in low cost markets such as Bangladesh, and runs its own stores—eliminating as many middlemen as possible in order to keep prices down. By 2008, H&M had over 1,500 stores in 32 countries and employed almost 70,000 employees worldwide.

As one of the world's most competitive fashion markets, Japan is also the world's second largest economy. Fashion-wise, Japanese consumers expect high quality merchandise and have a reputation for rejecting products with poor stitching, loose buttons, and inferior fabrics. H&M feels that items trendy in New York and Paris will also be trendy in Japan, and the company has employed quality managers in the Japanese locations so as to ensure product quality. Outsiders, however, wondered if anyone aside from those Japanese who have traveled internationally will know the H&M brand. If not, the trendy and possibly lower quality product would not be acceptable to the product-picky Japanese consumer and, thus, the H&M brand would not succeed in Japan.

Competition-wise, H&M was up against some strong international players. The H&M flagship store was a four-story shop with over 1,000 square meters of retail space, located very close to major competitors such as USA-based Gap, Zara out of Spain, and Japan's own Uniqlo. Additionally, the first Japanese H&M store was in the same shopping district as European designer boutiques such as Chanel, Christian Dior, and Giorgio Armani. In a market

© YOSHIKAZU TSUNO/AFP/GETTY IMAGES

IN 2008, H&M OPENED ITS FIRST RETAIL STORES IN JAPAN.

with a dearth of available real estate, H&M was able to acquire space that forced it to go head-to-head with the competition.

Response to the opening of H&M's first retail store was even greater than the company had anticipated. Shoppers waited in line for hours to get into the store—the average wait time was estimated to be two hours. Store visitors were estimated to number 8,000 per day. The company had to fly in additional employee help from locations in Europe. Even with the extra help, the company could not keep up with demand and consumers reported waiting in line only to enter the store and find that it did not have anything in the appropriate size. The overwhelming response to H&M's first store opening was repeated at the second store location in Harajuku, where it was reported that consumers were camping out two days before the opening.

The success of H&M showed the retail world that Japanese consumers did value fashion-trendy merchandise at a reasonable price. Importantly, the company was able to open new distribution outlets at a time when the entire world was concerned about difficult economic conditions.

SOURCES: "Hennes & Mauritz (H&M) in Japan—Hit or Mistake?" *Case Study Inc.*, September 2008, **http://www.casestudyinc .com/H&M-Japan-Case-Study.html**, retrieved February 9, 2009; "H&M Green Field Market Entry to Japan," *JapanStrategy-Blog*, September 22, 2008, **http://japanstrategy.com/ blog/2008/09/h-green-field-market-entry-to-japan.html**, retrieved February 9, 2009; Yrui Kageyama, "H&M Opens Shop in Pricey Japan Amid Downturn," *USA Today,* September 12, 2008, **http://www.usatoday.com/money/economy/2008-09-12- 213076897_x.htm**, retrieved February 9, 2009; Michael Fiorella, "H&M in Japan: Hit or Miss?" *Japan Marketing News*, December 30, 2006, **http://www.japanmarketingnews.com/2006/12/ in_japan_the_bi.html**, retrieved February 9, 2009; Yuri Kageyama, "H&M New Darling of Tokyo Fashion Scence," *The Japan Times*, November 8, 2008, **http://search.japantimes.com.jp/cgi-bin/ nn20081108f5.html**, retrieved February 9, 2009.

In addition to structure, functions performed by the various types of intermediaries have to be outlined. Retailers in Japan demand more from manufacturers and wholesalers than do U.S. retailers; for example, they expect returns of merchandise to be fully accepted even if there is no reason other than lack of sales. Retailers also expect significant amounts of financing and frequent delivery of products. Retailers, on their part, offer substantial services to their clientele and take great pains to build close relationships with their customers. As can be seen in Exhibit 13.3, which lists channel members in the Japanese cosmetics industry, functions are—and should be—clearly delineated. Manufacturers concentrate mainly on production and promotional activities; intermediaries work on logistics activities, financing, and communication with manufacturers and retailers; retailers focus on sales and promotional activities.

Changing existing distribution systems may be quite difficult. Porsche tried to change the way it sold automobiles in the United States from traditional independent franchised

Exhibit **13.3**

Examples of Function Performance in the Channel System for the Japanese Cosmetics Industry

	Channel Member	
Manufacturer	**Intermediary**	**Retail**
Production	Order taking	Selling
Advertising	Inventory maintenance	Organizing consumers
National sales promotion	Space control at the retail level	In-store promotion
Dealer aids	Product assortment	
Education of dealers	Dispatching of sales support personnel	
Financing	Area marketing	
	Financing	

SOURCE: Michael R. Czinkota, "Distribution of Consumer Products in Japan: An Overview," in *International Marketing Strategy: Environmental Assessment and Entry Strategies,* Michael R. Czinkota and Ilkka A. Ronkainen, eds. (Ft. Worth, TX: The Dryden Press, 1994), 293–307.

dealers to a "dealerless system." Whereas dealers buy cars for resale, Porsche would have instituted agents who would order cars as they sold them and work on an 8 percent commission rather than the normal 16 to 18 percent margin. After a dealer uproar, Porsche abandoned the plan. Wal-Mart has caused significant changes in supplier operating procedures with its demand that vendors forgo all other amenities and quote the lowest price. This has been traumatic in markets such as the United Kingdom, where suppliers and competitors have used the regulatory environment to exist in a less-competitive environment.[9] Wal-Mart will, however, work with suppliers on cost reduction. Similarly, direct sales by marketers through the Internet are raising concerns among distributors who feel that they lose out on these opportunities. Regardless of whether these are completely new sales or come from customers who would have used traditional channels before, intermediaries should be compensated for these sales in some way, such as through e-credits on their next purchase from the marketer, to acknowledge their role in developing the local market.

Foreign legislation affecting distributors and agents is an essential part of the distribution culture of a market. For example, legislation may require that foreign firms be represented only by firms that are 100 percent locally owned. Before China's entry into the WTO in late 2001, foreign companies were barred from importing their own products, distributing them, or providing after-sales service. These functions were to be performed by Chinese companies or Sino–foreign joint ventures. Now, these restrictions have been phased out. This means that General Motors China Group has regained control over its marketing. Up to now, Chinese companies have handled the importing, distributing, and selling, and GM's cars have often passed through four different entities before customers see them. GM is in the process of building a consistent network of dealers and will start providing financing, which has also become allowed.[10]

While distribution decisions have been mostly tactical and made on a market-by-market basis, marketing managers have to be cognizant of globalization in the distribution function as well. This is taking place in two significant ways.[11] Distribution formats are crossing borders, especially to newly emerging markets. While supermarkets accounted only for 8 percent of consumer nondurable sales in urban areas in Thailand in 1990, the figure today is over 50 percent. Other such formats include department stores, minimarts, and supercenters. The second globalization trend is the globalization of intermediaries themselves, either independently or through strategic alliances. Entities such as Toys 'Я' Us from the United States, Galeries Lafayette from France, Marks & Spencer from the United Kingdom, and Takashimaya and Isetan from Japan have expanded to both well-developed and newly emerging markets. Within the European Union, a growing number of EU-based retailers are merging and establishing a presence in other EU markets. These moves are partly in response to Wal-Mart's European expansion.[12] Some intermediaries are entering foreign markets by acquiring local

Exhibit **13.4**

Internationalization of Retailers

Approach	Objective	Example
Business exporter	Reconfigure retailing approach across markets with consistent core and focus on scale	Carrefour, IKEA, Makro, Wal-Mart
Concept exporter	Export concept but let local partners execute	Benetton
Skills exporter	Export unique skills (rather than entire concepts)	Price/Costco
Superior operator	Focus on operating capability; implemented through acquisition	Ahold, Tengelmann

SOURCES: Jody Evans, Alan Treadgold, and Felix T. Mavondo, "Psychic Distance and the Performance of International Retailers," *International Marketing Review* 17 (nos. 4 and 5, 2000): 373–391; and Denise Incandela, Kathleen McLaughlin, and Christiana Smith, "Retailers to the World," *The McKinsey Quarterly* 35 (no. 3, 1999): 84–97.

entities (e.g., Germany's Tengelmann and Holland's Ahold acquiring the U.S. chains A&P and Giant, respectively) or forming alliances. For example, in Mexico, joint ventures between Wal-Mart and Cifra, Fleming Cos. and Gigante, and Price/Costco and Comercial Mexicana are changing the distribution landscape by concentrating retail power. Beyond opportunity for marketers for more and broader-based sales, these entities are applying the same type of margin pressure marketers find in more developed markets. In many cases, marketers are providing new technologies to these intermediaries and helping to train them with the hope of establishing solid relationships that will withstand competition, especially from local entities that typically start beefing up their own operations.[13] The strategic options chosen by retailers are presented in Exhibit 13.4.

Competition

Channels used by competitors may be the only product distribution system that is accepted by both the trade and consumers. In this case, the international marketer's task is to use the structure effectively and efficiently, or even innovatively. This may mean, for example, that the exporter chooses a partner capable of developing markets rather than one who has existing contacts. The most obvious distributors may be content with the status quo in the market and be ready to push products that are the most profitable for them regardless of who made them. Two approaches may be applicable if those serving major customer prospects with similar product lines are not satisfactory. First, the exporter may form jointly owned sales companies with distributors (or with other exporters) to exercise more control. Second, the approach may be to seek a good company fit in terms of goals and objectives. In Asia, Lycos chose partners for their overall influence in the local market. In Japan, it teamed up with Sumitomo, an ultra-traditional trading company with a 250-year history, and in Korea with Mirae, a machinery and electronics firm.[14] Should a new approach be chosen, it must be carefully analyzed and tested against the cultural, political, and legal environments in which is to be introduced.

In some cases, the international marketer cannot manipulate the distribution variable. For example, in Sweden and Finland, all alcoholic beverages must be distributed through state monopoly–owned outlets. In Japan, the Japan Tobacco & Salt Public Corporation is a state monopoly that controls all tobacco imports and charges a 20 percent fee for distribution. In other cases, all feasible channels may be blocked by domestic competitors either through contractual agreements or through other means. U.S. suppliers of soda ash, which is used in glass, steel, and chemical products, have not been able to penetrate the Japanese market even though they offer a price advantage. The reason is the cartel-like condition developed by the Japan Soda Industry Association, which allegedly sets import levels, specifies which local trading company is to deal with each U.S. supplier, and buys the imports at lower U.S. prices for resale by its members at higher Japanese prices. Efforts by U.S. producers to distribute directly or through smaller, unaffiliated traders have faced strong resistance. The end users and traders fear alienating the domestic producers, on whom their business depends.

Company Objectives

A set of management considerations will have an effect on channel design. No channel of distribution can be properly selected unless it meets the requirements set by overall company objectives for market share and profitability. In distribution, this often calls for a compromise between cost and control objectives. While integrated channels (exporter owned and operated) may be preferred because they facilitate the protection of knowledge-based assets and provide needed high levels of customer service, the cost may be 15 to 35 percent of sales, whereas using distributors may drop the expense to 10 to 15 percent.

Often the use of multiple channels arises with the need to increase sales volume.[15] For example, in France, Xerox set up a chain of retail outlets in large cities to support its copier sales. To cover rural areas and smaller towns, Xerox withdrew its direct sales force and replaced it with independent distributors, concessionaires, who work on an exclusive basis. Rapid expansion can also be achieved through partnerships, as shown by the Starbucks example in Exhibit 13.5. Partnerships can be undertaken if appropriate controls are in place to secure expansion with relatively little investment. If expansion is too rapid and the adjustments made to local market conditions too extensive, a major asset—standardization and economies of scale and scope—can be lost.

Exhibit **13.5**

Distribution Expansion through Partnerships

	Where/what	Partners	
New channels (exclusive supply arrangements)	• Airlines • Airports • Bookstores • Cruise lines • Department stores • Hotels • Supermarkets	• United, Canadian • Host International • Barnes & Noble • Holland America • Nordstrom • Starwood Hotels • Kraft Foods	**Key success factors** • Starbucks invests very little capital in international expansion (<5% of revenue) • Local partners bear all business risk
New markets (through licenses with retailers)	• Japan • Malaysia • Philippines • Singapore • South Korea • Taiwan • Thailand	• Sazaby (joint venture) • Berjaya Coffee (licensee) • Restaurant Brands (licensee) • Rustan Coffee (licensee) • Bonvest Holdings (licensee) • ESCO (licensee) • President Group (joint venture) • Coffee Partners (licensee)	• Licensing allows stricter control over all operations than does franchising—for example, parent-company consultants visit each store once a month • Local partners contribute regulatory and cultural expertise—for example, on product adaptations
New products	• Ice cream • Bottled Frappuccino • Coffee-enhanced dark beer • Online catalog	• Dreyer's • PepsiCo • Red Hook Brewery • America Online	

SOURCES: Adapted from Ranjay Gulati, Sarah Huffman, and Gary Nelson, "The Barista Principle—Starbucks and the Rise of Relational Capital," *Strategy and Business* 7 (third quarter, 2002): 58–69; and Denise Incandela, Kathleen L. McLaughlin, and Christiana Smith, "Retailers to the World," *The McKinsey Quarterly* 35 (no. 3, 1999): 84–97. See also **http://www.starbucks.com**.

Character

The nature of the product, its character, will have an impact on the design of the channel. Generally, the more specialized, expensive, bulky, or perishable the product and the more after-sale service it may require, the more likely the channel is to be relatively short. Staple items, such as soap, tend to have longer channels.

The type of channel chosen must match the overall positioning of the product in the market. Changes in overall market conditions, such as currency fluctuations, may require changes in distribution as well. An increase in the value of the billing currency may cause a repositioning of the marketed product as a luxury item, necessitating an appropriate channel (such as an upper-grade department store) for its distribution.

Rules of thumb aside, particular products may be distributed in a number of ways even to the same target audience, as shown in Exhibit 13.6 for the PC industry. A dual channel may be used in which both intermediaries and a direct contact with customers are used. In some cases, a channel may extend beyond having one tier of distributors and resellers to include importers or agents. Another alternative, hybrid channels, features sharing of marketing functions, with the manufacturer handling promotion and customer generation, and the intermediaries, sales and distribution. The hybrid strategy is based more on cooperation and partnership, while the dual channel may result in conflict if disagreements arise as to who is to handle a specific customer. In either case, multiple channels are used to enhance sales performance in a foreign market.

Capital

The term *capital* is used to describe the financial requirements in setting up a channel system. The international marketer's financial strength will determine the type of channel and the basis on which channel relationships will be built. The stronger the marketer's finances, the more able the firm is to establish channels it either owns or controls. Intermediaries' requirements for beginning inventories, selling on a consignment basis, preferential loans, and need for training all will have an impact on the type of approach chosen by the international marketer. For example, an industrial goods manufacturer may find that potential distributors in a particular country lack the capability of servicing the product. The marketer then has two

Exhibit **13.6**

Distribution Alternatives: PCs in Europe

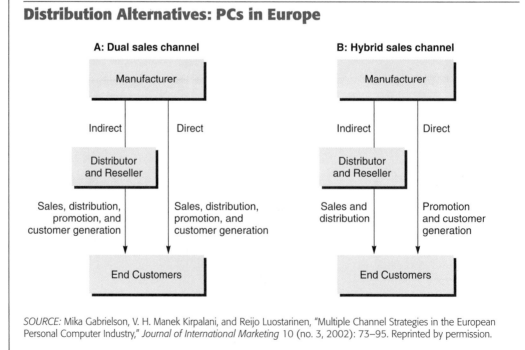

SOURCE: Mika Gabrielson, V. H. Manek Kirpalani, and Reijo Luostarinen, "Multiple Channel Strategies in the European Personal Computer Industry," *Journal of International Marketing* 10 (no. 3, 2002): 73–95. Reprinted by permission.

options: (1) set up an elaborate training program at headquarters or regionally, or (2) institute company-owned service centers to help distributors. Either approach will require a significant investment, but is necessary to ensure customer trust through superior execution of marketing programs. In developing markets, the lack of available intermediaries encourages the integration of distribution functions but requires direct investment in the market.[16]

Cost

Closely related to the capital dimension is cost—that is, the expenditure incurred in maintaining a channel once it is established. Costs will naturally vary over the life cycle of a relationship with a particular channel member, as well as over the life cycle of the products marketed. An example of the costs involved is promotional money spent by a distributor for the marketer's product. A cooperative advertising deal between the international marketer and the intermediary would typically split the costs of the promotional campaign executed in the local market.

Costs will vary in terms of the relative power of the manufacturer vis-à-vis its intermediaries. Consolidation among European retailers means that there are a fewer number of competitors, as well as a shifting in power. This consolidation includes not only large retailers such as Ahold and Migros but also smaller retailers that have joined forces to form buying groups. One of the most significant is Expert International GmbH, which has more than 7,400 participating retailers in 22 European, North American, South American, and Pacific countries. The concentrated distribution systems being developed by these giants are eroding the marketing strength of manufacturers, which lay in their networks of distribution depots that delivered direct to stores. Now, retailers want delivery to their central distribution centers. In addition, they are pushing stockholding costs to manufacturers by demanding more frequent deliveries, in smaller, mixed loads, with shorter delivery time.[17]

Costs may also be incurred in protecting the company's distributors against adverse market conditions. A number of U.S. manufacturers helped their distributors maintain competitive prices through subsidies when the exchange rate for the U.S. dollar caused pricing problems. Extra financing aid has been extended to distributors that have been hit with competitive adversity. Such support, although often high in monetary cost, will pay back manyfold through a smoother manufacturer–distributor relationship.

Coverage

The term *coverage* is used to describe both the number of areas in which the marketer's products are represented and the quality of that representation. Coverage is therefore two-dimensional, in that horizontal coverage and vertical coverage need to be considered in channel design. The number of areas to be covered depends on the dispersion of demand in the market and also on the time elapsed since the product's introduction to the market. Three different approaches are available:

1. Intensive coverage, which calls for distributing the product through the largest number of different types of intermediaries and the largest number of individual intermediaries of each type

2. Selective coverage, which entails choosing a number of intermediaries for each area to be penetrated

3. Exclusive coverage, which involves only one entity in a market

Generally, intensive and selective coverage call for longer channels using different types of intermediaries, usually wholesalers and agents. Exclusive distribution is conducive to more direct sales. For some products, such as ethnic or industrial products, customers are concentrated geographically and allow for more intensive distribution with a more direct channel. A company typically enters a market with one local distributor, but as volume expands, the distribution base often has to be adjusted. The advantages of a single distributor are listed in Exhibit 13.7.

Expanding distribution too quickly may cause problems. Benetton, one of Italy's major exporters of clothing, had planned to have 1,000 stores in the United States by 1990.

Exhibit 13.7

Advantages of a Single Distributor

1. One corporate presence eliminates confusion among buyers and local officials.
2. The volume of business that results when exports are consolidated will attract a larger/more qualified distributor. The distributor will thus have greater influence in its local business community.
3. Communication is less plagued by noise. This will have a positive effect in many areas, from daily information flows to supervising and training.
4. More effective coordination of the sales and promotional effort can be achieved through mutual learning.
5. Logistics flows are more economical.
6. A stronger presence can be maintained in smaller markets, or markets in which resources may dictate a holding mode, until more effective penetration can be undertaken.
7. Distributor morale and the overall principal–intermediary relationship are better through elimination of intrabrand competition.

SOURCE: Adapted from Business International Corporation, *201 Checklists: Decision Making in International Operations* (New York: Business International Corporation, 1980), 26–27.

The plan was abandoned because of concerns about oversaturation of certain urban areas and overprojection of retail sales. Rather, more emphasis is being put on customer service, and the number of stores in major North American cities was 50 in 2009.[18] Similarly, expanding distribution from specialty outlets to mass distribution may have an impact on the product's image and the after-sales service associated with it. The impact on channel relations may be significant if existing dealers perceive loss of sales as a result of such a move. This may be remedied by keeping the product lines in mass-distribution outlets different, or possibly developing a different brand for the new channels.

Control

The use of intermediaries will automatically lead to loss of some control over the marketing of the firm's products.[19] The looser the relationship is between the marketer and intermediaries, the less control the marketer can exert. The longer the channel, the more difficult it becomes for the marketer to have a final say in pricing, promotion, and the types of outlets in which the product will be made available.

In the initial stages of internationalization or specific market entry, an intermediary's specialized knowledge and working relationships are needed, but as exporters' experience base and sales in the market increase, many opt to establish their own sales offices. Use of intermediaries provides quick entry using an existing system in which complementary products provide synergistic benefits. Furthermore, payments are received from one entity rather than from multiple customers.

The issue of control correlates heavily with the type of product or service being marketed. In the case of industrial and high-technology products, control will be easier to institute because intermediaries are dependent on the marketer for new products and service. Where the firm's marketing strategy calls for a high level of service, integrated channels are used to ensure that the service does get performed.[20] Later on, an exporter may want to coordinate programs across markets on a regional basis, which is much easier if the channel is controlled.

The marketer's ability and willingness to exercise any type of power—whether reward, coercive, legitimate, referent, or expert—determines the extent of control. The exercise of control causes more incidents of conflict in channels of distribution than any other activity in the relationship. This points to the need for careful communication with foreign intermediaries about the marketer's intentions and also the need for certain control measures. These might include the marketer's need to be the sole source of advertising copy or to be in charge of all product-modification activities. Generally, the more control the marketer wishes to have, the more cost is involved in securing that control.

Continuity

Channel design decisions are the most long-term of the marketing mix decisions. Utmost care must therefore be taken in choosing the right type of channel, given the types of intermediaries available and any environmental threats that may affect the channel design. Occasionally, however, unpredictable events may occur. As an example, Cockspur, the largest distiller of rum in Barbados, negotiated an arrangement with one of the largest distributors in the United States. Almost immediately, the distributor was acquired by a company that thought liquor distribution did not fit its mission and thus eliminated the products and reassigned the salespeople. Years later, Cockspur was still without substantial distribution in the United States.[21]

Nurturing continuity rests heavily on the marketer because foreign distributors may have a more short-term view of the relationship. For example, Japanese wholesalers believe that it is important for manufacturers to follow up initial success with continuous improvement of the product. If such improvements are not forthcoming, competitors are likely to enter the market with similar, lower-priced products, and the wholesalers of the imported product will turn to the Japanese suppliers.

Continuity is also expressed through visible market commitment. Industries abroad may be quite conservative; distributors will not generally support an outsider until they are sure it is in the market to stay. Such commitments include sending in technical or sales personnel or offering training, and setting up wholly-owned sales subsidiaries from the start—and staffing them with locals to help communicate that the company is there for the long term.[22] Investment in distributors may be literal (resulting in co-ownership in the future) or abstract (resulting in more solid commitment in the relationship).

Communication

Communication provides the exchange of information that is essential to the functioning of the channel. Communication is an important consideration in channel design, and it gains more emphasis in international distribution because of various types of distances that may cause problems. In the buyer–seller relationships in international markets, the distance that is perceived to exist between a buyer and a seller has five aspects, all of which are amplified in the international setting:[23]

1. Social distance: the extent to which each of the two entities in a relationship is familiar with the other's ways of operating

2. Cultural distance: the degree to which the norms, values, or working methods between the two entities differ because of their separate national characteristics

3. Technological distance: the differences between the product or process technologies of the two entities

4. Time distance: the time that must elapse between establishing contact or placing an order and the actual transfer of the product or service involved

5. Geographical distance: the physical distance between the locations of the two entities

All these dimensions must be considered when determining whether to use intermediaries and, if they are to be used, what types to use.

Communication, if properly utilized, will assist the international marketer in conveying the firm's goals to the distributors, in solving conflict situations, and in marketing the product overall. Communication is a two-way process that does not permit the marketer to dictate to intermediaries. Cases are well known in which the marketer is not able to make the firm's marketing program functional. Prices may not be competitive; promotional materials may be obsolete or inaccurate and not well received overall. This may be compounded if the exporter tries to transplant abroad procedures and programs used domestically.[24] Solving these types of problems is important to the welfare of both parties.

Channels of distribution, because of their sequential positioning of the entities involved, are not conducive to noiseless communication. The marketer must design a channel and choose intermediaries that guarantee good information flow. Proper communication involves not only the passage of information between channel members but also a better understanding of each party's needs and goals. This can be achieved through personal visits, exchange of personnel, or distribution advisory councils. Consisting of members from all channel participants, advisory councils meet regularly to discuss opportunities and problems that may have arisen.

Selection of Intermediaries

Once the basic design of the channel has been determined, the international marketer must begin a search to fill the defined roles with the best available candidates, and must secure their cooperation.

Types of Intermediaries

Two basic decisions are involved in choosing the type of intermediaries to serve a particular market. First, the marketer must determine the type of relationship to have with intermediaries. The alternatives are distributorship and agency relationship. A **distributor** will purchase the product and will therefore exercise more independence than agencies. Distributors are typically organized along product lines and provide the international marketer with complete marketing services. **Agents** have less freedom of movement than distributors because they operate on a commission basis and do not usually physically handle the goods. This, in turn, allows the marketer control to make sure, for example, that the customer gets the most recent and appropriate product version. In addition to the business implications, the choice of type will have legal implications in terms of what the intermediary can commit its principal to and the ease of termination of the agreement.

Second, the international marketer must decide whether to utilize indirect exporting, direct exporting, or integrated distribution in penetrating a foreign market.[25] **Indirect exporting** requires dealing with another domestic firm that acts as a sales intermediary for the marketer, often taking over the international side of the marketer's operations. The benefits, especially in the short term, are that the exporter can use someone else's international channels without having to pay to set them up. But there may be long-term concerns in using this strategy if the marketer wants to actively and aggressively get into the market itself. Indirect exporting is only practiced by firms very early on in their internationalization process. With **direct exporting**, the marketer takes direct responsibility for its products abroad by either selling directly to the foreign customer or finding a local representative to sell its products in the market. The third category of export marketing strategy, **integrated exporting**, requires the marketer to make an investment in the foreign market for the purpose of selling its products in that market or more broadly. This investment could be the opening, for example, of a German or EU sales office, a distribution hub, or even an assembly operation or manufacturing facility. Although the last set of strategies indicates longer-term commitment to a market, it is riskier than the first two because the marketer is making a major financial investment. For example, if the exporter moves from an agency agreement to a sales office, its costs for that market are now fixed costs (i.e., will be incurred even if no sales are made) instead of the previous variable costs. Setting up even a modest office may be expensive.[26] The cost of an office manager and a secretary can easily reach $100,000, while a full-scale sales office will cost $500,000 on an annual basis. Real estate costs can be substantial if the office is in a main business district.

The major types of intermediaries are summarized in Exhibit 13.8. Care should be taken to understand conceptual differences that might exist from one market to another. For example, a **commissionario** may sell in his or her own name (as a distributor would) but for an undisclosed principal (an agency concept). Similarly, a **del credere agent** guarantees the solvency of the customer and may therefore be responsible to the supplier for payment by the customer.[27]

The respective strengths and weaknesses of various export intermediary types were discussed in Chapter 9.

Exhibit **13.8**

International Channel Intermediaries

Agents	
Foreign (Direct)	**Domestic (Indirect)**
Brokers	Brokers
Manufacturer's representatives	Export agents
Factors	EMCs
Managing agents	Webb-Pomerene associations
Purchasing agents	Commission agents
Distributors	
Distributors/dealers	Domestic wholesalers
Import jobbers	EMCs
Wholesalers/retailers	ETCs
	Complementary marketing

SOURCES: Peter B. Fitzpatrick and Alan S. Zimmerman, *Essentials of Export* Marketing (New York: American Management Association, 1985), 20; Bruce Seifert and John Ford, "Export Distribution Channels," *Columbia Journal of World Business* 24 (Summer 1989): 16; and **http://www.export.gov**.

Sources for Finding Intermediaries

Firms that have successful international distribution attest to the importance of finding top representatives.[28] This undertaking should be held in the same regard as recruiting and hiring within the company, because an ineffective foreign distributor can set an exporter back years; it is almost better to have no distributor than a bad one in a major market.

The approach can be either passive or active. Foreign operations for a number of smaller firms start through an unsolicited order; the same can happen with foreign distribution. Distributors, wherever they are, are always on the lookout for product representation that can be profitable and status enhancing. The initial contact may result from an advertisement or from a trade show the marketer has participated in. For example, Timberland has traditionally expanded to new markets by responding to intermediaries who have approached it.[29]

The marketer's best interest lies in taking an active role. The marketer should not simply use the first intermediary to show an interest in the firm. The choice should be a result of a careful planning process. The exporter should start by gaining an understanding of market conditions in order to define what is expected of an intermediary and what the exporter can offer in the relationship. At the same time, procedures need to be set for intermediary identification and evaluation.[30] The exporter does not have to do all of this independently; both governmental and private agencies can assist the marketer in locating intermediary candidates.

Governmental Agencies

The U.S. Department of Commerce has various services that can assist firms in identifying suitable representatives abroad. Some have been designed specifically for that purpose. A firm can subscribe to the department's Trade Opportunity Program (TOP), which matches product interests of over 70,000 foreign buyers with those indicated by the U.S. subscribers. The Country Directories of International Contacts (CDIC) provides the names and contact information for directories of importers, agents, trade associations, and government agencies on a country-by-country basis.[31] The government also provides a mechanism by which the marketer can indicate its interest in international markets. *The U.S. Exporters Yellow Pages* is a directory that includes information and display advertisements on more than 11,000 U.S. companies interested in exporting. *Commercial News USA* is a catalog-magazine distributed worldwide 6 times each year featuring advertisements by U.S. producers. Both help producers find export partners and locate export companies, freight forwarders, and other service firms that can facilitate export business.

Two services are specifically designed for locating foreign representatives. The Agent/ Distributor Service (ADS) locates foreign firms that are interested in export proposals submitted by U.S. firms and determines their willingness to correspond with the U.S. firm. Both U.S. and foreign commercial service posts abroad supply information on up to six representatives who meet these requirements. The International Company Profile (ICP) is a valuable service, especially when the screening of potential candidates takes place in markets where reliable data are not readily available. ICPs provide a trade profile of specific foreign firms. They also provide a general narrative report on the reliability of the foreign firm. All of the services are available for relatively small fees.[32] An example of an ICP report is provided in Exhibit 13.9. Furthermore, individual state agencies provide similar services. These are all available on an online basis.

Private Sources

The easiest approach for the firm seeking intermediaries is to consult trade directories. Country and regional business directories such as Kompass (Europe), Bottin International (worldwide), Foreign Trade Exchange (Northern Europe), and the Japan Trade Directory are good places to start. Company lists by country and line of business can be secured from Dun & Bradstreet, Reuben H. Donnelly, or Kellysearch. Telephone directories, especially the yellow page sections or editions, can provide distributor lists. Although not detailed, these listings will give addresses and an indication of the products sold.

The firm can solicit the support of some of its facilitating agencies, such as banks, advertising agencies, shipping lines, and airlines. All these have substantial international information networks and can put them to work for their clients. The services available will vary by agency, depending on the size of its foreign operations. Some of the major U.S. flagship carriers—for example, Northwest Airlines—have special staffs for this purpose within their cargo operations. Banks usually have the most extensive networks through their affiliates and correspondent banks. Similarly, the exporter may solicit the help of associations or chambers of commerce. For example, interest in China may warrant contacting American Chambers of Commerce in Beijing, Hong Kong, or Shanghai.

The marketer can take an even more direct approach by buying space to solicit representation. Advertisements typically indicate the type of support the marketer will be able to give to its distributor. An example of an advertisement for intermediaries placed in a trade medium is provided in Exhibit 13.10. For example, Regent Medical, a leading exporter of surgical gloves, may advertise for intermediaries in magazines such as *International Hospital Supplies* or on Web sites such as **http://www.hospitalmanagement.com**. Trade fairs are an important forum to meet potential distributors and to get data on intermediaries in the industry. Increasingly, marketers are using their own Web sites to attract international distributors and agents. The marketer may also deal directly with contacts from previous applications, launch new mail solicitations, use its own sales organization for the search, or communicate with existing customers to find prospective distributors. The latter may happen after a number of initial (unsolicited) sales to a market, causing the firm to want to enter the market on a more formal basis. If resources permit, the international marketer can use outside service agencies or consultants to generate a list of prospective representatives.

The purpose of using the sources summarized in Exhibit 13.11 is to generate as many prospective representatives as possible for the next step, screening.

Screening Intermediaries

In most firms, the evaluation of candidates involves both what to look for and where to go for the information. At this stage, the international marketer knows the type of distributor that is needed. The potential candidates must now be compared and contrasted against determining criteria. Although the criteria to be used vary by industry and by product, a good summary list is provided in Exhibit 13.12. Especially when various criteria are being weighed, these lists must be updated to reflect changes in the environment and the marketer's own situation. Some criteria can be characterized as determinant, in that they form the core dimensions along which candidates must perform well, whereas some criteria, although

Exhibit **13.9**

Sample Report from the International Company Profile

I. FOREIGN COMPANY CONTACT and SIZE INFORMATION:

China Power
Rm. 2301, Saxson Road
Beijing 1000301, China
Mr. Sam, President
Tel: 86-10-6606-3072
Fax: 86-10-6606-3071
1992
Sales: RMB 100,000,000
Employees: 80 including 15 at the headquarters

II. BACKGROUND AND PRODUCT INFORMATION:

Operation
The firm is mainly engaged in selling industrial automation products. It is also engaged in contracting factory automation system projects which consist of system design, programming, installation, and presales service. The firm started to provide services for machine tools refitting in the United States in 1996.

Company Background/History:
The firm is a wholly foreign owned enterprise registered in June of 1992 with the Municipal Administration for Industry & Commerce. The registered capital was USD1,250,000. The firm is a subsidiary of Can International Ltd., who owns 100% of the firm.
Business Size: small
Major Subsidiaries:
Name: China Power
Add: Rm. 22, Saxson Road, Beijing
Tel: 86-10-6606-3072
Ownership: 80% owned by the firm
Parent Company:
Name: ABZ Ltd., Hong Kong
Line of Business: Investment

Public Record:
According to management, an introduction to the firm and its products was included in editions of the following publications: The People's Daily Overseas Edition, the Science & Technology Daily, the Industrial & Commercial Times, the Worker's Daily, and the Computer World.

Location:
A site visit was made on September 19, 1996. The firm is located in a prime commercial area. It rents office space of 130 square meters at the address shown above. It occupies one floor in a ten-story building, the condition of which is good.

Key Company Officials:
Mr. Sam, President, born on October 24, 1958, is a graduate of Oxford University in 1982. He is now active in the firm's day to day operation in charge of the overall management. Prior to joining the firm, he was employed by the Ministry of Communications from 1982–1989 and China Harbor Engineering Co. 1989–1992.
Mr. Taylor, Vice President, was born in 1948. He joined the firm in 1995 and is currently active in the day to day operations responsible for marketing and sales. Prior to joining the firm, he was employed as Chief Representative from 1984–1995 by CROWE, a foreign plastic company merged by Miller Automation.
Ms. Young, Vice President, is currently active in the firm's day to day operations in charge of finance.

III. REFERENCES:

Foreign Firms Represented:
MILLER AUTOMATION for industrial automation products.
WILDWORLD WARE for Ministry of Machinery's industrial software.
ZXC for low voltage electrical components.
CONTON for industrial computer.
TBP for analyzing instruments.
TINNER for power station meter & instruments.
Bank References: The firm maintains banking relationships with the Industrial & Commercial Bank of China Beijing Branch. However, Mr. Sam declined to provide the account number.
Local Chamber/Trade Association:
Under current investigation, the firm is not known to be a member of any local chambers or trade associations. However, President Sam is a member of China Harbor Association and China Material Handling Association.
Trade References:
PURCHASE TERRITORY:
International: 100%
Import 90% from the U.S.A., 10% from Germany, Sweden and other countries
SALES TERRITORY: Local and International
Local: 95%; International: 5%
Exporting to South Africa

CUSTOMER TYPE:
Manufacturers: 100%
Major customers include Glass Bulb Co., Ltd.
Other customers include Iron & Steel Corporation.
PURCHASING AND SELLING ITEMS:
Purchasing Terms: L/C at sight T/T
Selling Terms: T/T
IMPORT & EXPORT: YES

IV. FINANCIAL DATA/CREDIT WORTHINESS INFORMATION:
Financial Highlights of the firm for the period January 1 to December 31, 1995 are shown below:
AMOUNT IN RMB
Sales 100,000,000
Total Assets 30,000,000
The firm declined to provide its financial statement due to "tax concerns."

V. MARKET INFORMATION AND OUTLOOK:
According to Mr. Sam, the firm is the sole "Gold Partner" of Miller Automation. Note: To be a "Gold Partner," the firm's sales volume should be more than 50 percent in the China market.

VI. SPECIAL REQUEST INFORMATION: n/a

VII. REPUTATION: Unknown

VIII. POST COMMENTS/EVALUATION:
As far as can be seen from the information supplied, the firm seems to be a satisfactory contact. EAJ Inc. may, however, wish to contact USFCS Hong Kong to obtain more information of China Power's parent company, Can International Ltd.

IX. SOURCES OF INFORMATION:
Dun & Bradstreet Report
NOTE: The information in this report has been supplied to the United States Government by commercial and government sources in the countries covered and its intended for the sole use of the purchaser. You are requested to honor the trust of these sources by not making secondary distribution of the data. While every effort is made to supply current and accurate information, the U.S. Government assumes no responsibility or liability for any decision based on the content of the ICP.

SOURCE: Example provided by Export Promotion Services, International Trade Administration, U.S. Department of Commerce.

Exhibit 13.10

Advertisement for an Intermediary

SOURCE: Courtesy of Del Monte Foods (**http://www.delmonte.com**).

important, may be used only in preliminary screening. This list should correspond closely to the exporter's own determinants of success—all the things that have to be done better to beat out competition.

Before signing a contract with a particular agent or a distributor, international marketers should satisfy themselves on certain key criteria. A number of these key criteria can be

Exhibit 13.11

Sources for Locating Foreign Intermediaries

1. Distributor inquiries
2. Home government (e.g., U.S. Department of Commerce)
   - Trade Opportunities Program
   - Commercial Service International Contacts
   - Country Directories of International Contacts
   - Agent/Distributor Service
   - International Company Profile
3. Host government
   - Representative offices
   - Import promotion efforts
4. Trade sources
   - Magazines, journals
   - Directories
   - Associations and Chambers of Commerce
   - Banks, advertising agencies, carriers
5. Field sales organizations
6. Customers
7. Direct-mail solicitation/contact of previous applicants
8. Trade fairs
9. Web sites
10. Independent consultants

Exhibit 13.12

Criteria for Choosing an International Distributor

Characteristics	Weight	Rating
Goals and strategies	—	—
Size of the firm	—	—
Financial strength	—	—
Reputation	—	—
Trading areas covered	—	—
Compatibility	—	—
Experience in products/with competitors	—	—
Sales organization	—	—
Physical facilities	—	—
Willingness to carry inventories	—	—
After-sales service capability	—	—
Use of promotion	—	—
Sales performance	—	—
Relations with local government	—	—
Communications	—	—
Overall attitude/commitment	—	—

easily quantified, thereby providing a solid base for comparisons between candidates, whereas others are qualitative and require careful interpretation and confidence in the data sources providing the information.

Performance

The financial standing of the candidate is one of the most important criteria, as well as a good starting point. This figure will show whether the distributor is making money and is able to perform some of the necessary marketing functions such as extension of credit to customers and risk absorption. Financial reports are not always complete or reliable, or they may lend themselves to interpretation differences, pointing to a need for third-party opinion. Many Latin American intermediaries lack adequate capital, a situation that can lead to more time spent managing credit than managing marketing strategy. Therefore, at companies like Xerox, assessment focuses on cash flow and the intermediary's ability to support its operations without outside help.[33]

Sales are another excellent indicator. What the distributor is presently doing gives an indication of how he or she could perform if chosen to handle the international marketer's product. The distributor's sales strength can be determined by analyzing management ability and the adequacy and quality of the sales team. If the intermediary is an importer or wholesaler, its ability to provide customer service to the next channel level is a critical determinant of future sales. Pernod Ricard selects its distribution partners based on their ability to have every needed product on hand and on time at retail locations.[34]

The distributor's existing product lines should be analyzed along four dimensions: competitiveness, compatibility, complementary nature, and quality. Quite often, international marketers find that the most desirable distributors in a given market are already handling competitive products and are therefore unavailable. In that case, the marketer can look for an equally qualified distributor handling related products. The complementary nature of products may be of interest to both parties, especially in industrial markets, where ultimate customers may be in the market for complete systems or one-stop shopping. The quality match for products is important for product positioning reasons; a high-quality product may suffer unduly from a questionable distributor reputation. The number of product lines handled gives the marketer an indication of the level of effort to expect from the distributor. Some distributors are interested in carrying as many products and product lines as possible to enhance their own standing, but they have the time and the willingness to actively sell only those that bring the best compensation. At this time, it is also important to check the candidate's physical facilities for handling the product. This is essential particularly for products that may be subject to quality changes, such as food products. The assessment should also include the candidate's marketing materials, including a possible Web site, for adequacy and appropriateness.

The distributor's market coverage must be determined. The analysis of coverage will include not only how much territory, or how many segments of the market, are covered, but also how well the markets are served. Again, the characteristics of the sales force and the number of sales offices are good quantitative indicators. To study the quality of the distributor's market coverage, the marketer can check whether the sales force visits executives, engineers, and operating people or concentrates mainly on purchasing agents. In some areas of the world, the marketer has to make sure that two distributors will not end up having territorial overlaps, which can lead to unnecessary conflict.

Professionalism

The distributor's reputation must be checked. This rather abstract measure takes its value from a number of variables that all should help the marketer forecast fit and effectiveness. The distributor's customers, suppliers, facilitating agencies, competitors, and other members of the local business community should be contacted for information on the business conduct of the distributor in such areas as buyer–seller relations and ethical behavior. This effort will shed light on variables that may be important only in certain parts of the world; for example, variables such as political clout, which is essential in certain developing countries.

The marketer must acknowledge the distributor as an independent entity with its own goals. The distributor's business strategy must therefore be determined, particularly what the distributor expects to get from the relationship and where the international marketer fits into those plans. Because a channel relationship is long term, the distributor's views on future expansion of the product line or its distribution should be clarified. This phase will also require a determination of the degree of help the distributor would need in terms of price, credit, delivery, sales training, communication, personal visits, product modification, warranty, advertising, warehousing, technical support, and after-sales service. Leaving uncertainties in these areas will cause major problems later.

Finally, the marketer should determine the distributor's overall attitude in terms of co-operation and commitment to the marketer. An effective way of testing this, and weeding out the less interested candidates, is to ask the distributor to assist in developing a local marketing plan or to develop one. This endeavor will bring out potential problem areas and will spell out which party is to perform the various marketing functions.[35]

A criteria list is valuable only when good data are available on each and every criterion. Although the initial screening can take place at the firm's offices, the three to five finalists should be visited. No better method of assessing distributors exists than visiting them, inspecting their facilities, and interviewing their various constituents in the market. A number of other critical data sources are important for firms without the resources for on-site inspection. The distributor's suppliers or firms not in direct competition can provide in-depth information. A bona fide candidate will also provide information through a local bank. Credit reports are available through the National Association of Credit Management, Dun & Bradstreet, and local credit-reporting agencies, as discussed in Chapter 11.

The Distributor Agreement

When the international marketer has found a suitable intermediary, a foreign sales agreement is drawn up.[36] The agreement can be relatively simple, but given the numerous differences in the market environments, certain elements are essential. The checklist presented in Exhibit 13.13 is the most comprehensive in stipulating the nature of the contract and the respective rights and responsibilities of the marketer and the distributor.

Contract duration is important, especially when an agreement is signed with a new distributor. In general, distribution agreements should be for a specified, relatively short period (one or two years). The initial contract with a new distributor should stipulate a trial period of either three or six months, possibly with minimum purchase requirements. Duration should be determined with an eye on the local laws and their stipulations on distributor agreements. These will be discussed later in conjunction with distributor termination.

Geographic boundaries for the distributor should be determined with care, especially by smaller firms. Future expansion of the product market might be complicated if a distributor claims rights to certain territories. The marketer should retain the right to distribute products independently, reserving the right to certain customers. For example, many marketers maintain a dual distribution system, dealing directly with certain large accounts. This type of arrangement should be explicitly stated in the agreement. Transshipments, sales to customers outside the agreed-upon territory or customer type, have to be explicitly prohibited to prevent the occurrence of parallel importation.

The payment section of the contract should stipulate the methods of payment as well as how the distributor or agent is to draw compensation. Distributors derive compensation from various discounts, such as the functional discount, whereas agents earn a specific commission percentage of net sales (such as 15 percent). Given the volatility of currency markets, the agreement should also state the currency to be used. The international marketer also needs to make sure that none of the compensation forwarded to the distributor is in violation of the Foreign Corrupt Practices Act or the OECD guidelines. A violation occurs if a payment is made to influence a foreign official in exchange for business favors, depending on the nature of the action sought. So-called grease or **facilitating payments**, such as a small fee to expedite paperwork through customs, are not considered violations.[37]

Product and conditions of sale need to be agreed on. The products or product lines included should be stipulated, as well as the functions and responsibilities of the intermediary in terms of carrying the goods in inventory, providing service in conjunction with them, and promoting them. Conditions of sale determine which party is to be responsible for some of the expenses involved, which will in turn have an effect on the price to the distributor. These conditions include credit and shipment terms.

Effective means of communication between the parties must be stipulated in the agreement if a marketer–distributor relationship is to succeed. The marketer should have access to all information concerning the marketing of his or her products in the distributor's territory, including past records, present situation assessments, and marketing research concerning the future. Communication channels should be formal for the distributor to voice

Exhibit **13.13**

Elements of a Distributor Agreement

A. Basic Components
1. Parties to the agreement
2. Statement that the contract supersedes all previous agreements
3. Duration of the agreement (perhaps a three- or six-month trial period)
4. Territory:
   a. Exclusive, nonexclusive, sole
   b. Manufacturer's right to sell direct at reduced or no commission to local government and old customers
5. Products covered
6. Expression of intent to comply with government regulations
7. Clauses limiting sales forbidden by U.S. Export Controls or practices forbidden by the Foreign Corrupt Practices Act

B. Manufacturer's Rights
1. Arbitration:
   a. If possible, in the manufacturer's country
   b. If not, before international Chamber of Commerce or American Arbitration Association, or using the London Court of Arbitration rules
   c. Definition of rules to be applied (e.g., in selecting the arbitration panel)
   d. Assurance that award will be binding in the distributor's country
2. Jurisdiction that of the manufacturer's country (the signing completed at home); if not possible, a neutral site such as Sweden or Switzerland
3. Termination conditions (e.g., no indemnification if due notice given)
4. Clarification of tax liabilities
5. Payment and discount terms
6. Conditions for delivery of goods
7. Nonliability for late delivery beyond manufacturer's reasonable control
8. Limitation on manufacturer's responsibility to provide information
9. Waiver of manufacturer's responsibility to keep lines manufactured outside the United States (e.g., licensees) outside of covered territory
10. Right to change prices, terms, and conditions at any time
11. Right of manufacturer or agent to visit territory and inspect books
12. Right to repurchase stock
13. Option to refuse or alter distributor's orders
14. Training of distributor personnel in the United States subject to:
    a. Practicality
    b. Costs to be paid by the distributor
    c. Waiver of manufacturer's responsibility for U.S. immigration approval

C. Distributor's Limitations and Duties
1. No disclosure of confidential information
2. Limitation of distributor's right to assign contract
3. Limitation of distributor's position as legal agent of manufacturer
4. Penalty clause for late payment
5. Limitation of right to handle competing lines
6. Placement of responsibility for obtaining customs clearance
7. Distributor to publicize designation as authorized representative in defined area
8. Requirement to move all signs or evidence identifying distributor with manufacturer if relationship ends
9. Acknowledgment by distributor of manufacturer's ownership of trademark, trade names, patents
10. Information to be supplied by the distributor:
    a. Sales reports
    b. Names of active prospects
    c. Government regulations dealing with imports
    d. Competitive products and competitors' activities
    e. Price at which goods are sold
    f. Complete data on other lines carried (on request)
11. Information to be supplied by distributor on purchasers

12. Accounting methods to be used by distributor
13. Requirement to display products appropriately
14. Duties concerning promotional efforts
15. Limitation of distributor's right to grant unapproved warranties, make excessive claims
16. Clarification of responsibility arising from claims and warranties
17. Responsibility of distributor to provide repair and other services
18. Responsibility to maintain suitable place of business
19. Responsibility to supply all prospective customers
20. Understanding that certain sales approaches and sales literature must be approved by manufacturer
21. Prohibition of manufacture or alteration of products
22. Requirement to maintain adequate stock, spare parts
23. Requirement that inventory be surrendered in event of a dispute that is pending in court
24. Prohibition of transshipments

SOURCE: Adapted from "Elements of a Distributor Agreement," *Business International,* March 29, 1963, 23–24. Some of the sections have been changed to reflect the present situation.

formal grievances. The contract should state the confidentiality of the information provided by either party and protect the intellectual property rights (such as patents) involved.

Channel Management

A channel relationship can be likened to a marriage in that it brings together two independent entities that have shared goals. For the relationship to work, each party must be clear about its expectations and openly communicate changes perceived in the other's behavior that might be contrary to the agreement. The closer the relationship is to a distribution partnership, the more likely marketing success will materialize. Conflict will arise, ranging from small grievances (such as billing errors) to major ones (rivalry over channel duties), but it can be managed to enhance the overall channel relationship. In some cases, conflict may be caused by an outside entity, such as gray markets, in which unauthorized intermediaries compete for market share with legitimate importers and exclusive distributors. Nevertheless, the international marketer must solve the problem.

The relationship has to be managed for the long term. An exporter may in some countries have a seller's market situation that allows it to exert pressure on its intermediaries for concessions, for example. However, if environmental conditions change, the exporter may find that the channel support it needs to succeed is not there because of the manner in which it managed channel relationships in the past.[38] Firms with harmonious relationships are typically those with more experience abroad and those that are proactive in managing the channel relationship. Harmonious relationships are also characterized by more trust, communication, and cooperation between the entities and, as a result, by less conflict and perceived uncertainty.[39]

As an exporter's operations expand, the need for coordination across markets may grow. Therefore, the exporter may want to establish distributor advisory councils to help in reactive measures (e.g., how to combat parallel importation) or proactive measures (e.g., how to transfer best practice from one distributor to another). Naturally, such councils are instrumental in building esprit de corps for the long-term success of the distribution system.

Factors in Channel Management

An excellent framework for managing channel relationships is shown in Exhibit 13.14. The complicating factors that separate the two parties fall into three categories: ownership; geographic, cultural, and economic distance; and different rules of law. Rather than lament their existence, both parties need to take strong action to remedy them. Often, the major step is acknowledgment that differences do indeed exist, followed by measures to build mutual trust.[40]

Exhibit **13.14**

Performance Problems and Remedies When Using Overseas Distributors

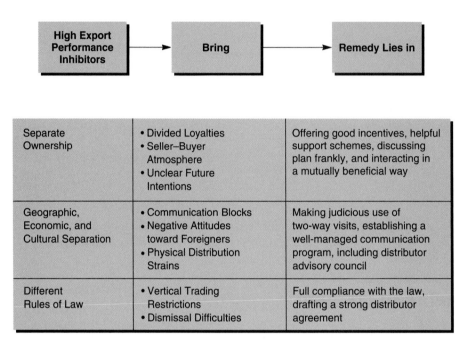

High Export Performance Inhibitors	→ Bring	→ Remedy Lies in

Separate Ownership	• Divided Loyalties • Seller–Buyer Atmosphere • Unclear Future Intentions	Offering good incentives, helpful support schemes, discussing plan frankly, and interacting in a mutually beneficial way
Geographic, Economic, and Cultural Separation	• Communication Blocks • Negative Attitudes toward Foreigners • Physical Distribution Strains	Making judicious use of two-way visits, establishing a well-managed communication program, including distributor advisory council
Different Rules of Law	• Vertical Trading Restrictions • Dismissal Difficulties	Full compliance with the law, drafting a strong distributor agreement

SOURCE: Adapted from Philip J. Rosson, "Success Factors in Manufacturer–Overseas Distributor Relationships in International Marketing," in *International Marketing Management,* ed. Erdener Kaynak (New York: Praeger, 1984), 91–107.

In international marketing, manufacturers and distributors are usually independent entities. Distributors typically carry the products of more than one manufacturer and judge products by their ability to generate revenue without added expense. The international marketer, in order to receive disproportionate attention for its concerns, may offer both monetary and psychological rewards.

Distance can be bridged through effective two-way communication. This should go beyond normal routine business communication to include innovative ways of sharing pertinent information. The international marketer may place one person in charge of distributor-related communications or put into effect an interpenetration strategy—that is, an exchange of personnel so that both organizations gain further insight into the workings of the other.[41] Cross-cultural differences in people's belief systems and behavior patterns have to be acknowledged and acted on for effective channel management. For example, in markets where individualism is stressed, local channel partners may seek arrangements that foster their own self-interest and may expect their counterparts to watch out for themselves. Conflict is seen as a natural phenomenon. In societies of low individualism, however, a common purpose is fostered between the partners.[42]

Economic distance manifests itself in exchange rates, for example. Instability of exchange rates can create serious difficulties for distributors in their trading activities, not only with their suppliers but also with their domestic customers. Manufacturers and distributors should develop and deploy mutually acceptable mechanisms that allow for some flexibility in interactions when unforeseen rate fluctuations occur.[43] For example, Harley Davidson has instituted a system of risk sharing in which it will maintain a single foreign currency price as long as the spot exchange rate does not move beyond a mutually agreed-upon rate. Should that happen, Harley Davidson and the distributor will share the costs or benefits of the change.

Laws and regulations in many markets may restrict the manufacturer in terms of control. For example, in the European Union, the international marketer cannot prevent a distributor from reexporting products to customers in another member country, even though the marketer has another distributor in that market. EU law insists on a single market where goods and services can be sold throughout the area without restriction. In 1998, VW was fined €90 million and in 2000 GM €43 million for taking steps to limit intra-EU imports. Even monitoring parallel imports may be considered to be in restraint of trade.

Most of the criteria used in selecting intermediaries can be used to evaluate existing intermediaries as well. If not conducted properly and fairly, however, evaluation can be a source of conflict. In addition to being given the evaluation results in order to take appropriate action, the distributor should be informed of the evaluative criteria and should be a part of the overall assessment process. Again, the approach should be focused on serving mutual benefits. For example, it is important that the exporter receive detailed market and financial performance data from the distributor. Most distributors identify these data as the key sources of power in distribution and may, therefore, be inherently reluctant to provide them in full detail. The exchange of such data is often the best indicator of a successful relationship.[44]

A part of the management process is channel adjustment. This can take the form of channel shift (eliminating a particular type of channel), channel modification (changing individual members while leaving channel structure intact), or role or relationship modification (changing functions performed or the reward structure) as a result of channel evaluation. The need for channel change should be well established and not executed hastily because it will cause a major distraction in the operations of the firm. Some companies have instituted procedures that require executives to consider carefully all of the aspects and potential results of change before execution.

Gray Markets

Gray markets, or **parallel importation**, refer to authentic and legitimately manufactured trademark items that are produced and purchased abroad but imported or diverted to the market by bypassing designated channels.[45] The IT industry estimates that gray market sales of IT products account for over $40 billion in revenue each year, collectively costing IT manufacturers up to $5 billion annually in lost profits.[46] Gray marketed products vary from inexpensive consumer goods (such as chewing gum) to expensive capital goods (such as excavation equipment). The phenomenon is not restricted to the United States; Japan, for example, has witnessed gray markets because of the high value of the yen and the subsidization of cheaper exports through high taxes. Japanese marketers thus often found it cheaper to go to Los Angeles to buy export versions of Japanese-made products. Gray markets are not a fringe phenomenon either; for example, 80 percent of the mobile phone market in Laos is supposedly furnished through sourcing or smuggling from Thailand.

A case history of the phenomenon is provided in Exhibit 13.15, which shows the flow of Seiko watches through authorized and unauthorized channels. Seiko is a good example of a typical gray market product in that it carries a well-known trademark. Unauthorized importers, such as Progress Trading Company in New York, and retailers, such as Kmart or Gem of the Day, buy Seiko watches around the world at advantageous prices and then sell them to consumers at substantial discounts over authorized Seiko dealers. Seiko has fought back, for example, by advertising warnings to consumers against buying gray market watches on the grounds that these products may be obsolete or worn-out models and that consumers might have problems with their warranties. Many gray marketers, however, provide their own warranty-related service and guarantee watches sold through them. Since watches have strong commercial potential online due to the power of their brand identities, gray-market watch Web sites are having the most impact on higher-priced watch lines selling for $1,000 retail. Authorized retailers are being forced to take bigger discounts to keep from losing sales.[47]

Various conditions allow unauthorized resellers to exist. The most important are price segmentation and exchange rate fluctuations. Competitive conditions may require the international marketer to sell essentially the same product at different prices in different markets or to different customers.[48] Because many products are priced higher in, for example, the United States, a gray marketer can purchase them in Europe or the Far East and offer discounts between 10 and 40 percent below list price when reselling them in the U.S. market.

Exhibit 13.15

Seiko's Authorized and Unauthorized Channels of Distribution

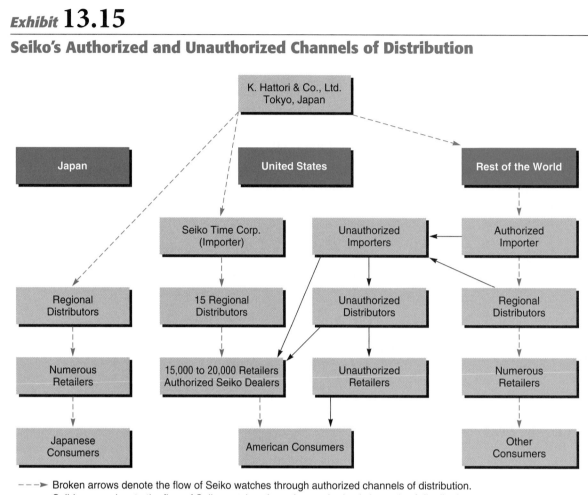

- - - → Broken arrows denote the flow of Seiko watches through authorized channels of distribution.
———→ Solid arrows denote the flow of Seiko watches through unauthorized channels of distribution.

SOURCE: Jack Kaikati, "Parallel Importation: A Growing Conflict in International Channels of Distribution," Symposium on Export-Import Interrelationships, Georgetown University, November 14–15, 1985.

Exchange rate fluctuations can cause price differentials and thus opportunities for gray marketers. For example, during the Asian financial crisis, gray marketers imported Caterpillar, Deere, and Komatsu construction and earth-moving equipment no longer needed for halted projects in markets such as Thailand and Indonesia—and usually never used—for as little as 60 percent of what U.S. dealers paid wholesale.[49] In some cases, gray markets emerge as a result of product shortages. For example, at one time, many U.S. computer manufacturers had to turn to gray marketers to secure their supply of DRAMs or else watch their production lines grind to a halt.[50] However, in these cases, the gray market goods typically cost more than those usually available through authorized suppliers. In other cases, if there are multiple production sites for the same product, gray markets can emerge due to negative perceptions about the country of origin.

Gray market flows have increased as current barriers to trade are being eliminated. As seen in *The International Marketplace 13.3,* the European Union has significant parallel importation due to significant price differentials in ethical drugs, which are in turn the result of differences in regulation, insurance coverage, medical practice, and exchange rates. Of the fifteen member countries, only Denmark grants manufacturers the freedom to price their ethical drugs. The share of parallel trade is estimated at 15 percent and is expected to grow since the European Commission is supporting the practice.[51] A similar controversy has emerged in the United States, where prescription drugs are priced higher than in Canada, and where some are advocating the reimportation of these drugs from Canada to the United States.

The Distribution of Counterfeit Pharmaceuticals

One of the biggest threats to the pharmaceutical industry is the distribution of counterfeit medicine. It was estimated that around seven percent of medicines distributed worldwide in 2008 were counterfeit. This estimate is low, however, compared to the distribution of counterfeit medicines in particular regions of the world. For example, it was estimated that 40 percent of medicines in South America and nearly 70 percent in West Africa were counterfeit. Counterfeit medicines pose severe risks to the people taking the medicine and cost pharmaceutical companies and governments millions of dollars annually.

The two major routes that counterfeiters tend to use to distribute fake medicines to patients internationally are parallel importation and online pharmacies. In 2007, three batches of counterfeit drugs were discovered in the pharmaceutical supply chain in the United Kingdom. Counterfeits of Lilly's Zyprexa (olanzapine), Sanofi-Aventis's Plavix (clopidogrel), and AstraZeneca's Casodex (bicalutaminde) had entered the country via parallel importation from France. Additionally, the increase in worldwide usage of the internet and rapid adoption of e-commerce enable the fairly easy sale of counterfeit medicines around the globe.

Manufacturers and distributors of pharmaceuticals have identified three major methods for stemming the flow of counterfeit medicines. One method is the use of technology. Using information technology solutions, companies could track the distribution of products throughout the supply chain. The most common form of tracking would be the barcode built into the labeling of all products. The information included on the barcode would be the pharmaceutical code, the supplier or importer code, size of the unit, the pharmaceutical product group code, and any special controls required for the product. More advanced than the basic barcode would be the use of auto ID technology such as the RFID. RFID tracking would enable the item, case, or pallet tagging of all products, again tracking them throughout the supply chain. Use of such technology, however, requires a major investment in well-designed, integrated supply chain systems in which all parties exploit the use of the technology.

The second method is a switch from the traditional wholesaler model in which pharmaceuticals are distributed through a network of wholesalers to a direct-to-pharmacy drug distribution model. In this new

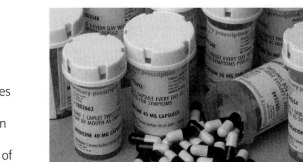

COUNTERFEIT PHARMACEUTICALS ARE
A HEALTH HAZARD WORLDWIDE.

distribution model, pharmaceutical manufacturers would enter into an exclusive agreement with a particular wholesaler to deliver its medicines to particular pharmacies. Essentially, the relationship is between the manufacturer and the pharmacy, with the wholesaler serving the delivery role in the channel of distribution. While this new form of distribution has been implemented in the United Kingdom, it has met considerable resistance as wholesalers try to convince the government that the direct-to-pharmacy model will lead to rising costs in the UK healthcare system and to diminished distribution service.

The third method that has been implemented, or is in the process of being implemented, by several pharmaceutical manufacturers is the use of dual pricing. With dual pricing, pharmaceuticals intended for export are sold at a premium compared to the drugs intended for domestic use. This helps prevent parallel importation from countries, such as Greece and Spain, where drugs are available at relatively lower costs. Thus, the distributors in Greece and Spain could not export to countries such as Germany and the United Kingdom, where prices are much higher, at the same price as they would sell internally. The European wholesalers association contends, however, that this type of dual pricing is anticompetitive.

Counterfeit pharmaceuticals are rapidly becoming a health hazard worldwide. Add the economics problem to this and one can see that it really is in the interests of the members of the distribution channel to create a deterrent to this potential global disaster. However, it does not appear that distributors are pleased with the current efforts put forth by the pharmaceutical companies.

SOURCES: Andre Grigianis, "Beating the Counterfeiters," New & Events, July 11, 2008, **http://www.ibs.net/uk/industries/ pharmaceutical/news/beating-the-counterfeiters .jsp**, retrieved February 9, 2009; "Anti-Counterfeiting Strategies—Combating Fake Pharmaceuticals," Datamonitor, Pharmaceutical Business Review, December 19, 2007, **http:// www.pharmaceutical-business-review.com/research/ anti_counterfeiting_strategies_combating_fake_ pharmaceuticals**, retrieved February 9, 2009; "Pharma Moving to More Restricted Drug Distribution, in Attempt to Guard Drug Supply," Biz Community, May 15, 2008, **http://medical**

.bizcommunity.com/Article/196/326/2499.html, retrieved February 9, 2009; "Wholesalers Threatened as Bib Pharma Adopts Direct-to-Pharmacy Drug Distribution," URCH Publishing, February 10, 2008, **http://www.urchpublishing.com/articles/ wholesalers_threatened_as_big_pharma_adopts_direct-to- pharmacy_drug_distribution_model.html**, retrieved February 9, 2009; "Changes to Pharma Distribution in the UK Potentially Problematic," The Infoshop, August 27, 2007, **http://www .businesswire.com/portal/site/google/?ndmViewId=news_ view&newsId=20070827005978&newsLang=en**, retrieved February 9, 2009.

Opponents and supporters of the practice disagree on whether the central issue is price or trade rights. Detractors typically cite the following arguments: (1) the gray market unduly hurts the legitimate owners of trademarks; (2) without protection, trademark owners will have little incentive to invest in product development; (3) gray marketers will "free ride" or take unfair advantage of the trademark owners' marketing and promotional activities; and (4) parallel imports can deceive consumers by not meeting product standards or their normal expectations of after-sale service. The bottom line is that gray market goods can severely under cut local marketing plans, erode long-term brand images, eat up costly promotion funds, and sour manufacturer–intermediary relations. The opponents scored a major victory when the European Court of Justice ruled in 2001 against Tesco, which imported cheap Levi jeans from the United States and sold them at prices well below those of other retailers. The decision backed Levi's claim that its image could be harmed if it lost control of import distribution. Tesco can continue sourcing Levi's products within the EU from the cheapest provider, but not from outside it.[52]

Proponents of parallel importation approach the issue from an altogether different point of view. They argue for their right to "free trade" by pointing to manufacturers that are both overproducing and overpricing in some markets. The main beneficiaries are consumers, who benefit from lower prices, and discount distributors, with whom some of the manufacturers do not want to deal and who have now, because of gray markets, found a profitable market niche.

Gray markets attract consumers with high price sensitivities. However, given the price–quality inference, quality may become a concern for the consumer, especially if they do not have relevant information about the brand and the intermediary. In addition, risk aversion will have a negative influence on consumers' propensity to buy gray-market goods. The likelihood of obtaining a counterfeit version, a deficient guarantee, or no service are foremost concerns.[53]

In response to the challenge, manufacturers have chosen various approaches. Despite the Supreme Court ruling in May 1988 to legitimize gray markets in the United States,[54] foreign manufacturers, U.S. companies manufacturing abroad, and authorized retailers have continued to fight the practice. In January 1991, the U.S. Customs Service enacted a new rule whereby trademarked goods that have been authorized for manufacture and sale abroad by U.S. trademark holders will no longer be allowed into the United States through parallel channels.[55] Those parallel importing goods of overseas manufacturers will not be affected. Recently, courts have taken exception to cases that have shown evidence of deception. For example, Lever Brothers won a long case to stop discounters from selling Sunlight brand dishwashing detergent, produced for the British market, in the United States. Because tap water is generally harder in Britain, formulation of the product there is different from Lever's U.S. version, which produces more lather. Lever reported lost sales and complaints from customers who bought the British brand and were disappointed.

The solution for the most part lies with the contractual relationships that tie businesses together. In almost all cases of gray marketing, someone in the authorized channel commits a diversion, thus violating the agreements signed. One of the standard responses is therefore disenfranchisement of such violators. This approach is a clear response to complaints from the authorized dealers who are being hurt by transshipments. Tracking down offenders is quite expensive and time-consuming, however. Some of the gray marketers can be added to the authorized dealer network if mutually acceptable terms can be reached, thereby increasing control of the channel of distribution.[56]

A one-price policy can eliminate one of the main reasons for gray markets. This means choosing the most efficient of the distribution channels through which to market the product, but it may also mean selling at the lowest price to all customers regardless of location and size. A meaningful one-price strategy must also include a way to reward the providers of other services, such as warranty repair, in the channel.

Other strategies have included producing different versions of products for different markets. For example, some electronics-goods companies are designing products so they will work only in the market for which they are designated. Some of the latest printers from Hewlett-Packard do not print if they are fed ink cartridges not bought in the same region as the printer. Nintendo's handheld game machines are sold in the United States with power adaptors that do not work in Europe.[57] Some companies have introduced price incentives to consumers. Hasselblad, the Swedish camera manufacturer, offers rebates to purchasers of legally imported, serial-numbered camera bodies, lenses, and roll-fill magazines. Many manufacturers promote the benefits of dealing with authorized dealers (and, thereby, the dangers of dealing with gray market dealers). For example, Rolex's message states that authorized dealers are the only ones who are capable of providing genuine accessories and who can ensure that the customer gets an authentic product and the appropriate warranty. Many pharmaceutical companies and the U.S. Food and Drug Administration have embarked on educational and promotional campaigns to call attention to buying drugs from abroad via Internet pharmacies.[58]

Termination of the Channel Relationship

Many reasons exist for the termination of a channel relationship, but the most typical are changes in the international marketer's distribution approach (for example, establishing a sales office), or a (perceived) lack of performance by the intermediary. On occasion, termination may result from either party not honoring agreements; for example, by selling outside assigned territories and initiating price wars.[59]

Channel relationships go through a life cycle. The concept of an international distribution life cycle is presented in Exhibit 13.16. Over time, the manufacturer's marketing capabilities increase while a distributor's ability and willingness to grow the manufacturer's

Exhibit 13.16

International Distribution Life Cycle

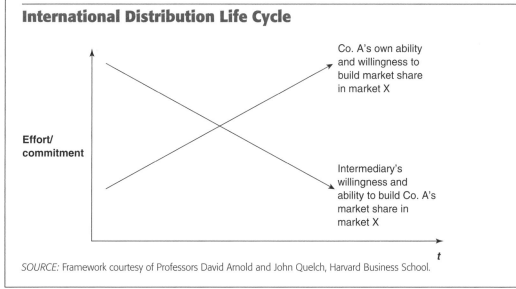

SOURCE: Framework courtesy of Professors David Arnold and John Quelch, Harvard Business School.

business in that market decreases. When a producer expands its market presence, it may expect more of a distributor's effort than the distributor is willing to make available. Furthermore, with expansion, the manufacturer may want to expand its product line to items that the distributor is neither interested in nor able to support. In some cases, intermediaries may not be interested in growing the business beyond a certain point (e.g., due to progressive taxation in the country) or as aggressively as the principal may expect (i.e., being more of an order-taker than an order-getter). As a marketer's operations expand, it may want to start to coordinate operations across markets for efficiency and customer-service reasons or to cater to global accounts—thereby needing to control distribution to a degree that independent intermediaries are not willing to accept, or requiring a level of service that they may not be able to deliver.

Independent distributors do remain long-run representatives of originators under certain circumstances. Some markets may not be considered strategic (e.g., due to size) or they may be culturally challenging (e.g., Saudi Arabia). The distributors may carry product lines that are complementary, thus enhancing the originator's efforts, and they may act more as partners by sharing information, or undertaking originator-specific projects in their or nearby markets to become "indispensable."[60]

If termination is a result of such a structural change, the situation has to be handled carefully. The effect of termination on the intermediary has to be understood, and open communication is needed to make the transition smooth. For example, the intermediary can be compensated for investments made, and major customers can be visited jointly to assure them that service will be uninterrupted.

Termination conditions are one of the most important considerations in the distributor agreement, because the just causes for termination vary and the penalties for the international marketer may be substantial. Just causes include fraud or deceit, damage to the other party's interest, or failure to comply with contract obligations concerning minimum inventory requirements or minimum sales levels. These must be spelled out carefully because local courts are often favorably disposed toward local businesses. In some countries, termination may not even be possible. In the EU and Latin America, terminating an ineffective intermediary is time-consuming and expensive. One year's average commissions are typical for termination without justification. A notice of termination has to be given three to six months in advance. In Austria, termination without just cause and/or failure to give notice of termination may result in damages amounting to average commissions for between 1 and 15 years.

The time to think about such issues is before the overseas distribution agreement is signed. It is especially prudent to find out what local laws say about termination and to check what type of experience other firms have had in the particular country. Careful preparation can allow the exporter to negotiate a termination without litigation. If the distributor's performance is unsatisfactory, careful documentation and clearly defined performance measures may help show that the distributor has more to gain by going quietly than by fighting.

E-Commerce

Increasingly, various marketing constituents are seeing the Web not only as a communication tool but as a builder of interactive relationships and as a device to sell products and services.[61] An important part of the economy, e-commerce is a fundamental component of developed markets. While in its infancy in emerging markets, e-commerce is supposedly on the cusp of a usage-explosion in these developing marketplaces. For example, China reportedly overtook the United States in 2008 with respect to the number of internet users in the country. By 2012, both B2C and B2B consumers are expected to be spending trillions of dollars online.[62]

Many companies willing to enter e-commerce will not have to do it on their own. Hub sites (also known as virtual malls, e-marketplaces, or digital intermediaries) will bring

HUB SITES SUCH AS EBAY BRING TOGETHER BUYERS, SELLERS, DISTRIBUTORS, AND TRANSACTION PAYMENT
PROCESSORS IN ONE SINGLE, INTERNATIONAL MARKETPLACE.

together buyers, sellers, distributors, and transaction payment processors in one single marketplace, making convenience the key attraction. With 1,400 of them in place,[63] entities such as Priceline.com (**http://www.priceline.com**), eBay (**http://www.ebay.com**), Shoplet (**http://www.shoplet.com**), Quadrem (**http://www.quadrem.com**), and ECnet (**http://www.ecnet.com**) are leading the way.

As soon as customers have the ability to access a company through the Internet, the company itself has to be prepared to provide 24-hour order taking and customer service, to acquire the regulatory and customs-handling expertise to deliver internationally, and to develop an in-depth understanding of marketing environments for the further development of the business relationship. The instantaneous interactivity of users' experience will also be translated into an expectation of expedient delivery of answers and products ordered. Many people living outside the United States who want to purchase online expect U.S.-style service. However, in many cases, they may find that shipping is not even available outside the United States.

The challenges faced in terms of response and delivery capabilities can be overcome by outsourcing services or by building international distribution networks. Air express carriers such as DHL, FedEx, and UPS offer full-service packages that leverage their own Internet infrastructure with customs clearance and e-mail shipment notification. If a company needs help in order fulfilment and customer support, logistics centers offer warehousing and inventory management services as well as same-day delivery from in-country stocks. DHL, for example, has more than 124,000 employees worldwide, operates in more than 220 countries and territories, and has 36 hubs, with key centers in Bahrain for the Middle East, Brussels for Europe, and Singapore for Asia-Pacific. Some companies elect to build their own international distribution networks. Both QVC, a televised shopping service, and amazon.com, an online retailer of books and consumer goods, have distribution centers in Britain and Germany to take advantage of the European Internet audience and to fulfill more quickly and cheaply the orders generated by their Web sites.

Transactions and the information they provide about the buyer allow for greater customization and for service by region, by market, or even by individual customer. One of the largest online sellers, Dell Computer, builds a Premier Page for its corporate customers, which is linked to the customer's intranet and thus allows approved employees to configure PCs, pay for them, and track their delivery status. Premier Pages also provide access to instant technical support and Dell sales representatives. Dell even offers a Tech Center

Wiki site so that customers can engage and keep up-to-date on the rapidly changing issues in information technology.[64]

Although English has long been perceived as the lingua franca of the Web, the share of non-English speakers worldwide increased to almost 70 percent by 2009. It has also been shown that Web users are three times more likely to buy when the offering is made in their own language.[65] However, not even the largest of firms can serve all markets with a full line of their products. Getting a Web site translated and running is an expensive proposition and, if done correctly, time-consuming as well. If the site is well developed, it will naturally lead to expectations that order fulfillment will be of equal caliber. Therefore, any worldwide Web strategy has to be tied closely with the company's overall growth strategy in world markets.

A number of hurdles and uncertainties are keeping some companies out of global markets or preventing them from exploiting these markets to their full potential. Some argue that the World Wide Web does not live up to its name, since it is mostly a tool for the United States and Europe. Yet, as Internet penetration levels increase in the near future, due to technological advances, improvements in many countries' Web infrastructures, and customer acceptance, e-business will become truly global. As a matter of fact, in some cases emerging markets may provide a chance to try out new approaches, because the markets and the marketers in them are not burdened by history.

The marketer has to be sensitive to the governmental role in e-commerce. No real consensus exists on the taxation of e-commerce, especially in the case of cross-border transactions. While the United States and the EU have agreed not to impose new taxes on sales through the Internet, there is no uniformity in the international taxation of transactions.[66] Other governments believe, however, that they have something to gain by levying new e-taxes. Until more firm legal precedents are established, international marketers should be aware of their potential tax liabilities and prepare for them, especially if they are considering substantial e-commerce investments. One likely scenario is an e-commerce tax system that closely resembles sales taxes at physical retail outlets. Vendors will be made responsible for collecting sales taxes and forwarding them to the governments concerned, most likely digitally. Another proposal involves the bit-tax, a variation of the Internet access tax.

In addition, any product traded will still be subject to government regulations.[67] For example, Virtual Vineyards has to worry about country-specific alcohol regulations, while software makers have to comply with U.S. software export regulations. Dell Computer was fined $50,000 by the U.S. Department of Commerce for shipping computers online to Iran, a country on the sanctions list due to its sponsorship of terrorism.

Governments will also have to come to terms with issues related to security, privacy, and access to the Internet.[68] The private sector argues for the highest possible ability to safeguard its databases, to protect cross-border transmission of confidential information, and to conduct secure financial transactions using global networks. This requires an unrestricted market for encryption products that operate globally. However, some governments, especially the United States, fear that encryption will enable criminals and terrorist organizations to avoid detection and tracking. Therefore, a strong argument is made in favor of limiting the extent of encryption.

Privacy issues have grown exponentially as a result of e-business. The European Union has a directive that introduced high standards of data privacy to ensure the free flow of data throughout its member states. Each individual has the right to review personal data, correct them, and limit their use. But more importantly, the directive also requires member states to block transmission of data to countries, including the United States, if those countries' domestic legislation does not provide an adequate level of protection. The issue between the United States and the EU will most likely be settled by companies, such as IBM, adopting global privacy policies for managing information online and getting certified by groups, such as Better Business Bureaus or TRUSTe, that are implementing privacy labeling systems to tell users when a site adheres to their privacy guidelines.[69] A register of such companies will also then have to be developed.

A related concern is the content of material on the Internet. While freedom of information across international lines is encouraged and easily achieved, some countries (such as China and Saudi Arabia) regulate information and others have quotas on domestically produced broadcasting. Regulations on advertising are also implemented.

For industries such as music and motion pictures, the Internet is both an opportunity and a threat.[70] It provides a new and efficient method of distribution and customization of products. At the same time, it can be a channel for intellectual property violations, through unauthorized postings on Web sites from which protected material can be downloaded. In addition, the music industry is concerned about a shift in the balance of economic power: if artists can deliver their works directly to customers via technologies such as MP3, what will be the role of labels and distributors? Many labels have switched to digital music and seen their profits increase with the new distribution mode.[71]

Summary

Channels of distribution consist of the marketing efforts and intermediaries that facilitate the movement of goods and services. Decisions that must be made to establish an international channel of distribution focus on channel design and the selection of intermediaries for the roles that the international marketer will not perform. The channel must be designed to meet the requirements of the intended customer base, coverage, long-term continuity of the channel once it is established, and the quality of coverage to be achieved. Having determined the basic design of the channel, the international marketer will then decide on the number of different types of intermediaries to use and how many of each type, or whether to use intermediaries at all, which would be the case in direct distribution using, for example, sales offices or e-commerce. The process is important because the majority of international sales involve distributors, and channel decisions are the most long-term of all marketing decisions. The more the channel operation resembles a team, rather than a collection of independent businesses, the more effective the overall marketing effort will be.

Key Terms

intermediaries	indirect exporting	del credere agent
distribution culture	direct exporting	facilitating payments
distributor	integrated exporting	parallel importation
agent	commissionario	

Questions for Discussion

1. Relate these two statements: "A channel of distribution can be compared to a marriage." "The number one reason given for divorce is lack of communication."

2. Channels of distribution tend to vary according to the level of economic development of a market. The more developed the economy, the shorter the channels tend to be. Why?

3. If a small exporter lacks the resources for an onsite inspection, what measures would you propose for screening potential distributors?

4. The international marketer and the distributor will have different expectations concerning the relationship. Why should these expectations be spelled out and clarified in the contract?

5. One method of screening candidates is to ask distributors for a sample marketing plan. What items would you want included in this plan?

6. Is gray marketing a trademark issue, a pricing issue, or a distribution issue?

Internet Exercises

1. Using the Web site of the U.S. Commercial Service (http://trade.gov/cs), assess the types of help available to an exporter in establishing distribution channels and finding partners in this endeavor.

2. The Alliance for Gray Market and Counterfeit Abatement (http://www.agmaglobal.org) has as its primary purpose to "mitigate gray marketing and counterfeiting of high-technology products." Is it appropriate to equate the two? Are the arguments by this industry coalition convincing?

Recommended Readings

Arikan, Akin. *Multichannel Marketing: Metrics and Methods for On and Offline Success.* Hoboken, NJ: Sybex, 2008.

Benfield, Scott and Stephen D. Griffith. *Disruption in the Channel: The New Realities of Distribution and Manufacturing in a Global Economy.* Camby, IN: Power Publishing, 2008.

Dent, Julian. *Distribution Channels: Understanding and Managing Channels to Market.* London: Kogan Page, 2008.

Fernandez, Mary Joy. *Analysis of Selected Aspects of the Multi-Channel Management and the International Distribution System.* Hamburg, Germany: Diplomica Verlag, 2008.

Rangan, V. Kasturi and Marie Bell. *Transforming Your Go-To-Market Strategy: The Three Disciplines of Channel Management.* Boston, MA: Harvard Business School Press, 2006.

Rushton, Alan and Steve Walker. *International Logistics and Supply Chain Outsourcing: From Local to Global.* London: Kogan Page, 2007.

HONEYLAND MANUKA HONEY FROM NEW ZEALAND

AN INTERNATIONAL NEW VENTURE

New Zealand's Economic Environment

New Zealand is a small island nation in the South Pacific south-east of Australia. Its landmass of 268 million square kilometers compares with the size of Oregon. With a slightly higher population than Oregon—just over four million (4.15 million in 2006)—New Zealand's domestic market is small. GDP per capita is about US$ 26,400 per year (2007), slightly more than half of that of the USA, with an annual economic growth rate of 3 percent in 2007. Virtually free access of overseas competitors to New Zealand's home market forces its numerous small and medium enterprises (SME[1]) to seek and develop international markets. Australia is its most important trading partner, accounting for 22 percent of New Zealand's exports, followed by the USA (11.5 percent) and Japan (9.2 percent). New Zealand relies for its economic viability mainly on the success of its SMEs, since these constitute up to 90.7 percent of all firms and provide about 50 percent of New Zealanders with work and income (Ministry of Economic Development, 2004). A 2002 report initiated by the New Zealand Treasury identified the two major constraints for economic growth in New Zealand: the distant geographic location from international markets and the difficulty of raising sufficient capital.

The Making of Honeyland and Its Products

Honeyland is an export business specializing in native New Zealand honeys. It was established in Palmerston North, a small town in the New Zealand Manawatu region in July 1986. The business started exporting right from its beginnings and has, in effect, never operated in the domestic New Zealand market, focusing on one international market only. The company supplies exclusively the lucrative Japanese market. The company is even by New Zealand's standards very small. It is literally a one (wo)man enterprise. That does not limit the success, though. From modest beginnings the enterprise has grown into a reasonable business that turns over more than NZ$500,000 (about U.S.$ 275,000) operating from a small office in the family home.

New Zealand honey is positioned as a health-promoting product, using New Zealand's clean and green image. The company strategically targets quality-conscious customers, especially those who have been to New Zealand for a holiday and know its spectacular landscape. New Zealand has a reputation for its beautiful and rather unspoilt natural environment, including its exotic plants. The majority of New Zealand's plants are indigenous, found growing naturally only in that part of the world. In particular, New Zealand has many flowering trees, such as the Pohutukawa, Kamahi, Manuka, Tawari, and Rewarewa. Native bush and forest honey, which is produced in this environment, has a reputation for being healthy and beneficial to human well-being. The honey that bees collect from the flowers of the New Zealand tea or Manuka tree is said to have a great taste and very beneficial healing properties.

The owner of Honeyland, Sue, a trained school teacher, became aware of the good reputation and health benefits of New Zealand honey early on. In the 1970s, she raised a young family while keeping bees in a few beehives in the back of her garden around the family home. Sue has always kept a friendly open home and entertained the many international friends of her teenage children and business partners of her husband. *"When I look back, our home was always an open home, long before other people actually were in the international world."* Many of these visitors were Japanese because Palmerston North has strong links to Japan through its Japanese-based

SOURCE: This case was contributed by Sabina Jaeger, Lecturer in International Business, AUT University, New Zealand, sabina.jaeger@aut.ac.nz.

'International Pacific College' and Massey University. Many young Japanese complete their high school and university education there. Attracted to the cultivated polite Japanese people, Sue chose her preferred market destination long before she started the company. Her interest in Japan and Japanese culture grew during visits when she accompanied her husband, a successful wool merchant, on his business trips. Soon Sue started looking for a business idea that would enable her to visit Japan on a regular basis without having to depend on her husband. The hobby of producing honey grew into a business idea.

Export Market Japan

The contacts with Japanese friends exposed her to their culture, way of life, and work. While on her trips in Japan she gradually built up an extensive network of friends and business partners. *"We had a real network of friends and acquaintances in Japan. I think that probably has been one of the great advantages, because some of them are students, some of them are old, they range from 15 years old to 90 years old. They are all around Japan and they enjoy different sorts of lifestyles. So that is a wonderful way of getting a feel for what a country is like."* Additionally, Sue undertook further preparation before starting up the enterprise. She began to learn the Japanese language because she understood the importance of language skills when doing business in Japan. It did not take long before she became convinced that New Zealand speciality honeys would be a suitable export product. Sue applied great care to understand the specifics of the Japanese market. One major hurdle she had to overcome was gaining access to Japanese distributors and retail businesses. She said that in the 1980s this was not easy for a businesswoman. Speaking the language, and with some support from her friends, she eventually overcame this difficulty. Sue modifies and markets her products to the special Japanese requirements.

Marketing Strategy

Honeyland's market can be distinguished into three different segments. One third of the business comes from sales through a supermarket chain that operates a "fixed price" strategy. Quality branded products are sold at a discount: *"It is a discount type store. Unbelievable, their whole layout is similar to the one of the 'two dollar' shop.[2] Like 1 dollar, 2 dollar, 3 dollar shop! It is primarily liquor.... So they use good brands to bring people in and sell them cheaply."* Another third of her business in-

volves supplying a Japanese honey company with New Zealand comb honey. This company brands the product under its own name. The third and most important segment of Honeyland's business derives from sales to a firm that is associated with Japan Travel Business (JTB). It targets the top range of the gift product industry with high returns selling gifts to returning travellers, various honeys in small gift packaging. *"The third part of my market is very much a niche market, a very top shelf specialty honey.... The niche market is going through my representative in Japan."* Japanese tourists spend their short holidays in New Zealand's surroundings. They experience the "great outdoors" enjoying the scenery doing bush walks and encounter many exotic plants among New Zealand's wild flora. It is part of Japanese culture that travellers take home a small gift to friends and family. Others like to have a piece of New Zealand as a memory for themselves. Honeyland provides a solution for those tourists who do not want to worry about purchasing presents when holidaying. Honeyland products are available in Japanese airport stores for tourists to pick up upon arrival back in Japan. Packaged in small, beautifully labeled containers, the distinctive New Zealand honeys have become a much appreciated gift in Japan.

Export Barriers

One of the biggest obstacles to Honeyland's growth is sourcing and securing the supply of quality honey. Thus, the New Zealand supply determines the extent of the company's involvement in the international market and limits business expansion. Annual variations in quality and quantity are natural occurrences of the product. Sue solved the supply difficulties by developing and maintaining a very good relationship with her domestic supplier. Their loyal commitment guarantees preferential supply even when overall stocks are low and they cannot deliver to other clients. Another problem is the management of organic export products. New Zealand has entered into an international treaty to protect plants and natural vegetation that requires strict export controls. New Zealand's Ministry of Agriculture and Fisheries (MAF) is the official body that looks after the treaty's enforcement. Export operations are difficult because MAF requires strict compliance with their phyto-sanitary and bio-security regulations, including the inspection of all exported organic products and detailed documentation. Careful planning and organization on the part of Honeyland is necessary to be able to meet the export deadlines. These problems have been solved through close attention to MAF regulations at the planning and strategy stages. Thus, Honeyland now organizes international trade around these requirements and uses these MAF certificates for quality differentiation.

Logistics

Access to reliable and cost-effective transportation is another issue with which Honeyland has to deal. New Zealand is far off the main shipping routes and transport costs are high compared to countries that are in the center of the world trade network. The large geographical distance between New Zealand and Japan is a big obstacle in itself. The normal shipping time to Japan is ten days on average. However, in reality it takes much longer for a shipment to arrive safely to the customer. Why is this? Honeyland usually ships out of Napier, a small rural town with international harbor facilities. Napier has turned out to be a convenient location since most of the honey is sourced and packaged regionally. The supplier loads the honey into sea containers onsite so transport costs and time inside New Zealand are minimized. However, using a small regional port also has disadvantages. Most of the drawbacks are related to capacity and frequency of transportation services, particularly during times when the general harvest season is underway. Around harvest time a variety of produce exporters usually compete for limited container space and shipping facilities.

There are other problems concerning logistics. The size of Honeyland's export unit is on average just one container load. To date (2008) the shipping of a "20 foot" standard container to Japan costs about NZ$ 4000 (U.S. $2200). This price includes the basic paperwork such as customs declaration. There may be times when customers require a more frequent delivery mode and then the size of the shipment can be less than one container. If containers are shared, the projected arrival time is less predictable than normally because a suitable load going to the same destination to fill up the remainder of the container has to be found. When shipping smaller quantities of high-priced niche products, Honeyland employs the services of a reliable international freight forwarder. Although utilizing the services of freight forwarders is more costly than organizing the shipping with the shipping company directly, it has the advantage that professional logistics services take care of all the formalities, including the customs declaration and the documentation of the bio-security requirement. They also ensure the necessary import license that is only valid for one year and has to be renewed in a timely fashion. If need be, they organize the clearing of customs at port in Japan swiftly, which reduces the order cycle time considerably.

Export Pricing

For the setting of export prices it is important to remember that Honeyland has no domestic sales and that only one export market is involved. Therefore, the price decision is straightforward since the export prices are based on the costs of sourcing the honeys as well as logistics. The prices for the Japanese customers are quoted and paid for in NZ$. Sue acknowledges that sufficiently large profit margins are critical to manage foreign exchange risk. Frequent currency fluctuations of the NZ$ affect profits and in the long term the business itself.

Risk Management

Sue believes in the benefits of maintaining long-term relationships with her clients. One factor that will most certainly upset Japanese clients is the renegotiating of prices. Sue knows this sensitivity. Therefore, she attempts to keep her prices fairly constant in spite of the New Zealand currency volatility. She does so even if that means that sometimes losses occur. Another important aspect of good business relationships is that it minimizes general risks, lowers transaction costs, and helps to avoid lengthy negotiations. For example, Honeyland experiences reliable payments on time and payment to the full amount. The company's excellent networks and culturally appropriate business practices practically guarantee that default situations hardly arise.

For Honeyland, the existing three Japanese business segments are a sufficiently large market because they account for Honeyland's entire export volume. A prerequisite for sustained good business relations with Japanese companies is that size and quality of the export ventures have to match expectations in order to create a good business fit and sustainability. *"Just from the beginning I realized three main factors in dealing with Japan: one is quality and guaranty of quality; two is supply ability—you must be*

Exhibit 1

Approximate Exchange Rates for the New Zealand Dollar

1 NZ $ buys	Nov-08	Jan-08	Jul-07	Jan-07	Jan-06	Jan-05
U.S. $	0.55	0.78	0.74	0.70	0.68	0.72
Japan Yen	52	85	95	82	80	74

SOURCE: New Zealand Reserve Bank.

Exhibit 2

New Zealand's Real Effective Exchange Rate, 1980–2004 (Index 2000=100)

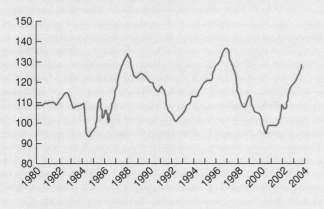

SOURCE: International Monetary Fund, International Financial Statistics

able to guarantee supply and that was very important with maintaining this relationship with this catalogue company.... And the third one was stability in price—so you have to take losses sometimes."

International Communications

Over the years, Honeyland has maintained mutually beneficial and trusting relationships with the same networks. Information technology, internet access, and email have allowed Sue to keep in regular contact with her network partners in between her regular visits to Japan. Often she is also busy with answering customers' queries and requests directly. *"There are daily emails from business partners; they have a habit of sending vast numbers of emails with queries, such as potential benefits of treating race horses with NZ Manuka honey to prevent stomach ulcers."* These kinds of queries have given Sue food for thought if she ever wanted to expand her business and develop other products. It is not astonishing that Honeyland has its own website for general information and marketing.

Conclusion

Sue says that she is very content with her business. She operates a lean and efficient enterprise with only minimal expenses and overheads. She does so single-handedly (no employees) from a small office room in her own home, and she has no immediate plans to change it. Honeyland is now one of the long-time successful "international new venture" businesses in New Zealand.

Questions for Discussion

1. Imagine that you are in charge of logistics for a small exporting business such as Honeyland. What are the difficulties you need to think about?
2. What are the specific contextual requirements when exporting from New Zealand?
3. Considering that Sue is under a significant time constraint, do you think that outsourcing the entire logistics would be a good move for Honeyland?
4. What would have been an alternative entry strategy for the Japanese market?
5. Do you think the company should expand or diversify?

Additional Resources for Research

For further information please see the following websites:

General information about New Zealand, including socio-economic details, supplied by the New Zealand Trade & Enterprise website which is government sponsored **http://www.marketnewzealand.com/MNZ/ aboutNZ/sectors/14436.aspx?Buyer=true**.

Economic overview, including some detailed economic data, New Zealand Treasury Report (2008) on the New Zealand economy **http://www.treasury.govt.nz/economy/overview/ 2008/nzefo-08-3.pdf**.

Report about New Zealand's export barriers, New Zealand Treasury Working Paper 02/10, *Growing Pains: New Zealand, Qualitative Evidence on Hurdles to Exporting Growth* by Simmons, G. **http://www.treasury.govt.nz/publications/ research-policy/wp/2002/02-10/twp02-10.pdf**.

Information about bio-security regulations for New Zealand's exporters exporting products of organic origin **http://www.biosecurity.govt.nz/commercial-exports/ animal-exports/export-requirements-omars/ omars-list**.

Information about New Zealand specialty food and beverages destined for export **http://www.marketnewzealand.com/MNZ/ aboutNZ/sectors/14413.aspx**.

Information about New Zealand's quality assurance program for bee products, including its certification **http://www.asurequality.com/auditing_and_ inspection/apiary.cfm**.

Information about Japanese customs requirements concerning import into Japan **http://www.customs.go.jp/english/summary/ import.htm**.

Info about the port facilities of Napier and useful details concerning transport and shipping vessels **http://www.portofnapier.co.nz/**.

DAVILA-BOND AND THE LATIN AMERICAN SWEATER MARKET

In the Summer of 2003, Charlie Davila-Bond was at yet another crossroads. As the General Manager of a major sweater exporter, Davila & Bond, Inc., based out of Quito, Ecuador, he was facing a number of international strategic issues. Since 1999 his importer in Chile had lost interest in Davila & Bond (D & Bond) products and there was a serious risk of a continued sales decline in Chile in the future. The Chilean dilemma stemmed from stiff international competition in the Chilean market. The economic crisis in Argentina had trickled over to Brazil and the devaluation of the Brazilian Real to the U.S. Dollar (now Ecuador's currency) had made the continuation of sales to Brazil unprofitable. Charlie's factory in Ecuador needed to operate at a high level of capacity to maintain profitability, due to extremely high fixed costs, such as loan payments on new equipment and employee salaries, and a drop in sales would have a major impact on D & Bond's performance. In order to diversify his international sales portfolio the decision was made to place more emphasis on Mexico, a large and potentially lucrative market. Sales to Mexico instantly jumped to over 25,000 sweaters (about l2 percent of D-B's total), which was promising.

Yet as Charlie looked at the numbers he noticed that his firm's reliance on the Ecuadorian market was still extremely heavy, with over 50 percent of the firm's sales coming from within the country. While the Ecuadorian climate in the mountains was ideal for lightweight sweaters,[1] the economic uncertainty of the country was at times mystifying and Ecuador had a chronic case of corruption and political unrest.

Would increased sales to Mexico help alleviate some of the uncertainty that D & Bond was experiencing? And were there underlying issues related to Ecuador's adoption of the U.S. Dollar that might dampen the potential in the Mexican market? Charlie knew that the time had come to redefine his international strategy. For years he and his family had dreamed of exporting to the United State, but with limited plant capacity and intensely narrow margins it seemed unrealistic. Perhaps Mexico could be an excellent stepping stone toward the ultimate goal of entry into the U.S. market.

Company History

In 1974, Fernando Davila, a native of Ecuador, and his Scottish wife, Rosalind Bond, opened a factory that made high-quality yarn in a valley just east of Quito, the national capital. Fernando had studied textile management at the University of Leicester, where he met Rosalind. They named the yarn manufacturing company Hilacril, which still exists today. The idea was to take high quality imported acrylic yarn, of various sizes, and spin it into a professionally woven product that could be used, by other firms, for clothing, upholstery, and car seat covers. By 1980 Hilacril began exporting to Colombia to increase sales. Although the margins were not very favorable, the company began to turn a reasonable profit.

After struggling with tight margins for a number of years, Fernando and Rosalind decided to open a weaving department in 1990. The objective of the weaving department was to utilize Hilacril yarn to create some finished products, which would eventually be sold directly to consumers and retailers. This strategy was extremely effective, and in 1997, now with their three sons home from university in the UK, the retail firm D & Bond was created to take further advantage of stronger margins by getting closer to the consumer.

While Fernando continued to head up the Hilacril arm of the family business, his wife Rosalind assumed the position of President of the final product–oriented D & Bond. Charlie, the oldest son, served as production manager for Hilacril and General Manager for D & Bond. The majority of his time was spent in the factory designing new products and ensuring that the firm's quality standards were met, but as his parents began to step aside as they prepared for retirement, Charlie had been essentially taking over the leadership position of the firm. Eduardo, the second son, was the salesman of the family, and he headed up all sales-related activities for both Hilacril and D & Bond. The youngest son, Fernando, a lawyer by training, was in charge of the D & Bond upholstery division. The final member of the management team was Jorge Perez, a veteran accountant and the C.F.O. for the firm.

It was Charlie's energy, vision, and zeal that truly brought D & Bond into international markets. Charlie spent eight years in Scotland, between prep school and university, and was anxious to return home and expand the family business. It took only four short years for Charlie's vision of a more integrated firm to come to fruition. And since the inception of the sweater retailer D & Bond, Charlie was instrumental in signing franchise agreements and pushing the product into new international markets.

As a manager Charlie had numerous strengths. He was always upbeat and energetic and could be found constantly joking with employees on the factory floor. Yet at the same time he commanded enormous respect due to his intricate knowledge of the retail sweater business. He used this knowledge and open communication style to

SOURCES: Christopher J. Robertson, Ph.D., Associate Professor, General Management Group, Northeastern University College of Business Administration; Marcelo Perez-Verzini, Research Assistant, General Management Group, Northeastern University College of Business Administration. The authors would like to thank Charlie Davila-Bond for his helpful comments and suggestions.

motivate workers. Charlie was also extremely creative and the majority of the firm's sweater designs were based on Charlie's ideas. He made a point of attending professions industry conferences, many in Europe, where he could learn about new manufacturing, design, and marketing techniques. Despite the fact that D & Bond was located in a very poor developing country with chronic economic problems, Charlie ran the company as if it were located in Milan, New York, or Paris. As a result of his accomplishments within Ecuador, Charlie was recognized in 2003 as an industry expert and appointed to a seat on the Ecuadorian Board of Textile Producers.

Hilacril Executive Officers

Name	Year of Birth	Year started with Business	Education	Position
Fernando Davila	1945	1974	B.A. Textile Management, University of Leicester, England	General Manager
Charles Davila-Bond	1969	1993	B.A. Marketing, Strathclyde University, Scotland; Graduate studies at La Universidad San Francisco de Quito	Production Manager
Eduardo Davila-Bond	1970	1991	Business degree from Harriot Watts University and Textile Management degree from University of Leicester	Sales Manager
Jorge Perez	1958	1975	B.A. Accounting and M.B.A., Escuela Polytecnica del Ejercito, Ecuador	Chief Financial Officer

D-Bond Executive Officers

Name	Year of Birth	Year started with Business	Education	Position
Rosalind Davila-Bond	1945	1997	Certified Midwife.	President
Charles Davila-Bond	1969	1993	B.A. Marketing, Strathclyde University, Scotland; Graduate studies at La Universidad San Francisco de Quito	General Manager
Eduardo Davila-Bond	1970	1991	Business degree from Harriot Watts University and Textile Management degree from University of Leicester	Sales Manager
Fernando Javier Davila-Bond	1974	2000	Law Degree, Robert Groden University, England; Advanced studies at La Universidad San Francisco de Quito	Manager of D-Bond Upholstery Division

The Ecuadorian Market[2]

Background

Ecuador had been a presidential democracy since 1979, but its institutions were fragile. Economic deterioration helped undermine the functioning of democracy. Lucio Gutiérrez, backed by left-wing and indigenous organizations, was inaugurated as president on January 15, 2003, taking over for Gustavo Noboa. At one point in 1999 the country held four Presidents in a twenty-four hour period during the ousting of former President Jamil Mahuad (for proposing dollarization), arguably the Latin American record for Presidents in one day. The country had a fragmented and polarized political system with numerous parties, despite reforms designed to prevent the proliferation of forces. Ecuador's largest political parties in terms of congressional representation are the centre-right PSC, the PRE, and the centre-left Izquierda Democrática (ID). All have held power at some time since the transition to democracy in 1979.

Exhibit 1

Composition of the Ecuadorian Congress, March 2003

	No. of seats
Partido Social Cristiano (PSC)	25
Izquierda Democrática (ID)	16
Partido Roldosista Ecuatoriano (PRE)	14
Independents	10
Partido Renovador Institucional Acción Nacional (PRIAN)	10
Movimiento Unidad Plurinacional Pachakútik-Nuevo País (MUPP-NP)	7
Partido Sociedad Patriótica 21 de Enero (PSP)	7
Movimiento Popular Democrático (MPD)	6
Democracia Popular (DP)	4
Patria Solidaria	1
Total	100

SOURCE: The Economist Intelligence Unit.

Economic Conditions/Business Environment

Ecuador had a long road ahead to become a stable international investment target. To achieve this goal, Ecuadorian officials have made important developments in recent years regarding economic openness and pursued a strategy that includes improving competitiveness and efficiency and matching these goals to international requirements. The Ecuadorian government also tried to consolidate this policy of openness by means of improving microeconomic management strategies in the productive and financial sectors, opening the real estate sector and the financial system to foreign investment, fostering a transparent privatization process, improving the administration of the state sector, and eliminating state interventionism.

Ecuador is a member of the Andean Community, which consists of Bolivia, Colombia, Ecuador, Peru, and Venezuela. The Andean Community was in the process of formally establishing a free trade zone. The Ecuadorian government signed complementary economic agreements with several Latin American countries, which included Argentina, Uruguay, Chile, Brazil, and Cuba.

U.S.–Andean Free Trade Agreement negotiations were under consideration and the goal was to sign a deal by the end of 2004. The accord would benefit the Andean nations by locking in more permanently the special access to the U.S. market that Andean nations enjoyed under the Andean Trade Preference Act, which was set to expire in 2006. The free trade agreement also would encourage reforms that would attract investment to the region and allow the Andean nations to remain competitive with other nations in the U.S. market.

Mexico and Ecuador started free trade negotiations in 1996 and that year drafted an agenda of issues related to market access, rules of origin, customs procedures, technical regulations, safeguards, as well as unfair trade practice. Ecuador withdrew from the talks as it said the terms of the possible agreement were not favorable. Both countries planned to restart talks to negotiate a free trade agreement in the near future.

Structure of the Economy

Oil and export agriculture were the main pillars of the Ecuadorean economy. Agriculture, forestry, and fishing accounted on average for 12.5 percent of GDP, 45 percent of exports, and over one-third of employment during the 1990s. The share of the oil and mining sector (dominated by the extraction of crude oil) as a proportion of national output averaged 12.1 percent of GDP in 1997–2001. Oil earnings represented 28 percent of central government fiscal revenue in 2001, and oil attracted the majority of long-term foreign investment. In the mid-1990s a border dispute with Peru evolved into a brief military conflict. The territory in question was known to have deep oil reserves. In general, the export sector is more developed than the rest of the economy. Exports accounted for an average of 35 percent of GDP

in 1997–2001. This increased the economy's vulnerability to external shocks, such as downturns in commodity prices.

Foreign Trade

Around 60 percent of Ecuador's export earnings came from oil and bananas. Other primary products accounted for most of the remainder, leaving the country vulnerable to external and climatic shocks. Dollarization exposed a lack of competitiveness in some export industries, and export volume growth had been weak in recent years, due in part to rising labor costs. Ecuador had also benefited from high oil prices since 2000. Recovery in consumer demand and the construction of a new oil pipeline, which was planned to traverse the Andes, had led to a rapid rise in imports of both capital and consumer goods, pushing the trade balance into deficit.

Exhibit 2

Ecuador: Exports–Imports*

Major exports 2002	% of total	Major imports 2002	% of total
Oil & oil products	41.0	Raw materials	36.1
Bananas & Plantain	19.3	Capital goods	31.4
Tinned fish	6.8	Consumer goods	28.0
Shrimp	5.0	Fuels & Lubricants	4.4
Leading markets 2002	% of total	Leading suppliers 2002	% of total
US	40.8	US	23.0
Peru	7.4	Colombia	14.0
Colombia	7.2	Brazil	6.3
Italy	5.8	Japan	6.1

*The Economist.

Trade Policy

According to the World Bank, Ecuador's weighted average tariff rate in 1999 was 11.1 percent.[3] Prior authorization from the corresponding Ministry was still needed to import processed foods, cosmetics, and other commodities. Agricultural commodities were occasionally prevented from entering Ecuador through the arbitrary use of sanitary rules as a way to restrict import quantities (and a method for soliciting bribes).

The customs system had three main problems: inefficiency, tax evasion, and outright corruption. Getting an imported container out of customs took weeks or months, unless the process was greased with money or influence. Some importers used loopholes to place merchandise in lower tariff categories. Some imports were passed through a tunnel, where they bypassed duties and entered the market as contraband. These and other skullduggeries, according to the Internal Revenue Service (SRI), cost the government from $600–800 million each year—let alone the millions they cost business.

Dollarization

Early in 2000, Ecuador, confronted with a serious economic and governance crisis, adopted the U.S. dollar as its national currency. The economic situation was appalling, with high inflation, government intervention in the banking system (which included the freezing of deposits to prevent further flight from the country), and large fiscal deficits. Politically, then President Mahaud was being challenged by a lack of congressional support for measures to stabilize the economic situation, a radicalized indigenous movement, and an agitated armed forces. In this environment, and as a policy of last resort, the government decided to adopt the U.S. dollar as its currency.[4] Another factor that related to dollarization was the tax structure. Taxes were subject to frequent change. The main taxes in Ecuador were a progressive income tax levied at a rate of up to 25 percent and a value-added tax (VAT) levied at 12 percent.

The Growth of D & Bond

By September of 2003, D & Bond was exporting sweaters and other woven items to five other countries in Latin America: Colombia, Mexico, Brazil, Bolivia, and Chile. The firm had also pursued, simultaneously, an aggressive retailing strategy with a combination of company-owned and franchised stores. Fourteen D & Bond retail stores (eight firm-owned) were operating in Ecuador, Colombia, and Bolivia. Three additional stores were scheduled to open in Ecuador by the end of 2004. As a result of the strong brand image and reputation that D & Bond built up through its high-quality sweaters, a number of franchising opportunities developed. In addition to the seven retail shops in Quito, D & Bond also owned one in Ambato, a small city about fifty miles south of Quito. Two stores were owned under a franchise agreement in Cuenca, a colonial city in the south of the country. Franchised retail stores were also present in other markets, with three in Colombia and one in Bolivia. Reflective of the D & Bond high-quality image, the stores were tastefully decorated with a European ambiance accentuated by British flags and classical music.

The basic terms of a franchise agreement were as follows: $40,000 was required up front for 120 days worth of merchandise; a $15,000 fee was charged to use the D & Bond name for four years; and approximately $20,000 to $30,000 was needed to set up the retail stores according to D & Bond standards (typically D & Bond would front the store set-up money with a stipulation for repayment within four years). In addition, D & Bond charged franchisees three percent of purchases for monthly publicity.

Exhibit **3**

P&L (in US$ thousands)

	2000	2001	2002
Revenues	4,895	5,800	4,959
Cost of Goods Sold	2,961	3,687	3,043
Gross Profit	1,934	2,113	1,916
Gross Margin	40%	36%	39%

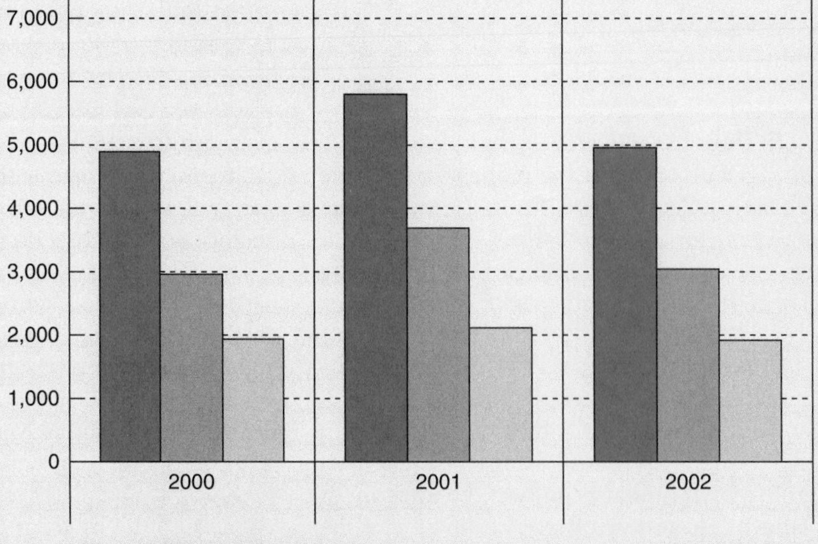

Revenues · Cost of Goods Sold · Gross Profit

Exhibit 4

P&L by Product Line

Products	Year 2000					Year 2001					Year 2002				
	Units Sold (000)	Net Sales (US $ 000)	Cost of Goods Sold (US $ 000)	Gross Profit (US $ 000)	Gross Margin	Units Sold (000)	Net Sales (US $ 000)	Cost of Goods Sold (US $ 000)	Gross Profit (US $ 000)	Gross Margin	Units Sold (000)	Net Sales (US $ 000)	Cost of Goods Sold (US $ 000)	Gross Profit (US $ 000)	Gross Margin
Sweaters	199	1,952	1,011	941	48%	253	2,405	1,417	988	41%	285	2,816	1,647	1,169	42%
Chales	42	319	155	164	51%	230	1,797	1,075	722	40%	215	1,622	1,026	596	37%
Fabries	201	536	325	211	39%	237	406	283	123	30%	96	310	211	99	32%
Yarns	454	2,088	1,470	618	30%	268	1,192	912	280	23%	51	211	160	51	24%
Total		4,895	2,961	1,934	40%		5,800	3,687	2,113	36%		4,959	3,043	1,915	39%

A decision was made in 2000 to gradually reduce emphasis on yarn production as a raw material and place more emphasis on finished product sales, primarily sweaters and shawls. From 2000 to 2002, yarn sales dropped from 42 percent of total sales to 4 percent, while sweaters and shawls experienced significant increases over the same period, with sweaters jumping from 40 to 57 percent and shawls up from 7 to 33 percent. The theory was that through vertical integration and the sale of finished products, profits would increase substantially over time. Yet production costs increased substantially due to the labor-intensive nature of sweater manufacturing and profits remained relatively flat.

D & Bond's marketing budget was close to US$ 100,000, or 2 percent of total sales, during the previous few years. Since 2004 the company has incorporated new products in its Ecuadorian stores. This was a new approach that involved other products not necessarily manufactured at their own factory, like Cumberland jackets, chinos, and women's shirts. Charlie noted that D & Bond was trying to leverage its name recognition in the home market, and he was also considering more of a push in the teenage market, primarily through magazine and television advertising.

The percentage of international sales hovered between 40 percent to 50 percent from 2000 to 2002, and the one major change was a six-fold increase in sales to Mexico and a ten percent decline in Colombian sales. Still, Colombia was the top export destination accounting for 24 percent of sales in 2002, followed by Mexico with 12 percent, Brazil with 3 percent, and Chile and Bolivia with 2 percent each. Political unrest and a weak economy in Bolivia likely meant the end to that market in the short run. And poor economic conditions throughout Latin America made market entry decisions very risky and complicated.

The sales increase in Mexico highlighted the potential of this market and how important it could be for future growth. In 2003, D & Bond had only one store and the company was engaged in the development of distribution channels. In 2004, Charlie Davila-Bond said, "We are developing our distributors. One of them sells with our brand name (D & Bond) and also with their private label to big wholesale chains like Liverpool, Palacio de Hierro, Costco, and Wal-Mart.[5] Our second distributor tackles the lower market all over Mexico, which has given us a great boost on sales. We have not decided on franchises yet. We sell over 90,000 items a year to the Mexican market. For the year 2005 we expect a sales increase of 20 percent for this market." The relevance of this market would definitely prompt a new approach with regards to production strategy. With respect to that, Charlie mentioned, "We have had some talks on the possibility in producing in Mexico, but nothing is definite yet. Mexico's labor costs are pretty similar to the Ecuadorian's, but labor laws are very difficult to handle."

Although D & Bond was clearly the market leader in Ecuador, Charlie perceived a number of small threats within the country. First, the importation of sweaters from China, South Korea, and Taiwan was on the rise. The producers in these countries had a major competitive advantage in labor costs, yet the quality of their sweaters was typically well below that of D & Bond. One local competitor, Fashionlana, had made a minor surge by copying the business model and manufacturing technique of D & Bond. Fashionlana had the same *supersoft* technology that D & Bond utilized, and they had recently opened three retail stores in Quito.

Production

Technology was a key ingredient to D & Bond's success. Through keen long-term vision, the firm purchased sophisticated weaving machines from Germany. While each of these machines cost over $100,000, the investment was well worth it in the mind of Charlie Davila-Bond, since the machines were run 24 hours a day, 364 days a year (every day except Christmas). D & Bond had plans for expanding its knitting department in 2004 with the acquisition of six new machines, in both gauges 7 and 12, from the German firm Stoll. Charlie commented, "The whole knitting project will increase our production 20 percent with a total investment of US$ 600,000." This investment would be financed directly by the German supplier over a period of three years. Also, for the year 2005, the company planned to buy a new weaving machine at a cost of US$ 250,000. This weaving machine would increase yarn production another 20 percent.

The raw synthetic yarn was also imported, typically from Peru or Germany, which enabled the firm to produce a high-quality range of products. Through *supersoft* technology and materials the result was a sweater that looked and felt like Cashmere but could be washed in a machine due to its synthetic nature. Moreover, Charlie and his staff of sweater designers traveled to seminars and fashion shows in the United States and Europe to generate ideas for new designs. A new state-of-the-art computer software design program had also been purchased to enhance the creation and production of new styles. Quality was a huge priority for D & Bond, and each final product went through a seven point quality check prior to shipment to ensure that the D & Bond reputation and image was maintained.

In the factory the firm employed 130 workers in the D & Bond knitting department, another 50 in weaving, and 70 in the Hilacril yarn division. In addition, about 40 employees worked in the various D & Bond–owned retail stores around the country. The typical factory worker worked fifty hours a week and earned $250 a month ($300 to $350 if production goals were met). This compared well to the local minimum wage of just under $150 a month and turnover was virtually nonexistent.

The Mexican Market[6]

Charlie was convinced that with just over 100 million consumers and a rising per capita income, Mexico could be an excellent market for D & Bond sweaters. The plan to open a D & Bond store was in place and the potential to engage in franchising looked promising. Charlie was extremely pleased with the distributor that he selected and he agreed to take on a second distributor, for "lower-end sales."

Mexico was the largest trading nation in Latin America and the eighth largest in the world. GDP growth had been strong since 1996 and foreign direct investment had surged into the country, partly due to Mexico's friendly investment climate, competitive labor costs, fully convertible currency, low taxation, and duty free access to the U.S. and Canada. Investment had been particularly strong from the major multinational manufacturers who set up operations in Mexico to supply the U.S. market free of duty. More investment was expected to be attracted with the recent entry into force of the EU/Mexico Free Trade Agreement. Mexico was now uniquely positioned to supply the two largest markets in the world, the EU and North America, tariff free.

Investors had few restrictions and investment approaches ranged from a branch office to a fully-owned subsidiary. Most investors set up a corporation (S.A). This required a minimum share of capital, at least two shareholders, and registration in the public register. All foreign investments had to receive prior authorization from the Ministry of Foreign Affairs. Labor costs in Mexico were very competitive. Skilled and semi-skilled labor was plentiful, although there were pressures in the border regions with the U.S. where plenty of job vacancies and a high turnover of staff existed. There were no controls on the remittance of profits or the repatriation of capital. There were some strategic areas of the economy, such as the oil industry, satellite communications, postal services, and minting, where foreign investment was prohibited.

There were no restrictions on a foreign investor's access to capital. Most financing from local sources was obtained from the privatized commercial banks. Interest rates were very high by international standards. Most investments however, both domestic and foreign, were sourced from private capital.

Mexico had a number of important ports on both its Atlantic and Pacific coasts, including Altamira, Ensenada, Mazatlan, Progreso, Salina Cruz, and Veracruz. There were plenty of warehouse facilities at most ports. Joint venture contracts were easily set up in Mexico. Such a contract did not create a business entity and operations were carried out by the active party. However, income and losses were divided between the two partners according to the contract.

With respect to patents and trademarks, Mexico was a signatory to the 1983 Union of Paris Convention for the Protection of Industrial Property. Patents were protected for a term of 20 years from the filing date. Non-use (unless justified by technical or economic reason) could result in the issue of a compulsory license. Trademarks were registered for ten years, renewable for further ten-year periods indefinitely. Mexico did have a significant problem with piracy in the music, alcoholic beverages, clothing and software industries, and some counterfeit/contraband difficulties with other consumer goods.

Looking to the Future

Although Charlie knew that the emphasis on international sales was an important factor in the growth of the firm, he also acknowledged that the Ecuadorian market was a mature cash cow. He clearly stated, "First, D & Bond must maintain its number one position in the Ecuadorian market." Yet at the same time, he went on, "We must also expand our image overall and increase our international sales." Indeed the tradeoff between balancing out the risk of relying too heavily on Ecuador while aggressively pursuing international sales (and perhaps losing ground at home) was the key to the future.

As Charlie examined his existing markets he still thought more growth in Mexico was almost a certainty. With a market of 100 million people and an income per capita triple that of Ecuador, the potential of selling more sweaters in Mexico was promising. Charlie mentioned that he even had some talks with a Mexican producer about the possibility of manufacturing there, but he was a little concerned about the complexity of Mexican labor laws. Elsewhere in Latin America, Brazil and Argentina seemed like viable possibilities. As relatively wealthy and large nations, with European fashion sense and an amenable climate, these markets looked like reasonable places to bolster sales in the future. For the moment, Charlie wanted to determine the best possible strategy for further penetration into the Mexican market. Would finding stronger distribution partners there be essential? What were the benefits and drawbacks of possibly getting involved in manufacturing in Mexico, perhaps through one of the Mexican maquilas? Compared to other potential markets in the world, Mexico's profile seemed to be an excellent fit, both culturally and economically, with D & Bond's international strategy (see Appendix 1).

Finally, the production issue was something Charlie had to address. Typically all of the sweaters for the year were sold by August. Expanding the plant was certainly an option, but labor costs in Ecuador had been creeping up and were no longer a competitive advantage. Did it make sense to outsource some part of his production to Mexico? And if so, could the D & Bond quality reputation be maintained? Also, franchising had gone well in recent years and the potential for establishing D & Bond stores in Mexico, Europe, or elsewhere remained strong. As the end of 2003 approached, Charlie knew that the time had come to take D & Bond to another level. The decisions he made would set the trajectory for the firm for years to come.

Exhibit 5

Sales Distribution by Market (in % of Sales Revenues)

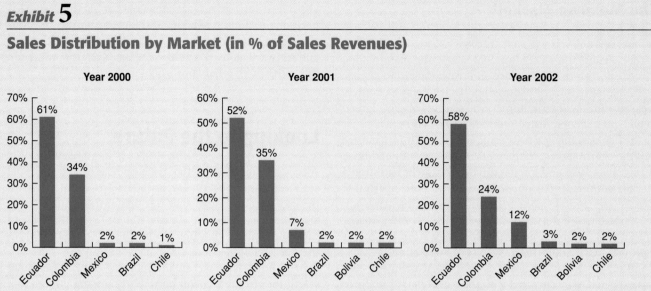

APPENDIX 1

Davila & Bond Current Markets

Country	Population[1]	GDP per Capita[1]	Household[1] income by percentage share	Corruption Perception Index[2] Ranking	Corruption Perception Index[2] Index
Mexico	101,879,171	$9,100	lowest 10%: 1.8% highest 10%: 36.6%	64	3.6
Colombia	40,349,388	$6,200	lowest 10%: 1% highest 10%: 44%	59	3.7
Ecuador	13,183,978	$2,900	lowest 10%: 2.2% highest 10%: 33.8%	113	2.2
Chile	15,328,467	$10,100	lowest 10%: 1.2% highest 10%: 41.3%	20	7.4
Bolivia	8,300,463	$2,600	lowest 10%: 2.3% highest 10%: 31.7%	106	2.3
Peru	27,483,864	$4,550	lowest 10%: 1.9% highest 10%: 34.3%	59	3.7
Potential Markets					
U.S.	290,342,554	$37,600	lowest 10%: 1.8% highest 10%: 30.5%	18	7.5
Canada	32,207,113	$29,400	lowest 10%: 2.8% highest 10%: 23.8%	11	8.7
U.K.	60,094,648	$25,300	lowest 10%: 2.3% highest 10%: 27.7%	11	8.7
Spain	40,217,413	$20,700	lowest 10%: 2.8% highest 10%: 25.2%	23	6.9
Brazil	182,032,604	$7,600	lowest 10%: 0.7% highest 10%: 48%	54	3.9
Argentina	38,740,807	$10,200	lowest 10%: NA% highest 10%: NA%	92	2.5

[1]CIA Factbook Y2001
[2]Transparency International Y2001

DR. ERIS: COSMETICS FROM POLAND

D r. Irena Eris is famous in Poland. In 1999 the Business Centre Club honored her with the title Business Woman of the Decade, in 2003 she was recognized for the creation of an internationally competitive Polish brand, and in 2004 she was placed on the list of influential women in Polish history that had turned the course of events, overcome stereotypes, and initiated new thinking. In 2005 she received the Economic Award of the President of Poland.

It all started in 1982 when Dr. Eris, a Ph.D. from the Faculty of Pharmacology at Berlin's Humboldt University, inherited the equivalent of six small Fiat cars. With this inheritance she and her husband opened a cottage workshop producing nourishing facial cream in 1983. The first cosmetic products were mixed in a makeshift machine made by a local locksmith friend.

The Polish Cosmetics Market

With its population of 40 million people, Poland is the eighth largest country in Europe. Its per-capita consumption is only one-fifth of the average of the pre-2004 European Union (EU) member countries. The key competitive factors are price, quality, and brand recognition. Packaging and advertising have become increasingly important. Poles tend to be risk averse when choosing everyday cosmetics. They prefer to buy a known brand from a known store. Purchasing decisions are determined by company reputation and brand recognition.

Poland has long traditions in the production of cosmetics. Max Faktor—born in Lódź, Poland, during the 1870s—became the founder of modern make-up, creating the global Max Factor brand. Helena Rubinstein, a Polish immigrant to the United States, is one of the biggest names in facial care. In the Communist Era, Poland was by far the largest cosmetics producer in the former socialist countries. The cosmetics of Pollena and Nivea were cherished by women and men of all ages. Poland was also a large market for cosmetics. Most of the cosmetics products were affordably priced. Only 5 percent represented luxury products, most of them imported. The collapse of the CMEA (Council for Mutual Economic Assistance) market at the beginning of the 1990s caused the market for Polish cosmetics to stagnate. Existing procurement and distribution networks in the domestic and foreign Soviet Bloc markets were dismantled. Market positions in the big Russian market and in the other markets of Central and Eastern Europe were lost.

Today, the cosmetics industry in Poland employs approximately 19,000 people. It has remained a key employer in a volatile labor market, but the transition process to a market-led economy has caused enormous job losses. The "shock therapy" approach to the privatization of state-owned enterprises led to the mushrooming of small domestic cosmetics companies; by the end of 2005 there were more than 470. Less than 15 percent of these employed more than 50 people. International cosmetics manufacturers were quick to enter the Polish cosmetics industry via acquisition of former state-owned companies or greenfield investment. They have big production capacity, premier facilities, established retail clout, and high brand recognition.

In the last 10 years the production of cosmetics in Poland has experienced steady annual growth (see Exhibit 1). In 2002 the market was valued at 1.85 billion Polish Zloty (PLN), the equivalent of US$450 million at the current exchange rate. The value of Polish cosmetics exports in 2002 was US$291 million, representing almost 10 percent growth over 2001. More than two-thirds of all exports went to former CMEA markets and about 30 percent to the European Union member countries. The major importers were Russia (18 percent of the total value of Polish exports), Hungary (14 percent), Lithuania (12 percent), Ukraine (11 percent), Germany (8 percent), and the United Kingdom (7 percent). Avon Cosmetics, Miraculum, Cussons Group, Kolastyna, Ziaja, Dr. Irena Eris, Polena Ewa, and L'Oréal are the biggest exporters.

Cosmetics imports come from Germany (23 percent), France (21 percent), the United Kingdom (17 percent), and Italy and Spain (6 percent each). Imported cosmetics sell at a price premium and enjoy high brand recognition.

Cosmetics manufacturers in Poland can be divided into four groups:

1. Producers owned by the Pollena conglomerate, owned by foreign investors (Beiersdorf, Cussons Group, and Unilever). They develop and introduce new products in the Polish market and upgrade the acquired cosmetic products.

2. Formerly state-owned cosmetics manufacturers, privatized and functioning independently (Pollena Ewa and Miraculum).

3. A large group of Polish private cosmetics firms established in the 1980s and 1990s (Inter-Fragrances, Dr. Irena Eris Cosmetics Laboratories, Kolastyna, Soraya, Dax Cosmetics, Dermika, and Ziaja).

4. New factories built by global cosmetics companies (Johnson & Johnson, L'Oréal, Avon, and Oriflame).

This case was developed by Svetla T. Marinova and Marin A. Marinov. It is intended to be used as a basis for classroom discussion rather than to illustrate either effective or ineffective handling of a business situation. The authors acknowledge the assistance of Dr. Irena Eris and her personal assistant Ms. Aleksandra Trzcinska in developing the case.

Exhibit 1

Market Size, US$ million

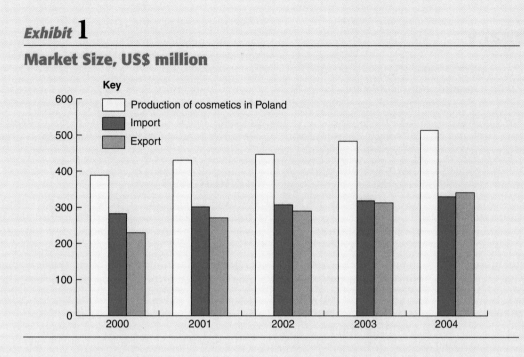

The strong domestic producers have established positions in the skin and body care product market segment and control about two-thirds of this market. The market leader is Beiersdorf-Lechia with almost a 30 percent share, followed by Johnson & Johnson (8 percent), Unilever (7 percent), Kolastyna (6.5 percent), and Dr. Irena Eris (5 percent).

The facial care cosmetics market segment is dominated by Dr. Irena Eris (16 percent), followed by Ziaja (10 percent), Oceanic (9 percent), and Cussons (8 percent). All foreign facial care brands have positioned themselves in the middle or premium sector of the market. For example, the U.S. firm Johnson & Johnson dominates the mid-market with 45 percent market share, while the French Garnier with its brand L'Oréal leads in the premium sector with more than 50 percent market share. The market pressure from foreign brands has pushed most of the Polish facial care brands into the low-price mass markets. The self-tanning cosmetics segment is dominated by L'Oréal with 27.5 percent, Beiersdorf with 25.3 percent, and Dr. Irena Eris with 12.2 percent market share.

Premium cosmetics brands are sold via specialized networks of stores such as Empik, Galeria Centrum, Ina Center, and French Sephora. The medium- and low-priced cosmetics are distributed via hypermarket and supermarket chains, drug stores, and specialty stores. Companies such as Avon, Oriflame, and Amway use direct selling. The largest distributor of cosmetics is Polbita, a privately owned company established in 1990. Polbita owns 20 percent of the cosmetics distribution system in Poland. Its store chain Drogeria Natura has more than 330 retail outlets.

Since 1988 almost all global and international cosmetics brands have entered the Polish market. They seek new market development and expansion. The best recognized foreign brands are: Christian Dior, Guerlain, Yves Saint Laurent, Yves Rocher, Yves Saint Rocher, L'Oréal, Laboratories Paris, Lancôme, Paloma Picasso, Guy Laroche, Giorgio Armani, Cacharel, Coty, Elizabeth Arden, Pierre Robert, Colgate Palmolive, Nivea, Jean Pierresand, Vichy Laboratories, Jade, Max Factor, Revlon, Maybelline, Biotherm, Givenchy, Nino Cerruti, Margaret Astor, and Rimmel. They have all set up their own exclusive stores and beauty salons. Aggressive advertising, new product development, and simultaneous product introduction in Paris and Warsaw reinforce their premium market position.

The ongoing process of market liberalization and EU enlargement has been favorable for the growing market presence of foreign cosmetics brands in Poland. The variety of products and services has led to a much greater consumer choice. This has increased the competitive pressure on Polish brands that are mostly too small to compete against global multinationals. One manager of a Polish medium-sized cosmetics company stated: "Small and medium-sized cosmetics companies do not have enough market power. I cannot see how they can compete successfully against the multinationals after the EU enlargement. It is unlikely that the Polish Government will protect us. It will not provide financial help for consolidation. Foreign giants will have no problem pushing us out of business. There will be more products, but Polish brands will gradually disappear."

Nevertheless, domestically owned cosmetics companies in Poland have been increasingly trying to gain market presence in the EU markets. Some managers believe that the EU enlargement can provide more opportunities for export and participation in partnerships with other cosmetics firms from the wider Europe.

The Company

Dr. Irena Eris Cosmetic Laboratories was set up in socialist Poland in 1982 with a monthly production output of 3,000 packages. Demand for Eris cosmetics constantly increased and the company expanded its operations rapidly.

The transition period with its diverse economic and political reforms created new opportunities for business growth. The increased productivity and profitability of the company in the early 1990s led to the launch of a new plant. Dr. Eris reinvested most of the company profits in product innovation and new technologies.

Presently, the company employs 350 employees and produces 300 types of products grouped into several product lines. The monthly output is approximately 1,000,000 units. All company cosmetics products meet the quality standards of the European Union and the U.S. Food and Drug Administration. Dr. Irena Eris holds ISO 9001 (since 1996) and Environment Management ISO 14001 (since 2001). Those certificates guarantee that its cosmetics are of global quality and their production is environmentally friendly.

Dr. Eris's focus is on innovation and R&D. Its R&D investment in 2004 was 3.4 percent of company turnover, growing to 4.6 percent in 2005. A large team of dermatologists, allergy specialists, biologists, and molecular biologists works on various projects at the company's Centre for Science and Research set up in 2001 (see Exhibit 2). R&D is the core of the company's strategy to develop scientifically advanced products.[1] Consumers who are interested in scientifically created cosmetics are the main targets.

Scientific research and innovative solutions are key to the brand positioning strategy of Dr. Irena Eris. All products are original and based on in-company research. This makes them distinctive and more difficult for competitors to copy. In the mid-1990s, Dr. Eris was the first in Europe to propose the use of vitamin K in cosmetics. More recently, it was the first company in the world to test and use the innovative complex FitoDHEA + folacin in its products.

Brand Image

The brand image of Dr. Irena Eris is built on respect for people, stressing their individual nature and the importance of cooperation. The brand development strategy reflects the value of interpersonal relationships within the company and with its clients. The brand value of Dr. Irena Eris is based on its holistic approach to the individual specific needs and preferences of customers. It offers an individual skin care program for home use and for use in specialised professional salons and spa hotels.

The brand has also gained international recognition. In 2005 it was nominated to the 2005 Beauty Awards for the best cosmetics introduced in the UK market. It was also awarded the Gold Glamour award by the British edition of Glamour.

The target segments of Dr. Irena Eris span all age groups. Users are women who prioritize cosmetic efficiency based on research. They wish to use high-quality products that are modern and pleasant to use. There are four segments (see Exhibit 3).

The company targets the economy segment with mass products. The premium segment is reached with

Exhibit 2

Structure of the R&D Department

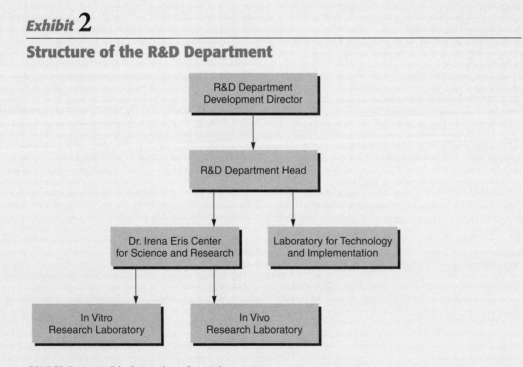

SOURCE: Dr. Irena Eris Cosmetics Laboratories.

Exhibit 3

Market Segments and Company Brands

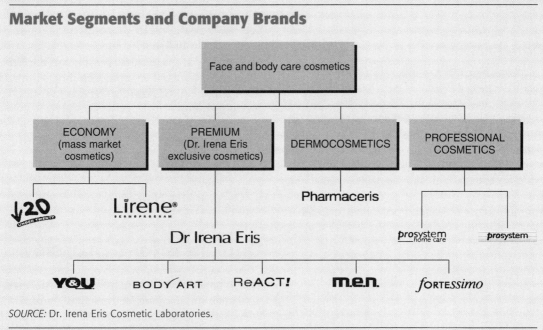

SOURCE: Dr. Irena Eris Cosmetic Laboratories.

innovative products. The dermocosmetics segment is served with health and hygienic products. Specialized products are designed for the professional segment. These segments are reached via 20,000 retail points of sale for widely distributed products and 1,000 points of sale for products destined for limited distribution via pharmacies, beauty salons, and centers.

Diversification

The company has diversified in related activities. Following the success of a four-star Spa Hotel, Dr. Irena Eris, in Krynica Zdrój in Poland, it has invested in a second Spa Hotel, Dr. Irena Eris Wzgórza Dylewskie, in Wysoka Wieś near Ostróda, which is to be completed in the first half of 2006. The Spa Hotels offer a comprehensive, tailor made skin treatment and revitalizing program. Skin treatment is complemented by a range of health improvement packages including exercises, massage, spa therapy and physical activities. The spa hotel concept promotes Dr. Eris as a modern lifestyle brand.

Moreover, the brand Dr. Irena Eris has been extended to the franchise chain Dr. Irena Eris Cosmetics Institutes. There are 22 of them established in the largest Polish cities. Such institutes were also opened in Moscow, Russia, and Bogota, Colombia. It is projected that ten new Institutes will serve clients in Poland and abroad by 2007. The Institutes offer several basic company treatments based on the Dr. Irena Eris Professional Program. The treatments are carried out using preparations from the company's own specialised line of cosmetics. They are exclusively used in beauty salons (Prosystem). The therapy is complemented by a line of products for subsequent home care (Prosystem

home care). The treatments are selected individually and preceded by obligatory skin diagnosis by dermatologists partnering with Dr. Irena Eris Cosmetic Institutes. The personnel of the Institutes consists of beauty therapists trained at the company's own center.

Marketing Communications

The marketing communications strategy of Dr. Irena Eris is consistent with its strategic focus on innovation. It is the Polish company with the highest advertising expenditure. In Poland the company advertises on national and regional state-owned and private TV channels, on billboards, and in fashion and women's magazines. Advertising and PR activities in the key international markets are generally standardized but adapted to the local language. Private TV channels are mostly used for the firm's international advertising campaigns. Next come advertisements in fashion magazines and in-store promotions. The company has strengthened its position in the professional segment by developing close relationships with leading business customers and participating in international fairs.

Dr. Irena Eris Cosmetic Laboratories donates PLN500,000 worth of products and money for charitable causes. It is a key contributor to the Always Healthy and Active Club programs set up to meet the needs of seven million adult Polish women. The program aims to increase the knowledge of mature women about health-related issues, and improve their general health and quality of life. In 2001, Dr. Eris was awarded the Summa Bonitas award from the foundation Zdążyć z pomocą for its corporate social responsibility.[2]

The 2004 sales of Dr. Irena Eris Cosmetics Laboratories were PLN97.6 million (€24 million) from domestic and export sales. This was 15 percent growth compared with the results in 2003. In 2004 after-tax profit was PLN7 million.

Internationalization

Most of the initial attempts to go international were driven by opportunities based on personal contacts. In 1989 the company started exporting its products. The debut was made in the vast U.S. market. The large Polish community in the U.S. formed a formidable basis for foreign market expansion. Personal relationships and contacts were of foremost importance. Currently, Dr. Eris cosmetics are available in over 1,000 specialized U.S. salons.

After tapping into the U.S. market, Dr. Eris turned her sights on the neighboring German and the former CMEA markets. Geographic proximity, low psychic distance, and previously strong positions of Polish cosmetics in these markets proved to help market entry and penetration.

Dr. Irena Eris developed its international presence systematically since the mid-1990s. Direct exporting has been the preferred mode of foreign market entry. Management has recognized the benefits of economies of scope and uses various sources of information in support of foreign market expansion. The firm works with a range of exclusive distributors. In 2004 Dr. Irena Eris products were introduced to the British market via the retailer Boots. The growth of exports has been substantial and in 2004 the company recorded an increase of international sales by 40 percent. By 2006 the products of Dr. Irena Eris were available in 24 countries around the globe. They are sold in beauty shops, pharmacies, supermarkets and beauty salons. Major markets are the United States, Lithuania, Russia, the Czech Republic, Hungary, the Slovak Republic, the Ukraine, Germany, Tasmania, Taiwan, and Singapore.

Franchising has been used for the company's international growth in the form of cosmetics institutes. Apart from the two franchise operation in Moscow and Bogota, an expansion of franchise operations is planned across Europe.

Questions for Discussion

1. What does the future hold for Polish small- and medium-sized cosmetics manufacturers? Do you agree with the statement of the Polish manager?

2. What should Dr. Irena Eris Cosmetics Laboratories do to secure its future as market leader in the facial cosmetics segment in the Polish market?

3. Explain the internationalization of Dr. Irena Eris Cosmetics Laboratories in the United States.

IMAGINARIUM

At the beginning of March 2001, Félix Tena was reviewing the internationalization process of his young company. Tena was the President and majority shareholder of Step Two, S.A., a company with headquarters in Zaragoza, Spain, that owned and operated Imaginarium, a retail chain of educational toy stores.

At the end of 2000, the chain consisted of 168 toy stores, 54 of which were owned and operated by Imaginarium, while 114 were franchised. There were 120 stores in Spain, and the other 48 were located in nine different countries. In the 2000 fiscal year, which had ended on January 31st, 2001, company sales had amounted to approximately €34 million, with after tax profits of €2.4 million.[1]

Background

After studying business administration in Spain, Tena had continued his studies in the United States. This had allowed him to witness first-hand the American ways of life and of doing business.

Upon his return to Spain he launched Publijuego, a small business venture in the educational toy sector. His first product was a board game similar to Monopoly, where the streets of a real city appeared on a board. This generated two sources of income, because he sold the individual board games to end users, and also the advertising space to different local businesses whose brands or retail emblems appeared on the board of the game. Tena subsequently sold 50% of Publijuego to some Italian partners, but the partnership was not successful, and the company was wound up in 1990.

At that time, Tena observed that mass merchandisers were becoming increasingly important players in the Spanish toy market. The market had been formerly dominated by small, independent, specialized toy stores who sold toys throughout the year.

This is a condensed version of the case "Imaginarium," prepared by Laureano Berasategui under the supervision of Professors Lluis G. Renart and Francesc Parés, as a basis for class discussion, rather than to illustrate either an effective or ineffective handling of an administrative situation. The complete version of the case (IESE code M-1173-E) is available from IESE Publishing, 08034 Barcelona, Spain, iesep@iesep.com. Both the original case and the present condensed version are Copyright © IESE, and cannot be further reproduced, stored in a retrieval system, used in a spreadsheet, or transmitted in any form or by any means—electronic, mechanical, photocopying, recording or otherwise—without the permission of IESE. The complete version of this case was the joint recipient of the prize in the "Marketing" category, in the 2004 edition of the European Case Writing Competition, organized every year by the European Foundation for Management Development (EFMD), Brussels, Belgium.

Toys Я Us, the "category killer," had opened its first store in Spain in Barcelona in 1991, and traditional small independent toy stores were fast disappearing from the Spanish retail scene. The mass merchandisers were changing the toy retail game by concentrating their sales efforts around the high Christmas season, when they temporarily allocated significant sales floor space to toys. They only bought and sold toys they knew would be backed by strong national TV campaigns. They all sold the same manufacturer-branded toys, and the main sales pitch was low prices. Toys received the same retail marketing treatment as any other packaged consumer product. No one seemed to place any importance on identifying and promoting the educational role that toys, as children's companions, should play.

This situation made a strong impact on Tena and he began to wonder whether anything could be done to change it. Perhaps he could find a different range or collection of toys that would transmit or contribute something new for children: imagination, relationships, opportunities to play with their parents, far from fads and from cartoon characters. He felt that children should be active participants rather than mere spectators.

Imaginarium: A New Business Concept

In November 1992, Tena decided to embark on a new entrepreneurial business venture by opening his first Imaginarium retail outlet in Zaragoza's old town district.[2] It was considered "a pilot store." The functional and decorative designs were created locally in Zaragoza, Spain.

Tena admitted that when developing this new business idea, some details about the retail toy trade in other countries had served as inspiration. But the overall Imaginarium business concept was the result of an original process and included full details of lighting, shelving, size and distribution of the retail store, range of toys offered, and so on.

The opening of the first pilot store implied a strategic change for Tena. As he put it, "I was no longer a manufacturer and seller of toys, but I had become a purchaser and a retailer. All the toys I sold in my store were bought from other manufacturers, after a very careful process of choice and selection." In order to do his toy procurement, he took advantage of his extensive knowledge and contacts in the toy industry. He also attended specialized international toy trade shows. The product range was chosen according to a system. On the one hand, he wanted to offer toys for children aged between birth and eight or nine; on the other hand, he defined a certain number of content and activity areas: preschool, games, music and theatre, dolls, manual work, science and nature, professions, movement, and so forth. An attempt was made to include toys at several price points or price levels within each cell or section of the toy matrix thus defined.

When preparing the opening of the first pilot store, Tena already had a clear idea that this one was going to be the first store of a retail chain. According to this idea, Tena already had set up separate "headquarters" with a team of two or three other people.[3] It was Tena's objective to help children learn, imagine, and discover. Some months later, this objective was summarized in what was to become the company's mission statement: "IMAGINARIUM: making a joyful contribution to the human development of boys and girls throughout the world."

Fine-tuning the New Business Concept

Early in 1993, Tena came across a Disney University leaflet announcing a one-week seminar soon to be held at the Disney Center in Florida.

This seminar helped him fine-tune his idea of the store and the business along the following lines:

- "Business involves putting on a show on a stage."
- "Customers should receive more they expect to receive."
- "Customers should feel an emotional experience."
- "Customers are our guests."

Another idea that occurred to Tena was that, in order to create a chain of retail stores that could easily be reproduced and multiplied, all the design details and operating procedures would have to be highly standardized. This required the preparation of highly detailed operating manuals that also reflected the "philosophy" or "concept" of the Imaginarium business.

In 1993, Tena decided to franchise Imaginarium, maintaining that almost all decisions would be made at company headquarters. This manifested itself in the merchandising details of the retail stores, the logistics operations, and the operating manuals prepared for the franchisees. The product range offered, shelving, and display stands in the Imaginarium stores were all determined in advance. Toys were not supplied in answer to orders placed at the discretion of the store managers or franchisees, but by means of automatic restocking procedures.

Opening the Next Four Stores

Based on the experience acquired in the pilot store in Zaragoza, Tena introduced some improvements in the model, and in September 1993 he proceeded to open four new stores: two in Madrid, and two in Barcelona. All of them were owned and operated by Imaginarium, and each one of them required an investment of about Euro 90,000.[4]

These efforts crystallized some of the conceptual and operational details that defined the character of Imaginarium. For instance, shop attendants were defined as "juególogas" ("toyologues" or toy experts, with a scientific connotation). They had to be able to advise parents about the toys they sold, and to look upon the children with an educator's understanding. The company therefore adopted very specific hiring policies, and many of the "toyologues" were graduates in education, psychology, sociology or related fields. The company provided them and their "guests" with data cards on each toy, containing detailed information regarding its use, recommended child age, the kinds of child-development benefits generated by that particular toy, and so on. Each toy purchased was wrapped, including a label with the name of the recipient child and a lollipop.

With a few exceptions, Imaginarium stores only sold toys manufactured according to its specifications, and under its own trademark and packaging. Generally speaking, it was not possible to find exactly the same toy anywhere else.

After the success of the 1993 openings, Tena was convinced that the store layout and overall business concept was sound. The subsequent evolution of the company's sales figures and forecasts shown below would seem to prove him right.[5]

Sales Revenue (in million Euros)
2000: 22.5
2001: 33.6 (as budgeted)
2002: 42.5 (forecast)

Note: Fiscal year ending on January 31st of the indicated year.

Opening of the First Franchised Stores

In 1994 Imaginarium opened seven new toy stores: five owned and operated by the company and two franchised. Quite spontaneously, people who had seen the first stores phoned the company requesting a license to open a franchised store. Tena thought this was terrific because it would allow him to grow faster. It would allow him to negotiate with his toy suppliers better terms of prices, exclusivity rights, etc. By growing fast, he might be able to preempt potential future competitors.

At the end of 1994 the British venture-capital company 3i (Investors In Industry) bought 35 percent of the shares of Step Two, S.A. At that time Tena thought he might be able to eventually open a total of about sixty toy stores throughout Spain. He was wrong, however, as this figure was exceeded in 1998, and doubled by 1999.

Opening the First Stores Abroad

In 1996, a Colombian entrepreneur applied for the Master Franchise for Colombia. Another entrepreneur requested the Master Franchise for Portugal.

Tena decided he would make Master Franchise agreements in some countries, provided the applicant appeared to be enthusiastic, and had sufficient financial resources and market knowledge to assure the opening of a number of toy stores by himself, or to subfranchise.

Tena decided that his first priority would be to expand his chain of educational toy stores in Southern Europe. In 1999 he opened his first three stores in France. Seven more were opened in year 2000. Out of these ten, nine were owned and operated by Imaginarium, and one was franchised. In Italy, four stores were opened in 2000. Only one was franchised.

Tena also decided that his second priority would be Latin America. By the end of year 2000, he had signed Master Franchise agreements with local entrepreneurs in Colombia (5 toy stores), Venezuela (5), Dominican Republic (2), Mexico (1), El Salvador (1), and Argentina (2).

The company was planning to open 25 new stores outside Spain in 2001, and a further 63 stores in 2002, thereby increasing the number of countries with Imaginarium stores to 18 by the end of 2002.

The Product Department

At the beginning of 2001, an external observer of the Imaginarium business would probably say that the Imaginarium business model and process started in the Product Department. Its manager was 35, and she was one of the few pioneers who had worked with Tena since his days at Publijuego.

Her vision was based on very few market surveys, a lot of personal observation, and lots of common sense. She took into account the age of target children, making sure the toys were educational, that they would play with the children, and were not sexist or racist or violent. Increasingly, toy manufacturers sent samples, which were stored in the "sample file" shelves in the Product Department, organized according to the same thematic sections in Imaginarium stores.

At the beginning of each year, right after the Christmas high season, she would attend a certain number of international toy trade shows. She insisted on the fact that their toys would always carry the Imaginarium brand, and (with very few exceptions) they were to be exclusively sold at Imaginarium stores. They developed and launched two toy collections per year, in Spring–Summer and in Fall–Winter. Each collection was made up of about 1,200 SKUs (stock keeping units). For the year 2000 collection, Imaginarium had some 110 different suppliers.

The Expansion and Projects Department

This department mission was to open new stores. Imaginarium might proactively open a new store, in a particular location, either fully owned or franchised. Alternatively, they might be reactive, when an entrepreneur requested a license to open a franchised store in a particular location. A strict, standardized eight-stage selection process had been set up for selecting future franchisees. The company's business know-how was transmitted by means of initial training courses, refresher courses, operation manuals, and ongoing communications and assistance.

Imaginarium insisted upon the fact that all stores were run and attended by specially qualified personnel (the "toyologues"). They were also given ongoing training to make sure that they were able to advise guests regarding the ideal product for each boy or girl. They had to be able to transmit the fundamental idea of the company's culture and mission in their day-to-day work: "To cheerfully contribute to the human development of children throughout the world in fun and creative ways."

Operations and Logistics

The Operations Department serviced each store as soon as it was ready to open. Stores were located in expensive premium locations. Therefore they were designed without a backroom or a storeroom. All available products were on the sales floor.

Toy manufacturers sent their orders to a central warehouse in Zaragoza. Most Imaginarium toy stores were staffed from about 8:30 a.m. to 10:30 p.m. At the close of each day's sales, each store sent out automatic sales records to Zaragoza, where restocking orders were prepared, loaded on a truck, and shipped in a few hours. In most cases, the restocking merchandise arrived early in the morning, in time to be placed on the shelves by the time the store opened again in the following morning. Resupply to stores located in France or Italy would normally take place every two or three days, and might take two days to reach their destination. Supplies were shipped to Latin America by full container load, every two weeks, consigned to the Master Franchisee.

An IT Department supported all business and logistics operations.

Imaginarium's Marketing Strategy

A clear business concept, retail store design and locations, capable and devoted retail store attendants, exclusive and branded products, and reasonable prices seemed to be the factors that drove Imaginarium's expansion, with limited media advertising.

The company spent a substantial proportion of its marketing funds producing and mailing two catalogues per year, mostly to Club Imaginarium members, as described below.

In August 1999 the company launched its first web page, but by late 2000, it was reconsidering its Internet strategy. It was clear to Imaginarium management that its goal was to promote multichannel sales, while including a high content of corporate values in each of the different sales channels. However, management had doubts as to whether the strategy was the right one. In particular, it worried about the potential negative reaction of franchised store owners who might dislike the fact that the company would start taking orders online. Tena insisted that the marketing department should develop a multichannel sales model where Internet sales would actually enhance sales in the Imaginarium brick-and-mortar stores.

Also, questions were raised regarding the strategic relationships between the store expansion strategy, the Internet strategy, and the relational marketing strategy, as developed by means of Club Imaginarium.

Club Imaginarium

Club Imaginarium was created with the initial purpose of having a "guest database" and of doing "something special." Its first members were registered in 1993. By early 2001, almost 400,000 families had registered. Registration cards were only available at Imaginarium stores, and registration required the signature of at least one of the parents.

Membership is awarded to a family. From the registration card, information was stored in the data base including names, addresses, birthdates, genders, postal address, telephone number, and e-mail address.

Up to 2001, membership or loyalty cards had not been issued to members of Club Imaginarium. Therefore, no distinction was made in the Imaginarium stores between occasional "guests" and registered members of the Club.

However, active Club members were identified when they went to an Imaginarium store in response to an invitation. Such invitations announced the opening of a new store or offered a free birthday gift on condition of making a minimum purchase. Club members were also informed that they could pick up a free copy of the new seasonal toy catalogue. On such occasions, Club members received a coded coupon which, if redeemed or used, allowed the company to know who had actively responded or participated.

Therefore, Imaginarium did not register its Club members' transactions (purchases), but could conclude which Club members were the most active and prticipated in the various activities and events to which they were invited.

The information thus gathered enabled the company to decide whether or not to include the "lapsed" or less active

Exhibit 1

Evolution of Imaginarium Retail Stores, 1992–2000

	1992	1993	1994	1995	1996	1997	1998	1999	2000	Total
Spain	1	4	11	22	32	50	67	96	119	119
Abroad:					3	6	14	27	49	49
Portugal					2	5	11	18	19	19
Colombia					1	1	2	3	5	5
Venezuela							1	2	5	5
Dominican Republic								1	2	2
France								3	10	10
Italy									4	4
Mexico									1	1
El Salvador									1	1
Argentina									2	2
Total number of stores in operation	1	4	11	22	35	56	81	123	168	168
Number of new countries with stores	1	1	1	1	3	3	4	6	10	10
Total number of company's own stores	1	4	9	15	20	26	31	38	54	54
Total number of franchise stores			2	7	15	30	50	85	114	114
Total number of own stores + franchise stores	1	1	11	22	35	56	81	123	168	168

The total of 168 stores includes those opened on December 31, 2000. The heading "Total number of company's own stores" includes the stores run directly by the franchiser Step Two, S.A., in Spain, plus the company's own stores in France and Italy. The heading "Total number of franchise stores" includes the franchise stores in Spain, France, and Italy, as well as the master franchisers' own stores in Portugal, Colombia, Venezuela, Mexico, El Salvador, and Argentina, plus the subfranchised stores in these six countries.

Exhibit 2

Step Two, S.A., Profit and Loss Account at 31 January 2001 (in Euros)

Income	33,592,942
Expenses	−29,996,474
Operating profit	3,596,468
Financial expenses and others	−510,423
Profits from ordinary activities	3,086,045
Extraordinary profits	65,080
Profits before tax	3,151,125
Corporate tax	−714,621
Fiscal-year profits	2,436,504

Step Two parent-company figures. They do not include the subsidiaries in Italy, France, and Switzerland, sales on the Internet, or franchise-store sales.

Club members in the types of promotional activities that entailed higher unit costs for the company, such as mailing to them the product catalogues twice every year. "Lapsed" Club members could be "restored" if they participated again in some activities or events.

According to the marketing manager of Imaginarium, "The more guests join the Club, the more they'll come to a store, the more they'll buy from us, and the more they will remember Imaginarium when they have to choose a toy store to buy from. The Club is of vital importance for managing our relationships with our members."

However, the managers of Imaginarium had for some time been giving thought to the idea of launching a loyalty card or a similar system or mechanism that would allow them to track and register the specific toy purchases made by each family member of the Club.

Such a loyalty card could be a multisponsor card, such as Travel Club, or it could be an exclusive Imaginarium card.[6] After consulting with companies specializing in such matters, the marketing manager of Imaginarium came to the conclusion that issuing and operating their own loyalty card could cost up to about 2 to 3 percent of Imaginarium turnover. This cost would include the cost of issuing and mailing the cards themselves, some incentives to be granted to members using the cards, and the administrative costs (maintaining the database, telephone operators to solve any incidents, mailings, e-mails, etc.).

Questions for Discussion

1. In planning the future of his company, Felix Tena asked himself the following questions:

   - A what speed should the business expand in terms of new stores?
   - Where should they be located?
   - Should the company open more stores of its own, or should it give priority to franchised stores?
   - In the latter option, should the company grant individual franchises, or rather, should agreements be reached with master franchises?
   - Given that the company already had educational toy stores open in ten countries, should they now concentrate on and aim at further penetrating these countries? Or rather, should they expand to other national markets?
   - What role should the Internet play in the company's future development?
   - How should they go about developing better relationships with the some 400,000 families, who are already members of Club Imaginarium?

JOEMARIN OY

Finland's first customers in the sailboat business are generally believed to have been the Vikings. More recently, ships and boats were exported as partial payment for World War II reparations. This long tradition in building sailboats is due, no doubt, to Finland's proximity to the sea, long coastline, and its 60,000 lakes. Among luxury sailing yachts, the Swan boats of Nautor Oy and the Finnclippers of Fiskars Oy are internationally known and admired. There are, however, over 100 other boat builders in Finland that turn out 10,000 sailing yachts yearly.

Although most of the Finnish sailboat companies are situated on the coast, for obvious reasons, Joemarin Oy is located in the town of Joensuu, roughly 450 kilometers northeast of Helsinki. Joemarin was founded in the town that lends part of its name to the company because of the efforts of Kehitysaluerahasto, which is the Development Area Foundation of the Finnish government. Kehitysaluerahasto provided a loan of 4 million Finnish marks to Joemarin, a privately owned company, to start its operations in the Joensuu area because of the town's high rate of unemployment.

The present product line consists of three types of fiberglass sailboats. The Joemarin 17 is a coastal sailing yacht with a new design approach (Exhibit 1). This approach is to provide a craft that enables a family to make weekend and holiday cruises in coastal waters and also offers exciting sailing. The sailboat is very fast. The Finnish Yacht Racing Association stated in its test in which the Joemarin 17 was judged to be the best in her class: "She is delicate, lively, spacious, and easy to steer. She is well balanced and has a high-quality interior. She is especially fast on the beat and lively to handle in a free wind."

The Joemarin 17, a small day cruiser with berths for two adults and two children, has a sail area of 130 square feet, weighs one-half ton, and has an overall length of a little over 17 feet. The hull is made of glass-reinforced plastic (GRP), and the mast and boom are made of aluminum. The boat has a drop keel that is useful when negotiating shallow anchorages or when lifting the boat on a trailer for transportation. The layout of the boat is shown in Exhibit 2.

The Joemarin 34 is a relatively large motor sailer that sleeps seven people in three separate compartments. The main saloon contains an adjustable dining table, a complete galley, and a navigator's compartment. The main saloon is separated from the fore cabin by a folding door. The aft cabin, which is entered by a separate companionway, contains a double berth, wardrobe, wash basin, and lockers. The toilet and shower are situated between the fore cabin and the main saloon. The boat has a sail area of 530 square feet, weighs

about five tons, and has an overall length of 33 feet 9 inches. A significant feature of the craft is that she is equipped with a 47 horsepower diesel engine.

The Joemarin 34 has the same design approach as the 17. She is well appointed, with sufficient space for seven people to live comfortably. An important feature is that the three separate living compartments allow for considerable privacy. In addition, however, the modern hull is quite sleek, making her an excellent sailing yacht.

The Joemarin 36 was designed for a different purpose. Whereas the 17 and 34 are oriented toward a family approach to sailing—combining the features of safety and comfortable accommodations with good sailing ability—the 36 is first and foremost a sailing craft. It does have two berths, a small galley, and toilet facilities, but the emphasis is on sailing and racing rather than comfort. The boat has a sail area of 420 square feet, weighs a little less than four tons, and has an overall length of 35 feet 10 inches. The boat is also equipped with a small (7 horsepower) diesel engine for emergency power situations. The Joemarin 36 is a traditional Swedish design and, therefore, is directed almost solely to the Swedish market.

The company was established in order to manufacture sailboats for export. The Finnish sailboat market is small because of the short sailing season. Nevertheless, the company has been successful in marketing the 17 in Finland, although this was difficult in the beginning because of the lack of boat dealers. To circumvent this problem, Joemarin persuaded a number of new car dealers throughout the country to handle the Joemarin 17 on an agency basis. This involved the company's providing one boat to each car dealer, who placed it in the showroom. The dealer then marketed the sailboats for a 15 percent sales commission.

Although many people scoffed at this idea, the system produced reasonable sales and also made the company known throughout Finland. This contributed to an arrangement with one of the largest cooperative wholesale-retail operations in Finland. Like most cooperatives, this organization began with agricultural products; however, the product range of the company now includes virtually every conceivable consumer product. The present contract states that the cooperative will purchase 80 Joemarin 17 boats per year for the next three years.

The Swedish market is served by a selling agent, although this representative has not been particularly effective. Because Sweden is also the home of many sailboat builders, the company has tried to market only the 36 in that country. In Denmark, France, Holland, Germany, and the United Kingdom, Joemarin has marketed the 34 through importers. These importers operate marinas in addition to new sailboat dealerships. They purchase the boats from Joemarin for their own accounts and mark

SOURCE: This case was prepared by James H. Sood of the American University. Reprinted with permission.

Exhibit **1**

Joemarin 17: Ideal for Family Cruising as Well as Exciting Racing

Exhibit **2**

The Layout of the Joemarin 17

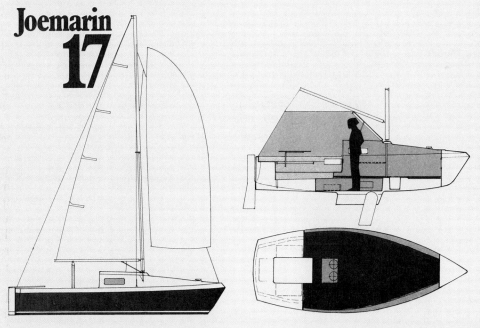

up the price by about 20 percent. In return for exclusive marketing rights in their respective countries, they agree to purchase a minimum number (usually three or four) of the 34 design per year. None of these importers is interested in marketing the 17 or the 36; the shipping cost for the 17 is too high compared with the value of the boat, and there is little customer interest in the 36.

Joemarin is planning to introduce a new sailboat. Whereas the present products were designed by people in the company who were relatively unknown (to the customers), the hull of the new sailboat has been designed by an internationally known boat designer. The cost of these design services was a $30,000 initial fee plus a $3,000 royalty fee to be paid for each boat produced. The new sailboat, the Joemarin 29, has an interior quite similar to that of the Joemarin 34. This is not unexpected because the same Joemarin people designed the interiors and decks of both sailboats.

The new boat is a motor sailer that sleeps six people in three separate compartments, is 28 feet 9 inches long, weighs 4 tons, and has a joined cabin space and a separate aft cabin, small galley, toilet and shower facilities, and a 12 horsepower diesel engine. Because of a new construction technique that greatly reduces the amount of fiberglass required, the variable costs to construct the boat are only 60 percent of the costs for the 34. With a preliminary selling price of €97,500, the Joemarin 29 is receiving favorable attention, and the company is concerned that sales may have an adverse effect on sales of the 34.

The company categorizes the marketing expenses as fixed costs because allocating these expenses to specific products is difficult. The major element of the program is participation in international boat shows in London, Paris, Hamburg, Amsterdam, Copenhagen, and Helsinki. The initial purpose of participating in these shows was to locate suitable importers in the target markets; however, this effort is maintained in order to support the marketing programs of the importers. The importers are also supported by advertising in the leading yachting magazines in the national markets. Joemarin's personal selling effort consists primarily of servicing the importers and agents and staffing the exhibitions at the boat shows. Most of the sales promotion costs are the result of the elaborate sales brochures that the company has developed for each boat. These brochures are printed in four colors on three folded pages of high-quality paper. The costs are greatly increased, however, by having to print a relatively small number of each brochure in Finnish, French, English, German, and Swedish. The brochures are provided to the agents and importers and are used at the boat shows.

The company is in the process of preparing its production and marketing plan for the coming year in order to arrange financing. The president is strongly committed to the continued growth of the company, and the market indications suggest that there is a reasonably strong demand for the 17 in Finland and for the 34 in most of the other national markets. The sales results of the previous and present years are shown in Exhibit 3; the profit statement for the present year is shown in Exhibit 4.

Exhibit 3

Joemarin Sales

	Last Year			Present Year		
	No.	Average Price[a]	Revenue	No.	Average Price[a]	Revenue
J/M-17	200	13,500	2,700,000	240	14,850	3,564,000
J/M-29	—	—	—	—	—	—
J/M-34	30	162,000	4,860,000	36	178,000	6,408,000
J/M-36	4	94,500	378,000	5	103,950	519,750
			7,938,000			10,491,750

[a]All prices are manufacturer's prices; prices and revenues are in euros: 1.00 € = U.S. $1.20.

Exhibit 4

Joemarin Profit Statement for Present Year

	In €	As a Percentage of Sales
Sales revenue	10,491,750[a]	
Variable costs (direct labor and materials)	6,755,000	65.0%
Fixed costs:		
Production (building expenses, production management salaries)	472,500	4.5
Product design costs (salaries, prototypes, testing, consultants)	661,500	6.4
Administration costs (salaries, insurance, office expenses)	324,000	3.1
Marketing costs (salaries, advertising, boat shows, sales promotion, travel expenses)	1,142,000	11.0
Total fixed costs	2,600,000	25.0%
Profit before taxes	1,136,750	10.0

[a]All prices are manufacturer's prices; prices and revenues are in euros: 1.00 € = U.S. $1.20.

Exhibit **5**

Shipping Costs for Joemarin 36 to Sweden, and for Joemarin 29 and 34 to Other Countries

Country	Present Exchange Rates in €	Expected Inflation Rates	Estimated Freight and Insurance Costs per Boat
Denmark	Danish Kroner = 0.1340	2.2%	€6,750
France	€	1.8	€9,500
Holland	€	2.1	€8,500
Sweden	Swedish Kroner = 0.1078	1.3	€5,000
United Kingdom	English Pound = 1.4716	2.0	€11,000
Germany	€	2.1	€8,500
Finland	€	1.1	–

SOURCE: Eurostat Newsrelease, January 19, 2006.

The main problem in developing the plan for next year is determining the price for each sailboat in each market. In previous years, Joemarin had established its prices in Finnish marks, on an ex-factory basis. Management has become convinced, however, that it must change the terms of its prices in order to meet competition in the foreign markets. Thus, the company has decided to offer CIF prices to its foreign customers in the currency of the foreign country. The use of truck ferries between Finland and Sweden, Denmark, and Germany is expected to make this pricing approach more competitive.

Joemarin would also like to assure its agents and importers that the prices will remain in effect for the entire year, but the financial manager is concerned about the possible volatility of exchange rates because of the varying rates of inflation in the market countries. The present exchange rates, the expected inflation rates in the market countries, and the estimated costs to ship the Joemarin 36 to Stockholm and the Joemarin 29 and 34 to the other foreign marinas are shown in Exhibit 5.

A second difficulty in pricing the product line in Joemarin is to establish a price for the 29 that will reflect the value of the boat but will not reduce the sales of the 34. There are three schools of thought concerning the pricing of motor sailers. The predominant theory is that price is a function of the overall length of the sailboat. A number of people, however, believe that the overall weight of the craft is a much more accurate basis. The third opinion argues that price is a function of the special features and equipment. Exhibit 6, which was prepared by a Swiss market research firm, shows the relationship between present retail prices and the length of new motor sailers in the West European market.

Exhibit **6**

Retail Price in the European Market of Sailing Yachts as a Function of Overall Length

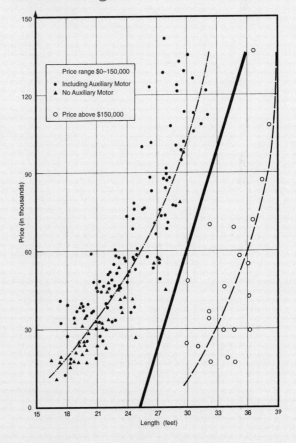

NOTE: All yachts to the right of the bold dividing line are priced above 150,000.

Questions for Discussion

1. Determine the optimal manufacturer's selling price in the Finnish market for the four Joemarin sailboats for the coming year.

2. Determine the CIF prices for the Joemarin 36 to the final customer in Sweden for the coming year. The agent's commission is 15 percent of the final selling price, and the final selling price should be in Swedish kroner.

3. Recommend a course of action for the company to take in regard to the Joemarin 36.

4. Determine the CIF prices, in the foreign currencies, for the Joemarin 29 and 34 to the importers in Denmark, France, Holland, the United Kingdom, and Germany for the coming year.

5. Develop a production and marketing plan for Joemarin for the coming year. What steps can the company take to ensure that the plan is in line with the demand for its products in its foreign markets?

THE GLOBAL MARKETING MIX

Part Four deals with global marketing activities. The core marketing concerns of the beginning internationalist and the multinational corporation are the same. Yet experienced marketers face challenges and opportunities that are different from those encountered by new entrants. They are able to expend more resources on international marketing efforts than are small- and medium-sized firms. In addition, their perspective can be more globally oriented. Multinational corporations also have more impact on individuals, economies, and governments. Therefore, they are much more subject to public scrutiny and need to be more concerned about repercussions from their activities. Yet their very size often enables them to be more influential in setting international marketing rules. The book concludes with a new chapter 19 which addresses emerging concern in the international marketing field and employment opportunities for its students.

CHAPTER FOURTEEN

GLOBAL PRODUCT MANAGEMENT AND BRANDING

Are Global Brands the Way to Go?

Pressure is on marketing managers to develop global approaches that increase growth and profit potential, while at the same time maintaining local appeal. If these two seemingly opposite demands could be coupled and the goal of being "global locally" met, one of the greatest challenges facing marketers could be solved. The cost of developing global programs is high in terms of intellectual and monetary investment, and the marketing challenges are commensurate. Externally, customer behavior similarities may not be sufficient. Internally, country management may object to cross-border efforts as an encroachment on decision making.

In the last few years, the global/local controversy has been most evident in branded consumer products. A number of companies have engaged in brand pruning efforts with the aim of reducing brand portfolios to manageable sizes. Preference has naturally been given to global brands given their prominent positions. (For example, according to Unilever executives, three-fourths of the company's business comes from 25 global brands.) Many local brands are being evaluated according to their potential as global candidates or as examples of best practice that could be applied elsewhere. The bottom line for global companies is that there aren't enough resources to go around for managing scores of local brands that are not truly different.

Global brands, like any facet of global marketing, are supposed to benefit from the scale and the scope that having a presence in multiple markets brings.

As global retailers gain more power, marketers may feel more pressure to have brands that can travel with their customers. Another justification for a global presence is fueled by the increasing similarity that consumers are displaying in terms of their consumption habits and preferences. It has also been argued that global brands are perceived to be more value-added for the consumer, either through better quality (as a function of worldwide acceptance) or by enhancing the consumer's self-perception as being cosmopolitan, sophisticated, and modern.

Internally, global branding can be seen as a tool to tighten organizational relationships using the transfer of best practice in brand management, as well as programs like brand stewardship through brand management teams at headquarters or designated centers of excellence. Concentrating resources and efforts on a limited number of brands should bring about improved results. For example, Unilever has singled out six brands for special attention in the personal care category, all of which have shown double-digit growth in the last years.

While the level and effects of globalization can be disputed, the critical question is whether a brand's image will carry over effectively to other markets. Efforts to standardize brand names by eliminating local brand names have met with consumer hostility, and globally branded items introduced into product lines have not always received enthusiastic support of country managers. Consumers' behavior may have converged, but some markets continue to have their own idiosyncrasies that can prove fatal to globalization efforts.

GLOBAL BRANDS, LIKE UNILEVER, MAY HAVE MORE SUCCESS IN HIGH-PROFILE,
HIGH-INVOLVEMENT PRODUCT CATEGORIES.

The ability of a global product to penetrate individual markets is determined to some extent by the product category in question. Global brands may have more success in high-profile, high-involvement categories, while consumers may still give local brands preference in purchasing everyday products.

SOURCES: Johny K. Johansson and Ilkka A. Ronkainen, "The Esteem of Global Brands," *Journal of Brand Management* 12 (number 5, 2005): 339–354; and Johny K. Johansson and Ilkka A. Ronkainen, "Are Global Brands the Right Choice for Your Company?" *Marketing Management,* March/April, 2004, 53–56.

Developing and managing a product portfolio in the global marketplace is both a great challenge and an attractive opportunity. While market conditions may warrant changes in individual product features, products and product lines should be managed for the greatest possible effect globally, regionally, and locally as shown in *The International Marketplace 14.1.* Global and regional products have to utilize best practice across borders, while local products should be monitored for possible use in other markets.

This chapter is divided into two parts to highlight these issues. The first part will focus on how the product development process can take into account the globalization of markets without compromising dimensions considered essential by local markets. To a large extent this means that the process is market-driven rather than determined by cost or convenience of manufacture. For example, Germany's Volkswagen operated for years under the philosophy that one car was good enough for the whole world, while U.S. marketing executives tried in vain to secure items such as cup holders or seatback release levers in cars destined for the U.S. market. Similarly, Japanese product-development engineers fought against the concept of a third row of seats for a sport utility vehicle, which is preferred by U.S. customers.[1]

The second half of the chapter features a discussion of product management, especially how marketers can utilize resources on a worldwide basis to exploit opportunities in product markets. Unilever, one of the world's largest food companies, often has to take a local view, given differences in the daily diet. Similarly, detergent formulas may have to differ between markets because washing habits, machines, clothes, and water quality vary. However, many strategic product decisions, such as branding, will benefit from worldwide experience and exposure applied to the local context. Some categories cross national borders quite well, such as ice cream, tea, and personal wash products, and translate to opportunities with a standard approach.[2] Unilever has cut the number of its brands from 1,600 to 400, and will focus efforts on 25 global brands, such as Axe.[3] These top 25 brands accounted for 70 percent of the company's sales in 2007.

Global Product Development

Product development is at the heart of the global marketing process. New products should be developed, or old ones modified, to cater to new or changing customer needs on a global or regional basis. At the same time, corporate objectives of technical feasibility and financial profitability must be satisfied.

To illustrate, Black & Decker, manufacturer of power tools for do-it-yourself household repairs, had done some remodeling of its own. The company earlier was the consummate customizer: the Italian subsidiary made tools for Italians, the British subsidiary for the British. At the same time, Japanese power tool makers, such as Makita Electric Works Ltd., saw the world differently. Makita was Black & Decker's first competitor with a global strategy. Makita management did not care that Germans prefer high-powered, heavy-duty drills and that U.S. consumers want everything lighter. They reasoned that a good drill at a low price will sell from Baden-Baden to Brooklyn. Using this strategy, Makita effectively cut into Black & Decker's market share. As a result, Black & Decker unveiled 50 new models—each standardized for world production. The company's current objective is to "establish itself as the preeminent global manufacturer and marketer" in its field.[4]

With competition increasingly able to react quickly when new products are introduced, worldwide planning at the product level provides a number of tangible benefits. A firm that adopts a worldwide approach is better able to develop products with specifications compatible on a worldwide scale. A firm that leaves product development to independent units will incur greater difficulties in transferring its experience and technology.

In many global corporations, each product is developed for potential worldwide usage, and unique market requirements are incorporated whenever technically feasible. Some design their products to meet the regulations and other key requirements in their major markets and then, if necessary, smaller markets' requirements are met on a country-by-country basis. For example, Nissan develops lead-country models that can, with minor changes, be made suitable for local sales in the majority of markets. For the remaining situations, the company also provides a range of additional models that can be adapted to the needs of local segments. Using this approach, Nissan has been able to reduce the number of basic models.[5] This approach also means that the new product can be introduced concurrently into all the firm's markets. Companies like 3M and Xerox develop most of their products with this objective in mind.

Some markets may require unique approaches to developing global products. At Gillette, timing is the only concession to local taste. Emerging markets, such as Eastern Europe and China, are first weaned on less-expensive products before they are sold the latest versions.[6] In a world economy where most of the growth is occurring in emerging markets, the traditional approach of introducing a global product may keep new products out of the hands of consumers due to their premium price. As a result, Procter & Gamble figures out what consumers in various countries can afford and then develops products they can pay for. For example, in Brazil, the company introduced a diaper called Pampers Uni, a less-expensive version of its mainstream product. The strategy is to create price tiers, generating brand loyalty early and then encouraging customers to trade up as their incomes and desire for better products grow.[7]

The main goal of the product development process, therefore, is not to develop a standard product or product line but to build adaptability into products and product lines that are being developed to achieve worldwide appeal. To accomplish the right balance, marketers need to develop basic capability for capturing consumer information within their country organizations. If consumers are willing to talk about their preferences, traditional approaches such as focus groups and interviews work well. Procter & Gamble, for example, generates Chinese consumer information using a 30-person market research team.[8]

The Product Development Process

The product development process begins with idea generation. Ideas may come from within the company—from the research and development staff, sales personnel, or almost anyone who becomes involved in the company's efforts. Intermediaries may suggest ideas because they are closer to the changing, and often different, needs of international customers. In franchising operations, franchisees are a source of many new products. For example, the McFlurry, McDonald's ice-cream dessert, was the brainchild of a Canadian operator.[9] Competitors are a major outside source of ideas. A competitive idea from abroad may be modified and improved to suit another market's characteristics. As an example, when the president of d-Con returned from a trip to Europe, he brought with him what would seem in the United States to be an unusual idea for packaging insecticides. In a market dominated by aerosols, the new idea called for offering consumers insect repellent in a "felt-tip pen."

For a number of companies, especially those producing industrial goods, customers provide the best source of ideas for new products.[10] Many new commercially important products are initially thought of and even prototyped by users rather than originators. They tend to be developed by **lead users**—companies, organizations, or individuals who are ahead of trends or have needs that go beyond what is available at present. For example, a car company in need of a new braking system may look for ideas from racing teams or even the aerospace industry, which has a strong incentive to stop its vehicles before they run out of runway.[11] Of the 30 products with the highest world sales, 70 percent trace their origins to manufacturing and marketing (rather than laboratories) via customer input.[12] Many companies work together with complementary-goods producers in developing new solutions; Whirlpool and Procter & Gamble developed new solutions for keeping people's clothes clean. With the increased diffusion of the Internet, chat rooms about products and features will become an important source of information pertinent to product development and adjustment. For example, Sony set up a Web site to support hackers who are interested in exploring and developing new types of games that could be played on the Sony PlayStation. In the field of industrial products, users are invited to use toolkits to design products and services that fit their own needs precisely.[13]

For some companies, procurement requisitions from governments and supranational organizations (for example, the United Nations) are a good source of new product ideas. When the United Nations Children's Fund (UNICEF) was looking for containers to transport temperature-sensitive vaccines in tropical climates, Igloo Corporation noticed that the technology from its picnic coolers could be used and adapted for UNICEF's use.[14] Facilitating agents, such as advertising agencies or market research organizations, can be instrumental in scanning the globe for new ideas. For example, DDB Worldwide used U.S. research company Market Access for "search-and-reapply" operations to keep clients informed about new ideas around the world, ranging from half-frozen mineral water in Korea to Argentine yogurt drinks containing cereal and fruit chunks.[15]

Most companies develop hundreds of ideas every year; for example, 3M may have 1,000 new product ideas competing for scarce development funds annually. Product ideas are screened on market, technical, and financial criteria: Is the market substantial and penetrable, can the product be mass produced, and if the answer to both of these questions is affirmative, can the company produce and market it profitably? Too often, companies focus on understanding only the current demand of the consumer. A repositioning of the concept may overcome an initial negative assessment; for example, in countries with no significant breakfast habit, cereal marketers present their products as snacks. Procter & Gamble created the perception that dandruff—traditionally a nonissue for the Chinese—is a social stigma and offered a product (Head & Shoulders antidandruff shampoo) to solve the problem. While the company still dominates the market, Unilever plans to wage a battle to garner a share of the market.[16]

A product idea that at some stage fails to earn a go-ahead is not necessarily scrapped. Most progressive companies maintain data banks of "miscellaneous opportunities." Often, data from these banks are used in the development of other products. One of the most famous examples concerns 3M. After developing a new woven fabric some 50 years ago, 3M's Commercial Office Supply Company did not know what to do with the technology. Among the applications rejected were seamless brassiere cups and disposable diapers. The fabric was finally used to make surgical and industrial masks.

All the development phases—idea generation, screening, product and process development, scale-up, and commercialization—should be global in nature with inputs into the process from all affected markets. If this is possible, original product designs can be adapted easily and inexpensively later on. The process has been greatly facilitated through the use of **computer-aided design (CAD)**. Some companies are able to design their products so that they meet most standards and requirements around the world, with minor modifications on a country-by-country basis. The product development process can be initiated by any unit of the organization, in the parent country or abroad. If the initiating entity is a subsidiary that lacks technical and financial resources for implementation, another entity of the firm is assigned the responsibility. Most often this is the parent and its central R&D department.

Global companies may have an advantage in being able to utilize resources from around the world. Otis Elevator Inc.'s product for high-rises, the Elevonic, is a good example of this. The elevator was developed by six research centers in five countries. Otis' group in Farmington, Connecticut, handled the systems integration, Japan designed the special motor drives that make the elevators ride smoothly, France perfected the door systems, Germany handled the electronics, and Spain took care of the small-geared components. The international effort saved more than $10 million in design costs and cut the development cycle from four years to two.[17]

In some cases, the assignment of product development responsibility may be based on a combination of special market and technical knowledge. When a major U.S. copier manufacturer was facing erosion of market share in the smaller copier segment in Europe because of Japanese incursions, its Japanese subsidiary was charged with developing an addition to the company's product line. This product, developed and produced outside the United States, has subsequently been marketed in the United States.

Even though the product development activity may take place in the parent country, all the affected units actively participate in development and market planning for a new product. For example, a subsidiary would communicate directly with the product division at the headquarters level and also with the international staff, who could support the subsidiary on the scene of the actual development activity. This often also involves the transfer of people from one location to another for such projects. For example, when Fiat wanted to build a car specifically for emerging markets, the task to develop the Palio was given to a 300-strong team that assembled in Turin, Italy. Among them were 120 Brazilians, ranging from engineers to shop-floor workers, as well as Argentines, Turks, and Poles.[18]

The activities of a typical global program are summarized in Exhibit 14.1. The managing unit has prime responsibility for accomplishing: (1) single-point worldwide technical development and design of a new product that conforms to the global design standard and global manufacturing and procurement standards, as well as transmittal of the completed design to each affected unit; (2) all other activities necessary to plan, develop, originate, introduce, and support the product in the managing unit, as well as direction and support to affected units to ensure that concurrent introductions are achieved; and (3) integration and coordination of all global program activities.

The affected units, on the other hand, have prime responsibility for achieving: (1) identification of unique requirements to be incorporated in the product goals and specifications as well as in the managing unit's technical effort; (2) all other activities necessary to plan, originate, introduce, and support products in affected units; and (3) identification of any nonconcurrence with the managing unit's plans and activities.

During the early stages of the product development process, the global emphasis is on identifying and evaluating the requirements of both the managing unit and the affected units and incorporating them into the plan. During the later stages, the emphasis is on the efficient development and design of a global product with a minimum of configuration differences and on the development of supporting systems capabilities in each of the participating units. The result of the interaction and communication is product development activity on a global basis, as well as products developed primarily to serve world markets. For example, Fiat's Palio is designed for the rough roads of the Brazilian interior rather than the smooth motorways of Italy. The car was also deliberately overengineered, because market research revealed that customers' future preferences were developing that way.

This approach effectively cuts through the standardized-versus-localized debate and offers a clear-cut way of determining and implementing effective programs in several

Exhibit 14.1

Global Program Management

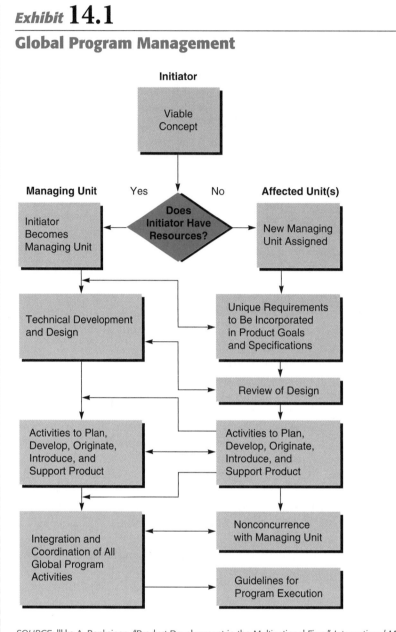

SOURCE: Ilkka A. Ronkainen, "Product Development in the Multinational Firm," *International Marketing Review* 1 (Winter 1983): 24–30.

markets simultaneously. It offers headquarters the opportunity to standardize certain aspects of the product while permitting maximum flexibility, whenever technically feasible, to differing market conditions. For instance, in terms of technical development, members of subsidiaries' staffs take an active part in the development processes to make sure that global specifications are built into the initial design of the product.[19]

The process has to be streamlined in terms of duration as well. In industries characterized by technological change, coming to market nine to twelve months late can cost a new product half its potential revenues. To cut down on development time, companies like NEC and Canon use multidisciplinary teams that stay with the project from start to finish, using a parallel approach toward product launch. Designers start to work before feasibility testing is over; manufacturing and marketing begin gearing up well before the design is finished. Such teams depend on computer systems for designing, simulating, and analyzing products. Toyota Motor Company estimates that it will, sometime in the future, develop a new automobile in one year (its RAV4 mini sport utility vehicle was brought to market in 24 months), whereas some of its competitors may spend as much as five years on the process.[20]

The challenge today is that no internal R&D effort can possibly predict, evaluate, and cover all possible configurations. Taking these new realities to heart, companies need to systematically tap into the capabilities of external knowledge and skills leaders, not just for state-of-the-art products but also for the continuous innovation and evolution of ideas (as argued in *The International Marketplace 14.2*).[21] At Procter & Gamble, the "connect-and-develop" model's objective is to identify promising ideas around the world, and apply the company's own R&D, manufacturing, and marketing capabilities to them to create better and cheaper products, faster.[22] A total of 45 percent of the initiatives in the company's product development portfolio have key elements from external constituents.

The International
MARKETPLACE
14.2

Outsourcing Innovation

The next step in outsourcing may be innovation. Underlying this phenomenon is a growing consensus that R&D spending is not generating enough return on the investment made. Companies can either cut costs or increase R&D productivity. As a result, little-known companies (such as those shown in the table below) are emerging as new powers in the technology industry.

At the minimum, most leading companies are turning toward a model of innovation that employs global networks of partners. These can include U.S. chipmakers, Taiwanese engineers, Indian software developers, and Chinese factories. IBM is offering the services of its research laboratories and a new global team of 1,200 engineers to help customers develop future products. Depending on their capabilities and needs, many companies can profitably outsource almost any elements in the innovation chain, from basic research to testing, and even to new-product introduction. Given the complexities of present-day technologies, no one company can master it all. Outsourcing some development makes sense so the company's own engineers can focus on next-generation technologies. Outsourcing is about the flexibility to put resources in the right places at the right time. For example, using a pre-designed platform can cut 70 percent of

development costs off a new model. As a rule of thumb, it takes $10 million and 150 staff to develop a new cell phone from scratch.

The danger of outsourcing R&D is creating competition. Motorola hired BenQ from Taiwan to design and manufacture mobile phones. Subsequently, BenQ started selling its phones in China under its brand name. Companies try to draw the line between mission-critical R&D and commodity work. What will be outsourced is routine, computer-like, spec-sheet based tasks, while work that entails artistry, creativity, and empathy with the customer will be performed at home. Motorola has announced that it will keep R&D spending at around 10 percent for the long term. Lucent has plans to keep its R&D staff at 9,000. However, most companies' new hiring will occur at their own labs abroad in China, India, and Eastern Europe. Some marketers are making their own R&D and design efforts a competitive tool; for example, each iPod has "Designed in California" etched on its back panel.

In today's global marketplace, there is a tendency to refer to smartsourcing instead of outsourcing. While outsourcing focuses on cost, smartsourcing suggests that a company is concerned not only with cost-cutting but also with developing true partners in innovation.

Company	Description	Key Products Designed
Cellon U.S.	Independent design house, spun off from Philips' cell-phone business, has big labs in China and France	Wireless handsets for Philips, Siemens, and Haier
Compal Taiwan	Top developer of computers; leading producer of mobile phones	Notebooks, cell phones for Motorola, Toshiba, Sony-Ericsson
Flextronics Singapore	Manufacturing services giant bought frog design to beef up design capabilities	Cell phones, printers, telecom equipment
Wipro India	World's largest contract R&D house for telecom, auto, and electronics	Telecom equipment, auto electronic systems, chips

SOURCES: Nitin Nohria, "Feed R&D—or Farm it Out," *Harvard Business Review* 83 (July/August 2005): 17–27; "Outsourcing Innovation," *Business Week*, March 21, 2005, 84–90; James B. Quinn, "Outsourcing Innovation: The New Engine of Growth," *Sloan Management Review* 41 (number 4, 2000): 13–29.

Firms using worldwide product management are better able to develop products that can be quickly introduced into any market.[23] Foreign market introduction can take the form of either production or marketing abroad. In general, the length of the lag will depend on (1) the product involved, with industrial products having shorter lags because of their more standardized general nature; (2) degree of newness; (3) customer characteristics—both demographics and psychographics; (4) geographic proximity; (5) firm-related variables— the number and type of foreign affiliations as well as overall experience in global marketing; and (6) degree of commitments of resources.

Many companies allow and encourage their research centers to devote part of their time purely to their own endeavors. These initiatives are both effective for the motivation of the local personnel and incubators for future regional and global products. For example, the current research and development activities of consumer-product companies, which tend to be centralized near world headquarters, will have to shift to take into account the increasing numbers of customers who live in emerging markets.

The Location of R&D Activities

In the past, many corporations located most of their product development operations within the parent corporation. However, a significant number of companies have started using foreign-based resources to improve their ability to compete internationally. At Asea Brown Boveri, for example, 80 percent of research was carried out in the company's Swiss, Swedish, and German offices only a few years ago, but now it is only half of the total. The company has established new research units in countries such as India and China to stay closer to markets to meet customer needs.[24] Dutch electronics giant Philips has fifteen research-and-development centers in China as part of the company's strategies aiming at satisfying demand for its products (such as low-end mobile phones) in China, India, Africa, South America, and Eastern Europe. These centers are integrated with the efforts of the R&D centers in Europe and the company's Innovation Campus in India.[25] While many endeavors may be set to deal with the local markets or similar regions, solutions may find broader acceptance in the world marketplace. For example, Campbell's R&D center in Hong Kong was initially set up to adjust the company's product offering to the Chinese market. It has since acquired a new role of transferring product concepts developed for the Asian market to the Americas and Europe, due to an increasing interest in ethnic foods. Savi Technology, a provider of real-time solutions for managing supply chains, established its R&D Center for IT Logistic Excellence in Singapore, because the city-state is a major starting point for many supply chains and Savi's major customers operate from there.[26]

Investments for R&D abroad are made for four general reasons: (1) to aid technology transfer from parent to subsidiary, (2) to develop new and improved products expressly for foreign markets, (3) to develop new products and processes for simultaneous application in world markets of the firm, and (4) to generate new technology of a long-term exploratory nature. The commitment of the firm to international operations increases from the first type of investment to the third and fourth, in which there is no or little bias toward headquarters performing the job.[27]

A survey of 209 multinationals in Europe, Japan, and North America shows that the trend towards internationalization of R&D is growing. The Japanese have the lowest degree of internationalization in their R&D efforts compared to their European and North American counterparts; the Europeans give their country operations abroad more responsibilities in product development.[28] In most cases, companies want to be closer to the customers they intend to serve. In some industries, such as pharmaceuticals, having localized R&D efforts is necessary due to heavy regulatory efforts by local or regional governments.

In truly global companies, the location of R&D is determined by the existence of specific skills, as seen in *The International Marketplace 14.3*. Placing R&D operations abroad may also ensure access to foreign scientific and technical personnel and information, either in industry or at leading universities. Investment in R&D facilities in the United States by non-U.S. companies is heavily concentrated in California's Silicon Valley, New Jersey, and North Carolina's Research Triangle Park.[29] The location decision may also be driven by the unique features of the market. For example, most of the major carmakers have design centers

Centers of Excellence

Local markets are absorbing bigger roles as marketers scan the world for ideas that will cross borders. The consensus among marketers is that many more countries are now capable of developing products and product solutions that can be applied on a worldwide basis. This realization has given birth to centers of excellence. A center of excellence is defined as an organizational unit that incorporates a set of capabilities that have been identified as an important source of value creation with the explicit intention that these capabilities be leveraged by and/or disseminated to other parts of the firm.

Colgate-Palmolive has set up centers of excellence around the world, clustering countries with geographic, linguistic, or cultural similarities to exploit the same marketing plans. Unilever is extending the innovation centers it opened for personal care products to its food businesses, starting with ice cream. In addition to innovation centers for oral care in Milan and hair care in Paris, there are now similar centers for developing product ideas, research, technology, and marketing expertise for ice-cream products in Rome; Hamburg; London; Paris; and Green Bay, Wisconsin; and in Bangkok for the Asian market.

Countries have an edge if there is strong local development in a particular product category, such as hair care in France and Thailand, creating an abundance of research and development talent. Local management or existing products with a history of sensitivity to the core competence also helps win a worldwide role for a country unit. For example, ABB Strömberg in Finland was assigned as a worldwide center of excellence for electric drivers, a category for which it is a recognized world leader.

Ford's centers of excellence have been established with two key goals in mind: to avoid duplicating efforts and to capitalize on the expertise of specialists on a worldwide basis. Located in several countries, the centers will work on key components for cars. One will, for example, work on certain kinds of engines. Another will engineer and develop common platforms—the suspension and other undercarriage components—for similar-sized cars. Designers in each market will then style exteriors and passenger compartments to appeal to local tastes. Each car will usually be built on the continent where it

is sold. Ford of Europe introduced the Focus, originally intended to replace the Escort. The one-year time lag between the two continents was to allow the same team of engineers to direct factory launches in both in Europe and North America. Five Ford design studios had to compromise on design proposals that ranged from a soft, rounded body to a sharply angular one. Although European operations maintained a leadership role, key responsibilities were divided. The U.S. side took over automatic transmissions, with Europe handling the manual version.

Centers of excellence do not necessarily have to be focused on products or technologies. For example, Corning has established a Center for Marketing Excellence where sales and marketing staff from all Corning's businesses, from glass to television components to electronic communications displays, will be able to find help with marketing intelligence, strategies, new product lines, and e-business. Procter & Gamble has six development hubs that are focused on finding products and technologies that are specialties of their regions. The China hub looks for new high-quality materials and cost innovations, while the India hub seeks out local talent in the sciences to solve problems, using tools such as computer modeling.

Whatever the format, centers of excellence have as the most important tasks to leverage and/or to transfer their current leading-edge capabilities, and to continually fine-tune and enhance those capabilities so that they remain state-of-the-art. Centers of excellence provide country organizations a critical tool by which to develop subsidiary-specific advantages to benefit the entire global organization.

SOURCES: Larry Huston and Nabil Sakkab, "Connect and Develop: Inside Procter & Gamble's Model for Innovation," *Harvard Business Review* 84 (March 2006): 58–66; Tony Frost, Julian Birkinshaw, and Prescott Ensign, "Centers of Excellence in Multinational Corporations," *Strategic Management Journal* 23 (November 2002): 997–1018; Karl J. Moore, "A Strategy for Subsidiaries: Centers of Excellence to Build Subsidiary-Specific Advantages," *Management International Review* 41 (third quarter, 2001): 275–290; Erin Strout, "Reinventing a Company," *Sales and Marketing Management* 152 (February 2000): 86–92; Karl Moore and Julian Birkinshaw, "Managing Knowledge in Global Service Firms: Centers of Excellence," *Academy of Management Executive* 12 (November 1998): 81–92; Laurel Wentz, "World Brands," *Advertising Age International,* September 1996, i1–i21; "Ford to Merge European, North American Car Units," *The Washington Post,* April 22, 1994, G1–2; "Percy Barnevik's Global Crusade," *Business Week Enterprise* 1993, 204–211; **http://www.colgate.com**; **http://www.abb.com**; **http://www.ford.com**; **http://www.pg.com**; and **http://www.corning.com**.

in California to allow for the monitoring of the technical, social, and aesthetic values of the fifth-largest car market in the world. Furthermore, the many technological innovations and design trends that have originated there give it a trendsetting image. Working with the most demanding customers (on issues such as quality) will give companies assurance of success in broader markets.[30]

Given the increasing importance of emerging and developing markets, many marketers believe that an intimate understanding of these new consumers can be achieved only through proximity. Consequently, Unilever has installed a network of innovation centers in 19 countries, many of which are emerging markets (such as Brazil, China, and Thailand). Hewlett-Packard's eInclusion initiative, which focused on rural markets, established a branch of its HP Labs in India charged with developing products and services explicitly for that market.[31] The e-inclusion idea has now been adopted by various organizations.

R&D centers are seen as highly desirable investments by host governments. Developing countries are increasingly demanding R&D facilities as a condition of investment or continued operation, to the extent that some companies have left countries where they saw no need for the added expense. Countries that have been known to have attempted to influence multinational corporations are Japan, India, Brazil, and France. The Chinese government has maintained a preference for foreign investors who have promised a commitment to technology transfer, especially in the form of R&D centers; Volkswagen's ability to develop its business in China is largely due to its willingness to do so. Some governments, such as Canada, have offered financial rewards to multinational corporations to start or expand R&D efforts in host markets. In addition to compliance with governmental regulation, local R&D efforts can provide positive publicity for the company involved. Internally, having local R&D may boost morale and elevate a subsidiary above the status of merely a manufacturing operation.[32]

In companies that still employ multidomestic strategies, product development efforts amount to product modifications—for example, making sure that a product satisfies local regulations. Local content requirements may necessitate major development input from the affected markets. In these cases, local technical people identify alternate, domestically available ingredients and prepare initial tests. More involved testing usually takes place at a regional laboratory or at headquarters.

The Organization of Global Product Development

The product development activity is undertaken by specific teams, whose task is to subject new products to tough scrutiny at specified points in the development cycle, to eliminate weak products before too much is invested in them and to guide promising prototypes from labs to the market.[33] Representatives of all the affected functional areas serve on each team to ensure the integrity of the project. A marketing team member is needed to assess the customer base for the new product, engineering to make sure that the product can be produced in the intended format, and finance to keep costs in control. An international team member should be assigned a permanent role in the product development process and not simply called in when a need arises. Organizational relationships have to be such that the firm's knowledge-based assets are easily transferable and transferred.[34]

In addition to having international representation on each product development team, some multinational corporations hold periodic meetings of purely international teams. A typical international team may consist of five members, each of whom also has a product responsibility (such as cable accessories) as well as a geographical responsibility (such as the Far East). Others may be from central R&D and domestic marketing planning. The function of international teams is to provide both support to subsidiaries and international input to overall planning efforts. A critical part of this effort is customer input before a new product design is finalized. This is achieved by requiring team members to visit key customers throughout the process. A key input of international team members is the potential for universal features that can be used worldwide as well as unique features that may be required for individual markets.

Such multidisciplinary teams maximize the payoff from R&D by streamlining decision making; that is, they reduce the need for elaborate reporting mechanisms and layers of committee approvals. With the need to slash development time, reduce overall material costs, and trim manufacturing processes, these teams can be useful. For example, in response to competition, Honeywell set up a multidisciplinary "tiger team" to build a thermostat in twelve months rather than the usual four years.[35]

Challenges to using teams or approaches that require cooperation between R&D centers are often language and cultural barriers. For example, pragmatic engineers in the United States may distrust their more theoretically thinking European counterparts. National rivalries may also inhibit the acceptance by others of solutions developed by one entity of the organization. Many companies have solved these problems with increased communication and exchange of personnel.[36]

With the costs of basic research rising and product life cycles shortening, many companies have joined forces in R&D. The U.S. government and many U.S.-based multinational corporations have seen this approach as necessary to restore technological competitiveness. In 1984, the United States passed the National Cooperative Research Act, which allows companies to collaborate in long-term R&D projects without the threat of antitrust suits. Since then, **R&D consortia** have been established to develop technologies ranging from artificial intelligence to those in semiconductor manufacturing, such as *Sematech*. Sematech's focus is on accelerating the commercialization of technology innovations into manufacturing solutions in semiconductors and emerging technologies.[37] *The United States Council for Automotive Research* was set up by GM, Ford, and Chrysler to work on new concepts for use in the automotive sector, such as new battery technology, safety features, and recycleability. A key focus of this collaboration is on the development of hybrid technology—designed to improve efficiency and conserve energy.[38] A group of consumer goods (e.g., Unilever and Kimberly-Clark) and technology firms (such as Intermec and Marconi) formed a consortium to speed up movement of goods in supply chains at rates faster than allowed by bar codes.[39] Similar consortia in the European Union are often heavily supported by the European Commission.

These consortia can provide the benefits and face the challenges of any strategic alliance. Countering the benefits of sharing costs and risks are management woes from mixing corporate cultures as well as varying levels of enthusiasm by the participants. As long as participants work on core technologies that each can then apply in their own way in their own fields, these consortia can work very effectively.

The Testing of New Product Concepts

The final stages of the product development process will involve testing the product in terms of both its performance and its projected market acceptance. Depending on the product, testing procedures range from reliability tests in the pilot plant to minilaunches, from which the product's performance in world markets will be estimated. Any testing will prolong full-scale commercialization and increase the possibility of competitive reaction. Further, the cost of test marketing is substantial—on the average, $1 to $1.5 million per market.

Because of the high rate of new product failure (estimated at 67–95 percent[40] and usually attributed to market or marketing reasons), most companies want to be assured that their product will gain customer acceptance. They therefore engage in testing or a limited launch of the product. This may involve introducing the product in one country—for instance, Belgium or Ireland—and basing the go-ahead decision for the rest of Europe on the performance of the product in that test market. Some countries are emerging as test markets for global products. Brazil is a test market used by Procter & Gamble and Colgate before rollout into the Latin American market. Unilever uses Thailand for a test market for the Asian market.

In many cases, companies rely too much on instinct and hunch in their marketing abroad, although in domestic markets they make extensive use of testing and research. Lack of testing has led to a number of major product disasters over the years. The most serious blunder is to assume that other markets have the same priorities and lifestyles as the domestic market. After a failure in introducing canned soups in Italy in the 1960s, Campbell Soup Company repeated the experience by introducing them in Brazil in 1979. Research conducted in Brazil after the failure revealed that women fulfill their roles as homemakers in part by such tasks as making soups from scratch. A similar finding had emerged in Italy more than 20 years earlier. However, when Campbell was ready to enter the Eastern and

Central European markets in the 1990s, it was prepared for this and was careful to position the product initially as a starter or to be kept for emergencies.

Other reasons for product failure are a lack of product distinctiveness, unexpected technical problems, and mismatches between functions.[41] Mismatches between functions may occur not only between, for example, engineering and marketing, but within the marketing function as well. Engineering may design features in the product that established distribution channels or selling approaches cannot exploit. Advertising may promise the customer something that the other functions within marketing cannot deliver.

The trend is toward a complete testing of the marketing mix. All the components of the brand are tested, including formulation, packaging, advertising, and pricing. Test marketing is indispensable because prelaunch testing is an artificial situation; it tells the researcher what people say they will do, not what they will actually do. Test marketing carries major financial risks, which can be limited only if the testing can be conducted in a limited area. Ideally, this would utilize localized advertising media—that is, broadcast and print media to which only a limited region would be exposed. However, localized media are lacking even in developed markets such as Western Europe.

Because test marketing in Europe and elsewhere is risky or even impossible, researchers have developed three research methods to cope with the difficulty. **Laboratory test markets** are the least realistic in terms of consumer behavior over time, but this method allows the participants to be exposed to television advertisements, and their reactions can be measured in a controlled environment. **Microtest marketing** involves a continuous panel of consumers serviced by a retail grocery operated by the research agency. The panelists are exposed to new products through high-quality color print ads, coupons, and free samples. Initial willingness to buy and repeat buying are monitored. **Forced distribution tests** are based on a continuously reporting panel of consumers, but they encounter new products in normal retail outlets. This is realistic, but competitors are immediately aware of the new product. An important criterion for successful testing is to gain the cooperation of key retailing organizations in the market. Mars Confectionery, which was testing a new chocolate malted-milk drink in Britain, could not get distribution in major supermarkets for test products. As a result, Mars changed its approach and focused its marketing on the home delivery market.[42] Faced with a similar fate, Panda, a small licorice maker from Finland, repositioned its product and sold it through health-care stores in Britain.

The Global Product Launch[43]

The impact of an effective global product launch can be great, but so can the cost of one that is poorly executed. High development costs as well as competitive pressures are forcing companies to rush products into as many markets as possible. But at the same time, a company can ill afford new products that are not effectively introduced, marketed, and supported in each market the company competes in.

A global product launch means introducing a product into countries in three or more regions within a narrow time frame. To achieve this, a company must undertake a number of measures. The country managers should be involved in the first stage of product strategy formulation to ensure that local and regional considerations are part of the overall corporate and product messages. More important, intercountry coordination of the rollout preparations will ultimately determine the level of success in the introduction. A product launch team (consisting of product, marketing, manufacturing, sales, service, engineering, and communication representatives) can also approach problems from an industry standpoint, as opposed to a home country perspective, enhancing product competitiveness in all markets.

Adequate consideration should be given to localization and translation requirements before the launch. This means that right messages are formulated and transmitted to key internal and external audiences. Support materials have to take into account both cultural and technical differences. The advantage of a simultaneous launch is that it boosts the overall momentum and attractiveness of the product by making it immediately available in key geographic markets.

Global product launches typically require more education and support of the sales channel than do domestic efforts or drawn-out efforts. This is due to the diversity of the distribution channels in terms of the support and education they may require before the launch.

A successfully executed global launch offers several benefits. First, it permits the company to showcase its technology in all major markets at the same time. Setting a single date for the launch functions as a strict discipline to force the entire organization to gear up quickly for a successful worldwide effort. A simultaneous worldwide introduction also solves the "lame duck" dilemma of having old models available in some markets while customers know of the existence of the new product. If margins are most lucrative at the early stages of the new product's life cycle, they should be exploited by getting the product to as many markets as possible from the outset. With product development costs increasing and product life cycles shortening, marketers have to consider this approach seriously. An additional benefit of a worldwide launch may be added publicity to benefit the marketer's efforts, as happened with the introductions worldwide of Microsoft's Windows 95, 98, 2000, and XP versions.

Management of the Product and Brand Portfolio

Most marketers have a considerable number of individual items in their product portfolios, consisting of different product lines, that is, grouping's of products managed and marketed as a unit. The options for a particular portfolio (or multiple portfolios) are to expand geographically to new markets or new segments and add to existing market operations through new product lines or new product business. The marketer will need to have a balanced product and market portfolio—a proper mix of new, growing, and mature products to provide a sustainable competitive advantage.[44] As seen in *The International Marketplace 14.4*, Heinz manages its product and brand portfolios very closely.

The assessment of the product portfolio will have to take into account various interlinkages both external and internal to the firm. Geographic interlinkages call attention to market similarities, especially to possibilities of extending operations across borders. Product-market interlinkages are manifested in common customers and competitors. Finally, the similarities in present-day operations should be assessed in terms of product lines, brands, and brand positionings. As a result of such an analysis, Mars has stayed out of the U.S. chocolate milk market, despite a product-company fit, because the market is dominated by Hershey and Nestlé. However, it has entered this particular market elsewhere, such as in Europe.

Analyzing the Product Portfolio

The specific approach chosen and variables included will vary by company, according to corporate objectives and characteristics as well as the nature of the product market. A product portfolio approach based on growth rates and market share positions allows the analysis of business entities, product lines, or individual products. Exhibit 14.2 represents the product-market portfolio of Company *A*, which markets the same product line in several countries. The company is a leader in most of the markets in which it has operations, as indicated by its relative market shares. It has two cash cows (United States and Canada), four stars (Germany, Great Britain, France, and Spain), and one "problem child" (Brazil). In the mature U.S. market, Company *A* has its largest volume but only a small market share advantage compared with competition. Company *A*'s dominance is more pronounced in Canada and in the EU countries.

At the same time, Company *B*, its main competitor, although not a threat in Company *A*'s major markets, does have a commanding lead in two fast-growing markets: Japan and Brazil. As this illustration indicates, an analysis should be conducted not only of the firm's own portfolio but also of competitors' portfolios, along with a projection of the firm's and the competitors' future international products/market portfolios. Building future scenarios based on industry estimates will allow Company *A* to take remedial long-term action to counter Company *B*'s advances. In this case, Company *A* should direct resources to build market share in fast-growing markets such as Japan and Brazil.

The International
MARKETPLACE

Brands at Heinz Reign Supreme in Worldwide Markets

In 1999, the H.J. Heinz Co. bought a majority stake in ABC, the leading Indonesian soy sauce maker. As the king of ketchup, the expansion into soy sauce made logical product-line sense. Unfortunately, Unilever also had its eye on Indonesia. In 2001, Unilever acquired a majority stake in Bango, the country's number 2 soy-sauce maker. As one of the world's leading food companies, Unilever was adding Bango to a strong line-up of brands in Indonesia—Blue Band, Royco, Sariwangi, Taro, and Wall's. Heinz was then faced with battling a global food giant that had deep roots in Indonesia.

But this was a battle worth fighting since soy sauce generated almost $7 billion in global sales annually. By 2005, Unilever's Bango brand had hurt sales of the ABC brand. With the Indonesian soy sauce market valued at around $182 million, ABC's share had dropped from 40 percent in 2001 to 33 percent in 2005. Bango's share had tripled to around 32 percent in the same time period.

Heinz realized that it was going to war over the Indonesian marketplace. One of the company's first moves was to hire someone to oversee research and development. One of the new R&D director's first tasks was to organize ABC. Much to the amazement of all, the director discovered that employees kept recipes in their heads—all employees were then ordered to write down recipes so that each batch of soy sauce would be consistent. Experts in packaging were also hired. Then, Heinz hired a marketing director—from Unilever, no less. Along with the experts in packaging, the new marketing director created ABC's first packaging upgrade in 15 years. A new metallic finish was applied to the soy sauce package so as to make ABC stand out on store shelves. Ultimately, a new pouring design and lighter packaging were added.

By 2008, ABC soy sauce had become one of the hottest brands in the Heinz product line. It skyrocketed to the world's second-largest soy sauce behind the Japanese Kikkoman brand. In 2007, ABC generated more than $200 million in sales worldwide. A vast majority of these sales came from Indonesia. The ABC label also

BOTH HEINZ AND UNILEVER HAVE ENTERED THE SOY SAUCE BUSINESS IN INDONESIA.

expanded to include a few side products like beverage syrup (for nonalcoholic drinks for the Muslim celebration of Ramadan) and chili sauce. As a label, overall sales increased 44 percent in a one-year time period.

But Heinz is not focused solely on ABC. It has emerged as an innovator, launching 200 new products in 2007–2008. In this early state of innovative growth, the company has only derived 11 percent of its sales from products introduced in the past three years; thus, there's much room for growth. Not only is the company innovating in the area of new product development, it is also taking its current products into new markets. Just as soy sauce was transported from Asia to America, Heinz sees growth opportunities for its flagship product, ketchup, to expand into Indonesian homes. The plan is for good product ideas to migrate across borders in this boundaryless world.

SOURCES: Steven Gray, "A Fight For Soy Sauce Crown," *Wall Street Journal*, April 20, 2007, **http://online.wsj.com/article/ SB117701231989075912.html?mod=dist_smartbrief%20**, retrieved December 11, 2008; Matthew Boyle, "How Heinz is Spicing up Sales," *Business Week*, August 2008, **http:// www.businessweek.com/magazine/content/08_36/ b4098028900467.htm?campaign_id=rss_daily**, retrieved December 11, 2008; Matthew Boyle, "The Ketchup King Prospers," *Business Week*, September 8, 2008, 28.

In expanding markets, any company not growing rapidly risks falling behind for good. Growth may mean bringing out new items or lines or having to adjust existing products. In the last ten years, General Motors invested over $5 billion in the Brazilian car market. GM is not going to be left unchallenged, however. Fiat, for example, is hoping to regain lost ground with the Palio.[45]

Portfolios should also be used to assess market, product, and business interlinkages.[46] This effort will allow the exploitation of increasing market similarities through corporate

Exhibit 14.2

Example of a Product-Market Portfolio

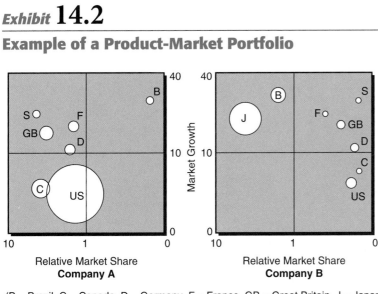

Company A   Company B

(B = Brazil, C = Canada, D = Germany, F = France, GB = Great Britain, J = Japan, S = Spain, US = United States)

SOURCE: Adapted from Jean-Claude Larréché, "The International Product-Market Portfolio," in *1978 AMA Educators' Proceedings* (Chicago: American Marketing Association, 1978), 276.

adjustments in setting up appropriate strategic business units (SBUs), and the standardization of product lines, products, and marketing programs.

The presentation in Exhibit 14.3 shows a market-product-business portfolio for a food company, such as Nestlé or Unilever. The interconnections are formed by common target markets served, sharing of research and development objectives, use of similar technologies, and the benefits that can be drawn from sharing common marketing experience. The example indicates possibilities within regions and between regions; frozen foods both in Europe and the United States, and ice cream throughout the three mega-markets.

Such assessments are integral in preparing future strategic outlines for different groups or units. For example, at Nestlé, ice cream was identified as an area of global development since the company already had a presence in a number of market areas and had identified others for their opportunity. The U.S. operations had to be persuaded to get more involved; they classified ice cream as a dairy product, whereas corporate planners saw it more as a frozen confectionery. U.S. operations produced machines and cones, and licensed brands to dairies, while corporate planners wanted to move over to self-manufacture and direct store delivery. Currently, Nestlé in the United States ranks second in the impulse–ice cream segment, and the machinery and cone businesses have been sold.[47]

Advantages of the Product Portfolio Approach

The major advantages provided by the product portfolio approach are as follows:

1. A global view of the competitive structure, especially when longer-term considerations are included

2. A guide for the formulation of a global marketing strategy based on the suggested allocation of scarce resources between product lines

3. A guide for the formulation of marketing objectives for specific markets based on an outline of the role of each product line in each of the markets served—for example, to generate cash or to block the expansion of competition

4. A convenient visual communication goal, achieved by integrating a substantial amount of information in an appealingly simple format including assessment of interlinkages between units and products

Exhibit **14.3**

Example of Market-Product-Business Portfolio

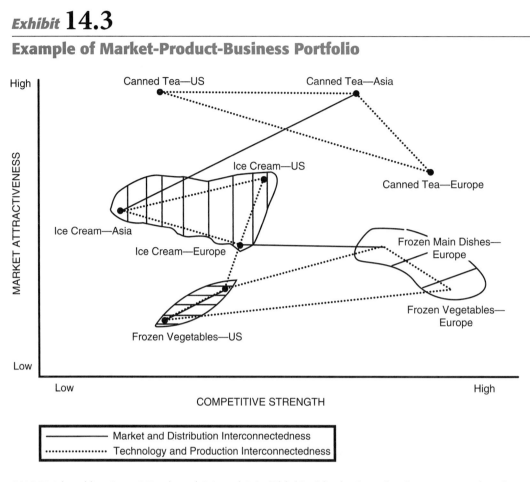

SOURCE: Adapted from Susan P. Douglas and C. Samuel Craig, "Global Portfolio Planning and Market Interconnectedness," *Journal of International Marketing 4* (no. 1, 1996): 93–110.

Before making strategic choices based on such a portfolio, the global marketer should consider the risks related to variables such as entry mode and exchange rates; management preferences for idiosyncratic objectives, such as concentrating on countries with similar market characteristics; and marketing costs. For example, the cost of entry into one market may be less because the company already has a presence there in another product category and the possibility exists that distribution networks may be shared. Similarly, ideas for new products and marketing programs can be leveraged across geographies based on both market characteristics and company position in those markets.[48]

The portfolio assessment also needs to be put into a larger context. For example, auto makers face dim prospects when it comes to markets in the United States, Europe, and Japan. Yet China experienced rapid growth in 2007. China displaced Germany as the world's third largest auto maker and surpassed Japan to become the second largest consumer of autos. Rising incomes in the country have led to consumers wanting a wider selection of autos to select from. Consumption of autos has occurred largely in the large cities within the country. However, it is expected that consumers in small- and mid-sized cities will demand autos that meet their driving needs, which will vary from those of consumers in the large cities. Auto manufacturers will have to determine the product portfolio that will meet these diverse needs.[49]

Disadvantages of the Product Portfolio Approach

The application of the product portfolio approach has a number of limitations. International competitive behavior does not always follow the same rules as in the firm's domestic market; for example, the major local competitor may be a government-owned firm whose main objective is to maintain employment. With European integration, many believed that the continent's $20 billion appliance business would consolidate into a handful of companies. Whirlpool was the major non-EU company that wanted to take advantage of the emerging opportunity and was expected to gain 20 percent of the market. However, its 12 percent share in the late 1990s was testimony that local companies were not standing still while foreigners invaded their turf. Whirlpool then shifted their orientation from local and regional to global by laying off workers, building up core businesses, and focusing on profits.[50]

The relationship between market share and profitability may be blurred by a number of factors in the marketing environment. Government regulations in every market have an impact on the products a company can market. For instance, major U.S. tobacco manufacturers estimated they could capture 30 percent of Japan's cigarette market of $10 billion a year if it were not for restrictions that apply only to non-Japanese producers.

Product lines offered will also be affected by various local content laws—those stipulating that a prescribed percentage of the value of the final product must be manufactured locally. Market tastes have an important impact on product lines. These not only may alter the content of a product but also may require an addition in a given market that is not available elsewhere. The Coca-Cola Company has market leadership in a product category unique to Japan: coffee-flavored soft drinks. The market came into existence some 20 years ago and grew rapidly, eventually accounting for 10 percent of soft-drink sales. The beverage is packaged like any other soft drink and is available through vending machines, which dispense hot cans in the winter and cold servings during warm weather. Although Coca-Cola executives have considered introducing "Georgia" in the United States, they are skeptical about whether the product would succeed, mainly because of declining coffee consumption and the lack of a vending machine network. Also, adoption of the concept by U.S. consumers is doubtful.

The fact that global firms produce the same products in different locations may have an impact on consumer perceptions of product risk and quality. If the product is produced in an emerging country, for example, the global marketer has to determine whether a well-known brand name can compensate for the concern a customer might feel. The situation may be more complicated for retailers importing from independent producers in developing nations under the retailer's private labels. In general, country-of-origin effects on product perceptions are more difficult to determine since the introduction of hybrid products.

Managing the Brand Portfolio

Branding is one of the major beneficiaries of a well-conducted portfolio analysis. Brands are important because they shape customer decisions and, ultimately, create economic value. Brand is a key factor behind the decision to purchase in both consumer and business-to-business situations, as shown in the results of a worldwide study summarized in Exhibit 14.4. On the average, brand was responsible for 18 percent of total purchase decisions, and the majority of the studies revealed a brand-loyal segment of individuals for whom the brand was the major influencing factor. In addition, strong brands are able to charge a price premium of 19 percent.[51] Gillette's Mach3, although priced more than 50 percent above its predecessor (Sensor Excel), was able to increase sales by 30 percent since rollout.[52] Research into the connection of brand strength and corporate performance at 130 multinational companies revealed that strong brands generate total returns to shareholders that are 1.9 percent above the industry average, while weaker brands lag behind the average by 3.1 percent.[53]

Brands are a major benefit to the customer as well. They simplify everyday choices, reduce the risk of complicated buying decisions, provide emotional benefits, and offer a sense of community. In technology (e.g., computer chips), where products change at an ever-increasing pace, branding is critical—far more so than in packaged goods, where a product may be more understandable because it stays the same or very similar over time. "Intel Inside," which derived from Intel's ad agency recommending "Intel, the Computer Inside" and the Japanese operation's "Intel In It," increased the company's brand awareness from 22 percent to 80 percent within two years of its introduction.[54]

Exhibit 14.4

Importance of Brand in Decision Making

Relative importance of brand

Type	Brand importance	Location of study
Electronics–computer	39%	Europe
Electrical utilities	25	US
Electronics–computer	26	US
Telecom–international calls	21	US
Airline	21	US
Telecom–inbound calls	20	US
Food beverage	20	US
Telecom–outbound calls	19	US
PFS–retail banking	18	Europe
Telecom–fixed lines	17	Asia
Telecom–mobile	16	US
PFS–retail banking	15	US
Telecom–fixed lines	15	US
Telecom–mobile	15	US
Telecom–fixed lines	14	Asia
HMO	14	US
PFS–mortgages	15	Europe
PFS–direct insurance	13	Europe
Car	12	Europe
Electronics–computer	12	US
Electronics–computer	12	US
Telecom–mobile	7	Europe

■ Consumer market   ▦ Business market

SOURCE: Adapted from David Court, Anthony Freeling, Mark Leiter, and Andre J. Parsons, "Uncovering the Value of Brands," *The McKinsey Quarterly* 32 (no. 4, 1996): 176.

STARBUCKS RELIED ON THE STRENGTH OF ITS BRAND IN BREAKING INTO NEW MARKETS, INCLUDING VIENNA, EUROPE'S CAFÉ CAPITAL.

The benefit of a strong brand name is, in addition to the price premium that awareness and loyalty allow, the ability to exploit the brand in a new market or a new product category. In a global marketplace, customers are aware of brands even though the products themselves may not be available. This was the case, for example, in many of the former Soviet Republics, before their markets opened up. Starbucks relied on the strength of its brand in breaking into new markets, including Vienna, Europe's café capital.[55]

Global marketers have three choices of branding within the global, regional, and local dimensions: brands can feature the corporate name, have family brands for a wide range of products or product variations, or have individual brands for each item in the product line. With the increase in strategic alliances, co-branding, in which two or more well-known brands are combined in an offer, has also become popular. Examples of these approaches include Heinz, which has a policy of using its corporate name in all its products, Procter & Gamble, which has a policy of stand-alone products or product lines, and Nestlé, which uses a mixture of Nestlé and Nes-designated brands and stand-alones. In the case of marketing alliances, the brand portfolio may be a combination of both partners'

Exhibit **14.5**

Best Global Brands for 2008

2008 Rank	2007 Rank	Brand	Country of Origin	Sector	2008 Brand Value ($m)	Change in Brand Value
1	1	Coca-Cola	United States	Beverages	66,667	2%
2	3	IBM	United States	Computer Services	59,031	3%
3	2	Microsoft	United States	Computer Software	59,007	1%
4	4	GE	United States	Diversified	53,086	3%
5	5	Nokia	Finland	Consumer Electronics	35,942	7%
6	6	Toyota	Japan	Automotive	34,050	6%
7	7	Intel	United States	Computer Hardware	31,261	1%
8	8	McDonald's	United States	Restaurants	31,049	6%
9	9	Disney	United States	Media	29,251	0%
10	20	Google	United States	Internet Services	25,590	43%
11	10	Mercedes-Benz	Germany	Automotive	25,577	9%
12	12	Hewlett-Packard	United States	Computer Hardware	23,509	6%
13	13	BMW	Germany	Automotive	23,298	8%
14	16	Gillette	United States	Personal Care	22,689	8%
15	15	American Express	United States	Financial Services	21,940	5%
16	17	Louis Vuitton	France	Luxury	21,602	6%
17	18	Cisco	United States	Computer Services	21,306	12%
18	14	Marlboro	United States	Tobacco	21,300	0%
19	11	Citi	United States	Financial Services	20,174	−14%
20	19	Honda	Japan	Automotive	19,079	6%
21	21	Samsung	Republic of Korea	Consumer Electronics	17,689	5%
22	New	H&M	Sweden	Apparel	13,840	New
23	27	Oracle	United States	Computer Software	13,831	11%
24	33	Apple	United States	Computer Hardware	13,724	24%
25	25	Sony	Japan	Consumer Electronics	13,583	5%

SOURCE: Interbrand, Best Global Brands List 2008, **http://www.interbrand.com**.

brands. General Mills' alliance with Nestlé in cereals, Cereal Partners Worldwide, features General Mills brands such as Trix and Nestlé brands such as Chocapic.[56]

Market power is usually in the hands of brand-name companies that have to determine the most effective use of this asset across markets. The value of brands can be seen in recent acquisitions where prices have been many times over the book value of the company purchased. Nestlé, for example, paid five times the book value for the British Rowntree, the owner of such brands as Kit Kat and After Eight. Many of the world's leading brands command high brand equity values, in other words, the price premium the brand commands times the extra volume it moves over what an average brand commands.[57]

An example of global rankings of brands is provided in Exhibit 14.5. This Interbrand-sponsored study rates brands on their value and their strength. Each ranked brand had to derive at least one-third of its earnings outside its home country, be recognizable beyond its established customer base, and have publicly available marketing and financial data. The ranking is truly on the strength of individual brands, not a portfolio of brands. Of the top 100 global brands in terms of brand value in 2007, 2 are Canadian, 9 are Asian, 37 are European, and 52 are based in the United States.

Brand Strategy Decisions

The goal of many marketers currently is to create consistency and impact, both of which are easier to manage with a single worldwide identity.[58] **Global brands** are a key way of reaching this goal. Global brands are those that reach the world's mega-markets and are perceived as the same brand by consumers and internal constituents.[59] While some of the global brands are completely standardized, some elements of the product may be adapted to local conditions. These adjustments include brand names (e.g., Tide, Whisper, and Clairol in North America are Ariel, Allways, and Wella in Europe), positioning (e.g., Ford Fiesta as a small car in Germany but a family vehicle in Portugal), or product versions sold under the same brand name (e.g., 9–13 different types of coffee sold under the Nescafé name in Northern Europe alone).[60]

Consumers all over the world associate global brands with three characteristics and evaluate their performance on them when making purchase decisions.[61] Global brands carry a strong quality signal suggested by their success across markets. Part of this is that great brands often represent great ideas and leading-edge technological solutions. Secondly, global brands compete on emotion, catering to aspirations that cut across cultural differences. Global brands may cater to needs to feel cosmopolitan, something that local brands cannot deliver. Global brands may also convey that their user has reached a certain status both professionally and personally. This type of recognition represents both perception and reality, enabling brands to establish credibility in markets.[62] The third reason consumers choose global brands is involvement in solving social problems linked to what they are marketing and how they conduct their business. Expectations that global marketers use their monetary and human resources to benefit society are uniform from developed to developing markets.

There are three main implications for the marketing manager to consider: (1) Don't hide globality. Given the benefits of globality, marketers should not be shy in communicating this feature of a brand. Creatively, this may mean referring to the leadership position of the brand around the world or referring to the extent of innovation or features that are possible only for a brand with considerable reach. Marketers intent on scaling down their brand portfolios and focusing on global offerings are able to invest in more marketing muscle and creative effort behind the sleeker set of offerings. (2) Tackle home-country bias. One of the marketing mantras is "being local on a global scale." Since some markets feature substantial preference for home-grown brands, it is imperative to localize some features of the marketing approach, possibly including even the brand name. One approach could be that a brand has a consistent global positioning but the name varies according to country language. An example is Mr. Clean becoming Mr. Propre in France. Many global brands have already localized to neutralize the home-country effect. (3) Satisfy the basics. Global brands signal quality and aspiration. However, taking a global approach to branding is not in itself the critical factor. What is critical is creating differentiation and familiarity as well as the needed margins and growth. The greater esteem that global brands enjoy is not sufficient in itself for pursuing this strategy. However, this dimension may tip the balance in ultimate strategy choice. At the same time, it is evident that globality should not be pursued at the cost of alienating local consumers by preemptively eliminating purely local brands or converging them under a global brand.[63]

Branding is an integral part of the overall identity management of the firm.[64] Global brands need to achieve a high degree of consistency in their delivery of customer service and how it is communicated across all consumer points of touch. Therefore, it is typically a centralized function to exploit to the fullest the brand's assets as well as to protect the asset from dilution by, for example, extending the brand to inappropriate new lines. The role of headquarters, strategic business unit management, global teams, or global managers charged with a product is to provide guidelines for the effort without hampering local initiative at the same time.[65] The "glocal" dimension can only be achieved by giving regional and local managers the power to interpret and express the message. In addition to the use of a global brand name from the very beginning, many marketers are consolidating their previously different brand names (often for the same or similar products) with global or regional brand names. For example, Mars replaced its Treets and Bonitas names with M&M worldwide and renamed its British best-seller, Marathon, with the Snickers name it uses in North and South America. The benefits in global branding are in marketing economies and higher acceptance of products by consumers and intermediaries. The drawbacks are in the loss of local flavor, especially when a local brand is replaced by a regional or global brand name. At these times, internal marketing becomes critical to instill ownership of the global brands in the personnel of the country organizations.[66]

An example of a brand portfolio is provided in Exhibit 14.6. It indicates four levels of brands at Nestlé: worldwide corporate and strategic brands, regional strategic brands,

Exhibit 14.6

Nestlé's Branding Tree

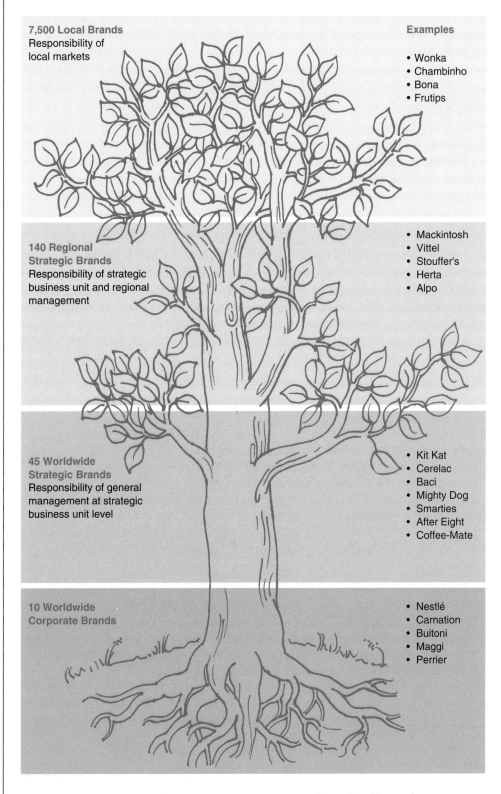

7,500 Local Brands
Responsibility of local markets

Examples
- Wonka
- Chambinho
- Bona
- Frutips

140 Regional Strategic Brands
Responsibility of strategic business unit and regional management

- Mackintosh
- Vittel
- Stouffer's
- Herta
- Alpo

45 Worldwide Strategic Brands
Responsibility of general management at strategic business unit level

- Kit Kat
- Cerelac
- Baci
- Mighty Dog
- Smarties
- After Eight
- Coffee-Mate

10 Worldwide Corporate Brands

- Nestlé
- Carnation
- Buitoni
- Maggi
- Perrier

SOURCE: "Daring, Defying to Grow," *Economist,* August 7, 2004, 55–58 figure adapted from Andrew J. Parsons, "Nestlé: The Visions of Local Managers," *The McKinsey Quarterly* (no. 2, 1996): 5–29.

and local brands. The worldwide brands are under the responsibility of SBU and general management, which establish a framework for each in the form of a planning policy document. These policies lay out the brand's positioning, labeling standards, packaging features, and other related marketing mix issues, such as a communications platform. The same principle applies to regional brands, where guidelines are issued and decisions made by SBU and regional management. Among the 7,500 local brands are 700 local strategic brands, such as Chambinho in Brazil, which are monitored by the SBUs for positioning and labeling standards. Nestlé is consolidating its efforts behind its corporate and strategic brands. This is taking place in various ways. When Nestlé acquired Rowntree, which had had a one-product one-brand policy, it added its corporate name to some of the products, such as Nestlé Kit Kat. Its refrigerated products line under the Chambourcy brand is undergoing a name change to Nestlé. Some of the products that do not carry the corporate name feature a Nestlé Seal of Guarantee on the back. About 40 percent of the company's sales come from products covered by the corporate brand.[67] L'Oreal is managed independently due to the fact that Nestlé is only a 26.4 percent owner in the corporation that in itself markets brands such as Maybelline, Helena Rubinstein, Garnier, and SoftSheen-Carson.[68]

Carefully crafted brand portfolios allow marketers to serve defined parts of specific markets. At Whirlpool, the Whirlpool brand name will be used as the global brand to serve the broad middle market segment, while regional and local brands will cover the others. For example, throughout Europe, the Bauknecht brand is targeted at the upper end of the market seeking a reputable German brand. Ignis and Laden are positioned as price value brands, Ignis Europe-wide, Laden in France. This approach applies to Whirlpool's other markets as well: in Latin America, Consul is the major regional brand.[69]

The brand portfolio needs to be periodically and regularly assessed. A number of global marketers are focusing their attention on "A" brands with the greatest growth potential. By continuing to dispose of noncore brands, the marketer can concentrate on the global ones and reduce production, marketing, storage, and distribution costs. It is increasingly difficult for the global company to manage purely local brands. The surge of private label products has also put additional pressure on "B" brands.[70]

However, before disposing of a brand, managers need to assess it in terms of current sales, loyalty, potential, and trends. For example, eliminating a local brand that may have a strong and loyal following, has been created by local management, and shows potential to be extended to nearby markets is not necessarily in the best interests of the company. Three approaches for purely local brands may work: a penetration price approach, a cultural approach positioning the product as a true defender of local culture, and a "chameleon" approach, in which the brand tries not to look local.[71] The number-one chewing gum brand in France for the past 25 years has been Cadbury Schweppes' Hollywood.

Private Brand Policies

The emergence of strong intermediaries has led to the significant increase in private brand goods, that is, the intermediaries' own branded products or "store brands." Two general approaches have been used: umbrella branding, where a number of products are covered using the same brand (often the intermediary's name), and separate brand names for individual products or product lines.

With price sensitivity increasing and brand loyalty decreasing, private brand goods have achieved a significant penetration in many countries. The overall penetration of private brand goods in the United Kingdom is 42 percent, in Germany 41 percent, in Finland 26 percent, and in France 32 percent.[72] Over the past 20 years, private brand sales in the United States have averaged 14 percent of supermarket sales. As both the trades and consumers become more sophisticated, private brands' market share is expected to reach U.K. levels in many parts of Europe and the world.

While private brand success can be shown to be affected strongly by economic conditions and the self-interest of retailers who want to improve their bottom lines through the contribution of private label goods, new factors have emerged to make the phenomenon more long-lived and significant in changing product choices worldwide. The level of private brand share will vary by country and by product category, reflecting variations in customer perceptions, intermediary strength, and behavior of leading branders.[73]

The improved quality of private brand products and the development of segmented private brand products have been major changes in the last ten years. While 60 percent of consumers still state that they prefer the comfort, security, and value of a manufacturer's brand over a private brand, as found in a DDB Needham survey,[74] a McKinsey survey found most consumers preferring such products also had no hesitation in buying the private brand.[75] Encouraged by this, private brands have been expanding to new product categories with the hope of increased acceptance by consumers.[76] Beyond just offering products, many retailers are focusing on a broader approach. For example, Tesco in the United Kingdom has focused on the design of its own-label products with the goal of projecting a more uniform image across product categories. Some premium private brand products have been developed to reposition manufacturer's brands. In Canada, for example, Loblaw's President's Choice brand and its regular private brand line squeeze national brands in between the two. Some U.S. chains have also started carrying this line of premium products.

European supermarket chains have had enormous success with private brands mainly due to their power over manufacturers. While the five largest operators in the United States command only 21 percent of supermarket sales, the figure in the United Kingdom is 62 percent, and in Finland the four leading wholesaler-led chains control over 90 percent. With the emergence of new types of intermediaries, such as mass merchandisers and warehouse clubs, this phenomenon will expand as these players exercise their procurement clout over manufacturers. Furthermore, many retailers believe that strong private brand programs can successfully differentiate their outlets and solidify shoppers' loyalty, thereby strengthening their position vis-à-vis manufacturers, and resulting in increasing profitability.[77]

The internationalization of retailers carrying or even focusing solely on private labels has given an additional boost to the phenomenon, such as German ALDI, which sells only its own private label goods in its stores throughout Europe, the United States (with over 1000 stores in 29 states), and Australia.[78] ALDI's focus is on cutting costs rather than sacrificing quality, permitting it to drive out low-quality brands that trade only on price.

With the increasing opportunities in the private brand categories, the marketing manager will have to make critical strategic choices, which are summarized in Exhibit 14.7. If the marketer operates in an environment where consumers have an absolute preference for manufacturers' brands and where product innovation is a critical factor of success, the marketer can refuse to participate. Brand leaders can attack private brands and thereby direct their ambitions on smaller competitors, which often may be local-only players. The argument

Exhibit 14.7

Private Brand Strategies

Strategy	Rationale	Circumstance
No participation	Refusal to produce private label	Heavily branded markets; high distinctiveness; technological advantage
Capacity filling	Opportunistic	
Market control	Influence category sales	High brand shares where distinctiveness is less; more switching by consumers
Competitive leverage	Stake in both markets	
Chief source of business	Major focus	Little or no differentiation by consumers
Dedicated producer	Leading cost position	

SOURCES: Adapted from Sabine Bonnot, Emma Carr, and Michael J. Reyner, "Fighting Brawn with Brains," *The McKinsey Quarterly* 40 (no. 2, 2000): 85–92; and François Glémet and Rafael Mira, "The Brand Leader's Dilemma," *The McKinsey Quarterly* 33 (no. 2, 1993): 4.

for strategic participation is that since the phenomenon cannot be eliminated, it is best to be involved. For example, Nestlé sells ice cream called Grandessa for ALDI through an acquired unit called Scholler.[79] Reasons include capacity filling, economies of scale, improved relationships with trade, and valuable information about consumer behavior and costs. The argument that profits from private brand manufacture can be used for promotion of the manufacturer's own brands may be eliminated by the relatively thin margins and the costs of having to set up a separate private brand manufacturing and marketing organization. Participation in the private brand category may, however, be inconsistent with the marketer's global brand and product strategy by raising questions about quality standards, by diluting management attention, and by affecting consumers' perception of the main branded business. Many marketers pursue a mixture of these strategies as a function of marketing and market conditions. Wilkinson Sword, for example, produces private brand disposable razors for the most dominant chain in Finland, the K-Group, thereby enabling it to compete on price against other branded products (especially the French Bic) and increasing its share of shelf space. While H.J. Heinz produces insignificant amounts for private brand distributors in the United States, most of its U.K. production is for private brand.

Summary

The global product planning effort must determine two critical decisions: (1) how and where the company's products should be developed, and (2) how and where the present and future product lines should be marketed.

In product development, multinational corporations are increasingly striving toward finding common denominators to rationalize worldwide production. This is achieved through careful coordination of the product development process by worldwide or regional development teams. No longer is the parent company the only source of new products. New product ideas emerge throughout the system and are developed by the entity most qualified to do so.

The global marketer's product line is not the same worldwide. The standard line items are augmented by local items or localized variations of products to better cater to the unique needs of individual markets. External variables such as competition and regulations often determine the final composition of the line and how broadly it is marketed.

Global marketers will also have to determine the extent to which they will use one of their greatest assets, brands, across national markets. Marketers will have to choose among global brands, regional brands, and purely local approaches as well as forgoing their own branding in favor of becoming a supplier for private brand efforts of retailers. Efficiencies of standardization must be balanced with customer preferences and internal issues of motivation at the country-market level.

Key Terms

lead users	laboratory test markets	global brands
computer-aided design (CAD)	microtest marketing	
R&D consortia	forced distribution tests	

Questions for Discussion

1. How can a company's product line reflect the maxim "think globally, act locally"?

2. Will a globally oriented company have an advantage over a multidomestic, or even a domestic, company in the next generation of new product ideas?

3. What factors should be considered when deciding on the location of research and development facilities?

4. What factors make product testing more complicated in the international marketplace?

5. What are the benefits of a coordinated global product launch? What factors will have to be taken into consideration before the actual launch?

6. Argue for and against the use of the corporate name in global branding.

Internet Exercises

1. Using the list of the world's leading brands (available at http://www.interbrand.com), evaluate why certain brands place high, some lower.

2. How is Gillette using its website (http://www.gillette.com) to attract the younger generation to its product portfolios.

Recommended Readings

Adamson, Allen P., and Martin Sorrell. *BrandSimple: How the Best Brands Keep it Simple and Succeed.* Hampshire, England: Palgrave-Macmillan, 2007.

Dhar, Mainak. *Brand Management 101: 101 Lessons from Real-World Marketing.* Hoboken, NJ: Wiley, 2007.

Estrin, Judy. *Closing the Innovation Gap: Reigniting the Spark of Creativity in a Global Economy.* Columbus, OH: McGraw-Hill, 2008.

Kapferer, Jean-Noel. *The New Strategic Brand Management: Creating and Sustaining Brand Equity Long Term.* London: Kogan Page, 2008.

Keller, Kevin Lane. *Strategic Brand Management.* Upper Saddle Creek, NJ: Prentice-Hall, 2007.

Koulopoulos, Thomas M., and Tom Roloff. *Smartsourcing: Driving Innovation and Growth through Outsourcing.* La Crosse, WI: Platinum Press, 2006.

Prahalad, C.K., and M.S. Krishnan. *The New Age of Innovation: Driving Cocreated Value through Global Networks.* Columbus, OH: McGraw-Hill, 2008.

Skarzynski, Peter, and Rowan Gibson. *Innovation to the Core: A Blueprint for Transforming the Way Your Company Innovates.* Boston, MA: Harvard Business School Press, 2008.

GLOBAL SERVICES

KTF as a Global Competitor in Service Innovation

KTF was established in Korea as Korea Telecom Freetel. KTF started commercial nationwide PCS services in 1997. The company began the era of public wireless communication services in Korea and was listed in the Guinness Book of World Records in 2000 for being the first company, worldwide, to record one million subscribers in the shortest period of time. Within its first three years of operation, KTF acquired over nine million subscribers. The company ranked first in mobile communications companies in BusinessWeek's top 100 global IT companies in 2006.

The key to this service provider's continued success has not been just in market development. KTF focused on sustaining its competitive edge by emphasizing service quality and telecommunications technologies.

With regard to technology, KTF has many "firsts" under its belt:

- Commercialized services for the first time anywhere in the world to broadcast the World Cup football games to mobile phones
- Began the era of video calling that enabled anyone to talk and see the other party by launching the first nationwide service
- Introduced various "daily life" services such as the first interactive text information service

KTF SEEKS TO ENHANCE THE QUALITY OF THE OVERALL CUSTOMER EXPERIENCE BY BEING FUN, CONVENIENT, AND ENJOYABLE.

With growing market saturation and consumer expectations, KTF knew that it had to adapt its marketing strategy to a more mature and knowledgeable marketplace. In 2007, the company transitioned to "design and emotional" marketing.

The intent of this strategy is to provide customers with a "good time" with KTF and its service offerings. Phrased as the company's "Good Time Management" philosophy, KTF seeks to enhance the quality of the overall customer experience. Management wants to make KTF fun, convenient, and enjoyable. KTF does so by helping the customer look good (fun), work well (convenient), and feel good (enjoyable). The company wants to be the consumer's personal hub in the digital world by providing optimal service, anytime and anywhere. The company's vision is stated as, "Create a far-reaching partnership with customers through the concept of a "Personal Life Hub" to be the world's top ICET (Information, Communication, Entertainment, and Transaction) corporation." The strategic themes underlying this vision are: (1) lead market through innovation, (2) creation of a new future lifestyle, and (3) strive to become a global corporation. The company has five core values as its foundation: all for customers, creativity, trust, innovation, and ownership.

Thus far, KTF has been able to generate a steady stream of revenue growth through services that stimulate the customer's emotions. While doing so, it has won the Korean Customer Satisfactions Award for five years in succession. KTF is spreading its customer message throughout the Asia-Pacific via partnerships with wireless communications companies in Australia, India, Indonesia, and Malaysia.

SOURCES: Won-Sik Lee and Bo-Young Kim, "Designed by KTF: A Telecoms Case Study," *Design Management Review*, Winter 2008, 53–58; **http://www.ktf.com**.

nternational services marketing is a major component of world business. This chapter will highlight marketing dimensions that are specific to services, with particular attention given to their international aspects. A discussion of the differences between the marketing of services and of goods will be followed by insights on the role of services in the United States and in the world economy. The chapter will explore the opportunities and new problems that have arisen from the increase in international services marketing, focusing particularly on the worldwide transformations of industries as a result of profound changes in the environment and in technology. The strategic responses to these transformations by both governments and firms will be described. Finally, the chapter will outline the initial steps that firms need to undertake in order to offer services internationally—and will look at the future of international services marketing.

Differences between Services and Goods

We rarely contemplate or analyze the precise role of services in our lives. As *The International Marketplace 15.1* shows, companies are recognizing that the race for global success demands service innovations. Services often accompany goods, but they are also, by themselves, an increasingly important part of our economy, domestically and internationally. One writer has contrasted services and products by stating that "a good is an object, a device, a thing; a service is a deed, a performance, an effort."[1] This definition, although quite general, captures the essence of the difference between goods and services. Services tend to be more intangible, personalized, and custom-made than goods. Services are also often marketed differently from goods. While goods are typically distributed to the customer, services can be transferred across borders or originated abroad, and the service provider can be transferred to the customer or the customer can be transferred to the service territory. Services also typically use a different approach to customer satisfaction. It has been stated that "service firms do not have products in the form of preproduced solutions to customers' problems; they have processes as solutions to such problems."[2]

Services are the fastest-growing sector of world trade, far outpacing the growth in the trade of goods. These major differences add dimensions to services that are not present in goods and thus call for a major differentiation.

Linkage between Services and Goods

Services may complement goods; at other times, goods may complement services. Offering goods that are in need of substantial technological support and maintenance may be useless if no proper assurance for service can be provided. For this reason, the initial contract of

Services as a Portion of Gross Domestic Product

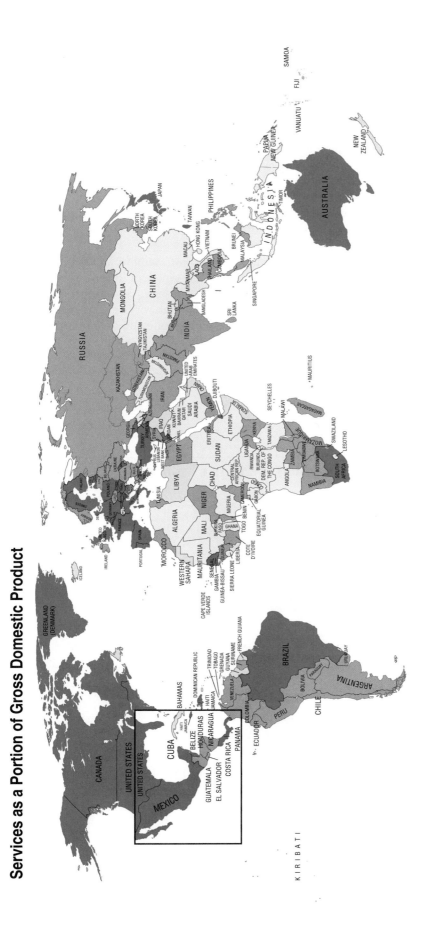

Services as a percentage of GDP

- 61% to 85%
- 41% to 60%
- 21% to 40%
- 0% to 20%
- No current data available

sale often includes important service dimensions. This practice is common in aircraft sales. When an aircraft is purchased, the buyer often contracts not only for the physical good—namely, the plane—but also for training of personnel, maintenance service, and the promise of continuous technological updates. Similarly, the sale of computer hardware is critically linked to the availability of proper servicing and software.

This linkage between goods and services can make international marketing efforts quite difficult. A foreign buyer, for example, may wish to purchase helicopters and contract for service support over a period of ten years. If the sale involves a U.S. firm, both the helicopter and the service sale will require an export license. Such licenses, however, are issued only for an immediate sale. Therefore, over the ten years, the seller will have to apply for an export license each time service is to be provided. Because the issuance of a license is often dependent on the political climate, the buyer and seller are haunted by uncertainty. As a result, sales may be lost to firms in countries that can unconditionally guarantee the long-term supply of support services.

Services can be just as dependent on goods. For example, an airline that prides itself on providing an efficient reservation system and excellent linkups with rental cars and hotel reservations could not survive without its airplanes. As a result, many offerings in the marketplace consist of a combination of goods and services. A graphic illustration of the tangible and intangible elements in the market offering of an airline is provided in Exhibit 15.1.

Exhibit **15.1**

Tangible and Intangible Offerings of Airlines

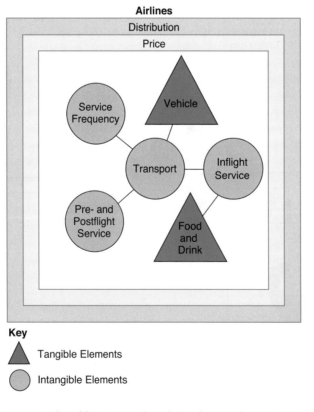

Key

▲ Tangible Elements

● Intangible Elements

SOURCE: Adapted from G. Lynn Shostack, "Breaking Free from Product Marketing," in *Services Marketing,* ed. Christopher H. Lovelock (Englewood Cliffs, NJ: Prentice-Hall, 1984), 40.

The simple knowledge that services and goods interact, however, is not enough. Successful managers must recognize that different customer groups will frequently view the service/goods combination differently. The type of use and usage conditions will also affect evaluations of the market offering. For example, the intangible dimension of "on-time arrival" by airlines may be valued differently by college students than by business executives. Similarly, a 20-minute delay will be judged differently by a passenger arriving at her final destination than by one who has just missed an overseas connection. As a result, adjustment possibilities in both the service and the goods area can be used as strategic tools to stimulate demand and increase profitability. For different offerings, service and goods elements may vary substantially. The marketer must identify the role of each and adjust all of them to meet the desires of the target customer group.

Stand-Alone Services

Services do not always come in unison with goods. Increasingly, they compete against goods and become an alternative offering. For example, rather than buy an in-house computer, the business executive can contract computing work to a local or foreign service firm. Similarly, the purchase of a car (a good) can be converted into the purchase of a service by leasing the car from an agency.

Services may also compete against each other. As an example, a store may have the option of offering full service to consumers who purchase there or of converting to the self-service format. With automated checkout services, consumers may self-serve all activities such as selection, transportation, packaging, and pricing.

Services differ from goods most strongly in their intangibility: They are frequently consumed rather than possessed. Even though the intangibility of services is a primary differentiating criterion, it is not always present. For example, publishing services ultimately result in a tangible good, namely, a book or an article. Similarly, construction services eventually result in a building, a subway, or a bridge. Even in those instances, however, the intangible component that leads to the final product is of major concern to both the producer of the service and the recipient of the ultimate output because it brings with it major considerations that are not traditional to goods.

One major difference concerns the storing of services. Because of their nature, services are difficult to inventory. If they are not used, the "brown around the edges" syndrome tends to result in high services perishability. Unused capacity in the form of an empty seat on an airplane, for example, becomes nonsaleable quickly. Once the plane has taken off, selling an empty seat is virtually impossible—except for an inflight upgrade from coach to first class—and the capacity cannot be stored for future usage. Similarly, the difficulty of keeping services in inventory makes it troublesome to provide service backup for peak demand. Constantly maintaining service capacity at levels necessary to satisfy peak demand would be very expensive. The marketer must therefore attempt to smooth out demand levels through price or promotion activities in order to optimize the use of capacity.

For many service offerings, the time of production is very close to or even simultaneous with the time of consumption. This fact points toward close customer involvement in the production of services. Customers frequently either service themselves or cooperate in the delivery of services. As a result, the service provider often needs to be physically present when the service is delivered. This physical presence creates both problems and opportunities, and it introduces a new constraint that is seldom present in the marketing of goods. For example, close interaction with the customer requires a much greater understanding of and emphasis on the cultural dimension. A good service delivered in a culturally unacceptable fashion is doomed to failure. Sensitivity to culture, beliefs, and preferences is imperative in the services industry. In some instances, the need to be sensitive to diverse customer groups in domestic markets can greatly assist a company in preparing for international market expansion. A common pattern of internationalization for service businesses is therefore to develop stand-alone business systems in each country. At the same time, however, some services have become "delocalized" as advances in modern technology have made it possible for firms to delink production and service processes and switch labor-intensive service performance to countries where qualified, low-cost labor is plentiful.

The close interaction with customers also points toward the fact that services often are custom-made. This contradicts the desire of a firm to standardize its offering; yet at the same time, it offers the service provider an opportunity to differentiate the service from the competition. The concomitant problem is that in order to fulfill customer expectations, **service consistency** is required. As with anything offered in real time, however, consistency is difficult to maintain over the long run. The human element in the service offering therefore takes on a much greater role than in the offering of goods. Errors can enter the system, and nonpredictable individual influences can affect the outcome of the service delivery. The issue of quality control affects the provider as well as the recipient of services. Efforts to increase such control through uniformity may sometimes be seen by customers as a reduction in service choices. The **quality perception** of service customers is largely determined by the behavior of the employees they contact. Customer-contact workers are therefore a key internal group whose skills must be addressed systematically through internal marketing, which takes place between firms and employees. The target groups of internal marketing are managers and employees of all levels who handle customer concerns. They must first be convinced that complaints contain business opportunities rather than dangers, and must therefore be handled in a positive and proactive manner. Second, achievement-based rewards should be established to create complaint management incentives for employees.[3]

Buyers have more problems in observing and evaluating services than goods. This is particularly true when a shopper tries to choose intelligently among service providers. Even when sellers of services are willing and able to provide more **market transparency** where the details of the service are clear, comparable, and available to all interested parties, the buyer's problem is complicated: Customers receiving the same service may use it differently and service quality may vary for each delivery. Since production lines cannot be established to deliver an identical service each time, and the quality of a service cannot be tightly controlled, the problem of service heterogeneity emerges, meaning that services may never be the same from one delivery to another.[4] For example, a teacher's advice, even if it is provided on the same day by the same person, may vary substantially depending on the student. Over time, even for the same student, the counseling may change. As a result, service offerings are not directly comparable, which makes quality measurements quite challenging. Therefore, the reputation of the service provider plays an overwhelming role in the customer choice process.

Services often require entirely new forms of distribution. Traditional channels are often multitiered and long and therefore slow. They often cannot be used because of the perishability of services. A weather news service, for example, either reaches its audience quickly or rapidly loses its value. As a result, direct delivery and short distribution channels are often required. When they do not exist—which is often the case domestically and even more so internationally—service providers need to be distribution innovators in order to reach their market.

All these aspects of services exist in both international and domestic settings. Their impact, however, takes on greater importance for the international marketer. For example, because of the longer distances involved, service perishability that may be an obstacle in domestic business becomes a barrier internationally. Similarly, the issue of quality control for international services may be much more difficult to deal with due to different service uses, changing expectations, and varying national regulations.

Because services are delivered directly to the user, they are frequently much more sensitive to cultural factors than are products. Sometimes their influence on the individual may even be considered with hostility abroad. For example, the showing of U.S. films in cinemas or television abroad is often attacked as an imposition of U.S. culture. National leaders who place strong emphasis on national cultural identity frequently denounce foreign services and attempt to hinder their market penetration. Even dimensions that one thinks to be highly standardized around the globe may need to be adapted. As an example, see Exhibit 15.2. As you can tell, many nations have developed their very own meaning of the symbol. Similarly, services are subject to many political vagaries occurring almost daily. Yet coping with these changes can become the service provider's competitive advantage.

Exhibit 15.2

Symbolism

What do people around the world call the "@" symbol, so prevalent in e-mail addresses? While in the United States most people say "at," in other countries it's referred to by different, and often humorous, names associated with what the @ reminds speakers of.

DOG

In Russia, the most common word for @ is *sobaka* or *sobachka*, meaning "dog" and "little doggie," respectively.

MONKEY

In countries such as Bulgaria, Poland, and Serbia, the @ symbol seems to remind speakers of a monkey with a long tail. They refer to it as *alpa* (Polish), *majmunkso* (Bulgarian), and *majmun* (Serbian). Another variation is "ape's tail," said as *aapstert* in Afrikaans, *apestaart* in Dutch, and *apsvans* in Swedish.

SNAIL

While traditional stamp and envelope mail is often referred to as "snail mail," many speakers insert a snail into their e-mail addresses. In Korea, @ is known as *dalphaengi* and in Italian it's *chiocciola* (both literally meaning "snail").

CAT

When Poles aren't referring to @ as a monkey, they know it as a curled up kitten (*kotek*). Similarly, Finns use the phrase *miuku mauku*.

FISH

A quite creative name for the @ is *zavinac*, or "rolled-up pickled herring," in Slovakia and the Czech Republic.

ELEPHANT

In Denmark, you would refer to @ as *snabel*, or elephant's trunk.

MOUSE

In China, the word "mouse" used in reference to a computer means more than that object you click and point with. *Xiao lao shu* ("little mouse") is also used for the symbol @.

WORM

In Hungary, the mental image of a *kukac* (literally "worm") is associated with @.

IMAGE SOURCE: © David Clark, used with permission.

The Role of Services in the U.S. Economy

Since the industrial revolution, the United States has seen itself as a primary international competitor in the area of production of goods. There has been a shift in this thinking, however, as the U.S. economy has increasingly become service oriented over time, as shown in Exhibit 15.3. The United States is now the world's largest services market. The U.S. services sector experienced strong GDP and employment growth in 2006.[5] The service sector now produces 83 percent of the U.S. GDP, employing 85 percent of the American workforce. The shift from goods-producing to service-providing employment is expected to account for almost 16 million new service-related jobs between 2006 and 2016, while the goods-producing industries are expected to experience an overall job loss.[6] Exhibits 15.4 and 15.5 show the breakdown of GDP and employment in services in the United States. As shown in the exhibits, infrastructure services are a significant component of overall services trade. **Infrastructure services** are services, such as telecommunications, insurance, banking, and logistics, that underpin an entire economy.

In addition, the United States is the world's leading exporter of services. That is, it sells the most services to customers in other countries. This means that people, information, and money cross national borders during the exchange process. This exchange is referred to as **cross-border transactions**. Total U.S. service exports grew from $6 billion in 1958 to $404 billion in 2006. With total cross-border exports at $2.8 trillion in 2006, the United States accounted for 14 percent of services exports worldwide.[7] International service trade has had very beneficial results for many firms and industries. For example, management consulting firms may derive more than half of their revenue from international sources, while large and small advertising agencies serve customers around the globe. The leading U.S. services exported in 2006 were (1) business, professional, and technical services (24 percent of services exports) and (2) travel services (21 percent of services exports).[8] Exhibit 15.6 shows U.S. exports.

Exhibit **15.3**

Employment in Industrial Sectors as a Percentage of the Total Labor Force

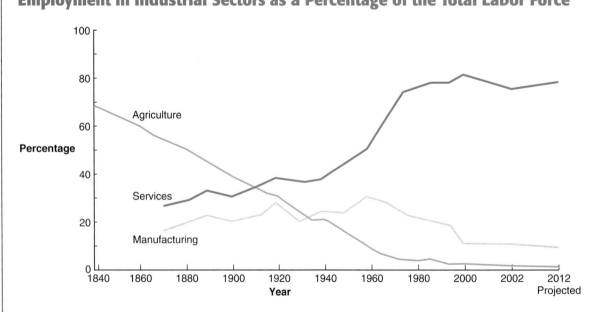

SOURCES: Bureau of Labor Statistics, "2002–12 Employment Projections," **http://www.bls.gov**, accessed May 18, 2006; Coalition of Service Industries, and Office of Service Industries, U.S. Department of Commerce, July 2002; Quarterly Labor Force Statistics, Paris, Organization for Economic Cooperation and Development, 1996, no. 2; and J.B. Quinn, "The Impacts of Technology on the Services Sector," *Technology and Global Industry: Companies and Nations in the World Economy*, by the National Academy of Sciences, Washington, DC.

Exhibit 15.4

U.S. Private-Sector Gross Domestic Product, by Sector, 2006

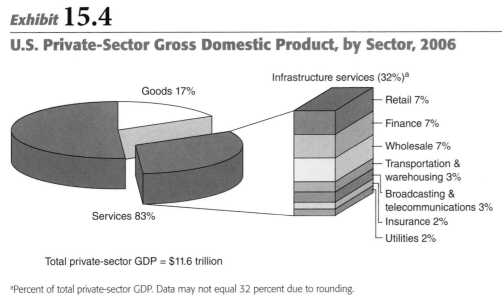

Total private-sector GDP = $11.6 trillion

[a]Percent of total private-sector GDP. Data may not equal 32 percent due to rounding.

SOURCE: U.S. Department of Commerce, Bureau of Economic Analysis, *Industry Economic Accounts database,* "Gross Domestic Product by Industry," October 2007.

Exhibit 15.5

U.S. Private-Sector Employment, by Sector, 2006

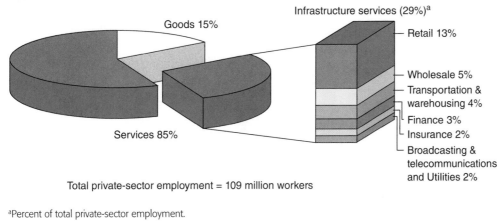

Total private-sector employment = 109 million workers

[a]Percent of total private-sector employment.

SOURCE: U.S. Department of Commerce, Bureau of Economic Analysis, *Industry Economic Accounts database,* "Full-Time Equivalent Employees by Industry," November 2007.

Large international growth and cross-border transactions, however, are not confined to U.S. service imports. The import of services into the United States is also high relative to other countries. Total services imported into the U.S. in 2006 were almost $308 billion. The growth in service imports was comprised largely of (1) travel services (23 percent of service imports), (2) transportation (21 percent of service imports), and (3) business, professional, and technical services (19 percent of service imports). Exhibit 15.7 shows U.S. imports.

As seen in Exhibit 15.8, the United States had a trade surplus in 2006 of around $96 billion. **Trade surplus** is a positive difference between exports and imports, while a **trade deficit** would occur if imports were greater than exports. The trade surplus of 2006 was the largest since services trade reporting began.[9]

Exhibit **15.6**

U.S. Exports of Services, by Industry, 2006[a]

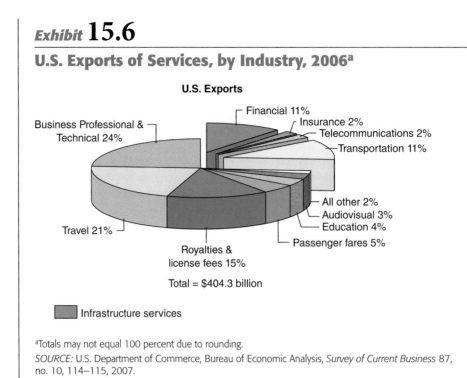

U.S. Exports

Financial 11%
Insurance 2%
Telecommunications 2%
Transportation 11%
Business Professional & Technical 24%
All other 2%
Audiovisual 3%
Education 4%
Passenger fares 5%
Travel 21%
Royalties & license fees 15%

Total = $404.3 billion

█ Infrastructure services

[a]Totals may not equal 100 percent due to rounding.

SOURCE: U.S. Department of Commerce, Bureau of Economic Analysis, *Survey of Current Business* 87, no. 10, 114–115, 2007.

Exhibit **15.7**

U.S. Imports of Services, by Industry, 2006[a]

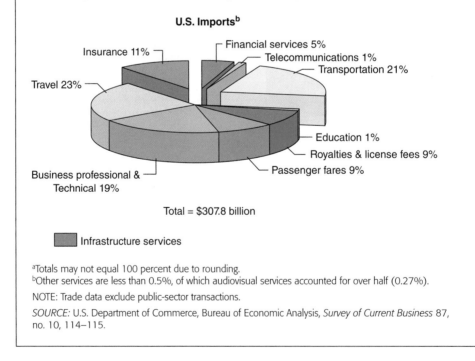

U.S. Imports[b]

Insurance 11%
Financial services 5%
Telecommunications 1%
Transportation 21%
Travel 23%
Education 1%
Royalties & license fees 9%
Passenger fares 9%
Business professional & Technical 19%

Total = $307.8 billion

█ Infrastructure services

[a]Totals may not equal 100 percent due to rounding.
[b]Other services are less than 0.5%, of which audiovisual services accounted for over half (0.27%).

NOTE: Trade data exclude public-sector transactions.

SOURCE: U.S. Department of Commerce, Bureau of Economic Analysis, *Survey of Current Business* 87, no. 10, 114–115.

The Role of Services in the World Economy

The rise of the service sector is a global phenomenon. According to the World Trade Organization (WTO), cross-border exports of services globally totaled $2.8 trillion in 2006.[10] Exhibit 15.9 shows cross-border service exports by countries and regions of the world. The

Exhibit **15.8**

U.S. Cross-Border Trade in Private Services: Exports, Imports, and Trade Balance, 1997–2006

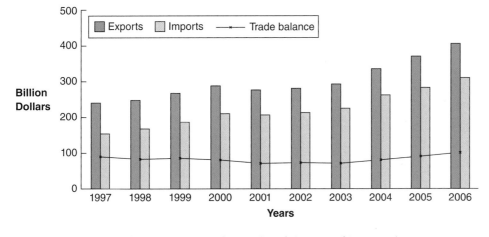

SOURCE: U.S. Department of Commerce, Bureau of Economic Analysis, *Survey of Current Business* 87, no. 10, 114–115.

Exhibit **15.9**

Global Cross-Border Exports of Services, by Exporting Country or Region, 2006

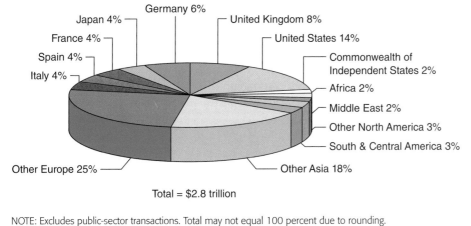

Total = $2.8 trillion

NOTE: Excludes public-sector transactions. Total may not equal 100 percent due to rounding.
SOURCE: World Trade Organization, *International Trade Statistics*, 2007, "World Exports of Commercial Services."

United States posted a trade surplus in 2006. Germany, however, posted the largest trade deficit of $50 billion in 2006.[11]

While there is a tendency to focus on large countries due to their impact on the world economy, the service sector has a significant impact on many of the small countries of the world. Exhibit 15.10 gives a listing of smaller countries worldwide where the service sector comprises at least 75 percent of the country's GDP. Additionally, Exhibit 15.11 shows how trade in services has become increasingly important worldwide. It is interesting to note the countries within each region (specific countries noted) that have benefited significantly from the fast-growing services trade.

Exhibit **15.10**

The Importance of the Service Sector

Country	Service as % of GDP
Jersey	97.00
Cayman Islands	95.40
Monaco	95.10
Macau	92.70
British Virgin Islands	92.00
Hong Kong	91.80
The Bahamas	90.00
Bermuda	89.00
Guernsey	87.00
Isle of Man	86.00
Luxembourg	86.00
Jordan	85.80
Nertherlands Antilles	84.00
Saint Martin	84.00
Palau	81.80
Virgin Islands	80.00
Saint Lucia	80.00
West Bank	79.00
Gaza Strip	79.00
Anguilla	78.00
Barbados	78.00
Fiji	77.60
Maldives	77.00
Panama	77.00
French Polynesia	76.90
Grenada	76.60
Lebanon	76.40
Greece	76.30
New Caledonia	76.20
Monterrat	75.70
Cook Islands	75.30
Latvia	75.20

SOURCE: CIA World Factbook 2008, "GDP—Composition by Sector—Services," **http://www.photius.com/rankings/ economy/gdp_composition_by_sector_services_2008_0.html**, retrieved February 3, 2009.

Unfortunately, the global credit crisis, as experienced in 2008 and 2009, can hit these smaller countries particularly hard. *The International Marketplace 15.2* describes the impact difficult economic times have on a relatively small country that depends upon the service sector for almost 70 percent of its GDP.

The hard hit taken by Iceland is not surprising given the role of banking in the global services sector. As late as 2006, conditions for global banks appeared favorable, with the global banking industry valued at $68.2 trillion. With profits at an all-time high of $788 billion, the industry had the highest absolute profits in the worldwide services sector.[12]

Exhibit **15.11**

Trade in Services is Becoming Increasingly Important

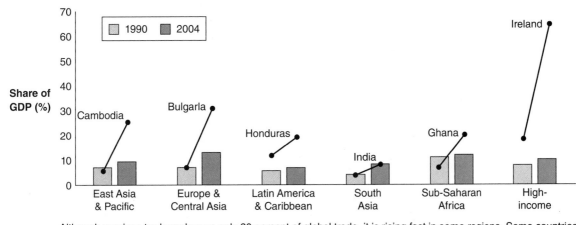

Although services trade makes up only 20 percent of global trade, it is rising fast in some regions, Some countries have benefited considerably from the fast-growing services trade.

SOURCE: International Monetary Fund Balance of Payments database, **http://devdata.worldbank.org/wdi 2006/content/section6.htm**.

The International MARKETPLACE

15.2

Iceland Goes Bankrupt

Only around 304,000 people live in the small country of Iceland. But the country became one of the largest casualties in the global financial crisis of 2008. In October of 2008, Iceland's government took control of the three major banks and shut down the country's stock exchange. At the same time, Iceland's prime minister began to raise the notion of "national bankruptcy."

Worldwide, people began to question what it meant for a country to go into bankruptcy. Essentially, Iceland could not pay its debts or raise foreign currency to pay for imports. For a country that relies heavily on the importation of necessary goods and services, this in and of itself evoked national panic. And Iceland's currency, the krona, was devalued to the point of 340 krona to the euro! As the financial collapse was unfolding, the British government even invoked anti-terrorism laws (placing Iceland in the same category as Al-Qaeda) in an effort to get money back that their citizens had deposited with Icelandic institutions.

Observers worldwide began to question how something like this could happen. Most people had never even considered the notion that a country could file bankruptcy. Analysts attributed the problem to the fact that the

Icelandic banking system, which was privatized in 2000, relied too heavily on external financing. The banks used such wholesale funding to gain entry into the local mortgage market and to acquire foreign financial firms. Most of the acquisitions took place in Britain and Scandinavia. By the beginning of 2007, this aggressive expansion had amassed $150 billion in the country's three main banks (Kaupthing Bank hf, Glithnir Banki hf, and Landsbanki Islands hf). This was eight times Iceland's GDP. The country had been transformed from one of Europe's poorest countries to one of the wealthiest.

Iceland is not a major player in any of the large currency trading blocs. Thus, there was very little incentive for a country or financial intermediary to step in and save them. Iceland looked to Russia for a 4 billion euro loan but was also very quick to clarify that there could be no strings attached (e.g., possible military cooperation). In November of 2008, the International Monetary Fund approved a $2 billion loan as part of an assistance package totaling approximately $10 billion.

In looking at the Iceland financial crisis, one has to wonder how such a small country acquired so much debt. Some now suggest that aggressive spenders in Iceland got caught up in a whirlwind of high risk ventures. In doing so, they also began buying the best food, the best clothes, the best cars, the best vacations, the best of everything—all on borrowed funds. The banks gave away too much money and landed everyone in a big mess with the devaluation of the krona. Unfortunately, all Icelanders, as well as many international investors, are now paying the price for these profligate Vikings.

SOURCES: Eric Pfanner, "Iceland, in Financial Collapse, is Likely to Need I.M.F. Help," *The New York Times*, October 10, 2008, **http://www.nytimes.com/2008/10/10/business/worldbusiness/10icebank.html?_r=1**, retrieved February 5, 2009; Kerry Capell, "The Stunning Collapse of Iceland," *Business Week*, October 9, 2008, **http://www.businessweek.com/globalbiz/content/oct2008/gb2008109_947306.htm**, retrieved February 5, 2009; "FACTBOX-Iceland Crisis: What does 'National Bankruptcy' Mean?" *Reuters*, October 14, 2008, **http://www.reuters.com/article/idUSLE43838820081014**, retrieved January 16, 2009; "Third Big Iceland Bank Files for U.S. Bankruptcy," December 9, 2008, **http://news.alibaba.com/article/detail/bank/10028592-1-third-big-iceland-bank-files.html**, retrieved January 16, 2009; Gary Davis, "Iceland Facing Bankruptcy," *Associated Content*, January 26, 2009, **http://www.associatedcontent.com/article/1421621/iceland_facing_bankruptcy.html**, retrieved February 5, 2009.

Other large service industries worldwide include insurance, telecommunications, retail, and logistics.

Global Transformation of Services

The rapid rise in international services marketing has been the result of major shifts in the business environment and innovations in technology. One primary change in the past decade has been the reduction of governmental regulation of services. This **deregulation** is clearly seen within the United States. In the mid-1970s, a philosophical decision was made to reduce government interference in the marketplace, in the hope that this would enhance competitive activity. As a consequence, some service sectors have benefited, and others have suffered, from the withdrawal of government intervention. The primary deregulated industries in the United States have been transportation, banking, and telecommunications. As a result, new competitors participate in the marketplace. Regulatory changes were initially thought to have primarily domestic effects, but they have rapidly spread internationally. For example, the 1984 deregulation of AT&T has given rise to the deregulation of Japan's telecommunications monopoly, NT&T. European deregulation followed in the mid-1990s.

Similarly, deregulatory efforts in the transportation sector have had international repercussions. New air carriers have entered the market to compete against established trunk carriers, and have done so successfully by pricing their services lower both nationally and internationally. In doing so, these airlines also affected the regulatory climate abroad. Obviously, a British airline can count only to a limited extent on government support to remain competitive with new low-priced fares offered by other carriers also serving the British market. As a result, the deregulatory movement has spread internationally and has fostered the emergence of new competition and new competitive practices. Because many of these changes resulted in lower prices, demand has been stimulated, leading to a rise in the volume of international services trade.

Another major change has been the decreased regulation of service industries by their industry groups. For example, business practices in fields such as healthcare, law, and accounting are becoming more competitive and aggressive. New economic realities require firms in these industries to search for new ways to attract market share. International markets are one frequently untapped possibility for market expansion and have therefore become a prime target for such service firms.

Technological advancement is another major factor in increasing service trade. Progress in technology offers new ways of doing business and permits businesses to expand their horizons internationally. For example, more rapid transmission of data has permitted financial institutions to expand their service delivery through a worldwide network. Again, were it not for advances in technology, such expansion would rarely have been possible or cost-effective.

Another result of these developments is that service industry expansion has not been confined to the traditional services that are labor-intensive and could therefore have been performed better in areas of the world where labor possesses a comparative advantage because of lower prices. Rather, technology-intensive services are the sunrise industries of the new century.

Increasingly, firms can reconfigure their service delivery in order to escape the location-bound dimension. Banks, for example, can offer their services through automatic teller machines or telephone banking. Consultants can advise via video conferences, and teachers can teach the world through multimedia classrooms. Physicians can perform operations in a distant country if proper computer linkages can drive roboticized medical equipment.

As a result, many service providers have the opportunity to become truly global marketers. To them, the traditional international market barrier of distance no longer matters. Knowledge, the core of many service activities, can offer a global reach without requiring a local presence. Service providers therefore may have only a minor need for local establishment, since they can operate without premises. You don't have to be there to do business! The effect of such a shift in service activities is major. Insurance and bank buildings in the downtowns of the world may soon become obsolete. Talented service providers see the demand for their performance increase while less capable ones will suffer from increased competition. Most important, consumers and society have a much broader range and quality of service choices available, and often at a lower cost.

International Trade Problems in Services

Together with the increasing importance of service marketing, new problems have beset the service sector. Even though many of these problems have been characterized as affecting mainly the negotiations between nations, they are of sufficient importance to the firm in its international activities to merit a brief review.

Data Collection Problems

The data collected on service trade are quite poor. Service transactions are often "invisible" statistically as well as physically. The fact that governments have precise data on the number of trucks exported, down to the last bolt, but little information on reinsurance flows, reflects past governmental inattention to services.

Only recently have policymakers recognized that the income generated and the jobs created through the sale of services abroad are just as important as income and jobs resulting from the production and exportation of goods. As a result, many governments are beginning to develop improved measuring techniques for the services sector. For example, the U.S. government has improved its estimates of services by covering more business, professional, and technical services and incorporating improved measurement of telecommunications services and insurance services. New data are also developed on travel and passenger fares, foreign students' expenditures in the United States, repairs and alterations of equipment, and noninterest income of banks.

It is easy to imagine how many data collection problems are encountered in countries lacking elaborate systems and unwilling to allocate funds for such efforts. The gathering of information is, of course, made substantially more difficult because services are intangible and therefore more difficult to measure and to trace than goods. The lack of service homogeneity does not make the task any easier. In an international setting, of course, an additional major headache is the lack of comparability between services categories as used by different national statistical systems. For example, while gas and electricity production and distribution are classified as goods by most governments, they are classified as services in the United States.[13]

Insufficient knowledge and information have led to a lack of transparency. As a result, governments have great difficulty gauging the effect of service transactions internationally or influencing service trade. Consequently, international services negotiations progress only slowly, and governmental regulations are often put into place without precise information as to their repercussions on actual trade performance.

Regulations and Service Trade Negotiations

Typical obstacles to services trade can be categorized into two major types: barriers to entry and problems in performing services. Governments often justify **barriers to entry** by referring to **national security** and economic security. For example, the impact of banking on domestic economic activity is given as a reason why banking should be carried out only by nationals or indeed be operated entirely under government control. Sometimes, the protection of service users is cited, particularly of bank depositors and insurance policyholders. Some countries claim that competition in societally important services is unnecessary, wasteful, and should be avoided. Another justification for barriers is the frequently used **infant industry** argument: "With sufficient time to develop on our own, we can compete in world markets." Often, however, this argument is used simply to prolong the ample licensing profits generated by restricted entry. Impediments to services consist of either tariff or nontariff barriers. Tariff barriers typically restrict or inhibit market entry for the service provider or consumer, while nontariff barriers tend to impede service performance. Yet, defining a barrier to service marketing is not always easy. For example, Germany gives an extensive written examination to prospective accountants (as do most countries) to ensure that licensed accountants are qualified to practice. Naturally, the examination is given in German. The fact that few U.S. accountants read and write German does not necessarily constitute a barrier to trade in accountancy services.

Even if barriers to entry are nonexistent or can be overcome, service companies have difficulty in performing effectively abroad once they have achieved access to the local market. One reason is that rules and regulations based on tradition may inhibit innovation. A more important reason is that governments aim to pursue social or cultural objectives through national regulations. Of primary importance here is the distinction between **discriminatory** and **nondiscriminatory regulations**. Regulations that impose larger operating costs on foreign service providers than on the local competitors, that provide subsidies to local firms only, or that deny competitive opportunities to foreign suppliers are a proper cause for international concern. The discrimination problem becomes even more acute when foreign firms face competition from government-owned or government-controlled enterprises. On the other hand, nondiscriminatory regulations may be inconvenient and may hamper business operations, but they offer less opportunity for international criticism.

For example, barriers to services destined for the U.S. market result mainly from **regulatory practices**. The fields of banking, insurance, and accounting provide some examples. These industries are regulated at both federal and state levels, and the regulations often pose formidable barriers to potential entrants from abroad. The chief complaint of foreign countries is not that the United States discriminates against foreign service providers but rather that the United States places more severe restrictions on them than do other countries. These barriers are, of course, a reflection of the decision-making process within the U.S. domestic economy and are unlikely to change in the near future. A coherent approach toward international commerce in services is hardly likely to emerge from the disparate decisions of agencies such as the Interstate Commerce Commission (ICC), the Federal Communications Commission (FCC), the Securities and Exchange Commission (SEC), and the many licensing agencies at the state level.

All these regulations make it difficult for the international service marketer to penetrate world markets. At the governmental level, services frequently are not recognized as a major facet of world trade or are viewed with suspicion because of a lack of understanding, and barriers to entry often result. To make progress in tearing them down, much educational work needs to be done. Unfortunately, the Doha Round WTO service negotiations have not yet achieved the desired level of success.[14]

Corporations and Involvement in International Services Marketing

Services and E-Commerce

Electronic commerce has opened up new horizons for global services reach and has drastically reduced the meaning of distance. For example, when geographic obstacles make the establishment of retail outlets cumbersome and expensive, firms can approach their customers via the World Wide Web. Government regulations that might be prohibitive to a transfer of goods may not have any effect on the international marketing of services. Also, regardless of size, companies are finding it increasingly easy to appeal to a global marketplace. The Internet can help service firms develop and transitional economies overcome two of the biggest tasks they face: gaining credibility in international markets and saving on travel costs. Little-known firms can become instantly "visible" on the Internet. Even a small firm can develop a polished and sophisticated Web presence and promotion strategy. Customers are less concerned about geographic location if they feel the firm is electronically accessible. An increasing number of service providers have never met their foreign customers except "virtually," online.[15]

Nonetheless, several notes of caution must be kept in mind. First, the penetration of the Internet has occurred at different rates in different countries. There are still many businesses and consumers who do not have access to electronic business media. Unless they are to be excluded from a company's focus, more traditional ways of reaching them must be considered. Also, firms need to prepare their Internet presence for global visitors. A multilingual website is a necessity in today's global world, since the Internet has become the default port of call for finding goods and services. Ten reasons for having a multilingual website are:[16]

1. To facilitate a shift away from English internet users
2. To use as a cost effective marketing tool
3. For access to new customers
4. To increase sales with little investment
5. To demonstrate that company is customer-centric
6. To generate trust by providing services in a customer's native tongue language
7. To demonstrate cultural sensitivity
8. To beat competition
9. To show that company thinks, works, and deals internationally
10. For more search engine access

With today's Web 2.0 internet technology, it is rather straightforward to publish in many different languages. A survey of 225 corporate websites across 21 industry categories found that it takes 20 languages to reach 90 percent of the web's worldwide users.[17] The most common website languages are (in decreasing order):[18]

- English
- French
- German
- Japanese
- Spanish (Spain)
- Chinese (simplified)
- Italian
- Spanish (Latin America)
- Korean
- Dutch
- Portuguese (Brazil)
- Polish
- Russian
- Chinese (traditional)
- French (Canada)
- Swedish
- Danish

Exhibit 15.12

Top 20 Global Web Sites 2008

1. Google	11. Deloitte
2. Wikipedia	12. American Express
3. Cisco Systems	13. Adobe
4. Volvo	14. Lenovo
5. Philips	15. Xbox
6. Caterpillar	16. Panasonic
7. Netvibes	17. IBM
8. Microsoft	18. 3M
9. HP	19. NIVEA
10. Nokia	20. XING

SOURCE: *The 2008 Web Globalization Report Card,* Byte Level Research (**www.bytelevel.com**).

- Portuguese (Portugal)
- Norwegian
- Czech
- Finnish

Exhibit 15.12 lists the top 20 global websites (both product and service providers) for 2008.

Services and Academia[19]

In the context of international services, it makes sense to briefly review the position of higher education. Academia has staunchly resisted accepting the notion of being part of any services "sector." University presidents, deans, and professors from around the world consistently assure the trade community that the problems they face are so specific and unique that wholesale approaches to anything in higher education would be heresy. However, academia is not exempt from influence by the same factors as other global services, such as demand and supply. Higher education is one of the largest service exports in the United States, with international students contributing $15.5 billion to the United States economy in the 2007–2008 academic year.[20]

With 623,805 international students studying in the United States during the 2007–2008 academic year, the top 10 countries tapping into this sector of U.S. services are:[21]

1. India
2. China
3. South Korea
4. Japan
5. Canada
6. Taiwan
7. Mexico
8. Turkey
9. Saudi Arabia
10. Thailand

Business management is the most popular field of study for international students, followed closely by engineering. The most prominent ports of interest in the United States are: California, New York, Texas, Massachusetts, Illinois, Florida, Pennsylvania, Michigan, Ohio, and Indiana.[22] But not all exporting of academic services occurs via international students studying in the United States. In 2007, there were 9,357 students enrolled in 19 U.S. university branch campuses abroad.[23]

At the same time, students in the United States require international knowledge acquisition. During the 2006–2007 academic year, 241,791 United States students studied abroad.[24] Keep in mind that only a decade before, less than 100,000 students studied abroad. The most popular destination point for United States students is Europe, with the United Kingdom drawing almost 33,000 U.S. students, followed closely by Italy, Spain, and France. The second most popular destination is Latin America, with Asia and the Oceania (Australia, New Zealand, and South Pacific Islands) close behind as destination points.[25]

Typical International Services

Although many firms are already active in the international service arena, others often do not perceive their existing competitive advantage. Numerous services have great potential for internationalization.

Financial institutions can offer some functions very competitively in the international field of banking services. Increased mergers and acquisitions on a global basis have led to the emergence of financial giants in Europe, Japan, and the United States. With the increased reach made possible by electronic commerce, they can develop direct linkages to clients around the world, offering tailor-made financial services and reduction in intermediation cost. Exhibit 15.13 provides an example of the international positioning of a bank.

Another area with great international potential is construction, design, and engineering services. Economies of scale work not only for machinery and material but also for areas such as personnel management and the overall management of projects. Particularly for international projects that are large scale and long term, the experience advantage could weigh heavily in favor of seasoned firms. The economic significance of these services far exceeds their direct turnover because they encourage subsequent demand for capital goods. For example, having an engineering consultant of a certain nationality increases the chances that contracts for the supply of equipment, technology, and know-how will be won by an enterprise of the same nationality, given the advantages enjoyed in terms of information, language, and technical specification.[26]

Firms in the fields of legal and accounting services can aid their domestic clients abroad through support activities; they can also aid foreign firms and countries in improving business and governmental operations. In computer and data services, international potential is growing rapidly. Knowledge of computer operations, data manipulations, data transmission, and data analysis are insufficiently exploited internationally by many small and medium-sized firms. For example, India is increasingly participating in the provision of international data services. Although some aspects of the data field are high-technology intensive, many operations still require skilled human service input. The coding and entering of data often has to be performed manually because appropriate machine-readable forms may be unavailable or not usable. Because of lower wages, Indian companies can offer data-entry services at a rate much lower than in more industrialized countries. As a result, data are transmitted in raw form to India where they are encoded on a proper medium and returned to the ultimate user. To some extent, this transformation can be equated to the value-added steps that take place in the transformation of a raw commodity into a finished product. Obviously, using its comparative advantage for this labor-intensive task, India can compete in the field of international services. The economic slowdown has not adversely affected India's IT sector. The Indian IT industry was looking at a 33 percent growth rate in 2008. By 2010, the sector was expected to become a $75 billion industry.[27]

Many opportunities exist in the field of teaching services. Both the academic and the corporate education sector have concentrated their work in the domestic market. Yet the teaching of knowledge is in high global demand and offers new opportunities for growth. Technology allows teachers to go global via video conferences, e-mail office hours, and Internet-relayed teaching materials. Removing the confinement of the classroom may well trigger the largest surge in learning that humankind has ever known.

Management consulting services can be provided by firms to institutions and corporations around the globe. Of particular value is management expertise in areas where firms

Exhibit 15.13

Financial Services Firm Positions Itself

EN ESPAÑA SOMOS ESPAÑOLES.

IN DEUTSCHLAND SIND WIR DEUTSCHE.

IN AUSTRALIA, WE ARE AUSTRALIAN.

日本では、日本人。

IN CANADA, WE ARE CANADIAN.

IN NEDERLAND ZIJN WE NEDERLANDS.

IN ENGLAND, WE ARE ENGLISH.

IN DER SCHWEIZ SIND WIR SCHWEIZER.

在香港我們是中國人。

IN AMERICA, WE ARE AMERICAN.

DI SINGAPURA KAMI IALAH ORANG SINGAPURA.

EN FRANCE, NOUS SOMMES FRANÇAIS.

AROUND THE WORLD WE ARE THE
CS FIRST BOSTON GROUP.

Announcing a worldwide investment banking firm that draws its strength from established investment banks in the world's financial capitals.

Operating as First Boston in the Americas, Credit Suisse First Boston in Europe and the Middle East, and CS First Boston Pacific in the Far East and Asia, the CS First Boston Group – together with Credit Suisse – offers unparalleled expertise in capital raising, mergers and acquisitions, securities sales, trading and research, asset management, and merchant banking.

So regardless of what language you speak, the words for powerful investment banking are the same all over the world – CS First Boston Group.

| CS First Boston Group | First Boston | Credit Suisse First Boston | CS First Boston Pacific |

SOURCE: Courtesy Credit Suisse First Boston LLC; **http://www.csfb.com**.

possess global leadership, be it in manufacturing or process activities. For example, companies with highly refined transportation or logistics activities can sell their management experience abroad. Yet consulting services are particularly sensitive to the cultural environment, and their use varies significantly by country and field of expertise.

All domestic service expenditures funded from abroad by foreign citizens also represent a service export. This makes tourism an increasingly important area of services trade. For example, every foreign visitor who spends foreign currency in a country contributes to an improvement in that nation's current account. The natural resources and beauty offered by so many countries contribute to travel and tourism becoming one of the world's leading growth service sectors.[28] While still expecting growth, real GDP sector growth was expected to slow with the economic conditions of 2008. Overall, the contribution of the travel and tourism economy to employment is expected to continue in a positive direction.

A proper mix in international services might also be achieved by pairing the strengths of different partners. For example, information technology expertise from one country could be combined with financial resources from another. The strengths of both partners can then be used to obtain maximum benefits. As seen in *The International Marketplace 15.3*, partnerships among service providers are even contributing to the future of greening the industry.

Combining international advantages in services may ultimately result in the development of an even newer and more drastic comparative lead. For example, if a firm has an international head start in such areas as high technology, information gathering, information processing, and information analysis, the major thrust of its international service might

---

The International MARKETPLACE

ENVIRONMENT & SUSTAINABILITY   15.3

Service Contractor Offers Sustainability in Trade Shows and Exhibitions

GES, with operations in 16 cities in the United States, eight cities in Canada, and four cities in the United Kingdom, provides exhibition and event services to a variety of companies worldwide. GES produces some of the world's leading trade shows and exhibitions, such as:

- International CES (consumer technology)
- Spring Fair Birmingham (launch for variety of new products and trends)
- Canadian International Auto Show (largest auto show in Canada)
- International Council of Shopping Centers (global trade association for shopping centers)
- MAGIC (fashion)
- WSA Show (footwear and accessories)
- CONEXPO-CON/AGG (construction industry)
- IFPE (power transmissions and motion control technologies)

GES is at the forefront in sustainability. The service contractor is dedicated to decreasing waste and using environmentally-friendly products as much as possible. As early as 1990, the company began recycling the carpet from its trade shows and exhibitions. Importantly, the company works closely with its vendors and clients to develop and use more eco-friendly, cost-effective alternatives.

One of the first company partners in the contractor's greening efforts was Nielsen Business Media's Sports Group. Nielsen Business Media, a part of the Nielsen Company, runs over 135 trade shows and conferences in over 30 industries across the globe. Events include: Outdoor Retailer Summer and Winter Markets, Action Sports Retailer September World Trade Expo, Health and Fitness Business Expo and Conference, Fly-Fishing Retailer World Trade Expo, and Interbike International Bicycle Expo.

The Sports Group at Nielsen Business Media was a natural sustainability partner since the environment

GES PROVIDES SOME OF THE WORLD'S LEADING TRADE SHOWS AND EXHIBITIONS; THE COMPANY IS AT THE FOREFRONT IN SUSTAINABILITY.

and sustainability already figured in the mindset of the exhibitors and the attendees to the various trade shows. All of the shows run by the Sports Group now have 100 percent recycled aisle carpet, recyclable badges for exhibitors (made with recycled paper and soy ink), biodegradable can liners, LED lighting for signs and backlighting, and recycling programs for exhibitors' materials. GES is dedicated to offering exhibitor services and products that decrease the carbon footprint.

Initially, GES found that sourcing the desired recyclable materials was neither easy nor inexpensive. However, raised awareness of environmental concerns has now made it easier to find the necessary resources. As a service provider, GES had to keep in mind that offering environmentally sustainable contractor services also meant that it had to be able to acquire the necessary supplies to do so. The goal for the company is to provide a service that offers environmental friendly booth rental packages for all of its trade shows and exhibits around the world.

SOURCES: Stephanie Corbin and Rachel Wimberly, "Service Contractors: Sustainability on the Floor," *Tradeshow Week,* April 21, 2008, **http://www.tradeshowweek.com/article/CA6552183.html**, retrieved February 2, 2009; **http://www.ges.com**; **http://www.nielsenbusinessmedia.com**.

not rely on providing these service components individually but rather on enabling clients, based on all resources, to make better decisions. If better decision-making is transferable to a wide variety of international situations, that in itself might become the overriding future competitive advantage of the firm in the international market.

Starting to Market Services Internationally

For many firms, participation in the Internet will offer the most attractive starting point in marketing services internationally. Setting up a Web site will allow visitors from any place on the globe to come see the offering. Of course, the most important problem will be communicating the existence of the site and enticing visitors to come. For that, very traditional advertising and communication approaches often need to be used. In some countries, for example, rolling billboards announce Web sites and their benefits. Overall, however, we need to keep in mind that not everywhere do firms and individuals have access to or make use of the new e-commerce opportunities.

For services that are delivered mainly in the support of or in conjunction with goods, the most sensible approach for the international novice is to follow the path of the good. For years, many large accounting and banking firms have done so by determining where their major multinational clients have set up new operations and then following them. Smaller service marketers who cooperate closely with manufacturing firms can determine where the manufacturing firms are operating internationally. Ideally, of course, it would be possible to follow clusters of manufacturers in order to obtain economies of scale internationally while, at the same time, looking for entirely new client groups abroad.

For service providers whose activities are independent from goods, a different strategy is needed. These individuals and firms must search for market situations abroad that are similar to the domestic market. Such a search should concentrate in their area of expertise. For example, a design firm learning about construction projects abroad can investigate the possibility of rendering its design services. Similarly, a management consultant learning about the plans of a foreign country or firm to computerize operations can explore the possibility of overseeing a smooth transition from manual to computerized activities. What is required is the understanding that similar problems are likely to occur in similar situations.

Another opportunity consists in identifying and understanding points of transition abroad. Just as U.S. society has undergone change, foreign societies are subject to a changing domestic environment. If, for example, new transportation services are introduced, an expert in containerization may wish to consider whether to offer service to improve the efficiency of the new system.

Leads for international service opportunities can also be gained by staying informed about international projects sponsored by domestic organizations such as the U.S. Agency for International Development, as well as international organizations such as the United Nations, the International Finance Corporation, or the World Bank. Very frequently, such projects are in need of support through services. Overall, the international service marketer needs to search for familiar situations or similar problems requiring similar solutions in order to formulate an effective international expansion strategy.

Strategic Implications of International Services Marketing

To be successful, the international service marketer must first determine the nature and the aim of the service offering—that is, whether the service will be aimed at people or at things, and whether the service act in itself will result in tangible or intangible actions. Exhibit 15.14 provides examples of such a classification that will help the marketer to better determine the position of the services effort.

During this determination, the marketer must consider other tactical variables that have an impact on the preparation of the service offering. The measurement of services capacity and delivery efficiency often remains highly qualitative rather than quantitative. In the field of communications, the intangibility of the service reduces the marketer's ability to provide samples. This makes communicating the service offer much more difficult than

Exhibit **15.14**

Understanding the Service Act

	Who or What Is the Direct Recipient of the Service?	
What Is the Nature of the Service Act?	**People**	**Possessions**
Tangible Actions	***People processing*** (services directed at people's bodies): Passenger transportation Healthcare Lodging Beauty salons Physical therapy Fitness center Restaurant/bars Barbers Funeral services	***Possessions processing*** (services directed at physical possessions): Freight transportation Repair and maintenance Warehousing/storage Office cleaning services Retail distribution Laundry and dry cleaning Refueling Landscaping/gardening Disposal/recycling
Intangible Actions	***Mental stimulus processing*** (services directed at people's mind): Advertising/PR Arts and entertainment Broadcasting/cable Management consulting Education Information services Music concerts Psychotherapy Religion Voice telephone	***Information processing*** (services directed at intangible assets): Accounting Banking Data processing Data transmission Insurance Legal services Programming Research Securities investment Software consulting

SOURCE: Christopher H. Loveclock and Jochen Wirtz, *Services Marketing: People, Technology, Strategy,* 5th ed., 15. © 2005. Reprinted by permission of Pearson Education, Inc., Upper Saddle River, NJ.

communicating an offer for a good. Brochures or catalogs explaining services often must show a "proxy" for the service in order to provide the prospective customer with tangible clues. A cleaning service, for instance, can show a picture of an individual removing trash or cleaning a window. Yet the picture will not fully communicate the performance of the service. Because of the different needs and requirements of individual consumers, the marketer must pay very close attention to the two-way flow of communication. Mass communication must often be supported by intimate one-on-one follow-up.

The role of personnel deserves special consideration in the international marketing of services. Because the customer interface is intense, proper provisions need to be made for training personnel both domestically and internationally. Major emphasis must be placed on appearance. The person delivering the service—rather than the service itself—will communicate the spirit, value, and attitudes of the service corporation. The service person is both the producer and the marketer of the service. Therefore, recruitment and training techniques must focus on dimensions such as customer relationship management and image projection as well as competence in the design and delivery of the service.[29]

This close interaction with the consumer will also have organizational implications. Whereas tight control over personnel may be desired, the individual interaction that is required points toward the need for an international decentralization of service delivery. This, in turn, requires both delegation of large amounts of responsibility to individuals and service "subsidiaries" and a great deal of trust in all organizational units. This trust, of course, can be greatly enhanced through proper methods of training and supervision. Sole ownership also helps strengthen trust. Research has shown that service firms, in their international expansion, tend greatly to prefer the establishment of full-control ventures. Only when costs escalate and the company-specific advantage diminishes will service firms seek out shared-control ventures.[30]

The areas of pricing and financing require special attention. Because services cannot be stored, much greater responsiveness to demand fluctuation must exist, and, therefore, much greater pricing flexibility must be maintained. At the same time, flexibility is countered by the desire to provide transparency for both the seller and the buyer of services in order to foster an ongoing relationship. The intangibility of services also makes financing more difficult. Frequently, even financial institutions with large amounts of international experience are less willing to provide financial support for international services than for products. The reasons are that the value of services is more difficult to assess, service performance is more difficult to monitor, and services are difficult to repossess. Therefore, customer complaints and difficulties in receiving payments are much more troublesome for a lender to evaluate for services than for products.

Finally, the distribution implications of international services must be considered. Usually, short and direct channels are required. Within these channels, closeness to the customer is of overriding importance in order to understand what the customer really wants, to trace the use of the service, and to aid the consumer in obtaining a truly tailor-made service.

Summary

Services are taking on an increasing importance in international marketing. They need to be considered separately from the marketing of goods because they no longer simply complement goods. Increasingly, goods complement services or are in competition with them. Because of service attributes such as intangibility, perishability, customization, and cultural sensitivity, the international marketing of services is frequently more complex than that of goods.

Services play a growing role in the global economy. As a result, international growth and competition in this sector outstrips that of merchandise trade and is likely to intensify in the future. Even though services are unlikely to replace production, the sector will account for the shaping of new comparative advantages internationally, particularly in light of new facilitating technologies that encourage electronic commerce.

The many service firms now operating domestically need to investigate the possibility of going global. The historical patterns in which service providers followed manufacturers abroad have become obsolete as stand-alone services have become more important to world trade. Management must therefore assess its vulnerability to international service competition and explore opportunities to provide its services around the world.

Key Terms

Intangibility
perishability
service capacity
customer involvement
service consistency

quality perception
market transparency
deregulation
barriers to entry
national security

infant industry
discriminatory/nondiscriminatory regulations
regulatory practices

Questions for Discussion

1. How has the Internet affected your service purchases?

2. Discuss the major reasons for the growth of international services.

3. How does the international sale of services differ from the sale of goods?

4. What are some of the international marketing implications of service intangibility?

5. Discuss the effects of cultural sensitivity on international services.

6. What are some ways for a firm to expand its services internationally?

7. How can a firm in a developing country participate in the international services boom?

8. Which services would be expected to migrate globally in the next decade? Why?

Internet Exercises

1. Find the most current data on the five leading export and import countries for commercial services. The information is available on the World Trade Organization site, http://www.wto.org. Click the statistics button.

2. What are the key U.S. services exports and imports? What is the current services trade balance? (http://www.bea.gov).

Recommended Readings

Alexander, Kern, and Mads Andenas. *The World Trade Organization and Trade in Services.* Leiden, The Netherlands: Martinus Nijhoff Publisher/Brill Academic, 2008.

Fisk, Raymond P., Stephen J. Grove, and Joby John. *Interactive Services Marketing.* Boston, Massachusetts: South-Western College Publishing, 2007.

Gronroos, Christian. *Service Management and Marketing: Customer Management in Service Competition.* Hoboken, New Jersey: Wiley, 2007.

Hefley, Bill, and Wendy Murphy. *Service Science, Management, and Engineering: Education for the 21st Century.* New York: Springer, 2008.

Lovelock, Christopher, and Jochen Wirtz. *Services Marketing.* Upper Saddle River, New Jersey: Prentice Hall, 2006.

Marchetti, Juan A., and Martin Roy. *Opening Markets for Trade in Services: Countries and Sectors in Bilateral and WTO Negotiations.* UK: Cambridge University Press, 2009.

Mattoo, Aaditya, Robert M. Stern, and Gianni Zanini. *A Handbook of International Trade in Services.* UK: Oxford University Press, 2007.

GLOBAL LOGISTICS AND MATERIALS MANAGEMENT

The International MARKETPLACE

ENVIRONMENT & SUSTAINABILITY

16.1

Environmental Sustainability: Greenhouse Gas and Logistics

The International Trade Centre (ITC) applauds a decision by the Soil Association to continue to allow African fresh fruits and vegetables flown to British markets to be certified as organic, without imposing additional trade standards that could be difficult to meet.

The Soil Association, Britain's largest organic certification body, made its ruling after an 18 month consultation with importers, exporters, and British consumers. It launched the probe into "food miles" because of consumer concerns that flying perishable, out-of-season produce can generate more greenhouse gas emissions than growing similar foods locally.

"The Soil Association has made the right decision and must be commended," said ITC Executive Director Patricia R. Francis. "Removing access to UK organic markets would have had a profound impact in some rural areas of Africa. Organic food exports are a dynamic driver of development in these communities; they pay for shelter, for children's education and health, and help improve the position of women," she said.

ITC strongly believes that it would be discriminatory to refuse organic certification for air-freighted goods while at the same time continuing to certify other energy-intensive products like beef arid vegetables grown under heated glasshouses.

Distance or means of transport are not always a reliable indicator of greenhouse gas emissions. Studies into Kenyan flowers flown to Europe, for example, suggest that their emissions may even be lower than flowers grown under glass in the Netherlands.

In opting not to impose additional requirements, the Soil Association concluded that organic agriculture's potential

© JEFFREY BLACKLER/ALAMY

THE SOIL ASSOCIATION, BRITAIN'S LARGEST ORGANIC CERTIFICATION BODY, RECENTLY RULED THAT AFRICAN FRESH FRUITS AND VEGETABLES FLOWN TO BRITISH MARKETS CAN BE CERTIFIED AS ORGANIC.

to alleviate poverty and enhance the local environment in developing countries had to be taken into consideration in the certification process.

Research published by ITC has shown that up to 20,000 livelihoods in Africa could be negatively affected by any move to limit access of air-freighted goods to the organic foods market in the UK.

"This decision adds a strong voice to concern over the ineffectiveness and inequity of food miles approaches to combating climate change. It focuses our attention on the need to find the most effective and non-discriminatory way to reduce carbon emissions without raising barriers to trade," Ms Francis said.

SOURCE: International Trade Centre, "ITC Applauds Soil Association Decision Backing African Organice Food Exports to Britain," February 6, 2009.

For the international firm, customer locations and sourcing opportunities are widely dispersed. The physical distribution and logistics aspects of international marketing therefore have great importance. To obtain and maintain favorable results from the complex international environment, the international logistics manager must coordinate activities globally, both within and outside of the firm. Neglect of logistics issues brings not only higher costs but also the risk of noncompetitiveness due to diminished market share, more expensive supplies, or lower profits. In an era of new trade opportunities in regions that may be suffering from major shortcomings in logistical infrastructure, competent logistics management is more important than ever before.

This chapter will focus on international logistics and supply chain management. Primary areas of concentration will be the linkages between the firm, its suppliers, and its customers, as well as transportation, inventory, packaging, and storage issues. The logistics management problems and opportunities that are particular to international marketing will also be highlighted.

A Definition of International Logistics

International logistics is the design and management of a system that controls the flow of materials into, through, and out of the international corporation. It encompasses the total movement concept by covering the entire range of operations concerned with goods movement, including therefore both exports and imports simultaneously. By taking a systems approach, the firm explicitly recognizes the linkages among the traditionally separate logistics components within and outside of the corporation. By incorporating the interaction with outside organizations and individuals such as suppliers and customers, the firm is able to build on jointness of purpose by all partners in the areas of performance, quality, and timing. As a result of implementing these systems considerations successfully, the firm can develop just-in-time (JIT) delivery for lower inventory costs, electronic data interchange (EDI) for more efficient order processing, and early supplier involvement (ESI) for better planning of goods development and movement. In addition, the use of such a systems approach allows a firm to concentrate on its core competencies and to form outsourcing alliances with other companies. For example, a firm can choose to focus on manufacturing and leave all aspects of order filling and delivery to an outside provider. By working closely with customers such as retailers, firms can also develop efficient customer response (ECR) systems which can track sales activity on the retail level. As a result, manufacturers can precisely coordinate production in response to actual shelf replenishment needs, rather than basing production on forecasts.

Two phases in the movement of materials are of major logistical importance. First is **materials management**, or the timely movement of raw materials, parts, and supplies into and through the firm. The second phase is **physical distribution**, which involves the movement of the firm's finished product to its customers. In both phases, movement is seen within the context of the entire process. Stationary periods (storage and inventory) are therefore included. The basic goal of logistics management is the effective coordination of both phases and their various components to result in maximum cost-effectiveness while maintaining service goals and requirements. Logistics is also increasingly concerned with the environment and sustainability, as shown in *The International Marketplace 16.1*.

The growth of logistics as a field has brought to the forefront three major concepts: the systems concept, the total cost concept, and the trade-off concept. The **systems concept** is based on the notion that materials-flow activities within and outside of the firm are so extensive and complex that they can be considered only in the context of their interaction. The systems concept stipulates that some components may have to work suboptimally to maximize the benefits of the system as a whole. The goal is to provide the firm, its suppliers, and its customers, both domestic and foreign, with the benefits of synergism expected from the coordinated application of size.

In order for the systems concept to work, information flows and partnership trust are instrumental. Logistics capability is highly information dependent, since information availability is key to planning and to process implementation. Long-term partnership and trust are required in order to forge closer links between firms and managers.

A logical outgrowth of the systems concept is the development of the **total cost concept**. To evaluate and optimize logistical activities, cost is used as a basis for measurement. The purpose of the total cost concept is to minimize the firm's overall logistics cost by implementing the systems concept appropriately.

Implementation of the total cost concept requires that the members of the system understand the sources of costs. To develop such understanding, a system of activity-based costing has been developed, which is a technique designed to more accurately assign the indirect and direct resources of an organization to the activities performed based on consumption.[1] In the international arena, the total cost concept must also incorporate the consideration of total after-tax profit, by taking the impact of national tax policies on the logistics function into account. The objective is to maximize after-tax profits rather than to minimize total cost.

The **trade-off concept**, finally, recognizes the linkages within logistics systems that result from the interaction of their components. For example, locating a warehouse near the customer may reduce the cost of transportation. However, the new warehouse will lead to increased storage costs and more inventory. Managers can maximize performance of logistics systems only by formulating decisions based on the recognition and analysis of such trade-offs. Consider a manufacturer building several different goods. The goods all use one or both of two parts, A and B, which the manufacturer buys in roughly equal amounts. Most of the goods produced use both parts. The unit cost of part A is $7, of part B, $10. Part B has more capabilities than part A; in fact, B can replace A. If the manufacturer doubles its purchases of part B, it qualifies for a discounted $8 unit price. For products that incorporate both parts, substituting B for A makes sense to qualify for the discount, since the total parts cost is $17 using A and B, but only $16 using Bs only. Part B should therefore become a standard part for the manufacturer. But departments building products that only use part A may be reluctant to accept the substitute part B because, even discounted, the cost of B exceeds that of A. Use of the trade-off concept will solve the problem.[2]

Supply Chain Management

The integration of these three concepts has resulted in the new paradigm of **supply chain management**, which encompasses the planning and management of all activities involved in sourcing and procurement, conversion, and logistics. It also includes coordination and collaboration with channel partners, which can be suppliers, intermediaries, third party service providers, and customers. In essence, supply chain management integrates supply and demand management within and across companies.[3]

Advances in information technology have been crucial to progress in supply chain management. Consider the example of Gestamp (Spain's leading supplier of metal components for car manufacturers), which used electronic data interchange technology to integrate inbound and outbound logistics between suppliers and customers. The company reports increased manufacturing productivity, reduced investment needs, increased efficiency of the billing process, and a lower rate of logistic errors across the supply process after implementing a supply chain management system.[4] *The International Marketplace 16.2* explains how such information technology works. Globalization has opened up supplier relationships for companies outside of the buyer's domestic market; however, the supplier's ability to provide satisfying goods and services will play the most critical role in securing long-term contracts. In addition, the physical delivery of goods often can be old-fashioned and slow. Nevertheless, the use of such strategic tools will be crucial for international

The International MARKETPLACE

16.2

RFID: Little Tags Can Make a World of Difference

Radio Frequency Identification (RFID) technology can change the way we think about supply chain management by permitting new levels of cost savings, efficiency, and business intelligence. RFID technology is a method of attaching small electronic tags to products and then installing transmitters, or readers of the tags, at several locations where tracking of the products may add value to the manufacturing and distribution process. These tags can signal market demand and allow for real-time production and delivery.

Although this technology has the potential to be useful in all industries, the large U.S. distributor Wal-Mart has been one of the main proponents of RFID development and has invested $3 billion in RFID during the past several years. By some estimates, Wal-Mart could save $8.35 billion each year using RFID! This large figure contains the savings from reduced stock-outs, theft, and inventory, and lower labor costs.

RFID technology can alter the supply chain management process in any organization that produces, moves, or sells physical goods. Hospitals, for instance, would be able to place tags on all patients, thus knowing exactly where they are located with information about them.

The technology is already used by Nestle. Nestle manufactures its candy bars through a complex process that involves storing the confectionaries on trays throughout the production period. For quality control purposes it is crucial that these trays undergo constant cleaning. Serious quality problems could arise if a few trays should miss their scheduled cleaning sessions. Escort Memory Systems offered Nestle a solution involving adhesive tags, the latest in RFID technology. The tags attach to Nestle's trays and remain attached until the end of the production cycle. At the beginning of the process, as the trays are first filled, information about weight and time is recorded on the tags. When the trays pass through Nestle's scales the actual weight is compared with the desired weight to reduce overfills. As this information is instantly linked to Nestle's system by RFID readers it is possible to track the locations of the trays at all times. Len Woods, Senior Control System Supervisor, commented, "If problems arise we are notified, enabling us to take remedial action well before any quality control issues arise."

SOURCES: "Escort Memory Systems Provides Material Handling Solution at Nestle," courtesy of Escort Memory Systems, **http://www.ems-rfid.com/pr/nestlepr.html**, accessed October 20, 2005; Ayman Abouseif, "How RFID can help optimize supply chain management," **www.ameinfo.com**, posted on August 21, 2005; "The Best Thing Since the Bar Code," The Economist, Feb. 6, 2003.

managers to develop and maintain key competitive advantages. An overview of the international supply chain is shown in Exhibit 16.1.

The Impact of International Logistics

Logistics costs comprise between 10 and 30 percent of the total landed cost of an international order.[5] International firms experience ongoing increases in their logistics cost. Surging fuel costs show no signs of dropping. Globalization has stretched the length of the value chain. Transportation providers have boosted their prices, both to offset fuel costs but also as a result of growing demand for their services and constraints in capacity. Increased security requirements for freight also have increased costs.[6]

Close collaboration with suppliers is required in order to develop a just-in-time inventory system, which in turn may be crucial to maintain manufacturing costs at a globally competitive level. Yet without electronic data interchange, such collaborations or alliances are severely handicapped. While most industrialized countries can offer the technological infrastructure for such computer-to-computer exchange of business information, the application of such a system in the global environment may be severely restricted. Often, it is not just the lack of technology that forms the key obstacle to modern logistics management, but rather the entire business infrastructure, ranging from ways of doing business in fields such as accounting and inventory tracking, to the willingness of businesses to collaborate with one another. A contrast between the United States and China is useful here.

For the U.S. economy, the total cost of distribution was close to 8.6 percent of nominal GDP in 2004. By contrast, China is still struggling to get demand and supply in line.

Exhibit **16.1**

The International Supply Chain

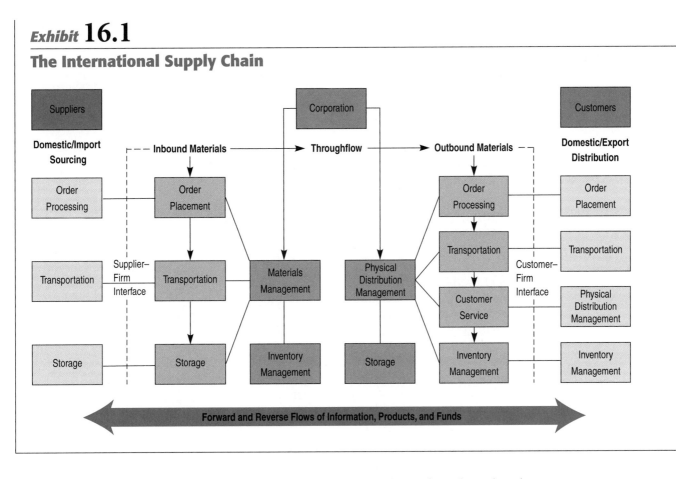

Forward and Reverse Flows of Information, Products, and Funds

The country is battling insufficient transportation systems, poor lines of supply, and intellectual property theft. The need for information development and exchange systems for integrated supplier–distributor alliances and for efficient communication systems is only poorly understood. As a result, total logistic costs for transportation, storage, and management activities incurred remain as much as 21 percent of GDP.[7]

The New Dimensions of International Logistics

In domestic operations, logistics decisions are guided by the experience of the manager, possible industry comparison, an intimate knowledge of trends, and the development of heuristics—or rules of thumb. The logistics manager in the international firm, on the other hand, frequently has to depend on educated guesses to determine the steps required to obtain a desired service level. Variations in locale mean variations in environment. Lack of familiarity with these variations leads to uncertainty in the decision-making process. By applying decision rules developed at home, the firm will be unable to adapt well to the new environment, and the result will be inadequate profit performance. The long-term survival of international activities depends on an understanding of the differences inherent in the international logistics field.

Basic differences in international logistics emerge because the corporation is active in more than one country. One example of a basic difference is distance. International marketing activities frequently require goods to be shipped farther to reach final customers. These distances in turn result in longer lead times, more opportunities for things to go wrong, more inventories—in short, greater complexity. **Currency variation** is a second basic difference in international logistics. The corporation must adjust its planning to incorporate different currencies and changes in exchange rates. The border-crossing process brings with it the need for conformance with national regulations, an inspection at customs, and proper documentation. As a result, additional intermediaries participate in the international logistics process. They include freight forwarders, customs agents, customs brokers, banks, and other financial intermediaries. The **transportation modes** may also be different. Most domestic transportation is either by truck or by rail, whereas the multinational corporation quite frequently ships its products by air or by sea. Airfreight and ocean freight have their own stipulations and rules that require new knowledge and skills. Since the logistics environment is different in each country, logistical responsibilities and requirements must also be seen from a country-specific perspective.

International Transportation Issues

International transportation is of major concern to the international firm because transportation determines how and when goods will be received. The transportation issue can be divided into three components: infrastructure, the availability of modes, and the choice of modes.

Transportation Infrastructure

In industrialized nations, firms can count on an established transportation network. Internationally, however, major infrastructural variations may be encountered. Some countries may have excellent inbound and outbound transportation systems but weak transportation links within the country. This is particularly true in former colonies, where the original transportation systems were designed to maximize the extractive potential of the countries. In such instances, shipping to the market may be easy, but distribution within the market may represent a very difficult and time-consuming task. It turns out that it costs more to ship a ton of wheat from Mombassa in Kenya to Kampala in Uganda than it does to ship the same ton of wheat from Chicago to Mombassa.[8] Such differences in logistics cost can have a major impact on a firm's ability to participate successfully in international trade.

The international marketer must therefore learn about existing and planned infrastructures abroad. In some countries, for example, railroads may be an excellent transportation mode, far surpassing the performance of trucking, whereas in others, the use of railroads for freight distribution may be a gamble at best. The future routing of pipelines must be determined before any major commitments are made to a particular location if the product is amenable to pipeline transportation. The transportation methods used to carry cargo to seaports or airports must also be investigated. Mistakes in the evaluation of transportation options can prove to be very costly. One researcher reported the case of a food processing firm that built a pineapple cannery at the delta of a river in Mexico. Since the pineapple plantation was located upstream, the company planned to float the ripe fruit down to the cannery on barges. To its dismay, the firm discovered that at harvest time the river current was far too strong for barge traffic. Since no other feasible alternative method of transportation existed, the plant was closed, and the new equipment was sold for a fraction of its original cost.[9]

Extreme variations also exist in the frequency of transportation services. For example, a particular port may not be visited by a ship for weeks or even months. Sometimes, only carriers with particular characteristics, such as small size, will serve a given location. All of these infrastructural concerns must be taken into account in the initial planning of the firm's transportation service. As *The International Marketplace 16.3* shows, shortcomings in infrastructure also present opportunities for international investments.

Availability of Modes

Even though goods are shipped abroad by rail or truck, international transportation frequently requires ocean or airfreight modes, which many corporations only rarely use domestically. In addition, combinations such as land bridges or sea bridges frequently permit the transfer of freight among various modes of transportation, resulting in intermodal movements. The international marketer must understand the specific properties of the different modes in order to use them intelligently.

Ocean Shipping

Water transportation is a key mode for international freight movements. An interruption of ocean-based transportation can have quite serious consequences for an economy. Three types of vessels operating in ocean shipping can be distinguished by their service: liner service, bulk service, and tramp or charter service. **Liner service** offers regularly scheduled passage on established routes. **Bulk service** mainly provides contractual services for

The International MARKETPLACE

16.3

Direct Logistics Investment in China

In recent years, many firms from around the world have expanded their investments in China's logistics market. In general, these investments have taken the form of establishing a commercial presence in China and/or building air hub facilities for the transportation, warehousing, and distribution of goods. In 2006, revenues for China's 3PL industry were slightly more than $37 billion, approximately equivalent to Japan, the world's third largest logistics market behind Europe and the United States. At the same time, China spent 21 percent of its GDP on logistic services in 2006, far higher than the 10 percent recorded for both the United States and Europe. The high cost of logistic services in China reflects the relative inefficiency of this sector due largely to the country's poor transportation infrastructure and burdensome regulatory environment.

Each of the largest global logistics and express delivery firms has a substantial presence in China—namely, DHL, FedEx, TNT (CEVA Logistics), and UPS. These firms have augmented the scale and scope of their operations in China following the country's relaxation of rules on foreign establishment and the expansion of air service rights. For example, German-based DHL has engaged in a long-term joint venture with Chinese state-owned firm Sinotrans Air Transportation Development Co., Ltd. (Sinotrans) focused on express delivery services, and recently took full ownership of a separate joint venture between Sinotrans and DHL-affiliate Exel Logistics. In addition, DHL invested $175 million to build a new air hub facility at Shanghai's Pudong International Airport, while at the same time establishing the DHL Logistics University, also in Shanghai. Overall, DHL has reportedly invested $900 million in China in the past few years. Similarly, FedEx has invested $150 million to build a new hub at Guangzhou's Baiyun International Airport to support its logistics and express delivery operations and, in 2007, acquired its Chinese joint-venture partner DTW's remaining 50 percent share for $400 million. Furthermore, having been awarded additional air traffic rights under a recently amended U.S.-China air transport agreement, FedEx now operates 30 weekly flights between the United States and major

EACH OF THE LARGEST GLOBAL LOGISTICS AND EXPRESS DELIVERY FIRMS, INCLUDING UPS, HAS A SUBSTANTIAL PRESENCE IN CHINA.

cities in China. Separately, in 2006, Netherlands-based TNT completed the purchase of China's Hoau Logistics Group for $135 million. The acquisition provided TNT with access to Hoau's 140 warehousing and distribution facilities across China, its extensive land-based transportation network, and its largely domestic customer base. Finally, UPS currently operates more than 60 warehousing and freight distribution facilities in China and, like DHL, plans to develop a new air hub in Shanghai's Pudong Airport to support its air cargo operations. UPS now operates approximately 21 non-stop weekly flights between the United States and China. Overall, UPS has reportedly invested $600 million in China over the past five years.

SOURCE: "Recent Trends in U.S. Services Trade," 2008 Annual Report, Washington, D.C., U.S. International Trade Commission, June 2008; Armstrong and Associates, July 2007, 2; Foster, "Logistics Inside China," September 2005; Malone, "DHL: The Long-Time China Player," October 2, 2006; Berman, "Global Logistics: DHL Buys Out Remaining Share of Sinotrans-Exel JV," December 14, 2007 (the establishment of the joint venture preceded the acquisition of then U.S.-based DHL by Germany's Deutsche Post World Net (DPWN) in 2002); "DHL to Set Up HQ for Sinotrans JV," Payload Asia, May 2006; "FedEx Completes Acquisition of Express Business of China's DTW Group," FedEx Express, February 28, 2007; **http://www.fedex.com**, accessed March 5, 2008; "TNT in Advanced Negotiations to Acquire Hoau, China's Leading Domestic Freight and Parcels Operator," TNT, 2005; "UPS and Shanghai to Announce First-Ever U.S. Air Hub in China," The Manufacturer, April 12, 2007; "UPS, FedEx Unveil New Asia Plans," UPS, July 14, 2005.

individual voyages or for prolonged periods of time. **Tramp service** is available for irregular routes and is scheduled only on demand.

In addition to the services offered by ocean carriers, the type of cargo a vessel can carry is also important. Most common are conventional (break bulk) cargo vessels, container ships, and roll-on-roll-off vessels. Conventional cargo vessels are useful for oversized and unusual cargoes but may be less efficient in their port operations. It is a reflection of the premium assigned to speed and ease of handling that has caused a decline in the use of general cargo vessels and a sharp increase in the growth of **container ships**. These carry standardized containers that greatly facilitate the loading and unloading of cargo and inter-modal transfers. Very large ships can carry 5000 standard containers. What a flood of goods!

A key concern is to reduce the time the ship has to spend in port, where money is spent but little income generated. Roll-on-roll-off (RORO) vessels are essentially oceangoing ferries. Trucks can drive onto built-in ramps and roll off at the destination. Another vessel similar to the RORO vessel is the LASH (lighter aboard ship) vessel. LASH vessels consist of barges stored on the ship and lowered at the point of destination. These individual barges can then operate on inland waterways, a feature that is particularly useful in shallow water.

The availability of a certain type of vessel, however, does not automatically mean that it can be used. The greatest constraint in international ocean shipping remains the lack of ports and port services. For example, modern container ships cannot serve some ports because the local equipment is unable to handle the resulting traffic. This problem is often found in developing countries, where local authorities lack the funds to develop facilities. In some instances, governments purposely limit the development of ports to impede the inflow of imports. Increasingly, however, nations recognize the importance of appropriate port structures and are developing such facilities in spite of the heavy investments necessary. If such investments are accompanied by concurrent changes in the overall infrastructure, transportation efficiency should, in the long run, more than recoup the original investment. Exhibit 16.2 shows a container ship.

Large investments in infrastructure are usually necessary to produce results. Selective allocation of funds to transportation tends to only shift bottlenecks to some other point in the infrastructure. If these bottlenecks are not removed, the consequences may be felt in the overall economic performance of the nation. A good example is provided by the Caribbean. Even though geographically close to the United States, many Caribbean nations are served poorly by ocean carriers. As a result, products that could be exported from the region to the United States are at a disadvantage because they take a long time to reach the U.S. market. For many products, quick delivery is essential because of required high levels of industry responsiveness to orders. From a regional perspective, maintaining adequate facilities is therefore imperative in order to remain on the list of areas and ports served by international carriers. Investment in leading-edge port technology can also provide an instrumental competitive edge and cause entire distribution systems to be reconfigured to take advantage of possible savings.

Exhibit **16.2**

Container Ship

© ISTOCKPHOTO.COM/DAN BARNES

Air Shipping

Airfreight is available to and from most countries. This includes the developing world, where it is often a matter of national prestige to operate a national airline. The tremendous growth in international airfreight is shown in Exhibit 16.3. The total volume of airfreight in relation to the total volume of shipping in international business remains quite small. Yet 40 percent of the world's manufactured exports by value travel by air.[10] Clearly, high-value items are more likely to be shipped by air, particularly if they have a high **density**, that is, a high weight-to-volume ratio.

Airlines make major efforts to increase the volume of airfreight by developing better, more efficient ground facilities, introducing airfreight containers, and marketing a wide variety of special services to shippers. In addition, some airfreight companies have specialized and become partners in the international logistics effort.

From the shipper's perspective, the products involved must be amenable to air shipment in terms of their size. In addition, the market situation for any given product must be evaluated. For example, airfreight may be needed if a product is perishable or if, for other reasons, it requires a short transit time. The level of customer service needs and expectations can also play a decisive role. The shipment of an industrial product that is vital to the ongoing operations of a customer may be much more urgent than the shipment of packaged consumer products.

Choice of Transport Modes

The international marketer must make the appropriate selection from the available modes of transportation. This decision, of course, will be heavily influenced by the needs of the firm and its customers. The manager must consider the performance of each mode on four dimensions: transit time, predictability, cost, and noneconomic factors.

Transit Time

The period between departure and arrival of the carrier varies significantly between ocean freight and airfreight. The 45-day transit time of an ocean shipment can be reduced to 12 hours if the firm chooses airfreight. The length of transit time will have a major impact on the overall operations of the firm. A short transit time may reduce or even eliminate the need for an overseas depot. Also, inventories can be significantly reduced if they

Exhibit **16.3**

International Airfreight, 1960–2027

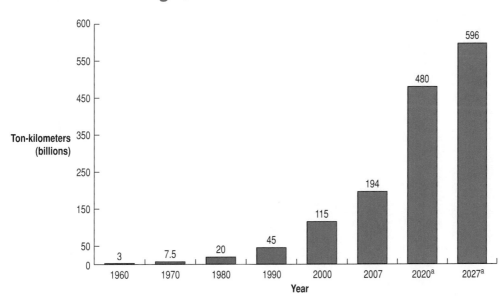

a = estimate

SOURCE: Civil Aviation Statistics of the World (Montreal: ICAO), **http://www.icao.org**; and *World Air Cargo Forecast,* Boeing Corporation, **http://www.boeing.com**, accessed March 3, 2009.

are replenished frequently. As a result, capital can be freed up and used to finance other corporate opportunities. Transit time can also play a major role in emergency situations. If the shipper is about to miss an important delivery date because of production delays, a shipment normally made by ocean freight can be made by air.

Perishable products require short transit times. Rapid transportation prolongs the shelf life in the foreign market. For products with a short life span, air delivery may be the only way to enter foreign markets successfully. International sales of cut flowers have reached their current volume only as a result of airfreight. At all times, the international marketing manager must understand the interactions between different components of the logistics process and their effect on transit times. Unless a smooth flow can be assured throughout the entire supply chain, bottlenecks will deny any timing benefits from specific improvements. For example, Levi Strauss, the blue jeans manufacturer, offered customers in some of its stores the chance to be measured by a body scanner to get custom-made jeans. Less than an hour after such measurement, a Levi factory began to cut the jeans of the customer's choice. Unfortunately, it then took ten days to get the finished product to the customer.[11]

Predictability

Providers of both ocean and airfreight service wrestle with the issue of **reliability**. Both modes are subject to the vagaries of nature, which may impose delays. Yet because reliability is a relative measure, the delay of one day for airfreight tends to be seen as much more severe and "unreliable" than the same delay for ocean freight. But delays tend to be shorter in absolute time for air shipments. As a result, arrival time via air is more predictable. This attribute has a major influence on corporate strategy. Due to the higher predictability of airfreight, inventory safety stock can be kept at lower levels. Greater predictability can also serve as a useful sales tool for foreign distributors, who are able to make more precise delivery promises to their customers. If inadequate harbor facilities exist, airfreight may again be the better

Exhibit 16.4

Loading a Tank on a Plane

© IAN PITMAN/ASSOCIATED PRESS

Shipping by airfreight has really taken off in the past 20 years. Even large and heavy items, such as this tank, are shipped to their destination by air.

alternative. Finally, merchandise shipped via air is likely to suffer less loss and damage from exposure of the cargo to movement. Therefore, once the merchandise arrives, it is more likely to be ready for immediate delivery—a facet that also enhances predictability.

Cost

A major consideration in choosing international transportation modes is the cost factor. International transportation services are usually priced on the basis of both **cost of the service** provided and the **value of the service** to the shipper. Because of the high value of the products shipped by air, airfreight is often priced according to the value of the service. In this instance, of course, price becomes a function of market demand and the monopolistic power of the carrier.

The international marketer must decide whether the clearly higher cost of airfreight can be justified. In part, this will depend on the cargo's properties. Bulky products may be too expensive to ship by air, whereas very compact products may be more amenable to airfreight transportation. High-priced items can absorb transportation costs more easily than low-priced goods because the cost of transportation as a percentage of total product cost will be lower. As a result, sending diamonds by airfreight is easier to justify than sending coal by air. In order to keep cost down, a shipper can join groups such as shippers-associations, which give the shipper more leverage in negotiations. Alternatively, a shipper can decide to mix modes of transportation in order to reduce overall cost and time delays. For example, part of the shipment route can be covered by air, while another portion can be covered by truck or ship.

The overall logistical considerations of the firm need to incorporate the product, the competition, and the environment. The manager must determine how important it is for merchandise to arrive on time, which will be different for DVDs of Oscar-nominated movies than for those that did poorly at the box office. The effect of transportation cost on price and the need for product availability abroad must be considered. Some firms may wish to use airfreight as a new tool for aggressive market expansion. Airfreight may also be considered a good way to begin operations in new markets without making sizable investments for warehouses and distribution centers.

Although costs are the major consideration in mode choice, an overall perspective must be employed. The manager must factor in all corporate activities that are affected by mode choice and explore the total cost effects of each alternative. The final selection of a mode will depend on the importance of different modal dimensions to the markets under consideration. A useful overall comparison between different modes of transportation is provided in Exhibit 16.5.

Exhibit 16.5

Evaluating Transportation Choices

Characteristics of Mode	Mode of Transportation				
	Air	Pipeline	Highway	Rail	Water
Speed (1 = fastest)	1	4	2	3	5
Cost (1 = highest)	1	4	2	3	5
Loss and Damage (1 = least)	3	1	4	5	2
Frequency* (1 = best)	3	1	2	4	5
Dependability (1 = best)	5	1	2	3	4
Capacity† (1 = best)	4	5	3	2	1
Availability (1 = best)	3	5	1	2	4

*Frequency: number of times mode is available during a given time period.

†Capacity: ability of mode to handle large or heavy goods.

SOURCE: Ronald H. Ballou, *Business Logistics: Supply Chain Management,* 5th ed. © 2004. Reprinted by permission of Prentice Hall, Upper Saddle River, NJ.

Noneconomic Factors

Often, noneconomic dimensions will enter into the selection process for a proper form of transportation. The transportation sector, nationally and internationally, both benefits and suffers from heavy government involvement. Carriers may be owned or heavily subsidized by governments. As a result, governmental pressure is exerted on shippers to use national carriers, even if more economical alternatives exist. Such preferential policies are most often enforced when government cargo is being transported. Restrictions are not limited to developing countries. For example, in the United States, all government cargo and all official government travelers must use national flag carriers when available.

For balance-of-payments reasons, international quota systems of transportation have been proposed. The United Nations Commission on International Trade and Development (UNCTAD), for example, has recommended a 40/40/20 treaty whereby 40 percent of the traffic between two nations is allocated to vessels of the exporting country, 40 percent to vessels of the importing country, and 20 percent to third-country vessels (40/40/20). However, stiff international competition among carriers and the price sensitivity of customers frequently render such proposals ineffective, particularly for trade between industrialized countries.

The International Shipment

International shipments usually involve not just one carrier but multiple types of carriers. The shipment must be routed to the port of export, where it is transferred to another mode of transportation—for example, from truck or rail to vessel. Documentation for international shipments is universally perceived as so complicated, especially by smaller firms, that it can be a trade barrier. Recognizing the impact both in terms of time and money that documentation can have, trading regions such as the European Union have greatly simplified their required documentation for shipments.

Documentation

In the most simple form of exporting, the only documents needed are a bill of lading and an export declaration. In most countries, these documents are available either from the government or from transportation firms. For example, an export declaration can be obtained in the United States from the Census Bureau (**http://www.census.gov/ foreign-trade/regulations/ forms**). A bill of lading can be obtained in Canada from a shipper, for example, Manitoulin Transport (**http://www.manitoulintransport.com**).

Most exports fit under a general license, which is a generalized authorization consisting simply of a number to be shown on the documents. Certain goods and data require a special validated license for export, as discussed in Chapter 5. For importation, the basic documents are a bill of lading and an invoice. Exhibit 16.6 provides a summary of the main documents used in international shipments.

The **bill of lading** is the most important document to the shipper, the carrier, and the buyer. It acknowledges receipt of the goods, represents the basic contract between the shipper and the carrier, and serves as evidence of title to the goods for collection by the purchaser. Various types of bills of lading exist. The inland bill of lading is a contract between the inland carrier and the shipper. Bills of lading may be negotiable instruments in that they may be endorsed to other parties (order bill) or may be nonnegotiable (straight). The **shipper's export declaration** states proper authorization for export and serves as a means for governmental data collection efforts.

The packing list, if used, lists in some detail the contents, the gross and net weights, and the dimensions of each package. Some shipments, such as corrosives, flammables, and poisons, require a **shipper's declaration for dangerous goods**. When the international marketer is responsible for moving the goods to the port of export, a dock receipt (for ocean freight) or a warehouse receipt (if the goods are stored) is issued before the issuance of the bill of lading. Collection documents must also be produced and always include a commercial

Exhibit **16.6**

Documentation for an International Shipment

A. Documents Required by the U.S. Government
   1. Shipper's export declaration
   2. Export license
B. Commercial Documents
   1. Commercial invoice
   2. Packing list
   3. Inland bill of lading
   4. Dock receipt
   5. Bill of lading or airway bill
   6. Insurance policies or certificates
   7. Shipper's declaration for dangerous goods
   8. Vessel loading observation inspection
   9. Letter of credit
C. Import Documents
   1. Import license
   2. Foreign exchange license
   3. Certificate of origin
   4. Consular invoice
   5. Customs invoice
   6. Customs notification

SOURCE: A Basic Guide to Exporting, 10th ed. U.S. Department of Commerce, Washington, D.C., 2009.

invoice (a detailed description of the transaction), often a **consular invoice or pro-forma invoice** (required by certain countries for data collection purposes), and a **certificate of origin** (required by certain countries to ensure correct tariffs). Insurance documents are produced when stipulated by the transaction. In certain countries, especially in Latin America, two additional documents are needed. An **import license** may be required for certain types or amounts of particular goods, while a **foreign exchange license** allows the importer to secure the needed hard currency to pay for the shipment. The exporter has to provide the importer with the data needed to obtain these licenses from governmental authorities and should make sure, before the actual shipment, that the importer has indeed secured the documents.

Two guidelines are critical in dealing with customs anywhere in the world: sufficient knowledge or experience in dealing with the customs service in question and sufficient preparation for the process. Whatever the required documents, their proper preparation and timing is of crucial importance, particularly since the major terrorist attacks of 2001. Many governments expect detailed information about cargo well in advance of its arrival in port. Improper or missing documents can easily delay payment or cause problems with customs.

Assistance with International Shipments

Several intermediaries provide services in the physical movement of goods. One very important distribution decision an exporter makes is the selection of an international freight forwarder. Such an **international freight forwarder** acts as an agent for the marketer in moving cargo to an overseas destination. Independent freight forwarders are regulated and, in the United States, should be certified by the Federal Maritime Commission. The forwarder advises the marketer on shipping documentation and packing costs and will prepare and review the documents to ensure that they are in order. Forwarders will also book the space aboard a carrier. They will make necessary arrangements to clear outbound goods with customs and, after clearance, forward the documents either to the customer or to the paying bank. A **customs broker** serves as an agent for an importer with authority to clear inbound goods through customs and ship them on to their destination. These functions are performed for a fee. Customs brokers are often regulated by their national customs service.

International Inventory Issues

Inventories tie up a major portion of corporate funds. As a result, capital used for inventory is not available for other corporate opportunities. Because annual **inventory carrying costs** (the expense of maintaining inventories) can easily comprise up to 25 percent or more of the value of the inventories themselves, proper inventory policies should be of major concern to the international marketing manager. Just-in-time inventory policies minimize the volume of inventory by making it available only when it is needed for the production process. Firms using such a policy will choose suppliers on the basis of their delivery and inventory performance. Proper inventory management may therefore become a determining variable in obtaining a sale.

In deciding the level of inventory to be maintained, the international marketer must consider three factors: the order cycle time, desired customer service levels, and the use of inventories as a strategic tool.

Order Cycle Time

The total time that passes between the placement of an order and the receipt of the merchandise is referred to as order cycle time. Two dimensions are of major importance to inventory management: the length of the total order cycle and its consistency. In international marketing, the order cycle is frequently longer than in domestic business. It comprises the time involved in order transmission, order filling, packing and preparation for shipment, and transportation. Order transmission time varies greatly internationally depending on whether telephone, fax, mail, or electronic order placement is used in communicating. The order filling time may also be increased because lack of familiarity with a foreign market makes the anticipation of new orders more difficult. Packing and shipment preparation require more detailed attention. Finally, of course, transportation time increases with the distances involved. As a result, total order cycle time can frequently approach a hundred days or more. Larger inventories may have to be maintained both domestically and internationally to bridge these time gaps.

Consistency, the second dimension of order cycle time, is also more difficult to maintain in international marketing. Depending on the choice of transportation mode, delivery times may vary considerably from shipment to shipment. This variation requires the maintenance of larger safety stocks in order to be able to fill demand in periods when delays occur.

The international marketer should attempt to reduce order cycle time and increase its consistency without an increase in total costs. This objective can be accomplished by altering methods of transportation, changing inventory locations, or improving any of the other components of the order cycle time, such as the way orders are transmitted. By shifting order placement from mail to telephone or to electronic data interchange (EDI), for example, a firm can reduce the order cycle time substantially.

Customer Service Levels

The level of customer service denotes the responsiveness that inventory policies permit for any given situation. Customer service is therefore a management-determined constraint within the logistics system. A customer service level of 100 percent could be defined as the ability to fill all orders within a set time—for example, three days. If within these three days only 70 percent of the orders can be filled, the customer service level is 70 percent. The choice of customer service level for the firm has a major impact on the inventories needed. In their domestic operations, U.S. companies frequently aim to achieve customer service levels of 95 to 98 percent. Often, such "homegrown" rules of thumb are then used in international inventory operations as well.

Managers may not realize that standards determined heuristically and based on competitive activity in the home market are often inappropriate abroad. Different locales have country-specific customer service needs and requirements. Service levels should not be oriented primarily around cost or customary domestic standards. Rather, the level chosen for use internationally should be based on customer expectations encountered in each market. These expectations are dependent on past performance, product desirability, customer sophistication, the competitive status of the firm, and whether a buyers' or sellers' market exists.

Because high customer service levels are costly, the goal should not be the highest customer service level possible but rather an acceptable level. Different customers have different priorities. Some will be prepared to pay a premium for speed. In industrial marketing, for example, even an eight-hour delay may be unacceptable for the delivery of a crucial product component, since it may mean a shutdown of the production process. Other firms may put a higher value on flexibility, and another group may see low cost as the most important issue. Flexibility and speed are expensive, so it is wasteful to supply them to customers who do not value them highly. The higher prices associated with higher customer service levels may reduce the competitiveness of a firm's product.

Inventory as a Strategic Tool

International inventories can be used by the international corporation as a strategic tool in dealing with currency valuation changes or hedging against inflation. By increasing inventories before an imminent devaluation of a currency, instead of holding cash, the corporation may reduce its exposure to devaluation losses. Similarly, in the case of high inflation, large inventories can provide an important inflation hedge. In such circumstances, the international inventory manager must balance the cost of maintaining high levels of inventories with the benefits accruing to the firm from hedging against inflation or devaluation. Many countries, for example, charge a property tax on stored goods. If the increase in tax payments outweighs the hedging benefits to the corporation, it would be unwise to increase inventories before a devaluation.

Despite the benefits of reducing the firm's financial risk, inventory management must still fall in line with the overall corporate market strategy. Only by recognizing the trade-offs, which may result in less than optimal inventory policies, can the corporation maximize the overall benefit.

International Storage Issues

Although international logistics is discussed as a movement or flow of goods, a stationary period is involved when merchandise becomes inventory stored in warehouses. Heated arguments can arise within a firm over the need for and utility of warehousing internationally. On the one hand, customers expect quick responses to orders and rapid delivery. Accommodating the customer's expectation may require locating many distribution centers around the world. On the other hand, warehousing space is expensive. In addition, the larger volume of inventory increases the inventory carrying cost. The international marketer must consider the trade-offs between service and cost to determine the appropriate levels of warehousing.

Storage Facilities

One important location decision is how many distribution centers to have and where to locate them. The availability of facilities abroad will differ from the domestic situation. For example, whereas public storage is widely available in some countries, such facilities may be scarce or entirely lacking in others. Also, the standards and quality of facilities abroad may often not be comparable to those offered at home. As a result, the storage decision of the firm is often accompanied by the need for large-scale, long-term investments. Despite the high cost, international storage facilities should be established if they support the overall marketing effort. In many markets, adequate storage facilities are imperative in order to satisfy customer demands and to compete successfully.

Once the decision is made to utilize storage facilities abroad, the warehouse conditions must be carefully analyzed. In some countries, warehouses have low ceilings. Packaging developed for the high stacking of products is therefore unnecessary. In other countries, automated warehousing is available. Proper bar coding of products and the use of package dimensions acceptable to the warehousing system are basic requirements. In contrast, in warehouses still stocked manually, weight limitations will be of major concern.

To optimize the logistics system, the marketer should analyze international product sales and then rank products according to warehousing needs. An **ABC analysis** classifies products that are most sensitive to delivery time as "A" products. "A" products would be stocked in all distribution centers, and safety stock levels would be kept high. Products for which immediate delivery is not urgent are classified as "B" products. They would be stored only at selected distribution centers around the world. Finally, "C" products for which short delivery time is not important, or for which there is little demand, are stocked only at headquarters. Should an urgent need for delivery arise, airfreight could be considered for rapid shipment. Classifying products through such an ABC analysis enables the international marketer to substantially reduce total international warehousing requirements and still maintain acceptable service levels.

Outsourcing

For many global firms the practice of outsourcing—which refers to the shifting of traditional corporate activities to parties outside of the firm and often outside of the country—is on the increase. German firms outsource to Hungary, French firms to Algeria, and U.S. firms to India. The decisive factors for choosing to outsource are the desire to reduce and control operating costs, to improve company focus, to gain access to world-class capabilities, and to free internal resources for other purposes.[12]

Our research into the future of outsourcing indicates continued growth and expansion of this practice.[13] An increasing portion of high-end, high value added services will be sourced from low labor cost but high labor skilled countries. The internationalization of the back office functions of multinational corporations will continue to grow. However, even sophisticated services will quickly move to low-cost locations. To remain competitive, firms in developed economies must change their strategy to focus on their ability to manage, coordinate, and define the interfaces between suppliers and customers. The challenge will be to effectively train the workers in the emerging markets to carry out their tasks while staying ahead of them in the ability to take on global coordination.

More manufacturing jobs will move to emerging markets. Firms will face the challenge to retain first-mover advantages through continued innovation. When cost pressures force firms to source globally, some will locate their own plants abroad, while others will outsource the needed inputs. Sourcing from abroad through independent suppliers on a contractual basis will have long-term consequences on the processes, competence, and capabilities of firms. In comparing the outsourcing networks of Japanese and U.S. companies, there is key concern that U.S. companies will gradually sever their value chain. In search of cost efficiency, they will increase their dependence on foreign suppliers for products that become technologically more sophisticated. The creation of new technology is a gradual and painstaking learning process of continual adjustment and refinement, as new productive methods are tested and adapted in light of a company's accumulated experience. Thus, overreliance on acquisitions and new technologies from other firms may not result in the same sustainable competitive advantage available through internal development. The manufacturing shift abroad may, therefore, shift current technology, design, and process advantages.[14] As some say, "It helps to develop and hang on to the blueprints."

Foreign Trade Zones

The existence of foreign trade zones can have a major effect on the international logistician, since production cost advantages may require a reconfiguration of storage, processing, and distribution strategies. Trade zones are considered, for purposes of tariff treatment, to be outside the customs territory of the country within which they are located. They are special areas and can be used for warehousing, packaging, inspection, labeling, exhibition, assembly, fabrication, or transshipment of imports without burdening the firm with duties.[15] Trade zones can be found at major ports of entry and also at inland locations near major production facilities. For example, Kansas City, Missouri, has one of the largest foreign trade zones in the United States. A listing of U.S. trade zones can be found at **http://www.trade.gov/ia**.

Foreign trade zones are designed to exclude the impact of duties from the location decision. This is done by exempting merchandise in the foreign trade zone from duty payment. The international firm can therefore import merchandise; store it in the foreign trade zone; and process, alter, test, or demonstrate it—all without paying duties. If the merchandise is subsequently shipped abroad (that is, reexported), no duty payments are ever due. Duty payments become due only if and when the merchandise is shipped into the country from the foreign trade zone.

One country that has used trade zones very successfully for its own economic development is China. Through the creation of *special economic zones* in which there are no tariffs, substantial tax incentives, and low prices for land and labor, the government has attracted many foreign investors bringing in billions of dollars. These investors have brought new equipment, technology, and managerial know-how and have therefore substantially increased the local economic prosperity.

Both parties to the arrangement benefit from foreign trade zones. The government maintaining the trade zone achieves increased employment. The firm using the trade zone obtains a spearhead in or close to the foreign market without incurring all of the costs customarily associated with such an activity. As a result, goods can be reassembled and large shipments can be broken down into smaller units. Also, goods can be repackaged when packaging weight becomes part of the duty assessment. Goods can also be given domestic "made-in" status if assembled in the foreign trade zone. Whenever use of a trade zone is examined, however, the marketer must keep the stability of rules, and the additional cost of storage, handling, and transportation in mind before making a decision.

International Packaging Issues

Packaging is instrumental in getting the merchandise to the ultimate destination in a safe, maintainable, and presentable condition. Packaging that is adequate for domestic shipping may be inadequate for international transportation because the shipment will be subject to the motions of the vessel on which it is carried. Added stress in international shipping also arises from the transfer of goods among different modes of transportation. Exhibit 16.7 provides examples of some sources of stress that are most frequently found in international transportation.

The responsibility for appropriate packaging rests with the shipper of goods. The U.S. Carriage of Goods by Sea Act of 1936 states: "Neither the carrier nor the ship shall be responsible for loss or damage arising or resulting from insufficiency of packing." The shipper must therefore ensure that the goods are prepared appropriately for international shipping. This is important because it has been found that "the losses that occur as a result of breakage, pilferage, and theft exceed the losses caused by major maritime casualties, which include fires, sinkings, and collision of vessels. Thus, the largest of these losses is a preventable loss."[16]

Packaging decisions must take into account differences in environmental conditions—for example, climate. When the ultimate destination is very humid or particularly cold, special provisions must be made to prevent damage to the product. The task becomes even more challenging when one considers that, in the course of long-distance transportation, dramatic changes in climate can take place.

Packaging issues need to be closely linked to overall strategic plans. The individual responsible for international packaging should utilize transportation modes as efficiently as possible. This requires appropriate package design, which takes into account the storage properties of the product. For example, John Deere was shipping its combines from the

Exhibit **16.7**

Stresses in Intermodal Movement

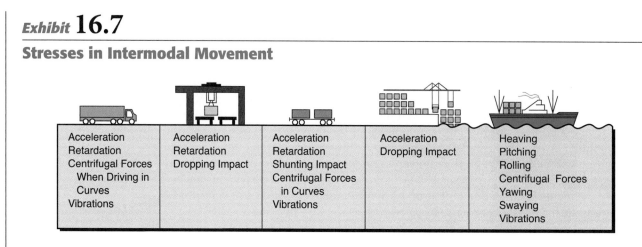

| Acceleration Retardation Centrifugal Forces When Driving in Curves Vibrations | Acceleration Retardation Dropping Impact | Acceleration Retardation Shunting Impact Centrifugal Forces in Curves Vibrations | Acceleration Dropping Impact | Heaving Pitching Rolling Centrifugal Forces Yawing Swaying Vibrations |

NOTE: Each transportation mode exerts a different set of stresses and strains on containerized cargoes. The most commonly overloaded are those associated with ocean transport.

SOURCE: Reprinted with permission from *Handling and Shipping Management,* September 1980 issue, p. 47; and David Greenfield, "Perfect Packing for Export," Copyright © 1980, Penton Publishing, Cleveland, OH.

United States to Australia for years at a shipping cost of $2,500 each. Each combine took up much more space than its footprint, since the harvesting arm stuck out on its side. Once the company decided to ship the harvesting arm unmounted, shipping costs were reduced by $1,000 per combine.

The weight of packaging must be considered, particularly when airfreight is used, since the cost of shipping is often based on weight. At the same time, packaging material must be sufficiently strong to permit stacking in international transportation. Another consideration is that, in some countries, duties are assessed according to the gross weight of shipments, which includes the weight of packaging. Obviously, the heavier the packaging, the higher the duties will be.

The shipper must pay sufficient attention to instructions provided by the customer for packaging. Requests by the customer that the weight of any one package should not exceed a certain limit, or that specific package dimensions should be adhered to, are usually made for a reason. Often they reflect limitations in transportation or handling facilities at the point of destination.

Although the packaging of a product is often used as a form of display abroad, international packaging can rarely serve the dual purpose of protection and display. Therefore, double packaging may be necessary. The display package is for future use at the point of destination; another package surrounds it for protective purposes.

One solution to the packaging problem in international logistics has been the development of intermodal containers—large metal boxes that fit on trucks, ships, railroad cars, and airplanes and ease the frequent transfer of goods in international shipments. In addition, containers offer greater safety from pilferage and damage. Of course, if merchandise from a containerized shipment is lost, frequently the entire container has been removed. Developed in different forms for both sea and air transportation, containers also offer better utilization of carrier space because of standardization of size. The shipper therefore may benefit from lower transportation rates.

Container traffic is heavily dependent on the existence of appropriate handling facilities, both domestically and internationally. In addition, the quality of inland transportation must be considered. If transportation for containers is not available and the merchandise must be removed and reloaded, the expected cost reductions may not materialize.

In some countries, rules for the handling of containers may be designed to maintain employment. For example, U.S. union rules obligate shippers to withhold containers from firms that do not employ members of the International Longshoreman Association for loading and unloading containers within a 50-mile radius of Atlantic or Gulf ports. Such restrictions can result in an onerous cost burden.

Overall, close attention must be paid to international packaging. The customer who ordered and paid for the merchandise expects it to arrive on time and in good condition. Even with replacements and insurance, the customer will not be satisfied if there are delays. This dissatisfaction will usually translate directly into lost sales.

Management of International Logistics

Because the very purpose of a multinational firm is to benefit from system synergism, a persuasive argument can be made for the coordination of international logistics at corporate headquarters. Without coordination, subsidiaries will tend to optimize their individual efficiency but jeopardize the overall performance of the firm.

Centralized Logistics Management

A significant characteristic of the centralized approach to international logistics is the existence of headquarters staff that retains decision-making power over logistics activities affecting international subsidiaries. Such an approach is particularly valuable in instances where corporations have become international by rapid growth and have lost the benefit of a cohesive strategy.

If headquarters exerts control, it must also take the primary responsibility for its decisions. Clearly, ill will may arise if local managers are appraised and rewarded on the basis of performance they do not control. This may be particularly problematic if headquarters staff suffers from a lack of information or expertise.

To avoid internal problems both headquarters staff and local logistics management should report to one person. This person, whether the vice president for international logistics or the president of the firm, can then become the final arbiter to decide the firm's priorities. Of course, this individual should also be in charge of determining appropriate rewards for managers, both at headquarters and abroad, so that corporate decisions that alter a manager's performance level will not affect the manager appraisal and evaluation. Further, this individual can contribute an objective view when inevitable conflicts arise in international logistics coordination. The internationally centralized decision-making process leads to an overall logistics management perspective that can dramatically improve profitability.

Decentralized Logistics Management

When a firm serves many international markets that are diverse in nature, total centralization would leave the firm unresponsive to local adaptation needs. If each subsidiary is made a profit center in itself, each one carries the full responsibility for its performance, which can lead to greater local management satisfaction and to better adaptation to local market conditions. Yet often such decentralization deprives the logistics function of the benefits of coordination. For example, whereas headquarters, referring to its large volume of total international shipments, may be able to extract bottom rates from transportation firms, individual subsidiaries by themselves may not have similar bargaining power. The same argument applies also to the sourcing situation, where the coordination of shipments by the purchasing firm may be much more cost-effective than individual shipments from many small suppliers around the world.

Once products are within a specific market, however, increased input from local logistics operations should be expected and encouraged. At the very least, local managers should be able to provide input into the logistics decisions generated by headquarters. Ideally, within a frequent planning cycle, local managers can identify the logistics benefits and constraints existing in their particular market and communicate them to headquarters. Headquarters can then either adjust its international logistics strategy accordingly or can explain to the manager why system optimization requires actions different from the ones recommended. Such a justification process will greatly help in reducing the potential for animosity between local and headquarters operations.

Contract Logistics

While the choice is open to maintain either centralized or decentralized in-house logistical management, a growing preference among international firms is to outsource, which means to employ outside logistical expertise. Often referred to as contract or **third-party (3PL) logistics**, it is a rapidly expanding industry. Most companies have outsourced at least one major logistics function such as customs clearance, transportation management, freight payment, warehouse management, shipment tracking, or other transportation-related functions. The main thrust behind the idea is that individual firms are experts in their industry and should therefore concentrate only on their operations. Third-party logistics providers, on the other hand, are experts solely at logistics, with the knowledge and means to perform efficient and innovative services for those companies in need. The goal is improved service at equal or lower cost.

Logistics providers' services vary in scope. For instance, some may use their own assets in physical transportation, while others subcontract out portions of the job. Certain other providers are not involved as much with the actual transportation as they are with developing systems and databases or consulting on administrative management services. In many instances, the partnership consists of working closely with established transport providers such as Federal Express or UPS. The concept of improving service, cutting costs, and unloading the daily management onto willing experts is driving the momentum of contract logistics.

One of the greatest benefits of contracting out the logistics function in a foreign market is the ability to take advantage of an existing network, complete with resources and experience. The local expertise and image are crucial when a business is just starting up. The prospect of newly entering a region, such as Europe, with different regions, business formats, and languages can be frightening without access to a seasoned and familiar logistics provider.

One of the main arguments leveled against contract logistics is the loss of the firm's control in the supply chain. Yet contract logistics does not and should not require the handing over of control. Rather, it offers concentration on one's specialization—a division of labor. The control and responsibility toward the customer remain with the firm.

The Supply Chain and the Internet

Many firms still use their Web sites as a marketing and advertising tool without expanding them to order-taking capabilities. That is changing rapidly. Global net e-commerce revenue is expected to surpass the $1 trillion dollar mark by 2012.[17]

Companies wishing to enter e-commerce do not have to do so on their own. Hub sites (also known as virtual malls or digital intermediaries) bring together buyers, sellers, distributors, and transaction payment processors in a single marketplace, making convenience the key attraction. Forrester Research estimates 2004 online commerce value to be $6.8 trillion, which comprises both business-to-business and business-to-consumer transactions.[18] The future is also growing brighter for hubs in the consumer-to-consumer market, where companies like eBay are setting high standards of profitability.

When customers have the ability to access a company through the Internet, a company itself has to be prepared for 24-hour order-taking and customer service, and to have the regulatory and customs-handling expertise for international delivery. The instantaneous interactivity that users experience will also be translated into an expectation of expedient delivery of answers and products ordered. As Internet penetration levels increase in the near future due to technological advances, improvements in many countries' Web infrastructures, and customer acceptance, e-business will become truly global.

Some companies elect to build their own international distribution networks. Both QVC, a televised shopping service, and amazon.com, an online retailer, have distribution centers in Britain and Germany to take advantage of the European Internet audience and to fulfill more quickly and cheaply the orders generated by their Web sites. Transactions and the information they provide about the buyers also allow for more customization and service by region, market, or even individual customer.

For industries such as music and motion pictures, the Internet is both an opportunity and a threat. The Web provides a new, efficient method of distribution and customization of products. Apple corporation uses the Web for both e-commerce and logistics purposes. The video iPod is a clever example of improved distribution techniques. Instead of making a trip to a store to purchase an audio CD a customer can now log into his Web account at iTunes, download the music and/or video files onto his computer, and then upload the files to the iPod, making the distribution aspect of logistics quicker and more efficient by giving the customer partial control of the process.

At the same time, the Web can be a channel for intellectual property violation through unauthorized posting and downloading on other sites. For example, Hollywood film production CEOs are concerned with the increasing piracy of DVDs. One of the reasons why it is so difficult to stop theft of intellectual property is because it is simple to download films illegally from various online sources. Currently companies lose tens of billions of dollars in sales each year due to such theft.

Logistics and Security

Firms worldwide have been exposed to the vicissitudes of terrorism, which often aims to disrupt the flow of supply and demand in order to damage economic systems. Governments are devoting major efforts to improved security measures such as the screening of shipments and shippers. International marketers may therefore have to redesign the movements of goods and services. Although a great portion of international transactions can today be conducted via e-mail or on the web, products still need to get to where the customers are. Companies require movement and storage of products to occur with the fewest number of impediments so that products reach customers on time.

Logistics systems are often the targets of attacks. These systems are the true soft spots of vulnerability for both nations and firms. Take the issue of sea ports: some 95 percent of all international trade shipments to the United States arrive by truck and rail. In most instances, the containers are secured by nothing more than a low cost seal that can be easily broken. Similar to imported merchandise, exported products also need to be protected by companies as they leave the country in order to prevent terrorists from contaminating shipments with the goal of destroying foreign markets together with the reputations of the exporting firms.

Security measures instigated by governments will affect the ability of firms to efficiently plan their international shipments. There is now more uncertainty and less control over the timing of arrivals and departures. There is also a much greater need for internal control and supervision of shipments. Cargo security will increasingly need to ensure both that nothing goes missing and also that nothing has been added to the shipment.[19]

Security measures for international shipments affect the ability of firms to efficiently plan their distributions. Increased inspections of containers used in international shipping, new security programs to protect ports, and other new protective policies are decreasing the efficiency and effectiveness of international shipping and logistics. In consequence, the costs of value chain and supply chain activities have increased substantially. There is now more uncertainty and less control over the timing of arrivals and departures. Companies may be inclined to produce more essential products themselves instead of relying on outside producers to deliver those products on time.

Similarly, costs may rise if companies should choose to purchase goods from suppliers located in close proximity, or from suppliers that are more familiar—and therefore apparently more safe—in order to reduce their vulnerability. Companies may also increase their inventory holdings (especially when inventory comes from an international producer) in hopes of protecting against delays caused by sudden heightened security measures against terrorism.[20] Holding more inventory or drawing goods from more than one source will increase the ability to meet the customer's demand at times when an outside producer is unable to deliver on time. Flexibility of supply chains is therefore a necessity when logistics security is at risk from terrorism.[21]

Exhibit 16.8

Pirate Attacks Increase Internationally

Dramatic rise in pirate attacks

Somalia, Nigeria and Indonesia remain international piracy hotspots.

Piracy-prone areas

Red Sea · India · Bangladesh · Gulf of Aden · Nigeria · Philippines · Somalia · Arabian Sea · Singapore · Peru · Brazil · Tanzania · Straits of Malacca · Indonesia

2008 Jan.-Sept.	Pirate raids 199	Vessels boarded 115	Crew members taken hostage 581
Q I	53	Vessels hijacked 31	Crew kidnapped 9
Q II	63	Vessels fired upon 23	Crew killed, missing 9, 7
Q III	83		

Source: AP, Reuters, International Maritime Bureau Graphic: Jutta Scheibe, Eeli Polli

© 2008 MCT

Firms with a just-in-time regimen are exploring alternative management strategies, because the process of moving goods has become more expensive. Some firms are considering replacing international shipments with domestic ones, where transportation via truck would replace transborder movement and eliminate the use of vulnerable international transportation. Further down the line are planning scenarios in which firms consider redesigning their logistics strategies to incorporate the effects of substantial and long-term interruptions of supplies and operations.

Another important security problem for logistics is shipping **piracy**. Even though pirates are often seen as legends from the past, piracy is very much a part of today's shipping security concerns. The 21st century freebooters are highly organized and heavily armed. The National Cargo Security Council estimates the global financial impact of cargo loss to exceed $50 billion annually.[22] Exhibit 16.8 shows the recent increase in pirate attacks.

Indonesian and Nigerian shores are the most treacherous areas of the world, as they are the primary choices for modern pirates.[23] Recent piracy maps completed by the International Chamber of Commerce can be seen at their Web site.[24] Companies conducting business in the surrounding areas have to face higher costs due to security measures undertaken to prevent severe cargo losses. In order to protect their revenues, export companies have been installing electric fences on their cargo ships. In spite of large corporate investments to build security, new attacks happen daily. You can track them at **http://www.cargolaw.com/presentations_casualties.html**.

Recycling and Reverse Logistics

By using logistics, the international marketer can play an increasingly important role in allowing the firm to operate in an environmentally conscious way. Environmental laws, expectations, and self-imposed goals set by firms are difficult to adhere to without a logistics orientation that systematically takes these concerns into account. Since laws and regulations differ across the world, the firm's efforts need to be responsive to a wide variety of requirements. One logistics orientation that has grown in importance due to environmental concerns is the development of **reverse distribution systems**. Such systems are instrumental in ensuring that the firm not only delivers the product to the market, but also can retrieve it from the market for subsequent use, recycling, or disposal. To a growing degree, the ability to develop such reverse logistics is a key determinant for market acceptance and profitability.

Traditionally businesses have focused on forward logistics even though product returns, an example of reverse logistics, have always been a fact of business life. With the growth of direct-to-consumer Internet sales, the reverse supply chain has exploded, amounting to over $100 billion per year—greater than the GDP of two-thirds of the world's countries! Industries facing the highest return volume are magazine/book publishing (50 percent), catalog retailers (18 to 35 percent), and greeting card companies (20 to 30 percent).[25] Just the disposal of returned merchandise alone can result in major headaches and costs.

Similar to forward logistics, reverse logistics require quality information and processes, and the ability to track both at all times. Reverse logistics, however, is also a complex customer service, inventory control, information management, cost accounting, and disposal process. Customers don't want to wait weeks before charges are removed from their credit cards, and returned goods idling in warehousing cause both higher carrying costs and the risk of obsolescence and shrinkage.

Reverse logistics management is highly specialized. Return and reclamation rates vary drastically between industries such as cosmetics or pharmaceuticals. The objectives of successful reverse logistics are the same: recovering the greatest value possible from returns, maintaining customer loyalty, controlling costs, and harvesting information to help reduce future returns. Successful reverse logistics greatly affects a company's bottom line. Idle electronic and computer parts in inventory lose 12 percent of value each month. Conversely, efficient management of returns can reduce companies' annual logistics costs by as much as 10 percent.

Society is beginning to recognize that retrieval should not be restricted to short-term consumer goods, such as bottles. Rather, it may be even more important to devise systems that enable the retrieval and disposal of long-term capital goods, such as cars, refrigerators, air conditioners, and industrial goods, with the least possible burden on the environment. Increasingly, governments establish rules that hold the manufacturer responsible for the ultimate disposal of the product at the end of its economic life. In Germany, for example, car manufacturers are required to take back their used vehicles for dismantling and recycling. The design of such long-term systems across the world may well be one of the key challenges and opportunities for the logistician and will require close collaboration with all other functions in the firm, such as design, production, and sales.

On the transportation side, logistics managers will need to expand their involvement in carrier and routing selection. Shippers of oil or other potentially hazardous materials are increasingly expected to ensure that the carriers used have excellent safety records and use only double-hulled ships. Society may even expect corporate involvement in choosing the route that the shipment will travel, preferring routes that are far from ecologically important and sensitive zones.

In the packaging field, environmental concerns are also growing on the part of individuals and governments. Increasingly, it is expected that the amount of packaging materials used is minimized and that the materials used are more environmentally friendly.

Companies need to learn how to simultaneously achieve environmental and economic goals. Esprit, the apparel maker, and The Body Shop, a British cosmetics producer, screen all their suppliers for environmental and socially responsible practices. ISO 14000 is a standard specifically targeted at encouraging international environmental practices by evaluating companies both at the organization level (management systems, environmental performance, and environmental auditing) and at the product level (life-cycle assessment, labeling, and product standards).[26] From the environmental perspective, those practices are desirable that bring about fewer shipments, less handling, and more direct movement. Such practices are to be weighed against optimal efficiency routings, including just-in-time inventory and quantity discount purchasing. For example, even though a just-in-time inventory system may connote highly desirable inventory savings, the resulting cost of frequent delivery, additional highway congestion, and incremental air pollution also needs to be factored into the planning horizon. Firms will need to assert leadership in such trade-off considerations in order to provide society with a better quality of life.

Summary

Competitiveness depends on cost efficiency. International logistics and supply chain management are of major importance because distribution comprises between 10 and 30 percent of the total landed cost of an international order.

International logistics is concerned with the flow of materials into, through, and out of the international corporation and includes materials management as well as physical distribution. The logistician must recognize the total systems demands of the firm in order to develop trade-offs between various logistics components. By taking a supply chain perspective, the marketing manager can develop logistics systems that are highly customer-focused and very cost-efficient. Implementation of such a system requires close collaboration between all members of the supply chain.

International logistics differs from domestic activities in that it deals with greater distances, new variables, and greater complexity because of country-specific differences. The international marketer needs to understand transportation infrastructures in other countries and modes of transportation such as ocean shipping and airfreight. The choice among these modes will depend on the customer's demands and the firm's transit time, predictability, and cost requirements. In addition, noneconomic factors such as government regulations weigh heavily in this decision.

Inventory management is another major consideration. Inventories abroad are expensive to maintain yet often crucial for international success. The marketer must evaluate requirements for order cycle times and customer service levels in order to develop an international inventory policy that can also serve as a strategic management tool.

The marketer must also deal with international storage issues and determine where to locate inventories. International warehouse space will have to be leased or purchased and decisions made about utilizing foreign trade zones.

International packaging is important because it ensures arrival of the merchandise at the ultimate destination in safe condition. In developing packaging requirements, the marketer must consider environmental concerns as well as climate, freight, and handling conditions.

International logistics management is growing in importance. The marketer must consider the benefits and the drawbacks that the information technology revolution has brought to supply chain and logistics activities. Increasingly, better implementation of change in logistics is key to defining a firm's competitiveness.

Security concerns have also greatly affected the planning and implementation of the logistics interface. In previous decades many governmental efforts were devoted to speeding up transactions across borders. Now national security concerns are forcing governments to construct new barriers to entry and conduct new inspections. Distribution and logistics are also susceptible to indirect effects of terrorism that may arise when, for instance, companies choose to hold more inventory because of the fear of not receiving shipments in time due to terrorist attacks. Flexibility of supply chains to allow for disruptions caused by terrorism is therefore a necessary component of conducting business in this day and age. Companies also will have to think about the need to build reverse logistics systems, when customer returns and recycling activities make such systems a necessity.

Key Terms

materials management	container ships	certificate of origin
physical distribution	density	import license
systems concept	reliability	foreign exchange license
total cost concept	cost of the service	international freight forwarder
trade-off concept	value of the service	customs broker
supply chain management	bill of lading	inventory carrying costs
currency variation	shipper's export declaration	ABC analysis
transportation modes	shipper's declaration for dangerous	third-party (3PL) logistics
liner service	goods	piracy
bulk service	consular invoice	reverse distribution systems
tramp service		

Questions for Discussion

1. What kind of transportation issues should a logistics manager consider when a firm is going international?

2. Why should customer service levels differ internationally? Is it, for example, ethical to offer a lower customer service level in developing countries than in industrialized countries?

3. How can an improved logistics infrastructure contribute to the economic development of China?

4. What are the major differences between centralized and decentralized logistics management?

5. What options are available for securing logistics systems from terrorism?

6. What steps can logisticians take to make their efforts more environmentally friendly?

Internet Exercises

1. What type of transportation information is available to exporters? Go to http://www.ups.com and http://www.marad.com and give examples of transportation links that an exporter would find helpful and explain why.

2. Determine the length of transit time a shipment takes between two international destinations. What else should you know before making a shipping decision? Go to http://www.apl.com and click on "Schedules."

Recommended Readings

A Basic Guide to Exporting. Washington D.C.: U.S. Department of Commerce, 2009.

Bowersox, David Closs, and M. Bixby Cooper. *Supply Chain Logistics Management*. New York: McGraw-Hill, 2009.

Christopher, Martin. *Logistics and Supply Chain Management and Lean Manufacturing Strategy*. London: Financial Times, 2006.

Coyle, John J., John Langley, Brian Gibson, and Robert A. Novack. *Supply Chain Management: A Logistics Perspective*. Mason, OH: South-Western College Publication, 2008.

Gourdin, Kent. *Global Logistics Management*. Oxford: Wiley, 2007.

Harvard Business Review on Supply Chain Management. Cambridge, MA: Harvard Business School Press, 2006.

Mangan, John., Chandra Lalwani, and Tim Butcher. *Global Logistics and Supply Chain Management*. Oxford: Wiley, 2008.

Murphy, Donald Wood, and David Parker. *Contemporary Logistics*, 9th ed., Prentice Hall, 2008.

Stauss, Bernd, and Wolfgang Seidel. *Complaint Management*. Mason, OH: Thomson/South-Western, 2005.

GLOBAL PRICING

The International MARKETPLACE

17.1

European Prices are Driven Down

The launch of a single currency taught car buyers the true meaning of pricing transparency. For years, identical cars cost 20 percent more in Germany and Austria than they did, for example, in Greece. It was not unusual for British consumers to take a train to Belgium if they needed a new car. Differences in local taxes and legally required features only partly explain the huge price disparity. The real cause lies in a dated exemption to Europe's antitrust laws, meant to protect local manufacturers from competition from low-priced imported vehicles. The exemption allows carmakers to sell exclusively through selected dealerships, each with its own sales territory. Dealerships, which are often manufacturer-owned, not only block out imports but are able to legally fix prices within their exclusive territories, usually based on what the market will bear. New regulations proposed by the EU aim to drive down prices across Europe by removing dealer exclusivity. Further, dealers will be able to sell outside their territories, opening up competition. While the auto industry is challenging the changes, one company, at least, sees the value of offering a single price across Europe. BMW recently announced a single basic sticker price in euros for its new 7-series. The companies plans to extend its pricing model across other brands.

Some argue that price differences can be maintained across Europe through product differentiation. Simpler products could be sold in less prosperous regions,

BMW RECENTLY ANNOUNCED A SINGLE BASIC STICKER PRICE IN EUROS FOR ITS NEW 7-SERIES.

whereas the more involved ones might go to markets that can afford them. At the minimum, prices will need to be coordinated to shield the company from the gray market challenge.

SOURCES: Mahmut Parlar and Kevin Weng, "Coordinating Pricing and Production Decisions in the Presence of Price Competition." *European Journal of Operational Research* 170 (number 1, 2006): 211–236; "EU Proposals to Overhaul Car Sales in Europe Come Under Immediate Fire in Biggest Market, Germany," *AP Worldstream,* February 5, 2002; "BMW to Charge the Same Basic Price for New 7-Series Throughout Europe," *AP Worldstream,* January 3, 2002; "Driving a Hard Bargain," *The Economist,* January 26, 2002 p. 55; "Car Prices Across Europe," *BBC News,* February 11, 2002, **http://www.bbc.co.uk**.

Successful pricing is a key element in the marketing mix. Many executives believe that developing a pricing capability is essential to business survival, and rank pricing as second only to the product variable in importance among the concerns to marketing managers.[1] This chapter will focus on price setting by multinational corporations that have direct inventories in other countries. This involves the pricing of sales to members of the corporate family as well as pricing within the individual markets in which the company operates. With increased economic integration and globalization of markets, the coordination of pricing strategies between markets becomes more important. At the same time, marketers may have to develop creative solutions to respond to financial crises, or to buyers who want to attach strings to their purchases (due to the size of the deal, or because they may not have the traditional means with which to pay for their purchases).

Transfer Pricing

Transfer pricing, or intracorporate pricing, is the pricing of sales to members of the extended corporate family. With rapid globalization and consolidation across borders, estimates have up to two-thirds of world trade taking place between related parties, including shipments and transfers from parent company to affiliates as well as trade between alliance partners.[2] This means that transfer pricing has to be managed in a world characterized by different tax rates, different foreign exchange rates, varying governmental regulations, and other economic and social challenges. Even in regions that are increasingly integrated, price differentials can play a pivoted role, as seen in *The International Marketplace 17.1*. Allocation of resources among the various units of the multinational corporation requires the central management of the corporation to establish the appropriate transfer price to achieve the following objectives:

1. Competitiveness in the international marketplace
2. Reduction of taxes and tariffs
3. Management of cash flows
4. Minimization of foreign exchange risks
5. Avoidance of conflicts with home and host governments
6. Internal concerns such as goal congruence and motivation of subsidiary managers[3]

Intracorporate sales can so easily change the consolidated global results that they compose one of the most important ongoing decision areas in the company. This is quite a change from the past when many executives dismissed internal pricing as the sole responsibility of the accounting department and as a compliance matter. Transfer pricing, when viewed from a company-wide perspective, enhances operational performance (including marketing), minimizes the overall tax burden, and reduces legal exposure both at home and abroad.[4] According to an annual survey, the portion of multinationals citing transfer pricing as the most important issue in terms of taxation has grown from one-half to two-thirds, and at the subsidiary level this importance is even more pronounced.[5]

Transfer prices can be based on costs or on market prices.[6] The cost approach uses an internally calculated cost with a percentage markup added. The market price approach is based on an established market selling price, and the products are usually sold at that price minus a discount to allow some margin of profit for the buying division. In general, cost-based prices are easier to manipulate because the cost base itself may be any one of these three: full cost, variable cost, or marginal cost.

Factors that have a major influence on intracompany prices are listed in Exhibit 17.1. Market conditions in general, and those relating to the competitive situation in particular, are typically mentioned as key variables in balancing operational goals and tax considerations. In some markets, especially in the Far East, competition may prevent the international marketer from pricing at will. Prices may have to be adjusted to meet local competition with lower labor costs. This practice may provide entry to the market and a reasonable profit to the affiliate. However, in the long term, it may also become a subsidy to an inefficient

Exhibit **17.1**

Influences on Transfer Pricing Decisions

1. Market conditions in target countries
2. Competition in target countries
3. Corporate taxes at home and in target countries
4. Economic conditions in target countries
5. Import restrictions
6. Customs duties
7. Price controls
8. Exchange controls
9. Reasonable profit for foreign affiliates

SOURCES: Compiled from Robert Feinschreiber, *Transfer Pricing Handbook* (New York: John Wiley & Sons, 2002), chapter 1 ("Business Facets of Transfer Pricing"); and Jane O. Burns, "Transfer Pricing Decisions in U.S. Multinational Corporations," *Journal of International Business Studies* 11 (Fall 1980): 23–39.

business. Further, tax and customs authorities may object because underpricing means that the seller is earning less income than it would otherwise receive in the country of origin and is paying duties on a lower base price on entry to the destination country.

Economic conditions in a market, especially the imposition of controls on movements of funds, may require the use of transfer pricing to allow the company to repatriate revenues. As an example, a U.S.-based multinational corporation with central procurement facilities required its subsidiaries to buy all raw materials from the parent; it began charging a standard 7 percent for its services, which include guaranteeing on-time delivery and appropriate quality. The company estimates that its revenue remittances from a single Latin American country, which had placed restrictions on remittances from subsidiaries to parent companies, increased by $900,000 after the surcharge was put into effect.[7]

A new dimension is emerging with the increase in e-commerce activity. Given a lack of clear understanding and agreement of tax authorities on taxation of electronic transfer pricing activities, companies have to be particularly explicit on how pricing decisions are made to avoid transfer-price audits.[8]

International transfer pricing objectives may lead to conflicting objectives, especially if the influencing factors vary dramatically from one market to another. For example, it may be quite difficult to perfectly match subsidiary goals with the global goals of the multinational corporation. Specific policies should therefore exist that would motivate subsidiary managers to avoid making decisions that would be in conflict with overall corporate goals. If transfer pricing policies lead to an inaccurate financial measure of the subsidiary's performance, this should be taken into account when a performance evaluation is made.

Use of Transfer Prices to Achieve Corporate Objectives

Three philosophies of transfer pricing have emerged over time: (1) cost-based (direct cost or cost-plus), (2) market-based (discounted "dealer" price derived from end market prices), and (3) **arm's-length price**, or the price that unrelated parties would have reached on the same transaction. The rationale for transferring at cost is that it increases the profits of affiliates, and their profitability will eventually benefit the entire corporation. In most cases, cost-plus is used, requiring every affiliate to be a profit center. Deriving transfer prices from the market is the most marketing-oriented method because it takes local conditions into account. Arm's-length pricing is favored by many constituents, such as governments, to ensure proper intracompany pricing. However, the method becomes difficult when sales to outside parties do not occur in a product category. Additionally, it is often difficult to convince external authorities that true negotiation occurs between two entities controlled by the same parent. In a study of 32 U.S.-based multinational corporations operating in Latin America, a total of 57 percent stated that they use a strategy of arm's-length pricing for their shipments, while the others used negotiated prices, cost-plus, or some other method.[9] Generally tax authorities will honor agreements among companies provided those agreements are commercially reasonable and the companies abide by the agreements consistently.[10]

The effect of environmental influences in overseas markets can be alleviated by manipulating transfer prices at least in principle. High transfer prices on goods shipped to a subsidiary and low ones on goods imported from it will result in minimizing the tax liability of a subsidiary operating in a country with a high income tax. The effective corporate tax rate in the United States is 40 percent (35 percent federal), while the average rate in the EU is 31.32 percent, in Latin America 30.2 percent, and in Asia 30.37 percent.[11] Many of the new members of the European Union have cut their rates the most; for example Poland and Slovakia to 19 percent. This may give multinationals a reason to report higher profits outside of the United States. On the other hand, a higher transfer price may have an effect on the import duty, especially if it is assessed on an ad valorem basis. Exceeding a certain threshold may boost the duty substantially when the product is considered a luxury and will have a negative impact on the subsidiary's competitive posture. Adjusting transfer prices for the opposite effects of taxes and duties is, therefore, a delicate balancing act.

Transfer prices may be adjusted to balance the effects of fluctuating currencies when one partner is operating in a low-inflation environment and the other in one of rampant inflation. Economic restrictions such as controls on dividend remittances and allowable deductions for expenses incurred can also be blunted. For example, if certain services performed by corporate headquarters (such as product development or strategic planning assistance) cannot be charged to the subsidiaries, costs for these services can be recouped by increases in the transfer prices of other product components. A subsidiary's financial and competitive position can be manipulated by the use of lower transfer prices. Start-up costs can be lowered, a market niche carved more quickly, and long-term survival guaranteed. Ultimately, the entire transfer price and taxation question is best dealt with at a time when the company is considering a major expansion or restructuring of operations. For example, if it fits the overall plan, a portion of a unit's R&D and marketing activities could be funded in a relatively low tax jurisdiction.

Transfer pricing problems grow geometrically as all of the subsidiaries with differing environmental concerns are added to the planning exercise, calling for more detailed intracompany data for decision making. Further, fluctuating exchange rates make the planning even more challenging. However, to prevent double taxation and meet arm's-length requirements, it is essential that the corporation's pricing practices be uniform. Many have adopted a philosophy that calls for an obligation to maintain a good-citizen fiscal approach (that is, recognizing the liability to pay taxes and duties in every country of operation and to avoid artificial tax-avoidance schemes) and a belief that the primary goal of transfer pricing is to support and develop commercial activities.[12] Some companies make explicit mention of this obligation of good citizenship in their corporate codes of conduct.

Transfer Pricing Challenges

Transfer pricing policies face two general types of challenges. The first is internal to the multinational corporation and concerns the motivation of those affected by the pricing policies of the corporation. The second, an external one, deals with relations between the corporation and tax authorities in both the home country and the host countries.

Performance Measurement

Manipulating intracorporate prices complicates internal control measures and, without proper documentation, will cause major problems. If the firm operates on a profit center basis, some consideration must be given to the effect of transfer pricing on the subsidiary's apparent profit performance and its actual performance. To judge a subsidiary's profit performance as not satisfactory when it was targeted to be a net source of funds can easily create morale problems. The situation may be further complicated by cultural differences in the subsidiary's management, especially if the need to subsidize less-efficient members of the corporate family is not made clear. An adjustment in the control mechanism is called for to give appropriate credit to divisions for their actual contributions. The method may range from dual bookkeeping to compensation in budgets and profit plans. Regardless of the method, proper organizational communication is necessary to avoid conflict between subsidiaries and headquarters.

Taxation

Transfer prices will by definition involve the tax and regulatory jurisdictions of the countries in which the company does business. Sales and transfers of tangible properties and transfers of intangibles such as patent rights and manufacturing know-how are subject to close review and to determinations about the adequacy of compensation received. This quite often puts the multinational corporation in a difficult position. U.S. authorities may think the transfer price is too low, whereas it may be perceived as too high by the foreign entity, especially if a less-developed country is involved. Section 482 of the Internal Revenue Code gives the Commissioner of the IRS vast authority to reallocate income between controlled foreign operations and U.S. parents and between U.S. operations of foreign corporations.

Before the early 1960s, the enforcement efforts under Section 482 were mostly domestic. However, since 1962, the U.S. government has attempted to stop U.S. companies from shifting U.S. income to their foreign subsidiaries in low- or no-tax jurisdictions and has affirmed the **arm's-length standard** as the principal basis for transfer pricing. Because unrelated parties normally sell products and services at a profit, an arm's-length price normally involves a profit to the seller.

A significant portion of Section 482 adjustments, including those resulting from the 1986 Tax Reform Act, have focused on licensing and other transfer of intangibles such as patents and trademarks. Historically, transfer pricing from a U.S. company's point of view has meant the shifting of income out of the United States, but, in cases of the U.S. having a lower corporate tax rate, the question now is how to use transfer pricing to shift profits into the United States. For example, Japan's corporate tax rate is 42 percent.

According to Section 482, there are six methods of determining an arm's-length price. The company can choose the approach as long as it is the procedure that provided the most accurate price for its unique situation.[13]

1. The comparable uncontrolled price method
2. The resale price method
3. The cost-plus method
4. The comparable profits method
5. The profit split method
6. Any other reasonable method

Beginning with the 1994 tax return, U.S. firms have had to disclose the pricing method they use so that the IRS can ascertain that the price was established using the arm's-length principle.[14] Guidelines of the OECD for transfer pricing are similar to those used by U.S. authorities.[15] Some experts who argue that the arm's-length standard is only applicable for commodities businesses have proposed a simpler system that allocates profits by a formula such as that of the state of California, which factors in percentages of world sales, assets, and other indicators. The rapid changes in international marketing caused by e-business will also have an impact on transfer pricing. Although transactions involving e-commerce represent new ways of conducting business, the fundamental economic relationships will remain the same. As a result, the existing principle of arm's length will probably be retained and adapted to address cross-border activities in a virtual economy.[16]

The starting point for testing the appropriateness of transfer prices is a comparison with *comparable uncontrolled* transactions, involving unrelated parties. Uncontrolled prices exist when (1) sales are made by members of the multinational corporation to unrelated parties, (2) purchases are made by members of the multinational corporation from unrelated parties, and (3) sales are made between two unrelated parties, neither of which is a member of the multinational corporation. In some cases, marketers have created third-party trading where none existed before. Instead of selling 100 percent of the product in a market to a related party, the seller can arrange a small number of direct transactions with unrelated parties to create a benchmark against which to measure related-party transactions.

If this method does not apply, the *resale* method can be used. This usually applies best to transfers to sales subsidiaries for ultimate distribution. The arm's-length approximation is arrived at by subtracting the subsidiary's profit from an uncontrolled selling price. The appropriateness of the amount is determined by comparison with a similar product being marketed by the multinational corporation.

The *cost-plus* approach is most applicable for transfers of components or unfinished goods to overseas subsidiaries. The arm's-length approximation is achieved by adding an appropriate markup for profit to the seller's total cost of the product.[17] The key is to apply such markups consistently over time and across markets.

The two methods focused on profits are based on the *functional analysis approach*. The functional analysis measures the profits of each of the related companies and compares them with the proportionate contribution to total income of the corporate group or comparable multinational marketers. It addresses the question of what profit would have been reported if the intercorporate transactions had involved unrelated parties. Understanding the functional interrelationships of the various parties (that is, which entity does what) is basic to determining each entity's economic contribution via-à-vis total income of the corporate group.

Such comparisons, however, are not always possible even under the most favorable circumstances and may remain burdened with arbitrariness.[18] Comparisons are impossible for products that are unique or when goods are traded only with related parties. Adjusting price comparisons for differences in the product mix, or for the inherently different facts and circumstances surrounding specific transactions between unrelated parties, undermines the reliance that can be placed on any such comparisons.

Since 1991, the Internal Revenue Service has been signing "advance pricing" agreements (APAs) with multinational corporations to stem the tide of unpaid U.S. income taxes. By January 1, 2006, a total of 631 such agreements were completed and 242 were under negotiation.[19] Since 1998, special provisions have been made for small-and medium-sized companies to negotiate such arrangements. Agreement on transfer pricing is set ahead of time, thus eliminating court challenges and costly audits. The harsh penalties have also caused companies to consider APAs. In the United States, a transfer pricing violation can result in a 40 percent penalty on the amount of underpayment, whereas in Mexico the penalty can reach 100 percent. The main criticism of this approach is the exorbitant amounts of staff time that each agreement requires as well as the amount of information that may have to be disclosed.[20] Some also argue that such agreements may result in worse transfer pricing systems, from the corporate point of view, because companies with effective intracompany bargaining processes may have to replace them with poorly designed ones to satisfy the tax authorities.[21] Some companies have expressed concern about sitting down with tax authorities in general, for fear of some other issues emerging. Additionally, in many countries all information disclosed to tax authorities under an APA might become available to the public. In general, the costs and concerns about APAs have been reduced considerably in the recent past. For example, more of the data needed are online, and software has been developed to address the issue. A study can be had for $15,000, and many of the big accounting firms include these studies as part of their global tax strategy services.[22] In cases in which a company is doing business in a country that has a bilateral tax treaty with the home government (e.g., the United States and Germany), the company can seek a bilateral APA that is negotiated simultaneously with the tax authorities of both countries.

The most difficult of cases are those involving intangibles, because comparables are absent in most cases.[23] The IRS requires that the price or royalty rate for any cross-border transfer be commensurate with income; that is, it must result in a fair distribution of income between the units. This requires marketers to analyze and attach a value to each business function (R&D, manufacturing, assembly, marketing services, and distribution). Comparable transactions, when available—or, if absent, industry norms—should be used to calculate the rates of return for each function. Take, for example, a subsidiary that makes a $100 profit on the sale of a product manufactured with technology developed and licensed by the U.S. parent. If the firm identifies rates of return for manufacturing and distribution of 30 percent and 10 percent, then $40 of the profit must be allocated to the subsidiary. The remaining $60 would be taxable income to the parent.[24] Needless to say, many of the analyses have to be quite subjective, especially in cases that involve the transfer of intellectual property, and may lead to controversies and disputes with tax authorities.[25]

Pricing within Individual Markets

Pricing within the individual markets in which the company operates is determined by (1) corporate objectives, (2) costs, (3) customer behavior and market conditions, (4) market structure, and (5) environmental constraints.[26] Because all these factors vary among the countries in which the multinational corporation might have a presence, the pricing policy is under pressure to vary as well. With price holding a position of importance with customers, a market-driven firm must be informed and sensitive to customer views and realities.[27] This is especially critical for those marketers wanting to position their products as premium alternatives.

Although many global marketers, both U.S.-based[28] and foreign-based,[29] emphasize nonprice methods of competition, they rank pricing high as a marketing tool overseas, even though the nondomestic pricing decisions are made at the middle management level in a majority of firms. Pricing decisions also tend to be made more at the local level, with coordination from headquarters in more strategic decision situations.[30] With increased trade liberalization and advanced economic integration, this coordination is becoming more important.

Corporate Objectives

Global marketers must set and adjust their objectives, both financial (such as return on investment) and marketing-related (such as maintaining or increasing market share), based on the prevailing conditions in each of their markets. Pricing may well influence the overall strategic moves of the company as a whole. This is well illustrated by the decision of many foreign-based companies, automakers for example, to begin production in the United States rather than to continue exporting. To remain competitive in the market, many have had to increase the dollar component of their output. Apart from trade barriers, many have had their market shares erode because of higher wages in their home markets, increasing shipping costs, and unfavorable exchange rates. Market share very often plays a major role in pricing decisions in that marketers may be willing to sacrifice immediate earnings for market share gain or maintenance. This is especially true in highly competitive situations;

© AFP PHOTO/JUNG YEON-JE/NEWSCOM

OVER THE PAST DECADE, KOREAN CONGLOMERATES SUCH AS HYUNDAI WERE ABLE TO PENETRATE AND CAPTURE THE LOW END OF MANY CONSUMER GOODS MARKETS IN BOTH THE UNITED STATES AND EUROPE BASED ON PRICE COMPETITIVENESS.

for example, during a period of extremely high competitive activity in Japan in the mainframe sector, the local Fujitsu's one-year net income was only 5 percent of sales, compared with IBM's 12.7 percent worldwide and 7.6 percent in Japan. In the longer term, situations of this type may require cross-subsidization from other geographic units.

Pricing decisions will also vary depending on the pricing situation. The basics of first-time pricing, price adjustment, and product line pricing as discussed earlier apply to pricing within nondomestic situations as well. For example, companies such as Kodak and Xerox, which introduce all of their new products worldwide within a very short time period, have an option of either skimming or penetration pricing. If the product is an innovation, the marketer may decide to charge a premium for the product. If, however, competition is keen or expected to increase in the near future, lower prices may be used to make the product more attractive to the buyers and the market less attractive to the competition. The Korean conglomerates (such as Daewoo, Goldstar, Hyundai, and Samsung) were able to penetrate and capture the low end of many consumer goods markets in both the United States and Europe based on price competitiveness over the past ten years (as shown in Exhibit 17.2). In the last few years, Chinese marketers have used similar pricing strategies to establish market positions. For example, Shanghai-based SVA Group sells LCD and plasma TV sets through channels such as Costco and Target at prices that are 30 percent below those of Panasonic from Japan.[31]

For the most part, the Koreans have competed in the world marketplace, especially against the Japanese, on price rather than product traits, with the major objective of capturing a foothold in various markets. For example, Samsung was able to gain access to U.S. markets when J.C. Penney was looking for lower-priced microwave ovens in the early 1980s. Samsung's ovens retailed for $299, whereas most models averaged between $350 and $400 at the time.[32] However, substantial strides in production technology and relentless marketing have started to make Korean products serious competitors in the medium to high price brackets as well.[33] In many cases, Koreans have been able to close the price gap and, in some cases, they have abandoned certain segments altogether. For example, in the compact refrigerator market, the Chinese have taken over.[34]

Price changes may be frequent if the company's objective is to undersell a major competitor. A marketer may, for example, decide to maintain a price level 10 to 20 percent below that of a major competitor; price changes would be necessary whenever the competitor made significant changes in its prices. Price changes may also be required because of changes in foreign exchange rates. Many marketers were forced to increase prices in the United States on goods of non-U.S. origin when the dollar weakened during the early to mid-1990s and since early 2002.

Exhibit **17.2**

The Price Edge Game

Product	Korean Brand			Japanese Brand			Chinese Brand
	1985	**1996**	**2008**	**1985**	**1996**	**2008**	**2008**
Subcompact Autos	Excel/Accent (Hyundai) $5,500	$9,079	$12,971	Sentra (Nissan) $7,600	$11,499	$15,483	Chery QQ (Chery) $7,500
DVD Videocassette Recorders	Samsung $270	$260	$99	Toshiba $350	$430	$49	N/A –
Compact Refridgerators	Goldstar $149	$150	N/A	Sanyo $265	$180	$130	Haier $89.99
13-inch Color TVs	Samsung $148	$179	$159	Hitachi/Sony $189	$229	$159	–
Microwave Ovens	Goldstar $149	$120	$95	Toshiba $180	$140	$100	Haier $85

SOURCE: Originally published in L. Helm, "The Koreans Are Coming," *Business Week*. December 23, 1985, 46–52; direct manufacturer/retailer inquries, December 1996. March 2000, and February 2006. In the absence of information/availability, a similar make/model has been used based on *Consumer Reports* data. **http://www.consumerreports.org**. The lowest price for each model was taken.

With longer-term unfavorable currency changes, marketers have to improve their efficiency and/or shift production bases. For example, Japanese car manufacturers transplanted more manufacturing into the United States to ensure that yen–dollar changes did not have as sharp an impact as they once did. Furthermore, design and production was improved so that profitability could be maintained even at 80 or 85 yen to the dollar. When 1996 yen values were over 110 to the dollar, Japanese companies were able to cut prices 1.1 percent for the 1997 model year, while their U.S. competitors increased them by 2.8 percent on the average.[35]

Product line pricing occurs typically in conjunction with positioning decisions. The global marketer may have a premium line as well as a standard line and, in some cases, may sell directly to retailers for their private label sales. Products facing mass markets have keener competition and smaller profit margins than premium products, which may well be priced more liberally because there is less competition. For example, for decades, Caterpillar's big ticket items virtually sold themselves. But environmental factors, such as the U.S. budget deficit, and the Asian crisis, resulted in fewer large-scale highway and construction projects. The company then expanded to smaller equipment to remain competitive globally.

Costs

Costs are frequently used as a basis for price determination largely because they are easily measured and provide a floor under which prices cannot go in the long term. These include procurement, manufacturing, logistics, and marketing costs, as well as overhead. Quality at an affordable price drives most procurement systems. The decision to turn to offshore suppliers may often be influenced by their lower prices, which enable the marketer to remain competitive.[36] Locating manufacturing facilities in different parts of the world may lower various costs, such as labor or distribution costs, although this may create new challenges. While a market may be attractive as far as labor costs are concerned, issues such as productivity, additional costs (such as logistics), and political risk will have to be factored in. Furthermore, a country may lose its attraction due to increasing costs (for example, the average industrial wage rose 110 percent in Korea in the 1990s), and the marketer may have to start the cycle anew by going to new markets (such as Indonesia or Vietnam).

Varying inflation rates will have a major impact on the administration of prices, especially because they are usually accompanied by government controls. The task of the parent company is to aid subsidiaries in their planning to ensure reaching margin targets despite unfavorable market conditions. Most experienced companies in the emerging markets generally have strong country managers who create significant value through their understanding of the local environment. Their ability to be more agile in a turbulent environment is a significant competitive advantage. Inflationary environments call for constant price adjustments; in markets with hyperinflation, pricing may be in a stable currency such as the U.S. dollar or the euro with daily translation into the local currency. In such volatile environments, the marketer may want to shift supply arrangements to cost-effective alternatives, pursue rapid inventory turnovers, shorten credit terms, and make sure contracts have appropriate safety mechanisms against inflation (e.g., choice of currency or escalator clause).

The opposite scenario may also be encountered; that is, prices cannot be increased due to economic conditions. Inflation has been kept in check in developed economies for a number of reasons. Globalization has increased the number of competitors, and the Internet has made it easy for customers to shop for the lowest prices. Big intermediaries, such as Wal-Mart, are demanding prices at near cost from their suppliers. In Europe, the advent of the euro has made prices even more transparent.[37] A survey of executives from 134 countries revealed that 59 percent of the respondents did not expect to be able to raise prices in the coming year.[38] Strategies for thriving in disinflationary times may include (1) target pricing, in which efficiencies are sought in production and marketing to meet price-driven costing; (2) value pricing, to move away from coupons, discounts, and promotions to everyday low prices; (3) stripping down products, to offer quality without all the frills; (4) adding value by introducing innovative products sold at a modest premium (accompanied by strong merchandising and promotion) but perceived by customers to be worth it; and (5) getting close to customers by using new technologies (such as the Internet and EDI) to track their needs and company costs more closely.[39]

Internally, controversy may arise in determining which manufacturing and marketing costs to include. For example, controversy may arise over the amounts of research and development to charge to subsidiaries or over how to divide the costs of a pan-regional advertising campaign when costs are incurred primarily on satellite channels and viewership varies dramatically from one market to the next.

Demand and Market Factors

Demand will set a price ceiling in a given market. Despite the difficulties in obtaining data on foreign markets and forecasting potential demand, the global marketer must make judgments concerning the quantities that can be sold at different prices in each foreign market. The global marketer must understand the **price elasticity of consumer demand** to determine appropriate price levels, especially if cost structures change. A status-conscious market that insists on products with established reputations will be inelastic, allowing for far more pricing freedom than a market where price-consciousness drives demand. Many U.S. and European companies have regarded Japan as a place to sell premium products at premium prices. With the increased information and travel that globalization has brought about, status-consciousness is being replaced by a more practical consumerist sensibility: top quality at competitive prices.

The marketer's freedom in making pricing decisions is closely tied to customer perceptions of the product offering and the marketing communication tied to it. Toyota is able to outsell Chevys, which are identical and both produced by NUMMI Inc., which is a joint venture between Toyota and GM, even though its version (the Corolla) is priced $2,000 higher on the average. Similarly, Korean automakers have had a challenging time in shedding their image as a risky purchase. For example, consumers who liked the Hyundai Santa Fe said they would pay $10,000 less because it was a Hyundai.[40] Hyundai has made major inroads into improving quality perceptions with its ten-year drive train warranty policy (which is very expensive, however). The high ratings from J.D. Power and Associates' Vehicle Dependability Studies have added validity to these perceptions.

Prices have to be set keeping in mind not only the ultimate consumers but also the intermediaries involved. The success of a particular pricing strategy will depend on the willingness of both the manufacturer and the intermediary to cooperate. For example, if the marketer wants to undercut its competition, it has to make sure that retailers' margins remain adequate and competitive to ensure appropriate implementation. At the same time, there is enormous pressure on manufacturers' margins from the side of intermediaries who are growing in both size and global presence. These intermediaries, such as the French Carrefour and the British Marks & Spencer, demand low-cost, direct-supply contracts, which many manufacturers may not be willing or able to furnish.[41] The only other option may be to resort to alternate distribution modes, which may be impossible.

Market Structure and Competition

Competition helps set the price within the parameters of cost and demand. Depending on the marketer's objectives and competitive position, it may choose to compete directly on price or elect for nonprice measures. If a pricing response is sought, the marketer can offer bundled prices (e.g., value deals on a combination of products) or loyalty programs to insulate the firm from a price war. Price cuts can also be executed selectively rather than across the board. New products can be introduced to counter price challenges. For example, when Japanese Kao introduced a low-priced diskette to compete against 3M, rather than drop its prices 3M introduced a new brand, Highland, that effectively flanked Kao's competitive incursion. Simply dropping the price on the 3M brand could have badly diluted its image. On the nonprice front, the company can opt to fight back on quality by adding and promoting value-adding features.[42]

If a company's position is being eroded by competitors who focus on price, the marketer may have no choice but to respond. For example, IBM's operation in Japan lost market share in mainframes largely because competitors undersold the company. A Japanese mainframe was typically listed at 10 percent less than its IBM counterpart, and it frequently carried an additional 10 to 20 percent discount beyond that. This created an extremely competitive market. IBM's reaction was to respond in kind with aggressive promotion of its own, with the result that it began regaining its lost share. Motorola and Nokia, the leading mobile phone makers, are facing tough conditions in the Korean market. In addition to being competitive in price and quality, local companies such as Samsung and Goldstar are quick to come up with new models to satisfy the fast-changing needs of consumers while providing better after-sales service, free of charge or at a marginal price, than the two global players.[43] In a market known for its ethnocentric consumers, the locals have won the battle.

In some cases, strategic realignment may be needed. To hold on to its eroding worldwide market share, Caterpillar has striven to shrink costs and move away from its old practice of competing only by building advanced, enduring machines and selling them at premium prices. Instead, the company has cut prices and used strategic alliances overseas to produce competitive equipment to better suit local and regional needs.

Some marketers can fend off price competition by emphasizing other elements of the marketing mix, even if they are at an absolute disadvantage in price. Singer Sewing Machine Co., which gains nearly half its $500 million in non-U.S. sales from developing countries, emphasizes its established reputation, product quality, and liberal credit terms, as well as other services (such as sewing classes), rather than compete head-on with lower-cost producers.[44] At $40 to $60, jeans are not affordable to the masses in developing countries. Arvind Mills, the world's fifth-largest denim maker, introduced "Ruf & Tuf" jeans—a ready-to-make kit of jeans components priced at $6 which could be assembled inexpensively by a local tailor.[45]

The pricing behavior of a global marketer may come under scrutiny in important market sectors, such as automobiles or retailing. If local companies lose significant market share to outsiders as a result of lower prices, they may ask for government interference against alleged dumping. Wal-Mart resigned from Mexico's National Retailers Association to protest an ethics code that members approved prohibiting price comparisons in ads by their members (on the basis of negative publicity for other retailers). Since ad campaigns are the key to Wal-Mart's "everyday low prices" strategy, it had no choice but to leave the organization.[46]

Environmental Constraints

Governments influence prices and pricing directly as well. In addition to policy measures, such as tariffs and taxes, governments may also elect to directly control price levels. Once under **price controls**, the global marketer has to operate as it would in a regulated industry. Setting maximum prices has been defended primarily on political grounds: It stops inflation and an accelerating wage-price spiral, and consumers want it. Supporters also maintain that price controls raise the income of the poor. Operating in such circumstances is difficult. Achieving change in prices can be frustrating; for example, a company may wait 30 to 45 days for an acknowledgment of a price-increase petition.

To fight price controls, multinational corporations can demonstrate that they are getting an unacceptable return on investment and that, without an acceptable profit opportunity, future investments will not be made and production perhaps will be stopped. These have been the arguments of U.S. and European pharmaceutical marketers in China.[47] Cadbury Schweppes sold its plant in Kenya because price controls made its operation unprofitable. At one time, Coca-Cola and PepsiCo withdrew their products from the shelves in Mexico until they received a price increase. Pakistani milk producers terminated their business when they could not raise prices, and Glaxo Wellcome, a pharmaceutical manufacturer, canceled its expansion plans in Pakistan because of price controls.

In general, company representatives can cite these consequences in arguing against price controls: (1) the maximum price often becomes the minimum price if a sector is allowed a price increase, because all businesses in the sector will take it regardless of cost justification; (2) the wage-price spiral advances vigorously in anticipation of controls; (3) labor often turns against restrictions because they are usually accompanied by an income policy or wage restrictions; (4) noninflationary wage increases are forestalled; (5) government control not only creates a costly regulatory body but also is difficult to enforce; (6) authorities raise less in taxes because less money is made; and (7) a government may have to bail out many companies with cheap loans or make grants to prevent bankruptcies and unemployment.[48] Once price controls are invoked, management will have to devote much time to resolving the many difficulties that controls present. The best interest of multinational corporations is therefore served by working with governments, especially in the developing countries, to establish an economic policy centered on a relatively free market without price controls. This means, for example, that pharmaceutical firms need to convince governments that their products greatly benefit the public and that their prices are reasonable. If the companies can point to R&D focused on solving local challenges, the argument can be made more convincingly.

Dealing with Financial Crises

A series of currency crises have shaken all emerging markets in the last ten years. The Asian crisis of July 1997, the Russian ruble collapse of August 1998, the fall of the Brazilian real in January 1999, and the Argentine default in 2001, have all provided a spectrum of emerging market economic failures, each with its own complex causes and challenging outlooks.

Causes of the Crises
Both the Mexican and Thai cases of currency devaluation led to regional effects in which international investors saw Mexico and Thailand as only the first domino in a long series of failures to come. For example, the historically stable Korean won fell from Won 900/US$ to Won 1,100/US$ in one month. The reasons for the crises were largely in three areas allowing comparison: corporate socialism, corporate governance, and banking stability and management. In 1997, business liabilities exceeded the capacities of government to bail businesses out, and practices such as lifetime employment were no longer sustainable. Many firms in the Far East were often controlled by families or groups related to the governing party of the country. The interests of stockholders and creditors were secondary in an atmosphere of cronyism. With the speculative investments made by many failing banks, banks themselves had to close, severely hampering the ability of businesses to obtain the necessary capital financing needed for operations. The pivotal role of banking liquidity was the focus of the International Monetary Fund's bail-out efforts.

The Asian crisis had global impact. What started as a currency crisis quickly became a region-wide recession.[49] The slowed economies of the region caused major reductions in world demand for many products, especially commodities. World oil markets, copper markets, and agricultural products all saw severe price drops as demand kept falling. These changes were immediately noticeable in declined earnings and growth prospects for other emerging economies. The problems of Russia and Brazil were reflections of those declines. In Argentina, the government defaulted on its debt, blocked Argentines from paying obligations to foreigners, and stopped pegging the peso to the U.S. dollar.[50]

Effects of the Crises
The collapse of the ruble in Russia and of Russia's access to international capital markets brought into question the benefits of a free-market economy, long championed by the advocates of Western-style democracy. While Russia is the sixth-most populous nation, a nuclear power, and the holder of a permanent seat in the Security Council of the United Nations, its economic status is in many ways that of a developing country. There is a growing middle class, particularly in the largest cities. Some Russian businesses had revealed glimmerings of respect for share holders, staff, and customers. Higher standards were encouraged by a growing international business presence. Many of these positive changes were put into jeopardy.

In Brazil, similar effects were felt. A total of 30 million consumers left the middle class. Many of the free-trade experiments within Mercosur were being reevaluated or endangered, especially by Brazilian moves in erecting tariff barriers. Many of the key sectors, such as automobiles, were hit by layoffs and suspended production. In Argentina, the supply of most foreign-made goods was choked off.

Consumer and Marketer Responses

Changes in the economic environment affect both consumers and marketers. Consumer confidence is eroded and marketers have to weigh their marketing strategies carefully. Some of these adjustments are summarized in Exhibit 17.3.

Recessions have an impact on consumer spending. For example, the 30 million Brazilians who, as a result of the real crisis, were no longer able to consume in a middle-class tradition were also lost to many marketers, such as McDonald's. Rather than buying hamburgers, they would consume more traditional and less expensive meals. Similarly, some consumption may turn not only toward local alternatives but even to generics. Especially hard hit may be big-ticket purchases, such as cars, furniture, and appliances, that may be put on long-term hold.

Marketers' responses to these circumstances have varied from abandoning markets to substantially increasing their efforts. While Daihatsu pulled out of Thailand, GM decided to stay, with a change in the car model to be produced and reduced production volume. Returning to a market having once abandoned it may prove to be difficult. For example, distribution channels may be blocked by competition, or suspicion about the long-term commitment of a returnee may surface among local partners. Deere & Co. would sell its farm

---

Exhibit **17.3**

Consumer and Marketer Adjustment to Financial Crisis

Consumer Adjustment to Financial Hardship	Marketer Adjustment to Financial Hardship

• General reactions
  Reduce consumption and wastefulness
  More careful decision making
  More search for information
	• Marketing-mix strategies
	  Withdraw from weak markets
	  Fortify in strong markets
	  Acquire weak competitors
	  Consider youth markets
	  Resale market for durables

• Product adjustments
  Necessities rather than luxuries
  Switch to cheaper brands or generics
  Local rather than foreign brands
  Smaller quantities/packages
	• Product strategies
	  Prune weak products
	  Avoid introducing new products in gaps
	  Flanker brands
	  Augment products with warranties
	  Adaptive positioning

• Price adjustments
  Life-cycle costs—durability/value
  Emphasis on economical prices
	• Pricing strategies
	  Improve quality while maintaining price
	  Reduce price while maintaining quality
	  Consider product life-cycle pricing

• Promotion adjustments
  Rational approach
  Reduced attraction to gifts
  Information rather than imagery
	• Promotion strategies
	  Maintain advertising budget
	  Focus on print media
	  Assurances through rational appeals
	  Expert endorsements
	  Advisory tone
	  Customer loyalty programs
	  Train sales force to handle objections

• Shopping adjustments
  Increased window shopping
  Preference for discount stores
  Fewer end-of-aisle purchases
	• Distribution strategies
	  Location is critical
	  Sell in discount and wholesale centers
	  Prune marginal dealers
	  Alternative channels

SOURCE: Compiled from Swee Hoon Ang, Siew Meng Leong, and Philip Kotler, "The Asian Apocalypse: Crisis Marketing for Consumers and Businesses," *Long Range Planning* 33 (February 2000): 97–119.

equipment in Argentina only if payment was in US$ or to customers with bank accounts abroad.[51] Manipulating the marketing mix is also warranted. Imported products are going to be more expensive, sometimes many times what the local versions cost. Therefore, emphasizing the brand name, the country of origin, and other benefits may convince the consumer of a positive value-price relationship. Adaptive positioning means recasting the product in a new light rather than changing the product itself. For example, Michelin changed its positioning from "expensive, but worth it" to "surprisingly affordable" in Asian markets affected by the crisis.[52] If the perceived prices are too high, the product and/or its packaging may have to be changed by making the product smaller or the number of units in a pack fewer. For example, Unilever reduced the size of its ice-cream packs, making them cheaper, and offers premiums in conjunction with the purchase of soap products (for example, buy three, get one free).[53] Nike's approach in Asia is described in *The International Marketplace 17.2*.

While marketers from North America and Europe may be faced by these challenges, local companies may have an advantage, not only at home but in inter national markets as well. Their lower prices give them an opportunity to expand outside their home markets or aggressively pursue expansion in new markets. Similarly, companies with sourcing in markets hit by currency crises may be able to benefit from lower procurement costs.

The most interesting approach in the face of challenges is to increase efforts in building market share. A number of U.S. companies in Mexico, such as Procter & Gamble, decided

---

The International
MARKETPLACE

17.2

Nike Does It (Even in a Crisis)

Nike's international revenues have gradually grown to be the majority of the company's $18.6 billion. Asia's share of the total is 18 percent. Asia is Nike's third largest market in terms of revenue and number one location in terms of manufacturing. While growth in Asia has been robust recently (for example, 22 percent in 2008), there have been some challenging times as well.

When the Asian financial crisis sapped the purchasing power in many communities, Nike started targeting teens living in the region's rural and suburban areas with a range of "entry-level" footwear. The Nike Play Series line, launched in India, Indonesia, Singapore, and Thailand, retailed for $25, roughly half of most Nike shoes and far less than the $150 charged for its top-range products.

Asian kids in rural areas might be playing sports with no shoes at all, so they cannot relate to Nike's high-end products. Nike Play Series was created to introduce them to the concept of different shoes for different sports. Even among those who purchase luxury products, sales fell 30 percent during the crisis in markets hardest hit.

Ads for the new product line used the slogan "It's My Turn" and depicted young Asian athletes (such as Singaporean soccer star Alvin Patrimonio) alongside images of major sports stars. Nike also built branded Play Zones in new or refurbished urban centers in Singapore, Kuala Lumpur, Bangkok, Manila, and Johor Bahru. Each included a multicourt facility where kids play everything from badminton

ASIA IS NIKE'S THIRD LARGEST MARKET IN TERMS OF REVENUE AND NUMBER ONE LOCATION IN TERMS OF MANUFACTURING. THIS ADVERTISEMENT IS FROM A RETAIL STORE IN BEIJING, CHINA.

to basketball, highlighted by "event days" with tournaments. In rural areas, Nike donated equipment such as basketball hoops and soccer goal posts to raise the profile of the Nike Play Series.

The experience in Asia has enabled Nike to transfer experiences to new product categories and new markets. For example, Nike launched a lower-priced shoe line in Wal-Mart stores using the Starter brand.

SOURCES: Nike 2008 annual report; "Nike Finds a Way to Go to Wal-Mart," *Advertising Age*, March 21, 2005, 1; "How Nike Got Its Game Back," *Business Week*, November 4, 2002, 129; Normandy Madden, "Nike Sells $25 Shoe Line in Recession-Hit Region," *Advertising Age*, November 1999, 17. See also **http://www.nikebiz.com**.

to invest more due to decreasing competition (that resulted from some competitors leaving) and the increased buying power of their currencies. This strategy is naturally based on the premise that the market will rebound in the foreseeable future, thus rewarding investments made earlier.

Pricing Coordination

The issue of standard worldwide pricing has been mostly a theoretical one because of the influence of the factors already discussed. However, coordination of the pricing function is necessary, especially in larger, regional markets such as the European Union, particularly after the introduction of the euro. With the increasing level of integration efforts around the world, and even discussion of common currency elsewhere, control and coordination of global and regional pricing takes on a new meaning.

With more global and regional brands in the global marketer's offering, control in pricing is increasingly important. Of course, this has to be balanced against the need for allowing subsidiaries latitude in pricing so that they may quickly react to specific market conditions.

Studies have shown that foreign-based multinational corporations allow their U.S. subsidiaries considerable freedom in pricing. This has been explained by the size and unique features of the market. Further, it has been argued that these subsidiaries often control the North American market (that is, a Canadian customer cannot get a better deal in the United States, and vice versa) and that distances create a natural barrier against arbitrage practices that would be more likely to emerge in Europe, although even with the common currency, different rules and standards, economic disparities, and information differences may make deal-hunting difficult.[54] However, recent experience has shown that pricing coordination has to be worldwide because parallel imports will surface in any markets in which price discrepancies exist, regardless of distances. Marketers who mainly sell to organizational customers, such as Nokia to telecommunications operators, have started using standard worldwide pricing.

The Euro and Marketing Strategy

On January 1, 1999, the euro (€) was officially launched by the European Union and it became the one and only currency of the 11 nations in the eurozone January 1, 2002. By 2009, the number of countries had grown to 16. Although the early focus was largely on managing the operational aspects of converting to the use of the euro for all business activities (such as preparing to account for sales and purchasing in euros as well as transforming internal accounting for areas such as R&D budgeting), the strategic issues are the most significant for the future.

In the longer term all firms will need to reexamine the positioning of their businesses. The potential advantages of a single-currency Europe (such as a more competitive market, both internally and externally) have been widely expounded, but the threats to businesses of all nationalities, sizes, and forms have not been so widely discussed. The threats are many. As barriers to the creation of a single domestic market are eliminated, more production and operating strategy decisions will be made on the basis of true-cost differentials (proximity to specific inputs, materials, immobile skills, or niche customers, for example). Consolidation will be the norm for many business units whose existence was in some way perpetuated by the uses of different currencies. This restructuring will have lasting effects on the European business landscape. For example, many marketers are streamlining their operations throughout Euroland and eliminating overlapping entities, such as distribution facilities.[55]

The euro pushes national markets closer together. First and foremost in this area is the transparency to consumers of a single currency and a single cross-border price. The euro combined with the growing use of e-business, for example, allows consumers in Barcelona to surf the Web for the cheapest source of fresh seafood delivered from anywhere within the

EU16. Although theoretically possible before, the quotation of prices by individual currency and complexity of payment often posed a barrier—somewhat real, somewhat imagined—to cross-border purchasing. This barrier no longer exists, as consumers are now able to demand the highest quality product and service at the lowest price from businesses throughout the European community.

A more troublesome result is pricing, both within the firm and to the marketplace. Within the firm, the transfer prices between business units of the firm, whether in-country or cross-border, will now be held to an even more rigorous standard of no differentiation. Transfer prices internationally, however, are one of the key factors in how firms reposition profits in order to reduce their global tax burdens. Without this veil of differences in currency of denomination, any differences in transfer prices across multinational units will be even more apparent (and will not be allowed by the European Commission).

The single currency has made prices completely transparent for all buyers. If discrepancies are not justifiable due to market differences such as consumption preferences, competition, or government interference, parallel importation may occur. The simplest solution would be to have one euro price throughout the market. However, given huge price differences of up to 100 percent, that solution would lead to significant losses in sales and profits, since a single price would likely be closer to the lower-priced countries' level. The recommended approach is a pricing corridor that considers existing country-specific prices while optimizing the profits at a pan-European level.[56] Such a corridor defines the maximum and minimum prices that country organizations can charge—enough to allow flexibility as a result of differences in price elasticities, competition, and positioning, but not enough to attract parallel imports that may start at price differences of 20 percent and higher.[57] This approach moves pricing authority away from country managers to regional management and requires changes in management systems and incentive structures.

In terms of specific pricing approaches, marketers should aim to lower prices as slowly as possible, especially for less price-sensitive customers. Alternatives include developing selective offers to price-sensitive customers using discounts and long-term contracts—measures that put considerably less downward pressure on prices across all customers. In addition, marketers can enhance the value of product and service offerings selectively, and thereby maintain price differentials across Europe.[58]

Multinational customers, such as Coca-Cola or IBM, like to drive hard bargains with their suppliers, seeking low and consistent prices worldwide. This can become a problem when some suppliers provide steep discounts in emerging markets such as China, while keeping prices higher in developed markets. Marketers should make sure that price differences reflect differences in quality or in the services provided. Many industrial companies try to coordinate panregional purchasing in Europe by empowering an individual or department to do so. However, many of them still have national structures whereby country organizations retain considerable say-so in what is bought. Marketers can take advantage of this separation of decision-making power and influence.

Countertrade

The Australian government declared that it would only purchase military equipment from the United States if the U.S. Navy and Marine Corps would buy lollipops from an Australian firm, Allen Sweets Ltd.[59] General Motors exchanged automobiles for a trainload of strawberries. As explained in *The International Marketplace 17.3*, an entire air force can be created with chickens. Or a nation may swap physicians in exchange for oil. All these are examples of countertrade activities carried out around the world.

Countertrade is a sale that encompasses more than an exchange of goods, services, or ideas for money. In the international market, countertrade transactions "are those transactions which have as a basic characteristic a linkage, legal or otherwise, between exports and imports of goods or services in addition to, or in place of, financial settlements."[60] Historically, countertrade was mainly conducted in the form of barter, which is a direct exchange of goods of approximately equal value, with no money involved. These transactions were

The International
MARKETPLACE

A Chicken-Based Air Force

The government of Thailand has announced a plan to expand its air force. The intent is to purchase a 12-plane squadron of Russian SU-30 fighter jets. The cost of these jets is about 35 billion baht: a very large government expenditure.

For many years, Thai producers of agricultural products have felt unable to crack the Russian market. Even though Russia imports about two million tons of chicken every year, about 80 percent of that comes from the United States, but none from Thailand. The Thai government has repeatedly asked Russia to open up its market to Thai chicken. It invited Russian inspectors to the country to examine the high levels of hygiene of Thai chicken plants, but the visit was cancelled due to the outbreak of avian influenza.

Prime Minister Thaksin Shinawatra wanted to put Thai chicken exports on the fast track. When shopping for new fighter jets, his government decided to offer chicken as payment for the planes. The cost of the planes just about equals the total annual chicken exports of Thailand. By successfully penetrating the Russian market,

Thai chicken exports could rise by 30 percent annually. In addition, there could also be large export increases for other agricultural exports, such as pork, rice, rubber, and shrimp. But chicken would be the key component to make the deal fly.

By taking this route to pay for imports, Thailand follows in the footsteps of many other governments. For example, in Latin America, Bolivia has announced that it plans to purchase $180 million worth of diesel fuel from Venezuela. The imports are to be paid for with shipments of soybeans and chicken. Cuba has been even more creative in its exchanges. To pay for its oil imports of 90,000 barrels per day, the Cuban government, which has a history of employing countertrade, has pledged to improve medical treatment and literacy in Venezuela, and is doing so by sending more than 30,000 physicians, sports coaches, and teachers.

SOURCES: Countertrade and Offsets, January 2009; Danna Harman, "Chavez Seeks Influence with Oil Diplomacy," *Christian Science Monitor*, August 25, 2005, **http://www.csmonitor.com**; "CPF Backs Chicken for Fighter Jets," *Knight-Ridder Tribune Business News*, December 24, 2005, **http://www.tmcnet.com**.

---

the very essence of business at times when no money—that is, a common medium of exchange—existed or was available or accepted. Money permits greater flexibility in trading activities. However, we see returns to the barter system as a result of economic circumstances. For example, because of tight financial constraints, Georgetown University, during its initial years of operation after 1789, charged its students part of the tuition in foodstuffs and required students to participate in the construction of university buildings. During periods of high inflation or currency devaluation, goods such as bread, meat, and gold were seen as much more useful and secure than paper money.

Countertrade transactions have therefore always arisen when economic circumstances have encouraged a direct exchange of goods over the use of money. Conditions that support such business activities are lack of money, lack of value of money, lack of acceptability of money as an exchange medium, or greater ease of transaction by using goods. However, the shrinking of established markets and the existence of a substantial product surplus are also conditions that foster countertrade.

These same reasons prevail in today's resurgence of countertrade activities. Throughout the past decades, the use of countertrade has steadily increased. In 1972, countertrade was used by only 15 countries. By 1983, the countries conducting countertrade transactions numbered 88, and by 2004 the number was 130.[61] Estimates of the total global countertrade volume vary widely. The United Nations estimates that countertrade transactions make up about 10 percent of world trade.[62]

Why Countertrade?

Many countries are deciding that countertrade transactions are more beneficial to them than transactions based on financial exchange alone. A primary reason is that world debt crises and exchange rate volatility have made ordinary trade financing very risky. Many in the developing world cannot obtain the trade credit or financial assistance necessary to afford desired imports. Heavily indebted nations, faced with the possibility of not being able to afford imports at all, resort to countertrade to maintain product inflow.

The use of countertrade permits the covert reduction of prices and therefore allows firms and governments to circumvent price and exchange controls. Particularly in commodity markets with operative cartel arrangements, such as oil or agriculture, this benefit may be very useful to a producer. For example, by using oil as a countertraded product for industrial equipment, a surreptitious discount (by using a higher price for the acquired products) may expand market share. In a similar fashion, the countertrading of products masks dumping activities.[63]

Countertrade is also often viewed by firms and nations alike as an excellent mechanism to gain entry into new markets. When a producer believes that marketing is not its strong suit, or that international competition is too strong, it often sees countertrade as useful. The producer often hopes that the party receiving the goods will serve as a new distributor, opening up new international marketing channels and ultimately expanding the original market. Conversely, markets with little cash can provide major opportunities for firms if they are willing to accept countertrade. A firm that welcomes countertrade welcomes new buyers and sets itself apart from the competition.

Countertrade also can provide stability for long-term sales. For example, if a firm is tied to a countertrade agreement, it will need to source the product from a particular supplier, whether or not it wants to do so. This stability is often highly valued because it eliminates, or at least reduces, vast swings in demand and thus allows for better planning.

Under certain conditions, countertrade can ensure the quality of an international transaction. In instances where the seller of technology is paid in output produced by the technology delivered, the seller's revenue depends on the success of the technology transfer and maintenance services in production. Therefore, the seller is more likely to be dedicated in the provision of services, maintenance, and general technology transfer.[64] In such instances, the second part of the transaction serves as a "hostage" that induces both trading partners to fulfill their contractual obligations. Particularly under conditions of limited legal protection, countertrade can be equated to an exchange of hostages that ensures that all parties involved live up to their agreement.[65]

In spite of all these apparent benefits of countertrade, there are strong economic arguments against this activity. These arguments are based mainly on efficiency grounds. As economist Paul Samuelson stated, "Instead of there being a double coincidence of wants, there is likely to be a want of coincidence; so that, unless a hungry tailor happens to find an undraped farmer, who has both food and a desire for a pair of pants, neither can make a trade."[66] Instead of trade balances being settled on a multilateral basis, with surpluses from one country being balanced by deficits with another, countertrade requires that accounts be settled on a country-by-country or even transaction-by-transaction basis. Trade then results only from the ability of two parties or countries to purchase specified goods from one another rather than from competition. As a result, uncompetitive goods may be marketed. In consequence, the ability of countries and their industries to adjust structurally to more efficient production may be restricted. Countertrade can therefore be seen as eroding the quality and efficiency of production and as lowering world consumption. These economic arguments notwithstanding, however, countries and companies see countertrade as an alternative that may be flawed but worthwhile to undertake. As far as the unilateral focus is concerned, it may well be that this restriction can be removed through electronic commerce. With growing ease of reach, it may well become possible to create an online global barter economy that addresses itself to those transactions that cannot be conducted on regular financial terms.

Types of Countertrade

Under the traditional types of **barter** arrangements, goods are exchanged directly for other goods of approximately equal value. However, simple barter transactions are less often used today.

Exhibit 17.4

Classification of Forms of Countertrade

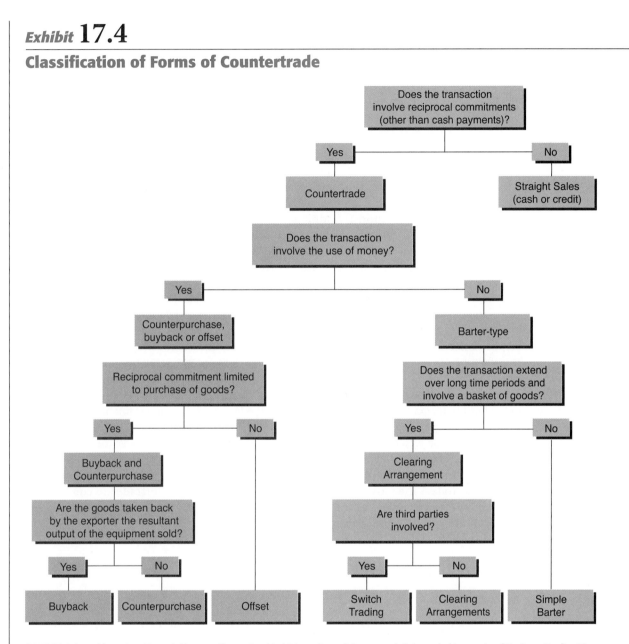

SOURCE: Adapted from Jean-François Hennart, "Some Empirical Dimensions of Countertrade," *Journal of International Business Studies* 21 (no. 2, 1990): 245.

Increasingly, participants in countertrade have resorted to more sophisticated versions of exchanging goods that often also include some use of money. Exhibit 17.4 provides an overview of the different forms of countertrade that are in use today. One refinement of simple barter is the **counterpurchase**, or parallel barter, agreement. The participating parties sign two separate contracts that specify the goods and services to be exchanged. Frequently, the exchange is not of precisely equal value; therefore, some amount of cash will be involved. However, because an exchange of goods for goods does take place, the transaction can rightfully be called barter.

Another common form of countertrade is the **buyback**, or compensation, arrangement. One party agrees to supply technology or equipment that enables the other party to produce goods with which the price of the supplied products or technology is repaid. One example of such a buyback arrangement is an agreement entered into by Levi Strauss and Hungary.

The company transferred the know-how and the Levi's trademark to Hungary. A Hungarian firm began producing Levi's products and marketing some of them domestically. The rest are marketed abroad by Levi Strauss, in compensation for the know-how.

A more refined form of barter, aimed at reducing the effect of the immediacy of the transaction, is called **clearing arrangements**. Here, clearing accounts are established in which firms can deposit and withdraw the results of their countertrade activities. These currencies merely represent purchasing power, however, and are not directly withdrawable in cash. As a result, each party can agree in a single contract to purchase goods or services of a specified value. Although the account may be out of balance on a transaction-by-transaction basis, the agreement stipulates that over the long term, a balance in the account will be restored. Frequently, the goods available for purchase with clearing account funds are tightly stipulated. In fact, funds have on occasion been labeled "apple clearing dollars" or "horseradish clearing funds." Additional flexibility can be given to the clearing account by permitting **switch-trading**, in which credits in the account can be sold or transferred to a third party. Doing so can provide creative intermediaries with opportunities for deal making by identifying clearing account relationships with major imbalances and structuring business transactions to reduce them.

Another key form of barter arrangement is called **offset**, which is the industrial compensation mandated by governments when purchasing defense-related goods and services in order to offset or counterbalance the effect of this purchase on the balance of payments. Offsets can include coproduction, licenses production, subcontractor production, technology transfer, or overseas investment. Typically, in order to secure the sale of military equipment, the selling companies have to offset the cost of the arms through investment in nonrelated industries. The offsets frequently reach or exceed the price of the defense equipment, to the delight of the buyer, but often to the chagrin of the home country government of the selling firms. U.S. weapons exporters alone are estimated to complete about $4 to $7 billion annually in defense offset transactions, which, according to some, may over time strengthen foreign competitors and adversely affect employment.[67]

With the increasing sophistication of countertrade, the original form of straight barter is used less today. The most frequently completed forms of countertrade are counterpurchase, buyback agreements, and, due to continued major military expenditures around the world, offsets.

Preparing for Countertrade

Early on in the countertrade process a firm needs to decide whether it wishes to use an outside countertrade intermediary or keep the management of the transaction in-house. Assistance from intermediaries can be quite expensive but relieves the firm of the need to learn a new expertise. Exhibit 17.5 provides a summary of the advantages and disadvantages of carrying out countertrade transactions within versus outsourcing them. If companies carry out countertrade transactions in-house, the profitability of countertrade can be high. However, developing an in-house capability for handling countertrade should be done with great caution.

First, the company needs to determine the import priorities of its products to the country or firm to which it is trying to sell. Goods that are highly desirable and necessary for a country mandating countertrade are less likely to be subject to countertrade requirements than imports of goods considered luxurious and unnecessary. As a next step, the company needs to incorporate possible countertrade cost into the pricing scheme. It is quite difficult to increase the price of goods once a "cash-deal" price has been quoted and a subsequent countertrade demand is presented.

At this stage, the most favored countertrade arrangement from the buyer's perspective should be identified. To do this, the company needs to determine the goals and objectives of the countertrading parties. These can consist of import substitution, preservation of hard currency, or export promotion.

Exhibit **17.5**

Organizing for Countertrade: In-House versus Third Parties

Advantages	Disadvantages
In-House	
· More profitable	· Accounting and legal expertise required
· Customer contact	· Reselling problems
· Greater control	· Recruitment and training costs
· More flexibility	· Less objectivity
· More learning	· Unexpected risks and demands for countertrade
Third Parties	
· Export specialists	· May be expensive
· Customer contacts	· Distanced from customer
· Reselling contacts	· Less flexibility
· Legal and accounting expertise	· Less confidentiality
· More objectivity	· Less learning

SOURCE: Adapted from Charles W. Neale, David D. Shipley, and J. Colin Dodds, "The Countertrading Experience of British and Canadian Firms," *Management International Review* 31 (no. 1, 1991): 33.

The next step is to match the strengths of the firm with current and potential countertrade situations. The company should explore whether any internal needs can fulfill a countertrade contract. This may mean that raw materials or intermediate products currently sourced from other suppliers could now be obtained from the countertrade partner. However, this assessment should not be restricted to the corporation itself. A firm may be able to use its distribution capabilities or its contacts with customers and suppliers to help with countertrade transactions. Based on the notion that the supplier benefits from the export taking place due to the countertrade, main contractors may demand that major suppliers participate in disposing of the countertraded goods. As a result, even companies that do not see themselves as international marketers may suddenly be confronted with countertrade demands.

At this point, the company can decide whether it should engage in countertrade transactions. The accounting and taxation aspects of the countertrade transactions should be considered because they can often be quite different from current procedures. The use of an accounting or tax professional is essential to comply with difficult and obscure tax regulations.

Next, all of the risks involved in countertrade must be assessed. This means that the goods to be obtained need to be specified, the delivery time for these goods needs to be determined, and the reliability of the supplier and the quality and consistency of the goods needs to be assessed. It is also useful to explore the impact of countertrade on future prices, both for the price of the specific goods obtained and for the world market price of the category of goods. For example, a countertrade transaction may appear to be quite profitable at the time of agreement. Because months or even years may pass before the transaction is actually consummated, however, world market prices can change. The effect of the countertrade transaction itself on market price should also be considered. Large-volume transactions may affect established prices. Such a situation not only may affect the profitability of a transaction but also can result in possible legal actions by other suppliers of similar products who feel injured.

When evaluating the countertraded products, it is useful to determine the impact of the countertraded products on the sales and profits of other complementary product lines currently marketed by the firm. Any repercussions from outside groups should also be investigated. Such repercussions may consist of antidumping actions brought about by competitors or reactions from totally unsuspected quarters. For example, McDonnell Douglas ran into strong opposition when it bartered an airplane for ham used in its employee cafeteria and as Christmas gifts. The local meat-packers' union complained vociferously that McDonnell Douglas was threatening the jobs of its members and went on strike.

Using all of the information obtained, the company can finally evaluate the length of the intended relationship with the countertrading partner and the importance of this relationship for future plans and goals. These parameters will be decisive for the final action because they may form constraints overriding short-term economic effects. Overall, management needs to remember that, in most instances, a countertrade transaction should remain a means for successful international marketing and not become an end in itself.

Summary

In a world of increasing competition, government regulation, accelerating inflation, and widely fluctuating exchange rates, global marketers must spend increasing amounts of time planning pricing strategy. Because pricing is the only revenue-generating element of the marketing mix, its role in meeting corporate objectives is enhanced. However, it comes under increasing governmental scrutiny as well, as evidenced by intracompany transfer pricing.

The three philosophies of transfer pricing that have emerged over time are cost-based, market-based, and arm's-length. Transfer pricing concerns are both internal and external to the company. Internally, manipulating transfer prices may complicate control procedures and documentation. Externally, problems arise from the tax and regulatory entities of the countries involved.

Pricing decisions are typically left to the local managers; however, planning assistance is provided by the parent company. Pricing in individual markets comes under the influence of environmental variables, each market with its own unique set. This set consists of corporate objectives, costs, customer behavior and market conditions, market structure, and environmental constraints.

Economic crises have hit many of the world's emerging markets in the last twenty years. In such a challenging environment, effective marketing planning and implementation take on additional significance. While withdrawal may be a feasible alternative, the consequences have to be assessed against the company's global operations. Marketers have found ways to grow market share even under such adverse circumstances.

The individual impact of these environmental variables and their interaction must be thoroughly understood by the global marketer, especially if regional, or even worldwide, coordination is attempted. Control and coordination are becoming more important with increasing economic integration.

Corporations use countertrade as a competitive tool to maintain or increase market share. The complexity of these transactions requires careful planning in order to avoid major corporate losses. Management must consider how the acquired merchandise will be disposed of, what the potential for market disruptions is, and to what extent the countertraded goods fit with the corporate mission.

Key Terms

arm's-length price	price controls	buyback
arm's-length standard	countertrade	clearing arrangements
price elasticity of consumer	barter	switch-trading
demand	counterpurchase	offset

Questions for Discussion

1. Comment on the pricing philosophy, "Sometimes price should be wrong by design."

2. The standard worldwide base price is most likely looked on by management as full-cost pricing, including an allowance for manufacturing overhead, general overhead, and selling expenses. What factors are overlooked?

3. In combating price controls, multinational corporations will deal with agency administrators rather than policymakers. How can they convince administrators that price relief is fair to the company and also in the best interest of the host country?

4. Which elements of pricing can be standardized?

5. Why do local price differences stay in place even with the euro as a common currency?

6. Discuss the advantages and drawbacks of countertrade.

Internet Exercises

1. The European Union promotes the benefits of the euro as a common currency for the 16 EU nations that have adopted it (see http://europa.eu.int/comm/economy_finance/euro/our_currency_en.htm). What are possible disadvantages of it?

2. Compare the services of the Global Offset and Countertrade Organization (http://www.countertrade.org) and the Asia-Pacific Countertrade Association (http://www.apca.net).

Recommended Reading

Ancheoli, Brian, Mark Levey and Kenneth Parker. *Tax Director's Guide to International Transfer Pricing.* Newton, MA: GBIS, 2008.

Brauer, Juergen. *Arms Trade and Economic Development: Theory and Policy in Offsets.* Oxford: Routledge, 2005.

Bureau of Industry and Security, U.S. Department of Commerce. *Offsets in Defense Trade,* 13th Annual Report. Washington, D.C.: December 2008.

Countertrade and Offsets, a twice monthly publication, http://www.cto-offset.com.

Global Offset and Counter Trade Organization, http://www.globaloffset.org.

Li, Jian, and Alan Paisey. *International Transfer Pricing.* New York: Palgrave McMillan, 2008.

Zurawicki, Leon. *International Countertrade.* New York: Pergamon Press, 2003.

GLOBAL PROMOTIONAL STRATEGIES

The International
MARKETPLACE

Global Sponsorship

In any given country, the majority of corporate sponsorship goes to sports. Of the nearly $43.5 billion spent worldwide for sponsorships in 2008, 69 percent was allocated to sports. Within sports, the two flagship events are the World Cup in soccer and the Olympic Games (both summer and winter). Sponsors want to align themselves with—and create—meaningful sports-related moments for consumers. At the same time, consumers associate sponsors of sports events with leadership, teamwork, and pursuit of excellence, as well as friendship. Under the "live Olympic" platform for Coca-Cola, a variety of marketing activities were rolled out by The Coca-Cola Company both globally and in selected countries around the world during the XX Winter Olympics in Torino, Italy, in 2006.

Sponsorships have been a cornerstone of the Coca-Cola Company's marketing efforts for 100 years, having started with using sports stars such as world champion cyclist Bobby Walthour in ads in 1903. Presently, the company is the world's biggest sports sponsor, with total sponsorship-related expenses at $1 billion annually. These activities span different types of sports and various geographies (as shown below).

Coca-Cola spent $26 million for its sponsorship of the World Cup in 2002, which gave it the right to use the World Cup logo/trademarks, exclusive positioning and branding around the event, as well as premium perimeter advertising positions at every game. Sponsorships include

a guarantee that no rival brands can be officially linked to the tournament or use the logo or trademarks. To assure exclusivity, FIFA (soccer's governing body) bought all key billboard advertising space around the main stadia for the tournament, and this space was offered to the sponsors first. In addition, every main sponsor got 250 tickets for each game of the tournament for promotional purposes or corporate entertainment (of key constituents, such as intermediaries or customers).

Each country organization within Coca-Cola decides which programs it wants to use during sponsorship depending on its goals, which are jointly set by local managers and headquarters. For example, in Rio de Janeiro, the company erected huge TV screens on which people could watch World Cup games. Given that Ecuador qualified for the tournament for the first time in its history, this fact was played up in local advertising. In Japan, the company used I-mode phones in addition to traditional media to create meaningful and relevant connections with the World Cup. Naturally, there is always substantial overlap in programs between markets, with headquarters' 20-person team in charge of the coordination effort. One example of this was an online World Cup game that headquarters created in conjunction with Yahoo! and then helped each interested country localize. Another global program was Coca-Cola Go! Stadium Art that allowed consumers and artists to compete to create ads that ran in the various stadia throughout the tournament. The company also joined forces with other sponsors for cross-promotional efforts, e.g., with Adidas to give away the Official Match Ball, with McDonald's for consumer promotions, and with Toshiba on a cyber cup tournament.

Although marketers have become far more demanding in terms of their sponsorships, the World Cup is one of the few global events available. Pulling out would mean a competitor stepping in (for example, when Vauxhall left in 1998, Hyundai took its place).

While measurement of the return on such investment is challenging, Coca-Cola evaluates such dimensions as the number of new corporate customers that sell Coke in their stores, the incremental amount of promotional/display activity, and new vending placement. The influence on the brand is the most difficult to establish; World Cup sponsorship has been suggested to have boosted its presence, especially in the emerging and developing markets.

Coca-Cola's Sports Sponsorships

Olympics (since 1928)

- Supports athletes and teams in nearly 200 countries in exchange for exclusive rights in nonalcoholic beverage category through 2020
- Official soft/sports drink (Coca-Cola, PowerAde)
- Runs marketing programs in over 130 countries

Soccer

- FIFA partner since 1974—signed landmark eight-year agreement through 2006 to be official soft/sports drink at Men's World Cup 2002/2006, Women's World Cup 1999/2003, Confederation Cup competitions, under 20/under 17 World Youth Championships
- Also sponsors Copa America, Asian Football Confederation, over 40 national teams

COCA-COLA SPONSORED THE BEIJING OLYMPICS IN 2008.

© ELIZABETH DALZIEL/ASSOCIATED PRESS

Basketball

- Signed 100-year agreement in 1998 for Sprite to be official soft drink of NBA/WNBA
- Advertising in over 100 countries

Others

- Coca-Cola Classic: official soft drink of National Football League
- Surge/PowerAde: official sports drink of National Hockey League
- Coca-Cola Classic/PowerAde: official soft drink/sports drink of Rugby World Cup
- Sponsor of International Paralympics/Special Olympics

SOURCES: **http://www.sponsorship.com**, accessed February 12, 2009; "'06 Outlook: Sponsorship Growth Back to Double Digits," *IEG Sponsorship Report,* December 26, 2005, 1, 4; "Still Waiting for That Winning Kick," *Business Week,* October 21, 2002, 116–118; "The Best Global Brands," *Business Week,* August 5, 2002, 92–94; "World Cup: Sponsors Need to Get in the Game," *Business Week,* June 17, 2002, 52; "World Cup Marketing," *Advertising Age Global,* March 2002, 17–30; and "Too Many Players on the Field," *Advertising Age,* December 10, 2001, 3.

The general requirements of effective marketing communications apply to the global marketer as well; however, the environments and the situations usually are more numerous and call for coordination of the promotional effort. Increasingly, marketers opt for varying degrees of panregional and integrative approaches to take advantage of similarities in markets they serve, as seen in *The International Marketplace 18.1.* All possible points of touch that the customer has with the marketer's brands have to be incorporated into the communications plan.

The technology is in place for global communication efforts, but difficult challenges still remain in the form of cultural, economic, ethnic, regulatory, and demographic differences in the various countries and regions. Standardization of any magnitude requires sound management systems and excellent communication to ensure uniform strategic and tactical thinking of all the professionals in the overseas marketing chain.[1] One marketer has suggested the development of a worldwide visual language that would be understandable and that would not offend cultural sensitivities.

This chapter will analyze the elements to be managed in promotional efforts in terms of environmental opportunities and constraints. A framework is provided for the planning of promotional campaigns. Although the discussion focuses mostly on advertising, other elements of the promotion mix, especially sales promotion and publicity, fit integrally into the planning model. Naturally, all of the mass selling methods have to be planned in conjunction with personal selling efforts. For example, personal selling often relies on updated direct e-mailing lists and promotional materials sent to prospects before the first sales call.

Planning Promotional Campaigns

The planning for promotional campaigns consists of the following seven stages, which usually overlap or take place concurrently, especially after the basics of the campaign have been agreed on:

1. Determine the target audience
2. Determine specific campaign objectives
3. Determine the budget
4. Determine media strategy
5. Determine the message
6. Determine the campaign approach
7. Determine campaign effectiveness[2]

The actual content of these stages will change by type of campaign situation; compare, for example, a local campaign for which headquarters provides support versus a global corporate image campaign.

The Target Audience

Global marketers face multiple audiences beyond customers. The expectations of these audiences have to be researched to ensure the appropriateness of campaign decision making. Consider the following publics with whom communication is necessary: suppliers, intermediaries, government, the local community, bankers and creditors, media organizations, shareholders, and employees. Each can be reached with an appropriate mix of tools. A multinational corporation that wants to boost its image with the government and the local community may sponsor events. One of the approaches available is **cause-related marketing**, in which the company, or one of its brands, is linked with a cause such as environmental protection or children's health. For example, Unilever's Funfit Program for its Persil washing powder brand in Europe creates resource packs for teachers to help boost children's fitness through physical education lessons. Microsoft launched a Web site in Singapore to further the use of information technology. For every page hit within the site, Microsoft donated one cent to three local charities. This type of activity can benefit a brand but must be backed by a genuine effort within the company to behave responsibly.[3]

Some campaigns may be targeted at multiple audiences. For example, British Airways' "Manhattan Landing" campaign (in which Manhattan Island takes to the air and lands in London) was directed not only at international business travelers but also at employees, the travel industry, and potential stockholders (the campaign coincided with the privatization of the airline). Once the repositioning was achieved, the airline focused on establishing its global stature with the "Face" campaign and switched later to service enhancements with "Sweet Dreams."[4] As companies such as airlines become more internationally involved, target audience characteristics change. American Airlines, which enjoys a huge domestic market, services 40 countries (130 with its alliance partners), generating a third of passenger miles compared with virtually none in 1980.[5]

An important aspect of research is to determine multimarket target audience similarities. If such exist, panregional or global campaigns can be attempted. Grey Advertising checks for commonalities in variables such as economic expectations, demographics, income, and education. Consumer needs and wants are assessed for common features. An increasing number of companies are engaging in **corporate image advertising** in support of their more traditional tactical product-specific and local advertising efforts.[6] Especially for multidivisional companies, an umbrella campaign may help either to boost the image of lesser-known product lines or make the company itself be understood correctly or perceived more positively. Companies may announce repositioning strategies through image campaigns to both external and internal constituents. GE's campaign, branded Ecomagination, is a company-wide initiative to push environmentally-friendly products. The plan is to double company revenues from eco-safe products to $20 billion by 2010. To go beyond the campaign, each of GE's 11 business units are to come up with at least five big environmental ideas capable of generating $100 million of revenue within the next three to five years.[7] Canon has used the approach to reposition itself as an information technology specialist instead of just a manufacturer of office automation machines, and as a serious contender to Xerox in the high end of the market.[8] Costs may also be saved in engaging in global image campaigning, especially if the same campaign or core concepts can be used across borders. A campaign example by Toyota is shown in Exhibit 18.1.

Exhibit **18.1**

An Example of a Corporate Image Campaign

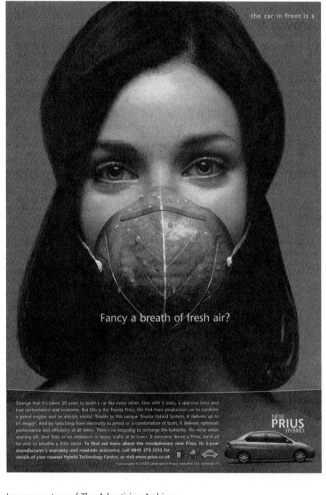

Image courtesy of The Advertising Archives

In some cases the product may be standard across markets but the product's positioning, and subsequently marketing communication, has to change. For example, Mars is a meal substitute in Britain but an energizer in continental Europe. The Ford Fiesta is a small car for the German market, but a family car in Portugal.[9] Audience similarities are more easily found in business markets.

Campaign Objectives

Nothing is more essential to the planning of international promotional campaigns than the establishment of clearly defined, measurable objectives. These objectives can be divided into overall global and regional objectives as well as local objectives. The objectives that are set at the local level are more specific and set measurable targets for individual markets. These objectives may be product- or service-related or related to the entity itself. Typical goals are to increase awareness, enhance image, and improve market share in a particular market. Whatever the objective, it has to be measurable for control purposes.

While FedEx is one the top three transportation companies in Latin America, it is not the household name it is in North America. The company wanted to increase brand awareness among its target audience of small- and medium-sized international shippers. Among large corporate clients, FedEx has no concerns and marketing to them is usually done through personal visits by the FedEx sales force. To reach the intended target, FedEx created a 30-second television spot featuring a soccer team's manager distressed over the fate of missing uniforms he had shipped to Madrid for a big match. Using soccer in the region is an effective way to cut through languages and cultures.[10]

There is a move by many governments to influence how their countries are perceived, to gain commercial or political advantage.[11] After 9/11, for example, the United States has needed to build a new level of understanding of how its values and policies are understood, especially in countries where resentment of its power and influence may be high. Part of this effort was a $10 million advertising campaign from McCann Erickson featuring stories of Muslim life in the United States. It ran on TV and radio from Indonesia through the Middle East. The campaign was based on the premise that Arab and U.S. cultures share family as a common core value. The Business for Diplomatic Action was founded by leading global companies on the premise that anti-American feelings would eventually hurt U.S. brands overseas.[12] The global economic debacle that struck in 2008 undermined substantially the trust the public had for government, firms, and the market economy. There may be, therefore, a substantial need for a future global campaign exercise to restore the belief of individuals in a newly devised corporate and government cooperation.

Local objectives are typically developed as a combination of headquarters (global or regional) and country organization involvement. Basic guidelines are initiated by headquarters, whereas local organizations set the actual country-specific goals. These goals are subject to headquarters approval, mainly to ensure consistency. Although some campaigns, especially global ones, may have more headquarters involvement than usual, local input is still quite important, especially to ensure appropriate implementation of the subsequent programs at the local level.

The Budget

The promotional budget links established objectives with media, message, and control decisions. Ideally, the budget would be set as a response to the objectives to be met, but resource constraints often preclude this approach. Many marketers use an objective task method, as a survey of 484 advertising managers for consumer goods in fifteen countries indicates (see Exhibit 18.2); however, realities may force compromises between ideal choices and resources available.[13] As a matter of fact, available funds may dictate the basis from which the objective task method can start. Furthermore, advertising budgets should be set on a market-by-market basis because of competitive differences across markets. When it comes to global image campaigns, for example, headquarters should provide country organizations extra funds for their implementation.

Exhibit **18.2**

Budgeting Methods for Promotional Programs

Budgeting Method	Percentage of Respondents Using this Method*	Major Differences	
		Lowest Percentages	Highest Percentages
Objective and task	64%	Sweden (36%)	Canada (87%)
		Argentina (44%)	Singapore (86%)
Percentage of sales	48	Germany (31%)	Brazil (73%)
			Hong Kong (70%)
Executive judgment	33	Finland (8%)	USA (64%)
		Germany (8%)	Denmark (51%)
			Brazil (46%)
			Great Britain (46%)
All-you-can-afford	12	Argentina (0%)	Sweden (30%)
		Israel (0%)	Germany (25%)
			Great Britain (24%)
Matched competitors	12	Denmark (0%)	Germany (33%)
		Israel (0%)	Sweden (33%)
			Great Britain (22%)
Same as last year plus a little more	9	Israel (0%)	
Same as last year	3		
Other	10	Finland (0%)	
		Germany (0%)	Canada (24%)
		Israel (0%)	Mexico (21%)

*Total exceeds 100 percent because respondents checked all budgeting methods that they used.

SOURCE: Nicolaos E. Synodinos, Charles F. Keown, and Laurence W. Jacobs, "Transnational Advertising Practices," *Journal of Advertising Research* 29 (April–May 1989): 43–50. © 1989, by the Advertising Research Foundation. Reprinted by permission.

Budgets can also be used as a control mechanism if headquarters retains final budget approval. In these cases, headquarters decision makers must have a clear understanding of cost and market differences to be able to make rational decisions.

In terms of worldwide ad spending, the leaders in 2007 were Procter & Gamble ($9.4 billion), Unilever ($5.3 billion), L'Oreal ($3.4 billion), General Motors ($3.3 billion), Toyota ($3.2 billion), Ford ($2.9 billion), Johnson & Johnson (2.4 billion), and Nestle (2.2 billion).[14] Geographic differences exist in spending; for example, while Procter & Gamble spent 45 percent of its budget in the United States, Unilever's spending there was only 17 percent. The top 100 advertisers incurred nearly half (48.8 percent) of their spending in the United States, with Europe second at 32.6 percent. Asia-Pacific was a distant third, commanding only 14 percent of measured media bought.[15]

Media Strategy

Target audience characteristics, campaign objectives, and the budget form the basis for the choice between media vehicles and the development of a media schedule. The major factors determining the choice of the media vehicles to be used are (1) the availability of the media in a given market, (2) the product or service itself, and (3) media habits of the intended audience.

Media Availability

Media spending, which totaled $478 billion in 2008, varies dramatically around the world. In absolute terms, the United States spends more money on advertising than most of the other major advertising nations combined. Other major spenders are Japan, the United Kingdom, Germany, Canada, and France.

Naturally, this spending varies by market. Countries devoting the highest percentage to television were Peru (84 percent), Mexico (73 percent), and Venezuela (67 percent). In some countries, the percentage devoted to print is still high: Kuwait (91 percent), Norway (77 percent), and Sweden (77 percent). Radio accounts for more than 20 percent of total measured media in only a few countries, such as Trinidad and Tobago, Nepal, and Honduras. Outdoor/transit advertising accounted for 48 percent of Bolivia's media spending but only 3 percent in Germany.[16] Cinema advertising is important in countries such as India and Nigeria. Until a few years ago, the prevailing advertising technique used by the Chinese consisted of outdoor boards and posters found outside factories. Today, the Internet is well on the way to establishing itself as a complementary advertising medium worldwide. The projection is that the Internet may have an 11.5 percent market share in world advertising by 2010, with Internet ad spending reaching $60 billion. Internet advertising constitutes 9 percent of advertising in Sweden and is expected to increase to 12 percent. China accounts for half of the Asia-Pacific region's Internet advertising and will constitute 77 percent of its projected growth. In addition to PCs, mobile phones and interactive TV will become delivery mechanisms.

The media available to the international marketer in major ad markets are summarized in Exhibit 18.3. The breakdown by media points to the enormous diversity in how media are used in a given market. These figures do not tell the whole story, however, which emphasizes the need for careful homework on the part of the international manager charged with media strategy. As an example, Brazil has five television networks, but one of them—TV Globo—corners 50 percent of all television advertising spending. Throughout Latin America, the tendency is to allocate half or more of total advertising budgets to television, with the most coveted spots on prime-time soap operas that attract viewers from Mexico to Brazil. In general, advertising in Latin America requires flexibility and creativity. Inflation rates have caused advertising rates to increase dramatically in countries like Argentina. In Mexico, advertisers can use the "French Plan," which protects participating advertisers from price increases during the year and additionally gives the advertiser two spots for the price of one. For these concessions, the advertiser must pay for the year's entire advertising schedule by October of the year before.

The major problems affecting global promotional efforts involve conflicting national regulations. Even within the EU there is no uniform legal standard. Conditions do vary from country to country, and ads must comply with national regulation. Most European countries either observe the Code of Advertising Practice of the International Chamber of Commerce or have their guidelines based on it.[17] Some of the regulations include limits on the amount of time available for advertisements; for example, in Italy, the state channels allow

Exhibit 18.3

Global Advertising Spending by Medium, 2004–2008 (in $ millions)

Medium	2004	2006	2008	2010
Television	141,510	155,659	176,069	198,894
Newspapers	113,729	122,559	131,724	134,829
Magazines	51,227	55,069	60,569	60,588
Radio	32,7114	34,941	38,134	41,032
Outdoor	21,892	24,916	29,289	31,249
Internet	14,093	22,433	29,902	60,888
Cinema	1,517	1,794	2,094	2,691
Total	376,683	417,371	467,781	530,171

SOURCE: "Ad Growth Stable with Healthy Hotspots," *Zenith Optimedia*, December 20, 2005, available at **http://www.zenithoptimedia.com**.

a maximum of 12 percent advertising per hour and 4 percent per week, and commercial stations allow 18 percent per hour and 15 percent per week. Furthermore, the leading Italian stations do not guarantee audience delivery when spots are bought. Strict separation between programs and commercials is almost a universal requirement, preventing U.S.-style sponsored programs. Restrictions on items such as comparative claims and gender stereotypes are prevalent; for example, Germany prohibits the use of superlatives such as "best."

Until now, with few exceptions, most nations have been very successful in controlling advertising that enters their borders. When commercials were not allowed on the state-run stations, advertisers in Belgium had been accustomed to placing their ads on the Luxembourg station. Radio Luxembourg has traditionally been used to beam messages to the United Kingdom. Currently, however, approximately half of the homes in Europe have access to additional television broadcasts through either cable or direct satellite, and television will no longer be restricted by national boundaries. The implications of this to global marketers are significant. The viewer's choice will be expanded, leading to competition among government-run public channels, competing state channels from neighboring countries, private channels, and pan-European channels.[18] This means that marketers need to make sure that advertising works not only within markets but across countries as well. As a consequence, media buying will become more challenging.

Product Influences

Marketers and advertising agencies are currently frustrated by wildly differing restrictions on how products can be advertised. Agencies often have to produce several separate versions to comply with various national regulations. Consumer protection in general has dominated the regulatory scene both in the European Union and the United States.[19] Changing and standardizing these regulations, even in an area like the EU, is a long and difficult process. While some countries have banned tobacco advertising altogether (e.g., France), some have voluntary restriction systems in place. For example, in the United Kingdom, tobacco advertising is not allowed in magazines aimed at very young women, but it is permitted in other women's magazines. Starting in 2003, tobacco companies were required to print vivid pictures of lung cancer victims and diseased organs on cigarette packets sold in the United Kingdom. The EU has developed union-wide regulation and has banned all forms of cross-border tobacco advertising effective 2005. This means no tobacco advertising in print, as well as on radio, the Internet, and Formula One racing. Existing regulations ban TV advertising. Tobacco marketers would be allowed to advertise on cinema, poster, and billboard sites, but can still be banned by national laws.[20] A summary of product-related regulations found in selected European countries is provided in Exhibit 18.4. Tobacco products, alcoholic beverages, and pharmaceuticals are the most heavily regulated products in terms of promotion.

However, the manufacturers of these products have not abandoned their promotional efforts. Altria Group (formerly Philip Morris) engages in corporate image advertising using its cowboy spokesperson. Some European cigarette manufacturers have diversified into the entertainment business (restaurants, lounges, movie theaters) and named them after their cigarette brands. AstraZeneca, a leading global pharmaceutical, funded a TV campaign run by the French Migraine Association, which discussed medical advances but made no mention of the company. Novo Nordisk has set up an Internet page on diabetes separate from its home page and established the World Diabetes Foundation awareness group.[21]

Certain products are subject to special rules. In the United Kingdom, for example, advertisers cannot show a real person applying an underarm deodorant; the way around this problem is to show an animated person applying the product. What is and is not allowable is very much a reflection of the country imposing the rules. Explicit advertisements of contraceptives are commonplace in Sweden, for example, but far less frequent in most parts of the world. A number of countries have varying restrictions on advertising of toys; Greece bans them altogether, and Belgium restricts their use before and after children's programming.

Beyond the traditional media, the international marketer may also consider **product placement** in movies, TV shows, games, or Web sites. Although there is disagreement about the effectiveness of the method beyond creating brand awareness,[22] products from makers such as BMW, Omega, Nokia, and Heineken have been placed in movies to help both parties to the deal: to create a brand definition for the product and a dimension of reality for the

Exhibit **18.4**

Restrictions on Advertisements for Specific Products in Selected European Countries

Country	Cigarette and Tobacco Products	Alcoholic Beverages	Pharmaceutical Products
United Kingdom	Banned in broadcast; approval required for showing brands of tobacco companies in any sponsored events	Banned in broadcast during or adjacent to children's programs Broadcast permitted in non–children's program airtime, with many regulations	Advertisements for prescription drugs prohibited Restriction applies; e.g., no promotion by celebrities allowed
Ireland	Banned for all cigarette and tobacco products in all forms of advertising, including any sponsorship of events	Broadcast targeting adults is allowed with many rules	Advertisements for prescription drugs prohibited Strict guideline applies to nonprescription drugs
Denmark	Banned in all forms of advertising	Permitted for beverages with alcohol content of less than 2.8% Strict conditions apply	Banned in TV broadcast for both prescription-only and nonprescription medicines Radio broadcast is permitted with strict guidelines
Portugal	Banned in all forms of advertising, except in automobile sports events with international prestige	Banned in TV and radio broadcast between 7 A.M. and 10:30 P.M. Banned in sponsoring events in which minors participate	Advertisements for prescription drugs prohibited Strict guideline applies to nonprescription drugs

SOURCE: "Study on the Evolution of New Advertising Techniques in UK, Ireland, Denmark and Portugal," *Bird & Bird Brussels,* June 17, 2002. Reprinted with permission.

film. The estimated size of the product-placement market in 2005 was $4.24 billion with forecasts for growth reaching $10 billion by 2010.[23] This is driven partly by the success of reality television and by a more empowered consumer who can skip traditional ads with the touch of a button.[24] GM used the action feature film "XXX" to reintroduce its Pontiac GTO. In some markets, product placement may be an effective method of attracting attention due to constraints on traditional media. In China, for example, most commercials on Chinese state-run television are played back-to-back in ten-minute segments, making it difficult for any 30-second ad to be singled out. Placing products in soap operas, such as "Love Talks," has been found to be an effective way to get to the burgeoning middle class in the world's most populous country.[25] Some marketers have started to create stand-alone entertainment vehicles around a brand, such as the BMW film series on the Internet.[26] Calls have been made to ban product placements, or at the very least clearly disclose them in credits. The European Commission will allow product placement in fiction (not in news or factual material), and requires clear labeling.[27]

Audience Characteristics

A major objective of media strategy is to reach the intended target audience with a minimum of waste. As an example, Amoco Oil Company wanted to launch a corporate image campaign in China in the hope of receiving drilling contracts. Identifying the appropriate decision makers was not difficult because they all work for the government. The selection of appropriate media proved to be equally simple because most of the decision makers overseeing petroleum exploration were found to read the vertical trade publications: *International Industrial Review, Petroleum Production,* and *Offshore Petroleum.*

If conditions are ideal, and they seldom are in international markets, the media strategist would need data on (1) media distribution, that is, the number of copies of the print medium or the number of sets for broadcast; (2) media audiences; and (3) advertising exposure. For instance, an advertiser interested in using television in Brazil would like to know that the top adult TV program is "O Clone," with an average audience share of 48 percent and a 30-second ad rate of $71,000. In markets where more sophisticated market research services are available, data on advertising perception and consumer response may be available. In many cases, advertisers have found circulation figures to be unreliable or even fabricated.

An issue related to audience characteristics is the move by some governments to protect their own national media from foreign ones. In Canada, for example, the government prevents foreign publishers from selling space to Canadian advertisers in so-called split-run editions that, in effect, have no local content. If U.S. publications, such as *Sports Illustrated,* were allowed to do it, Canadian publications would be threatened with insufficient amounts of advertising.[28]

Global Media

Media vehicles that have target audiences on at least three continents and for which the media buying takes place through a centralized office are considered to be **global media.**[29] Global media have traditionally been publications that, in addition to the worldwide edition, have provided advertisers the option of using regional editions. For example, *Time Europe* covers the Middle East, Africa, and, since 2003, Latin America. An Asian edition (*Time Asia*) is based in Hong Kong and a Canadian edition (*Time Canada*) is based in Toronto. The South Pacific edition, covering Australia, New Zealand, and the Pacific Islands, is based in Sydney. Different editions enable advertisers to reach a particular country, continent, or the world. In print media, global vehicles include dailies such as *International Herald Tribune,* weeklies such as *The Economist,* and monthlies such as *National Geographic.* Included on the broadcast side are BBC Worldwide TV, CNN, the Discovery Channel, and MTV. The Discovery Channel reaches more than 600 million subscribers in 160 countries in 35 languages through Discovery Channel–Europe, Discovery Channel–Latin America/Iberia, Discovery Channel–Asia, Discovery Canada, Discovery New Zealand, and several other language-tailored networks. The argument that global media drown out local content is not borne out in fact.[30] MTV as a global medium is profiled in *The International Marketplace 18.2,* and shows that one country's MTV looks very little like another's. While Italy, for example, is stylish and features food shows, Japan is very techie featuring a lot of wireless product.

Advertising in global media is dominated by major consumer ad categories, particularly airlines, financial services, telecommunications, automobiles, and tobacco. The aircraft industry represents business market advertisers. Companies spending in global media include AT&T, IBM, UBS, and General Motors. In choosing global media, media buyers consider the three most important media characteristics: targetability, client-compatible editorial, and editorial quality.[31] Some global publications have found that some parts of the globe are more appealing to advertisers than others; for example, some publications have eliminated editions in Africa (due to lack of advertising) and in Asia and Latin America (due to financial crises).

In broadcast media, panregional radio stations have been joined by television as a result of satellite technology. The pan-European satellite channels, such as Sky Channel and Super Channel, were conceived from the very beginning as advertising media. Many are skeptical about the potential of these channels, especially in the short term, because of the challenges of developing a cross-cultural following in Europe's still highly nationalistic markets.[32] Pan-European channels have had to cut back, whereas native language satellite channels like Tele 5 in France and RTL Plus in Germany have increased their viewership. The launch of STAR TV (see Exhibit 18.5) has increased the use of regional advertising campaigns in Asia. While this medium is still regarded as a corporate advertising vehicle, it has nonetheless attracted the interest of consumer goods manufacturers as well.[33]

The International MARKETPLACE

18.2

The World Wants Its MTV!

MTV has emerged as a significant global medium, with more than 440 million households in 167 countries subscribing to its services. The reason for its success is simple—MTV offers consistent, high-quality programming that reflects the tastes and lifestyle of young people.

Its balance of fashion, film, news, competitions, and comedy wrapped in the best music and strong visual identity has made it "the best bet to succeed as a pan-European thematic channel, with its aim to be in every household in Europe," according to *Music Week,* Britain's leading music trade paper. Given that 79 percent of the channel's viewers are in the elusive 16–34 age group, MTV is a force as an advertising medium for those who want to closely target their campaigns. MTV has proven to be the ultimate youth marketing vehicle for companies such as Wrangler, Wrigleys, Braun, Britvic, Levi Strauss, Pepsi, Pentax, and many others. Although many knockoffs have been started around the world, the enormous cost of building a worldwide music video channel will most likely protect MTV.

MTV's best response to threats from competition has been to make programming as local as possible. Its policy of 70 percent local content has resulted in some of the network's more creative shows, such as Brazil's month-long Rockgol which pitted musicians against record industry executives and Russia's Twelve Angry Viewers, a talk show focused on the latest videos.

Digital compression allows the number of services offered on a satellite feed to be multiplied. The network will use the new capacity to complement panregional programming and playlists, customizing them to local tastes in key areas. For example, MTV Asia has launched MTV India to have five hours of India-specific programming during the 24-hour satellite feed to the subcontinent.

Owned by Viacom, MTV's global network consists of the following entities:

- **MTV USA** is seen 24 hours a day on cable television in over 85 million U.S. television homes. Presented in stereo, MTV's overall on-air environment is unpredictable and irreverent, reflecting the cutting-edge spirit of rock 'n' roll that is the heart of its programming. Through its graphic look, VJs, music news, promotions,

interviews, concert tour information, specials, and documentaries, as well as its original strip programming, MTV has become an international institution of pop culture and the leading authority on rock music since it launched on August 1, 1981.

- **MTV Europe** reaches 43 territories (124 million households), 24 hours a day in stereo, via satellite, cable, and terrestrial distribution. The station acquires its own video clips, drawing from the domestic markets in individual European countries to discover bands making an international sound. It has its own team of VJs presenting shows specially tailored for the European market. The channel's programming mix reflects its diverse audience, with coverage of music, style, news, movie information, comedy, and more. MTV Europe has five local programming feeds and five local advertising windows—U.K./Ireland; MTV Central: (Austria, Germany, and Switzerland); MTV European (76 territories, including France and Israel); MTV Southern (Italy); and MTV Nordic (Sweden, Norway and others). It was launched August 1, 1987.

- **MTV Asia** was launched September 15, 1991. MTV Asia reaches over 138 million households in 21 territories. Programming is tailored to the musical tastes, lifestyles, and sensibilities of Asian audiences in three regions: MTV Mandarin, MTV Southeast Asia, and MTV India. Although Japan was originally launched in October 1984 under a licensing agreement, it was reintroduced in 2001 as a wholly-owned entity of MTV Networks International. The 24-hour music television channel and Web site feature original Japanese-language programming and reach 2.8 million households.

- **MTV Latin America** reaches 28 million households in 21 countries and territories. The network features a mix of U.S. and Latin music, regional production, music and entertainment news, artist interviews, concert coverage, and specials.

- **MTV Brazil** was launched in 1990 and is a joint venture of MTVNetworks and Abril S.A., Brazil's leading magazine publisher. The Portuguese-language network, viewed in 16 million households, is broadcast via UHF in São Paulo and via VHF in Rio de Janeiro.

- **MTV Russia**, launched in September 1998, is a free over-the-air service reaching more than 20 million homes in major cities. The entity was established with BIZ Enterprises in a multiyear licensing agreement. In 2000, MTV Networks International gained an equity position in MTV Russia. Programming includes music videos from Russian and international artists, as well as coverage of social issues relevant to Russian youth.

SOURCES: "MTV's Passage to India," *Fortune,* August 9, 2004, 116–125; Claudia Penteado, "MTV Breaks New Ground," *Advertising Age Global,* March 2002, 8; "MTV's World," *Business Week,* February 18, 2002, 81–84; "MTV Asia's Hit Man," *Advertising Age Global,* December 2001, 10; "Focus: Trends in TV," *Advertising Age International,* January 11, 1999, 33; "MTV Fights Back from Nadir to Hit High Notes in India," *Advertising Age International,* March 30, 1998, 10; "High Tech helps MTV Evolve," *World Trade,* June 1996, 10; "Will MTV Have to Share the Stage?" *Business Week,* February 21, 1994, 38; and **http://www.mtv.com**.

Exhibit **18.5**

Example of a Panregional Medium

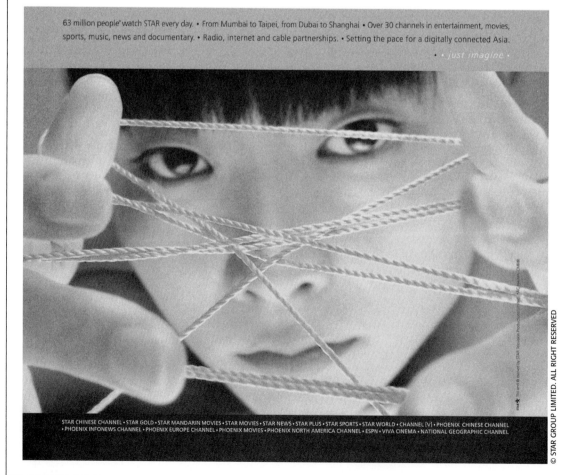

The alternative showing the most immediate promise is cable channels that cater to universal segments with converging tastes, such as MTV, Animal Planet, or the Cartoon Network, all of which feature both local content and localized versions of foreign content.

The Internet provides the international marketer with a global medium. U.S. marketers have been slow to react to its potential because their domestic market is so dominant. They have also been reluctant to adapt their Web sites but are willing to repeat what happened in the United States in these regions. One simple way of getting started is to choose a few key languages for the Web site. For example, Gillette decided to add German and Japanese to its Mach3 Web site after studying the number of Internet users in those countries.[34] If the marketer elects to have a global site and region-specific sites (e.g., organized by country), they all should have a similar look, especially in terms of the level of sophistication. Another method is to join forces with Internet service providers. Samsung has gained more global brand value than any other brand ranked over the last five years. A big contributor has been Samsung's bold Internet-marketing strategy, which had the company enter into long-term contracts with 425 high-traffic Web sites (such as *PC Magazine* and *USA Today*), negotiating for top banner position (as shown in Exhibit 18.6). Samsung now has right of first refusal for the position in perpetuity, and delivers a lower-cost Internet buy than its competitors in the consumer-electronics sector.[35]

The Promotional Message

The creative people must have a clear idea of the characteristics of the audience expected to be exposed to the message. In this sense, the principles of creating effective advertising are the same as in the domestic marketplace. The marketer must determine what the consumer is really buying—that is, the customer's motivations. These will vary, depending on the following:

1. The diffusion of the product or service into the market. For example, to penetrate Third World markets with business computers is difficult when few potential customers know how to type, or with Internet advertising when the infrastructure is lacking.

Exhibit **18.6**

Online Advertising

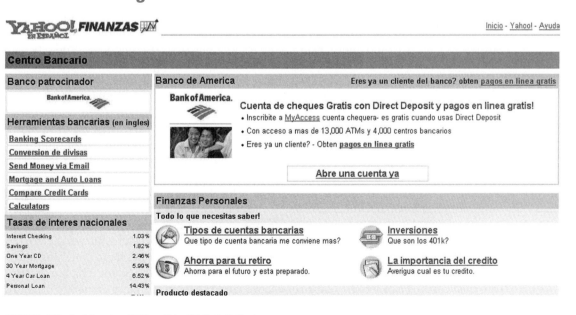

SOURCE: © Bank of American/PRNewsFoto (AP Topic Gallery).

2. The criteria on which the customer will evaluate the product. For example, in traditional societies, advertising the time-saving qualities of a product may not be the best approach, as Campbell Soup Company learned in Italy, Brazil, and Poland, where women felt inadequate as homemakers if they did not make soups from scratch.

3. The product's positioning. For example, Parker Pen's upscale market image around the world may not be profitable enough in a market that is more or less a commodity business. The solution is to create an image for a commodity product and make the public pay for it—for example, the positioning of Perrier in the United States as a premium mineral water.

The ideal situation in developing message strategy is to have a world brand—a product that is manufactured, packaged, and positioned the same around the world. Companies that have been successful with the global approach have shown flexibility in the execution of the campaigns. The idea may be global, but overseas subsidiaries then tailor the message to suit local market conditions and regulations. Executing an advertising campaign in multiple markets requires a balance between conveying the message and allowing for local nuances. The localization of global ideas can be achieved by various tactics, such as adopting a modular approach, localizing international symbols, and using international advertising agencies.[36]

Marketers may develop multiple broadcast and print ads from which country organizations can choose the most appropriate for their operations. This can provide local operations with cost savings and allow them to use their budgets on tactical campaigns (which may also be developed around the global idea). For example, the "Membership Has Its Privileges" campaign of American Express, which has run in 24 countries on TV and three more in print, was adjusted in some markets to make sure that "privileges" did not have a snob or elitist appeal, especially in countries with a strong caste or class system. An example of local adjustment in a global campaign for Marriott International is provided in Exhibit 18.7. While the ads share common graphic elements, two distinct approaches are evident. The top set of advertisements from the United States and Saudi Arabia is an example of a relatively standard approach, given the similarity in target audiences (i.e., the business traveler) and in the competitive conditions in the markets. The second set features ads for Latin American and German-speaking Europe. While the Latin advertisement stresses comfort, the German version focuses on results. While most of Marriott's ads translate the theme ("When you're comfortable you can do anything"), the German version keeps the original English-language theme.

Product-related regulations will affect advertising messages as well. When General Mills Toy Group's European subsidiary launched a product line related to G.I. Joe–type war toys and soldiers, it had to develop two television commercials, a general version for most European countries and another for countries that bar advertisements for products with military or violent themes. As a result, in the version running in Germany, Holland, and Belgium, Jeeps replaced the toy tanks, and guns were removed from the hands of the toy soldiers. Other countries, such as the United Kingdom, do not allow children to appear in advertisements.

Marketers may also want to localize their international symbols. Some of the most effective global advertising campaigns have capitalized on the popularity of pop music worldwide and used well-known artists in the commercials, such as Pepsi's use of Tina Turner. In some versions, local stars have been included with the international stars to localize the campaign. Aesthetics plays a role in localizing campaigns. The global marketer does not want to chance the censoring of the company's ads or risk offending customers. For example, even though importers of perfumes into Saudi Arabia want to use the same campaigns as are used in Europe, they occasionally have to make adjustments dictated by moral standards. In one case, the European version shows a man's hand clutching a perfume bottle and a woman's hand seizing his bare forearm. In the Saudi Arabian version, the man's arm is clothed in a dark suit sleeve, and the woman's hand is merely brushing his hand.

Exhibit 18.7

Local Adjustments in a Global Campaign

The International MARKETPLACE

18.3

Rethinking Agency Partners

Procter & Gamble Co. shifted global advertising duties for its Old Spice brand to Wieden + Kennedy, an independent ad firm based in Portland, Oregon, from Publicis Groupe's Saatchi and Saatchi for advertising and Starcom MediaVest for media planning and buying.

The account shift was the latest example of a small ad firm winning a big account at the expense of a global ad firm. Recently, Wieden and other small firms, such as Miami agency Crispin Porter + Bogusky, have won accounts with global marketers such as Coca-Cola and Volkswagen AG. A growing number of marketers believe small independents are more adept than bigger firms at using untraditional marketing methods that do not depend heavily on TV ads. Some also see smaller firms as better equipped to react to a rapidly changing media landscape because they are not bogged down by bureaucracy and the potential conflicts that abound in bulky conglomerates.

P&G said Wieden was given the account because of its extensive work on brands that target "young men." "They know the male consumer very well," said Tami Jones, a

spokeswoman for P&G. The Old Spice brand is sold in 30 markets around the world.

The Cincinnati consumer-product marketer also awarded media buying and planning duties in North America to Wieden. The move is a break from P&G's past practice of hiring different agencies to handle its creative work and its media planning and buying duties. P&G says Wieden will be given the media duties on a "test" basis in North America. Publicis Groupe's Starcom Mediavest will continue to handle media planning and buying on the brand outside of North America.

The fragmentation of audiences among an array of media options is forcing marketers to put less emphasis on traditional media such as TV and more on new media such as Web sites, video on demand, cable TV, e-mail, or iPod. Marketers are increasingly asking their marketing communications partners to include both creative and media placement recommendations. Having both under one roof makes things easier and more coordinated.

SOURCES: "Agencies Rethink Wall Between Creative, Media," *The Wall Street Journal*, March 1, 2006, B3; and "P&G Moves Old Spice Account to Small Independent Ad Firm," *The Wall Street Journal*, February 9, 2006, B7.

The use of one agency—or only a few agencies—ensures consistency. The use of one agency allows for coordination, especially when the global marketer's operations are decentralized. It also makes the exchange of ideas easier and may therefore lead, for example, to wider application of a modification or a new idea. For example, BP uses Ogilvy & Mather for its largely corporate-image based advertising. Companies such as Procter & Gamble and Unilever have each of their global brands under a single agency, such as Pampers handled by Saatchi & Saatchi, and Old Spice by Wieden + Kennedy (as shown in *The International Marketplace 18.3*).[37]

The environmental influences that call for these modifications, or in some cases totally unique approaches, are culture, economic development, and lifestyles. It is quite evident that customers prefer localized to foreign-sourced advertising.[38] Of the cultural variables, language is most apparent in its influence on promotional campaigns. The European Union alone has eleven languages: English, Finnish, French, German, Dutch, Danish, Italian, Greek, Spanish, Swedish, and Portuguese. Advertisers in the Arab world have sometimes found that the voices in a TV commercial speak in the wrong Arabic dialect. The challenge of language is often most pronounced in translating themes. For example, Coca-Cola's worldwide theme "Can't Beat the Feeling" is the equivalent of "I Feel Coke" in Japan, "Unique Sensation" in Italy, and "The Feeling of Life" in Chile. In Germany, where no translation really worked, the original English language theme was used. One way of getting around this is to have no copy or very little copy and to use innovative approaches, such as pantomime. Using any type of symbolism will naturally require adequate copy testing to determine how the target market perceives the message.

The stage of economic development—and therefore the potential demand for and degree of awareness of the product—may vary and differentiate the message from one market to another. Whereas developed markets may require persuasive messages (to combat other alternatives), a developing market may require a purely informative campaign. Campaigns may also have to be dramatically adjusted to cater to lifestyle differences in regions that are demographically quite similar. For example, N. W. Ayer's Bahamas tourism campaign for the European market emphasized clean water, beaches, and air. The exceptions are in Germany, where it focuses on sports activities, and in the United Kingdom, where it features humor.

The Campaign Approach

Many multinational corporations are staffed and equipped to perform the full range of promotional activities. In most cases, however, they will rely on the outside expertise of advertising agencies and other promotions-related companies such as media-buying companies and specialty marketing firms. In the organization of promotional efforts, a company has two basic decisions to make: (1) what type of outside services to use and (2) how to establish decision-making authority for promotional efforts.

Outside Services

Of all the outside promotion-related services, advertising agencies are by far the most significant. A list of the world's top 25 agencies and agency groups is given in Exhibit 18.8. Of the top 25 agencies, 13 are based in the United States, 6 in Japan and Korea, and 6 in the European Union. Size is typically measured in terms of revenue and billings. Billings are the cost of advertising time and space placed by the agency plus fees for certain extra services,

Exhibit **18.8**

Top 25 Marketing Organizations

Rank	Company	Headquarters	Net Revenue	% CHG
1	Omnicom Group	New York	$11,376.9	8.5
2	WPP Group	London	10,819.6	11.1
3	Interpublic Group of Cos.	New York	6,190.8	−1.3
4	Publicis Groupe	Paris	5,872.0	7.3
5	Dentsu	Tokyo	2,950.7	2.2
6	Havas	Suresnes, France	1,841.0	1.8
7	Aegis Group	London	1,825.8	15.7
8	Hakuhodo DY Holdings	Tokyo	1,337.0	−2.0
9	aQuantive (bought by Microsoft in Aug. '07)	Seattle	442.2	43.4
10	Asatsu-DK	Tokyo	430.0	−3.3
11	WDC Partners	Toronto/New York	423.7	16.6
12	Sapient Corp.	Cambridge, Mass.	406.0	27.1
13	Carlson Marketing	Minneapolis	390.0	5.4
14	Epsllon	Iming, Texas	300.0	62.7
15	Aspen Marketing Services	West Chicago, Ill.	278.0	16.3
16	Cheil Communications	Seoul	256.3	21.6
17	George P. Johnson Co.	Anburn Hills, Mich.	213.2	5.0
18	HealthSTAR Communications*	Woodbridge, N. J.	213.0	0.0
19	LBI International	Stockholm	212.4	15.3
20	Media Square*	London	196.0	47.5
21	inVenthy Communications (formerly inOhord)	Westerville, Ohio	191.7	62.5
22	Cossetle Communication Group	Quebec City	190.2	15.9
23	Harte-Hanics Direct	Langhome, Pa.	180.8	3.8
24	Clemenger Communications	Melbourne	174.1	4.9
25	Doner	Southfield, Mich.	173.1	5.4

Ranked by worldwide revenue. An asterisk "*" indicates estimate.

SOURCE: Top 25 Marketing Organizations, *"Advertising Age"* 2008 Issue.

which are converted by formula to correspond to media billings in terms of value of services performed. Agencies do not receive billings as income; in general, agency income is approximately 15 percent of billing.

Agencies form world groups for better coverage. One of the largest world holding groups, WPP Group, includes such entities as Ogilvy & Mather, J. Walter Thompson, Young & Rubicam, and Grey. Smaller advertising agencies have affiliated local agencies in foreign markets.

The choice of an agency will largely depend on the quality of coverage the agency will be able to give the multinational company. Global marketing requires global advertising, according to proponents of the globalization trend. The reason is not that significant cost savings can be realized through a single worldwide ad campaign but that such a global campaign is inseparable from the idea of global marketing. Some predict that the whole industry will be concentrated into a few huge multinational agencies. Agencies with networks too small to compete have become prime takeover targets in the creation of worldwide mega-agencies. Many believe that local, midsized agencies can compete in the face of globalization by developing local solutions and/or joining international networks.[39]

Although the forecast that six large agencies will eventually place most international advertising may be exaggerated, global marketing is the new wave and is having a strong impact on advertising. Major realignments of client–agency relationships have occurred due to mergers and to clients' reassessment of their own strategies toward more global or regional approaches.

Advertising agencies have gone through major geographic expansion in the last five years. The leader is McCann-Erickson, with advertising running in 130 countries, compared with 72 in 1991. In 2008, it handled the most international assignments of any group.[40] Some agencies, such as DDB Worldwide, were domestically focused in the early 1990s but have been forced to rethink with the globalization of their clients. As a result, by 2009 DDB Worldwide had more than 200 offices in over 90 countries.[41] New markets are also emerging, and agencies are establishing their presence in them. China's $30 billion ad market has competitors from around the world, including the WPP Group, whose activities grew by more than 31% in 2007 alone.[42]

A presentation of agency-client relationships is provided in Exhibit 18.9. The J. Walter Thompson agency, which serves 87 countries worldwide, has 28 accounts that it serves in more than ten countries including Kimberly-Clark, Nestlé, and Unilever. On the client side, Unilever assigns more business on an international basis, working with eight agency networks from four holding groups, than any other global marketer. In a study of 40 multinational marketers, 32.5 percent are using a single agency worldwide, 20 percent are using two, 5 percent are using three, 10 percent are using four, and 32.5 percent are using more than four agencies. Of the marketers using only one or two agencies, McCann-Erickson was the most popular with 17 percent of the companies.[43] While global media reviews (to consolidate all business to a single agency) are popular, most large companies typically use more than one agency, with the division of labor usually along product lines. For example, Matsushita Electric Industrial Company, an innovator in the consumer electronics industry, uses two major agencies. Dentsu handles everything involving portables, audio, and television. Grey Advertising handles the hi-fi area, the Technics label, and telephone products. Panasonic, one of Matsushita's U.S. brands, has a small agency for primarily nonconsumer items. Marketers are choosing specialized interactive shops over full-service agencies for Internet advertising. This is largely for pragmatic reasons due to conflicts, agencies' uneven coverage of the world (especially in emerging markets), and the marketers' own inability to make decisions from headquarters work on a global scale.[44]

The main concern arising from the use of mega-agencies is conflict. With only a few giant agencies to choose from, the global marketer may end up with the same agency as the main competitor. The mega-agencies believe they can meet any objections by structuring their companies as rigidly separate, watertight agency networks (such as the Interpublic Group) under the umbrella of a holding group. Following that logic, Procter & Gamble, a client of Saatchi & Saatchi, and Colgate-Palmolive, a client of Ted Bates, should not worry about falling into the same network's client base. However, when the Saatchi & Saatchi network purchased Ted Bates, Colgate-Palmolive left the agency.

Exhibit 18.9

Worldwide Agency–Client Relationships

Rank	Marketer	Dots/ Assignments	Arnold Worldwide	Bartle Bogle Hegarty	BBDO Worldwide	DDB Worldwide	Dems	Euro RSCG Worldwide	Fallon Worldwide	Foote Cone & Belding Worldwide	Grey Worldwide	Hakuhodo	JWT	Leo Burnett Worldwide	Lowe Worldwide	McCann Erickson Worldwide	Ogilvy & Mather Worldwide	Publicis	Saatchi & Saatchi	TBWA Worldwide	United Network	Y&R Advertising
1	Unilever	580	•	•							•		•	•		•	•	•		•		
2	Procter & Gamble Co.	309		•							•			•		•	•	•	•		•	
3	Nestle	290			•	•	•	•			•			•		•	•					
4	Altria Group	220				•		•			•		•	•			•					•
5	L'Oreal	201				•											•					
6	Johnson & Johnson	191				•										•	•	•		•		
7	Diageo	175	•	•			•				•			•						•		
8	Pfizer	165				•								•						•		
9	Novartis	159			•						•					•	•	•				
10	Kimberly-Clark Corp.	158									•											•
11	Mattel	156															•					•
12	PepsiCo	151		•	•			•														
13	Ford Motor Co.	135				•					•					•						•
14	GlaxoSmithKline	134	•		•			•								•	•					
15	General Mills	128														•		•				
16	Mars Inc.	121		•							•									•		
17	Coca-Cola Co.	114							•	•						•	•	•				
18	Sanofi-Aventis	107				•					•					•		•				
19	Siemens	98														•		•				
20	Tchibo Holding	97								•										•		
21	Reckitt Benckiser	96					•							•								
22	Royal Dutch Shell Group of Cos.	92					•								•							
23	Cadbury Schweppes	92					•				•					•		•				•
24	Motorola	90				•												•				
25	Henkel	88	•	•																•		

Ranking based on total assignments the advertisers awarded the agency networks in this report.

SOURCE: Reprinted with permission from the November 14, 2005, issue of *Advertising Age.* Copyright, Crain Communications Inc., 2006.

Despite the globalization trend, local agencies will survive as a result of governmental regulations. In Peru, for example, a law mandates that any commercial aired on Peruvian television must be 100 percent nationally produced. Local agencies also tend to forge ties with foreign agencies for better coverage and customer service and thus become part of the general globalization effort. A basic fear in the advertising industry is that accounts will be taken away from agencies that cannot handle world brands. An additional factor is contributing to the fear of losing accounts. In the past, many multinational corporations allowed local subsidiaries to make advertising decisions entirely on their own. Others gave subsidiaries an approved list of agencies and some guidance. Still others allowed local decisions subject only to headquarters' approval. Now the trend is toward centralization of all advertising decisions, including those concerning the creative product.

Decision-Making Authority

The alternatives for allocating decision-making authority range from complete centralization to decentralization. With complete centralization, the headquarters level is perceived to have all the right answers and has adequate power to impose its suggestions on all of its operating units. Decentralization involves relaxing most of the controls over foreign affiliates and allowing them to pursue their own promotional approaches.

Of 40 multinational marketers, 26 percent have centralized their advertising strategies, citing as their rationale the search for economies of scale, synergies, and brand consistency. Xerox's reason is that its technology is universal and opportunities abound for global messages. Centralization is also occurring at the regional level. GM's Opel division in Europe is seeking to unify its brand-building efforts with central direction. A total of 34 percent of the companies favor decentralization with regional input. This approach benefits from proximity to market, flexibility, cultural sensitivity, and faster response time. FedEx allows local teams to make advertising decisions as needed. The majority of marketers use central coordination with local input. While Ford Motor Company conceives brand strategy on a global level, ad execution is done at the regional level, and retail work is local.[45] However, multinational corporations are at various stages in their quest for centralization. Procter & Gamble and Gillette generally have an approved list of agencies, whereas Quaker Oats and Johnson & Johnson give autonomy to their local subsidiaries but will veto those decisions occasionally.

The important question is not who should make decisions but how advertising quality can be improved at the local level. Gaining approval in multinational corporations is an interactive approach using coordinated decentralization. This nine-step program, which is summarized in Exhibit 18.10, strives for development of common strategy but flexible execution. The approach maintains strong central control but at the same time capitalizes on the greatest asset of the individual markets: market knowledge. Interaction between the central authority and the local levels takes place at every single stage of the planning process. The central authority is charged with finding the commonalities in the data provided by the individual market areas. This procedure will avoid one of the most common problems associated with acceptance of plans—the NIH syndrome (not invented here)—by allowing for local participation by the eventual implementers.

A good example of this approach was Eastman Kodak's launch of its Ektaprint copier-duplicator line in eleven separate markets in Europe. For economic and organizational reasons, Kodak did not want to deal with different campaigns or parameters. It wanted the same ad graphics in each country, accompanied by the theme "first name in photography, last word in copying." Translations varied slightly from country to country, but the campaign was identifiable from one country to another. A single agency directed the campaign, which was more economical than campaigns in each country would have been and was more unified and identifiable through Europe. The psychological benefit of association of the Kodak name with photography was not lost in the campaign.

Agencies are adjusting their operations to centrally run client operations. Many accounts are now handled by a lead agency, usually in the country where the client is based. More and more agencies are moving to a strong international supervisor for global accounts. This supervisor can overrule local agencies and make personnel changes. Specialty units have emerged as well. For example, Ogilvy & Mather established the Worldwide Client Service organization at headquarters in New York, specializing in developing global campaigns for its clients.[46]

Measurement of Advertising Effectiveness

John Wanamaker reportedly said, "I know half the money I spend on advertising is wasted. Now, if I only knew which half." Whether or not advertising effectiveness can be measured, most companies engage in the attempt. Measures of advertising effectiveness should range from pretesting of copy appeal and recognition, to posttesting of recognition, all the way to sales effects. The measures most used are sales, awareness, recall, executive judgment, intention to buy, profitability, and coupon return, regardless of the medium used.[47]

Exhibit **18.10**

Coordinated Approach to Panregional Campaign Development

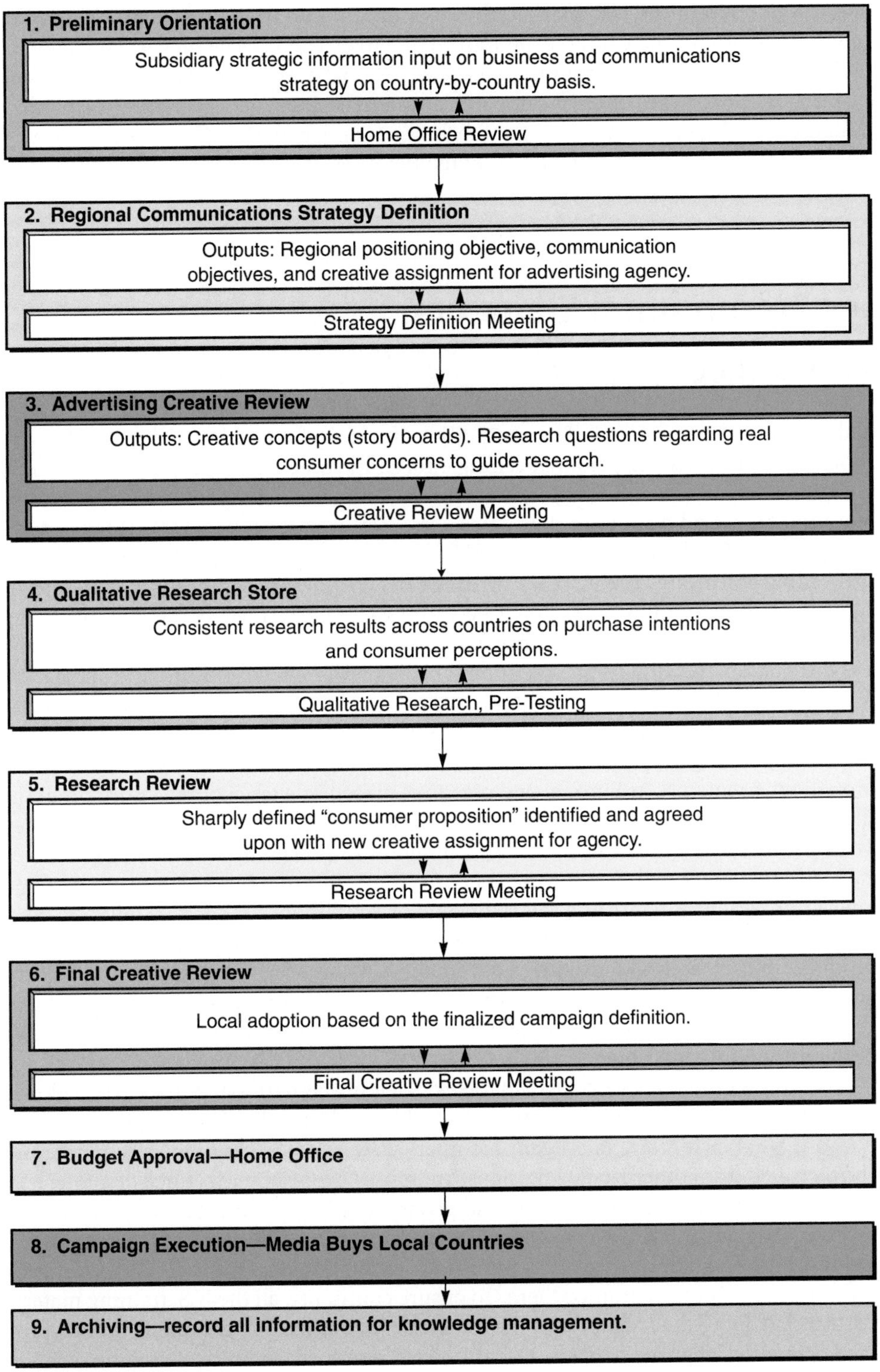

1. Preliminary Orientation

Subsidiary strategic information input on business and communications strategy on country-by-country basis.

Home Office Review

2. Regional Communications Strategy Definition

Outputs: Regional positioning objective, communication objectives, and creative assignment for advertising agency.

Strategy Definition Meeting

3. Advertising Creative Review

Outputs: Creative concepts (story boards). Research questions regarding real consumer concerns to guide research.

Creative Review Meeting

4. Qualitative Research Store

Consistent research results across countries on purchase intentions and consumer perceptions.

Qualitative Research, Pre-Testing

5. Research Review

Sharply defined "consumer proposition" identified and agreed upon with new creative assignment for agency.

Research Review Meeting

6. Final Creative Review

Local adoption based on the finalized campaign definition.

Final Creative Review Meeting

7. Budget Approval—Home Office

8. Campaign Execution—Media Buys Local Countries

9. Archiving—record all information for knowledge management.

SOURCES: Jae H. Pae, Saeed Samiee, and Susan Tai, "Global Advertising Strategy: The Moderating Role of Brand Familiarity and Execution Style," *International Marketing Review* 19 (no. 2, 2002): 176–189; Clive Nancarrow and Chris Woolston, "Pre-Testing International Press Advertising," *Qualitative Market Research: An International Journal* (1998): 25–38; and David A. Hanni, John K. Ryans, Jr., and Ivan R. Vernon, "Coordinating International Advertising: The Goodyear Case Revisited for Latin America," *Journal of International Marketing* 3 (no. 2, 1995): 83–98.

The technical side of these measurement efforts does not differ from that in the domestic market, but the conditions are different. Very often, syndicated services, such as A.C. Nielsen, are not available to the global marketer. If available, their quality may not be at an acceptable level. Testing is also quite expensive and may not be undertaken for the smaller markets. Compared with costs in the U.S. market, the costs of research in the international market are higher in relation to the overall expenditure on advertising.[48] The biggest challenge to advertising research will come from the increase of global and regional campaigns. Comprehensive and reliable measures of campaigns for a mass European market, for example, are difficult because audience measurement techniques and analysis differ for each country. Advertisers are pushing for universally accepted parameters to compare audiences in one country to those in another.

Other Promotional Elements

Personal Selling

Advertising is often equated with the promotional effort; however, a number of other efforts are used to support advertising. The marketing of industrial goods, especially of high-priced items, requires strong personal selling efforts. In some cases, personal selling may be truly global; for example, Boeing and Northrop-Grumman salespeople engage in sales efforts around the world from their domestic bases. However, most personal selling is done by the subsidiaries, with varying degrees of headquarters' involvement. In cases in which personal selling constitutes the primary thrust of the corporate promotional effort and in which global customer groups can be identified, unified and coordinated sales practices may be called for. When distribution is intensive, channels are long, or markets have tradition-oriented distribution, headquarters' role should be less pronounced and should concentrate mostly on offering help and guidance.[49] A pivotal role is played by the field sales manager as the organizational link between headquarters and the salespeople.[50]

Eastman Kodak developed a line-of-business approach to allow for standardized strategy throughout a region.[51] In Europe, one person is placed in charge of the entire program in each country, with responsibility for all sales and service teams. Typically, each customer is served by three representatives, each with a different responsibility. Sales representatives maintain ultimate responsibility for the account; they conduct demonstrations, analyze customer requirements, determine the right type of equipment for each installation, and obtain the orders. Service representatives install and maintain the equipment and retrofit new product improvements to existing equipment. Customer service representatives are the liaison between sales and service. They provide operator training on a continuing basis and handle routine questions and complaints. Each team is positioned to respond to any European customer within hours.

The training of the sales force usually takes place in the national markets, but global corporations' headquarters will have a say in the techniques used. For instance, when Kodak introduced the Ektaprint line, sales team members were selected carefully. U.S. personnel could be recruited from other Kodak divisions, but most European marketing personnel had to be recruited from outside the company and given intensive training. Sales managers and a select group of sales trainers were sent to the Rochester, New York, headquarters for six weeks of training. They then returned to Europe to set up programs for individual countries so that future teams could be trained there. To ensure continuity, all the U.S. training materials were translated into the languages of the individual countries. To maintain a unified program and overcome language barriers, Kodak created a service language consisting of 1,200 words commonly found in technical information.

Foreign companies entering the Japanese market face challenges in establishing a sales force. Recruitment poses the first major problem, since well-established, and usually local, entities have an advantage in attracting personnel. Many have, therefore, entered into joint ventures or distribution agreements to obtain a sales force. Companies can also expect to invest more in training and organizational culture-building activities than in the United States. These may bring long-term advantages in fostering loyalty to the company.[52]

Sales Promotion

Sales promotion has been used as the catchall term for promotion that does not fall under advertising, personal selling, or publicity. Sales promotion directed at consumers involves such activities as couponing, sampling, premiums, consumer education and demonstration activities, cents-off packs, point-of-purchase materials, and direct mail. The use of sales promotions as alternatives and as support for advertising is increasing worldwide. The appeal is related to several factors: cost and clutter of media advertising, simpler targeting of customers compared with advertising, and easier tracking of promotional effectiveness (for example, coupon returns provide a clear measure of effectiveness).

The success in Latin America of Tang, Kraft Foods' presweetened powder juice substitute, is for the most part traceable to successful sales promotion efforts. One promotion involved trading Tang pouches for free popsicles from Kraft Foods' Brazilian subsidiary. The company also placed coupons for free groceries in Tang pouches. In Puerto Rico, General Foods ran Tang sweepstakes. In Argentina, in-store sampling featured Tang pitchers and girls in orange Tang dresses. Decorative Tang pitchers were a hit throughout Latin America. Sales promotion directed at intermediaries, also known as trade promotion, includes activities such as trade shows and exhibits, trade discounts, and cooperative advertising.

For sales promotion to be effective, the campaign planned by manufacturers, or their agencies, must gain the support of the local retailer population. Coupons from consumers, for example, have to be redeemed and sent to the manufacturer or to the company handling the promotion. A.C. Nielsen tried to introduce cents-off coupons in Chile and ran into trouble with the nation's supermarket union, which notified its members that it opposed the project and recommended that coupons not be accepted. The main complaint was that an intermediary, like Nielsen, would unnecessarily raise costs and thus the prices to be charged to consumers. Also, some critics felt that coupons would limit individual negotiations because Chileans often bargain for their purchases.

Global marketers are well advised to take advantage of local or regional opportunities. In Brazil, gas delivery people are used to distribute product samples to households by companies such as Nestlé, Johnson & Johnson, and Unilever. The delivery people are usually assigned to the same district for years and have, therefore, earned their clientele's trust. For the marketers, distributing samples this way is not only effective, it is very economical: they are charged five cents for each unit distributed. The gas companies benefit as well in that their relationship with customers is enhanced through these "presents."[53]

Sales promotion tools fall under varying regulations, as can be seen from Exhibit 18.11. A particular level of incentive may be permissible in one market but illegal in another. The Northern European countries present the greatest difficulties in this respect because every promotion has to be approved by a government body. In France, a gift cannot be worth more than 4 percent of the retail value of the product being promoted, making certain promotions virtually impossible. Although competitions are allowed in most of Europe, to insist on receiving proofs of purchase as a condition of entry is not permitted in Germany.

Regulations such as these make truly global sales promotions rare and difficult to launch. Although only a few multinational brands have been promoted on a multiterritory basis, the approach can work. In general, such multicountry promotions may be suitable for products such as soft drinks, liquor, airlines, credit cards, and jeans, which span cultural divides. Naturally, local laws and cultural differences have to be taken into account at the planning stage. Although many of the promotions may be funded centrally, they will be implemented differently in each market so that they can be tied with the local company's other promotional activities. For example, Johnson & Johnson Vision Care offered trials of its one-day Acuvue contact lens throughout Europe, Africa, and the Middle East. The aim was to deliver the brand message of "Enhancing Everyday Experiences" and encourage consumers to book a sight test. The venue was a road-show event that adapted well to local market conditions. Professional lens fitters offered on-the-spot trials at gyms, sports clubs, and leisure centers. The program was devised and tested in Germany, and has since been executed in 18 different countries. The creative materials were translated into 14 languages and a virtual network using intranets ensured that all offices shared information and best practice.[54]

Exhibit **18.11**

Regulations Regarding Premiums, Gifts, and Competitions in Selected Countries

Country	Category	No Restrictions or Minor Ones	Authorized with Major Restrictions	General Ban with Important Exceptions	Almost Total Prohibition
Australia	Premiums	x			
	Gifts	x			
	Competitions		x		
Austria	Premiums				x
	Gifts		x		
	Competitions		x		
Canada	Premiums	x			
	Gifts	x			
	Competitions		x		
Denmark	Premiums			x	
	Gifts		x		
	Competitions			x	
France	Premiums	x			
	Gifts	x			
	Competitions	x			
Germany	Premiums				x
	Gifts		x		
	Competitions		x		
Hong Kong	Premiums	x			
	Gifts	x			
	Competitions	x			
Japan	Premiums		x		
	Gifts		x		
	Competitions		x		
Korea	Premiums		x		
	Gifts		x		
	Competitions		x		
United Kingdom	Premiums	x			
	Gifts	x			
	Competitions		x		
United States	Premiums	x			
	Gifts	x			
	Competitions	x			
Venezuela	Premiums		x		
	Gifts		x		
	Competitions		x		

SOURCE: Jean J. Boddewyn, *Premiums, Gifts, and Competitions,* 1988, published by International Advertising Association, 342 Madison Avenue, Suite 2000, NYC, NY 10017. Reprinted with permission.

In the province of Quebec in Canada, advertisers must pay a tax on the value of the prizes they offer in a contest, whether the prize is a trip, money, or a car. The amount of the tax depends on the geographical extent of the contest. If it is open only to residents of Quebec, the tax is 10 percent; if open to all of Canada, 3 percent; if worldwide, 1 percent. Subtle distinctions are drawn in the regulations between a premium and a prize. As an example, the Manic soccer team was involved with both McDonald's and Provigo Food stores. The team offered a dollar off the price of four tickets, and the stubs could be cashed for a special at McDonald's. Provigo was involved in a contest offering a year's supply of groceries. The Manic-McDonald's offer was a premium that involved no special tax; Provigo, however, was taxed because it was involved in a contest. According to the regulation, a premium is available to everyone, whereas a prize is available to a certain number of people among those who participate. In some cases, industries may self-regulate the use of promotional items.

Public Relations

Image—the way a multinational corporation relates to and is perceived by its key constituents—is a bottom-line issue for management. Public relations is the marketing communications function charged with executing programs to earn public understanding and acceptance, which means both internal and external communication. The function can further be divided into proactive and reactive forms.

Internal Public Relations

Especially in multinational corporations, internal communication is important to create an appropriate corporate culture.[55] The Japanese have perfected this in achieving a *wa* (we) spirit. Everyone in an organization is, in one way or another, in marketing and will require additional targeted information on issues not necessarily related to his or her day-to-day functions. A basic part of most internal programs is the employee publication produced and edited typically by the company's public relations or advertising department and usually provided in both hard-copy and electronic formats. Some have foreign-language versions. More often, as at ExxonMobil, each affiliate publishes its own employee publication. The better this vehicle can satisfy the information needs of employees, the less they will have to rely on others, especially informal sources such as the grapevine. Audiovisual media in the form of e-mails, films, videotapes, slides, and videoconferencing are being used, especially for training purposes. Some of the materials that are used internally can be provided to other publics as well; for example, booklets, manuals, and handbooks are provided to employees, distributors, and visitors to the company.

External Public Relations

External public relations (also known as marketing public relations) is focused on the interactions with customers. In the *proactive* context, marketers are concerned about establishing global identities to increase sales, differentiate products and services, and attract employees. These activities have been seen as necessary to compete against companies with strong local identities. External campaigns can be achieved through the use of corporate symbols, corporate advertising, customer relations programs, and publicity. For example, Black & Decker's corporate logo, which is in the shape and color of an orange hexagon, is used for all B&D products. Specific brand books are developed to guide marketing personnel worldwide on the proper use of these symbols to ensure a consistent global image. Exhibit 18.12 depicts an agricultural marketing publication, *The Furrow*, in three different language versions. Total circulation is 1.5 million in 11 languages in more than 45 countries.

Publicity, in particular, is of interest to the multinational corporation. Publicity is the securing of editorial space (as opposed to paid advertising) to further marketing objectives. Because it is editorial in content, the consuming public perceives it as more trustworthy than advertising. A good example of how publicity can be used to aid in advertising efforts was the introduction by Princess Lines of a new liner, the *Royal Princess*. Because of its innovative design and size, the *Royal Princess* was granted substantial press coverage, which was especially beneficial in the travel and leisure magazines. Such coverage does not come automatically but has to be coordinated and initiated by the public relations staff of the company.

Unanticipated developments in the marketplace can place the company in a position that requires *reactive* public relations, including anticipating and countering criticism. The criticisms range from general ones against all multinational corporations to more specific ones. They may be based on a market; for example, doing business with prison factories in China. They may concern a product; for example, Nestlé's practices of advertising and promoting infant formula in developing countries where infant mortality is unacceptably high. They may center on conduct in a given situation; for example, Union Carbide's perceived lack of response in the Bhopal disaster. The key concern is that, if not addressed, these criticisms

Exhibit 18.12

External Media: *The Furrow*

SOURCE: Courtesy of Deere & Co., Moline, IL, USA; **http://www.johndeere.com**.

can lead to more significant problems, such as the internationally orchestrated boycott of Nestlé's products. The six-year boycott did not so much harm earnings as it harmed image and employee morale.

Crisis management is becoming more formalized in companies, with specially assigned task forces ready to step in if problems arise. In general, companies must adopt policies that will allow them to effectively respond to pressure and criticism, which will continue to surface. Crisis management policies should have the following traits: (1) openness about corporate activities, with a focus on how these activities enhance social and economic performance; (2) preparedness to utilize the tremendous power of the multinational corporation in a responsible manner and, in the case of pressure, to counter criticisms swiftly; (3) integrity, which often means that the marketer must avoid not only actual wrongdoing but the mere appearance of it; and (4) clarity, which will help ameliorate hostility if a common language is used with those pressuring the corporation.[56] The marketer's role is one of enlightened self-interest; reasonable critics understand that the marketer cannot compromise the bottom line.

Complicating the situation often is the fact that groups in one market criticize what the marketer is doing in another market. For example, the Interfaith Center on Corporate Responsibility urged Colgate-Palmolive to stop marketing Darkie toothpaste under that brand name in Asia because of the term's offensiveness elsewhere in the world. Darkie toothpaste was sold in Thailand, Hong Kong, Singapore, Malaysia, and Taiwan and was packaged in a box that featured a likeness of Al Jolson in blackface.[57] Colgate-Palmolive redid the package and changed the brand name to Darlie. Levi Strauss decided to withdraw from $40 million worth of production contracts in China after consultations with a variety of sources, including human rights organizations, experts on China, and representatives of the U.S. government, led it to conclude that there was pervasive abuse of human rights.[58]

With growing and evolving interactive technology, consumers can find or initiate topics of interest on the Web and engage in online discussions that strongly affect their and others' views. This new form of communication, consumer-generated media (CGM), is growing at 30 percent per year. While these media can take multiple forms, the most prominent are online bulletin boards, blogs, podcasts, and Web sites for consumers to post complaints and compliments. The challenges for the global marketer include the new media's limitless reach, fast diffusion of news, and its very expressive and influential nature. To leverage CGM to the marketer's advantage, someone in the company needs to be put in charge of the phenomenon: to monitor the relevant information and then disseminate the important findings and take action when needed.[59] Some marketers are incorporating consumer-generated content into their promotion mixes. For example, Mercedes Benz encourages drivers to send digital photos of themselves living the Mercedes-Benz lifestyle for posting on the company's Web site.[60]

The public relations function can be handled in-house or with the assistance of an agency. The largest agencies are presented in Exhibit 18.13. The use and extent of public relations activity will vary by company and the type of activity needed. Product-marketing PR may work best with a strong component of control at the local level and a local PR firm, while crisis management—given the potential for worldwide adverse impact—will probably be controlled principally from a global center.[61] This has meant that global marketers funnel short-term projects to single offices for their local expertise while maintaining contact with the global agencies for their worldwide reach when a universal message is needed.

Exhibit 18.13

The Top Independent Public Relations Firms

Firm	2007 Net Fees	Employees
1. Edelman, New York	$395,494,858	2,860
2. Waggener Edstrom, Bellevue, WA	106,507,000	801
3. APCO Worldwide, Wash., DC	97,500,000	549
4. Ruder Finn Group, New York	93,549,000	590
5. Text 100 Int'l., San Francisco	60,000,000	550
6. Qorvis Comms., Wash., DC	30,497,000	86
7. Schwartz Comms., Waltham, MA	30,486,822	210
8. ICR (formerly Integrated Corp. Rels.), Westport, CT	24,645,933	95
9. Dan Klores Comms., New York	21,700,000	131
10. Regan Comms., Boston	21,014,000	74
11. Taylor, New York	20,141,000	110
12. Gibbs & Soell, New York	19,162,200	101
13. Bite Communications, San Francisco	16,000,000	84
14. Padilla Speer Beardsley, Minneapolis	14,740,080	95
15. Access Comms., San Francisco	14,171,456	64
16. WeissComm Partners, San Francisco	13,031,000	68
17. French/West/Vaughan, Raleign, NC	12,248,312	85
18. RF|Binder Partners, New York	12,220,000	70
19. Capstrat, Raleigh, NC	12,094,000	85
20. Peppercom, New York	11,815,773	69
21. 5W Public Relations, New York	11,581,939	79
22. Allison & Partners, San Francisco	11,535,700	71
23. Zeno Group, New York	11,494,595	55
24. M Booth & Assocs., New York	11,341,079	57
25. CRT/tanaka, Richmond, VA	11,322,874	71

SOURCE: **http://www.odwyerpr.com/pr_firm_rankings/independents.htm**, accessed February 12, 2009.

Some global corporations maintain public relations staffs in their main offices around the world, while others use the services of firms that are part of large worldwide agency groups such as Weber Shandwick (Interpublic Group of Companies), Fleishman Hillard (Omnicom Group), or Hill & Knowlton (WPP Group).

Sponsorship Marketing

Sponsorship involves the marketer's investment in events or causes. Sponsorship funds worldwide are directed for the most part at sports events (both individual and team sports) and cultural events (both in the popular and high-culture categories). Sponsorship spending is relatively even around the world: of the nearly $33.8 billion spent in 2006, North America contributed $13.4, Europe $9.6, Asia-Pacific $6.4, and Latin America $2.7 billion.[62] Examples range from Coca-Cola's sponsorship of the 2004 Olympic Games in Athens and Master Card's sponsorship of World Cup Soccer in 2006 in Germany to Visa's sponsoring of Eric Clapton's tour and Ford's sponsoring of the Montreux Detroit Jazz Festival. Sponsorship of events such as the Olympics is driven by the desire to be associated with a worldwide event that has a positive image, global reach, and a proven strategic positioning of excellence. The rising costs of sponsorship and the difficulty of establishing return on the investment has forced some marketers to bow out; for example, IBM after Sydney in 2000, and Xerox after Athens in 2004.[63]

The challenge is that an event may become embroiled in controversy, thus hurting the sponsors' images as well. Furthermore, in light of the high expense of sponsorship, marketers worry about **ambush marketing** by competitors. Ambush marketing is the unauthorized use of an event without the permission of the event owner. For example, an advertising campaign could suggest a presumed sponsorship relationship. During the Atlanta Olympic Games in 1996, some of the sponsors' competitors garnered a higher profile than the sponsors themselves. For example, Pepsi erected stands outside venues and plastered the town with signs. Nike secured substantial amounts of air time on radio and TV stations. Fuji bought billboards on the route from the airport into downtown Atlanta. None of the three contributed anything to the International Olympic Committee during this time.[64] In London in 2012, total costs are estimated to be $7 billion, and big sponsors may expect to pay as much as $80 million apiece. The ambush-marketing provisions of the London Olympics Bill will prohibit the uses of terms such as "gold," "summer," and "2012" in advertisements by nonsponsors.[65]

Cause-related marketing is a combination of public relations, sales promotion, and corporate philanthropy. This activity should not be developed merely as a response to a crisis, nor should it be a fuzzy, piecemeal effort to generate publicity; instead, marketers should have a social vision and a planned long-term social policy. For example, in Casanare, Colombia, where it is developing oil interests, British Petroleum invests in activities that support its business plan and contribute to the region's development. This has meant an investment of $10 million in setting up a loan fund for entrepreneurs, giving students technical training, supporting a center for pregnant women and nursing mothers, working on reforestation, building aqueducts, and helping to create jobs outside the oil industry.[66] Examples of IBM's contributions to local communities are provided in *The International Marketplace 18.4*. Cisco Systems' Networking Academy is an example of how a marketer can link philanthropic strategy, its competitive advantage, and broader social good. To address a chronic deficit in IT job applicants, the company created The Network Academy concept whereby it contributes networking equipment to schools. Cisco now operates 10,000 academies in secondary schools, community colleges, and community-based organizations in 150 countries. As the leading player in the field, Cisco stands to benefit the most from this improved labor pool. At the same time, Cisco has attracted worldwide recognition for this program, boosted its employee morale and partner goodwill, as well as generated a reputation for leadership in philanthropy.[67]

Increasingly, the United Nations is promoting programs to partner multinationals and NGOs (nongovernmental organizations) to tackle issues such as healthcare, energy, and biodiversity. For example, Merck and GlaxoSmithKline have partnered with UNICEF and the World Bank to improve access to AIDS care in the hardest hit regions of the world.[68]

The International
MARKETPLACE

 ENVIRONMENT & SUSTAINABILITY

18.4

Global Community Relations

A Roper survey found that 92 percent of the respondents feel that it is important for marketers to seek out ways to become good corporate citizens, and they are most interested in those who get involved in environmental, educational, and health issues. Many are worried that globalization has brought about a decline in corporate conduct and responsibility. However, many marketers have seen it as completely the opposite. Community relations is, as one chief executive put it, "food for the soul of the organization." It has become a strategic aspect of business and a fundamental ingredient for the long-term health of the enterprise. As a global company, IBM has a network of staff responsible for corporate responsibility throughout the 152 countries of operation. Major initiatives that address environmental concerns, support programs for the disabled, and support education reform have been pioneered by IBM around the world.

IBM's policy of good corporate citizenship means accepting responsibility as a participant in community and national affairs and striving to be among the most-admired companies in its host countries. IBM sponsors Worldwide Initiatives in Volunteerism, a $1 million–plus program to fund projects worldwide and promote employee volunteerism. In Thailand, for example, IBM provides equipment and personnel to universities and donates money to the nation's wildlife fund and environmental protection agency. The firm is one of only two companies with a U.S.-based parent to win the Garuda Award, which recognizes significant contributions to Thailand's social and economic development.

As part of its long-term strategy for growth in Latin America, IBM is investing millions of dollars in an initiative that brings the latest technology to local schools. IBM does not donate the computers (they are bought by governments, institutions, and other private firms), but it does provide the needed instruction and technological support. Some 800,000 children and 10,000 teachers have benefited from the program in ten countries. IBM

Latin America's technology-in-education initiative is a creative combination of marketing, social responsibility, and long-term relationship building that fits in with the company's goal of becoming a "national asset" in Latin American countries. In Venezuela, IBM teamed with the government to bring computers to the K–12 environment to enhance the learning process through technology.

Increased privatization and government cutbacks in social services in many countries offer numerous opportunities for companies to make substantive contributions to solving various global, regional, and local problems. Conservative governments in Europe are welcoming private-sector programs to provide job training for inner-city youth, to meet the needs of immigrants, and to solve massive pollution problems. And in Eastern and Central Europe, where the lines between the private and public sectors are just now being drawn, corporations have a unique opportunity to take a leadership role in shaping new societies. IBM Germany provided computer equipment and executive support to clean the heavily polluted River Elbe, which runs through the Czech Republic and Germany into the North Sea.

James Parkel, director of IBM's Office of Corporate Support Programs, summarizes the new expectations in the following way: "Employees don't want to work for companies that have no social conscience, customers don't want to do business with companies that pollute the environment or are notorious for shoddy products and practices, and communities don't welcome companies that are not good corporate citizens. Many shareholder issues are socially driven."

SOURCES: Michael E. Porter and Mark R. Kramer, "The Competitive Advantage of Corporate Philanthropy," *Harvard Business Review* 80 (December 2002): 56–68; Roger L. Martin, "The Virtue Matrix: Calculating the Return on Corporate Responsibility," *Harvard Business Review* 80 (March 2002): 68–75; Bradley K. Googins, "Why Community Relations Is a Strategic Imperative," *Strategy and Business* (third quarter, 1997): 64–67; "Consumers Note Marketers' Good Causes: Roper," *Advertising Age*, November 11, 1996, 51; Paul N. Bloom, Pattie Yu Hussein, and Lisa R. Szykman, "Benefiting Society and the Bottom Line," *Marketing Management*, Winter 1995, 8–18; and **http://www.ibm.com**.

Summary

As global marketers manage the various elements of the promotions mix in differing environmental conditions, decisions must be made about channels to be used in communication, the message, who is to execute or help execute the program, and how the success of the endeavor is to be measured. The trend is toward more harmonization of

strategy, at the same time allowing for flexibility at the local level and early incorporation of local needs into the promotional plans.

The effective implementation of the promotional program is a key ingredient in the marketing success of the firm. The promotional tools must be used within the opportunities and constraints posed by the communications channels as well as by the laws and regulations governing marketing communications.

Advertising agencies are key facilitators in communicating with the firm's constituent groups. Many marketers are realigning their accounts worldwide in an attempt to streamline their promotional efforts and achieve a global approach.

The use of other promotional tools, especially personal selling, tends to be more localized to fit the conditions of the individual markets. Decisions concerning recruitment,

training, motivation, and evaluation must be made at the affiliate level, with general guidance from headquarters.

An area of increasing challenge for global marketers is public relations. Global entities, by their very design, draw attention to their activities. The best interest of the marketer lies in anticipating problems with both internal and external constituencies and managing them, through communications, to the satisfaction of all parties. Community relations and cause-related marketing play important roles in this process.

Key Terms

cause-related marketing	product placement	consumer-generated media (CGM)
corporate image advertising	global media	ambush marketing

Questions for Discussion

1. MasterCard sponsors the World Cup and Visa the Olympics. Who gets the "better deal," since the expense of sponsorship is about the same for both?

2. Comment on the opinion that "practically speaking, neither an entirely standardized nor an entirely localized advertising approach is necessarily best."

3. What type of adjustments must advertising agencies make as more companies want "one sight, one sound, one sell" campaigns?

4. Assess the programmed management approach for coordinating international advertising efforts.

5. Discuss problems associated with measuring advertising effectiveness in foreign markets.

6. What is the role of community relations for a global marketer? How can the marketer treat even the anti-globals as customers?

Internet Exercises

1. The FIFA World Cup is a marketing platform from which a company can create awareness, enhance its image, and foster goodwill. FIFA offers sponsors a multitude of ways to promote themselves and their products in conjunction with the FIFA World Cup as well as other FIFA Events. Using FIFA's Web site (http://www.fifa.com), assess the different ways a sponsor can benefit from this association. Assess FIFA's attempts to curb ambush marketing.

2. A company wishing to engage in global markets through the Internet has to make sure that its regional/local Web sites are of the same caliber and consistent with its global site. Using Procter & Gamble as an example (http://www.pg.com/company/who_we_are/globalops.jhtml), evaluate whether its various sites abroad satisfy these criteria.

Recommended Readings

Beckwith, Sandra. *Complete Publicity Plans.* Avon, MA: Adams Media Corp., 2003.

De Mooij, Marieke K. *Global Marketing and Advertising: Understanding Cultural Paradoxes.* San Francisco, CA: Sage Publications, Inc., 2005.

Fullerton, Jamie, and Alice Kendrick. *Advertising's War on Terrorism.* Spokane, WA: Marquette Books, 2006.

Percy, Larry, and Richard Elliot. *Strategic Advertising Management.* Oxford University Press, 2008.

Shimp, Terence A. *Advertising, Promotions, and Other Aspects of Integrated Marketing Communications (8th edition),* Cincinnati, Ohio: South-Western, 2006.

Zenith Media. *Advertising Expenditure Forecasts.* London: Zenith Media, December 2008.

INTERNATIONAL MARKETING AND THE FUTURE

No Matter the Stress, Consumers Worldwide will Poke Fun: Literally and Immediately!

A worldwide economic crisis, wars on various fronts, and natural disasters have not stemmed people's desire to engage in humor at the expense of someone else. Of course, today's boundaryless world also means that everyone around the globe can engage in the humor, sometimes at the expense of the world's political leaders.

K&B Publishers is a French company founded in 2001. The company's strategy is to attract the largest possible target audience with high-quality products. The company's product offerings include a variety of interactive books about artists such as Elvis Presley, Jimi Hendrix, 50 Cent, and Céline Dion; illustrated books about Mylène Farmer, M. Pokora, and Madonna; and various biography, memoir, lifestyle, and humor publications. Basically, the company's collections cover fiction, societal topics, politics, and history. One particular offering in the fall of 2008, however, stirred up both national and international conversations on the Internet.

K&B published a voodoo manual and doll kit in the image of French President Nicolas Sarkozy. Popular belief about voodoo is that worshippers can stick pins in dolls, which represent enemies, and plant a curse on these enemies. Voodoo is considered to be a religion that originated in West Africa. It is practiced in parts of the Caribbean, especially Haiti, and parts of the southern United States. By virtue of K&B's offerings, voodoo can also be practiced in France or anywhere else that the voodoo manual and doll kit is shipped.

© BENOIT TESSIER/REUTERS/LANDOV

K&B PUBLISHED THIS VOODOO MANUAL AND DOLL KIT IN THE IMAGE OF FRENCH PRESIDENT NICOLAS SARKOZY.

President Sarkozy was not happy, however, to have his image portrayed in this format. He claimed that K&B, by selling the satirical biography with the voodoo doll, made unlawful commercial use of his image. As well, he claimed that the voodoo product offering could provoke violence against him. The doll has a light blue body and comes with a set of 12 needles and a manual explaining how to put a voodoo curse on the president.

President Sarkozy attempted to forestall K&B's efforts by asking the courts to ban the sale of the voodoo product. Citing freedom of expression in an October, 2008, ruling, the court allowed the continued sale of the dolls. Not only did K&B win that round in court, the dolls became a top-selling product on Amazon.com. Additionally, FNAC stores in Paris sold out of the K&B product within a day of the October hearing. President Sarkozy appealed the lower court ruling. In November, the appeals court upheld the lower court's ruling that the doll could not be blocked from the marketplace. However, the appeals court did award the president a symbolic euro in damages, ordered that a bright red sticker saying "Judicial Injunction" be placed on the package, and that a warning notice accompany the doll. The warning notice reads, "*It was ruled that the encouragement of the reader to poke the doll that comes with the needles in the kit, an activity whose subtext is physical harm, even if it is symbolic, constitutes an attack on the dignity of the person of Mr. Sarkozy.*" K&B expected to have 20,000 units of the voodoo manual and doll kit, with sticker and warning label, ready by December 2008.

In today's marketplace, the voodoo doll and accompanying lawsuits were picked up by many online communication sites. Many blogs posted comments. The sites ranged from the personal to newspaper blogs to sites maintained by lawyers in various countries. The range of discussion was equally wide—from religious zealots discussing voodoo to human rights advocates commenting on Sarkozy's right to dignity to comments about the fact that the president chose to engage in a lawsuit over such trivia. One has to wonder if the online communications is what fed the sales of the voodoo product, rather than people truly wanting to use voodoo against President Sarkozy. This example shows the power of interconnectivity in driving company sales—power that marketers are learning to harness to their advantage.

SOURCES: K&B Publishers, **http://www.kandb.fr**; "Sarkozy Fights Back Against Voodoo Doll," *Reuters*, October 21, 2008, **http://www.reuters.com/article/oddlyEnoughNews/ idUSTRE49K68X20081021**, retrieved January 16, 2009; Katrin Benhold, "Sarkozy Voodoo Doll Wins 'Right to Humor' in Court," *International Herald Tribune*, November 28, 2008, **http://www .iht.com/articles/2008/11/28/africa/sarko.php**, retrieved November 28, 2008; "Sarkozy Wins One Euro in Voodoo-Doll Case; Doll to Remain on Sale," **http://www.loweringthebar .net/2008/12/sarkozy-loses-voodoo-doll-case.html**, retrieved November 28, 2008; Gregory Viscusi and Heather Smith, "Sarkozy Voodoo Dolls Must Be Sold with Warning Label," *Bloomberg.com*, November 28, 2008, **http://www.bloomberg.com/apps /news?pid=20601090&sid=aad8a.Fze2YE&refer=france**, retrieved January 16, 2009.

Worldwide, marketers are faced with major external factors that can dramatically affect efforts toward marketplace success. The fragility of the global marketplace has been seen numerous times over the past few years—from the devastating tsunami in the Indian Ocean to the force with which Hurricane Katrina tore through New Orleans, Louisiana (USA), to the earthquake in Kashmir that took 75,000 lives and left 2.5 million homeless. We have seen how flat and boundaryless the world has become as images of these horrible natural disasters were brought into our homes almost immediately.

As though natural disasters are not enough, we have seen the disasters caused by political instability, marked by conflict in the Middle East, and economic disaster due to the collapse of major financial institutions, perilously high oil prices, and rising unemployment. The job for us, as marketers, is to better understand both the good and the bad of marketplace changes, while recognizing that "the forces of globalization can turn on a dime."[1] In a recent study, the functional area of marketing was noted as the second most critical business function for global success (behind logistics).[2] As portrayed in *The International Marketplace 19.1*, the power of information technology spawned sales of a product that otherwise might not have made an impression on other than a select few.

International marketers are faced constantly with global change. This is not a new situation, nor one to be feared, since change provides the opportunity for the emergence of new market positions. Recently, however, changes are occurring more frequently and more rapidly with the potential for more severe impact. Due to growing real-time access to knowledge about customers, suppliers, and competitors, the international marketing environment is increasingly characterized by high speed, bordering on instantaneity. The past has lost much of its value as a predictor of the future.

This chapter identifies critical issues that marketers need to understand for future success. The intent is to identify major trends or drivers that will affect a marketer's ability to make sound business decisions, as well as suggest critical areas of focus in marketing.

International Drivers—A Marketer's External Environment

The identification of global trends has been the focus of several recent studies. Various methods are used to spot these trends. The Economist Intelligence Unit conducted a survey of more than 260 senior global marketing executives and chief executive officers worldwide to understand challenges faced by global Chief Marketing Officers.[3] *Foreign Policy* and A.T. Kearney collaborated on the seventh annual edition of the Globalization Index that measures countries on their economic, personal, technological, and political integration.[4] In the latest of five international Delphi studies involving key global experts in policy, business, and research, Czinkota and Ronkainen (2009) identified important international business dimensions subject to change by 2020.[5]

Taken together these studies identify several major trends or drivers that will require considerable marketing attention. These drivers in the international marketplace are: demographic, technological development, culture, economic development, natural resources, and political/legal issues.

Demographic

Demographic characteristics have long been a foundation for marketing opinions, and trends in demography will remain critical to the future of marketing decisions. According to the Population Reference Bureau (PRB), the **demographic divide** is widening.[6] The demographic divide is the measure of the inequality in the population and health profiles between rich and poor countries. The world's population in 2008 was estimated at 6.7 billion and is expected to rise to 9.3 billion by 2050. According to PRB president Bill Butz, "Nearly all of the world population growth is now concentrated in the world's poorer countries. Even the small amount of overall growth in the wealthier nations will largely result from immigration."[7] Exhibit 19.1 shows the most populous countries in 2008 and expected most populous countries in 2050. Exhibit 19.2 provides a listing of the countries with the expected largest percent increases and decreases in population between 2008 and 2050.

Population numbers are also affected by changes in life expectancy. The longevity of our population is unprecedented.[8] Life expectancy is increasing and people have progressively more years to live. The phrase "60 is the new 40" will challenge marketers as never before. Exhibit 19.3 shows current and expected median indices worldwide.

Exhibit 19.1

Most Populous Countries, 2008 and 2050

2008		2050	
Country	**Population (millions)**	**Country**	**Population (millions)**
China	1,324.7	India	1,755.2
India	1,149.3	China	1,437.0
United States	304.5	United States	438.2
Indonesia	239.9	Indonesia	343.1
Brazil	195.1	Pakistan	295.2
Pakistan	172.8	Nigeria	282.2
Nigeria	148.1	Brazil	259.8
Bangladesh	147.3	Bangladesh	215.1
Russia	141.9	Congo, Dem. Rop.	189.3
Japan	127.7	Philippines	150.1

SOURCE: 2008 World Population Data Sheet, 2008 Population Reference Bureau, **http://www.prb.org/Publications/Datasheets/2008/2008wpds.aspx**, retrieved January 13, 2009.

Exhibit **19.2**

Largest Population Growth or Decline, 2008 to 2050

Largest Percent Increase		Largest Percent Decline	
Country	**Percent**	**Country**	**Percent**
Uganda	263	Bulgaria	−35
Niger	261	Swaziland	−33
Burundi	220	Georgia	−28
Liberia	216	Ukraine	−28
Guinea-Bissau	205	Japan	−25
Cong, Dem. Rep.	185	Moldova	−23
Timor Leste (East Timor)	179	Russia	−22
Mali	169	Serbia	−21
Somalia	166	Belarus	−20
Angola	155	Romania	−20
		Bosnia-Herzegovina	−20

NOTE: Exdudes countries with fewer than 1 million residents.

SOURCE: 2008 World Population Data Sheet, 2008 Population Reference Bureau, **http://www.prb.org/Publications/ Datasheets/2008/2008wpds.aspx**, retrieved January 13, 2009.

Exhibit **19.3**

Median Age for Major World Region

	2005	2045
WORLD	**28.1**	**37.1**
More developed regions	38.6	45.5
Less developed regions	25.6	35.7
Least developed regions	18.9	26.1
AFRICA	**18.9**	**26.1**
Eastern Africa	17.5	24.3
Middle Africa	16.8	21.6
Northern Africa	23	34.6
Southern Africa	23	28.6
Western Africa	17.6	25.6
ASIA	**27.7**	**39**
Eastern Asia	33.5	45.5
South-central Asia	23.5	35.6
Southeast Asia	25.7	38.8
Western Asia	23.6	24
EUROPE	**39**	**47.2**
Eastern Europe	37.5	47.3
Northern Europe	38.9	43.8
Southern Europe	39.8	50.4
Western Europe	40.7	46.7
LATIN AMERICA & THE CARIBBEAN	**25.9**	**38.5**
Central America	24	38.9
South America	26.4	38.4
NORTH AMERICA	**36.3**	**41.1**

SOURCE: Warren Sanderson and Sergei Scherbov, "Rethinking Age and Aging," *Population Bulletin* 63(4), 2008, 10.

The top ten most globalized countries according to The Globalization Index 2007 are: 1. Singapore; 2. Hong Kong; 3. The Netherlands; 4. Switzerland; 5. Ireland; 6. Denmark; 7. United States; 8. Canada; 9. Jordan; and 10. Estonia.[9] Eight of these top ten have land areas smaller than the state of Indiana in the United States, with seven having fewer than 8 million citizens. Mobility is key to such globalization growth.[10] Countries have to be able to step outside their borders to garner resources that might be lacking nationally (e.g., Singapore and The Netherlands lack natural resources) or to tap into larger size markets (e.g., Ireland has a limited domestic market size).

Technological Development

The electronic superhighway is probably one of the most critical, man-made drivers of the world. This highway has opened up routes between and among countries and consumers that were basically impassable or time-restrictive in the late twentieth century, creating a **"death of distance"**[11] with respect to how rapidly information is transferred around the globe. While immigration may be fueling population growth in the wealthiest nations, technology growth is fueling the business world. Historically, worker mobility was a critical human resources variable that involved changing physical environments. Today, worker mobility may mean as little as someone being on their computer at times that coincide with when a customer is on the computer on the other side of the world!

THE ELECTRONIC SUPERHIGHWAY HAS OPENED UP ROUTES BETWEEN AND AMONG COUNTRIES AND CONSUMERS.

Exhibit 19.4 provides a look at the number of internet users, by geographic regions of the world, in 2008. There is a correlation between globalization and internet bandwidth. That is, the more globalized the country, the more cybertraffic flows through the country. The United States is the biggest handler of international cybertraffic, with most E-mails trafficking between Latin America and Europe having to pass through the United States; London is the key gateway for cybertraffic destined for Europe.[12]

Technological developments over the past decade have led to dramatic changes in the way people think about communication and information sharing. As of the end of 2007, mobile telephone subscriptions worldwide were equal to half of the worldwide population,

Exhibit **19.4**

Internet Users in the World by Geographic Regions

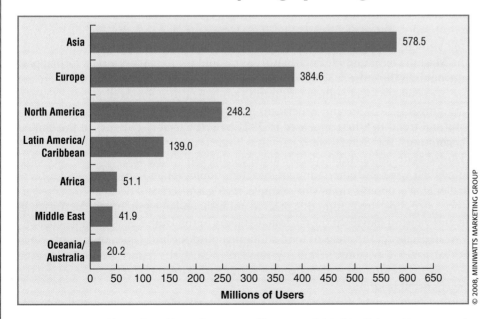

SOURCE: Internet World Stats, **http://www.internetworldstats.com/stats.htm**. Estimated Internet users is 1,463,632,361 for Q2 2008.

with mobile phones having the largest volume worldwide sales in the consumer electronics sector.[13] Many mature markets have over 100 percent mobile penetration (meaning that some owners have more than one phone, not that all members of that market's population own a phone). At the end of 2007, 59 countries had over 100 percent mobile penetration, while only 27 countries had mobile penetration under 10 percent.[14]

The difference in mobile penetration between mature and emerging markets is reflected in a critical ROI indicator—Average Revenue per User (ARPU). For example, the highest ARPU in the world is the Kuwaiti operator MTC, which has an ARPU of $71 per month. Other high ARPU generators are found in the United Kingdom, Japan, and Austria. On the low end, however, ARPUs in Sri Lanki, Bangladesh, Ukraine, and Pakistan are only around $3.[15]

Not only are technology advances leading to greater information sharing worldwide, there are advancements allowing new equipment to be more sophisticated and perform more functions at a lower cost.[16] For example, energy management and connectivity are the two major trends shaping the future of the business-to-business marketplace. Through the use of more intelligent and accurate control equipment, energy efficiency can bring huge cost savings and minimize greenhouse gas emissions. Additionally, the use of wired and wireless connectivity options will permit centralized control of resources to enable efficient use of energy resources in factories and office buildings, while also enabling seamless communications between manufacturing processes and management.[17]

Culture

Culture is the result of learned behavior and adjustments to new conditions. Cultures around the globe will become more and more similar with respect to macro issues such as accountability, performance expectations, freedom accorded within society, and product preferences. However, **cultural clashes** are expected at the micro level. For example, Americans will be exposed to large groups of Latinos and may even be confronted with becoming a regional minority. Similarly, western Europeans will see an influx and competitive activity from what used to be their communist neighbors.[18]

Cultural clashes are likely to occur, particularly with respect to religion. For example, there are over two million Muslims now residing in Great Britain. *Sharia* is the body of Islamic religious law based on the Koran (the Koran is comprised of the words and actions of the Prophet Mohammad and the rulings of Islamic scholars). *Sharia* has begun to enter prominently into British life. Informal neighborhood councils provide rules on family issues such as divorce, and banks offer mortgages that comply with *Sharia* rules.[19] The Archbishop of Canterbury stirred up much public sentiment when he called for the reexamination of the role of *Sharia* in British life in 2008. Interestingly, the Archbishop faced harsh rejoinders from both sides. Those of Christian heritage were outraged that the Archbishop may not have felt strongly enough that British laws should be based on Anglican values, while those in the Muslim community feared that Britain would try to make *Sharia* a formal part of law that would disallow the successful informal aspect of the *Sharia* councils. There are many more areas where local culture can inhibit globalization. For example, the French prefer home-grown agriculture and Americans fear foreign management of ports.[20]

One cultural trend that first appeared in 2001 after the terrorist attacks in the United States is "cocooning." This trend toward staying at home is now a worldwide phenomenon—from the United States to Australia, people are spending more time at home. They are basically bringing their work and entertainment into their homes rather than going out for these things. Challenging economic times (for example, high gas prices and declines in home values and stock portfolios) are behind this push to cut back on large purchases like traveling, eating out, and viewing movies at the cinema. Retailers in the United States report cocooning trend-related sales in the areas of food shopping, outdoor barbeque equipment, video games, and flat-panel televisions.[21] Similarly, retailers in Australia report the buying/renting of DVDs, meal-preparation ingredients, and outdoor furniture and accessories topping the cocoon-buyer's list of priorities.[22]

Cocooning is, of course, made easier by virtue of technological advances that enable tele-cocooning. People can literally purchase merchandise without leaving their homes, engage in social exchanges via social networking and matchmaking sites, and communicate with friends and relatives in real-time via text and Internet messaging.

Economic Development

The economy is an underlying hot spot in the growth and development of any international enterprise. Without a doubt, the **economic crisis** in 2008 rocked the world dramatically! Individuals and nations alike were hit hard by the collapse of financial markets. One of the hardest hit nations was Iceland, home to some 300,000 people. The collapse of the financial world of Iceland not only had ramifications for the individual well-being of Icelandic citizens, but also for world markets. As the events of Iceland's financial crisis unfolded, the relationship between Iceland and the United Kingdom was seriously damaged when the UK employed the same type of anti-terror laws it uses against foes like Al Qaeda to seize Icelandic bank funds.

While emerging markets are at great risk in a financial crisis such as that experienced in 2008, the International Monetary Fund's projection for 2009 gross domestic product growth in these markets was still above five percent, although they had declined collectively by more than 60 percent.[23] The emerging markets were vulnerable to the 2008 financial crisis in three major ways: 1. Exports of goods and services suffered; 2. Net imports of capital slowed; and 3. Banks had less money to lend.[24]

At the same time, trade-related endeavors comprise more than 25 percent of economic activities in the United States.[25] Seventy-five percent of the world's economy is accounted for by only five major regions: USA, EU, Japan, China, and Canada.[26] But the world economies are intertwined. Thus, economic stimuli put into play by any one nation will rapidly affect other countries and trigger responses.

Looking beyond the turmoil, international service organizations might become weaker. For example, the developmental role of the World Bank could diminish. Poor countries may feel that there is very little for them to gain from the institution. Similarly, the International Monetary Fund (IMF) may be outperformed by local and regional lending arrangements. The currently overwhelming power of richer countries in the IMF voting system tends to make the less-developed countries feel that they are not getting the same value as rich members. While all countries and companies have much to gain from strong country economies, they all have much to lose as well!

Natural Resources

A growing concern for planet Earth has prompted much interest and investment in the world's natural resources. Safeguarding the earth refers to protecting Earth's people, plants, animals, and natural systems. This global phenomenon is referred to in a variety of contexts: sustainable development, global warming, climate change, going green, renewable energy, bio-energy, and green revolution. From a natural resource perspective, futurists predict that we will be stretching our planet's capacity by 2050. Issues such as a growing and aging global population, urbanization, energy demand, and the food and water needed to nourish over nine billion people are close to the hearts and on the minds of organizations around the world.

Sustainability is the all-encompassing term generally utilized, and global corporations do not hesitate to promote their interests in sustainability. Here are a few excerpts from company websites:

> "The need for truly sustainable options for twenty-first century life remains one of the most critical challenges facing the global community." (**http://www.dupont.com**)

> "Our commitment to Sustainable Development, which we define as 'ensuring a better quality of life for everyone, now and for generations to come,' is an important part of how we fulfill P&G's Purpose." (**http://www.pg.com**)

> "Sustainability at Wrigley means driving business performance by advancing the well being of people and the planet, now and for generations to come." (**http://www.wrigley.com**)

A GROWING CONCERN FOR PLANET EARTH HAS PROMPTED INTEREST AND INVESTMENT IN THE WORLD'S NATURAL RESOURCES. IT HAS ALSO POPULARIZED RECYCLING, AS SHOWN IN THIS APPLE POSTER.

"Sustainability is about preserving the planet—land, air, water and people. From the 'big picture' issues like climate change by greenhouse gases, to local issues like coffee and cocoa farmers earning a decent wage, Kraft is finding ways to have positive impacts on the world we live in." (**http://www.kraft.com**)

"Kodak is committed to sustainability worldwide. We recognize that we have a role to play in helping society prosper by driving business growth in a responsible manner that creates value for all stakeholders." (**http://www.kodak.com**)

The rapid growth associated with emerging economies will lead to the further depletion of natural resources. There will be shortages in some resource areas due to the associated aspirations for economic progress and better lifestyles. From an economic perspective, scarcity will drive up prices for raw materials.

One of the biggest enigmas when it comes to sustainability is China. In less than five years, China's energy consumption grew at an average of 11 percent per year. It is the world's biggest emitter of carbon dioxide and is predicted to emit as much as the United States and Europe combined by 2030. At the same time, hundreds of thousands of people die from pollution-related cancer every year.[27] Even with these acknowledged issues, there is fear that China will demonstrate only limited concern toward the environment.[28]

The concern about our natural resources and sustainability has led to a variety of predictions for the future:[29]

- Governments will attempt to put more land into grain production and also use tools such as subsidies and price controls,

- Recycling and recovery will grow as vital business opportunities,

- Farming will regain its attractiveness and profitability as fuel production from food sources accelerates,

- The global shortage of potable water will be re-discovered as a key climate issue, leading to higher government investments in desalination and reverse osmosis technologies and more emphasis on water conversation, and

- There will be growing preference for energy-saving technologies and a reduction and limit to energy use.

These concerns will lead to the creation and expansion of sectors worldwide. For example, we can expect to see more focus upon the protection of public health and a growth in bio-technology, genomics, and nano-technology. Sustainable water-recycling technologies will spawn new industries. Government involvement in the oversight of issues and creation of new industries will be unprecedented.

Political and Legal

The globalization of markets has taken place against a backdrop of **political instability** and various perspectives on what is and is not legal. Looking ahead politically, the United States entered into a new political regime with the inauguration of a new president in 2009. This transpired as sectarian violence continued in Iraq, and Israeli soldiers and Palestinian militants fought on the outskirts of Gaza City. The 2008 round of the Doha global-free-trade talks still failed since the United States, India, and China could not agree on access to agricultural markets. The incoming United States secretary of state listed Mexico and all of Latin America at the bottom of her regional priorities, only ahead of Africa.

In a 2008 Delphi Study,[30] experts identified **terrorism** as a critical dimension of international business over the upcoming decade. Terrorism was seen as a facet of international life that would have to be managed, even if it could not be defeated. In this study, the root causes of terrorism were found to be policies toward immigration and the oftentimes dividing roles taken on by advocates of specific religions, cultures, regions, or races. Consumers worldwide were willing to change their consumption patterns if necessary for security considerations, and corporations expressed a willingness to not do business in countries that lacked law and order.

Ranking very closely behind terrorism in the Delphi Study is **corruption**. Strategic decision makers face pressure from stakeholders when it comes to social and ethical issues in business. Corruption serves as a major barrier to entry as international organizations attempt to move goods and services across borders. Regardless of market potential, corruption is a major detractor with respect to business development and prosperity. There is concern that corruption breeds corruption.[31] There is also the concern that future business leaders expect laws to guide their actions rather than utilizing a moral compass to determine right and wrong in decision making. Thus, while there are laws governing corruption, such as the U.S. Foreign Corrupt Practices Act, the business environment is at risk if cheating becomes a norm because "everyone else" is doing it.[32] *The International Marketplace 19.2* describes the impact corruption can have on economic wellbeing.

The International MARKETPLACE　　　19.2

Counterfeiting, Software Piracy, and Terrorism

Counterfeiting is a common form of corruption and cost businesses well over US $1 trillion in 2008. One of the most highly scrutinized areas of counterfeiting in today's business world is the theft of intellectual property. Intellectual property is the ownership of ideas, as well as the control over the tangible or virtual representation of those ideas. The piracy of this intellectual property has become a major form of illegal business.

Software is intellectual property, as are books, movies, and music. Music performers, authors, and software developers use copyright laws to protect their work and their investment in the field. Global software piracy has reached financial values of astronomical proportions. According to estimates by the Business Software Alliance, just under five percent of all software purchased annually is pirated, resulting in revenue losses in the billions of dollars. IDC, a global market intelligence and information technology and telecommunications advisory firm, estimated that a 10 percent reduction in worldwide software piracy over a four-year period would put US $400 billion back into economic growth. This economic growth would also add more than 1 million jobs and generate billions in new taxes.

Firms that expand globally with their intellectual property are increasingly mindful of the potential ramifications of software piracy, which range from multimillion dollar losses to the hindrance of future software development. The accessibility of software and the ease of duplicating it make it highly vulnerable to unauthorized copying.

The Business Software Alliance (BSA) delineates five common types of software piracy: end-user piracy, client-server overuse, Internet swapping, hard-disk loading, and commercial counterfeiting. *End-user piracy* occurs when a person reproduces copies of software without authorization. *Client-server overuse* happens when too many people on a network are using a central copy of a program at the same time—a company has to be licensed for the number of users who can access the program simultaneously. *Internet swapping*, or the downloading of unauthorized copies of copyrighted programs from the Internet, is illegal if the software is accessed via pirate websites or peer-to-peer networks. *Hard-disk loading* occurs when a reseller loads software illegally with the aim of making the machine more attractive to customers. *Commercial counterfeiting* of software is the illegal duplication of copyrighted programs with the express intent of directly imitating the copyrighted software. Creating, allowing others to create, or obtaining any unauthorized copy of software, regardless of commercial or financial benefit, is considered copyright infringement and can be prosecuted under civil and criminal law in many countries.

Interpol suggests a connection between counterfeiting and both organized crime and terrorism. The Secretary General of Interpol has gone so far as to imply that profit from pirated CDs in Central America funded Hezbollah terrorist efforts in the Middle East. Countries considered highly corrupt according to Transparency International tolerate high levels of software piracy.

Given the significant ramifications to the world economy, counterfeiting and the theft of intellectual property will be watched closely in the future. The global electronic village demands a revenue model that ensures adequate income to those developing intellectual property while simultaneously providing consumers with access to such intellectual content.

SOURCES: "Fighting Fakes: Foiling Counterfeit Products," *Business Week*, May 26, 2007, **http://feedroom.businessweek.com/?fr_story=FEEDROOM196813&rf=sitemap**; Frederik Balfour, "Fakes!" *Business Week*, February 7, 2005, i3919, 54–64; William F. Crittenden, Christopher J. Robertson, and Victoria L. Crittenden, "Hard Facts about Software Piracy," *Business Strategy Review*, Winter 2007, 30–33, **http://www.bsa.org**.

The Marketer of the Future—Strategic Efforts

International marketing in the future will have both similarities and differences with that of today. Marketers will still engage in critical marketing-mix decisions and will, as always, need to understand the intricacies of the marketplace in which business is being conducted. Looking ahead, there are five major areas of which marketers will have to be particularly more attentive. These are in balancing global and local expectations, innovation, collaborative partnerships, connecting with the world's customers, and technology-based marketing research.

The Balance between Global and Local

"Think Globally, Act Locally" has long been the mantra in the marketing world. While we are unlikely to see a major shift in this thinking, the balance between global marketing and local marketing has taken on new meaning in the twenty-first century. A major driver behind the precarious balance between global and local has been technology. In particular, the Internet has created a flat world. Customizing for local markets has become more difficult as online viewers access information originating in various countries. Most large companies manage this by asking viewers to select a country upon entry into the corporation's website. The key at the corporate level is to maintain consistency of appearance and product offerings for different country versions.

Within the company, the precarious balance between global and local has a huge impact on the company's organizational structure. If consumers across the globe are becoming more alike, then a centralized structure might make sense from both consistency and budgeting points of view. However, even global consumers have local preferences and, according to the CEO of Interbrand, "One of the big lessons is that in your local market you have a greater duty to stay fresh. People become bored quickly."[33] Thus, the trend is to have a centralized budgeting process with decentralized spending/allocation and centralized development of the marketing message and decentralization of the marketing mix.[34] Simultaneously, smaller firms will be able to benefit by focusing on niche markets, especially those abandoned by large companies where the global/local imbalance was too great.[35]

Marketers will continue to face pressure from a variety of stakeholders from both governments and non-governmental organizations (NGOs). Accounting systems will have to recognize and develop procedures for calculating worldwide value and performance. Corporate responsibility will be interpreted to include broad-based activities and profit sharing. Stakeholders will demand greater involvement and will play a major role in the global image building of the company. Corporate social responsibility (CSR) will have to look at global impact, since lapses in ethics or social responsibility could affect brand equity in a major way.[36]

Corporate and marketing actions taken locally will be observed globally! It will no longer be "global *versus* local," since the two will have to go hand-in-hand, appealing to consumers globally as well as locally. In thinking about marketing objectives, plans, and programs, marketers will have to begin thinking in terms of "global *and* local."

Innovation

Innovation cannot be emphasized enough when it comes to the future of marketing. Innovation has many meanings and areas of relevance—generating new ideas, exploiting new ideas, higher-quality goods and services, sustained growth, and new knowledge are just several examples of what innovation can refer to. Former British Prime Minister Tony Blair said, "The creativeness and inventiveness of our people is our country's greatest asset . . . in an increasingly global world, our ability to invent, design, and manufacture the goods and services that people want is more vital to our future prosperity than ever before."[37]

The domain of innovation is very broad—it does not just include developing new products and services. Eight different types of innovation have been identified:[38]

1. *Disruptive Innovation*—gets a great deal of attention, roots in technological discontinuities
2. *Application Innovation*—takes existing technologies into new markets to serve new purposes
3. *Product Innovation*—takes established offers in established markets to the next level
4. *Process Innovation*—makes processes for established offers in established markets more effective or efficient
5. *Experiential Innovation*—makes surface modifications that improve customers' experiences of established products or processes
6. *Marketing Innovation*—improves customer-touching processes
7. *Business Model Innovation*—reframes an established value proposition to the customer or a company's established role in the value chain or both
8. *Structural Innovation*—capitalizes on disruption to restructure industry relationships.

Different types of innovation occur at different points during a product category's life cycle. Exhibit 19.5 maps these eight types of innovation onto the life cycle of a product category. Companies cannot limit themselves to just one type of innovation. Competing in today's global economy demands that companies pursue a range of innovative efforts for continued growth and profitability.

The importance of innovation to the future of world business is stressed by the World Economic Forum. Exhibit 19.6 lists the 34 visionary companies the Forum selected as 2009 Technology Pioneers. The companies were selected for their accomplishment as innovators of the highest caliber.

Exhibit **19.5**

Aligning Innovation with the Life Cycle

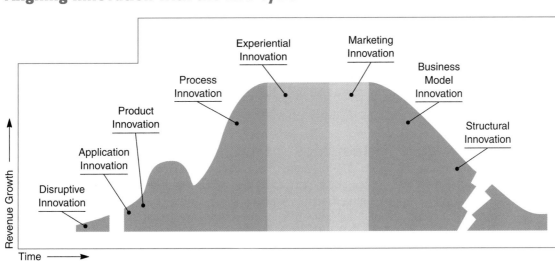

SOURCE: Geoffrey A. Moore, "Darwin and the Demon: Innovating within Established Enterprises," *Harvard Business Review*, July–August 2004, 90–91.

Exhibit **19.6**

Technology Pioneers 2009

Biotech/Health
AC Immune S.A., **http://www.acimmune.com**
Alnylam Pharmaceuticals, **http://www.alnylam.com**
BioMedica Diagnostics, **http://www.biomedicadiagnostics.com**
Intercell AG, **http://www.intercell.com**
Mobile Healthcare Inc., **http://www.lifewatcher.com**
MorphoSys AG, **http://www.morphosys.com**
Phase Forward, Inc., **http://www.phaseforward.com**
Proteus Biomedical, **http://www.proteusbiomed.com**

Energy/Environment
CURRENT Group, LLC, **http://www.currentgroup.com**
BrightSource Energy, Inc., **http://www.brightsourceenergy.com**
Cows to Kilowatts Partnership Limited, **http://www.biotec.or.th/biotechnology-en/newsdetail .asp?id=732**
GreenPeak Technologies, **http://www.greenpeak.com**
Lemnis Lighting, **http://www.lemnislighting.com**
NovaTorque, **http://www.novatorque.com**
RECYCLA Chile, **http://www.recycla.cl**
RecycleBank, LLC, **http://www.RecycleBank.com**
SemiLEDs Corporation, **http://www.semileds.com**
Virent Energy Systems, Inc., **http://www.virent.com**
ZPower, Inc., **http://www.zpowerbattery.com**

Information Technology
Advanced Track & Trace, **http://www.advancedtrackandtrace.com**
Brightcove Inc., **http://www.brightcove.com**
Etsy Inc., **http://www.etsy.com**
GameForge, **http://www.gameforge.de**
JiGrahak Mobility Solution Pvt. Ltd., **http://www.ngpay.com**
Mint.com, **http://www.mint.com**
Mojix, Inc., **http://www.mojix.com**
MPedigree, **http://www.mPedigree.org**
Nivio, **http://www.nivio.com**
Qifang Inc., **http://www.qifang.cn**
Slide, Inc., **http://www.slide.com**
SpinVox Ltd, **http://www.spinvox.com**
Tideway Systems, **http://www.tideway.com**
Ubiquisys Ltd, **http://www.ubiquisys.com**
TraceTracker Innovation ASA, **http://www.tracetracker.com**

SOURCE: World Economic Forum, **http://www.weforum.org/en/Communities/Technology%20Pioneers /SelectedTechPioneers/index.htm**, retrieved January 20, 2009.

Collaborative Partnerships

As described in *The International Marketplace 19.3*, partnering with outside companies in the formulation and implementation of customer-oriented, global marketing strategies is a necessity for companies in the twenty-first century.[39] Doing business in today's economic times is the result of collaboration across country and company boundaries. Companies realize that today's global marketplace requires a diversity of inputs. Those companies that have been able to manage successfully both across geographic and competitive boundaries are the ones that are able to advance in today's fast-paced business world.

Examples of successful cross-border and cross-company partnerships include:

- *Nokia*—customer research in Europe and Asia, design skills from Italy and USA, and substitutions for landlines in China and India

The International MARKETPLACE

ENVIRONMENT & SUSTAINABILITY 19.3

The Body Shop Partners with Daabon

Continuing with its efforts in responsible business practices, The Body Shop became the first cosmetics retailer to introduce sustainable palm oil into the global beauty-product industry. Spurred by growing concerns about the impact of palm oil plantations on biodiversity, The Body Shop partnered with Daabon, a certified organic producer in Colombia, to bring sustainable oil to the marketplace.

Palm oil is one of the world's most popular vegetable oils. It is a common ingredient in items such as cosmetics, household products, and foods. Two countries leading in palm oil production are Malaysia and Indonesia. Unfortunately, rapid expansion of palm oil production has come at the expense of biodiverse rainforests and carbon-rich peatlands that store greenhouse gases. It is estimated that at least 2000 million tons of carbon dioxide are released annually from just the logged and drained peatlands of Southeast Asia, accounting for eight percent of global emissions. Over 50 percent of new plantations in Southeast Asia are located on peatlands. As such, palm oil has become a major driver of global CO_2 emissions. In addition to the destruction of rainforests and global emissions issues, expansion of palm oil plantations endangers animal species such as orangutans in Borneo and Sumatra. While the new palm oil plantations create employment opportunities for local people, there is also considerable conflict over human rights violations.

The Body Shop decided that it needed to source its palm oil from a sustainable producer. Producing over 14.5 million bars of soap per annum that contain palm oil, the company needed a reliable source of the raw material—but a source that had concern for the environment in much the same way as that of The Body Shop.

Certified by the Rainforest Alliance, SA8000, Ecocert, and the Fairtrade Labelling Organization, Daabon is an organic family-run Colombian company that produces palm oil, coffee, bananas, and cocoa. Daabon's philosophy

THE BODY SHOP BECAME THE FIRST COSMETICS RETAILER TO INTRODUCE SUSTAINABLE PALM OIL TO THE GLOBAL BEAUTY PRODUCT INDUSTRY.

centers on organic agriculture, social accountability, traceability, and sustainability. It is the only company in the world that has vertically integrated the palm oil production process—from seeding to end products. The company has three organic palm oil plantations, for a total of 2,500 hectares of palm trees. The company is also organizing the development of 2,000 hectares owned by cooperatives of local farmers. Both Daabon and The Body Shop are members of the Malaysia-based Roundtable on Sustainable Palm Oil.

Conservation groups applauded the move by The Body Shop. However, it was only through the partnership with an international company that it was able to engage in such a promising effort. This was not something that the company could have done on its own. The future of sustainability may lie in global partnerships such as the one between The Body Shop and Daabon.

SOURCES: Louise Prance, "The Body Shop Produces First Cosmetics using Sustainable Palm Oil," *Decision News Media,* July 12, 2007, **http://www.cosmeticsdesign-europe.com/Formulation-Scuebce?The-Body-Shop-produces-first-cosmetics-using-sustainable-palm-oil**, retrieved January 6, 2009; Rhett A. Butler, "Environmental Concerns Mount as Palm Oil Production Surges," **http://news.mongabay.com/2007/0515-palm_oil.html**, retrieved January 6, 2009; **http://www.thebodyshop.com**; **http://www.daabon.com**.

- *Airbus*—wing aerodynamics from the United Kingdom, avionics from France, flight-control techniques from the USA, knowledge from regional carriers worldwide

- *SAP*—market knowledge from foreign customers to enable language, currency, and accounting differences

- *Starbucks*—Italian technology for espresso coffee roasting, the European concept for the café, USA expertise in retail concepts (e.g., fast-food service routines, logistics, staff training, incentive systems), and a Preferred Supplier Program for sustainable development

Companies that innovate across borders and across companies are referred to as **metanational innovators**.[40] Sometimes such partnerships result in companies becoming subsidiaries of major multinational companies. For example, Tom's of Maine is a niche-brand product known for its socially responsible production. The company was bought by Colgate-Palmolive in 2006, providing Colgate-Palmolive a much needed entry into the fast-growing U.S. market for natural personal care products.[41]

Connecting with the World's Customers

Historically, connecting with the customer meant that the company had one-way communications (via advertising, packaging, promotion). In today's world, however, consumers are likely to initiate contact with the company—two-way communication is a must for today's marketer and will become even more important in the future.

Interactive digital media is changing the landscape of a marketer's world.[42] Global brand building, changes in channel structure, and marketing messages are only the tip of the iceberg when it comes to the areas in which interactive digital media impact the future of marketing. The Economist Intelligence Unit explored the idea of the newly empowered individual customer over the next five years.[43] Over 50 percent of the corporate respondents to the survey reported that their companies were highly customer-centric and expected customers to be directly connected to the brand and the development process. According to the vice president of Web strategy of IBM, "We seek to engage with clients in the way they prefer to engage."[44]

Consumers worldwide are now connected to companies in a variety of ways. Marketers and consumers connect via:

- Company websites,
- Videoconferencing, webinars, Voice-over Internet Protocol (VoIP), Podcasts,
- Hand-held devices for product demonstration, mobile credit-card transaction terminals,
- The e-suite of touch processes—e-guests, e-invites, e-reminders, e-magazines, and e-newsletters, and
- Social networking sites, blogs, text messaging, YouTube

Nortel utilized connectivity with consumers to highlight their latest product line, engage customers on their website, and underscore the company's focus on sustainability. The company built an interactive energy calculator (**http://hyperconnectivity.com/en/saveenergy/**) that allowed visitors to input their own operations variables to calculate energy consumption and costs in 49 countries across the globe.[45]

The future of global marketing lies in connecting with consumers in every corner of the world—and doing so by identifying the consumer-preferred mode and location of connection and outpacing competitors who also want to connect. Thus, the battle for brand and product allegiance will take place, literally, in the hands of the consumer.

Technology-Based Marketing Research

Marketers will connect with consumers in ways almost unimaginable several years ago. The marketing message has truly become a two-way communication stream, and marketers will be engaging in new and exciting ways of gathering information about consumers. As mentioned in Chapter 8, traditional methods of marketing research have already migrated to Web 2.0. Polling on *social network sites* such as Facebook has already become somewhat mainstream in marketing research, with younger consumers worldwide very comfortable with this medium.

Companies are moving beyond social networking sites for polling into virtual worlds such as **Second Life**. Virtual worlds were introduced by Linden Labs at the beginning of the twenty-first century. Since then, marketing in virtual worlds has had its ups and downs. The expectation, however, is that Second Life will rebound and that virtual worlds will be ideal for conducting marketing research.[46] Virtual worlds are truly a worldwide phenomenon, with 60 percent of Second Life users residing outside the USA.[47] As with many Web 2.0 technologies, virtual worlds tend to appeal to the younger demographic since this group is

Exhibit **19.7**

Marketing Research Companies in Second Life

Beatenetworks **(http://www.beatenetworks.com)**
Market Truths **(http://www.sl.markettruths.com)**
Ibranz **(http://www.ibranz.com)**
PluggedIN **(http://www.pluggedinco.com)**
Sentient Services **(http://www.sentientservices.com)**
The Kalypso Agency **(http://www.thekalypsoagency.com)**

used to navigating virtual worlds on game consoles.[48] Exhibit 19.7 lists several marketing research companies that focus largely on virtual worlds for collecting consumer data. Additionally, the Social Research Foundation, a non-profit 301(c)3 organization, launched a virtual research panel in mid-2000 that has over 11 million registered users (**http://www .socialresearchfoundation.org**).

Another advancement that bodes well for the future of marketing research is video eye-tracking technology. Eye-tracking is precisely what the name implies—the technology tracks the eye's movement as it views images on a screen. From a marketing research perspective, the researcher can see what consumers are really viewing when they see an advertisement, a package design, or website. In the eye-tracking methodology, a person sits in front of a specialized computer screen and views marketing material; the computer tracks and records where the person looks and for how long the person looks at something. An eye-tracking marketing research report can provide:[49]

- The real-time scan path / eye movement and areas of focus,
- Static plots illustrating where the respondent looked, in what order, and for how long, and
- What was noticed or not noticed and what seemed to peak interest.

Researchers have preliminarily started using eye-tracking research to better understand the impact of specific consumer technologies on advertising. One eye-tracking study found that while an ad placed above the fold ("above the fold" refers to ads that are viewable without having to scroll down) on a website is visible to everyone visiting the site, only about 60 percent of the visitors actually see the ad. Only about 70 percent of visitors actually scroll below the fold and, even then, only about 25 percent of the viewers actually see the ads.[50]

Another groundbreaking study examined the concern that advertisers have with consumers using digital video recorders (DVRs) to fast-forward through commercials. Results from multiple eye-tracker studies found the following:[51]

- Fast-forwarding viewers constrain their vision to the center of the screen—thus brand information at the center of the screen is viewed more often than information placed elsewhere,
- Brand information found in the center of the screen is a strong predictor of ad recognition, and
- Advertisements with branding in the center do lead to increased brand attitude and choice behavior for the centrally-placed brand.

Using equipment to gauge consumer responses to stimuli opens the door for yet another piece of equipment to take on a research purpose—the functional magnetic resonance imaging (fMRI) scanning equipment. The fMRI is a non-invasive neural-imaging technique that basically looks inside the brain. By observing blood oxygen signals during an fMRI, marketing researchers can reliably predict, for example, whether a person will purchase a given product or whether the price of a product influences positive or negative responses about a product.[52]

Several global companies have used fMRI to gauge consumers' responses to advertising, branding, and choice behavior.[53] These include Daimler-Chrysler, Delta Airlines, General Motors, Hallmark, Home Depot, Motorola, and Procter & Gamble. But, the technique is not without its skeptics. One consumer group in the USA, Commercial Alert, has sought a congressional investigation of the technique. The fear is that marketing researchers will learn too much about neural activity and enable marketers of the future to more adequately trigger desired responses from consumers.[54]

Summary

External factors have always been out of a marketer's control. A good marketer, however, will learn how to identify opportunities in the external environment. Looking ahead, changes in the external environment do present many opportunities for the astute marketer, just as there will be numerous threats that have to be managed accordingly. The international, boundaryless marketplace is changing, and we as marketers have to stay ahead of those changes.

Key Terms

demographic divide

death of distance

cultural clashes

cocooning

economic crisis

sustainability

political instability

terrorism

corruption

innovation

metanational innovators

interactive digital media

Second Life

Questions for Discussion

1. What are the key drivers that today's marketer has to understand in planning for the international marketplace?

2. Why have smaller countries been able to be some of the top globalized countries?

3. What is the role of each international driver in implementing each of the strategic efforts?

4. Which of the international drivers and strategic efforts is likely to change more often and rapidly?

Internet Exercises

1. Identify a global online retail commerce and describe how it (1) targets specific countries and (2) engages the consumer in an interactive manner.

2. Identify five social networking sites and prepare a profile of the sites' users in terms of demographic characteristics (for example, gender, age, geographic location). How can an international marketer use this type of information?

Recommended Readings

Cowhey, Peter F., and Jonathan D. Aronson. *Transforming Global Information and Communication Markets.* Cambridge, MA: The MIT Press, 2009.

Esty, Daniel, and Andrew Winston. *Green to Gold: How Smart Companies Use Environmental Strategy to Innovate, Create Value, and Build Competitive Advantage.* Hoboken, NJ: Wiley, 2009.

Fisher-Buttinger, Claudia, and Christine Vallaster. *Connective Branding: Building Brand Equity in a Demanding World.* Hoboken, NJ: Wiley, 2008.

Hollis, Nigel. *The Global Brand: How to Create and Develop Lasting Brand Value in the World Market.* New York: Palgrave Macmillan, 2008.

Pacek, Nenad. *Emerging Markets: Lessons for Business Success and the Outlook for Different Markets.* London: Profile Books, 2007.

Prahalad, C.K., and M.S. Krishnan. *The New Age of Innovation: Driving Cocreated Value through Global Networks.* Columbus, OH: McGraw-Hill, 2008.

CAREERS IN INTERNATIONAL MARKETING

A career in international marketing does not consist only of jet-setting travel between Rome, London, and Paris. Globalists need to be well versed in the specific business functions and may wish to work at summer internships abroad, take language courses, and travel not simply for pleasure but to observe business operations abroad and to gain a greater understanding of different peoples and cultures. Taking on and successfully completing an international assignment is seen by managers as crucial for the development of professional, managerial, and intercultural skills and is highly likely to affect career advancement.[1]

Further Training

One option for the student on the road to more international involvement is to obtain further in-depth training by enrolling in graduate business school programs that specialize in international business education. A substantial number of universities around the world specialize in training international managers. According to the Institute of International Education, the number of U.S. students studying for a degree at universities abroad rose to more than 191,321 students in 2005. Furthermore, American students increasingly go abroad for business and economics degrees, not just for a semester or two. At the same time, business and management are the most popular fields of study for the 565,000 international students at American universities.[2] A review of college catalogues and of materials from groups such as the Academy of International Business will be useful here.

In addition, as the world becomes more global, more organizations are able to assist students interested in studying abroad or in gathering foreign work experience.

Apart from individual universities and their programs for study abroad, many nonprofit institutions stand ready to help and to provide informative materials. Exhibit 1 provides information about programs and institutions that can help with finding an international job.

Employment with a Large Firm

One career alternative in international marketing is to work for a large multinational corporation. These firms constantly search for personnel to help them in their international operations.

Many multinational firms, while seeking specialized knowledge like languages, expect employees to be firmly grounded in the practice and management of business. They rarely will hire a new employee at the starting level and immediately place him or her in a position of international responsibility. Usually, a new employee is expected to become thoroughly familiar with the company's internal operations before being considered for an international position. The reason a manager is sent abroad is that the company expects him or her to reflect the corporate spirit, to be tightly wed to the corporate culture, and to be able to communicate well with both local and corporate management personnel. In this liaison position, the manager will have to be exceptionally sensitive to both headquarters and local operations. As an intermediary, the expatriate must be empathetic and understanding, and yet fully prepared to implement the goals set by headquarters.

It is very expensive for companies to send an employee overseas. Typically, the annual cost of maintaining a manager overseas is about three times the cost of hiring a local manager. Companies want to be sure that the expenditure is worth the benefit they will receive, even though certainty is never possible.

Even if a position opens up in international operations, there is some truth in the saying that the best place to be in international business is on the same floor as the chairman at headquarters. Employees of firms that have taken the international route often come back to headquarters to find only a few positions available for them. Such encounters lead, of course, to organizational difficulties, as well as to financial pressures and family problems, all of which may add up to significant executive stress. Because family re-entry angst is the reason why 25 percent of expatriates quit within one year of their return, companies are paying increasing attention to the spouses and

Exhibit 1

Web Sites Useful in Gaining International Employment

Advancing Women
P.O. Box 6642
San Antonio, TX 78209 USA
(210) 822-8087
Web site: **http://www.advancingwomen.com/ networks/intlinks.html**
Provides international networking contacts for women.

AVOTEK Headhunters
Nieuwe Markt 54
6511 XL Nijmegen,
NETHERLANDS
Telephone: (31) 24 3221367
Fax: (31) 24 3240467
Web site: **http://www.avotek.n1**
Lists Web sites and addresses of jobs and agencies worldwide. Offers sale publications and other free reference materials.

Council Exchanges
Council on International Educational Exchange
633 3rd Avenue
New York, NY 10017
USA
Telephone: (212) 822-2600
Fax: (212) 822-2649
Web site: **http://www.ciee.org**
Paid work and internships overseas for college students and recent graduates. Also offers international volunteer projects, as well as teaching positions.

Datum Online
91 Charlotte Street
London W1P1LB
UK
Telephone: 44 171 255 1313/1314/1320
Fax: 44 (0) 171 255 1316
E-mail: admin@dutumeurope.com
http://www.datumeurope.com/
Online database providing all the resources to find IT, sales, and accountancy jobs across Europe.

Dialogue with Citizens
Internal Market Directorate General
MARKT A/04, C107 03/52
European Commission
Rue de la Loi, 200
B-1049 Brussels
BELGIUM
Telephone: (011) 322 299 5804
Fax: (011) 322 295 6695
Web site: **http://ec.europa.eu/youreurope/nav/en/ citizens/home.html**
Factsheets on EU citizens' rights regarding residence, education, working conditions and social security, rights as a consumer, and ways of enforcing these rights, etc. Easy-to-use

guides that give a general outline of EU citizens' rights and the possibilities offered by the European Single Market. A Signpost Service for citizens' practical problems.

Ed-U-Link Services
PO Box 2076
Prescott, AZ 86302
USA
Telephone: (520) 778-5581
Fax: (520) 776-0611
Web site: **http://www.edulink.com/JobOpeningsMair .html**
Provides listings of and assistance in locating teaching jobs abroad.

80 Days
Web site: **http://www.80days.com**
Links to Web sites with job listings worldwide, including volunteer work and teaching English as a foreign language. Has special section on Europe.

The Employment Guide's CareerWeb
150 West Brambleton Avenue
Norfolk, VA 23510
USA
Telephone: (800) 871-0800
Fax: (757) 616-1593
Web site: **http://www.employmentguide.com**
Online employment source with international listings, guides, publications, etc.

Escape Artist
EscapeArtist.com Inc.
Suite 832–1245
World Trade Center
Panama
Republic of PANAMA
Fax: (011) 507 317 0139
Web site: **http://www.escapeartist.com**
Web site for U.S. expatriates. Contains links on overseas jobs, living abroad, offshore investing, free magazine, etc.

EuroJobs
Heathefield House
303 Tarring Rd.
Worthing
West Sussex BN115JG
UK
Telephone: 44 (0) 1260 223144
Fax: 44 (0) 1260 223145
E-mail: medialinks@eurojobs.com
http://www.eurojobs.com
Lists vacant jobs all over Europe. Also includes the possibility of submitting CV to recruiters; employment tips and other services.

EURopean Employment Services—EURES
Employment and Social Affairs Directorate General
EMPL A/03, BU33 02/24
European Commission
Rue de la Loi, 200
B-1049 Brussels
BELGIUM
Telephone: (011) 322 299 6106
Fax: (011) 322 299 0508 or 295 7609
Web site: **http://europa.eu.int/eures**
Aims to facilitate the free movement of workers within the 17 countries of the European Economic Area. Partners in the network include public employment services, trade unions, and employer organizations. The Partnership is coordinated by the European Commission. For citizens of these 17 countries, provides job listings, background information, links to employment services, and other job-related Web sites in Europe.

Expat Network
International House
500 Purley Way
Croydon
Surrey CRO 4NZ
UK
Telephone: (44) 20 8760 5100
Fax: (44) 20 8760 0469
Web site: **http://www.expatnetwork.com**
Dedicated to expatriates worldwide, linking to overseas jobs, country profiles, healthcare, expatriate gift and bookshop, plus in-depth articles and industry reports on issues that affect expatriates. Over 5,000 members. Access is restricted for nonmembers.

Federation of European Employers (FedEE)
Superla House
127 Chiltern Drive
Surbiton
Surrey, KT5 8LS
UK
Telephone: (44) 20 8339 4134
Fax: (44) 13 5926 9900
Web site: **http://www.fedee.com**
FedEE's European Personnel Resource Centre is the most comprehensive and up-to-date source of pan-European national pay, employment law, and collective-bargaining data on the Web.

HotJobs.com
Hotjobs.com, Ltd.
406 West 31st Street
New York, NY 10001
USA
Telephone: (212) 699-5300
Fax: (212) 944-8962
Web site: **http://hotjobs.yahoo.com**
Contains international job listings, including Europe.

Jobpilot
75 Cannon Street
London C4N 5BN
UK
Telephone: (44) 20 7556 7044
Fax: (44) 20 7556 7501
Web site: **http://www.jobpilot.com**
"Europe's unlimited career market on the Internet."

Jobs.ac.uk
University of Warwick
Coventry CV4 7AL
UK
Telephone: 44 (0) 24 7657 2839
Fax: 44 (0)24 7657 2946
http://www.jobs.ac.uk/
Search jobs in science, research, academic, and related employment in the UK and abroad.

Monster.com
TMP Worldwide Global Headquarters
1633 Broadway
33rd Floor
New York, NY 10019
USA
Telephone: 1 800 MONSTER or (212) 977-4200
Fax: (212) 956-2142
Web site: **http://www.monster.com**
Global online network for careers and working abroad. Career resources (including message boards and daily chats). Over 800,000 jobs.

Organization of Women in International Trade
Web site: **http://www.owit.org**
Offers networking and opportunities in international trade. Has chapters worldwide.

OverseasJobs.com
AboutJobs.com Network
12 Robinson Road
Sagamore Beach, MA 02562
USA
Telephone: (508) 888-6889
Web site: **http://www.overseasjobs.com**
Job seekers can search the database by keywords or locations and post a resume online for employers to view.

PlanetRecruit.com
PlanetRecruit Ltd.
Alexandria House
Covent Garden
Cambridge CB1 2HR
UK
Telephone: (44) 87 0321 3660
Fax: (44) 87 0321 3661
Web site: **http://www.planetrecruit.com**
One of the world's largest UK and international recruitment

networks. Features accounting and finance, administrative and clerical, engineering, graduate and trainee, IT, media, new media and sales, marketing and public-relations jobs from about 60 countries.

The Riley Guide
Margaret F. Dikel
11218 Ashley Drive
Rockville, MD 20852
USA
Telephone: (301) 984-4229
Fax: (301) 984-6390
Web site: **http://www.rileyguide.com**
It is a directory of employment and career information sources and services on the Internet, providing instruction for job seekers and recruiters on how to use the Internet to their best advantage. Includes a section on working abroad, including in Europe.

SCI-IVS USA
814 NE 40th Street
Seattle, WA 98105
USA
Telephone: (206) 545-6585
Fax: (206) 545-6585
Web site: **http://www.sci-ivs.org**
Through various noncommercial partner organizations worldwide and through SCI international, national, and regional branch development, the U.S. branch of SCI participates in the SCI network, which exchanges over 5,000 volunteers each year in short-term (2–4 week) international group workcamps and in long-term (3–12 months) volunteer postings in over 60 countries.

Transitions Abroad Online: Work Abroad
PO Box 1300
Amherst, MA 01004-1300
Telephone: (800) 293-0373 or (413) 256-3414
Fax: (413) 256-0373

SOURCE: European Union, **http://www.eurunion.org**.

Web site: **http://www.transitionsabroad.com**
Contains articles from its bimonthly magazine; a listing of work abroad resources (including links); lists of key employers, internship programs, volunteer programs, and English-teaching openings.

Vacation Work Publications
9 Park End Street
Oxford, OXI 1HJ
UK
Web site: **http://www.vacationwork.co.uk**
Lists job openings abroad, in addition to publishing many books on the topic. Has an information exchange section and a links section.

Upseek.com
Telephone: (877) 587-5627
Web site: **http://www.upseek.com**
A global search engine that empowers job seekers in the online job search market. Provides job opportunities from the top career and corporate sites with some European listings.

Women in the Academy of International Business
Center for International Business Studies
Mays Business School, Texas A&M University
College Station, TX 77843
USA
Web site: **http://cibs.tamu.edu/waib**
Encourages networking, mentoring, and research by linking women faculty, administrators, and Ph.D. students in international business studies.

WWOOF International
PO Box 2675
Lewes BN7 1RB,
UK
Web site: **http://www.wwoof.org**
WWOOF International is dedicated to helping those who would like to work as volunteers on organic farms internationally.

---

children of employees. For example, about 15 percent of Fortune 500 firms offer support for children of employees relocated abroad.[3]

Employment with a Small or Medium-Sized Firm

A second alternative is to begin work in a small- or medium-sized firm. Some of these firms have only recently developed an international outlook, and the new employee will arrive on the "ground floor." Initial involvement will normally be in the export field—evaluating potential foreign customers, preparing quotes, and dealing with mundane activities such as shipping and transportation. With a very limited budget, the export manager will only occasionally visit foreign markets to discuss marketing strategy with foreign distributors. Most of the work will be done by E-mail, by fax, or by telephone. The hours are often long because of the need to reach contacts overseas, for example, during business hours in Hong Kong. Yet the possibilities for implementing creative business methods are virtually limitless, and the contribution made by the successful export manager will be visible in the firm's growing export volume.

Alternatively, international work in a small firm may involve importing—finding new low-cost sources for domestically sourced products. Decisions often must be based on limited information, and the import manager is faced with many uncertainties. Often, things do not work out as planned. Shipments are delayed, letters of credit are canceled, and products may not arrive in the form and shape anticipated. Yet the problems are always new and offer an ongoing challenge.

As a training ground for international marketing activities, there is probably no better place than a smaller firm. Ideally, the person with some experience may find work with an export trading or export-management company, concentrating virtually exclusively on the international arena.

Opportunities for Women in Global Firms

As firms become more involved in global business activities, the need for skilled global managers is growing. Concurrent with this increase in business activity is the ever growing presence and managerial role of women in international business.

Research conducted during the mid-1980s[4] indicated that women held 3.3 percent of the overseas positions in U.S. business firms. Five years prior to that time, almost no women were global managers in either expatriate or professional travel status. Thus, the 3.3 percent figure represented a significant increase. By 2000, 13 percent of expatriates in U.S. corporations were women.[5] The reason for the low participation of women in global management roles seems to have been the assumption that because of the subservient roles of women in Japan, Latin America, and the Middle East, neither local nor expatriate women would be allowed to succeed as managers. The error is that expatriates are not seen as local women, but rather as "foreigners who happen to be women," thus solving many of the problems that would be encountered by a local woman manager.

There appear to be some distinct advantages for a woman in a management position overseas. Among them are the advantages of added visibility and increased access to clients. Clients tend to assume that "expatriate women must be excellent, or else their companies would not have sent them."

It also appears that companies that are larger in terms of sales, assets, income, and employees send more women overseas than smaller organizations. Further, the number of women expatriates is not evenly distributed among industry groups. Industry groups that utilize greater numbers or percentages of women expatriates include banking, electronics, petroleum, publishing, diversified corporations, pharmaceuticals, and retailing and apparel.

For the future, it is anticipated that the upward trend previously cited reflects increased participation of women in global management roles in the future.

Self-Employment

A third alternative is to hang up a consultant's shingle or to establish a trading firm. Many companies are in dire need of help for their international marketing effort and are quite prepared to part with a portion of their profits to receive it. Yet in-depth knowledge and broad experience are required to make a major contribution to a company's international marketing effort or to run a trading firm successfully. Specialized services that might be offered by a consultant include international market research, international strategic planning, or, particularly desirable, beginning-to-end assistance in international market entry or international marketing negotiations.

The up-front costs in offering such a service are substantial and are not covered by turnover but rather have to be covered by profits. Yet the rewards are there. For an international marketing expert, the hourly billable rate typically is as high as $400 for experienced principals and $150 for staff. Whenever international travel is required, overseas activities are often billed at the daily rate of $3,000 plus expenses. The latter can add up quickly as the cost-per-diem map in Exhibit 2 shows. When trading on one's own, income and risk can be limitless. Even at these relatively high rates, solid groundwork must be completed before all the overhead is paid. The advantage is the opportunity to become a true international entrepreneur. Consultants and owners of trading firms work at a higher degree of risk than employees, but with the opportunity for higher rewards.

International marketing is complex and difficult, yet it affords many challenges and opportunities. "May you live in interesting times" is an ancient Chinese curse. For the international marketer, this curse is a call to action. Observing changes and analyzing how best to incorporate them into one's plans are the bread and butter of the international marketer. The frequent changes are precisely what makes international marketing so fascinating. It must have been international marketers who were targeted by the old Indian proverb, "When storms come about little birds seek to shelter, while eagles soar." May you be an eagle!

Exhibit 2

The Cost Per Diem in the World's Major Business Cities (in U.S. dollars)

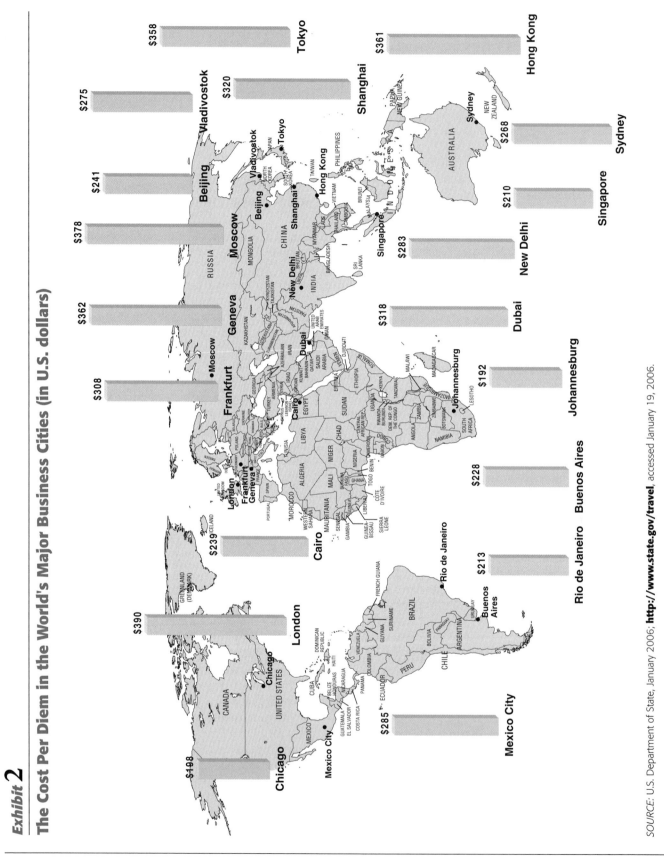

Chicago $198

London $390

Mexico City $285

Frankfurt $308

Geneva $362

Moscow $378

Vladivostok $275

Beijing $241

Tokyo $358

Shanghai $320

Hong Kong $361

Sydney $268

Singapore $210

New Delhi $283

Dubai $318

Cairo $239

Johannesburg $192

Buenos Aires $228

Rio de Janeiro $213

SOURCE: U.S. Department of State, January 2006; **http://www.state.gov/travel**, accessed January 19, 2006.

Recommended Readings

Carland, Maria, and Lisa Gihring. *Careers in International Affairs.* 7th ed. Washington, DC: Georgetown University Press, 2003.

Hult, G.T.M., and E.C. Lashbrooke, Jr. *Study Abroad: Perspective and Experiences from Business School.* Vol. 13. St. Louis: 2003.

Kocher, Eric, and Nina Segal. *International Jobs: Where They Are and How to Get Them.* 6th ed. Phoenix, AZ: Perseus Books Group, 2004.

Lauber, Daniel, and Kraig Rice. *International Job Finder: Where the Jobs Are Worldwide.* River Forest, IL: Planning/Communications, 2003.

Goldsmith, Marshall, Warren G. Bennis, John O'Neil, Cathy Greenberg, Maya Hu-Chan, and Alastair Roberston. *Global Leadership: The Next Generation.* London: Financial Times Prentice Hall, 2004.

POLAR-ADIDAS

Introduction

On Sunday, April 3, 2005, in a downtown hotel in Erlangen, Germany, Mr. Jorma Kallio, managing Director of Polar Electro Oy, a Finnish family-owned manufacturer or heart rate monitors, was preparing his opening speech to a group of some 100 Polar Electro employees and partners. He was in central Germany for an internal launch of a partnership between Polar Electro and adidas, the second largest sporting goods manufacturer in the world. The next day, on the premises of the expansive headquarters complex of adidas in Herzogenaurach, the partnership and "Project Fusion," the world's first completely integrated training system, would be introduced to marketing and sales personnel. The project had been under development for the last year and a half and kept confidential—only some 40 people within Polar Electro knew about it. Project Fusion was a new, complete solution for runners to be launched in 2006, consisting of adidas shoes with built-in electronics, running textiles that had built-in sensors, and watch-type sports computers that would display such information as heart rate data, speed, and distance to the runner (see Exhibit 1). The electronics technology was provided by Polar, but the textiles and shoes would be sold as premium adidas-branded goods.

Mr. Kallio was convinced that the partnership with adidas would be very beneficial for his company. First of all, becoming a trusted partner of adidas, an icon in sporting goods, was like a top-grade seal of approval for Polar. Polar would certainly benefit from the great brand equity that adidas owned. The majority of consumers around the world had heard of adidas, but selected few were aware of Polar. The adidas partnership would certainly raise consumer awareness of the Polar brand, something that Polar needed if it was to achieve its ambitious goals of both growing its sports-related business and extending from the core of serious sports into lifestyle applications. Second, the partnership could give a boost to the distribution of Polar goods. While Polar was represented through some 35,000 retailers in 50 countries, the channel power of adidas could not be ignored by wholesalers or retailers. Third, there was certainly a lot to learn from a successful company like adidas, be it in concept development or marketing processes.

There were some concerns, however. First of all, the sheer difference in size between the two companies: Polar's sales in 2004 had been 170 million euros, whereas adidas sales exceeded 5 billion euros, making it 30 times the size of Polar. The track record of alliances in general is not great and significant size differences between partners can cause difficulties in the relationship sooner or later. As an example, when adidas could appoint 5 people to a certain part of the project, Polar could afford two at most. Executives who were to implement the partnership, such as Christian Franke, Director of Brand Marketing at Polar, would have a lot on their plates. Another concern was the ability of Polar to perform in the relationship. Even though Kallio had full confidence in the capabilities of his managers, the fact that Polar was engaged in the development of very demanding high-tech electronics, whereas adidas would be responsible for shoes and textiles, was a factor that might bring surprises. His concern was that if there were unexpected difficulties in the development of electronics, the schedule of introducing new, jointly developed products with adidas might turn out to be frighteningly tight. A large company could hire an additional twenty R&D engineers if there were unexpected challenges in the development work, but for a company of Polar's size that would be financially an extreme solution. In terms of the classic risk of enabling and creating a future competitor, Kallio did not see it as very relevant in this case. He had full confidence in the partner, largely thanks to the solid personal relationship that existed between Kallio and key executives at adidas. Referring to the key executives in both of the companies, Kallio said: "We all understand and in fact love sports, so we talk the same language—that is a great starting point for the relationship."

About Partnership Agreements

The agreement with adidas comprised, first of all, joint development of technology for endeavors such as "Project Fusion." Polar is responsible for providing the

This case was authored by Hannu Seristö of the Helsinki School of Economics and Ilkka A. Ronkainen. For further information on the companies and their strategies, see **http://www.adidas-polar.com**; **http://www.polar.fi/polar/channels/eng/**; **http://www .adidas-group.com/en/home/welcome.asp**; and **http://www .nokia.com**. See also, "This Social Network is Up and Running," *Business Week*, November 17, 2008; and **www.micoach.com**.

Exhibit 1

Press Release on the Launch of Project Fusion

Helsinki/Herzogenaurach—August 4, 2005
adidas and Polar introduce the world's first completely integrated training system

Polar Electro, the innovative leader in heart rate monitoring, and adidas, one of the world's leading sports brands, have formed a partnership that will introduce the world's first completely integrated training system. Called "Project Fusion," it seamlessly integrates Polar heart rate and speed and distance monitoring equipment into adidas apparel and footwear.

The integration simplifies use and increases comfort, allowing the products to become part of the athlete. Included in the project are the adidas adiStar Fusion range of apparel (t-shirts, long sleeve shirts, bras, women's tops), the adidas adiStar Fusion shoe, Polar's s3™ Stride Sensor, The Polar WearLink™ transmitter, and The Polar RS800™ Running Computer.

How does it work? Special fibers bonded onto adidas tops work in conjunction with Polar's Wear Link™ technology to eliminate the need for a separate chest strap to monitor heart rate. Just snap the tiny Polar WearLink connector onto the front of the shirt and go. The data are sent to the Polar RS 800™ wrist-mounted running computer, which easily displays and records all information in real time. Simply put, your shirt talks to your running computer.

The adiStar Fusion shoe has a strategically placed cavity in the midsole which can house the very light Polar s3™ Stride Sensor, making it easier to use, more comfortable, and more consistently accurate than top-of-shoe systems. And you won't even know it's there when your shoe is talking to your running computer.

Information like speed and distance, chronograph functions, along with heart rate, are also shown on the RS800™ in real time. And when the workout is over, all data can be downloaded onto a computer so workouts can be easily managed and analyzed, meaning the whole system talks to you.

"The great thing about the system is that it's so easy to use," says Michael Birke, adidas Running Business Unit Manager. "By putting all the best equipment into one package, it's made training simpler, more comfortable, and more precise. The system is greater than the sum of its parts."

"An athlete can train more effectively with the right objective information," says Marco Suvilaakso, Running Segment Manager for Polar Electro. "This system caters to the individual, with precise and personalized feedback."

Purchasing the entire system—Polar RS 800™, Polar s3™ Stride Sensor, adiStar Fusion top, and adiStar Fusion shoe—will be around 640 Euros/680 Dollars. The products are available as separate pieces as well, and available in Spring of 2006.

© ADIDAS/WWW.PRESS-ADIDAS.COM

sensor, but joint work is needed particularly in fusing the textiles and sensor technology, which inevitably means shared engineering and industrial design. In shared engineering, a challenging issue typically is to decide which partner owns the jointly-created intellectual property. Also, as "Project Fusion" is a complete package, or solution, the industrial design has to be coordinated in terms of form and appearance. Rights concerning the design issues should normally be covered in partnership agreements.

Partnership agreements need to address the issues of exclusivity; that is, can certain technologies or solutions be offered to other companies beyond the main partners. Normally it is not recommended to lock oneself into one partner only, since it would compromise one's flexibility or stand-alone capability. On the other hand, exclusivity given to a partner is bound to enhance commitment and trust in the relationship.

The second part of the agreement deals with joint marketing efforts. Channels where there is joint presence and sales efforts have to be specified, including complementary marketing efforts (i.e., whereby Polar uses the adidas distribution system to get its products to the world marketplace). A considerable benefit for Polar is that adidas controls globally 145 flagship stores, such as adidas Originals Georgetown in Washington, D.C., Performance Store Abasto in Buenos Aires, adidas Concept Store Nevski in St. Petersburg, and adidas Originals Sydney. As for promotion, the choice of media for shared appearance and, for instance, joint web sites (such as **http://www.adidas-polar.com**) are important issues to address in the agreement.

In implementation, the management of the partnership should be clarified in the agreement. Whether there is, for example, a steering board composed of members from both partners, and who will serve as its chairperson, are some of the questions to settle. Also, determination of areas of responsibilities between the partners and the sharing of costs and revenues is normally a standard clause in an agreement of this sort. Finally, the agreements normally should address issues like the term and termination procedures of the partnership, and the settlement of disputes.

The Growth of Polar Electro Oy

The origins of the Finnish sports instruments producer Polar Electro can be traced back to the need of cross-country skiing coaches for a device to measure an athlete's heart rate during training sessions in the field, as opposed to this being possible only in a laboratory environment. There were no light, portable devices available, only large expensive laboratory equipment. Promoted by this need, professor Säynäjäkangas of the technology faculty at Oulu University started development work on technology that would make such measurements possible. Work was done partly with colleagues at the Oulu University, and eventually a company called Polar Electro was founded in Oulu in 1977, with Säynäjäkangas as the owner. The first heart rate monitor (HRM) was a battery-powered device that measured the heart rate from a fingertip. By the year 1982, the technology had advanced to the point that the first wireless heart rate monitor was ready. The first computer interface was introduced in 1984. The zone feature was launched in 1987, which was a predecessor to the so-called OwnZone feature of today. The principle is that the suitable intensity levels of training may vary daily due to factors such as fatigue, illness, or jetlag, and the athlete should check the right intensity levels before each training session.

In the 1980s, Polar Electro sought cooperation with top-level competitive athletes and world-class trainers and coaches. Relationships with leading universities and research institutes in the area of sports medicine were established. The target customers for Polar technology were competitive national and Olympic level athletes. From the very beginning the company was compelled to take a global look at the markets, because the chosen niche was narrow. Domestic market sales would have been in hundreds of units during the early years.

During this era, Polar Electro was first and foremost a technology company that conducted research, developed new technological solutions, and started to build manufacturing capacity for the large-scale production of heart rate monitors. Early on, the company benefited from financial support for promising high-technology start-ups in developing regions by Finnish government agencies. Products were sold mostly under other brands, through private label arrangements, particularly in the U.S. market, which was then the key market for Polar Electro. Marketing to the masses existed only in long-term plans. By the end of the 1980s, Polar Electro had grown to a company of one hundred employees with annual sales of almost 20 million dollars.

At this point, the target market was broadened from the original devices aimed at competitive top-level athletes. The first steps to the so-called fitness market were taken in 1987. New models were developed for ordinary people who wanted to monitor the intensity of training, through heart rate measurement, while they were exercising. The Polar brand became a focus of development in 1989. Polar's target was defined as being "anyone with a heart." Indeed, the company provided an HRM for race horses, which they continue to provide to this day.

Throughout the 1990s, Polar started to put more emphasis on marketing, partly driven by increasing competitive pressures. The heart rate monitor business had caught the attention of some big firms and entrepreneurs, all hoping to challenge Polar in this potentially sizeable business area. Large players like the U.S. watchmaker Timex and the Japanese electronics company Casio started to work on HRM products, and in Europe such companies as Sigma from Germany and Cardiosport from the U.K. introduced comparable HRMs. However, in terms of features, technology, quality, and even production costs, Polar was able to maintain its lead of a couple of years in this race. The building of an extensive international dealer network became the key focus of marketing efforts.

The key products by Polar in the 1990s comprised specific models for runners, bicyclists, and fitness users. Two special product groups were developed: Team Systems, to be used in the training of football or ice-hockey teams; and Educational Systems that were used in the physical education classes of school children, mostly in the United States, where the Federal Government provided support for schools that adopted innovative equipment to improve the quality of physical education. The largest product category for Polar was Fitness, because the products appealed to many different kinds of users. Several trailblazing technologies were introduced at this time, including the first integrated one-piece transmitter of heart rate measures in 1992; coded transmission of heart rate measures (from the chest transmitter unit to the wristwatch unit) in 1995; the first HRM combined with a bicycle computer, which had speed, cadence, and altitude measurement in 1996; personalized OwnZone training intensity zone and OwnCal energy consumption solutions in 1997; and the Polar fitness test, which provided a very accurate estimate of physical condition, even when measured while the person was not exercising but simply lying down for about 5 minutes, in 1999.

Polar Electro has used aggressive patenting policy to protect its inventions and intellectual property. In 2000, the company introduced a soft and very user-friendly textile transmitter belt to replace the traditional rather hard plastic model. The launch of a speed and distance measurement device in 2004 brought a new dimension to running computers: a pod attached to the running shoe measures acceleration and sends the information to the wrist unit with an accuracy of 99 percent. Now runners can see on their wrist units not only their heart rate and training intensity information, but also their real-time pace or speed and the distance covered. Competitors to this speed-and-distance technology include GPS-based running computers by the U.S. company Garmin and by Nike, developed with the Dutch electronics firm Philips. Outdoor computers were also launched in 2004. These wristwatch type devices have an electronic compass, barometer, altimeter, thermometer, and various watch and diary functions in addition to the advanced heart rate measurement features.

Polar spends some 10 percent of its sales on research and development, which takes place mostly in Oulu. The company benefits from the supply of high-quality engineers from the University of Oulu. Oulu is a city with a concentration of high-tech companies, particularly in the area of electronics (Nokia, the world's largest mobile-phone manufacturer, has a significant R&D and manufacturing presence in the city). The company also maintains collaborative ties with well-known institutes, such as Cooper Institute in Dallas, Texas, and leading universities in the areas of cardiology and sports medicine.

After-sales service is an essential component of the HRM business. The devices are rather complicated pieces of technology, and consumers often need support in installing software updates or setting up data transfer between the devices and the PC. These computers are also very personal objects, literally close to heart, and consumers typically want support immediately if they have a problem in the use of the equipment. The objective is to provide an answer to consumers' or retailers' questions within 24 hours, anywhere in the world. Competitors have not been able to match Polar's level in after-sales service, making Polar users very loyal customers.

Industrial design has been a focus in the last two years. The design and looks of the products were somewhat soulless until a new generation of more fashionable and colorful models was launched in 2004. In particular, female consumers were targeted with specific light and colorful fitness computers. Polar received international recognition for its improved design in 2004, when its new outdoor computer AXN 500 received an award in the German IF design competition.

Today, Polar Electro sees its mission as being to provide people the best solution to achieve their personal well-being, sports, and performance goals. The company exists to improve people's quality of life by generating innovative, high-quality, and user-friendly products. The Polar brand's essence is captured in the statement that "Polar is the leading brand and the true partner in improving human health and well-being through its understanding of personal physiology and the environment." Physiology refers to the monitoring of heart, and the environment refers to the measurement of altitude, direction, speed, distance, and temperature.

Most of Polar's €170 million in sales come from Western Europe and the United States, while the Asian market represents a very small share of business. Volume production is in the Far East, while the R&D and the manufacturing of the most advanced premium models remain in Oulu. Some 1,700 people work in Finland and in the 15 wholly-owned foreign marketing subsidiaries in the key world markets.

Polar may be a household name for competitive athletes and the most active exercisers, but the average consumer does not really know the brand. Potential markets include millions of people that could need and want a heart rate monitor. Driving this potential is an increasing realization by individuals, societies, and national economies that if people exercise more and are in better physical condition, the result is fewer health problems and lower consequent costs to the society. Populations particularly in Western Europe and Japan are aging, and the elderly want to stay active and healthy to lead rewarding lives after retirement. Obesity is increasingly a problem, particularly in North America, but also in Western Europe, and possibly soon in many Asian countries as well. Competition in the future is more in the area of marketing rather than in the pure development of technology. Design, trends, and fashion are becoming an essential part of this business, making HRMs a lifestyle product.

Polar Marketing

The heart rate monitor consists of two parts: the transmitter and the receiver. The transmitter is worn around one's chest, as close to the heart as possible to ensure accurate sensing of the heartbeat. Modern generation transmitters, provided only by Polar, are soft fabric belts where the sensors, or electrodes, are woven into the fabric, and the signal is sent to the receiver through a separate little unit that is snapped onto the belt. The fabric transmitters are much more comfortable to use than the old versions. The retail cost of a transmitter is in the region of 40 euros.

The receiver is like a sports wristwatch that functions mainly as the display for measured information. The receiver typically has heart rate measurement functions, watch and chronometer functions, and a variety of other features. The simplest models display only time and the current heart rate, whereas the most advanced models have several test features; a training diary and training program features; measure air pressure, altitude, and temperature; have compass functions; and display speed and distance information. The case of the receiver is typically made of different grades of plastics, but some expensive models are made of steel or titanium.

The basic heart rate monitors by Polar cost about 60 euros in retail, whereas the most advanced models with a titanium case can cost close to 500 euros. The cheapest heart rate monitors in the market, often by Asian manufacturers, can be bought for as little as 20 euros, but these are typically of poor quality, poor usability, and with no product support nor real warranty.

Polar heart rate monitors are distributed through sporting goods stores, specialty stores, department stores, and in some cases catalog sellers and online stores. The products are so rich in features that the expertise and professionalism of the sales personnel is a key factor in the sales process. As a result, Polar has committed significant resources to the training of sales people throughout the channel.

Polar provides extensive online support for its products. Software can be downloaded from the Polar website, and consumers can create their own training programs and diaries on the global web site (**http://www.polar.fi**).

Other Partnerships

In early 2004, a technology and marketing partnership between Nokia and Polar was made public. Polar offers a few heart rate monitor models that have the capability to communicate with a certain Nokia mobile phone, model 5140. This compatibility allows the user to transmit training data from the wrist computer to the mobile phone, and again send it via mobile phone network, for instance, to the PC of one's coach. So, for instance, a distance-runner who is training in the warm conditions of South Africa in January can easily send his daily training session information for analysis by his trainer in Northern Europe in order to get instructions for the following day's training. Nokia and Polar were very visible in a joint marketing campaign, with the theme "Training Mates," during the 2004 Tour de France.

A key product that had the Nokia compatibility is the running computer model S625X. It was launched in the summer 2004 and was a great success from the very beginning. The S625X has a speed-and-distance feature that is based on acceleration technology. Acceleration data are turned into information on distance covered and speed or pace of the runner, and then displayed on the wrist receiver. The accuracy is very high, with error rates of less than 1 percent (i.e., when running 10 kilometers, the error in the distance information is expected to be less than 100 meters). Runners love it and media have praised it.

Even though the product is relatively expensive (€400), it appears that S625X is becoming one of the most successful running computers Polar has ever made.

Growth Prospects of Polar

Polar Electro has many of the ingredients to grow and become a truly significant global company. It has a solid technological basis, processes in place, and very capable personnel. In its own niche market, it is the world market leader. However, it has to acknowledge its limited resources: there are numerous potential new business areas and an abundance of ideas, but the development of completely new products takes millions of euros. Brand marketing is obviously very important in the future, but doing that with a real impact can easily consume tens of millions of euros per year. Asia is undoubtedly the market for the future, as in almost every business, but the question is how to go there, since it appears to be quite different from Europe and North America: what products (adapted or not), which features, which markets (alone or with partners, or through which channels), are some of the key questions. Moreover, the human resources might turn out to be a challenge—there are limitless opportunities, but the current managers may not be able to handle all the new issues simultaneously. Both the owners and the management see the numerous avenues for growth, but there are a multitude of factors to assess when choosing the right path to follow.

In terms of financial benefits, it is perhaps too early to assess the value of these partnerships. For one thing, the measurement of inputs and outputs is not that simple. For instance, how do you measure accurately the management effort that has been put into the partnerships, and whether that effort could have been used more effectively somewhere else?

Mr. Kallio was convinced that the adidas partnership was very valuable for Polar especially in the long term. Some questions remained, however. How can a relatively small company make sure that it can perform in a relationship with a significantly larger partner like adidas, and not let the partner down? How can Polar make sure that it gets most of the possible value out of the partnerships—for instance, through learning from a more experienced company? How about assessing the inputs and outputs—how should Polar measure whether the relationship is producing value to the company?

Competitor Moves

In May of 2006, Nike launched Nike+, a technology that tracks data on every run—such as the elapsed time of the workout, the distance traveled, pace, or calories burned by the individual wearing the shoes—and displays it on a screen or broadcasts it through the headphones of an iPod. iTunes software could be used to view the walk or run history. The sensor and Sportband kit was announced in April 2008. The kit allows users to store run information without the iPod Nano. The Sportband consists of two parts: a rubber holding strap that is worn around the wrist and the receiver that resembles a USB key-disk. The receiver displays information comparable to that of the iPod kit on the built-in display. After a run, the receiver can be plugged straight into a USB port and the software will upload the run information automatically to the Nike+ website. By late 2008, Nike reports to have sold 1.3 million Nike+iPod Sport Kits and 500,000 Nike+ Sportbands. Runners have collectively logged 93 million miles on nikeplus.com.

Going up against Nike and the iPod, Samsung Mobile has teamed up with adidas for a product called miCoach that allows runners to upload heart rate and running data to a Web site via a mobile phone. Rather than just record information to download to a computer later, the phone, through the headphones, will give the runner information on the fly by simply tapping the screen. miCoach will offer over 220 training programs via a fitness Web site, ranging from weight loss to marathon running, and measure running speed within four zones to best suit training based on an initial assessment run.

Questions for Discussion

1. How does the alliance with adidas fit with Polar's growth objectives?

2. What are the pros and cons of having a company like adidas as an alliance partner?

3. By 2010, what is the likely outcome of this alliance (e.g., will Polar become part of adidas)?

LPP-RESERVED

Growth of a Fashion Retailer

In early March 2008, Marek Piechocki,[1] President and Chief Executive Officer of LPP S.A., and his management team, had to make their final decision about whether or not to buy Artman S.A. Until then, LPP S.A., with headquarters in Gdansk, Poland, had been operating three different chains of fast fashion clothing retail stores: Reserved, Cropp Town, and Esotiq.

All in all, by the end of 2007, LPP had a grand total of 345 retail stores occupying 149,000 square meters and located in nine different countries[2] in Central and Eastern Europe. The company had firm plans to open a further 89 new stores in 2008, including outlets in Romania and Bulgaira.

For several months now, Piechocki and his management team had been negotiating the possible acquisition of Artman S.A., owner of the fashion retail chain House.

The final buying price would be around 400 million Polish New Zlotys or PLN,[3] which was about 50 percent higher than the going market price of Artman's shares in the Warsaw stock exchange.

Should they go ahead with this purchase? Was the price too high?

The Origins of a Startup Venture

Marek Piechocki was born in Kartuzy, a small town located some 60 kilometers south of Gdansk. During the period 1980–1987, he studied Civil Engineering in Gdansk and also in Brunswick, near Hanover, in Germany.

When things started to change in 1989, after the unexpected fall of the Berlin wall, his friend Jerzy Lubianiec, came to him with the idea of flying to Singapore, buying electronic goods with cash, and personally taking them back into Poland.

Then, in 1990 they started importing finished sweaters from Turkey as personal luggage, which they sold to other retailers located in Poland. Initially they were operating under the business name "Mistral."[4]

In 1992 they started importing from China and also started creating their own designs, prepared by Piechocki himself. They started to use the brands "Ross" for jogging suits, "Henderson" for shirts and men's underwear, and "Promo Stars" for caps, tee shirts, blouses, polo shirts, and windbreakers. They also sold promotional goods for international brands like Coca-Cola and British Petroleum.

In 1993 their total turnover was around PLN 10 million, and they had about 15 employees (full time equivalent).

In 1995, the first hypermarket opened in Poland, shortly followed by many others. They were capable of generating a huge volume of business and therefore offered the opportunity of very fast growth for their suppliers.

In 1996, LPP started using the brand "Reserved" on "casual wear" garments sold directly to small retailers. LPP was importing garments and selling them under different brand names to several retail channels: small shops; wholesalers (who, in turn, sold the garments to retailers); directly to hypermarkets; and promotional garments sold either directly or indirectly to large corporate customers, usually embroidered with their particular logos. Also in 1996, they started re-exporting their garments to other Central and Eastern European countries, selling them to exclusive importer-distributors.

By about 1998, they made a key strategic decision: to start opening their own retail stores. The first one (80 square meters) was opened in 1999 in Szczecin. Its basic mission was to sell the garments that might have been returned by wholesalers or hypermarkets. Shortly afterwards they started using the brand "Reserved," which had been successfully registered in Poland.

The managers of LPP very quickly realized that customers also wanted a certain image, an atmosphere and other tangible or intangible characteristics, along with good personal service and personal attention. As Piechocki would say, "We sell EMOTIONS! We are fashion-orientated, selling what facilitates the expression of an image and a personality!"

LPP stopped directly supplying small retailers in 2000–2001. The line of sales to wholesalers also closed in 2002 because they were being killed by the mass retailers. And finally, LPP stopped selling to hypermarkets and other mass merchandisers in 2003, because this line of sales had become unprofitable. During the period 1996–2001 LPP exported from 8 percent to 12 percent of its total turnover to neighboring countries via exclusive national importer-distributors.

Going Public

By 2001, LPP already had 15 "Reserved" stores in major Polish cities. All but one of them were located in shopping malls.

Their fast rate of growth required funding, because a newly opened store required about 18 months to reach break-even level. Initially, they publicly offered 300,000 shares in the Warsaw Stock Exchange, at PLN 48 per share, which generated PLN 14.4 million. In 2003, the company decided to issue another 190,000 LPP shares (at a price of PLN 237 per share), which generated PLN 45 million.[5]

This case was prepared by IESE Prof. Lluis G. Renart as the basis for class discussion rather than to illustrate either effective or ineffective handling of an administrative situation. September 2008. This is a condensed version of the case "LPP-Reserved" (IESEM-1213-E) available in full length from IESE Publishing (**http://www.iesep.com**).

One of their financial advisers mentioned that, if they wanted the price of their shares to go steadily up, thereby increasing the total value of their company, it was imperative that they prepare LPP to have an international presence and not to limit its retail activity to Poland.

Further Expansion

In 2002, LPP was able to open some 30 new Reserved stores, including openings in Estonia, Czech Republic, Hungary, and Russia.

This substantial expansion provoked the need to install a powerful software system to manage the logistic and retail operations. Piechocki and his management team considered that they had no other choice but to strongly reinforce their IT capabilities, if they wanted to have hundreds of stores. The cost to LPP was huge, around PLN 15 million, equivalent to about one full year of the company's net profits.

Exploring Further Avenues for Growth

The most obvious avenue for growth was to open more stores within Poland.[6] The second avenue for growth was to open more stores in other countries.

They could also grow by enlarging the average size of the stores. In that sense, while their first store was only 80 square meters, they were soon opening new Reserved stores of about 200 square meters, then 400, and so on.[7]

The fourth avenue for growth could be to create new retail concepts, under different brands, focused on different segments of potential customers. Reserved stores sold garments and accessories for men, women, and children, with a target adult age of 19 to 30 years old. Their value proposition was to sell garments of a nicer quality and a more attractive design at relatively lower retail prices. They aimed at offering "a good deal" to a mass market audience, so that their customers might exclaim, "This is so nice and such good value!"

Finally, a fifth avenue for growth was to increase the ratio of sales per m^2, determining the productivity of the selling floor area. For instance, by the end of 2007, the sales figure per m^2 would be around PLN 900 per month (equivalent to about €270 per m^2 per month).

Launching "Cropp Town" and "Esotiq"

In order to implement the fourth avenue for growth, LPP launched Cropp Town, a different and separate chain of fashion retail stores, whose target were men and women in the 13 to 25 year old bracket. In 2003, LPP opened 30 Cropp Town stores. By the end of 2007, Cropp Town sales represented about 25 percent of total company turnover.

In a similar way, in the year 2005, LPP had launched Esotiq, a third retail chain, devoted to ladies underwear. By the end of 2007, 15 Esotiq stores had been opened, of about 100 square meters each.

The Triangular Playing Field: Negotiating with Shopping Mall Developers[8]

Obviously, in order to grow, the different fashion retail concepts operated by LPP had to be permanently attractive to their target potential customers. They attempted to do so by offering attractive good design, reasonable quality garments at affordable prices. This was easier said than done. Actually, sales in 2005 and 2006 had been somewhat below target, because those collections had turned out to be somewhat less attractive than expected.[9]

But one of the key ingredients of growth had to do with successfully negotiating and signing up new retail space leases in the new shopping malls sprouting all over Central and Eastern Europe.

Most of the new prime retail space was being created in modern shopping malls. Well-lit and with contemporary decoration, they allowed customers to shop while sheltered from the whether conditions outside and offered the advantages of availability of parking space, one-stop shopping, and the ability for families to combine shopping with food and entertainment.

Large fast fashion retail chains, therefore, had acquired a lot of power to negotiate their presence with the mall landowners for a number of reasons:

1. Because they could rent space for several retail stores in the same shopping mall, they could end up renting a significant percentage of the total retail space available in a given mall.

2. They were willing to pay relatively attractive rents[10] contingent upon many variables like negotiating power, total size and location of the new mall, and location of their stores within a specific mall. Fixed, minimum rents could go from about €15 per square meter per month, to a maximum as high as €40 per square meter per month. But they were also assessed to pay a percentage on sales, which could be as high as 10 percent. Very attractive chains frequently paid their leases as a percentage on sales, because it turned out to be higher than the minimum per square meter.

3. Fast fashion retail chains had become the real "anchors" of new shopping centers, making them attractive to fashion-sensitive consumers. They generated traffic for all the mall's tenants, including smaller, less attractive "functional" tenants like a pharmacy, a bookstore, or a florist.

4. They were able to sign long-term leases, sometimes as long as ten years. On the one hand, this could be risky

for a fashion retailer, because new, more modern shopping malls could be built in their vicinity, damaging their capacity to attract consumers. But a long term lease was very desirable to a shopping mall builder, because it allowed ample time to depreciate and extract value from its initial investment. On the other hand, if a fashion retailer failed to secure a lease in a new shopping mall, it would be almost impossible to secure space there for the next ten years or even longer!

Therefore, in order to be able to negotiate favorable long-term leases, or just to be able to sign the leases in new shopping malls, a fashion retail chain had to be large, successful, desirable, and if possible, possess an array of brands.

The Fashion Retail Sector in Central and Eastern Europe

At the end of 2007, the fashion retail market in Central and Eastern Europe was composed of local firms as well as multinational corporations. On the one hand, LPP major local competitors were Orsay (a feminine brand that operated in Poland, Czech Republic, Hungary, Ukraine, Russia and Bulgaria), House (a young fashion brand with 190 retail stores in Poland), and Diverse (a retail firm that operated 119 shops in Poland). On the other hand, both Spanish company Inditex (operating almost all this concepts: Zara, Bershka, Pull and Bear, Stradivarious, Massimo Dutti, Kiddy's Class, Oysho, and recently launched Zara Home selling home textiles and furnishings)[11] and Hennes & Mauritz (H&M) were already present in the region. Esoting competed mostly against Triumph (from Germany) and Atlantic and Key (from Poland).

Future "Organic" Growth Trends

At the end of 2007, Piechocki decided that the only sources to finance further development would be self-generated funds and bank credit ability. The amount of funds necessary to open a store depended on its size and brand; but the average was around €900 per square meter. This meant a financial need of about €1.62 million (or PLN 5.4 million) for each new 1,800 square meter Reserved retail store.

At the beginning of 2007, the existing software was capable of sustaining a huge amount of stores. The company was investing about PLN 120 million in a new 26,000 square meter distribution center. Plus, they were aware that they would have to build another of 40,000 square meters "very soon."

So far, LPP had never paid dividends to its shareholders. Piechocki thought that this policy could be sustainable, provided the company continued to grow very rapidly.

LPP managers thought that the company had a fairly low level of indebtedness, because the ratio between EBITDA and Bank credit outstanding at the end of each year had been the following (figures in PLN million):

		EBITDA	Bank Credit
2005	Actual	89	150
2006	Actual	93	200
2007	Actual	240	250
2008	Forecast	350	300

Piechocki estimated that with an EBITDA of PLN 350 million the company might have a bank borrowing capacity as high as maybe PLN 1 billion. The going interest rate for a bank loan in Poland was Wibor[12] + between 0.9 percent and 1.3 percent. In March 2008, the Wibor rate was around 6 percent, which meant that a large and profitable company like LPP could probably borrow money at a rate of around 7 percent.

Further Options for Growth: Launching New Retail Chains and/or Mergers and Acquisitions

By early 2008, Piechocki was convinced that the Central and Eastern European market had matured enough so as to make it very difficult to launch a completely new fashion retail chain due to the shortage of available new retail space to build stores—and the problems concerning minimum quantities of merchandise that would have to be ordered from the Asian suppliers, who usually required minimum orders of 1,000 pieces per garment style.

It would also be impossible to get rented space in already successful shopping malls, because they were fully occupied and no present tenants would be willing to abandon such good locations. At the same time, Piechocki considered that fashion retail structure was still fluid enough, because new shopping malls were being built in this market.

Therefore, his mind was mostly focused toward the possible acquisition of one or more existing fashion retail chains, which could be integrated into the LPP corporation.

Opportunities Identified to Buy an Existing Retail Chain

After considering a few potential candidates, Piechocki and this team decided to concentrate their efforts on the House retail chain, which belonged to the Polish fashion retailer Artman SA, a joint-stock company listed in the Warsaw Stock Exchange. The company's net sales in 2007 grew to PLN 259.8 million from PLN 205.6 million in 2005 (+26 percent), and net profits in 2007 increased to PLN 10.5 million from PLN 6.6 million in 2006 (+60 percent). About 60 percent of its turnover was generated through franchised stores, while in the case of LPP it was only around 10 percent.

House had around 190 stores, most of them located in Poland. It was also present in Russia, the Baltic States, Slovakia and the Czech Republic, and several other less important markets.

House was a very popular and well-recognized teenager brand representing fast changing street fashion. The core target audience was young people aged 13 to 25. It was positioned in the lower segment of the youth market (accessible, low price, average to low quality). Obviously House was a direct competitor for both LPP clothing brands, especially Cropp Town.

The Negotiation with Artman

Artman, S.A. was generating a net profit after tax of about 4.5 percent on sales, while LPP was generating a net profit after tax of about 10.5 percent. In view of this difference, Piechocki and his team reviewed four key elements that would be relatively difficult to change in the short run were they to purchase House: 1) rent levels paid by Artman were fairly similar to those paid by LPP—this could not be the reason for the lower profitability; 2) the locations of stores were also quite good; 3) the size and look of stores was also considered acceptable; and 4), the level of recognition and brand image was also quite good.

In view of this, Piechocki came to the conclusion that the difference in net profitability between Artman and LPP had to be due to internal inefficiencies.

The eventual purchase of Artman could be justified on several grounds:

First, Piechocki and his team thought that, by applying their proven retail management techniques and IT and logistics technologies, House profits could reach LPP's level. Second, they would expect to be instrumental in launching the House retail chain in more countries where LPP was already present. Third, they thought that, because of their larger size, if they were to purchase Artman, they could have more negotiating power with shopping center

Exhibit **1**

LPP Profit and Loss Statement and Balance Sheet 2004–2010

Group LPP S. A.

Profit & Loss Statement (million PLN)

Fiscal Year	2004	2005	2006	2007	2008F	2009F	2010F
Sales	547	686	815	1,274	1,681	2,301	3,259
Cost of Sales	251	312	366	521	675	899	1,234
Gross Margin	295	374	449	753	1,006	1,402	2,025
Operating Expenses	239	313	391	568	737	1,052	1,594
Operating Income	56	61	57	185	269	350	431
Financing & Other Income	−3	−9	−7	−20	−43	−55	−67
Income Taxes	11	12	10	31	45	59	73
Net Profit	43	40	41	135	181	236	291

Balance Sheet (million PLN)

Year Ended	Dec 31 2004	Dec 31 2005	Dec 31 2006	Dec 31 2007	Dec 31 2008F	Dec 31 2009F	Dec 31 2010F
Fixed Assets	137	195	217	288	427	554	766
Current Assets	175	239	319	409	560	746	1,020
Inventories	132	172	233	290	382	523	740
Accounts Receivable	25	38	50	61	100	117	129
Cash and Cash Equivalent (need for operation)	18	30	36	59	78	106	150
Total Assets	311	435	536	697	987	1,300	1,787
Equity	191	232	273	406	586	822	1,114
Long Term Debt	4	15	16	33	111	101	91
Short Term Debt	116	187	247	256	289	377	582
Short Term Bank Loans	72	128	124	57	26	17	72
Accounts Payable	37	54	118	167	220	301	426
Other	8	5	5	33	43	59	83
Total Liabilities	121	202	263	291	400	478	673
Total Liabilities and Equity	311	435	536	697	987	1,300	1,787

"F" = Forecast. This forecast includes only the financial information of the three existing LPP retail chains and their expected growth. It does not include any figures from a hypothetical purchase of Artman/House.

landlords, garment suppliers,[13] and franchise partners. Presumably, some House franchises could be either renegotiated, or taken over and directly operated by LPP. Finally, this acquisition could generate a certain number of synergies in different departments. This was contingent upon the decision to either maintain Artman as a separate operational company in its original HQ in Krakow or turn it into just one more LPP retail chain, operated from Gdansk.

In either of these two options, it was considered that a significant number of departments then operating in Krakow could be moved to Gdansk and be merged with the corresponding LPP departments.

Some economies of scale generated by the hypothetical merger would not only apply to House but might also apply to LPP's brands, for instance, by giving the LPP team of Regional Directors responsibility for the field supervision of the House stores.

As a result, LPP would continue to grow fast enough so as to postpone any distribution of dividends. Therefore, the company would have more retained earnings and less need for external financing.

The amount of profits after taxes generated by Artman in 2007 had been PLN 11 million, that is, 4.5 percent on sales.

The LPP management team estimated that, considering all the above described potential benefits, the amount of net profits after taxes generated by Artman could increase up to PLN 18 million in 2008; PLN 36 million in 2009; and PLN 50 million in 2010.

The only key drawback seemed to be the asking price: PLN 400 million, which was about 50 percent over the current stock exchange price of Artman shares. Should LPP go ahead and buy Artman/House?

Exhibit 2

LPP Value Chain

1. Development, Expansion	Searching for new space for development of retail chains (new markets, new cities). Analyzing potential growth sources and expansion, both domestically and internationally. Retail premises acquisition.
2. Planning	Preparing accurate and integrated merchandising and business plans for all brands and markets (pre-season planning) and support for merchandising department during the season (in-season planning).
3. Design of collections	Preparing collections according to latest fashion trends and specific plans for particular markets.
4. Sourcing, Production	Work with clothes suppliers all over the world for cheap, fast, and quality production of designed styles and quantities.
5. Merchandising	Defining the specific plans for particular brands and markets; ordering collections; merchandise management during the season; defining and implementation of pricing policy.
6. IT, Logistics	IT support, import and export logistics, warehouse management, and deliveries to the stores all over Europe.
7. Visual Merchandising, Sales	Ensure good presentation of collections and styles in the stores. Organizing sales process.
8. Marketing communication	Creating proper image of LPP brands in particular markets; marketing communication with target customer groups; sales support for commercial and merchandise department during the season.

INTERNATIONAL MARKETING AND THE NBA

Take a basketball player with a trait you can't teach—a physique of 296 pounds spread over 7 feet, 6 inches. Stir in sleek mid-range jump shots, smooth passing skills, shot-blocking ability, court speed, and a plethora of great moves. Add in charisma with a dash of humor. And one more thing: Make him from China, the world's most populous nation with an untapped market of 1.3 billion people. From central casting comes Yao Ming—"The Next Big Thing" for international services and global business.

A New Ming Dynasty?

Straight from China's Basketball Association, Yao was the first international player ever selected as the number one overall pick by the NBA's Houston Rockets. He became a solid contributor to the Rockets almost immediately and a standout in the NBA. In 2002 he had the highest field goal percentage in NBA history over a six-game stretch, making 31 of 35 shot attempts for an accuracy of 88.6 percent. He was honored as one of the best new players in the NBA and has been voted to the All-Star Team (a collection of the NBA's best players) every year that he has played. Despite suffering an injury that caused him to miss a quarter of the games in 2005, Yao still won accolades as a key player.

His NBA stardom stems not only from his talents but also from his personality. Yao's self-deprecating charisma and humor makes him hard to dislike. While describing a dunk he missed, Yao told his teammates, "When you have pitiful moments that makes the good moments more valuable." When fellow NBA star Shaquille O'Neal said to a reporter "Tell Yao Ming, 'Ching chong yang wah ah soh'" while making kung fu moves, Yao quipped that Chinese is "a very difficult language to learn." With his talent and personality, Yao is the literal and figurative center of attention, bestriding two continents and making hearts pound and cash registers ring in both.

Perhaps more significantly, Yao has broken the Hollywood portrayal of Asian males as inscrutable and subservient and dispelled the popular stereotype of Asian-Americans as bookish, slight, unathletic, and over achieving pre-med students.

The NBA Goes Global

Basketball is the world's number two team sport, behind soccer. NBA commissioner David Stern has been laying the groundwork for global penetration for nearly 15 years, broadcasting to and recruiting from the international scene.

U.S. fans have shown a strong positive response to the influx of players from Germany (Dallas's Nowitzki), Yugoslavia (Sacramento's Stojakovic), and Spain (Memphis's Gasol), propelling the NBA to increase global recruitment. "Yao came at the perfect time to the perfect league," noted Rich Thomaselli, sports marketing expert. "The NBA has wanted exponential global growth. Other foreign players have helped, but Yao, who is truly unique because of his size, personality, and background leads the way."

Global Expansion in China

In what better country to seek exponential global growth than in China, home to 1.3 billion people? The Rockets and NBA couldn't be more grateful for the "Ming Mania." Says Rockets President and CEO George Postolos, "It's incredible. In one week when we drafted Yao, we got more international attention than either of our two NBA championships. We think we're on our way to becoming the most-watched team in the world."

Postolos was right—the international viewership is astounding. Yao's NBA debut against the Indiana Pacers in October 2002 reached 287 million Chinese households—in contrast to the 105 million in the United States. A typical weeknight NBA game between two strong teams drew television viewership of 1.1 million Americans. But due to Yao Ming playing, an 8:00 a.m. broadcast game between the Rockets and the league's worst-ranked team, the Cavaliers, pulled in 6 million Chinese viewers. Another 11.5 million tuned in for a repeat of the game that night—even a live broadcast of an NBA finals game doesn't attract that size audience in the United States.

A decade ago, anyone in China was lucky to see one NBA game per week, usually from a month-old tape mailed to Beijing. Today, the NBA broadcasts 270 games on 24 Chinese networks. Basketball is the second most popular sport, with 75 percent of males aged 15 to 24 watching at least one game per week and describing themselves as "NBA fans." In 2004, the Houston Rockets and the Sacramento Kings traveled to Shanghai, Yao's hometown, and Beijing for two exhibition games. Tickets to the two events cost between US $35 and US $240. Despite an average Chinese annual per capita income of just over US $1,000, both events were quickly sold out. A reporter described the Ming mania as more closely resembling a Beatles appearance than an American sporting event.

This case was written by Daria Cherepennikova of Georgetown University, under the guidance of Professor Michael R. Czinkota.

Licensing Benefits

Yao's popularity in China has been highly lucrative for the NBA. The sales of NBA merchandise have doubled every year for the past several years. Surprisingly, the number one selling jersey in China is not Yao Ming's, but rather that of his teammate Tracy McGrady. In fact, Yao ranks a measly third after McGrady and Allen Iverson. One explanation is that most fans already purchased a Yao jersey and are now expanding their NBA memorabilia collection. Another explanation is that the NBA has transcended the power of Yao to become a force in Chinese society in and of itself. Commissioner, David Stern, is optimistic: "Over the next 20 years, the growth of the NBA in China will mirror or parallel growth in China." The Asian market isn't only watching, it's also buying.

For corporations, Yao is more than just the biggest Chinese import to hit the United States in years. He's the perfect vehicle for multinational corporations to approach 1.3 billion potential consumers. With the 2008 Olympics in Beijing, the country is on the fast track to modernize. Young people have growing purchasing power and are willing to spend; one of the best ways to capture their money has been through sports figures. For example, multimillion-dollar marketing campaigns featuring superstar celebrities like Michael Jordan and Tiger Woods showcase a wide range of products from watches and cars to sneakers and Hanes underwear. In the past, Asian athletes such as Michael Chang and Michelle Kwan have attained prominence. Marquee basketball players like Yao command the most lucrative and successful endorsements. He is a marketing figure that can dominate China's still-emerging market without competition.

Yao is everywhere both in the United States and in China: he sized up Austin Power's Mini-Me in TV ads for Apple computers; he played the confused New York tourist in a Visa commercial that double-featured Yogi Berra; and he graced *Sports Illustrated*'s cover twice in only four months in the United States. He has been featured prominently in *Time Magazine*'s English language Asia publication, including several cover stories from 2002 to 2005. In China, McDonald's pick of Yao as a spokesperson seems guaranteed to win the fast-food franchise a sizeable share of the Chinese market ahead of the 2008 Beijing Olympics. Reebok International and PepsiCo also signed Yao as their spokesperson, while Walt Disney wants Yao to make a prominent appearance at its Hong Kong theme park. Chinese companies, like cell phone provider Unicom, are also eager to sign Yao, one of the most recognizable figures in modern Chinese society, as their spokesperson.

"The Golden Bridge"

The NBA sees Yao as a cornerstone of its international expansion strategy. "Chinese citizens are closely following Yao for symbolic reasons not related to basketball," said Steven Lewis, an Asia expert at the Baker Institute for Public Policy. They are wondering: 'Yao is a Chinese person going abroad to live and work among foreigners.'" Along with their hometown hero, the Chinese are watching as their nation opens up to the world. In 2004, the Chinese government chose to recognize Yao as a national "model worker," a title normally reserved for employees of the Communist state and previously unfathomable for a Chinese multimillionaire living abroad. "[It] shows the development of society," said Yao after receiving the award.

Questions for Discussion

1. Discuss the following statement: "Yao Ming isn't just China's best basketball player. He's the most persuasive symbol of globalization."

2. Consider China's current issues, such as intellectual property rights and logistical infrastructure. How should an international marketer consider these concerns before entering the potentially profitable yet elusive Chinese market?

3. With more international players joining the ranks of NBA teams, should the NBA begin to position itself as an international basketball league? How would doing so affect its marketing potential within and outside of the United States?

Sources

Barron, David. "The Marketing Machine behind Yao Ming." *The Houston Chronicle*, November 3, 2002, Section A1.

"Basketball Star Yao Ming Goes Wireless." *Business Wire*, January 7, 2003; http://www.businesswire.com.

Kreidler, Mark. "Capitalism Thrives in China as McGrady Passes Yao." *ESPN.com*, February 1, 2006.

Law, Niki. "Yao Wows Fans." *South China Morning Post*, January 21, 2003, Section News, 5.

Luo, Michael. "Yao Ming Carries Asians to New Heights." *Associated Press*, February 6, 2003.

MacLeod, Calum. "China: The NFL's Next Frontier: The Hunt for 'Yao Fling' Continues." *USA Today*, February 3, 2006, 6B.

McCallum, Jack. "Sky Rocket." *Sports Illustrated*, February 10, 2003.

National Basketball Association. http://www.nba.com, accessed February 1, 2006.

"NBA Uses Yao to Court China." *The Standard*, October 27, 2004.

Pasick, Adam. "Rookie Yao Ming, Apple of Advertisers' Eye." *Reuthers News,* February 2, 2003.

Sandomir, Richard. "Yao in China: No. 1 in Hearts, No. 3 in Shirts." *The New York Times*, February 2, 2006, Section D, Column 5.

Thomsen, Ian. "The New Mr. Big." *Sports Illustrated,* October 28, 2002.

Wang, Gene. "The Golden Bridge." *The Washington Post,* February 27, 2003, Section D1.

BLOOD FREE DIAMONDS

The ancient Greeks called diamonds the tears of the gods. Today, we know that natural diamonds consist of highly compressed carbon molecules. They have become a symbol of beauty, power, wealth, and love. Nevertheless, diamonds and the diamond trade are plagued by a sad reality: the exploitation of people for diamond extraction and the use of diamond profits to fund terrorist activity and rebel groups.

Trade in diamonds is highly profitable. The stones are readily converted to cash, small and are easily transportable, not detectable by dogs, nor do they set off any metal detectors. Unfortunately, this makes them an easy target for money laundering activities by terrorist and rebel groups. In addition, their high value encourages some diamond producing countries to employ means of extraction that may violate human rights. Consider the case in Botswana where a rich diamond deposit was discovered on the land belonging to a tribal group, the Bushmen. The government forcibly resettled all 2,500 of them.

The Diamond Production Process: From Mine to Market

Diamonds are mined in several different ways: in open pits, underground, in alluvial mines (mines located in ancient creek beds where diamonds were deposited by streams), and in coastal and marine mines. Despite advances in technology, diamond excavation remains a labor-intensive process in most areas of the world. Over 156 million carats of diamonds are mined annually (one carat is the equivalent of 0.2 grams).

Once diamonds have been excavated, they are sorted, by hand, into grades. While there are thousands of categories and subcategories based on the size, quality, color, and shape of the diamonds, there are two broad categories of diamonds—gem grade and industrial grade. On average, close to 60 percent of the annual production is of gem quality. In addition to jewelry, gem quality stones are used for collections, exhibits, and decorative art objects. Industrial diamonds, because of their hardness and abrasive qualities, are often used in the medical field, in space programs, and for diamond tools.

After the diamonds have been sorted, they are transported to one of the world's four main diamond trading centers—Antwerp, Belgium, which is the largest; New York, U.S.A; Tel Aviv, Israel; and Mumbai, India. Daily, between five and ten million individual stones pass through the Antwerp trading center. After they have been purchased, the diamonds are sent off to be cut, polished, and/or otherwise processed. Five countries currently dominate the diamond processing industry—India, which is the largest (processing 9 out of every 10 diamonds); Israel; Belgium; Thailand; and the United States; with China emerging as a new processing center. Finally, the polished diamonds are sold by manufacturers, brokers, and dealers to importers and wholesalers all over the world, who in turn, sell to retailers. The total timeframe from the time of extraction to the time at which the diamond is sold to the end consumer is called the "pipeline," and it usually takes about 2 years.

The Not So Dazzling Side of the Diamond Trade

While women across the world may want a diamond on their finger, the industry's sparkling reputation has been tarnished. Reports have shown that profits from the diamond trade have financed deadly conflicts in African nations such as Angola, Sierra Leone, Congo, Cote d'Ivoire, and Liberia. In addition, reports by the Washington Post and Global Witness (**http://www.globalwitness.org**), a key organization in monitoring the global diamond trade, revealed that Al Qaeda used smuggled diamonds from Sierra Leone, most likely obtained via Liberia, to fund its terrorist activities. Diamonds that have been obtained in regions of the world plagued by war and violence are called "conflict diamonds" or "blood diamonds."

The use of diamonds for illicit activities has been widespread. During the Bush War of Angola in 1992, Jonas Savimbi, the head of a rebel movement called UNITA (National Union for the Total Independence of Angola), extended his organization into the vast diamond fields of the country. In less than one year, UNITA's diamond-smuggling network became the largest in the world—netting hundreds of million dollars a year with which they purchased weapons. Diamonds were also a useful tool for buying friends and supporters, and could be used as a means for stockpiling wealth.

Soon warring groups in other countries like Sierra Leone, Liberia, and the Democratic Republic of Congo adopted the same strategy. For example, the RUF (Revolutionary United Front) in Sierra Leone, a group that achieved international notoriety for hacking off the arms and legs of civilians and abducting thousands of children

This case was prepared by Daria Cherepennikova under the supervision of Professor Michael R. Czinkota of Georgetown University.

and forcing them to fight as soldiers, controlled the country's alluvial diamond fields and used them to fund their activities.

According to current diamond industry estimates, conflict diamonds make up between 2 and 4 percent of the annual global production of diamonds. However, human rights advocates disagree with that number. They argue that up to 20 percent of all diamonds on the market could be conflict diamonds.

The Kimberley Process

Diamonds are generally judged on the "Four Cs": cut, carat, color, and clarity; some have recently pushed for the addition of a "fifth C": conflict. On November 5, 2002, representatives from 52 countries, along with mining executives, diamond dealers, and members from advocacy groups, met in Interlaken, Switzerland, to sign an agreement that they hoped would eliminate conflict diamonds from international trade. The agreement was called the Kimberley Process and took effect on January 1, 2003.

The Kimberley Process is a United Nations–backed certification plan created to ensure that only legally mined rough diamonds, untainted by conflicts, reach established markets around the world. According to the plan, all rough diamonds passing through or into a participating country must be transported in sealed, tamper-proof containers and must be accompanied by a government-issued certificate guaranteeing the container's contents and origin. Customs officials in importing countries are required to certify that the containers have not been tampered with and are instructed to seize all diamonds that do not meet the certification requirements.

The agreement also stipulates that only those countries that subscribe to the new rules will be able to trade legally in rough diamonds. Countries that break the rules will be suspended and their diamond trading privileges will be revoked. Furthermore, individual diamond traders who disobey the rules will be subject to punishment under the laws of their own countries.

Critics Speak Out

Several advocacy groups have voiced concerns that the Kimberley Process remains open to abuse, and that it will not be enough to stop the flow of conflict diamonds. Many worry that bribery and forgery are inevitable and that corrupt government officials will render the scheme inoperable. Even those diamonds with certified histories attached may not be trustworthy. Alex Yearsley of Global Witness predicts that firms will "be a bit more careful with their invoices" as a result of the implementation of the Kimberley Process, but warns, "if you're determined, you can get around this process." His organization urges governments to implement stricter policies of internal control, for the diamond industry to publicize names of individuals in companies found to be involved in the conflict trade, and for the United Nations to consider implementing sanctions against diamonds from Cote d'Ivoire.

The General Accountability Office, the investigative arm of the U.S. Congress, also voiced concerns in a 2002 report: "[T]he period after rough diamonds enter the first foreign port until the final point of sale is covered by a system of voluntary industry participation and self-regulated monitoring and enforcement. These and other shortcomings provide significant challenges in creating an effective scheme to deter trade in conflict diamonds."

Government organizations and policy groups are not the only ones bringing the problem of conflict diamonds to light. Rapper Kanye West released a song entitled "Diamonds from Sierra Leone" after hearing about the atrocities of conflict diamonds in Africa. "This ain't Vietnam still/People lose hands, legs, arms for real," he raps. A Hollywood movie "The Blood Diamond," starring Leonardo DiCaprio, also features an ethical dilemma about buying and trading diamonds.

New Technologies Offer Solutions

Recently, a number of new technologies have emerged that, if adopted by the diamond industry worldwide, could change the way that diamonds are produced, traded, and sold. Several United States companies, using machines produced by Russian scientists, have been able to make industrial and gem-grade diamonds artificially. In terms of industrial-grade diamonds, which constitute at least 40 percent of all annual diamond production, this could mean tremendous cost savings for industries using industrial diamonds and the elimination of conflict diamonds from industrial uses. For gem-grade diamonds the viability of synthetic diamonds is questionable. Because of marketing campaigns by industry leader DeBeers Diamond Group, most consumers still feel that diamond gems are natural pieces of art and a rarity of nature. They are unwilling to trade that image for the mass-production view of synthetic diamonds.

Another emerging technology is laser engraving. Lasers make it possible to mark diamonds—either in their rough or cut stage—with a symbol, number, or bar code that can help to permanently identify that diamond. Companies who adopt the technology have an interesting marketing opportunity to create diamond brands. Intel, a manufacturer of computer chips, launched a mass marketing campaign "Intel Inside" to create brand awareness in the previously homogenous market where computer chips were a commodity. Consumers have positive associations with computers using Intel chips—and may only consider computers that have "Intel inside." Likewise, establishing brand awareness and building brand equity could add value to diamonds and help increase consumer comfort and confidence. Sirius Diamonds, a Vancouver-based cutting and polishing company, now microscopically laser-engraves a polar bear logo and an identification number on each gem it processes. Another company, 3Beams Technologies of the United States, is currently working on a system to embed a bar code inside a diamond (as opposed to on its surface) which would make it much more difficult to remove.

Another option is the "invisible fingerprint" invented by a Canadian security company called Identex. The technology works by electronically placing an invisible information package on each stone. The fingerprint can include any information that the producer desires such as the mine source and production date. The data can only be read by Identex's own scanners. Unfortunately, if the diamond is recut, the fingerprint will be lost, although it can be reapplied at any time. Though this represents a major drawback to the technology, the recutting of a diamond is expensive and typically reduces its size and value. The technology's creators believe that it will soon become an industry standard because it is a quick and cost-effective away to analyze a stone. The technology may supplement or even replace paper certification.

Lastly, processes are being developed to read a diamond's internal fingerprint—its unique sparkle and combination of impurities. The machine used to do this is called a Laser Raman Spectroscope (LRS). A worldwide database could identify a diamond's origin and track its journey from the mine to end consumer. However, creation of such a database requires large investments for equipment to cope with the volume of diamonds. Such investment will only happen if customers are willing to pay for such identification.

Questions for Discussion

1. In light of the conflict diamond issue, would you buy a diamond? Why or why not?

2. As a diamond retailer, what options do you have to ensure that the diamonds you sell are not conflict diamonds?

3. As a diamond producer, what steps can you take to prevent conflict diamonds from entering your supply chain?

4. Do you think the diamond industry as a whole has an ethical responsibility to combat the illicit trade in diamonds?

Sources

"A Crook's Best Friend." *The Economist*, January 4, 2003.

"Conflict and Security; Conflict Diamonds Are Forever." *Africa News*, November 8, 2002.

Cowell, Alan. "40 Nations in Accord on 'Conflict Diamonds.'" *The New York Times*, November 6, 2002.

DeBeers Group. http://www.debeersgroup.com (accessed February 13, 2006).

Duke, Lynne. "Diamond Trade's Tragic Flaw." *Washington Post*, April 29, 2001.

Finlayson, David. "Preserving Diamond's Integrity." *Vancouver Sun*, December 23, 2002.

Fowler, Robert R. "Final Report of the UN Panel of Experts on Violations of Security Council Sanctions Against UNITA." (S/2000/203) March 10, 2000.

Jha, Amarendra. "Diamond Pact Hits Surat Cutters." *The Times of India*, December 28, 2002.

Jones, Lucy. "Diamond Industry Rough to Regulate; Central African Republic Works to Monitor Gem Trade." *The Washington Times*, August 22, 2002.

"Making It Work: Why the Kimberley Process Must Do More to Stop Conflict Diamonds." Global Witness, November 2005.

Olson, Donald W. "Diamond, Industrial and Gemstones." U.S. Survey Minerals Yearbook, 2004. http://minerals.usgs.gov/minerals/pubs/ (accessed February 23, 2006).

Reeker, Philip T. "Implementing the Kimberley Process." January 2, 2003. http://www. diamonds.net (accessed February 22, 2006).

Rory M. O'Ferrall. "De Beers O'Ferrall Calls Kimberley End of Beginning." December 2, 2002. http://www. diamonds.net (accessed February 22, 2006).

Smillie, Ian. "The Kimberley Process: The Case for Proper Monitoring." Partnership Africa Canada, September 2002. http://www. partnershipafricacanada.org (accessed March 28, 2003).

Sparshott, Jeffrey. "WTO Targets 'Conflict Diamonds.'" *The Washington Times*, March 1, 2003.

"U.S.: Blood Diamond Plan Too Soft." *Associated Press Online*, June 18, 2002.

Watson, Andrea. "Tribes Face Death in Diamond Bonanza." *Sunday Express*, January 17, 2006.

NOVA SCOTIA

The U.S. Market for Canadian Travel Services

The more than 15 million Americans who travel to Canada annually constitute 28 percent of all departures from the United States. The U.S. market is of crucial importance to the Canadian tourism industry because 79 percent of all non-Canadian tourists are Americans, who spend approximately $13.5 billion a year on these trips.

Campaigns to lure tourists to a particular state or foreign country have increased dramatically. The Canadian Tourism Commission, the government tourist organization, has launched umbrella campaigns with themes such as "Come to the world next door" and "Keep Exploring" for Canada as a whole. The provinces conduct their own independent campaigns to segments they deem most attractive and profitable. For example, ads for Manitoba are mostly written for the outdoor vacationer.

Overall, U.S. visitors to Canada rate their stays higher in satisfaction and value than their vacations in the United States. The aided and unaided awareness of Canada declines gradually with greater distance from Canada. Therefore, it is not surprising to find the top seven states for Canada-bound travel to be New York, Michigan, Washington, California, Ohio, Massachusetts, and Pennsylvania. While Canada earns high marks on dimensions such as exploration and safety, the main reasons to reject Canada include bad weather, other more interesting and exotic places, unfavorable exchange rates, price of gasoline, and lack of interest ("been there, done that"). Canada gained more share of the U.S. market post 9-11, but has since been losing it again. For example, since 2002, Canada has lost 9 percent of leisure person-stays, representing $1.2 billion in foregone revenues.[1] The bottom line for Canada as a whole is that it needs a unique emotive element to separate it from competition.

The Commission sponsored a large-scale benefit-segmentation study of the American market for pleasure travel to Canada, the results of which are summarized in Exhibit 1. Segmenting the market by benefits provides many advantages over other methods. Segmenting by attitude toward Canada or by geographic area would be feasible if substantial variation occurred. This is not the case, however. Segmenting by benefits reveals what consumers were and are seeking in their vacations. Knowing this is central to planning effective marketing programs.

A Benefit-Matching Model

Exhibit 2 summarizes a strategic view for understanding tourism behavior and developing a marketing campaign. The model emphasizes the dominant need to define markets by benefits sought and the fact that separate markets seek unique benefits or activity packages. Membership in the segments will fluctuate from year to year; the same individuals may seek rest and relaxation one year and foreign adventure the next.

Identifying benefits is not enough, however. Competition (that is, other countries or areas) may present the same type of benefits to the consumers. Because travelers seriously consider only a few destinations, a sharp focus is needed for promoting a destination. This also means that a destination should avoid trying to be "everything to everybody" by promoting too many benefits. Combining all of these concerns calls for positioning, that is, generating a unique, differentiated image in the mind of the consumer.

Three destinations are shown in Exhibit 2. Each destination provides unique as well as similar benefits for travelers. Marketers have the opportunity to select one or two specific benefits from a set of benefits when developing a marketing program to attract visitors. The benefits selected for promotion can match or mismatch the benefits sought by specific market segments. The letters S, M, and N in the table express the degree of fit between the benefits provided and those sought. For example, a mismatch is promoting the wrong benefit to the wrong market, such as promoting the scenic mountain beauty of North Carolina to Tennessee residents.

The Case of Nova Scotia

Nova Scotia is one of ten provinces and two territories that make up Canada. Given its location, it is known as Canada's Ocean Playground (see Exhibit 3). For many Nova Scotians the sea is their main source of livelihood and leisure. For 200 years the sea has played an integral role in the history and economy of the province (see Exhibit 4). It was the abundant fisheries that drew settlers into the area. Today, many of their descendants work in a variety of professions related to the water, including tourism. The importance of tourism has increased with both the mining

SOURCE: This case was written by Arch G. Woodside and Ilkka A. Ronkainen for discussion purposes and not to exemplify correct or incorrect decision-making. The case is largely based on Arch G. Woodside, "Positioning a Province Using Travel Research", *Journal of Travel Research* 20 (Winter 1982): 2–6. For additional information, please see **http://www.gov.ns.ca** and **http://www.canadatourism.com**.

Exhibit 1

Benefit Segments of U.S. Travelers to Canada

Segment	Segment Contents	Size	Segment Objective
I.	Friends and relatives—nonactive visitor	29%	Seek familiar surroundings where they can visit friends.
II.	Friends and relatives—active city visitor	12%	Seek familiar surroundings where they can visit friends and relatives but are more inclined to participate in activities (i.e., sightseeing, shopping, cultural, entertainment).
III.	Family sightseers	6%	Look for new vacation place that would be a treat for the children and an enriching experience.
IV.	Outdoor vacationer	19%	Seek clean air, rest, quiet, and beautiful scenery. Many are campers, and availability of recreation facilities is important. Children also an important factor.
V.	Resort vacationer	19%	Most interested in water sports (for example, swimming) and good weather. Prefer a popular place with a big-city atmosphere.
VI.	Foreign vacationer	26%	Look for a place they have never been before with a foreign atmosphere and beautiful scenery. Money is not of major concern but good accommodation and service are. They want an exciting, enriching experience.

SOURCE: Shirley Young, Leland Ott, and Barbara Feigin, "Some Practical Considerations in Market Segmentation," *Journal of Marketing Research* 15 (August 1978): 405–412. Reprinted with permission.

Exhibit 2

Benefit Matching Model

Markets		Benefits Sought		Benefit Match		Benefits Provided		Destinations
A	→	A_s, B_s	→	S	→	A_p, B_p	→	X
B	→	B_s, C_s	→	M	→	C_p, D_p	→	Y
C	→	C_s, D_s	→	N	→	E_p, F_p	→	Z

S = supermatch; M = match; N = no match

SOURCE: Arch G. Woodside, "Positioning a Province Using Travel Research," *Journal of Travel Research* 20 (Winter 1982): 3.

and fishing sectors having difficulties from their resources drying up. Total tourism receipts exceed $1.22 billion and over 33,500 workers are employed directly and in spin-off jobs. More than a million people visit the province every year, with almost a quarter of these coming from outside of Canada, mainly the United States. Halifax was tenth among Canadian cities visited by tourists from the United States, with 264,000 overnight visits in 2004 (with Toronto as number 1 with 2,335,000 visits).

Canada as a whole has a rather vague and diffused image among Americans. This is particularly true of the Atlantic provinces. The majority of Nova Scotia's nonresident travelers reside in New England and the mid-Atlantic states of New York, Pennsylvania, and New Jersey. Most of these travelers include households with married couples having incomes substantially above the U.S. national average, that is, $50,000 and above. Such households represent a huge, accessible market—10 million households that are one to two

and a half days' drive from Halifax, the capital. Most households in this market have not visited the Atlantic provinces and have no plans to do so. Thus, the market exhibits three of the four requirements necessary to be a very profitable customer base for the province: size, accessibility, and purchasing power. The market lacks the intention to visit for most of the households described. Nova Scotia is not one of the destinations considered when the next vacation or pleasure trip is being planned. Worse still, Nova Scotia does not exist in the minds of its largest potential market.

In the past, Nova Scotia had a number of diverse marketing themes, such as "Good times are here," "International gathering of the clans," "The 375th anniversary of Acadia," "Seaside spectacular," and the most recent, "There's so much to sea." These almost annual changes in marketing strategy contributed to the present situation both by confusing the consumer as to what Nova Scotia is all about and by failing to create a focused image based on the relative strengths

Exhibit 3

Nova Scotia and Its Main Travel Markets

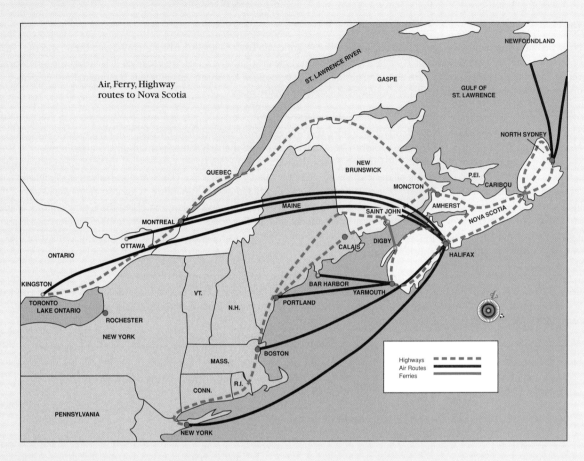

SOURCE: "Nova Scotia," *Travel Agent*, February 27, 1986, 14.

of the province. Some critics argue that Nova Scotia is not being promoted on its unique features but on benefits that other locations can provide as well or better.

Examples of Successful Positioning

Most North Atlantic passengers flying to Europe used to have a vague impression of Belgium. This presented a problem to the tourism authorities, who wanted travelers to stay for longer periods. Part of the problem was a former "Gateway to Europe" campaign that had positioned Belgium as a country to pass through on the way to somewhere else.

The idea for new positioning was found in the *Michelin Guides,* which rate cities as they do restaurants. The Benelux countries have six three-star cities (the highest ranking), of which five are in Belgium and only one (Amsterdam) is in the Netherlands. The theme generated was "In Belgium, there are five Amsterdams." This strategy was correct in three different ways: (1) it related Belgium to

a destination that was known to the traveler, Amsterdam; (2) the *Michelin Guides,* another entity already known to the traveler, gave the concept credibility; and (3) the "five cities to visit" made Belgium a bona fide destination.[2]

The state of Florida attracts far more eastern North American beach seekers than does South Carolina. Tourism officials in South Carolina had to find a way in which the state could be positioned against Florida.

The positioning theme generated was "You get two more days in the sun by coming to Myrtle Beach, South Carolina, instead of Florida." Florida's major beaches are a one-day drive beyond the Grand Strand of South Carolina—and one additional day back. Most travelers to Florida go in the May-to-October season when the weather is similar to that in South Carolina. Thus, more beach time and less driving time became the central benefit provided by the state.

Positioning Nova Scotia

The benefits of Nova Scotia as a Canadian travel destination cover segments III to VI of U.S. travelers (see Exhibit 1).

Exhibit 4

Nova Scotia Facts

The Land

Nova Scotia is surrounded by four bodies of water—the Atlantic, the Bay of Fundy, the Northumberland Strait, and the Gulf of St. Lawrence. Its average width of 70 miles (128 kilometers) means that no part of the province is far from the sea. Nova Scotia lies in the northern temperate zone and although it is surrounded by water, the climate is continental rather than maritime. The temperature extremes are moderated, however, by the ocean.

The History

The Micmac Indians inhabited Nova Scotia long before the first explorers arrived from Europe. The first visitors were Norsemen (in 1000), and, in 1497, Italian explorer John Cabot had noted the rich fishing grounds in the area. In the seventeenth century, all of Nova Scotia was settled by the French and formed a larger area known as Acadia. Feuds between the British and the French resulted in all of Acadia being ceded to the British in 1713. The British perceived the Acadians as a security threat and expelled them to Virginia and Louisiana. In 1783, there was an influx of loyalists from the newly independent New England states. Nova Scotia and three other provinces joined a federation called the Dominion of Canada in 1867. At the time, the province was known for international shipbuilding and trade in fish and lumber. The First and Second World Wars emphasized the importance of Halifax, Nova Scotia's capital, as a staging point for convoys and confirmed it as one of the world's major ports.

The People

Over 80 percent of Nova Scotia's population of 937,800 trace their ancestry to the British Isles, while 18 percent of residents are of French ancestry. The next largest groups by ancestry are German and Dutch. Almost 22,000 residents have Indian roots, primarily belonging to the Micmac nation.

The Economy

Nova Scotia's economy is highly diversified, having evolved from resource-based employment to manufacturing as well as business and personal services. The breakdown is as follows: (1) manufacturing/fish, 62 percent; (2) tourism, 12 percent; (3) forestry, 10 percent; (4) mining, 7 percent; (5) fishing, 5 percent; and (6) agriculture, 3 percent.

SOURCE: "Canadian Provinces and Territories," **http://www.canada.gc.ca**.

Those providing input to the planning process point out water activities, sea-side activities, camping, or scenic activities. The segment interested in foreign adventure could be lured by festivals and other related activities.

The planners' argument centers not so much on which benefits to promote but on which should be emphasized if differentiation is desired. The decision is important because of (1) the importance of the industry to the province and (2) the overall rise in competition for the travelers in Nova Scotia's market, especially competition by U.S. states.

Questions for Discussion

1. How would you position Nova Scotia to potential American travelers? Use the benefit-matching model to achieve your supermatch.

2. Constructively criticize past positioning attempts, such as "There's so much to sea."

3. What other variables, apart from positioning, will determine whether Americans will choose Nova Scotia as a destination?

THE F-18 HORNET OFFSET

In May 1992, the Finnish government's selection of the F/A-18 Hornet over the Swedish JAS-39 Gripen, the French Mirage 2000–5, and fellow American F-16 to modernize the fighter fleet of its air force was a major boost to McDonnell Douglas (MDC) in an otherwise quiet market. The deal would involve the sale of 57 F-18 Cs and 7 F-18 Ds at a cost of FIM 9.5 billion (approximately $2 billion). The Finnish version will have an "F" for "fighter" (rather than F/A) because the attack dimension is not included. Deliveries would take place between 1995 and 2000. Armaments would add another $1 billion to the deal.

© AP PHOTO/REMY DE LA MAUVINIERE

Winning the contract was critical since MDC had been on the losing side of two major aircraft competitions in the United States in 1991. In addition, one of its major projects with the U.S. Navy had been terminated (the A-12), and the government of the Republic of Korea had changed its mind to buy F-16 aircraft after it already had an agreement with MDC for F/A-18 Hornets.

However, the $3 billion was not earned without strings attached. Contractually, McDonnell Douglas and its main subcontractors (Northrop, General Electric, and General Motors's subsidiary Hughes), the "F-18 Team," were obligated to facilitate an equivalent amount of business for Finnish industry over a ten-year period (1992–2002) using various offset arrangements.

Offsets

Offsets are various forms of industrial and business activities required as a condition of purchase. They are an

SOURCES: This case was written by Ilkka A. Ronkainen and funded in part by a grant from the Business and International Education Program of the U.S. Department of Education. The assistance of the various organizations cited in the case is appreciated. Special thanks to David Danjczek, past chair of the Global Offset and Counter trade Association. For more information, see **http://www.boeing.com/defense-space/military/fa18/fa18 .htm**; **http://geae.net/geenginecenter/service_militaryavi.html**; **http://www.northgrum.com**; **http://www.hughes.com**.

obligation imposed on the seller in major (most often military hardware) purchases by or for foreign governments to minimize any trade imbalance or other adverse economic impact caused by the outflow of currency required to pay for such purchases. In wealthier countries, they are often used for establishing infrastructure. Two basic types of offset arrangements exist: direct and indirect (as seen in Exhibit 1). Although offsets have long been associated only with the defense sector, there are now increasing demands for offsets in commercial sales where the government is the purchaser or user.

From 1993 to 2004, 513 offset agreements totaling $77.2 billion were reported by U.S. defense exporters. Sales of aerospace defense systems made up 84 percent of all export contracts, totaling $64.8 billion. The average term for completing the offset agreements was 78–84 months. The agreements were concluded with a total of 41 nations, with 65.1 percent attributed to European nations. Although the average offset requirement is 99.1 percent for Europe, many countries require 100+ percent. Outside of Europe, the overall requirement is 46.6 percent; however, there are exceptions, such as South Africa's 116.7 percent average.

Direct offset consists of product-related manufacturing or assembly either for the purposes of the project in

Exhibit 1

The Offset Process

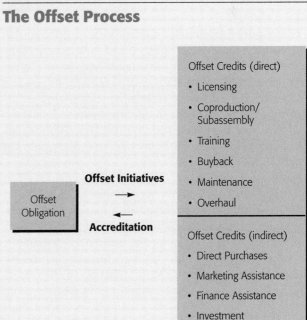

Offset Obligation

Offset Initiatives →

← Accreditation

Offset Credits (direct)
- Licensing
- Coproduction/ Subassembly
- Training
- Buyback
- Maintenance
- Overhaul

Offset Credits (indirect)
- Direct Purchases
- Marketing Assistance
- Finance Assistance
- Investment
- Technology Transfer

question only or for a longer-term partnership. The purchase, therefore, enables the purchaser to be involved in the manufacturing process. Various Spanish companies produce dorsal covers, rudders, aft fuselage panels, and speed brakes for the F/A-18s designated for the Spanish Air Force. In addition to coproduction arrangements, licensed production is prominent. Examples include Egypt producing U.S. M1-A1 tanks, China producing MDC's MD-82 aircraft, and Korea assembling the F-16 fighter. An integral part of these arrangements is the training of the local employees. Training is not only for production/assembly purposes but also for maintenance and overhaul of the equipment in the longer term. Some offsets have buyback provisions; that is, the seller is obligated to purchase output from the facility or operations it has set up or licensed. For example, Westland takes up an agreed level of parts and components from the Korean plant that produces Lynx Helicopters under license. In practice, therefore, direct offsets amount to technology transfer.

Indirect offsets are deals that involve products, investments, and so forth that are not to be used in the original sales contract but will satisfy part of the seller's "local" obligation. Direct purchases of raw materials, equipment, or supplies by the seller or its suppliers from the offset customer country present the clearest case of indirect offsets. These offset arrangements are analogous to counterpurchases and switch trading. Sellers faced with offset obligations work closely with their supplier base, some having goals of increasing supplier participation in excess of 50 percent. Teamwork does make the process more effective and efficient. There are various business activities taking place and procurement decisions being made by one of the sellers or its suppliers without offset needs that others may be able to use as offset credit to satisfy an indirect obligation.

Many governments see offsets as a mechanism to develop their indigenous business and industrial sectors. Training in management techniques may be attractive to both parties. The upgrading of skills may be seen by the government as more critical for improving international competitiveness than efforts focused only on hardware. For the seller, training is relatively inexpensive, but it provides good credits because of its political benefit.

An important dimension of the developmental effort will relate to exports. This may involve the analysis of business sectors showing the greatest foreign market potential, improving organizational and product readiness, conducting market research (e.g., estimating demand or assessing competition), identifying buyers or partners for foreign market development, or assisting in the export process (e.g., company visits, support in negotiations and reaching a final agreement, facilitating trial/sample shipments, handling documentation needs).

Sales are often won or lost on the availability of financing and favorable credit terms to the buyer. Financing packages put together by one of the seller's entities, if it is critical in winning the bid, will earn offset credits.

Buyer nations focusing on industrial development and technology transfer have negotiated contracts that call for offsetting the cost of their purchases through investments. Saudi Arabian purchases of military technology have recently been tied to sellers' willingness to invest in manufacturing plants, defense-related industries, or special-interest projects in the country. British Aerospace, for example, has agreed to invest in factories for the production of farm feed and sanitary ware.

Most often, the final offset deal includes a combination of activities, both direct and indirect vis-à-vis the sale, and no two offset deals are alike. With increasing frequency, governments may require "pre-deal counterpurchases" as a sign of commitment and ability to deliver should they be awarded the contract. Some companies, such as United Technologies, argue that there is limited advantage in carrying out offset activities in advance of the contract, unless the buyer agrees to a firm commitment. While none of the bidders may like it, buyers' market conditions give them very little choice to argue. Even if a bidder loses the deal, it can always attempt to sell its offset credits to the winner or use the credits in conjunction with other sales that one of its divisions may have. Some of the companies involved in the bidding in Finland maintain offset accounts with the Finnish government.

McDonnell's Deal with the Finnish Air Force

The F/A-18 Hornet is a twin-engine, twin-tail, multimission tactical aircraft that can be operated from aircraft carriers or from land bases (see Exhibit 2). It is both a fighter (air-to-air) and an attack (air-to-ground) aircraft. McDonnell Aircraft Company, a division of MDC, is the prime contractor for the F/A-18. Subcontractors include General Electric for the Hornet's smokeless F404 low-bypass turbofan engines, Hughes Aircraft Company for the APG-73 radar, and Northrop Corporation for the airframe. Approximately 1,100 F/A-18s have been delivered worldwide. Although it had been in use by the United States since 1983, it had been (and can continue to be) upgraded during its operational lifetime. Furthermore, it had proven its combat readiness in the Gulf War.

Only since June 1990 has the F/A-18 been available to countries that are not members of the North Atlantic Treaty Organization (NATO). The change in U.S. government position resulted from the rapidly changed East-West political situation. The attractive deals available in neutral countries such as Switzerland and Finland helped push the government as well. When the Finnish Air Force initiated its program in 1986, MDC was not invited to (and would not have been able to) offer a bid because of U.S. government restrictions. Finland is prohibited by World War II peace accords from having attack aircraft, hence the designation F-18.

Exhibit 2

F/A-18 Hornet Strike Fighter

Prime contractor	McDonnell Douglas
Principal subcontractor	Northrop Corporation
Type	Single- (C) and two-seat (D), twin-turbofan for fighter and attack missions
Power Plant	Two General Electric F404-GE-402 (enhanced performance engine)
Thrust	4,800 kp each (approx.)
Afterburning thrust	8,000 kp each (approx.)
Dimensions	
Length	17.07 m
Span	11.43 m
Wing area	37.16 m2
Height	4.66 m
Weights	
Empty	10,455 kg
Normal takeoff	16,650 kg
Maximum takeoff	22,328 kg
Wing loading	450 kg/m^2
Fuel (internal)	6,435 litre (4,925 kg)
Fuel (with external tanks)	7,687 litre
Armament	
Cannon	One General Electric M61A-1 Vulcan rotary-barrel 20-mm
Missiles	Six AIM-9 Sidewinder air-to-air
	Four AIM-7 Sparrow
	Six AIM-120 AMRAAM
Radar	AN/APG-73 multi-mode air-to-air and air-to-surface
Performance	
Takeoff distance	430 m
Landing distance	850 m
Fighter-mission radius	> 740 km
Maximum speed	1.8 Mach (1,915 km/h) at high altitude
	1.0 Mach at intermediate power
Service ceiling	15,240 m
Payload	7,710 kg
Used since	1983
Expected manufacturing lifetime	2000+
Users	USA, Australia, Canada, Spain, Switzerland, and Kuwait
Ordered quantity	1,168

The Finnish Government Position

The Finnish government's role in the deal had two critical dimensions: one related to the choice of the aircraft, the other related to managing the offset agreement in a fashion to maximize the benefit to the country's industry for the long term.

Selecting the Fighter

In 1986, the Finnish Air Force (FAF) decided to replace its aging Swedish-made Drakens and Soviet-made MIG-21s, which made up three fighter squadrons. At that time, the remaining service life of these aircraft was estimated to be 15 years, calling for the new squadrons to be operational by the year 2000 and to be up-to-date even in 2025. Finland, due to its strategic geographic location, has always needed a reliable air defense system. The position of neutrality adopted by Finland had favored split procurement between Eastern and Western suppliers until the collapse of the Soviet Union in December 1991 made it politically possible to purchase fighters from a single Western supplier.

The first significant contacts with potential bidders were made in 1988, and in February 1990, the FAF requested proposals from the French Dassault-Breguet, Sweden's Industrigruppen JAS, and General Dynamics in the United States for 40 fighters and trainer aircraft. In January 1991, the bid was amended to 60 fighters and seven trainers. Three months later, MDC joined the bidding, and by July 1991, binding bids were received from all four manufacturers.

During the evaluative period, the four bidders tried to gain favor for their alternative. One approach was the provision of deals for Finnish companies as "pre-deal counterpurchases." For example, General Dynamics negotiated for Vaisala (a major Finnish electronics firm) to become a subcontractor of specialty sensors for the F-16. Before the final decision, the Swedish bidder had arranged for deals worth $250 million for Finnish companies, the French for over $100 million, and General Dynamics for $40 million. MDC, due to its later start, had none to speak of. Other tactics were used as well. The Swedes pointed to long ties that the countries have had, and especially to the possibilities to develop them further on the economic front. As a matter of fact, offsets were the main appeal of the Swedish bid since the aircraft itself was facing development cost overruns and delays. The French reminded the Finnish government that choosing a European fighter might help in Finland's bid to join the European Union (EU) in 1995. Since the FAF preferred the U.S. AMRAAM missile system for its new fighters, the U.S. government cautioned that its availability depended on the choice of the fighter. The companies themselves also worked on making their bid sweeter: Just before the official announcement, General Dynamics improved its offer to include 67 aircraft for the budgeted sum and a guarantee of 125 percent offsets; that is, the amount of in-country participation would be 125 percent of the sale price paid by the Finnish government for the aircraft.

After extensive flight testing both in the producers' countries and in Finland (especially for winter conditions), the Hornet was chosen as the winner. Despite the high absolute cost of the aircraft (only 57 to be bought versus 60), the Hornet's cost-effectiveness relative to performance was high. The other alternatives were each perceived to have problems: The JAS-39 Gripen had the teething problems of a brand-new aircraft; the Mirage's model 2000–5 has not yet been produced; and the F-16 may be coming to the end of its product life cycle. The MIG-29 from the Soviet Union/Russia was never seriously in the running due to the political turmoil in that country. Some did propose purchasing the needed three squadrons from the stockpiles of the defunct East Germany (and they could have been had quite economically), but the uncertainties were too great for a strategically important product.

Working Out the Offsets

Typically, a specific committee is set up by the government to evaluate which arrangements qualify as part of the offset. In Finland's case, the Finnish Offset Committee (FOC) consists of five members with the Ministries of Defense, Foreign Affairs, and Industry and Trade represented. Its task is to provide recommendations as to which export contracts qualify and which do not. The Technical Working Group was set up to support its decision making, especially in cases concerning technology transfer. From 1977 to 1991, the procedures and final decisions were made by the Ministry of Defense; since then, the responsibility has been transferred to the Ministry of Trade and Industry (see Exhibit 3). The transfer was logical given the increased demands and expectations on the trade and technology fronts of the F/A-18 deal.

Exhibit 3

Offset Finnish Industry Output

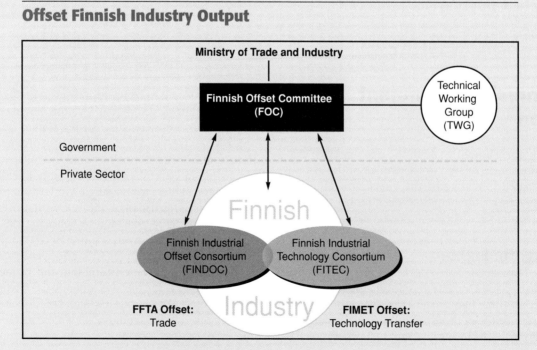

When the committee was established in 1977 in conjunction with a major military purchase, almost all contracts qualified until an export developmental role for offsets was outlined. The Finnish exporter is required to show that the offset agreement played a pivotal role in securing its particular contract.

Two different approaches are taken by the government to attain its developmental objective. First, the government will not make available (or give offset credit for) counterpurchasing goods that already have established market positions unless the counterpurchaser can show that the particular sale would not have materialized without its support (e.g., through distribution or financing). Second, the government will use compensation "multipliers" for the first time. While previous deals were executed on a one-on-one basis, the government now wants, through the use of multipliers, direct purchases to certain industries or types of companies. For example, in the case of small or medium-sized companies, a multiplier of two may be used; that is, a purchase of $500,000 from such a firm will satisfy a $1 million share of the counterpurchaser's requirement. Attractive multipliers also may be used that may generate long-term export opportunities or support Finland's indigenous arms or other targeted industry. Similarly, the seller may also insist on the use of multipliers. In the case of technology transfer, the seller may request a high multiplier because of the high initial cost of research and development that may have gone into the technology licensed or provided to the joint venture as well as its relative importance to the recipient country's economic development.

Finnish industry is working closely with the government on two fronts. The Finnish Industrial Offset Consortium (FINDOC) was established to collaborate with the Finnish Foreign Trade Association (a quasi-governmental organization) on trade development. FINDOC's 21 members represent 15 main business areas (e.g., aircraft, shipbuilding, pulp and paper machinery, and metal and engineering) and are among the main Finnish exporters. Their consortium was set up to take advantage of offset opportunities more efficiently and to provide a focal point for the F-18 Team's efforts. For example, MDC and FINDOC arranged for a familiarization trip to the United States for interested Finnish businesses in the fall of 1992. For those companies not in FINDOC, it is the task of the FFTA to provide information on possibilities to benefit from the deal. The Finnish Industrial Technology Consortium (FITEC) was established to facilitate technology transfer to and from the Finnish metal and engineering industries.

The F-18 Team's Position

The monies related to offset management and associated development are not generally allowed as a separate cost in the sales contract. Profit margins for aircraft sales are narrow, and any additional costs must be watched closely. Extraordinary demands by the buyer make bidding more challenging and time-consuming. For example, the customer may want extensive changes in the product without changes in the final price. Switzerland wanted major alterations made to the airframe and additional equipment, which made its total cost per plane higher than the price in Finland. In the experience of high-tech firms, the add-on for direct offsets ranges from 3 to 8 percent, which has to be incorporated into the feasibility plans. Offsets have to make good business sense and, once agreed to, successfully executed.

Competing for the Deal

In accepting the offer to bid for the FAF deal, the F-18 Team believed it had only a 5 percent chance to win the deal but, given its size, decided to go ahead. From the time it received a request to bid from the FAF, MDC had three months to prepare its proposal. The only main negative factor from the short preparation time was MDC's inability to arrange for "prepurchase" deals and generate goodwill with the constituents.

After two fact-finding missions to Finland, MDC established an office in Helsinki in August 1991. The decision to have a full-time office in Finland (compared to the competitors whose representatives were in Helsinki two days a week on the average) was made based on the experiences from Korea and Switzerland. MDC's approach was to be ready and able to help the customer in terms of information and be involved with all the constituents of the process, such as the testing groups of the FAF, the Ministry of Defense (owners of the program), and the Parliament (supporters of the program).

Beyond the technical merits of the Hornet, MDC's capabilities in meeting the pending offset obligations were a critical factor in winning the deal. MDC had by 1992 a total of 100 offset programs in 25 countries with a value of $8 billion, and its track record in administering them was excellent. Another factor in MDC's favor was its long-term relationship with Finnair, the national airline. Finnair's aircraft have predominantly come from MDC, from the DC-2 in 1941 to the MD-11 aircraft delivered in 1991.

Satisfying the Offset Obligation

Offset deals are not barter where the seller and the buyer swap products of equal value over a relatively short time period. The F-18 Team members had to complete the offset program by the year 2002 through a number of different elements including marketing assistance, export development, technology transfer, team purchases, and investment financing. One of the major beneficiaries of the offset arrangement was Patria Finnavitec, the only major aircraft manufacturer in Finland. Patria Finnavitec assembled the 57 C-versions in Finland and also counted on the F-18 Team's connections to open markets for its

Redigo trainer aircraft. The F-18 Team worked with Finnish companies to develop exports for their products and services by identifying potential buyers and introducing the two parties to each other. Purchases could come from within the contractor companies, suppliers to the F-18 contractors, and third parties. The motivation for completing offset projects was financial penalties for the prime team members if they did not meet contract deadlines.

However, no one in the F-18 Team or among its suppliers was obligated to engage in a given transaction just because Finland purchased fighters from McDonnell Douglas. The key point was that products must meet specifications, delivery dates, and price criteria to be successfully sold in any market. After an appropriate purchase had taken place, the F-18 Team received offset credit based on the Finnish-manufactured content of the transaction value as approved by the Finnish Offset Committee. For example, when Finnyards won the bid to build a passenger ferry for the Danish Stena Line, Northrop received offset credits due to its role in financing Finnyard's bid.

The offset obligations were not limited to the United States. The team had offset partners all over the world because the members operate worldwide. Furthermore, given the long time frame involved, there were no pressing time constraints on the members to earn offset credits.

Since 1992, the MDC office in Helsinki had two officers: one in charge of the aircraft, the other focused in offsets. Due to the worst recession in recent Finnish history, the response to the offset program was unprecedented, and the office was inundated with requests for information and deals.

Results

By October 2002 the program was complete, with Boeing having delivered all of the 64 aircraft early and satisfied the offset obligations ahead of schedule. A total of $3.345 billion of credits had been granted against the required minimum of $3 billion. Direct offsets accounted for 15 percent and indirect offsets 85 percent of the credits earned. Nearly 600 business transactions had been part of the indirect credits originating from 210 Finnish companies, 114 of which were small and medium-sized enterprises (SMEs). Exports had been directed at 30 different countries.

Politically, the deal enhanced Finnish–U.S. relations at a time of spectacular changes. Finnish industry was supported at a time when major shifts occurred in markets and their potential. The United States had become Finland's fourth largest trading partner, having surpassed Russia. While FINDOC companies generated, as expected, a substantial share (48 percent) of the business transactions, SMEs benefited as well. They generated 140 projects, for a total of nearly $500 million in sales. Some broke into world markets as a result of the offset deal.

Exports accounted for nearly two-thirds of the indirect offset credits. However, significant activity also centered on technology transfer and investments. For example, Aker Finnyards received technology transfers to allow it to move into the hovercraft market where it has already delivered its prototype vessel for the Finnish Navy. SMEs benefited through marketing assistance programs (which constituted 10 percent of the total credits). For example, groups of SME managers were able to use the facilities of General Electric Trading in New York while getting accustomed to the U.S. business climate and establishing relationships with intermediaries and clients.

Questions for Discussion

1. Why would the members of the F-18 Team, McDonnell Douglas, Northrop, General Electric, and Hughes, agree to such a deal rather than insist on a money-based transaction?

2. After the deal was signed, many Finnish companies expected that contracts and money would start rolling in by merely calling up McDonnell Douglas. What are the fundamental flaws of this thinking?

3. Why do seller governments typically take an unsupportive stance on countertrade arrangements?

4. Comment on this statement: "Offset arrangements involving overseas production that permit a foreign government or producer to acquire the technical information to manufacture all or part of a U.S.-origin article trade short-term sales for long-term loss of market position."

Recommended Readings

"Countertrade's Growth Continues." *BarterNews* 27 (1993): 54–55.

"Offsets in the Aerospace Industry." *BarterNews* 27 (1993): 56–57.

"Investing, Licensing, and Trading Conditions Abroad: Saudi Arabia." *Business International,* May 15, 1990, 5.

Jakubik, Maria, Irina Kabirova, Tapani Koivunen, Päivi Lähtevänoja, and Denice Stanfors. *Finnish Air Force Buying Fighters.* Helsinki School of Economics, September 24, 1993.

State Audit Office. *Offsets in the Procurement of Hornet Fighters.* Helsinki, Finland: Edita, 1999, chapter 1.

U.S. Department of Commerce. *Offsets in Defense Trade Tenth Study.* Washington, DC: Bureau of Industry and Security, December 2005, overview.

EQUAL EXCHANGE STRIVES FOR EQUALITY THROUGH FAIR TRADE

When you sip your cup of morning coffee—whether it's in your dorm room or in the trendy coffee shop down the street—you probably don't think about where it came from. Even if you're familiar with the jargon—*arabica beans, varietals, dark roast*—and even if you can name the major coffee-producing countries, such as Costa Rica and Colombia, you probably aren't thinking about the people who grow the beans thousands of miles away. But the coffee-growing business is so important in Central and South America that it provides many jobs for people who otherwise would be unemployed. When you buy a pound of gourmet coffee at $8 to $9 per pound, about 40 cents actually reaches the farmers who grew it. Where does the rest of the money go? To agents who offer the lowest possible price to buyers who then put their own brand labels on the coffee. The 20 million coffee farmers who are left in poverty call these middlemen "coyotes" because they are perceived to be preying on the poor.

Equal Exchange, Inc., a gourmet coffee company founded in 1986 in Canton, Massachusetts, is working to change these practices by engaging in its own ethically and socially responsible way of doing business. By adopting the concept of "fair trade," Equal Exchange buys coffee directly from the growers themselves, eliminating the middlemen. As a result, the growers gain as much as 50 cents more per pound. Because coffee is the leading source of foreign currency in Latin America, this arrangement is significant to the economy of the region. It is also significant to each individual coffee farmer. "We used to live in houses made of corn husks," recalls Don Miguel Sifontes, who operates a farm in El Salvador. "Now we have better work, better schools, homes of adobe, and a greater brotherhood of decision makers."

The concept of fair trade, first adopted in Europe about 15 years ago, illustrates the idea that businesses are responsible and accountable to their employees, their customers, and the general public. Equal Exchange growers receive better prices under exclusive agreements with farming cooperatives, customers are guaranteed high-quality coffee at fair prices, and the general public in the growers' regions benefits from projects that the farm cooperatives have undertaken with the additional income they make.

Typical projects are reforestation programs, training for doctors and nurses, and the building of new schools. Equal Exchange follows a strict set of fair trade guidelines in its purchase of coffee:

- *Buy directly from small farmer cooperatives.* These cooperatives are owned and run by the farmers themselves. Each cooperative governs the even distribution of income and services, such as education and healthcare. Buying direct means that profits go to the farmers rather than agents or other middlemen, reducing the need for growers to engage in more profitable activities, such as growing marijuana and other illegal endeavors, in order to survive.

- *Pay a fair price.* Equal Exchange pays a guaranteed minimum price for its coffee, regardless of how low the coffee market itself may drop. This price assures that farmers will be able to make a living wage during downturns. Of course, the price rises as the market rises.

- *Provide advance credit to growers.* Equal Exchange makes credit available to its farmers. Historically, credit was unavailable or offered only at extremely high rates, trapping farmers in debt. "When we sign a contract with producers, we pay up to 60 percent of the contract six months in advance," notes marketing manager Erbin Crowell. "If a hurricane hits, we share the risk." In fact, several years ago, a hurricane did hit—"Mitch" slammed into Nicaragua, causing deaths, injuries, and millions of dollars in damage. Equal Exchange worked with Lutheran World Relief to raise funds for residents who suffered because of the hurricane.

- *Encourage ecologically sustainable farming practices.* Equal Exchange helps growers use environmentally friendly farming methods, protecting both the local environment and consumers

SOURCE: Adapted from the video case (of the same name) by Louis E. Boone and David L. Kurtz, *Contemporary Business,* 10th ed. (Forth Worth, TX: Harcourt College Publishers, 2002), 80.

from toxic chemicals. In this way, the company demonstrates social responsibility not only to the health of workers and consumers but also to the local environment. The company pays a premium price for certified organic and shade-grown coffee, both of which are better for the environment.

Not surprisingly, Equal Exchange is also ethical in its conduct toward competitors. Recently, when specialty coffee giants Starbucks and Green Mountain announced that they were entering into fair trade agreements with farmers, Equal Exchange publicly congratulated them. "Believe it or not, we want more, not less competition," says Equal Exchange cofounder and coexecutive director Rink Dickinson. "That's because we know these farmers and their struggles. They urgently need more importers to pay a just price. So we encourage our fellow roasters to expand on the modest fair trade programs they've announced

so far." With this statement, Dickinson raised the bar of ethical standards in the coffee business—knowing that his company can clear it with ease.

Questions for Discussion

1. Is Equal Exchange trying to contravene the effect of market forces? Is it likely to succeed in the longer term?

2. Suppose Dickinson discovered that one of Equal Exchange's cooperatives was growing illegal products, selling coffee to competitors, or not paying fair wages to workers. What do you think he should do?

3. Visit Equal Exchange's Web site at http://www.equalexchange.com to learn about the company. What characteristics of the company do you think are most appealing to consumers?

LONELY PLANET PROVIDES GUIDANCE TO GLOBAL EXPLORERS

Lonely Planet has been global since before it was even a company—in its audience, its scope, and its foundation. The now ubiquitous guidebook brand got its start in 1973 when Brit Tony Wheeler and his wife, Maureen, holed up in Australia to write a pamphlet on their experiences traveling in Asia. The couple had met in their native Britain, found that they shared a love of adventure, and gotten married soon thereafter. For their honeymoon they chose to make a trip that no one at the time believed was possible—a journey from Britain across Europe and Asia via land all the way to Australia. They made it, but were stuck in Australia with 27 cents between the two of them. Tony made the best of the situation by writing the 94-page *Across Asia on the Cheap*, which sold 8,500 copies. From this suitably adventurous start, Lonely Planet ballooned into one of the powerhouses of the growing guidebook and phrasebook industry, with around 500 titles on 118 countries. Lonely Planet now represents one quarter of all English-language guidebooks sold in the world and has annual revenues in excess of $75 million.

The company has offices in London and Oakland, with its headquarters in Melbourne. It employs 500 office staff and around 300 on-the-road contributors. Thanks to these contributors from dozens of different countries, the company has a global scope and a global perspective, which helps the company successfully market worldwide. The huge diversity of languages, cultures, and interests across their consumer base makes marketing and developing a coherent brand image difficult. To cope with these hurdles, Lonely Planet works on maintaining a balance between consistency in branding and customizing marketing to suit specific target markets.

In 2007, the Wheelers finally relinquished control of the company when they sold it to BBC Worldwide, which is the commercial branch of the British Broadcasting Company. The addition of the BBC's extensive network of distribution channels has helped Lonely Planet to market itself more successfully, and to branch into complementary business areas such as Lonely Planet Images, Lonely Planet Television, Lonely Planet Foreign Rights Team, Lonely Planet Business Solutions unit, and Lonely Planet Foundation (which contributes 5 percent of all profits to international charities and has established a carbon offset program for printing and the travels of all employees). From the start, one of the fundamental tenets of the Lonely Planet brand has been that travel can truly change the world and make it a better place. Through the Lonely Planet Foundation, the Wheelers have tried to make profound differences in the places they visit. Their far-reaching message is being heard loud and clear as evidenced by the 4.3 million unique visitors clicking on **lonelyplanet.com** each month.

This marketing strategy of selective customization combined with relentless fact checking and updating, and a focus on hiring the best and most knowledgeable travel writers, has earned Lonely Planet a reputation for quality. Lonely Planet books are not only popular; they are considered by many to be the definitive guidebooks. In fact, Jay Garner, the first American administrator in Iraq, considers Lonely Planet such an authority on global travel that he used the book *Lonely Planet Iraq* to develop a list of historical sites worth saving. Another nod to the success of the brand is the fact that in Asia, imitation Lonely Planet guidebooks are now sold alongside imitation Gucci and Chanel handbags and Rolex watches.

No matter what criticisms people may have of Lonely Planet, this single guidebook brand has been responsible for the soaring popularity of adventure tourism worldwide. Because of Lonely Planet, there are surf camps in El Salvador, foreign-owned luxury resorts in Nicaragua, and remote villages in the heights of the Himalayas. Economies based on tourism are monuments to the success of lonely planets marketing strategy.

Lonely Planet continues its trek toward boundless success, due largely to the organization's clear vision of its target market. The Lonely Planet traveler is willing to embrace foreign food and culture, but still wants to do it comfortably and cheaply, if possible. The company reaches its customers through smart marketing strategies that balance a recognizable brand with customization to accommodate local tastes. Lonely Planet has never forgotten that there really is no such thing as global—that the world consists of thousands of different local populations. And Lonely Planet, by knowing clearly who comprises its market and by using smart marketing strategies, has grown from a pamphlet written in a cheap hostel to a huge global brand loved by millions of travelers the world over.

Questions for Discussion

1. Why is Lonely Planet a global success?

2. How has Lonely Planet been able to provide and market guidebooks that are useful across languages and cultures?

3. How could Lonely Planet guidebooks help marketers to develop effective marketing strategies in targeted foreign markets?

SOURCES: "About IDG," *International Data Group*, **http://www.idg .com/www/home.nsf/AboutIDGForm?OpenForm&region_WW**, accessed April 13, 2006; Sam Perkins and Neal Thornberry, "Corporate Entrepreneurship for Dummies," *Harvard Business School Publishing* (Case BAB114).

GREEN MOUNTAIN COFFEE ROASTERS

More than two decades ago, Robert Stiller visited a coffee shop in Waitsfield, Vermont, where he drank a cup that was so good he bought the coffee shop. Stiller, an entrepreneur, had recently sold another business and settled in Vermont because he was an avid skier. When he walked into the coffee shop—where the coffee was roasted on site—he smelled the sweet aroma of success. "I liked the idea that the product would be consumed, because if you do a great job, people will keep coming back," Stiller recalls. "I felt if you provide the best quality and service in whatever you pursue, you're going to do well." Within a few years, he'd bought a second coffee shop and founded Green Mountain Coffee Roasters, which—in addition to operating as retail shops—began wholesaling fresh-roasted coffee to restaurants and other outlets. When consumers complained of difficulty in going directly to the two Green Mountain Coffee shops and began to clamor for their favorite joe at home, the firm's mail-order business was born. Today, consumers can find all the flavors of Green Mountain Coffee in a variety of places—from restaurants and inns to doctors' offices and the Internet.

But just selling coffee isn't enough. Within two decades, the marketing environment had become amazingly complex. Competition from other firms like Starbucks is fierce, regulations govern international trade with coffee growers, economic factors affect how much consumers are willing to pay for premium coffee, and cultural factors may determine consumer preferences. Stiller and his executives must continually collect information about the marketing environment to provide the high-quality products that consumers want.

In addition, Green Mountain is well known for its ethical business practices and its commitment to social responsibility. Not long after Green Mountain was founded, a group of employees formed an environmental committee that became the foundation for the firm's social responsibility projects. The committee began with initiatives to turn off lights and turn down the heat in the company's offices to save energy. They then redesigned some of the firm's shipping boxes to reduce weight—which also reduced costs. Next they came up with the idea for Rain Forest Nut coffee, the sale of which helped develop public awareness of the depletion of rain forests in South America *and* raised money for the Rainforest Alliance and Conservation International. (Historically, rain forests have been cleared by coffee farmers to produce additional spaces for growing more coffee.) Consumers loved the taste of Rain Forest Nut coffee, as well as the philosophy behind it, and sales took off.

As Green Mountain got more and more involved with rain forest conservation, the firm developed alliances with coffee farmers, who agreed to specific conservation and quality criteria in return for guaranteed business. For example, to preserve the environment, the coffee is grown in the shade—this preserves habitats for certain birds and helps reduce global warming. Currently, Green Mountain is the world's largest supplier of double-certified coffee—products that meet qualifications for being organic as well as those of the Fair Trade initiative. Fair Trade certification signifies that coffee growers have been paid a fair price for their product, which means they can feed and clothe their families, send their children to school instead of requiring them to work in the fields, and use more environmentally sound farming practices.

Green Mountain donates 5 percent of its pretax earnings to nonprofit organizations and causes. The firm also creates alliances with these organizations or other companies for certain community projects. With the National Wildlife Federation, Green Mountain recently introduced two new shade-grown, Fair Trade coffees called National Wildlife Blend and National Wildlife Blend Decaf. Together, the two organizations are promoting the coffees as wells as the link between the shaded coffee environments and the health of migratory birds that live there. Green Mountain is also an active supporter of Coffee Kids, an organization that works to improve the quality of life for children and families in the coffee-growing communities. Some of the Coffee Kids programs have included education, healthcare, hurricane relief, and funding for small businesses.

SOURCES: Company Web site, **http://www.greenmountaincoffee .com**, accessed October 20, 2004; Adrienne Fox, "Green Mountain Coffee Roasters," in "50 Best Small & Medium Places to work," *HR Magazine*, July 2004, **http://www.shrm.org/hrmagazine**; "Green Mountain Coffee Roasters Ranked #9 on List of Best Medium Companies to Work for in America," *Business Wire*, June 29, 2004, **http://www.businesswire.com**; "Green Mountain Coffee Roasters Now #5 on *Business Ethics* Magazine's List of Best 100 Corporate Citizens," *Business Wire*, May 4, 2004; Virginia Lindaur Simmon, "Java Man," *Business People Vermont*, February 2, 2003, **http://www .vermontguides.com**.

All of the good business ethics and social responsibility projects in the world wouldn't amount to a hill of coffee beans if Green Mountain wasn't a great place to work. Green Mountain has been ranked by *Forbes* magazine as one of the "200 Best Small Companies in America" four years in a row, and *Business Ethics* recently ranked Green Mountain fifth overall in its list of "100 Best Corporate Citizens." Company culture embraces teamwork, personal growth, and fun. And Green Mountain pays its employees for time they spend volunteering for various social responsibility programs.

Ethics and social responsibility are an integral part of Green Mountain's overall marketing strategy, which seeks to promote the highest quality products in a way that preserves the natural environment and enhances the well-being of people in need around the world. "We have distinguished ourselves with our focus both on superior execution and being a responsible corporate citizen," says Robert Stiller, "and now we can leverage these positions to competitive advantage."

Questions for Discussion

1. What marketing approaches could Green Mountain adopt in order to expand its customer base?

2. How do international and domestic events affect Green Mountain's marketing strategy and sales?

3. How successful would Green Mountain be in South America?

DOC MARTENS MAKES STRIDES AROUND THE WORLD

Got a pair of Doc Martens in your closet? Maybe you're wearing them now. Perhaps you're wearing a pair of classic 1460 boots or a twin-strap sandal. Maybe your best friend is wearing a pair of guys' Grip Trax boots or even some wingtips. You're probably familiar with the distinctive yellow stitching, heel loop, and two-tone soles of Docs. The color names are pretty amazing, too—Bark Grizzly, Tan Analine, Aztec Crazy, Black Greasy. Even if you can't tell what colors these really are, you get curious. You scroll through the offerings online; you try on a pair in a shoe store. They look pretty clunky, but the Docs fit. When you walk around in them, your feet are really comfortable.

Doc Martens, or Docs or DMs, as they are often known, are officially named Dr. Martens, after their German inventor Dr. Klaus Maertens. Maertens, a physician in the German Army during World War II, injured his ankle on a ski trip to the Bavarian Alps in 1945. He'd been skiing in his uncomfortable army boots, and as he was recovering from his ankle injury, he spent a lot of time thinking about how to improve the boots. He came up with a design for a boot made of soft leather with air-padded soles.

Half a century later, consumers everywhere swear by their Docs. Now available in more than 250 styles of boots, sandals, and shoes, Doc Martens are worn by men, women, and children around the world. Madonna wears them, and so did Pope John Paul II, who had his own exclusive line in pure white. Police officers and postal carriers, construction and factory workers, students and supermodels all wear them. Docs are sold in 78 countries, with two-thirds of them bought by American consumers. The firm has offices in such diverse places as Australia, Poland, the Philippines, Singapore, Turkey, the United States, and the Ukraine. Even the United Arab Emirates boasts an office for Docs. People can buy them at retail stores or online from just about anywhere in the world. Unless you are stationed in Antarctica or climbing Mt. Everest, you can probably get a pair of Docs.

Since 1960, Doc Martens have been manufactured by R. Griggs, one of the two largest shoemakers in the United Kingdom (the other one is C&J Clark, maker of the Clarks brand). Despite its size, however, Griggs faces serious competition from other designer shoe manufacturers, as well as sports shoemakers such as Nike and Reebok. Because of fierce competition and uncertain economic conditions that have affected sales in the shoe industry in general, Griggs made the painful decision to move all of its manufacturing to China several years ago. Many companies in Europe have experienced similar pressures. Chinese manufacturers can produce goods cheaper than European facilities can. Since China is now considered a global trade power, having surpassed Taiwan and South Korea as the largest exporter of sport shoes to the United States, footwear companies everywhere are feeling the pinch. But Griggs marketers believe that the move was critical to the survival of its Dr. Martens brand.

In addition, the marketers behind the Doc Martens brand have changed their entire global strategy, rescinding foreign licenses and focusing more on marketing the brand than on manufacturing the boots. Now, all marketing and sales efforts are overseen from the firm's UK headquarters. When Docs were allowed to return to South Africa, for example, it was under a stricter agreement than the one that was previously in force. "We are importing the Doc Martens—we don't manufacture them," explains Stewart Franks, international brand director for South Africa's Jordan Footwear. "That will ensure that there is standard uniformity in the quality of the shoes themselves."

Perhaps the most innovative effort by Docs' marketers is the firm's current Web site. The site not only provides all the usual information and access to styles, but it also introduces "VEER: A Series of Documentaries," a program in conjunction with *Sports Illustrated* that is currently touring college campuses. Described as "6 films about people taking a different direction," the project focuses on six individuals who form the cutting edge of art, music, and other fields. Visitors to the site can click on each one of the films, download it, and watch it. They can follow Janette as she struggles to make it as a DJ or John, Adam, Mark, Whylee, or Ndidi as they make their way in various pursuits. The films have an edgy quality, as does the site itself, which features black-and-white photography. After 50 years, Doc Martens are cool again, on the feet of a new generation. You could say they are walking tall, around the world and back again.

SOURCES: Company Web site, **http://www.drmartens.com**, accessed October 30, 2004; "R. Griggs, Limited, Company Profile," *Hoover's Online*, **http://finance.yahoo.com**, accessed October 21, 2004; "Dr. Martens Shoes," *Onlineshoes.com*, **http://www.onlineshoes.com**, accessed October 21, 2004; "Doc Martens," *TheFreeDictionary.com*, **http://encyclopedia.thefreedictionary.com**, accessed October 21, 2004; Karin Schimke and Mzolisi Witbooi, "Cool Doc Martens Is Back with a Thump," *Cape Argus*, September 7, 2004, **http://www.capeargus.co.za**; Matt Forney, "Tug-of-War over Trade," *Time Europe*, February 23, 2004, **http://www.time.com/time/europe**; "Dr. Martens Moves to China," *BBC News*, October 24, 2002, **http://news.bbc.co.uk**.

Questions for Discussion

1. Dr. Martens are now manufactured in China. Should the company also market its shoes directly to Chinese shoppers?

2. Marketers for Doc Martens are using Internet technology to reach consumers via the documentaries presented on the Web site. Describe other creative ways they could use Internet technology to attract consumers.

3. Does the move to China affect Dr. Martens' image and risk exposure?

4. Do you think it was a good idea for Dr. Martens to rescind foreign licenses for its products at this time? Why or why not?

GOYA HELPS LATINOS MAINTAIN MEALTIME TRADITIONS

Eighty years ago, Latino immigrant Prudencio Unanue and his wife longed for the comfort foods of their home, so they started an import business to satisfy the need. However, a few years later, the Spanish Civil War broke out, and they could no longer obtain the foods they wanted for their business. So they began importing sardines from a cannery in Morocco. "He had to do something. He had four kids, and we had to eat," recalls his son, Joseph A. Unanue, now in his 70s. The elder Unanue bought the brand name, Goya, along with the sardines. The name cost an extra dollar. Throughout the years, Unanue added olive oil, olives, and other products the Latino community in America requested. During the 1960s, Goya began canning everything from beans to coconut juice. Today, Goya serves up entire menus of beans, rice, pasta, seasonings, beverages, and a variety of specialties.

On the surface, it might seem to be a simple matter to import and manufacture food products to serve what appears to be a niche community. But it isn't. First, the Latino population, including immigrants and descendants, now accounts for 13 percent of the U.S. population. By 2050, Latinos will make up about 25 percent of the population. Thus, Latino consumer tastes are becoming more and more a part of the mainstream, not to mention a huge segment of purchasing power. Second, there is no such thing as a single Latino population. Although Goya was originally founded to serve consumers of Spanish descent, American Latinos come from a variety of countries, from Puerto Rico and Mexico to Nicaragua and Cuba. Their cultures, family structures, attitudes, and tastes in food are different. "Latinos from different countries eat different foods," notes Andy Unanue, Joseph's son and likely successor as CEO. But Goya is ahead of other marketers in pinpointing the location of different populations. "We know which Latinos are moving into what regions before anybody else," says Andy.

Goya often ends up serving different groups of Latino consumers within the same geographical region. But its marketers know that Cubans prefer black beans, while Nicaraguans want small chili beans and Mexicans will buy pintos. So they provide all three—and more.

Changing roles in Latino families have also reflected a change in purchasing habits, and Goya has adeptly kept up with the times, serving both the young and the old. Latino seniors still want to create their own meals from scratch; they don't want packaged or prepared foods. So Goya offers a full complement of ingredients for this market. But "the younger people are busy, they are used to the microwave, and they want to eat those things they grew up on that they don't have time to make or can't make as well as their mothers," explains Mary Ann. So Goya provides a wide range of rice-and-bean mixes and other foods that can be prepared quickly by working mothers or fathers. The company Web site offers even more help for this new generation: a section with favorite recipes that includes menus for holiday celebrations and other occasions.

By being first to the grocery shelves decades ago, Goya established itself as the premiere Latino food brand, and it has been discovered by more and more non-Latino consumers who are becoming more interested in Latino foods. Moreover, Goya has managed to ward off attempts by larger companies to tread on its turf by simply producing higher-quality, more authentic products. "We firmly believe that Latinos like buying things they consider their own, that are authentic," remarks Andy Unanue. "And we are. We're Latino and we give them authenticity." Not only do Latino consumers prefer Goya's authenticity, but so do non-Latinos. Thus, after failed attempts to introduce their own Latino food lines, giants like Campbell's Soup are trying to compete by purchasing genuine Latino food businesses. Goya is watching carefully.

Goya remains a privately owned business steeped in strong family tradition, with no plans to change the way it operates. Although Goya products generally represent low-involvement purchase decisions, consumers relate strongly to the traditions these products represent. When they fill their shopping carts with Goya rice, olives, and salsa, they feel like members of a community.

Questions for Discussion

1. Evaluate an international expansion strategy for Goya.
2. Should Goya consider entering Latin American markets?
3. What are some of the research issues that Goya needs to consider when tracking Latino subgroups?

SOURCES: Goya Foods Web site, **http://www.goya.com**, accessed 4 March 2000; "Venezuela's Flood Victims Desperately Waiting for Aid," *PR Newswire*, 3 January 2000; Bill Saporito, "Food Fight," *Corporate Board Member*, Autumn 1999, **http://www.boardmember.com**; "Goya Foods," *Hispanic Online*, January/February 1999, **http://www.hispaniconline.com**.

GLOBAL MARKETING AT EVO

The ski and snowboard community is relatively small, so Evo—the Seattle-based snowboard, ski, skateboard, and wakeboard store—is always looking to maximize its exposure, and that means crossing borders and going global. The company started as an online outlet, selling close-outs and used gear to bargain hunters. Over the years, it expanded its offerings to include first-quality new stuff, trips to exotic locales, and a retail store in Seattle.

"There's a ton of really exciting things that happen here at a regional level that have an impact on the global community," says Molly Hawkins, head of marketing and PR at Evo. One of the most effective ways the firm reach its consumers is through advertisements and editorial pieces in the top snow sports magazines. Publications such as *Freeskier Magazine*, *Powder*, and *The Ski Journal* all have international circulations.

International exposure is nice, but selling the gear keeps the lights on. Expertise in e-commerce makes for a fairly easy transition into the global marketplace. Canada, not surprisingly, is one of Evo's largest international markets. "Our daily unique [web visitors] for example, are 64,000 from Canada," notes Molly. The United Kingdom, Germany, Australia, and Korea are also quite big for Evo with daily visitors to their Web sites in the 20,000 range—and that's in July!

But, here's the rub: all of the products Evo sells are name brand items that are for sale in local shops overseas. These brands often restrict the sales of their products to licensed resellers within a particular geographical zone. With the Internet, these rules become quite complicated. Evo can't stop someone in Japan from placing an order. The firm is working with its resellers to come up with a way to honor the contracts but still serve customers everywhere.

The world of business is becoming increasingly borderless, but there are still cultural issues to grapple with. Marketing is a particularly difficult thing to do globally. If language were the only hurdle, it would be fairly simple to translate. Unfortunately, even among English-speaking nations, cultural subtleties and colloquialisms can turn an innocent euphemism into a deeply offensive word. "I work with a lot of our vendors in marketing, looking for ways to co-promote their products through Evo," says Molly. "Like Rossignol, based out of Europe. Its business style and its designs and branding and marketing ideas are definitely, different." Molly and her staff tend to leave the marketing of the company pretty generic. Their main propositions: best brands, best prices, and a top-notch knowledge base really know no boundaries.

Evo has extended its commitment to a boundaryless world by offering extreme skiing and boarding expeditions to some of the world's most incredible destinations. "EvoTrip is such a natural extension of the Evo brand," says Bryce Phillips, Evo's founder, "and we're doing it with great activities—skiing, snowboarding, surfing."

"EvoTrip is definitely unique," says Molly. "There are other companies that are doing something similar, but our product is a little different in that we take people on extreme trips that people like Bryce and people here at Evo have actually been on. They know the intricacies of getting around these areas and so we offer experience. Our guys have that insider info, that connection."

"The reason why I get so excited about this concept is that it is near and dear to what all of us value," says Phillips. "It's just like, getting out there, learning more about different cultures, doing the activities in different parts of the world and seeing beautiful locations you might never have seen before." Through a partnership with online travel site JustFares.com—and local guides and professional athletes in each country—Evo will offer trips to South America, Japan, Indonesia, Switzerland, and many more locations. It's not all about the adventure, of course; sound business is behind it all. Every trip allows Evo's "ambassadors" to get in front of their potential customers in each of the countries they visit. No translations. No miscommunications. No boundaries.

Questions for Discussion

1. Why doesn't Evo need to tailor its marketing to different countries? Do you agree with their decision to present one marketing message? Why or why not?

2. What challenges do e-commerce companies face when selling their products abroad? Do you believe brands have the right to limit a company's right to sell internationally?

SOURCE: Video case (of the same name) from Louis E. Boone and David L. Kurtz, *Contemporary Marketing*, 14th ed. (Mason, OH: South-Western Cengage Learning, 2010), VC 7–8.

PART FOUR

VIDEO CASES

WHIRLPOOL AND THE GLOBAL APPLIANCE INDUSTRY

Within a few months after becoming CEO of Whirlpool Corp., David Whitwam met with his senior managers to plot a strategy for securing future company growth. At the time, Whirlpool was the market leader among U.S. appliance makers, but it generated only weak sales outside North America. Operating in a mature market, it faced the same low profit margins as major competitors like General Electric and Maytag. In addition to price wars, especially in mature markets, the industry had started to consolidate, and consumers were demanding more environmentally friendly products.

Whirlpool and Its Options

Whitwam and his management team explored several growth options, including diversifying into other industries experiencing more rapid growth, such as furniture or garden products; restructuring the company financially; and expanding vertically and horizontally. The group sharpened its focus to consider opportunities for expanding the appliance business beyond North American markets. After all, the basics of managing the appliance business and the product technologies are similar in Europe, North America, Asia, and Latin America. As Whitwam put it, "We were very good at what we did. What we needed was to enter appliance markets in other parts of the world and learn how to satisfy different kinds of customers."

Whirlpool industry data predicted that, over time, appliance manufacturing would become a global industry. As Whitwam saw it, his company had three options: "We could ignore the inevitable—a decision that would have condemned Whirlpool to a slow death. We could wait for globalization to begin and then try to react, which would have put us in a catch-up mode, technologically and organizationally. Or we could control our own destiny and try to shape the very nature of globalization in our industry. In short, we could force our competitors to respond to us."

Whitwam and his team chose the third option and set out on a mission to make Whirlpool "one company worldwide." They aimed much higher than simply marketing products or operating around the globe. For decades,

Whirlpool had sold some appliances in other countries to buyers who could afford them. Whitwam wanted to expand this reach by establishing a vision of a company that could leverage global resources to gain a long-term competitive advantage. In his words, this effort meant "having the best technologies and processes for designing, manufacturing, selling, and servicing your products at the lowest possible costs. Our vision at Whirlpool is to integrate our geographical businesses wherever possible, so that our most advanced expertise in any given area—whether it's refrigeration technology or distribution strategy—isn't confined to one location or one division. We want to be able to take the best capabilities we have and leverage them in all of our operations worldwide."

As its first step in transforming a largely domestic operation into a global powerhouse, Whirlpool purchased the European appliance business of Dutch consumer-goods giant, Philips Electronics. Philips had been losing market share for years, running its European operations as independent regional companies that made different appliances for individual markets. "When we bought this business," Whitwam recalls, "we had two automatic washer designs, one built in Italy and one built in Germany. If you as a consumer looked at them, they were basically the same machines. But there wasn't anything common about those two machines. There wasn't even a common screw."

The Whirlpool strategy called for reversing the decline in European market share and improving profitability by changing product designs and manufacturing processes and by switching to centralized purchasing. The change reorganized the national design and research staffs inherited from Philips into European product teams that worked closely with Whirlpool's U.S. designers. Redesigned models shared more parts, and inventory costs fell when Whirlpool consolidated warehouses from 36 to 8. The transformation

SOURCES: This case was compiled by Ilkka Ronkainen. Portions of this case were researched from material available at **http://www .whirlpool.com**. The Global Success Factors section is derived from a report on the global appliance industry by John Bonds, German Estrada, Peter Jacobs, JorgeHarb-Kallab, Paul Kunzer, and Karin Toth at Georgetown University, March 2000. See also Ilkka A. Ronkainen and Ivan Menezes, "Implementing Global Marketing Strategy," *International Marketing Review* 13 (no. 3, 1996): 56–63; and "The Right Way to Go Global: An Interview with Whirlpool CEO David Whitwam," *Harvard Business Review* 72 (March–April 1994): 134–145.

trimmed Philips's list of 1,600 suppliers by 50 percent, and it converted the national operations to regional companies.

Whitwam believed that the drive to become one company worldwide required making Whirlpool a global brand—a formidable task in Europe, where the name was not well-known. The company rebranded the Philips product lines, supported by a $135 million pan-European advertising campaign that initially presented both the Philips and Whirlpool names and eventually converted to Whirlpool alone.

Another important component of the Whirlpool global strategy—product innovation—sought to develop superior products based on consumer needs and wants. "We have to provide a compelling reason other than price for consumers to buy Whirlpool-built products," says Whitwam. "We can do that only by understanding the consumer better than anyone else does and then translating our understanding into clearly superior product designs, features, and after-sales support. Our goal is for consumers to prefer the Whirlpool brand because it offers greater overall value than competing products."

One successful product innovation led to the Whirlpool Crispwave microwave oven. Extensive research with European consumers revealed a desire for a microwave that could brown and crisp food. In response, Whirlpool engineers designed the VIP Crispwave, which can fry crispy bacon and cook a pizza with a crisp crust. The new microwave proved successful in Europe, and Whirlpool later introduced it in the United States.

Whirlpool's global strategy includes a goal to become the market leader in Asia, which will be the world's largest appliance market in the twenty-first century. In 1988, it began setting up sales and distribution systems in Asia to help it serve Asian markets and to make the firm more familiar with those markets and potential customers. The company established three regional offices: one in Singapore to serve Southeast Asia, a second in Hong Kong to handle the Chinese market, and a Tokyo office for Japan. Through careful analysis, Whirlpool marketers sought to match specific current products with Asian consumers. They studied existing and emerging trade channels and assessed the relative strengths and weaknesses of competitors in the Asian markets. The company set up joint ventures with five Asian manufacturers for four appliance lines with the highest market potential: refrigerators, washers, air conditioners, and microwave ovens. With a controlling interest in each of the joint ventures, the newly global company confidently expects to excel in the world's fastest-growing market.

Whirlpool has come a long way since embarking on its global strategy. By 2000, revenues had doubled to more than $10 billion. The company now reaches markets in more than 170 countries, leading the markets in both North America and Latin America. Whirlpool is number three in Europe and the largest Western appliance company in Asia. For building its integrated global network, "Whirlpool gets very high marks," says an industry analyst. "They are outpacing the industry dramatically."

Global Success Factors

From a global perspective, there are two success factors that affect all of the different geographic regions. The first key success factor on a global scale is successful branding. Each of the large global manufacturers has been very successful in developing a branding strategy. Most of these players sell a variety of brands, where each is targeted to certain quality and price levels. In addition, the strong brand reputation has been necessary for the major manufacturers either to expand operations into new regions or to launch new product lines. For example, Maytag did not have a line of products in the dishwasher category but had a large brand presence in the washer/dryer category. To expand its product line, Maytag decided to launch a new line of products in the dishwasher segment. Through a successful branding campaign, in less than two years Maytag captured the second-largest market share in the segment. It leveraged its successful brand image in one segment to quickly steal share from less successful competitors.

The second key success factor on a global scale is price sensitivity. Given the large cost of these goods, large-scale manufacturers have been able to lower prices to meet the demand of customers. While there is little price elasticity, some manufacturers have been able to raise prices on their high-end goods, but for the most part, most manufacturers have lowered prices, and thus margins, to stay competitive with other brands. With razor-thin margins across each segment, only manufacturers that have the size to realize economies of scale have been able to remain competitive and lower prices to meet demands of their customers. This price sensitivity and the need to continually lower prices made up one of the major forces driving the consolidation within the industry. Many smaller brands were not able to compete and therefore were sold to the larger appliance brands.

China and Asia

Aside from the global key success factors, two key success factors within China and Asia are very important. First, appliance manufacturers must have access to distribution channels and therefore the ability to provide the products across several different Chinese regions. The access to Chinese distribution channels can be very limiting for international corporations, whereas China-based companies, such as Kelon and Haier, have a definite competitive advantage.

Second, large appliance manufacturers must have a large scope of products for success. Specifically, it is the number of different segments in which a company sells products that will lead to success in China, not the scope of products within a given segment. Kelon manufactures 112 different types of air conditioners, but it is not a full-line supplier of appliances to its customers. Contrarily, Haier is a full-line supplier that manufactures products in each product segment and so provides its customers with a variety of appliances under one brand name.

The Japanese market has a different set of criteria for success than China and the rest of Asia. Instead, the Japanese market closely resembles certain aspects of the European and U.S. markets. Aside from the global success factors, success in the Japanese market is based on two key factors. First, due to the size of dwellings in Japan, innovation with regard to product size is very important. Japanese customers are looking for product innovations that will fit into smaller spaces while providing the most use of cabinet space. Second, to be successful in Japan, a manufacturer must sell a product that is very high in quality. Japanese customers are very demanding in regard to product quality, and they expect their products to last decades. Therefore, manufacturers selling products that are very high in quality will have a competitive advantage.

United States

Within the United States, two key success factors outside of the global factors are necessary for a company's success. First, a company must develop innovative products that incorporate new features while still operating efficiently. U.S. customers are very aware that energy consumption of a product will have a long-term effect on their utility bills, so they look for products that operate more efficiently. In addition, customers are willing to pay a premium for innovative features on a high-end product. Many manufacturers were surprised that Maytag was able to raise its prices for its front-loading washer not once, but twice. Customers were not as concerned with the price as they were concerned with the convenience of the product.

The second key success factor within the U.S. market is product quality, in respect to durability. U.S. consumers are willing to pay more for a product, but they expect it to operate for well over a decade with little to no maintenance. Therefore, for an appliance manufacturer to succeed in the United States, it must deliver products that are of high quality and of innovative design.

Europe

Outside of the two global success factors, the European market has two distinct factors that are required for success. First, to succeed in Europe, manufacturers must develop innovative products. In this context, innovative products are defined as products that are efficient and environmentally friendly. The "green" movement within Europe is very strong, and therefore a manufacturer that does not sell "eco-products" will not succeed when compared to a company that offers that type of product.

Second, quality is a key success factor for Europe. Similar to other markets, in this context quality refers to durability. European consumers are looking for products that are durable and will last over a long period of time. In this regard, the European market is very similar to the U.S., Japanese, and Latin American markets.

Latin America

Within Latin America, there are two additional success factors for a manufacturer to consider outside the global success factors. First, Latin American companies that provide excellent service to customers will have an advantage over the competition. The amount of time that the average consumer owns an appliance in Latin America is somewhat longer than in other global regions, so consumers are looking for excellent service. The economy in Latin America has had several challenges in recent history, and so consumers would much rather repair an existing product than buy a new appliance.

Second, quality is another success factor for Latin America. This key success factor ties directly into the service success factor. Initially, Latin Americans are looking for a durable product that will last for over a decade; then through customer service, the product will be repaired to extend its life for several more years.

Questions for Discussion

1. Whirlpool's marketing goal is to leverage resources across borders. How is this evident in its marketing approach? Consult http://www.whirlpool.com for additional information.

2. The challenge facing Whirlpool is not only external in catering to local customers' needs worldwide, but also internal—all the regional and local units have to "buy in" to the global vision. What types of particular issues (such as product or technology transfers) may arise, and how should they be dealt with?

3. Visit the Web site of the Association of Home Appliance Manufacturers, http://www.aham.org, and suggest some of the global trends among the major manufacturers of household appliances.

ESPN'S WORLDWIDE REACH

It began by mistake. Back in the late 1970s, Bill Rasmussen decided to launch a cable station to broadcast Connecticut-area sports. With the assistance of his partners, Rasmussen leased a building in Bristol from which to broadcast and then bought some satellite time. Only after signing the agreement did he learn that his satellite coverage was national—and his small-scale plan of New England sports coverage began to grow. The early name for the channel—Entertainment and Sports Programming Network—proved too much of a tongue twister and, in 1985, they settled on the ESPN acronym as the corporate name. The letters now stand for nothing—except a sports phenomenon.

Since those early days during which the network scrambled to televise whatever it could—from a men's pro, slow-pitch softball game to its first NHL game in 1979—the organization has grown dramatically, filling what Will Burkhardt of ESPN says is now a saturated market for televised sports in the United States and rapidly moving overseas. "We reach 150 to 155 million households around the world [excluding the United States]; that encompasses about 180 markets and territories," says Burkhardt. ESPN reaches all seven continents, including one of the scientific stations located in Antarctica. The expansion has taken place over the last 15 years, beginning when ESPN provided groundbreaking coverage of the America's Cup international sailing race from Australia in 1987. That race seemed to be a turning point not only for ESPN, but for cable broadcasting itself. From there, ESPN purchased a majority interest in the European Sports Network (called Eurosport) and began service to 25 Middle Eastern and North African nations. In addition to its Eurosport market, ESPN's largest international markets have become China, India, and Argentina.

Burkhardt notes that ESPN entered the international marketplace because of a "desire to grow outside of the U.S. borders and to take what we had learned in the United States in terms of people's passion for sport . . . and bring that to the international marketplace." This was around the same time that cable and satellite television were expanding around the world, so ESPN's timing seemed perfect.

However, marketing around the world isn't easy. For instance, although India has a huge middle-class population, middle class in that country means that a family might earn about $1,800 per year, as opposed to an American middle-class family's earnings of $35,000 per year. Thus, attracting viewers to pay for television is more difficult in India. In addition, the infrastructure for cable television is very different from that of the United States, which requires more effort for ESPN marketers. India has tens of thousands of cable entrepreneurs serving approximately 100 customers each, instead of a giant like AOL Time Warner, which serves 13 million. Still, ESPN thinks that serving India is worth the effort and tailors its programming to the single most-watched sport in the nation: cricket.

In the burgeoning South American markets, where sports fanatics thrive, viewers can watch all kinds of programming—Argentine rugby, Argentine polo, Brazilian basketball, and Brazilian tennis, to name a few. But Burkhardt emphasizes that ESPN starts with a regional marketing strategy, "building a bed of programming from which you then start to localize." Currently, most broadcasts are in English or the local language, but dealing with some countries' multiple local dialects is extremely difficult. In addition, consumers in smaller markets want to see broadcasters of their own nationality instead of ESPN's standard crew of broadcasters. "There is no question that people in Mexico would prefer all of our commentators to be Mexican, instead of some who are Argentine," remarks Burkhardt. ESPN simply can't afford to provide this degree of customization yet.

Ultimately, ESPN's goal is to reach as many households worldwide as possible, despite any difficulties in penetrating new markets. For example, the company landed a huge deal that gave it distribution rights in Latin America for all four rounds of the Masters Golf Tournament. ESPN Latin America alone is now distributed in more than 11 million households in 41 countries and territories, broadcasting in English, Spanish, and Portuguese.

In spite of victories like the Masters broadcast, perhaps one of the greatest challenges to ESPN is that the company must, in large part, make its pitch to cable and satellite television operators before its programming ever reaches the consumers themselves. Those operators conduct business in different ways, they lack rating systems, and some even replace ESPN programming with homegrown shows. Then there are political challenges, such as when ESPN was thrown off Chinese cable after the United States mistakenly bombed a Chinese embassy in Eastern Europe. And there are legal tangles in each country that need to be dealt with, as well. But sports is an international language that tries to provide entertainment without political ramifications, and people everywhere love to watch. "We're obviously not trying to promote any kind of political message through showing an American baseball game," says Burkhardt. And perhaps that is the key to ESPN's success—its ability to bring sport to everyone, everywhere, anytime.

SOURCES: Telephone interview with Will Burkhardt of ESPN, January 2000; "TV Listings," 8 February 2000, **http://www.espn.go.com**; "ESPN International Lands Masters for Latin America," company press release, 11 November 1999, **http://www.espn.go.com**; Michael Hiestand, "Did You Know? ESPN is 20 Today," USA Today, 7 September 1999, **http://www.usatoday.com**; "Looking Back, Back, Back...," company press release, 6 September 1999, **http://www.espn .go.com**; Rudy Martzke, "ESPN at 20," USA Today, 18 August 1999, 2c.

Questions for Discussion

1. How have environmental forces affected ESPN's worldwide marketing efforts?

2. Why is it important for ESPN to be global? What might be some barriers to trade for ESPN?

3. How would you describe ESPN's global marketing strategy?

4. Search ESPN's Web site at http://www.espn.go.com and summarize what it is doing in international markets.

BP: BEYOND PETROLEUM

Nearly a decade ago, two of the world's energy giants merged: British Petroleum and Amoco became BP. Consolidating the two organizations—and the two brands—was a massive undertaking. Getting the message out to the public that this was a new company with a new image was part of the marketing objective. With rising energy prices, public perception of oil companies in general has had its ups and downs, so BP marketers had their work cut out for them. But the merger offered the perfect opportunity to create a fresh image in consumers' minds.

Instead of focusing on selling products, BP marketers went straight to selling a new perception of the company itself by launching an ad campaign called "BP on the Street." "When you undertake an image campaign, it's critical that you know what you want to do," says BP spokesperson Kathy Leech. "We had two tasks. The first was informative. We had to let people know who BP was. The second was positioning. The goal was to lift BP from the negative aura that surrounds energy companies in the mind of the public. We positioned ourselves as a different kind of energy company."

The tag line of the new campaign was catchy: "Beyond Petroleum." But it also conveyed the message that BP is more than a company that sells fossil fuels. BP is interested in doing more than filling consumers' gas tanks. In fact, BP is willing to face head on some of the tough questions concerning the energy industry. "It is the responsibility of an energy company to provide heat, light, and mobility to people. But you have to recognize that there are environmental costs," says Leech. "And you have a responsibility to mitigate those effects as much as possible." BP was the first large energy company to acknowledge the existence of global warming and to take steps to reduce the impact of its operations on the environment. The firm has invested in new sources of energy such as solar and hydrogen, research in climate change, and energy security. These programs are featured in the advertising campaign, explaining to consumers why these activities are important to everyone.

If one part of the challenge is to make people aware of the new BP brand as well as its name, another part is to get them to relate to the message. So BP marketers created advertisements featuring real people voicing their concerns about energy issues. "The big issue in any sort of advertising is that people are cynical," admits Kathy Leech. "They are especially cynical about oil companies. By using real people [in the ads], speaking in unscripted situations, we hoped to cut through some of that cynicism."

The ads were originally launched in a few selected cities—Chicago; New York; Washington, D.C.; and London. The idea was to test some local markets and observe how viewers responded to the message. Although consumers liked the underlying principle, the ads were not wildly popular. "The first year, the ads came across as too negative," says Kathy Leech. "Consumers don't like negative advertising." So BP marketers went back to the drawing board and fine-tuned the ads. "The ads are now provocative without being negative," Leech continues. "Also, we are seeking a partnership with consumers. Rather than focusing on what BP is doing, we try to focus on what we can do together." BP has refined its ad campaign further, now targeting an audience that it refers to as opinion holders—those who vote, who follow decisions made by Congress, who may even write to their representatives. "You can't reach everyone," Leech explains. "Instead, we target people who are more informed, who other people go to for their information."

As the "BP on the Street" campaign moved from local advertising outlets to national and eventually international media, targeting its audience became even more important because it allowed BP to better monitor its advertising costs. The cost of advertising rises tremendously as media outlets expand. Despite this expansion, however, BP makes local adaptations wherever necessary. Leech notes that American consumers are receptive to British accents, but British consumers don't respond well to American speakers in commercials. German consumers don't care for "person on the street" ads, so BP creates an "expert on the street."

Because of the high cost of an advertising campaign, and because conveying the right message is so crucial, BP marketers track the progress of "BP on the Street" carefully. "We do what is called a key learning summary at the end of each period," says Leech. "We've made adjustments based on what we learn. For example, last year we found that we were presenting too many messages. So we scaled back."

Moving beyond petroleum is essential for an energy firm like BP to compete in the 21st century. As the firm transforms itself to meet new challenges, it also changes the messages it transmits to the public.

SOURCES: **http://www.bp.com**, accessed June 6, 2009; "Ogilvy Wins BP CO$_2$ Reduction Drive," *Marketing Week*, August 24, 2006, **http://www.mad.co.uk**; Wendy Melillo and Steve Miller, "Companies Find It's Not Easy Marketing Green," *Brandweek*, July 24, 2006, **http://www.brandweek.com**.

Questions for Discussion

1. What are the objectives of the "BP on the Street" advertising campaign? How would you categorize the campaign?

2. Would celebrity advertising be as effective for "BP on the Street" as the use of average citizens? Why or why not? If BP decided to include a celebrity spokesperson in its campaign, whom would you suggest and why?

3. What role do the "BP on the Street" advertisements play in BP's public relations efforts—domestic and international?

Chapter 1

1. Robert W. Armstrong and Jill Sweeney, "Industrial Type, Culture, Mode of Entry, and Perceptions of International Marketing Ethics Problems: A Cross-Culture Comparison," *Journal of Business Ethics* 13, 10: 775–785.

2. World Trade Organization, http://www.wto .org, Statistics Database, accessed November 20, 2008.

3. CIA, *The World Factbook,* http://www.cia. gov/cia/publications/factbook/index.html, accessed November 21, 2008.

4. UNEP 2005 (quoted in http://student.ulb .ac.be/~nroeck/index_files/Page2550.html), accessed October 17, 2005.

5. Mineral Management Services Report, http://www.mms.gov/ooc/press/2005/ press1031.htm, accessed November 22, 2008.

6. Eugene H. Fram and Riad Ajami, "Globalization of Markets and Shopping Stress: Cross-Country Comparisons," *Business Horizons* (January–February 1994): 17–23.

7. John J. Sviokla and Jeffrey F. Rayport, "Mapping the Marketspace: Information Technology and the New Marketing Environment," *Harvard Business School Bulletin* 71 (June 1995): 49–51.

8. Kaplan, E. and Teslik, L., Foreign Ownership of U.S. Infrastructure, Council on Foreign Relations, updated February 13, 2007.

9. Michael R. Czinkota and Sarah McCue, *The STAT-USA Companion to International Business,* Economics and Statistics Administration (U.S. Department of Commerce, Washington, DC, 2001), 16.

10. Peter R. Dickson and Michael R. Czinkota, "How the U.S. Can Be Number One Again: Resurrecting the Industrial Policy Debate," *The Columbia Journal of World Business* 31, 3 (Fall 1996): 76–87.

11. Howard Lewis III and J. David Richardson, *Why Global Commitment Really Matters* (Washington, DC: Institute for International Economics, 2001).

12. World Trade Organization, http://www.wto .org/english/thewto_e/minist_e/min99_e/ english/about_e/22fact_e.htm, accessed November 22, 2008.

13. Michael R., Czinkota, "Freedom and International Marketing: Janis Joplin's Candidacy as Patron of the Field," *Thunderbird International Business Review,* 47 (1), January–February 2005: 1–13.

14. *Cognetics,* Cambridge, MA, 1993.

15. Small & Medium-Sized Exporting Companies: Statistical Overview, 2003, http://ita.doc.gov/td/industry/otea/sme_ handbook/SME_index.htm, accessed December 1, 2008.

16. Michael Kutschker, "Internationalisierung der Wirtschaft," *Perspektiven der Internationalen Wirtschaft,* Wiesbaden, Gabler GmbH, 1999: 22.

Chapter 1 Appendix

1. American Marketing Association, Definition of Marketing, www.marketingpower.com, accessed Nov. 20, 2008.

2. Czinkota Michael R. and Masaaki Kotabe, *Marketing Management* (3rd ed.), (Cincinnati: Atomic Dog Publishing, 2005), 4–5.

3. Philip Kotler presents the eight Os in the eighth edition of *Marketing Management: Analysis, Planning, and Control* (Englewood Cliffs, NJ: Prentice-Hall, 1994), 174–175.

4. The four Ps were popularized originally by E. Jerome McCarthy. See William Perreault, Jr., Joseph Cannon and E. Jerome McCarthy, *Basic Marketing* 17th ed. (Burr Ridge, IL: Irwin/ McGraw-Hill, 2009).

5. Bert Rosenbloom, *Marketing Channels: A Management View,* 7th ed. custom (Mason, OH: Thomson Business & Professional Publishing, 2005.)

6. Robert Bartels, "Are Domestic and International Marketing Dissimilar?" *Journal of Marketing* 36 (July 1968): 56–61.

Chapter 2

1. Global Business Policy Council, *Globalization Ledger* (Washington, DC: A. T. Kearney, 2000), 3.

2. C. K. Prahalad and Stuart L. Hart, "The Fortune at the Bottom of the Pyramid," *Strategy and Business* (first quarter, 2002): 35–47.

3. www2.goldmansachs.com/ideas/brics/book/ BRICs-Chapter9.pdf.

4. "African Debt, European Doubt," *Economist,* April 8, 2000, 46.

5. "Who Will Join Europe's Club—and When?" *Economist,* April 8, 2000, 53–54.

6. Rahul Jacob, "The Big Rise," *Fortune,* May 30, 1994, 74–90.

7. Roger D. Blackwell, Paul W. Miniard, and James F. Engel, *Consumer Behavior* (Mason, OH: Thomson, 2001), 283.

8. *European Marketing Data and Statistics 2001* (London: Euromonitor, 2002), 380.

9. The World Bank, *World Development Indicators* (Washington, DC, 2000), 85. See also http://www.worldbank.org/data/ wdi2000.

10. "In India, Luxury Is Within Reach of Many," *The Wall Street Journal,* October 17, 1995, A17.

11. "Go West Westerners," *Business Week,* November 14, 2005, 60–61; and "A Booming Coast Breathes New Life into China's Inland," *The Wall Street Journal,* October 17, 2005, A1, A14.

12. Edward Tse, "The Right Way to Achieve Profitable Growth in the Chinese Market," *Strategy and Business* (second quarter, 1998): 10–21.

13. http://www.cellular-news.com/story/33811 .php.

14. "The Mobile Revolution: Global Scale is Critical," *Businessline,* January 10, 2006, 1; Tony Dennis, "Two Billion Mobile Phone Mark Reached," *The Inquirer,* September 18, 2005, available at http://www.theinquirer .net.

15. *Internet Domain Survey,* January 2008, available at http://www.isc.org.

16. http://www.internetworldstats.com/stats9 .htm.

17. "The Mad Grab for Piece of Air," *Business Week,* April 17, 2000, 152–154; and "Hello, Internet," *Business Week,* May 3, 1999, 170–175.

18. Jesse Berst, "It's Back: How Interactive TV Is Sneaking Back into Your Living Room," available at http://www.zdnet.com/ anchordesk/story/story_3368.html. See also, http://www.visiongain.com.

19. Rahul Jacob, "Asian Infrastructure: The Biggest Bet on Earth," *Fortune,* October 31, 1994, 139–150.

20. Global Business Policy Council, *Globalization Ledger* (Washington, DC: A.T. Kearney, April 2000).

21. Ben Crow and Alan Thomas, *Third World Atlas* (Milton Keynes, England: Open University Press, 1984), 85.

22. The World Bank, *World Development Report 1982* (New York: Oxford University Press, 1982), 63.

23. Ed Diener and Eunkook Suh, eds., *Culture and Subjective Well- Being,* (Boston: MIT Press, 2003), chapter 1; and "In Bhutan, Happiness is King," *The Wall Street Journal,* October 13, 2004, A14.

24. Ilkka A. Ronkainen, "Trading Blocs: Opportunity or Demise for International Trade?" *Multinational Business Review* 1 (Spring 1993): 1–9.

25. *The European Union: A Guide for Americans* (Washington, DC: Delegation of the European Commission to the United States, 2006), chapter 2. See http://www.eurunion. org/infores/euguide/euguide.htm.

26. See http://secretariat.efta.int.

27. "Nokia Closes Bochum, But Opens Cluj Factory," *Softpedia News,* January 15, 2008, available at http://news.softpedia.com.

28. "For U.S. Small Biz, Fertile Soil in Europe," *Business Week,* April 1, 2002, 55–56.

29. Gary C. Hufbauer and Jeffrey J. Schott, *NAFTA: An Eight-Year Appraisal* (Washington, DC: Institute for International Economics, 2003), Chapter 1.

30. Sidney Weintraub, *NAFTA at Three: A Progress Report* (Washington, DC: Center for Strategic and International Studies, 1997), 17–18.

31. John Cavanagh, Sarah Anderson, Jaime Serra, and J. Enrique Espinosa, "Happily Ever NAFTA," *Foreign Policy,* September/ October 2002, 58–65.

32. For annual trade information, see http://www.census.gov/foreign-trade.

33. "U.S. Trade with Mexico during the Third NAFTA Year," *International Economic Review* (Washington, DC: International Trade Commission, April 1997): 11.

34. "Fox and Bush, for Richer, for Poorer," *The Economist,* February 3, 2001, 37–38.

35. "Aerospace Suppliers Gravitate to Mexico," *The Wall Street Journal,* January 23, 2002, A17.

36. Laura Heller, "The Latin Market Never Looked So Bueno," *DSN Retailing Today,* June 10, 2002, 125–126.

37. "Retail Oasis," *Business Mexico,* April 2001, 15.

38. http://ec.europa.eu/external_relations/mexico/index_en.htm.

39. See, for example, http://www.crea-inc.org and http://www.maquilasolidarity.org.

40. "Americas: Critics Aside, Nafta Has Been a Boon To Mexico," *The Wall Street Journal,* January 9, 2004, A.11; and "NAFTA's Scorecard: So Far, So Good," *Business Week,* July 9, 2001, 54–56.

41. "Hogtied," *The Economist,* January 17, 2002, 35.

42. "Localizing Production," *Global Commerce,* August 20, 1997, 1.

43. "Latin America Fears Stagnation in Trade Talks with the United States," *The New York Times,* April 19, 1998, D1.

44. "Mexico, EU Sign Free-Trade Agreement," *The Wall Street Journal,* March 24, 2000, A15.

45. "Latin Lesson," *Far Eastern Economic Review,* January 4, 2001, 109.

46. Gilberto Meza, "Is the FTAA Floundering?" *Business Mexico,* February 2005, 46–48.

47. "The Americas: A Cautious Yes to Pan-American Trade," *The Economist,* April 28, 2001, 35–36.

48. "Regional Commonalities Help Global Ad Campaigns Succeed in Latin America," *Business International,* February 17, 1992, 47–52; and "Ripping Down the Walls across the Americas," *Business Week,* December 26, 1994, 78–80.

49. Michael R. Czinkota and Masaaki Kotabe, "America's New World Trade Order," *Marketing Management* 1 (Summer 1992): 49–56.

50. http://www.apec.org/apec/about_apec/scope_of_work.html.

51. "Afrabet Soup," *The Economist,* February 10, 2001, 77.

52. "Try, Try Again," *The Economist,* July 13, 2002, 41.

53. Josh Martin, "Gulf States to Adopt a Single Currency," *Middle East,* May 2002, 23–25.

54. Eric Friberg, Risto Perttunen, Chris tian Caspar, and Dan Pittard, "The Challenges of Europe 1992," *The McKinsey Quarterly* 21 (no. 2, 1988): 3–15.

55. "Lean, Mean, European," *The Economist,* April 29, 2000, 5–7.

56. Gianluigi Guido, "Implementing a Pan-European Marketing Strategy," *Long Range Planning* 24 (no. 5, 1991): 23–33.

57. "EU and US Approaches to Lobbying," *Euractiv.com,* February 15, 2005.

58. http://www.emdirectory.com.

59. James A. Gingrich, "Five Rules for Winning Emerging Market Consumers," *Strategy and Business* (second quarter, 1999): 19–33.

60. "GE Pins Hopes on Emerging Markets," *The Wall Street Journal,* March 2, 2005, A3, A10.

61. "Kremlin Blocks Big Acquisition by Siemens AG," *The Wall Street Journal,* April 14, 2005, A14, A16.

62. "China Seeks Its Own High-tech Standards," *CNN.com,* May 27, 2004; and "Despite Shelving WAPI, China Stands Firm on Chip Tax," *InfoWorld,* April 22, 2004.

63. "In Brazil, Thicket of Red Tape Spoils Recipe for Growth," *The Wall Street Journal,* May 24, 2005, A1, A9.

64. "China's Power Brands," *Business Week,* November 8, 2004, 77–84.

65. "The High-tech Threat from China," *Business Week,* January 31, 2005, 22.

66. "Let the Retail Wars Begin," *Business Week,* January 17, 2005, 44–45.

67. Guillermo D'Andrea, E. Alejandro Stengel, and Anne Goebel-Krstelj, "Six Truths About Emerging-Market Consumers," *Strategy and Business* 34 (Spring 2004): 58–69.

68. This section builds on Tarun Khanna, Krishna Palepu, and Jayant Sinha, "Strategies that Fit Emerging Markets," *Harvard Business Review* 83 (June 2005): 63–76 and James A. Gingrich, "Five Rules for Winning Emerging Market Consumers," *Strategy and Business* (second quarter, 1999): 19–33.

69. "Investing in Russia: A Symbiotic Process," *The Official Website of the 8th Annual U.S. Russian Investment Symposium,* June 27, 2001, available at http://www.uris.com.

70. "Dell Unveils New Computers Targeting Emerging Markets," *Marketing News,* September 15, 2008, 32.

71. "GM and VW: How Not to Succeed in China," *Business Week,* May 9, 2005, 94.

72. Orit Gadiesh, Philip Leung, and Til Vestring, "The Battle for China's Good-Enough Market," *Harvard Business Review* 85 (September 2007): 81–89.

73. "Cracking China's Market," *The Wall Street Journal,* January 9, 2003, B1, B4.

74. http://en.wahaha.com.cn/news/company/2005/06/03/wahaha750.html.

75. The World Bank considers $2,000 to be the minimum to sustain a decent life.

76. Dana James, "B2-4B Spells Profits," *Marketing News,* November 5, 2001, 1, 11–12.

77. http://www.hp.com/e-inclusion/en.

78. This framework is adapted from C. K. Prahalad and Stuart L. Hart, "The Fortune at the Bottom of the Pyramid," *Strategy and Business,* First Quarter, 2002, 35–47.

79. "Cell Phones Reshaping Africa," *CNN.com,* October 17, 2005; "Calling Across the Divide," *The Economist,* March 12, 2005, 74.

80. "Major victories for micro-finance," *Financial Times,* May 18, 2005, 10. See also http://www.planetfinance.org.

81. Cait Murphy, "The Hunt for Globalization That Works," *Fortune,* October 28, 2002, 163–176.

82. "And the Winners Are…," *The Economist,* September 18, 2004, 17; "The Digital Village," *Business Week,* June 28, 2004, 60–62; and Arundhati Parmar, "Indian Farmers Reap Web Harvest," *Marketing News,* June 1, 2004, 27, 31.

83. "Making the Web Worldwide," *The Economist,* September 28, 2004, 76.

84. "Laptop Program for Kids in Poor Countries Teams Up with Microsoft Windows," *Wall Street Journal,* May 16, 2008, B1.

85. "Cell Phones for the People," *Business Week,* November 14, 2005, 65.

86. C. K. Prahalad and Allen Hammond, "Serving the World's Poor, Profitably," *Harvard Business Review,* 80 (September 2002): 48–59.

87. "Drinks for Developing Countries," *The Wall Street Journal,* November 27, 2001, B1, B3.

Chapter 3

1. Henri Pirenne, *Economic and Social History of Medieval Europe* (New York: Harcourt, Brace, and World, 1933), 142–146.

2. Margaret P. Doxey, *Economic Sanctions and International Enforcement* (New York: Oxford University Press, 1980), 10.

3. Russian News and Information Agency, http://en.rian.ru, accessed November 23, 2008.

4. Thomas R. Graham, "Global Trade: War and Peace," *Foreign Policy* (Spring 1983): 124–137.

5. World Trade Organization, http://www.wto.org, accessed November 21, 2008.

6. WTO Trade Policy Review of the United States 2001, WTO Secretariat Summary, Press Release, September 17, 2001. http://www.wto.org/wto, accessed September 3, 2002.

7. *Business Guide to the Uruguay Round,* International Trade Centre and Commonwealth Secretariat, Geneva, 1995. http://www.intracen.org.

8. Michael R. Czinkota, "The World Trade Organization—Perspectives and Prospects," *Journal of International Marketing* 3 (no. 1, 1995): 85–92.

9. www.wto.org, accessed November 23, 2008.

10. IMF Backs Poverty Debt Write-off, BBC News, December 21, 2005, http://news.bbc.co.uk/2/hi/business/4550778.stm, accessed December 22, 2005.

11. IMF to launch new facility for emerging markets hit by crisis, International Monetary Fund, Washington D.C., October 29, 2008.

12. World Bank, Global Monitoring Report, Washington D.C., 2008.

13. Mordechai E. Kreinin, *International Economics: A Policy Approach,* 5th ed. (New York: Harcourt Brace Jovanovich, 1987), 12.

14. Lum, T. and Dick Nanto, *China's Trade with the United States and the World*, CRS Report to Congress, January 4, 2007.

15. Kreinin, *International Economics*, 6.

16. Gary Knight, and S. Tamer Cavusgil, "Innovation, Organizational Capabilities and the Born Global Firm," *Journal of International Business Studies*, 35, no. 2, 2004, 124–41.

17. Bureau of Economic Analysis, U.S. Department of Commerce, Washington, DC. http://www.bea.gov, accessed November 23, 2008.

18. Catherine L. Mann, *Is the U.S. Trade Deficit Sustainable?* September 1999, http://www.iie.com.

19. *U.S. Jobs Supported by Exports of Goods and Services*, U.S. Department of Commerce, Washington, DC., 2002.

20. Office of Industry and Trade Information, *Total jobs related to manufacturing employment*, U.S. Department of Commerce, Washington D.C., accessed November 23, 2008.

21. Michael R. Czinkota, "A National Export Development Strategy for New and Growing Businesses," remarks delivered to the National Economic Council, Washington, DC, August 6, 1993.

22. *Foreign Direct Investment in the United States*, Bureau of Economic Affairs, U.S. Department of Commerce, accessed November 23, 2008.

23. Zeile W., *U.S. Affiliates of Foreign Companies*, Survey of Current Business, U.S. Department of Commerce, August, 2002, pp. 149–166.

24. Erich Marquardt and Federico Bordonaro, "Economic Brief: French Protectionism," *Power and Interest News Report*, September 15, 2005, http://www.pinr.com/report.php?ac=view_report&report_id=367&language_id=1, accessed December 5, 2005.

25. Success for low-weight auto parts project, European Commission Research, www.ec.europa.eu/transport/news, accessed November 23, 2008.

26. Kym Anderson, Will Martin, and Dominique van der Mensbrugghe, *Distortions to World Trade: Impacts on Agricultural Markets and Farm Incomes* (Washington, DC: World Bank, November 30, 2005).

27. *Die Aussenwirtschaftsförderung der wichtigsten Konkurrenzländer der Bundesrepublik Deutschland—Ein internationaler Vergleich* (The export promotion of the most important countries competing with the Federal Republic of Germany—An international comparison) (Berlin: Deutsches Institut für Wirtschaftsforschung, June 1991).

28. Masaaki Kotabe and Michael R. Czinkota, "State Government Promotion of Manufacturing Exports: A Gap Analysis," *Journal of International Business Studies* (Winter 1992): 637–658.

29. *Publication 54, Tax Guide for US Citizens and Resident Aliens Abroad, 2008* (Washington, DC: Internal Revenue Service).

Chapter 4

1. Ernest Dichter, "The World Consumer," *Harvard Business Review* 40 (July–August 1962): 113–122; and Kenichi Ohmae, *Triad Power—The Coming Shape of Global Competition* (New York: The Free Press, 1985), 22–27.

2. "Rule No. 1: Don't Diss the Locals," *Business Week*, May 15, 1995, 8.

3. Alonso Martinez, Ivan De Souza, and Francis Liu, "Multinationals vs. Multilatinas," *Strategy and Business* (Fall, 2003): 56–67.

4. "Melting Pots," *The Washington Post*, January 6, 2006, H1, H4.

5. Mary O'Hara-Devereaux and Robert Johansen, *Global Work: Bridging Distance, Culture, and Time* (San Francisco: Jossey-Bass Publishers, 1994), 11.

6. Carla Rapoport, "Nestlé's Brand Building Machine," *Fortune*, September 19, 1994, 147–156.

7. Alfred Kroeber and Clyde Kluckhohn, *Culture: A Critical Review of Concepts and Definitions* (New York: Random House, 1985), 11.

8. Geert Hofstede, "National Cultures Revisited," *Asia-Pacific Journal of Management* 1 (September 1984): 22–24.

9. Edward T. Hall, *Beyond Culture* (Garden City, NY: Anchor Press, 1976), 15.

10. Kerry Capell, "How a Swedish Retailer Became a Global Cult Brand," *Business Week*, November 14, 2005, 96–106.

11. Marita von Oldenborgh, "What's Next for India?" *International Business*, January 1996, 44–47; and Ravi Vijh, "Think Global, Act Indian," *Export Today*, June 1996, 27–28.

12. "U.N. Body Endorses Cultural Protection," *The Washington Post*, October 21, 2005, A14.

13. "French Movies," http://www.understandfrance.org/France/FrenchMovies.html; "Subsidy Wars," *The Economist*, February 24, 2005, 76.

14. "India Digitizes Age-Old Wisdom," *The Washington Post*, January 8, 2006, A22.

15. "Britannia Rules the Airwaves," *Foreign Policy*, July/August 2005, 19.

16. "Asian Pop Stars Struggle to Find Cross-Cultural Groove," *The Wall Street Journal*, March 31, 2005, B1, B2.

17. "Multinational Firms Take Steps to Avert Boycotts Over War," *The Wall Street Journal*, April 4, 2003, A1, A4.

18. George P. Mundak, "The Common Denominator of Cultures," in *The Science of Man in the World*, ed. Ralph Linton (New York: Columbia University Press, 1945), 123–142.

19. "Euroteen Market Grabs U.S. Attention," *Marketing News*, October 22, 2001, 15; "Global Youth United," *Marketing News*, October 28, 2002, 1–2.

20. http://www.ethnologue.com.

21. David A. Ricks, *Blunders in International Business* (Malden, MA: Blackwell Publishers, 2000), Chapter 1.

22. David A. Hanni, John K. Ryans, and Ivan R. Vernon, "Coordinating International Advertising: The Goodyear Case Revisited for Latin America," *Journal of International Marketing* 3 (no. 2, 1995): 83–98.

23. "We Are Tous Québécois," *The Economist*, January 8, 2005, 39; "France: Mind Your Language," *The Economist*, March 23, 1996, 70–71.

24. "A World Empire by Other Means," *The Economist*, December 22, 2001, 65.

25. Rory Cowan, "The e Does Not Stand for English," *Global Business*, March 2000, L/22.

26. Margareta Bowen, "Business Translation," *Jerome Quarterly* 8 (August–September 1993): 5–9.

27. "Nokia Veti Pois Mainoskampanjansa," *Uutislehti 100*, June 15, 1998, 5.

28. "Sticky Issue," *The Economist*, August 24, 2002, 51.

29. Edward T. Hall, "The Silent Language of Overseas Business," *Harvard Business Review* 38 (May–June 1960): 87–96.

30. "Anywhere, Anytime," *The Wall Street Journal*, November 21, 2005, R6.

31. *World Almanac and the Book of Facts 2009* (Mahwah, NJ: Funk & Wagnalls, 2008), 707.

32. "Profit versus the Prophet: Islamic Law has Transformed Some Muslims into Creative Bankers." *Los Angeles Times*, February 10, 2008, M11.

33. "Out from Under," *Marketing News*, July 21, 2003, 1, 9.

34. "Islamic Businesses Emerge From the Shadows," *European Business Forum*, Winter, 2005, 58–61.

35. Roger D. Blackwell, Paul W. Miniard, and James F. Engel, *Consumer Behavior* (Mason, OH: Thomson, 2001), Chapter 10.

36. Y. H. Wong and Ricky Yee-kwong, "Relationship Marketing in China: Guanxi, Favoritism and Adaptation," *Journal of Business Ethics* 22 (no. 2, 1999): 107–118; and Tim Ambler, "Reflections in China: Re-Orienting Images of Marketing," *Marketing Management* 4 (no. 1, 1995): 23–30.

37. "Iran Unveils Islamic Twin Dolls to Fight Culture War," *AP Worldstream*, March 5, 2002.

38. Douglas McGray, "Japan's Gross National Cool," *Foreign Policy*, May/June 2002, 44.

39. Earl P. Spencer, "EuroDisney—What Happened?" *Journal of International Marketing* 3 (no. 3, 1995): 103–114.

40. "Disney's Great Leap into China," *Time*, July 18, 2005, 52–54.

41. Sergey Frank, "Global Negotiations: Vive Les Differences!" *Sales & Marketing Management* 144 (May 1992): 64–69.

42. See, for example, Terri Morrison, *Kiss, Bow, or Shake Hands: How to Do Business in Sixty Countries* (Holbrook, MA: Adams Media, 1994), or Roger Axtell, *Do's and Taboos around the World* (New York: John Wiley & Sons, 1993). For holiday observances, see http://www.religioustolerance.org/main_day.htm#cal and http://www.yahoo.com/society_and_culture/holidays_and_observances.

43. James A. Gingrich, "Five Rules for Winning Emerging Market Consumers," *Strategy and Business* (second quarter, 1999): 68–76.

44. "Feng Shui Strikes Chord," available at http://www.cnnfn.com/1999/09/11/life/q_fengshui/.

45. "Feng Shui Man Orders Sculpture out of the Hotel," *South China Morning Post,* July 27, 1992, 4.

46. "Year of the Mouse," *The Economist,* September 30, 2005, 58; "The Feng Shui Kingdom," *The New York Times,* April 25, 2005, A14.

47. "The New Life of O'Reilly," *Business Week,* June 13, 1994, 64–66; and "Heinz Aims to Export Taste for Ketchup," *The Wall Street Journal,* November 20, 1992, B1, B10.

48. "U.S. Superstores Find Japanese Are a Hard Sell," *The Wall Street Journal,* February 14, 2000, B1, B4.

49. "Why the Chinese Hate to Use Voice Mail," *The Wall Street Journal,* December 1, 2005, B1, B5.

50. The results of the Gallup study are available in "What the Chinese Want," *Fortune,* October 11, 1999, 229–234.

51. Kenichi Ohmae, "Managing in a Borderless World," *Harvard Business Review* 67 (May–June 1989): 152–161.

52. Joe Agnew, "Cultural Differences Probed to Create Product Identity," *Marketing News,* October 24, 1986, 22.

53. Joseph A. McKinney, "Joint Ventures of United States Firms in Japan: A Survey," *Venture Japan* 1 (no. 2, 1988): 14–19.

54. Peter MacInnis, "Guanxi or Contract: A Way to Understand and Predict Conflict between Chinese and Western Senior Managers in China-Based Joint Ventures," in Daniel E. McCarthy and Stanley J. Hille, eds., *Multinational Business Management and Internationalization of Business Enterprises* (Nanjing, China: Nanjing University Press, 1993), 345–351.

55. Tim Ambler, "Reflections in China: Re-Orienting Images of Marketing," *Marketing Management* 4 (Summer 1995): 23–30.

56. Jagdish N. Sheth and S. Prakash Sethi, "A Theory of Cross-Cultural Buying Behavior," in *Consumer and Industrial Buying Behavior,* eds. Arch G. Woodside, Jagdish N. Sheth, and Peter D. Bennett (New York: Elsevier North-Holland, 1977), 369–386.

57. Geert Hofstede, *Culture's Consequences: International Differences in Work-Related Values* (Beverly Hills, CA: Sage Publications, 1984).

58. Geert Hofstede and Michael H. Bond, "The Confucius Connection: From Cultural Roots to Economic Growth," *Organizational Dynamics* 16 (Spring 1988): 4–21.

59. "When Will It Fly?" *The Economist,* August 9, 2003, 51.

60. Sudhir H. Kale, "Grouping Euroconsumers: A Culture-Based Clustering Approach," *Journal of International Marketing* 3 (no. 3, 1995): 35–48.

61. Jan-Benedict Steenkamp and Frenkel ter Hofstede, "A Cross-National Investigation into the Individual and National Cultural Antecedents of Consumer Innovativeness," *Journal of Marketing* 63 (April 1999): 55–69.

62. Hong Cheng and John C. Schweitzer, "Cultural Values Reflected in Chinese and U.S. Television Commercials," *Journal of Advertising Research* 36 (May/June 1996): 27–45.

63. Sudhir H. Kale, "Distribution Channel Relationships in Diverse Cultures," *International Marketing Review* 8 (no. 3, 1991): 31–45.

64. Sengun Yeniyurt and Janell Townsend," Does Culture Explain Acceptance of New Products in a Country? An Empirical Investigation," *International Marketing Review* 20 (number 4, 2003): 377–397.

65. "Is E-Commerce Boundary-less? Effects of Individualism-Collectivism and Uncertainty Avoidance on Internet Shopping," *Journal of International Business Studies* 35 (number 6, 2004): 545–560.

66. "Exploring Differences in Japan, U.S. Culture," *Advertising Age International,* September 18, 1995, 1–8.

67. James A. Lee, "Cultural Analysis in Overseas Operations," *Harvard Business Review* 44 (March–April 1966): 106–114.

68. Peter B. Fitzpatrick and Alan S. Zimmerman, *Essentials of Export Marketing* (New York: American Management Organization, 1985), 16.

69. David Maxwell and Nina Garrett, "Meeting National Needs," *Change,* May/June 2002, 22–28.

70. W. Chan Kim and R. A. Mauborgne, "Cross-Cultural Strategies," *Journal of Business Strategy* 7 (Spring 1987): 28–37.

71. Mauricio Lorence, "Assignment USA: The Japanese Solution," *Sales & Marketing Management* 144 (October 1992): 60–66.

72. "Special Interest Group Operations," available at http://www.samsung.com; and "Sensitivity Kick," *The Wall Street Journal* (December 30, 1996), 1, 4.

73. Rosalie Tung, "Selection and Training of Personnel for Overseas Assignments," *Columbia Journal of World Business* 16 (Spring 1981): 68–78.

74. Maureen Lewis, "Why Cross-Cultural Training Simulations Work," *Journal of European Industrial Training* 29 (number 7, 2005): 593–598.

75. Simcha Ronen, "Training the International Assignee," in *Training and Career Development,* ed. I. Goldstein (San Francisco: Jossey-Bass, 1989), 426–440.

76. Nadeem Firoz and Taghi Ramin, "Understanding Cultural Variables is Critical to Success in International Business," *International Journal of Management* 21 (number 3, 2004): 307–324.

77. See, for example, Johnson & Johnson's credo at www.jnj.com/our_company/our_credo/index.htm.

78. 3M examples are adopted from John R. Engen, "Far Eastern Front," *World Trade,* December 1994, 20–24.

Chapter 5

1. Gary C. Hufbauer, Jeffery J. Schott, Kimberly Ann Elliott and Barbara Oegg. *Economic Sanctions Reconsidered,* 3rd ed. (Washington, DC: Peterson Institute, May 30, 2008).

2. Robin Renwick, *Economic Sanctions* (Cambridge, MA: Harvard University Press, 1981), 11.

3. "Sudan Sanctions," U.S. Department of the Treasury, http://www.ustreas.gov/offices/enforcement/ofac/programs/ascii/sudan.txt, July 25, 2008, accessed November 17, 2008.

4. "Sanctions on Sudan Now," Human Rights Watch, http://www.hrw.org/en/news/2008/04/01/sanctions-sudan-now, April 1, 2008, accessed November 17, 2008.

5. Gary C. Hufbauer, Jeffery J. Schott, Kimberly Ann Elliott, and Barbara Oegg, *Economic Sanctions Reconsidered,* 3rd ed. (Washington, DC: Peterson Institute, May 30, 2008).

6. Michael R. Czinkota and Erwin Dichtl, "Export Controls and Global Changes," *Der Markt* 37, 5 (1996): 148–155.

7. Kevin Gray, "Argentina Defends Export Taxes in Farm Conflict," Reuters, June 17, 2008, http://uk.reuters.com/article/latestCrisis/idUKN1738140020080617, accessed November 17, 2008.

8. Warren Hoge and Elaine Sciolino, "Security Council Adds Sanctions Against Iran," *New York Times,* March 4, 2008, http://www.nytimes.com/2008/03/04/world/middleeast/04nations.html, accessed November 17, 2008.

9. We are grateful to David Danjczek for his helpful comments.

10. E. M. Hucko, *Aussenwirtschaftsrecht-Kriegswaffenkontrollrecht, Textsammlung mit Einführung,* 4th ed. (Köln, Germany: Bundesanzeiger, 1993).

11. http://www.investorwords.com, accessed November 17, 2008.

12. Oil ship hijacked in Niger Delta," BBC News, May 14, 2008, http://news.bbc.co.uk/2/hi/africa/7400263.stm, accessed November 17, 2008.

13. See Trade Related Aspects of International Property Rights (TRIPS), http://www.wto.org.

14. Overseas Private Investment Corporation (OPIC), Washington, DC, http://www.opic.gov/insurance/details/rates/index.asp, accessed November 17, 2008.

15. "The present status of lawyers in Japanese legal system," Japan Business Expert, http://www.doing-japanbusiness.com/web/reg/reg.cgi?=1&acte=2, accessed November 17, 2008.

16. Surya Prakash Sinha, *What Is Law? The Differing Theories of Jurisprudence* (New York: Paragon House, 1989).

17. *National Trade Estimate Report on Foreign Trade Barriers* (Washington, DC, Office of the United States Trade Representative, 2008), http://www.ustr.gov, accessed November 24, 2008.

18. See office of the United States Trade Representative, Document Library, www.ustry.goy.

19. We are grateful to Professor Ed Soule of Georgetown University for this example.

20. "Brown Condemns Iceland over Banks," BBC News, October 10, 2008, http://news.bbc.co.uk/2/hi/uk_news/politics/7662027.stm, retrieved November 18, 2008.

21. Michael Czinkota and Gary Knight, "The Effects of Terrorism off International Marketing," *Anthology on Glocal Marketing,* ed. G. Svensson, 2009.

22. 2007 *Report on Terrorism,* National Counterterrorism Center, April 30, 2008, http://wits.nctc.gov/reports/crot2007/nctcannexfinal.pdf, accessed November 3, 2008.

23. Sheffi Jossi, *The Resilient Enterprise.* Cambridge, MA: MIT Press, 2005.

24. Michael Czinkota, and Gary Knight, "On the Front Line: Marketers Combat Global Terrorism," *Marketing Management,* May/June 2005, 33–39.

25. Michael R. Czinkota, "International Marketing and Terrorism Preparedness," testimony before the Congress of the United States, 109th Congress, Committee on Small Business, Washington, DC, November 1, 2005.

26. We are very grateful for input within this section from Professor Michael Moffett of Thunderbird University.

27. Michael R. Czinkota, Illka A. Ronkainen, and Bob Donath, *Mastering Global Markets* (Mason, OH: Thomson South-Western, 2004), 362.

28. Robert Sullivan, "Small Business Start-Up Guide," Chapter. 1: Prologue, http://www.isquarecom/prologue.cfm, accessed November 18, 2008.

29. Amy Kapczynski, "Strict International Patent Laws Hurt Developing Countries, *Yale Global,* http://yaleglobal.yale.eud/display.article?id=562, retrieved November 7, 2008.

30. Aoife White , "E.U. Changes Music Copyright Rules, Benefiting Online Stores," the Washington Post, July 17, 2008, p. D07.

31. James R. Hines, Jr., *Forbidden Payment: Foreign Bribery and American Business after 1977,* working paper 5266 (Cambridge, MA: National Bureau of Economic Research, September 1995), 1.

32. Magoroh Maruyama, "Bribing in Historical Context: The Case of Japan," *Human Systems Management* 15 (1996): 138–142.

33. Alix Stuart, "Keeping It to Themselves," *CFO Magazine,* April 1, 2008, http://www.cfo.com/article.cfm/10941670/c_10941875?f=insidecfo, retrieved November 18, 2008.

Part 1 Cases

China: Forging a Global Reputation

1. *Fisher-Price Recalls Licensed Character Toys Due To Lead Poisoning Hazard,* U.S. Consumer Product Safety Commission, Release #07-257, August 2, 2007, http://www.cpsc.gov/cpscpub/prerel/prhtml07/07257.html (accessed December 29, 2008).

2. "Mattel CEO: 'Rigorous standards' after massive toy recall," *CNN,* November 15, 2007, http://www.cnn.com/2007/US/08/14/recall/index.html (accessed December 29, 2008).

3. David Barboza, "Why Lead in Toy Paint? It's Cheaper," *New York Times,* September 27, 2007, http://www.nytimes.com/2007/09/11/business/worldbusiness/11lead.html (accessed December 5, 2008).

4. Barboza, "Why Lead in Toy Paint? It s Cheaper."

5. Louise Story and David Barboza, "Mattel Recalls 19 Million Toys Sent From China," *New York Times,* August 15, 2007, http://www.nytimes.com/2007/08/15/business/worldbusiness/15imports.html (accessed December 5, 2009).

6. David Barboza, "Owner of Chinese Toy Factory Commits Suicide," *New York Times,* August 14, 2007, http://www.nytimes.com/2007/08/14/business/worldbusiness/14toy.html?partner=rssnyt&emc=rss (accessed December 5, 2008).

7. "Chinese toy firms forced to close," *BBC,* October 14, 2008, http//news bbc co.uk/1/hi/world/asia-pacific/7670351.stm (accessed December 5, 2008).

8. Barboza, "Owner of Chinese Toy Factory Commits Suicide."

9. Barboza, "Why Lead in Toy Paint? It's Cheaper."

10. Jad Mouawad, "550, 000 More Chinese Toys Recalled for Lead," *New York Times,* September 27, 2007, http://www.nytimes.com/2007/09/27/business/27toys.html?ref=business (accessed December 5, 2008).

11. Barboza, "Why Lead in Toy Paint? It's Cheaper."

12. Donald Greenlees, "Toy Makers Mount Drive to Salvage China's Safety Reputation," *New York Times,* January 10, 2008, http://www.nytimes.com/2008/01/10/business/worldbusiness/10toys.html (accessed December 5, 2008).

13. Barboza, "Owner of Chinese Toy Factory Commits Suicide."

14. Greenlees, "Toys Makers Mount Drive to Salvage China's Safety Reputation."

15. Jim Yardley and David Barboza, "Despite Warnings, China's Regulators Failed to Stop Tainted Milk," *New York Times,* September 27, 2008, http://www.nytimes.com/2008/09/27/world/asia/27mi1k.html (accessed December 5, 2008).

16. Andrew Jacobs, "Chinese Release Increased Number in Tainted Milk Scandal," *New York Times,* December 2, 2008, http://www.nytimes.com/2008/12/03/world/asia/03milk.html (accessed December 5, 2008).

17. "EU limits imported Chinese food," *BBC,* September 25, 2008, http://news.bbc.co.uk/2/hi/europe/7635594.stm (accessed December 5, 2008).

18. "Soy: Starbucks In China Opts For Milk Substitutes," *ChinaCSR,* September 26, 2008, http://www.chinacsr.com/en/2008/09/26/3229-starbucks-in-china-opts-for-milk-substitutes/ (accessed December 29, 2008).

19. Wal-Mart acts over Chinese goods," *BBC,* October 22, 2008, http://news.bbc.co.uk/hi/business/7683686.stm (accessed December 5, 2008).

20. Yardley and Barboza, "Despite Warning, China's Regulators Failed to Stop Tainted Milk."

21. Ibid.

22. John Thornhill, "Trading Strains," *Financial Times,* October, 2008, http://www.ft.com/cms/s/0/6404deb6-8fe3-11dd-9890-0000779fd18c.html (accessed December 5, 2008).

23. "David Barboza, "No Flinching From Recalls as China's Exports Soars," *New York Times,* October 13, 2007, http://www.nytimes.com/2007/10/13/business/worldbusiness/13trade.html (accessed December 5, 2008).

24. Tom Mitchell, "Hasbro chairman calls for global toy rules," *Financial Times,* January 11, 2008, http://www.ft.com/cms/s/0/ec40a2e6-bf97-11dc-8052-0000779fd2ac.html?nclick_check=1 (accessed January 1, 2009).

The Catfish Dispute

1. Catfish Institute—http://catfishinstitute.com.

2. Elizabeth Becker, "Delta Farmers Want Copyright on Catfish," *New York Times,* January 16, 2002, Section A1.

3. Meredith Petran, "Catfish," *Restaurant Business,* New York, February 1, 2000.

4. Margot Cohen and Murray Hiebert, "Muddying the Waters," *Far Eastern Economic Review,* Hong Kong, December 6, 2001.

5. "The Vietnamese Invade: Catfish in the South," *The Economist,* October 6, 2001.

6. Philip Brasher, "When Is a Catfish Not a Catfish," *Washington Post,* December 27, 2001.

7. James Toedman, "Fighting Like Cats and Dogs Over Fish; It's U.S. vs. Vietnamese as Trade Battle Goes Global," *Newsday,* March 10, 2002 Sunday, F02.

8. "The Vietnamese invade: Catfish in the South."

9. "One of these negative advertisements, which ran in the national trade weekly Supermarket News, tells us in shrill tones, 'Never trust a catfish with a foreign accent!' This ad characterizes Vietnamese catfish as dirty and goes on to say, 'They've grown up flapping around in Third World rivers and dining on whatever they can get their fins on. . . . Those other guys probably couldn't spell U.S. even if they tried.'" Press release, Senator John McCain, December 18, 2001.

10. Philip Brasher, "When Is a Catfish Not a Catfish."

11. Ibid.

12. Margot Cohen and Murray Hiebert, "Muddying the Waters."

13. Elizabeth Becker, "Delta Farmers Want Copyright on Catfish."

14. Ibid.

15. Tim Brown, "South and Southeast, "Vietnam Embroiled in Catfish Controversy," *Marketing News,* October 22, 2001.

16. "The Vietnamese Invade: Catfish in the South."

17. Ibid.

18. James Toedman, "Fighting Like Cats and Dogs Over Fish."

19. Margot Cohen and Murray Hiebert, "Muddying the Waters."

Should Dubai Take Over U.S. Ports?

1. "Dubai: Business Partner of Terrorist Hotbed," *Wall Street Journal,* February 25–26, 2006.

2. "Dubai delays," *Globe and Mail,* February 24, 2006; http://www.theglobeandmail.com/servlet/story/RTGAM.2006224.wports0224/BNStory/Business.

3. D. Machalaba, "DP World's Ports Sale May Not Pinch," *Wall Street Journal,* March 11–12, 2006, p. A6.

4. http://www.ustreas.gov/press/releases/js4071.htm, accessed June 13, 2006.

5. Peter Overby, "Lobbyist's Last-Minute Bid Set Off Ports Controversy," *All Things Considered,* 8 March 2006, http://www.npr.org/templates/story/story.php?storyId=5252263; "Small Florida Firm Sowed Seed of Port Dispute," *Wall Street Journal,* February 28, page A3.

6. Ted Bridis, "United Arab Emirates Firm May Oversee 6 U.S. Ports," *Washington Post,* February 12, 2006, A17.

7. David E. Sanger, "Under Pressure, Dubai Company Drops Port Deal," *New York Times,* March 10, 2006, p. 1.

8. "Dubai: Business Partner of Terrorist Hotbed," *Wall Street Journal,* February 25–26, 2006, A9.

9. Greg Hitt and Sarah Ellison, "Dubai Firm Bows to Public Outcry," March 10–26, *Wall Street Journal,* A1.

10. Al-Issawi, Tarek, "Port Company Ignores Boycott," *Boston Globe,* March 3, 2006.

11. Much of the discussion in this section is based on: J.D. Haveman, Howard Shatz, and Ernesto Vilchis, "U.S. Port Security Policy after 9/11: Overview and Evaluation," *Journal of Homeland Security and Emergency Management,* 2 (no. 4, 2005): 1–24; and "Our Porous Port Protections," *New York Times,* March 10, 2006, A18.

12. "Dubai: Business partner of terrorist hotbed," *Wall Street Journal,* February 25–26, 2006, A9.

13. "Poll: Bush Ratings at All Time Low," http://www.cbsnews.com/stories/2006/02/27/opinion/polls/main1350874.shtml, accessed June 13, 2006.

14. "In Ports Furor, a Clash over Dubai," *Wall Street Journal,* February 23, 2006, A1.

15. Neil King, Jr., "DP World Tried to Soothe U.S. Waters," *Wall Street Journal,* March 14, 2006, A4.

16. S. E. Eizenstat, and M. C. Maiback, "Protect Our Heritage," *Wall Street Journal,* March 30, 2006, A14.

17. Eduardo Porter, "DP World and U.S. Trade: A Zero-Sum Game," *New York Times,* March 10, 2006, C1.

18. "US-UAE Postpone Free Trade Talks Amidst Ports Row," *Khaleej Times,* March 11, 2006.

19. Leslie Miller, "DP World Exec's Nomination Withdrawn," Associated Press, March 28, 2006, http://townhall.com/news/ap/online/gov/congress/D8GD00OO2.html.

20. "DP World Chief Says Dispute was 'Shock,'" *Financial Times,* March 22, 2006, 1.

21. Greg Ip and Neil King, "Ports Deal Shows Roadblocks for Globalization," *Wall Street Journal,* March 11–12, 2006, 1.

22. "Dubai Ports Debacle Darkens Mood of Investors in the Gulf," *Khaleej Times,* March 11, 2006.

23. Heather Timmons, "After Dubai Uproar, Emirates Air Holds No Grudges," *New York Times,* March 29, 2006, C1.

24. David Marchick, Testimony before the Senate Banking Committee, March 2006. N. King, "When Security, Foreign Investment Collide," *Wall Street Journal,* April 10, 2006, A4.

Chapter 6

1. Theodore Levitt, *The Marketing Imagination* (New York: Free Press, 1983), 20–49.

2. Michael R. Czinkota and Ilkka A. Ronkainen, "A Forecast of Globalization, International Business and Trade: Report from a Delphi Study," *Journal of World Business* 40 (Winter 2005): 111–123.

3. Jonathan Sprague, "China's Manufacturing Beachhead," *Fortune,* October 28, 2002, I192A–J.

4. Pankaj Ghemawat, "Regional Strategies for Global Leadership," *Harvard Business Review* 83 (December 2005): 98–108.

5. Bruce Greenwald and Judd Kahn, "All Strategy is Local," *Harvard Business Review* 83 (September 2005): 94–107.

6. This section draws from George S. Yip, *Total Global Strategy II* (Upper Saddle River, NJ: Prentice Hall, 2002), chapters 1 and 2; Jagdish N. Sheth and Atul Parvatiyar, "The Antecedents and Consequences of Integrated Global Marketing," *International Marketing Review* 18 (no. 1, 2001): 16–29; George S. Yip, "Global Strategy. . . . In a World of Nations?" *Sloan Management Review* 31 (Fall 1989): 29–41; and Susan P. Douglas and C. Samuel Craig, "Evolution of Global Marketing Strategy: Scale, Scope, and Synergy," *Columbia Journal of World Business* 24 (Fall 1989): 47–58.

7. Ernst Dichter, "The World Customer," *Harvard Business Review* 40 (July–August 1962): 113–122.

8. Kenichi Ohmae, *The Invisible Continent: Four Strategic Imperatives of the New Economy* (New York: Harper Business, 2001), chapter 1; Kenichi Ohmae, *The Borderless World: Power and Strategy in the Interlinked Economy* (New York: Harper Business, 1999), chapter 1; and Kenichi Ohmae, *Triad Power: The Coming Shape of Global Competition* (New York: Free Press, 1985), 22–27.

9. "BRICs and the Mobile Web," *Business Week,* October 13, 2008, 72.

10. Luciano Catoni, Nora Förisdal Larssen, James Nayor, and Andrea Zocchi, "Travel Tips for Retailers" *The McKinsey Quarterly* 38 (no. 3, 2002): 88–98.

11. Catherine George and J. Michael Pearson, "Riding the Pharma Roller Coaster," *The McKinsey Quarterly* 38 (no. 4, 2002): 89–98.

12. Nicholas Mockett, "Global M&A Trends in Paper, Packaging and Printing: 2003–2004," *PriceWaterhouseCoopers Forest & Paper Industry Practice,* available at http://www.pwc.com/forestry.

13. Stuart Crainer, "And the New Economy Winner Is . . . Europe," *Strategy and Business* 6 (second quarter, 2001): 40–47.

14. Suzy Wetlaufer, "Driving Change: An Interview with Ford Motor Company's Jacques Nasser," *Harvard Business Review* 77 (March–April 1999): 76–88.

15. "Telecommunications," *The Economist,* April 4, 2002, 102.

16. Daniel J. Isenberg, "The Global Entrepreneur," *Harvard Business Review* 86 (December 2008): 107–111; and Gary Knight. . . .

17. Gary Knight, Tage Koed Madsen, and Per Servais, "An Inquiry into Born-Global Firms in Europe and the USA," *International Marketing Review* 21 (November 6, 2004): 645–666; Oystein Moen and Per Servais, "Born Global or Gradual Global?" *Journal of International Marketing* 10 (no. 3, 2002): 49–72.

18. http://www.cochlear.com.

19. Nestlé data available at http://www.nestle.com/All_About/Glance/Introduction/Glance+Introduction.htm; and "A Dedicated Enemy of Fashion: Nestlé," *The Economist,* August 31, 2002, 51.

20. "Nestle to Keep Foot on Sales Accelerator," *Financial Times,* October 24, 2008, 14.

21. Jordan D. Lewis, *Trusted Partners: How Companies Build Mutual Trust and Win Together* (New York: The Free Press, 2000), 157.

22. Cait Murphy, "The Hunt for Globalization That Works," *Fortune,* October 28, 2002, 67–72.

23. "3 Big Carmakers to Create Net Site for Buying Parts," *The Washington Post,* February 26, 2000, E1, E8.

24. Myung-Su Chae and John S. Hill, "Determinants and Benefits of Global Strategic Planning Formality," *International Marketing Review* 17 (no. 6, 2000): 538–562.

25. Marcus Alexander and Harry Korine, "When you Shouldn't Go Global," *Harvard Business Review* 86 (December 2008): 70–77.

26. Edward Tse, Andrew Cainey, and Ronald Haddock, "Evolution on the Global Stage," *Strategy and Business Leading Ideas,* October 9, 2007.

27. "Computing's New Shape," *The Economist,* November 23, 2002, 11–12.

28. C. Samuel Craig and Susan P. Douglas, "Configural Advantage in Global Markets," *Journal of International Marketing* 8 (no. 1, 2000): 6–26.

29. Michael E. Porter, *Competitive Strategy: Techniques for Analyzing Industries and Competitors* (New York: Free Press, 1998), chapter 1.

30. "Europe's Car Makers Expect Tidy Profits," *The Wall Street Journal,* January 27, 2000, A16.

31. Lori Ioannou, "It's a Small World After All," *International Business,* February 1994, 82–88.

32. "Nokia Market Share Dives in Asia-Pacific," *Reuters,* December 4, 2008.

33. Pankaj Ghemawat and Thomas Hout, "Tomorrow's Global Giants? Not the Usual Suspects," *Harvard Business Review* 86 (November 2008): 80–89.

34. Michael Porter, *Competitive Advantage: Creating and Sustaining Superior Performance* (New York: Free Press, 1998), chapter 1.

35. Robert M. Grant, *Contemporary Strategy Analysis: Concepts, Techniques, Applications* (Oxford, England: Blackwell, 2005), chapter 7.

36. George S. Yip, *Total Global Strategy II* (Upper Saddle River, NJ: Prentice Hall, 2002), chapter 10.

37. The models referred to are GE/McKinsey, Shell International, and A. D. Little portfolio models.

38. "Company CV: Cereal Partners Worldwide," *Marketing,* November 29, 2001, 50. See also, http://www.generalmills.com/corporate/ company/cereal_partners.aspx.

39. "Tissue Titans Target Globally with Key Brands," *Advertising Age,* December 20, 1999, 4.

40. Richard Tomlinson, "Europe's New Computer Game," *Fortune,* February 21, 2000, 219–224.

41. Saeed Samiee and Kendall Roth, "The Influence of Global Marketing Standardization on Performance," *Journal of Marketing* 56 (April 1992): 1–17.

42. "Euroteen Market Grabs U.S. Attention," *Marketing News,* October 22, 2001, 15.

43. "The American Connection," *The Washington Post,* May 25, 2002, E1–E2.

44. Peter N. Child, Suzanne Heywood, and Michael Kliger, "Do Retail Brands Travel?" *The McKinsey Quarterly* 38 (no. 1, 2002): 73–77.

45. Aruna Chandra and John K. Ryans, "Why India Now?" *Marketing Management,* March/April 2002, 43–45.

46. C.K. Prahalad and Stuart L. Hart, "The Fortune at the Bottom of the Pyramid," *Strategy and Business* 7 (first quarter, 2002): 35–47.

47. Pankaj Ghemawat, "Managing Differences: The Central Challenge of Global Strategy," *Harvard Business Review* 85 (March 2007): 59–68.

48. Pascal Cagni, "Think Global, Act European," *Developments in Strategy and Business,* August 30, 2004, available at http://www .strategy-business.com/export/export. php?article_id=4510703.

49. Pankaj Ghemawat, "Regional Strategies for Global Leadership," *Harvard Business Review* 83 (December 2005): 98–108.

50. "Shania Reigns," *Time,* December 9, 2002, 80–85.

51. http://www.nokia.com/A402785.

52. Larry Greenemeier, "Offshore Outsourcing Grows to Global Proportions," *Information Week,* February 2002, 56–58.

53. "Philips Electronics to Make China One of Three Big Research Centers," *The Wall Street Journal,* December 20, 2002, B4.

54. W. Chan Kim and R. A. Mauborgne, "Becoming an Effective Global Competitor," *Journal of Business Strategy* 8 (January–February 1988): 33–37.

55. Gary Hamel and C. K. Prahalad, "Do You Really Have a Global Strategy?" *Harvard Business Review* 63 (July–August 1985): 75–82.

56. "Nokia Widens Lead in Wireless Market While Motorola, Ericsson Fall Back," *The Wall Street Journal,* February 8, 2000, B8.

57. Andreas F. Grein, C. Samuel Craig, and Hirokazu Takada, "Integration and Responsiveness: Marketing Strategies of Japanese and European Automobile Manufacturers," *Journal of International Marketing* 9 (no. 2, 2001): 19–50.

58. James A. Gingrich, "Five Rules for Winning Emerging Market Consumers," *Strategy and Business* (second quarter, 1999): 19–33.

59. "Does Globalization Have Staying Power?" *Marketing Management,* March/April 2002, 18–23.

60. Kamran Kashani, "Beware the Pitfalls of Global Marketing," *Harvard Business Review* 67 (September–October 1989): 91–98.

61. George S. Yip, Pierre M. Loewe, and Michael Y. Yoshino, "How to Take Your Company to the Global Market," *Columbia Journal of World Business* 23 (Winter 1988): 28–40.

62. George S. Yip and Tammy L. Madsen, "Global Account Management: The New Frontier in Relationship Marketing," *International Marketing Review* 13 (no. 3, 1996): 24–42.

63. David B. Montgomery and George S. Yip, "The Challenge of Global Customer Management," *Marketing Management,* Winter 2000, 22–29.

64. George Yip and Audrey Bink, "Managing Global Accounts," *Harvard Business Review* 85 (September 2007): 103–111.

65. Julian Birkinshaw, "Global Account Management: New Structures, New Tasks," *FT Mastering Management,* 2001, available at http://www.ftmastering.com/mmo/ mmo05_2.htm.

66. Ikujiro Nonaka and Hirotaka Takeuchi, *The Knowledge Creating Company* (New York: Oxford University Press, 1995), 115.

67. John A. Quelch and Helen Bloom, "Ten Steps to Global Human Resources Strategy," *Strategy and Business* 4 (first quarter, 1999): 18–29.

68. Pablo Haberer and Adrlan Kohan, "Building Global Champions in Latin America," *The McKinsev Quarterly,* March 2007, 35–41.

69. Meagan Dietz, Gordon Orr, and Jane Xing, "How Chinese Companies Can Succeed Abroad," *The McKinsey Quarterly* May 2008, 23–31.

70. This section draws from Niraj Dawar and Tony Frost, "Competing with the Giants: Survival Strategies for Local Companies in Emerging Markets," *Harvard Business Review* 77 (March–April 1999): 119–129; and Güliz Ger, "Localizing in the Global Village: Local Firms Competing in Global Markets," *California Management Review* 41 (Summer 1999): 64–83.

71. John H. Roberts, "Defensive Marketing: How a Strong Incumbent Can Protect Its Position," *Harvard Business Review* 83 (November 2005): 150–163.

72. Jonathan Ledgard, "Škoda Leaps to Market," *Strategy and Business* 10 (Fall 2005): 1–12.

73. Guillermo D'Andrea, E. Alejandro Stengel, and Anne Goebel-Krstelj, "6 Truths About Emerging-Market Consumers," *Strategy and Business* 10 (Spring 2004): 59–69.

74. Alonso Martinez, Ivan De Souza, and Francis Liu, "Multinationals vs. Multilatinas," *Strategy and Business* 9 (Fall 2003): 56–67.

75. "The Little Aircraft Company That Could," *Fortune,* November 14, 2005, 201–208.

76. "Chasing Desi Dollars," *Time Inside Business,* August 2005, A22–A24.

77. Ibsen Martínez, "Romancing the Globe," *Foreign Policy,* November/December 2005, 48–56.

78. http://www.jollibee.com.ph/corporate/ international.htm.

79. Arindam Bhattacharya and David Michael, "How Local Companies Keep Multinationals at Bay," *Harvard Business Review* 86 (March 2008): 85–95.

80. Douglas Ready, Linda Hill, and Jay Conger, "Winning the Race for Talent in Emerging Markets," *Harvard Business Review* 86 (November 2008): 62–71.

81. Sharon O'Donnell and Insik Jeong, "Marketing Standardization within Global Industries," *International Marketing Review* 17 (no. 1, 2000): 19–33.

Chapter 7

1. Lawrence M. Fischer, "Thought Leader," *Strategy and Business* 7 (fourth quarter, 2002): 115–123.

2. Robert J. Flanagan, "Knowledge Management in Global Organizations in the 21st Century," *HR Magazine* 44 (no. 11, 1999): 54–55.

3. "Partners in Wealth," *The Economist,* January 21, 2006, 16–17.

4. Michael Z. Brooke, *International Management: A Review of Strategies and Operations* (London: Hutchinson, 1986), 173–174; and "Running a Licensing Deparment," *Business International,* June 13, 1988, 177–178.

5. Jay R. Galbraith, *Designing the Global Corporation* (New York: Jossey-Bass, 2000), chapter 3.

6. William H. Davidson and Philippe C. Haspeslagh, "Shaping a Global Product Organization," *Harvard Business Review* 59 (March–April 1982): 69–76.

7. http://www.loctite.com/about/global_reach.html.

8. See, for example, Samuel Humes, *Managing the Multinational: Confronting the Global–Local Dilemma* (London, Prentice Hall, 1993), chapter 1.

9. Vijay Govindarajan, Anil K. Gupta, and C. K. Prahalad, *The Quest for Global Dominance: Transforming Global Presence into Global Competitive Advantage* (New York: Jossey-Bass, 2001), chapters 1 and 2.

10. "How Goodyear Sharpened Organization and Production for a Tough World Market," *Business International,* January 16, 1989, 11–14.

11. Michael J. Mol, *Ford Mondeo: A Model T World Car?* (Hershey, PA: Idea Group Publishing, 2002), 1–21.

12. Philippe Lasserre, "Regional Headquarters: The Spearhead for Asia Pacific Markets," *Long Range Planning* 29 (February 1996): 30–37; and John D. Daniels, "Bridging National and Global Marketing Strategies through Regional Operations," *International Marketing Review* 4 (Autumn 1987): 29–44.

13. "Boeing's Defense Unit to Divide Its Operations into 3 Segments," *The Wall Street Journal,* January 28, 2006, A5.

14. "The New Organization," *The Economist,* January 21, 2006, 3–5.

15. Daniel Robey, *Designing Organizations: A Macro Perspective* (Homewood, IL: Irwin, 1982), 327.

16. Christopher A. Bartlett and Sumantra Ghoshal, *Managing across Borders* (Cambridge, MA: Harvard Business School Press, 2002), chapter 10.

17. Spencer Chin, "Philips Shores Up the Dike," *EBN,* October 14, 2002, 4.

18. Milton Harris and Artur Raviv, "Organization Design," *Management Science* 48 (July 2002): 852–865.

19. John P. Workman, Jr., Christian Homburg, and Kjell Gruner, "Marketing Organization: Framework of Dimensions and Determinants," *Journal of Marketing* 62 (July 1998): 21–41; and John U. Farley, "Looking Ahead at the Marketplace: It's Global and It's Changing," in *Reflections on the Futures of Marketing,* Donald R. Lehman and Katherine E. Jocz, eds. (Cambridge, MA: Marketing Science Institute, 1995), 15–35.

20. William Taylor, "The Logic of Global Business," *Harvard Business Review* 68 (March–April 1990): 91–105.

21. C.K. Prahalad and Hrishi Bhattacharyya, "Twenty Hubs and No HQ," *Strategy and Business,* Spring 2008, 1–6.

22. Mohanbir Sawhney, "Don't Homogenize, Synchronize," *Harvard Business Review* 79 (July–August 2001): 100–108.

23. Gerard Fairtlough, *The Three Ways of Getting Things Done* (London: Triarchy Press, 2005), chapters 3 and 4.

24. Ilkka A. Ronkainen, "Thinking Globally, Implementing Successfully," *International Marketing Review* 13 (no. 3, 1996): 4–6.

25. "Why Multiple Headquarters Multiply," *The Wall Street Journal,* November 19, 2007, B1, B3.

26. Jack Neff, "Unilever Reorganization Shifts P&L Responsibility," *Advertising Age,* February 28, 2005, 13; "Despite Revamp, Unwieldy Unilever Falls Behind Rivals," *The Wall Street Journal,* January 3, 2005, A1, A5.

27. Russell Eisenstat, Nathaniel Foote, Jay Galbraith, and Danny Miller, "Beyond the Business Unit," *The McKinsey Quarterly* 37 (no. 1, 2001): 180–195.

28. "Country Managers," *Business Europe,* October 16, 2002, 3; John A. Quelch and Helen Bloom, "The Return of the Country Manager," *The McKinsey Quarterly* 33 (no. 2, 1996): 31–43; and Jon I. Martinez and John A. Quelch, "Country Managers: The Next Generation," *International Marketing Review* 13 (no. 3, 1996): 43–55.

29. Rodman Drake and Lee M. Caudill, "Management of the Large Multinational: Trends and Future Challenges," *Business Horizons* 24 (May–June 1981): 83–91.

30. Joe Studwell, *The China Dream* (New York: Atlantic Monthly Press, 2002), 104–105.

31. Goran Svensson, "'Glocalization' of Business Activities: A 'Glocal Strategy' Approach," *Management Decision* 39 (no. 1, 2001): 6–13.

32. Christopher A. Bartlett and Sumantra Ghoshal, "Matrix Management: Not a Structure, a Frame of Mind," *Harvard Business Review* 68 (July–August 1990): 138–145.

33. "Big and No Longer Blue," *The Economist,* January 21, 2006, 15; "Beyond Blue," *Business Week,* April 18, 2005, 68–76.

34. Carlos Ghosn, "Saving the Business without Losing the Company," *Harvard Business Review* 80 (January 2002): 37–45.

35. Karl Moore and Julian Birkinshaw, "Managing Knowledge in Global Service Firms," *Academy of Management Executive* 12 (no. 4, 1998): 81–92.

36. Julian Birkinshaw and Tony Sheehan, "Managing the Knowledge Life Cycle," *Sloan Management Review* 44 (Fall 2002): 75–83.

37. Noel Tichy, "The Teachable Point of View: A Primer," *Harvard Business Review* 77 (March–April 1999): 82–83.

38. "See Jack. See Jack Run Europe," *Fortune,* September 27, 1999, 127–136.

39. "GE Mentoring Program Turns Underlings into Teachers of the Web," *The Wall Street Journal,* February 15, 2000, B1, B16.

40. Richard Benson-Armer and Tsun-Yan Hsieh, "Teamwork across Time and Space," *The McKinsey Quarterly* 33 (no. 4, 1997): 18–27.

41. David A. Griffith and Michael G. Harvey, "An Intercultural Communication Model for Use in Global Interorganizational Networks," *Journal of International Marketing* 9 (no. 3, 2001): 87–103.

42. "Internet Software Poses Big Threat to Notes, IBM's Stake in Lotus," *The Wall Street Journal,* November 7, 1995, A1–5.

43. Linda S. Sanford and Dave Taylor, *Let Go to Grow* (Englewood Cliffs, NJ: Prentice-Hall, 2005), chapter 1.

44. Christopher A. Bartlett and Sumantra Ghoshal, "Tap Your Subsidiaries for Global Reach," *Harvard Business Review* 64 (November–December 1986): 87–94.

45. "The Zen of Nissan," *Business Week,* July 22, 2002, 46–49.

46. "Percy Barnevik's Global Crusade," *Business Week Enterprise 1993,* 204–211.

47. Michael D. White, "The Finnish Springboard," *World Trade,* January 1999, 48–49.

48. "A European Electronics Giant Races to Undo Mistakes in the U.S.," *The Wall Street Journal,* January 7, 2004, A1, A10.

49. Julian Birkinshaw and Neil Hood, "Unleash Innovation in Foreign Subsidiaries," *Harvard Business Review* 79 (March 2001): 131–137; and Julian Birkinshaw and Nick Fry, "Subsidiary Initiatives to Develop New Markets," *Sloan Management Review* 39 (Spring 1998): 51–61.

50. Vijay Govindarajan and Robert Newton, *Management Control Systems* (New York: McGraw-Hill/Irwin, 2000), chapter 1.

51. Anil Gupta and Vijay Govindarajan, "Organizing for Knowledge within MNCs," *International Business Review* 3 (no. 4, 1994): 443–457.

52. William G. Ouchi, "The Relationship between Organizational Structure and Organizational Control," *Administrative Science Quarterly* 22 (March 1977): 95–112.

53. Cheryl Nakata, "Activating the Marketing Concept in a Global Context," *International Marketing Review* 19 (no. 1, 2002): 39–64.

54. Laurent Leksell, *Headquarters-Subsidiary Relationships in Multinational Corporations* (Stockholm, Sweden: Stockholm School of Economics, 1981), chapter 5.

55. Henry P. Conn and George S. Yip, "Global Transfer of Critical Capabilities," *Business Horizons* 38 (January/February 1997): 22–31.

56. Arant R. Negandhi and Martin Welge, *Beyond Theory Z* (Greenwich, CT: JAI Press, 1984), 16.

57. Richard Pascale, "Fitting New Employees into the Company Culture," *Fortune,* May 28, 1994, 28–40.

58. http://www.nokia.com/A4433643.

59. Michael R. Czinkota and Ilkka A. Ronkainen, "International Business and Trade in the

Next Decade: Report from a Delphi Study," *Journal of International Business Studies* 28 (no. 4, 1997): 676–694.

60. Tsun-Yan Hsieh, Johanne La Voie, and Robert A. P. Samek, "Think Global, Hire Local," *The McKinsey Quarterly* 35 (no. 4, 1999): 92–101.

61. "Thinking for a Living," *The Economist,* January 21, 2006, 9–12.

62. R. J. Alsegg, *Control Relationships between American Corporations and Their European Subsidiaries,* AMA Research Study No. 107 (New York: American Management Association, 1971), 7.

63. Ron Edwards, Adlina Ahmad, and Simon Moss, "Subsidiary Autonomy: The Case of Multinational Subsidiaries in Malaysia," *Journal of International Business Studies* 33 (no. 1, 2002): 183–191.

64. John J. Dyment, "Strategies and Management Controls for Global Corporations," *Journal of Business Strategy* 7 (Spring 1987): 20–26.

65. Alfred M. Jaeger, "The Transfer of Organizational Culture Over seas: An Approach to Control in the Multinational Corporation," *Journal of International Business Studies* 14 (Fall 1983): 91–106.

66. Michael Goold and Andrew Campbell, "Do You Have a Well-Designed Organization?" *Harvard Business Review* 80 (March 2002): 117–124.

67. Michael C. Mankins and Richard Steele, "Turning Great Strategy into Great Performance," *Harvard Business Review* 83 (July–August 2005): 65–72.

Chapter 8

1. Naresh K. Malhotra, Mark Peterson, and Susan Bardi Kleiser, "Marketing Research: A State-of-the-Art Review and Directions for the Twenty-First Century," *Journal of the Academy of Marketing Science* 27 (no. 2, 1999): 160–183.

2. Marketing Definitions, http://marketingpower .com, Web site of the American Marketing Association, accessed December 2, 2008.

3. Naresh Malhotra, *Marketing Research: An Applied Orientation* and SPSS 14.0 Student CD 5th ed. (Upper Saddle River, NJ: Prentice-Hall, 2006).

4. C. Samuel Craig and Susan P. Douglas, *International Marketing Research,* 3rd ed. (Chichester: John Wiley and Sons, 2006).

5. Nina L. Reynolds, "Benchmarking International Marketing Research Practice in UK Agencies—Preliminary Evidence," *Benchmarking* 7 (no. 5, 2000): 343–359.

6. For an excellent exposition on measuring the value of research, see Gilbert A. Churchill, Jr., and Dawn Iacobucci, *Marketing Research: Methodological Foundations,* 9th ed. (Mason, OH: South-Western, 2005).

7. For an excellent online diagnostic tool, see Tamer S. Cavusgil's CORE (Company Readiness to Export), Michigan State University, http://globaledge.msu.edu/ diagtools/, accessed December 2, 2008.

8. Tamer S. Cavusgil, Tunga Kiyak, and Sengun Yeniyurt, "Complementary Approaches to Preliminary Foreign Market Opportunity Assessment: Country Clustering and Country Ranking," *Industrial Marketing Management,* December 24, 2003, 616.

9. "MP Backs Federal Action over China Fruit Trade Stance," *Australian Broadcasting Corporation,* http://www.abc.net.au/news/ stories/2005/09/15/1460594.htm, accessed December 2, 2008.

10. Michael R. Czinkota, *International Marketing and Accessability,* U.S. Department of Commerce, Washington D.C., 2007.

11. Michael R. Czinkota, "International Information Cross-Fertilization in Marketing: An Empirical Assessment," *European Journal of Marketing,* 34 (2000).

12. European Society for Opinion and Marketing Research (ESOMAR), "Marketing Research Expenditures up Worldwide by 5.1%," http://www.esomar.nl, accessed December 2, 2008.

13. Salah S. Hassan and A. Coskun Samli, "The New Frontiers of Intermarket Segmentation," in *Global Marketing: Perspectives and Cases,* eds. Salah S. Hassan and Roger D. Blackwell (Fort Worth, TX: The Dryden Press, 1994), 76–100.

14. Michael R. Czinkota and Masaaki Kotabe, "Product Development the Japanese Way," in *Trends in International Business: Critical Perspectives,* eds. M. Czinkota and M. Kotabe (Oxford, England: Blackwell Publishers, 1998), 153–158.

15. R. Nishikawa, "New Product Planning at Hitachi," *Long Range Planning* 22 (1989): 20–24.

16. For an excellent example, see Alan Dubinsky, Marvin Jolson, Masaaki Kotabe, and Chae Lim, "A Cross-National Investigation of Industrial Salespeople's Ethical Perceptions," *Journal of International Business Studies* 22 (1991): 651–670.

17. Raymond A. Jussaume, Jr., and Yoshiharu Yamada, "A Comparison of the Viability of Mail Surveys in Japan and the United States," *Public Opinion Quarterly* 54 (1990): 219–228.

18. Camille P. Schuster and Michael J. Copeland, "Global Business Exchanges: Similarities and Differences around the World," *Journal of International Marketing* (Number 2, 1999): 63–80.

19. Kavil Ramachandran, "Data Collection for Management Research in Developing Countries," in *The Management Research Handbook,* eds. N. Craig Smith and Paul Dainty (London: Routledge, 1991), 304.

20. Tamer S. Cavusgil, Seyda Deligonul, and Attila Yaprak, "International Marketing as a Field of Study: A Critical Assessment of Earlier Development and a Look Forward," *Journal of International Marketing,* 13 (no. 4, 2005): 1–27.

21. Gilbert A. Churchill, Jr., and Dawn Iacobucci, *Marketing Research: Methodological Foundations,* 9th ed. (Mason, OH: South-Western, 2005).

22. Kathleen Brewer Doran, "Lessons Learned in Cross-Cultural Research of Chinese and North American Consumers," *Journal of Business Research,* 55 (2002): 823–829.

23. C. Samuel Craig and Susan P. Douglas, *International Marketing Research,* 3rd ed. (Chichester: John Wiley and Sons, 2006).

24 Jason Freedman, Evan Konwiser, Emily Nielsten, and Colin Van Ostern, "Market Research: Web 1.0 in a Web 2.0 World. How can we Listen Instead of Asking Questions?" Glassmeyer/McNamee Center for Digital Strategies, Tuck School of Business at Dartmouth, March 2008, http://mba.tuck .dartmouth.edu/digital/Research/ ResearchProjects/ResearchMarketWeb.pdf, retrieved January 11, 2009.

25. Janet Ilieva, Steve Baron, and Nigel M. Healey, "On-line Surveys in Marketing Research: Pros and Cons," *International Journal of Marketing Research* 44 (no. 3, 2002): 361–376.

26. David Luna, Laura A. Peracchio, and Maria D. de Juan, "Cross-Cultural and Cognitive Aspects of Web Site Navigation," *Journal of the Academy of Marketing Science* 30 (no. 4, 2002): 397–410.

27. "Web-based Surveys Help Customers Evolve with Your Products," *ATX Dialogue,* February, 2004, http://www.broadviewnet .com/BVN/Default.asp, accessed December 2, 2008.

28. Michael Stanat, "Facebook: The Future of Market Research?" *Market Intelligence, Research Trends,* October 2007, http:// marketintelligences.com/2007/10/19/ facebook-the-future-of-niarket-research .aspx, retrieved January 11, 2009.

29. "Eric Pfanner, "AOL to Buy Social Networking Site Bebo," *International Herald Tribune,* March 13, 2008, http://www.iht .com/articles/2008/03/13/technology/aol .php, retrieved January 11, 2009.

30. http://www.vizu.com/solutions/power-polls/ index.htm, retrieved Jan. 13, 2009.

31. Ray Poynter, "Facebook: The Future of Networking with Customers," *International Journal of Market Research,* 50 (1), 2008, http://mrs.org.uk/publications/ijmr_ viewpoints/poynter.htm., retrieved January 13, 2009.

32. Freedman, Konwiser, Nielsten, and Ostern, 2008.

33. "Stanat, 2007; Freedman, Konwiser, Nielsten, and Ostern, 2008.

34. Freedman, Konwiser, Nielsten, and Ostern, 2008.

35. http://www.communispace.com/.

36. Thomas C. Kinnear and James R. Taylor, *Marketing Research: An Applied Approach,* 5th ed. (New York: McGraw-Hill, 1996).

37. Peter Clarke, "The Echelon Questions," *Electronic Engineering Times,* March 6, 2000, 36.

38. Andre L. Delbecq, Andrew H. Van de Ven, and David H. Gustafson, *Group Techniques for Program Planning* (Glenview, IL: Scott, Foresman, 1975), 83.

39. David Rutenberg, "Playful Plans," Queen's University working paper, 1991.

Chapter 9

1. Howard Lewis III and J. David Richardson, *Why Global Commitment Really Matters!* (Washington, DC: Institute for International Economics, 2001).

2. Tiger Li, "The Impact of the Marketing-R&D Interface on New Product Export Performance: A Contingency Analysis," *Journal of International Marketing* 7 (no. 1, 1999): 10–33.

3. Michael L. Ursic and Michael R. Czinkota, "An Experience Curve Explanation of Export Expansion," in *International Marketing Strategy: Environmental Assessment and Entry Strategies* (Fort Worth, TX: The Dryden Press, 1994), 133–141.

4. C. P. Rao, M. Krishna Erramilli, and Gopala K. Ganesh, "Impact of Domestic Recession on Export Marketing Behaviour," *International Marketing Review* 7 (1990): 54–65.

5. Shawna O'Grady and Henry W. Lane, "The Psychic Distance Paradox," *Journal of International Business Studies* 27 (no. 2, 1996): 309–333.

6. Aviv Shoham and Gerald S. Albaum, "Reducing the Impact of Barriers to Exporting: A Managerial Perspective," *Journal of International Marketing* 3 (4, 1995): 85–105.

7. Michael R. Czinkota, "U.S. Exporters in the Global Marketplace: An Analysis of the Strengths and Vulnerabilities of Small and Medium-Sized Manufacturers," Testimony before the 107th Congress of the United States, House of Representatives, Committee on Small Business, Washington, DC, April 24, 2002.

8. Shaoming Zou and S. Tamer Cavusgil, "The GMS: A Broad Conceptualization of Global Marketing Strategy and Its Effect on Firm Performance," *Journal of Marketing,* October 2002, 40–56.

9. Yoo S. Yang, Robert P. Leone, and Dana L. Alden, "A Market Expansion Ability Approach to Identify Potential Exporters," *Journal of Marketing* 56 (January 1992): 84–96.

10. S. Tamer Cavusgil and Shaoming Zou, "Marketing Strategy–Performance Relationship: An Investigation of the Empirical Link in Export Marketing Ventures," *Journal of Marketing* 58 (no. 1, 1994): 1–21.

11. Michael R. Czinkota, "Export Promotion: A Framework for Finding Opportunity in Change," *Thunderbird International Business Review,* May–June 2002, 315–324.

12. Oystein Moen and Per Servais, "Born Global or Gradual Global? Examining the Export Behavior of Small and Medium-Sized Enterprises," *Journal of International Marketing* 10 (no. 3, 2002): 49–72.

13. Masaaki Kotabe and Michael R. Czinkota, "State Government Promotion of Manufacturing Exports: A Gap Analysis," *Journal of International Business Studies* (Winter 1992): 637–658.

14. Andrew B. Bernard and J. Bradford Jensen, *Exceptional Exporter Performance: Cause Effect or Both,* Census Research Data Center, Pittsburgh, Carnegie Mellon University, 1997.

15. Daniel C. Bello and Nicholas C. Williamson, "Contractual Arrangement and Marketing Practices in the Indirect Export Channel," *Journal of International Business Studies* 16 (Summer 1985): 65–82.

16. Mike W. Peng and Anne Y. Ilinitch, "Export Intermediary Firms: A Note on Export Development Research," *Journal of International Business Studies* 3 (1998): 609–620.

17. Current Export Trade Certificate of Review Holders http://www.ita.doc.go, accessed Jan, 13, 2009.

18. Alibaba Corporate company overview, htttp://www.alibaba.com, accessed December 16, 2008.

19. Farok J. Contractor and Sumit K. Kundu, "Franchising versus Company-Run Operations: Modal Choice in the Global Hotel Sector," *Journal of International Marketing* 6 (no. 2, 1998): 28–53.

20. Martin F. Connor, "International Technology Licensing," Seminars in International Trade, National Center for Export-Import Studies, Washington, DC.

21. Pamela M. Deese and Sean Wooden, "Managing Intellectual Property in Licensing Agreements," *Franchising World* 33 (September 2001): 66–67.

22. Josh Martin, "Profitable Supply Chain Supporting Franchises," *Journal of Commerce,* Global Commerce Section (March 11, 1998): 1C.

23. George W. Russell, "Into the Frying Pan," *Asian Business* 37 (October 2001): 28–29.

24. Leonard N. Swartz, "International Trends in Retailing," Arthur Andersen, December 1999.

25. Farok J. Contractor, "Economic and Environmental Reasons for the Continuing Growth in Alliances and Interfirm Cooperation," in *Emerging Issues in International Business Research,* eds. M. Kotabe and P. Aulakh (Northampton, MA: Elgar Publishing, 2002).

26. Marko Grünhagen and Carl L. Witte, "Franchising as an Export Product and Its Role as an Economic Development Tool for Emerging Economies," *Enhancing Knowledge Development in Marketing,* vol. 13, eds. W. Kehoe and J. Lindgren, Jr. (Chicago: American Marketing Association, 2002), 414–415.

27. United Nations, Foreign Direct Investment http://www.unctad.org, accessed Dec. 16, 2008.

28. 2007 Year-end U.S. Net Investment Position, Bureau of Economic Analysis, U.S. Department of Commerce, Washington, DC, June 27, 2008.

29. *Multinational Corporations in World Development* (New York: United Nations, 1973), 23.

30. Scott DeCarlo and Brian Zajac, "The World's Biggest Companies," Forbes, April 2, 2008, http://www.forbes.com, accessed December 17, 2008.

31. Bernard L. Simonin, "Transfer of Marketing Know-How in International Strategic Alliances: An Empirical Investigation of the Role and Antecedents of Knowledge Ambiguity," *Journal of International Business Studies* 30 (3, 1999): 463–490.

32. Howard Lewis III and David Richardson, *Why Global Commitment Really Matters!* (Washington, DC: Institute for International Economics, 2001).

33. Detlev Nitsch, Paul Beamish, and Shige Makino, "Characteristics and Performance of Japanese Foreign Direct Investment in Europe," *European Management Journal* 13 (3, 1995): 276–285.

34. Michael R. Czinkota, "From Bowling Alone to Standing Together," *Marketing Management,* March/April 2002, 12–16.

35. Jack N. Behrman, "Transnational Corporations in the New International Economic Order," *Journal of International Business Studies* 12 (Spring-Summer 1981): 29–42.

36. Michael R. Czinkota, "Success of Globalization Rests on Good Business Reputations," *The Japan Times,* October 12, 2002, 19.

37. Prasad Padmanabhan and Kang Rae Cho, "Decision Specific Experience in Foreign Ownership and Establishment Strategies: Evidence from Japanese Firms," *Journal of International Business Studies* 30 (1, 1999): 25–44.

38. Isaiah Frank, *Foreign Enterprise in Developing Countries* (Baltimore: Johns Hopkins University, 1980).

39. W. G. Friedman and G. Kalmanoff, *Joint International Business Ventures* (New York: Columbia University Press, 1961).

40. Holton, "Making International Joint Ventures Work," 7.

41. Oded Shenkar and Shmuel Ellis, "Death of the 'Organization Man': Temporal Relations in Strategic Alliances," *The International Executive* 37 (6, November/December 1995): 537–553.

42. Jordan D. Lewis, *Partnerships for Profit: Structuring and Managing Strategic Alliances* (New York: Free Press, 1990), 85–87.

43. http://www.pepsco.com, accessed January 14, 2009.

44. Lawrence S. Welch and Anubis Pacifico, "Management Contracts: A Role in Internationalization?" *International Marketing Review* 7 (1990): 64–74.

45. http://www.eads.com, accessed January 13, 2009.

Part 2 Cases

Starting an Import/Export Business

1. "How to Start an Import/Export Business," Entrepreneur.com, http://www.entrepreneur.com/startingabusiness/businessideas/startupkits/article41846.html, accessed October 1, 2008.

2. Trade offices are set up to promote the economic interests of the respective country. They typically assist people with import/export to their country. The trade counselor is the head of the trade office. For information on trade in Vietnam, visit http://www.vietnamustrade.org.

3. http://www.discus.org.

4. http://www.commerce.gov.

5. For Country Commercial Guides, visit http://www.buyusa.gov/home/export.html and select the country from the drop down menu that says "Find Export Information By Country."

6. http://www.usitc.gov.

7. "Branded Distilled Spirits: FAS Value by Country Name and FAS Value for Vietnam," Report published by the U.S. International Trade Commission, 2008, http://www.dataweb.usitc.gov/scripts/REPORT.asp, accessed January 15, 2009.

8. "Vietnam Retail Food Sector 2007," Report published by USDA Foreign Agriculture Service, 2007, http://www.fas.usda.gov/GainFiles/200711/146293084.pdf, accessed October 1, 2008.

9. To find the nearest office go to http://www.export.gov and click "Find a Local Office." on the left hand menu.

10. Commercial attaches are assistants to the trade counselor and also work to promote trade with the respective country.

11. If you're using the EAC, they can do additional due diligence for you on your distributors. Even if you're not using the EAC, they may provide you with free information on a particular distributor.

Water from Iceland

1. "Feeling thrifty, the thirsty reach for tap water," *MSNBC,* June 17, 2008 http://www.msnbc.msn.com/id/25211545, accessed November 28, 2008.

2. "Tappening," http://www.tappening.comWhy_Tap_Water.

3. "Feeling thrifty, the thirsty reach for tap water."

Chapter 10

1. Jeffrey E. Garten, "Globalization without Tears: A New Social Compact for CEOs," *Strategy and Business* (fourth quarter, 2002): 36–45.

2. "For U.S. Small Biz, Fertile Soil in Europe," *Business Week,* April 1, 2002, 57.

3. Jill G. Klein, Richard Ettenson, and Marlene Morris, "The Animosity Model of Foreign Product Purchase: An Empirical Test in the People's Republic of China," *Journal of Marketing* 62 (January 1998): 89–100.

4. http://www.levistrauss.com/Brands/Dockers.aspx, accessed April 5, 2009.

5. Stephanie Nall, "American Exports Chicken Out," *World Trade,* September 1998, 44–45.

6. Thomas L. Friedman, *The Lexus and the Olive Tree: Understanding Globalization* (New York: Anchor Books, 2000), chapters 3 and 15.

7. S. Tamer Cavusgil and Shaoming Zou, "Marketing Strategy–Performance Relationship: An Investigation of the Empirical Link in Export Market Ventures," *Journal of Marketing* 58 (January 1994): 1–21.

8. Jean L. Johnson and Wiboon Arunthanes, "Ideal and Actual Product Adaptation in U.S. Exporting Firms," *International Marketing Review* 12 (number 3, 1995): 31–46.

9. Dana James, "B2–4B Spells Profits," *Marketing News,* November 5, 2001, 1, 11–12.

10. "Star Power," *Fortune,* February 6, 2006, 61.

11. Jean-Noël Kapferer, *Survey among 210 European Brand Managers* (Paris: Euro-RSCG, 1998).

12. Carl A. Sohlberg, "The Perennial Issue of Adaptation or Standardization of International Marketing Communication: Organizational Contingencies and Performance," *Journal of International Marketing* 10 (no. 3, 2002): 1–21.

13. "EU/Country Briefing," *Business Europe,* April 21, 1999, 9–11.

14. "Trading Places," *The Economist,* November 22, 2001, 58.

15. "U.S. and EU at Odds over Jet Noise," *The Washington Post,* January 19, 2000, E1, E10.

16. "Google Under the Gun," *Time,* February 13, 2006, 53–54; "Microsoft Revises Policy on Shutting Down Blogs," *The Wall Street Journal,* February 1, 2006, B10; and "Here Be Dragons," *The Economist,* January 28, 2006, 59.

17. Erika Morphy, "Cutting the Cost of Compliance," *Export Today* 12 (January 1996): 14–18.

18. James D. Southwick, "Addressing Market Access Barriers in Japan through the WTO: A Survey of Typical Japan Market Access Issues and the Possibility to Address Them through WTP Dispute Resolution Procedures," *Law and Policy in International Business* 31 (Spring 2000): 923–976.

19. "In Global Food-Trade Skirmish, Safety Is the Weapon of Choice," *Wall Street Journal,* December 15, 2004, A1, A8; and "EU Nears Stricter GMO Food Labels," *The Wall Street Journal,* July 5, 2002, A8.

20. Davis Goodman, "Thinking Export? Think ISO 9000," *World Trade,* August 1998, 48–49.

21. *ISO Survey 2007,* available at http://www.iso.org/iso/home.htm, accessed April 6, 2009.

22. Enrique Sierra, "The New ISO 14000 Series: What Exporters Should Know," *Trade Forum* (no. 3, 1996): 16–31.

23. Kirk Loncar, "Look Before You Leap," *World Trade,* June 1997, 92–93.

24. Drew Martin and Paul Herbig, "Marketing Implications of Japan's Social-Cultural Underpinnings," *Journal of Brand Management* 9 (January 2002): 171–179.

25. Jennifer Aaker, "Dimensions of Measuring Brand Personality," *Journal of Marketing Research* 34 (August 1997): 347–356.

26. http://www.sesameworkshop.org. accessed April 6, 2009

27. "The Simpsons Exported to Middle East—Minus Bacon, Beer," *ABC News,* October 18, 2005.

28. James A. Gingrich, "Five Rules for Winning Emerging Market Consumers," *Strategy and Business* (second quarter, 1999): 35–42.

29. "Tech's Future," *Business Week,* September 27, 2004, 82–89.

30. "Holding the Fries—At the Border," *Business Week,* December 14, 1998, 8.

31. "Exporting to Survive," *Time Global Business,* September 2002, A20–A22.

32. "Dubbing in Product Plugs," *The Wall Street Journal,* December 6, 2004, B1, B5.

33. Robert Gray, "Local on a Global Scale," *Marketing,* September 27, 2001, 22–23.

34. Jean-Noël Kapferer, "Is There Really No Hope for Local Brands?" *Journal of Brand Management* 9 (January 2002): 163–170.

35. Alan Mitchell, "Few Brands Can Achieve a Truly Global Presence," *Marketing Week,* February 7, 2002, 32–33.

36. "The Best Global Brands," *Business Week,* August 5, 2002, 92–108.

37. "Mozart's Genius Extends to Selling Lederhosen in Japan," *The Wall Street Journal Europe,* January 6, 1992, Section 1.1.

38. NameLab, Inc. (http://www.namelab.com/), accessed April 6, 2009.

39. Barry M. Tarnef, "How to Protect Your Goods in Transit without Going Along for a Ride," *Export Today* 9 (May 1993): 55–57.

40. Jesse Wilson, "Are Your Spanish Translations Culturally Correct?" *Export Today* 10 (May 1994): 68–69.

41. "The Perils of Packaging: Nestlé Aims for Easier Openings," *The Wall Street Journal,* November 17, 2005, B1, B5.

42. Dan McGinn, "Vodka with Punch," http://www.wetfeet.com/MBA.aspx, September/October 2002, 34–36. accessed April 6, 2009.

43. Guillermo D'Andrea, E. Alejandro Stengel, and Anne Goebel-Krstelj, "Six Truths About Emerging-Market Consumers," *Strategy and Business* 34 (Spring 2004): 58–69.

44. http://www.tetrapak.com/Pages/default.aspx, accessed April 6, 2009.

45. "Waste Not," *Business Europe,* February 20, 2002, 4.

46. Thomas J. Madden, Kelly Hewett, and Martin S. Roth, "Managing Images in Different Cultures: A Cross-National Study of Color Meanings and Preferences," *Journal of International Marketing* 8 (no. 4, 2000): 90–107.

47. "How the Swedish Retailer Became a Global Cult Brand," *Business Week,* November 14, 2005, 96–106.

48. "Riding the Theme Park Wave," *World Trade,* October 1999, 86.

49. http://www.ita.doc.gov/media/Publications/pdf/current2002FINAL.pdf, accessed April 6, 2009.

50. "Why Don't We Use the Metric System?" *Fortune,* May 29, 2000, 56–57.

51. Carla Kruytbosch, "The Minds behind the Winners," *International Business,* January 1994, 56–70.

52. "Awash in Export Sales," *Export Today* 5 (February 1989): 11.

53. Ian Wilkinson and Nigel Barrett, "In Search of Excellence in Exports: An Analysis of the 1986 Australian Export Award Winners," paper given at the Australian Export Award presentations, Sydney, November 28, 1986.

54. "EU Lifts the Hood on Chinese Autos," *The Wall Street Journal,* October 7, 2005, A14.

55. Thomas H. Stevenson and Frank C. Barnes, "Fourteen Years of ISO 9000: Impact, Criticisms, Costs, and Benefits," *Business Horizons* 44 (May/June 2001): 45–51.

56. "Keeping Cool in China," *The Economist,* April 6, 1996, 73–74.

57. Martin S. Roth and Jean B. Romeo, "Matching Product Category and Country Image Perceptions: A Framework for Managing Country-of-Origin Effects," *Journal of International Business Studies* 23 (third quarter, 1992): 477–497.

58. Warren J. Bilkey and Erik Nes, "Country-of-Origin Effects on Product Evaluations," *Journal of International Business Studies* 13 (Spring–Summer 1982): 88–99.

59. Johny K. Johansson, Ilkka A. Ronkainen, and Michael R. Czinkota, "Negative Country-of-Origin Effects: The Case of the New Russia," *Journal of International Business Studies* 25 (first quarter, 1994): 1–21.

60. Johny K. Johansson, "Determinants and Effects of the Use of 'Made in' Labels," *International Marketing Review* 6 (1989): 47–58.

61. Philip Kotler and David Gertner, "Country as Brand, Product, and Beyond: A Place Marketing and Brand Management Perspective," *Journal of Brand Management* 9 (April 2002): 249–261.

62. "Push for 'Made In' Tags Grows in EU," *The Wall Street Journal,* November 7, 2005, A6; and "Breaking a Taboo, High Fashion Starts Making Goods Overseas," *The Wall Street Journal,* September 27, 2005, A1, A10.

63. Roger J. Calantone, Daekwan Kim, Jeffrey B. Schmidt, and S. Tamer Cavusgil, "The Influence of Internal and External Firm Factors on International Product Adaptation Strategy and Export Performance: A Three-Country Comparison," *Journal of Business Research* 59 (number 2, 2006): 176–185.

64. Arnold Schuh, "Global Standardization as a Success Formula for Marketing in Central Eastern Europe," *Journal of World Business* 35 (Summer 2000): 133–148.

65. http://www.uschamber.com/ip, accessed April 6, 2009.

66. Business Software Alliance, *Fifth Annual BSA and IDC Global Software Piracy Study* (Washington, DC: BSA, 2007), 1; see also http://www.bsa.org/GlobalHome.aspx, accessed April 6, 2009.

67. Ilkka A. Ronkainen, "Imitation as the Worst Kind of Flattery: Product Counterfeiting," *Trade Analyst* 2 (July–August 1986): 2.

68. Ilkka A. Ronkainen and Jose-Luis Guerrero-Cusumano, "Correlates of Intellectual Property Violation," *Multinational Business Review* 9 (no. 1, 2001): 59–65.

69. "China Vice Commerce Minister Pledges to Crack Down on Piracy," *Jiji Press English News Service,* July 29, 2004; Amanda R. Evansburg, Mark J. Fiore, Vanessa Watson, and Brooke K. Welch, "Video Game Maker Wins Copyright Judgement," *Intellectual Property and Technology Law Journal,* 15 (number 9): 19; and "In Pursuit of Pokémon Pirates," *The Wall Street Journal,* November 8, 1999, B1, B4.

70. http://www.wipo.int/portal/index.html.en, accessed April 6, 2009.

71. "Piracy Fight Strains U.S.–China Ties," *The Wall Street Journal,* January 27, 2006, A2.

72. "Patently Problematic," *The Economist,* September 14, 2002, 86.

73. "Lubricating a Crackdown," *Export Today,* June 1999, 29.

74. Michael G. Harvey and Ilkka A. Ronkainen, "International Counterfeiters: Marketing Success without the Cost and the Risk," *Columbia Journal of World Business* 20 (Fall 1985): 37–45.

75. Pankaj Ghemawat, "Distance Still Matters: The Hard Reality of Global Expansion," *Harvard Business Review* 79 (September 2001): 137–147.

76. Kenneth Cukier, "In Defence of Creativity," *RSA Journal,* December 2005, 18–21.

Chapter 11

1. Julie Demers, "Enhanced Export Pricing Strategies," *CMA Management* 77 (June/July 2003): 52–53.

2. "The Secret of U.S. Exports: Great Products," *Fortune,* January 10, 2000, 154A–J.

3. James A. Gingrich, "Five Rules for Winning Emerging Market Consumers," *Strategy and Business* (second quarter, 1999), 35–46.

4. David Arnold, "Seven Rules of International Distribution," *Harvard Business Review* 78 (November/December 2000): 131–137.

5. Matthew Myers, S. Tamer Cavusgil, and Adamantios Diamantopoulos, "Antecedents and Actions of Export Pricing Strategy: A Conceptual Framework and Research Propositions," *European Journal of Marketing* 36 (numbers 1/2, 2002): 159–189.

6. Matthew B. Myers, and S. Tamer Cavusgil, "Export Pricing Strategy-Performance Relationship: A Conceptual Framework," *Advances in International Marketing* 8 (1996): 159–178.

7. Howard Forman and Richard A. Lancioni, "International Industrial Pricing Strategic Decisions and the Pricing Manager: Some Key Issues," Professional Pricing Society, October 9, 1999, at http://members-pricingsociety.com/articles/international-industrial-pricing.pdf

8. John A. Boyd, "How One Company Solved Its Export Pricing Problems," *Small Business Forum,* Fall 1995, 28–38.

9. Matthew Myers, "The Pricing of Export Products: Why Aren't Managers Satisfied with the Results," *Journal of World Business* 32 (number 3, 1997): 277–289.

10. S. Tamer Cavusgil, "Unraveling the Mystique of Export Pricing," *Business Horizons* 31 (May–June 1988): 54–63.

11. Thomas T. Nagle and Reed K. Holden, *The Strategy and Tactics of Pricing: A Guide to Profitable Decision Making* (Englewood Cliffs, NJ: Prentice-Hall, 2002), chapter 3.

12. Luis Felipe Lages and David B. Montgomery, "Effects of Export Assistance on Pricing Strategy Adaptation and Export Performance," *MSI Reports,* issue 3, 2004, 67–88.

13. Mary Anne Raymond, John F. Tanner, Jr., and Jonghoon Kim, "Cost Complexity of Pricing Decisions for Exporters in Developing and Emerging Markets," *Journal of International Marketing* 9 (no. 3, 2001): 19–40.

14. Barbara Stöttinger, "Strategic Export Pricing: A Long and Winding Road," *Journal of International Marketing* 9 (no. 1, 2001): 40–63.

15. "Keeping Time with the Global Market," *World Trade,* December 1999, 82–83.

16. "What's in a Name," *Economist,* February 2, 1991, 60.

17. Al D'Amico, "Duty Drawback: An Overlooked Customs Refund Program," *Export Today* 9 (May 1993): 46–48. See also http://www.cbp.gov, accessed July 29, 2009.

18. Michael D. White, "Money-Back Guarantees," *World Trade,* September 1999, 74–77.

19. International Chambers of Commerce, *Incoterms 2000* (Paris: ICC Publishing, 2000). See also http://www.iccwbo.org, accessed March 03, 2009.

20. Kevin Reilly, "Exporters Must Ensure Coordination of Incoterms and Documentary Requirements for LC Payment," *Business Credit* 107 (number 6, 2005): 48–50.

21. Alexandra Woznik and Edward G. Hinkelman, *A Basic Guide to Exporting* (Novate, CA: World Trade Press, 2000), chapter 10.

22. "Getting Paid: Or What's a Transaction For?" *World Trade,* September 1999, 42–52; and Chase Manhattan Bank, *Dynamics of Trade Finance* (New York: Chase Manhattan Bank, 1984): 10–11.

23. David K. Eiteman, Arthur I. Stonehill, and Michael H. Moffett, *Multinational Business Finance* (Reading, MA: Addison-Wesley, 2002), 460–488.

24. International Chamber of Commerce, *Uniform Customs and Practice for Documentary Credits* (New York: ICC Publishing Corp., 2002).

25. Vincent M. Maulella, "Payment Pitfalls for the Unwary," *World Trade,* April 1999, 76–79.

26. Erika Morphy, "Form vs. Format," *Export Today,* 15 (August 1999): 47–52.

27. Erika Morphy, "Paper's Last Stand," *Global Business,* May 2001, 36–39.

28. "Ready Cash?" *Global Business,* September 2000, 45. See also http://www.tradecard.com, accessed February 25, 2009.

29. Richard Barovick, "The Changing World of Trade Finance," *World Trade,* April 2004, 18–24.

30. Tom Beube, "Cashing in on China," *World Trade,* October 2005, 64–66.

31. http://www.cofacerating.com, accessed July 25, 2009.

32. Michael S. Tomczyk, "How Do You Collect When Foreign Customers Don't Pay?" *Export Today* 9 (November–December 1993): 33–35.

33. James Welsh, "Covering Your Bets on Credit and Collections," *World Trade,* February 1999, 28–29; and Ron Siegel and Mark Stoyas, "Foreign Collections," *Export Today* 11 (April 1995): 44–46.

34. Guido Schultz, "Foreign Exchange Strategies for Coping with Currency Volatility," *World Trade,* January 2005, 10.

35. Saied Mahdavi, "Do German, Japanese, and U.S. Export Prices Asymmetrically Respond to Exchange Rate Changes?" *Contemporary Economic Policy* 18 (January 2000): 70–81.

36. Paul R. Krugman, "Pricing-to-Market When the Exchange Rate Changes," in S. W. Arndt and J. D. Robinson, eds., *Real-Financial Linkages among Open Economies* (Cambridge, MA: MIT Press, 1987), 49–70.

37. "Did U.S. Car Makers Err by Raising Prices When the Yen Rose?" *The Wall Street Journal,* April 18, 1988, A1, A14.

38. Michael H. Moffett, "Harley Davidson: Hedging Hogs," in Michael R. Czinkota, Ilkka A. Ronkainen, and Michael H. Moffett, *International Business 2003 Update* (Mason, OH: Thomson, 2003), 634–637.

39. "Turning Small into a Big Advantage," *Business Week,* July 13, 1998, 42–44.

40. "Competitive Exports, Sky High Imports," *Financial Mail,* October 2, 1998, 19.

41. Chi Lo, "Asia's Competitive Endgame: Life after China's WTO Entry," *The China Business Review,* January–February 2002, 22–36.

42. See, for example, http://www.jetro.org, February 25, 2009.

43. "How to Choose a Trade Bank," *World Trade,* accessed April 2004, 20.

44. http://www.commerzbank.com, accessed February 25, 2009.

45. Lawrence W. Tuller, "Beyond the LC," *Export Today,* 12 (August 1996): 70–74.

46. Daniel S. Levine, "Factoring Pays Off," *World Trade,* September 1998, 79–80.

47. Ray Pereira, "International Factoring," *World Trade,* December 1999, 68–69.

48. Mary Ann Ring, "Innovative Export Financing," *Business America,* January 11, 1993, 12–14.

49. The authors acknowledge the assistance of Craig O'Connor of the Export-Import Bank of the United States.

50. "EXIM-Bank Program Summary," in *Export-Import Bank of the United States* (Washington, DC: EXIM Bank, 1985), 1; updated for 2006.

51. Robert Frewen, "Are Your International Credit Terms Cutting Your Throat?" *World Trade,* January 2001, 71–73.

52. Joshua Kurlantzick, "What Uncle Sam Can Do For You," *World Trade,* February 2004, 18–22.

53. Claude Cellich, "Business Negotiations: Making the First Offer," *International Trade Forum* 14 (no. 2, 2001): 12–16.

54. Global Insight Advisory Services Group, *The Economic Contribution of Equipment Leasing to the U.S. Economy,* July 25, 2005, 4; see also http://www.ELFA.online.org, accessed February 28, 2009.

55. Elnora M. Uzzelle, "American Equipment Leasing Companies Should Consider the International Arena," *Business America,* June 28, 1993, 11–12.

56. http://www.elcamino.com, accessed February 25, 2009.

57. "Steeling Jobs," *Time Global Business,* February 2002, B6–B12.

58. Thomas Russell, "Antidumping, Round 2," *Furniture Today,* January 2, 2006, 1–2.

59. "Politics and Economics: EU's Punitive Tariffs May Last Even as U.S. Eases Main Irritant," *The Wall Street Journal,* February 3, 2006, A6.

60. http://www.wto.org, accessed March 3, 2009.

61. ibid.

62. Delener Nejdet, "An Ethical and Legal Synthesis of Dumping: Growing Concerns in International Marketing," *Journal of Business Ethics* 17 (November 1998): 1747–1753.

Chapter 12

1. Wilbur Schramm and Donald F. Roberts, *The Process and Effects of Mass Communications* (Urbana: University of Illinois Press, 1971), 12–17.

2. John L. Graham and Persa Economou, "Introduction to the Symposium on International Business Negotiations," *Journal of International Business Studies* 29 (no. 4, 1998): 661–663.

3. Joel Reedy, Shauna Schullo, and Kenneth Zimmerman, *Electronic Marketing* (Mason, OH: South-Western, 2003), chapter 17.

4. "What's Working for Other American Companies," *International Sales & Marketing,* November 22, 1996, 5.

5. George Field, Hotaka Katahira, and Jerry Wind, *Leveraging Japan: Marketing to the New Asia* (Hoboken, NJ: Jossey-Bass, 1999), chapter 10.

6. "Overseas Call Centers Can Cost Firms Goodwill," *Marketing News,* April 15, 2004, 21; and "Lost in Translation," *The Economist,* November 29, 2003, 58.

7. John A. Quelch and Lisa R. Klein, "The Internet and International Marketing," *Sloan Management Review* 38 (Spring 1996): 60–75.

8. Terence Brake, Danielle Walker, and Thomas Walker, *Doing Business Internationally: The Guide to Cross-Cultural Success* (New York: McGraw-Hill Trade, 1994), chapters 1 and 2.

9. Courtney Fingan, "Table Manners," *Global Business,* July 2000, 48–52.

10. Nina Reynolds, Antonis Simintiras, and Efi Vlachou, "International Business Negotiations: Present Knowledge and Direction for Future Research," *International Marketing Review* 20 (number 3, 2003): 236–261.

11. Nurit Zaidman, "Stereotypes of International Managers: Content and Impact on Business Interactions," *Group and Organization Management* 25 (March 2000): 45–66.

12. Xiaohua Lin and Stephen J. Miller, "Negotiation Approaches: Direct and Indirect Effect of National Culture," *International Marketing Review* 20 (number 3, 2003): 286–303.

13. Arnold Pachtman, "Getting to 'Hao!'" *International Business,* July/August 1998, 24–26.

14. Claude Cellich, "FAQ . . . About Business Negotiations on the Internet," *International Trade Forum,* 15 (no. 1, 2001): 10–11.

15. Pervez N. Ghauri, "Guidelines for International Business Negotiations," *International Marketing Review* 4 (Autumn 1986): 72–82.

16. "Negotiating in Europe," *Hemispheres,* July 1994, 43–47.

17. Virginia J. Rehberg, "Kuwait: Reality Sets In," *Export Today* 7 (December 1991): 56–58.

18. Catherine H. Tinsley and Madan M. Pillutla, "Negotiating in the United States and Hong Kong," *Journal of International Business Studies* 29 (no. 4, 1998): 711–728.

19. Claude Cellich, "Negotiations for Export Business: Elements for Success," *International Trade Forum* 9 (no. 4, 1995): 20–27.

20. Jackie Mayfield, Milton Mayfield, Drew Martin, and Paul Herbig, "How Location Impacts International Business Negotiations," *Review of Business* 19 (Winter 1998): 21–24.

21. "Stay-at-Home Careers?" *Global Business,* January 2001, 62.

22. Rajesh Kumar and Verner Worm, "Social Capital and the Dynamics of Business Negotiations Between the Northern Europeans and the Chinese," *International Marketing Review* 20 (number 3, 2003): 262–285.

23. Framework for this section adapted from John L. Graham and Roy A. Herberger, Jr., "Negotiators Abroad—Don't Shoot from the Hip," *Harvard Business Review* 61 (July–August 1983): 160–168.

24. Sally Stewart and Charles F. Keown, "Talking with the Dragon: Negotiating in the People's Republic of China," *Columbia Journal of World Business* 24 (Fall 1989): 68–72.

25. Hokey Min and William P. Galle, "International Negotiation Strategies of U.S. Purchasing Professionals," *International Journal of Purchasing and Materials Management* 29 (Summer 1993): 41–53.

26. Frank L. Acuff, "Just Call Me Mr. Ishmael," *Export Today* 11 (July 1995): 14–15.

27. Andrea Kirby, "Doing Business in Asia," *Credit Management,* October 2002, 24–25.

28. Kathy Schmidt, "How to Speak So You're Open to Interpretation," *Presentations* 13 (December 1999): 126–127.

29. Berry J. Kesselman and Bryan Batson, "China: Clause and Effect," *Export Today* 12 (June 1996): 18–26.

30. Ilkka A. Ronkainen, "Project Exports and the CMEA," in *International Marketing Management,* ed. Erdener Kaynak (New York: Praeger, 1984), 305–317.

31. Richard D. Lewis, *When Cultures Collide* (London: Nicholas Brealey Publishing, 2000), chapter 17.

32. Y. H. Wong and Thomas K. Leung, *Guanxi: Relationship Marketing in a Chinese Context* (Binghamton, NY: Haworth Press, 2001), chapter 3.

33. Richard Lewis, *Absolut Book: The Absolut Vodka Advertising Story* (New York: Journey Editions, 1996); and Richard W. Lewis, *Absolut Sequel: The Absolut Advertising Story Continues* (New York: Periplus Editions, 2005). For the latest ads in the series, see http://absolut.com/us, accessed April 6, 2009.

34. "Absolut Vodka Gaining U.S. Market Share," Reuters, Food Industry News, March 3, 2007, http://www.flex-news-food.com/pages/7743/Spirts/Sweden/absolut-yodka-gaining-us-market-share.html, retrieved February 7, 2009.

35. Mike Beirne and Eric Newman, "Beer, Wine, and Liquor Superbrands 2008," *Brandweek* http://brandweek.com/bw/superbrands/article_beerwineliquor.html, retrieved February 8, 2009.

36. Gary Levin, "Russian Vodka Plans U.S. Rollout," *Advertising Age,* November 11, 1991, 4.

37. John Helyar, "Will Harley-Davidson Hit the Wall?" *Fortune,* August 12, 2002, 120–124.

38. Lara Sowinski, "Breaking All the Rules," *World Trade,* May 2002, 16–19. See also http://www.ernieball.com/, accessed April 6, 2009.

39. http://thinkglobal.US, accessed April 6, 2009.

40. http://realpages.com/sites/businessbuilder/ad_options/find_guia.html, accessed April 6, 2009, assessed April 6, 2009.

41. Sean Callahan, "McCann-Erickson Offers B-to-B Clients the World," *Business Marketing,* January 2000, 35.

42. *The Handbook of International Direct and E-Marketing* (London: Kogan Page Ltd., 2001), chapter 1.

43. Hope Katz Gibbs, "Mediums for the Message," *Export Today,* 15 (June 1999): 22–27.

44. Deborah Begum, "U.S. Retailers Find Mail-Order Happiness in Japan," *World Trade,* 13 (May 1996): 22–25.

45. William McDonald, "International Direct Marketing in a Rapidly Changing World," *Direct Marketing* 61 (March 1999): 44–47.

46. Hope Katz Gibbs, "It's Your Call," *Export Today* 13 (May 1997): 46–51. For examples, see Brendan Reid, "Call Center Showcase," *Call Center Magazine* 15 (March 2002): 40–41. See also http://www.callcenterops.com/index.php, accessed April 6, 2009.

47. Sam Bloomfield, "Reach Out and Touch Someone Far, Far Away," *World Trade,* April 1999, 80–84.

48. Melanie May, "The World is DM's Oyster," *Marketing Direct,* December 2005, 38–43.

49. For a discussion on marketing on the Internet, see K. Douglas Hoffman, Michael R. Czinkota, Peter R. Dickson, Patrick Dunne, Abbie Griffith, Michael D. Hutt, John H. Lindgren, Robert F. Lusch, Ilkka A. Ronkainen, Bert Rosenbloom, Jagdish N. Sheth, Terence A. Shimp, Judy A. Siguaw, Penny M. Simpson, Thomas W. Speh, and Joel E. Urbany, *Marketing: Best Practices* (Mason, OH: South-Western, 2003), chapter 15.

50. P. Rajan Varadarajan and Manjit Yadav, "Marketing Strategy and the Internet," *Academy of Marketing Science* 30 (Fall 2002): 296–312.

51. "International in Internet Closes U.S. Lead," *Marketing News,* February 14, 2000, 7.

52. Byte Level Research LLC, "Byte Level Research announces Best global web sites of 2008," March 12, 2008, http://www.byelevel.com/News/reportcard2008.html, retrieved February 5, 2009.

53. Gerry Dempsey, "A Hands-On Guide for Multilingual Web Sites," *World Trade,* September 1999, 68–70.

54. V. Kanti Prasad, K. Ramamurthy, and G. M. Naidu, "The Influence of Internet-Marketing Integration on Marketing Competencies and Export Performance," *Journal of International Marketing* 9 (no. 4, 2001): 82–110.

55. Lewis Rose, "Before You Advertise on the Net—Check the International Marketing Laws," *Bank Marketing,* May 1996, 40–42.

56. "Marketers Aim New Ads at Video iPod Users," *The Wall Street Journal,* January 31, 2006, B1.

57. Thomas V. Bonoma, "Get More Out of Your Trade Shows," *Harvard Business Review* 61 (January–February 1983): 137–145.

58. "It's Show Time," *Marketing News,* August 15, 2005, 9. See also, http://www.exhibitsurveys.com/, accessed April 6, 2009.

59. Kathleen V. Schmidt, "Trading Plätze," *Marketing News,* July 19, 1999, 11.

60. http://www.3gsmworldcongress.com/, accessed April 6, 2009.

61. Richard B. Golik, "The Lure of Foreign Trade Shows," *International Business,* March 1996, 16–20.

62. http://www.messe.de/27711 for "Trade Shows as a B2B Communication Tool," accessed April 6, 2009.

63. "IMB '97 a Hit: Cologne Show Draws 30,000 Manufacturers from 100 Countries," *Apparel Industry Magazine,* August 1997, 16–26.

64. Bob Lamons, "Involve Your Staff in Trade Shows for Better Results," *Marketing News,* March 1, 1999, 9–10.

65. "Philips under the Big Top," *Advertising Age,* December 1, 2003, 3, 36.

66. Liz Lee-Kelley, David Gilbert, and Nada F. Al-Shehabi, "Virtual Exhibitions; An Exploratory Study of Middle East Exhibitors' Dispositions," *International Marketing Review* 21 (number 6, 2004): 634–644.

67. http://www.buyusa.gov/home, accessed April 6, 2009.

68. Charlene Solomon, "Managing an Overseas Sales Force," *World Trade,* April 1999, S4–S6.

69. Sergio Román and Salvador Ruiz, "A Comparative Analysis of Sales Training in Europe: Implications for International Sales Negotiations," *International Marketing Review* 20 (number 3, 2003): 304–326.

70. For a detailed discussion of the expatriate phenomenon, see Michael R. Czinkota, Ilkka A. Ronkainen, and Michael H. Moffett, *International Business*: (Mason, OH: South-Western, 2005), chapter 19.

71. Lisa Bertagnoli, "Selling Overseas Complex Endeavor," *Marketing News,* July 30, 2001, 4.

Chapter 13

1. Donald V. Fites, "Make Your Dealers Your Partners," *Harvard Business Review* 74 (March/April 1996): 84–95.

2. Rod B. McNaughton, "Foreign Market Channel Integration Decisions of Canadian Computer Software Firms," *International Business Review* 5 (no. 1, 1996): 23–52.

3. Peter N. O'Farrell, Paul A. Wood, and Jiang Zheng, "Internationalization of Business Services: An Interregional Analysis," *Regional Studies* 30 (no. 2, 1998): 101–118.

4. Øystein Moen, Iver Endresen, and Morten Gavlen, "Use of the Internet in International Marketing: A Case Study of Small Computer Software Firms," *Journal of International Marketing* 11 (number 4, 2003): 129–149.

5. Rajiv Vaidyanathan and Praveen Aggarwal, "Strategic Brand Alliance: Implications of Ingredient Branding for National and Private Label Brands," *The Journal of Product and Brand Management* 9 (no. 4, 2000): 214–228.

6. Erin Anderson, George S. Day, and V. Kasturi Rangan, "Strategic Channel Design," *Sloan Management Review* 39 (Summer 1997): 59–69.

7. Rajshkhtar Javalgi and Rosemary Ramsey, "Strategic Issues of E-Commerce as an Alternative Global Distribution System," *International Marketing Review* 18 (no. 4, 2001): 376–391.

8. Michael R. Czinkota and Jon Woronoff, *Unlocking Japan's Market* (Rutland, VT: Tuttle Co., 1993).

9. Stephen J. Arnold and John Fernie, "Wal-Mart in Europe: Prospects for the UK," *International Marketing Review* 17 (nos. 4 and 5, 2000): 416–432.

10. "China's Car Makers: Flattened by Falling Tariffs," *Business Week,* December 3, 2001, 51; and Mike Dunne, "Car Loans: Ready, Set, Go?" *Automotive News International,* September 1, 2000, 33.

11. Nicholas Alexander and Hayley Myers, "The Retail Internationalization Process," *International Marketing Review* 17 (nos. 4 and 5, 2000): 334–353.

12. "European Retailing: French Fusion," *The Economist,* September 4, 1999, 68–69.

13. Vijay Govindarajan and Anil K. Gupta, "Taking Wal-Mart Global: Lessons from Retailing's Giant," *Strategy and Business* 4 (fourth quarter, 1999): 14–25.

14. "For U.S. Internet Portals, the Next Big Battleground Is Overseas," *The Wall Street Journal,* March 23, 2000, B1, B4.

15. Rod B. McNaughton, "The Use of Multiple Channels by Small Knowledge-Intensive Firms," *International Marketing Review* 19 (no. 2, 2002): 190–203.

16. Goitom Tesfom, Clemens Lutz, and Pervez Ghauri, "Comparing Export Marketing Channels: Developed versus Developing Countries," *International Marketing Review* 21 (numbers 4/5, 2004): 409–422.

17. http://www.expert.org, accessed February 25, 2009.

18. Mark J. Barela, "United Colors of Benetton: An Examination of the Triumphs and Controversies of a Multinational Clothing Company," *Journal of International Marketing* 11 (number 4, 2003): 113–128; Sandra Dolbow, "Benetton Bounces Back," *Brandweek,* February 12, 2001, 1, 8. www .benetton.com, accessed February 25, 2009.

19. Erin Anderson and Hubert Gatignon, "Modes of Foreign Entry: A Transaction Cost Analysis and Propositions," *Journal of International Business Studies* 17 (Fall 1986): 1–26.

20. George Balabanis, "Determinants of Intermediaries' Service-Mix Configurations," *International Marketing Review* 22 (number 4, 2005): 436–459.

21. We are indebted to Dr. James H. Sood of the American University for this example.

22. Andrea Knox, "The European Minefield," *World Trade,* November 1999, 36–40.

23. Soumava Bandyopadhyay and Robert H. Robicheaux, "Dealer Satisfaction through Relationship Marketing across Cultures," *Journal of Marketing Channels* 6 (no. 2, 1997): 35–55.

24. Daniel C. Bello and David I. Gilliland, "The Effect of Output Controls, Process Controls, and Flexibility on Export Channel Performance," *Journal of Marketing* 61 (January 1997): 22–38.

25. For a discussion of the basic forms, see http:// www.export.gov/exportbasics/index .asp., accessed February 25, 2009.

26. "It Could Be Worse," *International Business,* April 1996, 8.

27. Peter B. Fitzpatrick and Alan S. Zimmerman, *Essentials of Export Marketing* (New York: American Management Association, 1985), 43.

28. S. Tamer Cavusgil, Poh-Lin Yeoh, and Michel Mitri, "Selecting Foreign Distributors: An Export Systems Approach," *Industrial Marketing Management* 24 (Winter 1995): 297–304.

29. Sherrie E. Zhan, "Booting Up in Santiago," *World Trade,* July 1999, 30–34.

30. "Five Steps to Finding the Right Business Partners Abroad," *World Trade,* March 1999, 86–87.

31. Both TOP and CDIC are available on the National Trade Data Bank at http://www .stat-usa.gov, accessed February 25, 2009.

32. U.S. Department of Commerce, *2003–2004 Export Programs Guide* (Washington, D.C.: Department of Commerce, 2004). Also available through http://www.ita.doc.gov/tic.

33. Joseph V. Barks, "Penetrating Latin America," *International Business,* February 1996, 78–80.

34. Lara L. Sowinski, "Pernod Ricard Toasts Its U.S. Distribution Partners," *World Trade,* August 2002, 24–25.

35. Keysuk Kim and Changho Oh, "On Distributor Commitment in Marketing Channels for Industrial Products: Contrast between the United States and Japan," *Journal of International Marketing* 10 (no. 1, 2002): 72–97.

36. For a detailed discussion, see International Chambers of Commerce, *The ICC Model Distributorship Contract* (Paris: ICC Publishing, 2002), chapters 1–3; http://www .iccwbo.org, accessed February 25, 2009.

37. Michael G. Harvey and Ilkka A. Ronkainen, "The Three Faces of the Foreign Corrupt Practices Act: Retain, Reform, or Repeal," in *1984 AMA Educators' Proceedings* (Chicago: American Marketing Association, 1984), 290–294.

38. Gary L. Frazier, James D. Gill, and Sudhir H. Kale, "Dealer Dependence Levels and Reciprocal Actions in a Channel of Distribution in a Developing Country," *Journal of Marketing* 53 (January 1989): 50–69.

39. Leonidas C. Leonidou, Constantine S. Katsikeas, and John Hadjimarcou, "Building Successful Export Business Relationships: A Behavioral Perspective," *Journal of International Marketing* 10 (no. 3, 2002): 96–115.

40. Chun Zhang, S. Tamer Cavusgil, and Anthony S. Roath, "Manufacturer Governance of Foreign Distributor Relationships: Do Relational Norms Enhance Competitiveness in the Export Market?" *Journal of International Business Studies* 34 (number 6, 2003): 550–580.

41. Bert Rosenbloom, *Marketing Channels: A Management View* (Mason, OH: South-Western, 2003), Chapter 9.

42. Sudhir H. Kale and Roger P. McIntyre, "Distribution Channel Relationships in Diverse Cultures," *International Marketing Review* 8 (1991): 31–45.

43. Constantine S. Katsikeas and Tevfik Dalgic, "Importing Problems Experienced by Distributors: The Importance of Level-of-Import Development," *Journal of International Marketing* 3 (no. 2, 1995): 51–70.

44. David Arnold, "Seven Rules of International Distribution," *Harvard Business Review* 78 (November–December 2000): 131–137.

45. Ilkka A. Ronkainen and Linda van de Gucht, "Making a Case for Gray Markets," *Journal of Commerce,* January 6, 1987, 13A.

46. http://www.agmaglobal.org.

47. Jeff Prine, "Time On-Line, the New Global Grey Market," *Modern Jeweler,* November 1998, 45–48.

48. Frank V. Cespedes, E. Raymond Corey, and V. Kasturi Rangan, "Gray Markets: Causes and Cures," *Harvard Business Review* 66 (July–August 1988): 75–82.

49. "The Earth Is Shifting under Heavy Equipment," *Business Week,* April 6, 1998, 44.

50. "How the Gray Marketeers Are Cashing In on DRAM Shortages," *Electronic Business,* June 1, 1988, 18–19.

51. Peggy E. Chaudry and Michael G. Walsh, "Managing the Gray Market in the European Union: The Case of the Pharmaceutical Industry," *Journal of International Marketing* 3 (no. 3, 1995): 11–33; and "Parallel Trade and Comparative Pricing of Medicines: Poor Choice for Patients," *Pfizer Forum,* 1996.

52. "European Court Supports Levi Strauss in Tesco Case," *The Wall Street Journal,* November 21, 2001, A11.

53. Jen-Hung Huang, Bruce C.Y. Lee, and Shu Hsun Ho, "Consumer Attitude toward Gray Market Goods," *International Marketing Review* 21 (number 6, 2004): 598–614.

54. "A Red-Letter Day for Gray Marketeers," *Business Week,* June 13, 1988, 30.

55. Ellen Klein and J. D. Howard, "Strings Attached," *North American International Business* 6 (May 1991): 54–55.

56. For a comprehensive discussion on remedies, see Robert E. Weigand, "Parallel Import Channel—Options for Preserving Territorial Integrity," *Columbia Journal of World Business* 26 (Spring 1991): 53–60; and S. Tamer Cavusgil and Ed Sikora, "How Multinationals Can Counter Gray Market Imports," *Columbia Journal of World Business* 23 (Winter 1988): 75–85.

57. "Electronics with Borders: Some Work Only in the U.S.," *The Wall Street Journal,* January 17, 2005, B1, B5.

58. See, for example, "Buying prescription medicine online: A consumer safety Guide," http://www.fda.gov/cder/consumerinfo/ buyonlineGuide_text.htm.

59. Hong Liu and Yen Po Wang, "Co-ordination of International Channel Relationships," *Journal of Business and Industrial Marketing* 14 (no. 2, 1999): 130–150.

60. David Arnold, *The Mirage of Global Markets* (Upper Saddle River, NJ: Prentice-Hall, 2003), 149–150.

61. Anna Morgan-Thomas and Susan Bridgewater, "Internet and Exporting: Determinants of Success in Virtual Export Channels," *International Marketing Review* 21 (numbers 4/5, 2004): 393–408.

62. 2008 Global Digital Economy-M-Commerce, E-Commerce, and E-payments, http://www .companiesandmarkets.com/summary-Market-Report/2008-Global-Digital-Economy-M-Commerce,-E-Commerce-and-E-payments-64392.asp, retrieved February 15, 2009.

63. "Shopping for a Marketplace," *Global Business,* February 2001, 36–37.

64. The Dell Tech Center. Wiki, http://www .premier.dell.com.

65. Hope Katz Gibbs, "Taking Global Local," *Global Business,* December 1999, 44–50.

66. Christia Victor and Wen-Jang Jih, "Fair or Not? The Taxation of E-Commerce," *Information Systems Management* 23 (number 1, 2006): 68–73.

67. Aldo Forgione, "The Good, the Bad, the Ugly: The Frontiers of Internet Law," *Journal of Internet Law* 9 (July 2005): 25–31.

68. "E-Commerce Firms Start to Rethink Opposition to Privacy Regulation as Abuses, Anger Rise," *The Wall Street Journal,* January 6, 2000, A24.

69. Amy Zuckerman, "Order in the Courts?" *World Trade,* September 2001, 26–28.

70. "Music Piracy Poses a Threat to Regional Artists," *The Wall Street Journal,* June 4, 2002, B10.

71. "Warner Music's Earnings Surge 92% on Digital Sales, Lower Costs," *The Wall Street Journal,* February 15, 2006, B3.

Part 3 Cases

Honeyland Manuka Honey from New Zealand:

An international new venture

1. In New Zealand SMEs are firms with between 0 and 20 employees. This makes the New Zealand SME much smaller than its counterpart in the USA.

2. A "two dollar shop" is a retail outlet where all sales items are offered at the same ($2) price. These types of shops appeared in New Zealand in the late 1990s and have become very popular. They attract a lot of customers, especially those with little disposable income or bargain hunters. Most sales items are perceived as worth more than the purchase price.

Davila-Bond and the Latin American Sweater Market

1. In Quito the people say the there are four seasons in every day: the morning is like Spring, noon Summer, early evening Fall and midnight Winter.

2. Part of this section has been drawn from: *The Economist* Intelligence Unit Research.

3. Index of Economic Freedom—Heritage Foundation.

4. World Bank—Crisis and Dollarization in Ecuador.

5. Wal-Mart is the most important retailer in Mexico with sales of 11.8 US$ billion in 2003 and 671 units distributed over 68 cities nationwide. It employs approx 110,755 staff with 24,378,536 square feet in supermarket space, and 60,342 restaurant seats.

6. Part of this section was based on research drawn from the UK Trade and Investment Office.

Dr. Eris: Cosmetics from Poland

1. More details about the research program can be obtained from: http://www .drirenaeris.pl/badania/en/badania.php and http://www.drirenaeris.pl/en/kosmetyki_ skladniki.php.

2. For more information, see http://www .businessweek.com/magazine/content/ 04_19/b3882011.htm.

Imaginarium

1. During the period December 2000—January 2001, the rate of Exchange was around 0.9 U.S. dollars per 1 Euro.

2. The first Imaginarium store was open in the area popularly known as "The Tube." It was an area with very narrow streets, equipped with old and somewhat dilapidated buildings. It was far from what would normally be considered a prime shopping area.

3. Another indication of Tena's intention to open a chain of franchised toy stores was the fact that in 1992, he opened a franchise store for a clothing and accessories chain. This allowed him to acquire first-hand experience in managing a franchised store. This clothing store was subsequently sold.

4. The Euro currency was not actually to be launched until 1999. This figure is given here as the equivalent amount in Euros of the former Spanish Pesetas invested. In January 1999, the Euro was formally launched with an exchange rate of 1 Euro = 1.19 U.S. Dollars. Subsequently, the exchange rate fell to about 1 Euro = 0.90 U.S. Dollars in early 2001.

5. These are the sales figures of the parent company Step Two, S.A. They do not include the sales of the subsidiaries in Italy and France, online sales, or the downstream sales of the retail franchisees.

6. This was a Spanish loyalty card similar to Air Miles, with multiple sponsor, such as a supermarket chain, a telephone company, a chain of gas stations, or a leading Spanish bank. It was estimated that it would cost Imaginarium about 1 percent on retail sales.

Chapter 14

1. "Tailoring World's Cars to U.S. Tastes," *The Wall Street Journal,* January 15, 2001, B1; and "Auto Marketers Gas Up for World Car Drive," *Advertising Age,* January 16, 1995, 1–16.

2. "Introduction to Unilever," available at http:// www.unilever.com, accessed February 25, 2009.

3. "Cutting into P&G Turf," *Advertising Age,* October 18, 2004, 16; "Daring, Defying to Grow," *The Economist,* August 7, 2004, 55–58; and Jack Neff, "Unilever, C-P to Ax Big Brands," *Advertising Age,* April 21, 2003, 1, 45.

4. Black & Decker's Vision Statement is available at http://www.bdk.com/, accessed February 25, 2009.

5. "The Zen of Nissan," *Business Week,* July 22, 2002, 18–20.

6. "Blade-runner," *The Economist,* April 10, 1993, 68.

7. Bill Saporito, "Behind the Tumult at P&G," *Fortune,* March 7, 1994, 74–82.

8. Edward Tse, "Competing in China: An Integrated Approach," *Strategy and Business* 3 (fourth quarter, 1998): 45–52.

9. Ben Van Houten, "Foreign Interpreter," *Restaurant Business,* November 1, 1999, 32.

10. Eric von Hippel, *The Sources of Innovation* (Oxford, England: Oxford University Press, 1997), chapter 1.

11. Eric von Hippel, Stefan Thomke, and Mary Sonnack, "Creating Breakthroughs at 3M," *Harvard Business Review* 77 (September–October 1999): 47–57.

12. "Could America Afford the Transistor Today?" *Business Week,* March 7, 1994, 80–84.

13. Eric von Hippel and Ralph Katz, "Shifting Innovation to Users via Toolkits," *Management Science* 48 (July 2002): 821–833.

14. David DeVoss, "The $3 Billion Question," *World Trade,* September 1998, 34–39.

15. Laurel Wentz, "World Brands," *Advertising Age International,* September 1996, i1–i21.

16. Normandy Madden, "Unilever takes Aim at Dandruff, as well as P&G in China," *Advertising Age,* April 30, 2007, p. 48.

17. "The Stateless Corporation," *Business Week,* May 14, 1990, 98–106.

18. "A Car Is Born," *Economist,* September 13, 1997, 68–69.

19. Ilkka A. Ronkainen, "Product Development in the Multinational Firm," *International Marketing Review* 1 (Winter 1983): 24–30.

20. Durward K. Sobek, Jeffrey K. Liker, and Allen C. Ward, "Another Look at How Toyota Integrates Product Development," *Harvard Business Review* 76 (July–August 1998): 36–49.

21. James B. Quinn, "Outsourcing Innovation: The New Engine of Growth," *Sloan Management Review* 41 (number 4, 2000): 13–29.

22. Larry Huston and Nabil Sakkab, "Connect and Develop: Inside Procter & Gamble's Model for Innovation," *Harvard Business Review* 84 (March 2006): 58–66.

23. Georges LeRoy, *Multinational Product Strategies: A Typology for Analysis of Worldwide Product Innovation Diffusion* (New York: Praeger, 1976), 1–3.

24. "ABB Opens R&D Center in Beijing," *China Business Daily News,* April 4, 2005; and Imperial and ABB Set to Pool R&D Expertise," *Professional Engineering* 17 (number 21, 2004): 45.

25. "8 Multinationals Found R&D Centers in Shanghai," *China Business Daily News,* May 27, 2005.

26. "Savi Launches Global R&D Center in Singapore," *Transportation & Distribution,* July 2002, 16.

27. Robert Ronstadt, "International R&D: The Establishment and Evolution of Research and Development Abroad by U.S. Multinationals," *Journal of International Business Studies* 9 (Spring–Summer 1978): 7–24.

28. Guido Reger, "Internationalization of Research and Development in Western European, Japanese, and North American Multinationals," *International Journal of Entrepreneurship and Innovation Management* 2 (nos. 2/3, 2002): 164–185.

29. Manuel G. Serapio and Donald H. Dalton, "Foreign R&D Facilities in the United States," *Research and Technology Management,* November–December 1993, 33–39.

30. Michelle Fellman, "Auto Researchers' Focus on Customers Can Help Drive Sales in Other Industries," *Marketing News,* January 4, 1999, 12.

31. C. K. Prahalad and Allen Hammond, "Serving the World's Poor, Profitably," *Harvard Business Review* 80 (September 2002): 48–57.

32. Lester C. Krogh, "Managing R&D Globally: People and Financial Considerations," *Research & Technology Management* 14 (July–August 1994): 25–28.

33. Rajesh Sethi, Daniel Smith, and C. Whan Park, "Cross-Functional Product Development Teams, Creativity, and the Innovativeness of New Consumer Products," *Journal of Marketing Research* 38 (February 2001): 73–85.

34. Julian Birkinshaw, "Managing Internal R&D Networks in Global Firms—What Sort of Knowledge Is Involved?" *Long Range Planning* 35 (June 2002): 245–267.

35. "Manufacturers Strive to Slice Time Needed to Develop Products," *The Wall Street Journal,* February 23, 1988, 1, 24.

36. Gloria Barczak and Edward McDonough III, "Leading Global Product Development Teams," *Research Technology Management* 46 (number 6, 2003): 14–22.

37. http://www.sematech.org/corporate/index.htm, accessed February 25, 2009.

38. http://www.uscar.org, accessed February 25, 2009.

39. "Consortium Forms RFID Center of Excellence," *Transportation & Distribution,* August 2002, 10.

40. A.C. Nielsen, "New-Product Introduction—Successful Innovation/Failure: Fragile Boundary," *A.C. Nielsen BASES,* June 24, 1999, 1; Robert G. Cooper and Elko J. Kleinschmidt, "New Product Processes at Leading Industrial Firms," *Industrial Marketing Management* 14 (May 1991): 137–147; and David S. Hopkins, "Survey Finds 67% of New Products Fail," *Marketing News,* February 8, 1986, 1.

41. Eric Berggren and Thomas Nacher, "Introducing New Products Can Be Hazardous to Your Company," *The Academy of Management Executive* 15 (August 2001): 92–101.

42. Laurel Wentz, "Mars Widens Its Line in U.K.," *Advertising Age,* May 16, 1988, 37.

43. Veronica Wong, "Antecedents of International New Product Rollout Timeliness," *International Marketing Review* 19 (no. 2, 2002): 120–132; Robert Michelet and Laura Elmore, "Launching Your Product Globally," *Export Today* 6 (September 1990): 13–15; and Laura Elmore and Robert Michelet, "The Global Product Launch," *Export Today* 6 (November–December 1990): 49–52.

44. George S. Day, "Diagnosing the Product Portfolio," *Journal of Marketing* 41 (April 1977): 9–19.

45. "Even Rivals Concede GM Has Deftly Steered Road to Success in Brazil," *The Wall Street Journal,* February 25, 1999, A1, A8.

46. Susan P. Douglas and C. Samuel Craig, "Global Portfolio Planning and Market Interconnectedness," *Journal of International Marketing* 4 (no. 1, 1996): 93–110.

47. Andrew J. Parsons, "Nestlé: The Visions of Local Managers," *The McKinsey Quarterly* 36 (no. 2, 1996): 5–29.

48. C. Samuel Craig and Susan P. Douglas, "Configural Advantage in Global Markets," *Journal of International Marketing* 8 (no. 1, 2000): 6–26.

49. "China's Auto Sales set to Rise 15%," *Asia TimesOnLine,* January 18, 2007. http://www.atimes.com/atimes/China_Business/IA18Cb03.html, retrieved February 14, 2009.

50. "Whirlpool Expected Easy Going in Europe, and It Got a Big Shock," *The Wall Street Journal,* April 10, 1998, A1, A6.

51. David C. Court, Anthony Freeling, Mark G. Leiter, and Andrew J. Parsons, "Uncovering the Value of Brands," *The McKinsey Quarterly* 32 (no. 4, 1996): 176–178.

52. Christine Bittar, "Cutting Edge," *Brandweek,* February 4, 2002, 16.

53. David C. Court, Mark G. Leiter, and Mark A. Loch, "Brand Leverage," *The McKinsey Quarterly* 35 (no. 2, 1999): 100–110.

54. Tobi Elkin, "Intel Inside at 10," *Advertising Age,* April 30, 2001, 4, 31.

55. "Starbucks: Keeping the Brew Hot," *Business Week Online,* August 6, 2001.

56. http://www.nestle.com/MediaCenter/PressReleases/AllPressReleases/AcquisitionUncleTobysAustralia-23May06.htm?Tab=2006, accessed February 25, 2009.

57. David A. Aaker, *Managing Brand Equity: Capitalizing on the Value of a Brand Name* (New York: Free Press, 1995), 21–33.

58. "Global Brands," *Business Week,* August 1, 2005, 45–46.

59. Johny K. Johansson and Ilkka A. Ronkainen, "Are Global Brands the Right Choice for Your Company?" *Marketing Management,* March/April, 2004, 53–56.

60. Jean-Noël Kapferer, "The Post-Global Brand," *Journal of Brand Management* 12 (number 5, 2005): 319–324.

61. Douglas B. Holt, John A. Quelch, and Earl L. Taylor, "How Global Brands Compete," *Harvard Business Review* 82 (September 2004): 68–75.

62. Interbrand, *Going Global: Global Branding-Risks and Rewards* (New York: Interbrand, October 2005): 1–7.

63. Johny K. Johansson and Ilkka A. Ronkainen, "The Esteem of Global Brands," *Journal of Brand Management* 12 (number 5, 2005): 339–354.

64. Bernd Schmitt and Alexander Simonson, *Marketing Aesthetics: The Strategic Management of Brands, Identity, and Image* (New York: Free Press, 1997), chapter 1.

65. David Aaker and Erich Joachimsthaler, "The Lure of Global Branding," *Harvard Business Review* 77 (November/December 1999): 137–144; for an interesting application, see Anand P. Raman, "The Global Brand Face-Off," *Harvard Business Review* 81 (June 2003): 35–45.

66. Colin Mitchell, "Selling the Brand Inside," *Harvard Business Review* 80 (January 2002): 99–105.

67. Andrew J. Parsons, "Nestlé: The Visions of Local Managers," *The McKinsey Quarterly* 36 (no. 2, 1996): 5–29.

68. Richard Tomlinson, "L'Oreal's Global Makeover," *Fortune,* September 30, 2002, 141–146.

69. Ilkka A. Ronkainen and Ivan Menezes, "Implementing Global Marketing Strategy: An Interview with Whirlpool Corporation," *International Marketing Review* 13 (no. 3, 1996): 56–63.

70. "Unilever's Goal: Power Brands," *Advertising Age,* January 3, 2000, 1, 12; and "Why Unilever B-Brands Must Be Cast Aside," *Marketing,* June 10, 1999, 13.

71. Jean-Noël Kapferer, "Is There Really No Hope for Local Brands?" *Journal of Brand Management* 9 (January 2002): 163–170.

72. Private Label Manufacturers Association; available at http://www.plmainternational.com/plt/plten.html, accessed February 25, 2009.

73. David Dunne and Chakravarthi Narasimhan, "The New Appeal of Private Labels," *Harvard Business Review* 77 (May–June 1999): 41–52; and John A. Quelch and David Harding, "Brands versus Private Labels," *Harvard Business Review* 74 (January–February 1996): 99–109.

74. "Shoot Out at the Check-Out," *The Economist,* June 5, 1993, 69–72.

75. François Glémet and Rafael Mira, "The Brand Leader's Dilemma," *The McKinsey Quarterly* 33 (no. 2, 1993): 3–15.

76. "Like My Pants? Pssst, They're Wal-Mart," *The Wall Street Journal,* September 3, 2002, B1.

77. Varun Mudgil, "The Big Two Build on Private Label," *Retail World,* July 22, 2002, 3.

78. Alan Treadgold, "ALDI—A Four-Letter Word That Promises Fierce Competition," *Retail World,* August 16, 2002, 6; see also http://www.aldi.us, accessed February 25, 2009.

79. "Nestlé Set to Enter Euro Own-Label Market," *Marketing Week,* August 9, 2001, 7.

Chapter 15

1. Leonard L. Berry, "Services Marketing Is Different," in *Services Marketing,* ed. Christopher H. Lovelock (Englewood Cliffs, NJ: Prentice-Hall, 1984), 30.

2. Christian Grönroos, "Marketing Services: The Case of a Missing Product," *Journal of Business & Industrial Marketing* 13 (no. 4/5, 1998): 322–338.

3. Bernd Stauss, and Wolfgang Seidel, *Complaint Management: The Heart of CRM* (Chicago: American Marketing Association, 2005). 232–234.

4. Pierre Berthon, Leyland Pitt, Constantine S. Katsikeas, and Jean Paul Berthon, "Virtual Services Go International: International Services in the Marketspace," *Journal of International Marketing* 7 (no. 3, 1999): 84–106.

5. United States International Trade Commission, "Recent Trends in U.S. Services Trade," 2008 Annual Report, June 2008, Publication No. 4015.

6. Bureau of Labor Statistics, "Tomorrow's Jobs," Occupational Outlook Handbook, 2008–09 Edition, United States Department of Labor, http://www.bls.gov/oco/oco2003.htm, retrieved February 3, 2009.

7. United States International Trade Commission.

8. Ibid.

9. Ibid.

10. WTO, "World Exports of Commercial Services by Region and Selected Economy, 1996–2006," International Trade Statistics.

11. Ibid.

12. United States International Trade Commission.

13. Terry Clark, Daniel Rajaratnam, and Timothy Smith, "Toward a Theory of International Services: Marketing Intangibles in a World of Nations," *Journal of International Marketing* 4 (no. 2, 1995): 2–28.

14. United States International Trade Commission.

15. Dorothy Riddle. "Using the Internet for Service Exporting: Tips for Service Firms, "*International Trade Forum*, 1 (1999): 19–21.

16. Neil Payne, "10 Reasons why you need a Multilingual Website," May 10, 2008, Buzzle.com, http://www.buzzle.com/editorials/5-10-2005-69742.asp, retrieved February 5, 2009.

17. Byte Level Research LLC, "Byte Level Research Announces Best Global Web Sites of 2008," March 12, 2008, http://www.bytelevel.com/news/reportcard2008.html, retrieved February 5, 2009.

18. Jim DeLaHunt, "Web 2.0 goes to Babel: Multilingual Websites and User-Supplied Content." September 9, 2008, http://jdlh.com/en/doc/2008web/2babel.html, retrieved February 5, 2009.

19. Michael R. Czinkota, "Loosening the Shackles: the Future of Global Higher Education," testimony at WTO Symposium on Cross-Border Supply of Services, Geneva, 2005, http://www.wto.org.

20. Institute of International Education, "International Students of U.S. Campuses at All-Time High," http://opendoors.iienetwork.org/?p=131590, retrieved February 5, 2009.

21. Ibid.

22. Ibid.

23. Institute of International Education, http://opendoors.iienetwork.org/file_depot/0-10000000/0-10000/3390/folder/69364/

BranchCampus2007Analysis.pdf, retrieved February 5, 2009.

24. Institute of International Education, "U.S. Study Abroad up 8 percent, Continuing Decade-Long Growth," http://opendoors.iienetwork.org/?p=131592, retrieved February 5, 2009.

25. Ibid.

26. "Engineering, Technical, and Other Services to Industry," Synthesis Report, Organization for Economic Cooperation and Development, Paris, 1988.

27. "India's Software Exports to Cross $40 bn," rediff.com, February 11, 2008, http://www.rediff.com/money/2008/feb/11nass.htm, retrieved February 6, 2009.

28. World Travel & Tourism Council, "Economic Impact," http://www.wttc.org/eng/About_WTTC/, retrieved February 5, 2009.

29. Paul G. Patterson and Muris Cicic, "A Typology of Service Firms in International Markets: An Empirical Investigation," *Journal of International Marketing* 3 (no. 4, 1995): 57–83.

30. M. Krishna Erramilli and C.P. Rao, "Service Firms' International Entry-Mode Choice: A Modified Transaction-Cost Analysis Approach," *Journal of Marketing* 57 (July 1993): 19–38.

Chapter 16

1. Bernard LaLonde and James Ginter, "Activity-Based Costing: Best Practices," *Paper #606,* The Supply Chain Management Research Group, Ohio State University, September 1996.

2. Toshiro Hiromoto, "Another Hidden Edge: Japanese Management Accounting," in *Trends in International Business: Critical Perspectives,* ed. M. Czinkota and M. Kotabe (Oxford, England: Blackwell, 1998), 217–222.

3. Council of Supply Chain Management Professionals, http://www.cscmp.org/ accessed March 3, 2009.

4. Accenture Global, http://www.accenture.com/global/services/by_subject/supply_chain_mgmt/client_successes/enhancedmanagement.htm, accessed February 25, 2009.

5. Richard T. Hise, "The Implications of Time-Based Competition on International Logistics Strategies," *Business Horizons,* September/October 1995, 39–45.

6. Tonya Vinas, "IW Value-Chain Survey: A Map of the World," *Industry Week,* September 1, 2005, http://www.industrywerek.com, accessed February 25, 2009.

7. Song Ze, "Reduce the High Cost of Logistic Services," *China Economic Net,* October 31, 2005, http://en.ce.cn/Insight/200510/31/t20051031_5066381.shtml, accessed February 23, 2009.

8. "Logistics in Africa," *The Economist,* October 18, 2008, 76.

9. David A. Rick, *Blunders in International Business,* 4th ed. (Oxford, England: Blackwell, 2006).

10. http://www.iata.org, accessed February 25, 2009.

11. "Survey: E-Management," *The Economist,* November 11, 2000, 36.

12. Top Ten Outsourcing Survey, The Outsourcing Institute, www.outsourcing.com, accessed February 25, 2009.

13. Michael R. Czinkota and Ilkka A. Ronkainen, "A Forecast of Globalization, International Business, and Trade: Report from a Delphi Study," *Journal of World Business* 40 (2005), 111–123.

14. Kotabe Masaaki, "Efficiency vs. Effectiveness Orientation of Global Sourcing Strategy: A Comparison of U.S. and Japanese Multinational Companies," *Academy of Management Executive* 12 (number 4, 1999), 107–119.

15. Patriya S. Tansuhaj and George C. Jackson, "Foreign Trade Zones: A Comparative Analysis of Users and Non-Users," *Journal of Business Logistics* 10 (1989): 15–30.

16. Charles A. Taft, *Management of Physical Distribution and Transportation,* 7th ed. (Homewood, IL: Irwin, 1984), 324.

17. David W. Gardner, "Prediction: One Trillion Dollar Online Commerce Market by 2012," *TechWeb News,* September 21, 2005, http://www.techweb.com/wire/ebiz/171000869, accessed December 5, 2005.

18. "An Exploratory Investigation of Global Perspective on E-Commerce, Internet, and Digital Economy," Thailand Electronic Commerce Resource Center, http://www.ecommerce.or.th/nceb2002/paper/42-Investigation.pdf, accessed February 25, 2009.

19. Michael Czinkota and Gary Knight, "Managing the terrorist threat," European Business Forum, http://www.ebfonline.com/main_feat/in_depth.asp?id=526, accessed December 8, 2005.

20. Michael R. Czinkota, "International Marketing and Terrorism Preparedness," testimony before the Congress of the United States, 109th Congress, Washington, DC, November 1, 2005.

21. Yossi Sheffi and James B. Rice Jr., "A Supply Chain View of the Resilient Enterprise," *MIT Sloan Management Review,* 47 (number 1, 2005), 41–48.

22. Hayes, Tom, "The Full Cost of Cargo Losses, January 2008, http://www.inboundlogistics.com, accessed February 25, 2009.

23. Frank Stern and Kirk Turner, "Piracy Threat Continues," Allianz Group Portal, Global Risks Report, March 2005.

24. International Chamber of Commerce, Piracy Report, http://www.icc-ccs.org/ accessed February 25, 2009.

25. Robert Malone, "Reverse Side of Logistics: The Business of Returns," *Forbes,* November 2005.

26. Haw-Jan Wu and Steven C. Dunn, "Environmentally Responsible Logistics Systems," *International Journal of Physical Distribution and Logistics Management* 2 (1995): 20–38.

Chapter 17

1. Shantanu Dutta, Mark Bergen, Daniel Levy, Mark Ritson, and Mark Zbaracki, "Pricing as a Strategic Capability," *Sloan Management Review* 43 (Spring 2002): 61–66; and Saeed Samiee, "Elements of Marketing Strategy: A Comparative Study of U.S. and Non–U.S. Based Companies," *International Marketing Review* 1 (Summer 1982): 119–126.

2. Victor H. Miesel, Harlow H. Higinbotham, and Chun W. Yi, "International Transfer Pricing: Practical Solutions for Intercompany Pricing," *International Tax Journal* 28 (Fall 2002): 1–22.

3. Wagdy M. Abdallah, "How to Motivate and Evaluate Managers with International Transfer Pricing Systems," *Management International Review* 29 (1989): 65–71.

4. Sherif Assef and Surjya Mitra, "Making the Most of Transfer Pricing," *Insurance Executive*, Summer 1999, 2–4.

5. Ernst & Young, *Transfer Pricing 2007–2008 Global Surveys* (New York: Ernst & Young, November 2008), available at http://www.ey.com, accessed February 7, 2009.

6. Robert Feinschreiber, *Transfer Pricing Handbook* (New York: John Wiley & Sons, 2002), chapter 2 ("Practical Aspects of Transfer Pricing").

7. "How to Free Blocked Funds via Supplier Surcharges," *Business International*, December 7, 1984, 387.

8. Wagdy Abdallah, "Global Transfer Pricing of Multinationals and E-Commerce in the 21st Century," *Multinational Business Review* 10 (Fall 2002): 62–71.

9. Robert Grosse, "Financial Transfers in the MNE: The Latin American Case," *Management International Review* 26 (1986): 33–44.

10. Erika Morphy, "Spend and Tax Politics," *Export Today* 15 (April 1999): 50–56.

11. KPMG, *Corporate Tax Rate Survey* 2007 (New York: KPMG, accessed January 31, 2007), available at http://www.kpmg.com.

12. Michael P. Casey, "International Transfer Pricing," *Management Accounting* 66 (October 1985): 31–35.

13. Thomas H. Stevenson and David W.E. Cabell, "Integrating Transfer Pricing Policy and Activity-Based Costing," *Journal of International Marketing* 10 (number 4, 2002): 77–88.

14. Weston Anson, "An Arm's Length View of Transfer Pricing," *International Tax Review* (December 1999): 7–9; and "Pricing Foreign Transactions," *Small Business Reports* (April 1993): 65–66.

15. Organization for Economic Cooperation and Development, *Transfer Pricing Guidelines for Multinational Enterprises and Tax Administrations* (Paris, France, 1999), 14–15.

16. Brad Rolph and Jay Niederhoffer, "Transfer Pricing and E-Commerce," *International Tax Review* (September 1999): 34–39.

17. Robert B. Stack, Maria de Castello, and Natan J. Leyva, "Transfer Pricing in the United States and Latin America," *Tax Management International Journal* 31 (no. 1, 2002): 24–43.

18. Victor H. Miesel, Harlow H. Higinbotham, and Chun W. Yi, "International Transfer Pricing: Practical Solutions for Intercompany Pricing—Part II," *International Tax Journal* 29 (Winter 2003): 1–23.

19. Internal Revenue Service, *APA Quarterly Report* (Washington, DC: Department of the Treasury; see http://www.irs.gov/irm/part32/ch04s01.html, accessed February 7, 2009.

20. Stephane Gelin and Alan Baudeneau, "France Updates Transfer Pricing Rules," *Global Business*, February 2000, 62.

21. "Pricing Yourself into a Market," *Business Asia*, December 21, 1992, 1.

22. "Knocking on the IRS's Door," *Export Today* 15 (April 1999): 52–53.

23. Paul Burns, "U.S. Transfer Pricing Developments," *International Tax Review* 13 (no. 4, 2002): 48–49.

24. "MNCs Face Tighter Net over Transfer Pricing Rules," *Business International*, October 31, 1988, 337–338.

25. Phillip Beutel, Steven Schwartz, and Bryan Ray, "Beware the Transfer Pricing Gap," *Managing Intellectual Property*, June 2005, 33–38.

26. Kent B. Monroe, *Pricing: Making Profitable Decisions* (New York: McGraw-Hill, 2003), 12.

27. Douglas W. Vorhies, Michael Harker, and C. P. Rao, "The Capabilities and Performance Advantages of Market-Driven Firms," *European Journal of Marketing* 33 (nos. 11/12, 1999): 1171–1202.

28. J. J. Boddewyn, Robin Soehl, and Jacques Picard, "Standardization in International Marketing: Is Ted Levitt in Fact Right?" *Business Horizons* 29 (November–December 1986): 69–75.

29. Saeed Samiee, "Pricing in Marketing Strategies of U.S.- and Foreign-Based Companies," *Journal of Business Research* 15 (March 1987): 17–30.

30. For an example of pricing processes by multinational marketers, see John U. Farley, James M. Hulbert, and David Weinstein, "Price Setting and Volume Planning by Two European Industrial Companies: A Study and Comparison of Decision Processes," *Journal of Marketing* 44 (Winter 1980): 46–54.

31. "The China Price," *Business Week*, December 6, 2004, 102–112.

32. Ira C. Magaziner and Mark Patinkin, "Fast Heat: How Korea Won the Microwave War," *Harvard Business Review* 67 (January–February 1989): 83–92.

33. "Ford, GM Square Off over Daewoo Motor; The Question Is: Why?" *The Wall Street Journal*, February 14, 2000, A1, A13.

34. Jonathan Sprague, "Haier Reaches Higher," *Fortune*, September 16, 2002, 43–46.

35. "Detroit Is Getting Sideswiped by the Yen," *Business Week*, November 11, 1996, 54.

36. Mark Bernstein, "Expanding Capacity While Facing Global Pricing Puts Cummins' Supply Chain to the Test," *World Trade*, February 2006, 34–36.

37. "The Price Is Wrong," *The Economist*, May 25, 2002, 59.

38. "Global Survey of Business Executives: Inflation and Pricing," *The McKinsey Quarterly*, April 2007, available at http://www.mckinseyquarterly.com.

39. "Stuck!" *Business Week*, November 15, 1993, 146–155.

40. "Hyundai Gets Hot," *Business Week*, December 17, 2001, 84–86.

41. Richard Tomlinson, "Who's Afraid of Wal-Mart?" *Fortune*, June 26, 2000, 58–62.

42. Akshay R. Rao, Mark E. Bergen, and Scott Davis, "How to Fight a Price War," *Harvard Business Review* 78 (March–April 2000): 107–116.

43. "Domestic Electronic Products Overtaking Foreign Goods," *Korea Times*, May 12, 1996, 8.

44. Louis Kraar, "How to Sell to Cashless Buyers," *Fortune*, November 7, 1988, 147–154.

45. C. K. Prahalad and Stuart L. Hart, "The Fortune at the Bottom of the Pyramid," *Strategy and Business* 7 (first quarter, 2002): 35–47.

46. "Wal-Mart Quits Retailers Group," *Advertising Age*, October 21, 2002, 16.

47. Wang Yuguan and Jiang Song, "China: A Future Star for Foreign Pharma Companies," *Pharmaceutical Executive*, August 1999, 78–87.

48. Victor H. Frank, "Living with Price Control Abroad," *Harvard Business Review* 63 (March–April 1984): 137–142.

49. Pam Woodall, "Survey: East Asian Economies: Six Deadly Sins," *Economist*, March 7, 1998, S12–14.

50. "The Long Road Back: A Survey of Argentina," *The Economist*, June 5, 2004, 1–12.

51. "In Argentina, Going Without," *The Washington Post*, February 19, 2002, E1–E2.

52. Swee Hon Ang, Siew Meng Long, and Philip Kotler, "The Asian Apocalypse: Crisis Marketing for Consumers and Businesses," *Long Range Planning* 33 (February 2000): 97–119.

53. "Asia's Sinking Middle Class," *Far Eastern Economic Review*, April 9, 1998, 12–13.

54. "Borders and Barriers," *The Economist—A Survey of European Business and the Euro*, December 1, 2001, 10–11.

55. "One Currency—But 15 Economies," *Business Week*, December 31, 2001, 59.

56. "Even After Shift to Euro, One Price Won't Fit All," *The Wall Street Journal Europe*, December 28, 1998, 1.

57. Stephen A. Butscher, "Maximizing Profits in Euroland," *Journal of Commerce*, May 5, 1999, 5.

58. Johan Ahlberg, Nicklas Garemo, and Tomas Nauclér, "The Euro: How to Keep Your Prices Up and Your Competitors Down," *The McKinsey Quarterly* 35 (no. 2, 1999): 112–118.

59. Travis K. Taylor, "Using Offsets in Procurement as an Economic Development Strategy," Working Paper for presentation at the International Conference on Defence Offsets and Economic Development, Alfred University, College of Business, September 2002.

60. "Current Activities of International Organizations in the Field of Barter and Barter-like Transactions," *Report of the Secretary General*, United Nations, General Assembly, 1984, 4.

61. David Hew, "What is Offset, Countertrade, and Structured Finance," Asia-Pacific Countertrade Association, 2004, http://www.apca.net.

62. United Nations, *Trade Facilitation and Electronic Commerce*, available at http://www.unescap.org/tid/publication/part_six2184.pdf.

63. Dorothy A. Paun, Larry D. Compeau, and Dhruv Grewal, "A Model of the Influence of Marketing Objectives on Pricing Strategies in International Countertrade," *Journal of Public Policy and Marketing* 16 (no. 1, 1997): 69–82.

64. Rolf Mirus and Bernard Yeung, "Why Countertrade? An Economic Perspective," *The International Trade Journal* 7 (no. 4, 1993): 409–433.

65. Chong Ju Choi, Soo Hee Lee, and Jai Boem Kim, "A Note on Countertrade: Contractual Uncertainty and Transaction Governance in Emerging Economies," *Journal of International Business Studies* 30 (no. 1, 1999): 189–202.

66. Paul Samuelson, Economics, 11th ed. (New York: McGraw-Hill, 1980), 260.

67. Bureau of Industry and Security, U.S. Department of Commerce, *Offsets in Defense Trade, 10th Annual Report*, Washington D.C., January 2006, table 2-1.

Chapter 18

1. Carl Arthur Sohlberg, "The Perennial Issue of Adaptation or Standardization of International Marketing Communication: Organizational Contingencies and Performance," *Journal of International Marketing* 10 (no. 3, 2002): 1–21.

2. Framework adapted from Dean M. Peebles and John K. Ryans, *Management of International Advertising: A Marketing Approach* (Boston: Allyn & Bacon, 1984), 72–73.

3. "Why P&G Is Linking Brands to Good Causes," *Marketing*, August 26, 1999, 11; and "Microsoft's Singapore Site Ties Page Views to Charity," *Advertising Age International*, October 1999, 4.

4. "The Material Years 1982–1992," *Marketing*, July 4, 2002, 22–23.

5. http://www.aa.com.

6. "Corporate Campaigns Attract Bigger Slices of Advertising Pie," *Advertising Age International*, March 8, 1999, 2.

7. Jonah Bloom, "GE: The Marketing Giant Lights Up with Imagination," *Creativity,*

October 2005, 63; and Matthew Creamer, "GE Sets Aside Big Bucks to Show Off Some Green," *Advertising Age*, May 9, 2005, 7.

8. William J. Holstein, "Canon Takes Aim at Xerox," *Fortune*, October 14, 2002, 215–220.

9. Jean-Noël Kapferer, "The Post-Global Brand," *Journal of Brand Management* 12 (number 5, 2005): 319–324.

10. Paula Andruss, "FedEx Kicks Up Brand through Humor," *Marketing News*, July 30, 2001, 4–5.

11. Chris Powell, "Are Countries Brands?" *Advertising Age Global,* December 2001, 5.

12. "Brand America," *Marketing News*, April 15, 2005, 33; and Ira Tenowitz, "Beers Draws Mixed Reviews after One Year," *Advertising Age*, September 23, 2002, 3, 57.

13. J. Enrique Bigne, "Advertising Budget Practices: A Review," *Journal of Current Issues and Research in Advertising* 17 (Fall 1995): 17–32.

14. "100 Leading Global Advertisers Report" *Advertising Age*, December 2008.

15. R. Craig Endicott, "Global Marketing," *Advertising Age*, November 14, 2005, 1–3.

16. Compiled from Leo Burnett, *Worldwide Advertising and Media Fact Book* (Chicago: Triumph Books, 1994).

17. http://www.iccwbo.org/policy/marketing/id8532/index.html, accessed February 12, 2009.

18. European Media: Flirtation and Frustration," *The Economist,* December 9, 1999, 85–86.

19. Ross D. Petty, "Advertising Law in the United States and European Union," *Journal of Public Policy and Marketing* 16 (Spring 1997): 2–13.

20. "Tobacco Advertising: European Commission Takes Action Against Two Noncompliant EU Member States," *European Commission Press Releases,* February 1, 2006.

21. "Pushing Pills: In Europe, Prescription-Drug Ads Are Banned," *The Wall Street Journal,* March 15, 2002, B1.

22. Pola B. Gupta and Kenneth R. Lord, "Product Placement in Movies: The Effect of Prominence and Mode on Audience Recall," *Journal of Current Issues and Research in Advertising* 20 (Spring 1998): 47–60.

23. Global Product Placement Market Forecast 2006–2010, *PQ Media.*

24. "Value of Product Placement Market Exploded 30.5% to $3.46 Billion in 2004," *PQ Media,* March 29, 2005, available at http://www.pqmedia.com/about-press-2005327.html.placement, accessed February 12, 2009.

25. "Chinese TV Discovers Product Placement," *The Wall Street Journal,* January 26, 2000, B12.

26. Hank Kim, "Madison Avenue Melds Pitches and Content," *Advertising Age*, October 7, 2002, 1, 14–16.

27. "Lights, Camera, Brands," *The Economist,* October 29, 2005, 61–62.

28. "Canada Moves toward New Laws on Magazines," *Advertising Age International*, January 11, 1999, 29.

29. "Global Media," *Advertising Age International*, February 8, 1999, 23.

30. Benjamin Compaine, "Global Media," *Foreign Policy,* November/December 2002, 20–28.

31. David W. Stewart and Kevin J. McAuliffe, "Determinants of International Media Buying," *Journal of Advertising* 17 (Fall 1988): 22–26.

32. "Eurosport Posts Big Victory: First Profit Since Rocky Start," *Advertising Age International,* March 30, 1998, 17.

33. Michael Cooper, "TV: The Local Imperative," *Campaign,* April 21, 2000, 44–45.

34. "The Internet," *Advertising Age International,* June 1999, 42.

35. "Global Brands," *Business Week Online Extra,* August 1, 2005, available at www.businessweek.com/magazine/content/05_31/b3945098.htm.

36. "Global Marketing Campaigns with a Local Touch," *Business International,* July 4, 1988, 205–210.

37. R. Craig Endicott, "Global Marketing," *Advertising Age*, November 14, 2005, 17; and Jack Neff, "P&G Flexes Muscle for Global Branding," *Advertising Age*, June 3, 2002, 53.

38. Jae H. Pae, Saeed Samiee, and Susan Tai, "Global Advertising Strategy: The Moderating Role of Brand Familiarity and Execution Style," *International Marketing Review* 19 (no. 2, 2002): 176–189.

39. "So What Was the Fuss About?" *The Economist,* June 22, 1996, 59–60.

40. http://www.mccann.com, accessed February 23, 2009.

41. http://www.ddb.com, accessed February 23, 2009.

42. http://www.wpp.com, Annual Report, 2007.

43. "U.S. Multinationals," *Advertising Age International*, June 1999, 39.

44. Richard Linnett, "Global Media Reviews Not So Worldly," *Advertising Age*, August 19, 2002, 1, 32.

45. "Centralization," *Advertising Age International*, June 1999, 40.

46. *Global Vision* (New York: Ogilvy & Mather, 1994), 8. See also http://www.ogilvy.com.

47. Debra A. Williamson, "ARF to Spearhead Study on Measuring Web Ads," *Advertising Age,* February 10, 1997, 8; and Gerard J. Tellis and Doyle L. Weiss, "Does TV Advertising Really Affect Sales? The Role of Measures, Models, and Data Aggregation," *Journal of Advertising* 24 (Fall 1995): 1–12.

48. Joseph T. Plummer, "The Role of Copy Research in Multinational Advertising," *Journal of Advertising Research* 26 (October–November 1986): 11–15.

49. John S. Hill, Richard R. Still, and Unal O. Boya, "Managing the Multinational Sales Force," *International Marketing Review* 8 (1991): 19–31.

50. Artur Baldauf, David W. Cravens, and Nigel F. Piercy, "Examining the Consequences of Sales Management Control Strategies in European Field Sales Organizations," *International Marketing Review* 18 (no. 5, 2001): 474–508.

51. Joseph A. Lawton, "Kodak Penetrates the European Copier Market with Customized Marketing Strategy and Product Changes," *Marketing News,* August 3, 1984, 1, 6. See also http://www.kodak.com.

52. Robert B. Money and John L. Graham, "Salesperson Performance, Pay, and Job Satisfaction: Tests of a Model Using Data Collected in the United States and Japan," *Journal of International Business Studies* 30 (no. 1, 1999): 149–172.

53. "Fuel and Freebies," *The Wall Street Journal,* June 10, 2002, B1, B6.

54. Robert McLuhan, "Face to Face with Global Consumers," *Marketing,* August 22, 2002, 34.

55. Tim R. V. Davis, "Integrating Internal Marketing with Participative Management," *Management Decision* 39 (no. 2, 2001): 121–138.

56. Oliver Williams, "Who Cast the First Stone?" Harvard Business Review 62 (September–October 1984): 151–160.

57. "Church Group Gnashes Colgate-Palmolive," *Advertising Age,* March 24, 1986, 46.

58. "Levi to Sever Link with China; Critics Contend It's Just a PR Move," *Marketing News,* June 7, 1993, 10.

59. Christopher Hart and Pete Blackshaw, "Internet Inferno," *Marketing Management,* January/February 2006, 19–25; and Christopher Hart and Pete Blackshaw, "Communication Breakdown," *Marketing Management,* November/December 2005, 24–30.

60. Allison Enright, "Spin (Out of) Control," *Marketing News,* February 15, 2006, 19–20.

61. Michael Carberry, "Global Public Relations," keynote speech at Public Relations Association of Puerto Rico's Annual Convention, San Juan, September 17, 1993.

62. "'06 Outlook: Sponsorship Growth Back to Double Digits," *IEG Sponsorship Report,* December 26, 2005, 1, 4.

63. Rich Thomaselli, "No Fun in Games," *Advertising Age,* August 9, 2004, 1, 21.

64. "Olympic Torch Burns Sponsors' Fingers," *Financial Times,* December 13, 1999, 6.

65. "War Minus the Shooting," *The Economist,* February 18, 2006, 62–63.

66. Bradley K. Googins, "Why Community Relations Is a Strategic Imperative," *Strategy and Business* 2 (third quarter, 1997): 64–67.

67. Michael E. Porter and Mark R. Kramer, "The Competitive Advantage of Corporate Philanthropy," *Harvard Business Review* 80 (December 2002): 56–68. See also http://www.cisco.com/web/about/ac227/about_cisco_corp_citi_net_academies.html.

68. "Business Scales World Summit," *The Wall Street Journal,* August 28, 2002, A12, A13.

Chapter 19

1. A.T. Kearney/FOREIGN POLICY, "The Globalization Index 2007," November/December 2007, http://www.atkearney.com/main.taf?p=5,4,1,127,2 and http://www.foreignpolicy.com/story/cms.php?story_id=3995, retrieved December 10, 2008.

2. Michael R. Czinkota and Ilkka A. Ronkainen, "Trends and Indications in International Business: Topics for Future Research," *Management International Review,* Spring 2009.

3. Rob Garretson, "Future Tense: The Global CMO," Report from the Economist Intelligence Unit, Sponsored by Google, September 2008.

4. A.T. Kearney/*Foreign Policy*, 2007.

5. Czinkota and Ronkainen, 2009.

6. Population Reference Bureau, "2008 World Population Data Sheet," August 19, 2008, http://www.prb.org/Publicatons/Datasheets/2008/2008wpds.aspx?p=1, retrieved January 14, 2009.

7. Ibid.

8. Warren Sanderson and Sergei Scherbov, "Rethinking Age and Aging," *Population Bulletin*, 63 (4), 2008, http://www.prb.org, retrieved January 13, 2009.

9. A.T. Kearney/*Foreign Policy*, 2007.

10. Czinkota and Ronkainen, 2009.

11. Ron Smith, "7 Revolutions for Global Sustainability," *Delta Farm Press*, December 3, 2008, http://deltafarmpress.com/news/global-sustainability-1203/, retrieved January 16, 2009.

12. A.T. Kearney/*Foreign Policy*, 2007.

13. Tarmo Virki, "Global Cell Phone Use at 50 Percent," *Reuters*, November 29, 2007, http://www.reuters.com/article/technologyNews/idUSL2917209520071129, retrieved January 16, 2009.

14. Informa Telecoms & Media, "Global Mobile Penetration Hits 50% Today," http://mobileactive.org/global-mobile-penetration, retrieved January 16, 2009.

15. Ibid.

16. Czinkota and Ronkainen, 2009.

17. Bruno Baylac and Gordon Padkin, "Industrial Market Trends: Changes Shaping the Industry for 2008," *Industrial Embedded Systems*, December 17, 2007, http://www.industrial-embedded.com/articles/id/?2395, retrieved January 14, 2009.

18. Czinkota and Ronkainen, 2009.

19. Karla Adam, "Archbishop Defends Remarks on Islamic Law in Britain," *The Washington Post*, February 12, 2008, http://www.washingtonpost.com/wp-dyn/content/article/2008/02/11/AR2008021102783.html, retrieved January 16, 2009.

20. A.T. Kearney/*Foreign Policy*, 2007.

21. Tom Ryan, "Turning Point 2008: Cocooning Makes a Comeback," *RetailWire*, December 17, 2008, http://www.retailwire.com/Discussions/Sngl_Discussion.cfm/13439, retrieved January 14, 2009.

22. Lema Samandar, "Aussies Cocooning in Hard Economic Times," *The Sydney Morning Herald*, December 1, 2008, http://news.smh.com.au/business/aussies-cocooning-in-hard-economic-times-20081201-6om3.html, retrieved January 14, 2009.

23. Daniel Grana, "Emerging Markets Still Offer Opportunities," *Investment News*, November 16, 2008, http://www.investmentnews.com/apps/pbcs.dll/article?AID=/20081116/REG/311179992, retrieved November 28, 2008.

24. DELHI, "A Taxonomy of Trouble," *The Economist*, October 23, 2008, http://www.economist.com/finance/displayStory.cfm?source=hptextfeature&story_id=12481004, retrieved November 28, 2008.

25. Michael R. Czinkota and Maureen R. Smith, "Economic Stimulus Plans must Incorporate International Trade," *The Korea Times*, January 20, 2009.

26. Ibid.

27. Richard King, "Global Sustainability: The Asian Perspective," *BusinessLife.com*, http://www.businesslife.com/articles.php?id=955, retrieved January 16, 2009.

28. Czinkota and Ronkainen, 2009.

29. Ibid.

30. Ibid.

31. Victoria L. Crittenden, Richard C. Hanna, and Robert A. Peterson, "Business Students' Attitudes toward Unethical Behavior," *Marketing Letters*, 20 (1), 2008, pp. 1–14.

32. Victoria L. Crittenden, Richard C. Hanna, and Robert A. Peterson, "The Cheating Culture: A Global Societal Phenomenon," *Business Horizons*, 2009.

33. Jack Ewing, "Brands: Moving Overseas to Move Upmarket," *Business Week*, September 18, 2008, http://www.businessweek.com/magazine/content/08_39/b4101060110428.htm?chan=magazine+channel_special+report, retrieved January 20, 2009.

34. Garretson, 2008.

35. Czinkota and Ronkainen, 2009.

36. Ibid.

37. Innovation Report, "Competing in the Global Economy: The Innovation Challenge," December 2003, foreword.

38. Geoffrey A. Moore, "Darwin and the Demon: Innovating Within Established Enterprises," *Harvard Business Review*, July–August 2004, pp. 86–92.

39. Victoria L. Crittenden, "The Rebuilt Marketing Machine," *Business Horizons*, September 2005, 409–420.

40. José Santos, Yves Doz, and Peter Williamson, "Is your Innovation Process Global?" *MIT Sloan Management Review*, Summer 2004, 31–37.

41. Chris Reidy, "Colgate will buy Tom's of Maine," Boston Globe, March 22, 2006, http://www.boston.com/business/articles/2006/03/22/colgate_will_buy_toms_of_maine/, retrieved January 22, 2009.

42. Garretson, 2008.

43. Ibid.

44. Jon Brodkin, "IBM Opens Sales Center in Second Life," *Network World*, May 15, 2007, http://www.networkworld.com/news/2007/051507-ibm-second-life.html, retrieved December 5, 2008.

45. Garretson, 2008.

46. Tim Ferguson, "Virtual Worlds set for Second Coming," Silcon.com, October 27, 2008, http://networks.silicon.com/webwatch/0,39024876,39285821,00.htm, retrieved January 22, 2009.

47. Arianne Cohen, "The Second Life of Second Life," *Fast Company*, September 17, 2008, http://www.fastcompany.com/magazine/129/the-second-life-of-second-life.html, retrieved January 22, 2009.

48. C.G. Lynch, "Companies Explore Virtual Worlds as Collaboration Tools," http://www.cio.com/article/180301/Companies_Explore_Virtual_Worlds_As_Collaboration_Tools, retrieved January 22, 2009.

49. Dave Sattler, "Eye Tracking Marketing Research," Sattler New Media Marketing, August 22, 2007, http://davesattler.blogspot.com/2007/08/eye-tracking-marketing-research.html, retrieved January 22, 2009.

50. Tameka Kee, "Only 25% of Viewers see Web Ads Below the Fold," *Media Post News*, April 8, 2008, http://www.mediapost.com/publications/index.cfm?fuseaction=Articles.san&s=80131&Nid=41300&p=415480, retrieved January 22, 2009.

51. S. Adam Brasel and James Gips, "Breaking through Fast-Forwarding: Brand Information and Visual Attention," *Journal of Marketing*, November 2008, 31–48.

52. Joan O'C. Hamilton, "This is Your Brain on Bargains," *Stanford Magazine*, November/December 2008, http://www.stanfordalumni.org/news/magazine/2008/novdec/features/brainbuy.html, retrieved January 11, 2009.

53. Hilke Plassman, Tim Ambler, Sven Braeutigam, and Peter Kenning, "What can Advertisers learn from Neuroscience?" *International Journal of Advertising* 26(2), 2007, 151–175.

54. Robert Lee Hotz, "You Know You Want It, or Do You? Marketing and the Brain," *Seattle Times*, March 26, 2005, http://seattletimes.nwsource.com/html/nationworld/2002220525_brain26.html, retrieved January 11, 2009.

Chapter 19 Appendix

1. Gunter K. Stahl, Edwin L. Miller, and Rosalie L. Tung, "Toward the Boundaryless Career: A Closer Look at the Expatriate Career Concept and the Perceived Implications of an International Assignment," *Journal of World Business* 37 (2002): 216–227.

2. Institute of International Education, *Open Doors*, Internet Document, January 20, 2006. http://www.iie.org.

3. Joann S. Lublin, "To Smooth a Transfer Abroad, a New Focus on Kids," *The Wall Street Journal*, January 26, 1999, B1, B14.

4. Nancy J. Adler, "Women in International Management: Where are They?" *California Management Review 26*, 4 (1984): 78–89.

5. "U.S. Women in Global Business Face Glass Borders," *Catalyst Perspective*, November 2000, http://www.catalystwomen.org.

Part 4 Cases

LPP-Reserved

1. To be pronounced "Pijotski" (The "j" sounding like the h in "house" in English).

2. Namely: Poland, Russia, Ukraine, Lithuania, Estonia, Latvia, Czech Republic, Slovakia, and Hungary.

3. The going currency rate of exchange was about 3.3 Polish New Zlotys (PLN) to 1 Euro.

4. They did not change the name to LPP until November 1995. LPP meant "Lubianiec, Piechocki, and Partners," even though this full name was never actually used. Over the years, different people would come up with different creative, funny interpretations of these initials, like "Lots of Profit and Potential" or "Lots of Permanent Problems"!

5. As could be seen form the web page of the Warsaw stock Exchange (http://www.gpw.pl), the evolution of the LPP shares had been approximately the following: By the end of 2001: 65 PLN per share; by the end of 2002: 187 PLN; by the end of 2003: 536 PLN; by the end of 2004: 532 PLN; by the end of 2005: 760 PLN; by the end of 2006: 740 PLN; by the end of 2007: 2668 PLN; and by the end of February 2008: 2,250 PLN.

6. LPP marketing executives estimated that they could profitably operate a Reserved store in populations of 80,000 people, or multiples of that. If so, the potential number of Reserved stores that could be opened and operated in Poland could be as high as 250–300.

7. Over the years the size of their Reserved stores would grow to about 1,800/2,000 meter square each.

8. At the time of writing this case, the main Fashion Shopping Mall Developers active in Central and Eastern Europe were: ECE Projekt Management, with headquarters in Hamburg, Germany (www.ece.de); Apsys Development, with headquarters in Paris, France (www.apsys-international.com); Multi Development Corporation B.V., with headquarters in Gouda, The Netherlands (www.multi-development.com); TriGranit Development Corporation, with headquarters in Budapest, Hungary (www.trigranit.com); and the Swedish corporation IKEA (www.ikea.com).

9. At end of 2007, LPP operated under a system of 8 collections or introductions per year, which they called "intakes": 2 in Spring, 2 in Summer, 2 in Fall, and 2 in Winter. The new garments and related merchandise composing and intake would remain in the retail store for about 6 weeks. The new merchandise was not shipped to the store "all at once," but following a pattern of "constant replenishment," which meant that customers were likely to find "something new on the shelves," every time they visited a particular store again.

10. Frequently they agreed to pay a fixed minimum rent per meter square or a percentage on sales, whichever was higher.

11. According to Spanish newspaper *El Pais* (13 February 2008), at the end of January 2008, Inditex had a worldwide total of 3,691 retail stores in 68 countries, with a total sales surface of 1.914.493 meter square. The breakdown was as follows: 1,131 Zara stores; 230 Kiddy's Class; 519 Pull and Bear; 426 Massimo Dutti; 512 Bershka; 381 Stradivarius; 290 Oysho; and 204 Zara Home. In total, 560 new stores had been opened in 2007.

12. Warsaw Interbank Offered Rate.

13. In 2007 it was estimated that LPP had bought garments from about 230 different suppliers, most of them located in the Orient. About 70 percent of them could be considered as fairly permanent.

Nova Scotia

1. Canadian Tourism Commission *Changing, U.S. Travel Trends to Canada,* February 3, 2006, available at http://www.canadatourism.com.

2. Al Ries and Jack Trout, *Positioning: The Battle for Your Mind* (New York: McGraw-Hill, 2000), 171–178.

A

ABC analysis A classification of products and warehousing system based on sensitivity to delivery time; those most sensitive to delivery time are classified as "A" products; those less sensitive as "B," and those least sensitive as "C" products.

absorption A pricing approach in which foreign currency appreciation/depreciation is not reflected (either entirely or partially) in the target market price.

accidental exporters Firms which become international due to unsolicited orders, such as those placed via a Web site, requiring export; unplanned participation in the international market.

acculturation Adjusting and adapting to a specific culture other than one's own.

adaptation A process where a firm, usually experienced in exporting, adjusts its overall strategy and outlook to incorporate early-on global concerns such as tariffs, exchange rates, culture, and other variables.

agent An intermediary for the distribution of goods who earns a commission on sales. *See also* distributor

ambush marketing The unauthorized use of an event without the permission of the event owner; for example, an advertising campaign that suggests a sponsorship relationship.

antidumping duty A duty imposed on imports alleged to be "dumped"—or sold at less than fair market value— on a domestic marketplace.

antidumping laws Laws prohibiting below-cost sales of products.

area structure An approach to organization based on geographical areas.

area studies Environmental briefings and cultural orientation programs; factual preparation for living or working in another culture.

arm's length price A basis for intracompany transfer pricing: The price that unrelated parties would have arrived at for the same transaction.

arm's length standard A principle basis for transfer pricing favored by governments to stop companies from shifting income to foreign subsidiaries in low- or no-tax jurisdictions.

augmented features Elements added to a core product or service that serve to distinguish it from competing products or services.

awareness One of the key corporate export stages in which the firm becomes of aware of the international opportunities when unsolicited export orders or other international stimuli continue over time.

B

back-translation The translation of a foreign language version back to the original language by a person different from the one who made the first translation; an approach used to detect omissions and avoid language blunders.

backward innovation Simplifying a product or service due to lack of purchasing power or usage conditions.

banker's acceptance A method of payment for exported goods: When a time draft, with a specified term of maturity, is drawn on and accepted by a bank, it becomes a banker's acceptance, which is sold in the short-term money market. *See also* documentary collection; discounting

barriers to entry Obstacles to trade created by governments and market conditions.

barter Exchange of goods for other goods of equal value.

best practice An idea which has saved money or time, or a process that is more efficient than existing ones; best practices are usually established by councils appointed by a company.

bilateral negotiations Trade agreements carried out mainly between two nations.

bill of lading A document that acknowledges receipt of the goods, represents the basic contract between the shipper and the carrier, and serves as evidence of title to the goods for collection by the purchaser; required for export.

black hole A situation that the international marketer has to work its way out of; a company may be in a "black hole" because it has read the market incorrectly or because government may restrict its activities.

born global Newly founded firm that, from its inception, is established as an international business.

boycotts Refusing to purchase from or trade with a company because of political or ideological differences.

brain drain Foreign direct investors attracting the best and brightest employees from a domestic firm; said to be depriving domestic firms of talent.

brand Name, term, symbol, sign, or design used by a firm to differentiate its offerings from those of its competitors.

budgets Short-term financial guidelines in such areas as investment, cash, and personnel. *See also* plans

built environment The structures created by human activities; most evident in cities.

bulk service Ocean freight service that mainly provides contractual services for individual voyages for prolonged periods of time.

bureaucratic controls A limited and explicit set of regulations and rules that outline desired levels of performance. *See also* cultural controls

buyback A form of countertrade: A compensation arrangement whereby one party agrees to supply

683

technology or equipment that enables the other party to produce goods with which the price of the supplied technology or equipment is repaid.

C

cash in advance A method of payment for exported goods: The most favorable term to the exporter; not widely used, except for smaller, custom orders, or first-time transactions, or situations in which the exporter has reason to doubt the importer's ability to pay.

cause-related marketing Marketing that links a company or brand with a cause, such as environmental protection or children's health.

centralization When a firm maintains tight controls and strategic decision making is concentrated at headquarters. *See also* coordinated decentralization

certificate of origin A document required by certain countries to ensure correct tariffs are paid.

change agent The introduction into a culture of new products or ideas or practices, which may lead to changes in consumption.

chill effect A sharp reduction in demand for both consumer and industrial goods due to buyer uncertainty about the state of their nation's economy.

clearing arrangements Clearing accounts for deposit and withdrawal of results of countertrade activities.

climate A natural feature that has profound impact on economic activity within a place.

cocooning A cultural trend toward staying at home and turning away from the world and anything new.

code law A comprehensive set of written statutes; countries with code law try to spell out all possible legal rules explicitly; based on Roman law and found in a majority of nations.

commercial risk Term referring primarily to an overseas buyer suspected of insolvency or protracted payment default.

commissionario An intermediary for the distribution of goods who may sell in its own name (as a distributor would), but for an undisclosed principal (an agency concept).

common law Based on tradition and depends less on written statutes and codes than on precedent and custom.

common market Goods and services, including labor, capital, and technology, are freely exchanged among member countries; restrictions are removed on immigration and cross-border investment; member countries adopt common trade policies with nonmembers.

complementary strengths The differing strengths of partners that help in building a profitable joint venture, for example, often the partners have different product, geographic, or functional strengths, which the alliance can build on in order to achieve success with a new strategy or in a new market. They can then either operate jointly as equals or have one partner piggyback by making use of the other's strengths.

computer-aided design (CAD) A combination of hardware and software that allows for the design of products.

concentration A market expansion policy characterized by focusing on and developing a small number of markets. *See also* diversification

confiscation Transfer of ownership from a foreign firm to the host country without compensation to the owner.

consignment selling A method of payment that allows the importer to defer payment until the imported goods are actually sold.

consular invoice/proforma invoice Documents required by certain countries in order to prepare tax and duty payments.

consumer-generated media (CGM) Online bulletin boards, blogs, podcasts, and other Web sites at which consumers can post product complaints and compliments.

container ships Cargo vessels that carry standardized containers, which greatly facilitate the loading and unloading of cargo and intermodal transfers.

contender A local company whose assets are transferable, allowing it to compete head-on with established global players worldwide.

content analysis A research technique investigating the content of communication in a society; for example, counting the number of times preselected words, themes, symbols, or pictures appear in a given medium.

contributor A role of a country organization; a subsidiary with a distinctive competence, such as product development or regional expertise.

coordinated decentralization Overall corporate strategy is provided from headquarters (centralized decision making) but subsidiaries are free to implement it within the range established in consultation between headquarters and the subsidiaries.

core product Product or service in its simplest, generic state; other tangible and augmented features may be added to distinguish a core product or service from its competitors.

corporate governance The relationships among stakeholders used to determine and control the strategic direction and performance of an organization.

corporate image advertising An umbrella marketing communications plan to make the company itself be correctly understood or perceived more positively.

corruption The misuse of one's influence, capabilities, or funds in order to provide or obtain preferential treatment.

cost of the service One of the major considerations in choosing international transportation modes. Generally depends on the burden the international shipper or service provider can bear. Should therefore be seen in the context of product value. *See also* value of the service

cost-plus method A pricing strategy based on the true cost of a product (inclusive of domestic and foreign marketing costs).

counterpurchase A form of countertrade that is a parallel barter agreement: The participating parties sign two separate contracts that specify goods and services to be exchanged (some cash may be exchanged to compensate for differences in value).

countertrade Transactions in which purchases are tied to sales and sales to purchases.

countervailing duties A duty imposed on imports alleged to be priced at less than fair market value, due to subsidization of an industry by a foreign government.

cross-subsidization The use of resources accumulated in one part of the world to compete for market share in another part of the world.

cultural assimilator A program in which trainees must respond to scenarios of specific situations in a particular country.

cultural clashes Conflicts arising due to differences in cultures, especially differences in religion.

cultural controls Informal rules and regulations that are the result of shared beliefs and expectations among the members of an organization. *See also* bureaucratic controls

cultural convergence The growing similarity of attitudes and behaviors across cultures.

cultural imperialism The imposition of a foreign viewpoint, non-local perspective, or civilization on a people.

cultural knowledge Broad, multi-faceted knowledge acquired through living in a certain culture.

cultural universals Characteristics common to all cultures, such as body adornments, courtship, etiquette, family gestures, joking, mealtimes, music, personal names, status differentiation, and so on.

culture An integrated system of learned behavior patterns that are distinguishing characteristics of members of any given society.

currency variation Changes in exchange rates which can affect the purchases and profitability of the international firm.

customer involvement The degree of participation of the recipient in the production of a service.

customer relationship management Exporter's strategy to increase perceived attention to the foreign customer through call-center technologies, customer-service departments, and the company's Web site.

customer structure An approach to organization that is based on the customer groups that are served—for example, consumers versus businesses versus governments.

customs broker An agent for an importer with authority to clear inbound goods through customs and ship them on to their destination.

customs union Nation members of customs unions agree to set aside trade barriers and also establish common trade policies with nonmember nations.

D

data equivalence A consideration that ensures comparative structure in survey questions by taking into account cultural variations.

database marketing A form of direct marketing in which database information (developed through direct mail or the Internet) allows the creation of an individual relationship with each customer or prospect.

death of distance A phrase coined by Frances Cairncross, which suggests that distance may no longer be a limiting factor in people's ability to communicate and interact.

decentralization When a firm grants its subsidiaries a high degree of autonomy; controls are relatively loose and simple. *See also* coordinated decentralization

decoding The process by which the receiver of a message transforms an "encoded" message from symbols into thought.

defender A local company that has assets that give it a competitive advantage only in its home market.

del credere agent An intermediary for the distribution of goods who guarantees the solvency of the customer and may therefore be responsible to the supplier for payment by the customer.

demographic divide The measure of the inequality in the population and its age distribution between rich and poor countries.

density Weight-to-volume ratio of a good; high-density goods are more likely to be shipped as airfreight, rather than ocean freight.

deregulation Reduction of governmental involvement in the marketplace.

derived demand Business opportunities resulting from the move abroad by established customers and suppliers.

direct exporting A distribution channel in which the marketer takes direct responsibility for its products abroad by either selling directly to the foreign customer or finding a local representative to sell its products in the market. *See also* indirect exporting

direct/indirect questions In designing a survey questionnaire, the degree of societal sensitivity must be taken into account when determining the directness or indirectness of questions.

discounting When a time draft, a method of payment for exported goods with a specified term of maturity, is drawn on and accepted by a bank, it may be converted into cash by the exporter by discounting; the draft is sold to a bank at a discount from face value. *See also* banker's acceptance

discriminatory/nondiscriminatory regulations Regulations that impose larger operating costs on foreign service providers than on local competitors, provide subsidiaries to local firms only, or deny competitive advantages to foreign suppliers are discriminatory. Nondiscriminatory regulations may be inconvenient and may hamper business operations, but they offer less opportunity for international criticism.

distribution culture Existing channel structures and philosophies for distribution of goods.

distributor An intermediary that purchases goods for resale through its own channels. *See also* agent

diversification A market expansion policy characterized by growth in a relatively large number of markets. *See also* concentration

documentary collection A method of payment for exported goods: The seller ships the goods and the shipping documents and the draft demanding payment are presented to the importer through a bank acting as the seller's agent; the draft, also known as the bill of exchange, may be a sight draft or a time draft.

dodger A local company that sells out to a global player or becomes part of an alliance.

domestication Gaining control over the assets of a foreign firm by demanding partial transfer of ownership and management responsibility to the host country.

downstream change As a good flows from a commodity to becoming a specific product, changes in composition, sophistication and value can take place which help its competitiveness.

draft A method of payment for exported goods: Similar to a personal check; an order by one party to pay another; "documentary" drafts must be accompanied by specified shipping documents; "clean" drafts do not require documentation; also known as the "bill of exchange." *See also* documentary collection

dual pricing Differentiation of domestic and export prices.

dual-use items Goods that are useful for both military and civilian purposes.

duty drawbacks A refund of up to 99 percent of duties paid on imports when they are re-exported or incorporated into articles that are subsequently exported within five years of the importation.

E

e-commerce Offering goods and services over the Web.

economic blocs Groups of nations that integrate economic and political activities.

economic crisis A situation in which the economy of a country experiences a sudden downturn often brought on by a financial crisis. An economy facing an economic crisis will most likely experience a falling GDP, a drying up of liquidity and rising/falling prices due to inflation/deflation.

economic union Integration of economic policies among member countries; monetary policies, taxation, and government spending are harmonized.

economies of scale Production condition where an increase in the quantity of the product results in a decrease of the production cost per unit.

efficiency seekers Firms that attempt to obtain the most economic sources of production in their foreign direct investment strategy.

embargoes Governmental actions that terminate the free flow of trade in goods, services, or ideas, imposed for adversarial and political purposes.

encoding The process by which a sender converts a message into a symbolic form that will be properly understood by the receiver.

Environmental Superfund A fund to cover the costs of domestic safety regulations and made up from fees imposed on U.S. chemical manufacturers, based upon volume of production.

ethnocentrism The belief that one's own culture is superior to others.

European Union Effective January 1, 1994; formed by the ratification of the Maastricht Treaty; set the foundation for economic and monetary union among member countries and the establishment of the euro, a common currency.

evaluation One of the key corporate export stages in which the firms conduct an assessment of their export efforts and often makes the

decision whether or not to continue with the effort.

experiential knowledge Knowledge acquired only by being involved in a culture other than one's own.

export consortia Legislation that permits domestic firms to work together, in a manner similar to Japanese *sogoshoshas, to* overcome trade barriers through cooperative efforts.

export control systems Governmental policy designed to deny or at least delay the acquisition of strategically important goods by adversaries.

export license Written authorization to send a product abroad.

export trading company (ETC) Legal construct designed to encourage small and medium-sized companies that are encouraged to participate in the international marketplace.

expropriation Seizure of foreign assets by a government with payment of compensation to the owners.

extender A company that is able to exploit its success at home as a platform for expansion elsewhere; this calls for markets or segments that are similar in terms of customer preferences.

F

facilitating payments Small fees paid to expedite paperwork through customs; also called "grease"; not considered in violation of the Foreign Corrupt Practices Act or OECD guidelines.

factor mobility The loosening of restrictions on the trade of capital, labor, and technology among nations.

factoring A trade financing method; companies known as factoring houses may purchase an exporter's receivables for a discounted price; factors also provide the exporter with a complete financial package combining credit protection, accounts receivable bookkeeping, and collection services.

factual information Objective knowledge of a culture obtained from others through communication, research, and education.

feedback Responses to communications that seek to generate awareness, evoke a positive attitude, or increase purchases; collection and analysis of feedback is necessary to analyze the success of communication efforts.

field experience Placing a trainee in a different cultural environment for a limited time; for example, living with a host family of the nationality to which the trainee will be assigned.

financial incentives Special funding legislated by government to attract foreign investments.

fiscal incentives Special funding legislated by government to attract foreign investments.

focus groups Eight to twelve consumers representing the proposed target market audience, brought together to discuss motivations and behavior.

forced distribution tests A group of consumers reports on new products they encounter in normal retail outlets. *See also* laboratory test markets; microtest marketing

foreign affiliate A U.S. firm of which foreign entities own at least 10 percent.

foreign availability High-technology products that are available worldwide, from many sources.

foreign direct investment (FDI) Capital funds flow from abroad; company is held by noncitizens; foreign ownership is typically undertaken for longer-term participation in an economic activity.

foreign exchange license A license that may be required by certain countries for an importer to secure the needed hard currency to pay for an import shipment; the exporter has to provide the importer with the data needed to obtain these licenses from governmental authorities and should make sure that the importer has indeed secured the documents.

foreign-market opportunity analysis Basic information needed to identify and compare key alternatives when a firm plans to launch international activities.

forfaiting A trade financing technique; the importer pays the exporter with bills of exchange or promissory notes guaranteed by a leading bank in the importer's country; the exporter can sell them to a third party at a discount from their face value for immediate cash.

Fortress Europe Term expressing the fear that unified European nations will raise barriers to trade with other nations, including setting rules about domestic content and restricting imports.

forward exchange market A method used to counter challenges in currency movements; the exporter enters into an agreement for a rate at which it will buy the foreign currency at a future date; the rate is expressed as either a premium or a discount on the current spot rate.

franchising A business model in which a parent company (the franchiser) grants another, independent entity (the franchisee) the right to do business in a specified manner. This right can take the form of selling the franchiser's products or using its name, production, preparation, and marketing techniques, or its business approach.

free trade area The least restrictive and loosest form of economic integration among nations; goods and services are freely traded among member countries.

functional lubrication Bribes that are not imposed by individual greed, but that serve to "grease the wheels" of bureaucratic processes; amounts tend to be small, the "express fee" is standardized, and the money is passed along to the party in charge of processing a document.

functional structure An approach to organization that emphasizes the basic tasks of the firm—for example, manufacturing, sales, and research and development.

futures A method used to counter problems of currency movements; in the currency futures market, for example, a buyer agrees to buy futures on the British pound sterling, which implies an obligation to buy in the future at a prespecified price. *See also* option

G

Generalized System of Preferences (GPS) A method by which many developed countries help developing nations to improve their economic condition by providing for the duty-free importation of a wide range of products.

geologic characteristics The characteristics of a place relating to its natural attributes.

global account management Account programs extended across countries, typically for the most important customers, to build relationships.

global brands Brands that reach the world's megamarkets and are perceived as the same brand by consumers and internal constituents.

global media Media vehicles that have target audiences on at least three continents.

glocalization Building in organizational flexibility to allow for local/regional adjustments in global strategic planning and implementation; uniformity is sought in strategic elements such as positioning of a product; care is taken to localize tactical elements, such as distribution.

gray market Distribution channels uncontrolled by producers; goods may enter the marketplace in ways not desired by their manufacturers.

Group of Five Five industrialized nations regarded as economic superpowers: The United States, Britain, France, Germany, and Japan.

Group of Seven Seven industrialized nations regarded as economic superpowers: The United States, Britain, France, Germany, Japan, Italy, and Canada.

Group of Ten Ten industrialized nations regarded as economic superpowers: The United States, Britain, France, Germany, Japan, Italy, Canada, the Netherlands, Belgium, and Sweden.

H

high context cultures Cultures in which the context is at least as important as what is actually said;

for example, Japan and Saudi Arabia have cultures in which what is not said can carry more meaning than what is said.

household All the persons, both related and unrelated, who occupy a housing unit.

hydrology Rivers, lakes, and other bodies of water influence the kinds of economic activities that occur in a place.

I

implementors A role of a country organization; although implementors are usually placed in smaller, less-developed countries, they provide the opportunity to capture economies of scale and scope that are the basis of a global strategy.

import license A license that may be required by certain countries for particular types or amounts of imported goods.

import substitution A policy that requires a nation to produce goods that were formerly imported.

Incoterms Internationally accepted standard definitions for terms of sale, covering variable methods of transportation and delivery between country of origin and country of destination, and set by the International Chamber of Commerce (ICC) since 1936.

in-depth studies Market research tools that gather detailed data used to study consumer needs across markets.

indirect exporting A distribution channel that requires dealing with another domestic firm that acts as a sales intermediary for the marketer, often taking over the international side of the marketer's operations. *See also* direct exporting

infant industry Relatively new firms are sometimes seen as deserving of protection which allows the industry to "grow up" before having to compete with "adult" global industries.

inflation The increase in consumer prices compared with a previous period.

infrastructures Economic, social, financial, and marketing support

systems, from housing to banking systems to communications networks.

innate exporters Start-up exporters; firms founded for the express purpose of marketing abroad; also described as "born global."

innovation the generation of new ideas (or) adaptation of new ideas towards the provision of higher-quality goods and services, sustained growth, and new knowledge.

intangibility Cannot be seen, touched, or held. A key difference between goods and services.

integrated exporting An export marketing strategy in which the marketer takes direct responsibility for its products abroad by either selling directly to the foreign customer or finding a local representative to sell its products in the market.

integrated marketing communications Coordinating various promotional strategies according to target market and product characteristics, the size of budget, the type of international involvement, and control considerations.

intellectual property (IP) A legal entitlement of exclusive rights to use an idea, piece of knowledge or invention.

intellectual property rights Safeguarding rights by providing the originators of an idea or process with a proprietary compensation, at least, in order to encourage quick dissemination of innovations.

interactive digital media a digital media platform that enables customers to be directly connected to the brand and the development process.

interest The stage in the key corporate export stages where the awareness created in the first stage leads the management to gradually become interested in international activities.

intermediaries Independent distributors of goods, operating primarily at a local level. *See also* distributor; agent

international comparative research Research carried out

between nations, particularly those with similar environments, where the impact of uncontrollable macrovariables is limited.

international freight forwarder An agent who provides services in moving cargo to an overseas destination; independent freight forwarders are regulated in the United States and should be certified by the Federal Maritime Commission.

international marketing The process of planning and conducting transactions across national borders to create exchanges that satisfy the objectives of individuals, governments, and organizations.

interpretive knowledge Knowledge that requires comprehensive fact finding and preparation, and an ability to appreciate the nuances of different cultural traits and patterns.

intranet A company network that integrates a company's information assets into a single and accessible system using Internet-based technologies such as e-mail, newsgroups, and the World Wide Web.

inventory carrying costs The expense of maintaining inventories.

J

joint ventures Collaborations of two or more organizations for more than a transitory period, in which the partners share assets, risks, and profits.

K

Kyoto Protocol An international compact signed in 1997 that calls for reductions in the emissions of carbon dioxide and five other greenhouse gases.

L

laboratory test markets Participants are exposed to a product and their reactions measured in a controlled environment. *See also* microtest marketing; forced distribution tests

lead users Companies, organizations, or individuals who are ahead of trends or have needs that go beyond what is available at the present time.

letter of credit A method of payment for exported goods: an instrument issued by a bank at the request of a buyer; the bank promises to pay a specified amount of money on presentation of documents stipulated in the letter of credit, usually the bill of lading, consular invoice, and a description of the goods.

licensing An agreement in which one firm (the licensor) permits another firm (the licensee) to use its intellectual property in exchange for compensation designated as a royalty.

liner service Ocean freight service that offers regular scheduled passage on established routes.

lobbyists Well-connected individuals and firms that help companies influence the governmental decision-making process by providing access to policymakers and legislators.

low context cultures Cultures in which most information is contained explicitly in words; for example, North American cultures.

M

management contract An agreement where the supplier brings together a package of skills that will provide for the ongoing operation of the client's facilities.

mandatory/discretionary product adaptation Ensuring a product or service to meet prevailing legal and regulatory, social, economic, and climatic conditions in the market. Motivation for such adaptations does not have to be government fiat, but can also be a sense of corporate social responsibility.

maquiladoras Mexican plants that make goods and parts or process food for export to the United States.

marginal cost method A pricing strategy that considers only the direct cost of producing and selling products for export as the floor beneath which prices cannot be set; overhead costs are disregarded, allowing an exporter to lower prices

to be competitive in markets that otherwise might not be accessed.

market pricing Determining the initial price of a product by comparison to competitors' prices.

market seekers Firms that search for better opportunities for entry and expansion in their foreign direct investment strategy.

market transparency Clarity of the offering made to the customer; transparency in service delivery is often difficult to ensure, because services may be customized to individual needs.

market-differentiated pricing Export pricing based on the dynamic, changing conditions of each marketplace.

master franchising system A system wherein foreign partners are selected and awarded the franchising rights to territory in which they, in turn, can subfranchise.

materials management The timely movement of raw materials, parts, and supplies into and through a firm.

matrix structure An approach to organization based on the coordination of product and geographic dimensions of planning and implementing strategy.

metanational innovators Companies that innovate across borders and across companies.

microfinance Programs in developing markets that allow consumers, with no property as collateral, to borrow sums averaging $100 to make purchases, and to have access to retail banking services.

microtest marketing A panel of consumers is exposed to new products through a retail grocery operated by a research agency. *See also* laboratory test markets; forced distribution tests

mixed aid credits Loans to domestic businesses designed to overcome barriers to export and composed partially of commercial interest rates and partially of highly subsidized developmental aid interest rates.

mixed structure An approach to organization that combines one or more possible structures (see

product, functional, process, and customer structures); also called a hybrid structure.

multilateral negotiations Trade agreements carried out among a number of nations.

N

national security Protecting the welfare—economic, cultural, or military—of a nation's p eople; tariffs, barriers to entry, and other obstacles to trade often are established to ensure such protection.

noise Extraneous and distracting stimuli that interfere with the communication of a message.

nonfinancial incentives Support such as guaranteed government purchases; special protection from competition through tariffs; import quotas, and local content requirements designed to attract foreign investments.

nontariff barriers Barriers to trade that are more subtle than tariff barriers; for example, these barriers may be government or private-sector "buy domestic" campaigns, preferential treatment of domestic bidders over foreign bidders, or the establishment of standards that are not common to foreign goods or services.

not-invented-here syndrome (NIH) Local resistance or decline in morale caused by the perception that headquarters is not sensitive to local needs.

O

offset A form of countertrade: Industrial compensation mandated by governments when purchasing defense-related goods and services in order to equalize the effect of the purchase on the balance of payments.

open account A method of payment, also known as open terms; exporter selling on open account removes both real and psychological barriers to importing; however, no written evidence of the debt exists and there is no guarantee of payment.

operating risk Exposing ongoing operations of a firm to political risk in another nation.

opportunity costs Costs resulting from the foreclosure of other sources of profit, such as exports or direct investment; for example, when licensing eliminates options.

option A method used to counter challenges in currency movements; gives the holder the right to buy or sell foreign currency at a prespecified price on or up to a prespecified date. *See also* futures

outcome The results of meeting objectives that seek to generate awareness, evoke a positive attitude, or increase purchases.

overinvest Tendency in the initial acquisition process to buy more land, space, and equipment than is needed immediately to accommodate future growth.

ownership risk Exposing property and life to political risk in another nation.

P

parallel importation Authentic and legitimately manufactured trademark items that are produced and purchased abroad but imported or diverted to the markets by bypassing designated channels; also called "gray market."

pass-through A pricing approach in which foreign currency appreciation/depreciation is reflected in a commensurate amount in the target market price.

Pax Romana "The Roman Peace," referring to the common coinage, trading activities, and communication networks established and protected throughout a vast empire.

penetration pricing Introducing a product at an initial low price to generate sales volume and achieve high market share.

perishability The rapidity with which a service or good loses value or becomes worthless; unused capacity in the form of an empty seat on an airplane, for example, quickly becomes nonsaleable.

physical distribution The movement of a firm's finished product to its customers.

Physical Quality of Life Index (PQLI) A composite measure of the level of welfare in a country, including life expectancy, infant mortality, and adult literacy rates.

piggyback In a joint venture, one partner can piggyback by making use of the other's strengths.

piracy A contemporary security concern for shipping; annual cargo crime losses are estimated at $30–$50 billion internationally.

plans Formalized long-range financial programs with more than a one-year horizon. *See also* budget

political instability Conditions which lead to frequent and major changes in the government and its rules within a country.

political risk The risk of loss when investing in a given country caused by changes in a country's political structure or policies, such as tax laws, tariffs, expropriation of assets, or restriction in repatriation of profits.

political union Unification of policies among member nations and establishment of common institutions.

population The human element of the environment.

portfolio investment An international investment flow that focuses on the purchase of stocks and bonds.

positioning The presentation of a product or service to evoke a positive and differentiated mental image in the consumers' perception.

predatory dumping Dumping—or selling goods overseas for less than in the exporter's home market or at a price below the cost of production, or both—that is termed "predatory" because it is used deliberately to increase the exporter's market share and undermine domestic industries.

price controls Government regulations that set maximum or minimum prices; governmental imposition of limits on price changes.

price elasticity of consumer demand Adjusting prices to current conditions: for example, a status-conscious market that insists on products with established reputations will be inelastic, allowing for more pricing freedom than a price-conscious market.

price escalation The higher cost of a product resulting from the costs of exporting and marketing in a foreign country.

price manipulation Adjusting prices of exported goods to compensate for changing currency rates.

pricing-to-market Destination-specific adjustment of mark-ups in response to exchange-rate changes. *See also* pass-through; absorption

process structure An approach to organization that uses processes as a basis for structure; common in the energy and mining industries, where one entity may be in charge of exploration worldwide and another may be responsible for the actual mining operation.

product placement Creating brand awareness by arranging to have a product shown or used in visual media such as movies, television, games, or Web sites.

product structure An approach to organization that gives worldwide responsibility to strategic business units for the marketing of their product lines.

profit repatriation Transfer of business gains from a local market to another country by the foreign direct.

promotional mix The tools an international marketer has available to form a total communications program for use in a targeted market: advertising, personal selling, publicity, sales promotion, and sponsorship.

protectionistic legislation An important bargaining tool; however, legislated protectionism can result in the destruction of the international trade and investment framework.

proxy variable A substitute for a variable that one cannot directly measure.

psychological distance Perceived distance from a firm to a foreign market, caused by cultural variables, legal factors, and other societal norms; a market that is geographically close may seem to be psychologically distant.

pull strategies Promotional strategies in a targeted market relying primarily on mass communication tools, mainly advertising; appropriate for consumer-oriented products with large target audiences and long channels of distribution.

purchasing power parities (PPP) A measure of how many units of currency are needed in one country to buy the amount of goods and services that one unit of currency will buy in another country.

push strategies Promotional strategies in a targeted market relying primarily on personal selling; higher cost per contact, but appropriate for selling where there are shorter channels of distribution and smaller target populations.

Q

qualitative data Data is gathered to better understand situations, behavioral patterns, and underlying dimensions.

quality perception The evaluative impression that customers develop of a service, largely determined by the behavior of the employees that they contact.

quantitative data Data is amassed to assess statistical significance; surveys are appropriate research instruments.

quota systems Control of imports through quantitative restraints.

R

R&D consortia/research Companies that collaborate in long-term research and development projects to create technologies without the threat of antitrust suits.

R&D costs Costs resulting from the research and development of licensed technology.

realism check A step in the analysis of data in which the researcher determines what facts may have inadvertently skewed the responses; for example, if Italian responders report that very little spaghetti is consumed in Italy, the researcher may find that the responders were distinguishing between store-bought and homemade spaghetti.

reference groups A person or group of people that significantly influences an individual's attitude and behavior.

regulatory practices The primary source of barriers to services destined for the U.S. market; fields such as banking, insurance, and accounting are regulated at both federal and state levels, often posing formidable barriers to entrants from abroad.

reliability The vagaries of nature can impose delays on transportation services; these delays tend to be shorter in absolute time for air shipments, which are considered more predictable.

research specifications In the centralized approach to coordinating international marketing, specifications such as focus, thrust, and design are directed by the home office to the local country operations for implementation.

resource seekers Firms that search for either natural resources or human resources in their foreign direct investment strategy.

reverse distribution systems Logistics that ensure that a firm can retrieve its goods from the market for subsequent use, recycling, or disposal.

S

safety-valve activity The use of overseas sales as a way to balance inventories or compensate for overproduction in the short term.

Sarbanes-Oxley Act Law enacted in the United States in 2002, in the wake of major corporate corruption scandals (such as Enron and WorldCom), intended to protect investors by improving the accuracy and reliability of corporate disclosures.

scenario analysis Evaluating corporate plans under different conditions, such as variations in economic growth rates, import penetration, population growth, and political stability over medium- to long-term periods.

Second Life A virtual world introduced by Linden Labs at the beginning of the twenty-first century which can be used by marketers 'to explore the market for goods and services'.

self-reference criterion The unconscious reference to one's own cultural values in comparison to other cultures.

seminar missions Promotional event in which eight to ten firms are invited to participate in a one- to four-day forum; a soft-sell approach aimed at expanding sales abroad.

sensitivity training An approach based on the assumption that understanding and accepting oneself is critical to understanding a person from another culture.

service capacity Ability to supply service on demand, including the planning of backup during peak periods; similar to an inventory of goods.

service consistency Uniformity or standardization in the offering of a service; unlike products, services are often subject to individual influences and the need to customize to satisfy unique customer interactions.

shipper's declaration for dangerous goods Required for shipments such as corrosives, flammables, and poisons.

shipper's export declaration A document that states proper authorization for export and serves as a means for governmental data collection efforts.

Single European Act Ratified in 1987 by twelve European countries to free the exchange of goods, services, capital, and people among member countries.

skimming Offering a product at an initial high price to achieve the highest possible sales contribution in a short time period; as more market segments are identified, the price is gradually lowered.

social desirability A guidepost or motivation or activity which makes an entity acceptable or even in demand in social or interpersonal relations. It is related to social acceptance, social approval, popularity, social status, leadership qualities, or any quality making him a socially desirable companion.

social stratification The division of a particular population into classes.

soft power The goal is to have people want to engage in a certain course of action, rather than forcing them to do things.

sogoshosha Large Japanese trading companies, such as Sumitomo, Mitsubishi, Mutsui, and C. Itoh.

soils Variations in the soils found in different geographic regions (and their interactions with climate) have a profound impact on agricultural production.

solo exhibitions Promotional event, generally limited to one or a few product themes and held only when market conditions warrant them; aimed at expanding sales abroad.

standard worldwide price A price-setting strategy in which a product is offered at the same price regardless of the geography of the buyer.

strategic alliances A special form of joint ventures, consisting of arrangements between two or more companies with a common business objective. They are more than the traditional customer–vendor relationship, but less than an outright acquisition.

strategic leader A role of a country organization; a highly competent national subsidiary located in a strategically critical market.

structured/unstructured questions In a survey questionnaire, structured questions typically allow the respondent only limited option in reply; unstructured (or open-ended) questions permit the capture of more in-depth information, but they also increase the potential for interviewer bias.

supply chain management An integration of the three major concepts of the logistics in which a series of value-adding activities connect a company's supply side with its demand side. *See also* systems concept; total cost concept; and trade-off concept

sustainability As given in the Brundtland Report (WCED 1987), sustainability or sustainable development is an activity that meets present needs without compromising the ability of future generations to meet their needs.

switch-trading Credits in a clearing account (established for countertrading) can be sold or transferred to a third party.

systems concept One of three major concepts of the logistics of international management, based on the notion that materials-flow activities within and outside of the firm are so extensive and complex that they can be considered only in the context of their interaction. *See also* total cost concept and trade-off concept

T

tariffs Import control mechanisms that raise prices through placement of a tax.

telemarketing Promotional tool that is growing worldwide as customers become more accustomed to calling toll-free numbers and more willing to receive calls from marketers.

terminology Specific designations or definitions of terms, used by trade bodies (such as the WTO) or in trade agreements; these terms can often have unintended or distorted applications in political discourse.

terrain The geology of a place expressed in terms of its regional characteristics; terrain plays a role in population, resources, travel, and trade.

terrorism The systematic use (or threat) of violence aimed at attaining a political goal and conveying a political message.

theocracy A legal perspective that holds faith and belief as its key focus and is a mix of societal, legal, and spiritual guidelines.

third-party (3PL) logistics The outsourcing of logistical management, which is a rapidly expanding industry.

total cost concept One of three major concepts of the logistics of international management, in which cost is used as a basis for measurement; the purpose of the total cost concept is to minimize the firm's overall logistics cost by implementing the systems concept appropriately. *See also* systems concept and trade-off concept

trade deficit A trade deficit occurs when a country imports more goods and services than it exports.

trade mission A promotional event aimed at expanding sales abroad; may be a country-specific, industry organized, or government-approved event. *See also* seminar missions

trade promotion authority Assures that the U.S. executive branch may reach international agreements that will not be subject to minute amendments by Congress; gives Congress the right to accept or reject trade treaties and agreements.

trade sanctions Governmental actions that inhibit the free flow of trade in goods, services, or ideas, imposed for adversarial and political purposes.

trade surplus Trade conditions under which exports exceed imports.

trademark licensing The ownership of the name or logo of a designer, literary character, sports team, or movie star, for example, which can be used on merchandise.

trade-off concept One of three major concepts of the logistics of international management, which recognizes that linkages within logistics systems lead to interactions; for example, locating a warehouse near the customer may reduce the cost of transportation, but requires investment in a new warehouse. *See also* systems concept and total cost concept

tramp service Ocean freight service that is available for irregular routes and is scheduled only on demand.

transfer costs Costs incurred in negotiating licensing agreements; all variable costs resulting from transfer of a technology to a licensee, and all ongoing costs of maintaining the agreement.

transfer risk Exposing the transfer of funds to political risk across international borders.

translation-retranslation approach Reducing problems in the wording of questions by translating the question into a foreign language and having a second translator return the foreign text to the researcher's native language.

transportation modes Choices among airfreight and ocean freight, pipeline, rail, and trucking.

triad The megamarkets of North American, Europe, and Asia-Pacific.

trial A stage in which a firm begins to explore the feasibility of exporting and actually conducts international trade activities. Also known as exploratory stage.

U

unintentional dumping Dumping—or selling goods overseas for less than in the exporter's home market or at a price below the cost of production, or both—that is termed "unintentional" because the lower price is due to currency fluctuations.

urbanization Descriptions of urbanization range from densely-populated cities to built-up areas to small towns with proclaimed legal limits.

V

value of the service One of the major considerations in choosing international transportation modes generally depends upon the value that the shipper will gain from using the service. *See also* cost of the service

value-added tax (VAT) A tax on the value added to goods and services charged as a percentage of price at each stage in the production and distribution chain.

video/catalog exhibitions Promotional tool coordinating product presentations from several companies in one catalog or video; aimed at expanding sales abroad.

virtual trade shows Electronic promotional tool enabling exporters to promote their products and services over the Internet and to have electronic presence without actually attending an overseas trade show; aimed at expanding U.S. sales abroad.

voluntary restraint agreements Nontariff import control mechanisms consisting of self-imposed restrictions and cutbacks aimed at avoiding punitive trade actions from a host.

W

Web-based research Surveys and other data collection techniques administered using the resources of the Internet.

The United Nations and
The Advancement of Women, 1945-1996

The United Nations
Blue Books Series, Volume VI, revised edition

The United Nations and

The Advancement
of Women

1945-1996

**With an introduction by
Boutros Boutros-Ghali,
Secretary-General of the United Nations**

Department of Public Information
United Nations, New York

Published by the United Nations
Department of Public Information
New York, NY 10017

Editor's note:

Each of the United Nations documents and other materials reproduced in this book ("Texts of documents", pages 103-823) has been assigned a number (e.g. Document 1, Document 2, etc.). This number is used throughout the Introduction and other parts of this book to guide readers to the document texts. For other documents mentioned in the book but not reproduced, the United Nations document symbol (e.g., E/CN.14/714) is provided. With this symbol, such documents can be consulted at the Dag Hammarskjöld Library at United Nations Headquarters in New York, at other libraries in the United Nations system or at libraries around the world which have been designated as depository libraries for United Nations documents. *The United Nations and the Advancement of Women, 1945-1996* is a revision of *The United Nations and the Advancement of Women, 1945-1995*, updated to incorporate the outcome of the Fourth World Conference on Women held in September 1995. The information contained in this volume is correct as at 15 March 1996.

Copyright © 1995 and 1996 United Nations

The United Nations and the Advancement of Women, 1945-1996
The United Nations Blue Books Series
Volume VI
ISBN 92-1-100603-1
United Nations Publication
Sales No. E. 96.I.9

Printed by the United Nations Reproduction Section
New York, NY

Contents